Tables of Planetary Phenomena

Books by Neil F. Michelsen

The American Ephemeris 1931-1980 & Book of Tables
The American Ephemeris 1901-1930
The American Ephemeris 1941-1950
The American Ephemeris 1951-1960
The American Ephemeris 1961-1970
The American Ephemeris 1971-1980
The American Ephemeris 1981-1990
The American Ephemeris 1991-2000
The American Ephemeris for the 20th Century, 1900 to 2000 at Noon
The American Ephemeris for the 20th Century, 1900 to 2000 at Midnight
The American Ephemeris for the 21st Century, 2000 to 2050 at Noon
The American Ephemeris for the 21st Century, 2000 to 2050 at Midnight
The American Sidereal Ephemeris 1976-2000
*The American Sidereal Ephemeris 2001-2025**
The American Heliocentric Ephemeris 1901-2000
*The American Heliocentric Ephemeris 2001-2050**
The American Midpoint Ephemeris 1986-1990
The American Midpoint Ephemeris 1990-1995
*The American Midpoint Ephemeris 1996-2000**
*The American Midpoint Ephemeris 2001-2005**
The American Book of Tables
The Koch Book of Tables
The Michelsen Book of Tables
The Uranian Transneptune Ephemeris 1850-2050
Comet Halley Ephemeris 1901-1996
Search for the Christmas Star (with Maria Kay Simms)
The Asteroid Ephemeris (with Zipporah Dobyns and Rique Pottenger)
Tables of Planetary Phenomena

Tables of
Planetary Phenomena

Third Edition

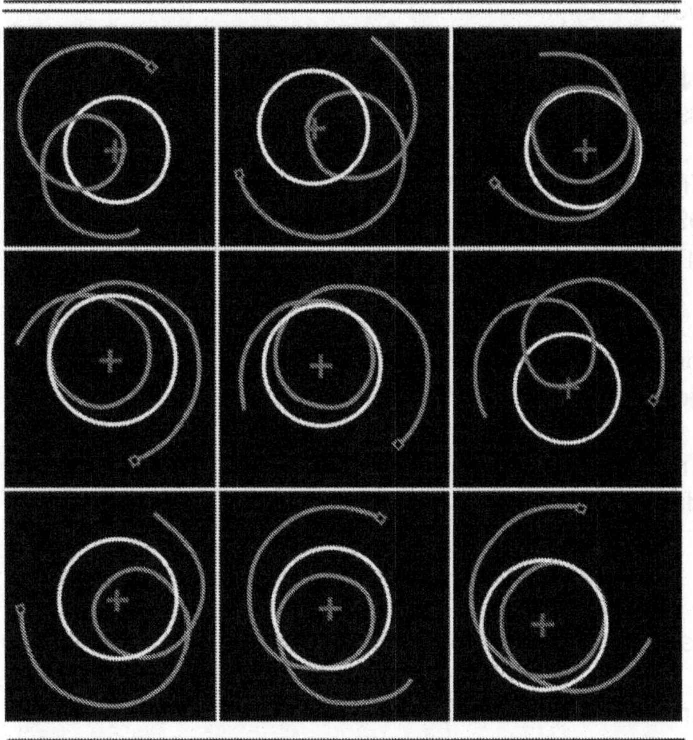

Neil F. Michelsen

Revisions by Rique Pottenger

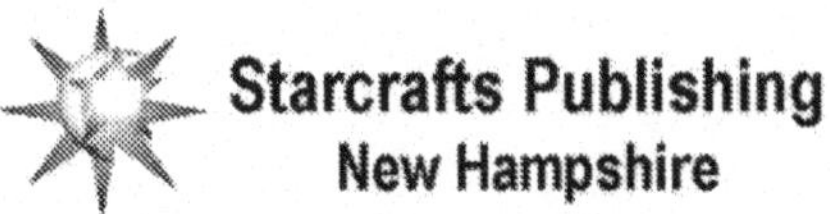

TABLES OF PLANETARY PHENOMENA

THIRD EDITION
First printing 2007

FIRST EDITION (published by ACS Publications)
First printing 1990

SECOND EDITION REVISED 1995
First printing 1995
Second printing 2003

Compiled and programmed by Neil F. Michelsen
Revisions by Rique Pottenger

Cover Design and Illustrations by Maria Kay Simms
Planetary Mandalas by Neil F. Michelsen

International Standard Book Number: 978-0-9762422-4-6

Library of Congress Control Number: 2007932721

Published by Starcrafts Publishing, Starcrafts LLC
PO Box 446, Exeter, NH 03833-0446
http://www.starcraftspublishing.com

Printed in the United States of America

In Memoriam

Neil F. Michelsen

May 11, 1931 —May 15, 1990

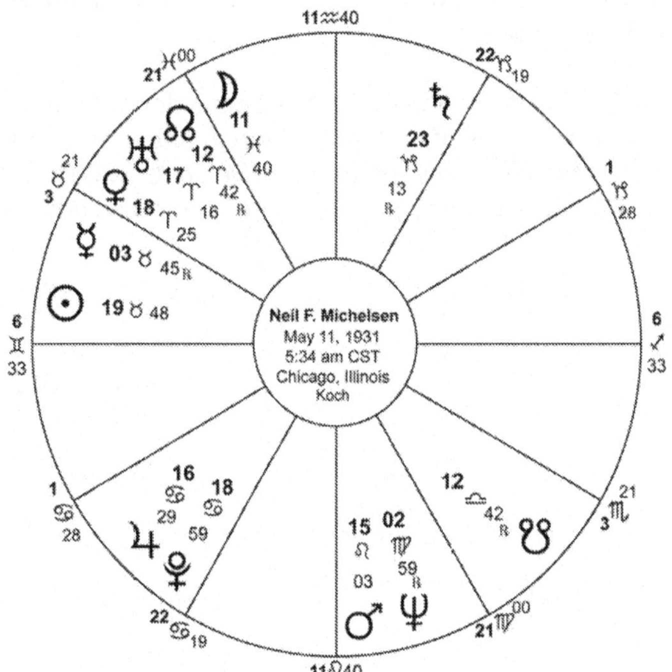

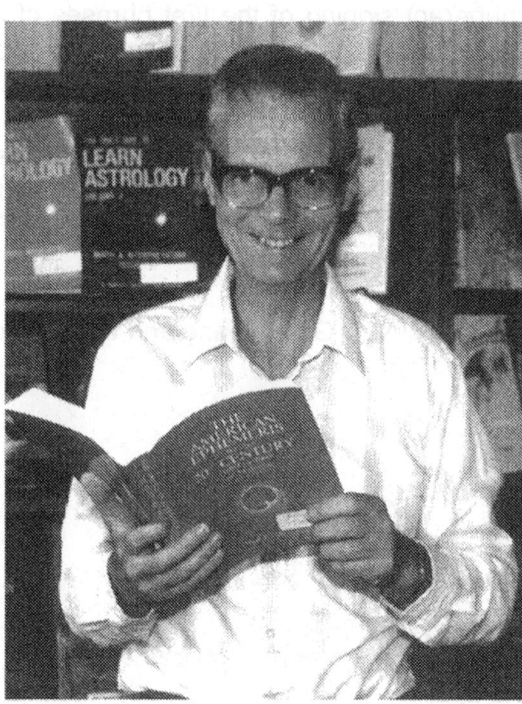

Neil dictated his final article for this book on the evening of his birthday May 11,1990, just a few days before he left this life. He had not yet completed what he had intended to write for this page, the acknowledgments of those who had assisted him in the completion of this work. And so, instead this page became the space that his staff at ACS Publications used to acknowledge him for his numerous contributions. Even though this book is now being republished by The Michelsen-Simms Family Trust- and many of those who signed the original acknowledgment article have gone their separate ways, their tribute is repeated here, both because of their contributions to the original publication of this work and also for the benefit of new readers' understanding of the history.

Neil F. Michelsen was a man of science. With his degree in mathematics and his incredible programming skills, he was one of the greatest technicians of our field. He defined accuracy in many astrological calculations. From the Astro Computing Natal Charts to his continually refined and enhanced ephemerides and books of tables, he insisted upon the highest degree of accuracy possible. Other programmers in astrology measured themselves against the standards set by Neil. His reference books are simply the best available.

Yet Neil F. Michelsen was, above all, a man of tremendous love and compassion. Everyone knows he had a soft heart that could be counted upon to contribute to a number of people, causes and ideals.

ideals. He gave computer time, technical expertise, money, his personal time, encouragement and caring to many astrologers, wholistic health practitioners, dowsers, new age philosophers, psychics and people in all walks of life. He was always ready to listen and ready to give assistance. He had friends all over the world who will miss his caring, support and concern as much as his incredible gifts to the world of astrology.

Neil's strong love of family and friends extended to his staff, whom he treated like family. Always eager to help in any way possible, he guided and inspired our individual growth, as well as the integrity of his business as a whole, and cheered us on when we made progress. How we will miss his exhuberant signing of the first phrases of Handel's "The Hallelujah Chorus" that rang through our building whenever something especially good had just happened!

This book, *Tables of Planetary Phenomena*, is Neil's last reference work. Amid considerable pain in his final days, he labored to finish the articles and tables. *Tables of Planetary Phenomena* is an enduring memorial to Neil. Although it is his final book, it embodies his incredible creative spirit and drive to contribute to the world. The legacy of Neil F. Michelsen will continue to enrich people the world over for many, many years ahead.

Thank you, Neil. Go in peace and with our love.

—The ACS Staff.

Table of Contents

General Information about the Tables 1

Part 1: Potpourri
Do We Know Where the Planets Really Are?
Article: *Where are Uranus, Neptune and Pluto?* 4
How Many Different Kinds of Stations Can a Planet Have?
Article: *More Stations Than You Ever Knew About!* 6
Table: *Mercury Stations in 8 Coordinate Systems 1990-1999* 7
What Causes the Seasons?
Article: *Cardinal Ingresses of the Sun* 9
Table: *Equinoxes and Solstices* 9

Part 2: The Sun is Not the Center of the Solar System!
Articles:
The Sun is Retrograde? Yes! 14
Where is the Center of the Solar System? 16
Table: *Center of Mass Distance from the Sun's Center and Aspects to Heliocentric Jupiter* 18

Part 3: Eclipses
Article: *Eclipses* 22
Tables:
Solar and Lunar Eclipses 1700-2050 23
Solar and Lunar Eclipses in Zodiacal Order 1700-2050 30
Solar Annular and Total Eclipses in Sequence by Maximum Duration 38

Part 4: Planetary Distances
Planetary Distances from Sun
Article: *Planetary Distance* 42
Tables:
Earth Perihelion/Aphelion 1837-2020 43
Mars and the Outer Planets in Perihelion and Aphelion 1700-2050 44
Moon Distance from Earth
Table: *Moon Perigee/Apogee 1900-2020* 46

Part 5: Ingresses
Article: *Ingresses* 56
by Maritha Pottenger & Zipporah Dobyns
Tables:
Chiron Ingresses 1900-2020 57
Ceres Ingresses 1900-2020 57
Pallas Ingresses 1990-2020 58
Vesta Ingresses 1900-2020 59
Pluto Ingresses 501 BC-2100 63
Neptune Ingresses 501 BC-2100 64
Uranus Ingresses 501 BC-2100 66
Saturn Ingresses 501 BC-2100 69
Jupiter Ingresses 501 BC-2100 75

Part 6: Outer Planet Phenomena

Article: *Outer Planet Phenomena—A Commentary on the Tables* 88
by David Dukelow
Tables:
Outer Planet Conjunctions 501 BC-2100 90
♃ ♄ ♅ ♆ ♇ *0°, 45°, 90°, 120°, 135° and 180° aspects 1700-2050* 94
♂ ♃ ♄ ♅ ♆ ♇ *0 Declination /Latitude 1700-2050* 104

Part 7: Planetary Stations

Article: *Planetary Stations in Longitude* 108
Tables: *Planetary Stations in Longitude 1700-2050* 109

Part 8: Planetary Clusters

Article: *Planetary Clusters* 128
Table: *5 or More Planets within 20° Arc 1700-2050* 129

Part 9: Moon Phases

Article: *The Lunar Cycle: An 8-Fold Cycle of Transformation* 152
by Maria Kay Simms
Table: *The 8 Phases of the Moon 1900-2020* 157

Part 10: High Energy Solar System Phenomena

Sunspots
Article: *Sunspots* 198
Tables:
Yearly Mean Sunspot Numbers 1700-1988 200
Daily Sunspot Numbers 1930-1989 201
Major Magnetic Storms: Ap 1932-1989*
Article: *Major Magnetic Storms Ap* 1932-1989* 216
Tables
Major Magnetic Storms: Ap 1932-1989 Summary* 217
Major Magnetic Storms: Ap 1932-1989* 217
Major Magnetic Storms: Ap 1932-1989 by Severity* 220

Part 11: Planetary Mandalas

Introduction 227
Graphs and Mandalas
Solar System Barycenter Plots at 20-year Intervals 1540-2040 229
Figures 1-24
Geocentric Planetary Orbits Showing Retrograde Motion 233
Figures 25-30
Planetary Mandalas using the Major Planets 234
Figures 31-48
One Planet as Viewed from Another 237
Figures 49-60
Planetary Mandalas involving the Asteroids 239
Figures 61-84
Planetary Mandalas involving the Uranian Planets 243

Part 12: Appendix

Planetary Patterns and the Dow Jones Industrial Average 246

General Information about the Tables

How Did This Book Come About?

I started Astro Computing Services in 1972 and even in that first year people would ask me for special calculations, services that sometimes were of general interest and sometimes were not. The general-interest requests became candidates for standard ACS reports.

I always had a problem on deciding how to handle narrow interest requests. Usually, I would quote some price significantly less than my time was worth because I wanted to be helpful to those in the astrological community working on special projects. Over the years, as my business grew, I had less and less time that I could devote to special projects so I had to turn down more and more such requests.

In the early 80s I contracted with Gary Duncan to start work on a Phenomena Program that would provide for the formulation of special requests using a generalized astronomical input language that would glue together a myriad of astronomical calculation routines that I and my co-workers had developed over the years. The language includes Boolean operators so that one can make conditional search requests —such as for the person who says "only give me the dates when the Sun is in Aries, Mars in Leo and Mercury retrograde."

The calculation functions include:
ARC—2 or more within a specific number of degrees
ASP—any arbitrary angle between 2 planets
POS—any body reaching a given position
STA —any body reaching a station
SHO—show the position of any body if another criteria is met
DST—distance from Sun or Earth
SGN—one or more bodies within a given sign

The positions could not only be in celestial longitude but in any one of 8 other measurements—geo latitude, declination, right ascension, radius vector, helio longitude, latitude, radius vector, and geocentric daily motion.

Gary started the Phenomena Program specifying syntax and Boolean structure but Rique Pottenger and I actually put the calculation flesh on the bare bones and enhanced its function significantly over the years.

Now ACS could handle special requests economically and not require my or Rique's special attention. But lo, many of the special requests were similar, so the idea for this book was born. Let's have astronomical data of general interest available in a reference book that, hopefully, will have broad appeal.

Calendar

The Gregorian calendar was instituted by Pope Gregory XIII in 1582 for regulating Easter and the ecclesiastical calendar. This reform of the Julian calendar had three parts:

1) to restore the vernal equinox to March 21, 10 days were omitted from the calendar so that the day after 1582 October 4 was 1582 October 15. The sequence of the days of the week was unchanged.

2) to adopt a different rule for leap year to correct the Julian calendar "drift" of about 3 days every four hundred years since the mean Julian year of 365.25 days exceeds the solar year by 11m 14s. Only the centurial years divisible by 400 have leap years, so 1700, 1800 and 1900 do not have leap years but the year 2000 will.

3) to fix rules for determining Easter in the new calendar.

The dates of adoption of the Gregorian calendar differ from country to country with predominately Catholic countries being the first.

Most of the tables in this book start no earlier than 1700. Those that start in the astronomical year -500, equivalent to 501 BC, use the Gregorian calendar for specifying dates of the phenomena even though that calendar did not come into existence until more than 1000 years later.

Time

The times listed in every table except the eclipse tables are based on the Greenwich meridian, time zone 0, and are for Ephemeris Time (ET) , not Universal Time (UT). The eclipse tables were calculated for Universal Time.

Both sidereal time and Universal Time depend upon the rotation of the Earth on its axis. It wasn't until the 20th century that astronomers discovered that this rotation is not uniform and that in the current time period the Earth's rotation is slowing down. This results in the practice of adding "leap seconds" to our civil clock to keep equal intervals of sidereal time corresponding to equal intervals of angular motion of the Earth on its axis. Since sidereal and Universal Time are not uniform, they are not suitable to be used in determining the position of the planets.

Starting in 1960, the uniform measure of time used by astronomers was called Ephemeris Time. It was determined by the dynamical theories of the laws of motion of bodies in the solar system. Since 1984, a refinement based on atomic clocks, called dynamical time has been used replacing Ephemeris Time. Dynamical time is actually a "family" of time scales beyond the scope of this introduction to define.

Accuracy of Tables

The planetary positions used to calculate the tables in this book are based on the Jet Propulsion Laboratories (JPL) export ephemerides identified as DE200/LE200. The ephemerides were calculated by a simultaneous numerical integration of the Sun, Moon, Mercury thru Pluto, Ceres, Pallas, Vesta, Iris and Bamberga and the librational motion of the Moon. The XYZ coordinates are aligned with the equator and equinox of J2000.0.

The reduction of the XYZ's to apparent positions used by astrologers, as well as astronomers, is given in the *Astronomical Almanac* on pages B36 through B38. After implementing these procedures on my computer, I compared my results to those printed in the *Astronomical Almanac*. My results agreed with the almanac results to the last decimal in all but a few cases. Further examination showed that when my result differed by one unit in the least significant digit, that next non-printed digit was within one unit of the almanac result considering rounding/truncation.

However, the accuracy of the JPL theory for Uranus, Neptune and Pluto as compared to observation is discussed in the next article entitled "Where Are Uranus, Neptune and Pluto?"

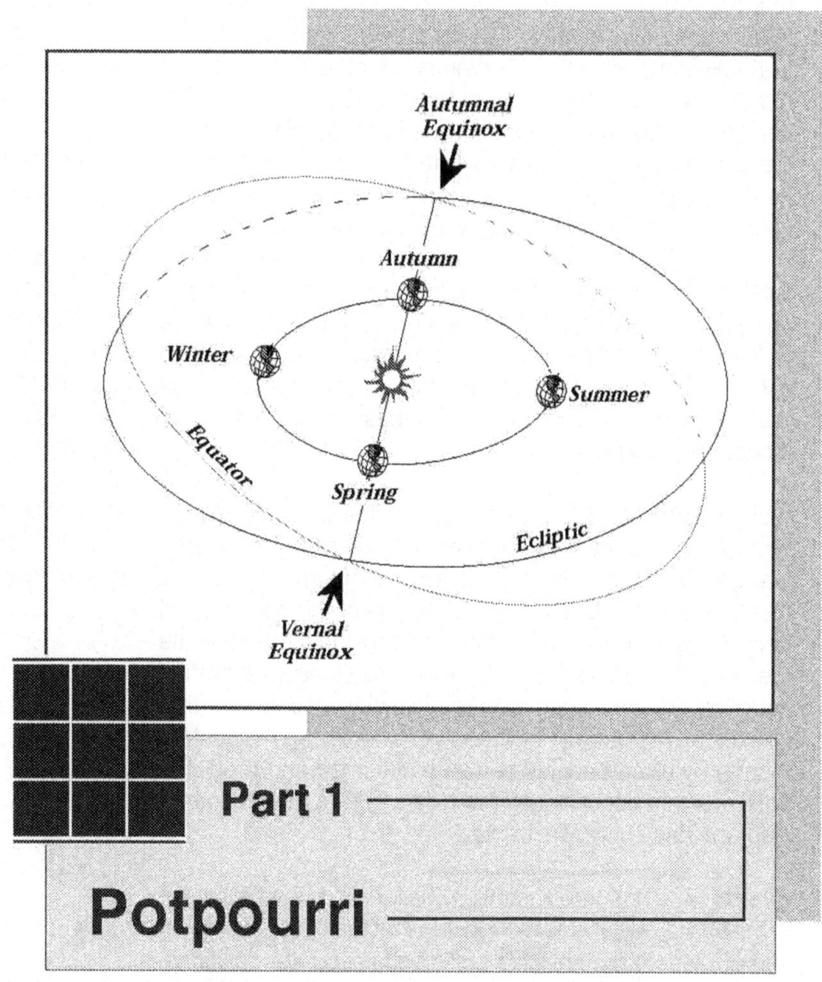

Part 1

Potpourri

- *Do We Know Where the Planets Really Are?*
- *How Many Different Kinds of Stations Can a Planet Have?*
- *What Causes the Seasons?*

Where Are Uranus, Neptune and Pluto?

Neptune was discovered with a telescope on September 23, 1846, by two astronomers, Galle and d'Arrest, at the Berlin Observatory using the predicted position calculated by Urbain Jean Joseph Leverrier. This discovery was made on the very first night of their search!

Simultaneously, as Leverrier, in France, was calculating the theoretical orbit of the planet perturbing the orbit of Uranus, John Couch Adams, in England, was using a different mathematical approach to solving the same problem. Both men had great difficulty persuading the astronomers in their respective countries to search for this planet with their telescopes. Since the actual discovery was made by astronomers at the Berlin Observatory, it is clear that Leverrier, out of frustration, had to go outside his country to find an astronomer willing to do this. Adams actually had his theoretical position calculated a little ahead of Leverrier, but he encountered the same lack of cooperation in England. Later both men were credited with Neptune's discovery.

Isn't it interesting that the astronomers who actually observed the planet for the first time in their telescope are known only to historians? Isn't it astounding that these astronomers found Neptune on the very first night of their search! Would that Neptune was so easy to keep track of in its post-discovery years!

A planetary theory is a series of equations/formulas that can be used to predict both the past and future positions of a planet. Obviously, the foundation in constructing such a theory is the actual observed positions of the body over a period of time. The longer the time period, the more accurate the theory tends to be. However, Neptune has baffled astronomers who specialize in celestial mechanics (that branch of astronomy that concerns itself with planetary theory) by discrepancies between observed and predicted positions that occur only a few years after a new theory of Neptune has been constructed.

Even today, Neptune presents a challenge. In the beginning of the space age, it was recognized that the optical observation of planets did not give sufficiently accurate positions, particularly in regard to distance, to adequately plan interplanetary space missions.

The Jet Propulsion Laboratory (JPL) in Pasadena, California, was and is in the forefront of mission planning. They use radar ranging data and information from space flybys to continually refine the planetary theories of the bodies in our solar system. However, when the ephemerides they constructed were compared to observational data, some uncorrectable problems showed up. For example, it is not possible to fit all the observational data of Uranus without a systematic difference between the ephemerides and the observations. The Uranus ephemeris is based on observational data only from 1900 onward. It differs from the pre-1900 observational data by both a periodic and secular deviation. The cumulative effect of periodic perturbations is zero. However, a secular perturbation is a steady monotonic change that, no matter how small, becomes important over time.

Of course, there does not exist a full orbit of post-discovery positional data for either Neptune or Pluto. When all the post-discovery observations of Neptune are included in a theory, the observations tend to deviate about 10 years after the ephemeris calculation. The observational data for Pluto covers only about one quarter of the orbital period of that planet and can have mean errors of about 2 arc seconds. Therefore the accuracy of the Pluto ephemeris is limited and is less satisfactory with increasing time from this century.

In the Table on the opposite page are some examples of the discrepancies between the current JPL data which is used in the national ephemerides of both the United States and Great Britain compared with the theory of the outer planets it superseded contained in Vol. XXII of the *Astronomical Papers prepared for the use of the American Ephemeris and Nautical Almanac (APAE).*

While the absolute differences are not great except for Neptune, these differences in position have enormous consequences for the times of phenomena.

Discrepancies between JPL and APAE

	LONGITUDE			LATITUDE			SPEED	GEO DISTANCE
Jan 1, 1 BC 0h0m0s Ephemeris Time Gregorian								
JPL URN	352.3412	22 Pi 20	28	-0.7112	0-42	40.22	0.0257	20.21934937
V22 URN	352.3243	22 Pi 19	27	-0.7108	0-42	38.96	0.0257	20.22058497
DELTA	0.0169	1'	1"	-0.0004	0'	1"	0.0000	–0.00123560
JPL NEP	227.6026	17 Sc36	10	1.7188	1 43	7.80	0.0255	30.88945488
V22 NEP	227.7790	17 Sc46	44	1.7160	1 42	57.44	0.0257	30.89317661
DELTA	–0.1764	–10'	35"	0.0028	0'	10"	–0.0002	–0.00372173
JPL PLU	175.0406	25 Vi 2	26	17.3928	17 23	34.14	–0.0021	29.86300978
V22 PLU	175.0258	25 Vi 1	33	17.3927	17 23	33.66	–0.0020	29.86356108
DELTA	0.0148	0'	53"	0.0001	0'	0"	–0.0001	–0.00055130
Jan 1, 1700 0h0m0s Ephemeris Time Gregorian								
JPL URN	98.7193	8 Ca43	10	0.3621	0 21	43.70	–0.0434	17.81365543
V22 URN	98.7190	8 Ca43	9	0.3623	0 21	44.19	–0.0433	17.81377165
DELTA	0.0003	0'	1"	-0.0002	0'	1"	–0.0001	–0.00011622
JPL NEP	2.8167	2 Ar 49	0	–1.4885	–1 29	18.65	0.0106	29.98805000
V22 NEP	2.8122	2 Ar 48	44	–1.4886	–1 29	18.82	0.0106	29.98839073
DELTA	0.0045	0'	16"	0.0001	0'	0"	0.0000	–0.00034073
JPL PLU	130.7569	10 Le45	25	7.2477	7 14	51.56	–0.0199	36.00603030
V22 PLU	130.7552	10 Le45	19	7.2469	7 14	49.01	–0.0199	36.00636365
DELTA	0.0017	0'	6"	0.0008	0'	3"	0.0000	–0.00033335
Jan 1, 1800 0h0m0s Ephemeris Time Gregorian								
JPL URN	177.1267	27 Vi 7	36	0.7690	0 46	8.31	0.0003	18.04782372
V22 URN	177.1271	27 Vi 7	38	0.7690	0 46	8.39	0.0003	18.04780150
DELTA	–0.0004	0'	1"	0.0000	0'	0"	0.0000	0.00002222
JPL NEP	226.6224	16 Sc37	20	1.7471	1 44	49.61	0.0249	30.89087441
V22 NEP	226.6196	16 Sc37	11	1.7471	1 44	49.66	0.0250	30.89032745
DELTA	0.0028	0'	10"	0.0000	0'	0"	–0.0001	0.00054696
JPL PLU	331.4174	1 Pi 25	3	–12.1130	12 6	46.81	0.0191	41.52199307
V22 PLU	331.4163	1 Pi 24	59	–12.1126	12 6	45.49	0.0191	41.52156867
DELTA	0.0011	0'	4"	–0.0004	0'	1"	0.0000	0.00042440
Jan 1, 1900 0h0m0s Ephemeris Time Gregorian								
JPL URN	250.1392	10 Sg 8	21	0.0634	0 3	48.26	0.0552	19.83785646
V22 URN	250.1392	10 Sg 8	21	0.0633	0 3	48.05	0.0552	19.83783928
DELTA	0.0000	0'	0"	0.0001	0'	0"	0.0000	0.00001718
JPL NEP	85.2186	25 Ge13	7	–1.2996	–1 17	58.70	–0.0273	28.92020656
V22 NEP	85.2186	25 Ge13	7	–1.2996	–1 17	58.62	–0.0272	28.92015623
DELTA	0.0000	0'	0"	0.0000	0'	0"	–0.0001	0.00005033
JPL PLU	75.2518	15 Ge15	6	–9.7767	–9 46	36.07	–0.0173	46.07954639
V22 PLU	75.2517	15 Ge15	6	–9.7768	–9 46	36.41	–0.0173	46.07939868
DELTA	0.0001	0'	0"	0.0001	0'	0"	0.0000	0.00014771
Jan 1, 2000 0h0m0s Ephemeris Time Gregorian								
JPL URN	314.7841	14 Aq47	3	–0.6584	0-39	30.39	0.0501	20.72221570
V22 URN	314.7829	14 Aq46	58	–0.6584	0-39	30.10	0.0502	20.72225939
DELTA	0.0012	0'	4"	0.0000	0'	0"	–0.0001	–0.00004369
JPL NEP	303.1754	3 Aq10	32	0.2351	0 14	6.42	0.0355	31.02103619
V22 NEP	303.1790	3 Aq10	44	0.2350	0 14	5.96	0.0355	31.02014411
DELTA	–0.0036	0'	13"	0.0001	0'	0"	0.0000	0.00089208
JPL PLU	251.4362	11 Sg26	10	10.8546	10 51	16.52	0.0352	31.06888015
V22 PLU	251.4351	11 Sg26	6	10.8548	10 51	17.26	0.0352	31.06899656
DELTA	0.0011	0'	4"	–0.0002	0'	1"	0.0000	–0.00011641

More Stations Than You Ever Knew About!

I'm not talking about radio or TV stations but stations such as those in longitude when a planet is about to go either direct or retrograde—the familiar stations used by all astrologers. A planet has a position in several different coordinate systems summarized in the following table:

Heliocentric	Geocentric	Equatorial
longitude latitude radius vector (distance from Sun)	longitude latitude radius vector (distance from Earth)	right ascension declination radius vector (same as geocentric)

At a given instant of time, the three coordinates in each system fix a body in space. In addition, each coordinate has a speed or velocity component since the body is moving through space over time. When the velocity in geocentric longitude of a planet is zero, we say the planet is at a station—for that instant it is not moving forward or backward in the ecliptic plane as seen from the Earth.

Since each of the other coordinates has a velocity component, each coordinate has stations! Since the radius vector in the geocentric longitude/latitude system is the same as that of the equatorial system, we have a total of eight coordinates that can have stations in velocity.

The station in heliocentric latitude/declination occurs when a planet has reached a maximum distance north/south of the ecliptic/equator and is about to change direction to start moving toward the ecliptic/equator. Geocentric stations can also occur at times other than when a planet has reached its maximum distance in latitude/declination.

The station in radius vector occurs when a planet has reached its maximum distance from the Sun/Earth and is about to start moving closer again. A station in radius vector also occurs when the planet has moved as close to the Sun/Earth as it can in its orbit and is about to start moving further away.

The elliptical motion of a planet about the Sun is always counterclockwise and, while the velocity is faster when the planet is closer to the Sun and slower when farther away (one of the laws of motion discovered by Kepler), the velocity is never zero. Therefore, a planet cannot have a station in heliocentric longitude analogous to a station in geocentric longitude. So our original eight is reduced by one to seven coordinates that can have stations.

I do want to add one more station in what is called a planet's geocentric daily motion. A planet moving in geocentric longitude will move from its station to a maximum velocity, either direct or retrograde. From that instant it will start slowing down until it is at its next station, when it starts accelerating again to its maximum velocity in longitude. The station in geocentric daily motion is that instant when the planet has reached its maximum velocity, either direct or retrograde, and is about to slow down.

Each of the other coordinates has velocity stations—when the rate of change in their motion is zero—but we won't present or use them in the report that follows.

The abbreviations used in this report are:

Description	Abbr.	Example from report
Stationary Direct	D	see Geocentric latitude example
Stationary Retrograde	℞	see Declination example
Geocentric longitude	GLon	1990 Jan 20 4:33 GLon 9♑42 D
Heliocentric longitude	HLon	does not occur
Right Ascension	RAsc	1990 Jan 20 2:47 RAsc 18h41 D
Geocentric latitude	GLat	1990 Aug31 19:27 GLat 4S29 D
Heliocentric latitude	HLat	1990 Jun 5 6:55 HLat 7S00 D
Declination	Decl	1990 Jul 1 10:55 Decl 24N22 ℞
Geocentric radius vector	Grv	1990 Jul 4 6:31 Grv 1.32906
Heliocentric radius vector	Hrv	1990 Aug11 23:14 Hrv 0.46670
Geocentric daily motion	Gdm	1990 Sep 7 9:53 Gdm –0.98970

When a station in latitude/declination is listed, with an "℞" it means that the planet has been moving in a northerly direction, has reached its farthest north position and is about to change direction and "retrograde" to the south. Motion to the north is "direct," to the south is "retrograde."

Stations in radius vector and geocentric daily motion are not shown with a "D" or "℞". The decimal number listed after "Grv" or "Hrv" is the distance in astronomical units (AUs) where 1.0 is the distance from the Earth to the Sun. Since our table has only Mercury stations, the Hrv will always be between .30 and .467—Mercury is the closest planet to the Sun. The number after "Gdm" is the instantaneous speed in degrees per day. At maximum speed in direct motion the number will be positive, of course. When the planet is moving retrograde, the maximum motion will be listed as negative, since its motion is "backwards" at that time.

This report about stations is presented so astrologers can investigate whether there is value in using this additional information in natal, horary, mundane, predictive, etc., work.

Mercury Stations in 8 Coordinate Systems 1990–1999

Year	Month	Day	Time	System	Value	Motion
1990	Jan	4	1:04	Hrv	.30750	
		9	8:10	Gdm	-1.34144	
		9	23:26	Grv	.66941	
		10	4:31	Decl	19S18	℞
		14	5:48	GLat	3N24	℞
		14	6:37	HLat	7N00	℞
		20	2:47	RAsc	18h41	D
		20	4:33	GLon	9♑42	D
	Feb	3	13:54	Decl	21S33	D
		17	0:43	Hrv	.46670	
	Mar	5	10:49	GLat	2S10	D
		9	7:40	HLat	7S00	D
		12	21:23	Grv	1.36679	
		25	0:39	Gdm	2.02568	
	Apr	2	0:19	Hrv	.30750	
		12	5:52	HLat	7N00	℞
		18	12:29	GLat	2N58	℞
		21	6:36	Decl	19N47	℞
		23	6:55	GLon	17♉32	℞
		23	15:22	RAsc	2h57	℞
	May	4	14:33	Gdm	-.63591	
		6	10:54	Grv	.55769	
		15	23:59	Hrv	.46670	
		16	6:52	RAsc	2h26	D
		17	2:03	GLon	7♉55	D
		21	0:28	Decl	11N11	D
		27	11:45	GLat	3S38	D
	Jun	5	6:55	HLat	7S00	D
		28	23:38	Hrv	.30750	
	Jul	1	4:45	Gdm	2.18138	
		1	10:55	Decl	24N22	℞
		4	6:31	Grv	1.32906	
		9	5:08	HLat	7N00	℞
		12	3:50	GLat	1N51	℞
	Aug	11	23:14	Hrv	.46670	
		24	23:50	RAsc	11h30	℞
		25	14:09	GLon	23♍34	℞
		27	17:38	Decl	1S17	D
		31	19:27	GLat	4S29	D
	Sep	1	6:11	HLat	7S00	D
		5	9:28	Grv	.63024	
		7	9:53	Gdm	-.98970	
		16	16:15	RAsc	10h43	D
		17	12:07	GLon	9♍35	D
		21	11:19	Decl	7N47	℞
		24	22:54	Hrv	.30750	
	Oct	5	0:04	GLat	1N55	℞
		5	4:24	HLat	7N00	℞
		10	2:04	Gdm	1.76328	
		28	19:01	Grv	1.43707	
	Nov	7	22:31	Hrv	.46670	
		28	5:27	HLat	7S00	D
		28	23:41	GLat	2S27	D
		30	16:21	Decl	25S52	D
	Dec	14	18:31	RAsc	18h44	℞
		14	21:09	GLon	10♑01	℞
		21	22:11	Hrv	.30750	
		24	10:27	Gdm	-1.37816	
		24	16:40	Grv	.67567	
		31	7:25	GLat	3N09	℞
		31	22:39	Decl	20S11	℞
1991	Jan	1	3:39	HLat	7N00	℞
		3	17:53	GLon	23♐42	D
		3	18:31	RAsc	17h33	D
		25	8:28	Decl	22S53	D
	Feb	3	21:46	Hrv	.46670	
		20	23:35	GLat	2S07	D
		22	16:15	Grv	1.38759	
		24	4:42	HLat	7S00	D
	Mar	9	18:25	Gdm	1.95199	
		19	21:26	Hrv	.30750	
		30	2:54	HLat	7N00	℞
	Apr	4	17:14	RAsc	1h43	℞
		4	18:10	GLon	29♈01	℞
		4	21:57	Decl	14N10	℞
		5	4:37	GLat	3N15	℞
		15	16:14	Gdm	-.74012	
		18	3:39	Grv	.57363	
		27	5:46	RAsc	1h08	D
		28	9:50	GLon	17♈59	D
	May	2	21:01	Hrv	.46670	
		3	4:34	Decl	5N12	D
		14	22:36	GLat	3S14	D
		23	3:57	HLat	7S00	D
	Jun	15	20:41	Hrv	.30750	
		16	16:43	Gdm	2.19925	
		17	16:45	Grv	1.32353	
		21	21:21	Decl	24N52	℞
		26	2:09	HLat	7N00	℞
		29	13:45	GLat	1N55	℞
	Jul	29	20:16	Hrv	.46670	
	Aug	7	3:54	RAsc	10h25	℞
		7	23:59	GLon	5♍55	℞
		11	16:04	Decl	5N28	D
		17	1:28	GLat	4S47	D
		18	16:22	Grv	.61091	
		19	3:12	HLat	7S00	D
		21	0:49	Gdm	-.87390	
		30	19:50	RAsc	9h39	D
		31	14:36	GLon	23♌03	D
	Sep	6	1:42	Decl	12N52	℞
		11	19:56	Hrv	.30750	
		22	1:25	HLat	7N00	℞
		22	7:57	GLat	1N51	℞
		24	2:42	Gdm	1.84775	
	Oct	11	6:32	Grv	1.42090	
		25	19:33	Hrv	.46669	
	Nov	15	2:27	HLat	7S00	D
		16	9:36	GLat	2S38	D
		21	7:25	Decl	25S35	D
		28	17:02	GLon	24♐12	℞
		28	18:26	RAsc	17h34	℞
	Dec	8	12:43	Grv	.67827	
		8	14:37	Gdm	-1.38517	
		8	19:12	Hrv	.30750	
		17	16:24	GLat	2N54	℞
		18	1:51	Decl	18S47	℞
		18	11:13	GLon	7♐55	D
		18	11:42	RAsc	16h27	D
		19	0:41	HLat	7N00	℞
1992	Jan	16	23:31	Decl	23S44	D
		21	18:48	Hrv	.46670	
	Feb	4	13:29	Grv	1.40906	
		8	11:42	GLat	2S05	D
		11	1:43	HLat	7S00	D
		22	4:36	Gdm	1.87026	
	Mar	5	18:27	Hrv	.30750	
		15	23:58	HLat	7N00	℞
		16	15:12	RAsc	0h37	℞
		17	0:33	GLon	11♈19	℞
		18	10:58	Decl	7N32	℞
		21	8:59	GLat	3N31	℞
		27	11:25	Gdm	-.86715	
		30	0:53	Grv	.59404	
	Apr	8	1:18	RAsc	23h55	D
		9	6:27	GLon	28♓44	D
		14	13:04	Decl	1S17	D
		18	18:04	Hrv	.46670	
	May	1	14:51	GLat	2S55	D
		9	0:58	HLat	7S00	D
		31	5:06	Grv	1.32184	
	Jun	1	4:40	Gdm	2.20186	
		1	17:42	Hrv	.30750	
		11	13:43	Decl	25N17	℞
		11	23:13	HLat	7N00	℞
		16	0:22	GLat	2N01	℞
	Jul	15	17:18	Hrv	.46670	
		19	3:28	RAsc	9h16	℞
		20	0:55	GLon	17♌29	℞
		26	5:48	Decl	11N47	D
		30	13:31	Grv	.59030	
	Aug	1	1:54	GLat	4S57	D
		2	1:03	Gdm	-.75883	
		5	0:13	HLat	7S00	D
		12	12:47	RAsc	8h30	D
		13	2:54	GLon	5♌58	D
		21	4:32	Decl	17N05	℞
		28	16:57	Hrv	.30750	
	Sep	7	14:45	Gdm	1.92976	
		7	22:28	HLat	7N00	℞
		8	15:60	GLat	1N48	℞
		22	13:00	Grv	1.40124	
	Oct	11	16:34	Hrv	.46670	
		31	23:27	HLat	7S00	D
	Nov	2	16:59	GLat	2S52	D
		7	19:38	Decl	24S13	D
		11	9:50	GLon	8♐23	℞
		11	14:02	RAsc	16h25	℞
		21	9:15	Grv	.67742	
		21	18:44	Gdm	-1.36401	
		24	16:13	Hrv	.30750	
	Dec	1	5:32	RAsc	15h22	D
		1	7:32	GLon	22♏12	D
		2	0:59	Decl	15S48	℞
		3	8:48	GLat	2N39	℞
		4	21:44	HLat	7N00	℞
1993	Jan	7	15:51	Hrv	.46669	
		7	17:39	Decl	24S20	D
		16	17:49	Grv	1.42822	
		25	23:23	GLat	2S05	D
		27	22:43	HLat	7S00	D
	Feb	5	3:16	Gdm	1.78443	
		20	15:29	Hrv	.30750	
		27	9:08	RAsc	23h34	℞
		27	22:55	GLon	24♓13	℞
	Mar	2	6:25	Decl	0N32	℞
		2	20:60	HLat	7N00	℞
		7	4:06	GLat	3N40	℞
		9	23:02	Gdm	-.99852	
		12	5:32	Grv	.61546	
		21	13:15	RAsc	22h46	D
		22	13:45	GLon	10♓17	D
		28	7:37	Decl	7S33	D
	Apr	5	15:06	Hrv	.46670	
		19	8:14	GLat	2S40	D
		25	21:59	HLat	7S00	D
	May	14	15:39	Grv	1.32396	
		17	16:11	Gdm	2.18900	
		19	14:44	Hrv	.30750	
		29	20:15	HLat	7N00	℞
	Jun	2	15:27	Decl	25N35	℞
		3	11:37	GLat	2N09	℞
		30	23:03	RAsc	8h00	℞
	Jul	1	15:30	GLon	28♋15	℞
		2	14:21	Hrv	.46670	
		12	4:05	Grv	.57089	
		13	1:10	Decl	16N41	D
		14	8:20	Gdm	-.65750	
		17	1:29	GLat	4S56	D
		22	21:14	HLat	7S00	D
		25	14:17	RAsc	7h16	D
		25	20:51	GLon	18♋09	D
	Aug	7	17:57	Decl	20N07	℞
		15	13:59	Hrv	.30750	
		23	11:14	Gdm	2.00512	
		25	19:30	HLat	7N00	℞
		27	0:12	GLat	1N46	℞
	Sep	4	16:40	Grv	1.38069	
		28	13:37	Hrv	.46670	
	Oct	18	20:30	HLat	7S00	D
		20	19:28	GLat	3S09	D
		24	5:43	Decl	21S18	D
		25	22:41	GLon	22♏31	℞
		26	3:25	RAsc	15h17	℞
	Nov	5	3:59	Grv	.67325	
		5	21:02	Gdm	-1.31712	
		11	13:15	Hrv	.30750	
		14	23:36	RAsc	14h20	D
		15	5:40	GLon	6♏32	D
		16	15:54	Decl	11S36	℞
		20	7:31	GLat	2N25	℞
		21	18:46	HLat	7N00	℞
	Dec	25	12:54	Hrv	.46670	
		30	5:15	Grv	1.44253	
		30	11:48	Decl	24S49	D
1994	Jan	13	10:54	GLat	2S07	D
		14	19:46	HLat	7S00	D
		19	10:46	Gdm	1.69913	
	Feb	7	12:33	Hrv	.30750	
		10	17:60	RAsc	22h34	℞
		11	8:31	GLon	7♓35	℞
		14	11:51	Decl	6S16	℞
		17	18:02	HLat	7N00	℞
		20	18:41	GLat	3N44	℞
		21	0:00	Gdm	-1.12013	
		22	19:33	Grv	.63521	
	Mar	4	12:25	RAsc	21h37	D
		5	5:50	GLon	22♒38	D
		11	17:23	Decl	13S02	D
		23	12:11	Hrv	.46670	
	Apr	7	0:56	GLat	2S28	D
		12	19:02	HLat	7S00	D
		27	20:17	Grv	1.33017	
	May	3	0:58	Gdm	2.16109	
		6	11:48	Hrv	.30750	
		16	17:18	HLat	7N00	℞
		21	23:03	GLat	2N19	℞
		24	23:13	Decl	25N37	℞
	Jun	12	12:22	RAsc	6h36	℞
		12	17:49	GLon	8♋25	℞
		19	11:26	Hrv	.46670	
		23	16:09	Grv	.55614	
		25	0:25	Gdm	-.58595	
	Jul	2	6:19	Decl	18N43	D
		2	6:51	GLat	4S44	D
		6	19:44	GLon	29♊25	D
		6	19:52	RAsc	5h58	D
		9	18:17	HLat	7S00	D
		27	11:22	Decl	22N01	℞
	Aug	2	11:04	Hrv	.30750	
		8	13:40	Gdm	2.07074	
		12	16:33	HLat	7N00	℞
		14	8:33	GLat	1N46	℞
		17	23:13	Grv	1.36172	
	Sep	15	10:42	Hrv	.46670	
	Oct	5	17:33	HLat	7S00	D
		7	14:06	GLat	3S30	D
		8	18:23	Decl	16S58	D
		9	6:45	GLon	6♏29	℞
		9	9:08	RAsc	14h12	℞
		19	18:37	Grv	.66571	
		20	19:37	Gdm	-1.24695	
		29	10:19	Hrv	.30750	
		29	17:05	RAsc	13h19	D
		30	4:07	GLon	20♎49	D
	Nov	1	3:59	Decl	6S34	℞
		7	10:41	GLat	2N14	℞
		8	15:49	HLat	7N00	℞
		27	4:52	Gdm	1.57396	
	Dec	7	19:48	Gdm	1.56896	
		12	9:58	Hrv	.46670	
		12	21:47	Grv	1.45030	
		22	6:20	Decl	25S13	D
		31	22:20	GLat	2S10	D
1995	Jan	1	13:03	Gdm	1.62041	
		1	16:49	HLat	7S00	D
		25	9:35	Hrv	.30750	
		25	12:29	RAsc	21h33	℞
		26	1:17	GLon	21♒16	℞
		30	7:45	Decl	12S23	℞

Mercury Stations in 8 Coordinate Systems 1990–1999

Month	Day	Time	System	Value	Station
Feb	4	11:03	Gdm	-1.22424	
	4	15:05	HLat	7N00	℞
	5	19:00	Grv	.65163	
	6	8:40	GLat	3N40	℞
	15	18:56	RAsc	20h30	D
	16	5:08	GLon	5♒37	D
	24	3:51	Decl	17S23	D
Mar	10	9:15	Hrv	.46670	
	25	16:24	GLat	2S19	D
	30	16:05	HLat	7S00	D
Apr	10	15:15	Grv	1.34087	
	18	7:03	Gdm	2.11861	
	23	8:53	Hrv	.30750	
May	3	14:21	HLat	7N00	℞
	9	9:21	GLat	2N32	℞
	14	18:43	Decl	24N51	℞
	24	9:03	GLon	18♊22	℞
	24	15:47	RAsc	5h09	℞
Jun	5	4:11	Grv	.54932	
	5	6:15	Gdm	-.55979	
	6	8:32	Hrv	.46670	
	17	6:13	RAsc	4h35	D
	17	6:59	GLon	9♊49	D
	17	18:59	Decl	17N37	D
	18	1:30	GLat	4S21	D
	26	15:21	HLat	7S00	D
Jul	17	10:11	Decl	23N12	℞
	20	8:09	Hrv	.30749	
	24	20:34	Gdm	2.12436	
	30	13:36	HLat	7N00	℞
	31	14:00	Grv	1.34602	
Aug	1	17:12	GLat	1N47	℞
Sep	2	7:47	Hrv	.46670	
	22	6:20	RAsc	13h09	℞
	22	9:16	GLon	20♎11	℞
	22	14:36	HLat	7S00	D
	22	20:32	Decl	11S28	D
	23	22:22	GLat	3S53	D
Oct	3	2:32	Grv	.65473	
	4	12:22	Gdm	-1.15725	
	13	9:04	RAsc	12h19	D
	14	0:48	GLon	5♎00	D
	16	7:24	Hrv	.30750	
	16	15:07	Decl	1S03	℞
	25	16:27	GLat	2N05	℞
	26	12:52	HLat	7N00	℞
Nov	6	15:10	Gdm	1.63674	
	25	16:51	Grv	1.45078	
	29	7:02	Hrv	.46670	
Dec	14	2:29	Decl	25S33	D
	19	9:45	GLat	2S15	D
	19	13:51	HLat	7S00	D
1996 Jan	9	12:26	RAsc	20h29	℞
	9	21:52	GLon	5♒10	℞
	12	6:40	Hrv	.30750	
	16	13:10	Decl	17S20	℞
	19	5:44	Gdm	-1.30551	
	20	2:45	Grv	.66409	
	22	12:07	HLat	7N00	℞
	23	1:24	GLat	3N31	℞
	30	6:02	RAsc	19h21	D
	30	10:18	GLon	19♑07	D
Feb	10	14:44	Decl	20S22	D
	25	6:19	Hrv	.46670	
Mar	12	6:38	GLat	2S13	D
	16	13:07	HLat	7S00	D
	22	22:37	Grv	1.35618	
Apr	2	8:48	Gdm	2.06274	
	9	5:56	Hrv	.30750	
	19	11:23	HLat	7N00	℞
	25	15:52	GLat	2N48	℞
	29	23:30	Decl	22N15	℞
May	3	22:41	GLon	28♉39	℞
	4	9:43	RAsc	3h44	℞
	15	10:50	Gdm	-.59182	
	16	17:07	Grv	.55204	
	23	5:36	Hrv	.46670	
	27	7:29	RAsc	3h13	D
	27	19:03	GLon	19♉39	D
	30	21:03	Decl	14N06	D
Jun	3	14:11	GLat	3S54	D
	12	12:23	HLat	7S00	D
Jul	6	5:13	Hrv	.30749	
	6	16:12	Decl	23N59	℞
	9	6:17	Gdm	2.16464	
	13	14:08	Grv	1.33415	
	16	10:39	HLat	7N00	℞
	19	2:12	GLat	1N49	℞
Aug	19	4:51	Hrv	.46670	
Sep	3	19:40	RAsc	12h06	℞
	4	5:48	GLon	3♎29	℞
	5	17:20	Decl	5S10	D
	8	11:38	HLat	7S00	D
	8	19:26	GLat	4S16	D
	15	1:37	Grv	.64018	
	16	20:57	Gdm	-1.05266	
	25	22:10	RAsc	11h19	D
	26	17:10	GLon	19♍00	D
	30	1:58	Decl	4N36	℞
Oct	2	4:27	Hrv	.30749	
	11	23:31	GLat	1N58	℞
	12	9:54	HLat	7N00	℞
	19	4:53	Gdm	1.71532	
Nov	7	11:21	Grv	1.44396	
	15	4:06	Hrv	.46670	
Dec	5	0:42	Decl	25S48	D
	5	10:53	HLat	7S00	D
	5	21:01	GLat	2S22	D
	23	14:34	RAsc	19h23	℞
	23	19:47	GLon	19♑14	℞
	29	3:43	Hrv	.30750	
1997 Jan	2	5:50	Gdm	-1.36038	
	2	17:13	Grv	.67252	
	6	20:04	Decl	20S02	℞
	7	23:20	GLat	3N18	℞
	8	9:09	HLat	7N00	℞
	12	20:17	RAsc	18h13	D
	12	20:42	GLon	2♑58	D
	30	2:16	Decl	22S11	D
Feb	11	3:21	Hrv	.46670	
	27	19:52	GLat	2S09	D
Mar	3	10:08	HLat	7S00	D
	4	20:38	Grv	1.37541	
	18	5:45	Gdm	1.99525	
	27	2:58	Hrv	.30750	
Apr	6	8:25	HLat	7N00	℞
	12	14:21	GLat	3N05	℞
	14	1:28	Decl	17N36	℞
	15	0:02	GLon	9♉39	℞
	15	4:48	RAsc	2h25	℞
	26	3:18	Gdm	-.67706	
	28	8:01	Grv	.56373	
May	7	18:11	RAsc	1h53	D
	8	18:06	GLon	29♈28	D
	10	2:38	Hrv	.46670	
	13	3:17	Decl	8N47	D
	21	18:52	GLat	3S28	D
	30	9:24	HLat	7S00	D
Jun	23	2:14	Hrv	.30750	
	24	17:38	Gdm	2.19051	
	26	21:37	Grv	1.32627	
	27	0:34	Decl	24N35	℞
Jul	3	7:41	HLat	7N00	℞
	6	11:44	GLat	1N52	℞
Aug	6	1:54	Hrv	.46670	
	17	2:42	RAsc	11h03	℞
	17	19:50	GLon	16♍14	℞
	20	13:11	Decl	1N34	D
	25	6:17	GLat	4S37	D
	26	8:40	HLat	7S00	D
	28	14:21	Grv	.62232	
	30	18:40	Gdm	-.93955	
Sep	9	5:50	RAsc	10h17	D
	10	1:44	GLon	2♍42	D
	14	14:02	Decl	10N00	℞
	19	1:30	Hrv	.30750	
	29	6:56	HLat	7N00	℞
	29	7:12	GLat	1N53	℞
Oct	2	21:19	Gdm	1.79967	
	21	1:48	Grv	1.43072	
Nov	2	1:09	Hrv	.46670	
	22	7:55	HLat	7S00	D
	23	7:44	GLat	2S31	D
	26	15:33	Decl	25S50	D
Dec	7	16:06	RAsc	18h15	℞
	7	16:57	GLon	3♑22	℞
	16	0:44	Hrv	.30750	
	17	9:10	Gdm	-1.38558	
	17	11:55	Grv	.67716	
	25	3:56	GLat	3N03	℞
	25	23:46	Decl	19S48	℞
	26	6:11	HLat	7N00	℞
	27	11:42	GLon	17♐04	D
	27	12:34	RAsc	17h05	D
1998 Jan	21	9:26	Decl	23S16	D
	29	0:23	Hrv	.46670	
Feb	14	15:33	Grv	1.39677	
	15	8:22	GLat	2S06	D
	18	7:10	HLat	7S00	D
Mar	2	20:31	Gdm	1.91832	
	14	0:00	Hrv	.30750	
	24	5:26	HLat	7N00	℞
	27	14:48	RAsc	1h14	℞
	27	19:43	GLon	21♈30	℞
	28	14:13	Decl	11N28	℞
	30	1:22	GLat	3N22	℞
Apr	7	13:13	Gdm	-.79366	
	10	2:35	Grv	.58189	
	19	2:11	RAsc	0h37	D
	20	7:32	GLon	9♈47	D
	25	7:54	Decl	2N30	D
	26	23:39	Hrv	.46670	
May	9	8:44	GLat	3S06	D
	17	6:25	HLat	7S00	D
Jun	9	23:20	Hrv	.30750	
	10	5:17	Gdm	2.20177	
	10	9:07	Grv	1.32229	
	17	13:03	Decl	25N03	℞
	20	4:42	HLat	7N00	℞
	23	21:54	GLat	1N57	℞
Jul	23	22:56	Hrv	.46669	
	30	5:11	RAsc	9h57	℞
	31	2:29	GLon	28♌16	℞
Aug	4	15:46	Decl	8N13	D
	10	9:32	GLat	4S52	D
	10	16:55	Grv	.60216	
	13	3:12	Gdm	-.82453	
	13	5:40	HLat	7S00	D
	23	5:17	RAsc	9h11	D
	23	22:36	GLon	15♌58	D
	30	7:54	Decl	14N45	℞
Sep	5	22:36	Hrv	.30750	
	16	3:58	HLat	7N00	℞
	16	15:08	GLat	1N49	℞
	17	4:04	Gdm	1.88363	
Oct	3	10:33	Grv	1.41280	
	19	22:12	Hrv	.46669	
Nov	9	4:56	HLat	7S00	D
	10	16:50	GLat	2S43	D
	16	1:05	Decl	25S11	D
	21	11:47	GLon	17♐33	℞
	21	14:34	RAsc	17h05	℞
Dec	1	8:35	Grv	.67831	
	1	13:44	Gdm	-1.38078	
	2	21:51	Hrv	.30750	
	11	6:11	RAsc	15h59	D
	11	6:31	GLon	1♐18	D
	11	10:35	Decl	17S42	℞
	11	16:07	GLat	2N47	℞
	13	3:13	HLat	7N00	℞
1999 Jan	13	2:44	Decl	24S00	D
	15	21:27	Hrv	.46670	
	27	14:48	Grv	1.41761	
Feb	2	20:21	GLat	2S05	D
	5	4:12	HLat	7S00	D
	15	2:58	Gdm	1.83453	
	28	21:06	Hrv	.30750	
Mar	9	21:28	RAsc	0h10	℞
	10	9:12	GLon	4♈03	℞
	11	2:28	HLat	7N00	℞
	12	5:14	Decl	4N36	℞
	16	1:17	GLat	3N36	℞
	20	15:39	Gdm	-.92260	
	23	2:51	Grv	.60315	
Apr	1	5:44	RAsc	23h26	D
	2	9:20	GLon	20♓52	D
	7	20:05	Decl	3S58	D
	13	20:42	Hrv	.46670	
	27	1:52	GLat	2S48	D
May	4	3:27	HLat	7S00	D
	24	21:02	Grv	1.32218	
	26	16:40	Gdm	2.19792	
	27	20:21	Hrv	.30750	
Jun	7	1:44	HLat	7N00	℞
	8	9:01	Decl	25N25	℞
	11	8:45	GLat	2N04	℞
Jul	10	19:58	Hrv	.46670	
	12	3:21	RAsc	8h45	℞
	12	23:34	GLon	9♌29	℞
	20	21:04	Decl	14N05	D
	23	11:09	Grv	.58170	
	25	21:07	Gdm	-.71448	
	26	8:56	GLat	4S58	D
	31	2:43	HLat	7S00	D
Aug	5	16:19	RAsc	8h00	D
	6	3:28	GLon	28♋35	D
	15	21:41	Decl	18N30	℞
	23	19:39	Hrv	.30750	
Sep	1	20:37	Gdm	1.96278	
	3	1:00	HLat	7N00	℞
	3	23:14	GLat	1N47	℞
	15	15:05	Grv	1.39252	
Oct	6	19:16	Hrv	.46670	
	27	1:59	HLat	7S00	D
	28	22:32	GLat	2S59	D
Nov	2	11:06	Decl	23S11	D
	5	3:00	GLon	1♐44	℞
	5	7:45	RAsc	15h56	℞
	15	4:45	Grv	.67607	
	15	17:29	Gdm	-1.34726	
	19	18:55	Hrv	.30750	
	25	0:21	RAsc	14h56	D
	25	3:56	GLon	15♏37	D
	26	5:10	Decl	14S10	℞
	28	11:25	GLat	2N33	℞
	30	0:16	HLat	7N00	℞

Cardinal Ingresses of the Sun

The equinoxes and solstices mark the Sun's ingresses into the cardinal signs and the four seasons. The June and December solstices, when the day is longest and shortest in the northern hemisphere, respectively, represent a station when the increasing (or decreasing) daylight reaches its maximum (minimum) and the length of the day begins to decrease (increase) until the next solstice. There is more daylight at the June solstice in the northern hemisphere because the Sun is at its maximum north declination. So the day that has the longest period of daylight is also the day on which the Sun reaches its northern station and declination. The Sun can be directly overhead only as far north as the Tropic of Cancer.

The equinoxes in March and September mark the two days of the year when the length of the day is equal to the length of the night. This is also the time when the Sun is at 0 declination. Any body at 0 declination is on the celestial equator (the imaginary extension of the Earth's equator into space). The March equinox occurs at that instant when the Sun's path on the plane of the ecliptic intersects the celestial equator crossing from south to north. This intersection also defines the 0° Aries point. In September the Sun enters Libra when it is at 0 declination, this time crossing the celestial equator from north to south.

Each century, I summarize the shortest and longest of each of the four seasons, the average length of each season, and the earliest and latest starting times of each season.

Equinoxes and Solstices

Year	March Equinox		June Solstice		September Equinox		December Solstice	
1601	20	14:35:38	21	15:46:00	23	3:07:56	21	16:32:54
1602	20	20:21:58	21	21:34:20	23	8:56:58	21	22:19:56
1603	21	2:10:15	22	3:19:37	23	14:45:26	22	4:16:06
1604	20	8:04:38	21	9:11:04	22	20:37:01	21	10:07:08
1605	20	13:43:33	21	14:53:48	23	2:28:35	21	16:02:51
1606	20	19:36:53	21	20:50:39	23	8:20:11	21	21:57:15
1607	21	1:38:43	22	2:41:50	23	14:07:20	22	3:46:12
1608	20	7:25:51	21	8:18:36	22	19:57:02	21	9:41:12
1609	20	13:21:12	21	14:16:23	23	1:50:34	21	15:28:35
1610	20	19:09:53	21	20:08:49	23	7:35:07	21	21:15:37
1611	21	0:58:13	22	1:54:30	23	13:18:47	22	3:07:31
1612	20	6:51:06	21	7:45:45	22	19:08:44	21	8:51:40
1613	20	12:29:31	21	13:26:51	23	0:58:15	21	14:36:42
1614	20	18:15:54	21	19:18:04	23	6:48:19	21	20:24:06
1615	21	0:09:04	22	1:06:52	23	12:34:31	22	2:12:40
1616	20	5:47:17	21	6:38:07	22	18:19:02	21	8:06:02
1617	20	11:33:51	21	12:30:01	23	0:10:40	21	13:55:43
1618	20	17:24:10	21	18:19:36	23	5:54:19	21	19:42:27
1619	20	23:15:05	21	23:59:47	23	11:37:01	22	1:32:35
1620	20	5:10:58	21	5:52:17	22	17:29:50	21	7:20:24
1621	20	10:54:17	21	11:38:46	22	23:19:11	21	13:09:08
1622	20	16:41:49	21	17:34:02	23	5:08:52	21	19:00:55
1623	20	22:38:56	21	23:30:10	23	10:59:09	22	0:53:57
1624	20	4:23:33	21	5:05:57	22	16:46:36	21	6:44:15
1625	20	10:12:44	21	11:00:26	22	22:44:45	21	12:33:53
1626	20	16:07:07	21	16:55:30	23	4:35:05	21	18:22:32
1627	20	21:55:50	21	22:35:50	23	10:18:42	22	0:15:57
1628	20	3:47:10	21	4:28:46	22	16:13:26	21	6:09:59
1629	20	9:30:47	21	10:14:07	22	22:00:21	21	11:59:20
1630	20	15:19:33	21	16:03:52	23	3:47:04	21	17:48:46
1631	20	21:18:49	21	21:56:23	23	9:36:15	21	23:38:09
1632	20	3:04:30	21	3:30:35	22	15:19:49	21	5:24:28
1633	20	8:50:09	21	9:23:17	22	21:12:42	21	11:12:16
1634	20	14:39:29	21	15:18:16	23	2:57:47	21	16:58:47
1635	20	20:25:17	21	20:56:10	23	8:35:29	21	22:45:36
1636	20	2:12:34	21	2:45:51	22	14:29:55	21	4:33:24
1637	20	7:55:05	21	8:30:40	22	20:18:31	21	10:17:17
1638	20	13:40:14	21	14:17:26	23	2:06:39	21	16:05:58
1639	20	19:32:57	21	20:09:13	23	7:58:22	21	22:01:15
1640	20	1:16:18	21	1:43:57	22	13:42:21	21	3:54:35
1641	20	7:04:08	21	7:35:21	22	19:36:20	21	9:47:44
1642	20	13:00:22	21	13:32:05	23	1:25:44	21	15:39:36
1643	20	18:57:54	21	19:13:23	23	7:07:04	21	21:28:29
1644	20	0:51:56	21	1:07:35	22	13:04:58	21	3:21:08
1645	20	6:40:57	21	7:02:00	22	18:55:29	21	9:10:24
1646	20	12:29:34	21	12:53:41	23	0:40:58	21	14:58:36
1647	20	18:23:04	21	18:50:05	23	6:34:55	21	20:52:49
1648	20	0:09:35	21	0:28:07	22	12:20:32	21	2:38:18
1649	20	5:53:50	21	6:16:28	22	18:15:26	21	8:24:25
1650	20	11:43:29	21	12:11:07	23	0:06:47	21	14:15:00
1651	20	17:31:42	21	17:46:46	23	5:43:39	21	20:02:18
1652	19	23:14:15	20	23:32:24	22	11:36:21	21	1:55:32
1653	20	4:58:40	21	5:20:14	22	17:22:52	21	7:44:23
1654	20	10:47:09	21	11:02:56	22	23:02:07	21	13:27:27
1655	20	16:40:56	21	16:53:37	23	4:54:45	21	19:21:15
1656	19	22:30:40	20	22:32:16	22	10:37:41	21	1:06:20
1657	20	4:14:37	21	4:21:24	22	16:27:43	21	6:53:47
1658	20	10:05:37	21	10:21:45	22	22:19:56	21	12:47:33
1659	20	15:58:43	21	16:02:59	23	3:58:00	21	18:33:13
1660	19	21:45:36	20	21:52:43	22	9:56:26	21	0:24:54
1661	20	3:34:00	21	3:46:46	22	15:51:49	21	6:15:06
1662	20	9:24:53	21	9:34:39	22	21:37:13	21	12:01:55
1663	20	15:15:55	21	15:28:10	23	3:34:34	21	18:03:04
1664	19	21:04:42	20	21:10:33	22	9:21:36	20	23:56:02
1665	20	2:52:01	21	2:58:28	22	15:11:44	21	5:45:20
1666	20	8:45:24	21	8:55:35	22	21:05:48	21	11:39:38
1667	20	14:43:50	21	14:35:46	23	2:42:54	21	17:23:14
1668	19	20:30:29	20	20:22:13	22	8:36:20	20	23:12:40
1669	20	2:14:32	21	2:15:44	22	14:26:14	21	5:02:22
1670	20	8:02:40	21	8:01:38	22	20:03:39	21	10:43:41
1671	20	13:48:34	21	13:49:23	23	1:54:42	21	16:35:49
1672	19	19:33:45	20	19:28:36	22	7:39:59	20	22:21:04
1673	20	1:18:55	21	1:12:27	22	13:27:52	21	4:02:10
1674	20	7:04:01	21	7:05:53	22	19:22:11	21	9:56:51
1675	20	12:57:27	21	12:46:32	23	0:59:20	21	15:44:51
1676	19	18:40:47	20	18:30:12	22	6:51:09	20	21:37:46
1677	20	0:26:50	21	0:24:33	22	12:45:06	21	3:33:19
1678	20	6:24:32	21	6:12:51	22	18:25:30	21	9:15:59
1679	20	12:18:16	21	12:04:07	23	0:21:57	21	15:12:55
1680	19	18:10:55	20	17:52:49	22	6:13:20	20	21:05:36
1681	20	0:00:55	20	23:44:44	22	12:02:15	21	2:51:03
1682	20	5:49:01	21	5:44:33	22	17:59:28	21	8:49:11
1683	20	11:46:50	21	11:30:26	22	23:40:17	21	14:35:33
1684	19	17:32:19	20	17:14:17	22	5:33:54	20	20:22:24
1685	19	23:15:31	20	23:07:29	22	11:32:10	21	2:15:56
1686	20	5:07:53	21	4:53:14	22	17:10:42	21	7:56:54
1687	20	10:51:40	21	10:36:53	22	23:01:26	21	13:54:49
1688	19	16:37:00	20	16:18:31	22	4:48:04	20	19:47:29
1689	19	22:24:45	20	22:01:55	22	10:29:08	21	1:27:42
1690	20	4:12:47	21	3:53:44	22	16:21:48	21	7:21:03
1691	20	10:11:33	21	9:36:34	22	21:59:29	21	13:04:50
1692	19	15:57:20	20	15:20:11	22	3:47:25	20	18:49:42
1693	19	21:37:28	20	21:15:08	22	9:42:22	21	0:44:01
1694	20	3:31:19	21	3:06:22	22	15:20:38	21	6:24:46
1695	20	9:17:53	21	8:52:32	22	21:12:54	21	12:18:14
1696	19	15:03:58	20	14:38:37	22	3:08:29	20	18:11:22

Equinoxes and Solstices

Year	March Equinox		June Solstice		September Equinox		December Solstice	
1697	19	20:55:51	20	20:27:55	22	8:57:21	20	23:53:17
1698	20	2:41:41	21	2:21:24	22	14:55:33	21	5:53:22
1699	20	8:38:30	21	8:08:03	22	20:39:00	21	11:48:02
1700	20	14:27:05	21	13:52:36	23	2:28:44	21	17:38:11

	Year	Shortest	Year	Longest	Mean	Year	Earliest	Year	Latest
Spring	1692	92.9742	1606	93.0512	93.0129	1697	79.8721	1604	81.3365
Summer	1601	93.4736	1700	93.5251	93.4983	1697	172.8527	1604	174.3827
Fall	1602	89.5576	1700	89.6316	89.5966	1697	266.3732	1604	267.8590
Winter	1689	89.1092	1603	89.1599	89.1350	1697	355.9953	1604	357.4216

Year	March Equinox		June Solstice		September Equinox		December Solstice	
1701	20	20:10:46	21	19:45:56	23	8:25:55	21	23:36:06
1702	21	2:12:46	22	1:37:42	23	14:06:43	22	5:19:02
1703	21	8:05:11	22	7:22:07	23	19:55:59	22	11:10:06
1704	20	13:49:47	21	13:08:35	23	1:48:32	21	17:04:46
1705	20	19:42:24	21	19:00:39	23	7:31:08	21	22:43:43
1706	21	1:24:53	22	0:51:03	23	13:21:52	22	4:36:35
1707	21	7:18:35	22	6:36:01	23	19:03:33	22	10:23:50
1708	20	13:04:55	21	12:17:07	23	0:50:15	21	16:02:43
1709	20	18:41:18	21	18:05:58	23	6:47:04	21	21:55:49
1710	21	0:35:02	21	23:55:43	23	12:26:53	22	3:39:01
1711	21	6:19:36	22	5:36:38	23	18:13:16	22	9:32:08
1712	20	11:59:46	21	11:19:56	23	0:06:54	21	15:30:42
1713	20	17:55:13	21	17:10:41	23	5:50:53	21	21:11:29
1714	20	23:44:22	21	22:59:48	23	11:43:39	22	3:05:50
1715	21	5:43:23	22	4:47:58	23	17:30:30	22	8:59:08
1716	20	11:35:51	21	10:36:35	22	23:18:31	21	14:43:19
1717	20	17:15:51	21	16:31:14	23	5:16:39	21	20:41:48
1718	20	23:13:59	21	22:27:27	23	10:59:44	22	2:27:08
1719	21	5:04:18	22	4:12:17	23	16:48:33	22	8:17:18
1720	20	10:47:13	21	9:57:25	22	22:47:39	21	14:13:15
1721	20	16:42:07	21	15:50:21	23	4:35:07	21	19:54:13
1722	20	22:27:17	21	21:38:12	23	10:26:21	22	1:49:55
1723	21	4:18:09	22	3:22:11	23	16:11:20	22	7:46:31
1724	20	10:08:47	21	9:07:11	22	21:55:21	21	13:29:23
1725	20	15:48:16	21	14:53:40	23	3:47:24	21	19:22:08
1726	20	21:46:48	21	20:45:30	23	9:28:52	22	1:04:53
1727	21	3:38:40	22	2:28:29	23	15:12:29	22	6:49:48
1728	20	9:15:51	21	8:11:45	22	21:06:32	21	12:44:48
1729	20	15:08:06	21	14:07:08	23	2:50:57	21	18:25:22
1730	20	20:52:24	21	19:54:08	23	8:38:31	22	0:15:22
1731	21	2:41:17	22	1:37:19	23	14:26:23	22	6:08:41
1732	20	8:33:47	21	7:24:33	22	20:15:50	21	11:49:28
1733	20	14:11:36	21	13:10:53	23	2:10:58	21	17:43:29
1734	20	20:06:10	21	19:04:37	23	7:57:34	21	23:36:35
1735	21	1:59:30	22	0:49:52	23	13:42:45	22	5:27:54
1736	20	7:38:44	21	6:32:14	22	19:38:23	21	11:28:37
1737	20	13:39:43	21	12:30:52	23	1:27:49	21	17:13:55
1738	20	19:34:11	21	18:20:03	23	7:17:01	21	23:04:14
1739	21	1:27:50	22	0:06:47	23	13:06:56	22	5:01:09
1740	20	7:23:23	21	6:00:16	22	18:54:49	21	10:44:00
1741	20	13:02:02	21	11:49:31	23	0:45:49	21	16:35:37
1742	20	18:54:54	21	17:43:37	23	6:31:05	21	22:23:07
1743	21	0:47:12	21	23:28:48	23	12:15:53	22	4:05:38
1744	20	6:22:13	21	5:06:41	22	18:11:02	21	9:57:55
1745	20	12:13:17	21	11:00:33	23	0:00:16	21	15:41:01
1746	20	17:58:36	21	16:44:41	23	5:44:46	21	21:30:39
1747	20	23:42:09	21	22:22:45	23	11:30:39	22	3:28:49
1748	20	5:34:03	21	4:10:44	22	17:16:09	21	9:12:26
1749	20	11:15:53	21	9:54:24	22	23:04:28	21	15:02:27
1750	20	17:11:39	21	15:44:56	23	4:49:54	21	20:50:43
1751	20	23:08:27	21	21:33:42	23	10:34:20	22	2:37:11
1752	20	4:47:32	21	3:16:42	22	16:27:49	21	8:32:48
1753	20	10:40:58	21	9:17:23	22	22:19:15	21	14:20:22
1754	20	16:34:11	21	15:10:03	23	4:07:24	21	20:09:33
1755	20	22:22:30	21	20:51:50	23	9:58:54	22	2:05:58
1756	20	4:17:57	21	2:46:18	22	15:53:53	21	7:51:30
1757	20	10:00:56	21	8:33:51	22	21:45:46	21	13:42:42
1758	20	15:51:25	21	14:25:09	23	3:34:10	21	19:37:58
1759	20	21:46:52	21	20:14:28	23	9:19:38	22	1:28:16
1760	20	3:25:06	21	1:52:05	22	15:09:59	21	7:22:10
1761	20	9:19:24	21	7:47:36	22	21:00:39	21	13:08:03
1762	20	15:15:34	21	13:36:47	23	2:45:16	21	18:52:41

Year	March Equinox		June Solstice		September Equinox		December Solstice	
1763	20	21:00:53	21	19:13:59	23	8:29:52	22	0:45:53
1764	20	2:51:09	21	1:07:23	22	14:19:37	21	6:30:47
1765	20	8:30:59	21	6:53:06	22	20:03:32	21	12:15:08
1766	20	14:17:09	21	12:39:52	23	1:47:54	21	18:04:40
1767	20	20:12:04	21	18:28:02	23	7:34:06	21	23:48:29
1768	20	1:48:06	21	0:03:33	22	13:24:39	21	5:37:37
1769	20	7:37:23	21	5:59:20	22	19:18:32	21	11:27:39
1770	20	13:30:48	21	11:50:51	23	1:04:51	21	17:19:05
1771	20	19:16:03	21	17:28:12	23	6:51:02	21	23:18:16
1772	20	1:10:39	20	23:23:23	22	12:45:40	21	5:08:57
1773	20	7:01:48	21	5:14:00	22	18:34:59	21	10:56:37
1774	20	12:57:04	21	11:04:18	23	0:23:45	21	16:49:19
1775	20	18:56:24	21	17:00:25	23	6:14:38	21	22:40:08
1776	20	0:37:17	20	22:43:24	22	12:05:13	21	4:31:40
1777	20	6:26:21	21	4:41:29	22	17:58:54	21	10:21:12
1778	20	12:21:35	21	10:35:25	22	23:46:05	21	16:08:22
1779	20	18:06:18	21	16:09:24	23	5:31:41	21	21:59:03
1780	19	23:54:00	20	21:59:55	22	11:26:52	21	3:45:08
1781	20	5:37:39	21	3:46:42	22	17:12:53	21	9:31:40
1782	20	11:22:26	21	9:27:25	22	22:53:42	21	15:22:50
1783	20	17:12:38	21	15:15:11	23	4:39:11	21	21:14:04
1784	19	22:53:52	20	20:51:59	22	10:23:52	21	3:01:05
1785	20	4:43:16	21	2:42:45	22	16:13:43	21	8:47:16
1786	20	10:42:00	21	8:37:18	22	22:00:35	21	14:35:02
1787	20	16:28:56	21	14:13:28	23	3:42:28	21	20:26:02
1788	19	22:16:35	20	20:09:17	22	9:38:16	21	2:16:13
1789	20	4:05:09	21	2:04:13	22	15:26:25	21	8:02:52
1790	20	9:54:24	21	7:49:57	22	21:11:56	21	13:52:53
1791	20	15:48:57	21	13:44:02	23	3:08:10	21	19:45:15
1792	19	21:32:59	20	19:26:37	22	9:00:55	21	1:34:19
1793	20	3:20:24	21	1:19:45	22	14:55:41	21	7:27:39
1794	20	9:16:38	21	7:16:15	22	20:46:49	21	13:24:21
1795	20	15:04:20	21	12:50:58	23	2:28:19	21	19:18:15
1796	19	20:54:04	20	18:42:33	22	8:24:17	21	1:09:56
1797	20	2:47:50	21	0:34:55	22	14:11:04	21	6:54:13
1798	20	8:39:01	21	6:16:31	22	19:50:28	21	12:41:16
1799	20	14:31:04	21	12:09:13	23	1:41:09	21	18:32:11
1800	20	20:11:55	21	17:51:54	23	7:25:52	22	0:16:31

	Year	Shortest	Year	Longest	Mean	Year	Earliest	Year	Latest
Spring	1798	92.9010	1701	92.9828	92.9412	1797	80.1166	1704	81.5762
Summer	1707	93.5191	1796	93.5707	93.5444	1797	173.0242	1704	174.547
Fall	1709	89.6311	1799	89.7021	89.6656	1797	266.5910	1704	268.0754
Winter	1796	89.0665	1703	89.1154	89.0916	1797	356.2877	1704	357.7116

Year	March Equinox		June Solstice		September Equinox		December Solstice	
1801	21	1:55:48	21	23:42:06	23	13:13:28	22	6:02:04
1802	21	7:48:17	22	5:35:46	23	19:02:33	22	11:50:58
1803	21	13:34:07	22	11:08:27	24	0:43:51	22	17:36:15
1804	20	19:17:31	21	16:56:28	23	6:40:06	21	23:24:27
1805	21	1:04:46	21	22:49:48	23	12:29:19	22	5:13:37
1806	21	6:52:33	22	4:30:21	23	18:08:15	22	11:04:17
1807	21	12:41:46	22	10:21:11	24	0:02:02	22	17:01:12
1808	20	18:29:49	21	16:06:28	23	5:51:30	21	22:50:03
1809	21	0:22:09	21	21:57:01	23	11:42:27	22	4:38:03
1810	21	6:20:50	22	3:55:56	23	17:37:04	22	10:34:21
1811	21	12:13:22	22	9:36:43	23	23:20:24	22	16:25:32
1812	20	17:59:17	21	15:29:12	23	5:16:10	21	22:16:40
1813	20	23:50:00	21	21:27:55	23	11:07:56	22	4:07:40
1814	21	5:43:06	22	3:09:52	23	16:46:47	22	9:51:40
1815	21	11:30:32	22	8:58:32	23	22:42:20	22	15:43:36
1816	20	17:16:07	21	14:44:35	23	4:33:02	21	21:30:27
1817	20	23:00:42	21	20:30:12	23	10:18:26	22	3:16:52
1818	21	4:49:54	22	2:23:16	23	16:09:31	22	9:14:30
1819	21	10:38:49	22	7:58:05	23	21:47:14	22	15:02:09
1820	20	16:23:49	21	13:42:36	23	3:37:59	21	20:48:24
1821	20	22:15:33	21	19:37:25	23	9:28:18	22	2:36:00
1822	21	4:09:26	22	1:19:01	23	15:03:41	22	8:18:20
1823	21	9:54:46	22	7:08:40	23	20:56:23	22	14:11:26
1824	20	15:38:52	21	12:58:42	23	2:46:40	21	19:59:28
1825	20	21:25:37	21	18:47:10	23	8:31:40	22	1:43:08
1826	21	3:16:20	22	0:42:00	23	14:28:32	22	7:39:40
1827	21	9:08:05	22	6:21:12	23	20:13:49	22	13:27:44
1828	20	14:53:18	21	12:07:53	23	2:09:51	21	19:18:40

Equinoxes and Solstices

Year	March Equinox		June Solstice		September Equinox		December Solstice	
1829	20	20:42:13	21	18:05:05	23	8:04:57	22	1:15:23
1830	21	2:36:53	21	23:48:23	23	13:41:35	22	7:05:05
1831	21	8:26:20	22	5:36:44	23	19:35:01	22	13:01:43
1832	20	14:16:38	21	11:27:03	23	1:27:54	21	18:51:50
1833	20	20:11:59	21	17:16:43	23	7:12:23	22	0:33:39
1834	21	2:04:22	21	23:11:44	23	13:06:53	22	6:30:08
1835	21	7:55:45	22	4:54:53	23	18:49:15	22	12:18:19
1836	20	13:39:03	21	10:41:12	23	0:38:05	21	18:02:29
1837	20	19:23:23	21	16:37:01	23	6:31:24	21	23:53:24
1838	21	1:17:02	21	22:18:44	23	12:07:07	22	5:33:25
1839	21	6:59:28	22	4:00:34	23	17:59:12	22	11:22:06
1840	20	12:40:44	21	9:47:49	22	23:52:56	21	17:12:38
1841	20	18:28:16	21	15:33:23	23	5:33:48	21	22:55:39
1842	21	0:13:05	21	21:22:02	23	11:25:36	22	4:55:32
1843	21	6:04:32	22	3:02:31	23	17:09:18	22	10:47:39
1844	20	11:53:51	21	8:46:02	22	22:57:21	21	16:31:04
1845	20	17:43:41	21	14:42:14	23	4:53:45	21	22:26:52
1846	20	23:45:38	21	20:30:44	23	10:31:12	22	4:12:16
1847	21	5:32:12	22	2:18:15	23	16:22:26	22	10:05:02
1848	20	11:17:54	21	8:14:17	22	22:20:04	21	15:59:53
1849	20	17:12:46	21	14:07:06	23	4:03:39	21	21:40:51
1850	20	23:02:01	21	19:58:53	23	10:00:17	22	3:37:35
1851	21	4:54:12	22	1:42:54	23	15:50:37	22	9:28:44
1852	20	10:41:19	21	7:28:28	22	21:40:25	21	15:12:35
1853	20	16:23:59	21	13:22:16	23	3:36:17	21	21:10:52
1854	20	22:19:53	21	19:07:19	23	9:12:02	22	2:58:21
1855	21	4:05:16	22	0:47:43	23	14:58:25	22	8:47:25
1856	20	9:49:09	21	6:35:51	22	20:53:27	21	14:38:39
1857	20	15:45:13	21	12:25:06	23	2:32:33	21	20:15:41
1858	20	21:31:51	21	18:12:34	23	8:22:09	22	2:09:56
1859	21	3:18:29	21	23:55:57	23	14:07:54	22	8:00:56
1860	20	9:04:38	21	5:42:07	22	19:52:46	21	13:41:20
1861	20	14:46:35	21	11:33:45	23	1:46:52	21	19:33:55
1862	20	20:42:44	21	17:19:35	23	7:26:19	22	1:18:46
1863	21	2:30:03	21	23:01:59	23	13:16:26	22	7:06:04
1864	20	8:10:07	21	4:51:56	22	19:16:20	21	13:03:36
1865	20	14:05:59	21	10:46:10	23	0:59:34	21	18:49:38
1866	20	19:54:44	21	16:34:04	23	6:50:35	22	0:49:27
1867	21	1:46:29	21	22:19:51	23	12:42:43	22	6:47:00
1868	20	7:43:46	21	4:09:59	22	18:31:16	21	12:28:02
1869	20	13:32:09	21	10:04:24	23	0:28:00	21	18:23:34
1870	20	19:32:03	21	15:56:19	23	6:09:35	22	0:13:11
1871	21	1:19:47	21	21:41:53	23	11:56:10	22	5:59:09
1872	20	6:57:23	21	3:31:55	22	17:53:30	21	11:53:32
1873	20	12:52:26	21	9:25:04	22	23:35:10	21	17:32:36
1874	20	18:37:59	21	15:07:12	23	5:22:55	21	23:22:08
1875	21	0:21:16	21	20:47:01	23	11:15:00	22	5:15:54
1876	20	6:09:58	21	2:32:14	22	16:58:44	21	10:54:22
1877	20	11:47:55	21	8:18:00	22	22:48:10	21	16:50:20
1878	20	17:42:39	21	14:03:46	23	4:26:35	21	22:41:18
1879	20	23:31:57	21	19:44:24	23	10:09:19	22	4:24:29
1880	20	5:13:37	21	1:31:44	22	16:06:46	21	10:18:18
1881	20	11:13:54	21	7:28:12	22	21:50:10	21	16:00:33
1882	20	17:04:38	21	13:16:41	23	3:37:45	21	21:53:40
1883	20	22:49:48	21	19:03:31	23	9:32:20	22	3:52:06
1884	20	4:44:34	21	0:59:06	22	15:21:17	21	9:33:35
1885	20	10:29:39	21	6:50:54	22	21:16:12	21	15:27:32
1886	20	16:26:26	21	12:41:15	23	3:04:34	21	21:19:56
1887	20	22:18:31	21	18:27:24	23	8:54:19	22	3:04:56
1888	20	3:56:00	21	0:14:27	22	14:53:48	21	9:03:15
1889	20	9:50:54	21	6:10:04	22	20:38:13	21	14:51:58
1890	20	15:41:05	21	11:53:59	23	2:22:38	21	20:44:59
1891	20	21:24:56	21	17:32:39	23	8:13:53	22	2:40:36
1892	20	3:22:04	20	23:23:33	22	13:59:39	21	8:19:23
1893	20	9:08:28	21	5:10:06	22	19:46:20	21	14:07:26
1894	20	14:59:23	21	10:56:54	23	1:27:34	21	19:58:19
1895	20	20:49:18	21	16:44:09	23	7:10:31	22	1:38:45
1896	20	2:23:26	20	22:28:17	22	13:03:36	21	7:29:26
1897	20	8:16:14	21	4:23:26	22	18:49:02	21	13:12:51
1898	20	14:06:33	21	10:07:11	23	0:34:38	21	18:59:13
1899	20	19:45:48	21	15:45:40	23	6:30:11	22	0:56:15
1900	21	1:39:05	21	21:39:51	23	12:20:16	22	6:41:39

	Year	Shortest	Year	Longest	Mean	Year	Earliest	Year	Latest
Spring	1895	92.8298	1802	92.9080	92.8686	1897	80.3446	1804	81.8038
Summer	1802	93.5603	1899	93.6142	93.5881	1897	173.1829	1804	174.7059
Fall	1805	89.6974	1894	89.7714	89.7354	1897	266.7840	1804	268.2778
Winter	1891	89.0277	1802	89.0738	89.0506	1897	356.5506	1804	357.9753

Year	March Equinox		June Solstice		September Equinox		December Solstice	
1901	21	7:23:40	22	3:27:53	23	18:09:02	22	12:36:42
1902	21	13:16:40	22	9:15:15	23	23:55:27	22	18:35:38
1903	21	19:14:54	22	15:05:04	24	5:43:49	23	0:20:34
1904	21	0:58:42	21	20:51:30	23	11:40:22	22	6:14:06
1905	21	6:57:41	22	2:51:32	23	17:30:07	22	12:03:53
1906	21	12:52:59	22	8:41:59	23	23:15:11	22	17:53:29
1907	21	18:33:11	22	14:23:12	24	5:09:06	22	23:51:46
1908	21	0:27:27	21	20:19:16	23	10:58:30	22	5:33:40
1909	21	6:13:12	22	2:05:47	23	16:44:46	22	11:20:03
1910	21	12:03:08	22	7:48:58	23	22:31:00	22	17:12:00
1911	21	17:54:38	22	13:35:49	24	4:17:49	22	22:53:29
1912	20	23:29:38	21	19:17:11	23	10:08:19	22	4:45:00
1913	21	5:18:16	22	1:09:48	23	15:53:04	22	10:35:12
1914	21	11:11:03	22	6:55:22	23	21:34:07	22	16:22:45
1915	21	16:51:37	22	12:29:43	24	3:24:09	22	22:16:08
1916	20	22:47:14	21	18:24:47	23	9:15:07	22	3:58:55
1917	21	4:37:37	22	0:14:42	23	15:00:32	22	9:46:04
1918	21	10:26:01	22	6:00:00	23	20:46:02	22	15:41:54
1919	21	16:19:31	22	11:53:58	24	2:35:46	22	21:27:29
1920	20	21:59:42	21	17:40:13	23	8:28:31	22	3:17:23
1921	21	3:51:26	21	23:36:04	23	14:20:10	22	9:07:51
1922	21	9:49:00	22	5:27:07	23	20:09:59	22	14:57:21
1923	21	15:29:10	22	11:03:10	24	2:03:59	22	20:53:41
1924	20	21:20:33	21	16:59:48	23	7:58:42	22	2:45:53
1925	21	3:12:36	21	22:50:23	23	13:43:48	22	8:37:04
1926	21	9:01:36	22	4:30:27	23	19:27:02	22	14:33:46
1927	21	14:59:31	22	10:22:36	24	1:17:21	22	20:18:55
1928	20	20:44:40	21	16:06:51	23	7:05:55	22	2:04:05
1929	21	2:35:16	21	22:01:02	23	12:52:44	22	7:53:10
1930	21	8:30:11	22	3:53:15	23	18:36:22	22	13:39:58
1931	21	14:06:43	22	9:28:29	24	0:23:43	22	19:30:00
1932	20	19:54:00	21	15:23:03	23	6:16:18	22	1:14:40
1933	21	1:43:31	21	21:12:15	23	12:01:34	22	6:57:55
1934	21	7:28:20	22	2:48:20	23	17:45:36	22	12:49:50
1935	21	13:18:10	22	8:38:20	23	23:38:35	22	18:37:32
1936	20	18:58:16	21	14:22:03	23	5:26:23	22	0:27:06
1937	21	0:45:29	21	20:12:25	23	11:13:21	22	6:22:05
1938	21	6:43:30	22	2:04:00	23	16:59:56	22	12:13:49
1939	21	12:28:53	22	7:39:51	23	22:49:52	22	18:06:24
1940	20	18:24:10	21	13:36:51	23	4:46:00	21	23:55:10
1941	21	0:20:49	21	19:33:44	23	10:33:11	22	5:44:35
1942	21	6:11:04	22	1:16:42	23	16:16:54	22	11:40:00
1943	21	12:03:04	22	7:12:46	23	22:12:11	22	17:29:33
1944	20	17:49:03	21	13:02:45	23	4:02:05	21	23:15:16
1945	20	23:37:40	21	18:52:32	23	9:50:14	22	5:04:02
1946	21	5:33:09	22	0:44:48	23	15:41:06	22	10:53:48
1947	21	11:13:09	22	6:19:18	23	21:29:06	22	16:43:15
1948	20	16:57:16	21	12:11:04	23	3:22:11	21	22:33:46
1949	20	22:48:32	21	18:03:15	23	9:06:20	22	4:23:23
1950	21	4:35:39	21	23:36:33	23	14:44:04	22	10:13:51
1951	21	10:26:14	22	5:25:20	23	20:37:22	22	16:00:35
1952	20	16:14:16	21	11:13:04	23	2:24:11	21	21:43:40
1953	20	22:01:01	21	17:00:28	23	8:06:25	22	3:31:59
1954	21	3:53:56	21	22:54:34	23	13:55:47	22	9:24:53
1955	21	9:35:38	22	4:31:54	23	19:41:25	22	15:11:26
1956	20	15:20:50	21	10:24:17	23	1:35:35	21	21:00:01
1957	20	21:17:01	21	16:21:04	23	7:26:37	22	2:49:10
1958	21	3:06:22	21	21:57:27	23	13:09:24	22	8:40:16
1959	21	8:55:05	22	3:50:20	23	19:09:00	22	14:34:53
1960	20	14:43:14	21	9:42:52	23	0:59:25	21	20:26:30
1961	20	20:32:41	21	15:30:41	23	6:43:01	22	2:20:03
1962	21	2:30:07	21	21:24:42	23	12:35:48	22	8:15:51
1963	21	8:20:17	22	3:04:37	23	18:24:06	22	14:02:29
1964	20	14:10:28	21	8:57:25	23	0:17:16	21	19:50:09
1965	20	20:05:22	21	14:56:18	23	6:06:37	22	1:41:03
1966	21	1:53:33	21	20:34:00	23	11:43:46	22	7:28:48

Equinoxes and Solstices

Year	March Equinox		June Solstice		September Equinox		December Solstice	
1967	21	7:37:27	22	2:23:29	23	17:38:42	22	13:16:58
1968	20	13:22:40	21	8:13:56	22	23:26:51	21	19:00:26
1969	20	19:08:46	21	13:55:44	23	5:07:34	22	0:44:23
1970	21	0:57:01	21	19:43:20	23	10:59:39	22	6:36:22
1971	21	6:38:51	22	1:20:18	23	16:45:36	22	12:24:38
1972	20	12:22:08	21	7:06:54	22	22:33:29	21	18:13:38
1973	20	18:13:11	21	13:01:20	23	4:21:53	22	0:08:28
1974	21	0:07:23	21	18:38:23	23	9:59:12	22	5:56:44
1975	21	5:57:27	22	0:27:13	23	15:55:59	22	11:46:21
1976	20	11:50:23	21	6:25:00	22	21:48:59	21	17:35:57
1977	20	17:43:05	21	12:14:35	23	3:30:04	21	23:23:58
1978	20	23:34:23	21	18:10:24	23	9:26:14	22	5:21:48
1979	21	5:22:47	21	23:57:02	23	15:17:15	22	11:10:37
1980	20	11:10:33	21	5:47:53	22	21:09:33	21	16:56:57
1981	20	17:03:43	21	11:45:33	23	3:06:05	21	22:51:25
1982	20	22:56:44	21	17:23:53	23	8:47:05	22	4:39:03
1983	21	4:39:39	21	23:09:35	23	14:42:31	22	10:30:50
1984	20	10:25:15	21	5:03:09	22	20:33:48	21	16:23:44
1985	20	16:14:39	21	10:45:03	23	2:08:22	21	22:08:35
1986	20	22:03:37	21	16:30:54	23	7:59:48	22	4:03:04
1987	21	3:52:54	21	22:11:41	23	13:46:12	22	9:46:49
1988	20	9:39:33	21	3:57:29	22	19:29:47	21	15:28:50
1989	20	15:29:12	21	9:53:58	23	1:20:33	21	21:22:58
1990	20	21:20:14	21	15:33:46	23	6:56:28	22	3:07:58
1991	21	3:02:54	21	21:19:45	23	12:49:04	22	8:54:37
1992	20	8:49:02	21	3:15:08	22	18:43:46	21	14:44:13
1993	20	14:41:38	21	9:00:44	23	0:23:29	21	20:26:49
1994	20	20:29:01	21	14:48:33	23	6:20:14	22	2:23:44
1995	21	2:15:27	21	20:35:24	23	12:14:01	22	8:17:50
1996	20	8:04:07	21	2:24:46	22	18:01:08	21	14:06:56
1997	20	13:55:42	21	8:20:58	22	23:56:49	21	20:08:05
1998	20	19:55:35	21	14:03:38	23	5:38:15	22	1:57:31
1999	21	1:46:53	21	19:50:10	23	11:32:34	22	7:44:52
2000	20	7:36:19	21	1:48:46	22	17:28:39	21	13:38:30

	Year	Shortest	Year	Longest	Mean	Year	Earliest	Year	Latest
Spring	1999	92.7523	1901	92.8363	92.7948	1997	80.5803	1904	82.0408
Summer	1906	93.6064	1999	93.6544	93.6298	1997	173.3479	1904	174.8691
Fall	1901	89.7692	1998	89.8467	89.8067	1997	266.9978	1904	268.4864
Winter	1996	88.9905	1906	89.0341	89.0115	1997	356.8389	1904	358.2598

Year	March Equinox		June Solstice		September Equinox		December Solstice	
2001	20	13:31:47	21	7:38:47	22	23:05:32	21	19:22:34
2002	20	19:17:13	21	13:25:28	23	4:56:28	22	1:15:26
2003	21	1:00:50	21	19:11:32	23	10:47:53	22	7:04:53
2004	20	6:49:42	21	0:57:56	22	16:30:54	21	12:42:40
2005	20	12:34:29	21	6:47:12	22	22:24:14	21	18:36:01
2006	20	18:26:39	21	12:26:56	23	4:04:27	22	0:23:11
2007	21	0:08:30	21	18:07:30	23	9:52:18	22	6:08:54
2008	20	5:49:23	21	0:00:27	22	15:45:34	21	12:04:51
2009	20	11:44:44	21	5:46:37	22	21:19:41	21	17:47:53
2010	20	17:33:18	21	11:29:30	23	3:10:07	21	23:39:33
2011	20	23:21:49	21	17:17:36	23	9:05:44	22	5:31:09
2012	20	5:15:32	20	23:09:55	22	14:50:05	21	11:12:43
2013	20	11:03:02	21	5:05:04	22	20:45:15	21	17:12:07
2014	20	16:58:12	21	10:52:21	23	2:30:11	21	23:04:08
2015	20	22:46:16	21	16:39:02	23	8:21:40	22	4:49:04
2016	20	4:31:19	20	22:35:18	22	14:22:15	21	10:45:18
2017	20	10:29:46	21	4:25:17	22	20:02:56	21	16:29:05
2018	20	16:16:35	21	10:08:26	23	1:55:14	21	22:23:52
2019	20	21:59:34	21	15:55:23	23	7:51:18	22	4:20:34
2020	20	3:50:45	20	21:44:49	22	13:31:47	21	10:03:28
2021	20	9:38:37	21	3:33:18	22	19:22:13	21	16:00:26
2022	20	15:34:33	21	9:14:59	23	1:04:50	21	21:49:21
2023	20	21:25:35	21	14:58:58	23	6:51:07	22	3:28:30
2024	20	3:07:32	20	20:52:08	22	12:44:47	21	9:21:42
2025	20	9:02:37	21	2:43:24	22	18:20:28	21	15:04:13
2026	20	14:47:05	21	8:25:38	23	0:06:21	21	20:51:22
2027	20	20:25:49	21	14:11:58	23	6:02:51	22	2:43:17
2028	20	2:18:16	20	20:03:08	22	11:46:26	21	8:20:48
2029	20	8:03:06	21	1:49:25	22	17:39:38	21	14:15:14
2030	20	13:53:13	21	7:32:26	22	23:28:01	21	20:10:46
2031	20	19:42:06	21	13:18:16	23	5:16:26	22	1:56:41
2032	20	1:23:01	20	19:09:54	22	11:12:00	21	7:57:04
2033	20	7:23:51	21	1:02:16	22	16:52:48	21	13:47:08
2034	20	13:18:38	21	6:45:19	22	22:40:42	21	19:35:08
2035	20	19:03:52	21	12:34:16	23	4:40:04	22	1:32:00
2036	20	1:03:58	20	18:33:22	22	10:24:27	21	7:14:01
2037	20	6:51:24	21	0:23:35	22	16:14:13	21	13:08:53
2038	20	12:41:46	21	6:10:32	22	22:03:25	21	19:03:28
2039	20	18:33:11	21	11:58:34	23	3:50:45	22	0:41:44
2040	20	0:12:51	20	17:47:32	22	9:46:04	21	6:34:00
2041	20	6:07:58	20	23:37:01	22	15:27:43	21	12:19:30
2042	20	11:54:29	21	5:17:00	22	21:12:43	21	18:05:14
2043	20	17:28:58	21	10:59:33	23	3:08:07	22	0:02:25
2044	19	23:21:44	20	16:52:19	22	8:49:03	21	5:44:47
2045	20	5:08:49	20	22:35:06	22	14:34:07	21	11:36:19
2046	20	10:59:04	21	4:15:52	22	20:22:57	21	17:29:42
2047	20	16:53:53	21	10:04:43	23	2:09:19	21	23:08:28
2048	19	22:35:04	20	15:55:10	22	8:01:53	21	5:03:31
2049	20	4:29:52	20	21:48:34	22	13:43:52	21	10:53:26
2050	20	10:20:52	21	3:34:19	22	19:29:48	21	16:39:59
2051	20	16:00:27	21	9:19:54	23	1:28:38	21	22:35:25
2052	19	21:57:23	20	15:17:32	22	7:17:03	21	4:18:34
2053	20	3:48:45	20	21:05:30	22	13:07:38	21	10:11:16
2054	20	9:35:49	21	2:48:32	22	19:00:52	21	16:11:21
2055	20	15:30:02	21	8:41:19	23	0:50:12	21	21:57:04
2056	19	21:12:33	20	14:29:40	22	6:40:56	21	3:53:03
2057	20	3:09:22	20	20:20:32	22	12:24:46	21	9:44:22
2058	20	9:06:32	21	2:05:36	22	18:09:56	21	15:26:30
2059	20	14:45:47	21	7:48:47	23	0:05:03	21	21:19:29
2060	19	20:40:02	20	13:47:12	22	5:49:48	21	3:03:02
2061	20	2:27:53	20	19:33:51	22	11:32:59	21	8:50:26
2062	20	8:09:06	21	1:12:59	22	17:21:31	21	14:44:18
2063	20	14:00:50	21	7:03:35	22	23:09:55	21	20:22:49
2064	19	19:40:21	20	12:47:22	22	4:58:43	21	2:10:27
2065	20	1:29:52	20	18:34:11	22	10:44:20	21	8:02:30
2066	20	7:21:34	21	0:18:11	22	16:28:48	21	13:47:19
2067	20	12:55:24	21	5:57:47	22	22:21:24	21	19:44:52
2068	19	18:50:45	20	11:55:35	22	4:08:36	21	1:34:31
2069	20	0:46:54	20	17:43:10	22	9:53:44	21	7:23:55
2070	20	6:36:45	20	23:24:26	22	15:46:40	21	13:21:11
2071	20	12:36:33	21	5:22:43	22	21:39:40	21	19:05:49
2072	19	18:23:00	20	11:15:44	22	3:29:44	21	0:57:56
2073	20	0:15:16	20	17:08:56	22	9:17:14	21	6:52:40
2074	20	6:10:50	20	23:00:28	22	15:05:49	21	12:37:16
2075	20	11:48:37	21	4:42:27	22	21:00:50	21	18:29:05
2076	19	17:40:51	20	10:38:49	22	2:52:19	21	0:15:29
2077	19	23:33:12	20	16:25:35	22	8:37:59	21	6:02:57
2078	20	5:12:58	20	22:00:03	22	14:26:38	21	12:00:05
2079	20	11:02:49	21	3:51:29	22	20:15:23	21	17:46:15
2080	19	16:46:21	20	9:36:20	22	1:58:38	20	23:35:03
2081	19	22:36:30	20	15:18:37	22	7:40:03	21	5:24:47
2082	20	4:32:54	20	21:05:36	22	13:25:18	21	11:07:01
2083	20	10:12:52	21	2:46:14	22	19:13:57	21	16:55:42
2084	19	16:01:48	20	8:42:56	22	1:01:30	20	22:43:41
2085	19	21:55:58	20	14:35:18	22	6:45:58	21	4:31:12
2086	20	3:37:45	20	20:12:04	22	12:34:40	21	10:25:08
2087	20	9:30:48	21	2:08:29	22	18:30:52	21	16:11:04
2088	19	15:19:37	20	7:59:18	22	0:20:52	20	21:58:47
2089	19	21:09:12	20	13:45:34	22	6:09:31	21	3:54:40
2090	20	3:04:33	20	19:38:35	22	12:02:04	21	9:46:19
2091	20	8:44:37	21	1:21:41	22	17:53:34	21	15:41:16
2092	19	14:36:19	20	7:17:42	21	23:44:34	20	21:34:41
2093	19	20:37:19	20	13:09:54	22	5:31:45	21	3:23:36
2094	20	2:24:25	20	18:45:09	22	11:19:22	21	9:16:08
2095	20	8:17:46	21	0:41:41	22	17:14:00	21	15:03:43
2096	19	14:05:49	20	6:33:42	21	22:57:38	20	20:49:07
2097	19	19:51:18	20	12:16:16	22	4:38:43	21	2:40:19
2098	20	1:43:20	20	18:05:54	22	10:27:10	21	8:23:47
2099	20	7:20:41	20	23:44:37	22	16:14:01	21	14:07:17
2100	20	13:06:39	21	5:35:09	22	22:03:26	21	19:53:52

	Year	Shortest	Year	Longest	Mean	Year	Earliest	Year	Latest
Spring	2094	92.6811	2005	92.7588	92.7201	2097	79.8273	2004	81.2845
Summer	2001	93.6436	2094	93.6904	93.6686	2097	172.5113	2004	174.0402
Fall	2004	89.8415	2097	89.9178	89.8789	2097	266.1936	2004	267.6881
Winter	2092	88.9549	2002	88.9963	88.9751	2097	356.1113	2004	357.5296

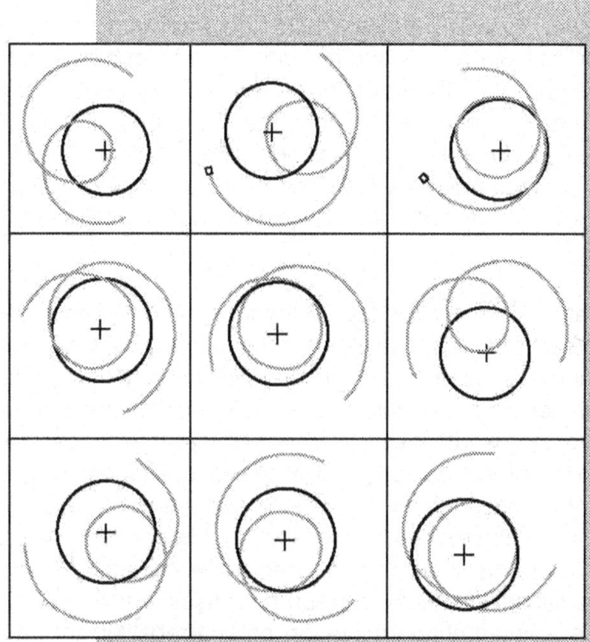

Part 2

The Sun is Not the Center of the Solar System!

The Sun Retrograde? Yes!

The center of the solar system is not the center of the Sun! The mass of the planets is about 1/750 the mass of the Sun, and the center of mass of the solar system, called the **solar system barycenter**, can move from close to the center of the Sun to as far as one solar radius outside the surface of the Sun!

Therefore, all bodies in the solar system orbit about the barycenter, including the Sun itself. This motion is counterclockwise, and from the heliocentric point of view all planetary motion is direct, of course, since retrograde motion is only a perception when planets are viewed from Earth.

However, massive Jupiter in configuration with the other three "gas giants" —Saturn, Uranus and Neptune— can cause the Sun to move clockwise with respect to the barycenter; hence, its motion is then retrograde! This is a rare event and has happened only seven times in the last 3400 years! As this is written, we are in such a period which started April 28, 1989, and will last through December 23, 1990.

The last two times this happened were in 1810-12 and 1632-33. Weather and climate after 1810 were more extreme than anything ever experienced since. 1816 was the year without a summer when the northeastern US and western Europe had freezing weather every month of the year. A succession of cold summers and short growing seasons triggered famines in places such as Switzerland and the Ukraine. J. D. Post in the *Journal of Interdisciplinary History* (1973) said: "The years 1812-1817 introduced three decades of economic pause punctuated by recurring crises, distress, social upheaval, international migration, political rebellion and pandemic disease."

The climate of the 1630s and 40s was also extreme. The River Thames froze solid during this time and the people of London held "frost fairs" on the ice. This has not happened for at least 150 years. There were also short growing seasons, and the winter of 1641 was one of the three worst of the entire century for the American colonies. Also, this period had one of the most intensive concentrations of volcanic activity of the past 500 years.

Whether the next decade or two will mirror the decades following the last two Sun retrograde periods is difficult to predict on the basis of just a look at those two times alone. However, it is interesting to note that the political upheavals in China, Russia, eastern Europe and South Africa are climaxing during our current Sun retrograde period! And San Diego is having the worst drought since records were kept starting in 1850 — we had less than three inches of rain in 1989. And this comes on top of two drought years, 1987 and 1988.

Western Europe's 1989 summer was the hottest on record and its 1988 summer was its wettest. The winter of 89-90 in the midwest and eastern part of the US was the coldest on record. Both Northern and Southern California are having droughts for an unprecedented three years in a row.

In 1992, the U.S. experienced extreme flooding of the Mississippi and other rivers. Some of the towns in the flood plains of Illinois, Missouri and other areas were simply destroyed. St. Louis and other cities had considerable damage. Evacuations were necessary in several areas. In 1993, the East Coast had an extremely severe winter. Temperatures were cold enough to kill a number of people. As of this writing (Spring 1994), it appears our climate extremes are continuing.

See figures 5, 14 and 23 in the mandala section for the Sun Retrograde periods in 1632, 1811 and 1990.

The eleven occurrences of Sun Retrograde between -1400 and 3000 are shown by Jupiter entering a heliocentric 270° square to the barycenter and leaving a 90° square. The "Cs 0.04128" says that the center of mass of the solar system was at its "station," in this case the minimum distance from the Sun's center. (C = Center of Mass, s = Station. 0.04128 is in units of a solar radius, and in this particular case .04128 is about 1/24th of a solar radius.)

Less than 2 days later, on September 8, -55, Jupiter made a 180° aspect to the Center of Mass, which indicates the maximum Sun Retrograde period.

The conjunction and the station are all within 100 hours of each other; most are much less than that.

References

James H. Shirley, "When the Sun Goes Backward: Solar Motion, Volcanic Activity, and Climate, 1990-2000," *Cycles Magazine*, V39 4:113-119. Reprinted in both the 1988 and 1989 *Foundation for the Study of Cycles Annual Conference Proceedings*.

11 Sun Retrograde Periods -1400 (1401 BC) – 3000 AD

				♃ To Barycenter		♃ Heliocentric Longitude
-55	Feb	12	4:14	♃ 270	C	9♑01
	Aug	8	12:11	♃ 225	C	24♑35
	Sep	6	21:11		Cs	0.04128
		8	14:22	♃ 180	C	27♑21
	Oct	12	17:57	♃ 135	C	0♒23
-54	May	24	23:04	♃ 90	C	20♒34
123	Dec	22	2:21	♃ 270	C	10♒55
124	Jul	7	1:32	♃ 225	C	28♒49
	Aug	13	5:13		Cs	0.05275
		14	9:30	♃ 180	C	2♓18
	Sep	23	20:13	♃ 135	C	5♓59
125	May	9	18:23	♃ 90	C	26♓46
302	Nov	25	6:37	♃ 270	C	15♓49
303	May	31	4:32	♃ 225	C	2♈52
	Jul	3	7:47	♃ 180	C	5♈52
		3	14:24		Cs	0.04507
	Aug	4	13:60	♃ 135	C	8♈48
304	Feb	19	8:10	♃ 90	C	26♈42
482	Jan	28	5:38	♃ 270	C	29♈36
	Apr	5	16:56	♃ 225	C	5♉37
		9	3:10		Cs	0.01855
		9	9:27	♃ 180	C	5♉57
		13	2:32	♃ 135	C	6♉17
	Jun	18	5:44	♃ 90	C	12♉08
1632	Jan	27	11:52	♃ 270	C	24♈48
	Jul	31	18:58	♃ 225	C	11♉44
	Aug	14	12:32	♃ 180	C	12♉59
		15	7:05		Cs	0.02168
		26	13:46	♃ 135	C	14♉04
	Nov	19	11:26	♃ 90	C	21♉42
1810	Jul	5	14:37	♃ 270	C	14♉02
1811	Apr	13	14:13	♃ 225	C	9♊13
	Jun	3	12:35	♃ 180	C	13♊41
		7	15:46		Cs	0.06355
	Jul	17	9:07	♃ 135	C	17♊30
1812	Jan	15	23:02	♃ 90	C	3♋10
1989	Apr	28	8:14	♃ 270	C	14♊51
1990	Feb	26	2:02	♃ 225	C	10♋55
	Apr	20	10:20	♃ 180	C	15♋23
		23	22:35		Cs	0.06514
	Jun	7	12:31	♃ 135	C	19♋23
	Dec	23	1:30	♃ 90	C	5♌37
2168	Jun	8	13:26	♃ 270	C	23♋39
2169	Mar	5	9:37	♃ 225	C	15♌32
	Apr	5	3:27	♃ 180	C	17♌59
		6	13:22		Cs	0.03493
	May	3	14:00	♃ 135	C	20♌15
	Oct	14	2:15	♃ 90	C	3♍05
2308	Jun	24	18:26	♃ 270	C	12♉19
	Dec	10	16:24	♃ 225	C	27♉38
2309	Jan	2	6:43		Cs	0.03305
		2	8:05	♃ 180	C	29♉40
		24	18:34	♃ 135	C	1♊41
	Jul	10	14:10	♃ 90	C	16♊30
2487	Mar	4	4:09	♃ 270	C	10♊09
	Sep	20	9:39	♃ 225	C	27♊48
	Oct	20	3:29	♃ 180	C	0♋22
		20	8:19		Cs	0.04017
	Nov	18	5:50	♃ 135	C	2♋53
2488	May	24	19:16	♃ 90	C	18♋56
2666	Jun	18	15:11	♃ 270	C	25♋45
	Aug	26	14:36	♃ 225	C	1♌29
		28	11:33		Cs	0.00858
		28	13:29	♃ 180	C	1♌39
		30	10:50	♃ 135	C	1♌48
	Oct	12	14:48	♃ 90	C	5♌21

Where Is the Center of the Solar System?

The center of the solar system is not the center of the Sun! The mass of the planets is about 1/750 the mass of the Sun and the center of mass of the solar system can move from close to the center of the Sun to up to one solar radius outside the surface of the Sun! Where the **solar system barycenter** is at any given moment is determined by the configuration of planets as they revolve around the Sun—but now you know it is really the barycenter they revolve around! (See the related article in this book, "The Sun Retrograde? Yes!")

The planet that most determines the barycenter's position is Jupiter, the most massive body in our system outside the Sun itself. It has more mass than all the rest of the bodies in our system combined! Yes, more than all the other planets with their many moons, the over 4000 asteroids whose orbits are known, the countless other asteroids too small to bother with, the comets and the dust between the planets.

The other three large planets, Saturn, Uranus and Neptune, also have significant influence on the movement of the barycenter. As all the bodies in our solar system revolve about the barycenter, their changing configurations result in barycenter motion with respect to the Sun that is illustrated in the first graphs in the mandala of this book.

The barycenter and the Sun's center can be closer than .01 solar radius and as far apart as 2.22 solar radii. The actual distance is less important than the proximity of the barycenter to the Sun's surface and the time span of that proximity.

The Sun's surface is a boundary determined by the balance of forces between the compression of the Sun's mass due to gravity and the expansion of that mass due to heat and the thermonuclear furnace that powers the Sun. The Sun's surface is an everchanging configuration of flares, eruptions, spots, prominences and features. In short, the Sun's surface is unstable!

Chaos theory says that a small disturbing force applied to an unstable boundary can cause a large resultant force totally out of proportion to the magnitude of the disturbing force. A simple mechanical analogy is a huge ten-ton rock, balanced precariously on a mountainside, which can be sent crashing down by a small 80-pound boy giving it a gentle push.

The solar system barycenter is the disturbing force on the Sun's surface.

As you can see from the graphs, the angle of the path of the barycenter as it passes through the Sun's surface is usually acute. But occasionally that angle is shallow enough so that its path parallels the Sun's surface, remaining close for a longer period of time. Occasionally, the barycenter will even move back across the Sun's surface without ever moving very far away after its first intersection.

Theodor Landscheidt calls these periods **major instability events**. His arbitrary but useful limits for such events are when the barycenter remains within the range of .9 to 1.1 solar radii for at least 2.5 years and/or between .8 and 1.2 solar radii for at least 5.5 years.

Scanning from -1400, the instability events meeting those criteria are shown in the following table.

.8 to 1.2 Solar Radii			.9 to 1.1 Solar Radii		
from	to	span	from	to	span
–1365 Jul 10	–1359 Feb 8	5.58	–1364 Jul 12	–1361 Oct 7	3.24
–1333 Aug 16	–1327 Nov 15	6.25	–1331 Apr 9	–1327 Jan 24	3.79
			–1185 Aug 23	–1182 Sep 17	3.07
–1155 Sep 27	–1148 Dec 13	7.21	–1151 Jan 4	–1148 Apr 19	3.29
–977 Nov 22	–969 Dec 16	8.07			
–898 Mar 16	–889 Mar 14	8.99			
–798 Jun 21	–790 Nov 22	8.42			
–759 Sep 18	–750 Jun 15	8.74			
–719 Mar 19	–710 Apr 2	9.04	–718 Mar 31	–715 Apr 19	3.05
–619 Apr 28	–611 Nov 4	8.52	–618 Jun 6	–611 Feb 27	6.73
–580 Oct 27	–571 Nov 6	9.03	–579 Sep 26	–571 Jan 17	7.31
–540 Mar 10	–531 Jan 20	8.86	–540 Dec 31	–532 Jun 6	7.43
–440 May 12	–432 Nov 11	8.50	–439 Mar 29	–433 Nov 18	6.64
–401 Nov 13	–391 May 26	9.53	–397 Nov 11	–392 Jun 20	4.61
–361 Mar 14	–353 Aug 13	8.42	–361 Dec 28	–354 Nov 25	6.91
–261 Jul 4	–252 Oct 2	9.25			
–217 Jan 5	–212 Dec 10	5.93	–216 Feb 7	–212 Jan 5	3.91
–182 Mar 21	–174 Jan 6	7.80	–181 Feb 10	–175 Mar 18	6.10
–115 Dec 20	–108 Dec 19	7.00			
–77 Jul 8	–67 May 2	9.82	–76 Nov 14	–72 Apr 5	3.39
–38 Jul 4	–32 Feb 22	5.64	–37 Jun 2	–33 Feb 27	3.74
–3 Jul 1	4 Apr 18	6.80	–1 Jan 1	3 Jun 17	4.46
64 Sep 18	72 Jan 22	7.34	67 Oct 5	71 Mar 24	3.47
102 Nov 15	112 Jul 23	9.69	103 Aug 23	109 Mar 20	5.57
			142 Oct 17	145 Nov 16	3.08
243 Aug 12	251 Apr 27	7.71	244 Sep 1	250 Jan 16	5.38
281 Nov 15	291 Sep 18	9.84	286 Apr 19	291 Mar 14	4.90
422 Apr 12	430 Dec 6	8.65			
460 Oct 11	470 Sep 7	9.91	466 Feb 6	470 Feb 15	4.02
500 Aug 29	508 Jun 10	7.78			
			645 Sep 3	648 Oct 10	3.10
1428 Mar 14	1434 Jul 16	6.34	1429 Feb 13	1432 Aug 12	3.49
			1465 Sep 22	1469 Mar 12	3.47
1606 Apr 25	1614 Jun 4	8.11	1606 Dec 21	1609 Jun 28	2.52
			1610 Feb 25	1612 Oct 29	2.67
1644 Jan 13	1650 Feb 18	6.10	1644 Jul 24	1648 Sep 24	4.17
1784 Sep 25	1794 Jan 5	9.28	1789 Jul 31	1793 Jan 19	3.47
1823 Jan 23	1832 Dec 4	9.86	1823 Jul 27	1828 Apr 29	4.76
1864 Oct 20	1870 Dec 17	6.16	1867 Nov 5	1870 Feb 28	2.32*
1932 Jun 30	1938 Mar 16	5.71	1933 Nov 28	1937 Mar 24	3.32
1967 May 31	1973 Apr 9	5.86	1968 Jun 6	1972 Jul 8	4.09
2002 Mar 27	2011 Sep 22	9.49	2002 Oct 17	2011 Jan 28	8.28
			2045 Jan 31	2048 Jan 5	2.93
2110 Jun 4	2117 Jul 22	7.13	2111 Oct 27	2116 Oct 8	4.95
2146 Aug 24	2152 May 25	5.75	2147 Jul 3	2151 Aug 30	4.16
2181 Jul 31	2190 Aug 17	9.05	2182 Mar 15	2189 Aug 1	7.38
2288 Jul 5	2296 Oct 9	8.26	2289 Jun 16	2296 Feb 13	6.66
2325 Dec 25	2331 Aug 29	5.68	2326 Oct 28	2330 Oct 20	3.98
2360 Dec 18	2370 Apr 19	9.33			
2466 Nov 19	2475 Nov 11	8.98	2467 Aug 2	2475 Apr 4	7.67
2505 Jun 4	2515 Feb 14	9.70	2506 Apr 26	2510 Feb 20	3.82
2546 Feb 21	2554 Apr 7	8.12	2550 Jul 6	2553 Jul 12	3.02
2645 Aug 8	2654 Nov 23	9.29	2649 Nov 15	2654 Mar 25	4.36
2685 Jan 12	2694 Mar 1	9.13	2685 Nov 24	2693 Jun 17	7.56
2725 Jul 17	2732 Dec 20	7.43	2726 Sep 27	2731 Dec 13	5.21
2824 Jul 12	2833 Dec 18	9.44	2829 Oct 31	2833 Feb 28	3.33
2864 May 27	2873 Apr 4	8.85	2865 Feb 4	2872 Feb 19	7.04
2904 Jul 17	2911 Jul 9	6.98	2905 Jul 6	2910 Mar 27	4.72
			2938 Jun 25	2941 Jan 12	2.55

I have shown the 1867 to 1870 .9 to 1.1 event with an asterisk since Landscheidt calculated that event as having a duration of 2.6 years whereas my result shows 2.32 years. This illustrates both the difficulty two researchers have in getting similar results when using different astronomical theories and the arbitrariness of choosing 2.5 and 5.5 years as cutoffs.

Why should we be interested in these events as defined above?

In his book, *Sun-Earth-Man: A Mesh of Cosmic Oscillations*, Landscheidt details some of the historical, cultural, artistic, economic and scientific changes that occurred during the five instability events starting with the one of 1789 and ending with the one that began in 1968. He characterizes these periods as ones involving upheaval of the old order and structures, and the emergence of new ones. While that is certainly true of those time periods, it is certainly not uniquely true.

A second reason for our interest is his discovery(?), observation, correlation of these instability events with "phase shifts" in certain cycles, particularly those involving the heliocentric conjunction of Jupiter with the barycenter. As examples, he presents graphs of US stock prices from 1830 to 1942, German share prices from 1951 to 1985, US immigration from 1824 to 1950 and others. Each graph demonstrates that in one phase Jupiter conjunct the barycenter will show maximums, but following an instability event the phase shifts and Jupiter conjunct the barycenter will then show minimums. These "phase shifts" are delimited by the instability events!

In addition to the cycles that Landscheidt correlates with psychological implications (stock prices, immigration, etc.), he shows how solar events, purely physical in nature, can be predicted, using center of mass, center of Sun, and Jupiter/Saturn/Uranus/Neptune configurations. Landscheidt has used these parameters to predict energetic solar activity, including X-ray flares.

The table at right shows the Jupiter/barycenter conjunctions for the period 1500 through 2049.

The three Jupiter/barycenter oppositions which mark the height of the Sun retrograde period are included.

References

Theodor Landscheidt, *Sun-Earth-Man: A Mesh of Cosmic Oscillations* (London: Urania Trust, 1989).

———, "Conjunctions of Jupiter with the Center of Mass: A Cosmic Indicator of Turning Points in Economic Cycles" (Proceedings, Foundation for the Study of Cycles Annual Conference, Irvine, California, 1988a), 79-81.

———, "Multidisciplinary Forecast of Stock Prices" (Proceedings, Foundation for the Study of Cycles Annual Conference, Irvine, California, 1988b), 75- 78.

———, "Foundations of Astrology in the Third Millenium" (Paper presented at the 6th International Astrological Research Conference, London, November 20-22, 1987).

———, "Long-Range Prediction of Energetic Solar Eruptions and Their Terrestrial Effects" (Paper presented at the Second International Astrological Research Conference, London, November 28-29, 1981 (*Correlation* 1,2,3)).

———, "Modulation of the Sun's Rotation, Energetic Solar Eruptions, Geomagnetic Storms, Weather, Abundance of Wild Life, and Economic Cycles by Conjunctions of Sun, Jupiter, and the Center of Mass of the Solar System" (Paper presented at the 5th International Astrological Research Conference, London, November 22-23, 1986).

———, "Prediction of Energetic Solar Eruptions and Their Terrestrial Effects by Constellations of Planets," *Astrology'84* (New York: The National Astrology Society, 1984), 25-35.

———, "Decipherment of the Rosetta Stone of Planetary Functions in the Solar System" (Paper presented at the 4th International Astrological Research Conference, London, October 27-28, 1984).

Rhodes W. Fairbridge & John E. Sanders, "The Sun's Orbit, AD 750-2050: Basis for New Perspectives on Planetary Dynamics and Earth-Moon Linkage," Article 26. (*Climate History, Periodicity, and Predictability*, edited by Rampino, Sanders, Newman. New York: Van Nostrand Reinhold Company, 1987).

Jupiter/Barycenter 1500-2049

1501	Mar	22	1:47	0	10♈25	1795	Apr	7	6:49	0	23♑05
1516	Feb	5	8:27	0	17♋10	1803	Sep	15	5:03	0	14♎20
1524	May	30	1:48	0	22♓57	1811	Jun	3	12:35	180	13♊41
1533	Feb	16	20:27	0	13♐49	1819	Sep	9	22:32	0	15♒21
1544	Nov	26	18:04	0	11♐32	1834	Nov	23	5:20	0	6♊05
1554	Jul	16	14:40	0	8♎50	1843	Mar	4	15:33	0	8♒05
1563	May	4	4:19	0	11♋39	1850	Nov	26	23:12	0	8♎06
1573	Aug	23	12:25	0	22♉59	1859	Mar	16	20:46	0	24♊59
1584	Jun	6	12:38	0	17♈41	1873	Apr	10	2:10	0	0♍43
1593	Oct	9	16:52	0	25♑13	1881	Nov	21	4:05	0	21♉51
1602	Apr	7	22:28	0	17♎19	1891	Mar	2	19:06	0	26♒11
1615	Dec	22	2:21	0	9♐36	1901	Oct	13	1:55	0	16♑52
1624	Jul	21	8:07	0	7♍53	1912	Jan	22	20:38	0	0♐16
1632	Aug	14	12:32	180	12♉59	1920	Oct	24	10:37	0	3♍51
1640	Nov	18	0:09	0	15♑18	1930	May	1	16:30	0	24♊16
1656	Feb	13	22:33	0	6♉06	1942	Apr	16	6:25	0	27♊28
1664	May	7	7:04	0	7♑56	1951	May	17	15:44	0	26♓27
1671	Nov	1	10:45	0	3♍54	1959	Aug	15	2:57	0	4♐01
1680	Feb	27	21:20	0	16♉44	1967	Oct	28	15:21	0	21♌55
1694	Sep	26	5:60	0	10♌56	1970	Jan	6	22:14	0	23♎09
1703	Feb	23	16:56	0	22♈38	1974	Jun	23	12:47	0	6♓11
1712	Mar	17	19:21	0	21♑13	1982	Oct	31	18:51	0	19♏54
1723	Feb	5	21:41	0	21♐56	1990	Apr	20	10:20	180	15♋23
1733	Mar	17	3:25	0	2♏02	1998	Jul	21	23:56	0	17♓57
1742	Jan	19	13:05	0	7♌42	2013	Aug	19	13:13	0	3♋44
1752	Jan	7	14:47	0	9♊59	2021	Dec	24	18:19	0	8♓35
1763	Apr	3	0:07	0	19♉51	2030	Feb	1	14:28	0	15♏01
1772	Jul	27	5:51	0	25♒31	2038	Jun	10	19:14	0	6♌41
1780	Nov	17	4:36	0	8♏56						

Center of Mass Distance from the Sun's Center and Aspects to Heliocentric Jupiter

1451	Apr 2	15:37	C@	1.1000
	Jul 9	13:47	C@	1.0000
	Oct 11	7:22	C@	0.9000
1452	Jan 11	6:51	C@	0.8000
1453	Sep 30	11:29	315	8♈52
	Nov 14	9:34	Cs	0.05962
	17	8:29	0	13♈16
1454	Jan 11	6:36	45	18♈17
1455	Oct 20	1:04	C@	0.8000
1456	Jan 28	3:47	C@	0.9000
	May 15	18:15	C@	1.0000
	Sep 6	17:22	C@	1.1000
	Nov 27	15:12	45	19♋54
1457	Jan 7	3:09	C@	1.2000
1460	Sep 2	18:25	Cs	1.72905
1462	Feb 14	17:58	0	17♐36
1465	Feb 4	9:42	C@	1.2000
	Sep 22	16:41	C@	1.1000
1466	Aug 26	16:16	C@	1.0000
1467	Apr 25	18:34	Cs	0.97832
	Dec 25	16:16	C@	1.0000
1469	Mar 12	19:57	C@	1.1000
1470	Apr 23	3:30	C@	1.2000
1471	Sep 10	19:06	Cs	1.25756
1473	Jan 20	20:47	C@	1.2000
	Nov 10	11:38	C@	1.1000
1474	Jun 6	22:56	C@	1.0000
	Nov 20	16:02	C@	0.9000
1475	Apr 18	4:22	C@	0.8000
1477	May 1	1:58	0	4♈40
	Jun 13	15:16	Cs	0.26416
1478	Feb 1	17:33	45	29♈55
1479	Apr 11	22:12	C@	0.8000
	Jul 16	14:34	C@	0.9000
	Oct 21	1:27	C@	1.0000
1480	Jan 25	12:21	C@	1.1000
	May 6	1:57	C@	1.2000
	Oct 5	18:46	45	24♋07
1485	May 11	11:47	Cs	2.20574
	Jun 20	16:20	0	7♐00
1488	Dec 15	12:56	315	26♓55
1490	Jan 1	17:38	C@	1.2000
	Apr 2	8:12	C@	1.1000
	Jun 29	15:11	C@	1.0000
	Sep 24	17:20	C@	0.9000
	Dec 19	2:33	C@	0.8000
1492	Oct 5	3:22	315	28♋16
	Nov 3	14:50	Cs	0.04484
	10	8:45	0	1♌10
	Dec 31	23:48	45	5♌17
1495	Jan 11	8:43	C@	0.8000
	May 11	0:50	C@	0.9000
	Sep 16	3:09	C@	1.0000
1496	Feb 2	13:22	C@	1.1000
	May 2	19:11	45	8♏46
	Jul 2	0:12	C@	1.2000
1499	Sep 13	9:05	Cs	1.57992
1501	Mar 22	1:47	0	10♈25
1504	Apr 3	17:55	C@	1.2000
1505	Jun 25	21:09	Cs	1.16360
1506	Aug 5	16:30	C@	1.2000
1509	Oct 12	20:45	Cs	1.35741
1512	Jan 4	14:35	C@	1.2000
	Aug 9	2:47	C@	1.1000
1513	Jan 31	13:15	C@	1.0000
	Jul 7	20:46	C@	0.9000
	Nov 29	5:22	C@	0.8000
1516	Feb 5	8:27	0	17♋10
	27	21:50	Cs	0.32722
1517	Jun 25	23:43	45	27♌24
1518	Apr 14	13:48	C@	0.8000
	Aug 15	14:25	C@	0.9000
	Dec 15	18:47	C@	1.0000
1519	Apr 18	11:11	C@	1.1000
	Aug 23	8:35	C@	1.2000
	31	12:42	45	27♎57
1524	May 9	12:20	Cs	.98272
	30	1:48	0	22♓57
1528	Dec 31	19:30	315	17♌47
1529	Feb 14	10:19	C@	1.2000
	Jun 29	5:00	C@	1.1000
	Nov 13	23:09	C@	1.0000
1530	Mar 28	7:12	C@	0.9000
	Aug 11	1:51	C@	0.8000
1531	May 28	7:33	315	24♎44
1532	Dec 31	11:19	Cs	0.35123
1533	Feb 16	20:27	0	13♐49
1535	Sep 8	13:58	C@	0.8000
1536	Mar 9	22:48	C@	0.9000
	Sep 19	22:29	C@	1.0000
1537	May 2	14:36	C@	1.1000
1538	Jan 24	13:35	C@	1.2000
1544	May 8	16:52	Cs	.46109
	Nov 26	18:04	0	11♐32
1549	Jun 5	23:25	C@	1.2000
1550	Feb 18	15:49	C@	1.1000
	Oct 8	18:04	C@	1.0000
1551	May 9	1:12	C@	0.9000
	Dec 5	14:17	C@	0.8000
1554	Jul 16	14:40	0	8♎50
	Sep 23	18:12	Cs	0.45360
1557	Mar 10	19:60	C@	0.8000
	Aug 19	12:24	C@	0.9000
1558	Jan 27	1:10	C@	1.0000
	Jul 3	21:31	C@	1.1000
	Dec 15	12:46	C@	1.2000
1563	May 4	4:19	0	11♋39
	Aug 9	22:53	Cs	.74603
1568	Oct 28	10:52	C@	1.2000
1569	May 20	13:29	C@	1.1000
	Nov 30	4:39	C@	1.0000
1570	Jun 18	2:15	C@	0.9000
1571	Jan 8	0:19	C@	0.8000
1573	Apr 21	5:27	Cs	0.57100
	Aug 23	12:25	0	22♉59
1576	Feb 23	14:16	C@	0.8000
1577	Jan 5	14:25	C@	0.9000
	Nov 17	19:05	C@	1.0000
1578	Oct 1	14:13	C@	1.1000
1579	Aug 13	7:03	C@	1.2000
1584	Jun 6	12:38	0	17♈41
1585	Feb 12	2:39	Cs	.68126
1589	Sep 26	17:28	C@	1.2000
1590	Mar 18	21:09	C@	1.1000
	Aug 21	0:10	C@	1.0000
	Nov 30	11:07	315	1♏15
1591	Jan 17	23:29	C@	0.9000
	Jun 7	13:42	C@	0.8000
1592	Jul 1	0:59	315	16♐28
1593	Oct 9	16:52	0	25♑13
	28	14:55	Cs	0.24157
1594	Sep 13	9:03	45	24♒58
1595	Dec 26	21:56	C@	0.8000
1596	Apr 22	8:21	C@	0.9000
	Aug 3	17:08	45	27♈52
	21	12:33	C@	1.0000
	Dec 24	21:48	C@	1.1000
1597	May 11	1:40	C@	1.2000
1601	May 9	22:12	Cs	.72269
1602	Apr 7	22:28	0	17♎19
1606	Apr 25	2:03	C@	1.2000
	Dec 21	3:41	C@	1.1000
1607	Oct 10	11:49	C@	1.0000
1609	Jun 28	19:51	C@	0.9000
	Aug 11	10:09	Cs	0.89960
	Oct 4	13:40	Cs	0.89970
1610	Jan 2	18:10	Cs	0.89949
	Feb 25	4:41	C@	0.9000
1611	Oct 20	12:01	Cs	0.91702
1612	Oct 29	4:18	C@	0.9000
1614	Jun 4	16:10	C@	0.8000
1615	Dec 22	2:21	0	9♐36
1616	Dec 24	2:42	Cs	0.59422
1618	Aug 26	9:19	C@	0.8000
1619	Jan 23	14:12	C@	0.9000
	Jun 9	12:02	C@	1.0000
	Oct 16	4:32	C@	1.1000
1620	Feb 20	11:20	C@	1.2000
1624	Jul 21	8:07	0	7♍53
1625	Mar 30	16:20	Cs	2.08182
1629	Jan 8	18:35	315	15♑11
	Nov 14	16:14	C@	1.2000
1630	Feb 17	13:06	C@	1.1000
	May 21	6:15	C@	1.0000
	Aug 16	18:57	C@	0.9000
	Nov 9	20:41	C@	0.8000
1632	Jan 27	11:52	270	24♈48
	Jul 31	18:58	225	11♉44
	Aug 14	12:32	180	12♉59
	15	7:05	Cs	0.02168
	26	13:46	135	14♉04
	Nov 19	11:26	90	21♉42
1634	Jun 30	20:44	C@	0.8000
	Oct 7	17:16	C@	0.9000
1635	Jan 17	5:18	C@	1.0000
	May 5	16:41	C@	1.1000
	Aug 30	16:19	C@	1.2000
1636	Jan 23	11:19	45	28♌10
1639	Aug 10	15:24	Cs	1.81260
1640	Nov 18	0:09	0	15♑18
1644	Jan 13	21:43	C@	1.2000
	Jul 24	15:55	C@	1.1000
1645	Mar 23	8:10	C@	1.0000
1646	May 24	2:56	Cs	0.93007
1647	Sep 11	4:17	C@	1.0000
1648	Sep 24	15:41	C@	1.1000
1650	Feb 18	21:01	C@	1.2000
	Sep 17	22:19	Cs	1.21252
1651	Jun 3	10:58	C@	1.2000
1652	Jul 24	2:20	C@	1.1000
1653	Mar 12	6:42	C@	1.0000
	Sep 11	3:24	C@	0.9000
1654	Feb 13	14:26	C@	0.8000
1656	Feb 13	22:33	0	6♉06
	Apr 8	15:37	Cs	0.33926
1657	May 5	6:52	45	15♊44
1658	Feb 13	7:28	C@	0.8000
	May 29	14:24	C@	0.9000
	Sep 12	21:22	C@	1.0000
	Dec 28	0:27	C@	1.1000
1659	Apr 15	14:32	C@	1.2000
	25	20:36	45	15♌06
1664	Apr 22	9:35	Cs	2.14595
	May 7	7:04	0	7♑56
1667	Sep 27	14:50	315	28♈08
1668	Oct 15	8:12	C@	1.2000
1669	Jan 17	18:48	C@	1.1000
	Apr 21	22:53	C@	1.0000
	Jul 23	15:36	C@	0.9000
	Oct 23	17:12	C@	0.8000
1671	Sep 3	15:34	315	29♌22
	Oct 23	14:38	Cs	0.06476
	Nov 1	10:45	0	3♍54
1672	Jan 20	7:45	45	10♍02
1674	Feb 5	22:39	C@	0.8000
	Jun 8	17:53	C@	0.9000
	Oct 17	2:01	C@	1.0000
1675	Mar 6	14:55	C@	1.1000
	Jul 9	3:15	45	17♐25
	Aug 3	10:02	C@	1.2000
1678	Dec 20	19:57	Cs	1.60256
1680	Feb 27	21:20	0	16♉44
1685	Jun 4	22:49	Cs	1.20206
1688	Mar 24	14:22	Cs	1.23716
1689	Jun 30	8:34	C@	1.2000
1690	Aug 10	11:34	C@	1.1000
1691	Apr 29	12:04	C@	1.0000
	Dec 3	9:59	C@	0.9000
1692	Jun 13	10:17	C@	0.8000
1694	Sep 26	5:60	0	10♌56
	Nov 14	22:23	Cs	0.45357
1697	Jan 26	23:43	C@	0.8000
	Jun 20	18:31	C@	0.9000
	Nov 14	4:40	C@	1.0000
1698	Apr 5	5:15	C@	1.1000
	Aug 27	5:11	C@	1.2000
1703	Feb 23	16:56	0	22♈38
	Apr 12	15:59	Cs	1.90565
1708	Mar 5	7:55	C@	1.2000
	Jul 30	2:26	C@	1.1000
	Oct 30	1:17	315	13♎32
	Dec 24	18:11	C@	1.0000
1709	May 15	4:20	C@	0.9000
	Oct 2	17:27	C@	0.8000
1710	Mar 10	12:12	315	21♏24
1712	Feb 20	8:29	Cs	0.34301
	Mar 17	19:21	0	21♑13
1714	Aug 30	11:08	C@	0.8000
1715	Feb 9	13:36	C@	0.9000
	Aug 3	23:32	C@	1.0000
1716	Feb 12	8:06	C@	1.1000
	Sep 23	17:03	C@	1.2000
1721	Jun 18	7:52	Cs	1.50972
	Sep 27	20:22	Cs	1.50899
1722	Jan 9	10:36	Cs	1.50949
1723	Feb 5	21:41	0	21♐56
1727	Sep 13	11:07	C@	1.2000
1728	Jun 23	22:16	C@	1.1000
1729	Mar 11	5:34	C@	1.0000
	Nov 10	23:17	C@	0.9000
1730	Jul 1	2:07	C@	0.8000
1733	Mar 17	3:25	0	2♏02
	Jun 13	9:54	Cs	0.46530
1735	Nov 26	8:36	C@	0.8000
1736	May 3	23:39	C@	0.9000
	Oct 6	6:48	C@	1.0000
1737	Mar 12	19:10	C@	1.1000
	Aug 16	18:49	C@	1.2000
1742	Jan 19	13:05	0	7♌42
	Feb 28	19:44	Cs	1.75900
1747	May 7	20:59	C@	1.2000
	Nov 9	13:54	C@	1.1000
1748	May 12	11:43	C@	1.0000
	Nov 13	7:21	C@	0.9000
1749	May 31	23:07	C@	0.8000
1751	Jul 11	6:23	Cs	0.58878
1752	Jan 7	14:47	0	9♊59
1754	Jun 6	14:43	C@	0.8000
1755	Jul 6	18:12	C@	0.9000
1756	Aug 25	15:29	C@	1.0000
1757	Oct 6	17:04	C@	1.1000
1758	Oct 9	14:20	C@	1.2000
1763	Apr 3	0:07	0	19♉51
1764	May 4	16:10	Cs	1.70110
1768	Nov 21	8:45	C@	1.2000
1769	Apr 24	18:09	C@	1.1000
	Jun 5	3:28	315	20♏15
	Sep 9	7:30	C@	1.0000
1770	Jan 19	13:59	C@	0.9000
	May 23	2:49	C@	0.8000
1771	Dec 20	0:44	315	6♒06
1772	Jul 27	5:51	0	25♒31
	Aug 3	1:07	Cs	0.16641
1773	Jan 23	18:41	45	11♓47
1774	Aug 16	15:03	C@	0.8000
	Nov 28	22:56	C@	0.9000
1775	Mar 17	14:30	C@	1.0000
	Jul 10	20:03	C@	1.1000
	Aug 20	7:06	45	6♊58
	Nov 7	2:55	C@	1.2000

Center of Mass Distance from the Sun's Center and Aspects to Heliocentric Jupiter

1780	Jan 24	21:17	Cs	1.81348
	Nov 17	4:36	0	8♏56
1784	Sep 25	0:36	C@	1.2000
1785	Mar 20	21:21	C@	1.1000
	Oct 4	2:51	C@	1.0000
1786	May 29	17:22	C@	0.9000
1787	Oct 4	22:49	Cs	0.81668
1789	Jul 31	2:31	C@	0.9000
1791	May 23	8:56	Cs	0.96951
1793	Jan 19	9:37	C@	0.9000
1794	Jan 5	21:02	C@	0.8000
1795	Apr 7	6:49	0	23♑05
1796	Feb 27	20:43	Cs	0.59290
1797	Sep 12	15:35	C@	0.8000
1798	Jan 31	13:51	C@	0.9000
	Jun 12	11:43	C@	1.0000
	Oct 13	16:04	C@	1.1000
1799	Feb 13	19:55	C@	1.2000
1803	Sep 15	5:03	0	14♎20
1804	Apr 8	0:14	Cs	2.10750
1807	Oct 12	7:14	315	13♒36
1808	Sep 29	5:28	C@	1.2000
	Dec 28	12:36	C@	1.1000
1809	Mar 26	9:43	C@	1.0000
	Jun 20	23:57	C@	0.9000
	Sep 11	18:02	C@	0.8000
1810	Jul 5	14:37	270	14♉02
1811	Apr 13	14:13	225	9♊13
	Jun 3	12:35	180	13♊41
	7	15:46	Cs	0.06355
	Jul 17	9:07	135	17♊30
1812	Jan 15	23:02	90	3♋10
1813	Apr 20	9:18	C@	0.8000
	Jul 27	8:28	C@	0.9000
	Nov 7	14:59	C@	1.0000
1814	Feb 21	16:14	C@	1.1000
	Jun 15	12:43	C@	1.2000
1815	Mar 24	14:48	45	5♎09
1818	Aug 8	8:48	Cs	1.86468
1819	Sep 9	22:32	0	15♒21
1823	Jan 23	4:43	C@	1.2000
	Jul 27	21:33	C@	1.1000
1824	Mar 15	9:49	C@	1.0000
1825	Jul 9	9:32	Cs	0.91330
1827	Feb 10	14:28	C@	1.0000
1828	Apr 29	14:56	C@	1.1000
1829	Sep 12	9:33	Cs	1.15398
1830	Dec 29	21:01	C@	1.1000
1831	Nov 2	2:56	C@	1.0000
1832	Jun 5	20:55	C@	0.9000
	Dec 4	2:45	C@	0.8000
1834	Nov 23	5:20	0	6♊05
1835	Feb 7	4:45	Cs	0.42941
1836	Dec 14	9:48	C@	0.8000
1837	Apr 14	6:42	C@	0.9000
	Aug 11	22:03	C@	1.0000
	Dec 10	16:18	C@	1.1000
1838	Apr 9	8:00	C@	1.2000
1843	Mar 4	15:33	0	8♒05
	Apr 4	10:16	Cs	2.07028
1846	Aug 14	0:02	315	1♊43
1847	Aug 13	5:43	C@	1.2000
	Nov 27	1:40	C@	1.1000
1848	Mar 7	6:57	C@	1.0000
	Jun 16	20:04	C@	0.9000
	Sep 25	0:54	C@	0.8000
1850	Aug 18	19:04	315	0♎31
	Nov 17	0:16	Cs	0.09755
	26	23:12	0	8♎06
1851	Mar 30	16:17	45	17♎27
1853	Mar 27	21:20	C@	0.8000
	Jul 29	9:08	C@	0.9000
	Dec 6	18:12	C@	1.0000
1854	Apr 23	16:27	C@	1.1000
	Aug 14	6:03	45	25♑09
	Sep 17	15:52	C@	1.2000
1858	Apr 4	23:50	Cs	.62927
1859	Mar 16	20:46	0	24♊59
1864	Oct 20	22:02	C@	1.2000
1867	Nov 5	16:41	C@	1.1000
1869	Mar 25	10:54	C@	1.0000
1870	Feb 28	14:24	C@	0.9000
	Dec 17	10:33	C@	0.8000
1873	Apr 10	2:10	0	0♍43
1873	Jul 30	12:06	Cs	0.55858
1875	Oct 7	12:57	C@	0.8000
1876	Apr 6	22:51	C@	0.9000
	Sep 24	1:51	C@	1.0000
1877	Mar 7	13:58	C@	1.1000
	Aug 16	13:24	C@	1.2000
1881	Nov 21	4:05	0	21♉51
1882	Apr 9	13:14	Cs	.84444
1887	Mar 15	10:27	C@	1.2000
	Aug 15	5:21	C@	1.1000
1888	Jan 12	8:05	C@	1.0000
	Jun 3	4:05	C@	0.9000
	Oct 20	22:05	C@	0.8000
1891	Feb 12	22:20	Cs	0.34475
	Mar 2	19:06	0	26♒11
1893	Jul 12	15:14	C@	0.8000
	Dec 15	19:17	C@	0.9000
1894	Jun 6	6:34	C@	1.0000
	Dec 7	16:56	C@	1.1000
1895	Jul 10	10:07	C@	1.2000
1900	Jun 10	3:06	Cs	.53125
1901	Oct 13	1:55	0	16♑52
1906	May 31	5:28	C@	1.2000
1907	Mar 30	5:14	C@	1.1000
1908	Jan 1	1:38	C@	1.0000
	Sep 7	8:42	C@	0.9000
1909	May 4	12:10	C@	0.8000
1912	Jan 22	20:38	0	0♐16
	Apr 29	6:40	Cs	0.43505
1914	Sep 4	1:10	C@	0.8000
1915	Jan 29	9:20	C@	0.9000
	Jun 20	14:41	C@	1.0000
	Nov 11	9:04	C@	1.1000
1916	Apr 9	2:12	C@	1.2000
1920	Oct 24	10:37	0	3♍51
	Nov 24	16:24	Cs	1.78785
1925	Oct 23	3:54	C@	1.2000
1926	Apr 15	4:38	C@	1.1000
	Oct 2	5:46	C@	1.0000
1927	Mar 25	6:10	C@	0.9000
	Oct 2	18:38	C@	0.8000
1929	Sep 3	4:25	Cs	0.60707
1930	May 1	16:30	0	24♊16
1932	Jun 30	2:12	C@	0.8000
1933	Nov 28	23:08	C@	0.9000
1935	Oct 13	13:17	C@	1.0000
1937	Mar 24	23:35	C@	1.1000
1938	Mar 16	23:42	C@	1.2000
1942	Apr 16	6:25	0	27♊28
1943	Nov 13	14:16	Cs	1.75908
1948	Jan 23	8:13	C@	1.2000
	26	5:48	315	12♐47
	Jun 3	17:45	C@	1.1000
	Sep 30	19:28	C@	1.0000
1949	Jan 23	17:01	C@	0.9000
	May 11	14:41	C@	0.8000
1951	Feb 21	9:38	315	18♓40
	May 17	15:44	0	26♓27
	19	12:24	Cs	0.08436
	Aug 4	6:20	45	3♈39
1953	Apr 21	11:07	C@	0.8000
	Jul 28	0:33	C@	0.9000
	Nov 4	9:17	C@	1.0000
1954	Feb 17	11:21	C@	1.1000
1954	Jun 8	13:09	C@	1.2000
	Sep 5	13:02	45	13♋59
1958	Oct 8	0:09	Cs	1.90045
1959	Aug 15	2:57	0	4♐01
1963	May 17	13:50	C@	1.2000
	Oct 12	14:47	C@	1.1000
1964	Mar 14	0:29	C@	1.0000
	Sep 6	11:33	C@	0.9000
1965	Apr 18	7:33	C@	0.8000
1966	Apr 18	14:09	Cs	0.73851
1967	May 31	3:20	C@	0.8000
	Oct 28	15:21	0	21♌55
1968	Jun 6	13:15	C@	0.9000
1969	Oct 22	12:58	C@	1.0000
1970	Jan 6	22:14	0	23♎09
	Jul 7	5:55	Cs	1.01702
1971	Apr 21	20:26	C@	1.0000
1972	Jul 8	7:34	C@	0.9000
1973	Apr 9	23:01	C@	0.8000
1974	Jun 23	12:47	0	6♓11
1975	Mar 16	19:35	Cs	0.59400
1976	Sep 9	19:50	C@	0.8000
1977	Jan 26	6:30	C@	0.9000
	Jun 7	7:53	C@	1.0000
	Oct 8	21:13	C@	1.1000
1978	Feb 9	14:38	C@	1.2000
1982	Oct 31	18:51	0	19♏54
1983	Mar 29	1:13	Cs	2.09781
1986	Jul 29	3:22	315	13♓54
1987	Jul 30	17:10	C@	1.2000
	Oct 29	21:55	C@	1.1000
1988	Jan 25	12:30	C@	1.0000
	Apr 20	11:42	C@	0.9000
	Jul 15	3:30	C@	0.8000
1989	Apr 28	8:14	270	14♊51
1990	Feb 26	2:02	225	10♋55
	Apr 20	10:20	180	15♋23
	23	22:35	Cs	0.06514
	Jun 7	12:31	135	19♋23
	Dec 23	1:30	90	5♌37
1992	Apr 1	5:11	C@	0.8000
	Jul 11	3:59	C@	0.9000
	Oct 24	17:26	C@	1.0000
1993	Feb 11	13:30	C@	1.1000
	Jun 5	19:10	C@	1.2000
1994	May 20	18:44	45	11♏21
1997	Aug 22	17:50	Cs	1.87943
1998	Jul 21	23:56	0	17♓57
2002	Mar 27	0:34	C@	1.2000
	Oct 17	9:10	C@	1.1000
2003	Jul 4	14:23	C@	1.0000
2004	Oct 25	1:55	Cs	0.92455
2006	Sep 8	6:25	C@	1.0000
2008	Sep 1	4:29	Cs	1.07800
2010	Apr 4	7:12	C@	1.0000
2011	Jan 28	23:38	C@	0.9000
	Sep 22	10:37	C@	0.8000
2013	Aug 19	13:13	0	3♋44
	Nov 11	0:07	Cs	0.53126
2015	Oct 8	4:34	C@	0.8000
2016	Mar 1	11:38	C@	0.9000
	Jul 21	12:32	C@	1.0000
	Dec 9	11:20	C@	1.1000
2017	Apr 25	7:42	C@	1.2000
2021	Dec 24	18:19	0	8♓35
2022	Feb 17	9:40	Cs	1.98159
2025	Sep 11	18:23	315	10♋03
2026	Jul 16	21:34	C@	1.2000
	Nov 13	22:09	C@	1.1000
2027	Mar 7	6:57	C@	1.0000
	Jun 27	15:57	C@	0.9000
	Oct 16	16:02	C@	0.8000
2029	Aug 31	3:20	315	3♏14
2030	Jan 24	11:23	Cs	0.13312
	Feb 1	14:28	0	15♏01
	Jul 18	16:54	45	27♏54
2032	Jun 4	11:14	C@	0.8000
	Oct 2	23:34	C@	0.9000
2033	Feb 7	17:15	C@	1.0000
	Jun 19	16:42	C@	1.1000
	Aug 30	11:57	45	2♓50
	Nov 8	14:39	C@	1.2000
2037	Oct 26	1:23	Cs	1.66594
2038	Jun 10	19:14	0	6♌41
2043	Oct 20	3:54	C@	1.2000
2045	Jan 31	1:46	C@	1.1000
2046	Jul 31	18:19	C@	1.0000
2048	Jan 5	14:31	C@	0.9000
2049	Apr 16	23:05	C@	0.8000

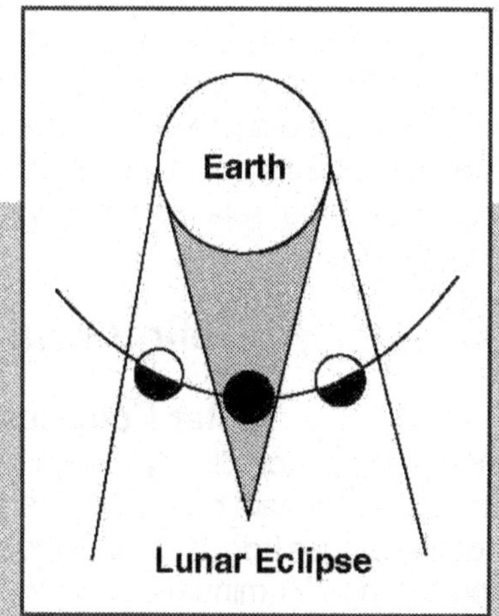

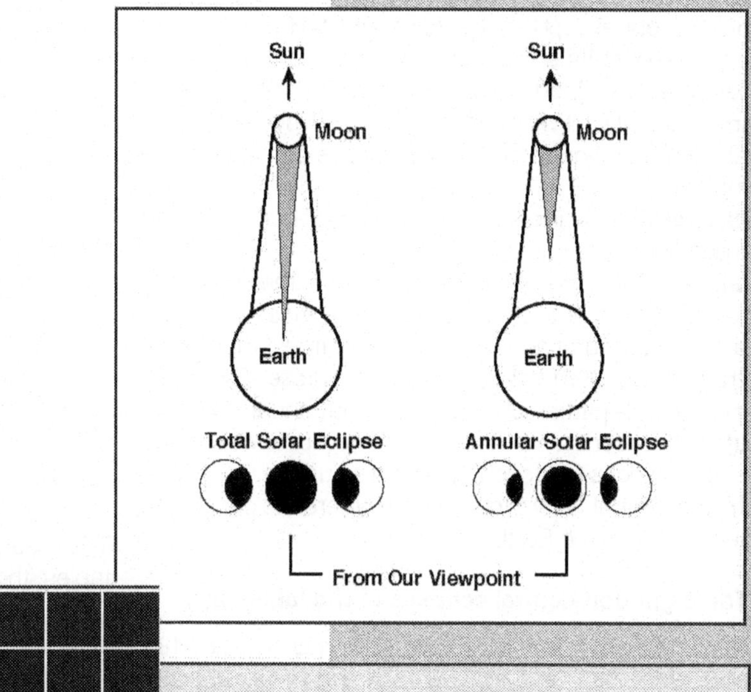

Part 3

Eclipses

Eclipses

The solar and lunar eclipse tables in this book cover the 351 years from 1700-2050. The first table lists the 1684 eclipses in chronological sequence. The second table lists those same eclipses in zodiacal sequence. The third and last table lists the annular and total solar eclipses by the duration time of the maximum eclipse.

Definitions

Solar Eclipses

Total: The Moon completely covers the solar disk as seen from a shadow path on the Earth's surface. The duration of totality ranges from less than one second to a maximum approaching $7\frac{1}{2}$ minutes.

Annular: From the Latin *annulus*, a ring. An annular eclipse would be total except that the Moon is too far from the Earth for the apex of its shadow to touch the Earth's surface. Therefore, the Moon will not entirely hide the Sun so a narrow ring of light will surround the dark New Moon. The maximum duration of an annular eclipse can exceed 12 minutes.

Annular-total: An eclipse that is total for part of its path and annular for the remainder.

Partial: The Moon does not completely cover the solar disk. The magnitude of a partial eclipse is a measure of the maximum obscuration of the Sun. The largest magnitude in the tables is .996 for the July 3, 1750, eclipse. The smallest magnitude partial eclipse of .001 is on January 5, 1935.

Annular: Non-central: a rare annular eclipse where the center line does not touch the Earth's surface.

Total: Non-central: a rare total eclipse where the center line does not touch the Earth's surface.

The eight non-central eclipses in the tables are					
1928	May 19	●	13:23:56	T non-C	28♉18
1950	Mar 18	●	15:31:31	A non-C	27♓28
1957	Apr 30	●	0:04:54	A non-C	9♉23
1957	Oct 23	●	4:53:28	T non-C	29♎31
1967	Nov 2	●	5:38:17	T non-C	9♏07
2014	Apr 29	●	6:03:32	A non-C	8♉51
2043	Apr 9	●	18:56:47	T non-C	19♈49
2043	Oct 3	●	3:00:47	A non-C	9♎48

Lunar eclipses

Total: Where the Moon is entirely immersed in the umbral shadow of the Earth.

Partial: Where the Moon enters the umbral shadow of the Earth, but is not entirely immersed in it.

Appulse: Also known as penumbral eclipse, where the Moon only enters the penumbral shadow of the Earth.

Summary of Eclipses by Type		
Solar Eclipses	●	**Abbreviation in Table**
Total	229	T
Annular/total	45	AT
Annular	265	A
Partial	295	P
Non-central	8	T non-C or A non-C
Lunar Eclipses	●	**Abbreviation In Table**
Total	250	T
Partial	287	P
Appulses	313	A

Astrologers are interested in the sign and degree of eclipses so the second table sorts the eclipses in zodiacal order.

Summary of Eclipses by Sign					
	Solar	**Lunar**		**Solar**	**Lunar**
♈	70	67	♎	66	69
♉	66	67	♏	68	72
♊	67	70	♐	68	69
♋	73	71	♑	67	74
♌	76	70	♒	69	76
♍	73	73	♓	71	72
				834	850

The maximum number of eclipses in a year is seven. The ten maximum years in the tables are: 1749, 1805, 1861, 1879, 1908, 1917, 1935, 1973, 1982 and 2038.

The least number of solar eclipses in a year is two. In both 1978 and 1989 the two solar eclipses were partial ones. The greatest number of solar eclipses in a year is five. In the tables, those years are 1805 and 1935.

The greatest number of lunar eclipses in a year is five. In the tables, those years are 1749 and 1879.

Since the least number of solar or lunar eclipses in a calendar year is two, any year with five of one type will be a year with seven eclipses altogether since there must be two eclipses of the other type in that same year.

Meeus in his *Canon of Solar Eclipses –2003 to +2526* lists 39 total solar eclipses having a duration of at least 7m. Three of those are in our tables—1937, 1955, and 1973. The eclipse of longest duration of 7m29s will be in 2186.

For that same period of time, Meeus lists 10 annular eclipses of 12m or more. Our tables have two of those—1955 and 1973.

The eclipse pattern tends to repeat in cycles of 18 years, 11 days and 8 hours. This cycle, called Saros, was known to the ancients and was possibly used by them to help predict eclipses.

Solar and Lunar Eclipses 1700–2050

Date		Time	Type	Position
1700				
Feb 18	●	23:49:29	P 0.374	0♓26
Mar 5	○	7:37	T 1.703	14♍47
Aug 14	●	16:59:00	P 0.700	21♌44
29	○	13:01	T 1.583	6♓03
Sep 13	●	0:34:10	P 0.300	20♍08
1701				
Feb 7	●	23:04:47	A 9m53s	19♒03
22	○	23:30	P 0.463	4♍07
Aug 4	●	9:31:38	T 5m06s	11♌36
18	○	13:32	P 0.234	25♒08
1702				
Jan 14	○	1:33	A 0.499	23♋39
28	●	1:37:03	A 4m14s	7♒46
Feb 12	○	14:21	A 0.145	23♌21
Jul 9	○	9:41	A 0.890	16♑38
24	●	21:38:44	AT 0m01s	1♌19
1703				
Jan 3	○	6:58	P 0.624	12♋22
17	●	11:24:17	T 0m50s	26♑45
Jun 29	○	1:13	T 1.352	6♑27
Jul 14	●	2:36:25	P 0.758	20♋47
Dec 8	●	15:41:25	P 0.428	15♐56
23	○	6:30	T 1.758	0♋49
1704				
Jan 7	●	2:14:42	P 0.318	15♑56
Jun 2	●	13:02:31	A 4m26s	11♊51
17	○	18:26	T 1.058	26♐21
Nov 27	●	5:33:47	A 0m01s	5♐06
Dec 11	○	7:11	P 0.534	19♊20
1705				
May 8	○	21:48	A 0.229	18♏06
22	●	19:54:59	AT 1m32s	1♊22
Jun 7	○	8:39	A 0.576	16♐07
Nov 1	○	3:13	A 0.325	8♉39
16	●	13:22:59	A 5m31s	24♏03
30	○	14:50	A 0.398	8♊10
1706				
Apr 28	○	1:32	P 0.470	7♏18
May 12	●	9:35:01	T 4m07s	21♉06
Oct 21	○	18:58	P 0.632	28♈00
Nov 5	●	14:23:49	A 7m02s	12♏46
1707				
Apr 2	●	18:12:18	P 0.508	12♈18
17	○	1:39	T 1.818	26♎19
May 2	●	2:28:09	P 0.434	10♉55
Sep 25	●	23:04:57	P 0.160	2♎08
Oct 11	○	10:25	T 1.840	17♈24
25	●	14:17:14	P 0.253	1♏30
1708				
Mar 22	●	6:51:29	A 0m46s	1♈43
Apr 5	○	5:38	P 0.496	15♎24
Sep 14	●	9:00:14	T 2m10s	21♍31
29	○	21:01	P 0.422	6♈39
1709				
Feb 24	○	6:51	A 0.573	5♍41
Mar 11	●	12:18:27	A 6m28s	20♓48
25	○	16:43	A 0.272	4♎44
Aug 20	○	8:28	A 0.414	27♒07
Sep 4	●	0:32:19	T 5m47s	11♍12
19	○	0:31	A 0.064	25♓41
1710				
Feb 13	○	22:50	P 0.833	24♌59
28	●	12:07:21	A 8m00s	9♓33
Aug 9	○	9:56	P 0.760	16♒18
24	●	17:17:08	T 4m00s	0♍59
1711				
Jan 18	●	22:23:25	P 0.308	28♑18
Feb 3	○	12:31	T 1.631	14♌07
17	●	13:30:07	P 0.092	28♒19
Jul 15	●	19:22:00	P 0.822	22♋28
29	○	17:50	T 1.489	5♒46
1712				
Jan 8	●	9:58:30	T 1m48s	17♑21
23	○	19:47	P 0.253	2♌57
Jul 3	●	22:34:49	A 5m18s	11♋53
18	○	8:22	P 0.168	25♑32
Dec 13	○	0:54	A 0.160	21♊22
28	●	1:24:47	T 4m15s	6♑32
1713				
Jan 11	○	20:15	A 0.054	21♋28
Jun 8	○	18:28	P 0.309	17♐44
22	●	23:15:31	A 5m23s	1♋12
Dec 2	○	3:17	P 0.415	9♊58
17	●	16:04:13	AT 0m56s	25♐42
1714				
May 13	●	18:39:22	P 0.101	22♉30
29	○	7:05	T 1.647	7♐24
Jun 12	●	4:39:54	P 0.698	20♊41
Nov 7	●	9:04:21	P 0.173	14♏37
21	○	13:02	T 1.784	28♉55
Dec 7	●	1:27:02	P 0.142	14♐39
1715				
May 3	●	9:36:21	T 4m14s	12♉15
18	○	12:29	P 0.590	26♏46
Oct 27	●	9:02:39	A 7m02s	3♏21
Nov 11	○	4:00	P 0.710	18♉08
1716				
Apr 6	○	21:22	A 0.207	17♎17
22	●	2:28:25	T 5m44s	2♉01
May 6	○	12:58	A 0.291	15♏53
Oct 1	○	9:10	A 0.380	8♈24
15	●	10:07:31	A 5m10s	22♎10
30	○	19:42	A 0.419	7♉25
1717				
Mar 27	○	3:14	P 0.601	6♎24
Apr 11	●	16:34:31	AT 0m39s	21♈38
Sep 20	○	17:54	P 0.606	27♓38
Oct 4	●	18:08:18	AT 0m56s	11♎22
1718				
Mar 2	●	7:31:27	P 0.329	11♓25
16	○	15:54	T 1.758	25♍43
Aug 26	●	0:41:36	P 0.584	2♍19
Sep 9	○	19:52	T 1.702	16♓40
24	●	8:34:10	P 0.389	0♎53
1719				
Feb 19	●	6:52:49	A 9m00s	0♓07
Mar 6	○	7:59	P 0.504	15♍07
Aug 15	●	16:59:43	T 4m27s	22♌07
29	○	20:24	P 0.364	5♓42
1720				
Jan 25	○	10:04	A 0.483	4♌49
Feb 8	●	9:52:22	A 3m40s	18♒53
23	○	22:48	A 0.166	4♍25
Jul 19	○	16:55	A 0.760	27♑05
Aug 4	●	4:38:05	A 0m27s	11♌48
18	○	2:32	A 0.121	25♒01
1721				
Jan 13	○	15:08	P 0.609	23♋33
27	●	20:05:01	T 1m07s	7♒56
Jul 9	○	8:40	T 1.217	16♑55
24	●	9:06:45	P 0.899	1♌13
Dec 19	●	0:31:44	P 0.417	27♐08
1722				
Jan 2	○	14:33	T 1.771	12♋00
17	●	11:06:59	P 0.325	27♑08
Jun 13	●	19:40:11	P 0.908	22♊17
29	○	1:49	T 1.194	6♑48
Dec 8	●	14:07:27	A 0m28s	16♐16
22	○	15:28	P 0.548	0♋31
1723				
May 20	○	4:52	A 0.096	28♏38
Jun 3	●	3:05:05	T 2m05s	11♊51
18	○	15:45	A 0.707	26♐34
Nov 12	○	11:42	A 0.298	19♉42
27	●	21:28:06	A 6m12s	5♐09
Dec 11	○	23:26	A 0.417	19♊20
1724				
May 8	○	8:20	P 0.341	17♏53
22	●	17:09:59	T 4m33s	1♊39
Nov 1	○	3:26	P 0.586	9♉00
15	●	22:07:27	A 7m15s	23♏48
1725				
Apr 13	●	2:11:13	P 0.419	23♈04
27	○	8:37	T 1.711	6♏57
May 12	●	10:12:08	P 0.545	21♉31
Oct 6	●	6:39:32	P 0.092	12♎55
21	○	18:35	T 1.830	28♈19
Nov 4	●	22:02:41	P 0.304	12♏29
1726				
Apr 2	●	14:38:07	A 0m51s	12♈32
16	○	13:06	P 0.597	26♎08
Sep 25	●	16:51:35	T 2m07s	2♎16
Oct 11	○	4:40	P 0.490	17♈29
1727				
Mar 7	○	15:16	A 0.530	16♍41
22	●	19:47:46	A 6m19s	1♈39
Apr 6	○	0:42	A 0.351	15♎32
Aug 31	○	15:12	A 0.288	7♓42
Sep 15	●	8:27:22	T 5m33s	21♍53
30	○	7:40	A 0.156	6♈26
1728				
Feb 25	○	7:24	P 0.798	6♍02
Mar 10	●	19:38:46	A 7m25s	20♓30
Aug 19	○	16:49	P 0.629	26♒50
Sep 4	●	0:59:13	T 3m44s	11♍37
1729				
Jan 29	●	6:48:29	P 0.299	9♒28
Feb 13	○	20:58	T 1.655	25♌13
27	●	21:26:53	P 0.135	9♓20
Jul 26	●	2:10:27	P 0.675	2♌55
Aug 9	○	1:05	T 1.623	16♒16
24	●	13:48:22	P 0.007	1♍14
1730				
Jan 18	●	18:45:05	T 1m59s	28♑33
Feb 3	○	3:56	P 0.270	14♌05
Jul 15	●	4:58:58	A 5m13s	22♋17
29	○	15:50	P 0.302	6♒01
Dec 24	○	8:58	A 0.150	2♋32
1731				
Jan 8	●	10:17:35	T 4m11s	17♑45
23	○	4:14	A 0.071	2♌38
Jun 20	○	1:50	P 0.169	28♐11
Jul 4	●	5:46:16	A 5m15s	11♋36
Dec 13	○	11:38	P 0.407	21♊08
29	●	0:46:44	AT 0m39s	6♑55
1732				
Jun 8	○	14:06	T 1.505	17♐53
22	●	11:38:40	P 0.846	1♋07
Nov 17	●	16:58:36	P 0.139	25♏41
Dec 1	○	21:40	T 1.768	10♊04
17	●	9:46:48	P 0.147	25♐50
1733				
May 13	●	17:18:18	T 4m07s	22♉50
28	○	19:08	P 0.732	7♐15
Nov 6	●	16:40:03	A 6m54s	14♏20
21	○	12:41	P 0.734	29♉14
1734				
Apr 18	○	4:32	A 0.112	28♎00
May 3	●	10:15:46	T 5m46s	12♉40
17	○	19:38	A 0.425	26♏25
Oct 12	○	17:08	A 0.312	19♈15
26	●	17:53:17	A 5m08s	3♏06
Nov 11	○	4:10	A 0.448	18♉28
1735				
Apr 7	○	10:57	P 0.529	17♎12
23	●	0:11:25	AT 0m44s	2♉19
Oct 2	○	1:19	P 0.513	8♈24
16	●	2:10:23	AT 1m02s	22♎14
1736				
Mar 12	●	15:05:44	P 0.273	22♓22
27	○	0:06	T 1.822	6♎36
Apr 11	●	7:17:56	P 0.075	21♈39
Sep 5	●	8:30:15	P 0.478	12♍57
20	○	2:51	T 1.809	27♓21
Oct 4	●	16:41:23	P 0.467	11♎42
1737				
Mar 1	●	14:35:07	A 8m04s	11♓07
16	○	16:22	P 0.554	26♍04
Aug 26	●	0:31:58	T 3m45s	2♍42
Sep 9	○	3:24	P 0.483	16♓20
1738				
Feb 4	○	18:29	A 0.460	15♌58
18	●	18:02:21	A 3m03s	29♒58
Mar 6	○	7:07	A 0.198	15♍25
Jul 31	○	0:13	A 0.635	7♒34
Aug 15	●	11:40:01	A 1m00s	22♌18
29	○	9:51	A 0.243	5♓36
1739				
Jan 24	○	23:14	P 0.589	4♌42
Feb 8	●	4:41:02	T 1m28s	19♒04
Jul 20	○	16:09	T 1.084	27♑23
Aug 4	●	15:40:45	A 3m59s	11♌40
Dec 30	●	9:21:55	P 0.406	8♑20
1740				
Jan 13	○	22:33	T 1.789	23♋10
28	●	19:54:47	P 0.339	8♒19
Jun 24	●	2:18:45	P 0.770	2♋43
Jul 9	○	9:13	T 1.328	17♑15
Dec 18	●	22:43:08	A 0m53s	27♐27
1741				
Jan 1	○	23:47	P 0.562	11♋42
Jun 13	●	10:12:38	T 2m35s	22♊18
28	○	22:48	A 0.843	7♑00
Nov 22	○	20:19	A 0.280	0♊49
Dec 8	●	5:37:49	A 6m51s	16♐18
22	○	8:05	A 0.430	0♋32
1742				
May 19	○	14:58	P 0.200	28♏24
Jun 3	●	0:39:45	T 5m00s	12♊08
Nov 12	○	12:02	P 0.552	20♉03
27	●	5:58:48	A 7m26s	4♐54
1743				
Apr 24	●	10:00:00	P 0.315	3♉44
May 8	○	15:26	T 1.583	17♏32
23	●	17:48:44	P 0.667	2♊03
Oct 17	●	14:25:31	P 0.039	23♎48
Nov 2	○	2:52	T 1.783	9♉18
16	●	5:58:13	P 0.342	23♏31
1744				
Apr 12	●	22:15:13	A 0m58s	23♈17
26	○	20:29	P 0.709	6♏47
Oct 6	●	0:51:12	T 2m05s	13♎05
21	○	12:26	P 0.546	28♈23
1745				
Mar 17	○	23:37	A 0.479	27♍37
Apr 2	●	3:09:07	A 6m13s	12♈28
16	○	8:35	A 0.438	26♎16
Sep 10	○	22:02	A 0.172	18♓19
25	●	16:28:44	T 5m21s	2♎38
Oct 10	○	14:57	A 0.238	17♈15
1746				
Mar 7	○	15:52	P 0.755	17♍03
22	●	3:02:37	A 6m51s	1♈22
Aug 30	○	23:48	P 0.507	7♓24
Sep 15	●	8:46:25	T 3m23s	22♍17
1747				
Feb 9	●	15:11:02	P 0.286	20♒35
25	○	5:18	T 1.687	6♍17
Mar 11	●	5:17:56	P 0.187	20♓18
Aug 6	●	9:01:06	P 0.534	13♌23
20	○	8:27	T 1.748	26♒49
Sep 4	●	21:07:45	P 0.109	11♍51
1748				
Jan 30	●	3:29:00	T 2m12s	9♒43
Feb 14	○	11:58	P 0.296	25♌10
Jul 25	●	11:26:49	A 5m12s	2♌43
Aug 8	○	23:23	P 0.429	16♒32
1749				
Jan 3	○	17:03	A 0.139	13♋43

Solar and Lunar Eclipses 1700–2050

18	●	19:08:45	T 4m07s	28♑57
Feb 2	○	12:09	A 0.093	13♌45
Jun 30	○	9:09	P 0.028	8♑39
Jul 14	●	12:19:09	A 4m45s	22♋01
29	○	16:31	A 0.064	6♒22
Dec 23	○	20:02	P 0.402	2♋19
1750				
Jan 8	●	9:28:33	AT 0m24s	18♑07
Jun 19	○	21:03	T 1.357	28♐20
Jul 3	●	18:38:41	P 0.996	11♋33
Nov 29	●	0:57:57	P 0.113	6♐47
Dec 13	○	6:22	T 1.758	21♊15
28	●	18:06:40	P 0.151	7♑01
1751				
May 25	●	0:55:01	T 3m54s	3♊22
Jun 9	○	1:42	P 0.882	17♐43
Nov 18	●	0:25:45	A 6m46s	25♏22
Dec 2	○	21:27	P 0.751	10♊23
1752				
Apr 28	○	11:35	A 0.006	8♏38
May 13	●	17:56:16	T 5m42s	23♉15
28	○	2:14	A 0.568	6♐55
Oct 23	○	1:13	A 0.254	0♉11
Nov 6	●	1:48:01	A 5m03s	14♏06
21	○	12:44	A 0.470	29♉34
1753				
Apr 17	○	18:33	P 0.445	27♎55
May 3	●	7:39:28	AT 0m48s	12♉57
Oct 12	○	8:51	P 0.433	19♈15
26	●	10:21:48	AT 1m08s	3♏11
1754				
Mar 23	●	22:28:44	P 0.203	3♈13
Apr 7	○	8:08	T 1.851	17♎24
22	●	14:25:44	P 0.167	2♉19
Sep 16	●	16:25:28	P 0.382	23♍39
Oct 1	○	9:58	T 1.727	8♈06
16	●	0:57:33	P 0.532	22♎35
1755				
Mar 12	●	22:09:20	A 7m06s	22♓03
28	○	0:36	P 0.617	6♎57
Sep 6	●	8:09:33	T 3m00s	13♍20
20	○	10:34	P 0.589	27♓01
1756				
Feb 16	○	2:48	A 0.428	27♌03
Mar 1	●	2:06:56	A 2m24s	10♓59
16	○	15:18	A 0.240	26♍21
Aug 10	○	7:37	A 0.517	18♒04
25	●	18:46:04	A 1m38s	2♍51
Sep 8	○	17:19	A 0.355	16♓15
1757				
Feb 4	○	7:17	P 0.566	15♌50
18	●	13:14:00	T 1m52s	0♓09
Jul 30	○	23:40	P 0.953	7♒52
Aug 14	●	22:16:32	A 4m36s	22♌09
1758				
Jan 9	●	18:13:30	P 0.397	19♑34
24	○	6:34	T 1.807	4♌20
Feb 8	●	4:40:36	P 0.355	19♒28
Jul 5	●	8:57:32	P 0.630	13♋08
20	○	16:37	T 1.461	27♑43
Dec 30	●	7:20:00	A 1m15s	8♑39
1759				
Jan 13	○	8:06	P 0.576	22♋53
Jun 24	●	17:20:46	T 2m60s	2♋45
Jul 10	○	5:49	A 0.980	17♑27
Dec 4	○	5:02	A 0.269	11♊58
19	●	13:49:51	A 7m25s	27♐28
1760				
Jan 2	○	16:47	A 0.441	11♋44
May 29	○	21:33	P 0.053	8♐54
Jun 13	●	8:09:01	T 5m27s	22♊37
Nov 22	○	20:41	P 0.524	1♊09
Dec 7	●	13:53:29	A 7m37s	16♐01
1761				
May 4	●	17:42:58	P 0.203	14♉23
18	○	22:12	T 1.449	28♏04
Jun 3	●	1:22:22	P 0.794	12♊34
Nov 12	○	11:16	T 1.745	20♉21
26	●	14:00:12	P 0.373	4♐37
1762				
Apr 24	●	5:41:57	A 1m08s	3♉58
May 8	○	3:45	P 0.832	17♏23
Oct 17	●	9:00:21	T 2m02s	23♎58
Nov 1	○	20:20	P 0.590	9♉21
1763				
Mar 29	○	7:49	A 0.414	8♎29
Apr 13	●	10:19:17	A 6m11s	23♈11
27	○	16:20	A 0.537	6♏57
Sep 22	○	5:03	A 0.071	29♓01
Oct 7	●	0:38:50	T 5m10s	13♎28
21	○	22:22	A 0.307	28♈08
1764				
Mar 18	○	0:11	P 0.698	27♍58
Apr 1	●	10:17:01	A 6m20s	12♈10
Sep 10	○	6:58	P 0.399	18♓02
25	●	16:41:29	T 3m01s	3♎03
1765				
Feb 19	●	23:28:20	P 0.264	1♓39
Mar 7	○	13:29	T 1.732	17♍16
21	●	13:01:30	P 0.253	1♈11
Aug 16	●	15:53:43	P 0.400	23♌53
30	○	15:55	T 1.863	7♓25
Sep 15	●	4:32:19	P 0.201	22♍31
1766				
Feb 9	●	12:09:28	T 2m28s	20♒51
24	○	19:53	P 0.332	6♍13
Aug 5	●	17:56:42	A 5m15s	13♌11
20	○	7:01	P 0.549	27♒05
1767				
Jan 15	○	1:08	A 0.128	24♋53
30	●	3:56:40	T 4m06s	10♒08
Feb 13	○	19:59	A 0.124	24♌50
Jul 11	○	16:27	A 0.851	19♑05
25	●	18:55:33	A 4m21s	2♌27
Aug 10	○	0:03	A 0.182	16♒53
1768				
Jan 4	○	4:29	P 0.401	13♋31
19	●	18:09:15	AT 0m13s	29♑19
Jun 30	○	3:56	T 1.206	8♑46
Jul 14	●	1:40:43	AT 0m29s	21♋59
Dec 9	●	9:01:17	P 0.093	17♐55
23	○	15:07	T 1.752	2♋27
1769				
Jan 8	●	2:26:28	P 0.153	18♑13
Jun 4	●	8:28:17	T 3m36s	13♊52
19	○	8:11	T 1.037	28♐08
Nov 28	●	8:18:22	A 6m39s	6♐28
Dec 13	○	6:17	P 0.761	21♊34
1770				
May 25	●	1:29:57	T 5m32s	3♊47
Jun 8	○	8:45	A 0.718	17♐22
Nov 3	○	9:24	A 0.208	11♉10
17	●	9:51:38	A 4m56s	25♏09
Dec 2	○	21:22	A 0.482	10♊43
1771				
Apr 29	○	2:04	P 0.351	8♏35
May 14	●	14:59:48	AT 0m49s	23♉31
Oct 23	○	16:30	P 0.365	0♉09
Nov 6	●	18:40:48	AT 1m13s	14♏12
1772				
Apr 3	●	5:43:35	P 0.123	14♈01
17	○	16:05	T 1.766	28♎09
May 2	●	21:26:27	P 0.268	12♉56
Sep 27	●	0:28:02	P 0.299	4♎25
Oct 11	○	17:14	T 1.643	18♈56
26	●	9:21:03	P 0.585	3♏32
1773				
Mar 23	●	5:36:42	A 6m13s	2♈55
Apr 7	○	8:43	P 0.691	17♎45
Sep 16	●	15:52:08	T 2m18s	24♍01
30	○	17:53	P 0.683	7♈46
1774				
Feb 26	○	10:59	A 0.386	8♍06
Mar 12	●	10:05:00	A 1m43s	21♓56
27	○	23:19	A 0.295	7♎13
Aug 21	○	15:06	A 0.409	28♒38
Sep 6	●	1:57:26	A 2m20s	13♍28
20	○	0:57	A 0.454	26♓58
1775				
Feb 15	○	15:11	P 0.531	26♌54
Mar 1	●	21:39:04	T 2m20s	11♓11
Aug 11	○	7:15	P 0.830	18♒23
26	●	4:59:24	A 5m16s	2♍42
1776				
Jan 21	●	3:02:13	P 0.385	0♒45
Feb 4	○	14:30	T 1.785	15♌27
19	●	13:19:53	P 0.380	0♓33
Jul 15	●	15:39:15	P 0.494	23♋33
31	○	0:02	T 1.591	8♒12
Aug 14	●	5:22:39	P 0.044	21♌52
1777				
Jan 9	●	15:55:21	A 1m32s	19♑51
23	○	16:24	P 0.594	4♌03
Jul 5	●	0:29:14	T 3m18s	13♋11
20	○	12:49	P 0.109	27♑53
Dec 14	○	13:49	A 0.263	23♊09
29	●	22:03:12	A 7m53s	8♑39
1778				
Jan 13	○	1:29	A 0.452	22♋56
Jun 10	○	4:01	A 0.966	19♐20
24	●	15:34:39	T 5m53s	3♋04
Dec 4	○	5:28	P 0.505	12♊19
18	●	21:53:36	A 7m45s	27♐11
1779				
May 16	●	1:17:25	P 0.080	24♉57
30	○	4:52	T 1.306	8♐33
Jun 14	●	8:51:11	P 0.928	23♊02
Nov 23	○	19:45	T 1.717	1♊27
Dec 7	●	22:08:38	P 0.396	15♐45
1780				
May 4	●	13:00:26	A 1m21s	14♉35
18	○	10:58	P 0.962	27♏57
Oct 27	●	17:18:12	T 1m60s	4♏55
Nov 12	○	4:20	P 0.623	20♉23
1781				
Apr 8	○	15:55	A 0.339	19♎17
23	●	17:21:10	A 6m13s	3♉51
May 8	○	0:01	A 0.646	17♏34
Oct 17	●	8:55:43	T 4m59s	24♎21
Nov 1	○	5:56	A 0.364	9♉05
1782				
Mar 29	○	8:23	P 0.631	8♎50
Apr 12	●	17:24:31	A 5m51s	22♈54
Sep 21	○	14:17	P 0.303	28♓45
Oct 7	●	0:43:03	T 2m37s	13♎52
1783				
Mar 3	●	7:40:11	P 0.231	12♓40
18	○	21:31	T 1.789	28♍11
Apr 1	●	20:38:22	P 0.330	12♈00
Aug 27	●	22:51:46	P 0.276	4♍27
Sep 10	○	23:33	T 1.759	18♓04
26	●	12:04:01	P 0.281	3♎15
1784				
Feb 20	●	20:45:21	T 2m44s	1♓56
Mar 7	○	3:39	P 0.379	17♍11
Aug 16	●	0:31:36	A 5m23s	23♌40
30	○	14:46	P 0.660	7♓41
1785				
Jan 25	○	9:11	A 0.113	6♌03
Feb 9	●	12:40:25	T 4m07s	21♒16
24	○	3:42	A 0.165	5♍52
Jul 21	○	23:46	A 0.713	29♑33
Aug 5	●	1:37:06	A 4m01s	12♌55
20	○	7:38	A 0.295	27♒26
1786				
Jan 14	○	12:56	P 0.398	24♋42
30	●	2:45:10	AT 0m05s	10♒28
Jul 11	○	10:47	T 1.053	19♑12
25	●	8:46:18	T 0m59s	2♌26
Dec 20	●	17:07:01	P 0.077	29♐05
1787				
Jan 3	○	23:53	T 1.747	13♋39
19	●	10:42:57	P 0.159	29♑23
Jun 15	●	15:59:06	T 3m09s	24♊21
30	○	14:39	T 1.195	8♑34
Dec 9	●	16:15:19	A 6m32s	17♐36
24	○	15:08	P 0.770	2♋46
1788				
Jun 4	●	8:59:14	T 5m16s	14♊17
18	○	15:15	A 0.873	27♐48
Nov 13	○	17:42	A 0.172	22♉13
27	●	18:02:37	A 4m46s	6♐16
Dec 13	○	6:04	A 0.489	21♊53
1789				
May 9	○	9:28	P 0.246	19♏11
24	●	22:11:42	AT 0m46s	4♊02
Nov 3	○	0:17	P 0.309	11♉07
17	●	3:08:19	AT 1m19s	25♏16
1790				
Apr 14	●	12:47:54	P 0.029	24♈43
28	○	23:53	T 1.669	8♏49
May 14	●	4:17:05	P 0.384	23♉28
Oct 8	●	8:38:33	P 0.229	15♎15
23	○	0:40	T 1.573	29♈50
Nov 6	●	17:52:55	P 0.625	14♏34
1791				
Apr 3	●	12:54:55	A 5m21s	13♈42
18	○	16:41	P 0.778	28♎29
Sep 27	●	23:42:13	T 1m36s	4♎46
Oct 12	○	1:23	P 0.761	18♈37
1792				
Mar 8	○	19:02	A 0.335	19♍05
22	●	17:57:19	A 1m02s	2♈49
Apr 7	○	7:12	A 0.361	18♎01
Aug 31	○	22:42	A 0.308	9♓14
Sep 16	●	9:13:36	A 3m02s	24♍08
30	○	8:43	A 0.542	7♈44
1793				
Feb 25	○	22:59	P 0.490	7♍56
Mar 12	●	5:59:52	T 2m52s	22♓10
Aug 21	○	14:55	P 0.712	28♒57
Sep 5	●	11:47:09	A 6m02s	13♍17
1794				
Jan 31	●	11:48:31	P 0.368	11♒56
Feb 14	○	22:21	T 1.755	26♌32
Mar 1	●	21:53:43	P 0.414	11♓35
Jul 26	●	22:24:14	P 0.360	4♌00
Aug 11	○	7:29	T 1.716	18♒43
25	●	12:08:40	P 0.171	2♍24
1795				
Jan 21	●	0:28:58	A 1m45s	1♒02
Feb 4	○	0:39	P 0.617	15♌12
Jul 16	●	7:41:21	T 3m26s	23♋38
31	○	19:50	P 0.239	8♒22
Dec 25	○	22:37	A 0.259	4♋21
1796				
Jan 10	●	6:14:38	A 8m15s	19♑50
24	○	10:09	A 0.466	4♌07
Jun 20	○	10:28	A 0.809	29♐46
Jul 4	●	23:02:40	T 6m02s	13♋31
Dec 14	○	14:16	P 0.491	23♊30
29	●	5:54:43	A 7m51s	8♑21
1797				
Jun 9	○	11:30	T 1.159	19♐01
24	●	16:17:57	T 2m47s	3♋29
Dec 4	○	4:18	T 1.697	12♊36
18	●	6:21:35	P 0.414	26♐55
1798				
May 15	●	20:10:20	A 1m36s	25♉08
29	○	18:07	T 1.099	8♐27

Solar and Lunar Eclipses 1700–2050

Date		Time	Type	Position
Nov 8	●	1:44:26	T 1m59s	15♏57
23	☽	12:25	P 0.647	1♊28
1799				
Apr 19	☽	23:52	A 0.251	0♏00
May 5	●	0:12:54	A 6m20s	14♉27
19	☽	7:36	A 0.764	28♏08
Oct 28	●	17:21:33	T 4m50s	5♏19
Nov 12	☽	13:38	A 0.409	20♉06
1800				
Apr 9	☽	16:26	P 0.550	19♎38
24	●	0:23:46	A 5m26s	3♉33
Oct 2	☽	21:46	P 0.220	9♈31
18	●	8:51:32	T 2m14s	24♎45
1801				
Mar 14	●	15:45:13	P 0.187	23♓37
30	☽	5:24	T 1.840	9♎02
Apr 13	●	4:07:46	P 0.421	22♈45
Sep 8	●	5:54:17	P 0.162	15♍03
22	☽	7:19	T 1.667	28♓47
Oct 7	●	19:42:14	P 0.351	14♎03
1802				
Mar 4	●	5:14:09	T 3m02s	12♓57
19	☽	11:15	P 0.442	28♍05
Aug 28	●	7:11:39	A 5m35s	4♍12
Sep 11	☽	22:36	P 0.762	18♓21
1803				
Feb 6	☽	17:10	A 0.092	17♌10
21	●	21:18:27	T 4m10s	2♓21
Mar 8	☽	11:17	A 0.217	16♍50
Aug 3	☽	7:05	A 0.579	10♒02
17	●	8:24:44	A 3m47s	23♌25
Sep 1	☽	15:19	A 0.400	8♓03
1804				
Jan 26	☽	21:21	P 0.392	5♌53
Feb 11	●	11:16:14	A 0m00s	21♒36
Jul 22	☽	17:38	P 0.901	29♑38
Aug 5	●	15:56:55	T 1m20s	12♌55
1805				
Jan 1	●	1:14:31	P 0.064	10♑16
15	☽	8:41	T 1.742	24♋52
30	●	18:56:43	P 0.168	10♒32
Jun 26	●	23:27:18	P 0.936	4♋48
Jul 11	☽	21:05	T 1.355	18♑58
26	●	6:14:01	P 0.141	2♌44
Dec 21	●	0:17:16	A 6m27s	28♐46
1806				
Jan 5	☽	0:02	P 0.775	13♋59
Jun 16	●	16:24:08	T 4m55s	24♊45
30	☽	21:44	A 1.032	8♑13
Nov 26	☽	2:05	A 0.145	3♊19
Dec 10	●	2:19:21	A 4m32s	17♐25
25	☽	14:48	A 0.492	3♋05
1807				
May 21	☽	16:49	P 0.135	29♏44
Jun 6	●	5:18:14	AT 0m38s	14♊31
Nov 15	☽	8:10	P 0.265	22♉09
29	●	11:41:52	AT 1m26s	6♐23
1808				
May 10	☽	7:38	T 1.564	19♏26
25	●	11:02:18	P 0.506	3♊59
Oct 19	●	16:55:09	P 0.169	26♎08
Nov 3	☽	8:13	T 1.515	10♉47
18	●	2:29:46	P 0.656	25♏38
1809				
Apr 14	●	20:06:52	A 4m35s	24♈26
30	☽	0:33	P 0.873	9♏10
Oct 9	●	7:38:23	T 1m02s	15♎36
23	☽	9:02	P 0.827	29♈30
1810				
Mar 21	☽	2:54	A 0.269	29♍59
Apr 4	●	1:41:01	A 0m21s	13♈38
19	☽	14:54	A 0.441	28♎44
Sep 13	☽	6:27	A 0.220	19♓54
28	●	16:37:07	A 3m45s	4♎52
Oct 12	☽	16:39	A 0.617	18♈35
1811				
Mar 10	☽	6:37	P 0.434	18♍54
24	●	14:11:55	T 3m27s	3♈03
Sep 2	☽	22:42	P 0.604	9♓34
17	●	18:43:27	A 6m51s	23♍56
1812				
Feb 12	●	20:28:23	P 0.342	23♒03
27	☽	6:05	T 1.714	7♍33
Mar 13	●	6:19:12	P 0.459	22♓34
Aug 7	●	5:15:33	P 0.234	14♌28
22	☽	15:01	T 1.832	29♒17
Sep 5	●	19:03:52	P 0.287	13♍00
1813				
Feb 1	●	8:58:10	A 1m52s	12♒12
15	☽	8:50	P 0.649	26♌18
Jul 27	●	14:55:18	T 3m27s	4♌05
Aug 12	☽	2:53	P 0.365	18♒52
1814				
Jan 6	☽	7:28	A 0.257	15♋34
21	●	14:24:29	A 8m28s	1♒00
Feb 4	☽	18:47	A 0.484	15♌17
Jul 2	☽	16:51	A 0.650	10♑11
17	●	6:30:11	T 6m34s	23♋58
Dec 26	☽	23:08	P 0.483	4♋43
1815				
Jan 10	●	13:56:48	A 7m56s	19♑32
Jun 21	☽	18:06	T 1.008	29♐27
Jul 6	●	23:42:48	T 3m13s	13♋56
Dec 16	☽	12:55	T 1.685	23♊47
30	●	14:38:19	P 0.427	8♑07
1816				
May 27	●	3:13:08	A 1m53s	5♊39
Jun 10	☽	1:14	T 1.241	18♐56
Nov 19	●	10:17:06	T 1m59s	27♏01
Dec 4	☽	20:35	P 0.663	12♊36
1817				
May 1	☽	7:44	A 0.155	10♏41
16	●	6:57:57	A 6m30s	25♉00
30	☽	15:07	A 0.888	8♐40
Nov 9	●	1:53:36	T 4m42s	16♏21
23	☽	21:27	A 0.444	1♊11
1818				
Apr 21	☽	0:20	P 0.457	0♏22
May 5	●	7:15:31	A 5m05s	14♉09
Oct 14	☽	5:25	P 0.151	20♈21
29	●	17:06:52	T 1m51s	5♏42
1819				
Mar 25	●	23:44:11	P 0.133	4♈30
Apr 10	☽	13:08	T 1.757	19♎50
24	●	11:31:41	P 0.523	3♉26
Sep 19	●	13:03:27	P 0.060	25♍44
Oct 3	☽	15:13	T 1.587	9♈34
19	●	3:26:59	P 0.409	24♎55
1820				
Mar 14	●	13:36:58	T 3m20s	23♓55
29	☽	18:42	P 0.517	8♎56
Sep 7	●	13:59:40	A 5m49s	14♍48
22	☽	6:35	P 0.851	29♓05
1821				
Feb 17	☽	1:05	A 0.062	28♌14
Mar 4	●	5:49:56	T 4m14s	13♓23
18	☽	18:45	A 0.281	27♍45
Aug 13	☽	14:26	A 0.450	20♒33
27	●	15:19:25	A 3m38s	3♍58
Sep 11	☽	23:05	A 0.497	18♓42
1822				
Feb 6	☽	5:43	P 0.380	17♌01
21	●	19:40:24	A 0m02s	2♓40
Aug 3	☽	0:30	P 0.753	10♒06
16	●	23:14:18	T 1m32s	23♌26
1823				
Jan 12	●	9:19:49	P 0.048	21♑27
26	☽	17:25	T 1.731	6♌02
Feb 11	●	3:02:46	P 0.186	21♒39
Jul 8	●	6:56:08	P 0.796	15♋15
23	☽	3:32	T 1.512	29♑24
Aug 6	●	13:45:26	P 0.275	13♌14
1824				
Jan 1	●	8:20:50	A 6m21s	9♑57
16	☽	8:54	P 0.783	25♋12
Jun 26	●	23:46:17	T 4m24s	5♋12
Jul 11	☽	4:15	P 0.133	18♑38
Dec 6	☽	10:32	A 0.124	14♊28
20	●	10:40:20	A 4m15s	28♐35
1825				
Jan 4	☽	23:32	A 0.493	14♋18
Jun 1	☽	0:06	P 0.015	10♐15
16	●	12:18:48	AT 0m25s	24♊58
Nov 25	☽	16:09	P 0.231	3♊15
Dec 9	●	20:21:31	AT 1m34s	17♐33
1826				
May 21	☽	15:15	T 1.446	29♏59
Jun 5	●	17:38:51	P 0.641	14♊27
Oct 31	●	1:20:20	P 0.122	7♏07
Nov 14	☽	15:56	T 1.471	21♉49
29	●	11:13:55	P 0.677	6♐46
1827				
Apr 26	●	3:10:59	A 3m53s	5♉06
May 11	☽	8:17	P 0.980	19♏47
Oct 20	●	15:41:50	AT 0m30s	26♎29
Nov 3	☽	16:52	P 0.880	10♉29
1828				
Mar 31	☽	10:39	A 0.192	10♎50
Apr 14	●	9:19:24	AT 0m18s	24♈23
29	☽	22:28	A 0.532	9♏25
Sep 23	☽	14:05	A 0.130	0♈29
Oct 9	●	0:07:33	A 4m26s	15♎40
23	☽	0:44	A 0.679	29♈29
1829				
Mar 20	☽	14:08	P 0.368	29♍48
Apr 3	●	22:18:23	T 4m05s	13♈54
Sep 13	☽	6:33	P 0.505	20♓14
28	●	1:46:40	A 7m43s	4♎39
1830				
Feb 23	●	5:04:01	P 0.310	4♓08
Mar 9	☽	13:43	T 1.663	18♍32
24	●	14:38:31	P 0.515	3♈28
Aug 18	●	12:13:24	P 0.117	24♌59
Sep 2	☽	22:38	T 1.803	9♓54
17	●	2:08:00	P 0.393	23♍39
1831				
Feb 12	●	17:21:34	A 1m57s	23♒19
26	☽	16:56	P 0.690	7♍20
Aug 7	●	22:15:49	T 3m20s	14♌35
23	☽	9:60	P 0.483	29♒24
1832				
Jan 17	☽	16:18	A 0.252	26♋46
Feb 1	●	22:30:03	A 8m35s	12♒09
16	☽	3:20	A 0.508	26♌24
Jul 12	☽	23:16	A 0.493	20♑36
27	●	14:00:55	T 6m46s	4♌27
Aug 11	☽	14:15	A 0.066	18♒41
1833				
Jan 6	☽	7:60	P 0.473	15♋55
20	●	21:56:44	A 8m00s	0♒42
Jul 2	☽	0:43	P 0.857	9♑53
17	●	7:07:51	T 3m30s	24♋23
Dec 26	☽	21:33	T 1.675	4♋58
1834				
Jan 9	●	22:55:19	P 0.442	19♑18
Jun 7	●	10:08:30	P 0.930	16♊07
21	☽	8:20	T 1.387	29♐23
Nov 30	●	18:56:26	T 2m02s	8♐09
Dec 16	☽	4:48	P 0.675	23♊46
1835				
May 12	☽	15:29	A 0.049	21♏17
27	●	13:35:33	A 6m44s	5♊29
Jun 10	☽	22:36	P 0.068	19♐09
Nov 20	●	10:31:48	T 4m35s	27♏26
Dec 5	☽	5:20	A 0.472	12♊17
1836				
May 1	☽	8:07	P 0.353	11♏01
15	●	14:01:28	A 4m47s	24♉42
Oct 24	☽	13:15	P 0.097	1♉16
Nov 9	●	1:29:15	T 1m29s	16♏43
1837				
Apr 5	●	7:35:19	P 0.065	15♈19
20	☽	20:41	T 1.660	0♏32
May 4	●	18:48:18	P 0.638	14♉03
Oct 13	☽	23:17	T 1.519	20♈26
29	●	11:19:13	P 0.454	5♏51
1838				
Mar 25	●	21:52:06	T 3m39s	4♈49
Apr 10	☽	1:59	P 0.608	19♎42
Sep 18	●	20:55:46	A 6m06s	25♍28
Oct 3	☽	14:41	P 0.929	9♈53
1839				
Feb 28	☽	8:54	A 0.023	9♍16
Mar 15	●	14:13:33	T 4m20s	24♓20
30	☽	2:03	A 0.359	8♎35
Aug 24	☽	21:52	A 0.328	1♓07
Sep 7	●	22:23:17	A 3m34s	14♍34
23	☽	6:57	A 0.583	29♓26
1840				
Feb 17	☽	14:02	P 0.362	28♌07
Mar 4	●	3:58:13	A 0m03s	13♓42
Aug 13	☽	7:23	P 0.607	20♒36
27	●	6:37:23	T 1m45s	4♍00
1841				
Jan 22	●	17:24:00	P 0.032	2♒37
Feb 6	☽	2:07	T 1.718	17♌12
21	●	11:03:47	P 0.210	2♓43
Jul 18	●	14:25:01	P 0.656	25♋42
Aug 2	☽	10:01	T 1.668	9♒51
16	●	21:20:15	P 0.406	23♌45
1842				
Jan 11	●	16:25:29	A 6m15s	21♑08
26	☽	17:44	P 0.793	6♌23
Jul 8	●	7:06:17	T 4m06s	15♋38
22	☽	10:47	P 0.292	29♑04
Dec 17	☽	19:02	A 0.108	25♊39
31	●	19:04:14	A 3m54s	9♑47
1843				
Jan 16	☽	8:14	A 0.495	25♋30
Jun 12	☽	7:22	A 0.872	20♐44
27	●	19:16:54	AT 0m08s	5♋25
Jul 11	☽	16:50	A 0.022	18♑31
Dec 7	☽	0:11	P 0.203	14♊22
21	●	5:03:17	T 1m43s	28♐44
1844				
May 31	☽	22:51	T 1.326	10♐32
Jun 16	●	0:13:13	P 0.778	24♊53
Nov 10	●	9:51:31	P 0.085	18♏09
24	☽	23:45	T 1.436	2♊53
Dec 9	●	20:01:30	P 0.692	17♐56
1845				
May 6	●	10:08:48	A 3m15s	15♉42
21	☽	15:54	T 1.096	0♐21
Oct 30	●	23:51:46	AT 0m02s	7♏27
Nov 14	☽	0:49	P 0.922	21♉30
1846				
Apr 11	☽	18:11	A 0.100	21♎36
25	●	16:50:20	AT 0m54s	5♉04
May 11	☽	5:54	A 0.635	20♏01
Oct 4	☽	22:21	A 0.078	11♈27
20	●	7:46:02	A 5m05s	26♎33
Nov 3	☽	8:59	A 0.729	10♉29
1847				
Mar 31	☽	21:27	P 0.286	10♎37
Apr 15	●	6:16:03	T 4m44s	24♈39
Sep 24	☽	14:34	P 0.418	0♈59
Oct 9	●	9:00:13	A 8m35s	15♎27
1848				
Mar 5	●	13:31:24	P 0.266	15♓09
19	☽	21:12	T 1.599	29♍26

Solar and Lunar Eclipses 1700–2050

Date		Time	Type	Position
Apr 3	●	22:48:56	P 0.583	14♈18
Aug 28	●	19:18:11	P 0.009	5♍32
Sep 13	☽	6:19	T 1.700	20♓34
27	●	9:21:09	P 0.488	4♎23
1849				
Feb 23	●	1:38:00	A 1m58s	4♓23
Mar 9	☽	0:56	P 0.741	18♍19
Aug 18	●	5:40:40	T 3m07s	25♌07
Sep 2	☽	17:10	P 0.594	10♓00
1850				
Jan 28	☽	1:06	A 0.244	7♌58
Feb 12	●	6:29:27	A 8m35s	23♒15
26	☽	11:48	A 0.542	7♍27
Jul 24	☽	5:40	A 0.337	1♒02
Aug 7	●	21:33:44	T 6m50s	14♌56
22	☽	20:55	A 0.199	29♒13
1851				
Jan 17	☽	16:51	P 0.464	27♋08
Feb 1	●	5:54:16	A 8m01s	11♒50
Jul 13	☽	7:22	P 0.707	20♑18
28	●	14:33:31	T 3m41s	4♌51
1852				
Jan 7	☽	6:11	T 1.666	16♋11
21	●	7:12:04	P 0.458	0♒28
Jun 17	●	16:59:42	P 0.783	26♊34
Jul 1	☽	15:26	T 1.533	9♑50
Dec 11	●	3:40:35	T 2m05s	19♐20
26	☽	13:03	P 0.681	4♋57
1853				
Jun 6	●	20:07:12	A 6m59s	15♊57
21	☽	6:02	P 0.206	29♐37
Nov 30	●	19:15:29	T 4m28s	8♐34
Dec 15	☽	13:18	A 0.492	23♊26
1854				
May 12	☽	15:46	P 0.239	21♏38
26	●	20:42:42	A 4m32s	5♊12
Nov 4	☽	21:13	P 0.054	12♉15
20	●	9:56:47	AT 1m07s	27♏48
1855				
May 2	☽	4:05	T 1.551	11♏11
16	●	2:01:00	P 0.762	24♉37
Oct 25	☽	7:29	T 1.464	1♉21
Nov 9	●	19:17:39	P 0.489	16♏51
1856				
Apr 5	●	6:00:50	T 3m56s	15♈39
20	☽	9:07	P 0.710	0♏24
Sep 29	●	3:59:33	A 6m21s	6♎11
Oct 13	☽	22:54	P 0.996	20♈44
1857				
Mar 25	●	22:29:27	T 4m28s	5♈14
Apr 9	☽	9:13	A 0.450	19♎21
Sep 4	☽	5:22	A 0.215	11♓43
18	●	5:35:54	A 3m34s	25♍14
Oct 3	☽	14:57	A 0.658	10♈13
1858				
Feb 27	☽	22:14	P 0.332	9♍09
Mar 15	●	12:05:17	A 0m02s	24♓38
Aug 24	☽	14:21	P 0.471	1♓08
Sep 7	●	14:09:18	T 1m50s	14♍37
1859				
Feb 3	●	1:22:26	P 0.008	13♒44
17	☽	10:43	T 1.694	28♌18
Mar 4	●	18:54:39	P 0.246	13♓42
Jul 29	●	21:56:43	P 0.521	6♌11
Aug 13	☽	16:34	T 1.815	20♒20
28	●	5:01:50	P 0.526	4♍20
1860				
Jan 23	●	0:27:18	A 6m07s	2♒17
Feb 7	☽	2:30	P 0.811	17♌32
Jul 18	●	14:26:13	T 3m39s	26♋06
Aug 1	☽	17:25	P 0.445	9♒31
Dec 28	☽	3:34	A 0.095	6♋50
1861				
Jan 11	●	3:29:12	A 3m30s	20♑58
26	☽	16:54	A 0.500	6♌41
Jun 22	☽	14:35	A 0.740	1♑11
Jul 8	●	2:10:15	A 0m14s	15♋50
21	☽	23:50	A 0.169	28♑58
Dec 17	☽	8:19	P 0.184	25♊32
31	●	13:48:56	T 1m55s	9♑57
1862				
Jun 12	☽	6:21	T 1.196	21♐01
27	●	6:42:11	P 0.922	5♋18
Nov 21	●	18:29:32	P 0.058	29♏15
Dec 6	☽	7:40	T 1.411	14♊00
21	●	4:52:53	P 0.702	29♐08
1863				
May 17	●	17:00:32	P 0.861	26♉15
Jun 1	☽	23:26	T 1.219	10♐52
Nov 11	●	8:08:51	A 0m22s	18♏28
25	☽	8:56	P 0.952	2♊36
1864				
May 6	●	0:16:38	AT 1m25s	15♉42
21	☽	13:12	A 0.748	0♐34
Oct 15	☽	6:31	A 0.023	22♈18
30	●	15:30:22	A 5m41s	7♏29
Nov 13	☽	17:21	A 0.768	21♉31
1865				
Apr 11	☽	4:38	P 0.193	21♎23
25	●	14:08:26	T 5m23s	5♉21
Oct 4	☽	22:40	P 0.341	11♈47
19	●	16:21:05	A 9m27s	26♎18
1866				
Mar 16	●	21:51:14	P 0.212	26♓06
31	☽	4:33	T 1.523	10♎16
Apr 15	●	6:51:31	P 0.664	25♈04
Sep 24	☽	14:07	T 1.607	1♈17
Oct 8	●	16:44:14	P 0.569	15♎10
1867				
Mar 6	●	9:46:40	A 1m57s	15♓23
20	☽	8:49	P 0.804	29♍15
Aug 29	●	13:13:00	T 2m51s	5♍41
Sep 14	☽	0:26	P 0.695	20♓39
1868				
Feb 8	☽	9:50	A 0.229	19♌06
23	●	14:21:25	A 8m30s	4♓18
Mar 8	☽	20:10	A 0.585	18♍27
Aug 3	☽	12:09	A 0.189	11♒29
18	●	5:12:04	T 6m47s	25♌29
Sep 2	☽	3:41	A 0.324	9♓47
1869				
Jan 28	☽	1:38	P 0.451	8♌19
Feb 11	●	13:46:34	A 8m02s	22♒56
Jul 23	☽	14:03	P 0.560	0♒44
Aug 7	●	22:01:00	T 3m49s	15♌21
1870				
Jan 17	☽	14:46	T 1.657	27♋22
31	●	15:26:18	P 0.478	11♒37
Jun 28	●	23:46:41	P 0.634	6♋59
Jul 12	☽	22:34	T 1.677	20♑17
28	●	11:02:25	P 0.074	5♌07
Dec 22	●	12:27:30	T 2m11s	0♑31
1871				
Jan 6	☽	21:17	P 0.689	16♋08
Jun 18	●	2:35:00	A 7m13s	26♊23
Jul 2	☽	13:28	P 0.343	10♑05
Dec 12	●	4:03:36	T 4m23s	19♐44
26	☽	21:19	A 0.507	4♋37
1872				
May 22	☽	23:18	P 0.115	2♐11
Jun 6	●	3:20:01	A 4m20s	15♊40
Nov 15	☽	5:20	P 0.023	23♉17
30	●	18:29:31	AT 0m47s	8♐56
1873				
May 12	☽	11:20	T 1.429	21♏47
26	●	9:08:53	P 0.897	5♊08
Nov 4	☽	15:51	T 1.422	12♉21
20	●	3:22:50	P 0.514	27♏55
1874				
Apr 16	●	14:00:53	T 4m11s	26♈24
May 1	☽	16:03	P 0.828	11♏02
Oct 10	●	11:13:34	A 6m28s	16♎59
25	☽	7:16	T 1.050	1♉41
1875				
Apr 6	●	6:37:27	T 4m37s	16♈04
20	☽	16:15	A 0.554	0♏03
Sep 15	☽	12:57	A 0.111	22♓23
29	●	12:58:10	A 3m36s	5♎58
Oct 14	☽	23:03	A 0.723	21♈05
1876				
Mar 10	☽	6:22	P 0.294	20♍08
25	●	20:05:07	A 0m01s	5♈32
Sep 3	☽	21:23	P 0.342	11♓44
17	●	21:49:16	T 1m53s	25♍18
1877				
Feb 27	☽	19:16	T 1.664	9♍22
Mar 15	●	2:38:11	P 0.292	24♓39
Aug 9	●	5:30:23	P 0.389	16♌41
23	☽	23:12	T 1.685	0♓52
Sep 7	●	12:48:45	P 0.638	14♍58
1878				
Feb 2	●	8:27:52	A 5m59s	13♒25
17	☽	11:11	P 0.834	28♌39
Jul 29	●	21:47:19	T 3m11s	6♌34
Aug 13	☽	0:08	P 0.591	20♒01
1879				
Jan 8	☽	12:04	A 0.081	18♋02
22	●	11:53:11	A 3m03s	2♒09
Feb 7	☽	1:29	A 0.511	17♌50
Jul 3	☽	21:51	A 0.610	11♑38
19	●	9:04:35	A 0m38s	26♋17
Aug 2	☽	6:58	A 0.310	9♒27
Dec 28	☽	16:26	P 0.166	6♋42
1880				
Jan 11	●	22:34:29	T 2m07s	21♑09
Jun 22	☽	13:51	T 1.064	1♑29
Jul 7	●	13:10:32	A 5m46s	15♋43
Dec 2	●	3:11:30	P 0.037	10♐23
16	☽	15:39	T 1.391	25♊09
31	●	13:45:06	P 0.710	10♑20
1881				
May 27	●	23:48:40	P 0.737	6♊45
Jun 12	☽	6:54	T 1.349	21♐22
Nov 21	●	16:31:11	A 0m43s	29♏33
Dec 5	☽	17:09	P 0.975	13♊44
1882				
May 17	●	7:36:30	T 1m50s	26♉16
Jun 1	☽	20:22	A 0.872	11♐04
Nov 10	●	23:22:24	A 5m57s	18♏30
25	☽	1:51	A 0.797	2♊38
1883				
Apr 22	☽	11:39	P 0.085	2♏04
May 6	●	21:53:53	T 5m58s	15♉59
Oct 16	☽	6:54	P 0.276	22♈40
30	●	23:50:58	A 9m43s	7♏14
1884				
Mar 27	●	6:02:12	P 0.144	6♈59
Apr 10	☽	11:47	T 1.434	21♎01
25	●	14:46:21	P 0.756	5♉46
Oct 4	☽	22:02	T 1.526	12♈05
19	●	0:17:46	P 0.639	26♎02
1885				
Mar 16	●	17:45:46	A 1m55s	26♓20
30	☽	16:34	P 0.880	10♎06
Sep 8	●	20:51:56	T 2m31s	16♍19
24	☽	7:48	P 0.787	1♈21
1886				
Feb 18	☽	18:29	A 0.206	0♍13
Mar 5	●	22:05:30	A 8m20s	15♓17
20	☽	4:24	A 0.639	29♍23
Aug 14	☽	18:42	A 0.049	21♒58
29	●	12:55:27	T 6m36s	6♍04
Sep 13	☽	10:35	A 0.439	20♓25
1887				
Feb 8	☽	10:22	P 0.432	19♌28
22	●	21:33:07	A 8m01s	3♓59
Aug 3	☽	20:49	P 0.419	11♒12
19	●	5:32:09	T 3m50s	25♌53
1888				
Jan 28	☽	23:20	T 1.645	8♌33
Feb 11	●	23:38:18	P 0.503	22♒44
Jul 9	●	6:30:58	P 0.483	17♋25
23	☽	5:45	T 1.819	0♒44
Aug 7	●	18:05:49	P 0.198	15♌35
1889				
Jan 1	●	21:16:55	T 2m17s	11♑44
17	☽	5:30	P 0.697	27♋19
Jun 28	●	9:00:06	A 7m22s	6♋47
Jul 12	☽	20:54	P 0.481	20♑32
Dec 22	●	12:54:19	T 4m18s	0♑56
1890				
Jan 6	☽	5:21	A 0.521	15♋47
Jun 3	☽	6:45	A 0.949	12♐42
17	●	9:55:09	A 4m09s	26♊06
Jul 2	☽	14:09	A 0.102	10♑26
Nov 26	☽	13:34	P 0.002	4♊23
Dec 12	●	3:05:31	AT 0m29s	20♐05
1891				
May 23	☽	18:29	T 1.300	2♐20
Jun 6	●	16:15:39	A 0m06s	15♊37
Nov 16	☽	0:19	T 1.388	23♉24
Dec 1	●	11:31:11	P 0.533	9♐01
1892				
Apr 26	●	21:55:25	T 4m19s	7♉05
May 11	☽	22:53	P 0.955	21♏37
Oct 20	●	18:36:11	P 0.905	27♎51
Nov 4	☽	15:45	T 1.093	12♉41
1893				
Apr 16	●	14:36:17	T 4m47s	26♈49
30	☽	23:09	A 0.671	10♏41
Sep 25	☽	20:39	A 0.019	3♈07
Oct 9	●	20:30:28	A 3m41s	16♎46
25	☽	7:16	A 0.775	2♉00
1894				
Mar 21	☽	14:21	P 0.242	1♎03
Apr 6	●	3:53:46	AT 0m01s	16♈20
Sep 15	☽	4:32	P 0.226	22♓23
29	●	5:39:07	T 1m55s	6♎04
1895				
Mar 11	☽	3:39	T 1.620	20♍21
26	●	10:09:38	P 0.353	5♈30
Aug 20	●	13:09:18	P 0.267	27♌14
Sep 4	☽	5:57	T 1.553	11♓27
18	●	20:44:06	P 0.737	25♍40
1896				
Feb 13	●	16:23:16	A 5m48s	24♒31
28	☽	19:46	P 0.867	9♍43
Aug 9	●	5:09:04	T 2m43s	17♌03
23	☽	6:57	P 0.731	0♓33
1897				
Jan 18	☽	20:33	A 0.066	29♋14
Feb 1	●	20:15:20	A 2m34s	13♒18
17	☽	9:58	A 0.528	28♌56
Jul 14	☽	5:05	A 0.479	22♑05
29	●	15:57:03	A 1m05s	6♌43
Aug 12	☽	14:09	A 0.447	19♒57
1898				
Jan 8	☽	0:35	P 0.151	17♋54
22	●	7:19:17	T 2m21s	2♒21
Jul 3	☽	21:17	P 0.928	11♑56
18	●	19:36:58	A 6m10s	26♋07
Dec 13	●	11:58:10	P 0.023	21♐33
27	☽	23:42	T 1.378	6♋20
1899				
Jan 11	●	22:38:07	P 0.716	21♑33
Jun 8	●	6:33:42	P 0.608	17♊13
23	☽	14:18	T 1.482	1♑50
Dec 3	●	0:57:27	A 1m01s	10♐41
17	☽	1:26	P 0.992	24♊53
1900				

Solar and Lunar Eclipses 1700–2050

Date		Time	Type	Position
May28	☉	14:53:56	T 2m10s	6♊47
Jun 13	☽	3:28	A 1.001	21♐33
Nov22	☉	7:19:43	A 6m42s	29♏34
Dec 6	☽	10:26	A 0.818	13♊46
1901				
May 3	☽	18:31	A 1.043	12♏42
18	☉	5:33:48	T 6m29s	26♉34
Oct 27	☽	15:15	P 0.221	3♉36
Nov11	☉	7:28:21	A 11m01s	18♏13
1902				
Apr 8	☉	14:05:02	P 0.064	17♈48
22	☽	18:53	T 1.333	1♏43
May 7	☉	22:34:15	P 0.859	16♉24
Oct 17	☽	6:03	T 1.457	22♈57
31	☉	8:00:16	P 0.696	6♏58
1903				
Mar 29	☉	1:35:20	A 1m53s	7♈12
Apr 12	☽	0:13	P 0.968	20♎53
Sep 21	☉	4:39:48	T 2m12s	27♍01
Oct 6	☽	15:18	P 0.865	12♈08
1904				
Mar 2	☽	3:02	A 0.175	11♍16
17	☉	5:40:40	A 8m07s	26♓13
31	☽	12:32	A 0.704	10♎15
Sep 9	☉	20:44:16	T 6m20s	16♍42
24	☽	17:35	A 0.544	1♈06
1905				
Feb 19	☽	18:50	P 0.405	0♍34
Mar 6	☉	5:12:20	A 7m58s	14♓59
Aug15	☽	3:41	P 0.287	21♒42
30	☉	13:07:19	T 3m46s	6♍28
1906				
Feb 9	☽	7:47	T 1.625	19♌41
23	☉	7:43:13	P 0.539	3♓48
Jul 21	☉	13:14:14	P 0.336	27♋50
Aug 4	☽	13:00	T 1.779	11♒13
20	☉	1:12:41	P 0.315	26♌06
1907				
Jan 14	☉	6:05:37	T 2m25s	22♑56
29	☽	13:38	P 0.711	8♌28
Jul 10	☉	15:24:26	A 7m22s	17♋12
25	☽	4:22	P 0.615	1♒00
1908				
Jan 3	☉	21:45:13	T 4m14s	12♑09
18	☽	13:21	A 0.537	26♋57
Jun 14	☽	14:06	A 0.813	23♐11
28	☉	16:29:41	A 3m60s	6♋32
Jul 13	☽	21:34	A 0.229	20♑53
Dec 7	☽	21:55	A 1.034	15♊31
23	☉	11:44:17	AT 0m12s	1♑17
1909				
Jun 4	☽	1:29	T 1.158	12♐49
17	☉	23:18:26	AT 0m24s	26♊04
Nov27	☽	8:54	T 1.366	4♊31
Dec12	☉	19:44:35	P 0.542	20♐11
1910				
May 9	☉	5:42:02	T 4m15s	17♉43
24	☽	5:34	T 1.095	2♐08
Nov 2	☉	2:08:20	P 0.852	8♏47
17	☽	0:21	T 1.125	23♉44
1911				
Apr 28	☉	22:27:09	T 4m57s	7♉30
May13	☽	5:56	A 0.799	21♏15
Oct 22	☉	4:12:48	A 3m47s	27♎39
Nov 6	☽	15:36	A 0.815	13♉00
1912				
Apr 1	☽	22:14	P 0.182	11♎54
17	☉	11:34:07	AT 0m02s	27♈05
Sep26	☽	11:45	P 0.118	3♈05
Oct 10	☉	13:35:58	T 1m55s	16♎52
1913				
Mar22	☽	11:58	T 1.568	1♎17
Apr 6	☉	17:32:50	P 0.424	16♈19
Aug31	☉	20:51:52	P 0.151	7♍49
Sep15	☽	12:48	T 1.430	22♓04
30	☉	4:45:32	P 0.825	6♎25
1914				
Feb 25	☉	0:12:42	A 5m35s	5♓34
Mar 12	☽	4:13	P 0.911	20♍42
Aug21	☉	12:34:08	T 2m15s	27♌36
Sep 4	☽	13:55	P 0.858	11♓07
1915				
Jan 31	☽	4:57	A 0.045	10♌23
Feb 14	☉	4:33:02	A 2m03s	24♒25
Mar 1	☽	18:19	A 0.555	9♍58
Jul 26	☽	12:24	A 0.354	2♒33
Aug10	☉	22:52:06	A 1m33s	17♌12
24	☽	21:27	A 0.575	0♓29
1916				
Jan 20	☽	8:39	P 0.133	29♋03
Feb 3	☉	16:00:03	T 2m36s	13♒31
Jul 15	☽	4:46	P 0.794	22♑24
30	☉	2:05:52	A 6m24s	6♌34
Dec24	☉	20:45:55	P 0.012	2♑45
1917				
Jan 8	☽	7:44	T 1.364	17♋30
23	☉	7:28:12	P 0.726	2♒45
Jun 19	☉	13:15:55	P 0.473	27♊39
Jul 4	☽	21:39	T 1.618	12♑17
19	☉	2:42:22	P 0.086	25♋51
Dec14	☉	9:26:56	A 1m16s	21♐50
28	☽	9:46	T 1.006	6♋04
1918				
Jun 8	☉	22:07:21	T 2m23s	17♊16
24	☽	10:28	P 0.130	2♑00
Dec 3	☉	15:21:39	A 7m06s	10♐40
17	☽	19:06	A 0.834	24♊57
1919				
May15	☽	1:14	A 0.910	23♏15
29	☉	13:08:33	T 6m51s	7♊06
Nov 7	☽	23:44	P 0.178	14♉37
22	☉	15:13:50	A 11m36s	29♏17
1920				
May 3	☽	1:51	T 1.219	12♏21
18	☉	6:14:33	P 0.974	26♉59
Oct 27	☽	14:11	T 1.399	3♉53
Nov10	☉	15:51:53	P 0.742	17♏58
1921				
Apr 8	☉	9:14:37	A 1m50s	18♈00
22	☽	7:44	T 1.068	1♏35
Oct 1	☉	12:35:34	T 1m52s	7♎47
16	☽	22:54	P 0.932	22♈59
1922				
Mar 13	☽	11:28	A 0.132	22♍15
28	☉	13:05:03	A 7m50s	7♈04
Apr 11	☽	20:32	A 0.781	21♎03
Sep 21	☉	4:40:08	T 5m59s	27♍25
Oct 6	☽	0:43	A 0.636	11♈52
1923				
Mar 3	☽	3:32	P 0.370	11♍37
17	☉	12:44:34	A 7m51s	25♓55
Aug 26	☽	10:39	P 0.163	2♓14
Sep 10	☉	20:47:05	T 3m37s	17♍06
1924				
Feb 20	☽	16:09	T 1.599	0♍47
Mar 5	☉	15:43:55	P 0.582	14♓49
Jul 31	☉	19:57:58	P 0.192	8♌17
Aug 14	☽	20:20	T 1.652	21♒44
30	☉	8:22:35	P 0.425	6♍40
1925				
Jan 24	☉	14:53:40	T 2m32s	4♒08
Feb 8	☽	21:42	P 0.730	19♌35
Jul 20	☉	21:48:19	A 7m14s	27♋37
Aug 4	☽	11:53	P 0.746	11♒30
1926				
Jan 14	☉	6:36:34	T 4m11s	23♑21
28	☽	21:20	A 0.555	8♌06
Jun 25	☽	21:25	A 0.675	3♑38
Jul 9	☉	23:05:37	A 3m39s	16♋57
25	☽	4:60	A 0.354	1♒22
Dec 19	☽	6:20	A 1.026	26♊41
1927				
Jan 3	☉	20:22:27	A 0m02s	12♑29
Jun 15	☽	8:24	T 1.012	23♐17
29	☉	6:23:01	T 0m50s	6♋31
Dec 8	☽	17:35	T 1.351	15♊40
24	☉	3:59:14	P 0.549	1♑21
1928				
May19	☉	13:23:56	T non-C	28♉18
Jun 3	☽	12:10	T 1.242	12♐37
17	☉	20:27:01	P 0.038	26♊21
Nov12	☉	9:48:01	P 0.808	19♏47
27	☽	9:01	T 1.149	4♊51
1929				
May 9	☉	6:10:10	T 5m07s	18♉07
23	☽	12:37	A 0.937	1♐47
Nov 1	☉	12:04:46	A 3m54s	8♏35
17	☽	0:03	A 0.846	24♉03
1930				
Apr 13	☽	5:58	P 0.106	22♎40
28	☉	19:03:09	AT 0m02s	7♉45
Oct 7	☽	19:07	P 0.025	13♈52
21	☉	21:43:29	T 1m55s	27♎46
1931				
Apr 2	☽	20:08	T 1.502	12♎08
18	☉	0:45:09	P 0.511	27♈02
Sep12	☉	4:40:58	P 0.047	18♍28
26	☽	19:48	T 1.321	2♈46
Oct 11	☉	12:55:15	P 0.901	17♎15
1932				
Mar 7	☉	7:55:25	A 5m19s	16♓33
22	☽	12:32	P 0.967	1♎38
Aug31	☉	20:03:16	T 1m45s	8♍10
Sep14	☽	21:01	P 0.975	21♓46
1933				
Feb10	☽	13:17	A 0.018	21♌31
24	☉	12:46:15	A 1m31s	5♓29
Mar12	☽	2:33	A 0.592	20♍57
Aug 5	☽	19:46	A 0.232	13♒02
21	☉	5:48:47	A 2m03s	27♌42
Sep 4	☽	4:52	A 0.695	11♓05
1934				
Jan30	☽	16:42	P 0.112	10♌12
Feb14	☉	0:38:17	T 2m52s	24♒38
Jul 26	☽	12:15	P 0.661	2♒52
Aug10	☉	8:37:24	A 6m33s	17♌01
1935				
Jan 5	☉	5:35:15	P 0.001	13♑58
19	☽	15:47	T 1.350	28♋41
Feb 3	☉	16:15:56	P 0.739	13♒55
Jun 30	☉	19:59:16	P 0.338	8♋05
Jul 16	☽	4:60	T 1.754	22♑44
30	☉	9:16:04	P 0.232	6♌17
Dec25	☉	17:59:25	A 1m30s	3♑02
1936				
Jan 8	☽	18:10	T 1.017	17♋16
Jun 19	☉	5:20:06	T 2m32s	27♊44
Jul 4	☽	17:25	P 0.267	12♑26
Dec13	☉	23:27:47	A 7m07s	21♐49
28	☽	3:49	A 0.845	6♋09
1937				
May25	☽	7:51	A 0.770	3♐47
Jun 8	☉	20:40:38	T 7m04s	17♊36
Nov18	☽	8:19	P 0.144	25♉40
Dec 2	☉	23:05:22	A 11m13s	10♐22
1938				
May14	☽	8:44	T 1.097	22♏56
29	☉	13:49:55	T 4m04s	7♊31
Nov 7	☽	22:26	T 1.353	14♉53
21	☉	23:52:02	P 0.778	29♏01
1939				
Apr 19	☉	16:45:27	A 1m49s	28♈44
May 3	☽	15:11	T 1.177	12♏15
Oct 12	☉	20:39:57	T 1m33s	18♎37
28	☽	6:36	P 0.988	3♉54
1940				
Mar 23	☽	19:48	A 0.079	3♎10
Apr 7	☉	20:20:56	A 7m30s	17♈52
22	☽	4:26	A 0.868	1♏47
Oct 1	☉	12:43:41	T 5m36s	8♎11
16	☽	8:01	A 0.716	22♈42
1941				
Mar 13	☽	11:55	P 0.323	22♍36
27	☉	20:07:43	A 7m41s	6♈46
Sep 5	☽	17:47	P 0.051	12♓50
21	☉	4:33:37	T 3m22s	27♍48
1942				
Mar 3	☽	0:21	T 1.561	11♍48
16	☉	23:36:41	P 0.639	25♓45
Aug12	☉	2:44:47	P 0.056	18♌46
26	☽	3:48	T 1.534	2♓18
Sep10	☉	15:39:06	P 0.523	17♍17
1943				
Feb 4	☉	23:37:45	T 2m35s	15♒18
20	☽	5:38	P 0.762	0♍39
Aug 1	☉	4:15:48	A 6m58s	8♌03
15	☽	19:28	P 0.870	22♒01
1944				
Jan 25	☉	15:26:16	T 4m09s	4♒33
Feb 9	☽	5:14	A 0.579	19♌13
Jul 6	☽	4:40	A 0.533	14♑05
20	☉	5:42:46	A 3m42s	27♋22
Aug 4	☽	12:26	A 0.478	11♒51
Dec29	☽	14:49	A 1.022	7♋53
1945				
Jan 14	☉	5:01:15	A 0m15s	23♑41
Jun 25	☽	15:14	P 0.859	3♑43
Jul 9	☉	13:27:17	T 1m16s	16♋57
Dec19	☽	2:20	T 1.342	26♊51
1946				
Jan 3	☉	12:15:41	P 0.553	12♑32
May30	☉	20:59:57	P 0.887	8♊49
Jun 14	☽	18:39	T 1.398	23♐03
29	☉	3:51:28	P 0.180	6♋48
Nov23	☉	17:36:46	P 0.776	0♐50
Dec 8	☽	17:48	T 1.164	16♊00
1947				
May20	☉	13:47:19	T 5m14s	28♉42
Jun 3	☽	19:15	P 0.020	12♐16
Nov12	☉	20:05:09	A 3m59s	19♏36
28	☽	8:34	A 0.868	5♊09
1948				
Apr 23	☽	13:39	P 0.023	3♏23
May 9	☉	2:25:34	AT 0m00s	18♉22
Oct 18	☽	2:35	A 1.014	24♈43
Nov 1	☉	5:58:49	T 1m56s	8♏44
1949				
Apr 13	☽	4:11	T 1.425	22♎56
28	☉	7:48:23	P 0.609	7♉41
Oct 7	☽	2:56	T 1.224	13♈32
21	☉	21:12:30	P 0.964	28♎08
1950				
Mar18	☉	15:31:31	A non-C	27♓28
Apr 2	☽	20:44	T 1.033	12♎29
Sep12	☉	3:38:16	T 1m14s	18♍49
26	☽	4:17	T 1.078	2♈28
1951				
Mar 7	☉	20:53:10	A 0m59s	16♓29
23	☽	10:37	A 0.642	1♎52
Aug17	☽	3:14	A 0.119	23♒33
Sep 1	☉	12:51:21	A 2m36s	8♍17
15	☽	12:27	A 0.803	21♓45
1952				
Feb11	☽	0:39	P 0.083	21♌19
25	☉	9:11:05	T 3m09s	5♓43
Aug 5	☽	19:47	P 0.532	13♒22
20	☉	15:13:05	A 6m40s	27♌31
1953				
Jan 29	☽	23:47	T 1.331	9♌49
Feb14	☉	0:58:59	P 0.760	25♒03

Solar and Lunar Eclipses 1700–2050

Date		Time	Type	Position
Jul 11	●	2:43:38	P 0.202	18♋30
26	☽	12:21	T 1.863	3♒12
Aug 9	●	15:54:32	P 0.373	16♌45
1954				
Jan 5	●	2:31:27	A 1m42s	14♑14
19	☽	2:32	T 1.032	28♋27
Jun 30	●	12:32:05	T 2m35s	8♋10
Jul 16	☽	0:20	P 0.405	22♑52
Dec 25	●	7:36:11	A 7m39s	2♑59
1955				
Jan 8	☽	12:33	A 0.855	17♋21
Jun 5	☽	14:23	A 0.622	14♐15
20	●	4:10:11	T 7m08s	28♊05
Nov 29	☽	16:59	P 0.119	6♊47
Dec 14	●	7:01:54	A 12m09s	21♐31
1956				
May 24	☽	15:31	P 0.965	3♐27
Jun 8	●	21:20:08	T 4m44s	18♊01
Nov 18	☽	6:48	T 1.317	25♉56
Dec 2	●	8:00:04	P 0.805	10♐08
1957				
Apr 30	●	0:04:54	A non-C	9♉23
May 13	☽	22:31	T 1.298	22♏50
Oct 23	●	4:53:28	T non-C	29♎31
Nov 7	☽	14:27	T 1.030	14♉53
1958				
Apr 4	☽	3:60	A 0.013	14♎02
19	●	3:26:44	A 7m07s	28♈34
May 3	☽	12:13	P 0.009	12♏27
Oct 12	●	20:54:55	T 5m11s	19♎01
27	☽	15:27	A 0.782	3♉36
1959				
Mar 24	☽	20:11	P 0.264	3♎31
Apr 8	●	3:23:35	A 7m25s	17♈33
Sep 17	☽	1:03	A 0.987	23♓29
Oct 2	●	12:26:27	T 3m02s	8♎34
1960				
Mar 13	☽	8:28	T 1.515	22♍47
27	●	7:24:34	P 0.706	6♈38
Sep 5	☽	11:21	T 1.424	12♓54
20	●	22:59:22	P 0.614	27♍58
1961				
Feb 15	●	8:19:15	T 2m45s	26♒26
Mar 2	☽	13:28	P 0.801	11♍41
Aug 11	●	10:46:14	A 6m35s	18♌31
26	☽	3:08	P 0.986	2♓35
1962				
Feb 5	●	0:12:04	T 4m08s	15♒43
19	☽	13:03	A 0.612	0♍18
Jul 17	☽	11:54	A 0.392	24♑32
31	●	12:24:58	A 3m33s	7♌49
Aug 15	☽	19:57	A 0.596	22♒22
1963				
Jan 9	☽	23:19	A 1.018	19♋04
25	●	13:36:36	A 0m25s	4♒52
Jul 6	☽	22:02	P 0.706	14♑09
20	●	20:35:37	T 1m40s	27♋24
Dec 30	☽	11:07	T 1.335	8♋03
1964				
Jan 14	●	20:29:31	P 0.559	23♑43
Jun 10	●	4:33:33	P 0.755	19♊19
25	☽	1:06	T 1.556	3♑29
Jul 9	●	11:17:16	P 0.322	17♋15
Dec 4	●	1:31:21	P 0.752	11♐56
19	☽	2:37	T 1.175	27♊11
1965				
May 30	●	21:16:55	T 5m15s	9♊13
Jun 14	☽	1:49	P 0.177	22♐43
Nov 23	●	4:14:15	A 4m02s	0♐40
Dec 8	☽	17:10	A 0.882	16♊18
1966				
May 4	☽	21:11	A 0.916	14♏02
20	●	9:38:24	A 0m04s	28♉55
Oct 29	☽	10:12	A 0.952	5♉38
Nov 12	●	14:22:50	T 1m58s	19♏45
1967				
Apr 24	☽	12:06	T 1.336	3♏39
May 9	●	14:42:09	P 0.720	18♉17
Oct 18	☽	10:15	T 1.143	24♈22
Nov 2	●	5:38:17	T non-C	9♏07
1968				
Mar 28	●	22:59:51	P 0.899	8♈19
Apr 13	☽	4:47	T 1.112	23♎17
Sep 22	●	11:18:06	T 0m40s	29♍30
Oct 6	☽	11:42	T 1.169	13♈14
1969				
Mar 18	●	4:54:18	A 0m26s	27♓25
Apr 2	☽	18:32	A 0.703	12♎43
Aug 27	☽	10:48	A 0.013	4♓07
Sep 11	●	19:58:19	A 3m11s	18♍53
25	☽	20:10	A 0.901	2♈28
1970				
Feb 21	☽	8:30	P 0.046	2♍23
Mar 7	●	17:37:49	T 3m28s	16♓44
Aug 17	☽	3:23	P 0.408	23♒53
31	●	21:54:49	A 6m48s	8♍04
1971				
Feb 10	☽	7:45	T 1.308	20♌56
25	●	9:37:26	P 0.787	6♓08
Jul 22	●	9:31:08	P 0.069	28♋56
Aug 6	☽	19:43	T 1.728	13♒41
20	●	22:38:50	P 0.508	27♌15
1972				
Jan 16	●	11:02:37	A 1m53s	25♑25
30	☽	10:53	T 1.050	9♌36
Jul 10	●	19:45:53	T 2m36s	18♋37
26	☽	7:16	P 0.543	3♒19
1973				
Jan 4	●	15:45:37	A 7m49s	14♑10
18	☽	21:17	A 0.865	28♋33
Jun 15	☽	20:50	A 0.468	24♐42
30	●	11:37:57	T 7m04s	8♋32
Jul 15	☽	11:39	A 0.104	22♑42
Dec 10	☽	1:44	P 0.101	17♊57
24	●	15:02:00	A 12m02s	2♑40
1974				
Jun 4	☽	22:16	P 0.827	13♐57
20	●	4:47:20	T 5m09s	28♊30
Nov 29	☽	15:13	T 1.290	7♊03
Dec 13	●	16:12:29	P 0.827	21♐16
1975				
May 11	●	7:16:44	P 0.864	20♉00
25	☽	5:48	T 1.425	3♐23
Nov 3	●	13:15:06	P 0.959	10♏30
18	☽	22:23	T 1.064	25♉55
1976				
Apr 29	●	10:23:30	A 6m41s	9♉13
May 13	☽	19:54	P 0.122	23♏03
Oct 23	●	5:12:58	T 4m47s	29♎56
Nov 6	☽	23:01	A 0.838	14♉34
1977				
Apr 4	☽	4:18	P 0.193	14♎22
18	●	10:30:42	A 7m04s	28♈16
Sep 27	☽	8:29	A 0.901	4♈13
Oct 12	●	20:26:39	T 2m37s	19♎24
1978				
Mar 24	☽	16:22	T 1.452	3♎41
Apr 7	●	15:02:58	P 0.788	17♈26
Sep 16	☽	19:04	T 1.327	23♓35
Oct 2	●	6:27:54	P 0.691	8♎43
1979				
Feb 26	●	16:54:16	T 2m49s	7♓30
Mar 13	☽	21:08	P 0.854	22♍38
Aug 22	●	17:21:48	A 6m03s	29♌01
Sep 6	☽	10:54	T 1.094	13♓12
1980				
Feb 16	●	8:53:11	T 4m08s	26♒50
Mar 1	☽	20:45	A 0.654	11♍19
Jul 27	☽	19:08	A 0.253	5♒00
Aug 10	●	19:11:30	A 3m23s	18♌17
26	☽	3:30	A 0.709	2♓56
1981				
Jan 20	☽	7:50	A 1.013	0♌16
Feb 4	●	22:08:31	A 0m33s	16♒01
Jul 17	☽	4:47	P 0.549	24♑35
31	●	3:45:44	T 2m03s	7♌51
1982				
Jan 9	☽	19:56	T 1.331	19♋16
25	●	4:41:59	P 0.566	4♒53
Jun 21	●	12:03:42	P 0.617	29♊47
Jul 6	☽	7:31	T 1.718	13♑54
20	●	18:43:50	P 0.464	27♋43
Dec 15	●	9:31:18	P 0.735	23♐05
30	☽	11:29	T 1.182	8♋24
1983				
Jun 11	●	4:42:41	T 5m11s	19♊43
25	☽	8:22	P 0.335	3♑09
Dec 4	●	12:30:22	A 4m01s	11♐47
20	☽	1:49	A 0.889	27♊29
1984				
May 15	☽	4:40	A 0.807	24♏38
30	●	16:44:47	A 0m11s	9♊26
Jun 13	☽	14:26	A 0.064	22♐35
Nov 8	☽	17:55	A 0.899	16♉36
22	●	22:53:22	T 1m60s	0♐50
1985				
May 4	☽	19:56	T 1.237	14♏19
19	●	21:28:42	P 0.841	28♉50
Oct 28	☽	17:42	T 1.074	5♉17
Nov 12	●	14:10:31	T 1m59s	20♏08
1986				
Apr 9	●	6:20:27	P 0.824	19♈07
24	☽	12:43	T 1.202	4♏00
Oct 3	●	19:05:19	AT 0m00s	10♎16
17	☽	19:18	T 1.245	24♈05
1987				
Mar 29	●	12:48:52	AT 0m08s	8♈18
Apr 14	☽	2:19	A 0.777	23♎30
Sep 23	●	3:11:26	A 3m49s	29♍34
Oct 7	☽	4:01	A 0.986	13♈15
1988				
Mar 3	☽	16:13	A 1.091	13♍23
18	●	1:58:01	T 3m47s	27♓42
Aug 27	☽	11:05	P 0.292	4♓28
Sep 11	●	4:43:33	A 6m57s	18♍40
1989				
Feb 20	☽	15:35	T 1.275	2♍00
Mar 7	●	18:07:44	P 0.827	17♓09
Aug 17	☽	3:08	T 1.598	24♒12
31	●	5:30:50	P 0.634	7♍48
1990				
Jan 26	●	19:30:25	A 2m03s	6♒35
Feb 9	☽	19:11	T 1.075	20♌44
Jul 22	●	3:02:09	T 2m33s	29♋04
Aug 6	☽	14:12	P 0.677	13♒48
1991				
Jan 15	●	23:52:54	A 7m36s	25♑20
30	☽	5:59	A 0.881	9♌43
Jun 27	☽	3:15	A 0.312	5♑07
Jul 11	●	19:06:04	T 6m53s	18♋59
26	☽	18:08	A 0.254	3♒08
Dec 21	☽	10:33	P 0.088	29♊08
1992				
Jan 4	●	23:04:40	A 10m58s	13♑51
Jun 15	☽	4:57	P 0.682	24♐23
30	●	12:10:25	T 5m20s	8♋56
Dec 9	☽	23:44	T 1.271	18♊12
24	●	0:30:44	P 0.842	2♑27
1993				
May 21	●	14:19:13	P 0.735	0♊32
Jun 4	☽	13:00	T 1.562	13♐53
Nov 13	●	21:44:50	P 0.928	21♏32
29	☽	6:26	T 1.088	7♊00
1994				
May 10	●	17:11:27	A 6m14s	19♉49
25	☽	3:30	P 0.243	3♐37
Nov 3	●	13:39:07	T 4m24s	10♏54
18	☽	6:44	A 0.881	25♉35
1995				
Apr 15	☽	12:18	P 0.111	25♎09
29	●	17:32:22	A 6m37s	8♉56
Oct 8	☽	16:04	A 0.825	15♈00
24	●	4:32:31	T 2m10s	0♏17
1996				
Apr 4	☽	0:10	T 1.380	14♎32
17	●	22:37:13	P 0.880	28♈11
Sep 27	☽	2:54	T 1.239	4♈18
Oct 12	●	14:02:04	P 0.758	19♎31
1997				
Mar 9	●	1:23:50	T 2m50s	18♓31
24	☽	4:39	P 0.919	3♎32
Sep 2	●	0:03:48	P 0.899	9♍34
16	☽	18:47	T 1.191	23♓53
1998				
Feb 26	●	17:28:27	T 4m09s	7♓55
Mar 13	☽	4:20	A 0.708	22♍16
Aug 8	☽	2:25	A 0.120	15♒29
22	●	2:06:10	A 3m14s	28♌48
Sep 6	☽	11:10	A 0.812	13♓33
1999				
Jan 31	☽	16:18	A 1.003	11♌25
Feb 16	●	6:33:37	A 0m39s	27♒08
Jul 28	☽	11:34	P 0.397	5♒02
Aug 11	●	11:03:08	T 2m23s	18♌21
2000				
Jan 21	☽	4:44	T 1.325	0♌27
Feb 5	●	12:49:24	P 0.580	16♒01
Jul 1	●	19:32:35	P 0.477	10♋15
16	☽	13:56	T 1.768	24♑19
31	●	2:13:05	P 0.603	8♌11
Dec 25	●	17:34:58	P 0.723	4♑15
2001				
Jan 9	☽	20:21	T 1.189	19♋36
Jun 21	●	12:03:46	T 4m56s	0♋11
Jul 5	☽	14:55	P 0.495	13♑34
Dec 14	●	20:52:01	A 3m53s	22♐56
30	☽	10:29	A 0.893	8♋41
2002				
May 26	☽	12:03	A 0.689	5♐10
Jun 10	●	23:44:21	A 0m22s	19♊54
24	☽	21:27	A 0.209	3♑02
Nov 20	☽	1:47	A 0.860	27♉39
Dec 4	●	7:31:14	T 2m04s	11♐58
2003				
May 16	☽	3:40	T 1.128	24♏55
31	●	4:08:20	A 3m37s	9♊19
Nov 9	☽	1:19	T 1.018	16♉15
23	●	22:49:19	T 1m58s	1♐14
2004				
Apr 19	●	13:34:05	P 0.737	29♈50
May 4	☽	20:30	T 1.304	14♏39
Oct 14	●	2:59:22	P 0.928	21♎06
28	☽	3:04	T 1.308	5♉00
2005				
Apr 8	●	20:35:50	AT 0m42s	19♈06
24	☽	9:55	A 0.865	4♏12
Oct 3	●	10:31:46	A 4m31s	10♎19
17	☽	12:03	P 0.062	24♈07
2006				
Mar 14	☽	23:48	A 1.030	24♍20
29	●	10:11:21	T 4m07s	8♈35
Sep 7	☽	18:51	P 0.184	15♓05
22	●	11:40:15	A 7m09s	29♍20
2007				
Mar 3	☽	23:21	T 1.233	13♍01
19	●	2:31:56	P 0.876	28♓07
Aug 28	☽	10:37	T 1.476	4♓46
Sep 11	●	12:31:23	P 0.751	18♍24
2008				
Feb 7	●	3:55:07	A 2m12s	17♒45

Solar and Lunar Eclipses 1700–2050

Date		Time	Type	Position
21	☽	3:25	T 1.106	1♍50
Aug 1	☉	10:21:09	T 2m27s	9♌32
16	☽	21:10	P 0.808	24♒17
2009				
Jan 26	☉	7:58:43	A 7m54s	6♒30
Feb 9	☽	14:38	A 0.899	20♌52
Jul 7	☽	9:39	A 0.156	15♑32
22	☉	2:35:23	T 6m39s	29♋27
Aug 6	☽	0:39	A 0.402	13♒35
Dec31	☽	19:23	P 0.076	10♋20
2010				
Jan 15	☉	7:06:39	A 11m07s	25♑01
Jun 26	☽	11:39	P 0.537	4♑50
Jul 11	☉	19:33:37	T 5m20s	19♋24
Dec21	☽	8:17	T 1.256	29♊22
2011				
Jan 4	☉	8:50:42	P 0.858	13♑38
Jun 1	☉	21:16:13	P 0.601	11♊02
15	☽	20:13	T 1.700	24♐22
Jul 1	☉	8:38:30	P 0.097	9♋12
Nov25	☉	6:20:20	P 0.905	2♐37
Dec10	☽	14:32	T 1.106	18♊08
2012				
May20	☉	23:52:51	A 5m36s	0♊21
Jun 4	☽	11:03	P 0.370	14♐08
Nov13	☉	22:11:53	T 4m02s	21♏57
28	☽	14:33	A 0.915	6♊40
2013				
Apr 25	☽	20:08	P 0.015	5♏51
May10	☉	0:25:19	A 6m03s	19♉31
25	☽	4:10	A 0.015	3♐58
Oct 18	☽	23:50	A 0.765	25♈51
Nov 3	☉	12:46:35	AT 1m40s	11♏16
2014				
Apr 15	☽	7:46	T 1.291	25♎17
29	☉	6:03:32	A non-C	8♉51
Oct 8	☽	10:55	T 1.166	15♈07
23	☉	21:44:38	P 0.811	0♏24
2015				
Mar 20	☉	9:45:45	T 2m47s	29♓28
Apr 4	☽	12:00	T 1.001	14♎21
Sep 13	☉	6:54:17	P 0.788	20♍11
28	☽	2:47	T 1.276	4♈38
2016				
Mar 9	☉	1:57:18	T 4m10s	18♓56
23	☽	11:47	A 0.775	3♎10
Sep 1	☉	9:07:01	A 3m05s	9♍21
16	☽	18:54	A 0.908	24♓13
2017				
Feb 11	☽	0:44	A 0.988	22♌34
26	☉	14:53:31	A 0m44s	8♓12
Aug 7	☽	18:21	P 0.246	15♒30
21	☉	18:25:39	T 2m40s	28♌53
2018				
Jan 31	☽	13:30	T 1.315	11♌38
Feb 15	☉	20:51:31	P 0.599	27♒07
Jul 13	☉	3:01:16	P 0.337	20♋42
27	☽	20:22	T 1.609	4♒45
Aug 11	☉	9:46:25	P 0.737	18♌41
2019				
Jan 6	☉	1:41:39	P 0.715	15♑26
21	☽	5:12	T 1.195	0♌49
Jul 2	☉	19:23:07	T 4m33s	10♋38
16	☽	21:31	P 0.653	24♑00
Dec26	☉	5:17:53	A 3m39s	4♑07
2020				
Jan 10	☽	19:10	A 0.895	19♋53
Jun 5	☽	19:25	A 0.568	15♐41
21	☉	6:40:14	A 0m38s	0♋21
Jul 5	☽	4:30	A 0.354	13♑29
Nov30	☽	9:43	A 0.828	8♊44
Dec14	☉	16:13:37	T 2m10s	23♐08
2021				
May26	☽	11:19	T 1.009	5♐28
Jun 10	☉	10:42:04	A 3m51s	19♊47
Nov19	☽	9:03	P 0.974	27♉17
Dec 4	☉	7:33:35	T 1m55s	12♐22
2022				
Apr 30	☉	20:41:36	P 0.640	10♉29
May16	☽	4:12	T 1.414	25♏16
Oct 25	☉	11:00:19	P 0.862	2♏01
Nov 8	☽	10:59	T 1.359	15♉59
2023				
Apr 20	☉	4:16:55	AT 1m16s	29♈50
May 5	☽	17:23	A 0.964	14♏51
Oct 14	☉	17:59:39	A 5m17s	21♎08
28	☽	20:14	P 0.122	5♉03
2024				
Mar 25	☽	7:13	A 0.956	5♎13
Apr 8	☉	18:17:28	T 4m28s	19♈24
Sep 18	☽	2:44	P 0.085	25♓46
Oct 2	☉	18:45:12	A 7m25s	10♎04
2025				
Mar 14	☽	6:59	T 1.178	23♍58
29	☉	10:47:34	P 0.938	9♈00
Sep 7	☽	18:12	T 1.362	15♓24
21	☉	19:42:02	P 0.855	29♍05
2026				
Feb 17	☉	12:12:02	A 2m20s	28♒50
Mar 3	☽	11:34	T 1.151	12♍51
Aug 12	☉	17:46:02	T 2m18s	20♌02
28	☽	4:13	P 0.930	4♓51
2027				
Feb 6	☉	15:59:46	A 7m51s	17♒38
20	☽	23:13	A 0.927	1♍58
Jul 18	☽	16:03	A 0.001	25♑57
Aug 2	☉	10:06:48	T 6m23s	9♌55
17	☽	7:14	A 0.546	24♒04
2028				
Jan 12	☽	4:13	P 0.066	21♋33
26	☉	15:07:58	A 10m27s	6♒11
Jul 6	☽	18:20	P 0.389	15♑15
22	☉	2:55:39	T 5m10s	29♋50
Dec31	☽	16:52	T 1.246	10♋34
2029				
Jan 14	☉	17:12:47	P 0.871	24♑50
Jun 12	☉	4:05:06	P 0.458	21♊30
26	☽	3:22	T 1.844	4♑49
Jul 11	☉	15:36:18	P 0.230	19♋37
Dec 5	☉	15:02:53	P 0.891	13♐46
20	☽	22:42	T 1.117	29♊18
2030				
Jun 1	☉	6:28:10	A 5m21s	10♊50
15	☽	18:33	P 0.502	24♐38
Nov25	☉	6:50:35	T 3m44s	3♐02
Dec 9	☽	22:28	A 0.941	17♊47
2031				
May 7	☽	3:51	A 0.881	16♏31
21	☉	7:15:03	A 5m25s	0♊04
Jun 5	☽	11:44	A 0.129	14♐30
Oct 30	☽	7:46	A 0.716	6♉47
Nov 14	☉	21:06:29	AT 1m08s	22♏17
2032				
Apr 25	☽	15:14	T 1.191	6♏00
May 9	☉	13:25:41	A 0m22s	19♉29
Oct 18	☽	19:03	T 1.103	25♈59
Nov 3	☉	5:33:12	P 0.856	11♏21
2033				
Mar 30	☉	18:01:33	T 2m37s	10♈21
Apr 14	☽	19:13	T 1.094	25♎06
Sep 23	☉	13:53:28	P 0.689	0♎51
Oct 8	☽	10:55	T 1.350	15♈26
2034				
Mar 20	☉	10:17:44	T 4m09s	29♓53
Apr 3	☽	19:06	A 0.854	13♎59
Sep 12	☉	16:18:26	A 2m58s	19♍59
28	☽	2:47	P 0.014	4♈57
2035				
Feb 22	☽	9:05	A 0.965	3♍39
Mar 9	☉	23:04:52	A 0m46s	19♓12
Aug 19	☽	1:11	P 0.104	26♒00
Sep 2	☉	1:55:44	T 2m54s	9♍28
2036				
Feb 11	☽	22:12	T 1.299	22♌47
27	☉	4:45:46	P 0.629	8♓10
Jul 23	☉	10:31:06	P 0.199	1♌10
Aug 7	☽	2:52	T 1.454	15♒13
21	☉	17:24:43	P 0.862	29♌14
2037				
Jan 16	☉	9:47:55	P 0.705	26♑36
31	☽	14:01	T 1.207	11♌59
Jul 13	☉	2:39:35	T 3m58s	21♋04
27	☽	4:09	P 0.810	4♒26
2038				
Jan 5	☉	13:46:10	A 3m18s	15♑19
21	☽	3:49	A 0.899	1♌05
Jun 17	☽	2:44	A 0.442	26♐10
Jul 2	☉	13:31:53	A 0m60s	10♋47
16	☽	11:35	A 0.500	23♑56
Dec11	☽	17:44	A 0.805	19♊52
26	☉	0:59:07	T 2m19s	4♑20
2039				
Jun 6	☽	18:53	P 0.885	15♐59
21	☉	17:11:51	A 4m05s	0♋12
Nov30	☽	16:55	P 0.943	8♊22
Dec15	☉	16:22:43	T 1m52s	23♐32
2040				
May11	☉	3:42:02	P 0.531	21♉04
26	☽	11:45	T 1.535	5♐49
Nov 4	☉	19:08:01	P 0.808	12♏59
18	☽	19:04	T 1.397	27♉01
2041				
Apr 30	☉	11:51:19	T 1m51s	10♉31
May16	☽	0:42	P 0.064	25♏26
Oct 25	☉	1:35:20	A 6m07s	2♏01
Nov 8	☽	4:34	P 0.170	16♉03
2042				
Apr 5	☽	14:29	A 0.868	16♎02
20	☉	2:16:28	T 4m51s	0♉09
Sep 29	☽	10:45	A 0.953	6♈31
Oct 14	☉	1:59:40	A 7m44s	20♎52
2043				
Mar 25	☽	14:31	T 1.114	4♎52
Apr 9	☉	18:56:47	T non-C	19♈49
Sep 19	☽	1:51	T 1.256	26♓04
Oct 3	☉	3:00:47	A non-C	9♎48
2044				
Feb 28	☉	20:23:36	A 2m27s	9♓54
Mar 13	☽	19:37	T 1.203	23♍50
Aug 23	☉	1:15:58	T 2m04s	0♍35
Sep 7	☽	11:20	T 1.046	15♓26
2045				
Feb 16	☉	23:55:04	A 7m32s	28♒43
Mar 3	☽	7:42	A 0.962	13♍01
Aug 12	☉	17:41:37	T 6m06s	20♌25
27	☽	13:54	A 0.682	4♓36
2046				
Jan 22	☽	13:02	P 0.053	2♌45
Feb 5	☉	23:05:25	A 9m16s	17♒18
Jul 18	☽	1:05	P 0.246	25♑42
Aug 2	☉	10:20:12	T 4m51s	10♌19
2047				
Jan 12	☽	1:25	T 1.234	21♋46
26	☉	1:32:17	P 0.891	6♒00
Jun 23	☉	10:51:23	P 0.313	1♋56
Jul 7	☽	10:35	T 1.751	15♑17
22	☉	22:35:16	P 0.361	0♌04
Dec16	☉	23:49:07	P 0.882	24♐56
2048				
Jan 1	☽	6:53	T 1.128	10♋28
Jun 11	☉	12:57:49	A 4m58s	21♊17
26	☽	2:01	P 0.639	5♑06
Dec 5	☉	15:34:24	T 3m28s	14♐11
20	☽	6:27	A 0.962	28♊56
2049				
May17	☽	11:26	A 0.764	27♏06
31	☉	13:58:57	A 4m45s	10♊34
Jun 15	☽	19:13	A 0.251	24♐59
Nov 9	☽	15:51	A 0.681	17♉47
25	☉	5:32:46	AT 0m38s	3♐23
2050				
May 6	☽	22:31	T 1.077	16♏37
20	☉	20:41:50	AT 0m21s	0♊02
Oct 30	☽	3:21	T 1.054	6♉56
Nov14	☉	13:29:53	P 0.887	22♏22

Solar and Lunar Eclipses in Zodiacal Order 1700–2050

1828	Sep 23	☽	14:05:00	A 0.130	0♈29
1847	Sep 24	☽	14:34:00	P 0.418	0♈59
1904	Sep 24	☽	17:35:00	A 0.544	1♈06
1765	Mar 21	●	13:01:30	P 0.253	1♈11
1866	Sep 24	☽	14:07:00	T 1.607	1♈17
1885	Sep 24	☽	7:48:00	P 0.787	1♈21
1746	Mar 22	●	3:02:37	A 6m51s	1♈22
1727	Mar 22	●	19:47:46	A 6m19s	1♈39
1708	Mar 22	●	6:51:29	A 0m46s	1♈43
1950	Sep 26	☽	4:17:00	T 1.078	2♈28
1969	Sep 25	☽	20:10:00	A 0.901	2♈28
1931	Sep 26	☽	19:48:00	T 1.321	2♈46
1792	Mar 22	●	17:57:19	A 1m02s	2♈49
1773	Mar 23	●	5:36:42	A 6m13s	2♈55
1811	Mar 24	●	14:11:55	T 3m27s	3♈03
1912	Sep 26	☽	11:45:00	P 0.118	3♈05
1893	Sep 25	☽	20:39:00	A 0.019	3♈07
1754	Mar 23	●	22:28:44	P 0.203	3♈13
1830	Mar 24	●	14:38:31	P 0.515	3♈28
1977	Sep 27	☽	8:29:00	A 0.901	4♈13
1996	Sep 27	☽	2:54:00	T 1.239	4♈18
1819	Mar 25	●	23:44:11	P 0.133	4♈30
2015	Sep 28	☽	2:47:00	T 1.276	4♈38
1838	Mar 25	●	21:52:06	T 3m39s	4♈49
2034	Sep 28	☽	2:47:00	P 0.014	4♈57
1857	Mar 25	●	22:29:27	T 4m28s	5♈14
1895	Mar 26	●	10:09:38	P 0.353	5♈30
1876	Mar 25	●	20:05:07	A 0m01s	5♈32
1727	Sep 30	☽	7:40:00	A 0.156	6♈26
2042	Sep 29	☽	10:45:00	A 0.953	6♈31
1960	Mar 27	●	7:24:34	P 0.706	6♈38
1708	Sep 29	☽	21:01:00	P 0.422	6♈39
1941	Mar 27	●	20:07:43	A 7m41s	6♈46
1884	Mar 27	●	6:02:12	P 0.144	6♈59
1922	Mar 28	●	13:05:03	A 7m50s	7♈04
1903	Mar 29	●	1:35:20	A 1m53s	7♈12
1792	Sep 30	☽	8:43:00	A 0.542	7♈44
1773	Sep 30	☽	17:53:00	P 0.683	7♈46
1754	Oct 1	☽	9:58:00	T 1.727	8♈06
1987	Mar 29	●	12:48:52	AT 0m08s	8♈18
1968	Mar 28	●	22:59:51	P 0.899	8♈19
1716	Oct 1	☽	9:10:00	A 0.380	8♈24
1735	Oct 2	☽	1:19:00	P 0.513	8♈24
2006	Mar 29	●	10:11:21	T 4m07s	8♈35
2025	Mar 29	●	10:47:34	P 0.938	9♈00
1800	Oct 2	☽	21:46:00	P 0.220	9♈31
1819	Oct 3	☽	15:13:00	T 1.587	9♈34
1838	Oct 3	☽	14:41:00	P 0.929	9♈53
1857	Oct 3	☽	14:57:00	A 0.658	10♈13
2033	Mar 30	●	18:01:33	T 2m37s	10♈21
1846	Oct 4	☽	22:21:00	A 0.078	11♈27
1865	Oct 4	☽	22:40:00	P 0.341	11♈47
1922	Oct 6	☽	0:43:00	A 0.636	11♈52
1783	Apr 1	●	20:38:22	P 0.330	12♈00
1884	Oct 4	☽	22:02:00	T 1.526	12♈05
1903	Oct 6	☽	15:18:00	P 0.865	12♈08
1764	Apr 1	●	10:17:01	A 6m20s	12♈10
1707	Apr 2	●	18:12:18	P 0.508	12♈18
1745	Apr 2	●	3:09:07	A 6m13s	12♈28
1726	Apr 2	●	14:38:07	A 0m51s	12♈32
1968	Oct 6	☽	11:42:00	T 1.169	13♈14
1987	Oct 7	☽	4:01:00	A 0.986	13♈15
1949	Oct 7	☽	2:56:00	T 1.224	13♈32
1810	Apr 4	●	1:41:01	A 0m21s	13♈38
1791	Apr 3	●	12:54:55	A 5m21s	13♈42
1930	Oct 7	☽	19:07:00	P 0.025	13♈52
1829	Apr 3	●	22:18:23	T 4m05s	13♈54
1772	Apr 3	●	5:43:35	P 0.123	14♈01
1848	Apr 3	●	22:48:56	P 0.583	14♈18
1995	Oct 8	☽	16:04:00	A 0.825	15♈00
2014	Oct 8	☽	10:55:00	T 1.166	15♈07
1837	Apr 5	●	7:35:19	P 0.065	15♈19
2033	Oct 8	☽	10:55:00	T 1.350	15♈26
1856	Apr 5	●	6:00:50	T 3m56s	15♈39
1875	Apr 6	●	6:37:27	T 4m37s	16♈04
1913	Apr 6	●	17:32:50	P 0.424	16♈19
1894	Apr 6	●	3:53:46	AT 0m01s	16♈20
1745	Oct 10	☽	14:57:00	A 0.238	17♈15
1707	Oct 11	☽	10:25:00	T 1.840	17♈24
1978	Apr 7	●	15:02:58	P 0.788	17♈26
1726	Oct 11	☽	4:40:00	P 0.490	17♈29
1959	Apr 8	●	3:23:35	A 7m25s	17♈33
1902	Apr 8	●	14:05:02	P 0.064	17♈48
1940	Apr 7	●	20:20:56	A 7m30s	17♈52
1921	Apr 8	●	9:14:37	A 1m50s	18♈00
1810	Oct 12	☽	16:39:00	A 0.617	18♈35
1791	Oct 12	☽	1:23:00	P 0.761	18♈37
1772	Oct 11	☽	17:14:00	T 1.643	18♈56
2005	Apr 8	●	20:35:50	AT 0m42s	19♈06
1986	Apr 9	●	6:20:27	P 0.824	19♈07
1734	Oct 12	☽	17:08:00	A 0.312	19♈15
1753	Oct 12	☽	8:51:00	P 0.433	19♈15
2024	Apr 8	●	18:17:28	T 4m28s	19♈24
2043	Apr 9	●	18:56:47	T non-C	19♈49
1818	Oct 14	☽	5:25:00	P 0.151	20♈21
1837	Oct 13	☽	23:17:00	T 1.519	20♈26
1856	Oct 13	☽	22:54:00	P 0.996	20♈44
1875	Oct 14	☽	23:03:00	A 0.723	21♈05
1717	Apr 11	●	16:34:31	AT 0m39s	21♈38
1736	Apr 11	●	7:17:56	P 0.075	21♈39
1864	Oct 15	☽	6:31:00	A 0.023	22♈18
1883	Oct 16	☽	6:54:00	P 0.276	22♈40
1940	Oct 16	☽	8:01:00	A 0.716	22♈42
1801	Apr 13	●	4:07:46	P 0.421	22♈45
1782	Apr 12	●	17:24:31	A 5m51s	22♈54
1902	Oct 17	☽	6:03:00	T 1.457	22♈57
1921	Oct 16	☽	22:54:00	P 0.932	22♈59
1725	Apr 13	●	2:11:13	P 0.419	23♈04
1763	Apr 13	●	10:19:17	A 6m11s	23♈11
1744	Apr 12	●	22:15:13	A 0m58s	23♈17
1986	Oct 17	☽	19:18:00	T 1.245	24♈05
2005	Oct 17	☽	12:03:00	P 0.062	24♈07
1967	Oct 18	☽	10:15:00	T 1.143	24♈22
1828	Apr 14	●	9:19:24	AT 0m18s	24♈23
1809	Apr 14	●	20:06:52	A 4m35s	24♈26
1847	Apr 15	●	6:16:03	T 4m44s	24♈39
1790	Apr 14	●	12:47:54	P 0.029	24♈43
1948	Oct 18	☽	2:35:00	A 1.014	24♈43
1866	Apr 15	●	6:51:31	P 0.664	25♈04
2013	Oct 18	☽	23:50:00	A 0.765	25♈51
2032	Oct 18	☽	19:03:00	T 1.103	25♈59
1874	Apr 16	●	14:00:53	T 4m11s	26♈24
1893	Apr 16	●	14:36:17	T 4m47s	26♈49
1931	Apr 18	●	0:45:09	P 0.511	27♈02
1912	Apr 17	●	11:34:07	AT 0m02s	27♈05
1706	Oct 21	☽	18:58:00	P 0.632	28♈00
1763	Oct 21	☽	22:22:00	A 0.307	28♈08
1996	Apr 17	●	22:37:13	P 0.880	28♈11
1977	Apr 18	●	10:30:42	A 7m04s	28♈16
1725	Oct 21	☽	18:35:00	T 1.830	28♈19
1744	Oct 21	☽	12:26:00	P 0.546	28♈23
1958	Apr 19	●	3:26:44	A 7m07s	28♈34
1939	Apr 19	●	16:45:27	A 1m49s	28♈44
1828	Oct 23	☽	0:44:00	A 0.679	29♈29
1809	Oct 23	☽	9:02:00	P 0.827	29♈30
1790	Oct 23	☽	0:40:00	T 1.573	29♈50
2004	Apr 19	●	13:34:05	P 0.737	29♈50
2023	Apr 20	●	4:16:55	AT 1m16s	29♈50
1771	Oct 23	☽	16:30:00	P 0.365	0♉09
2042	Apr 20	●	2:16:28	T 4m51s	0♉09
1752	Oct 23	☽	1:13:00	A 0.254	0♉11
1836	Oct 24	☽	13:15:00	P 0.097	1♉16
1855	Oct 25	☽	7:29:00	T 1.464	1♉21
1874	Oct 25	☽	7:16:00	T 1.050	1♉41
1893	Oct 25	☽	7:16:00	A 0.775	2♉00
1716	Apr 22	●	2:28:25	T 5m44s	2♉01
1735	Apr 23	●	0:11:25	AT 0m44s	2♉19
1754	Apr 22	●	14:25:44	P 0.167	2♉19
1819	Apr 24	●	11:31:41	P 0.523	3♉26
1800	Apr 24	●	0:23:46	A 5m26s	3♉33
1901	Oct 27	☽	15:15:00	P 0.221	3♉36
1958	Oct 27	☽	15:27:00	A 0.782	3♉36
1743	Apr 24	●	10:00:00	P 0.315	3♉44
1781	Apr 23	●	17:21:10	A 6m13s	3♉51
1920	Oct 27	☽	14:11:00	T 1.399	3♉53
1939	Oct 28	☽	6:36:00	P 0.988	3♉54
1762	Apr 24	●	5:41:57	A 1m08s	3♉58
2004	Oct 28	☽	3:04:00	T 1.308	5♉00
2023	Oct 28	☽	20:14:00	P 0.122	5♉03
1846	Apr 25	●	16:50:20	AT 0m54s	5♉04
1827	Apr 26	●	3:10:59	A 3m53s	5♉06
1985	Oct 28	☽	17:42:00	T 1.074	5♉17
1865	Apr 25	●	14:08:26	T 5m23s	5♉21
1966	Oct 29	☽	10:12:00	A 0.952	5♉38
1884	Apr 25	●	14:46:21	P 0.756	5♉46
2031	Oct 30	☽	7:46:00	A 0.716	6♉47
2050	Oct 30	☽	3:21:00	T 1.054	6♉56
1892	Apr 26	●	21:55:25	T 4m19s	7♉05
1716	Oct 30	☽	19:42:00	A 0.419	7♉25
1911	Apr 28	●	22:27:09	T 4m57s	7♉30
1949	Apr 28	●	7:48:23	P 0.609	7♉41
1930	Apr 28	●	19:03:09	AT 0m02s	7♉45
1705	Nov 1	☽	3:13:00	A 0.325	8♉39
2014	Apr 29	●	6:03:32	A non-C	8♉51
1995	Apr 29	●	17:32:22	A 6m37s	8♉56
1724	Nov 1	☽	3:26:00	P 0.586	9♉00
1781	Nov 1	☽	5:56:00	A 0.364	9♉05
1976	Apr 29	●	10:23:30	A 6m41s	9♉13
1743	Nov 2	☽	2:52:00	T 1.783	9♉18
1762	Nov 1	☽	20:20:00	P 0.590	9♉21
1957	Apr 30	●	0:04:54	A non-C	9♉23
1827	Nov 3	☽	16:52:00	P 0.880	10♉29
1846	Nov 3	☽	8:59:00	A 0.729	10♉29
2022	Apr 30	●	20:41:36	P 0.640	10♉29
2041	Apr 30	●	11:51:19	T 1m51s	10♉31
1808	Nov 3	☽	8:13:00	T 1.515	10♉47
1707	May 2	●	2:28:09	P 0.434	10♉55
1789	Nov 3	☽	0:17:00	P 0.309	11♉07
1770	Nov 3	☽	9:24:00	A 0.208	11♉10
1715	May 3	●	9:36:21	T 4m14s	12♉15
1854	Nov 4	☽	21:13:00	P 0.054	12♉15
1873	Nov 4	☽	15:51:00	T 1.422	12♉21
1734	May 3	●	10:15:46	T 5m46s	12♉40
1892	Nov 4	☽	15:45:00	T 1.093	12♉41
1772	May 2	●	21:26:27	P 0.268	12♉56
1753	May 3	●	7:39:28	AT 0m48s	12♉57
1911	Nov 6	☽	15:36:00	A 0.815	13♉00
1837	May 4	●	18:48:18	P 0.638	14♉03
1818	May 5	●	7:15:31	A 5m05s	14♉09
1761	May 4	●	17:42:58	P 0.203	14♉23
1799	May 5	●	0:12:54	A 6m20s	14♉27
1976	Nov 6	☽	23:01:00	A 0.838	14♉34
1780	May 4	●	13:00:26	A 1m21s	14♉35
1919	Nov 7	☽	23:44:00	P 0.178	14♉37
1938	Nov 7	☽	22:26:00	T 1.353	14♉53
1957	Nov 7	☽	14:27:00	T 1.030	14♉53
1845	May 6	●	10:08:48	A 3m15s	15♉42
1864	May 6	●	0:16:38	AT 1m25s	15♉42
1883	May 6	●	21:53:53	T 5m58s	15♉59
2022	Nov 8	☽	10:59:00	T 1.359	15♉59
2041	Nov 8	☽	4:34:00	P 0.170	16♉03
2003	Nov 9	☽	1:19:00	T 1.018	16♉15
1902	May 7	●	22:34:15	P 0.859	16♉24
1984	Nov 8	☽	17:55:00	A 0.899	16♉36
1910	May 9	●	5:42:02	T 4m15s	17♉43
2049	Nov 9	☽	15:51:00	A 0.681	17♉47
1929	May 9	●	6:10:10	T 5m07s	18♉07
1715	Nov 11	☽	4:00:00	P 0.710	18♉08
1967	May 9	●	14:42:09	P 0.720	18♉17
1948	May 9	●	2:25:34	AT 0m00s	18♉22
1734	Nov 11	☽	4:10:00	A 0.448	18♉28
2032	May 9	●	13:25:41	A 0m22s	19♉29
2013	May 10	●	0:25:19	A 6m03s	19♉31
1723	Nov 12	☽	11:42:00	A 0.298	19♉42
1994	May 10	●	17:11:27	A 6m14s	19♉49

Solar and Lunar Eclipses in Zodiacal Order 1700–2050

1975	May 11	☌	7:16:44	P 0.864	20♉00
1742	Nov 12	☍	12:02:00	P 0.552	20♉03
1799	Nov 12	☍	13:38:00	A 0.409	20♉06
1761	Nov 12	☍	11:16:00	T 1.745	20♉21
1780	Nov 12	☍	4:20:00	P 0.623	20♉23
2040	May 11	☌	3:42:02	P 0.531	21♉04
1706	May 12	☌	9:35:01	T 4m07s	21♉06
1845	Nov 14	☍	0:49:00	P 0.922	21♉30
1725	May 12	☌	10:12:08	P 0.545	21♉31
1864	Nov 13	☍	17:21:00	A 0.768	21♉31
1826	Nov 14	☍	15:56:00	T 1.471	21♉49
1807	Nov 15	☍	8:10:00	P 0.265	22♉09
1788	Nov 13	☍	17:42:00	A 0.172	22♉13
1714	May 13	☌	18:39:22	P 0.101	22♉30
1733	May 13	☌	17:18:18	T 4m07s	22♉50
1752	May 13	☌	17:56:16	T 5m42s	23♉15
1872	Nov 15	☍	5:20:00	P 0.023	23♉17
1891	Nov 16	☍	0:19:00	T 1.388	23♉24
1790	May 14	☌	4:17:05	P 0.384	23♉28
1771	May 14	☌	14:59:48	AT 0m49s	23♉31
1910	Nov 17	☍	0:21:00	T 1.125	23♉44
1929	Nov 17	☍	0:03:00	A 0.846	24♉03
1855	May 16	☌	2:01:00	P 0.762	24♉37
1836	May 15	☌	14:01:28	A 4m47s	24♉42
1779	May 16	☌	1:17:25	P 0.080	24♉57
1817	May 16	☌	6:57:57	A 6m30s	25♉00
1798	May 15	☌	20:10:20	A 1m36s	25♉08
1994	Nov 18	☍	6:44:00	A 0.881	25♉35
1937	Nov 18	☍	8:19:00	P 0.144	25♉40
1975	Nov 18	☍	22:23:00	T 1.064	25♉55
1956	Nov 18	☍	6:48:00	T 1.317	25♉56
1863	May 17	☌	17:00:32	P 0.861	26♉15
1882	May 17	☌	7:36:30	T 1m50s	26♉16
1901	May 18	☌	5:33:48	T 6m29s	26♉34
1920	May 18	☌	6:14:33	P 0.974	26♉59
2040	Nov 18	☍	19:04:00	T 1.397	27♉01
2021	Nov 19	☍	9:03:00	P 0.974	27♉17
2002	Nov 20	☍	1:47:00	A 0.860	27♉39
1928	May 19	☌	13:23:56	T non-C	28♉18
1947	May 20	☌	13:47:19	T 5m14s	28♉42
1985	May 19	☌	21:28:42	P 0.841	28♉50
1714	Nov 21	☍	13:02:00	T 1.784	28♉55
1966	May 20	☌	9:38:24	A 0m04s	28♉55
1733	Nov 21	☍	12:41:00	P 0.734	29♉14
1752	Nov 21	☍	12:44:00	A 0.470	29♉34
2050	May 20	☌	20:41:50	AT 0m21s	0♊02
2031	May 21	☌	7:15:03	A 5m25s	0♊04
2012	May 20	☌	23:52:51	A 5m36s	0♊21
1993	May 21	☌	14:19:13	P 0.735	0♊32
1741	Nov 22	☍	20:19:00	A 0.280	0♊49
1760	Nov 22	☍	20:41:00	P 0.524	1♊09
1817	Nov 23	☍	21:27:00	A 0.444	1♊11
1705	May 22	☌	19:54:59	AT 1m32s	1♊22
1779	Nov 23	☍	19:45:00	T 1.717	1♊27
1798	Nov 23	☍	12:25:00	P 0.647	1♊28
1724	May 22	☌	17:09:59	T 4m33s	1♊39
1743	May 23	☌	17:48:44	P 0.667	2♊03
1863	Nov 25	☍	8:56:00	P 0.952	2♊36
1882	Nov 25	☍	1:51:00	A 0.797	2♊38
1844	Nov 24	☍	23:45:00	T 1.436	2♊53
1825	Nov 25	☍	16:09:00	P 0.231	3♊15
1806	Nov 26	☍	2:05:00	A 0.145	3♊19
1751	May 25	☌	0:55:01	T 3m54s	3♊22
1770	May 25	☌	1:29:57	T 5m32s	3♊47
1808	May 25	☌	11:02:18	P 0.506	3♊59
1789	May 24	☌	22:11:42	AT 0m46s	4♊02
1890	Nov 26	☍	13:34:00	P 0.002	4♊23
1909	Nov 27	☍	8:54:00	T 1.366	4♊31
1928	Nov 27	☍	9:01:00	T 1.149	4♊51
1873	May 26	☌	9:08:53	P 0.897	5♊08
1947	Nov 28	☍	8:34:00	A 0.868	5♊09
1854	May 26	☌	20:42:42	A 4m32s	5♊12
1835	May 27	☌	13:35:33	A 6m44s	5♊29
1816	May 27	☌	3:13:08	A 1m53s	5♊39
2012	Nov 28	☍	14:33:00	A 0.915	6♊40
1881	May 27	☌	23:48:40	P 0.737	6♊45
1900	May 28	☌	14:53:56	T 2m10s	6♊47
1955	Nov 29	☍	16:59:00	P 0.119	6♊47
1993	Nov 29	☍	6:26:00	T 1.088	7♊00
1974	Nov 29	☍	15:13:00	T 1.290	7♊03
1919	May 29	☌	13:08:33	T 6m51s	7♊06
1938	May 29	☌	13:49:55	T 4m04s	7♊31
1705	Nov 30	☍	14:50:00	A 0.398	8♊10
2039	Nov 30	☍	16:55:00	P 0.943	8♊22
2020	Nov 30	☍	9:43:00	A 0.828	8♊44
1946	May 30	☌	20:59:57	P 0.887	8♊49
1965	May 30	☌	21:16:55	T 5m15s	9♊13
2003	May 31	☌	4:08:20	A 3m37s	9♊19
1984	May 30	☌	16:44:47	A 0m11s	9♊26
1713	Dec 2	☍	3:17:00	P 0.415	9♊58
1732	Dec 1	☍	21:40:00	T 1.768	10♊04
1751	Dec 2	☍	21:27:00	P 0.751	10♊23
2049	May 31	☌	13:58:57	A 4m45s	10♊34
1770	Dec 2	☍	21:22:00	A 0.482	10♊43
2030	Jun 1	☌	6:28:10	A 5m21s	10♊50
2011	Jun 1	☌	21:16:13	P 0.601	11♊02
1704	Jun 2	☌	13:02:31	A 4m26s	11♊51
1723	Jun 3	☌	3:05:05	T 2m05s	11♊51
1759	Dec 4	☍	5:02:00	A 0.269	11♊58
1742	Jun 3	☌	0:39:45	T 5m00s	12♊08
1835	Dec 5	☍	5:20:00	A 0.472	12♊17
1778	Dec 4	☍	5:28:00	P 0.505	12♊19
1761	Jun 3	☌	1:22:22	P 0.794	12♊34
1797	Dec 4	☍	4:18:00	T 1.697	12♊36
1816	Dec 4	☍	20:35:00	P 0.663	12♊36
1881	Dec 5	☍	17:09:00	P 0.975	13♊44
1900	Dec 6	☍	10:26:00	A 0.818	13♊46
1769	Jun 4	☌	8:28:17	T 3m36s	13♊52
1862	Dec 6	☍	7:40:00	T 1.411	14♊00
1788	Jun 4	☌	8:59:14	T 5m16s	14♊17
1843	Dec 7	☍	0:11:00	P 0.203	14♊22
1826	Jun 5	☌	17:38:51	P 0.641	14♊27
1824	Dec 6	☍	10:32:00	A 0.124	14♊28
1807	Jun 6	☌	5:18:14	AT 0m38s	14♊31
1908	Dec 7	☍	21:55:00	A 1.034	15♊31
1891	Jun 6	☌	16:15:39	A 0m06s	15♊37
1872	Jun 6	☌	3:20:01	A 4m20s	15♊40
1927	Dec 8	☍	17:35:00	T 1.351	15♊40
1853	Jun 6	☌	20:07:12	A 6m59s	15♊57
1946	Dec 8	☍	17:48:00	T 1.164	16♊00
1834	Jun 7	☌	10:08:30	P 0.930	16♊07
1965	Dec 8	☍	17:10:00	A 0.882	16♊18
1899	Jun 8	☌	6:33:42	P 0.608	17♊13
1918	Jun 8	☌	22:07:21	T 2m23s	17♊16
1937	Jun 8	☌	20:40:38	T 7m04s	17♊36
2030	Dec 9	☍	22:28:00	A 0.941	17♊47
1973	Dec 10	☍	1:44:00	P 0.101	17♊57
1956	Jun 8	☌	21:20:08	T 4m44s	18♊01
2011	Dec 10	☍	14:32:00	T 1.106	18♊08
1992	Dec 9	☍	23:44:00	T 1.271	18♊12
1964	Jun 10	☌	4:33:33	P 0.755	19♊19
1704	Dec 11	☍	7:11:00	P 0.534	19♊20
1723	Dec 11	☍	23:26:00	A 0.417	19♊20
1983	Jun 11	☌	4:42:41	T 5m11s	19♊43
2021	Jun 10	☌	10:42:04	A 3m51s	19♊47
2038	Dec 11	☍	17:44:00	A 0.805	19♊52
2002	Jun 10	☌	23:44:21	A 0m22s	19♊54
1714	Jun 12	☌	4:39:54	P 0.698	20♊41
1731	Dec 13	☍	11:38:00	P 0.407	21♊08
1750	Dec 13	☍	6:22:00	T 1.758	21♊15
2048	Jun 11	☌	12:57:49	A 4m58s	21♊17
1712	Dec 13	☍	0:54:00	A 0.160	21♊22
2029	Jun 12	☌	4:05:06	P 0.458	21♊30
1769	Dec 13	☍	6:17:00	P 0.761	21♊34
1788	Dec 13	☍	6:04:00	A 0.489	21♊53
1722	Jun 13	☌	19:40:11	P 0.908	22♊17
1741	Jun 13	☌	10:12:38	T 2m35s	22♊18
1760	Jun 13	☌	8:09:01	T 5m27s	22♊37
1779	Jun 14	☌	8:51:11	P 0.928	23♊02
1777	Dec 14	☍	13:49:00	A 0.263	23♊09
1853	Dec 15	☍	13:18:00	A 0.492	23♊26
1796	Dec 14	☍	14:16:00	P 0.491	23♊30
1834	Dec 16	☍	4:48:00	P 0.675	23♊46
1815	Dec 16	☍	12:55:00	T 1.685	23♊47
1787	Jun 15	☌	15:59:06	T 3m09s	24♊21
1806	Jun 16	☌	16:24:08	T 4m55s	24♊45
1844	Jun 16	☌	0:13:13	P 0.778	24♊53
1899	Dec 17	☍	1:26:00	P 0.992	24♊53
1918	Dec 17	☍	19:06:00	A 0.834	24♊57
1825	Jun 16	☌	12:18:48	AT 0m25s	24♊58
1880	Dec 16	☍	15:39:00	T 1.391	25♊09
1861	Dec 17	☍	8:19:00	P 0.184	25♊32
1842	Dec 17	☍	19:02:00	A 0.108	25♊39
1909	Jun 17	☌	23:18:26	AT 0m24s	26♊04
1890	Jun 17	☌	9:55:09	A 4m09s	26♊06
1928	Jun 17	☌	20:27:01	P 0.038	26♊21
1871	Jun 18	☌	2:35:00	A 7m13s	26♊23
1852	Jun 17	☌	16:59:42	P 0.783	26♊34
1926	Dec 19	☍	6:20:00	A 1.026	26♊41
1945	Dec 19	☍	2:20:00	T 1.342	26♊51
1964	Dec 19	☍	2:37:00	T 1.175	27♊11
1983	Dec 20	☍	1:49:00	A 0.889	27♊29
1917	Jun 19	☌	13:15:55	P 0.473	27♊39
1936	Jun 19	☌	5:20:06	T 2m32s	27♊44
1955	Jun 20	☌	4:10:11	T 7m08s	28♊05
1974	Jun 20	☌	4:47:20	T 5m09s	28♊30
2048	Dec 20	☍	6:27:00	A 0.962	28♊56
1991	Dec 21	☍	10:33:00	P 0.088	29♊08
2029	Dec 20	☍	22:42:00	T 1.117	29♊18
2010	Dec 21	☍	8:17:00	T 1.256	29♊22
1982	Jun 21	☌	12:03:42	P 0.617	29♊47
2001	Jun 21	☌	12:03:46	T 4m56s	0♋11
2039	Jun 21	☌	17:11:51	A 4m05s	0♋12
2020	Jun 21	☌	6:40:14	A 0m38s	0♋21
1722	Dec 22	☍	15:28:00	P 0.548	0♋31
1741	Dec 22	☍	8:05:00	A 0.430	0♋32
1703	Dec 23	☍	6:30:00	T 1.758	0♋49
1732	Jun 22	☌	11:38:40	P 0.846	1♋07
1713	Jun 22	☌	23:15:31	A 5m23s	1♋12
2047	Jun 23	☌	10:51:23	P 0.313	1♋56
1749	Dec 23	☍	20:02:00	P 0.402	2♋19
1768	Dec 23	☍	15:07:00	T 1.752	2♋27
1730	Dec 24	☍	8:58:00	A 0.150	2♋32
1740	Jun 24	☌	2:18:45	P 0.770	2♋43
1759	Jun 24	☌	17:20:46	T 2m60s	2♋45
1787	Dec 24	☍	15:08:00	P 0.770	2♋46
1778	Jun 24	☌	15:34:39	T 5m53s	3♋04
1806	Dec 25	☍	14:48:00	A 0.492	3♋05
1797	Jun 24	☌	16:17:57	T 2m47s	3♋29
1795	Dec 25	☍	22:37:00	A 0.259	4♋21
1871	Dec 26	☍	21:19:00	A 0.507	4♋37
1814	Dec 26	☍	23:08:00	P 0.483	4♋43
1805	Jun 26	☌	23:27:18	P 0.936	4♋48
1852	Dec 26	☍	13:03:00	P 0.681	4♋57
1833	Dec 26	☍	21:33:00	T 1.675	4♋58
1824	Jun 26	☌	23:46:17	T 4m24s	5♋12
1862	Jun 27	☌	6:42:11	P 0.922	5♋18
1843	Jun 27	☌	19:16:54	AT 0m08s	5♋25
1917	Dec 28	☍	9:46:00	T 1.006	6♋04
1936	Dec 28	☍	3:49:00	A 0.845	6♋09
1898	Dec 27	☍	23:42:00	T 1.378	6♋20
1927	Jun 29	☌	6:23:01	T 0m50s	6♋31
1908	Jun 28	☌	16:29:41	A 3m60s	6♋32
1879	Dec 28	☍	16:26:00	P 0.166	6♋42
1889	Jun 28	☌	9:00:06	A 7m22s	6♋47
1946	Jun 29	☌	3:51:28	P 0.180	6♋48
1860	Dec 28	☍	3:34:00	A 0.095	6♋50
1870	Jun 28	☌	23:46:41	P 0.634	6♋59
1944	Dec 29	☍	14:49:00	A 1.022	7♋53
1963	Dec 30	☍	11:07:00	T 1.335	8♋03
1935	Jun 30	☌	19:59:16	P 0.338	8♋05
1954	Jun 30	☌	12:32:05	T 2m35s	8♋10
1982	Dec 30	☍	11:29:00	T 1.182	8♋24
1973	Jun 30	☌	11:37:57	T 7m04s	8♋32
2001	Dec 30	☍	10:29:00	A 0.893	8♋41

Solar and Lunar Eclipses in Zodiacal Order 1700–2050

1992	Jun	30	☉	12:10:25	T 5m20s	8♋56
2011	Jul	1	☉	8:38:30	P 0.097	9♋12
2000	Jul	1	☉	19:32:35	P 0.477	10♋15
2009	Dec	31	☽	19:23:00	P 0.076	10♋20
2048	Jan	1	☽	6:53:00	T 1.128	10♋28
2028	Dec	31	☽	16:52:00	T 1.246	10♋34
2019	Jul	2	☉	19:23:07	T 4m33s	10♋38
2038	Jul	2	☉	13:31:53	A 0m60s	10♋47
1750	Jul	3	☉	18:38:41	P 0.996	11♋33
1731	Jul	4	☉	5:46:16	A 5m15s	11♋36
1741	Jan	1	☽	23:47:00	P 0.562	11♋42
1760	Jan	2	☽	16:47:00	A 0.441	11♋44
1712	Jul	3	☉	22:34:49	A 5m18s	11♋53
1722	Jan	2	☽	14:33:00	T 1.771	12♋00
1703	Jan	3	☽	6:58:00	P 0.624	12♋22
1758	Jul	5	☉	8:57:32	P 0.630	13♋08
1777	Jul	5	☉	0:29:14	T 3m18s	13♋11
1768	Jan	4	☽	4:29:00	P 0.401	13♋31
1796	Jul	4	☉	23:02:40	T 6m02s	13♋31
1787	Jan	3	☽	23:53:00	T 1.747	13♋39
1749	Jan	3	☽	17:03:00	A 0.139	13♋43
1815	Jul	6	☉	23:42:48	T 3m13s	13♋56
1806	Jan	5	☽	0:02:00	P 0.775	13♋59
1825	Jan	4	☽	23:32:00	A 0.493	14♋18
1823	Jul	8	☉	6:56:08	P 0.796	15♋15
1814	Jan	6	☽	7:28:00	A 0.257	15♋34
1842	Jul	8	☉	7:06:17	T 4m06s	15♋38
1880	Jul	7	☉	13:10:32	A 5m46s	15♋43
1890	Jan	6	☽	5:21:00	A 0.521	15♋47
1861	Jul	8	☉	2:10:15	A 0m14s	15♋50
1833	Jan	6	☽	7:60:00	P 0.473	15♋55
1871	Jan	6	☽	21:17:00	P 0.689	16♋08
1852	Jan	7	☽	6:11:00	T 1.666	16♋11
1926	Jul	9	☉	23:05:37	A 3m39s	16♋57
1945	Jul	9	☉	13:27:17	T 1m16s	16♋57
1907	Jul	10	☉	15:24:26	A 7m22s	17♋12
1964	Jul	9	☉	11:17:16	P 0.322	17♋15
1936	Jan	8	☽	18:10:00	T 1.017	17♋16
1955	Jan	8	☽	12:33:00	A 0.855	17♋21
1888	Jul	9	☉	6:30:58	P 0.483	17♋25
1917	Jan	8	☽	7:44:00	T 1.364	17♋30
1898	Jan	8	☽	0:35:00	P 0.151	17♋54
1879	Jan	8	☽	12:04:00	A 0.081	18♋02
1953	Jul	11	☉	2:43:38	P 0.202	18♋30
1972	Jul	10	☉	19:45:53	T 2m36s	18♋37
1991	Jul	11	☉	19:06:04	T 6m53s	18♋59
1963	Jan	9	☽	23:19:00	A 1.018	19♋04
1982	Jan	9	☽	19:56:00	T 1.331	19♋16
2010	Jul	11	☉	19:33:37	T 5m20s	19♋24
2001	Jan	9	☽	20:21:00	T 1.189	19♋36
2029	Jul	11	☉	15:36:18	P 0.230	19♋37
2020	Jan	10	☽	19:10:00	A 0.895	19♋53
2018	Jul	13	☉	3:01:16	P 0.337	20♋42
1703	Jul	14	☉	2:36:25	P 0.758	20♋47
2037	Jul	13	☉	2:39:35	T 3m58s	21♋04
1713	Jan	11	☽	20:15:00	A 0.054	21♋28
2028	Jan	12	☽	4:13:00	P 0.066	21♋33
2047	Jan	12	☽	1:25:00	T 1.234	21♋46
1768	Jul	14	☉	1:40:43	AT 0m29s	21♋59
1749	Jul	14	☉	12:19:09	A 4m45s	22♋01
1730	Jul	15	☉	4:58:58	A 5m13s	22♋17
1711	Jul	15	☉	19:22:00	P 0.822	22♋28
1759	Jan	13	☽	8:06:00	P 0.576	22♋53
1778	Jan	13	☽	1:29:00	A 0.452	22♋56
1740	Jan	13	☽	22:33:00	T 1.789	23♋10
1721	Jan	13	☽	15:08:00	P 0.609	23♋33
1776	Jul	15	☉	15:39:15	P 0.494	23♋33
1795	Jul	16	☉	7:41:21	T 3m26s	23♋38
1702	Jan	14	☽	1:33:00	A 0.499	23♋39
1814	Jul	17	☉	6:30:11	T 6m34s	23♋58
1833	Jul	17	☉	7:07:51	T 3m30s	24♋23
1786	Jan	14	☽	12:56:00	P 0.398	24♋42
1805	Jan	15	☽	8:41:00	T 1.742	24♋52
1767	Jan	15	☽	1:08:00	A 0.128	24♋53
1824	Jan	16	☽	8:54:00	P 0.783	25♋12
1843	Jan	16	☽	8:14:00	A 0.495	25♋30
1841	Jul	18	☉	14:25:01	P 0.656	25♋42
1917	Jul	19	☉	2:42:22	P 0.086	25♋51
1860	Jul	18	☉	14:26:13	T 3m39s	26♋06
1898	Jul	18	☉	19:36:58	A 6m10s	26♋07
1879	Jul	19	☉	9:04:35	A 0m38s	26♋17
1832	Jan	17	☽	16:18:00	A 0.252	26♋46
1908	Jan	18	☽	13:21:00	A 0.537	26♋57
1851	Jan	17	☽	16:51:00	P 0.464	27♋08
1889	Jan	17	☽	5:30:00	P 0.697	27♋19
1870	Jan	17	☽	14:46:00	T 1.657	27♋22
1944	Jul	20	☉	5:42:46	A 3m42s	27♋22
1963	Jul	20	☉	20:35:37	T 1m40s	27♋24
1925	Jul	20	☉	21:48:19	A 7m14s	27♋37
1982	Jul	20	☉	18:43:50	P 0.464	27♋43
1906	Jul	21	☉	13:14:14	P 0.336	27♋50
1954	Jan	19	☽	2:32:00	T 1.032	28♋27
1973	Jan	18	☽	21:17:00	A 0.865	28♋33
1935	Jan	19	☽	15:47:00	T 1.350	28♋41
1971	Jul	22	☉	9:31:08	P 0.069	28♋56
1916	Jan	20	☽	8:39:00	P 0.133	29♋03
1990	Jul	22	☉	3:02:09	T 2m33s	29♋04
1897	Jan	18	☽	20:33:00	A 0.066	29♋14
2009	Jul	22	☉	2:35:23	T 6m39s	29♋27
2028	Jul	22	☉	2:55:39	T 5m10s	29♋50
2047	Jul	22	☉	22:35:16	P 0.361	0♌04
1981	Jan	20	☽	7:50:00	A 1.013	0♌16
2000	Jan	21	☽	4:44:00	T 1.325	0♌27
2019	Jan	21	☽	5:12:00	T 1.195	0♌49
2038	Jan	21	☽	3:49:00	A 0.899	1♌05
2036	Jul	23	☉	10:31:06	P 0.199	1♌10
1721	Jul	24	☉	9:06:45	P 0.899	1♌13
1702	Jul	24	☉	21:38:44	AT 0m01s	1♌19
1786	Jul	25	☉	8:46:18	T 0m59s	2♌26
1767	Jul	25	☉	18:55:33	A 4m21s	2♌27
1731	Jan	23	☽	4:14:00	A 0.071	2♌38
1748	Jul	25	☉	11:26:49	A 5m12s	2♌43
1805	Jul	26	☉	6:14:01	P 0.141	2♌44
2046	Jan	22	☽	13:02:00	P 0.053	2♌45
1729	Jul	26	☉	2:10:27	P 0.675	2♌55
1712	Jan	23	☽	19:47:00	P 0.253	2♌57
1794	Jul	26	☉	22:24:14	P 0.360	4♌00
1777	Jan	23	☽	16:24:00	P 0.594	4♌03
1813	Jul	27	☉	14:55:18	T 3m27s	4♌05
1796	Jan	24	☽	10:09:00	A 0.466	4♌07
1758	Jan	24	☽	6:34:00	T 1.807	4♌20
1832	Jul	27	☉	14:00:55	T 6m46s	4♌27
1739	Jan	24	☽	23:14:00	P 0.589	4♌42
1720	Jan	25	☽	10:04:00	A 0.483	4♌49
1851	Jul	28	☉	14:33:31	T 3m41s	4♌51
1870	Jul	28	☉	11:02:25	P 0.074	5♌07
1804	Jan	26	☽	21:21:00	P 0.392	5♌53
1823	Jan	26	☽	17:25:00	T 1.731	6♌02
1785	Jan	25	☽	9:11:00	A 0.113	6♌03
1859	Jul	29	☉	21:56:43	P 0.521	6♌11
1935	Jul	30	☉	9:16:04	P 0.232	6♌17
1842	Jan	26	☽	17:44:00	P 0.793	6♌23
1878	Jul	29	☉	21:47:19	T 3m11s	6♌34
1916	Jul	30	☉	2:05:52	A 6m24s	6♌34
1861	Jan	26	☽	16:54:00	A 0.500	6♌41
1897	Jul	29	☉	15:57:03	A 1m05s	6♌43
1962	Jul	31	☉	12:24:58	A 3m33s	7♌49
1981	Jul	31	☉	3:45:44	T 2m03s	7♌51
1850	Jan	28	☽	1:06:00	A 0.244	7♌58
1943	Aug	1	☉	4:15:48	A 6m58s	8♌03
1926	Jan	28	☽	21:20:00	A 0.555	8♌06
2000	Jul	31	☉	2:13:05	P 0.603	8♌11
1924	Jul	31	☉	19:57:58	P 0.192	8♌17
1869	Jan	28	☽	1:38:00	P 0.451	8♌19
1907	Jan	29	☽	13:38:00	P 0.711	8♌28
1888	Jan	28	☽	23:20:00	T 1.645	8♌33
2008	Aug	1	☉	10:21:09	T 2m27s	9♌32
1972	Jan	30	☽	10:53:00	T 1.050	9♌36
1991	Jan	30	☽	5:59:00	A 0.881	9♌43
1953	Jan	29	☽	23:47:00	T 1.331	9♌49
2027	Aug	2	☉	10:06:48	T 6m23s	9♌55
1934	Jan	30	☽	16:42:00	P 0.112	10♌12
2046	Aug	2	☉	10:20:12	T 4m51s	10♌19
1915	Jan	31	☽	4:57:00	A 0.045	10♌23
1999	Jan	31	☽	16:18:00	A 1.003	11♌25
1701	Aug	4	☉	9:31:38	T 5m06s	11♌36
2018	Jan	31	☽	13:30:00	T 1.315	11♌38
1739	Aug	4	☉	15:40:45	A 3m59s	11♌40
1720	Aug	4	☉	4:38:05	A 0m27s	11♌48
2037	Jan	31	☽	14:01:00	T 1.207	11♌59
1785	Aug	5	☉	1:37:06	A 4m01s	12♌55
1804	Aug	5	☉	15:56:55	T 1m20s	12♌55
1766	Aug	5	☉	17:56:42	A 5m15s	13♌11
1823	Aug	6	☉	13:45:26	P 0.275	13♌14
1747	Aug	6	☉	9:01:06	P 0.534	13♌23
1749	Feb	2	☽	12:09:00	A 0.093	13♌45
1730	Feb	3	☽	3:56:00	P 0.270	14♌05
1711	Feb	3	☽	12:31:00	T 1.631	14♌07
1812	Aug	7	☉	5:15:33	P 0.234	14♌28
1831	Aug	7	☉	22:15:49	T 3m20s	14♌35
1850	Aug	7	☉	21:33:44	T 6m50s	14♌56
1795	Feb	4	☽	0:39:00	P 0.617	15♌12
1814	Feb	4	☽	18:47:00	A 0.484	15♌17
1869	Aug	7	☉	22:01:00	T 3m49s	15♌21
1776	Feb	4	☽	14:30:00	T 1.785	15♌27
1888	Aug	7	☉	18:05:49	P 0.198	15♌35
1757	Feb	4	☽	7:17:00	P 0.566	15♌50
1738	Feb	4	☽	18:29:00	A 0.460	15♌58
1877	Aug	9	☉	5:30:23	P 0.389	16♌41
1953	Aug	9	☉	15:54:32	P 0.373	16♌45
1822	Feb	6	☽	5:43:00	P 0.380	17♌01
1934	Aug	10	☉	8:37:24	A 6m33s	17♌01
1896	Aug	9	☉	5:09:04	T 2m43s	17♌03
1803	Feb	6	☽	17:10:00	A 0.092	17♌10
1841	Feb	6	☽	2:07:00	T 1.718	17♌12
1915	Aug	10	☉	22:52:06	A 1m33s	17♌12
1860	Feb	7	☽	2:30:00	P 0.811	17♌32
1879	Feb	7	☽	1:29:00	A 0.511	17♌50
1980	Aug	10	☉	19:11:30	A 3m23s	18♌17
1999	Aug	11	☉	11:03:08	T 2m23s	18♌21
1961	Aug	11	☉	10:46:14	A 6m35s	18♌31
2018	Aug	11	☉	9:46:25	P 0.737	18♌41
1942	Aug	12	☉	2:44:47	P 0.056	18♌46
1868	Feb	8	☽	9:50:00	A 0.229	19♌06
1944	Feb	9	☽	5:14:00	A 0.579	19♌13
1887	Feb	8	☽	10:22:00	P 0.432	19♌28
1925	Feb	8	☽	21:42:00	P 0.730	19♌35
1906	Feb	9	☽	7:47:00	T 1.625	19♌41
2026	Aug	12	☉	17:46:02	T 2m18s	20♌02
2045	Aug	12	☉	17:41:37	T 6m06s	20♌25
1990	Feb	9	☽	19:11:00	T 1.075	20♌44
2009	Feb	9	☽	14:38:00	A 0.899	20♌52
1971	Feb	10	☽	7:45:00	T 1.308	20♌56
1952	Feb	11	☽	0:39:00	P 0.083	21♌19
1933	Feb	10	☽	13:17:00	A 0.018	21♌31
1700	Aug	14	☉	16:59:00	P 0.700	21♌44
1776	Aug	14	☉	5:22:39	P 0.044	21♌52
1719	Aug	15	☉	16:59:43	T 4m27s	22♌07
1757	Aug	14	☉	22:16:32	A 4m36s	22♌09
1738	Aug	15	☉	11:40:01	A 1m00s	22♌18
2017	Feb	11	☽	0:44:00	A 0.988	22♌34
2036	Feb	11	☽	22:12:00	T 1.299	22♌47
1702	Feb	12	☽	14:21:00	A 0.145	23♌21
1803	Aug	17	☉	8:24:44	A 3m47s	23♌25
1822	Aug	16	☉	23:14:18	T 1m32s	23♌26
1784	Aug	16	☉	0:31:36	A 5m23s	23♌40
1841	Aug	16	☉	21:20:15	P 0.406	23♌45
1765	Aug	16	☉	15:53:43	P 0.400	23♌53
1767	Feb	13	☽	19:59:00	A 0.124	24♌50
1710	Feb	13	☽	22:50:00	P 0.833	24♌59
1830	Aug	18	☉	12:13:24	P 0.117	24♌59
1849	Aug	18	☉	5:40:40	T 3m07s	25♌07
1748	Feb	14	☽	11:58:00	P 0.296	25♌10
1729	Feb	13	☽	20:58:00	T 1.655	25♌13
1868	Aug	18	☉	5:12:04	T 6m47s	25♌29

Solar and Lunar Eclipses in Zodiacal Order 1700–2050

Year	Date		Time	Type	Position
1887	Aug 19	☉	5:32:09	T 3m50s	25♌53
1906	Aug 20	☉	1:12:41	P 0.315	26♌06
1813	Feb 15	☽	8:50:00	P 0.649	26♌18
1832	Feb 16	☽	3:20:00	A 0.508	26♌24
1794	Feb 14	☽	22:21:00	T 1.755	26♌32
1775	Feb 15	☽	15:11:00	P 0.531	26♌54
1756	Feb 16	☽	2:48:00	A 0.428	27♌03
1895	Aug 20	☉	13:09:18	P 0.267	27♌14
1971	Aug 20	☉	22:38:50	P 0.508	27♌15
1952	Aug 20	☉	15:13:05	A 6m40s	27♌31
1914	Aug 21	☉	12:34:08	T 2m15s	27♌36
1933	Aug 21	☉	5:48:47	A 2m03s	27♌42
1840	Feb 17	☽	14:02:00	P 0.362	28♌07
1821	Feb 17	☽	1:05:00	A 0.062	28♌14
1859	Feb 17	☽	10:43:00	T 1.694	28♌18
1878	Feb 17	☽	11:11:00	P 0.834	28♌39
1998	Aug 22	☉	2:06:10	A 3m14s	28♌48
2017	Aug 21	☉	18:25:39	T 2m40s	28♌53
1897	Feb 17	☽	9:58:00	A 0.528	28♌56
1979	Aug 22	☉	17:21:48	A 6m03s	29♌01
2036	Aug 21	☉	17:24:43	P 0.862	29♌14
1886	Feb 18	☽	18:29:00	A 0.206	0♍13
1962	Feb 19	☽	13:03:00	A 0.612	0♍18
1905	Feb 19	☽	18:60:00	P 0.405	0♍34
2044	Aug 23	☉	1:15:58	T 2m04s	0♍35
1943	Feb 20	☽	5:38:00	P 0.762	0♍39
1924	Feb 20	☽	16:09:00	T 1.599	0♍47
1710	Aug 24	☉	17:17:08	T 4m00s	0♍59
1729	Aug 24	☉	13:48:22	P 0.007	1♍14
2008	Feb 21	☽	3:26:00	T 1.106	1♍50
2027	Feb 20	☽	23:13:00	A 0.927	1♍58
1989	Feb 20	☽	15:35:00	T 1.275	2♍00
1718	Aug 26	☉	0:41:36	P 0.584	2♍19
1970	Feb 21	☽	8:30:00	P 0.046	2♍23
1794	Aug 25	☉	12:08:40	P 0.171	2♍24
1737	Aug 26	☉	0:31:58	T 3m45s	2♍42
1775	Aug 26	☉	4:59:24	A 5m16s	2♍42
1756	Aug 25	☉	18:46:04	A 1m38s	2♍51
2035	Feb 22	☽	9:05:00	A 0.965	3♍39
1821	Aug 27	☉	15:19:25	A 3m38s	3♍58
1840	Aug 27	☉	6:37:23	T 1m45s	4♍00
1701	Feb 22	☽	23:30:00	P 0.463	4♍07
1802	Aug 28	☉	7:11:39	A 5m35s	4♍12
1859	Aug 28	☉	5:01:50	P 0.526	4♍20
1720	Feb 23	☽	22:48:00	A 0.166	4♍25
1783	Aug 27	☉	22:51:46	P 0.276	4♍27
1848	Aug 28	☉	19:18:11	P 0.009	5♍32
1709	Feb 24	☽	6:51:00	A 0.573	5♍41
1867	Aug 29	☉	13:13:00	T 2m51s	5♍41
1785	Feb 24	☽	3:42:00	A 0.165	5♍52
1728	Feb 25	☽	7:24:00	P 0.798	6♍02
1886	Aug 29	☉	12:55:27	T 6m36s	6♍04
1766	Feb 24	☽	19:53:00	P 0.332	6♍13
1747	Feb 25	☽	5:18:00	T 1.687	6♍17
1905	Aug 30	☉	13:07:19	T 3m46s	6♍28
1924	Aug 30	☉	8:22:35	P 0.425	6♍40
1831	Feb 26	☽	16:56:00	P 0.690	7♍20
1850	Feb 26	☽	11:48:00	A 0.542	7♍27
1812	Feb 27	☽	6:05:00	T 1.714	7♍33
1989	Aug 31	☉	5:30:50	P 0.634	7♍48
1913	Aug 31	☉	20:51:52	P 0.151	7♍49
1793	Feb 25	☽	22:59:00	P 0.490	7♍56
1970	Aug 31	☉	21:54:49	A 6m48s	8♍04
1774	Feb 26	☽	10:59:00	A 0.386	8♍06
1932	Aug 31	☉	20:03:16	T 1m45s	8♍10
1951	Sep 1	☉	12:51:21	A 2m36s	8♍17
1858	Feb 27	☽	22:14:00	P 0.332	9♍09
1839	Feb 28	☽	8:54:00	A 0.023	9♍16
2016	Sep 1	☉	9:07:01	A 3m05s	9♍21
1877	Feb 27	☽	19:16:00	T 1.664	9♍22
2035	Sep 2	☉	1:55:44	T 2m54s	9♍28
1997	Sep 2	☉	0:03:48	P 0.899	9♍34
1896	Feb 28	☽	19:46:00	P 0.867	9♍43
1915	Mar 1	☽	18:19:00	A 0.555	9♍58
1709	Sep 4	☉	0:32:19	T 5m47s	11♍12
1904	Mar 2	☽	3:02:00	A 0.175	11♍16
1980	Mar 1	☽	20:45:00	A 0.654	11♍19
1728	Sep 4	☉	0:59:13	T 3m44s	11♍37
1923	Mar 3	☽	3:32:00	P 0.370	11♍37
1961	Mar 2	☽	13:28:00	P 0.801	11♍41
1942	Mar 3	☽	0:21:00	T 1.561	11♍48
1747	Sep 4	☉	21:07:45	P 0.109	11♍51
2026	Mar 3	☽	11:34:00	T 1.151	12♍51
1736	Sep 5	☉	8:30:15	P 0.478	12♍57
1812	Sep 5	☉	19:03:52	P 0.287	13♍00
2007	Mar 3	☽	23:21:00	T 1.233	13♍01
2045	Mar 3	☽	7:42:00	A 0.962	13♍01
1793	Sep 5	☉	11:47:09	A 6m02s	13♍17
1755	Sep 6	☉	8:09:33	T 3m00s	13♍20
1988	Mar 3	☽	16:13:00	A 1.091	13♍23
1774	Sep 6	☉	1:57:26	A 2m20s	13♍28
1839	Sep 7	☉	22:23:17	A 3m34s	14♍34
1858	Sep 7	☉	14:09:18	T 1m50s	14♍37
1700	Mar 5	☽	7:37:00	T 1.703	14♍47
1820	Sep 7	☉	13:59:40	A 5m49s	14♍48
1877	Sep 7	☉	12:48:45	P 0.638	14♍58
1801	Sep 8	☉	5:54:17	P 0.162	15♍03
1719	Mar 6	☽	7:59:00	P 0.504	15♍07
1738	Mar 6	☽	7:07:00	A 0.198	15♍25
1885	Sep 8	☉	20:51:56	T 2m31s	16♍19
1727	Mar 7	☽	15:16:00	A 0.530	16♍41
1904	Sep 9	☉	20:44:16	T 6m20s	16♍42
1803	Mar 8	☽	11:17:00	A 0.217	16♍50
1746	Mar 7	☽	15:52:00	P 0.755	17♍03
1923	Sep 10	☉	20:47:05	T 3m37s	17♍06
1784	Mar 7	☽	3:39:00	P 0.379	17♍11
1765	Mar 7	☽	13:29:00	T 1.732	17♍16
1942	Sep 10	☉	15:39:06	P 0.523	17♍17
1849	Mar 9	☽	0:56:00	P 0.741	18♍19
2007	Sep 11	☉	12:31:23	P 0.751	18♍24
1868	Mar 8	☽	20:10:00	A 0.585	18♍27
1931	Sep 12	☉	4:40:58	P 0.047	18♍28
1830	Mar 9	☽	13:43:00	T 1.663	18♍32
1988	Sep 11	☉	4:43:33	A 6m57s	18♍40
1950	Sep 12	☉	3:38:16	T 1m14s	18♍49
1969	Sep 11	☉	19:58:19	A 3m11s	18♍53
1811	Mar 10	☽	6:37:00	P 0.434	18♍54
1792	Mar 8	☽	19:02:00	A 0.335	19♍05
2034	Sep 12	☉	16:18:26	A 2m58s	19♍59
1700	Sep 13	☉	0:34:10	P 0.300	20♍08
1876	Mar 10	☽	6:22:00	P 0.294	20♍08
2015	Sep 13	☉	6:54:17	P 0.788	20♍11
1895	Mar 11	☽	3:39:00	T 1.620	20♍21
1914	Mar 12	☽	4:13:00	P 0.911	20♍42
1933	Mar 12	☽	2:33:00	A 0.592	20♍57
1708	Sep 14	☉	9:00:14	T 2m10s	21♍31
1727	Sep 15	☉	8:27:22	T 5m33s	21♍53
1922	Mar 13	☽	11:28:00	A 0.132	22♍15
1998	Mar 13	☽	4:20:00	A 0.708	22♍16
1746	Sep 15	☉	8:46:25	T 3m23s	22♍17
1765	Sep 15	☉	4:32:19	P 0.201	22♍31
1941	Mar 13	☽	11:55:00	P 0.323	22♍36
1979	Mar 13	☽	21:08:00	P 0.854	22♍38
1960	Mar 13	☽	8:28:00	T 1.515	22♍47
1754	Sep 16	☉	16:25:28	P 0.382	23♍39
1830	Sep 17	☉	2:08:00	P 0.393	23♍39
2044	Mar 13	☽	19:37:00	T 1.203	23♍50
1811	Sep 17	☉	18:43:27	A 6m51s	23♍56
2025	Mar 14	☽	6:59:00	T 1.178	23♍58
1773	Sep 16	☉	15:52:08	T 2m18s	24♍01
1792	Sep 16	☉	9:13:36	A 3m02s	24♍08
2006	Mar 14	☽	23:48:00	A 1.030	24♍20
1857	Sep 18	☉	5:35:54	A 3m34s	25♍14
1876	Sep 17	☉	21:49:16	T 1m53s	25♍18
1838	Sep 18	☉	20:55:46	A 6m06s	25♍28
1895	Sep 18	☉	20:44:06	P 0.737	25♍40
1718	Mar 16	☽	15:54:00	T 1.758	25♍43
1819	Sep 19	☉	13:03:27	P 0.060	25♍44
1737	Mar 16	☽	16:22:00	P 0.554	26♍04
1756	Mar 16	☽	15:18:00	A 0.240	26♍21
1903	Sep 21	☉	4:39:48	T 2m12s	27♍01
1922	Sep 21	☉	4:40:08	T 5m59s	27♍25
1745	Mar 17	☽	23:37:00	A 0.479	27♍37
1821	Mar 18	☽	18:45:00	A 0.281	27♍45
1941	Sep 21	☉	4:33:37	T 3m22s	27♍48
1764	Mar 18	☽	0:11:00	P 0.698	27♍58
1960	Sep 20	☉	22:59:22	P 0.614	27♍58
1802	Mar 19	☽	11:15:00	P 0.442	28♍05
1783	Mar 18	☽	21:31:00	T 1.789	28♍11
2025	Sep 21	☉	19:42:02	P 0.855	29♍05
1867	Mar 20	☽	8:49:00	P 0.804	29♍15
2006	Sep 22	☉	11:40:15	A 7m09s	29♍20
1886	Mar 20	☽	4:24:00	A 0.639	29♍23
1848	Mar 19	☽	21:12:00	T 1.599	29♍26
1968	Sep 22	☉	11:18:06	T 0m40s	29♍30
1987	Sep 23	☉	3:11:26	A 3m49s	29♍34
1829	Mar 20	☽	14:08:00	P 0.368	29♍48
1810	Mar 21	☽	2:54:00	A 0.269	29♍59
2033	Sep 23	☉	13:53:28	P 0.689	0♎51
1718	Sep 24	☉	8:34:10	P 0.389	0♎53
1894	Mar 21	☽	14:21:00	P 0.242	1♎03
1913	Mar 22	☽	11:58:00	T 1.568	1♎17
1932	Mar 22	☽	12:32:00	P 0.967	1♎38
1951	Mar 23	☽	10:37:00	A 0.642	1♎52
1707	Sep 25	☉	23:04:57	P 0.160	2♎08
1726	Sep 25	☉	16:51:35	T 2m07s	2♎16
1745	Sep 25	☉	16:28:44	T 5m21s	2♎38
1764	Sep 25	☉	16:41:29	T 3m01s	3♎03
1940	Mar 23	☽	19:48:00	A 0.079	3♎10
2016	Mar 23	☽	11:47:00	A 0.775	3♎10
1783	Sep 26	☉	12:04:01	P 0.281	3♎15
1959	Mar 24	☽	20:11:00	P 0.264	3♎31
1997	Mar 24	☽	4:39:00	P 0.919	3♎32
1978	Mar 24	☽	16:22:00	T 1.452	3♎41
1848	Sep 27	☉	9:21:09	P 0.488	4♎23
1772	Sep 27	☉	0:28:02	P 0.299	4♎25
1829	Sep 28	☉	1:46:40	A 7m43s	4♎39
1709	Mar 25	☽	16:43:00	A 0.272	4♎44
1791	Sep 27	☉	23:42:13	T 1m36s	4♎46
1810	Sep 28	☉	16:37:07	A 3m45s	4♎52
2043	Mar 25	☽	14:31:00	T 1.114	4♎52
2024	Mar 25	☽	7:13:00	A 0.956	5♎13
1875	Sep 29	☉	12:58:10	A 3m36s	5♎58
1894	Sep 29	☉	5:39:07	T 1m55s	6♎04
1856	Sep 29	☉	3:59:33	A 6m21s	6♎11
1717	Mar 27	☽	3:14:00	P 0.601	6♎24
1913	Sep 30	☉	4:45:32	P 0.825	6♎25
1736	Mar 27	☽	0:06:00	T 1.822	6♎36
1755	Mar 28	☽	0:36:00	P 0.617	6♎57
1774	Mar 27	☽	23:19:00	A 0.295	7♎13
1921	Oct 1	☉	12:35:34	T 1m52s	7♎47
1940	Oct 1	☉	12:43:41	T 5m36s	8♎11
1763	Mar 29	☽	7:49:00	A 0.414	8♎29
1959	Oct 2	☉	12:26:27	T 3m02s	8♎34
1839	Mar 30	☽	2:03:00	A 0.359	8♎35
1978	Oct 2	☉	6:27:54	P 0.691	8♎43
1782	Mar 29	☽	8:23:00	P 0.631	8♎50
1820	Mar 29	☽	18:42:00	P 0.517	8♎56
1801	Mar 30	☽	5:24:00	T 1.840	9♎02
2043	Oct 3	☉	3:00:47	A non-C	9♎48
2024	Oct 2	☉	18:45:12	A 7m25s	10♎04
1885	Mar 30	☽	16:34:00	P 0.880	10♎06
1904	Mar 31	☽	12:32:00	A 0.704	10♎15
1866	Mar 31	☽	4:33:00	T 1.523	10♎16
1986	Oct 3	☉	19:05:19	AT 0m00s	10♎16
2005	Oct 3	☉	10:31:46	A 4m31s	10♎19
1847	Mar 31	☽	21:27:00	P 0.286	10♎37
1828	Mar 31	☽	10:39:00	A 0.192	10♎50
1717	Oct 4	☉	18:08:18	AT 0m56s	11♎22
1736	Oct 4	☉	16:41:23	P 0.467	11♎42
1912	Apr 1	☽	22:14:00	P 0.182	11♎54
1931	Apr 2	☽	20:08:00	T 1.502	12♎08
1950	Apr 2	☽	20:44:00	T 1.033	12♎29
1969	Apr 2	☽	18:32:00	A 0.703	12♎43
1725	Oct 6	☉	6:39:32	P 0.092	12♎55

Solar and Lunar Eclipses in Zodiacal Order 1700–2050

1744	Oct	6	●	0:51:12	T 2m05s	13♎05
1763	Oct	7	●	0:38:50	T 5m10s	13♎28
1782	Oct	7	●	0:43:03	T 2m37s	13♎52
2034	Apr	3	☽	19:06:00	A 0.854	13♎59
1958	Apr	4	☽	3:60:00	A 0.013	14♎02
1801	Oct	7	●	19:42:14	P 0.351	14♎03
2015	Apr	4	☽	12:00:00	T 1.001	14♎21
1977	Apr	4	☽	4:18:00	P 0.193	14♎22
1996	Apr	4	☽	0:10:00	T 1.380	14♎32
1866	Oct	8	●	16:44:14	P 0.569	15♎10
1790	Oct	8	●	8:38:33	P 0.229	15♎15
1708	Apr	5	☽	5:38:00	P 0.496	15♎24
1847	Oct	9	●	9:00:13	A 8m35s	15♎27
1727	Apr	6	☽	0:42:00	A 0.351	15♎32
1809	Oct	9	●	7:38:23	T 1m02s	15♎36
1828	Oct	9	●	0:07:33	A 4m26s	15♎40
2042	Apr	5	☽	14:29:00	A 0.868	16♎02
1893	Oct	9	●	20:30:28	A 3m41s	16♎46
1912	Oct	10	●	13:35:58	T 1m55s	16♎52
1874	Oct	10	●	11:13:34	A 6m28s	16♎59
1735	Apr	7	☽	10:57:00	P 0.529	17♎12
1931	Oct	11	●	12:55:15	P 0.901	17♎15
1716	Apr	6	☽	21:22:00	A 0.207	17♎17
1754	Apr	7	☽	8:08:00	T 1.851	17♎24
1773	Apr	7	☽	8:43:00	P 0.691	17♎45
1792	Apr	7	☽	7:12:00	A 0.361	18♎01
1939	Oct	12	●	20:39:57	T 1m33s	18♎37
1958	Oct	12	●	20:54:55	T 5m11s	19♎01
1781	Apr	8	☽	15:55:00	A 0.339	19♎17
1857	Apr	9	☽	9:13:00	A 0.450	19♎21
1977	Oct	12	●	20:26:39	T 2m37s	19♎24
1996	Oct	12	●	14:02:04	P 0.758	19♎31
1800	Apr	9	☽	16:26:00	P 0.550	19♎38
1838	Apr	10	☽	1:59:00	P 0.608	19♎42
1819	Apr	10	☽	13:08:00	T 1.757	19♎50
2042	Oct	14	●	1:59:40	A 7m44s	20♎52
1903	Apr	12	☽	0:13:00	P 0.968	20♎53
1884	Apr	10	☽	11:47:00	T 1.434	21♎01
1922	Apr	11	☽	20:32:00	A 0.781	21♎03
2004	Oct	14	●	2:59:22	P 0.928	21♎06
2023	Oct	14	●	17:59:39	A 5m17s	21♎08
1865	Apr	11	☽	4:38:00	P 0.193	21♎23
1846	Apr	11	☽	18:11:00	A 0.100	21♎36
1716	Oct	15	●	10:07:31	A 5m10s	22♎10
1735	Oct	16	●	2:10:23	AT 1m02s	22♎14
1754	Oct	16	●	0:57:33	P 0.532	22♎35
1930	Apr	13	☽	5:58:00	P 0.106	22♎40
1949	Apr	13	☽	4:11:00	T 1.425	22♎56
1968	Apr	13	☽	4:47:00	T 1.112	23♎17
1987	Apr	14	☽	2:19:00	A 0.777	23♎30
1743	Oct	17	●	14:25:31	P 0.039	23♎48
1762	Oct	17	●	9:00:21	T 2m02s	23♎58
1781	Oct	17	●	8:55:43	T 4m59s	24♎21
1800	Oct	18	●	8:51:32	T 2m14s	24♎45
1819	Oct	19	●	3:26:59	P 0.409	24♎55
2033	Apr	14	☽	19:13:00	T 1.094	25♎06
1995	Apr	15	☽	12:18:00	P 0.111	25♎09
2014	Apr	15	☽	7:46:00	T 1.291	25♎17
1884	Oct	19	●	0:17:46	P 0.639	26♎02
1726	Apr	16	☽	13:06:00	P 0.597	26♎08
1808	Oct	19	●	16:55:09	P 0.169	26♎08
1745	Apr	16	☽	8:35:00	A 0.438	26♎16
1865	Oct	19	●	16:21:05	A 9m27s	26♎18
1707	Apr	17	☽	1:39:00	T 1.818	26♎19
1827	Oct	20	●	15:41:50	AT 0m30s	26♎29
1846	Oct	20	●	7:46:02	A 5m05s	26♎33
1911	Oct	22	●	4:12:48	A 3m47s	27♎39
1930	Oct	21	●	21:43:29	T 1m55s	27♎46
1892	Oct	20	●	18:36:11	P 0.905	27♎51
1753	Apr	17	☽	18:33:00	P 0.445	27♎55
1734	Apr	18	☽	4:32:00	A 0.112	28♎00
1949	Oct	21	●	21:12:30	P 0.964	28♎08
1772	Apr	17	☽	16:05:00	T 1.766	28♎09
1791	Apr	18	☽	16:41:00	P 0.778	28♎29
1810	Apr	19	☽	14:54:00	A 0.441	28♎44
1957	Oct	23	●	4:53:28	T non-C	29♎31
1976	Oct	23	●	5:12:58	T 4m47s	29♎56
1799	Apr	19	☽	23:52:00	A 0.251	0♏00
1875	Apr	20	☽	16:15:00	A 0.554	0♏03
1995	Oct	24	●	4:32:31	T 2m10s	0♏17
1818	Apr	21	☽	0:20:00	P 0.457	0♏22
1856	Apr	20	☽	9:07:00	P 0.710	0♏24
2014	Oct	23	●	21:44:38	P 0.811	0♏24
1837	Apr	20	☽	20:41:00	T 1.660	0♏32
1707	Oct	25	●	14:17:14	P 0.253	1♏30
1921	Apr	22	☽	7:44:00	T 1.068	1♏35
1902	Apr	22	☽	18:53:00	T 1.333	1♏43
1940	Apr	22	☽	4:26:00	A 0.868	1♏47
2022	Oct	25	●	11:00:19	P 0.862	2♏01
2041	Oct	25	●	1:35:20	A 6m07s	2♏01
1883	Apr	22	☽	11:39:00	P 0.085	2♏04
1734	Oct	26	●	17:53:17	A 5m08s	3♏06
1753	Oct	26	●	10:21:48	AT 1m08s	3♏11
1715	Oct	27	●	9:02:39	A 7m02s	3♏21
1948	Apr	23	☽	13:39:00	P 0.023	3♏23
1772	Oct	26	●	9:21:03	P 0.585	3♏32
1967	Apr	24	☽	12:06:00	T 1.336	3♏39
1986	Apr	24	☽	12:43:00	T 1.202	4♏00
2005	Apr	24	☽	9:55:00	A 0.865	4♏12
1780	Oct	27	●	17:18:12	T 1m60s	4♏55
1799	Oct	28	●	17:21:33	T 4m50s	5♏19
1818	Oct	29	●	17:06:52	T 1m51s	5♏42
1837	Oct	29	●	11:19:13	P 0.454	5♏51
2013	Apr	25	☽	20:08:00	P 0.015	5♏51
2032	Apr	25	☽	15:14:00	T 1.191	6♏00
1744	Apr	26	☽	20:29:00	P 0.709	6♏47
1725	Apr	27	☽	8:37:00	T 1.711	6♏57
1763	Apr	27	☽	16:20:00	A 0.537	6♏57
1902	Oct	31	●	8:00:16	P 0.696	6♏58
1826	Oct	31	●	1:20:20	P 0.122	7♏07
1883	Oct	30	●	23:50:58	A 9m43s	7♏14
1706	Apr	28	☽	1:32:00	P 0.470	7♏18
1845	Oct	30	●	23:51:46	AT 0m02s	7♏27
1864	Oct	30	●	15:30:22	A 5m41s	7♏29
1771	Apr	29	☽	2:04:00	P 0.351	8♏35
1929	Nov	1	●	12:04:46	A 3m54s	8♏35
1752	Apr	28	☽	11:35:00	A 0.006	8♏38
1948	Nov	1	●	5:58:49	T 1m56s	8♏44
1910	Nov	2	●	2:08:20	P 0.852	8♏47
1790	Apr	28	☽	23:53:00	T 1.669	8♏49
1967	Nov	2	●	5:38:17	T non-C	9♏07
1809	Apr	30	☽	0:33:00	P 0.873	9♏10
1828	Apr	29	☽	22:28:00	A 0.532	9♏25
1975	Nov	3	●	13:15:06	P 0.959	10♏30
1817	May	1	☽	7:44:00	A 0.155	10♏41
1893	Apr	30	☽	23:09:00	A 0.671	10♏41
1994	Nov	3	●	13:39:07	T 4m24s	10♏54
1836	May	1	☽	8:07:00	P 0.353	11♏01
1874	May	1	☽	16:03:00	P 0.828	11♏02
1855	May	2	☽	4:05:00	T 1.551	11♏11
2013	Nov	3	●	12:46:35	AT 1m40s	11♏16
2032	Nov	3	●	5:33:12	P 0.856	11♏21
1939	May	3	☽	15:11:00	T 1.177	12♏15
1920	May	3	☽	1:51:00	T 1.219	12♏21
1958	May	3	☽	12:13:00	P 0.009	12♏27
1725	Nov	4	●	22:02:41	P 0.304	12♏29
1901	May	3	☽	18:31:00	A 1.043	12♏42
1706	Nov	5	●	14:23:49	A 7m02s	12♏46
2040	Nov	4	●	19:08:01	P 0.808	12♏59
1966	May	4	☽	21:11:00	A 0.916	14♏02
1752	Nov	6	●	1:48:01	A 5m03s	14♏06
1771	Nov	6	●	18:40:48	AT 1m13s	14♏12
1985	May	4	☽	19:56:00	T 1.237	14♏19
1733	Nov	6	●	16:40:03	A 6m54s	14♏20
1790	Nov	6	●	17:52:55	P 0.625	14♏34
1714	Nov	7	●	9:04:21	P 0.173	14♏37
2004	May	4	☽	20:30:00	T 1.304	14♏39
2023	May	5	☽	17:23:00	A 0.964	14♏51
1716	May	6	☽	12:58:00	A 0.291	15♏53
1798	Nov	8	●	1:44:26	T 1m59s	15♏57
1817	Nov	9	●	1:53:36	T 4m42s	16♏21
2031	May	7	☽	3:51:00	A 0.881	16♏31
2050	May	6	☽	22:31:00	T 1.077	16♏37
1836	Nov	9	●	1:29:15	T 1m29s	16♏43
1855	Nov	9	●	19:17:39	P 0.489	16♏51
1762	May	8	☽	3:45:00	P 0.832	17♏23
1743	May	8	☽	15:26:00	T 1.583	17♏32
1781	May	8	☽	0:01:00	A 0.646	17♏34
1724	May	8	☽	8:20:00	P 0.341	17♏53
1920	Nov	10	●	15:51:53	P 0.742	17♏58
1705	May	8	☽	21:48:00	A 0.229	18♏06
1844	Nov	10	●	9:51:31	P 0.085	18♏09
1901	Nov	11	●	7:28:21	A 11m01s	18♏13
1863	Nov	11	●	8:08:51	A 0m22s	18♏28
1882	Nov	10	●	23:22:24	A 5m57s	18♏30
1789	May	9	☽	9:28:00	P 0.246	19♏11
1808	May	10	☽	7:38:00	T 1.564	19♏26
1947	Nov	12	●	20:05:09	A 3m59s	19♏36
1966	Nov	12	●	14:22:50	T 1m58s	19♏45
1827	May	11	☽	8:17:00	P 0.980	19♏47
1928	Nov	12	●	9:48:01	P 0.808	19♏47
1846	May	11	☽	5:54:00	A 0.635	20♏01
1985	Nov	12	●	14:10:31	T 1m59s	20♏08
1911	May	13	☽	5:56:00	A 0.799	21♏15
1835	May	12	☽	15:29:00	A 0.049	21♏17
1993	Nov	13	●	21:44:50	P 0.928	21♏32
1892	May	11	☽	22:53:00	P 0.955	21♏37
1854	May	12	☽	15:46:00	P 0.239	21♏38
1873	May	12	☽	11:20:00	T 1.429	21♏47
2012	Nov	13	●	22:11:53	T 4m02s	21♏57
2031	Nov	14	●	21:06:29	AT 1m08s	22♏17
2050	Nov	14	●	13:29:53	P 0.887	22♏22
1957	May	13	☽	22:31:00	T 1.298	22♏50
1938	May	14	☽	8:44:00	T 1.097	22♏56
1976	May	13	☽	19:54:00	P 0.122	23♏03
1919	May	15	☽	1:14:00	A 0.910	23♏15
1743	Nov	16	●	5:58:13	P 0.342	23♏31
1724	Nov	15	●	22:07:27	A 7m15s	23♏48
1705	Nov	16	●	13:22:59	A 5m31s	24♏03
1984	May	15	☽	4:40:00	A 0.807	24♏38
2003	May	16	☽	3:40:00	T 1.128	24♏55
1770	Nov	17	●	9:51:38	A 4m56s	25♏09
1789	Nov	17	●	3:08:19	AT 1m19s	25♏16
2022	May	16	☽	4:12:00	T 1.414	25♏16
1751	Nov	18	●	0:25:45	A 6m46s	25♏22
2041	May	16	☽	0:42:00	P 0.064	25♏26
1808	Nov	18	●	2:29:46	P 0.656	25♏38
1732	Nov	17	●	16:58:36	P 0.139	25♏41
1734	May	17	☽	19:38:00	A 0.425	26♏25
1715	May	18	☽	12:29:00	P 0.590	26♏46
1816	Nov	19	●	10:17:06	T 1m59s	27♏01
2049	May	17	☽	11:26:00	A 0.764	27♏06
1835	Nov	20	●	10:31:48	T 4m35s	27♏26
1854	Nov	20	●	9:56:47	AT 1m07s	27♏48
1873	Nov	20	●	3:22:50	P 0.514	27♏55
1780	May	18	☽	10:58:00	P 0.962	27♏57
1761	May	18	☽	22:12:00	T 1.449	28♏04
1799	May	19	☽	7:36:00	A 0.764	28♏08
1742	May	19	☽	14:58:00	P 0.200	28♏24
1723	May	20	☽	4:52:00	A 0.096	28♏38
1938	Nov	21	●	23:52:02	P 0.778	29♏01
1862	Nov	21	●	18:29:32	P 0.058	29♏15
1919	Nov	22	●	15:13:50	A 11m36s	29♏17
1881	Nov	21	●	16:31:11	A 0m43s	29♏33
1900	Nov	22	●	7:19:43	A 6m42s	29♏34
1807	May	21	☽	16:49:00	P 0.135	29♏44
1826	May	21	☽	15:15:00	T 1.446	29♏59
1845	May	21	☽	15:54:00	T 1.096	0♐21
1864	May	21	☽	13:12:00	A 0.748	0♐34
1965	Nov	23	●	4:14:15	A 4m02s	0♐40
1946	Nov	23	●	17:36:46	P 0.776	0♐50
1984	Nov	22	●	22:53:22	T 1m60s	0♐50
2003	Nov	23	●	22:49:19	T 1m58s	1♐14
1929	May	23	☽	12:37:00	A 0.937	1♐47
1910	May	24	☽	5:34:00	T 1.095	2♐08

Solar and Lunar Eclipses in Zodiacal Order 1700–2050

1872	May 22	☽	23:18:00	P 0.115	2♐11
1891	May 23	☽	18:29:00	T 1.300	2♐20
2011	Nov 25	●	6:20:20	P 0.905	2♐37
2030	Nov 25	●	6:50:35	T 3m44s	3♐02
1975	May 25	☽	5:48:00	T 1.425	3♐23
2049	Nov 25	●	5:32:46	AT 0m38s	3♐23
1956	May 24	☽	15:31:00	P 0.965	3♐27
1994	May 25	☽	3:30:00	P 0.243	3♐37
1937	May 25	☽	7:51:00	A 0.770	3♐47
2013	May 25	☽	4:10:00	A 0.015	3♐58
1761	Nov 26	●	14:00:12	P 0.373	4♐37
1742	Nov 27	●	5:58:48	A 7m26s	4♐54
1704	Nov 27	●	5:33:47	A 0m01s	5♐06
1723	Nov 27	●	21:28:06	A 6m12s	5♐09
2002	May 26	☽	12:03:00	A 0.689	5♐10
2021	May 26	☽	11:19:00	T 1.009	5♐28
2040	May 26	☽	11:45:00	T 1.535	5♐49
1788	Nov 27	●	18:02:37	A 4m46s	6♐16
1807	Nov 29	●	11:41:52	AT 1m26s	6♐23
1769	Nov 28	●	8:18:22	A 6m39s	6♐28
1826	Nov 29	●	11:13:55	P 0.677	6♐46
1750	Nov 29	●	0:57:57	P 0.113	6♐47
1752	May 28	☽	2:14:00	A 0.568	6♐55
1733	May 28	☽	19:08:00	P 0.732	7♐15
1714	May 29	☽	7:05:00	T 1.647	7♐24
1834	Nov 30	●	18:56:26	T 2m02s	8♐09
1798	May 29	☽	18:07:00	T 1.099	8♐27
1779	May 30	☽	4:52:00	T 1.306	8♐33
1853	Nov 30	●	19:15:29	T 4m28s	8♐34
1817	May 30	☽	15:07:00	A 0.888	8♐40
1760	May 29	☽	21:33:00	P 0.053	8♐54
1872	Nov 30	●	18:29:31	AT 0m47s	8♐56
1891	Dec 1	●	11:31:11	P 0.533	9♐01
1956	Dec 2	●	8:00:04	P 0.805	10♐08
1825	Jun 1	☽	0:06:00	P 0.015	10♐15
1937	Dec 2	●	23:05:22	A 11m13s	10♐22
1880	Dec 2	●	3:11:30	P 0.037	10♐23
1844	May 31	☽	22:51:00	T 1.326	10♐32
1918	Dec 3	●	15:21:39	A 7m06s	10♐40
1899	Dec 3	●	0:57:27	A 1m01s	10♐41
1863	Jun 1	☽	23:26:00	T 1.219	10♐52
1882	Jun 1	☽	20:22:00	A 0.872	11♐04
1983	Dec 4	●	12:30:22	A 4m01s	11♐47
1964	Dec 4	●	1:31:21	P 0.752	11♐56
2002	Dec 4	●	7:31:14	T 2m04s	11♐58
1947	Jun 3	☽	19:15:00	P 0.020	12♐16
2021	Dec 4	●	7:33:35	T 1m55s	12♐22
1928	Jun 3	☽	12:10:00	T 1.242	12♐37
1890	Jun 3	☽	6:45:00	A 0.949	12♐42
1909	Jun 4	☽	1:29:00	T 1.158	12♐49
2029	Dec 5	●	15:02:53	P 0.891	13♐46
1993	Jun 4	☽	13:00:00	T 1.562	13♐53
1974	Jun 4	☽	22:16:00	P 0.827	13♐57
2012	Jun 4	☽	11:03:00	P 0.370	14♐08
2048	Dec 5	●	15:34:24	T 3m28s	14♐11
1955	Jun 5	☽	14:23:00	A 0.622	14♐15
2031	Jun 5	☽	11:44:00	A 0.129	14♐30
1714	Dec 7	●	1:27:02	P 0.142	14♐39
2020	Jun 5	☽	19:25:00	A 0.568	15♐41
1779	Dec 7	●	22:08:38	P 0.396	15♐45
1703	Dec 8	●	15:41:25	P 0.428	15♐56
2039	Jun 6	☽	18:53:00	P 0.885	15♐59
1760	Dec 7	●	13:53:29	A 7m37s	16♐01
1705	Jun 7	☽	8:39:00	A 0.576	16♐07
1722	Dec 8	●	14:07:27	A 0m28s	16♐16
1741	Dec 8	●	5:37:49	A 6m51s	16♐18
1770	Jun 8	☽	8:45:00	A 0.718	17♐22
1806	Dec 10	●	2:19:21	A 4m32s	17♐25
1825	Dec 9	●	20:21:31	AT 1m34s	17♐33
1787	Dec 9	●	16:15:19	A 6m32s	17♐36
1751	Jun 9	☽	1:42:00	P 0.882	17♐43
1713	Jun 8	☽	18:28:00	P 0.309	17♐44
1732	Jun 8	☽	14:06:00	T 1.505	17♐53
1768	Dec 9	●	9:01:17	P 0.093	17♐55
1844	Dec 9	●	20:01:30	P 0.692	17♐56
1816	Jun 10	☽	1:14:00	T 1.241	18♐56
1797	Jun 9	☽	11:30:00	T 1.159	19♐01
1835	Jun 10	☽	22:36:00	P 0.068	19♐09
1778	Jun 10	☽	4:01:00	A 0.966	19♐20
1852	Dec 11	●	3:40:35	T 2m05s	19♐20
1871	Dec 12	●	4:03:36	T 4m23s	19♐44
1890	Dec 12	●	3:05:31	AT 0m29s	20♐05
1909	Dec 12	●	19:44:35	P 0.542	20♐11
1843	Jun 12	☽	7:22:00	A 0.872	20♐44
1862	Jun 12	☽	6:21:00	T 1.196	21♐01
1974	Dec 13	●	16:12:29	P 0.827	21♐16
1881	Jun 12	☽	6:54:00	T 1.349	21♐22
1955	Dec 14	●	7:01:54	A 12m09s	21♐31
1898	Dec 13	●	11:58:10	P 0.023	21♐33
1900	Jun 13	☽	3:28:00	A 1.001	21♐33
1936	Dec 13	●	23:27:47	A 7m07s	21♐49
1917	Dec 14	●	9:26:56	A 1m16s	21♐50
1984	Jun 13	☽	14:26:00	A 0.064	22♐35
1965	Jun 14	☽	1:49:00	P 0.177	22♐43
2001	Dec 14	●	20:52:01	A 3m53s	22♐56
1946	Jun 14	☽	18:39:00	T 1.398	23♐03
1982	Dec 15	●	9:31:18	P 0.735	23♐05
2020	Dec 14	●	16:13:37	T 2m10s	23♐08
1908	Jun 14	☽	14:06:00	A 0.813	23♐11
1927	Jun 15	☽	8:24:00	T 1.012	23♐17
2039	Dec 15	●	16:22:43	T 1m52s	23♐32
2011	Jun 15	☽	20:13:00	T 1.700	24♐22
1992	Jun 15	☽	4:57:00	P 0.682	24♐23
2030	Jun 15	☽	18:33:00	P 0.502	24♐38
1973	Jun 15	☽	20:50:00	A 0.468	24♐42
2047	Dec 16	●	23:49:07	P 0.882	24♐56
2049	Jun 15	☽	19:13:00	A 0.251	24♐59
1713	Dec 17	●	16:04:13	AT 0m56s	25♐42
1732	Dec 17	●	9:46:48	P 0.147	25♐50
2038	Jun 17	☽	2:44:00	A 0.442	26♐10
1704	Jun 17	☽	18:26:00	T 1.058	26♐21
1723	Jun 18	☽	15:45:00	A 0.707	26♐34
1797	Dec 18	●	6:21:35	P 0.414	26♐55
1721	Dec 19	●	0:31:44	P 0.417	27♐08
1778	Dec 18	●	21:53:36	A 7m45s	27♐11
1740	Dec 18	●	22:43:08	A 0m53s	27♐27
1759	Dec 19	●	13:49:51	A 7m25s	27♐28
1788	Jun 18	☽	15:15:00	A 0.873	27♐48
1769	Jun 19	☽	8:11:00	T 1.037	28♐08
1731	Jun 20	☽	1:50:00	P 0.169	28♐11
1750	Jun 19	☽	21:03:00	T 1.357	28♐20
1824	Dec 20	●	10:40:20	A 4m15s	28♐35
1843	Dec 21	●	5:03:17	T 1m43s	28♐44
1805	Dec 21	●	0:17:16	A 6m27s	28♐46
1786	Dec 20	●	17:07:01	P 0.077	29♐05
1862	Dec 21	●	4:52:53	P 0.702	29♐08
1834	Jun 21	☽	8:20:00	T 1.387	29♐23
1815	Jun 21	☽	18:06:00	T 1.008	29♐27
1853	Jun 21	☽	6:02:00	P 0.206	29♐37
1796	Jun 20	☽	10:28:00	A 0.809	29♐46
1870	Dec 22	●	12:27:30	T 2m11s	0♑31
1889	Dec 22	●	12:54:19	T 4m18s	0♑56
1861	Jun 22	☽	14:35:00	A 0.740	1♑11
1908	Dec 23	●	11:44:17	AT 0m12s	1♑17
1927	Dec 24	●	3:59:14	P 0.549	1♑21
1880	Jun 22	☽	13:51:00	T 1.064	1♑29
1899	Jun 23	☽	14:18:00	T 1.482	1♑50
1918	Jun 24	☽	10:28:00	P 0.130	2♑00
1992	Dec 24	●	0:30:44	P 0.842	2♑27
1973	Dec 24	●	15:02:00	A 12m02s	2♑40
1916	Dec 24	●	20:45:55	P 0.012	2♑45
1954	Dec 25	●	7:36:11	A 7m39s	2♑59
1935	Dec 25	●	17:59:25	A 1m30s	3♑02
2002	Jun 24	☽	21:27:00	A 0.209	3♑02
1983	Jun 25	☽	8:22:00	P 0.335	3♑09
1964	Jun 25	☽	1:06:00	T 1.556	3♑29
1926	Jun 25	☽	21:25:00	A 0.675	3♑38
1945	Jun 25	☽	15:14:00	P 0.859	3♑43
2019	Dec 26	●	5:17:53	A 3m39s	4♑07
2000	Dec 25	●	17:34:58	P 0.723	4♑15
2038	Dec 26	●	0:59:07	T 2m19s	4♑20
2029	Jun 26	☽	3:22:00	T 1.844	4♑49
2010	Jun 26	☽	11:39:00	P 0.537	4♑50
2048	Jun 26	☽	2:01:00	P 0.639	5♑06
1991	Jun 27	☽	3:15:00	A 0.312	5♑07
1703	Jun 29	☽	1:13:00	T 1.352	6♑27
1712	Dec 28	●	1:24:47	T 4m15s	6♑32
1722	Jun 29	☽	1:49:00	T 1.194	6♑48
1731	Dec 29	●	0:46:44	AT 0m39s	6♑55
1741	Jun 28	☽	22:48:00	A 0.843	7♑00
1750	Dec 28	●	18:06:40	P 0.151	7♑01
1815	Dec 30	●	14:38:19	P 0.427	8♑07
1806	Jun 30	☽	21:44:00	A 1.032	8♑13
1739	Dec 30	●	9:21:55	P 0.406	8♑20
1796	Dec 29	●	5:54:43	A 7m51s	8♑21
1787	Jun 30	☽	14:39:00	T 1.195	8♑34
1749	Jun 30	☽	9:09:00	P 0.028	8♑39
1758	Dec 30	●	7:20:00	A 1m15s	8♑39
1777	Dec 29	●	22:03:12	A 7m53s	8♑39
1768	Jun 30	☽	3:56:00	T 1.206	8♑46
1842	Dec 31	●	19:04:14	A 3m54s	9♑47
1852	Jul 1	☽	15:26:00	T 1.533	9♑50
1833	Jul 2	☽	0:43:00	P 0.857	9♑53
1824	Jan 1	●	8:20:50	A 6m21s	9♑57
1861	Dec 31	●	13:48:56	T 1m55s	9♑57
1871	Jul 2	☽	13:28:00	P 0.343	10♑05
1814	Jul 2	☽	16:51:00	A 0.650	10♑11
1805	Jan 1	●	1:14:31	P 0.064	10♑16
1880	Dec 31	●	13:45:06	P 0.710	10♑20
1890	Jul 2	☽	14:09:00	A 0.102	10♑26
1879	Jul 3	☽	21:51:00	A 0.610	11♑38
1889	Jan 1	●	21:16:55	T 2m17s	11♑44
1898	Jul 3	☽	21:17:00	P 0.928	11♑56
1908	Jan 3	●	21:45:13	T 4m14s	12♑09
1917	Jul 4	☽	21:39:00	T 1.618	12♑17
1936	Jul 4	☽	17:25:00	P 0.267	12♑26
1927	Jan 3	●	20:22:27	A 0m02s	12♑29
1946	Jan 3	●	12:15:41	P 0.553	12♑32
2020	Jul 5	☽	4:30:00	A 0.354	13♑29
2001	Jul 5	☽	14:55:00	P 0.495	13♑34
2011	Jan 4	●	8:50:42	P 0.858	13♑38
1992	Jan 4	●	23:04:40	A 10m58s	13♑51
1982	Jul 6	☽	7:31:00	T 1.718	13♑54
1935	Jan 5	●	5:35:15	P 0.001	13♑58
1944	Jul 6	☽	4:40:00	A 0.533	14♑05
1963	Jul 6	☽	22:02:00	P 0.706	14♑09
1973	Jan 4	●	15:45:37	A 7m49s	14♑10
1954	Jan 5	●	2:31:27	A 1m42s	14♑14
2028	Jul 6	☽	18:20:00	P 0.389	15♑15
2047	Jul 7	☽	10:35:00	T 1.751	15♑17
2038	Jan 5	●	13:46:10	A 3m18s	15♑19
2019	Jan 6	●	1:41:39	P 0.715	15♑26
2009	Jul 7	☽	9:39:00	A 0.156	15♑32
1704	Jan 7	●	2:14:42	P 0.318	15♑56
1702	Jul 9	☽	9:41:00	A 0.890	16♑38
1721	Jul 9	☽	8:40:00	T 1.217	16♑55
1740	Jul 9	☽	9:13:00	T 1.328	17♑15
1712	Jan 8	●	9:58:30	T 1m48s	17♑21
1759	Jul 10	☽	5:49:00	A 0.980	17♑27
1731	Jan 8	●	10:17:35	T 4m11s	17♑45
1750	Jan 8	●	9:28:33	AT 0m24s	18♑07
1769	Jan 8	●	2:26:28	P 0.153	18♑13
1843	Jul 11	☽	16:50:00	A 0.022	18♑31
1824	Jul 11	☽	4:15:00	P 0.133	18♑38
1805	Jul 11	☽	21:05:00	T 1.355	18♑58
1767	Jul 11	☽	16:27:00	A 0.851	19♑05
1786	Jul 11	☽	10:47:00	T 1.053	19♑12
1834	Jan 9	●	22:55:19	P 0.442	19♑18
1815	Jan 10	●	13:56:48	A 7m56s	19♑32
1758	Jan 9	●	18:13:30	P 0.397	19♑34
1796	Jan 10	●	6:14:38	A 8m15s	19♑50
1777	Jan 9	●	15:55:21	A 1m32s	19♑51
1870	Jul 12	☽	22:34:00	T 1.677	20♑17
1851	Jul 13	☽	7:22:00	P 0.707	20♑18
1889	Jul 12	☽	20:54:00	P 0.481	20♑32

Solar and Lunar Eclipses in Zodiacal Order 1700–2050

Year	Month	Day	Type	Time	Magnitude	Position
1832	Jul	12	☽	23:16:00	A 0.493	20♑36
1908	Jul	13	☽	21:34:00	A 0.229	20♑53
1861	Jan	11	●	3:29:12	A 3m30s	20♑58
1842	Jan	11	●	16:25:29	A 6m15s	21♑08
1880	Jan	11	●	22:34:29	T 2m07s	21♑09
1823	Jan	12	●	9:19:49	P 0.048	21♑27
1899	Jan	11	●	22:38:07	P 0.716	21♑33
1897	Jul	14	☽	5:05:00	A 0.479	22♑05
1916	Jul	15	☽	4:46:00	P 0.794	22♑24
1973	Jul	15	☽	11:39:00	A 0.104	22♑42
1935	Jul	16	☽	4:60:00	T 1.754	22♑44
1954	Jul	16	☽	0:20:00	P 0.405	22♑52
1907	Jan	14	●	6:05:37	T 2m25s	22♑56
1926	Jan	14	●	6:36:34	T 4m11s	23♑21
1945	Jan	14	●	5:01:15	A 0m15s	23♑41
1964	Jan	14	●	20:29:31	P 0.559	23♑43
2038	Jul	16	☽	11:35:00	A 0.500	23♑56
2019	Jul	16	☽	21:31:00	P 0.653	24♑00
2000	Jul	16	☽	13:56:00	T 1.768	24♑19
1962	Jul	17	☽	11:54:00	A 0.392	24♑32
1981	Jul	17	☽	4:47:00	P 0.549	24♑35
2029	Jan	14	●	17:12:47	P 0.871	24♑50
2010	Jan	15	●	7:06:39	A 11m07s	25♑01
1991	Jan	15	●	23:52:54	A 7m36s	25♑20
1972	Jan	16	●	11:02:37	A 1m53s	25♑25
1712	Jul	18	☽	8:22:00	P 0.168	25♑32
2046	Jul	18	☽	1:05:00	P 0.246	25♑42
2027	Jul	18	☽	16:03:00	A 0.001	25♑57
2037	Jan	16	●	9:47:55	P 0.705	26♑36
1703	Jan	17	●	11:24:17	T 0m50s	26♑45
1720	Jul	19	☽	16:55:00	A 0.760	27♑05
1722	Jan	17	●	11:06:59	P 0.325	27♑08
1739	Jul	20	☽	16:09:00	T 1.084	27♑23
1758	Jul	20	☽	16:37:00	T 1.461	27♑43
1777	Jul	20	☽	12:49:00	P 0.109	27♑53
1711	Jan	18	●	22:23:25	P 0.308	28♑18
1730	Jan	18	●	18:45:05	T 1m59s	28♑33
1749	Jan	18	●	19:08:45	T 4m07s	28♑57
1861	Jul	21	☽	23:50:00	A 0.169	28♑58
1842	Jul	22	☽	10:47:00	P 0.292	29♑04
1768	Jan	19	●	18:09:15	AT 0m13s	29♑19
1787	Jan	19	●	10:42:57	P 0.159	29♑23
1823	Jul	23	☽	3:32:00	T 1.512	29♑24
1785	Jul	21	☽	23:46:00	A 0.713	29♑33
1804	Jul	22	☽	17:38:00	P 0.901	29♑38
1852	Jan	21	●	7:12:04	P 0.458	0♒28
1833	Jan	20	●	21:56:44	A 8m00s	0♒42
1869	Jul	23	☽	14:03:00	P 0.560	0♒44
1888	Jul	23	☽	5:45:00	T 1.819	0♒44
1776	Jan	21	●	3:02:13	P 0.385	0♒45
1814	Jan	21	●	14:24:29	A 8m28s	1♒00
1907	Jul	25	☽	4:22:00	P 0.615	1♒00
1795	Jan	21	●	0:28:58	A 1m45s	1♒02
1850	Jul	24	☽	5:40:00	A 0.337	1♒02
1926	Jul	25	☽	4:60:00	A 0.354	1♒22
1879	Jan	22	●	11:53:11	A 3m03s	2♒09
1860	Jan	23	●	0:27:18	A 6m07s	2♒17
1898	Jan	22	●	7:19:17	T 2m21s	2♒21
1915	Jul	26	☽	12:24:00	A 0.354	2♒33
1841	Jan	22	●	17:24:00	P 0.032	2♒37
1917	Jan	23	●	7:28:12	P 0.726	2♒45
1934	Jul	26	☽	12:15:00	P 0.661	2♒52
1991	Jul	26	☽	18:08:00	A 0.254	3♒08
1953	Jul	26	☽	12:21:00	T 1.863	3♒12
1972	Jul	26	☽	7:16:00	P 0.543	3♒19
1925	Jan	24	●	14:53:40	T 2m32s	4♒08
2037	Jul	27	☽	4:09:00	P 0.810	4♒26
1944	Jan	25	●	15:26:16	T 4m09s	4♒33
2018	Jul	27	☽	20:22:00	T 1.609	4♒45
1963	Jan	25	●	13:36:36	A 0m25s	4♒52
1982	Jan	25	●	4:41:59	P 0.566	4♒53
1980	Jul	27	☽	19:08:00	A 0.253	5♒00
1999	Jul	28	☽	11:34:00	P 0.397	5♒02
1711	Jul	29	☽	17:50:00	T 1.489	5♒46
2047	Jan	26	●	1:32:17	P 0.891	6♒00
1730	Jul	29	☽	15:50:00	P 0.302	6♒01
2028	Jan	26	●	15:07:58	A 10m27s	6♒11
1749	Jul	29	☽	16:31:00	A 0.064	6♒22
2009	Jan	26	●	7:58:43	A 7m54s	6♒30
1990	Jan	26	●	19:30:25	A 2m03s	6♒35
1738	Jul	31	☽	0:13:00	A 0.635	7♒34
1702	Jan	28	●	1:37:03	A 4m14s	7♒46
1757	Jul	30	☽	23:40	P 0.953	7♒52
1721	Jan	27	●	20:05:01	T 1m07s	7♒56
1776	Jul	31	☽	0:02:00	T 1.591	8♒12
1740	Jan	28	●	19:54:47	P 0.339	8♒19
1795	Jul	31	☽	19:50:00	P 0.239	8♒22
1879	Aug	2	☽	6:58:00	A 0.310	9♒27
1729	Jan	29	●	6:48:29	P 0.299	9♒28
1860	Aug	1	☽	17:25:00	P 0.445	9♒31
1748	Jan	30	●	3:29:00	T 2m12s	9♒43
1841	Aug	2	☽	10:01:00	T 1.668	9♒51
1803	Aug	3	☽	7:05:00	A 0.579	10♒02
1822	Aug	3	☽	0:30:00	P 0.753	10♒06
1767	Jan	30	●	3:56:40	T 4m06s	10♒08
1786	Jan	30	●	2:45:10	AT 0m05s	10♒28
1805	Jan	30	●	18:56:43	P 0.168	10♒32
1887	Aug	3	☽	20:49:00	P 0.419	11♒12
1906	Aug	4	☽	13:00:00	T 1.779	11♒13
1868	Aug	3	☽	12:09:00	A 0.189	11♒29
1925	Aug	4	☽	11:53:00	P 0.746	11♒30
1870	Jan	31	●	15:26:18	P 0.478	11♒37
1851	Feb	1	●	5:54:16	A 8m01s	11♒50
1944	Aug	4	☽	12:26:00	A 0.478	11♒51
1794	Jan	31	●	11:48:31	P 0.368	11♒56
1832	Feb	1	●	22:30:03	A 8m35s	12♒09
1813	Feb	1	●	8:58:10	A 1m52s	12♒12
1933	Aug	5	☽	19:46:00	A 0.232	13♒02
1897	Feb	1	●	20:15:20	A 2m34s	13♒18
1952	Aug	5	☽	19:47:00	P 0.532	13♒22
1878	Feb	2	●	8:27:52	A 5m59s	13♒25
1916	Feb	3	●	16:00:03	T 2m36s	13♒31
2009	Aug	6	☽	0:39:00	A 0.402	13♒35
1971	Aug	6	☽	19:43:00	T 1.728	13♒41
1859	Feb	3	●	1:22:26	P 0.008	13♒44
1990	Aug	6	☽	14:12:00	P 0.677	13♒48
1935	Feb	3	●	16:15:56	P 0.739	13♒55
2036	Aug	7	☽	2:52:00	T 1.454	15♒13
1943	Feb	4	●	23:37:45	T 2m35s	15♒18
1998	Aug	8	☽	2:25:00	A 0.120	15♒29
2017	Aug	7	☽	18:21:00	P 0.246	15♒30
1962	Feb	5	●	0:12:04	T 4m08s	15♒43
1981	Feb	4	●	22:08:31	A 0m33s	16♒01
2000	Feb	5	●	12:49:24	P 0.580	16♒01
1729	Aug	9	☽	1:05:00	T 1.623	16♒16
1710	Aug	9	☽	9:56:00	P 0.760	16♒18
1748	Aug	8	☽	23:23:00	P 0.429	16♒32
1767	Aug	10	☽	0:03:00	A 0.182	16♒53
2046	Feb	5	●	23:05:25	A 9m16s	17♒18
2027	Feb	6	●	15:59:46	A 7m51s	17♒38
2008	Feb	7	●	3:55:07	A 2m12s	17♒45
1756	Aug	10	☽	7:37:00	A 0.517	18♒04
1775	Aug	11	☽	7:15:00	P 0.830	18♒23
1832	Aug	11	☽	14:15:00	A 0.066	18♒41
1794	Aug	11	☽	7:29:00	T 1.716	18♒43
1813	Aug	12	☽	2:53:00	P 0.365	18♒52
1720	Feb	8	●	9:52:22	A 3m40s	18♒53
1701	Feb	7	●	23:04:47	A 9m53s	19♒03
1739	Feb	8	●	4:41:02	T 1m28s	19♒04
1758	Feb	8	●	4:40:36	P 0.355	19♒28
1897	Aug	12	☽	14:09:00	A 0.447	19♒57
1878	Aug	13	☽	0:08:00	P 0.591	20♒01
1859	Aug	13	☽	16:34:00	T 1.815	20♒20
1821	Aug	13	☽	14:26:00	A 0.450	20♒33
1747	Feb	9	●	15:11:02	P 0.286	20♒35
1840	Aug	13	☽	7:23:00	P 0.607	20♒36
1766	Feb	9	●	12:09:28	T 2m28s	20♒51
1785	Feb	9	●	12:40:25	T 4m07s	21♒16
1804	Feb	11	●	11:16:14	A 0m00s	21♒36
1823	Feb	11	●	3:02:46	P 0.186	21♒39
1905	Aug	15	☽	3:41:00	P 0.287	21♒42
1924	Aug	14	☽	20:20:00	T 1.652	21♒44
1886	Aug	14	☽	18:42:00	A 0.049	21♒58
1943	Aug	15	☽	19:28:00	P 0.870	22♒01
1962	Aug	15	☽	19:57:00	A 0.596	22♒22
1888	Feb	11	●	23:38:18	P 0.503	22♒44
1869	Feb	11	●	13:46:34	A 8m02s	22♒56
1812	Feb	12	●	20:28:23	P 0.342	23♒03
1850	Feb	12	●	6:29:27	A 8m35s	23♒15
1831	Feb	12	●	17:21:34	A 1m57s	23♒19
1951	Aug	17	☽	3:14:00	A 0.119	23♒33
1970	Aug	17	☽	3:23:00	P 0.408	23♒53
2027	Aug	17	☽	7:14:00	A 0.546	24♒04
1989	Aug	17	☽	3:08:00	T 1.598	24♒12
2008	Aug	16	☽	21:10:00	P 0.808	24♒17
1915	Feb	14	●	4:33:02	A 2m03s	24♒25
1896	Feb	13	●	16:23:16	A 5m48s	24♒31
1934	Feb	14	●	0:38:17	T 2m52s	24♒38
1720	Aug	18	☽	2:32:00	A 0.121	25♒01
1953	Feb	14	●	0:58:59	P 0.760	25♒03
1701	Aug	18	☽	13:32:00	P 0.234	25♒08
2035	Aug	19	☽	1:11:00	P 0.104	26♒00
1961	Feb	15	●	8:19:15	T 2m45s	26♒26
1747	Aug	20	☽	8:27:00	T 1.748	26♒49
1728	Aug	19	☽	16:49:00	P 0.629	26♒50
1980	Feb	16	●	8:53:11	T 4m08s	26♒50
1766	Aug	20	☽	7:01:00	P 0.549	27♒05
1709	Aug	20	☽	8:28:00	A 0.414	27♒07
2018	Feb	15	●	20:51:31	P 0.599	27♒07
1999	Feb	16	●	6:33:37	A 0m39s	27♒08
1785	Aug	20	☽	7:38:00	A 0.295	27♒26
1711	Feb	17	●	13:30:07	P 0.092	28♒19
1774	Aug	21	☽	15:06:00	A 0.409	28♒38
2045	Feb	16	●	23:55:04	A 7m32s	28♒43
2026	Feb	17	●	12:12:02	A 2m20s	28♒50
1793	Aug	21	☽	14:55:00	P 0.712	28♒57
1850	Aug	22	☽	20:55:00	A 0.199	29♒13
1812	Aug	22	☽	15:01:00	T 1.832	29♒17
1831	Aug	23	☽	9:60:00	P 0.483	29♒24
1738	Feb	18	●	18:02:21	A 3m03s	29♒58
1719	Feb	19	●	6:52:49	A 9m00s	0♓07
1757	Feb	18	●	13:14:00	T 1m52s	0♓09
1700	Feb	18	●	23:49:29	P 0.374	0♓26
1915	Aug	24	☽	21:27:00	A 0.575	0♓29
1776	Feb	19	●	13:19:53	P 0.380	0♓33
1896	Aug	23	☽	6:57:00	P 0.731	0♓33
1877	Aug	23	☽	23:12:00	T 1.685	0♓52
1839	Aug	24	☽	21:52:00	A 0.328	1♓07
1858	Aug	24	☽	14:21:00	P 0.471	1♓08
1765	Feb	19	●	23:28:20	P 0.264	1♓39
1784	Feb	20	●	20:45:21	T 2m44s	1♓56
1923	Aug	26	☽	10:39:00	P 0.163	2♓14
1942	Aug	26	☽	3:48:00	T 1.534	2♓18
1803	Feb	21	●	21:18:27	T 4m10s	2♓21
1961	Aug	26	☽	3:08:00	P 0.986	2♓35
1822	Feb	21	●	19:40:24	A 0m02s	2♓40
1841	Feb	21	●	11:03:47	P 0.210	2♓43
1980	Aug	26	☽	3:30:00	A 0.709	2♓56
1906	Feb	23	●	7:43:13	P 0.539	3♓48
1887	Feb	22	●	21:33:07	A 8m01s	3♓59
1969	Aug	27	☽	10:48:00	A 0.013	4♓07
1830	Feb	23	●	5:04:01	P 0.310	4♓08
1868	Feb	23	●	14:21:25	A 8m30s	4♓18
1849	Feb	23	●	1:38:00	A 1m58s	4♓23
1988	Aug	27	☽	11:05:00	P 0.292	4♓28
2045	Aug	27	☽	13:54:00	A 0.682	4♓36
2007	Aug	28	☽	10:37:00	T 1.476	4♓46
2026	Aug	28	☽	4:13:00	P 0.930	4♓51
1933	Feb	24	●	12:46:15	A 1m31s	5♓29
1914	Feb	25	●	0:12:42	A 5m35s	5♓34
1738	Aug	29	☽	9:51:00	A 0.243	5♓36
1719	Aug	29	☽	20:24:00	P 0.364	5♓42
1952	Feb	25	●	9:11:05	T 3m09s	5♓43
1700	Aug	29	☽	13:01:00	T 1.583	6♓03
1971	Feb	25	●	9:37:26	P 0.787	6♓08

Solar and Lunar Eclipses in Zodiacal Order 1700–2050

1746	Aug 30	☽	23:48:00	P 0.507	7♓24
1765	Aug 30	☽	15:55:00	T 1.863	7♓25
1979	Feb 26	☉	16:54:16	T 2m49s	7♓30
1784	Aug 30	☽	14:46:00	P 0.660	7♓41
1727	Aug 31	☽	15:12:00	A 0.288	7♓42
1998	Feb 26	☉	17:28:27	T 4m09s	7♓55
1803	Sep 1	☽	15:19:00	A 0.400	8♓03
2036	Feb 27	☉	4:45:46	P 0.629	8♓10
2017	Feb 26	☉	14:53:31	A 0m44s	8♓12
1792	Aug 31	☽	22:42:00	A 0.308	9♓14
1729	Feb 27	☉	21:26:53	P 0.135	9♓20
1710	Feb 28	☉	12:07:21	A 8m00s	9♓33
1811	Sep 2	☽	22:42:00	P 0.604	9♓34
1868	Sep 2	☽	3:41:00	A 0.324	9♓47
1830	Sep 2	☽	22:38	T 1.803	9♓54
2044	Feb 28	☉	20:23:36	A 2m27s	9♓54
1849	Sep 2	☽	17:10:00	P 0.594	10♓00
1756	Mar 1	☉	2:06:56	A 2m24s	10♓59
1933	Sep 4	☽	4:52:00	A 0.695	11♓05
1737	Mar 1	☉	14:35:07	A 8m04s	11♓07
1914	Sep 4	☽	13:55:00	P 0.858	11♓07
1775	Mar 1	☉	21:39:04	T 2m20s	11♓11
1718	Mar 2	☉	7:31:27	P 0.329	11♓25
1895	Sep 4	☽	5:57:00	T 1.553	11♓27
1794	Mar 1	☉	21:53:43	P 0.414	11♓35
1857	Sep 4	☽	5:22:00	A 0.215	11♓43
1876	Sep 3	☽	21:23:00	P 0.342	11♓44
1783	Mar 3	☉	7:40:11	P 0.231	12♓40
1941	Sep 5	☽	17:47:00	P 0.051	12♓50
1960	Sep 5	☽	11:21:00	T 1.424	12♓54
1802	Mar 4	☉	5:14:09	T 3m02s	12♓57
1979	Sep 6	☽	10:54:00	T 1.094	13♓12
1821	Mar 4	☉	5:49:56	T 4m14s	13♓23
1998	Sep 6	☽	11:10:00	A 0.812	13♓33
1840	Mar 4	☉	3:58:13	A 0m03s	13♓42
1859	Mar 4	☉	18:54:39	P 0.246	13♓42
1924	Mar 5	☉	15:43:55	P 0.582	14♓49
1905	Mar 6	☉	5:12:20	A 7m58s	14♓59
2006	Sep 7	☽	18:51:00	P 0.184	15♓05
1848	Mar 5	☉	13:31:24	P 0.266	15♓09
1886	Mar 5	☉	22:05:30	A 8m20s	15♓17
1867	Mar 6	☉	9:46:40	A 1m57s	15♓23
2025	Sep 7	☽	18:12:00	T 1.362	15♓24
2044	Sep 7	☽	11:20:00	T 1.046	15♓26
1756	Sep 8	☽	17:19:00	A 0.355	16♓15
1737	Sep 9	☽	3:24:00	P 0.483	16♓20
1951	Mar 7	☉	20:53:10	A 0m59s	16♓29
1932	Mar 7	☉	7:55:25	A 5m19s	16♓33
1718	Sep 9	☽	19:52:00	T 1.702	16♓40
1970	Mar 7	☉	17:37:49	T 3m28s	16♓44
1989	Mar 7	☉	18:07:44	P 0.827	17♓09
1764	Sep 10	☽	6:58:00	P 0.399	18♓02
1783	Sep 10	☽	23:33:00	T 1.759	18♓04
1745	Sep 10	☽	22:02:00	A 0.172	18♓19
1802	Sep 11	☽	22:36:00	P 0.762	18♓21
1997	Mar 9	☉	1:23:50	T 2m50s	18♓31
1821	Sep 11	☽	23:05:00	A 0.497	18♓42
2016	Mar 9	☉	1:57:18	T 4m10s	18♓56
2035	Mar 9	☉	23:04:52	A 0m46s	19♓12
1810	Sep 13	☽	6:27:00	A 0.220	19♓54
1829	Sep 13	☽	6:33:00	P 0.505	20♓14
1747	Mar 11	☉	5:17:56	P 0.187	20♓18
1886	Sep 13	☽	10:35:00	A 0.439	20♓25
1728	Mar 10	☉	19:38:46	A 7m25s	20♓30
1848	Sep 13	☽	6:19:00	T 1.700	20♓34
1867	Sep 14	☽	0:26:00	P 0.695	20♓39
1709	Mar 11	☉	12:18:27	A 6m28s	20♓48
1951	Sep 15	☽	12:27:00	A 0.803	21♓45
1932	Sep 14	☽	21:01:00	P 0.975	21♓46
1774	Mar 12	☉	10:05:00	A 1m43s	21♓56
1755	Mar 12	☉	22:09:20	A 7m06s	22♓03
1913	Sep 15	☽	12:48:00	T 1.430	22♓04
1793	Mar 12	☉	5:59:52	T 2m52s	22♓10
1736	Mar 12	☉	15:05:44	P 0.273	22♓22
1875	Sep 15	☽	12:57:00	A 0.111	22♓23
1894	Sep 15	☽	4:32:00	P 0.226	22♓23
1812	Mar 13	☉	6:19:12	P 0.459	22♓34
1959	Sep 17	☽	1:03:00	A 0.987	23♓29
1978	Sep 16	☽	19:04:00	T 1.327	23♓35
1801	Mar 14	☉	15:45:13	P 0.187	23♓37
1997	Sep 16	☽	18:47:00	T 1.191	23♓53
1820	Mar 14	☉	13:36:58	T 3m20s	23♓55
2016	Sep 16	☽	18:54:00	A 0.908	24♓13
1839	Mar 15	☉	14:13:33	T 4m20s	24♓20
1858	Mar 15	☉	12:05:17	A 0m02s	24♓38
1877	Mar 15	☉	2:38:11	P 0.292	24♓39
1709	Sep 19	☽	0:31:00	A 0.064	25♓41
1942	Mar 16	☉	23:36:41	P 0.639	25♓45
2024	Sep 18	☽	2:44:00	P 0.085	25♓46
1923	Mar 17	☉	12:44:34	A 7m51s	25♓55
2043	Sep 19	☽	1:51:00	T 1.256	26♓04
1866	Mar 16	☉	21:51:14	P 0.212	26♓06
1904	Mar 17	☉	5:40:40	A 8m07s	26♓13
1885	Mar 16	☉	17:45:46	A 1m55s	26♓20
1774	Sep 20	☽	0:57:00	A 0.454	26♓58
1755	Sep 20	☽	10:34:00	P 0.589	27♓01
1736	Sep 20	☽	2:51:00	T 1.809	27♓21
1969	Mar 18	☉	4:54:18	A 0m26s	27♓25
1950	Mar 18	☉	15:31:31	A non-C	27♓28
1717	Sep 20	☽	17:54:00	P 0.606	27♓38
1988	Mar 18	☉	1:58:01	T 3m47s	27♓42
2007	Mar 19	☉	2:31:56	P 0.876	28♓07
1782	Sep 21	☽	14:17:00	P 0.303	28♓45
1801	Sep 22	☽	7:19:00	T 1.667	28♓47
1763	Sep 22	☽	5:03:00	A 0.071	29♓01
1820	Sep 22	☽	6:35:00	P 0.851	29♓05
1839	Sep 23	☽	6:57:00	A 0.583	29♓26
2015	Mar 20	☉	9:45:45	T 2m47s	29♓28
2034	Mar 20	☉	10:17:44	T 4m09s	29♓53

Solar Annular and Total Eclipses in Sequence by Maximum Duration

1955	Dec 14	●	7:01:54	A 12m09s	21♐31
1973	Dec 24	●	15:02:00	A 12m02s	2♑40
1919	Nov 22	●	15:13:50	A 11m36s	29♏17
1937	Dec 2	●	23:05:22	A 11m13s	10♐22
2010	Jan 15	●	7:06:39	A 11m07s	25♑ 1
1901	Nov 11	●	7:28:21	A 11m01s	18♏13
1992	Jan 4	●	23:04:40	A 10m58s	13♑51
2028	Jan 26	●	15:07:58	A 10m27s	6♒11
1701	Feb 7	●	23:04:47	A 9m53s	19♒ 3
1883	Oct 30	●	23:50:58	A 9m43s	7♏14
1865	Oct 19	●	16:21:05	A 9m27s	26♎18
2046	Feb 5	●	23:05:25	A 9m16s	17♒18
1719	Feb 19	●	6:52:49	A 9m00s	0♓ 7
1850	Feb 12	●	6:29:27	A 8m35s	23♒15
1847	Oct 9	●	9:00:13	A 8m35s	15♎27
1832	Feb 1	●	22:30:03	A 8m35s	12♒ 9
1868	Feb 23	●	14:21:25	A 8m30s	4♓18
1814	Jan 21	●	14:24:29	A 8m28s	1♒ 0
1886	Mar 5	●	22:05:30	A 8m20s	15♓17
1796	Jan 10	●	6:14:38	A 8m15s	19♑50
1904	Mar 17	●	5:40:40	A 8m07s	26♓13
1737	Mar 1	●	14:35:07	A 8m04s	11♓ 7
1869	Feb 11	●	13:46:34	A 8m02s	22♒56
1887	Feb 22	●	21:33:07	A 8m01s	3♓59
1851	Feb 1	●	5:54:16	A 8m01s	11♒50
1833	Jan 20	●	21:56:44	A 8m00s	0♒42
1710	Feb 28	●	12:07:21	A 8m00s	9♓33
1905	Mar 6	●	5:12:20	A 7m58s	14♓59
1815	Jan 10	●	13:56:48	A 7m56s	19♑32
2009	Jan 26	●	7:58:43	A 7m54s	6♒30
1777	Dec 29	●	22:03:12	A 7m53s	8♑39
2027	Feb 6	●	15:59:46	A 7m51s	17♒38
1923	Mar 17	●	12:44:34	A 7m51s	25♓55
1796	Dec 29	●	5:54:43	A 7m51s	8♑21
1922	Mar 28	●	13:05:03	A 7m50s	7♈ 4
1973	Jan 4	●	15:45:37	A 7m49s	14♑10
1778	Dec 18	●	21:53:36	A 7m45s	27♐11
2042	Oct 14	●	1:59:40	A 7m44s	20♎52
1829	Sep 28	●	1:46:40	A 7m43s	4♎39
1941	Mar 27	●	20:07:43	A 7m41s	6♈46
1954	Dec 25	●	7:36:11	A 7m39s	2♑59
1760	Dec 7	●	13:53:29	A 7m37s	16♐ 1
1991	Jan 15	●	23:52:54	A 7m36s	25♑20
2045	Feb 16	●	23:55:04	A 7m32s	28♒43
1940	Apr 7	●	20:20:56	A 7m30s	17♈52
1742	Nov 27	●	5:58:48	A 7m26s	4♐54
2024	Oct 2	●	18:45:12	A 7m25s	10♎ 4
1959	Apr 8	●	3:23:35	A 7m25s	17♈33
1759	Dec 19	●	13:49:51	A 7m25s	27♐28
1728	Mar 10	●	19:38:46	A 7m25s	20♓30
1907	Jul 10	●	15:24:26	A 7m22s	17♋12
1889	Jun 28	●	9:00:06	A 7m22s	6♋47
1724	Nov 15	●	22:07:27	A 7m15s	23♏48
1925	Jul 20	●	21:48:19	A 7m14s	27♋37
1871	Jun 18	●	2:35:00	A 7m13s	26♊23
2006	Sep 22	●	11:40:15	A 7m09s	29♍20
1955	Jun 20	●	4:10:11	T 7m08s	28♊ 5
1958	Apr 19	●	3:26:44	A 7m07s	28♈34
1936	Dec 13	●	23:27:47	A 7m07s	21♐49
1918	Dec 3	●	15:21:39	A 7m06s	10♐40
1755	Mar 12	●	22:09:20	A 7m06s	22♓ 3
1977	Apr 18	●	10:30:42	A 7m04s	28♈16
1973	Jun 30	●	11:37:57	T 7m04s	8♋32
1937	Jun 8	●	20:40:38	T 7m04s	17♊36
1715	Oct 27	●	9:02:39	A 7m02s	3♏21
1706	Nov 5	●	14:23:49	A 7m02s	12♏46
1853	Jun 6	●	20:07:12	A 6m59s	15♊57
1943	Aug 1	●	4:15:48	A 6m58s	8♌ 3
1988	Sep 11	●	4:43:33	A 6m57s	18♍40
1733	Nov 6	●	16:40:03	A 6m54s	14♏20
1991	Jul 11	●	19:06:04	T 6m53s	18♋59
1919	May 29	●	13:08:33	T 6m51s	7♊ 6
1811	Sep 17	●	18:43:27	A 6m51s	23♍56
1746	Mar 22	●	3:02:37	A 6m51s	1♈22
1741	Dec 8	●	5:37:49	A 6m51s	16♐18

1850	Aug 7	●	21:33:44	T 6m50s	14♌56
1970	Aug 31	●	21:54:49	A 6m48s	8♍ 4
1868	Aug 18	●	5:12:04	T 6m47s	25♌29
1832	Jul 27	●	14:00:55	T 6m46s	4♌27
1751	Nov 18	●	0:25:45	A 6m46s	25♏22
1835	May 27	●	13:35:33	A 6m44s	5♊29
1900	Nov 22	●	7:19:43	A 6m42s	29♏34
1976	Apr 29	●	10:23:30	A 6m41s	9♉13
1952	Aug 20	●	15:13:05	A 6m40s	27♌31
2009	Jul 22	●	2:35:23	T 6m39s	29♋27
1769	Nov 28	●	8:18:22	A 6m39s	6♐28
1995	Apr 29	●	17:32:22	A 6m37s	8♉56
1886	Aug 29	●	12:55:27	T 6m36s	6♍ 4
1961	Aug 11	●	10:46:14	A 6m35s	18♌31
1814	Jul 17	●	6:30:11	T 6m34s	23♋58
1934	Aug 10	●	8:37:24	A 6m33s	17♌ 1
1787	Dec 9	●	16:15:19	A 6m32s	17♐36
1817	May 16	●	6:57:57	A 6m30s	25♉ 0
1901	May 18	●	5:33:48	T 6m29s	26♉34
1874	Oct 10	●	11:13:34	A 6m28s	16♎59
1709	Mar 11	●	12:18:27	A 6m28s	20♓48
1805	Dec 21	●	0:17:16	A 6m27s	28♐46
1916	Jul 30	●	2:05:52	A 6m24s	6♌34
2027	Aug 2	●	10:06:48	T 6m23s	9♌55
1856	Sep 29	●	3:59:33	A 6m21s	6♎11
1824	Jan 1	●	8:20:50	A 6m21s	9♑57
1904	Sep 9	●	20:44:16	T 6m20s	16♍42
1799	May 5	●	0:12:54	A 6m20s	14♉27
1764	Apr 1	●	10:17:01	A 6m20s	12♈10
1727	Mar 22	●	19:47:46	A 6m19s	1♈39
1842	Jan 11	●	16:25:29	A 6m15s	21♑ 8
1994	May 10	●	17:11:27	A 6m14s	19♉49
1781	Apr 23	●	17:21:10	A 6m13s	3♉51
1773	Mar 23	●	5:36:42	A 6m13s	2♈55
1745	Apr 2	●	3:09:07	A 6m13s	12♈28
1723	Nov 27	●	21:28:06	A 6m12s	5♐ 9
1763	Apr 13	●	10:19:17	A 6m11s	23♈11
1898	Jul 18	●	19:36:58	A 6m10s	26♋ 7
2041	Oct 25	●	1:35:20	A 6m07s	2♏ 1
1860	Jan 23	●	0:27:18	A 6m07s	2♒17
2045	Aug 12	●	17:41:37	T 6m06s	20♌25
1838	Sep 18	●	20:55:46	A 6m06s	25♍28
2013	May 10	●	0:25:19	A 6m03s	19♉31
1979	Aug 22	●	17:21:48	A 6m03s	29♌ 1
1796	Jul 4	●	23:02:40	T 6m02s	13♋31
1793	Sep 5	●	11:47:09	A 6m02s	13♍17
1922	Sep 21	●	4:40:08	T 5m59s	27♍25
1878	Feb 2	●	8:27:52	A 5m59s	13♒25
1883	May 6	●	21:53:53	T 5m58s	15♉59
1882	Nov 10	●	23:22:24	A 5m57s	18♏30
1778	Jun 24	●	15:34:39	T 5m53s	3♋ 4
1782	Apr 12	●	17:24:31	A 5m51s	22♈54
1820	Sep 7	●	13:59:40	A 5m49s	14♍48
1896	Feb 13	●	16:23:16	A 5m48s	24♒31
1709	Sep 4	●	0:32:19	T 5m47s	11♍12
1880	Jul 7	●	13:10:32	A 5m46s	15♋43
1734	May 3	●	10:15:46	T 5m46s	12♉40
1716	Apr 22	●	2:28:25	T 5m44s	2♉ 1
1752	May 13	●	17:56:16	T 5m42s	23♉15
1864	Oct 30	●	15:30:22	A 5m41s	7♏29
2012	May 20	●	23:52:51	A 5m36s	0♊21
1940	Oct 1	●	12:43:41	T 5m36s	8♎11
1914	Feb 25	●	0:12:42	A 5m35s	5♓34
1802	Aug 28	●	7:11:39	A 5m35s	4♍12
1727	Sep 15	●	8:27:22	T 5m33s	21♍53
1770	May 25	●	1:29:57	T 5m32s	3♊47
1705	Nov 16	●	13:22:59	A 5m31s	24♏ 3
1760	Jun 13	●	8:09:01	T 5m27s	22♊37
1800	Apr 24	●	0:23:46	A 5m26s	3♉33
2031	May 21	●	7:15:03	A 5m25s	0♊ 4
1865	Apr 25	●	14:08:26	T 5m23s	5♉21
1784	Aug 16	●	0:31:36	A 5m23s	23♌40
1713	Jun 22	●	23:15:31	A 5m23s	1♋12
2030	Jun 1	●	6:28:10	A 5m21s	10♊50
1791	Apr 3	●	12:54:55	A 5m21s	13♈42

1745	Sep 25	●	16:28:44	T 5m21s	2♎38
2010	Jul 11	●	19:33:37	T 5m20s	19♋24
1992	Jun 30	●	12:10:25	T 5m20s	8♋56
1932	Mar 7	●	7:55:25	A 5m19s	16♓33
1712	Jul 3	●	22:34:49	A 5m18s	11♋53
2023	Oct 14	●	17:59:39	A 5m17s	21♎ 8
1788	Jun 4	●	8:59:14	T 5m16s	14♊17
1775	Aug 26	●	4:59:24	A 5m16s	2♍42
1965	May 30	●	21:16:55	T 5m15s	9♊13
1766	Aug 5	●	17:56:42	A 5m15s	13♌11
1731	Jul 4	●	5:46:16	A 5m15s	11♋36
1947	May 20	●	13:47:19	T 5m14s	28♉42
1730	Jul 15	●	4:58:58	A 5m13s	22♋17
1748	Jul 25	●	11:26:49	A 5m12s	2♌43
1983	Jun 11	●	4:42:41	T 5m11s	19♊43
1958	Oct 12	●	20:54:55	T 5m11s	19♎ 1
2028	Jul 22	●	2:55:39	T 5m10s	29♋50
1763	Oct 7	●	0:38:50	T 5m10s	13♎28
1716	Oct 15	●	10:07:31	A 5m10s	22♎10
1974	Jun 20	●	4:47:20	T 5m09s	28♊30
1734	Oct 26	●	17:53:17	A 5m08s	3♏ 6
1929	May 9	●	6:10:10	T 5m07s	18♉ 7
1701	Aug 4	●	9:31:38	T 5m06s	11♌36
1846	Oct 20	●	7:46:02	A 5m05s	26♎33
1818	May 5	●	7:15:31	A 5m05s	14♉ 9
1752	Nov 6	●	1:48:01	A 5m03s	14♏ 6
1742	Jun 3	●	0:39:45	T 5m00s	12♊ 8
1781	Oct 17	●	8:55:43	T 4m59s	24♎21
2048	Jun 11	●	12:57:49	A 4m58s	21♊17
1911	Apr 28	●	22:27:09	T 4m57s	7♉30
2001	Jun 21	●	12:03:46	T 4m56s	0♋11
1770	Nov 17	●	9:51:38	A 4m56s	25♏ 9
1806	Jun 16	●	16:24:08	T 4m55s	24♊45
2046	Aug 2	●	10:20:12	T 4m51s	10♌19
2042	Apr 20	●	2:16:28	T 4m51s	0♉ 9
1799	Oct 28	●	17:21:33	T 4m50s	5♏19
1976	Oct 23	●	5:12:58	T 4m47s	29♎56
1893	Apr 16	●	14:36:17	T 4m47s	26♈49
1836	May 15	●	14:01:28	A 4m47s	24♉42
1788	Nov 27	●	18:02:37	A 4m46s	6♐16
2049	May 31	●	13:58:57	A 4m45s	10♊34
1749	Jul 14	●	12:19:09	A 4m45s	22♋ 1
1956	Jun 8	●	21:20:08	T 4m44s	18♊ 1
1847	Apr 15	●	6:16:03	T 4m44s	24♈39
1817	Nov 9	●	1:53:36	T 4m42s	16♏21
1875	Apr 6	●	6:37:27	T 4m37s	16♈ 4
1757	Aug 14	●	22:16:32	A 4m36s	22♌ 9
1835	Nov 20	●	10:31:48	T 4m35s	27♏26
1809	Apr 14	●	20:06:52	A 4m35s	24♈26
2019	Jul 2	●	19:23:07	T 4m33s	10♋38
1724	May 22	●	17:09:59	T 4m33s	1♊39
1854	May 26	●	20:42:42	A 4m32s	5♊12
1806	Dec 10	●	2:19:21	A 4m32s	17♐25
2005	Oct 3	●	10:31:46	A 4m31s	10♎19
2024	Apr 8	●	18:17:28	T 4m28s	19♈24
1857	Mar 25	●	22:29:27	T 4m28s	5♈14
1853	Nov 30	●	19:15:29	T 4m28s	8♐34
1719	Aug 15	●	16:59:43	T 4m27s	22♌ 7
1828	Oct 9	●	0:07:33	A 4m26s	15♎40
1704	Jun 2	●	13:02:31	A 4m26s	11♊51
1994	Nov 3	●	13:39:07	T 4m24s	10♏54
1824	Jun 26	●	23:46:17	T 4m24s	5♋12
1871	Dec 12	●	4:03:36	T 4m23s	19♐44
1767	Jul 25	●	18:55:33	A 4m21s	2♌27
1872	Jun 6	●	3:20:01	A 4m20s	15♊40
1839	Mar 15	●	14:13:33	T 4m20s	24♓20
1892	Apr 26	●	21:55:25	T 4m19s	7♉ 5
1889	Dec 22	●	12:54:19	T 4m18s	0♑56
1910	May 9	●	5:42:02	T 4m15s	17♉43
1824	Dec 20	●	10:40:20	A 4m15s	28♐35
1712	Dec 28	●	1:24:47	T 4m15s	6♑32
1908	Jan 3	●	21:45:13	T 4m14s	12♑ 9
1821	Mar 4	●	5:49:56	T 4m14s	13♓23
1715	May 3	●	9:36:21	T 4m14s	12♉15
1702	Jan 28	●	1:37:03	A 4m14s	7♒46

Solar Annular and Total Eclipses in Sequence by Maximum Duration

Year	Date		Time	Type	Duration	Position
1926	Jan 14	●	6:36:34	T	4m11s	23♑21
1874	Apr 16	●	14:00:53	T	4m11s	26♈24
1731	Jan 8	●	10:17:35	T	4m11s	17♑45
2016	Mar 9	●	1:57:18	T	4m10s	18♓56
1803	Feb 21	●	21:18:27	T	4m10s	2♓21
2034	Mar 20	●	10:17:44	T	4m09s	29♓53
1998	Feb 26	●	17:28:27	T	4m09s	7♓55
1944	Jan 25	●	15:26:16	T	4m09s	4♒33
1890	Jun 17	●	9:55:09	A	4m09s	26♊ 6
1980	Feb 16	●	8:53:11	T	4m08s	26♒50
1962	Feb 5	●	0:12:04	T	4m08s	15♒43
2006	Mar 29	●	10:11:21	T	4m07s	8♈35
1785	Feb 9	●	12:40:25	T	4m07s	21♒16
1749	Jan 18	●	19:08:45	T	4m07s	28♑57
1733	May 13	●	17:18:18	T	4m07s	22♉50
1706	May 12	●	9:35:01	T	4m07s	21♉ 6
1842	Jul 8	●	7:06:17	T	4m06s	15♋38
1767	Jan 30	●	3:56:40	T	4m06s	10♒ 8
2039	Jun 21	●	17:11:51	A	4m05s	0♋12
1829	Apr 3	●	22:18:23	T	4m05s	13♈54
1938	May 29	●	13:49:55	T	4m04s	7♊31
2012	Nov 13	●	22:11:53	T	4m02s	21♏57
1965	Nov 23	●	4:14:15	A	4m02s	0♐40
1983	Dec 4	●	12:30:22	A	4m01s	11♐47
1785	Aug 5	●	1:37:06	A	4m01s	12♌55
1710	Aug 24	●	17:17:08	T	4m00s	0♍59
1908	Jun 28	●	16:29:41	A	3m60s	6♋32
1947	Nov 12	●	20:05:09	A	3m59s	19♏36
1739	Aug 4	●	15:40:45	A	3m59s	11♌40
2037	Jul 13	●	2:39:35	T	3m58s	21♋ 4
1856	Apr 5	●	6:00:50	T	3m56s	15♈39
1929	Nov 1	●	12:04:46	A	3m54s	8♏35
1842	Dec 31	●	19:04:14	A	3m54s	9♑47
1751	May 25	●	0:55:01	T	3m54s	3♊22
2001	Dec 14	●	20:52:01	A	3m53s	22♐56
1827	Apr 26	●	3:10:59	A	3m53s	5♉ 6
2021	Jun 10	●	10:42:04	A	3m51s	19♊47
1887	Aug 19	●	5:32:09	T	3m50s	25♌53
1987	Sep 23	●	3:11:26	A	3m49s	29♍34
1869	Aug 7	●	22:01:00	T	3m49s	15♌21
1988	Mar 18	●	1:58:01	T	3m47s	27♓42
1911	Oct 22	●	4:12:48	A	3m47s	27♎39
1803	Aug 17	●	8:24:44	A	3m47s	23♌25
1905	Aug 30	●	13:07:19	T	3m46s	6♍28
1810	Sep 28	●	16:37:07	A	3m45s	4♎52
1737	Aug 26	●	0:31:58	T	3m45s	2♍42
2030	Nov 25	●	6:50:35	T	3m44s	3♐ 2
1728	Sep 4	●	0:59:13	T	3m44s	11♍37
1944	Jul 20	●	5:42:46	A	3m42s	27♋22
1893	Oct 9	●	20:30:28	A	3m41s	16♎46
1851	Jul 28	●	14:33:31	T	3m41s	4♌51
1720	Feb 8	●	9:52:22	A	3m40s	18♒53
2019	Dec 26	●	5:17:53	A	3m39s	4♑ 7
1926	Jul 9	●	23:05:37	A	3m39s	16♋57
1860	Jul 18	●	14:26:13	T	3m39s	26♋ 6
1838	Mar 25	●	21:52:06	T	3m39s	4♈49
1821	Aug 27	●	15:19:25	A	3m38s	3♍58
2003	May 31	●	4:08:20	A	3m37s	9♊19
1923	Sep 10	●	20:47:05	T	3m37s	17♍ 6
1875	Sep 29	●	12:58:10	A	3m36s	5♎58
1769	Jun 4	●	8:28:17	T	3m36s	13♊52
1857	Sep 18	●	5:35:54	A	3m34s	25♍14
1839	Sep 7	●	22:23:17	A	3m34s	14♍34
1962	Jul 31	●	12:24:58	A	3m33s	7♌49
1861	Jan 11	●	3:29:12	A	3m30s	20♑58
1833	Jul 17	●	7:07:51	T	3m30s	24♋23
2048	Dec 5	●	15:34:24	T	3m28s	14♐11
1970	Mar 7	●	17:37:49	T	3m28s	16♓44
1813	Jul 27	●	14:55:18	T	3m27s	4♌ 5
1811	Mar 24	●	14:11:55	T	3m27s	3♈ 3
1795	Jul 16	●	7:41:21	T	3m26s	23♋38
1980	Aug 10	●	19:11:30	A	3m23s	18♌17
1746	Sep 15	●	8:46:25	T	3m23s	22♍17
1941	Sep 21	●	4:33:37	T	3m22s	27♍48
1831	Aug 7	●	22:15:49	T	3m20s	14♌35
1820	Mar 14	●	13:36:58	T	3m20s	23♓55
2038	Jan 5	●	13:46:10	A	3m18s	15♑19
1777	Jul 5	●	0:29:14	T	3m18s	13♋11
1845	May 6	●	10:08:48	A	3m15s	15♉42
1998	Aug 22	●	2:06:10	A	3m14s	28♌48
1815	Jul 6	●	23:42:48	T	3m13s	13♋56
1969	Sep 11	●	19:58:19	A	3m11s	18♍53
1878	Jul 29	●	21:47:19	T	3m11s	6♌34
1952	Feb 25	●	9:11:05	T	3m09s	5♓43
1787	Jun 15	●	15:59:06	T	3m09s	24♊21
1849	Aug 18	●	5:40:40	T	3m07s	25♌ 7
2016	Sep 1	●	9:07:01	A	3m05s	9♍21
1879	Jan 22	●	11:53:11	A	3m03s	2♒ 9
1738	Feb 18	●	18:02:21	A	3m03s	29♒58
1959	Oct 2	●	12:26:27	T	3m02s	8♎34
1802	Mar 4	●	5:14:09	T	3m02s	12♓57
1792	Sep 16	●	9:13:36	A	3m02s	24♍ 8
1764	Sep 25	●	16:41:29	T	3m01s	3♎ 3
1755	Sep 6	●	8:09:33	T	3m00s	13♍20
1759	Jun 24	●	17:20:46	T	2m60s	2♋45
2034	Sep 12	●	16:18:26	A	2m58s	19♍59
2035	Sep 2	●	1:55:44	T	2m54s	9♍28
1934	Feb 14	●	0:38:17	T	2m52s	24♒38
1793	Mar 12	●	5:59:52	T	2m52s	22♓10
1867	Aug 29	●	13:13:00	T	2m51s	5♍41
1997	Mar 9	●	1:23:50	T	2m50s	18♓31
1979	Feb 26	●	16:54:16	T	2m49s	7♓30
2015	Mar 20	●	9:45:45	T	2m47s	29♓28
1797	Jun 24	●	16:17:57	T	2m47s	3♋29
1961	Feb 15	●	8:19:15	T	2m45s	26♒26
1784	Feb 20	●	20:45:21	T	2m44s	1♓56
1896	Aug 9	●	5:09:04	T	2m43s	17♌ 3
2017	Aug 21	●	18:25:39	T	2m40s	28♌53
2033	Mar 30	●	18:01:33	T	2m37s	10♈21
1977	Oct 12	●	20:26:39	T	2m37s	19♎24
1782	Oct 7	●	0:43:03	T	2m37s	13♎52
1972	Jul 10	●	19:45:53	T	2m36s	18♋37
1951	Sep 1	●	12:51:21	A	2m36s	8♍17
1916	Feb 3	●	16:00:03	T	2m36s	13♒31
1954	Jun 30	●	12:32:05	T	2m35s	8♋10
1943	Feb 4	●	23:37:45	T	2m35s	15♒18
1741	Jun 13	●	10:12:38	T	2m35s	22♊18
1897	Feb 1	●	20:15:20	A	2m34s	13♒18
1990	Jul 22	●	3:02:09	T	2m33s	29♋ 4
1936	Jun 19	●	5:20:06	T	2m32s	27♊44
1925	Jan 24	●	14:53:40	T	2m32s	4♒ 8
1885	Sep 8	●	20:51:56	T	2m31s	16♍19
1766	Feb 9	●	12:09:28	T	2m28s	20♒51
2044	Feb 28	●	20:23:36	A	2m27s	9♓54
2008	Aug 1	●	10:21:09	T	2m27s	9♌32
1907	Jan 14	●	6:05:37	T	2m25s	22♑56
1756	Mar 1	●	2:06:56	A	2m24s	10♓59
1999	Aug 11	●	11:03:08	T	2m23s	18♌21
1918	Jun 8	●	22:07:21	T	2m23s	17♊16
1898	Jan 22	●	7:19:17	T	2m21s	2♒21
2026	Feb 17	●	12:12:02	A	2m20s	28♒50
1775	Mar 1	●	21:39:04	T	2m20s	11♓11
1774	Sep 6	●	1:57:26	A	2m20s	13♍28
2038	Dec 26	●	0:59:07	T	2m19s	4♑20
2026	Aug 12	●	17:46:02	T	2m18s	20♌ 2
1773	Sep 16	●	15:52:08	T	2m18s	24♍ 1
1889	Jan 1	●	21:16:55	T	2m17s	11♑44
1914	Aug 21	●	12:34:08	T	2m15s	27♌36
1800	Oct 18	●	8:51:32	T	2m14s	24♎45
2008	Feb 7	●	3:55:07	A	2m12s	17♒45
1903	Sep 21	●	4:39:48	T	2m12s	27♍ 1
1748	Jan 30	●	3:29:00	T	2m12s	9♒43
1870	Dec 22	●	12:27:30	T	2m11s	0♑31
2020	Dec 14	●	16:13:37	T	2m10s	23♐ 8
1995	Oct 24	●	4:32:31	T	2m10s	0♏17
1900	May 28	●	14:53:56	T	2m10s	6♊47
1708	Sep 14	●	9:00:14	T	2m10s	21♍31
1880	Jan 11	●	22:34:29	T	2m07s	21♑ 9
1726	Sep 25	●	16:51:35	T	2m07s	2♎16
1852	Dec 11	●	3:40:35	T	2m05s	19♐20
1744	Oct 6	●	0:51:12	T	2m05s	13♎ 5
1723	Jun 3	●	3:05:05	T	2m05s	11♊51
2044	Aug 23	●	1:15:58	T	2m04s	0♍35
2002	Dec 4	●	7:31:14	T	2m04s	11♐58
1990	Jan 26	●	19:30:25	A	2m03s	6♒35
1981	Jul 31	●	3:45:44	T	2m03s	7♌51
1933	Aug 21	●	5:48:47	A	2m03s	27♌42
1915	Feb 14	●	4:33:02	A	2m03s	24♒25
1834	Nov 30	●	18:56:26	T	2m02s	8♐ 9
1762	Oct 17	●	9:00:21	T	2m02s	23♎58
1984	Nov 22	●	22:53:22	T	1m60s	0♐50
1780	Oct 27	●	17:18:12	T	1m60s	4♏55
1985	Nov 12	●	14:10:31	T	1m59s	20♏ 8
1816	Nov 19	●	10:17:06	T	1m59s	27♏ 1
1798	Nov 8	●	1:44:26	T	1m59s	15♏57
1730	Jan 18	●	18:45:05	T	1m59s	28♑33
2003	Nov 23	●	22:49:19	T	1m58s	1♐14
1966	Nov 12	●	14:22:50	T	1m58s	19♏45
1849	Feb 23	●	1:38:00	A	1m58s	4♓23
1867	Mar 6	●	9:46:40	A	1m57s	15♓23
1831	Feb 12	●	17:21:34	A	1m57s	23♒19
1948	Nov 1	●	5:58:49	T	1m56s	8♏44
2021	Dec 4	●	7:33:35	T	1m55s	12♐22
1930	Oct 21	●	21:43:29	T	1m55s	27♎46
1912	Oct 10	●	13:35:58	T	1m55s	16♎52
1894	Sep 29	●	5:39:07	T	1m55s	6♎ 4
1885	Mar 16	●	17:45:46	A	1m55s	26♓20
1861	Dec 31	●	13:48:56	T	1m55s	9♑57
1972	Jan 16	●	11:02:37	A	1m53s	25♑25
1903	Mar 29	●	1:35:20	A	1m53s	7♈12
1876	Sep 17	●	21:49:16	T	1m53s	25♍18
1816	May 27	●	3:13:08	A	1m53s	5♊39
2039	Dec 15	●	16:22:43	T	1m52s	23♐32
1921	Oct 1	●	12:35:34	T	1m52s	7♎47
1813	Feb 1	●	8:58:10	A	1m52s	12♒12
1757	Feb 18	●	13:14:00	T	1m52s	0♓ 9
2041	Apr 30	●	11:51:19	T	1m51s	10♉31
1818	Oct 29	●	17:06:52	T	1m51s	5♏42
1921	Apr 8	●	9:14:37	A	1m50s	18♈ 0
1882	May 17	●	7:36:30	T	1m50s	26♉16
1858	Sep 7	●	14:09:18	T	1m50s	14♍37
1939	Apr 19	●	16:45:27	A	1m49s	28♈44
1712	Jan 8	●	9:58:30	T	1m48s	17♑21
1932	Aug 31	●	20:03:16	T	1m45s	8♍10
1840	Aug 27	●	6:37:23	T	1m45s	4♍ 0
1795	Jan 21	●	0:28:58	A	1m45s	1♒ 2
1843	Dec 21	●	5:03:17	T	1m43s	28♐44
1774	Mar 12	●	10:05:00	A	1m43s	21♓56
1954	Jan 5	●	2:31:27	A	1m42s	14♑14
2013	Nov 3	●	12:46:35	AT	1m40s	11♏16
1963	Jul 20	●	20:35:37	T	1m40s	27♋24
1756	Aug 25	●	18:46:04	A	1m38s	2♍51
1798	May 15	●	20:10:20	A	1m36s	25♉ 8
1791	Sep 27	●	23:42:13	T	1m36s	4♎46
1825	Dec 9	●	20:21:31	AT	1m34s	17♐33
1939	Oct 12	●	20:39:57	T	1m33s	18♎37
1915	Aug 10	●	22:52:06	A	1m33s	17♌12
1822	Aug 16	●	23:14:18	T	1m32s	23♌26
1777	Jan 9	●	15:55:21	A	1m32s	19♑51
1705	May 22	●	19:54:59	AT	1m32s	1♊22
1933	Feb 24	●	12:46:15	A	1m31s	5♓29
1935	Dec 25	●	17:59:25	A	1m30s	3♑ 2
1836	Nov 9	●	1:29:15	T	1m29s	16♏43
1739	Feb 8	●	4:41:02	T	1m28s	19♒ 4
1807	Nov 29	●	11:41:52	AT	1m26s	6♐23
1864	May 6	●	0:16:38	AT	1m25s	15♉42
1780	May 4	●	13:00:26	A	1m21s	14♉35
1804	Aug 5	●	15:56:55	T	1m20s	12♌55
1789	Nov 17	●	3:08:19	AT	1m19s	25♏16
2023	Apr 20	●	4:16:55	AT	1m16s	29♈50
1945	Jul 9	●	13:27:17	T	1m16s	16♋57
1917	Dec 14	●	9:26:56	A	1m16s	21♐50
1758	Dec 30	●	7:20:00	A	1m15s	8♑39
1950	Sep 12	●	3:38:16	T	1m14s	18♍49
1771	Nov 6	●	18:40:48	AT	1m13s	14♏12

Solar Annular and Total Eclipses in Sequence by Maximum Duration

Year	Date		Time	Type	Duration	Position
2031	Nov 14	●	21:06:29	AT	1m08s	22♏17
1762	Apr 24	●	5:41:57	A	1m08s	3♉58
1753	Oct 26	●	10:21:48	AT	1m08s	3♏11
1854	Nov 20	●	9:56:47	AT	1m07s	27♏48
1721	Jan 27	●	20:05:01	T	1m07s	7♒56
1897	Jul 29	●	15:57:03	A	1m05s	6♌43
1809	Oct 9	●	7:38:23	T	1m02s	15♎36
1792	Mar 22	●	17:57:19	A	1m02s	2♈49
1735	Oct 16	●	2:10:23	AT	1m02s	22♎14
1899	Dec 3	●	0:57:27	A	1m01s	10♐41
1738	Aug 15	●	11:40:01	A	1m00s	22♌18
2038	Jul 2	●	13:31:53	A	0m60s	10♋47
1951	Mar 7	●	20:53:10	A	0m59s	16♓29
1786	Jul 25	●	8:46:18	T	0m59s	2♌26
1744	Apr 12	●	22:15:13	A	0m58s	23♈17
1717	Oct 4	●	18:08:18	AT	0m56s	11♎22
1713	Dec 17	●	16:04:13	AT	0m56s	25♐42
1846	Apr 25	●	16:50:20	AT	0m54s	5♉ 4
1740	Dec 18	●	22:43:08	A	0m53s	27♐27
1726	Apr 2	●	14:38:07	A	0m51s	12♈32
1927	Jun 29	●	6:23:01	T	0m50s	6♋31
1703	Jan 17	●	11:24:17	T	0m50s	26♑45
1771	May 14	●	14:59:48	AT	0m49s	23♉31
1753	May 3	●	7:39:28	AT	0m48s	12♉57
1872	Nov 30	●	18:29:31	AT	0m47s	8♐56
2035	Mar 9	●	23:04:52	A	0m46s	19♓12
1789	May 24	●	22:11:42	AT	0m46s	4♊ 2
1708	Mar 22	●	6:51:29	A	0m46s	1♈43
2017	Feb 26	●	14:53:31	A	0m44s	8♓12
1735	Apr 23	●	0:11:25	AT	0m44s	2♉19
1881	Nov 21	●	16:31:11	A	0m43s	29♏33
2005	Apr 8	●	20:35:50	AT	0m42s	19♈ 6
1968	Sep 22	●	11:18:06	T	0m40s	29♍30
1999	Feb 16	●	6:33:37	A	0m39s	27♒ 8
1731	Dec 29	●	0:46:44	AT	0m39s	6♑55
1717	Apr 11	●	16:34:31	AT	0m39s	21♈38
2049	Nov 25	●	5:32:46	AT	0m38s	3♐23
2020	Jun 21	●	6:40:14	A	0m38s	0♋21
1879	Jul 19	●	9:04:35	A	0m38s	26♋17
1807	Jun 6	●	5:18:14	AT	0m38s	14♊31
1981	Feb 4	●	22:08:31	A	0m33s	16♒ 1
1827	Oct 20	●	15:41:50	AT	0m30s	26♎29
1890	Dec 12	●	3:05:31	AT	0m29s	20♐ 5
1768	Jul 14	●	1:40:43	AT	0m29s	21♋59
1722	Dec 8	●	14:07:27	A	0m28s	16♐16
1720	Aug 4	●	4:38:05	A	0m27s	11♌48
1969	Mar 18	●	4:54:18	A	0m26s	27♓25
1963	Jan 25	●	13:36:36	A	0m25s	4♒52
1825	Jun 16	●	12:18:48	AT	0m25s	24♊58
1909	Jun 17	●	23:18:26	AT	0m24s	26♊ 4
1750	Jan 8	●	9:28:33	AT	0m24s	18♑ 7
2032	May 9	●	13:25:41	A	0m22s	19♉29
2002	Jun 10	●	23:44:21	A	0m22s	19♊54
1863	Nov 11	●	8:08:51	A	0m22s	18♏28
2050	May 20	●	20:41:50	AT	0m21s	0♊ 2
1810	Apr 4	●	1:41:01	A	0m21s	13♈38
1828	Apr 14	●	9:19:24	AT	0m18s	24♈23
1945	Jan 14	●	5:01:15	A	0m15s	23♑41
1861	Jul 8	●	2:10:15	A	0m14s	15♋50
1768	Jan 19	●	18:09:15	AT	0m13s	29♑19
1908	Dec 23	●	11:44:17	AT	0m12s	1♑17
1984	May 30	●	16:44:47	A	0m11s	9♊26
1987	Mar 29	●	12:48:52	AT	0m08s	8♈18
1843	Jun 27	●	19:16:54	AT	0m08s	5♋25
1891	Jun 6	●	16:15:39	A	0m06s	15♊37
1786	Jan 30	●	2:45:10	AT	0m05s	10♒28
1966	May 20	●	9:38:24	A	0m04s	28♉55
1840	Mar 4	●	3:58:13	A	0m03s	13♓42
1930	Apr 28	●	19:03:09	AT	0m02s	7♉45
1927	Jan 3	●	20:22:27	A	0m02s	12♑29
1912	Apr 17	●	11:34:07	AT	0m02s	27♈ 5
1858	Mar 15	●	12:05:17	A	0m02s	24♓38
1845	Oct 30	●	23:51:46	AT	0m02s	7♏27
1822	Feb 21	●	19:40:24	A	0m02s	2♓40
1894	Apr 6	●	3:53:46	AT	0m01s	16♈20
1876	Mar 25	●	20:05:07	A	0m01s	5♈32
1704	Nov 27	●	5:33:47	A	0m01s	5♐ 6
1702	Jul 24	●	21:38:44	AT	0m01s	1♌19
1986	Oct 3	●	19:05:19	AT	0m00s	10♎16
1948	May 9	●	2:25:34	AT	0m00s	18♉22
1804	Feb 11	●	11:16:14	A	0m00s	21♒36

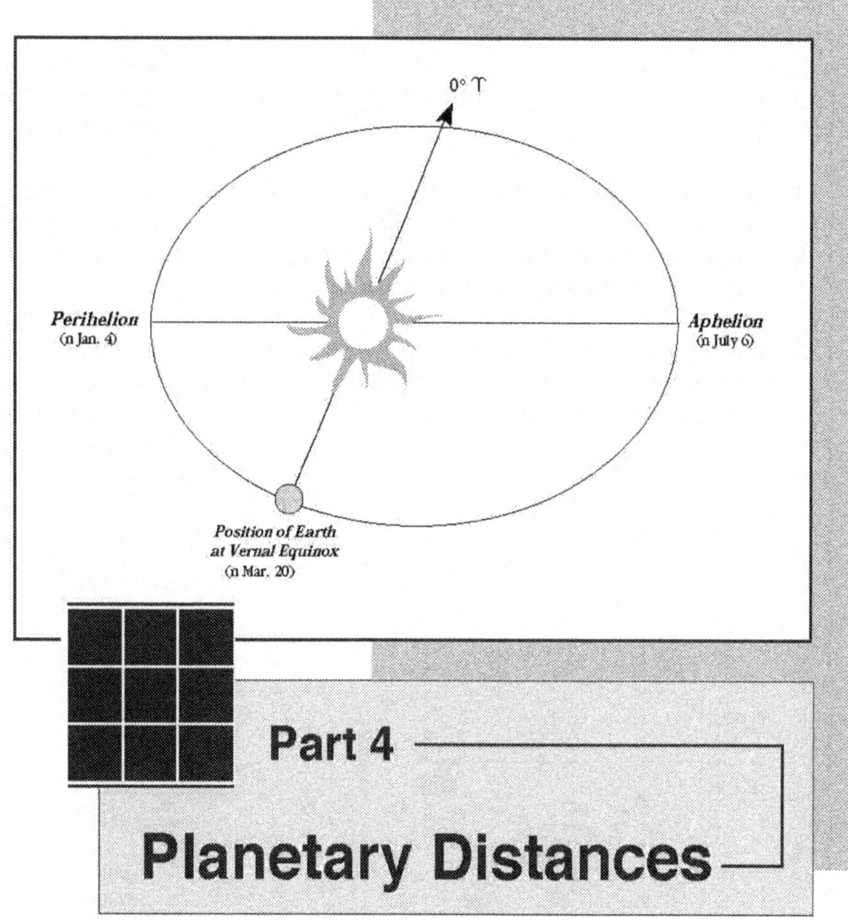

Part 4
Planetary Distances

- *Planetary Distances from Sun*
- *Moon Distance from Earth*

Planetary Distance

All permanent bodies in the solar system have elliptical orbits. Major planets, asteroids and comets orbit the Sun. Satellites of planets orbit the planet of which they are a satellite! An obvious characteristic of elliptical motion is that the distance between a revolving body and its primary is constantly changing.

When a planet or asteroid is at its maximum distance from the Sun it is at its **aphelion**. When a planet is at its mimimum distance from the Sun it is at its **perihelion**. When the Moon is at its maximum distance from the Earth it is at its **apogee**, and at its minimum distance it is at its **perigee**. Clearly, "helion" comes from *helios*, the Sun, and "gee" comes from *geo*, the Earth.

The three laws of orbital motion discovered by Johannes Kepler are:

1. The orbit of each planet is an ellipse with the Sun at one of its foci.
2. Each planet revolves so that the line joining it to the Sun sweeps out equal areas in equal intervals of time.
3. The squares of the periods of any two planets are in the same proportion as the cubes of their mean distances from the Sun.

As a consequence of the second law, the body is moving at its slowest orbital velocity when it is farthest away from its primary, and fastest when it is at its closest. Further, when a planet is at its perihelion or aphelion, it is at its "station" in terms of its movement away from or toward the Sun.

From the Earth Perihelion/Aphelion Table on the following page, you can see that in this century aphelion occurs in early July and perihelion occurs in early January. So now you know why the Sun moves faster through Sagittarius, Capricorn and Aquarius than it does through Gemini, Cancer and Leo.

Another interesting consequence of the times of year that the Earth's perihelion-aphelion occur is that the northern hemisphere's winters are about 3% warmer than the southern hemisphere's. The Sun is closer to the Earth during our winter, and due to the inverse square law of electromagnetic radiation, the light from the Sun is stronger during the northern hemisphere winter and weaker during the summer. The opposite, of course, is true for the southern hemisphere.

It is interesting to note that the Moon's perigee shows a much greater variation about a mean value than does the apogee. The apogee narrow range is from 404,000 to 406,000 kilometers from the Earth. The perigee can vary from 355,000 to over 370,000 kilometers.

Earth Perihelion/Aphelion 1837–2020 • Distance in Astronomical Units

1837	Jul	2	8:45	A	1.01681
1838	Jan	2	4:00	P	0.98325
	Jul	1	5:21	A	1.01674
	Dec	31	23:17	P	0.98323
1839	Jul	4	6:22	A	1.01676
	Dec	31	12:05	P	0.98324
1840	Jul	1	12:31	A	1.01683
1841	Jan	1	21:08	P	0.98319
	Jul	1	17:54	A	1.01676
	Dec	31	1:08	P	0.98318
1842	Jul	3	16:01	A	1.01679
1843	Jan	1	10:56	P	0.98324
	Jul	1	18:58	A	1.01681
1844	Jan	2	10:03	P	0.98319
	Jul	2	23:53	A	1.01678
	Dec	30	15:09	P	0.98321
1845	Jul	2	21:27	A	1.01682
1846	Jan	2	1:40	P	0.98326
	Jul	1	10:39	A	1.01674
1847	Jan	1	9:34	P	0.98322
	Jul	4	10:05	A	1.01672
	Dec	31	11:59	P	0.98324
1848	Jul	1	22:02	A	1.01680
1849	Jan	2	4:02	P	0.98323
	Jul	1	7:43	A	1.01674
	Dec	31	10:36	P	0.98323
1850	Jul	3	21:16	A	1.01676
	Dec	31	21:15	P	0.98329
1851	Jul	2	2:09	A	1.01680
1852	Jan	2	13:31	P	0.98321
	Jul	2	11:06	A	1.01676
	Dec	30	16:56	P	0.98319
1853	Jul	3	4:48	A	1.01681
1854	Jan	1	17:25	P	0.98323
	Jul	1	11:14	A	1.01677
1855	Jan	1	19:56	P	0.98320
	Jul	4	5:38	A	1.01675
	Dec	31	13:17	P	0.98323
1856	Jul	2	8:38	A	1.01683
1857	Jan	2	4:39	P	0.98325
	Jul	1	7:27	A	1.01675
	Dec	31	19:09	P	0.98323
1858	Jul	4	4:23	A	1.01674
	Dec	31	14:20	P	0.98327
1859	Jul	2	11:26	A	1.01678
1860	Jan	2	22:09	P	0.98322
	Jul	1	20:37	A	1.01674
	Dec	31	2:21	P	0.98321
1861	Jul	3	11:19	A	1.01679
1862	Jan	1	7:14	P	0.98327
	Jul	1	16:21	A	1.01677
1863	Jan	2	2:18	P	0.98324
	Jul	3	23:25	A	1.01673
	Dec	31	11:57	P	0.98322
1864	Jul	2	18:04	A	1.01682
1865	Jan	1	23:13	P	0.98323
	Jul	1	5:26	A	1.01677
1866	Jan	1	5:22	P	0.98319
	Jul	4	3:10	A	1.01674
	Dec	31	13:13	P	0.98325
1867	Jul	2	20:22	A	1.01680
1868	Jan	3	4:07	P	0.98324
	Jul	1	14:11	A	1.01676
	Dec	31	9:47	P	0.98322
1869	Jul	3	21:10	A	1.01678
	Dec	31	17:20	P	0.98328
1870	Jul	2	1:36	A	1.01675
1871	Jan	2	10:10	P	0.98324
	Jul	3	11:25	A	1.01670
	Dec	31	19:05	P	0.98321
1872	Jul	3	0:59	A	1.01679
1873	Jan	1	19:58	P	0.98326
	Jul	1	6:10	A	1.01676
1874	Jan	1	14:09	P	0.98323
	Jul	3	23:20	A	1.01673
	Dec	31	8:08	P	0.98326
1875	Jul	3	6:25	A	1.01681
1876	Jan	3	0:30	P	0.98324
	Jul	1	8:37	A	1.01677
	Dec	31	17:13	P	0.98317
1877	Jul	4	0:13	A	1.01678
	Dec	31	11:52	P	0.98324
1878	Jul	2	8:37	A	1.01678
1879	Jan	2	20:11	P	0.98323
	Jul	2	21:45	A	1.01673
1880	Jan	1	3:45	P	0.98322
	Jul	3	11:37	A	1.01680
1881	Jan	1	9:39	P	0.98328
	Jul	1	16:01	A	1.01676
1882	Jan	1	22:05	P	0.98325
	Jul	3	21:27	A	1.01670
	Dec	31	11:39	P	0.98326
1883	Jul	3	16:20	A	1.01676
1884	Jan	3	1:26	P	0.98327
	Jul	1	4:30	A	1.01675
1885	Jan	1	3:57	P	0.98322
	Jul	3	22:25	A	1.01674
	Dec	31	5:23	P	0.98328
1886	Jul	2	16:41	A	1.01677
1887	Jan	2	20:04	P	0.98327
	Jul	2	10:36	A	1.01673
1888	Jan	1	6:56	P	0.98320
	Jul	3	17:17	A	1.01680
	Dec	31	16:46	P	0.98324
1889	Jul	1	20:43	A	1.01679
1890	Jan	2	6:35	P	0.98321
	Jul	3	6:08	A	1.01673
	Dec	31	19:20	P	0.98322
1891	Jul	4	0:54	A	1.01680
1892	Jan	2	22:44	P	0.98327
	Jul	1	9:44	A	1.01679
1893	Jan	1	13:35	P	0.98322
	Jul	4	1:50	A	1.01674
	Dec	31	4:17	P	0.98327
1894	Jul	3	5:09	A	1.01674
1895	Jan	2	23:30	P	0.98328
	Jul	2	6:01	A	1.01670
1896	Jan	1	18:17	P	0.98322
	Jul	3	20:50	A	1.01675
	Dec	31	10:16	P	0.98328
1897	Jul	2	3:36	A	1.01677
1898	Jan	2	12:14	P	0.98327
	Jul	2	15:00	A	1.01671
	Dec	31	22:04	P	0.98324
1899	Jul	4	8:56	A	1.01679
1900	Jan	2	6:27	P	0.98326
	Jul	2	13:23	A	1.01679
1901	Jan	2	20:20	P	0.98319
	Jul	4	16:22	A	1.01674
1902	Jan	1	7:24	P	0.98323
	Jul	4	12:60	A	1.01677
1903	Jan	4	0:44	P	0.98327
	Jul	3	4:11	A	1.01674
1904	Jan	3	4:14	P	0.98322
	Jul	5	1:25	A	1.01677
1905	Jan	1	4:28	P	0.98328
	Jul	3	15:45	A	1.01677
1906	Jan	3	16:35	P	0.98327
	Jul	3	7:07	A	1.01669
1907	Jan	2	7:28	P	0.98323
	Jul	5	15:47	A	1.01676
1908	Jan	2	22:60	P	0.98327
	Jul	2	18:55	A	1.01678
1909	Jan	3	5:40	P	0.98323
	Jul	4	4:11	A	1.01672
1910	Jan	1	10:53	P	0.98326
	Jul	4	22:36	A	1.01676
1911	Jan	3	15:02	P	0.98330
	Jul	3	6:35	A	1.01674
1912	Jan	3	10:44	P	0.98321
	Jul	4	23:16	A	1.01675
1913	Jan	1	2:22	P	0.98324
	Jul	3	23:53	A	1.01677
1914	Jan	3	20:52	P	0.98326
	Jul	2	23:16	A	1.01672
1915	Jan	2	18:05	P	0.98322
	Jul	5	21:24	A	1.01677
1916	Jan	2	12:40	P	0.98329
	Jul	3	5:25	A	1.01679
1917	Jan	3	10:56	P	0.98325
	Jul	3	19:14	A	1.01671
1918	Jan	1	16:59	P	0.98325
	Jul	5	7:45	A	1.01672
1919	Jan	3	8:25	P	0.98331
	Jul	3	9:29	A	1.01672
1920	Jan	3	21:49	P	0.98323
	Jul	4	14:10	A	1.01672
1921	Jan	1	4:30	P	0.98326
	Jul	4	8:06	A	1.01676
1922	Jan	3	16:57	P	0.98330
	Jul	2	21:44	A	1.01672
1923	Jan	2	23:24	P	0.98323
	Jul	6	0:20	A	1.01676
1924	Jan	2	1:55	P	0.98325
	Jul	3	13:22	A	1.01681
1925	Jan	3	15:42	P	0.98322
	Jul	3	4:58	A	1.01673
1926	Jan	2	3:36	P	0.98321
	Jul	5	13:59	A	1.01675
1927	Jan	3	1:38	P	0.98330
	Jul	3	18:07	A	1.01676
1928	Jan	4	6:49	P	0.98325
	Jul	4	10:49	A	1.01672
1929	Jan	1	7:60	P	0.98327
	Jul	4	21:09	A	1.01674
1930	Jan	3	12:21	P	0.98332
	Jul	3	1:04	A	1.01669
1931	Jan	3	10:38	P	0.98324
	Jul	5	22:30	A	1.01671
1932	Jan	2	3:22	P	0.98328
	Jul	3	20:31	A	1.01678
1933	Jan	3	18:52	P	0.98327
	Jul	2	19:47	A	1.01673
1934	Jan	2	9:31	P	0.98325
	Jul	5	18:38	A	1.01674
1935	Jan	2	7:34	P	0.98330
	Jul	4	1:52	A	1.01677
1936	Jan	4	9:51	P	0.98322
	Jul	3	19:56	A	1.01673
1937	Jan	1	14:16	P	0.98321
	Jul	5	3:50	A	1.01676
1938	Jan	3	8:03	P	0.98329
	Jul	3	4:08	A	1.01674
1939	Jan	3	22:12	P	0.98323
	Jul	5	19:54	A	1.01674
1940	Jan	2	5:27	P	0.98327
	Jul	4	9:48	A	1.01679
1941	Jan	3	18:10	P	0.98329
	Jul	2	22:53	A	1.01672
1942	Jan	2	19:16	P	0.98325
	Jul	6	0:05	A	1.01669
1943	Jan	2	4:36	P	0.98331
	Jul	4	10:28	A	1.01673
1944	Jan	4	17:37	P	0.98326
	Jul	3	5:34	A	1.01671
1945	Jan	1	22:46	P	0.98325
	Jul	5	10:02	A	1.01673
1946	Jan	2	17:52	P	0.98333
	Jul	3	10:39	A	1.01673
1947	Jan	4	2:44	P	0.98325
	Jul	5	10:38	A	1.01672
1948	Jan	2	5:11	P	0.98324
	Jul	4	17:29	A	1.01678
1949	Jan	3	13:31	P	0.98326
	Jul	2	20:45	A	1.01674
1950	Jan	3	6:17	P	0.98323
	Jul	5	22:31	A	1.01672
1951	Jan	2	3:52	P	0.98329
	Jul	4	20:55	A	1.01677
1952	Jan	4	20:42	P	0.98328
	Jul	3	2:19	A	1.01673
1953	Jan	2	6:38	P	0.98324
	Jul	5	18:20	A	1.01671
1954	Jan	2	8:20	P	0.98332
	Jul	3	19:55	A	1.01671
1955	Jan	4	12:21	P	0.98326
	Jul	4	22:03	A	1.01669
1956	Jan	2	13:24	P	0.98325
	Jul	5	1:12	A	1.01676
1957	Jan	3	6:31	P	0.98331
	Jul	3	0:22	A	1.01674
1958	Jan	3	13:25	P	0.98326
	Jul	5	19:55	A	1.01670
1959	Jan	2	0:18	P	0.98328
	Jul	5	6:34	A	1.01676
1960	Jan	4	18:53	P	0.98326
	Jul	2	21:34	A	1.01674
1961	Jan	2	16:48	P	0.98321
	Jul	5	19:54	A	1.01672
1962	Jan	2	4:49	P	0.98330
	Jul	4	4:48	A	1.01674
1963	Jan	4	19:37	P	0.98327
	Jul	4	13:27	A	1.01672
1964	Jan	2	20:45	P	0.98326
	Jul	5	12:07	A	1.01675
1965	Jan	2	19:17	P	0.98332
	Jul	3	8:22	A	1.01672
1966	Jan	3	22:48	P	0.98327
	Jul	5	11:51	A	1.01666
1967	Jan	2	5:55	P	0.98329
	Jul	5	14:29	A	1.01673
1968	Jan	4	18:03	P	0.98329
	Jul	2	19:57	A	1.01673
1969	Jan	3	1:06	P	0.98325
	Jul	5	19:54	A	1.01671
1970	Jan	1	21:10	P	0.98331
	Jul	4	14:51	A	1.01675
1971	Jan	4	18:32	P	0.98327
	Jul	4	4:15	A	1.01673
1972	Jan	3	4:14	P	0.98322
	Jul	5	16:59	A	1.01675
1973	Jan	2	12:00	P	0.98328
	Jul	3	14:59	A	1.01675
1974	Jan	4	9:41	P	0.98326
	Jul	5	1:28	A	1.01668
1975	Jan	2	12:56	P	0.98329
	Jul	6	2:35	A	1.01674
1976	Jan	4	11:05	P	0.98332
	Jul	3	3:20	A	1.01673
1977	Jan	3	9:54	P	0.98326
	Jul	5	20:29	A	1.01666
1978	Jan	1	23:20	P	0.98331
	Jul	5	0:18	A	1.01671
1979	Jan	4	22:36	P	0.98330
	Jul	3	21:05	A	1.01670
1980	Jan	3	14:45	P	0.98326
	Jul	5	17:44	A	1.01673
1981	Jan	2	1:42	P	0.98332
	Jul	3	23:05	A	1.01675
1982	Jan	4	11:20	P	0.98329
	Jul	4	13:30	A	1.01668
1983	Jan	2	15:18	P	0.98326
	Jul	6	9:59	A	1.01674
1984	Jan	3	21:58	P	0.98328
	Jul	3	6:22	A	1.01676
1985	Jan	3	19:54	P	0.98322
	Jul	5	10:17	A	1.01669
1986	Jan	2	4:55	P	0.98328
	Jul	5	10:06	A	1.01674
1987	Jan	4	23:03	P	0.98330
	Jul	4	1:01	A	1.01674
1988	Jan	4	0:00	P	0.98325
	Jul	5	23:57	A	1.01672
1989	Jan	1	21:54	P	0.98331
	Jul	4	11:34	A	1.01672
1990	Jan	4	17:23	P	0.98330
	Jul	4	5:06	A	1.01665
1991	Jan	3	2:59	P	0.98328
	Jul	6	15:27	A	1.01670
1992	Jan	3	15:03	P	0.98332
	Jul	3	12:08	A	1.01674
1993	Jan	4	3:05	P	0.98328
	Jul	4	22:20	A	1.01667
1994	Jan	2	5:55	P	0.98330
	Jul	5	19:18	A	1.01672
1995	Jan	4	11:06	P	0.98330
	Jul	4	2:17	A	1.01674
1996	Jan	4	7:26	P	0.98322
	Jul	5	19:01	A	1.01672
1997	Jan	1	23:18	P	0.98327
	Jul	4	19:21	A	1.01675
1998	Jan	4	21:16	P	0.98330
	Jul	3	23:51	A	1.01670
1999	Jan	3	13:01	P	0.98328
	Jul	6	22:51	A	1.01672
2000	Jan	3	5:19	P	0.98332
	Jul	3	23:52	A	1.01674
2001	Jan	4	8:53	P	0.98329
	Jul	4	13:38	A	1.01664
2002	Jan	2	14:10	P	0.98329
	Jul	6	3:48	A	1.01669
2003	Jan	4	5:04	P	0.98332
	Jul	4	5:40	A	1.01673
2004	Jan	4	17:43	P	0.98326
	Jul	5	10:55	A	1.01669
2005	Jan	2	0:36	P	0.98330
	Jul	5	4:58	A	1.01674
2006	Jan	4	15:30	P	0.98333
	Jul	3	23:11	A	1.01670
2007	Jan	3	19:45	P	0.98326
	Jul	6	23:53	A	1.01671
2008	Jan	2	23:52	P	0.98328
	Jul	4	7:41	A	1.01675
2009	Jan	4	15:31	P	0.98327
	Jul	4	1:43	A	1.01667
2010	Jan	3	0:09	P	0.98329
	Jul	6	11:31	A	1.01670
2011	Jan	3	18:32	P	0.98334
	Jul	4	14:56	A	1.01674
2012	Jan	5	0:33	P	0.98328
	Jul	5	3:35	A	1.01668
2013	Jan	2	4:38	P	0.98329
	Jul	5	14:46	A	1.01671
2014	Jan	4	11:60	P	0.98333
	Jul	4	0:14	A	1.01668
2015	Jan	4	6:37	P	0.98328
	Jul	6	19:41	A	1.01668
2016	Jan	2	22:50	P	0.98330
	Jul	4	16:26	A	1.01675
2017	Jan	4	14:19	P	0.98331
	Jul	3	20:12	A	1.01668
2018	Jan	3	5:35	P	0.98328
	Jul	6	16:48	A	1.01670
2019	Jan	3	5:22	P	0.98330
	Jul	4	22:14	A	1.01675
2020	Jan	5	7:49	P	0.98324
	Jul	4	11:36	A	1.01669

Mars and the Outer Planets in Perihelion and Aphelion 1700–2050

Pluto in Perihelion

Year	Date	Time	Distance	Position
1741	Aug 26	9:21	29.64978	10♏51
1989	Sep 4	23:26	29.65596	14♏40

Pluto in Aphelion

Year	Date	Time	Distance	Position
1866	Jun 2	15:08	49.30336	13♉46

Neptune in Perihelion

Year	Date	Time	Distance	Position
1711	Dec 15	12:26	29.81685	1♉24
1720	Aug 17	6:60	29.81008	20♉48
1876	Aug 26	8:41	29.81485	3♉31
1886	Jul 8	23:16	29.81742	25♉36
2042	Sep 3	9:16	29.80644	8♉35
2049	Dec 31	13:53	29.81672	24♉59
2050	Jun 30	8:52	29.81678	26♉05

The perihelion entries for the high degrees of Taurus are local minima and do not correspond to a perihelion

Neptune in Aphelion

Year	Date	Time	Distance	Position
1794	May 17	5:30	30.32087	2♏58
1800	May 24	0:00	30.32173	15♏58
1803	Dec 22	8:34	30.32727	23♏43
1959	Jul 17	1:00	30.33173	6♏05
1968	Nov 21	8:31	30.32406	26♏17

The aphelion entries for the high degrees of Scorpio are local maxima and do not correspond to an aphelion

Uranus in Perihelion

Year	Date	Time	Distance	Position
1714	Apr 29	10:52	18.29549	15♍11
1798	Mar 3	6:24	18.28900	15♍29
1882	Mar 23	22:45	18.28065	16♍44
1966	May 22	2:41	18.28479	18♍33
2050	Aug 16	22:55	18.28302	20♍47

Uranus in Aphelion

Year	Date	Time	Distance	Position
1756	Nov 26	20:39	20.08928	18♓06
1841	Mar 15	12:23	20.09758	20♓22
1925	Apr 1	5:38	20.09732	21♓41
2009	Feb 27	1:34	20.09888	22♓28

Saturn in Perihelion

Year	Date	Time	Distance	Position
1709	Jan 17	10:56	9.00627	29♊39
1738	May 8	10:26	9.00195	27♊53
1767	Dec 27	8:40	9.01362	0♋44
1797	Apr 19	23:50	9.00742	29♊07
1826	Nov 30	8:35	9.01948	1♋43
1856	Mar 23	16:02	9.01091	0♋08
1885	Oct 21	8:44	9.02575	2♋27
1915	Feb 21	9:46	9.01353	1♋09
1944	Sep 8	2:32	9.02885	3♋07
1974	Jan 8	6:40	9.01531	1♋52
2003	Jul 26	16:27	9.03090	3♋51
2032	Nov 28	15:35	9.01492	2♋42

Saturn in Aphelion

Year	Date	Time	Distance	Position
1723	Sep 2	19:45	10.09010	28♐28
1753	Mar 29	14:53	10.06991	0♑18
1782	Aug 22	22:23	10.08213	29♐52
1812	Feb 24	20:50	10.06007	1♑01
1841	Aug 5	16:17	10.07585	1♑09
1871	Jan 4	15:59	10.05154	1♑19
1900	Jul 9	22:26	10.06987	2♑14
1929	Nov 11	21:24	10.04668	1♑37
1959	May 29	21:56	10.06641	2♑57
1988	Sep 11	10:16	10.04440	1♑45
2018	Apr 17	11:26	10.06565	3♑43
2047	Jul 15	7:03	10.04616	1♑59

Jupiter in Perihelion

Year	Date	Time	Distance	Position
1702	Oct 4	14:14	4.94791	9♈35
1714	Aug 7	0:31	4.94974	9♈08
1726	Jun 17	23:03	4.95349	9♈20
1738	May 4	13:25	4.95341	10♈01
1750	Mar 28	0:15	4.94887	11♈12
1762	Jan 30	11:30	4.94767	10♈53
1773	Dec 1	16:04	4.94905	10♈18
1785	Oct 11	5:12	4.95267	10♈23
1797	Aug 27	12:26	4.95287	11♈01
1809	Jul 24	1:15	4.94934	12♈23
1821	May 30	0:13	4.94791	12♈10
1833	Mar 29	15:59	4.94863	11♈26
1845	Feb 4	20:09	4.95207	11♈24
1856	Dec 22	8:24	4.95266	12♈04
1868	Nov 18	5:29	4.95021	13♈31
1880	Sep 25	7:27	4.94851	13♈24
1892	Jul 24	18:53	4.94843	12♈33
1904	Jun 1	21:22	4.95167	12♈25
1916	Apr 18	1:14	4.95261	13♈02
1928	Mar 15	12:45	4.95126	14♈32
1940	Jan 23	13:03	4.94942	14♈34
1951	Nov 21	3:59	4.94841	13♈38
1963	Sep 26	18:04	4.95133	13♈22
1975	Aug 12	12:33	4.95264	13♈58
1987	Jul 10	6:09	4.95242	15♈29
1999	May 20	10:15	4.95047	15♈36
2011	Mar 17	17:03	4.94839	14♈38
2023	Jan 20	11:44	4.95101	14♈18
2034	Dec 5	16:57	4.95268	14♈51
2046	Nov 1	11:42	4.95342	16♈17

Jupiter in Aphelion

Year	Date	Time	Distance	Position
1708	Sep 3	0:43	5.45556	9♎14
1720	Jul 9	21:03	5.45410	9♎03
1732	May 25	22:40	5.45178	9♎39
1744	Apr 20	18:32	5.45512	11♎00
1756	Mar 1	13:39	5.45664	11♎14
1767	Dec 29	23:57	5.45626	10♎26
1779	Nov 4	2:01	5.45507	10♎10
1791	Sep 19	4:05	5.45262	10♎41
1803	Aug 16	17:39	5.45509	12♎07
1815	Jun 28	17:19	5.45653	12♎24
1827	Apr 27	0:45	5.45667	11♎35
1839	Mar 2	3:33	5.45574	11♎19
1851	Jan 14	3:49	5.45319	11♎44
1862	Dec 10	6:21	5.45473	13♎08
1874	Oct 24	6:31	5.45602	13♎34
1886	Aug 22	15:12	5.45680	12♎43
1898	Jun 27	3:51	5.45618	12♎25
1910	May 10	19:57	5.45355	12♎43
1922	Apr 5	8:38	5.45416	14♎04
1934	Feb 19	6:39	5.45522	14♎38
1945	Dec 18	23:27	5.45671	13♎48
1957	Oct 23	8:45	5.45641	13♎29
1969	Sep 3	19:21	5.45374	13♎42
1981	Jul 28	6:12	5.45351	14♎52
1993	Jun 14	23:11	5.45428	15♎35
2005	Apr 14	21:46	5.45652	14♎49
2017	Feb 17	7:20	5.45652	14♎30
2028	Dec 28	2:45	5.45386	14♎36
2040	Nov 18	9:58	5.45292	15♎36

Mars in Perihelion

Year	Date	Time	Distance	Position
1700	Oct 31	1:55	1.38178	0♓30
1702	Sep 18	6:53	1.38179	0♓39
1704	Aug 5	2:16	1.38190	0♓35
1706	Jun 23	2:32	1.38162	0♓37
1708	May 10	7:13	1.38167	0♓46
1710	Mar 28	5:51	1.38188	0♓46
1712	Feb 13	1:34	1.38181	0♓43
1713	Dec 31	5:15	1.38172	0♓50
1715	Nov 18	2:54	1.38193	0♓49
1717	Oct 4	23:31	1.38167	0♓47
1719	Aug 23	5:21	1.38157	0♓56
1721	Jul 10	7:15	1.38181	1♓01
1723	May 28	2:30	1.38188	0♓57
1725	Apr 14	3:07	1.38171	1♓00
1727	Mar 2	4:41	1.38188	1♓05
1729	Jan 16	23:06	1.38178	1♓00
1730	Dec 5	2:27	1.38156	1♓07
1732	Oct 22	5:42	1.38172	1♓13
1734	Sep 9	2:52	1.38185	1♓12
1736	Jul 27	1:10	1.38170	1♓11
1738	Jun 14	5:26	1.38179	1♓19
1740	Apr 30	23:33	1.38184	1♓13
1742	Mar 19	0:12	1.38154	1♓16
1744	Feb 4	5:21	1.38161	1♓25
1745	Dec 22	3:38	1.38184	1♓25
1747	Nov 8	23:11	1.38177	1♓22
1749	Sep 26	3:25	1.38168	1♓30
1751	Aug 14	0:54	1.38187	1♓29
1753	Jun 30	22:50	1.38162	1♓28
1755	May 19	3:52	1.38156	1♓36
1757	Apr 5	4:20	1.38179	1♓39
1759	Feb 20	23:46	1.38180	1♓36
1761	Jan 8	1:29	1.38166	1♓40
1762	Nov 26	1:55	1.38186	1♓44
1764	Oct 12	20:24	1.38170	1♓39
1766	Aug 31	1:13	1.38148	1♓47
1768	Jul 18	4:40	1.38167	1♓53
1770	Jun 5	0:52	1.38181	1♓51
1772	Apr 21	23:20	1.38164	1♓51
1774	Mar 10	3:04	1.38174	1♓58
1776	Jan 25	21:18	1.38178	1♓53
1777	Dec 12	22:32	1.38151	1♓56
1779	Oct 31	2:46	1.38161	2♓04
1781	Sep 17	1:06	1.38178	2♓04
1783	Aug 4	21:50	1.38167	2♓02
1785	Jun 22	2:37	1.38166	2♓11
1787	May 9	22:31	1.38183	2♓08
1789	Mar 26	20:34	1.38155	2♓07
1791	Feb 12	2:01	1.38152	2♓17
1792	Dec 30	2:01	1.38176	2♓19
1794	Nov 16	20:52	1.38176	2♓14
1796	Oct 3	23:14	1.38159	2♓20
1798	Aug 21	23:42	1.38178	2♓22
1800	Jul 9	19:45	1.38160	2♓19
1802	May 28	0:20	1.38144	2♓27
1804	Apr 14	2:33	1.38165	2♓33
1806	Mar 1	22:17	1.38176	2♓30
1808	Jan 17	21:34	1.38160	2♓31
1809	Dec 5	0:18	1.38174	2♓37
1811	Oct 22	18:01	1.38171	2♓31
1813	Sep 8	21:05	1.38142	2♓36
1815	Jul 28	1:55	1.38155	2♓44
1817	Jun 13	23:33	1.38175	2♓44
1819	May 1	20:04	1.38163	2♓41
1821	Mar 19	0:22	1.38164	2♓50
1823	Feb 3	19:49	1.38178	2♓46
1824	Dec 21	18:33	1.38150	2♓47
1826	Nov 8	23:22	1.38149	2♓56
1828	Sep 25	23:15	1.38168	2♓58
1830	Aug 13	19:25	1.38164	2♓54
1832	Jun 30	23:22	1.38154	3♓01
1834	May 18	21:59	1.38176	3♓02
1836	Apr 4	17:33	1.38154	2♓58

Mars in Aphelion

Year	Date	Time	Distance	Position
1701	Oct 9	15:15	1.66552	0♍33
1703	Aug 27	13:39	1.66563	0♍33
1705	Jul 14	18:01	1.66567	0♍40
1707	Jun 1	16:19	1.66564	0♍41
1709	Apr 18	15:51	1.66563	0♍43
1711	Mar 6	17:58	1.66557	0♍48
1713	Jan 21	16:50	1.66553	0♍48
1714	Dec 9	13:14	1.66553	0♍46
1716	Oct 26	14:52	1.66564	0♍50
1718	Sep 13	15:55	1.66574	0♍53
1720	Jul 31	15:32	1.66572	0♍55
1722	Jun 18	17:51	1.66558	1♍00
1724	May 5	17:02	1.66551	1♍01
1726	Mar 23	13:16	1.66553	0♍59
1728	Feb 8	13:28	1.66563	1♍02
1729	Dec 26	16:16	1.66567	1♍07
1731	Nov 13	13:12	1.66567	1♍07
1733	Sep 30	14:40	1.66567	1♍10
1735	Aug 18	16:47	1.66565	1♍15
1737	Jul 5	14:35	1.66556	1♍14
1739	May 23	12:11	1.66559	1♍13
1741	Apr 9	15:22	1.66570	1♍19
1743	Feb 25	13:44	1.66572	1♍20
1745	Jan 12	14:21	1.66569	1♍23
1746	Nov 30	15:59	1.66559	1♍27
1748	Oct 17	13:46	1.66558	1♍27
1750	Sep 4	11:01	1.66567	1♍25
1752	Jul 22	14:47	1.66573	1♍32
1754	Jun 9	14:47	1.66569	1♍34
1756	Apr 26	12:50	1.66569	1♍34
1758	Mar 14	14:59	1.66563	1♍39
1760	Jan 30	14:41	1.66559	1♍41
1761	Dec 17	10:58	1.66557	1♍39
1763	Nov 4	11:00	1.66567	1♍41
1765	Sep 21	13:19	1.66578	1♍45
1767	Aug 9	12:13	1.66581	1♍47
1769	Jun 26	14:33	1.66569	1♍52
1771	May 14	14:47	1.66561	1♍54
1773	Mar 31	11:30	1.66561	1♍52
1775	Feb 16	10:12	1.66568	1♍53
1777	Jan 3	13:49	1.66575	1♍59
1778	Nov 21	11:19	1.66574	1♍59
1780	Oct 8	11:42	1.66574	2♍01
1782	Aug 26	14:17	1.66573	2♍06
1784	Jul 13	13:06	1.66563	2♍07
1786	May 31	9:39	1.66562	2♍06
1788	Apr 17	12:04	1.66574	2♍10
1790	Mar 5	11:43	1.66577	2♍12
1792	Jan 21	10:57	1.66575	2♍14
1793	Dec 8	12:58	1.66566	2♍18
1795	Oct 26	11:34	1.66563	2♍19
1797	Sep 12	8:16	1.66571	2♍17
1799	Jul 31	10:48	1.66580	2♍22
1801	Jun 18	12:46	1.66578	2♍26
1803	May 6	9:57	1.66578	2♍26
1805	Mar 23	11:59	1.66573	2♍31
1807	Feb 8	12:40	1.66567	2♍34
1808	Dec 26	9:27	1.66564	2♍32
1810	Nov 13	7:54	1.66571	2♍32
1812	Sep 30	11:02	1.66584	2♍37
1814	Aug 18	9:50	1.66589	2♍39
1816	Jul 5	11:32	1.66577	2♍43
1818	May 23	12:29	1.66567	2♍46
1820	Apr 9	9:46	1.66565	2♍45
1822	Feb 25	7:04	1.66570	2♍45
1824	Jan 13	10:24	1.66579	2♍50
1825	Nov 30	9:10	1.66579	2♍52
1827	Oct 18	8:12	1.66582	2♍53
1829	Sep 4	11:02	1.66582	2♍58
1831	Jul 23	11:05	1.66573	3♍00
1833	Jun 9	7:21	1.66569	2♍58
1835	Apr 27	8:33	1.66579	3♍01
1837	Mar 14	9:54	1.66584	3♍05

Mars and the Outer Planets in Perihelion and Aphelion 1700–2050

Mars in Perihelion

Year	Date	Time	Distance	Longitude
1838	Feb 20	22:17	1.38141	3♓07
1840	Jan 8	23:57	1.38164	3♓12
1841	Nov 25	19:04	1.38172	3♓07
1843	Oct 13	19:07	1.38152	3♓10
1845	Aug 30	22:25	1.38167	3♓16
1847	Jul 18	17:16	1.38161	3♓11
1849	Jun 4	20:18	1.38139	3♓17
1851	Apr 22	23:54	1.38155	3♓24
1853	Mar 9	20:32	1.38172	3♓22
1855	Jan 25	17:46	1.38158	3♓21
1856	Dec 12	21:48	1.38162	3♓29
1858	Oct 30	16:28	1.38170	3♓24
1860	Sep 16	17:12	1.38137	3♓27
1862	Aug 4	23:03	1.38141	3♓37
1864	Jun 21	22:30	1.38166	3♓38
1866	May 9	17:46	1.38161	3♓34
1868	Mar 26	20:60	1.38152	3♓41
1870	Feb 11	18:46	1.38172	3♓40
1871	Dec 30	15:06	1.38148	3♓37
1873	Nov 16	19:51	1.38138	3♓46
1875	Oct 4	21:18	1.38158	3♓50
1877	Aug 21	17:31	1.38162	3♓47
1879	Jul 9	19:14	1.38147	3♓51
1881	May 26	20:40	1.38168	3♓56
1883	Apr 13	14:34	1.38157	3♓50
1885	Feb 28	17:55	1.38134	3♓57
1887	Jan 16	21:20	1.38152	4♓03
1888	Dec 3	17:39	1.38166	4♓01
1890	Oct 21	15:38	1.38149	4♓00
1892	Sep 7	20:47	1.38154	4♓10
1894	Jul 26	15:47	1.38161	4♓05
1896	Jun 12	16:38	1.38135	4♓08
1898	Apr 30	21:05	1.38142	4♓16
1900	Mar 18	19:09	1.38163	4♓16
1902	Feb 3	15:01	1.38154	4♓13
1903	Dec 22	18:50	1.38149	4♓20
1905	Nov 8	15:30	1.38166	4♓18
1907	Sep 26	13:22	1.38137	4♓17
1909	Aug 13	19:14	1.38131	4♓26
1911	Jul 1	20:31	1.38157	4♓30
1913	May 18	15:23	1.38160	4♓26
1915	Apr 5	16:42	1.38144	4♓30
1917	Feb 20	17:23	1.38163	4♓34
1919	Jan 8	12:15	1.38148	4♓29
1920	Nov 25	16:15	1.38129	4♓37
1922	Oct 13	19:21	1.38147	4♓43
1924	Aug 30	16:19	1.38159	4♓41
1926	Jul 18	15:31	1.38143	4♓42
1928	Jun 4	19:04	1.38155	4♓49
1930	Apr 22	12:48	1.38157	4♓43
1932	Mar 9	14:09	1.38128	4♓47
1934	Jan 25	18:49	1.38138	4♓56
1935	Dec 13	16:26	1.38159	4♓55
1937	Oct 30	12:31	1.38147	4♓52
1939	Sep 17	17:31	1.38142	5♓01
1941	Aug 4	14:05	1.38159	4♓58
1943	Jun 22	12:30	1.38133	4♓58

Mars in Aphelion

Year	Date	Time	Distance	Longitude
1839	Jan 30	8:07	1.66584	3♍06
1840	Dec 17	10:15	1.66575	3♍11
1842	Nov 4	9:50	1.66570	3♍12
1844	Sep 21	6:25	1.66576	3♍10
1846	Aug 9	7:17	1.66585	3♍13
1848	Jun 26	10:35	1.66584	3♍19
1850	May 14	7:31	1.66583	3♍18
1852	Mar 31	8:42	1.66580	3♍21
1854	Feb 16	10:05	1.66573	3♍25
1856	Jan 4	7:32	1.66570	3♍25
1857	Nov 21	4:44	1.66574	3♍23
1859	Oct 9	7:45	1.66589	3♍29
1861	Aug 26	7:23	1.66596	3♍31
1863	Jul 14	8:12	1.66588	3♍35
1865	May 31	9:54	1.66575	3♍38
1867	Apr 18	8:02	1.66573	3♍38
1869	Mar 5	4:39	1.66575	3♍36
1871	Jan 21	7:01	1.66586	3♍41
1872	Dec 8	7:38	1.66587	3♍44
1874	Oct 26	5:22	1.66589	3♍44
1876	Sep 12	7:60	1.66589	3♍49
1878	Jul 31	9:07	1.66581	3♍53
1880	Jun 17	5:32	1.66573	3♍51
1882	May 5	5:00	1.66582	3♍52
1884	Mar 22	7:37	1.66589	3♍57
1886	Feb 7	5:19	1.66590	3♍57
1887	Dec 26	7:03	1.66584	4♍01
1889	Nov 12	7:31	1.66577	4♍04
1891	Sep 30	4:30	1.66581	4♍03
1893	Aug 17	3:47	1.66590	4♍04
1895	Jul 5	7:45	1.66592	4♍11
1897	May 22	5:29	1.66590	4♍11
1899	Apr 9	5:29	1.66589	4♍13
1901	Feb 25	7:31	1.66582	4♍18
1903	Jan 13	5:54	1.66578	4♍18
1904	Nov 30	2:19	1.66579	4♍16
1906	Oct 18	4:25	1.66593	4♍19
1908	Sep 4	5:22	1.66602	4♍23
1910	Jul 23	5:05	1.66596	4♍25
1912	Jun 9	7:08	1.66583	4♍30
1914	Apr 27	6:06	1.66579	4♍31
1916	Mar 14	2:32	1.66581	4♍29
1918	Jan 30	3:23	1.66591	4♍32
1919	Dec 18	5:39	1.66594	4♍37
1921	Nov 4	2:38	1.66595	4♍36
1923	Sep 22	4:41	1.66596	4♍40
1925	Aug 9	6:45	1.66589	4♍45
1927	Jun 27	3:51	1.66580	4♍44
1929	May 14	1:44	1.66586	4♍43
1931	Apr 1	4:57	1.66596	4♍49
1933	Feb 16	3:01	1.66598	4♍50
1935	Jan 4	3:51	1.66593	4♍53
1936	Nov 21	5:06	1.66584	4♍57
1938	Oct 9	2:43	1.66586	4♍56
1940	Aug 26	0:43	1.66595	4♍55
1942	Jul 14	4:25	1.66598	5♍01
1944	May 31	3:43	1.66597	5♍03

Mars in Perihelion

Year	Date	Time	Distance	Longitude
1945	May 9	17:22	1.38130	5♓06
1947	Mar 27	17:18	1.38152	5♓08
1949	Feb 11	12:50	1.38151	5♓05
1950	Dec 30	15:19	1.38139	5♓11
1952	Nov 16	14:51	1.38160	5♓13
1954	Oct 4	10:20	1.38140	5♓09
1956	Aug 21	15:29	1.38123	5♓18
1958	Jul 9	18:33	1.38145	5♓24
1960	May 26	14:04	1.38156	5♓20
1962	Apr 13	13:07	1.38138	5♓21
1964	Feb 29	16:12	1.38151	5♓27
1966	Jan 16	10:20	1.38149	5♓22
1967	Dec 4	12:19	1.38123	5♓27
1969	Oct 21	16:25	1.38135	5♓35
1971	Sep 8	14:30	1.38152	5♓34
1973	Jul 26	11:39	1.38139	5♓32
1975	Jun 13	16:09	1.38141	5♓41
1977	Apr 30	11:22	1.38154	5♓36
1979	Mar 18	10:23	1.38125	5♓37
1981	Feb 2	15:48	1.38126	5♓46
1982	Dec 21	15:08	1.38151	5♓48
1984	Nov 7	10:13	1.38148	5♓44
1986	Sep 25	13:42	1.38133	5♓51
1988	Aug 12	13:04	1.38154	5♓52
1990	Jun 30	9:29	1.38133	5♓49
1992	May 17	14:04	1.38120	5♓58
1994	Apr 4	15:44	1.38141	6♓02
1996	Feb 20	11:20	1.38149	5♓59
1998	Jan 7	11:25	1.38133	6♓01
1999	Nov 25	13:27	1.38150	6♓06
2001	Oct 12	7:27	1.38141	6♓00
2003	Aug 30	11:05	1.38115	6♓07
2005	Jul 17	15:41	1.38130	6♓15
2007	Jun 4	12:38	1.38148	6♓13
2009	Apr 21	9:47	1.38133	6♓12
2011	Mar 9	14:07	1.38138	6♓20
2013	Jan 24	8:58	1.38149	6♓16
2014	Dec 12	8:27	1.38121	6♓17
2016	Oct 29	13:13	1.38124	6♓25
2018	Sep 16	12:54	1.38144	6♓27
2020	Aug 3	9:04	1.38138	6♓24
2022	Jun 21	13:08	1.38130	6♓32
2024	May 8	10:44	1.38150	6♓31
2026	Mar 26	7:09	1.38126	6♓29
2028	Feb 11	12:14	1.38116	6♓38
2029	Dec 29	13:17	1.38140	6♓41
2031	Nov 16	8:09	1.38145	6♓37
2033	Oct 3	9:15	1.38124	6♓41
2035	Aug 21	11:35	1.38141	6♓45
2037	Jul 8	6:53	1.38132	6♓41
2039	May 26	10:21	1.38111	6♓48
2041	Apr 12	13:36	1.38129	6♓54
2043	Feb 28	9:56	1.38144	6♓52
2045	Jan 15	7:43	1.38130	6♓51
2046	Dec 3	11:22	1.38138	6♓59
2048	Oct 20	5:38	1.38142	6♓54
2050	Sep 7	7:14	1.38111	6♓58

Mars in Aphelion

Year	Date	Time	Distance	Longitude
1946	Apr 18	2:23	1.66597	5♍04
1948	Mar 5	4:45	1.66591	5♍09
1950	Jan 21	4:09	1.66586	5♍10
1951	Dec 9	0:21	1.66584	5♍08
1953	Oct 26	0:58	1.66596	5♍11
1955	Sep 13	3:15	1.66607	5♍16
1957	Jul 31	2:12	1.66604	5♍17
1959	Jun 18	4:12	1.66592	5♍22
1961	May 5	4:03	1.66586	5♍23
1963	Mar 23	0:38	1.66586	5♍22
1965	Feb 6	23:51	1.66594	5♍23
1966	Dec 26	3:06	1.66600	5♍29
1968	Nov 12	0:15	1.66601	5♍28
1970	Sep 30	1:14	1.66603	5♍32
1972	Aug 17	4:02	1.66598	5♍37
1974	Jul 5	2:10	1.66589	5♍37
1976	May 21	22:60	1.66591	5♍35
1978	Apr 9	1:53	1.66603	5♍40
1980	Feb 25	1:14	1.66605	5♍42
1982	Jan 12	0:52	1.66602	5♍44
1983	Nov 30	2:42	1.66592	5♍48
1985	Oct 17	1:04	1.66591	5♍48
1987	Sep 3	22:16	1.66599	5♍48
1989	Jul 22	0:53	1.66604	5♍53
1991	Jun 9	1:58	1.66602	5♍56
1993	Apr 25	23:22	1.66604	5♍56
1995	Mar 14	1:34	1.66599	6♍01
1997	Jan 29	1:54	1.66592	6♍03
1998	Dec 16	22:21	1.66590	6♍01
2000	Nov 2	21:18	1.66599	6♍01
2002	Sep 21	0:34	1.66613	6♍07
2004	Aug 7	23:31	1.66614	6♍09
2006	Jun 26	1:09	1.66603	6♍13
2008	May 13	1:55	1.66594	6♍16
2010	Mar 30	23:09	1.66594	6♍15
2012	Feb 15	21:01	1.66598	6♍15
2014	Jan 3	0:25	1.66606	6♍21
2015	Nov 20	22:36	1.66606	6♍21
2017	Oct 7	22:08	1.66609	6♍23
2019	Aug 26	1:15	1.66606	6♍28
2021	Jul 13	0:27	1.66596	6♍29
2023	May 30	20:33	1.66594	6♍27
2025	Apr 16	22:13	1.66606	6♍31
2027	Mar 4	23:07	1.66610	6♍35
2029	Jan 19	21:32	1.66609	6♍36
2030	Dec 7	23:35	1.66601	6♍40
2032	Oct 24	22:54	1.66598	6♍41
2034	Sep 11	19:57	1.66605	6♍40
2036	Jul 29	21:17	1.66611	6♍43
2038	Jun 17	0:00	1.66611	6♍48
2040	May 3	21:00	1.66611	6♍47
2042	Mar 21	22:41	1.66607	6♍52
2044	Feb 6	23:56	1.66600	6♍55
2045	Dec 24	21:00	1.66596	6♍55
2047	Nov 11	18:27	1.66601	6♍54
2049	Sep 28	21:46	1.66617	6♍59

Moon Perigee/Apogee 1900–2020 • Distance in Kilometers

Year	Month	Day	Time	Distance
1900	Jan	3	17:05	P 362958
		19	16:33	A 405800
	Feb	1	0:00	P 358386
		16	1:01	A 406410
	Mar	1	12:07	P 356707
		15	1:19	A 406471
		29	23:29	P 358275
	Apr	11	10:06	A 405886
		27	4:29	P 362421
	May	9	2:13	A 404909
		24	17:34	P 367486
	Jun	5	20:54	A 404260
		19	2:28	P 369467
	Jul	3	15:23	A 404437
		15	13:40	P 365411
		31	8:40	A 405317
	Aug	12	11:01	P 360551
		27	22:27	A 406267
	Sep	9	18:35	P 357354
		24	4:09	A 406653
	Oct	8	5:18	P 356915
		21	6:38	A 406364
	Nov	5	16:08	P 359556
		17	18:37	A 405540
	Dec	3	19:51	P 364646
		15	13:30	A 404645
		30	15:38	P 369823
1901	Jan	12	10:52	A 404330
		24	11:35	P 368043
	Feb	9	7:22	A 404808
		21	2:35	P 362491
	Mar	8	23:35	A 405655
		21	10:01	P 358392
	Apr	5	6:41	A 406240
		18	21:12	P 357097
	May	2	8:16	A 406258
		17	6:41	P 358755
		29	17:37	A 405616
	Jun	14	11:07	P 362734
		26	9:09	A 404653
	Jul	11	23:44	P 367619
		24	3:09	A 404074
	Aug	6	8:08	P 369582
		20	22:19	A 404332
	Sep	1	19:34	P 365447
		17	16:36	A 405268
		29	18:08	P 360452
	Oct	15	7:11	A 406209
		28	2:55	P 357217
	Nov	11	11:56	A 406539
		25	15:53	P 356946
	Dec	8	14:15	A 406239
		24	2:57	P 359898
1902	Jan	5	3:46	A 405404
		21	5:28	P 365208
	Feb	1	23:49	A 404511
		16	17:54	P 370020
	Mar	1	20:54	A 404233
		13	20:41	P 367620
		29	16:16	A 404757
	Apr	10	13:03	P 362347
		26	7:16	A 405643
	May	8	19:32	P 358502
		23	14:36	A 406246
	Jun	6	4:53	P 357236
		19	16:56	A 406236
	Jul	4	14:05	P 358766
		17	1:25	A 405596
	Aug	1	18:27	P 362659
		13	16:25	A 404695
		29	7:31	P 367650
	Sep	10	10:35	A 404209
		23	13:04	P 369671
	Oct	8	6:19	A 404561
		20	1:50	P 365167
	Nov	5	1:34	A 405541
		17	2:35	P 359923
	Dec	2	15:60	A 406433
		15	13:33	P 356767
		29	18:45	A 406708
1903	Jan	13	2:31	P 356875
		25	22:15	A 406381
	Feb	10	13:12	P 360254
		22	13:05	A 405474
	Mar	10	12:44	P 365636
		22	8:35	A 404550
	Apr	5	18:37	P 369862
		19	4:27	A 404294
	May	1	5:09	P 367166
		16	22:49	A 404852
		28	21:31	P 362124
	Jun	13	13:05	A 405754
		26	2:20	P 358409
	Jul	10	20:30	A 406342
		24	11:37	P 357171
	Aug	6	22:52	A 406288
		21	21:03	P 358735
	Sep	3	7:05	A 405631
		19	1:52	P 362790
		30	22:39	A 404747
	Oct	16	15:23	P 368031
		28	18:00	A 404288
	Nov	10	14:04	P 369692
		25	14:49	A 404647
	Dec	7	8:51	P 364631
		23	10:11	A 405572
1904	Jan	4	12:27	P 359435
		19	22:52	A 406366
	Feb	2	0:00	P 356722
		16	0:25	A 406601
	Mar	1	12:53	P 357328
		14	6:02	A 406203
		29	21:51	P 360870
	Apr	10	21:39	A 405218
		26	18:42	P 366017
	May	8	16:25	A 404300
		22	22:10	P 369767
	Jun	5	11:22	A 404105
		17	12:40	P 367089
	Jul	3	5:07	A 404727
		15	4:04	P 362198
		30	20:07	A 405665
	Aug	12	9:16	P 358486
		27	4:16	A 406236
	Sep	9	19:22	P 357186
		23	5:58	A 406152
	Oct	8	5:37	P 358797
		20	14:15	A 405507
	Nov	5	12:08	P 363073
		17	6:48	A 404656
	Dec	3	0:00	P 368539
		15	3:25	A 404243
		27	17:01	P 369543
1905	Jan	12	0:48	A 404635
		23	18:40	P 364177
	Feb	8	19:47	A 405554
		20	23:46	P 359237
	Mar	8	7:00	A 406334
		21	10:45	P 356877
	Apr	4	8:55	A 406559
		18	22:15	P 357612
	May	1	15:30	A 406109
		17	4:59	P 361052
		29	6:02	A 405135
	Jun	14	0:36	P 365989
		25	23:59	A 404303
	Jul	10	5:07	P 369648
		23	18:33	A 404212
	Aug	4	19:44	P 367044
		20	12:43	A 404926
	Sep	1	11:08	P 362024
		17	4:22	A 405906
		29	17:17	P 358117
	Oct	14	12:28	A 406443
		28	4:08	P 356804
	Nov	10	12:58	A 406329
		25	16:02	P 358703
	Dec	7	22:14	A 405683
		23	22:22	P 363401
1906	Jan	4	16:08	A 404819
		20	5:39	P 368940
	Feb	1	13:09	A 404402
		13	22:12	P 368976
	Mar	1	9:41	A 404791
		13	4:33	P 363584
		29	2:44	A 405695
	Apr	10	9:16	P 358979
		25	12:42	A 406462
	May	8	19:16	P 356891
		22	15:19	A 406652
	Jun	6	4:47	P 357734
		18	22:16	A 406143
	Jul	4	11:12	P 361151
		16	12:12	A 405161
	Aug	1	6:45	P 366073
		13	5:38	A 404364
		27	9:42	P 369753
	Sep	10	0:40	A 404326
		22	0:14	P 366862
	Oct	7	19:58	A 405065
		19	17:57	P 361588
	Nov	4	11:54	A 405997
		17	1:31	P 357698
	Dec	1	18:15	A 406442
		15	14:23	P 356751
		28	18:29	A 406299
1907	Jan	13	2:10	P 359143
		25	6:01	A 405587
	Feb	10	7:01	P 364105
		22	0:53	A 404653
	Mar	9	8:25	P 369287
		21	21:45	A 404218
	Apr	3	4:53	P 368532
		18	17:04	A 404620
		30	13:35	P 363405
	May	16	9:05	A 405539
		28	17:25	P 359125
	Jun	12	19:01	A 406307
		26	2:02	P 357157
	Jul	9	22:18	A 406463
		24	11:54	P 357945
	Aug	6	4:57	A 405935
		21	18:53	P 361296
	Sep	2	18:55	A 404986
		18	15:22	P 366317
		30	13:02	A 404256
	Oct	14	14:19	P 370091
		28	9:14	A 404294
	Nov	9	5:54	P 366698
		25	5:21	A 405071
	Dec	7	2:32	P 361235
		22	21:24	A 405965
1908	Jan	4	12:33	P 357524
		19	2:11	A 406364
	Feb	2	1:26	P 356925
		15	3:19	A 406203
	Mar	1	12:40	P 359580
		13	16:02	A 405437
		29	14:58	P 364484
	Apr	10	10:23	A 404513
		25	12:18	P 369244
	May	8	5:46	A 404158
		20	13:37	P 368283
	Jun	5	0:15	A 404657
		16	22:02	P 363368
	Jul	2	16:27	A 405647
		15	0:34	P 359099
		30	3:05	A 406438
	Aug	12	9:29	P 357004
		26	6:23	A 406570
	Sep	9	19:56	P 357716
		22	12:07	A 406043
	Oct	8	3:25	P 361228
		20	2:11	A 405134
	Nov	5	0:19	P 366586
		16	21:40	A 404457
		30	15:19	P 370233
	Dec	14	18:49	A 404532
		26	13:30	P 366112
1909	Jan	11	14:46	A 405292
		23	13:11	P 360621
	Feb	8	4:56	A 406125
		20	23:35	P 357249
	Mar	7	8:09	A 406499
		21	11:19	P 357064
	Apr	3	11:05	A 406281
		18	20:36	P 359900
	May	1	0:00	A 405445
		16	20:40	P 364691
		28	17:31	A 404525
	Jun	12	15:58	P 369152
		25	12:02	A 404220
	Jul	7	20:04	P 368087
		23	6:13	A 404768
	Aug	4	3:57	P 363177
		19	22:42	A 405777
	Sep	1	7:06	P 358837
		16	9:26	A 406527
		29	17:03	P 356757
	Oct	13	11:37	A 406599
		28	4:20	P 357708
	Nov	9	17:51	A 406047
		25	13:22	P 361624
	Dec	7	9:42	A 405106
		23	8:46	P 367256
1910	Jan	4	6:14	A 404397
		17	13:21	P 370191
	Feb	1	3:34	A 404443
		12	22:11	P 365540
		28	22:41	A 405162
	Mar	12	23:25	P 360385
		28	11:08	A 405959
	Apr	10	8:37	P 357482
		24	14:15	A 406312
	May	8	19:35	P 357521
		21	18:32	A 406033
	Jun	6	3:11	P 360291
		18	7:05	A 405176
	Jul	4	2:46	P 364894
		16	0:00	A 404307
		30	22:22	P 369285
	Aug	12	18:47	A 404080
		25	1:22	P 368190
	Sep	9	13:45	A 404702
		21	10:20	P 363130
	Oct	7	7:09	A 405741
		19	15:13	P 358678
	Nov	3	18:06	A 406446
		17	2:28	P 356665
		30	18:57	A 406479
	Dec	15	15:36	P 357891
		28	2:22	A 405921
1911	Jan	13	0:00	P 362108
		24	19:48	A 404964
	Feb	9	16:29	P 367748
		21	16:33	A 404273
	Mar	6	16:55	P 369895
		21	13:01	A 404370
	Apr	2	8:06	P 365236
		18	6:40	A 405139
		30	8:52	P 360393
	May	15	18:44	A 405973
		28	17:21	P 357618
	Jun	11	22:40	A 406322
		26	2:43	P 357576
	Jul	9	2:52	A 406019
		24	10:29	P 360224
	Aug	5	14:33	A 405194
		21	10:32	P 364845
	Sep	2	7:09	A 404402
		17	6:03	P 369427
		30	2:21	A 404274
	Oct	12	6:31	P 368098
		27	22:40	A 404971
	Nov	8	18:15	P 362673
		24	16:29	A 406003
	Dec	7	0:45	P 358123
		22	1:60	A 406635
1912	Jan	4	13:37	P 356381
		18	2:02	A 406642
	Feb	2	1:57	P 358054
		14	11:11	A 406025
	Mar	1	8:55	P 362557
		13	4:47	A 405006
		28	20:60	P 367981
	Apr	10	0:38	A 404317
		22	22:21	P 369439
	May	7	20:06	A 404448
		19	16:51	P 364911
	Jun	4	12:44	A 405246
		16	16:35	P 360249
	Jul	2	0:31	A 406085
		15	0:00	P 357522
		29	4:50	A 406400
	Aug	12	9:30	P 357502
		25	8:32	A 406061
	Sep	9	18:01	P 360252
		21	20:25	A 405235
	Oct	7	18:59	P 365116
		19	14:02	A 404463
	Nov	3	10:52	P 369840
		16	10:29	A 404353
		28	10:47	P 367752
	Dec	14	7:12	A 405029
		26	2:39	P 362082
1913	Jan	11	0:23	A 405977
		23	11:20	P 357837
	Feb	7	7:44	A 406536
		21	0:00	P 356609
	Mar	6	8:38	A 406507
		21	11:28	P 358634
	Apr	2	19:35	A 405796
		18	16:19	P 363082
		30	12:57	A 404742
	May	16	1:24	P 368139
		28	7:52	A 404096
	Jun	10	4:58	P 369296
		25	2:24	A 404299
	Jul	6	23:59	P 364928
		22	19:31	A 405154
	Aug	3	23:23	P 360317
		19	8:05	A 406005
	Sep	1	6:59	P 357543
		15	12:20	A 406285
		29	18:04	P 357502
	Oct	12	15:27	A 405934
		28	3:28	P 360402
	Nov	9	4:02	A 405131
		25	4:57	P 365548
	Dec	6	23:19	A 404395
		21	14:13	P 370217
1914	Jan	3	20:44	A 404325
		15	18:18	P 367327
		31	17:17	A 405015
	Feb	12	13:34	P 361726

Moon Perigee/Apogee 1900–2020 • Distance in Kilometers

		28	9:11	A 405953
	Mar	12	22:32	P 357826
		27	15:34	A 406511
	Apr	10	9:50	P 356854
		23	17:50	A 406447
	May	8	19:49	P 358866
		21	4:29	A 405707
	Jun	5	23:08	P 363139
		17	20:55	A 404706
	Jul	3	7:40	P 368044
		15	15:07	A 404159
		28	12:02	P 369243
	Aug	12	9:43	A 404464
		24	6:24	P 364830
	Sep	9	3:20	A 405393
		21	6:23	P 360015
	Oct	6	16:38	A 406244
		19	15:46	P 357114
	Nov	2	19:43	A 406474
		17	3:35	P 357225
		29	22:44	A 406115
	Dec	15	14:07	P 360537
		27	12:47	A 405296
1915	Jan	12	13:58	P 366013
		24	8:39	A 404543
	Feb	7	13:18	P 370206
		21	5:44	A 404473
	Mar	5	3:01	P 366663
		21	0:58	A 405159
	Apr	1	23:50	P 361294
		17	15:22	A 406083
		30	7:08	P 357723
	May	14	21:18	A 406626
		28	17:27	P 356928
	Jun	11	0:33	A 406507
		26	1:50	P 358966
	Jul	8	10:50	A 405730
		24	4:56	P 363221
	Aug	5	2:35	A 404745
		20	13:54	P 368176
	Sep	1	21:17	A 404244
		14	15:28	P 369255
		29	16:41	A 404591
	Oct	11	12:08	P 364493
		27	11:01	A 405511
	Nov	8	14:19	P 359533
		23	23:40	A 406278
	Dec	7	0:58	P 356839
		21	0:55	A 406444
1916	Jan	4	14:18	P 357438
		17	5:30	A 406048
	Feb	2	0:00	P 361165
		13	21:32	A 405145
		29	20:54	P 366635
	Mar	12	17:35	A 404346
		26	13:11	P 370055
	Apr	9	13:41	A 404284
		21	11:41	P 366325
	May	7	7:42	A 404994
		19	7:50	P 361305
	Jun	3	21:33	A 405934
		16	14:40	P 357948
	Jul	1	4:12	A 406462
		15	0:01	P 357155
		28	7:29	A 406308
	Aug	12	9:13	P 359119
		24	17:29	A 405538
	Sep	9	13:18	P 363393
		21	9:36	A 404604
	Oct	6	22:23	P 368535
		19	5:02	A 404178
		31	18:39	P 369344
	Nov	16	1:41	A 404590
		27	19:48	P 364165
	Dec	13	20:53	A 405509
		26	0:11	P 359218
1917	Jan	10	8:26	A 406219
		23	12:30	P 356842
	Feb	6	8:43	A 406367
		21	0:56	P 357768
	Mar	5	15:09	A 405925
		21	9:03	P 361604
	Apr	2	7:06	A 404992
		18	2:45	P 366834
		30	2:05	A 404248
	May	13	18:31	P 369793
		27	21:25	A 404282
	Jun	8	20:25	P 366205
		24	14:59	A 405079
	Jul	6	15:42	P 361295
		22	5:09	A 406072
	Aug	3	22:05	P 357838
		18	12:22	A 406596
	Sep	1	7:43	P 356924
		14	14:54	A 406419
		29	17:53	P 358932
	Oct	12	0:32	A 405669
		27	22:49	P 363498
	Nov	8	17:43	A 404777
		24	5:51	P 368922
	Dec	6	14:18	A 404394
		18	22:13	P 369015
1918	Jan	3	11:21	A 404816
		15	4:58	P 363494
		31	5:19	A 405691
	Feb	12	11:13	P 358759
		27	14:46	A 406355
	Mar	12	22:58	P 356787
		26	15:23	A 406479
	Apr	10	9:44	P 358028
		22	23:11	A 405957
	May	8	15:50	P 361888
		20	14:35	A 404989
	Jun	5	7:34	P 366912
		17	8:36	A 404279
		30	23:19	P 369625
	Jul	15	3:07	A 404369
		27	2:22	P 366035
	Aug	11	21:07	A 405206
		23	22:01	P 361052
	Sep	8	11:41	A 406187
		21	4:38	P 357545
	Oct	5	18:16	A 406645
		19	16:08	P 356762
	Nov	1	20:04	A 406427
		17	3:05	P 359127
		29	7:11	A 405649
	Dec	15	8:17	P 364093
		27	1:51	A 404719
1919	Jan	11	10:11	P 369485
		23	23:29	A 404305
	Feb	5	3:09	P 368528
		20	19:59	A 404694
	Mar	4	14:52	P 363062
		20	12:22	A 405532
	Apr	1	21:08	P 358778
		16	20:34	A 406176
		30	7:14	P 357168
	May	13	22:18	A 406263
		28	17:17	P 358463
	Jun	10	6:27	A 405690
		25	22:33	P 362168
	Jul	7	21:28	A 404742
		23	14:16	P 367061
	Aug	4	15:16	A 404100
		18	5:14	P 369793
	Sep	1	10:16	A 404271
		13	8:02	P 366068
		29	5:05	A 405169
	Oct	11	4:47	P 360915
		26	20:42	A 406143
	Nov	8	13:51	P 357379
		23	2:29	A 406541
	Dec	7	2:28	P 356784
		20	3:54	A 406310
1920	Jan	4	14:33	P 359480
		16	16:45	A 405512
	Feb	1	18:16	P 364640
		13	12:12	A 404575
		28	13:32	P 369694
	Mar	12	9:02	A 404201
		24	11:58	P 368121
	Apr	9	4:23	A 404652
		21	0:41	P 362922
	May	6	20:04	A 405540
		19	5:48	P 358872
	Jun	3	4:32	A 406207
		16	15:15	P 357260
		30	6:58	A 406271
	Jul	15	0:09	P 358421
		27	14:15	A 405697
	Aug	12	5:39	P 362073
		24	4:25	A 404806
	Sep	8	22:30	P 367106
		20	22:49	A 404254
	Oct	4	9:49	P 369923
		18	18:48	A 404513
		30	14:33	P 365755
	Nov	15	14:27	A 405447
		27	13:59	P 360350
	Dec	13	5:30	A 406370
		26	0:11	P 356911
1921	Jan	9	9:12	A 406711
		23	13:39	P 356730
	Feb	5	11:46	A 406450
		21	0:05	P 359824
	Mar	5	1:45	A 405575
		21	1:00	P 365042
	Apr	1	21:02	A 404605
		16	15:07	P 369591
		29	16:40	A 404257
	May	11	20:14	P 367702
		27	10:48	A 404745
	Jun	8	8:43	P 362711
		24	1:44	A 405656
	Jul	6	12:53	P 358754
		21	10:29	A 406309
	Aug	3	21:57	P 357146
		17	12:46	A 406329
	Sep	1	7:19	P 358372
		13	19:52	A 405736
		29	13:54	P 362219
	Oct	11	10:45	A 404852
		27	6:34	P 367532
	Nov	8	6:07	A 404318
		21	9:45	P 370008
	Dec	6	3:10	A 404580
		17	21:40	P 365196
1922	Jan	2	23:07	A 405459
		15	0:00	P 359857
		30	12:27	A 406289
	Feb	12	10:58	P 356897
		26	14:42	A 406592
	Mar	12	23:44	P 357173
		25	19:32	A 406262
	Apr	10	8:29	P 360414
		22	10:05	A 405311
	May	8	7:08	P 365400
		20	4:19	A 404356
	Jun	3	19:10	P 369554
		16	23:27	A 404076
		29	3:12	P 367654
	Jul	14	17:26	A 404634
		26	15:31	P 362769
	Aug	11	8:59	A 405584
		23	19:52	P 358780
	Sep	7	18:20	A 406222
		21	5:25	P 357124
	Oct	4	19:52	A 406207
		19	16:47	P 358418
	Nov	1	3:03	A 405623
		17	0:00	P 362510
		28	19:28	A 404764
	Dec	14	15:40	P 368056
		26	16:05	A 404264
1923	Jan	8	11:41	P 369877
		23	13:29	A 404557
	Feb	4	7:07	P 364736
		20	8:22	A 405440
	Mar	4	10:46	P 359677
		19	20:28	A 406268
	Apr	1	21:33	P 357034
		15	23:07	A 406565
		30	8:18	P 357427
	May	13	4:46	A 406188
		28	15:59	P 360549
	Jun	9	18:30	A 405249
		25	13:38	P 365362
	Jul	7	11:46	A 404373
		22	2:03	P 369472
	Aug	4	6:17	A 404197
		16	9:49	P 367613
	Sep	1	0:50	A 404851
		12	22:31	P 362553
		28	17:28	A 405841
	Oct	11	3:31	P 358366
		26	2:39	A 406439
	Nov	8	15:02	P 356723
		22	2:54	A 406390
	Dec	7	2:51	P 358334
		19	11:03	A 405796
1924	Jan	4	10:15	P 362865
		16	4:32	A 404911
		31	21:34	P 368471
	Feb	13	1:21	A 404402
		25	15:50	P 369340
	Mar	11	22:06	A 404695
		23	17:13	P 364166
	Apr	8	15:19	A 405571
		20	20:25	P 359424
	May	6	2:07	A 406390
		19	5:11	P 357034
	Jun	2	5:26	A 406655
		16	15:12	P 357512
		29	11:14	A 406222
	Jul	14	22:16	P 360624
		27	0:17	A 405275
	Aug	11	20:06	P 365466
		23	17:45	A 404431
	Sep	7	7:07	P 369656
		20	12:54	A 404301
	Oct	2	14:05	P 367447
		18	8:21	A 404976
		30	4:57	P 362091
	Nov	15	1:06	A 405916
		27	12:34	P 357938
	Dec	12	8:38	A 406419
		26	0:59	P 356681
1925	Jan	8	8:23	A 406339
		23	13:32	P 358803
	Feb	4	19:05	A 405673
		20	19:13	P 363562
	Mar	4	13:31	A 404712
		20	1:03	P 368831
	Apr	1	9:46	A 404192
		13	22:06	P 368950
		29	5:01	A 404513
	May	11	1:32	P 364015
		26	21:39	A 405418
	Jun	8	3:44	P 359564
		23	8:36	A 406242
	Jul	6	12:21	P 357267
		20	12:28	A 406478
	Aug	3	22:22	P 357678
		16	17:59	A 406025
	Sep	1	5:46	P 360758
		13	7:03	A 405108
		29	4:44	P 365730
	Oct	11	1:03	A 404330
		25	12:29	P 370048
	Nov	7	21:47	A 404273
		19	19:39	P 367260
	Dec	5	18:13	A 404983
		17	14:17	P 361712
1926	Jan	2	10:42	A 405886
		14	23:46	P 357756
		29	16:26	A 406348
	Feb	12	12:28	P 356870
		25	17:11	A 406249
	Mar	12	23:45	P 359211
		25	4:51	A 405529
	Apr	10	2:36	P 363899
		21	22:50	A 404583
	May	7	5:39	P 368801
		19	17:55	A 404145
	Jun	1	6:23	P 368728
		16	12:23	A 404564
		28	9:37	P 363979
	Jul	14	4:51	A 405546
		26	11:13	P 359508
	Aug	10	16:37	A 406397
		23	19:54	P 357060
	Sep	6	20:21	A 406605
		21	6:09	P 357425
	Oct	4	1:05	A 406149
		19	15:08	P 360697
		31	14:41	A 405260
	Nov	16	14:17	P 366030
		28	9:50	A 404520
	Dec	12	13:44	P 370255
		26	7:05	A 404491
1927	Jan	7	2:50	P 366657
		23	3:15	A 405184
	Feb	4	0:31	P 361100
		19	18:08	A 406034
	Mar	4	10:08	P 357509
		18	22:17	A 406471
	Apr	1	22:02	P 356995
		15	0:45	A 406319
		30	6:56	P 359506
	May	12	12:35	A 405530
		28	8:25	P 364092
	Jun	9	5:23	A 404589
		24	9:56	P 368764
	Jul	7	0:00	A 404204
		19	12:14	P 368580
	Aug	3	18:26	A 404674
		15	15:44	P 363784
		31	11:19	A 405673
	Sep	12	17:51	P 359210
		27	23:10	A 406480
	Oct	11	3:11	P 356787
		25	1:49	A 406622
	Nov	8	15:27	P 357421
		21	6:50	A 406139
	Dec	7	0:50	P 361117
		18	22:25	A 405211
1928	Jan	3	22:55	P 366722
		15	18:55	A 404428
		29	11:25	P 370299
	Feb	12	16:10	A 404370
		24	11:24	P 366113
	Mar	11	11:07	A 405033
		23	10:33	P 360900
	Apr	8	0:20	A 405861

Moon Perigee/Apogee 1900–2020 • Distance in Kilometers

		20	19:25	P 357737
	May	5	4:39	A 406281
		19	5:31	P 357424
	Jun	1	8:04	A 406075
		16	14:01	P 359858
		28	19:41	A 405269
	Jul	14	15:12	P 364281
		26	12:04	A 404376
	Aug	10	16:55	P 368932
		23	6:36	A 404069
	Sep	4	17:19	P 368713
		20	1:54	A 404620
	Oct	1	22:08	P 363707
		17	20:13	A 405650
		30	1:43	P 359008
	Nov	14	8:11	A 406411
		27	13:29	P 356683
	Dec	11	9:18	A 406512
		26	2:22	P 357605
1929	Jan	7	15:37	A 406018
		23	11:52	P 361604
	Feb	4	8:21	A 405063
		20	6:27	P 367190
	Mar	4	4:46	A 404300
		17	14:15	P 370042
	Apr	1	1:04	A 404303
		12	21:32	P 365823
		28	19:09	A 405027
	May	10	20:11	P 360901
		26	7:55	A 405897
	Jun	8	3:18	P 357836
		22	12:58	A 406320
	Jul	6	13:06	P 357428
		19	16:17	A 406090
	Aug	3	21:25	P 359747
		16	2:53	A 405313
		31	23:13	P 364226
	Sep	12	19:24	A 404492
		28	0:51	P 369106
	Oct	10	14:42	A 404275
		22	21:56	P 368619
	Nov	7	11:02	A 404892
		19	5:44	P 363206
	Dec	5	5:26	A 405914
		17	11:60	P 358438
1930	Jan	1	15:55	A 406602
		15	0:13	P 356397
		28	16:05	A 406675
	Feb	12	13:05	P 357779
		25	0:17	A 406116
	Mar	12	20:34	P 362026
		24	17:25	A 405095
	Apr	9	11:20	P 367414
		21	12:54	A 404333
	May	4	18:42	P 369648
		19	7:55	A 404376
		31	5:29	P 365522
	Jun	16	0:55	A 405138
		28	3:06	P 360743
	Jul	13	13:47	A 406015
		26	10:03	P 357707
	Aug	9	18:56	A 406403
		23	20:01	P 357312
	Sep	5	21:51	A 406136
		21	4:46	P 359770
	Oct	3	8:45	A 405352
		19	7:38	P 364532
		31	2:09	A 404544
	Nov	15	6:33	P 369582
		27	23:04	A 404339
	Dec	10	1:33	P 368274
		25	19:59	A 404930
1931	Jan	6	14:45	P 362610
		22	13:30	A 405869
	Feb	3	22:39	P 358160
		18	21:43	A 406489
	Mar	4	10:42	P 356646
		17	22:40	A 406528
	Apr	1	22:18	P 358331
		14	8:30	A 405880
		30	3:24	P 362516
	May	12	1:07	A 404831
		27	16:27	P 367579
	Jun	8	19:60	A 404118
		22	0:59	P 369557
	Jul	6	14:33	A 404235
		18	12:19	P 365548
	Aug	3	7:51	A 405058
		15	9:49	P 360784
		30	21:32	A 405954
	Sep	12	17:33	P 357679
		27	2:48	A 406303
	Oct	11	4:21	P 357286
		24	4:52	A 406021
	Nov	8	15:04	P 359925
		20	16:48	A 405254
	Dec	6	18:11	P 364976
		18	11:40	A 404469
1932	Jan	2	10:56	P 369988
		15	9:02	A 404297
		27	8:49	P 367840
	Feb	12	5:39	A 404911
		24	1:13	P 362254
	Mar	10	22:07	A 405854
		23	9:05	P 358159
	Apr	7	5:38	A 406480
		20	20:26	P 356857
	May	4	7:47	A 406488
		19	5:54	P 358521
		31	17:20	A 405812
	Jun	16	10:17	P 362542
		28	8:51	A 404812
	Jul	13	22:58	P 367497
		26	2:49	A 404197
	Aug	8	7:40	P 369536
		22	21:55	A 404418
	Sep	3	18:53	P 365431
		19	16:02	A 405313
	Oct	1	17:24	P 360433
		17	6:10	A 406204
		30	2:03	P 357211
	Nov	13	10:09	A 406499
		27	14:42	P 357012
	Dec	10	12:04	A 406203
		26	1:18	P 360078
1933	Jan	7	1:25	A 405409
		23	2:45	P 365453
	Feb	3	21:18	A 404597
		18	10:54	P 370037
	Mar	3	18:12	A 404422
		15	17:32	P 367199
		31	13:21	A 405037
	Apr	12	11:09	P 361853
		28	4:04	A 405976
	May	10	17:51	P 358050
		25	11:16	A 406589
	Jun	8	3:13	P 356902
		21	14:10	A 406547
	Jul	6	12:24	P 358591
		18	23:27	A 405836
	Aug	3	16:45	P 362621
		15	14:43	A 404848
		31	5:29	P 367678
	Sep	12	9:05	A 404273
		25	10:20	P 369617
	Oct	10	4:47	A 404533
		22	0:07	P 365074
	Nov	6	23:56	A 405418
		19	1:05	P 359921
	Dec	4	13:25	A 406220
		17	12:03	P 356948
		31	15:11	A 406448
1934	Jan	15	0:58	P 357244
		27	18:56	A 406114
	Feb	12	11:20	P 360722
		24	10:07	A 405228
	Mar	12	9:48	P 366063
		24	5:42	A 404374
	Apr	7	11:20	P 369967
		21	1:36	A 404221
	May	3	1:37	P 366903
		18	20:01	A 404872
		30	19:19	P 361871
	Jun	15	10:25	A 405833
		28	0:40	P 358244
	Jul	12	18:09	A 406436
		26	10:18	P 357094
	Aug	8	21:08	A 406360
		23	20:02	P 358711
	Sep	5	5:60	A 405654
		21	1:02	P 362795
	Oct	2	21:57	A 404715
		18	14:29	P 368067
		30	17:29	A 404209
	Nov	12	12:43	P 369735
		27	14:23	A 404527
	Dec	9	7:52	P 364718
		25	9:43	A 405412
1935	Jan	6	11:39	P 359605
		21	22:09	A 406165
	Feb	3	23:36	P 356951
		17	23:02	A 406377
	Mar	4	11:53	P 357575
		17	4:30	A 405997
	Apr	1	20:21	P 361117
		13	19:47	A 405083
		29	16:07	P 366232
	May	11	14:19	A 404284
		25	16:25	P 369752
	Jun	8	9:10	A 404229
		20	9:58	P 366797
	Jul	6	2:59	A 404975
		18	2:27	P 361837
	Aug	2	18:07	A 405993
		15	8:02	P 358098
		30	2:27	A 406591
	Sep	12	18:16	P 356817
		26	4:35	A 406488
	Oct	11	4:29	P 358514
		23	13:14	A 405794
	Nov	8	10:51	P 362926
		20	5:55	A 404885
	Dec	5	22:22	P 368488
		18	2:32	A 404411
		30	15:15	P 369421
1936	Jan	15	0:00	A 404736
		26	17:33	P 364042
	Feb	11	18:11	A 405578
		23	22:37	P 359156
	Mar	10	4:27	A 406289
		23	9:17	P 356914
	Apr	6	5:39	A 406479
		20	20:23	P 357807
	May	3	12:14	A 406022
		19	2:32	P 361371
		31	2:44	A 405076
	Jun	15	21:15	P 366318
		27	20:40	A 404312
	Jul	11	20:60	P 369660
		25	15:11	A 404311
	Aug	6	15:48	P 366654
		22	9:17	A 405097
	Sep	3	8:39	P 361580
		19	0:47	A 406104
	Oct	1	15:17	P 357771
		16	8:35	A 406629
		30	2:26	P 356641
	Nov	12	9:42	A 406481
		27	14:32	P 358732
	Dec	9	20:03	A 405756
		25	20:53	P 363546
1937	Jan	6	14:33	A 404794
		22	3:21	P 369081
	Feb	3	11:47	A 404283
		15	19:43	P 368970
	Mar	3	8:14	A 404585
		15	2:54	P 363641
		31	1:00	A 405408
	Apr	12	7:45	P 359199
		27	10:25	A 406107
	May	10	17:47	P 357271
		24	12:32	A 406264
	Jun	8	3:16	P 358201
		20	19:30	A 405763
	Jul	6	9:26	P 361623
		18	9:32	A 404836
	Aug	3	4:05	P 366477
		15	3:05	A 404142
		29	3:16	P 369882
	Sep	11	22:34	A 404226
		23	21:17	P 366680
	Oct	9	17:49	A 405073
		21	16:07	P 361401
	Nov	6	10:07	A 406071
		19	0:21	P 357567
	Dec	3	16:49	A 406535
		17	13:36	P 356668
		30	17:38	A 406373
1938	Jan	15	1:31	P 359085
		27	5:36	A 405619
	Feb	12	6:19	P 364074
		24	0:37	A 404649
	Mar	11	7:37	P 369287
		23	21:28	A 404184
	Apr	5	4:10	P 368582
		20	16:45	A 404554
	May	2	12:50	P 363516
		18	8:37	A 405436
		30	16:38	P 359270
	Jun	14	18:15	A 406165
		28	1:06	P 357311
	Jul	11	20:59	A 406302
		26	10:41	P 358116
	Aug	8	3:08	A 405798
		23	17:13	P 361505
	Sep	4	16:46	A 404922
		20	12:40	P 366540
	Oct	2	10:46	A 404307
		16	7:46	P 370060
		30	6:57	A 404474
	Nov	11	3:20	P 366333
		27	3:03	A 405354
	Dec	9	1:04	P 360795
		24	18:55	A 406298
1939	Jan	6	11:20	P 357106
		20	23:25	A 406705
	Feb	4	0:13	P 356615
		17	1:27	A 406510
	Mar	4	11:18	P 359427
		16	14:38	A 405672
	Apr	1	13:22	P 364451
		13	9:08	A 404668
		28	10:04	P 369229
	May	11	4:29	A 404234
		23	11:52	P 368201
	Jun	7	23:01	A 404650
		19	20:34	P 363306
	Jul	5	14:29	A 405556
		17	23:30	P 359119
	Aug	2	0:18	A 406271
		15	7:49	P 357164
		29	2:51	A 406363
	Sep	12	18:08	P 358038
		25	8:39	A 405837
	Oct	11	1:20	P 361661
		22	23:14	A 404963
	Nov	7	21:20	P 367004
		19	18:39	A 404356
	Dec	3	7:03	P 370223
		17	15:52	A 404516
		29	10:24	P 365765
1940	Jan	14	11:47	A 405341
		26	11:12	P 360319
	Feb	11	1:51	A 406202
		23	22:02	P 357101
	Mar	9	5:12	A 406574
		23	10:02	P 357062
	Apr	5	9:05	A 406314
		20	19:30	P 359975
	May	2	22:48	A 405408
		18	19:38	P 364781
		30	16:34	A 404421
	Jun	14	14:46	P 369239
		27	11:13	A 404056
	Jul	9	18:40	P 368186
		25	5:26	A 404548
	Aug	6	2:43	P 363349
		21	21:54	A 405501
	Sep	3	6:01	P 359108
		18	8:25	A 406202
	Oct	1	16:06	P 357100
		15	10:04	A 406254
		30	3:24	P 358072
	Nov	11	16:05	A 405733
		27	12:08	P 361971
	Dec	9	7:54	A 404874
		25	6:22	P 367539
1941	Jan	6	4:25	A 404294
		19	7:55	P 370123
	Feb	3	1:47	A 404486
		14	20:19	P 365300
	Mar	2	21:04	A 405325
		14	22:18	P 360141
		30	9:48	A 406194
	Apr	12	7:46	P 357235
		26	13:27	A 406565
	May	10	18:48	P 357270
		23	18:09	A 406261
	Jun	8	2:21	P 360064
		20	6:46	A 405366
	Jul	6	1:54	P 364727
		17	23:51	A 404459
	Aug	1	21:40	P 369192
		14	18:24	A 404195
		27	0:44	P 368155
	Sep	11	13:15	A 404778
		23	9:37	P 363101
	Oct	9	6:23	A 405770
		21	14:25	P 358650
	Nov	5	16:40	A 406427
		19	1:28	P 356677
	Dec	2	16:50	A 406441
		17	14:12	P 358008
		30	0:02	A 405902
1942	Jan	14	22:20	P 362339
		26	17:18	A 405002
	Feb	11	12:34	P 367961
		23	13:52	A 404404
	Mar	8	10:52	P 369634
		23	10:09	A 404601
	Apr	4	5:42	P 364760
		20	3:35	A 405446
	May	2	7:03	P 359904
		17	15:23	A 406311
		30	15:39	P 357213

Moon Perigee/Apogee 1900–2020 • Distance in Kilometers

Year	Month	Day	Time	Distance
	Jun	13	19:25	A 406651
		28	1:03	P 357316
	Jul	11	0:22	A 406296
		26	8:48	P 360125
	Aug	7	12:37	A 405389
		23	8:46	P 364859
	Sep	4	5:33	A 404508
		19	3:25	P 369449
	Oct	2	0:52	A 404290
		14	4:23	P 368005
		29	21:02	A 404891
	Nov	10	16:40	P 362610
		26	14:22	A 405827
	Dec	8	23:44	P 358207
		23	22:46	A 406385
1943	Jan	6	12:05	P 356664
		19	22:21	A 406369
	Feb	4	0:17	P 358487
		16	8:03	A 405754
	Mar	4	6:43	P 363027
		16	1:53	A 404780
		31	16:49	P 368325
	Apr	12	22:05	A 404180
		25	16:25	P 369305
	May	10	17:15	A 404416
		22	14:04	P 364638
	Jun	7	9:59	A 405295
		19	14:37	P 360034
	Jul	4	21:60	A 406173
		17	22:41	P 357401
	Aug	1	2:43	A 406487
		15	8:22	P 357452
		28	7:07	A 406112
	Sep	12	17:07	P 360243
		24	19:32	A 405232
	Oct	10	18:08	P 365138
		22	13:26	A 404408
	Nov	6	9:41	P 369887
		19	10:02	A 404256
	Dec	1	9:39	P 367804
		17	6:46	A 404893
		29	1:46	P 362206
1944	Jan	13	23:56	A 405799
		26	10:33	P 358038
	Feb	10	6:47	A 406322
		23	23:26	P 356847
	Mar	8	7:14	A 406286
		23	10:15	P 358880
	Apr	4	17:52	A 405616
		20	14:25	P 363323
	May	2	10:56	A 404657
		17	21:53	P 368300
		30	5:40	A 404144
	Jun	12	0:25	P 369111
		27	0:11	A 404484
	Jul	8	21:53	P 364596
		24	17:23	A 405443
	Aug	5	21:57	P 359938
		21	6:05	A 406350
	Sep	3	5:48	P 357155
		17	10:36	A 406634
	Oct	1	16:56	P 357167
		14	14:12	A 406248
		30	2:15	P 360187
	Nov	11	3:03	A 405389
		27	3:29	P 365467
	Dec	8	22:25	A 404592
		23	11:43	P 370156
1945	Jan	5	19:44	A 404456
		17	16:57	P 367192
	Feb	2	15:57	A 405073
		14	12:25	P 361613
	Mar	2	7:08	A 405933
		14	21:12	P 357801
		29	12:31	A 406435
	Apr	12	8:08	P 356971
		25	14:27	A 406349
	May	10	17:41	P 359136
		23	1:09	A 405615
	Jun	7	20:18	P 363494
		19	17:34	A 404660
	Jul	5	2:37	P 368311
		17	11:45	A 404196
		30	5:39	P 369020
	Aug	14	6:20	A 404587
		26	3:20	P 364400
	Sep	11	0:00	A 405568
		23	4:10	P 359610
	Oct	8	12:55	A 406425
		21	13:56	P 356859
	Nov	4	15:56	A 406635
		19	2:02	P 357169
	Dec	1	20:01	A 406222
		17	12:41	P 360643
		29	10:57	A 405311
1946	Jan	14	12:20	P 366178
		26	7:14	A 404463
	Feb	9	10:00	P 370281
		23	4:23	A 404304
	Mar	7	1:07	P 366678
		22	23:40	A 404907
	Apr	3	22:16	P 361438
		19	13:28	A 405755
	May	2	5:37	P 358031
		16	18:48	A 406244
		30	15:57	P 357362
	Jun	12	21:44	A 406111
		28	0:15	P 359443
	Jul	10	8:08	A 405363
		26	2:57	P 363671
	Aug	7	0:00	A 404459
		22	10:11	P 368509
	Sep	3	18:49	A 404073
		16	10:17	P 369186
	Oct	1	14:25	A 404543
		13	9:44	P 364294
		29	9:05	A 405556
	Nov	10	12:51	P 359372
		25	22:05	A 406368
	Dec	9	0:03	P 356732
		22	23:35	A 406535
1947	Jan	6	13:38	P 357364
		19	4:56	A 406107
	Feb	3	23:35	P 361114
		15	21:14	A 405164
	Mar	3	20:10	P 366612
		15	17:19	A 404334
		29	12:31	P 370069
	Apr	12	13:23	A 404242
		24	10:58	P 366406
	May	10	7:19	A 404917
		22	7:05	P 361434
	Jun	6	20:60	A 405817
		19	13:49	P 358093
	Jul	4	3:12	A 406312
		17	23:26	P 357308
		31	5:54	A 406156
	Aug	15	7:49	P 359302
		27	15:29	A 405431
	Sep	12	11:18	P 363619
		24	7:22	A 404590
	Oct	9	18:29	P 368713
		22	2:44	A 404290
	Nov	3	14:09	P 369099
		18	23:41	A 404821
		30	17:54	P 363752
	Dec	16	18:30	A 405818
		28	23:21	P 358777
1948	Jan	13	5:48	A 406556
		26	11:17	P 356466
	Feb	9	6:22	A 406696
		24	0:00	P 357532
	Mar	7	13:31	A 406198
		23	7:35	P 361517
	Apr	4	5:46	A 405187
		20	0:58	P 366825
	May	2	0:49	A 404363
		15	16:10	P 369743
		29	20:03	A 404315
	Jun	10	18:52	P 366128
		26	13:17	A 405029
	Jul	8	14:12	P 361266
		24	2:52	A 405939
	Aug	5	20:30	P 357921
		20	9:12	A 406399
	Sep	3	6:00	P 357162
		16	11:20	A 406203
	Oct	1	16:01	P 359319
		13	21:23	A 405468
		29	20:27	P 363950
	Nov	10	14:38	A 404629
		26	0:48	P 369243
	Dec	8	11:21	A 404327
		20	17:13	P 368764
1949	Jan	5	8:27	A 404829
		17	2:36	P 363150
	Feb	2	2:21	A 405754
		14	9:29	P 358528
	Mar	1	11:43	A 406432
		14	21:35	P 356715
		28	12:53	A 406540
	Apr	12	8:33	P 358067
		24	21:37	A 405959
	May	10	14:47	P 361967
		22	13:31	A 404922
	Jun	7	6:31	P 366992
		19	7:45	A 404151
	Jul	2	22:01	P 369710
		17	2:21	A 404184
		29	1:05	P 366163
	Aug	13	20:22	A 404965
		25	20:52	P 361270
	Sep	10	10:53	A 405895
		23	3:38	P 357848
	Oct	7	17:06	A 406314
		21	15:13	P 357111
	Nov	3	18:25	A 406099
		19	2:05	P 359475
	Dec	1	5:27	A 405374
		17	6:43	P 364411
		29	0:04	A 404550
1950	Jan	13	6:03	P 369668
		25	21:41	A 404277
	Feb	7	0:09	P 368326
		22	18:15	A 404807
	Mar	6	13:26	P 362809
		22	10:50	A 405746
	Apr	3	20:10	P 358523
		18	19:25	A 406438
	May	2	6:25	P 356903
		15	21:43	A 406520
		30	16:28	P 358207
	Jun	12	6:06	A 405913
		27	21:41	P 361957
	Jul	9	21:07	A 404925
		25	13:24	P 366924
	Aug	6	14:53	A 404245
		20	4:39	P 369727
	Sep	3	9:49	A 404378
		15	7:19	P 366029
	Oct	1	4:28	A 405232
		13	4:03	P 360873
		28	19:37	A 406155
	Nov	10	12:57	P 357354
		25	0:34	A 406512
	Dec	9	1:17	P 356835
		22	1:36	A 406280
1951	Jan	6	12:52	P 359655
		18	14:18	A 405515
	Feb	3	15:36	P 364893
		15	9:35	A 404652
	Mar	2	7:08	P 369766
		15	6:14	A 404378
		27	8:21	P 367715
	Apr	12	1:24	A 404921
		23	23:01	P 362426
	May	9	16:49	A 405863
		22	4:02	P 358408
	Jun	6	1:06	A 406543
		19	13:33	P 356917
	Jul	3	3:59	A 406579
		17	22:56	P 358241
		30	12:01	A 405937
	Aug	15	3:58	P 362038
		27	2:40	A 404958
	Sep	11	20:33	P 367148
		23	21:18	A 404314
	Oct	7	6:47	P 369888
		21	17:17	A 404480
	Nov	2	12:45	P 365661
		18	12:39	A 405318
		30	12:27	P 360347
	Dec	16	3:01	A 406150
		28	23:11	P 357092
1952	Jan	12	5:43	A 406440
		26	12:06	P 357099
	Feb	8	8:27	A 406169
		23	22:44	P 360293
	Mar	6	22:59	A 405312
		22	22:38	P 365480
	Apr	3	18:10	A 404410
		18	8:32	P 369763
	May	1	13:48	A 404165
		13	16:20	P 367463
		29	8:01	A 404754
	Jun	10	6:24	P 362456
		25	23:14	A 405729
	Jul	8	11:10	P 358581
		23	8:10	A 406403
	Aug	5	20:40	P 357061
		19	11:01	A 406405
	Sep	3	6:19	P 358338
		15	18:46	A 405766
	Oct	1	13:04	P 362217
		13	10:03	A 404829
		29	5:41	P 367562
	Nov	10	5:37	A 404249
		23	8:22	P 370047
	Dec	8	2:45	A 404472
		19	20:41	P 365274
1953	Jan	4	22:40	A 405312
		16	23:13	P 360016
	Feb	1	11:46	A 406100
		14	10:10	P 357112
		28	13:32	A 406378
	Mar	14	22:45	P 357409
		27	17:59	A 406061
	Apr	12	7:00	P 360653
		24	8:13	A 405175
	May	10	4:42	P 365620
		22	2:12	A 404334
	Jun	5	13:45	P 369591
		18	21:13	A 404190
	Jul	1	0:10	P 367372
		16	15:15	A 404874
		28	13:47	P 362403
	Aug	13	6:54	A 405909
		25	18:35	P 358384
	Sep	9	16:22	A 406578
		23	4:17	P 356746
	Oct	6	18:18	A 406547
		21	15:38	P 358133
	Nov	3	1:55	A 405915
		18	23:06	P 362366
		30	18:31	A 404995
	Dec	16	13:53	P 368014
		28	15:09	A 404431
1954	Jan	10	9:38	P 369761
		25	12:21	A 404653
	Feb	6	5:56	P 364602
		22	6:44	A 405458
	Mar	6	9:32	P 359597
		21	17:56	A 406214
	Apr	3	20:03	P 357073
		17	19:46	A 406470
	May	2	6:25	P 357621
		15	1:23	A 406081
		30	13:36	P 360875
	Jun	11	15:08	A 405165
		27	10:12	P 365716
	Jul	9	8:24	A 404355
		23	18:28	P 369575
	Aug	6	2:56	A 404268
		18	5:29	P 367255
	Sep	2	21:43	A 404994
		14	19:57	P 362121
		30	13:56	A 406014
	Oct	13	1:33	P 358022
		27	22:40	A 406604
	Nov	10	13:22	P 356568
		23	23:26	A 406525
	Dec	9	1:25	P 358368
		21	8:50	A 405855
1955	Jan	6	8:50	P 363013
		18	2:59	A 404874
	Feb	2	19:33	P 368621
		15	0:02	A 404274
		27	13:18	P 369358
	Mar	14	20:44	A 404483
		26	15:33	P 364238
	Apr	11	13:43	A 405281
		23	18:55	P 359649
	May	9	0:04	A 406032
		22	3:44	P 357408
	Jun	5	2:51	A 406260
		19	13:44	P 357973
	Jul	2	8:34	A 405832
		17	20:38	P 361094
		29	21:56	A 404938
	Aug	14	17:45	P 365880
		26	15:15	A 404194
	Sep	10	1:14	P 369843
		23	10:34	A 404190
	Oct	5	10:42	P 367278
		21	6:17	A 404979
	Nov	2	3:08	P 361900
		17	23:28	A 405994
		30	11:25	P 357801
	Dec	15	7:16	A 406522
		29	0:13	P 356584
1956	Jan	11	7:36	A 406426
		26	12:54	P 358728
	Feb	7	18:43	A 405721
		23	18:32	P 363512
	Mar	6	13:16	A 404725
		22	0:19	P 368815
	Apr	3	9:30	A 404175
		15	21:28	P 368992
	May	1	4:42	A 404465
		13	0:49	P 364115
		28	21:13	A 405332
	Jun	10	2:58	P 359694
		25	7:53	A 406117
	Jul	8	11:26	P 357404
		22	11:12	A 406330

Moon Perigee/Apogee 1900–2020 • Distance in Kilometers

Year	Month	Day	Time	Distance
	Aug	5	21:13	P 357834
		18	16:11	A 405895
	Sep	3	4:11	P 360956
		15	4:55	A 405044
	Oct	1	2:15	P 365958
		12	23:06	A 404375
		27	6:05	P 370072
	Nov	9	19:30	A 404444
		21	16:52	P 366900
	Dec	7	15:53	A 405258
		19	12:46	P 361268
1957	Jan	4	8:10	A 406216
		16	22:34	P 357332
		31	13:45	A 406689
	Feb	14	11:12	P 356553
		27	15:11	A 406559
	Mar	14	22:22	P 359050
		27	3:21	A 405768
	Apr	12	1:00	P 363858
		23	21:31	A 404740
	May	9	3:32	P 368791
		21	16:36	A 404221
	Jun	3	4:32	P 368654
		18	10:53	A 404559
		30	8:07	P 363916
	Jul	16	2:57	A 405455
		28	9:40	P 359521
	Aug	12	13:58	A 406228
		25	18:16	P 357212
	Sep	8	16:52	A 406391
		23	4:24	P 357738
	Oct	5	21:39	A 405932
		21	13:08	P 361132
	Nov	2	11:30	A 405075
		18	11:18	P 366465
		30	6:52	A 404402
	Dec	14	5:22	P 370320
		28	4:12	A 404459
1958	Jan	8	23:55	P 366322
		25	0:21	A 405222
	Feb	5	22:59	P 360800
		21	15:09	A 406106
	Mar	6	8:34	P 357354
		20	19:24	A 406547
	Apr	3	20:45	P 356981
		16	22:44	A 406357
	May	2	5:50	P 359564
		14	11:18	A 405503
		30	7:24	P 364166
	Jun	11	4:28	A 404497
		26	8:53	P 368841
	Jul	8	23:17	A 404054
		21	10:55	P 368674
	Aug	5	17:43	A 404470
		17	14:31	P 363944
	Sep	2	10:37	A 405416
		14	16:48	P 359462
		29	22:18	A 406175
	Oct	13	2:17	P 357109
		27	0:24	A 406293
	Nov	10	14:33	P 357767
		23	5:10	A 405836
	Dec	9	0:00	P 361449
		20	20:41	A 404985
1959	Jan	5	20:42	P 367001
		17	17:07	A 404329
		31	5:34	P 370264
	Feb	14	14:22	A 404418
		26	9:24	P 365865
	Mar	14	9:26	A 405207
		26	9:22	P 360639
	Apr	10	22:57	A 406112
		23	18:31	P 357468
	May	8	3:44	A 406556
		22	4:42	P 357149
	Jun	4	7:36	A 406328
		19	13:08	P 359610
	Jul	1	19:18	A 405483
		17	14:16	P 364100
		29	11:40	A 404550
	Aug	13	16:03	P 368828
		26	6:09	A 404205
	Sep	7	16:35	P 368659
		23	1:22	A 404714
	Oct	4	21:23	P 363656
		20	19:23	A 405695
	Nov	2	0:55	P 358958
		17	6:40	A 406404
		30	12:27	P 356680
	Dec	14	7:02	A 406480
		29	0:58	P 357713
1960	Jan	10	13:12	A 405998
		26	9:48	P 361837
	Feb	7	5:46	A 405093
		23	2:44	P 367424
	Mar	6	2:02	A 404417
		19	7:17	P 369836
	Apr	2	22:27	A 404518
		14	18:53	P 365353
		30	15:60	A 405319
	May	12	18:17	P 360409
		28	4:30	A 406224
	Jun	10	1:33	P 357422
		24	9:33	A 406641
	Jul	8	11:22	P 357164
		21	13:36	A 406364
	Aug	5	19:44	P 359647
		18	0:51	A 405506
	Sep	2	21:29	P 364248
		14	17:45	A 404595
		29	22:21	P 369150
	Oct	12	13:12	A 404286
		24	19:35	P 368536
	Nov	9	9:25	A 404808
		21	4:05	P 363141
	Dec	7	3:24	A 405733
		19	10:29	P 358518
1961	Jan	3	12:56	A 406343
		16	23:12	P 356678
		30	12:32	A 406389
	Feb	14	11:27	P 358215
		26	21:15	A 405830
	Mar	14	18:29	P 362504
		26	14:31	A 404850
	Apr	11	7:33	P 367785
		23	10:01	A 404177
	May	6	12:08	P 369573
		21	5:05	A 404328
	Jun	2	2:32	P 365259
		17	22:25	A 405176
		30	1:06	P 360524
	Jul	15	11:18	A 406099
		28	8:32	P 357578
	Aug	11	16:50	A 406491
		25	18:53	P 357254
	Sep	7	20:25	A 406192
		23	3:53	P 359753
	Oct	5	7:51	A 405357
		21	6:49	P 364546
	Nov	2	1:34	A 404499
		17	5:26	P 369625
		29	22:38	A 404252
	Dec	12	0:24	P 368319
		27	19:34	A 404806
1962	Jan	8	13:52	P 362723
		24	12:58	A 405705
	Feb	5	21:52	P 358349
		20	20:49	A 406287
	Mar	6	9:49	P 356872
		19	21:17	A 406315
	Apr	3	21:06	P 358568
		16	6:46	A 405702
	May	2	1:34	P 362753
		13	23:20	A 404742
		29	13:05	P 367760
	Jun	10	17:46	A 404157
		23	19:37	P 369412
	Jul	8	12:17	A 404410
		20	10:01	P 365216
	Aug	5	5:40	A 405343
		17	8:18	P 360396
	Sep	1	19:27	A 406297
		14	16:20	P 357282
		29	0:52	A 406654
	Oct	13	3:12	P 356944
		26	3:28	A 406340
	Nov	10	13:50	P 359711
		22	15:43	A 405515
	Dec	8	16:43	P 364902
		20	10:41	A 404666
1963	Jan	4	8:26	P 369945
		17	7:60	A 404426
		29	7:21	P 367707
	Feb	14	4:18	A 404964
		26	0:02	P 362141
	Mar	13	20:05	A 405826
		26	7:43	P 358133
	Apr	10	2:37	A 406390
		23	18:45	P 356976
	May	7	4:20	A 406372
		22	3:49	P 358793
	Jun	3	13:55	A 405698
		19	7:34	P 362911
	Jul	1	5:28	A 404741
		16	18:27	P 367810
		28	23:46	A 404206
	Aug	11	0:28	P 369383
		25	18:34	A 404511
	Sep	6	15:36	P 365020
		22	12:37	A 405462
	Oct	4	15:08	P 360036
		20	2:31	A 406363
	Nov	2	0:14	P 356959
		16	6:20	A 406641
		30	13:09	P 356961
	Dec	13	9:18	A 406297
		29	0:00	P 360185
1964	Jan	9	23:48	A 405414
		26	1:14	P 365620
	Feb	6	19:54	A 404508
		21	8:00	P 370139
	Mar	5	16:54	A 404247
		17	15:35	P 367231
	Apr	2	11:56	A 404784
		14	9:34	P 361999
		30	2:22	A 405648
	May	12	16:22	P 358354
		27	9:02	A 406204
	Jun	10	1:48	P 357327
		23	11:33	A 406144
	Jul	8	10:55	P 359064
		20	20:52	A 405460
	Aug	5	14:57	P 363072
		17	12:13	A 404549
	Sep	2	2:17	P 368030
		14	6:42	A 404091
		27	4:42	P 369588
	Oct	12	2:36	A 404478
		23	22:03	P 364880
	Nov	8	22:04	A 405463
		21	0:00	P 359754
	Dec	6	11:54	A 406317
		19	11:08	P 356831
1965	Jan	2	14:06	A 406552
		17	0:18	P 357152
		29	18:25	A 406189
	Feb	14	10:41	P 360650
		26	9:50	A 405266
	Mar	14	9:05	P 366020
		26	5:28	A 404381
	Apr	9	10:45	P 369968
		23	1:19	A 404197
	May	5	0:57	P 366972
		20	19:39	A 404814
	Jun	1	18:34	P 361985
		17	9:53	A 405735
		30	0:00	P 358372
	Jul	14	17:12	A 406302
		28	9:17	P 357229
	Aug	10	19:34	A 406219
		25	18:42	P 358881
	Sep	7	4:00	A 405552
		22	23:32	P 363015
	Oct	4	19:43	A 404699
		20	10:57	P 368265
	Nov	1	15:11	A 404313
		14	7:36	P 369516
		29	12:03	A 404752
	Dec	11	5:52	P 364301
		27	7:17	A 405717
1966	Jan	8	10:17	P 359157
		23	19:26	A 406502
	Feb	5	22:21	P 356567
		19	20:32	A 406709
	Mar	6	10:33	P 357328
		19	2:46	A 406276
	Apr	3	18:52	P 361019
		15	18:23	A 405284
	May	1	14:23	P 366220
		13	12:60	A 404403
		27	14:04	P 369717
	Jun	10	7:47	A 404267
		22	8:20	P 366723
	Jul	8	1:21	A 404929
		20	0:57	P 361801
	Aug	4	15:56	A 405861
		17	6:27	P 358167
		31	23:16	A 406390
	Sep	14	16:36	P 357047
		28	1:01	A 406263
	Oct	13	2:41	P 358897
		25	9:55	A 405582
	Nov	10	8:36	P 363383
		22	2:53	A 404721
	Dec	7	17:54	P 368840
		19	23:57	A 404327
1967	Jan	1	9:44	P 369206
		16	21:09	A 404734
		28	15:05	P 363709
	Feb	13	15:16	A 405634
		25	20:52	P 358924
	Mar	13	1:30	A 406367
		26	7:50	P 356828
	Apr	9	3:11	A 406544
		23	19:12	P 357828
	May	6	10:39	A 406034
		22	1:31	P 361431
	Jun	3	1:41	A 405023
		18	20:17	P 366385
		30	19:52	A 404198
	Jul	14	19:51	P 369740
		28	14:29	A 404143
	Aug	9	14:33	P 366770
		25	8:38	A 404876
	Sep	6	7:32	P 361776
		22	0:06	A 405833
	Oct	4	14:21	P 358051
		19	7:33	A 406319
	Nov	2	1:36	P 356969
		15	8:10	A 406169
		30	13:34	P 359064
	Dec	12	18:23	A 405491
		28	19:23	P 363852
1968	Jan	9	12:48	A 404632
		24	23:42	P 369273
	Feb	6	9:57	A 404262
		18	16:23	P 368774
	Mar	5	6:27	A 404706
		17	1:24	P 363375
	Apr	1	23:32	A 405636
		14	6:43	P 358923
		29	9:09	A 406388
	May	12	16:55	P 356984
		26	11:50	A 406546
	Jun	10	2:24	P 357920
		22	19:04	A 406011
	Jul	8	8:30	P 361393
		20	9:07	A 405043
	Aug	5	3:07	P 366326
		17	2:38	A 404308
		31	2:27	P 369802
	Sep	13	22:04	A 404352
		25	20:31	P 366621
	Oct	11	17:09	A 405153
		23	15:20	P 361337
	Nov	8	8:58	A 406097
		20	23:56	P 357523
	Dec	5	14:47	A 406516
		19	12:24	P 356708
1969	Jan	1	15:12	A 406347
		17	0:00	P 359256
		29	3:04	A 405619
	Feb	14	3:42	P 364334
		25	22:12	A 404714
	Mar	13	1:45	P 369405
		25	18:36	A 404343
	Apr	7	0:01	P 368199
		22	13:40	A 404807
	May	4	10:35	P 363021
		20	5:18	A 405747
	Jun	1	14:46	P 358803
		16	14:43	A 406491
		29	23:48	P 356958
	Jul	13	17:47	A 406604
		28	8:58	P 357928
	Aug	10	0:44	A 406035
		25	15:32	P 361472
	Sep	6	14:55	A 405071
		22	10:46	P 366595
	Oct	4	9:12	A 404364
		18	4:29	P 370049
	Nov	1	5:27	A 404437
		13	1:27	P 366238
		29	1:18	A 405220
	Dec	10	23:59	P 360786
		26	16:32	A 406072
1970	Jan	8	9:51	P 357284
		22	20:00	A 406424
	Feb	5	23:10	P 356984
		18	22:07	A 406216
	Mar	6	9:30	P 359895
		18	11:39	A 405394
	Apr	3	10:47	P 364896
		15	6:15	A 404456
		30	4:15	P 369455
	May	13	1:38	A 404126
		25	7:34	P 367993
	Jun	9	20:14	A 404645
		21	18:08	P 363056
	Jul	7	11:53	A 405622
		19	21:44	P 358940
	Aug	3	21:57	A 406365
		17	6:30	P 357065
		31	1:04	A 406445
	Sep	14	17:09	P 357994

Moon Perigee/Apogee 1900–2020 • Distance in Kilometers

Year	Month	Day	Time	Distance
		27	7:32	A 405876
	Oct	13	0:31	P 361651
		24	22:33	A 404950
	Nov	9	20:29	P 367031
		21	18:10	A 404298
	Dec	5	5:35	P 370259
		19	15:28	A 404420
		31	9:26	P 365830
1971	Jan	16	11:21	A 405207
		28	10:25	P 360463
	Feb	13	1:11	A 406027
		25	21:16	P 357304
	Mar	12	4:03	A 406371
		26	9:02	P 357286
	Apr	8	7:33	A 406118
		23	18:02	P 360209
	May	5	20:55	A 405270
		21	17:18	P 365005
	Jun	2	14:24	A 404392
		17	9:47	P 369319
		30	8:56	A 404163
	Jul	12	15:13	P 367919
		28	3:11	A 404782
	Aug	9	0:52	P 362978
		24	19:45	A 405823
	Sep	6	4:40	P 358701
		21	6:19	A 406558
	Oct	4	14:55	P 356714
		18	8:18	A 406599
	Nov	2	2:13	P 357780
		14	14:49	A 406030
		30	10:48	P 361829
	Dec	12	6:51	A 405108
		28	4:36	P 367507
1972	Jan	9	3:25	A 404461
		22	5:31	P 370020
	Feb	6	0:37	A 404580
		17	19:02	P 365166
	Mar	4	19:25	A 405338
		16	21:02	P 360060
	Apr	1	7:18	A 406132
		14	6:15	P 357271
		28	10:05	A 406456
	May	12	16:56	P 357465
		25	14:41	A 406136
	Jun	10	0:04	P 360395
		22	3:22	A 405260
	Jul	7	23:03	P 365103
		19	20:29	A 404412
	Aug	3	14:59	P 369372
		16	15:03	A 404236
		28	20:05	P 367834
	Sep	13	9:54	A 404895
		25	6:56	P 362679
	Oct	11	2:55	A 405921
		23	12:24	P 358313
	Nov	7	12:53	A 406572
		21	0:00	P 356522
	Dec	4	13:25	A 406560
		19	12:47	P 358045
		31	21:55	A 405950
1973	Jan	16	20:60	P 362489
		28	15:45	A 404956
	Feb	13	10:45	P 368118
		25	12:36	A 404270
	Mar	10	8:16	P 369673
		25	8:52	A 404388
	Apr	6	4:03	P 364837
		22	2:07	A 405157
	May	4	5:34	P 360126
		19	13:33	A 405954
	Jun	1	14:13	P 357581
		15	17:02	A 406254
		30	0:00	P 357768
	Jul	12	21:50	A 405901
		28	7:16	P 360588
	Aug	9	10:08	A 405044
		25	6:38	P 365272
	Sep	6	3:09	A 404263
		20	22:10	P 369682
	Oct	3	22:56	A 404171
		16	0:48	P 367852
		31	19:01	A 404893
	Nov	12	14:49	P 362417
		28	12:42	A 405911
	Dec	10	22:37	P 358058
		25	21:27	A 406501
1974	Jan	8	11:20	P 356551
		21	21:36	A 406472
	Feb	6	0:00	P 358393
		18	7:43	A 405821
	Mar	6	6:03	P 362957
		18	1:39	A 404813
	Apr	2	16:07	P 368292
		14	21:51	A 404183
		27	15:53	P 369332
	May	12	16:57	A 404387
		24	13:23	P 364723
	Jun	9	9:34	A 405229
		21	13:52	P 360147
	Jul	6	21:19	A 406067
		19	21:48	P 357521
	Aug	3	1:29	A 406353
		17	7:13	P 357590
		30	5:20	A 405990
	Sep	14	15:35	P 360433
		26	17:25	A 405170
	Oct	12	15:48	P 365370
		24	11:09	A 404450
	Nov	8	3:45	P 369959
		21	7:42	A 404422
	Dec	3	6:37	P 367449
		19	4:23	A 405163
		31	0:12	P 361756
1975	Jan	15	21:20	A 406126
		28	9:16	P 357604
	Feb	12	3:59	A 406663
		25	22:08	P 356519
	Mar	11	5:05	A 406601
		26	8:49	P 358704
	Apr	7	16:17	A 405861
		23	12:51	P 363275
	May	5	9:34	A 404820
		20	19:54	P 368297
	Jun	2	4:20	A 404225
		14	22:21	P 369044
		29	23:01	A 404481
	Jul	11	20:22	P 364528
		27	15:33	A 405355
	Aug	8	20:27	P 359942
		24	3:34	A 406179
	Sep	6	4:12	P 357294
		20	7:10	A 406413
	Oct	4	15:15	P 357475
		17	10:43	A 406021
	Nov	2	0:23	P 360621
		14	0:00	A 405190
		30	0:44	P 365911
	Dec	11	19:29	A 404456
		26	3:51	P 370291
1976	Jan	8	16:53	A 404406
		20	13:31	P 366876
	Feb	5	13:05	A 405100
		17	10:22	P 361314
	Mar	4	4:13	A 406003
		16	19:38	P 357638
		31	9:44	A 406512
	Apr	14	6:51	P 356940
		27	12:29	A 406394
	May	12	16:37	P 359178
		25	0:00	A 405599
	Jun	9	19:21	P 363555
		21	16:41	A 404582
	Jul	7	1:39	P 368377
		19	11:01	A 404061
	Aug	1	4:24	P 369106
		16	5:41	A 404401
		28	2:11	P 364544
	Sep	12	23:26	A 405331
		25	3:10	P 359842
	Oct	10	12:10	A 406141
		23	13:04	P 357161
	Nov	6	14:40	A 406325
		21	1:11	P 357494
	Dec	3	18:26	A 405931
		19	11:32	P 360959
		31	9:16	A 405094
1977	Jan	16	10:13	P 366449
		28	5:26	A 404370
	Feb	11	4:04	P 370285
		25	2:33	A 404358
	Mar	8	23:17	P 366425
		24	21:57	A 405090
	Apr	5	21:01	P 361160
		21	11:57	A 406022
	May	4	4:40	P 357739
		18	17:45	A 406540
	Jun	1	15:05	P 357064
		14	21:09	A 406388
		29	23:48	P 359174
	Jul	12	7:42	A 405601
		28	1:59	P 363475
	Aug	8	23:49	A 404654
		24	9:11	P 368396
	Sep	5	18:20	A 404227
		18	9:27	P 369114
	Oct	3	13:49	A 404653
		15	8:57	P 364223
		31	8:11	A 405614
	Nov	12	12:01	P 359304
		27	20:28	A 406370
	Dec	10	23:30	P 356716
		24	21:10	A 406508
1978	Jan	8	12:11	P 357468
		21	2:24	A 406086
	Feb	5	21:32	P 361348
		17	18:34	A 405184
	Mar	5	16:38	P 366863
		17	14:28	A 404434
		31	4:55	P 369933
	Apr	14	10:22	A 404440
		26	7:60	P 365949
	May	12	4:06	A 405194
		24	5:02	P 360941
	Jun	8	17:32	A 406131
		21	11:58	P 357673
	Jul	5	23:31	A 406623
		19	21:41	P 357037
	Aug	2	3:01	A 406424
		17	6:08	P 359199
		29	13:20	A 405621
	Sep	14	9:36	P 363648
		26	5:40	A 404689
	Oct	11	16:08	P 368778
		24	1:15	A 404295
	Nov	5	11:34	P 369024
		20	22:07	A 404730
	Dec	2	16:14	P 363687
		18	16:31	A 405630
		30	21:51	P 358858
1979	Jan	15	2:57	A 406289
		28	9:46	P 356747
	Feb	11	2:53	A 406397
		25	22:30	P 357967
	Mar	10	10:24	A 405897
		26	5:33	P 361993
	Apr	7	2:52	A 404925
		22	21:48	P 367214
	May	4	22:17	A 404189
		18	9:11	P 369740
	Jun	1	17:14	A 404250
		13	15:41	P 365882
		29	10:36	A 405057
	Jul	11	12:07	P 361045
		27	0:27	A 406020
	Aug	8	18:58	P 357784
		23	7:08	A 406488
	Sep	6	4:52	P 357093
		19	9:54	A 406265
	Oct	4	15:08	P 359294
		16	20:31	A 405482
	Nov	1	19:40	P 363958
		13	14:05	A 404593
		28	23:46	P 369281
	Dec	11	10:55	A 404252
		23	16:03	P 368803
1980	Jan	8	8:02	A 404718
		20	1:44	P 363254
	Feb	5	1:50	A 405603
		17	8:42	P 358704
	Mar	3	10:51	A 406243
		16	20:42	P 356929
		30	11:32	A 406335
	Apr	14	7:20	P 358293
		26	19:53	A 405784
	May	12	12:60	P 362201
		24	11:27	A 404830
	Jun	9	3:26	P 367187
		21	5:30	A 404182
	Jul	4	16:16	P 369614
		19	0:04	A 404351
		30	22:53	P 365835
	Aug	15	18:09	A 405244
		27	19:17	P 360876
	Sep	12	8:44	A 406236
		25	2:23	P 357440
	Oct	9	15:01	A 406666
		23	14:04	P 356763
	Nov	5	16:51	A 406421
		21	0:51	P 359259
	Dec	3	4:16	A 405639
		19	5:15	P 364342
		30	23:20	A 404747
1981	Jan	15	3:38	P 369640
		27	20:37	A 404403
	Feb	8	22:42	P 368197
		24	16:52	A 404855
	Mar	8	12:11	P 362699
		24	8:49	A 405712
	Apr	5	18:47	P 358499
		20	16:27	A 406338
	May	4	4:43	P 357020
		17	18:13	A 406388
	Jun	1	14:24	P 358480
		14	2:38	A 405780
		29	19:06	P 362335
	Jul	11	17:42	A 404829
		27	9:18	P 367270
	Aug	8	11:30	A 404226
		21	20:32	P 369658
	Sep	5	6:29	A 404445
		17	3:50	P 365639
	Oct	3	1:07	A 405358
		15	1:45	P 360481
		30	16:05	A 406293
	Nov	12	11:08	P 357105
		26	20:35	A 406637
	Dec	11	0:00	P 356784
		23	22:47	A 406362
1982	Jan	8	11:32	P 359764
		20	12:29	A 405511
	Feb	5	14:11	P 365060
		17	8:14	A 404556
	Mar	4	4:39	P 369884
		17	5:00	A 404200
		29	6:25	P 367761
	Apr	14	0:05	A 404668
		25	21:29	P 362577
	May	11	15:16	A 405537
		24	2:36	P 358708
	Jun	7	23:00	A 406159
		21	12:10	P 357334
	Jul	5	1:33	A 406173
		19	21:34	P 358705
	Aug	1	9:33	A 405555
		17	2:19	P 362482
		29	0:16	A 404651
	Sep	13	17:47	P 367512
		25	18:60	A 404123
	Oct	9	0:41	P 369906
		23	15:10	A 404421
	Nov	4	10:15	P 365469
		20	10:50	A 405366
	Dec	2	11:01	P 360171
		18	1:33	A 406258
		30	22:17	P 356960
1983	Jan	14	4:41	A 406561
		28	11:26	P 356989
	Feb	10	7:59	A 406263
		25	22:05	P 360201
	Mar	9	22:45	A 405370
		25	21:55	P 365417
	Apr	6	17:56	A 404437
		21	7:59	P 369747
	May	4	13:32	A 404162
		16	15:44	P 367519
	Jun	1	7:40	A 404716
		13	5:42	P 362553
		28	22:43	A 405651
	Jul	11	10:21	P 358690
		26	7:14	A 406287
	Aug	8	19:40	P 357178
		22	9:28	A 406277
	Sep	6	5:01	P 358491
		18	16:47	A 405670
	Oct	4	11:15	P 362432
		16	7:50	A 404813
	Nov	1	2:27	P 367776
		13	3:18	A 404349
		26	2:29	P 369864
	Dec	11	0:25	A 404691
		22	18:34	P 364855
1984	Jan	7	20:12	A 405613
		19	21:50	P 359560
	Feb	4	8:60	A 406436
		17	8:53	P 356717
	Mar	2	10:54	A 406712
		16	21:24	P 357152
		29	16:07	A 406344
	Apr	14	5:31	P 360545
		26	6:44	A 405381
	May	12	2:59	P 365605
		24	0:51	A 404457
	Jun	7	11:24	P 369567
		20	19:51	A 404230
	Jul	2	22:40	P 367298
		18	13:38	A 404830
		30	12:15	P 362362
	Aug	15	4:48	A 405778
		27	17:01	P 358446
	Sep	11	13:25	A 406374
		25	2:39	P 356965
	Oct	8	14:44	A 406315
		23	13:53	P 358511
	Nov	4	22:44	A 405692

Moon Perigee/Apogee 1900–2020 • Distance in Kilometers

Year	Month	Day	Time	Distance
		20	21:01	P 362827
	Dec	2	15:29	A 404815
		18	9:55	P 368391
		30	12:16	A 404329
1985	Jan	12	3:29	P 369590
		27	9:30	A 404638
	Feb	8	3:23	P 364273
		24	3:53	A 405508
	Mar	8	7:45	P 359358
		23	15:04	A 406291
	Apr	5	18:37	P 356976
		19	17:21	A 406540
	May	4	5:14	P 357625
		16	23:53	A 406103
	Jun	1	12:35	P 360921
		13	14:06	A 405124
		29	9:16	P 365770
	Jul	11	7:37	A 404256
		25	17:28	P 369644
	Aug	8	2:17	A 404116
		20	4:17	P 367360
	Sep	4	21:08	A 404792
		16	18:53	P 362300
	Oct	2	13:20	A 405763
		15	0:39	P 358283
		29	21:47	A 406313
	Nov	12	12:33	P 356876
		25	22:01	A 406227
	Dec	11	0:29	P 358682
		23	7:15	A 405601
1986	Jan	8	7:22	P 363307
		20	1:16	A 404718
	Feb	4	16:14	P 368821
		16	22:32	A 404256
	Mar	1	9:32	P 369174
		16	18:55	A 404609
		28	13:56	P 363961
	Apr	13	12:01	A 405518
		25	17:49	P 359355
	May	10	22:38	A 406329
		24	2:50	P 357099
	Jun	7	1:59	A 406562
		21	12:50	P 357673
	Jul	4	8:02	A 406103
		19	19:40	P 360849
		31	21:26	A 405165
	Aug	16	16:43	P 365721
		28	14:45	A 404378
	Sep	11	23:57	P 369754
		12	0:11	P 369754
		25	10:00	A 404331
	Oct	7	9:51	P 367201
		23	5:33	A 405073
	Nov	4	2:20	P 361817
		19	22:16	A 406029
	Dec	2	10:30	P 357742
		17	5:08	A 406507
		30	23:29	P 356615
1987	Jan	13	5:02	A 406401
		28	11:11	P 358899
	Feb	9	16:04	A 405714
		25	15:58	P 363781
	Mar	9	10:28	A 404776
		24	19:04	P 368977
	Apr	6	6:32	A 404317
		18	16:37	P 368643
	May	4	1:34	A 404700
		15	22:46	P 363625
		31	17:52	A 405626
	Jun	13	1:02	P 359222
		28	4:16	A 406429
	Jul	11	9:37	P 357047
		25	7:49	A 406621
	Aug	8	19:29	P 357646
		21	13:38	A 406126
	Sep	6	2:31	P 360928
		18	3:00	A 405188
	Oct	4	0:25	P 366025
		15	21:31	A 404424
		30	2:45	P 370090
	Nov	12	17:60	A 404398
		24	14:52	P 366812
	Dec	10	14:10	A 405115
		22	11:12	P 361263
1988	Jan	7	5:52	A 405981
		19	21:04	P 357512
	Feb	3	10:30	A 406396
		17	9:39	P 356919
	Mar	1	11:53	A 406251
		16	20:38	P 359519
		29	0:24	A 405473
	Apr	13	22:58	P 364312
		25	18:40	A 404509
	May	10	22:28	P 369065
		23	13:46	A 404094
	Jun	4	23:50	P 368483
		20	8:08	A 404540
	Jul	2	5:34	P 363669
		18	0:24	A 405514
		30	7:52	P 359335
	Aug	14	11:44	A 406320
		27	16:57	P 357106
	Sep	10	15:06	A 406476
		25	3:26	P 357686
	Oct	7	20:32	A 405977
		23	12:20	P 361116
	Nov	4	10:50	A 405070
		20	10:28	P 366484
	Dec	2	6:24	A 404353
		16	3:57	P 370354
		30	3:49	A 404374
1989	Jan	10	22:57	P 366383
		27	0:00	A 405100
	Feb	7	22:12	P 360936
		23	14:30	A 405944
	Mar	8	7:46	P 357545
		22	18:18	A 406354
	Apr	5	19:45	P 357195
		18	21:12	A 406166
	May	4	4:24	P 359788
		16	9:24	A 405364
	Jun	1	5:11	P 364390
		13	2:17	A 404461
		28	4:24	P 368960
	Jul	10	20:58	A 404149
		23	6:59	P 368431
	Aug	7	15:26	A 404694
		19	12:32	P 363573
	Sep	4	8:24	A 405732
		16	15:24	P 359050
	Oct	1	20:06	A 406529
		15	1:06	P 356714
		28	22:17	A 406639
	Nov	12	13:22	P 357473
		25	3:47	A 406136
	Dec	10	22:47	P 361310
		22	19:35	A 405219
1990	Jan	7	18:58	P 366977
		19	16:03	A 404492
	Feb	2	2:52	P 370179
		16	13:09	A 404505
		28	8:03	P 365737
	Mar	16	7:47	A 405213
		28	8:03	P 360561
	Apr	12	20:30	A 406040
		25	16:58	P 357507
	May	10	0:22	A 406431
		24	2:50	P 357342
	Jun	6	4:04	A 406184
		21	10:54	P 359947
	Jul	3	15:51	A 405354
		19	11:17	P 364495
		31	8:17	A 404477
	Aug	15	10:09	P 369075
		28	2:50	A 404218
	Sep	9	11:14	P 368381
		24	22:22	A 404804
	Oct	6	18:38	P 363247
		22	16:00	A 405823
	Nov	3	23:23	P 358626
		19	2:59	A 406529
	Dec	2	10:48	P 356531
		16	3:37	A 406585
		31	0:00	P 357751
1991	Jan	12	10:58	A 406037
		28	8:30	P 361984
	Feb	9	4:15	A 405041
		25	1:07	P 367580
	Mar	9	0:48	A 404280
		22	4:43	P 369899
	Apr	5	21:14	A 404304
		17	17:13	P 365442
	May	3	14:39	A 405033
		15	16:48	P 360631
		31	2:52	A 405871
	Jun	13	0:11	P 357780
		27	7:25	A 406244
	Jul	11	10:02	P 357605
		24	11:11	A 405966
	Aug	8	18:20	P 360103
		20	22:39	A 405155
	Sep	5	19:35	P 364663
		17	15:26	A 404340
	Oct	2	18:00	P 369418
		15	11:01	A 404160
		27	15:45	P 368398
	Nov	12	7:28	A 404808
		24	2:16	P 362942
	Dec	10	1:46	A 405822
		22	9:22	P 358358
1992	Jan	6	11:41	A 406471
		19	22:28	P 356551
	Feb	2	11:50	A 406510
		17	10:49	P 358101
		29	20:57	A 405916
	Mar	16	17:48	P 362413
		28	14:18	A 404902
	Apr	13	6:51	P 367732
		25	9:47	A 404200
	May	8	11:42	P 369585
		23	4:47	A 404319
	Jun	4	1:53	P 365330
		19	22:00	A 405130
	Jul	2	0:22	P 360619
		17	10:38	A 406012
		30	7:39	P 357678
	Aug	13	15:37	A 406373
		27	17:46	P 357375
	Sep	9	18:37	A 406080
		25	2:24	P 359930
	Oct	7	5:44	A 405298
		23	4:36	P 364780
	Nov	3	23:35	A 404538
		18	23:55	P 369741
		19	0:03	P 369741
	Dec	1	20:18	A 404410
		13	21:13	P 367972
		29	17:09	A 405069
1993	Jan	10	12:12	P 362268
		26	10:19	A 406028
	Feb	7	20:34	P 357908
		22	17:54	A 406628
	Mar	8	8:29	P 356533
		21	18:58	A 406632
	Apr	5	19:40	P 358384
		18	5:05	A 405951
	May	4	0:00	P 362698
		15	21:54	A 404908
		31	11:10	P 367760
	Jun	12	16:24	A 404240
		25	17:26	P 369357
	Jul	10	10:49	A 404410
		22	8:26	P 365148
	Aug	7	3:53	A 405256
		19	6:47	P 360391
	Sep	3	17:02	A 406125
		16	14:45	P 357412
		30	21:20	A 406426
	Oct	15	1:35	P 357244
		27	23:58	A 406103
	Nov	12	12:01	P 360147
		24	12:35	A 405301
	Dec	10	14:10	P 365359
		22	7:46	A 404513
1994	Jan	6	1:22	P 370142
		19	5:10	A 404360
		31	3:40	P 367409
	Feb	16	1:28	A 404980
		27	22:22	P 361846
	Mar	15	17:14	A 405891
		28	6:06	P 357962
	Apr	11	23:45	A 406468
		25	17:25	P 356933
	May	9	2:21	A 406423
		24	2:44	P 358818
	Jun	5	12:39	A 405693
		21	6:37	P 362956
	Jul	3	4:36	A 404676
		18	17:34	P 367866
		30	23:05	A 404086
	Aug	12	23:09	P 369464
		27	17:58	A 404341
	Sep	8	14:28	P 365150
		24	12:04	A 405244
	Oct	6	14:10	P 360249
		22	1:53	A 406098
	Nov	3	23:54	P 357240
		18	5:12	A 406347
	Dec	2	12:20	P 357270
		15	7:48	A 406019
		30	23:16	P 360489
1995	Jan	11	22:10	A 405204
		27	23:35	P 365887
	Feb	8	18:07	A 404417
		23	2:18	P 370181
	Mar	8	15:02	A 404303
		20	13:14	P 366974
	Apr	5	10:08	A 404973
		17	8:15	P 361705
	May	3	0:45	A 405926
		15	15:23	P 358045
		30	7:49	A 406516
	Jun	13	0:54	P 357010
		26	10:50	A 406441
	Jul	11	9:58	P 358779
		23	20:20	A 405717
	Aug	8	13:55	P 362866
		20	11:42	A 404761
	Sep	5	1:10	P 367912
		17	6:09	A 404260
		30	3:41	P 369505
	Oct	15	1:57	A 404602
		26	21:12	P 364792
	Nov	11	21:07	A 405530
		23	23:15	P 359670
	Dec	9	10:14	A 406324
		22	10:04	P 356804
1996	Jan	5	11:33	A 406526
		19	23:20	P 357252
	Feb	1	15:45	A 406163
		17	8:38	P 360888
		29	7:05	A 405273
	Mar	16	5:42	P 366291
		28	2:33	A 404463
	Apr	11	2:57	P 369909
		24	22:33	A 404374
	May	6	21:54	P 366532
		22	16:23	A 405070
	Jun	3	16:23	P 361495
		19	6:22	A 406032
	Jul	1	22:25	P 357950
		16	13:33	A 406598
		30	7:29	P 356953
	Aug	12	16:29	A 406478
		27	17:01	P 358781
	Sep	9	1:45	A 405735
		24	21:53	P 363054
	Oct	6	17:59	A 404790
		22	8:44	P 368350
	Nov	3	13:40	A 404309
		16	4:45	P 369460
	Dec	1	10:30	A 404652
		13	4:10	P 364238
		29	5:23	A 405521
1997	Jan	10	8:46	P 359237
		25	16:45	A 406224
	Feb	7	20:52	P 356850
		21	17:07	A 406396
	Mar	8	8:57	P 357763
		20	23:44	A 405958
	Apr	5	16:56	P 361501
		17	15:29	A 405001
	May	3	11:15	P 366627
		15	10:10	A 404209
		29	7:02	P 369787
	Jun	12	4:60	A 404184
		24	4:56	P 366494
	Jul	9	22:57	A 404944
		21	23:14	P 361581
	Aug	6	13:34	A 405935
		19	4:54	P 358023
	Sep	2	21:14	A 406479
		16	15:28	P 356971
		29	23:29	A 406330
	Oct	15	1:51	P 358862
		27	9:03	A 405603
	Nov	12	7:50	P 363383
		24	2:21	A 404695
	Dec	9	16:56	P 368874
		21	23:34	A 404262
1998	Jan	3	8:33	P 369240
		18	20:46	A 404634
		30	14:14	P 363804
	Feb	15	14:46	A 405495
		27	20:05	P 359090
	Mar	15	0:41	A 406189
		28	6:58	P 357030
	Apr	11	1:52	A 406347
		25	18:01	P 358045
	May	8	8:56	A 405861
		24	0:00	P 361660
	Jun	4	23:51	A 404925
		20	17:26	P 366594
	Jul	2	17:35	A 404219
		16	13:51	P 369700
		30	12:09	A 404298
	Aug	11	11:47	P 366448
		27	6:22	A 405147
	Sep	8	5:53	P 361377
		23	21:57	A 406169
	Oct	6	13:04	P 357639
		21	5:20	A 406669
	Nov	4	0:26	P 356614
		17	6:27	A 406493
	Dec	2	12:19	P 358847

Moon Perigee/Apogee 1900–2020 • Distance in Kilometers

Year	Month	Day	Time	km
		14	17:08	A 405757
		30	17:55	P 363785
1999	Jan	11	11:41	A 404828
		26	21:25	P 369258
	Feb	8	8:49	A 404385
		20	14:36	P 368654
	Mar	8	5:03	A 404750
		20	0:06	P 363267
	Apr	4	21:34	A 405596
		17	5:17	P 358897
	May	2	6:16	A 406278
		15	15:13	P 357098
		29	8:17	A 406398
	Jun	13	0:25	P 358191
		25	15:33	A 405858
	Jul	11	6:02	P 361780
		23	5:41	A 404924
	Aug	7	23:41	P 366705
		19	23:36	A 404262
	Sep	2	17:60	P 369819
		16	18:47	A 404390
		28	16:47	P 366253
	Oct	14	13:51	A 405254
		26	12:60	P 360954
	Nov	11	5:30	A 406216
		23	22:08	P 357279
	Dec	8	11:04	A 406625
		22	10:54	P 356659
2000	Jan	4	12:24	A 406418
		19	23:01	P 359362
	Feb	1	1:16	A 405608
		17	2:22	P 364495
		28	20:53	A 404614
	Mar	14	23:36	P 369533
		27	17:26	A 404166
	Apr	8	22:13	P 368258
		24	12:27	A 404557
	May	6	9:03	P 363172
		22	3:55	A 405427
	Jun	3	13:21	P 359094
		18	12:58	A 406113
	Jul	1	22:30	P 357364
		15	15:32	A 406201
		30	7:39	P 358380
	Aug	11	22:28	A 405652
		27	14:01	P 361910
	Sep	8	12:37	A 404759
		24	8:19	P 366963
	Oct	6	6:59	A 404168
		19	21:51	P 370115
	Nov	3	3:24	A 404376
		14	23:13	P 366048
		30	23:45	A 405273
	Dec	12	22:35	P 360603
		28	15:06	A 406192
2001	Jan	10	8:57	P 357135
		24	19:00	A 406563
	Feb	7	22:30	P 356853
		20	21:40	A 406332
	Mar	8	8:50	P 359780
		20	11:25	A 405473
	Apr	5	10:03	P 364812
		17	6:01	A 404504
	May	2	3:42	P 369419
		15	1:21	A 404144
		27	7:01	P 368033
	Jun	11	19:53	A 404628
		23	17:26	P 363135
	Jul	9	11:23	A 405566
		21	20:57	P 359029
	Aug	5	21:03	A 406269
		19	5:32	P 357161
	Sep	1	23:23	A 406330
		16	15:53	P 358133
		29	5:33	A 405787
	Oct	14	23:12	P 361861
		26	20:19	A 404934
	Nov	11	17:28	P 367257
		23	15:50	A 404392
	Dec	6	22:37	P 370117
		21	13:04	A 404631
2002	Jan	2	7:10	P 365408
		18	8:48	A 405504
		30	8:57	P 360000
	Feb	14	22:21	A 406363
		27	19:55	P 356900
	Mar	14	1:15	A 406707
		28	7:36	P 357015
	Apr	10	5:31	A 406408
		25	16:30	P 360088
	May	7	19:20	A 405482
		23	15:36	P 364986
	Jun	4	12:59	A 404520
		19	7:32	P 369309
	Jul	2	7:32	A 404208
		14	13:23	P 367848
		30	1:37	A 404742
	Aug	10	23:43	P 362928
		26	17:44	A 405694
	Sep	8	3:08	P 358748
		23	3:28	A 406352
	Oct	6	13:20	P 356923
		20	4:44	A 406360
	Nov	4	0:34	P 358154
		16	11:31	A 405796
	Dec	2	8:47	P 362293
		14	3:52	A 404913
		30	0:59	P 367902
2003	Jan	11	0:35	A 404343
		23	22:28	P 369898
	Feb	7	22:06	A 404551
		19	16:21	P 364848
	Mar	7	16:36	A 405381
		19	19:12	P 359819
	Apr	4	4:30	A 406209
		17	4:47	P 357160
	May	1	7:41	A 406530
		15	15:44	P 357454
		28	13:06	A 406168
	Jun	12	23:30	P 360425
		25	2:20	A 405232
	Jul	10	22:09	P 365145
		22	19:44	A 404327
	Aug	6	14:03	P 369433
		19	14:26	A 404100
		31	18:53	P 367926
	Sep	16	9:21	A 404712
		28	5:54	P 362837
	Oct	14	2:22	A 405692
		26	11:31	P 358552
	Nov	10	12:05	A 406301
		23	23:31	P 356812
	Dec	7	12:05	A 406279
		22	11:51	P 358344
2004	Jan	3	20:22	A 405707
		19	19:34	P 362772
		31	14:02	A 404805
	Feb	16	7:41	P 368323
		28	10:44	A 404256
	Mar	12	3:57	P 369506
		27	6:58	A 404519
	Apr	8	2:18	P 364548
		24	0:20	A 405403
	May	6	4:24	P 359813
		21	12:01	A 406264
	Jun	3	13:15	P 357252
		17	16:00	A 406575
	Jul	1	23:11	P 357449
		14	21:10	A 406192
		30	6:15	P 360327
	Aug	11	9:33	A 405290
		27	5:32	P 365107
	Sep	8	2:35	A 404463
		22	20:54	P 369589
	Oct	5	22:19	A 404326
		18	0:00	P 367758
	Nov	2	18:14	A 404996
		14	13:58	P 362315
		30	11:24	A 405953
	Dec	12	21:40	P 357985
		27	19:13	A 406489
2005	Jan	10	10:05	P 356576
		23	18:53	A 406445
	Feb	7	22:25	P 358566
		20	4:58	A 405805
	Mar	8	3:30	P 363234
		19	23:03	A 404846
	Apr	4	11:12	P 368493
		16	18:48	A 404302
		29	10:14	P 369028
	May	14	13:43	A 404598
		26	10:42	P 364243
	Jun	11	6:09	A 405505
		23	11:48	P 359677
	Jul	8	17:40	A 406363
		21	19:56	P 357161
	Aug	4	21:46	A 406632
		19	5:28	P 357397
	Sep	1	2:36	A 406213
		16	13:55	P 360409
		28	15:23	A 405306
	Oct	14	14:01	P 365452
		26	9:32	A 404492
	Nov	10	0:30	P 370010
		23	6:13	A 404368
	Dec	5	4:30	P 367365
		21	2:43	A 405013
2006	Jan	1	23:03	P 361751
		17	19:09	A 405884
		30	7:47	P 357783
	Feb	14	0:52	A 406359
		27	20:38	P 356887
	Mar	13	1:49	A 406278
		28	7:07	P 359173
	Apr	9	13:19	A 405550
		25	10:32	P 363735
	May	7	6:43	A 404571
		22	15:26	P 368608
	Jun	4	1:32	A 404080
		16	17:01	P 368919
	Jul	1	20:18	A 404447
		13	17:40	P 364290
		29	13:03	A 405405
	Aug	10	18:36	P 359752
		26	1:22	A 406269
	Sep	8	2:53	P 357177
		22	5:25	A 406501
	Oct	6	14:17	P 357415
		19	9:36	A 406074
	Nov	4	0:00	P 360596
		15	23:28	A 405194
	Dec	2	0:00	P 365923
		13	19:03	A 404416
		28	2:29	P 370323
2007	Jan	10	16:30	A 404333
		22	12:33	P 366927
	Feb	7	12:40	A 404991
		19	9:35	P 361439
	Mar	7	3:36	A 405853
		19	18:49	P 357818
	Apr	3	8:40	A 406330
		17	5:50	P 357140
		30	10:57	A 406210
	May	15	15:12	P 359394
		27	22:09	A 405460
	Jun	12	17:14	P 363781
		24	14:29	A 404538
	Jul	9	21:43	P 368528
		22	8:41	A 404148
	Aug	3	23:54	P 368891
		19	3:22	A 404617
		31	0:04	P 364171
	Sep	15	21:11	A 405642
		28	1:44	P 359420
	Oct	13	9:53	A 406492
		26	11:51	P 356758
	Nov	9	12:33	A 406672
		24	0:00	P 357194
	Dec	6	16:56	A 406235
		22	10:12	P 360819
2008	Jan	3	8:04	A 405330
		19	8:30	P 366431
		31	4:20	A 404532
	Feb	14	1:08	P 370219
		28	1:19	A 404443
	Mar	10	21:50	P 366299
		26	20:18	A 405092
	Apr	7	19:41	P 361082
		23	9:34	A 405943
	May	6	3:08	P 357773
		20	14:27	A 406403
	Jun	3	13:14	P 357256
		16	17:34	A 406228
	Jul	1	21:39	P 359515
		14	4:12	A 405452
		29	23:34	P 363883
	Aug	10	20:26	A 404555
		26	3:58	P 368696
	Sep	7	15:01	A 404212
		20	3:29	P 368886
	Oct	5	10:34	A 404719
		17	6:04	P 363825
	Nov	2	4:52	A 405723
		14	9:59	P 358976
		29	16:54	A 406480
	Dec	12	21:53	P 356567
		26	17:45	A 406602
2009	Jan	10	10:49	P 357502
		23	0:10	A 406118
	Feb	7	20:18	P 361490
		19	17:04	A 405128
	Mar	7	15:10	P 367018
		19	13:18	A 404297
	Apr	2	2:26	P 370013
		16	9:14	A 404229
		28	6:22	P 366041
	May	14	2:52	A 404915
		26	3:36	P 361155
	Jun	10	16:05	A 405787
		23	10:38	P 358020
	Jul	7	21:36	A 406232
		21	20:26	P 357465
	Aug	4	0:45	A 406028
		19	4:49	P 359642
		31	11:03	A 405268
	Sep	16	7:52	P 364056
		28	3:27	A 404431
	Oct	13	12:25	P 369067
		25	23:28	A 404166
	Nov	7	7:25	P 368903
		22	20:13	A 404732
	Dec	4	14:22	P 363483
		20	14:56	A 405730
2010	Jan	1	20:45	P 358685
		17	1:43	A 406435
		30	9:02	P 356598
	Feb	13	2:12	A 406541
		27	21:52	P 357830
	Mar	12	10:06	A 406008
		28	4:51	P 361879
	Apr	9	2:39	A 405001
		24	21:05	P 367141
	May	6	22:02	A 404235
		20	8:49	P 369733
	Jun	3	16:56	A 404264
		15	15:04	P 365934
	Jul	1	10:12	A 405034
		13	11:23	P 361119
		28	23:50	A 405955
	Aug	10	18:07	P 357861
		25	5:55	A 406389
	Sep	8	3:48	P 357193
		21	8:05	A 406166
	Oct	6	13:42	P 359459
		18	18:22	A 405427
	Nov	3	17:32	P 364193
		15	11:46	A 404629
		30	18:55	P 369430
	Dec	13	8:32	A 404404
		25	12:17	P 368466
2011	Jan	10	5:33	A 404975
		22	0:00	P 362792
	Feb	6	23:16	A 405924
		19	7:19	P 358251
	Mar	6	7:51	A 406583
		19	19:20	P 356578
	Apr	2	9:03	A 406657
		17	5:52	P 358093
		29	18:04	A 406039
	May	15	11:25	P 362139
		27	9:57	A 405002
	Jun	12	1:34	P 367190
		24	4:07	A 404270
	Jul	7	13:53	P 369569
		21	22:55	A 404355
	Aug	2	21:15	P 365762
		18	16:25	A 405160
		30	17:45	P 360861
	Sep	15	6:24	A 406065
		28	0:51	P 357558
	Oct	12	11:44	A 406434
		26	12:27	P 357057
	Nov	8	13:21	A 406177
		23	23:34	P 359691
	Dec	6	1:10	A 405414
		22	2:50	P 364801
2012	Jan	2	20:27	A 404577
		17	21:19	P 369886
		30	17:48	A 404321
	Feb	11	18:41	P 367922
		27	14:04	A 404861
	Mar	10	9:59	P 362404
		26	6:02	A 405776
	Apr	7	17:08	P 358319
		22	13:48	A 406419
	May	6	3:23	P 356958
		19	16:13	A 406449
	Jun	3	13:19	P 358489
		16	1:23	A 405787
	Jul	1	18:11	P 362368
		13	16:51	A 404778
		29	8:27	P 367316
	Aug	10	10:52	A 404121
		23	19:25	P 369728
	Sep	7	5:56	A 404293
		19	2:44	P 365752
	Oct	5	0:37	A 405160
		17	0:50	P 360673
	Nov	1	15:30	A 406050
		14	10:20	P 357366
		28	19:33	A 406362
	Dec	12	23:28	P 357075
		25	21:20	A 406098
2013	Jan	10	10:26	P 360053
		22	10:52	A 405309

Moon Perigee/Apogee 1900–2020 • Distance in Kilometers

Year	Month	Day	Time	Distance
	Feb	7	12:15	P 365320
		19	6:26	A 404470
	Mar	5	23:12	P 369957
		19	3:06	A 404260
		31	3:49	P 367504
	Apr	15	22:28	A 404862
		27	20:03	P 362270
	May	13	13:33	A 405825
		26	1:32	P 358378
	Jun	9	21:38	A 406486
		23	11:11	P 356997
	Jul	7	0:40	A 406490
		21	20:34	P 358403
	Aug	3	8:54	A 405832
		19	1:15	P 362264
		30	23:55	A 404881
	Sep	15	16:34	P 367392
		27	18:23	A 404306
	Oct	10	23:10	P 369814
		25	14:27	A 404555
	Nov	6	9:21	P 365363
		22	9:49	A 405442
	Dec	4	10:08	P 360071
		19	23:48	A 406269
2014	Jan	1	21:12	P 356925
		16	1:59	A 406532
		30	9:57	P 357085
	Feb	12	5:11	A 406231
		27	20:02	P 360442
	Mar	11	19:53	A 405363
		27	18:41	P 365705
	Apr	8	14:56	A 404498
		23	0:31	P 369765
	May	6	10:22	A 404316
		18	11:58	P 367103
	Jun	3	4:21	A 404953
		15	3:21	P 362066
		30	19:12	A 405930
	Jul	13	8:23	P 358264
		28	3:31	A 406567
	Aug	10	17:52	P 356900
		24	6:12	A 406524
	Sep	8	3:21	P 358391
		20	14:24	A 405844
	Oct	6	9:37	P 362480
		18	6:03	A 404895
	Nov	3	0:22	P 367879
		15	1:49	A 404336
		27	23:11	P 369827
	Dec	12	23:12	A 404581
		24	16:49	P 364800
2015	Jan	9	18:22	A 405407
		21	20:19	P 359647
	Feb	6	6:28	A 406150
		19	7:23	P 357000
	Mar	5	7:37	A 406385
		19	19:50	P 357586
	Apr	1	13:02	A 406012
		17	3:38	P 361025
		29	3:52	A 405082
	May	15	0:09	P 366024
		26	22:22	A 404244
	Jun	10	4:50	P 369711
		23	17:06	A 404130
	Jul	5	18:59	P 367094
		21	11:03	A 404834
	Aug	2	10:02	P 362142
		18	2:30	A 405848
		30	15:28	P 358294
	Sep	14	11:28	A 406464
		28	1:34	P 356878
	Oct	11	13:19	A 406388
		26	13:04	P 358468
	Nov	7	21:55	A 405721
		23	20:17	P 362819
	Dec	5	14:60	A 404798
		21	8:59	P 368417
2016	Jan	2	11:54	A 404274
		15	2:18	P 369619
		30	9:08	A 404551
	Feb	11	2:34	P 364361
		27	3:24	A 405383
	Mar	10	6:58	P 359514
		25	14:17	A 406125
	Apr	7	17:45	P 357167
		21	16:04	A 406351
	May	6	4:04	P 357830
		18	22:10	A 405933
	Jun	3	10:54	P 361143
		15	12:02	A 405023
	Jul	1	6:36	P 365985
		13	5:20	A 404268
		27	11:38	P 369662
	Aug	10	0:00	A 404262
		22	1:15	P 367050
	Sep	6	18:50	A 405054
		18	17:08	P 361899
	Oct	4	11:04	A 406096
		16	23:49	P 357861
		31	19:27	A 406662
	Nov	14	11:21	P 356515
		27	20:08	A 406554
	Dec	12	23:43	P 358461
		25	5:54	A 405870
2017	Jan	10	5:54	P 363241
		22	0:07	A 404914
	Feb	6	14:03	P 368816
		18	21:23	A 404375
	Mar	3	7:35	P 369062
		18	17:31	A 404648
		30	12:34	P 363857
	Apr	15	10:05	A 405474
		27	16:22	P 359331
	May	12	19:51	A 406210
		26	1:09	P 357208
	Jun	8	22:19	A 406401
		23	10:51	P 357942
	Jul	6	4:29	A 405934
		21	17:19	P 361239
	Aug	2	18:00	A 405024
		18	13:21	P 366123
		30	11:25	A 404306
	Sep	13	16:04	P 369859
		27	6:46	A 404346
	Oct	9	5:52	P 366856
		25	2:20	A 405154
	Nov	6	0:00	P 361438
		21	18:55	A 406131
	Dec	4	8:42	P 357497
		19	1:31	A 406603
2018	Jan	1	22:03	P 356566
		15	2:13	A 406464
		30	9:56	P 358998
	Feb	11	14:18	A 405699
		27	14:43	P 363935
	Mar	11	9:12	A 404676
		26	17:18	P 369106
	Apr	8	5:26	A 404142
		20	14:43	P 368714
	May	6	0:28	A 404457
		17	21:17	P 363778
	Jun	2	16:38	A 405316
		15	0:00	P 359503
		30	2:45	A 406061
	Jul	13	8:21	P 357436
		27	5:48	A 406223
	Aug	10	18:16	P 358082
		23	11:24	A 405745
	Sep	8	1:08	P 361351
		20	0:49	A 404876
	Oct	5	22:34	P 366393
		17	19:24	A 404226
		31	20:16	P 370204
	Nov	14	16:01	A 404337
		26	12:14	P 366622
	Dec	12	12:26	A 405175
		24	9:47	P 361065
2019	Jan	9	4:28	A 406117
		21	20:12	P 357345
	Feb	5	9:31	A 406556
		19	8:60	P 356766
	Mar	4	11:28	A 406391
		19	19:59	P 359379
	Apr	1	0:11	A 405577
		16	22:14	P 364205
		28	18:27	A 404581
	May	13	21:52	P 369009
		26	13:30	A 404135
	Jun	7	23:21	P 368504
		23	7:47	A 404546
	Jul	5	4:54	P 363728
		21	0:00	A 405481
	Aug	2	7:06	P 359402
		17	10:50	A 406245
		30	16:00	P 357181
	Sep	13	13:33	A 406378
		28	2:12	P 357804
	Oct	10	18:32	A 405899
		26	10:38	P 361315
	Nov	7	8:35	A 405057
		23	7:38	P 366718
	Dec	5	4:03	A 404445
		18	20:18	P 370264
2020	Jan	2	1:23	A 404580
		13	20:31	P 365960
		29	21:33	A 405392
	Feb	10	20:40	P 360463
		26	11:35	A 406278
	Mar	10	6:23	P 357126
		24	15:22	A 406692
	Apr	7	18:18	P 356910
		20	19:02	A 406462
	May	6	2:52	P 359656
		18	7:44	A 405582
	Jun	3	3:30	P 364367
		15	0:50	A 404595
		30	2:13	P 368958
	Jul	12	19:34	A 404198
		25	5:02	P 368361
	Aug	9	13:53	A 404657
		21	10:57	P 363516
	Sep	6	6:27	A 405606
		18	13:52	P 359087
	Oct	3	17:22	A 406322
		17	0:00	P 356912
		30	18:44	A 406395
	Nov	14	11:44	P 357842
		27	0:29	A 405894
	Dec	12	20:53	P 361774
		24	16:36	A 405010

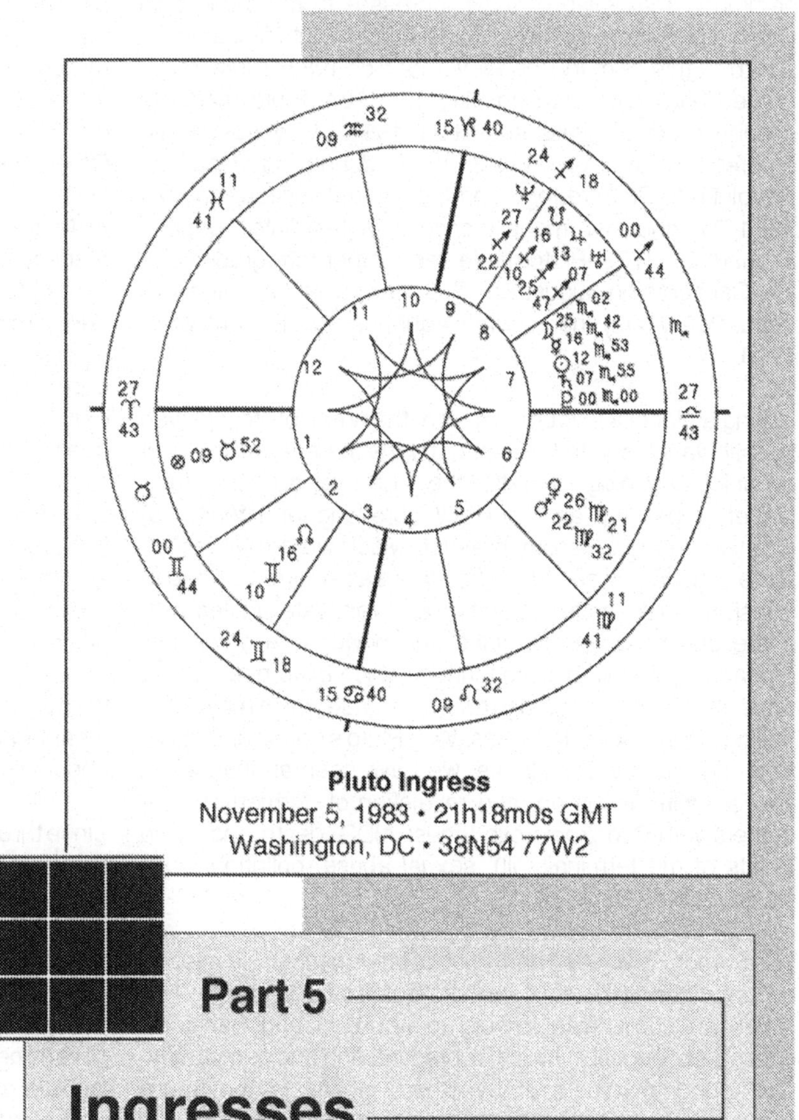

Pluto Ingress
November 5, 1983 • 21h18m0s GMT
Washington, DC • 38N54 77W2

Part 5

Ingresses

Ingresses

by Maritha Pottenger & Zipporah Dobyns

An ingress refers to the moment a planet leaves one sign to enter another. Due to the retrograde cycles, outer planets commonly make two or three ingresses to the same sign within a brief period of time. For example, Pluto first entered Scorpio (this century) on November 5, 1983. Pluto retrograded back into Libra on May 18, 1984. Pluto made its second Scorpio ingress August 28, 1984. By contrast, Pluto entered Aquarius on April 3, 1777 (during our American Revolution). Pluto retrograded back into Capricorn on May 28, 1777, and then made a second ingress into Aquarius January 26, 1778. Pluto made yet another retrograde back into Capricorn on August 21, 1778. Pluto's third and final (for about 250 years) ingress into Aquarius was December 1, 1778.

During a planet's sojourn in a sign, the areas of life signified by that planet tend to be colored by the themes of the sign it occupies. Astrologers watch the sign cycles of the outer planets especially (as they show more long-term concerns) for clues to broad, societal issues which we are all facing. Pluto is generally seen as a key to areas where we need to transform, transmute, refurbish and renovate, to learn to share pleasures, possessions and power with our fellow humans. Pluto symbolizes matters which have been swept under the carpet and hidden away, garbage which may come boiling out into consciousness. With Pluto's transit of Scorpio from the mid-80s to mid-90s, we have seen an increasing concern with, focus on, and revelation of, formerly secret matters with Scorpionic overtones: AIDS, death and dying (rights of the terminally ill), sexual abuse, pollution, toxic waste, debts and greed.

The French Revolution and much of our American Revolution occurred during Pluto's transit of Aquarius (1777-1797). The American public was striving to refurbish and transform concepts of equality, justice, representation and democracy. Our founding fathers and mothers looked to the future (Aquarius) and transformed humanitarian principles.

Marilyn Waram's *Book of Neptune* contains an excellent description—complete with historical examples—of how Neptune's sign placement depicts illusions the world must face. We may react with dread and fear when our illusions are questioned—or glorify the illusion (perhaps ending up martyrs or victims). We often go through periods of confusion until—by the end of a transit—we have clarified our values in that area.

For example, Neptune was in Sagittarius during the 1970s and early 1980s (January 4, 1970-May 3, 1970, and November 6, 1970-January 19, 1984, plus June 23-November 21, 1984). During this transit, people pursued a search for ultimate "Truth" in a big way. Eastern concepts, gurus and ideals were sought out—abroad and at home. Some people turned to fundamentalist religions (Christian, Moslem, etc.) as the water (Neptune) urge to cling to the familiar past overrode the fire (Sagittarius) urge to seek expanded Truth. Others welcomed the foreign ideas.

As Marilyn Waram points out (page 64): "A businessman who meditated in 1970 would have been looked upon with suspicion. Halfway through the transit of Neptune through Sagittarius, Transcendental Meditation was being taught everywhere imaginable, even in small towns and villages. By the end of the transit, meditation had become respectable; it had gained mainstream acceptance as an excellent method of dealing with stress."

The path of religions was not all pure or peaceful during Neptune's sojourn in Sagittarius. The abuses and misuses of a number of cults were revealed during this period. Certain religious organizations had taken advantage of the human desire to "believe" and to "belong." "Deprogramming" their victims was in vogue for a time. Some people drifted away from their churches; others reached a firmer, clearer sense of meaning and purpose in life. Either way, veils and illusions about spirituality and selflessness were often confronted.

Since three of the outer planets entered the sign of Capricorn, some of the most dramatic political events of recorded history have occurred. Gorbachev became the leader of Russia in March 1985, soon after Neptune entered Capricorn. His radical changes in the Soviet Union were finally accepted as genuine; and after 1988, when Saturn and Uranus also entered Capricorn (the sign of the executive branch of government), the pace of change accelerated. The totalitarian rule of Communists in the countries of eastern Europe was overthrown in a few months in the fall of 1989 after Gorbachev made it clear that he would not use Soviet forces to maintain power there. But he was unwilling to allow Soviet republics the same freedom. We might suspect that with the movement of Saturn, Uranus and Neptune into Aquarius (the sign of democracy) during the 1990s, any remaining totalitarian rulers will be challenged.

In addition to considering the general "astrological weather" faced by everyone when a planet transits each sign, ingresses are a part of the tool kit of astrologers who seek to understand the world (*mundo*). Mundane astrologers focus primarily on large-scale issues which confront countries or

(continued on page 62)

Chiron Ingresses 1900–2020

Year	Date	Time	Sign
1901	Jan 13	1:33	♑
	Aug 8	16:05	℞ ♐
	Sep 30	1:03	♑
1904	Apr 22	14:04	♒
	May 20	13:29	℞ ♑
1905	Jan 13	2:05	♒
1910	Mar 20	8:49	♓
	Aug 29	9:51	℞ ♒
1911	Jan 15	9:44	♓
1918	Mar 31	10:57	♈
	Oct 22	16:21	℞ ♓
1919	Jan 28	18:04	♈
1926	May 25	2:06	♉
	Oct 20	7:43	℞ ♈
1927	Mar 25	11:27	♉
1933	Jun 7	2:29	♊
	Dec 22	7:29	℞ ♉
1934	Mar 23	14:15	♊
1937	Aug 27	17:28	♋
	Nov 23	1:54	℞ ♊
1938	May 28	12:44	♋
1940	Sep 30	3:55	♌
	Dec 27	4:47	℞ ♋
1941	Jun 16	18:41	♌
1943	Jul 26	22:49	♍
1944	Nov 18	3:35	♎
1945	Mar 24	2:31	℞ ♍
	Jul 22	16:44	♎
1946	Nov 10	7:23	♏
1948	Nov 28	13:09	♐
1951	Feb 9	1:41	♑
	Jun 18	12:51	℞ ♐
	Nov 8	16:37	♑
1955	Jan 27	16:41	♒
1960	Mar 26	13:55	♓
	Aug 19	6:12	℞ ♒
1961	Jan 21	2:04	♓
1968	Apr 1	7:20	♈
	Oct 18	22:17	℞ ♓
1969	Jan 30	8:29	♈
1976	May 28	11:22	♉
	Oct 13	22:33	℞ ♈
1977	Mar 28	19:16	♉
1983	Jun 21	14:03	♊
	Nov 29	13:08	℞ ♉
1984	Apr 11	4:28	♊
1988	Jun 21	9:44	♋
1991	Jul 21	18:55	♌
1993	Sep 3	21:28	♍
1995	Sep 9	16:48	♎
1996	Dec 29	12:10	♏
1997	Apr 4	16:24	℞ ♎
	Sep 3	3:01	♏
1999	Jan 7	9:06	♐
	Jun 1	12:52	℞ ♏
	Sep 22	0:04	♐
2001	Dec 11	23:06	♑
2005	Feb 21	22:09	♒
	Jul 31	20:37	℞ ♑
	Dec 6	6:32	♒
2010	Apr 20	20:03	♓
	Jul 19	18:16	℞ ♒
2011	Feb 9	3:54	♓
2018	Apr 17	15:24	♈
	Sep 25	15:03	℞ ♓
2019	Feb 18	15:60	♈

Ceres Ingresses 1900–2020

Year	Date	Time	Sign
1900	Mar 19	12:28	♒
1901	Jan 19	3:21	♓
	Apr 6	6:02	♈
	Jun 30	7:50	♉
	Nov 20	3:22	℞ ♈
1902	Jan 14	10:54	♉
	Apr 20	2:02	♊
	Jun 30	17:15	♋
	Sep 10	9:41	♌
1903	Jun 12	1:38	♍
	Aug 25	18:00	♎
	Nov 1	0:45	♏
1904	Jan 11	10:10	♐
	Nov 4	8:17	♑
1905	Jan 21	19:09	♒
	Apr 11	22:46	♓
1906	Feb 11	18:56	♈
	Apr 29	5:24	♉
	Jul 16	18:26	♊
1907	May 2	5:24	♋
	Jul 12	5:15	♌
	Sep 16	17:15	♍
	Nov 27	7:42	♎
1908	Sep 2	0:15	♏
	Nov 14	18:15	♐
1909	Jan 27	3:24	♑
	Nov 27	4:57	♒
1910	Feb 16	3:44	♓
	May 6	2:20	♈
1911	Mar 4	3:32	♉
	May 18	23:02	♊
	Jul 30	17:35	♋
	Oct 29	19:08	♌
1912	Jan 6	3:14	℞ ♋
	May 1	19:59	♌
	Jul 19	5:47	♍
	Sep 23	22:44	♎
	Nov 30	10:56	♏
1913	Mar 5	16:54	♐
	Apr 19	3:08	℞ ♏
	Sep 12	18:20	♐
	Dec 4	21:01	♑
1914	Feb 18	13:38	♒
	Jun 4	3:01	♓
	Jul 18	12:52	℞ ♒
	Dec 20	0:15	♓
1915	Mar 12	15:25	♈
	May 28	14:45	♉
1916	Mar 18	19:00	♊
	Jun 3	15:12	♋
	Aug 11	8:34	♌
	Oct 21	23:13	♍
1917	Jul 24	6:43	♎
	Oct 5	1:20	♏
	Dec 13	6:37	♐
1918	Mar 4	14:58	♑
	Jul 7	15:60	℞ ♐
	Sep 23	18:53	♑
	Dec 27	21:60	♒
1919	Mar 14	21:18	♓
	Jun 16	22:06	♈
	Sep 13	18:25	℞ ♓
1920	Jan 9	3:44	♈
	Apr 3	4:16	♉
	Jun 16	13:43	♊
	Sep 8	21:08	♋
1921	Jan 6	16:18	℞ ♊
	Mar 18	17:44	♋
	Jun 13	21:16	♌
	Aug 20	6:15	♍
	Oct 25	2:49	♎
1922	Jan 10	6:12	♏
	May 5	18:51	℞ ♎
	Jul 17	16:30	♏
	Oct 18	22:48	♐
	Dec 31	16:07	♑
1923	Mar 22	6:47	♒
1924	Jan 21	13:43	♓
	Apr 7	17:02	♈
	Jul 3	5:19	♉
	Nov 10	19:42	℞ ♈
1925	Jan 20	11:51	♉
	Apr 22	0:60	♊
	Jul 2	14:03	♋
	Sep 12	19:45	♌
1926	Jun 15	2:42	♍
	Aug 27	12:15	♎
	Nov 2	12:17	♏
1927	Jan 13	4:18	♐
	Nov 6	18:25	♑
1928	Jan 23	19:32	♒
	Apr 13	9:29	♓
1929	Feb 13	2:54	♈
	Apr 30	11:19	♉
	Jul 18	17:30	♊
1930	May 4	8:44	♋
	Jul 14	1:46	♌
	Sep 18	19:23	♍
	Nov 30	15:36	♎
1931	Sep 5	12:36	♏
	Nov 17	12:21	♐
1932	Jan 29	22:46	♑
	Nov 28	22:30	♒
1933	Feb 17	6:04	♓
	May 7	12:12	♈
1934	Mar 5	20:04	♉
	May 20	11:25	♊
	Aug 1	18:40	♋
	Nov 7	7:57	♌
	Dec 24	0:30	℞ ♋
1935	May 7	3:18	♌
	Jul 22	16:05	♍
	Sep 27	2:42	♎
	Dec 3	20:29	♏
1936	Sep 15	18:15	♐
	Dec 6	9:08	♑
1937	Feb 20	0:34	♒
	Jun 14	20:06	♓
	Jul 5	1:03	℞ ♒
	Dec 22	3:52	♓
1938	Mar 14	1:22	♈
	May 30	8:26	♉
1939	Mar 22	5:21	♊
	Jun 6	5:47	♋
	Aug 13	23:18	♌
	Oct 25	6:02	♍
1940	Jul 26	8:02	♎
	Oct 6	10:07	♏
	Dec 14	14:43	♐
1941	Mar 7	6:08	♑
	Jun 30	8:29	℞ ♐
	Sep 27	18:11	♑
	Dec 29	9:00	♒
1942	Mar 16	10:18	♓
	Jun 21	9:57	♈
	Sep 5	20:41	℞ ♓
1943	Jan 12	2:51	♈
	Apr 5	18:52	♉
	Jun 19	5:29	♊
	Sep 13	3:36	♋
	Dec 30	12:34	℞ ♊
1944	Mar 23	3:36	♋
	Jun 15	9:23	♌
	Aug 21	11:39	♍
	Oct 26	10:19	♎
1945	Jan 12	23:57	♏
	Apr 28	0:59	℞ ♎
	Jul 21	22:00	♏
	Oct 20	8:24	♐
1946	Jan 1	23:01	♑
	Mar 24	10:49	♒
	Sep 1	22:26	℞ ♑
	Oct 7	8:59	♒
1947	Jan 23	3:32	♓
	Apr 10	5:18	♈
	Jul 7	3:01	♉
	Nov 4	4:37	℞ ♈
1948	Jan 25	18:08	♉
	Apr 23	12:49	♊
	Jul 3	22:56	♋
	Sep 14	15:02	♌
1949	Jun 17	7:53	♍
	Aug 28	22:04	♎
	Nov 3	19:49	♏
1950	Jan 14	23:21	♐
	Nov 8	10:39	♑
1951	Jan 25	2:53	♒
	Apr 16	6:39	♓
1952	Feb 15	14:31	♈
	May 1	19:43	♉
	Jul 20	21:17	♊
1953	May 6	16:10	♋
	Jul 16	3:06	♌
	Sep 21	3:22	♍
	Dec 4	12:29	♎
1954	Sep 8	1:25	♏
	Nov 19	7:34	♐
1955	Jan 31	19:32	♑
	Dec 1	15:55	♒
1956	Feb 19	9:50	♓
	May 9	1:31	♈
1957	Mar 7	15:41	♉
	May 22	3:35	♊
	Aug 4	1:02	♋
1958	May 11	5:48	♌
	Jul 25	3:31	♍
	Sep 29	8:03	♎
	Dec 6	8:21	♏
1959	Sep 19	14:21	♐
	Dec 8	22:01	♑
1960	Feb 22	13:34	♒
	Dec 24	3:28	♓
1961	Mar 15	8:18	♈
	May 31	22:25	♉
1962	Mar 24	9:32	♊
	Jun 7	20:10	♋
	Aug 15	17:38	♌
	Oct 28	0:47	♍
1963	Jul 29	23:28	♎
	Oct 9	8:31	♏
	Dec 17	13:25	♐
1964	Mar 11	3:54	♑
	Jun 21	11:49	℞ ♐
	Oct 2	3:49	♑
	Dec 31	2:23	♒
1965	Mar 18	2:31	♓
	Jun 26	15:16	♈
	Aug 28	14:45	℞ ♓
1966	Jan 14	15:32	♈
	Apr 7	4:37	♉
	Jun 20	17:46	♊
	Sep 16	15:51	♋
	Dec 22	12:35	℞ ♊
1967	Mar 28	3:31	♋
	Jun 18	4:53	♌
	Aug 24	5:16	♍
	Oct 29	12:35	♎
1968	Jan 18	23:33	♏
	Apr 16	19:21	℞ ♎
	Jul 27	15:51	♏
	Oct 22	15:51	♐
1969	Jan 4	0:28	♑
	Mar 27	16:30	♒
	Aug 19	16:19	℞ ♑
	Oct 16	22:58	♒
1970	Jan 25	0:08	♓
	Apr 11	21:49	♈
	Jul 10	10:13	♉
	Oct 27	13:42	℞ ♈
1971	Jan 29	14:52	♉
	Apr 26	4:12	♊
	Jul 6	15:02	♋
	Sep 18	2:30	♌
1972	Jun 20	15:26	♍
	Aug 31	7:50	♎
	Nov 6	4:41	♏
1973	Jan 18	5:60	♐
	Nov 11	2:27	♑
1974	Jan 27	3:54	♒
	Apr 19	1:51	♓
1975	Feb 17	16:06	♈
	May 4	20:07	♉
	Jul 25	5:47	♊
1976	May 9	20:50	♋
	Jul 18	22:25	♌
	Sep 24	5:06	♍
	Dec 9	17:23	♎
1977	Apr 12	23:04	℞ ♍
	Jun 8	1:26	♎
	Sep 10	20:42	♏
	Nov 21	7:50	♐
1978	Feb 2	22:32	♑
	Dec 3	15:50	♒
1979	Feb 20	21:54	♓
	May 12	5:24	♈
1980	Mar 10	3:10	♉
	May 24	10:45	♊
	Aug 7	2:24	♋
1981	May 15	16:47	♌
	Jul 27	22:15	♍
	Oct 1	18:19	♎
	Dec 9	0:26	♏
1982	Sep 22	6:39	♐
	Dec 10	10:28	♑
1983	Feb 24	2:54	♒
	Dec 27	3:18	♓
1984	Mar 16	18:41	♈
	Jun 2	20:10	♉
1985	Mar 27	1:42	♊
	Jun 9	22:25	♋
	Aug 18	1:21	♌
	Oct 31	18:06	♍
1986	Aug 1	21:45	♎
	Oct 11	10:26	♏
	Dec 19	13:22	♐
1987	Mar 16	7:28	♑
	Jun 14	4:44	℞ ♐
	Oct 6	15:55	♑
1988	Jan 2	12:46	♒
	Mar 19	12:10	♓

Ceres Ingresses 1900–2020

Year	Date	Time	Sign
	Jul 2	11:49	♈
	Aug 19	22:57 ℞	♓
1989	Jan 16	20:01	♈
	Apr 8	13:57	♉
	Jun 22	9:43	♊
	Sep 21	6:07	♋
	Dec 13	8:24 ℞	♊
1990	Apr 1	8:58	♋
	Jun 20	10:52	♌
	Aug 26	9:53	♍
	Nov 1	3:60	♎
1991	Jan 26	2:44	♏
	Apr 4	19:30 ℞	♎
	Aug 3	2:27	♏
	Oct 26	1:04	♐
1992	Jan 7	1:20	♑
	Mar 30	20:58	♒
	Aug 10	2:08 ℞	♑
	Oct 22	20:13	♒
1993	Jan 26	13:31	♓
	Apr 13	9:18	♈
	Jul 13	19:46	♉
	Oct 20	4:53 ℞	♈

Year	Date	Time	Sign
1994	Feb 2	2:41	♉
	Apr 28	0:06	♊
	Jul 8	15:25	♋
	Sep 21	6:04	♌
1995	Jun 25	8:14	♍
	Sep 4	0:51	♎
	Nov 9	19:06	♏
1996	Jan 22	19:12	♐
	Nov 13	11:07	♑
1997	Jan 28	23:07	♒
	Apr 21	15:60	♓
	Oct 11	12:05 ℞	♒
	29	4:48	♓
1998	Feb 19	16:33	♈
	May 6	20:58	♉
	Jul 28	17:15	♊
1999	Jan 2	21:52 ℞	♉
	Jan 30	16:25	♊
	May 13	13:48	♋
	Jul 22	5:28	♌
	Sep 27	16:03	♍
	Dec 15	4:38	♎
2000	Mar 31	9:59 ℞	♍

Year	Date	Time	Sign
	Jun 15	15:47	♎
	Sep 12	20:22	♏
	Nov 22	19:27	♐
2001	Feb 4	15:32	♑
	Dec 5	11:39	♒
2002	Feb 22	10:09	♓
	May 14	12:47	♈
2003	Mar 13	11:07	♉
	May 27	12:35	♊
	Aug 10	18:00	♋
2004	May 18	17:35	♌
	Jul 29	18:18	♍
	Oct 3	7:44	♎
	Dec 10	18:27	♏
2005	Sep 24	2:03	♐
	Dec 11	13:31	♑
2006	Feb 25	10:35	♒
	Dec 29	0:26	♓
2007	Mar 19	5:03	♈
	Jun 5	18:31	♉
2008	Mar 29	9:03	♊
	Jun 11	15:43	♋
	Aug 19	21:07	♌

Year	Date	Time	Sign
	Nov 3	16:46	♍
2009	Aug 3	19:03	♎
	Oct 12	18:09	♏
	Dec 20	20:08	♐
2010	Mar 19	13:10	♑
	Jun 7	19:25 ℞	♐
	Oct 8	23:52	♑
2011	Jan 3	14:24	♒
	Mar 21	16:16	♓
	Jul 11	6:41	♈
	Aug 10	14:27 ℞	♓
2012	Jan 19	17:58	♈
	Apr 9	20:16	♉
	Jun 23	22:29	♊
	Sep 26	6:03	♋
	Dec 4	10:31 ℞	♊
2013	Apr 4	21:43	♋
	Jun 22	11:48	♌
	Aug 28	9:53	♍
	Nov 3	13:42	♎
2014	Feb 3	15:23	♏
	Mar 22	17:24 ℞	♎
	Aug 7	3:06	♏

Year	Date	Time	Sign
	Oct 27	21:47	♐
2015	Jan 8	15:08	♑
	Apr 3	11:47	♒
	Aug 4	0:32 ℞	♑
	Oct 27	15:01	♒
2016	Jan 28	18:13	♓
	Apr 14	14:20	♈
	Jul 17	2:59	♉
	Oct 13	12:29 ℞	♈
2017	Feb 4	23:31	♉
	Apr 29	15:20	♊
	Jul 10	11:25	♋
	Sep 24	5:10	♌
2018	Jun 28	8:24	♍
	Sep 6	5:54	♎
	Nov 11	21:08	♏
2019	Jan 25	17:32	♐
	Nov 16	4:14	♑
2020	Jan 31	7:38	♒
	Apr 23	19:36	♓
	Sep 27	10:11 ℞	♒
	Nov 9	12:20	♓

Pallas Ingresses 1900–2020

Year	Date	Time	Sign
1900	Jan 24	7:08	♑
	Dec 16	2:54	♒
1901	Mar 15	21:55	♓
1902	Feb 22	15:35	♈
	May 8	13:02	♉
	Jul 14	20:18	♊
	Sep 20	3:46	♋
1903	May 12	22:33	♌
	Jul 16	16:48	♍
	Sep 18	22:56	♎
	Nov 24	19:55	♏
1904	Feb 17	11:56	♐
	Apr 30	10:30 ℞	♏
	Sep 18	7:54	♐
	Dec 8	3:00	♑
1905	Feb 25	3:06	♒
1906	Feb 2	20:58	♓
	May 6	7:58	♈
	Nov 8	8:48 ℞	♓
	Dec 17	23:17	♈
1907	Mar 17	22:30	♉
	May 14	22:16	♊
	Jul 5	8:11	♋
	Aug 24	9:53	♌
	Oct 17	13:48	♍
1908	Jan 17	13:54	♎
	26	12:31 ℞	♍
	Jul 22	0:53	♎
	Oct 4	3:45	♏
	Dec 11	22:05	♐
1909	Feb 28	19:43	♑
	Jun 23	22:16 ℞	♐
	Oct 11	23:06	♑
1910	Jan 11	17:24	♒
	Apr 12	19:58	♓
	Sep 7	9:29 ℞	♒
	Dec 14	14:46	♓
1911	Mar 20	20:13	♈
	Jun 10	10:46	♉
1912	Mar 6	18:23	♊
	May 1	12:36	♋
	Jun 23	12:59	♌
	Aug 18	8:51	♍
	Oct 18	8:15	♎
	Dec 30	9:35	♏
1913	May 3	7:22 ℞	♎

Year	Date	Time	Sign
	Jul 30	10:36	♏
	Oct 23	19:35	♐
1914	Jan 4	5:32	♑
	Mar 30	17:02	♒
	Jul 15	19:15 ℞	♑
	Nov 23	14:01	♒
1915	Feb 26	15:33	♓
	Jun 15	10:33	♈
	Aug 25	9:29 ℞	♓
1916	Feb 2	3:29	♈
	Apr 16	17:06	♉
	Jun 17	9:56	♊
	Aug 12	15:58	♋
	Oct 8	5:51	♌
1917	Jun 19	4:33	♍
	Aug 29	0:34	♎
	Nov 4	8:40	♏
1918	Jan 15	9:03	♐
	Nov 19	0:32	♑
1919	Feb 6	20:07	♒
	Jun 7	16:09	♓
	23	13:38 ℞	♒
1920	Jan 16	0:01	♓
	Apr 15	7:32	♈
	Aug 10	0:41	♉
	Sep 9	9:45 ℞	♈
1921	Feb 20	13:23	♉
	Apr 21	0:13	♊
	Jun 11	4:30	♋
	Jul 31	10:20	♌
	Sep 23	1:39	♍
	Nov 26	3:36	♎
1922	Apr 22	14:27 ℞	♍
	Jun 13	12:21	♎
	Sep 14	22:07	♏
	Nov 24	3:51	♐
1923	Feb 4	17:20	♑
	Dec 25	17:13	♒
1924	Mar 23	16:26	♓
1925	Mar 2	17:21	♈
	May 18	5:13	♉
	Jul 29	20:43	♊
1926	Mar 28	23:13	♋
	May 29	14:30	♌
	Jul 28	20:46	♍
	Sep 29	12:26	♎

Year	Date	Time	Sign
	Dec 6	10:03	♏
1927	Oct 3	6:35	♐
	Dec 18	6:58	♑
1928	Mar 6	18:50	♒
	Sep 3	5:30 ℞	♑
	Oct 19	13:41	♒
1929	Feb 10	5:06	♓
	May 16	7:06	♈
	Oct 10	21:12 ℞	♓
1930	Jan 7	11:17	♈
	Mar 27	23:38	♉
	May 25	20:24	♊
	Jul 17	9:47	♋
	Sep 6	12:43	♌
	Nov 2	10:06	♍
1931	Aug 6	6:03	♎
	Oct 15	17:56	♏
	Dec 23	16:14	♐
1932	Mar 22	8:11	♑
	May 21	11:17 ℞	♐
	Oct 26	19:01	♑
1933	Jan 20	1:46	♒
	Apr 24	0:03	♓
	Aug 18	1:18 ℞	♒
	Dec 26	8:35	♓
1934	Mar 28	22:24	♈
	Jun 23	13:59	♉
	Dec 2	23:03 ℞	♈
1935	Jan 8	13:12	♉
	Mar 25	8:25	♊
	May 17	2:16	♋
	Jul 7	15:03	♌
	Aug 31	7:52	♍
	Oct 31	11:43	♎
1936	Jan 24	3:28	♏
	Mar 22	16:11 ℞	♎
	Aug 19	14:39	♏
	Nov 3	23:13	♐
1937	Jan 14	10:04	♑
	Apr 19	20:13	♒
	Jun 16	20:26 ℞	♑
	Dec 5	9:19	♒
1938	Mar 6	18:42	♓
1939	Feb 12	14:38	♈
	Apr 28	2:57	♉
	Jul 1	9:59	♊

Year	Date	Time	Sign
	Aug 30	17:35	♋
	Nov 9	0:54	♌
1940	Jan 4	4:57 ℞	♋
	Apr 21	20:56	♌
	Jul 4	4:29	♍
	Sep 8	16:46	♎
	Nov 14	8:23	♏
1941	Jan 29	6:25	♐
	Jun 1	4:53 ℞	♏
	Sep 1	2:24	♐
	Nov 28	5:31	♑
1942	Feb 14	20:20	♒
1943	Jan 24	0:41	♓
	Apr 24	21:24	♈
1944	Mar 4	22:08	♉
	May 2	8:04	♊
	Jun 22	13:26	♋
	Aug 11	15:07	♌
	Oct 4	6:33	♍
	Dec 11	23:21	♎
1945	Mar 15	9:27 ℞	♍
	Jul 6	22:04	♎
	Sep 24	9:05	♏
	Dec 2	6:22	♐
1946	Feb 14	9:27	♑
	Jul 28	5:16 ℞	♐
	Sep 17	16:38	♑
1947	Jan 1	17:09	♒
	Mar 31	19:14	♓
	Oct 6	19:31 ℞	♒
	Nov 22	12:10	♓
1948	Mar 9	18:06	♈
	May 27	4:30	♉
	Aug 15	16:57	♊
	Dec 13	7:27 ℞	♉
1949	Feb 5	18:50	♊
	Apr 15	2:29	♋
	Jun 10	8:09	♌
	Aug 7	3:23	♍
	Oct 7	18:10	♎
	Dec 16	0:47	♏
1950	Oct 12	2:31	♐
	Dec 24	19:17	♑
1951	Mar 15	8:35	♒
	Aug 13	3:03 ℞	♑
	Nov 5	16:29	♒

Year	Date	Time	Sign
1952	Feb 16	12:46	♓
	May 24	19:28	♈
	Sep 23	13:04 ℞	♓
1953	Jan 17	15:39	♈
	Apr 4	7:38	♉
	Jun 3	2:29	♊
	Jul 26	18:43	♋
	Sep 17	3:52	♌
	Nov 17	20:17	♍
1954	Feb 18	14:44 ℞	♌
	May 26	6:27	♍
	Aug 15	3:27	♎
	Oct 22	22:22	♏
	Dec 31	9:11	♐
1955	Nov 5	1:35	♑
1956	Jan 26	13:24	♒
	May 2	23:15	♓
	Aug 3	14:15 ℞	♒
1957	Jan 2	5:18	♓
	Apr 3	12:13	♈
	Jul 4	10:49	♉
	Nov 1	17:56 ℞	♈
1958	Jan 29	21:14	♉
	Apr 4	9:44	♊
	May 26	5:01	♋
	Jul 16	1:48	♌
	Sep 8	4:43	♍
	Nov 8	19:39	♎
1959	Aug 30	6:13	♏
	Nov 11	11:37	♐
1960	Jan 21	17:50	♑
	Dec 11	17:25	♒
1961	Mar 11	18:05	♓
1962	Feb 18	11:19	♈
	May 4	9:09	♉
	Jul 9	17:58	♊
	Sep 12	8:28	♋
1963	May 7	7:55	♌
	Jul 12	23:12	♍
	Sep 15	18:27	♎
	Nov 21	9:50	♏
1964	Feb 10	0:05	♐
	May 11	6:59 ℞	♏
	Sep 12	7:53	♐
	Dec 3	19:45	♑
1965	Feb 20	5:11	♒

Pallas Ingresses 1900–2020

Year	Date	Time	Sign
1966	Jan 29	0:41	♓
	Apr 30	16:17	♈
1967	Mar 12	21:40	♉
	May 10	3:28	♊
	Jun 30	13:29	♋
	Aug 19	16:07	♌
	Oct 12	14:35	♍
	Dec 27	20:42	♎
1968	Feb 19	16:54 ℞	♍
	Jul 16	13:53	♎
	Sep 30	1:19	♏
	Dec 7	13:19	♐
1969	Feb 21	16:40	♑
	Jul 7	7:24 ℞	♐
	Oct 2	8:53	♑
1970	Jan 6	10:49	♒
	Apr 6	2:43	♓
	Sep 20	3:10 ℞	♒
	Dec 4	20:16	♓
1971	Mar 15	11:30	♈
	Jun 3	14:20	♉
	Sep 2	22:01	♊
	Nov 8	23:24 ℞	♉
1972	Feb 25	10:02	♊
	Apr 24	9:47	♋
	Jun 17	14:03	♌
	Aug 13	3:55	♍
	Oct 13	7:48	♎
	Dec 23	7:34	♏
1973	May 20	9:03 ℞	♎
	Jul 17	11:59	♏
	Oct 17	23:30	♐
	Dec 29	14:24	♑
1974	Mar 21	17:59	♒
	Jul 30	1:15 ℞	♑
	Nov 14	7:23	♒
1975	Feb 20	15:00	♓
	Jun 2	12:04	♈
	Sep 11	2:37 ℞	♓
1976	Jan 25	5:54	♈
	Apr 9	19:47	♉
	Jun 9	14:33	♊
	Aug 3	13:11	♋
	Sep 26	17:07	♌
	Dec 11	2:55	♍
1977	Jan 12	16:52 ℞	♌
	Jun 8	16:39	♍
	Aug 22	4:39	♎
	Oct 29	2:51	♏
1978	Jan 7	16:06	♐
	Nov 11	23:41	♑
1979	Jan 31	16:25	♒
	May 14	17:14	♓
	Jul 20	7:03 ℞	♒
1980	Jan 8	23:52	♓
	Apr 8	14:40	♈
	Jul 16	22:47	♉
	Oct 9	17:04 ℞	♈
1981	Feb 10	10:13	♉
	Apr 12	17:56	♊
	Jun 3	5:45	♋
	Jul 23	19:29	♌
	Sep 15	16:46	♍
	Nov 17	10:32	♎
1982	Sep 7	18:01	♏
	Nov 18	0:26	♐
1983	Jan 28	15:45	♑
	Dec 19	1:08	♒
1984	Mar 17	3:03	♓
1985	Feb 24	4:29	♈
	May 10	21:28	♉
	Jul 19	5:16	♊
	Oct 1	6:27	♋
	Dec 24	18:51 ℞	♊
1986	Mar 10	13:26	♋
	May 19	20:23	♌
	Jul 21	11:00	♍
	Sep 22	23:43	♎
	Nov 29	5:01	♏
1987	Mar 4	8:31	♐
	Apr 10	2:24 ℞	♏
	Sep 24	16:06	♐
	Dec 11	20:08	♑
1988	Feb 28	10:15	♒
1989	Feb 3	22:52	♓
	May 7	23:46	♈
	Oct 28	21:22 ℞	♓
	Dec 24	21:30	♈
1990	Mar 20	16:43	♉
	May 18	7:19	♊
	Jul 9	9:08	♋
	Aug 29	0:39	♌
	Oct 23	6:20	♍
1991	Jul 28	21:03	♎
	Oct 9	1:09	♏
	Dec 16	14:02	♐
1992	Mar 6	22:16	♑
	Jun 11	18:43 ℞	♐
	Oct 16	18:31	♑
1993	Jan 13	10:34	♒
	Apr 14	15:29	♓
	Sep 1	13:59 ℞	♒
	Dec 16	19:50	♓
1994	Mar 22	3:24	♈
	Jun 13	8:54	♉
1995	Mar 14	3:23	♊
	May 7	16:09	♋
	Jun 29	3:50	♌
	Aug 23	13:59	♍
	Oct 23	15:12	♎
1996	Jan 7	22:02	♏
	Apr 16	0:34 ℞	♎
	Aug 8	1:27	♏
	Oct 27	11:39	♐
1997	Jan 7	1:58	♑
	Apr 4	1:57	♒
	Jul 7	8:06 ℞	♑
	Nov 26	4:45	♒
1998	Feb 27	17:56	♓
	Jun 20	3:30	♈
	Aug 17	1:17 ℞	♓
1999	Feb 4	2:23	♈
	Apr 20	0:46	♉
	Jun 21	21:20	♊
	Aug 18	18:09	♋
	Oct 17	19:07	♌
2000	Feb 19	15:18 ℞	♋
	Mar 26	3:07	♌
	Jun 25	9:30	♍
	Sep 2	5:54	♎
	Nov 8	7:03	♏
2001	Jan 20	17:41	♐
	Jun 21	8:41 ℞	♏
	Aug 16	22:40	♐
	Nov 21	23:40	♑
2002	Feb 8	18:54	♒
2003	Jan 17	6:21	♓
	Apr 17	16:20	♈
2004	Feb 25	5:47	♉
	Apr 24	16:31	♊
	Jun 15	4:58	♋
	Aug 4	15:52	♌
	Sep 27	13:41	♍
	Dec 2	18:42	♎
2005	Apr 1	3:58 ℞	♍
	Jun 26	21:55	♎
	Sep 19	5:33	♏
	Nov 27	14:07	♐
2006	Feb 8	11:50	♑
	Dec 27	11:58	♒
2007	Mar 25	23:36	♓
2008	Mar 4	2:03	♈
	May 20	13:27	♉
	Aug 4	6:50	♊
2009	Apr 6	6:06	♋
	Jun 4	2:20	♌
	Aug 2	5:25	♍
	Oct 3	11:34	♎
	Dec 11	5:32	♏
2010	Oct 7	13:33	♐
	Dec 20	22:18	♑
2011	Mar 10	8:46	♒
	Aug 24	13:02 ℞	♑
	Oct 27	3:46	♒
2012	Feb 12	5:12	♓
	May 18	4:14	♈
	Oct 3	23:14 ℞	♓
2013	Jan 10	16:11	♈
	Mar 30	11:03	♉
	May 29	2:40	♊
	Jul 21	12:42	♋
	Sep 11	13:48	♌
	Nov 10	0:30	♍
2014	Mar 5	23:35 ℞	♌
	May 16	19:29	♍
	Aug 11	2:59	♎
	Oct 19	12:38	♏
	Dec 27	14:51	♐
2015	Apr 9	0:47	♑
	30	20:15 ℞	♐
	Oct 31	10:49	♑
2016	Jan 22	19:11	♒
	Apr 26	8:27	♓
	Aug 12	6:44 ℞	♒
	Dec 28	0:17	♓
2017	Mar 30	4:31	♈
	Jun 27	1:50	♉
	Nov 16	5:34 ℞	♈
2018	Jan 20	0:29	♉
	Mar 30	0:54	♊
	May 21	12:48	♋
	Jul 11	21:38	♌
	Sep 4	10:47	♍
	Nov 5	1:19	♎
2019	Aug 26	7:54	♏
	Nov 8	9:43	♐
2020	Jan 18	10:16	♑
	Apr 30	1:11	♒
	Jun 3	0:16 ℞	♑
	Dec 7	12:17	♒

Juno Ingresses 1900–2020

Year	Date	Time	Sign
1900	Jan 19	18:12	♒
	Apr 1	5:28	♓
	Jun 20	3:03	♈
	Oct 18	16:17 ℞	♓
	Nov 30	16:40	♈
1901	Feb 15	13:18	♉
	Apr 10	23:46	♊
	Jun 2	21:35	♋
	Jul 28	10:32	♌
	Sep 28	10:45	♍
	Dec 28	12:18	♎
1902	Feb 14	22:05 ℞	♍
	Jul 25	1:02	♎
	Oct 24	4:50	♏
1903	Jan 28	17:12	♐
	May 21	6:16 ℞	♏
	Sep 17	2:13	♐
	Dec 19	7:06	♑
1904	Mar 10	14:33	♒
	Dec 26	6:39	♓
1905	Feb 25	5:26	♈
	Apr 19	14:40	♉
	Jun 9	15:51	♊
	Jul 31	9:14	♋
	Sep 26	18:34	♌
1906	Jun 24	11:29	♍
	Sep 14	4:49	♎
	Dec 7	20:25	♏
1907	Nov 6	8:59	♐
1908	Feb 2	9:41	♑
	Dec 12	15:57	♒
1909	Feb 18	19:03	♓
	Apr 21	7:50	♈
	Jun 20	16:20	♉
	Aug 26	2:00	♊
1910	Apr 9	19:50	♋
	Jun 14	4:51	♌
	Aug 19	2:56	♍
	Oct 31	2:47	♎
1911	Sep 19	20:02	♏
	Dec 18	13:35	♐
1912	Nov 12	18:20	♑
1913	Jan 30	7:10	♒
	Apr 15	12:47	♓
1914	Jan 4	19:50	♈
	Mar 5	6:36	♉
	Apr 26	8:13	♊
	Jun 17	0:55	♋
	Aug 10	17:45	♌
	Oct 12	6:04	♍
1915	Aug 7	13:49	♎
	Nov 2	14:14	♏
1916	Feb 16	3:11	♐
	Apr 23	2:29 ℞	♏
	Sep 29	10:40	♐
	Dec 27	21:36	♑
1917	Mar 25	4:06	♒
	Aug 28	3:12 ℞	♑
	Oct 12	17:38	♒
1918	Jan 10	7:07	♓
	Mar 11	2:09	♈
	May 4	3:13	♉
	Jun 25	5:47	♊
	Aug 17	13:51	♋
	Oct 20	9:27	♌
1919	Feb 6	15:14 ℞	♋
	Apr 6	13:27	♌
	Jul 9	17:28	♍
	Sep 24	19:01	♎
	Dec 20	4:11	♏
1920	May 9	18:51 ℞	♎
	Aug 2	5:11	♏
	Nov 14	14:26	♐
1921	Feb 13	9:36	♑
	Jul 31	16:46 ℞	♐
	Sep 15	10:48	♑
	Dec 24	15:17	♒
1922	Mar 2	21:31	♓
	May 6	2:14	♈
	Jul 12	0:31	♉
1923	Feb 25	12:55	♊
	Apr 29	3:40	♋
	Jun 28	5:44	♌
	Aug 30	19:28	♍
	Nov 12	7:40	♎
1924	Sep 28	18:18	♏
	Dec 27	5:42	♐
1925	Nov 23	0:42	♑
1926	Feb 9	8:17	♒
	May 1	0:23	♓
1927	Jan 22	10:46	♈
	Mar 19	7:12	♉
	May 9	14:15	♊
	Jun 29	22:45	♋
	Aug 23	15:43	♌
	Oct 27	13:19	♍
1928	Aug 18	21:41	♎
	Nov 11	14:33	♏
1929	Oct 11	5:41	♐
1930	Jan 6	13:35	♑
	Apr 12	4:11	♒
	Jul 18	12:22 ℞	♑
	Nov 7	22:28	♒
1931	Jan 22	15:44	♓
	Mar 23	10:17	♈
	May 17	17:17	♉
	Jul 10	18:26	♊
	Sep 5	23:55	♋
1932	May 7	14:17	♌
	Jul 22	20:30	♍
	Oct 5	6:58	♎
1933	Jan 5	6:38	♏
	Apr 9	6:17 ℞	♎
	Aug 21	2:05	♏
	Nov 24	19:28	♐
1934	Mar 1	3:22	♑
	Jun 24	13:11 ℞	♐
	Oct 11	11:43	♑
1935	Jan 5	8:54	♒
	Mar 15	12:45	♓
	May 23	0:40	♈
	Aug 22	5:05	♉
	Oct 2	16:43 ℞	♈
1936	Jan 15	8:36	♉
	Mar 20	2:02	♊
	May 15	2:60	♋
	Jul 11	10:26	♌
	Sep 11	17:27	♍
	Nov 27	6:45	♎
1937	Apr 5	5:40 ℞	♍
	Jun 29	3:58	♎
	Oct 9	20:36	♏
1938	Jan 8	15:29	♐
	Jul 6	14:17 ℞	♏
	Aug 13	19:52	♐
	Dec 4	11:12	♑
1939	Feb 21	15:44	♒
	May 27	3:47	♓
	Aug 11	18:53 ℞	♒
	Dec 2	3:56	♓
1940	Feb 7	17:08	♈
	Apr 1	17:32	♉
	May 22	13:32	♊
	Jul 12	17:22	♋
	Sep 5	19:21	♌
	Nov 15	20:34	♍
1941	Feb 16	9:35 ℞	♌
	May 29	23:43	♍
	Aug 30	10:41	♎
	Nov 22	6:06	♏

Juno Ingresses 1900–2020

Year	Date	Time	Sign
1942	Oct 22	18:37	♐
1943	Jan 17	12:22	♑
	Nov 25	9:03	♒
1944	Feb 4	1:52	♓
	Apr 4	5:36	♈
	May 31	2:53	♉
	Jul 27	2:21	♊
	Oct 2	20:21	♋
	Dec 29	22:45 ℞	♊
1945	Mar 2	19:50	♋
	May 26	0:58	♌
	Aug 4	1:28	♍
	Oct 16	5:07	♎
1946	Feb 4	5:02	♏
	Mar 1	13:36 ℞	♎
	Sep 3	23:22	♏
	Dec 4	20:36	♐
1947	Mar 24	18:28	♑
	May 20	6:40 ℞	♐
	Oct 28	0:35	♑
1948	Jan 17	2:42	♒
	Mar 28	7:53	♓
	Jun 13	10:60	♈
1949	Feb 11	3:16	♉
	Apr 7	7:09	♊
	May 30	9:11	♋
	Jul 24	21:32	♌
	Sep 24	11:48	♍
	Dec 17	16:18	♎
1950	Mar 1	5:16 ℞	♍
	Jul 18	20:39	♎
	Oct 19	20:07	♏
1951	Jan 21	22:30	♐
	Jun 1	9:31 ℞	♏
	Sep 9	17:16	♐
	Dec 15	5:32	♑
1952	Mar 5	23:39	♒
	Dec 22	5:40	♓
1953	Feb 22	1:23	♈
	Apr 16	12:35	♉
	Jun 6	10:20	♊
	Jul 27	19:30	♋
	Sep 22	4:41	♌
1954	Jun 18	17:45	♍
	Sep 9	19:57	♎
	Dec 2	13:39	♏
1955	Nov 1	15:33	♐
1956	Jan 28	7:41	♑
	Dec 8	9:11	♒
1957	Feb 15	5:32	♓
	Apr 17	14:36	♈
	Jun 16	4:57	♉
	Aug 18	14:58	♊
1958	Apr 3	12:07	♋
	Jun 9	12:30	♌
	Aug 14	19:15	♍
	Oct 26	5:01	♎
1959	Sep 14	7:49	♏
	Dec 13	11:04	♐
1960	Nov 7	7:19	♑
1961	Jan 25	17:09	♒
	Apr 9	20:47	♓
	Jul 23	0:15	♈
	Aug 19	1:57 ℞	♓
	Dec 28	9:13	♈
1962	Feb 28	9:37	♉
	Apr 22	0:19	♊
	Jun 12	22:28	♋
	Aug 6	16:30	♌
	Oct 7	15:59	♍
1963	Aug 2	7:29	♎
	Oct 29	5:35	♏
1964	Feb 6	4:45	♐
	May 6	5:56 ℞	♏
	Sep 23	3:37	♐
	Dec 23	9:07	♑
1965	Mar 18	20:19	♒
1966	Jan 5	18:45	♓
	Mar 7	5:13	♈
	Apr 30	7:60	♉
	Jun 21	7:43	♊
	Aug 13	6:26	♋
	Oct 13	18:32	♌
1967	Jul 5	9:14	♍
	Sep 21	1:21	♎
	Dec 15	0:10	♏
1968	May 22	4:51 ℞	♎
	Jul 23	1:41	♏
	Nov 10	8:51	♐
1969	Feb 8	0:05	♑
	Dec 20	13:45	♒
1970	Feb 27	5:02	♓
	May 2	0:18	♈
	Jul 6	7:32	♉
1971	Feb 18	18:54	♊
	Apr 24	22:08	♋
	Jun 24	15:15	♌
	Aug 27	8:14	♍
	Nov 8	1:33	♎
1972	Sep 24	12:31	♏
	Dec 22	18:20	♐
1973	Nov 18	18:27	♑
1974	Feb 5	9:55	♒
	Apr 25	7:41	♓
1975	Jan 17	15:44	♈
	Mar 15	6:50	♉
	May 5	17:13	♊
	Jun 26	1:25	♋
	Aug 19	14:07	♌
	Oct 22	7:46	♍
1976	Aug 14	8:01	♎
	Nov 7	10:35	♏
1977	Mar 14	1:30	♐
	22	4:58 ℞	♏
	Oct 6	7:50	♐
1978	Jan 2	11:43	♑
	Apr 4	15:02	♒
	Jul 30	18:31 ℞	♑
	Oct 31	21:60	♒
1979	Jan 18	17:27	♓
	Mar 19	16:35	♈
	May 13	18:28	♉
	Jul 6	8:15	♊
	Aug 31	7:58	♋
1980	Apr 30	21:20	♌
	Jul 18	15:51	♍
	Oct 1	10:26	♎
	Dec 29	14:52	♏
1981	Apr 19	8:13 ℞	♎
	Aug 14	20:07	♏
	Nov 20	21:10	♐
1982	Feb 23	1:41	♑
	Jul 4	16:26 ℞	♐
	Oct 4	21:47	♑
1983	Jan 1	22:26	♒
	Mar 12	3:37	♓
	May 18	18:51	♈
	Aug 8	1:04	♉
	Oct 25	1:11 ℞	♈
1984	Jan 6	3:31	♉
	Mar 15	13:51	♊
	May 11	6:52	♋
	Jul 7	19:30	♌
	Sep 8	0:12	♍
	Nov 21	21:33	♎
1985	Apr 18	3:39 ℞	♍
	Jun 18	22:09	♎
	Oct 5	17:32	♏
1986	Jan 3	19:05	♐
	Nov 30	16:52	♑
1987	Feb 17	22:37	♒
	May 19	1:01	♓
	Aug 24	3:31 ℞	♒
	Nov 26	4:41	♓
1988	Feb 4	6:14	♈
	Mar 29	11:17	♉
	May 19	4:46	♊
	Jul 9	2:56	♋
	Sep 1	16:24	♌
	Nov 8	13:48	♍
1989	Mar 2	20:33 ℞	♌
	May 20	9:15	♍
	Aug 25	20:45	♎
	Nov 17	13:52	♏
1990	Oct 18	0:16	♐
1991	Jan 13	3:47	♑
	May 4	7:04	♒
	Jun 15	19:48 ℞	♑
	Nov 20	9:35	♒
1992	Jan 31	10:31	♓
	Mar 31	13:11	♈
	May 26	23:10	♉
	Jul 21	21:27	♊
	Sep 22	19:13	♋
1993	May 20	4:03	♌
	Jul 30	9:38	♍
	Oct 11	12:42	♎
1994	Jan 17	18:21	♏
	Mar 22	0:01 ℞	♎
	Aug 28	17:59	♏
	Nov 30	1:49	♐
1995	Mar 12	16:50	♑
	Jun 4	14:06 ℞	♐
	Oct 21	19:52	♑
1996	Jan 12	21:54	♒
	Mar 23	21:34	♓
	Jun 6	13:58	♈
1997	Feb 5	20:18	♉
	Apr 3	4:15	♊
	May 26	14:44	♋
	Jul 21	5:27	♌
	Sep 20	13:04	♍
	Dec 9	13:32	♎
1998	Mar 13	10:45 ℞	♍
	Jul 12	0:11	♎
	Oct 15	8:36	♏
1999	Jan 15	12:03	♐
	Jun 14	1:12 ℞	♏
	Aug 31	8:57	♐
	Dec 10	19:12	♑
2000	Mar 1	2:04	♒
	Dec 17	12:33	♓
2001	Feb 18	14:39	♈
	Apr 13	7:25	♉
	Jun 3	5:01	♊
	Jul 24	10:06	♋
	Sep 18	3:20	♌
	Dec 22	14:60	♍
	29	7:10 ℞	♌
2002	Jun 13	4:35	♍
	Sep 5	19:16	♎
	Nov 27	20:06	♏
2003	Oct 27	23:02	♐
2004	Jan 23	10:36	♑
	Dec 3	21:57	♒
2005	Feb 11	16:14	♓
	Apr 14	0:34	♈
	Jun 12	2:32	♉
	Aug 12	15:29	♊
2006	Mar 28	12:08	♋
	Jun 5	9:42	♌
	Aug 11	1:50	♍
	Oct 22	1:21	♎
2007	Sep 9	3:20	♏
	Dec 8	20:02	♐
2008	Nov 2	0:51	♑
2009	Jan 21	12:08	♒
	Apr 4	20:11	♓
	Jul 3	2:09	♈
	Sep 14	22:43 ℞	♓
	Dec 19	22:05	♈
2010	Feb 23	11:45	♉
	Apr 17	17:07	♊
	Jun 8	21:15	♋
	Aug 2	17:11	♌
	Oct 3	6:58	♍
2011	Jul 27	23:32	♎
	Oct 25	1:54	♏
2012	Jan 29	14:09	♐
	May 17	6:28 ℞	♏
	Sep 16	17:43	♐
	Dec 19	3:31	♑
2013	Mar 13	7:28	♒
2014	Jan 1	7:21	♓
	Mar 3	10:03	♈
	Apr 26	14:16	♉
	Jun 17	11:07	♊
	Aug 9	1:39	♋
	Oct 7	21:29	♌
2015	Jun 30	23:10	♍
	Sep 17	10:02	♎
	Dec 10	7:50	♏
2016	Jun 7	23:52 ℞	♎
	Jul 8	2:56	♏
	Nov 6	9:38	♐
2017	Feb 3	6:54	♑
	Dec 16	19:30	♒
2018	Feb 23	20:22	♓
	Apr 28	7:54	♈
	Jul 1	8:55	♉
	Sep 30	0:41	♊
	Oct 24	6:45 ℞	♉
2019	Feb 11	4:32	♊
	Apr 20	16:51	♋
	Jun 21	2:51	♌
	Aug 24	0:13	♍
	Nov 4	2:39	♎
2020	Sep 20	11:15	♏
	Dec 18	17:24	♐

Vesta Ingresses 1900–2020

Year	Date	Time	Sign
1900	Feb 14	13:17	♉
	Apr 30	16:53	♊
	Jul 9	3:36	♋
	Sep 21	2:43	♌
1901	Jun 27	4:20	♍
	Aug 30	20:60	♎
	Oct 28	2:32	♏
	Dec 23	21:28	♐
1902	Feb 22	5:13	♑
	Nov 4	2:04	♒
1903	Jan 13	4:56	♓
	Mar 17	6:35	♈
	May 21	9:46	♉
	Aug 7	2:17	♊
	Dec 8	14:30 ℞	♉
1904	Feb 20	18:21	♊
	May 18	0:59	♋
	Jul 26	0:20	♌
	Oct 1	2:41	♍
	Dec 16	7:37	♎
1905	Apr 6	11:11 ℞	♍
	Jun 11	1:25	♎
	Aug 29	8:26	♏
	Oct 27	17:19	♐
	Dec 22	13:10	♑
1906	Feb 17	0:50	♒
	Apr 20	8:08	♓
1907	Jan 16	13:40	♈
	Mar 29	20:11	♉
	Jun 5	23:49	♊
	Aug 18	17:33	♋
1908	May 31	8:01	♌
	Aug 7	3:05	♍
	Oct 7	15:08	♎
	Dec 7	6:01	♏
1909	Feb 13	22:38	♐
	Oct 22	10:24	♑
	Dec 23	8:43	♒
1910	Feb 20	12:24	♓
	Apr 23	7:57	♈
	Jul 6	0:51	♉
	Nov 17	12:00 ℞	♈
1911	Jan 12	23:06	♉
	Apr 14	15:11	♊
	Jun 24	0:41	♋
	Sep 2	2:20	♌
	Nov 28	8:04	♍
1912	Feb 5	7:08 ℞	♌
	Jun 1	5:45	♍
	Aug 12	5:53	♎
	Oct 10	13:18	♏
	Dec 5	14:46	♐
1913	Jan 31	9:34	♑
	Apr 5	22:57	♒
	Dec 23	15:01	♓
1914	Feb 28	13:46	♈
	May 4	16:07	♉
	Jul 14	19:15	♊
1915	Apr 30	4:54	♋
	Jul 10	12:28	♌
	Sep 14	0:38	♍
	Nov 19	13:20	♎
1916	Aug 2	22:21	♏
	Oct 8	8:15	♐
	Dec 5	0:59	♑
1917	Jan 30	11:53	♒
	Mar 30	21:32	♓
	Jun 10	23:57	♈
	Oct 11	21:13 ℞	♓
	Dec 14	10:36	♈
1918	Mar 12	12:10	♉
	May 20	23:26	♊
	Jul 30	10:12	♋
	Oct 29	0:35	♌
	Dec 31	16:43 ℞	♋
1919	May 8	18:16	♌
	Jul 21	14:52	♍
	Sep 21	12:51	♎
	Nov 19	6:54	♏
1920	Jan 18	15:06	♐

Vesta Ingresses 1900–2020

Year	Date	Time	℞	Sign
	Apr 9	3:10		♑
	Jun 2	10:49	℞	♐
	Sep 22	23:55		♑
	Dec 4	12:32		♒
1921	Feb 3	22:34		♓
	Apr 6	8:30		♈
	Jun 12	23:11		♉
1922	Mar 26	9:54		♊
	Jun 7	22:47		♋
	Aug 15	12:58		♌
	Oct 27	2:55		♍
1923	Jul 23	5:28		♎
	Sep 23	19:05		♏
	Nov 19	9:52		♐
1924	Jan 14	1:18		♑
	Mar 13	0:12		♒
	May 30	1:41		♓
	Aug 11	9:32	℞	♒
	Nov 26	7:56		♓
1925	Feb 11	7:04		♈
	Apr 18	17:35		♉
	Jun 26	6:30		♊
	Sep 20	22:42		♋
	Dec 9	22:40	℞	♊
1926	Apr 6	19:37		♋
	Jun 23	17:22		♌
	Aug 28	6:11		♍
	Oct 30	9:23		♎
1927	Jan 6	15:37		♏
	Sep 17	11:26		♐
	Nov 18	10:52		♑
1928	Jan 15	0:08		♒
	Mar 13	10:42		♓
	May 17	6:50		♈
1929	Feb 20	21:16		♉
	May 5	2:01		♊
	Jul 13	11:51		♋
	Sep 27	6:19		♌
1930	Jul 3	2:29		♍
	Sep 4	22:47		♎
	Nov 2	5:37		♏
	Dec 29	14:38		♐
1931	Mar 2	0:09		♑
	Nov 12	21:14		♒
1932	Jan 18	15:55		♓
	Mar 20	23:33		♈
	May 25	5:53		♉
	Aug 14	6:17		♊
	Nov 21	12:47	℞	♉
1933	Mar 1	7:27		♊
	May 22	12:31		♋
	Jul 30	6:39		♌
	Oct 6	6:01		♍
	Dec 28	5:57		♎
1934	Mar 12	12:57	℞	♍
	Jun 24	23:50		♎
	Sep 4	20:04		♏
	Nov 2	7:27		♐
	Dec 27	23:14		♑
1935	Feb 22	18:53		♒
	Apr 27	19:19		♓
1936	Jan 23	9:59		♈
	Apr 2	12:41		♉
	Jun 9	10:09		♊
	Aug 23	13:22		♋
1937	Jun 5	19:10		♌
	Aug 11	22:47		♍
	Oct 12	19:06		♎
	Dec 13	16:13		♏
1938	Feb 27	11:41		♐
	May 21	9:49	℞	♏
	Aug 15	9:17		♐
	Oct 29	17:23		♑
	Dec 28	23:12		♒
1939	Feb 25	14:30		♓
	Apr 28	14:60		♈
	Jul 14	13:48		♉
	Oct 28	23:02	℞	♈
1940	Jan 25	11:22		♉
	Apr 18	10:39		♊
	Jun 27	11:12		♋
	Sep 6	11:24		♌
1941	Jun 10	9:35		♍
	Aug 18	6:14		♎
	Oct 16	2:44		♏
	Dec 11	6:35		♐
1942	Feb 6	18:54		♑
	Apr 16	2:12		♒
	Aug 20	12:24	℞	♑
	Sep 30	13:20		♒
	Dec 30	0:31		♓
1943	Mar 5	7:30		♈
	May 9	3:23		♉
	Jul 20	9:13		♊
1944	May 4	15:50		♋
	Jul 14	4:54		♌
	Sep 18	3:57		♍
	Nov 25	18:19		♎
1945	Aug 12	10:29		♏
	Oct 14	17:17		♐
	Dec 10	14:24		♑
1946	Feb 4	20:35		♒
	Apr 5	17:36		♓
	Jun 21	9:18		♈
	Sep 20	5:33	℞	♓
	Dec 26	20:15		♈
1947	Mar 17	10:01		♉
	May 25	6:45		♊
	Aug 4	9:33		♋
1948	May 15	10:39		♌
	Jul 25	22:53		♍
	Sep 25	16:50		♎
	Nov 23	21:24		♏
1949	Jan 24	20:41		♐
	Oct 3	11:10		♑
	Dec 10	2:44		♒
1950	Feb 8	12:38		♓
	Apr 10	19:09		♈
	Jun 18	10:22		♉
1951	Mar 31	22:55		♊
	Jun 12	9:58		♋
	Aug 20	8:50		♌
	Nov 3	12:50		♍
1952	Apr 8	17:27	℞	♌
	19	12:28		♍
	Jul 28	20:04		♎
	Sep 28	1:29		♏
	Nov 23	7:58		♐
1953	Jan 18	1:47		♑
	Mar 18	22:43		♒
	Jun 23	5:53		♓
	Jul 10	0:44	℞	♒
	Dec 4	23:34		♓
1954	Feb 15	21:56		♈
	Apr 22	19:21		♉
	Jun 30	19:30		♊
	Oct 3	22:59		♋
	Nov 21	12:16	℞	♊
1955	Apr 13	22:24		♋
	Jun 28	9:40		♌
	Sep 1	21:17		♍
	Nov 4	19:26		♎
1956	Jan 15	23:59		♏
	May 17	5:42	℞	♎
	Jun 29	23:16		♏
	Sep 23	8:47		♐
	Nov 22	14:38		♑
1957	Jan 18	15:02		♒
	Mar 18	2:15		♓
	May 23	2:25		♈
1958	Feb 26	9:19		♉
	May 9	6:01		♊
	Jul 17	19:19		♋
	Oct 3	21:16		♌
1959	Feb 17	4:02	℞	♋
	Apr 11	10:51		♌
	Jul 8	7:28		♍
	Sep 9	10:13		♎
	Nov 6	16:58		♏
1960	Jan 3	14:27		♐
	Mar 8	7:22		♑
	Nov 18	9:09		♒
1961	Jan 22	5:51		♓
	Mar 25	4:53		♈
	May 29	21:53		♉
	Aug 24	7:52		♊
	Nov 5	6:23	℞	♉
1962	Mar 9	3:34		♊
	May 26	23:10		♋
	Aug 3	12:16		♌
	Oct 11	8:04		♍
1963	Jan 16	15:39		♎
	Feb 13	3:59	℞	♍
	Jul 3	21:54		♎
	Sep 10	0:18		♏
	Nov 6	19:57		♐
1964	Jan 1	9:22		♑
	Feb 27	14:10		♒
	May 3	14:48		♓
1965	Jan 28	0:36		♈
	Apr 6	19:22		♉
	Jun 13	16:42		♊
	Aug 29	15:42		♋
1966	Jan 26	4:03	℞	♊
	Mar 7	12:26		♋
	Jun 10	16:40		♌
	Aug 16	7:31		♍
	Oct 17	11:15		♎
	Dec 19	15:49		♏
1967	Mar 22	9:14		♐
	Apr 16	11:50	℞	♏
	Aug 27	11:57		♐
	Nov 4	15:20		♑
1968	Jan 2	19:43		♒
	Mar 1	5:14		♓
	May 2	16:38		♈
	Jul 23	15:49		♉
	Oct 10	12:07	℞	♈
1969	Feb 2	5:32		♉
	Apr 22	19:35		♊
	Jul 1	11:08		♋
	Sep 11	7:02		♌
1970	Jun 16	20:43		♍
	Aug 22	23:37		♎
	Oct 20	15:50		♏
	Dec 16	2:39		♐
1971	Feb 12	15:24		♑
	Apr 28	3:07		♒
	Jul 20	20:22	℞	♑
	Oct 19	8:17		♒
1972	Jan 4	22:33		♓
	Mar 9	1:23		♈
	May 12	18:46		♉
	Jul 25	11:03		♊
1973	May 9	11:22		♋
	Jul 18	7:43		♌
	Sep 22	16:26		♍
	Dec 2	13:56		♎
1974	Aug 19	17:34		♏
	Oct 20	5:60		♐
	Dec 15	16:54		♑
1975	Feb 10	0:48		♒
	Apr 11	17:47		♓
	Jul 6	17:33		♈
	Aug 27	11:59	℞	♓
1976	Jan 5	5:29		♈
	Mar 21	5:56		♉
	May 28	13:44		♊
	Aug 8	9:50		♋
1977	May 21	22:40		♌
	Jul 30	22:08		♍
	Sep 30	17:16		♎
	Nov 29	14:59		♏
1978	Feb 2	2:21		♐
	Oct 12	16:51		♑
	Dec 16	0:31		♒
1979	Feb 13	13:56		♓
	Apr 15	18:31		♈
	Jun 24	17:15		♉
1980	Apr 5	2:10		♊
	Jun 15	15:25		♋
	Aug 24	0:39		♌
	Nov 10	16:38		♍
1981	Mar 6	10:59	℞	♌
	May 15	22:55		♍
	Aug 4	5:19		♎
	Oct 3	15:02		♏
	Nov 28	20:19		♐
1982	Jan 24	0:35		♑
	Mar 26	14:12		♒
	Dec 13	16:15		♓
1983	Feb 21	4:10		♈
	Apr 27	9:49		♉
	Jul 5	21:12		♊
1984	Apr 19	10:30		♋
	Jul 2	3:37		♌
	Sep 5	19:09		♍
	Nov 9	21:57		♎
1985	Jan 28	18:54		♏
	Apr 13	20:56	℞	♎
	Jul 20	1:25		♏
	Sep 30	14:23		♐
	Nov 28	9:21		♑
1986	Jan 23	22:19		♒
	Mar 23	12:02		♓
	May 30	4:15		♈
1987	Mar 3	21:39		♉
	May 13	15:05		♊
	Jul 22	12:07		♋
	Oct 12	5:11		♌
1988	Jan 27	14:24	℞	♋
	Apr 24	10:23		♌
	Jul 13	4:23		♍
	Sep 13	18:38		♎
	Nov 11	5:58		♏
1989	Jan 9	0:57		♐
	Mar 19	1:36		♑
	Jul 17	5:57	℞	♐
	Aug 29	13:42		♑
	Nov 25	7:10		♒
1990	Jan 27	6:00		♓
	Mar 29	17:19		♈
	Jun 3	20:04		♉
	Sep 9	0:43		♊
	Oct 15	7:40	℞	♉
1991	Mar 15	23:30		♊
	May 31	11:37		♋
	Aug 8	2:55		♌
	Oct 17	9:21		♍
1992	Jul 11	21:52		♎
	Sep 15	2:10		♏
	Nov 11	6:44		♐
1993	Jan 5	18:01		♑
	Mar 4	10:24		♒
	May 12	12:06		♓
	Sep 19	4:27	℞	♒
	Nov 3	8:60		♓
1994	Feb 2	12:58		♈
	Apr 11	3:07		♉
	Jun 18	2:38		♊
	Sep 5	16:28		♋
1995	Jan 5	20:09	℞	♊
	Mar 22	12:49		♋
	Jun 15	21:04		♌
	Aug 21	2:25		♍
	Oct 22	16:17		♎
	Dec 26	14:42		♏
1996	Sep 5	0:59		♐
	Nov 9	5:34		♑
1997	Jan 6	11:19		♒
	Mar 5	15:37		♓
	May 7	16:13		♈
	Aug 7	2:38		♉
	Sep 20	0:41	℞	♈
1998	Feb 9	13:26		♉
	Apr 27	7:00		♊
	Jul 5	20:16		♋
	Sep 16	23:45		♌
1999	Jun 23	11:29		♍
	Aug 28	0:21		♎
	Oct 25	10:15		♏
	Dec 21	2:05		♐
2000	Feb 18	15:58		♑
	May 16	11:01		♒
	Jun 20	4:35	℞	♑
	Oct 28	18:31		♒
2001	Jan 8	22:11		♓
	Mar 13	5:35		♈
	May 17	1:09		♉
	Jul 31	16:32		♊
	Dec 21	8:44	℞	♉
2002	Feb 9	11:57		♊
	May 14	6:36		♋
	Jul 22	15:38		♌
	Sep 27	13:31		♍
	Dec 10	15:07		♎
2003	Apr 22	7:29	℞	♍
	May 30	16:49		♎
	Aug 26	6:40		♏
	Oct 25	9:05		♐
	Dec 20	10:08		♑
2004	Feb 14	19:22		♒
	Apr 16	10:02		♓
2005	Jan 11	9:47		♈
	Mar 25	15:47		♉
	Jun 1	16:42		♊
	Aug 13	11:03		♋
2006	May 27	10:50		♌
	Aug 4	5:21		♍
	Oct 5	0:10		♎
	Dec 4	12:46		♏
2007	Feb 9	18:55		♐
	Oct 19	8:05		♑
	Dec 20	19:31		♒
2008	Feb 17	22:37		♓
	Apr 19	8:20		♈
	Jun 30	5:14		♉
	Dec 5	2:57	℞	♈
	27	11:39		♉
2009	Apr 9	23:38		♊
	Jun 19	18:30		♋
	Aug 28	13:06		♌
	Nov 19	14:18		♍
2010	Feb 16	2:50	℞	♌
	May 26	15:17		♍
	Aug 9	6:25		♎
	Oct 8	2:13		♏
	Dec 3	7:47		♐
2011	Jan 28	23:38		♑
	Apr 2	12:42		♒
	Dec 20	8:04		♓
2012	Feb 25	19:18		♈
	Apr 30	17:01		♉
	Jul 9	21:44		♊
2013	Apr 25	1:13		♋

Vesta Ingresses 1900–2020

Jul 6 10:18 ♌	Mar 28 18:15 ♓	Oct 20 1:59 ♌	Apr 2 3:19 ♑	2020 Mar 21 5:40 ♊
Sep 10 5:26 ♍	Jun 6 21:33 ♈	2017 Jan 10 16:51 ℞ ♋	Jun 13 10:46 ℞ ♐	Jun 3 19:19 ♋
Nov 15 14:05 ♎	Oct 25 8:23 ℞ ♓	May 3 0:34 ♌	Sep 18 5:09 ♑	Aug 11 11:42 ♌
2014 Jul 31 0:17 ♏	Dec 3 19:14 ♈	Jul 17 23:36 ♍	Dec 1 21:11 ♒	Oct 22 8:10 ♍
Oct 6 14:57 ♐	2016 Mar 8 1:11 ♉	Sep 18 8:08 ♎	2019 Feb 1 11:25 ♓	
Dec 3 12:11 ♑	May 16 18:48 ♊	Nov 16 4:36 ♏	Apr 3 15:47 ♈	
2015 Jan 28 20:05 ♒	Jul 25 21:44 ♋	2018 Jan 15 5:13 ♐	Jun 9 10:16 ♉	

(continued from page 56)

people as a whole. The most-used tools are horoscopes calculated for the exact instant the Sun or Moon makes an ingress into the four cardinal signs. (The Sun's ingress into cardinal signs from 1601-2100 is provided in tables on pages 9-12.)

Horoscopes are erected for the latitude and longitude of the capital city of whatever country (or countries) the astrologer wishes to consider. The solar ingress charts are applicable for about three months each. Within that three month period, each lunar ingress into a cardinal sign focuses on a particular week. Naturally, the house placements and aspects to the angles will vary considerably, depending on the location used for the ingress chart. Astrologers interested in local conditions could erect ingress charts for their town of residence.

The solar ingress chart (Sun into 0 Aries) for 1939 (March 21 at 12:28:53 ET) had Pluto within one degree of the Ascendant for both London, England, and Paris, France. (That chart for Berlin, Germany, had Saturn within two degrees of the MC.) Mars was also within 7 minutes of arc to the exact square to the Sun.

Tradition suggests that the (solar) Aries ingress is the most significant and can be considered symbolic of the entire year ahead. It is also possible that each (solar) cardinal ingress could be used for one year—until the next one in the same sign— but limiting the focus to issues indicated by the sign involved: Aries for assertion, war, action, etc.; Cancer for domestic issues, commodities, homes, real estate, etc.; Libra for relationships, negotiations, aesthetics, etc.; and Capricorn for bureaucratic and governmental structures and power, natural law and general earth conditions (perhaps including earthquakes).

Although traditional mundane astrology focuses on the Sun and Moon for ingress charts, the other planets are used in other patterns. The entry of a planet into north declination offers another kind of ingress. When considering war prospects (a Martian issue), for example, mundane astrologers might look at a chart erected for the moment Mars enters north declination. The chart is significant until Mars completes its declination cycle and once again enters north declination. (Pages 104-106 provide tables of planets entering north and south declination.)

Astrologers also calculate charts for planetary conjunctions. Solar eclipses when the Sun and Moon are conjunct and lunar eclipses when the Sun and Moon are on opposite sides of the Earth were probably the most important astrological phenomena in the ancient world. (Pages 23-40 provide eclipse data.) Another conjunction chart, the Mars-Saturn conjunction chart, is considered a key to possible war or other threats to an established government. The chart remains valid until the next Mars-Saturn conjunction. Outer planet conjunction charts can be used to examine issues pertinent to those outer planets.

Due to retrograde cycles, planetary conjunctions can also occur more than once within a short period of time. The tradition is that each conjunction chart is valid until the next conjunction, which means that the chart of the **final** conjunction would last the longest. Both declination and conjunction charts (like ingresses) are set up for the latitude and longitude of your personal locality (if that is your focus) or for the capital city of the country whose future you are considering.

Astrologers can explore the nature of any planet making an ingress and/or the nature of the sign which that planet is entering. For example, it may or may not be significant, but scanning the ingress tables of the "big four" asteroids reveals that three of the four (Ceres, Juno and Vesta) made an ingress into Virgo in October of 1962 (the month of the Cuban Missile Crisis). Some people associate Virgo with "Mother Russia" both for the sickle (used by Ceres to harvest Virgoan wheat and also found on the Soviet flag) and for the linkage between Virgo and "workers of the world." Such tidbits are what makes astrology fascinating. Working with ingresses (and other cycle charts) offers a rich field of exploration for astrologers.

Pluto Ingresses –500 (501 BC)—2100

Year	Date	Time	℞	Sign
-490	Nov 1	12:16		♎
-489	Mar 14	3:45	℞	♍
-489	Aug 28	21:19		♎
-478	Nov 6	17:11		♏
-477	May 18	17:03	℞	♎
-477	Sep 1	23:34		♏
-465	Dec 7	6:43		♐
-464	Jun 13	5:13	℞	♏
-464	Oct 7	8:46		♐
-449	Mar 7	5:48		♑
-449	Apr 28	16:40	℞	♐
-449	Dec 29	4:28		♑
-448	Jul 22	1:15	℞	♐
-448	Nov 1	23:44		♑
-429	Mar 20	12:13		♒
-429	Jun 14	21:05	℞	♑
-428	Jan 24	15:35		♒
-428	Aug 22	0:31	℞	♑
-428	Dec 3	18:22		♒
-404	Mar 23	21:27		♓
-404	Aug 11	10:26	℞	♒
-403	Feb 7	9:25		♓
-403	Oct 14	19:15	℞	♒
-403	Dec 13	23:13		♓
-375	Apr 23	1:26		♈
-375	Sep 10	9:55	℞	♓
-374	Mar 11	10:27		♈
-374	Nov 7	5:37	℞	♓
-373	Jan 20	1:33		♈
-344	Jun 12	6:18		♉
-344	Sep 18	4:47	℞	♈
-343	Apr 26	18:36		♉
-343	Nov 11	7:52	℞	♈
-342	Mar 14	18:21		♉
-314	Jul 7	1:37		♊
-314	Oct 26	7:38	℞	♉
-313	May 20	23:43		♊
-313	Dec 23	11:59	℞	♉
-312	Apr 1	10:01		♊
-289	Jul 21	1:16		♋
-289	Dec 19	4:34	℞	♊
-288	May 31	9:41		♋
-271	Oct 7	15:21		♌
-271	Nov 27	8:36	℞	♋
-270	Jul 28	23:58		♌
-269	Feb 23	1:51	℞	♋
-269	May 28	6:51		♌
-256	Sep 7	18:44		♍
-255	Mar 12	17:02	℞	♌
-255	Jul 5	14:21		♍
-244	Oct 6	0:08		♎
-243	Apr 18	7:58	℞	♍
-243	Jul 29	18:02		♎
-233	Dec 17	19:01		♏
-232	Mar 21	18:24	℞	♎
-232	Oct 10	14:15		♏
-220	Dec 26	11:17		♐
-219	May 14	16:29	℞	♏
-219	Oct 28	17:06		♐
-204	Feb 29	1:35		♑
-204	May 3	2:26	℞	♐
-204	Dec 25	0:46		♑
-203	Jul 26	4:11	℞	♐
-203	Oct 28	2:06		♑
-184	Feb 15	0:36		♒
-184	Jul 24	2:31	℞	♑
-184	Dec 27	18:43		♒
-160	Mar 19	18:09		♓
-160	Aug 16	21:53	℞	♒
-159	Feb 3	2:01		♓
-159	Oct 29	8:00	℞	♒
-159	Nov 30	4:06		♓
-132	May 19	14:01		♈
-132	Aug 12	4:48	℞	♓
-131	Mar 31	2:59		♈
-131	Oct 8	6:53	℞	♓
-130	Feb 16	11:03		♈
-100	May 15	9:60		♉
-100	Oct 21	9:47	℞	♈
-99	Apr 3	16:39		♉
-99	Dec 25	16:52	℞	♈
-98	Feb 2	20:52		♉
-70	Jun 28	21:37		♊
-70	Nov 6	8:33	℞	♉
-69	May 15	5:33		♊
-68	Jan 4	4:29	℞	♉
-68	Mar 23	21:36		♊
-45	Aug 24	5:10		♋
-45	Nov 10	22:24	℞	♊
-44	Jun 27	17:14		♋
-43	Jan 16	16:38	℞	♊
-43	May 6	22:46		♋
-25	Aug 8	13:60		♌
-24	Feb 7	0:03	℞	♋
-24	Jun 11	11:55		♌
-11	Oct 18	21:58		♍
-10	Jan 19	7:44	℞	♌
-10	Aug 13	23:59		♍
1	Dec 6	21:13		♎
2	Jan 29	18:09	℞	♍
2	Sep 20	6:30		♎
3	Jun 5	6:23	℞	♍
3	Jun 16	11:07		♎
13	Nov 23	21:46		♏
14	Apr 21	1:57	℞	♎
14	Sep 21	12:25		♏
26	Feb 20	6:16		♐
26	Mar 13	9:16	℞	♏
26	Nov 27	1:27		♐
27	Jun 30	22:23	℞	♏
27	Sep 21	12:14		♐
42	Jan 1	2:56		♑
42	Jul 16	3:06	℞	♐
42	Nov 6	1:54		♑
60	Mar 28	15:40		♒
60	Jun 3	3:26	℞	♑
61	Jan 27	9:30		♒
61	Aug 16	1:11	℞	♑
61	Dec 7	14:55		♒
84	Mar 24	22:51		♓
84	Aug 8	23:23	℞	♒
85	Feb 7	10:16		♓
85	Oct 14	3:51	℞	♒
85	Dec 12	23:30		♓
112	May 1	10:47		♈
112	Sep 1	3:46	℞	♓
113	Mar 18	2:52		♈
113	Oct 27	9:59	℞	♓
114	Jan 30	7:04		♈
143	Jun 11	22:41		♉
143	Sep 20	12:11	℞	♈
144	Apr 25	22:21		♉
144	Nov 12	10:11	℞	♈
145	Mar 13	22:42		♉
174	Jun 24	22:28		♊
174	Nov 8	21:05	℞	♉
175	May 11	19:09		♊
176	Jan 7	22:08	℞	♉
176	Mar 18	17:31		♊
200	Jul 29	19:06		♋
200	Dec 7	5:13	℞	♊
201	Jun 10	15:53		♋
202	Feb 18	10:33	℞	♊
202	Apr 6	22:00		♋
220	Aug 24	8:23		♌
221	Jan 15	6:59	℞	♋
221	Jun 30	13:04		♌
235	Sep 26	18:27		♍
236	Feb 15	22:36	℞	♌
236	Jul 26	18:28		♍
247	Nov 22	6:04		♎
248	Feb 16	6:50	℞	♍
248	Sep 12	12:08		♎
259	Nov 15	2:46		♏
260	May 4	3:41	℞	♎
260	Sep 10	15:41		♏
272	Jan 9	16:43		♐
272	Apr 28	20:29	℞	♏
272	Nov 7	11:10		♐
287	Jan 18	14:36		♑
287	Jun 22	14:45	℞	♐
287	Nov 25	3:58		♑
305	Mar 14	10:46		♒
305	Jun 21	18:43	℞	♑
306	Jan 19	11:54		♒
306	Sep 2	9:18	℞	♑
306	Nov 24	17:60		♒
328	Apr 9	16:52		♓
328	Jul 24	16:47	℞	♒
329	Feb 19	13:07		♓
329	Sep 25	8:40	℞	♒
330	Jan 1	10:14		♓
356	Apr 20	18:57		♈
356	Sep 13	8:32	℞	♓
357	Mar 9	4:46		♈
357	Nov 12	18:24	℞	♓
358	Jan 15	7:10		♈
387	May 22	15:43		♉
387	Oct 13	0:39	℞	♈
388	Apr 9	14:30		♉
388	Dec 8	5:19	℞	♈
389	Feb 18	3:02		♉
418	Jun 21	4:25		♊
418	Nov 13	1:23	℞	♉
419	May 9	0:42		♊
420	Jan 13	3:35	℞	♉
420	Mar 14	4:37		♊
444	Sep 21	23:20		♋
444	Oct 8	19:51	℞	♊
445	Jul 9	3:48		♋
445	Dec 29	23:42	℞	♊
446	May 22	7:30		♋
465	Sep 11	12:45		♌
465	Dec 23	10:23	℞	♋
466	Jul 16	7:31		♌
467	Mar 15	21:59	℞	♋
467	May 8	8:47		♌
481	Sep 8	19:34		♍
482	Mar 8	15:37	℞	♌
482	Jul 8	21:22		♍
493	Nov 16	5:04		♎
494	Feb 20	3:22	℞	♍
494	Sep 9	11:55		♎
505	Nov 12	9:49		♏
506	May 8	7:57	℞	♎
506	Sep 8	6:55		♏
517	Dec 24	22:52		♐
518	May 19	0:03	℞	♏
518	Oct 25	17:03		♐
532	Feb 21	16:24		♑
532	May 12	14:42	℞	♐
532	Dec 19	23:46		♑
533	Aug 9	0:32	℞	♐
533	Oct 15	11:25		♑
550	Mar 14	8:01		♒
550	Jun 20	20:59	℞	♑
551	Jan 18	11:40		♒
551	Sep 3	15:05	℞	♑
551	Nov 22	2:18		♒
573	Mar 12	6:26		♓
573	Aug 25	20:38	℞	♒
574	Jan 25	15:39		♓
600	Apr 20	13:18		♈
600	Sep 14	2:19	℞	♓
601	Mar 8	14:22		♈
601	Nov 15	6:01	℞	♓
602	Jan 13	3:30		♈
630	Jul 12	3:34		♉
630	Aug 19	21:42	℞	♈
631	May 12	9:37		♉
631	Oct 24	23:07	℞	♈
632	Mar 31	3:43		♉
633	Jan 3	18:02	℞	♈
633	Jan 23	16:55		♉
662	Jun 21	19:01		♊
662	Nov 12	13:39	℞	♉
663	May 9	17:21		♊
664	Jan 11	15:47	℞	♉
664	Mar 16	1:01		♊
689	Aug 14	2:07		♋
689	Nov 18	14:52	℞	♊
690	Jun 23	16:15		♋
691	Jan 20	9:31	℞	♊
691	May 4	4:54		♋
711	Aug 5	20:18		♌
712	Feb 9	16:56	℞	♋
712	Jun 10	20:42		♌
727	Aug 31	12:47		♍
728	Mar 24	11:51	℞	♌
728	Jun 26	10:01		♍
739	Nov 23	17:20		♎
740	Feb 14	23:35	℞	♍
740	Sep 13	21:48		♎
751	Nov 18	12:30		♏
752	Apr 29	22:24	℞	♎
752	Sep 14	2:23		♏
763	Dec 21	1:12		♐
764	May 25	1:00	℞	♏
764	Oct 20	5:13		♐
778	Jan 22	22:53		♑
778	Jun 17	13:19	℞	♐
778	Nov 28	4:54		♑
795	Mar 27	1:22		♒
795	Jun 7	14:14	℞	♑
796	Jan 25	16:44		♒
796	Aug 22	7:25	℞	♑
796	Dec 1	15:02		♒
817	Apr 13	16:36		♓
817	Jul 19	7:59	℞	♒
818	Feb 21	9:39		♓
818	Sep 21	23:26	℞	♒
819	Jan 3	4:42		♓
844	Apr 24	6:22		♈
844	Sep 7	22:31	℞	♓
845	Mar 11	15:46		♈
845	Nov 6	16:11	℞	♓
846	Jan 19	12:38		♈
874	Jun 22	11:00		♉
874	Sep 7	10:19	℞	♈
875	May 3	0:50		♉
875	Nov 3	13:22	℞	♈
876	Mar 21	4:42		♉
906	Jun 22	11:05		♊
906	Nov 11	20:30	℞	♉
907	May 10	15:13		♊
908	Jan 9	19:19	℞	♉
908	Mar 18	4:26		♊
934	Jul 24	17:24		♋
934	Dec 11	15:49	℞	♊
935	Jun 8	1:38		♋
936	Feb 20	10:02	℞	♊
936	Apr 4	13:02		♋
956	Aug 24	1:36		♌
957	Jan 12	21:29	℞	♋
957	Jul 2	11:43		♌
972	Oct 31	20:03		♍
973	Jan 2	16:53	℞	♌
973	Aug 22	18:54		♍
974	Apr 7	3:20	℞	♌
974	Jun 13	6:33		♍
985	Dec 7	10:31		♎
986	Jan 27	23:24	℞	♍
986	Sep 20	21:34		♎
987	May 22	19:41	℞	♍
987	Jun 28	4:33		♎
997	Nov 30	0:51		♏
998	Apr 12	3:26	℞	♎
998	Sep 26	11:08		♏
1009	Dec 24	16:57		♐
1010	May 20	11:44	℞	♏
1010	Oct 24	7:31		♐
1024	Jan 8	21:37		♑
1024	Jul 7	20:02	℞	♐
1024	Nov 11	11:19		♑
1041	Feb 9	10:09		♒
1041	Jul 31	8:12	℞	♑
1041	Dec 20	10:36		♒
1062	Mar 31	13:07		♓
1062	Aug 4	2:14	℞	♒
1063	Feb 11	10:43		♓
1063	Oct 11	13:59	℞	♒
1063	Dec 16	21:16		♓
1088	May 8	9:57		♈
1088	Aug 23	12:02	℞	♓
1089	Mar 22	11:47		♈
1089	Oct 20	10:55	℞	♓
1090	Feb 4	14:30		♈
1118	Jun 21	2:17		♉
1118	Sep 11	0:16	℞	♈
1119	May 2	18:57		♉
1119	Nov 6	9:06	℞	♈
1120	Mar 20	19:53		♉
1150	Jun 25	18:28		♊
1150	Nov 8	5:41	℞	♉
1151	May 13	19:59		♊
1152	Jan 3	15:53	℞	♉
1152	Mar 24	12:51		♊
1178	Sep 12	19:32		♋
1178	Oct 19	3:18	℞	♊
1179	Jul 9	12:56		♋
1179	Dec 30	1:57	℞	♊
1180	May 23	19:18		♋
1201	Sep 19	8:34		♌
1201	Dec 14	16:04	℞	♋
1202	Jul 23	15:35		♌
1203	Feb 25	20:52	℞	♋
1203	May 26	22:24		♌
1218	Oct 23	22:33		♍
1219	Jan 12	6:47	℞	♌
1219	Aug 19	14:22		♍
1220	Apr 15	5:14	℞	♌
1220	Jun 5	1:11		♍
1232	Oct 3	16:28		♎
1233	Apr 19	19:34	℞	♍
1233	Jul 27	20:11		♎
1243	Dec 25	5:11		♏
1244	Mar 13	6:49	℞	♎
1244	Oct 13	19:02		♏
1256	Jan 4	19:24		♐
1256	May 4	12:18	℞	♏
1256	Nov 1	19:20		♐
1269	Dec 31	15:46		♑
1270	Jul 18	15:02	℞	♐
1270	Nov 1	11:50		♑
1286	Mar 5	19:08		♒
1286	Jun 29	19:38	℞	♑
1287	Jan 10	19:20		♒
1287	Sep 23	20:18	℞	♑
1287	Nov 1	8:18		♒
1307	Mar 27	1:52		♓
1307	Aug 10	5:06	℞	♒
1308	Feb 7	11:14		♓
1308	Oct 23	3:51	℞	♒
1308	Dec 4	13:16		♓
1332	Jun 8	13:09		♈

Pluto Ingresses –500 (501 BC)–2100

Year	Date	Time		Sign
1332	Jul 21	16:47	℞	♓
1333	Apr 7	16:51		♈
1333	Sep 29	3:25	℞	♓
1334	Feb 23	4:01		♈
1362	Jun 20	8:36		♉
1362	Sep 9	21:42	℞	♈
1363	May 1	22:38		♉
1363	Nov 5	9:48	℞	♈
1364	Mar 20	2:15		♉
1394	Jun 29	9:37		♊
1394	Nov 2	5:39	℞	♉
1395	May 16	21:06		♊
1395	Dec 27	4:12	℞	♉
1396	Mar 29	23:15		♊
1423	Aug 11	14:04		♋
1423	Nov 22	7:54	℞	♊
1424	Jun 22	15:51		♋
1425	Jan 19	20:37	℞	♊
1425	May 5	4:09		♋
1447	Aug 11	23:38		♌
1448	Jan 29	2:22	℞	♋
1448	Jun 20	17:04		♌
1464	Oct 18	5:02		♍
1465	Jan 17	10:08	℞	♌
1465	Aug 16	17:08		♍
1466	Apr 21	13:04	℞	♌
1466	May 31	10:09		♍
1478	Oct 21	8:17		♎
1479	Mar 25	3:26	℞	♍
1479	Aug 19	13:14		♎
1490	Nov 5	9:15		♏
1491	May 19	5:57	℞	♎
1491	Aug 28	22:09		♏
1502	Jan 31	19:02		♐
1502	Apr 5	13:21	℞	♏
1502	Nov 19	15:52		♐
1503	Jul 31	17:50	℞	♏
1503	Aug 23	6:51		♐
1516	Jan 2	19:05		♑
1516	Jul 18	20:03	℞	♐
1516	Nov 2	3:14		♑
1532	Feb 12	4:47		♒
1532	Jul 29	16:02	℞	♑
1532	Dec 21	0:41		♒
1552	Mar 30	17:25		♓
1552	Aug 4	16:05	℞	♒
1553	Feb 10	1:24		♓
1553	Oct 15	11:51	℞	♒
1553	Dec 12	10:19		♓
1577	May 4	15:50		♈
1577	Aug 28	16:57	℞	♓
1578	Mar 19	7:43		♈
1578	Oct 27	5:33	℞	♓
1579	Jan 30	4:23		♈
1606	Jul 7	21:16		♉
1606	Aug 22	20:34	℞	♈
1607	May 10	1:30		♉
1607	Oct 26	18:39	℞	♈
1608	Mar 28	10:40		♉
1638	Jul 9	1:52		♊
1638	Oct 22	17:27	℞	♉
1639	May 24	18:15		♊
1639	Dec 15	12:14	℞	♉
1640	Apr 10	5:58		♊
1668	Jul 24	4:18		♋
1668	Dec 8	22:43	℞	♊
1669	Jun 8	22:35		♋
1670	Feb 10	18:04	℞	♊
1670	Apr 13	7:38		♋
1692	Sep 2	12:39		♌
1692	Dec 30	9:56	℞	♋
1693	Jul 12	13:15		♌
1694	Mar 15	7:52	℞	♋
1694	May 8	20:55		♌
1710	Oct 17	17:05		♍
1711	Jan 19	0:30	℞	♌
1711	Aug 17	3:09		♍
1712	Apr 19	14:58	℞	♌
1712	Jun 1	17:29		♍
1724	Nov 14	7:11		♎
1725	Feb 22	8:43	℞	♍
1725	Sep 9	16:53		♎
1736	Dec 5	21:24		♏
1737	Apr 4	19:50	℞	♎
1737	Oct 1	12:33		♏
1748	Dec 10	6:22		♐
1749	Jun 8	18:13	℞	♏
1749	Oct 6	21:05		♐
1762	Jan 7	17:36		♑
1762	Jul 8	22:22	℞	♐
1762	Nov 9	6:25		♑
1777	Apr 3	21:50		♒
1777	May 28	11:03	℞	♑
1778	Jan 26	17:08		♒
1778	Aug 21	2:58	℞	♑
1778	Dec 1	10:37		♒
1797	Apr 11	5:11		♓
1797	Jul 21	10:20	℞	♒
1798	Feb 17	18:44		♓
1798	Sep 28	19:43	℞	♒
1798	Dec 26	6:08		♓
1822	Apr 16	10:06		♈
1822	Sep 19	19:21	℞	♓
1823	Mar 3	6:14		♈
1851	May 20	8:54		♉
1851	Oct 14	19:01	℞	♈
1852	Apr 7	11:09		♉
1852	Dec 12	4:36	℞	♈
1853	Feb 14	4:35		♉
1882	Jul 21	20:38		♊
1882	Oct 9	9:47	℞	♉
1883	Jun 2	0:30		♊
1883	Dec 4	22:44	℞	♉
1884	Apr 19	23:41		♊
1912	Sep 10	16:08		♋
1912	Oct 20	8:41	℞	♊
1913	Jul 9	22:18		♋
1913	Dec 28	4:26	℞	♊
1914	May 26	20:37		♋
1937	Oct 7	12:18		♌
1937	Nov 25	9:03	℞	♋
1938	Aug 3	17:59		♌
1939	Feb 7	12:56	℞	♋
1939	Jun 14	4:50		♌
1956	Oct 20	6:18		♍
1957	Jan 15	2:39	℞	♌
1957	Aug 19	4:27		♍
1958	Apr 11	14:52	℞	♌
1958	Jun 10	18:56		♍
1971	Oct 5	6:18		♎
1972	Apr 17	7:46	℞	♍
1972	Jul 30	11:43		♎
1983	Nov 5	21:18		♏
1984	May 18	14:19	℞	♎
1984	Aug 28	4:59		♏
1995	Jan 17	9:59		♐
1995	Apr 21	2:08	℞	♏
1995	Nov 10	19:40		♐
2008	Jan 26	3:45		♑
2008	Jun 14	3:47	℞	♐
2008	Nov 27	2:06		♑
2023	Mar 23	15:24		♒
2023	Jun 11	6:16	℞	♑
2024	Jan 21	2:36		♒
2024	Sep 1	20:37	℞	♑
2024	Nov 19	23:43		♒
2043	Mar 9	3:47		♓
2043	Aug 31	23:32	℞	♒
2044	Jan 19	12:51		♓
2066	Jun 18	19:06		♈
2066	Jul 10	17:56	℞	♓
2067	Apr 9	2:58		♈
2067	Sep 27	10:35	℞	♓
2068	Feb 23	18:49		♈
2095	Jun 9	13:21		♉
2095	Sep 20	13:03	℞	♈
2096	Apr 23	5:13		♉
2096	Nov 14	6:20	℞	♈
2097	Mar 10	8:14		♉

Neptune Ingresses –500 (501 BC)–2100

Year	Date	Time		Sign
-500	Dec 1	12:09		♏
-499	Apr 9	1:45	℞	♎
-499	Oct 4	10:26		♏
-486	Dec 16	23:22		♐
-485	May 30	6:43	℞	♏
-485	Oct 20	8:42		♐
-472	Mar 21	19:15		♑
-472	Apr 14	10:15	℞	♐
-472	Dec 28	7:59		♑
-471	Jul 28	8:20	℞	♐
-471	Oct 26	2:25		♑
-458	Mar 3	22:15		♒
-458	Jul 9	5:58	℞	♑
-457	Jan 3	9:03		♒
-445	May 27	2:03		♓
-445	Jun 12	4:15	℞	♒
-444	Feb 27	15:53		♓
-444	Sep 26	16:15	℞	♒
-444	Dec 24	13:19		♓
-431	Apr 19	15:21		♈
-431	Sep 25	16:24	℞	♓
-430	Feb 19	3:44		♈
-418	Jun 12	5:02		♉
-418	Sep 28	22:50	℞	♈
-417	Apr 10	8:49		♉
-404	May 30	8:43		♊
-404	Dec 23	11:31	℞	♉
-403	Mar 26	15:18		♊
-391	Jul 27	7:52		♋
-391	Dec 15	12:35	℞	♊
-390	May 28	21:06		♋
-377	Jul 31	15:57		♌
-376	Feb 21	10:50	℞	♋
-376	May 27	16:05		♌
-364	Oct 12	13:40		♍
-363	Jan 23	16:20	℞	♌
-363	Aug 12	10:14		♍
-350	Oct 26	1:45		♎
-349	Mar 15	21:22	℞	♍
-349	Aug 29	9:43		♎
-336	Nov 11	14:02		♏
-335	May 2	15:22	℞	♎
-335	Sep 14	15:19		♏
-322	Nov 29	5:21		♐
-321	Jun 23	13:59	℞	♏
-321	Sep 28	4:37		♐
-308	Feb 12	3:20		♑
-308	May 23	21:01	℞	♐
-308	Dec 11	10:12		♑
-294	Feb 13	8:52		♒
-294	Aug 1	9:42	℞	♑
-294	Dec 17	1:23		♒
-281	Apr 17	23:06		♓
-281	Jul 23	4:08	℞	♒
-280	Feb 12	18:27		♓
-267	Apr 3	22:43		♈
-267	Oct 17	3:06	℞	♓
-266	Jan 31	20:33		♈
-254	May 24	11:11		♉
-254	Oct 20	9:30	℞	♈
-253	Mar 25	16:13		♉
-241	Jul 20	11:19		♊
-241	Oct 20	7:14	℞	♉
-240	May 15	7:09		♊
-239	Feb 4	13:37	℞	♉
-239	Feb 12	23:35		♊
-227	Jul 10	7:25		♋
-226	Jan 6	9:07	℞	♊
-226	May 10	11:01		♋
-214	Sep 17	1:16		♌
-214	Dec 20	9:54	℞	♋
-213	Jul 15	17:09		♌
-200	Sep 22	23:57		♍
-199	Feb 18	3:54	℞	♌
-199	Jul 26	17:02		♍
-186	Oct 8	7:43		♎
-185	Apr 11	7:36	℞	♍
-185	Aug 9	16:10		♎
-172	Jan 8	2:47		♏
-172	Feb 25	13:26	℞	♎
-172	Oct 26	5:58		♏
-171	May 31	21:04	℞	♎
-171	Aug 22	2:40		♏
-158	Jan 12	18:24		♐
-158	Apr 24	12:37	℞	♏
-158	Nov 12	18:15		♐
-144	Jan 21	23:24		♑
-144	Jun 20	9:45	℞	♐
-144	Nov 24	13:21		♑
-131	Apr 21	10:19		♒
-131	May 14	17:29	℞	♑
-130	Jan 27	4:54		♒
-130	Aug 27	12:08	℞	♑
-130	Nov 24	20:55		♒
-117	Mar 26	21:13		♓
-117	Aug 17	12:12	℞	♒
-116	Jan 26	22:05		♓
-104	May 26	4:34		♈
-104	Aug 12	7:37	℞	♓
-103	Mar 19	3:04		♈
-103	Nov 16	17:01	℞	♓
-102	Jan 3	14:33		♈
-90	May 8	5:30		♉
-90	Nov 12	19:53	℞	♈
-89	Mar 7	17:52		♉
-77	Jun 29	18:25		♊
-77	Nov 14	12:22	℞	♉
-76	Apr 29	16:03		♊
-64	Sep 6	2:45		♋
-64	Oct 31	13:01	℞	♊
-63	Jun 25	3:43		♋
-62	Feb 2	18:51	℞	♊
-62	Apr 17	3:53		♋
-50	Aug 27	2:08		♌
-49	Jan 15	15:19	℞	♋
-49	Jun 28	23:45		♌
-36	Sep 4	19:10		♍
-35	Mar 15	5:12	℞	♌
-35	Jul 5	11:49		♍
-23	Nov 26	5:54		♎
-22	Feb 7	22:55	℞	♍
-22	Sep 20	22:15		♎
-21	May 14	3:09	℞	♍
-21	Jul 10	17:33		♎
-9	Dec 7	10:53		♏
-8	Mar 31	21:08	℞	♎
-8	Oct 8	3:48		♏
5	Dec 21	7:44		♐
6	May 21	19:28	℞	♏
6	Oct 25	1:42		♐
20	Jan 2	18:31		♑
20	Jul 17	14:58	℞	♐
20	Nov 2	12:11		♑
33	Mar 12	2:54		♒
33	Jun 26	23:37	℞	♑
34	Jan 9	15:15		♒
47	Mar 8	6:26		♓
47	Sep 10	21:23	℞	♒
48	Jan 7	8:56		♓
60	Apr 30	11:10		♈
60	Sep 9	18:43	℞	♓
61	Mar 1	11:57		♈
73	Jun 28	19:32		♉
73	Sep 8	10:44	℞	♈
74	Apr 20	5:30		♉
74	Dec 12	0:29	℞	♈
75	Feb 6	21:05		♉
87	Jun 10	6:18		♊
87	Dec 6	16:58	℞	♉
88	Apr 9	12:21		♊
100	Aug 7	14:15		♋
100	Dec 2	6:01	℞	♊
101	Jun 7	12:21		♋
114	Aug 8	8:03		♌
115	Feb 9	3:36	℞	♋
115	Jun 8	10:01		♌
127	Oct 22	10:14		♍
128	Jan 14	23:23	℞	♌
128	Aug 17	21:20		♍
129	Apr 21	23:02	℞	♌
129	May 31	3:52		♍
141	Oct 31	4:56		♎
142	Mar 9	16:16	℞	♍
142	Sep 2	16:26		♎
155	Nov 16	10:06		♏
156	Apr 27	8:03	℞	♎
156	Sep 18	15:15		♏
169	Dec 1	19:28		♐
170	Jun 19	3:01	℞	♏
170	Oct 1	20:16		♐
183	Feb 17	10:40		♑
183	May 18	14:13	℞	♐
183	Dec 15	20:04		♑
184	Aug 28	19:16	℞	♐
184	Sep 24	19:16		♑
197	Feb 17	18:10		♒
197	Jul 24	0:47	℞	♑
197	Dec 21	18:04		♒
210	Apr 28	13:14		♓
210	Jul 11	2:30	℞	♒
211	Feb 19	0:10		♓
211	Oct 14	23:43	℞	♒
211	Dec 9	15:31		♓
224	Apr 11	16:50		♈
224	Oct 5	10:46	℞	♓
225	Feb 10	23:45		♈
237	Jun 2	21:43		♉
237	Oct 8	21:20	℞	♈
238	Apr 3	6:05		♉
250	Aug 4	4:24		♊

Neptune Ingresses –500 (501 BC)–2100

250 Oct 4 9:46 ℞ ♉	538 Sep 5 11:50 ℞ ♒	811 Aug 23 5:01 ♏	1111 Apr 14 5:55 ℞ ♌	1398 Jan 28 14:51 ℞ ♉
251 May 24 6:16 ♊	539 Jan 11 18:38 ♓	824 Jan 14 7:14 ♐	1111 Jun 8 23:15 ♍	1398 Feb 19 16:09 ♊
252 Jan 6 1:45 ℞ ♉	551 May 8 4:21 ♈	824 Apr 21 12:40 ℞ ♏	1123 Nov 1 22:06 ♎	1410 Jul 8 17:19 ♋
252 Mar 14 15:04 ♊	551 Sep 2 20:01 ℞ ♓	824 Nov 12 20:54 ♐	1124 Mar 8 19:24 ℞ ♍	1411 Jan 10 6:03 ℞ ♊
264 Jul 17 11:17 ♋	552 Mar 6 16:56 ♈	838 Jan 23 14:35 ♑	1124 Sep 3 3:29 ♎	1411 May 8 7:56 ♋
264 Dec 27 9:58 ℞ ♊	564 Jul 11 19:10 ♉	838 Jun 16 16:57 ℞ ♐	1137 Nov 15 20:40 ♏	1423 Sep 8 11:10 ♌
265 May 18 22:38 ♋	564 Aug 25 16:14 ℞ ♈	838 Nov 27 1:57 ♑	1138 Apr 28 21:17 ℞ ♎	1424 Jan 1 1:30 ℞ ♋
277 Sep 25 1:30 ♌	565 Apr 25 6:47 ♉	852 Jan 31 20:57 ♒	1138 Sep 18 20:44 ♏	1424 Jul 8 5:46 ♌
277 Dec 11 16:30 ℞ ♋	565 Dec 1 1:27 ℞ ♈	852 Aug 18 4:53 ℞ ♑	1151 Dec 3 10:24 ♐	1437 Sep 11 5:43 ♍
278 Jul 20 13:19 ♌	566 Feb 17 5:32 ♉	852 Dec 1 2:01 ♒	1152 Jun 17 20:53 ℞ ♏	1438 Mar 5 5:57 ℞ ♌
279 Mar 15 22:32 ℞ ♋	578 Jun 15 2:32 ♊	865 Apr 4 4:21 ♓	1152 Oct 2 10:57 ♐	1438 Jul 13 12:60 ♍
279 May 7 1:22 ♌	578 Nov 30 2:22 ℞ ♉	865 Aug 4 15:10 ℞ ♒	1165 Feb 20 5:44 ♑	1450 Dec 3 7:56 ♎
291 Sep 27 18:19 ♍	579 Apr 16 1:20 ♊	866 Feb 3 4:35 ♓	1165 May 14 23:40 ℞ ♐	1451 Jan 31 14:42 ℞ ♍
292 Feb 12 4:21 ℞ ♌	591 Aug 12 13:32 ♋	878 Jun 22 7:02 ♈	1165 Dec 17 15:12 ♑	1451 Sep 24 5:07 ♎
292 Jul 30 4:09 ♍	591 Nov 26 19:04 ℞ ♊	878 Jul 14 4:00 ℞ ♓	1166 Aug 22 13:24 ℞ ♐	1452 May 4 4:41 ℞ ♍
305 Oct 11 14:02 ♎	592 Jun 9 21:33 ♋	879 Mar 28 11:58 ♈	1166 Oct 2 8:37 ♑	1452 Jul 17 2:51 ♎
306 Apr 6 11:03 ℞ ♍	605 Aug 10 7:49 ♌	879 Oct 26 17:38 ℞ ♓	1179 Feb 23 0:11 ♒	1464 Dec 9 15:37 ♏
306 Aug 13 12:15 ♎	606 Feb 6 5:46 ℞ ♋	880 Jan 23 7:57 ♈	1179 Jul 19 0:37 ℞ ♑	1465 Mar 27 23:39 ℞ ♎
319 Jan 14 3:57 ♏	606 Jun 10 19:42 ♌	892 May 17 12:26 ♉	1179 Dec 27 1:30 ♒	1465 Oct 10 12:44 ♏
319 Feb 19 4:53 ℞ ♎	618 Oct 23 21:14 ♍	892 Oct 25 23:52 ℞ ♈	1192 May 14 10:21 ♓	1478 Dec 24 22:46 ♐
319 Oct 29 3:06 ♏	619 Jan 13 12:05 ℞ ♌	893 Mar 19 2:55 ♉	1192 Jun 21 9:07 ℞ ♒	1479 May 16 15:57 ℞ ♏
320 May 28 4:38 ℞ ♎	619 Aug 19 16:53 ♍	905 Jul 12 11:13 ♊	1193 Feb 24 10:17 ♓	1479 Oct 28 12:52 ♐
320 Aug 25 2:28 ♏	620 Apr 18 7:08 ℞ ♌	905 Oct 28 11:34 ℞ ♉	1193 Sep 29 21:47 ℞ ♒	1493 Jan 7 7:32 ♑
333 Jan 15 20:04 ♐	620 Jun 3 11:13 ♍	906 May 10 18:43 ♊	1193 Dec 21 13:40 ♓	1493 Jul 8 11:19 ℞ ♐
333 Apr 20 22:36 ℞ ♏	632 Oct 30 12:34 ♎	919 Jul 3 4:20 ♋	1206 Apr 20 19:01 ♈	1493 Nov 9 17:12 ♑
333 Nov 14 15:25 ♐	633 Mar 10 11:26 ℞ ♍	920 Jan 18 18:06 ℞ ♊	1206 Sep 23 2:00 ℞ ♓	1506 Mar 27 0:58 ♒
347 Jan 24 16:38 ♑	633 Sep 2 2:02 ♎	920 Apr 29 22:01 ♋	1207 Feb 20 19:24 ♈	1506 Jun 11 5:12 ℞ ♑
347 Jun 17 22:11 ℞ ♐	646 Nov 15 21:34 ♏	932 Sep 1 18:36 ♌	1219 Jun 16 15:52 ♉	1507 Jan 19 10:09 ♒
347 Nov 27 21:24 ♑	647 Apr 28 20:40 ℞ ♎	933 Jan 6 14:33 ℞ ♋	1219 Sep 22 19:46 ℞ ♈	1507 Sep 15 23:32 ℞ ♑
361 Jan 30 18:19 ♒	647 Sep 19 3:35 ♏	933 Jul 3 19:12 ♌	1220 Apr 12 11:12 ♉	1507 Nov 8 15:43 ♒
361 Aug 21 8:01 ℞ ♑	660 Dec 2 4:49 ♐	946 Sep 7 20:21 ♍	1233 Jun 1 12:15 ♊	1520 Mar 21 12:33 ♓
361 Nov 30 5:40 ♒	661 Jun 18 5:08 ℞ ♏	947 Mar 10 10:39 ℞ ♌	1233 Dec 18 21:21 ℞ ♉	1520 Aug 23 1:14 ℞ ♒
374 Apr 1 8:34 ♓	661 Oct 2 12:09 ♐	947 Jul 9 4:18 ♍	1234 Mar 30 10:55 ♊	1521 Jan 22 6:15 ♓
374 Aug 10 15:20 ℞ ♒	674 Feb 18 3:14 ♑	959 Nov 28 5:14 ♎	1246 Jul 25 18:41 ♋	1533 May 24 10:33 ♈
375 Jan 31 17:30 ♓	674 May 17 10:44 ℞ ♐	960 Feb 6 1:41 ℞ ♍	1246 Dec 16 20:52 ℞ ♊	1533 Aug 14 17:27 ℞ ♓
387 Jun 8 0:40 ♈	674 Dec 16 14:04 ♑	960 Sep 20 20:07 ♎	1247 May 27 4:04 ♋	1534 Mar 18 16:20 ♈
387 Jul 31 11:21 ℞ ♓	675 Aug 25 18:44 ℞ ♐	961 May 10 7:36 ℞ ♍	1259 Oct 7 12:12 ♌	1534 Nov 21 1:20 ℞ ♓
388 Mar 24 8:03 ♈	675 Sep 29 14:36 ♑	961 Jul 11 17:01 ♎	1259 Nov 28 17:25 ℞ ♋	1535 Jan 1 12:15 ♈
388 Nov 4 1:26 ℞ ♓	688 Feb 20 22:50 ♒	973 Dec 6 21:49 ♏	1260 Jul 24 23:50 ♌	1547 May 8 20:18 ♉
389 Jan 15 14:42 ♈	688 Jul 20 20:18 ℞ ♑	974 Mar 31 7:39 ℞ ♎	1261 Mar 1 15:13 ℞ ♋	1547 Nov 10 21:53 ℞ ♈
401 May 13 21:38 ♉	688 Dec 24 2:37 ♒	974 Oct 8 9:23 ♏	1261 May 18 6:37 ♌	1548 Mar 8 2:53 ♉
401 Nov 2 8:38 ℞ ♈	701 May 6 4:40 ♓	987 Dec 21 10:11 ♐	1273 Sep 29 17:20 ♍	1560 Jun 28 23:22 ♊
402 Mar 14 21:16 ♉	701 Jul 2 12:17 ℞ ♒	988 May 20 13:27 ℞ ♏	1274 Feb 7 15:04 ℞ ♌	1560 Nov 12 11:19 ℞ ♉
414 Jul 5 18:56 ♊	702 Feb 22 10:00 ♓	988 Oct 23 22:28 ♐	1274 Aug 1 14:14 ♍	1561 Apr 29 17:53 ♊
414 Nov 5 4:42 ℞ ♉	702 Oct 7 3:10 ℞ ♒	1002 Jan 4 14:21 ♑	1287 Oct 11 4:58 ♎	1573 Aug 31 18:50 ♋
415 May 5 17:01 ♊	702 Dec 16 21:55 ♓	1002 Jul 15 13:44 ℞ ♐	1288 Apr 3 6:11 ℞ ♍	1573 Nov 5 18:21 ℞ ♊
427 Sep 20 1:28 ♋	715 Apr 17 13:25 ♈	1002 Nov 5 19:10 ♑	1288 Aug 12 3:54 ♎	1574 Jun 22 3:05 ♋
427 Oct 17 3:49 ℞ ♊	715 Sep 29 17:39 ℞ ♓	1015 Mar 19 1:54 ♒	1301 Jan 14 3:11 ♏	1575 Feb 7 19:49 ℞ ♊
428 Jun 28 7:07 ♋	716 Feb 17 11:01 ♈	1015 Jun 20 14:24 ℞ ♑	1301 Feb 17 8:14 ℞ ♎	1575 Apr 11 20:02 ♋
429 Jan 24 9:20 ℞ ♊	728 Jun 9 13:52 ♉	1016 Jan 14 17:06 ♒	1301 Oct 28 10:44 ♏	1587 Aug 20 0:07 ♌
429 Apr 23 23:17 ♋	728 Oct 1 0:36 ℞ ♈	1016 Oct 5 16:22 ℞ ♑	1302 May 27 5:36 ℞ ♎	1588 Jan 24 0:09 ℞ ♋
441 Aug 30 1:01 ♌	729 Apr 8 11:16 ♉	1016 Oct 19 0:18 ♒	1302 Aug 25 8:56 ♏	1588 Jun 20 14:05 ♌
442 Jan 9 19:48 ℞ ♋	741 Aug 17 12:49 ♊	1029 Mar 14 10:56 ♓	1315 Jan 16 17:57 ♐	1600 Nov 5 13:53 ♍
442 Jul 1 13:46 ♌	741 Sep 20 12:01 ℞ ♉	1029 Sep 1 17:02 ℞ ♒	1315 Apr 19 15:13 ℞ ♏	1600 Dec 29 2:20 ℞ ♌
455 Sep 6 21:06 ♍	742 May 28 11:10 ♊	1030 Jan 14 22:12 ♓	1315 Nov 15 9:41 ♐	1601 Aug 24 22:54 ♍
456 Mar 10 18:44 ℞ ♌	742 Dec 28 21:04 ℞ ♉	1042 May 12 20:38 ♈	1316 Aug 2 19:36 ℞ ♏	1602 Apr 2 4:30 ℞ ♌
456 Jul 7 8:59 ♍	743 Mar 23 4:29 ♊	1042 Aug 28 0:25 ℞ ♓	1316 Aug 20 17:39 ♐	1602 Jun 18 1:09 ♍
468 Nov 27 8:02 ♎	755 Jul 22 12:51 ♋	1043 Mar 11 10:30 ♈	1329 Jan 26 14:43 ♑	1614 Nov 6 5:21 ♎
469 Feb 4 15:49 ℞ ♍	755 Dec 23 7:28 ℞ ♊	1056 Apr 29 22:04 ♉	1329 Jun 12 16:16 ℞ ♐	1615 Mar 2 12:50 ℞ ♍
469 Sep 21 5:23 ♎	756 May 22 21:40 ♋	1056 Nov 22 9:22 ℞ ♈	1329 Nov 29 19:29 ♑	1615 Sep 7 7:21 ♎
470 May 9 2:47 ℞ ♍	768 Sep 29 15:42 ♌	1057 Feb 25 5:34 ♉	1343 Feb 4 7:18 ♒	1628 Nov 19 11:04 ♏
470 Jul 13 6:55 ♎	768 Dec 6 23:50 ℞ ♋	1069 Jun 19 23:54 ♊	1343 Aug 13 15:60 ℞ ♑	1629 Apr 21 13:43 ℞ ♎
482 Dec 7 11:24 ♏	769 Jul 22 14:25 ♌	1069 Nov 23 12:03 ℞ ♉	1343 Dec 6 13:39 ♒	1629 Sep 22 15:19 ♏
483 Mar 30 13:56 ℞ ♎	770 Mar 10 15:27 ℞ ♋	1070 Apr 21 12:24 ♊	1356 Apr 9 17:51 ♓	1642 Dec 6 9:46 ♐
483 Oct 8 23:49 ♏	770 May 11 20:08 ♌	1082 Aug 18 9:20 ♋	1356 Jul 28 20:43 ℞ ♒	1643 Jun 11 1:19 ℞ ♏
496 Dec 21 8:27 ♐	782 Sep 27 17:15 ♍	1082 Nov 20 3:45 ℞ ♊	1357 Feb 7 6:04 ♓	1643 Oct 8 1:59 ♐
497 May 19 8:49 ℞ ♏	783 Feb 12 8:52 ℞ ♌	1083 Jun 15 0:34 ♋	1370 Apr 3 6:50 ♈	1656 Feb 29 15:45 ♑
497 Oct 25 0:11 ♐	783 Jul 30 20:12 ♍	1084 Mar 8 1:31 ℞ ♊	1370 Oct 17 3:42 ℞ ♓	1656 May 3 4:05 ℞ ♐
511 Jan 4 22:06 ♑	796 Oct 9 22:01 ♎	1084 Mar 13 12:10 ♋	1371 Jan 31 16:58 ♈	1656 Dec 21 16:28 ♑
511 Jul 15 4:09 ℞ ♐	797 Apr 6 11:01 ℞ ♍	1096 Aug 12 0:53 ♌	1383 May 25 9:28 ♉	1657 Aug 6 14:54 ℞ ♐
511 Nov 6 6:28 ♑	797 Aug 11 9:55 ♎	1097 Feb 1 6:03 ℞ ♋	1383 Oct 18 5:54 ℞ ♈	1657 Oct 15 0:46 ♑
524 Mar 15 20:13 ♒	810 Jan 9 22:41 ♏	1097 Jun 13 2:32 ♌	1384 Mar 25 19:18 ♉	1670 Mar 1 13:48 ♒
524 Jun 22 10:43 ℞ ♑	810 Feb 21 17:43 ℞ ♎	1109 Oct 26 21:12 ♍	1396 Jul 20 2:47 ♊	1670 Jul 8 3:25 ℞ ♑
525 Jan 12 3:43 ♒	810 Oct 27 3:44 ♏	1110 Jan 10 7:56 ℞ ♌	1396 Oct 17 19:04 ℞ ♉	1671 Jan 1 22:22 ♒
538 Mar 11 23:54 ♓	811 May 30 0:05 ℞ ♎	1110 Aug 21 7:02 ♍	1397 May 15 8:31 ♊	1684 Mar 3 10:04 ♓

Neptune Ingresses –500 (501 BC)—2100

Year	Date	Time	℞	Sign
1684	Sep 14	15:48	℞	♒
1685	Jan 1	23:48		♓
1697	Apr 30	9:23		♈
1697	Sep 8	11:28	℞	♓
1698	Mar 1	18:28		♈
1710	Jul 3	15:42		♉
1710	Sep 3	23:52	℞	♈
1711	Apr 22	16:33		♉
1711	Dec 8	7:01	℞	♈
1712	Feb 12	6:41		♉
1724	Jun 11	15:04		♊
1724	Dec 3	20:04	℞	♉
1725	Apr 12	11:34		♊
1737	Aug 6	11:48		♋
1737	Dec 2	22:44	℞	♊
1738	Jun 6	4:27		♋
1751	Aug 2	23:19		♌
1752	Feb 16	8:43	℞	♋
1752	May 31	2:32		♌
1764	Oct 9	12:12		♍
1765	Jan 27	6:27	℞	♌
1765	Aug 9	4:57		♍
1778	Oct 18	12:37		♎
1779	Mar 25	6:52	℞	♍
1779	Aug 20	22:55		♎
1792	Nov 2	16:29		♏
1793	May 15	5:34	℞	♎
1793	Sep 2	16:32		♏
1806	Jan 28	1:32		♐
1806	Apr 6	20:53	℞	♏
1806	Nov 21	16:02		♐
1807	Jul 11	3:45	℞	♏
1807	Sep 12	19:30		♐
1820	Feb 5	0:23		♑
1820	Jun 2	2:36	℞	♐
1820	Dec 6	18:42		♑
1834	Feb 13	5:02		♒
1834	Jul 31	5:05	℞	♑
1834	Dec 17	8:50		♒
1847	Apr 26	3:17		♓
1847	Jul 11	22:42	℞	♒
1848	Feb 17	23:55		♓
1848	Oct 15	17:44	℞	♒
1848	Dec 6	17:45		♓
1861	Apr 13	20:37		♈
1861	Oct 1	5:34	℞	♓
1862	Feb 14	0:34		♈
1874	Jun 8	15:21		♉
1874	Sep 30	22:41	℞	♈
1875	Apr 7	21:53		♉
1887	Aug 16	4:54		♊
1887	Sep 20	20:00	℞	♉
1888	May 26	18:40		♊
1888	Dec 27	17:40	℞	♉
1889	Mar 22	1:49		♊
1901	Jul 19	23:59		♋
1901	Dec 25	13:27	℞	♊
1902	May 21	13:37		♋
1914	Sep 23	20:26		♌
1914	Dec 14	20:38	℞	♋
1915	Jul 19	13:34		♌
1916	Mar 19	15:23	℞	♋
1916	May 2	10:49		♌
1928	Sep 21	12:04		♍
1929	Feb 19	11:25	℞	♌
1929	Jul 24	15:03		♍
1942	Oct 3	16:59		♎
1943	Apr 17	10:59	℞	♍
1943	Aug 2	19:08		♎
1955	Dec 24	15:19		♏
1956	Mar 12	1:57	℞	♎
1956	Oct 19	9:26		♏
1957	Jun 15	20:13	℞	♎
1957	Aug 6	8:20		♏
1970	Jan 4	19:53		♐
1970	May 3	1:35	℞	♏
1970	Nov 6	16:30		♐
1984	Jan 19	2:52		♑
1984	Jun 23	1:16	℞	♐
1984	Nov 21	13:18		♑
1998	Jan 29	2:46		♒
1998	Aug 23	0:27	℞	♑
1998	Nov 28	1:09		♒
2011	Apr 4	13:37		♓
2011	Aug 5	3:12	℞	♒
2012	Feb 3	18:53		♓
2025	Mar 30	11:45		♈
2025	Oct 22	10:17	℞	♓
2026	Jan 26	17:14		♈
2038	May 21	23:55		♉
2038	Oct 21	12:51	℞	♈
2039	Mar 23	20:19		♉
2051	Jul 16	12:06		♊
2051	Oct 22	23:39	℞	♉
2052	May 12	10:17		♊
2065	Jul 3	7:21		♋
2066	Jan 14	20:56	℞	♊
2066	May 1	21:57		♋
2078	Sep 1	9:45		♌
2079	Jan 6	9:53	℞	♋
2079	Jul 3	6:13		♌
2092	Sep 4	15:05		♍
2093	Mar 11	13:15	℞	♌
2093	Jul 5	13:06		♍

Uranus Ingresses –500 (501 BC)—2100

Year	Date	Time	℞	Sign
-495	Jun 30	9:55		♉
-495	Sep 14	22:30	℞	♈
-494	Apr 11	18:01		♉
-488	Jul 22	11:17		♊
-488	Oct 24	16:50	℞	♉
-487	May 5	23:25		♊
-481	Jul 19	21:50		♋
-480	Jan 7	10:37	℞	♊
-480	May 4	4:10		♋
-475	Sep 21	1:44		♌
-475	Dec 25	1:06	℞	♋
-474	Jul 4	12:04		♌
-468	Aug 23	6:20		♍
-462	Oct 15	21:56		♎
-461	Apr 13	7:11	℞	♍
-461	Jul 31	18:39		♎
-455	Jan 1	15:05		♏
-455	Mar 9	19:39	℞	♎
-455	Oct 12	5:07		♏
-448	Jan 10	4:46		♐
-448	May 5	5:17	℞	♏
-448	Oct 29	10:04		♐
-441	Feb 24	5:04		♑
-441	May 18	3:33	℞	♐
-441	Dec 10	10:55		♑
-433	Feb 6	18:13		♒
-433	Aug 21	1:06	℞	♑
-433	Nov 26	22:58		♒
-426	Apr 24	14:15		♓
-426	Jul 20	4:03	℞	♒
-425	Feb 8	8:06		♓
-418	Apr 12	16:28		♈
-418	Oct 13	13:08	℞	♓
-417	Jan 31	1:22		♈
-411	Jun 3	6:45		♉
-411	Oct 15	0:20	℞	♈
-410	Mar 23	13:56		♉
-404	Jun 29	3:24		♊
-404	Nov 20	9:37	℞	♉
-403	Apr 17	4:26		♊
-397	Jul 3	1:46		♋
-396	Feb 6	16:31	℞	♊
-396	Apr 6	4:39		♋
-391	Aug 31	5:01		♌
-390	Jan 18	11:40	℞	♋
-390	Jun 17	8:43		♌
-385	Oct 30	15:54		♍
-384	Jan 12	16:55	℞	♌
-384	Aug 8	17:14		♍
-378	Oct 1	3:26		♎
-377	May 13	14:53	℞	♍
-377	Jul 3	23:07		♎
-372	Dec 8	20:22		♏
-371	Apr 5	19:37	℞	♎
-371	Sep 26	23:38		♏
-365	Dec 22	16:05		♐
-364	May 28	19:09	℞	♏
-364	Oct 12	5:12		♐
-357	Jan 31	16:14		♑
-357	Jun 14	11:43	℞	♐
-357	Nov 23	11:27		♑
-349	Jan 20	4:43		♒
-342	Mar 30	9:01		♓
-342	Aug 17	23:24	℞	♒
-341	Jan 20	14:51		♓
-334	Mar 24	20:15		♈
-334	Nov 22	0:18	℞	♓
-334	Dec 25	6:15		♈
-327	May 13	21:30		♉
-327	Nov 10	9:37	℞	♈
-326	Mar 1	19:27		♉
-320	Jun 9	22:32		♊
-320	Dec 16	21:40	℞	♉
-319	Mar 25	8:55		♊
-314	Sep 16	20:50		♋
-314	Oct 25	2:26	℞	♊
-313	Jun 16	5:60		♋
-307	Aug 13	17:30		♌
-306	Feb 11	20:12	℞	♋
-306	May 27	18:51		♌
-301	Oct 7	10:22		♍
-300	Feb 8	4:10	℞	♌
-300	Jul 24	10:28		♍
-295	Dec 21	3:08		♎
-294	Jan 18	21:27	℞	♍
-294	Sep 17	1:51		♎
-288	Nov 21	20:06		♏
-287	Apr 30	2:20	℞	♎
-287	Sep 10	14:14		♏
-281	Dec 6	16:03		♐
-280	Jun 25	18:32	℞	♏
-280	Sep 20	8:19		♐
-273	Jan 13	22:54		♑
-273	Jul 10	17:50	℞	♐
-273	Nov 4	17:38		♑
-266	Mar 16	14:04		♒
-266	Jun 28	11:48	℞	♑
-265	Jan 3	14:40		♒
-258	Mar 11	1:13		♓
-258	Sep 15	10:07	℞	♒
-258	Dec 30	4:25		♓
-251	May 21	8:40		♈
-251	Aug 23	10:32	℞	♓
-250	Mar 7	14:15		♈
-243	Apr 25	22:06		♉
-243	Dec 20	4:42	℞	♈
-242	Jan 25	11:16		♉
-236	May 23	17:32		♊
-230	Aug 14	8:28		♋
-230	Dec 2	2:02	℞	♊
-229	May 30	4:08		♋
-223	Jul 28	6:01		♌
-222	Mar 28	9:10	℞	♋
-222	Apr 17	13:20		♌
-217	Sep 19	9:53		♍
-216	Mar 5	7:03	℞	♌
-216	Jul 4	13:30		♍
-211	Nov 16	0:13		♎
-210	Feb 26	0:09	℞	♍
-210	Aug 31	20:38		♎
-204	Nov 5	8:60		♏
-203	May 26	20:58	℞	♎
-203	Aug 18	13:04		♏
-197	Nov 22	2:39		♐
-190	Dec 29	11:34		♑
-189	Aug 11	15:12	℞	♐
-189	Oct 9	3:38		♑
-182	Feb 23	19:07		♒
-182	Jul 25	13:27	℞	♑
-182	Dec 17	12:32		♒
-174	Feb 22	9:37		♓
-174	Oct 25	22:50	℞	♒
-174	Nov 24	9:39		♓
-167	Apr 27	22:15		♈
-167	Sep 21	9:18	℞	♓
-166	Feb 17	9:57		♈
-160	Jun 25	19:29		♉
-160	Sep 18	6:24	℞	♈
-159	Apr 8	21:02		♉
-153	Jul 24	20:40		♊
-153	Oct 22	6:18	℞	♉
-152	May 6	19:34		♊
-146	Jul 24	13:58		♋
-146	Dec 29	13:02	℞	♊
-145	May 10	23:44		♋
-140	Oct 5	12:54		♌
-140	Dec 6	23:51	℞	♋
-139	Jul 12	7:50		♌
-133	Sep 2	18:54		♍
-132	Apr 8	3:56	℞	♌
-132	Jun 5	17:16		♍
-127	Oct 26	9:17		♎
-126	Mar 25	19:53	℞	♍
-126	Aug 13	19:44		♎
-120	Oct 20	14:47		♏
-113	Jan 18	8:04		♐
-113	Apr 24	10:12	℞	♏
-113	Nov 4	21:01		♐
-106	Mar 1	3:35		♑
-106	May 10	20:10	℞	♐
-106	Dec 12	7:23		♑
-98	Feb 5	21:47		♒
-98	Aug 23	3:19	℞	♑
-98	Nov 25	13:20		♒
-91	Apr 19	16:29		♓
-91	Jul 26	3:24	℞	♒
-90	Feb 5	7:47		♓
-83	Apr 9	12:34		♈
-83	Oct 18	22:54	℞	♓
-82	Jan 27	0:38		♈
-76	Jun 1	4:27		♉
-76	Oct 18	0:27	℞	♈
-75	Mar 21	19:12		♉
-69	Jul 1	22:19		♊
-69	Nov 19	7:49	℞	♉
-68	Apr 19	6:14		♊
-62	Jul 7	8:08		♋
-61	Jan 28	4:24	℞	♊
-61	Apr 16	7:35		♋
-56	Sep 8	20:35		♌
-55	Jan 7	16:38	℞	♋
-55	Jun 25	10:49		♌
-50	Nov 23	13:14		♍
-50	Dec 18	11:53	℞	♌
-49	Aug 18	0:47		♍
-43	Oct 9	14:02		♎
-42	Apr 23	12:24	℞	♍
-42	Jul 22	4:47		♎
-37	Dec 20	8:36		♏
-36	Mar 24	9:39	℞	♎
-36	Oct 4	9:34		♏
-30	Dec 27	22:57		♐
-29	May 22	14:58	℞	♏
-29	Oct 18	17:22		♐
-22	Feb 3	9:45		♑
-22	Jun 11	11:30	℞	♐
-22	Nov 25	14:04		♑
-15	Apr 25	13:12		♒
-15	May 15	1:11	℞	♑
-14	Jan 19	16:39		♒
-7	Mar 27	14:57		♓
-7	Aug 22	1:19	℞	♒
-6	Jan 17	22:20		♓
1	Mar 22	23:51		♈
1	Dec 6	1:20	℞	♓
1	Dec 12	3:59		♈
8	May 13	1:22		♉
8	Nov 12	1:59	℞	♈
9	Feb 28	21:35		♉
15	Jun 13	13:23		♊
15	Dec 13	18:15	℞	♉
16	Mar 29	11:33		♊
22	Jun 21	0:31		♋
28	Aug 21	15:31		♌
29	Jan 30	16:08	℞	♋
29	Jun 7	6:11		♌
34	Oct 18	12:20		♍
35	Jan 26	2:16	℞	♌
35	Aug 1	21:23		♍
41	Sep 23	20:59		♎
47	Nov 28	22:22		♏
48	Apr 19	12:33	℞	♎
48	Sep 16	17:56		♏
54	Dec 9	13:05		♐
55	Jun 18	20:15	℞	♏
55	Sep 26	10:26		♐
62	Jan 14	5:13		♑
62	Jul 8	10:00	℞	♐
62	Nov 4	23:01		♑
69	Mar 14	11:25		♒
69	Jun 29	1:04	℞	♑
70	Jan 2	0:41		♒
77	Mar 7	22:18		♓
77	Sep 18	15:08	℞	♒
77	Dec 26	0:47		♓
84	May 18	16:02		♈
84	Aug 24	13:34	℞	♓
85	Mar 5	17:59		♈
92	Apr 25	11:57		♉
92	Dec 17	5:18	℞	♈
93	Jan 26	23:24		♉
99	May 28	1:46		♊
100	Jan 16	2:15	℞	♉
100	Feb 27	0:54		♊
105	Aug 24	13:48		♋

Uranus Ingresses –500 (501 BC)—2100

Year	Date	Time	℞	Sign
105	Nov 20	15:14	℞	♊
106	Jun 6	7:20		♋
112	Aug 6	20:57		♌
113	Feb 25	21:47	℞	♋
113	May 16	11:39		♌
118	Sep 30	7:08		♍
119	Feb 19	0:58	℞	♌
119	Jul 17	14:21		♍
124	Dec 2	0:09		♎
125	Feb 7	19:59	℞	♍
125	Sep 10	7:56		♎
131	Nov 13	7:50		♏
132	May 14	11:32	℞	♎
132	Aug 29	1:50		♏
138	Nov 25	7:03		♐
139	Jul 29	8:19	℞	♏
139	Aug 21	16:30		♐
145	Dec 29	12:41		♑
146	Aug 9	1:18	℞	♐
146	Oct 9	19:08		♑
153	Feb 22	5:10		♒
153	Jul 25	16:26	℞	♑
153	Dec 16	0:44		♒
161	Feb 19	19:19		♓
168	Apr 26	19:11		♈
168	Sep 20	20:45	℞	♓
169	Feb 16	10:36		♈
175	Jun 28	18:35		♉
175	Sep 15	5:25	℞	♈
176	Apr 9	17:58		♉
182	Aug 3	15:15		♊
182	Oct 9	16:48	℞	♉
183	May 12	18:29		♊
189	Aug 2	13:30		♋
189	Dec 15	10:54	℞	♊
190	May 20	11:08		♋
196	Jul 23	5:57		♌
202	Sep 15	10:17		♍
203	Mar 14	6:04	℞	♌
203	Jun 29	20:01		♍
208	Nov 10	10:49		♎
209	Mar 6	3:59	℞	♍
209	Aug 27	17:27		♎
215	Oct 30	18:20		♏
216	Jun 15	16:40	℞	♎
216	Aug 1	10:11		♏
222	Jan 29	22:27		♐
222	Apr 11	7:04	℞	♏
222	Nov 11	9:51		♐
229	Mar 7	0:42		♑
229	May 4	16:30	℞	♐
229	Dec 14	18:39		♑
237	Feb 5	11:53		♒
237	Aug 21	16:13	℞	♑
237	Nov 25	6:24		♒
244	Apr 16	22:24		♓
244	Jul 27	9:36	℞	♒
245	Feb 3	8:38		♓
252	Apr 9	1:08		♈
252	Oct 17	12:46	℞	♓
253	Jan 26	19:36		♈
259	Jun 4	0:07		♉
259	Oct 14	16:44	℞	♈
260	Mar 23	15:58		♉
266	Jul 8	22:09		♊
266	Nov 8	17:31	℞	♉
267	Apr 26	10:51		♊
273	Jul 16	7:18		♋
274	Jan 9	11:14	℞	♊
274	May 1	8:48		♋
279	Sep 28	20:21		♌
279	Dec 15	15:22	℞	♋
280	Jul 8	7:21		♌
286	Aug 30	21:19		♍
287	Apr 15	22:50	℞	♌
287	May 30	9:23		♍
292	Oct 23	17:45		♎
293	Mar 28	15:33	℞	♍
293	Aug 10	16:58		♎
299	Jan 12	21:33		♏
299	Feb 25	3:12	℞	♎
299	Oct 15	22:23		♏
306	Jan 7	17:54		♐
306	May 8	18:11	℞	♏
306	Oct 28	4:55		♐
313	Feb 9	4:07		♑
313	Jun 4	15:27	℞	♐
313	Nov 30	1:00		♑
321	Jan 21	13:22		♒
328	Mar 27	6:26		♓
328	Aug 22	19:25	℞	♒
329	Jan 17	18:41		♓
336	Mar 23	18:42		♈
336	Nov 29	19:10	℞	♓
336	Dec 18	20:37		♈
343	May 16	15:07		♉
343	Nov 9	6:44	℞	♈
344	Mar 4	15:26		♉
350	Jun 19	19:36		♊
350	Dec 4	15:44	℞	♉
351	Apr 7	12:12		♊
357	Jun 30	1:13		♋
358	Feb 12	23:30	℞	♊
358	Apr 1	0:44		♋
363	Sep 5	23:14		♌
364	Jan 12	15:31	℞	♋
364	Jun 21	22:55		♌
369	Nov 15	3:14		♍
369	Dec 26	13:35	℞	♌
370	Aug 15	17:15		♍
376	Oct 8	0:14		♎
377	Apr 25	7:57	℞	♍
377	Jul 19	12:08		♎
382	Dec 14	12:17		♏
383	Mar 31	15:56	℞	♎
383	Sep 30	23:51		♏
389	Dec 20	1:07		♐
390	Jun 2	3:52	℞	♏
390	Oct 9	20:30		♐
397	Jan 20	9:32		♑
397	Jun 29	14:33	℞	♐
397	Nov 11	22:04		♑
404	Mar 19	5:33		♒
404	Jun 23	18:36	℞	♑
405	Jan 5	1:46		♒
412	Mar 8	12:57		♓
412	Sep 17	22:57	℞	♒
412	Dec 27	1:06		♓
419	May 20	21:57		♈
419	Aug 24	10:12	℞	♓
420	Mar 6	14:10		♈
427	Apr 28	19:24		♉
427	Dec 11	1:39	℞	♈
428	Feb 4	8:24		♉
434	Jun 1	23:59		♊
435	Jan 2	23:13	℞	♉
435	Mar 11	18:48		♊
440	Sep 8	1:14		♋
440	Nov 2	22:56	℞	♊
441	Jun 13	7:23		♋
447	Aug 17	16:03		♌
448	Feb 7	2:14	℞	♋
448	Jun 1	1:58		♌
453	Oct 14	1:33		♍
454	Jan 30	11:08	℞	♌
454	Jul 29	15:25		♍
460	Sep 21	7:40		♎
466	Nov 23	10:22		♏
467	Apr 27	6:10	℞	♎
467	Sep 11	21:07		♏
473	Dec 2	22:10		♐
474	Jul 1	5:04	℞	♏
474	Sep 14	16:59		♐
481	Jan 2	21:26		♑
481	Jul 27	10:33	℞	♐
481	Oct 19	6:12		♑
488	Feb 25	20:41		♒
488	Jul 20	5:33	℞	♑
488	Dec 18	9:12		♒
496	Feb 20	23:05		♓
496	Oct 29	0:30	℞	♒
496	Nov 18	12:55		♓
503	Apr 29	0:01		♈
503	Sep 20	16:44	℞	♓
504	Feb 18	13:47		♈
510	Jul 3	8:42		♉
510	Sep 10	8:17	℞	♈
511	Apr 13	8:37		♉
517	Aug 15	8:23		♊
517	Sep 27	14:02	℞	♉
518	May 17	6:51		♊
524	Aug 11	14:49		♋
524	Dec 4	13:17	℞	♊
525	May 28	10:35		♋
531	Aug 1	22:52		♌
532	Mar 10	16:59	℞	♋
532	May 3	18:15		♌
537	Sep 24	22:37		♍
538	Feb 25	7:21	℞	♌
538	Jul 12	1:17		♍
543	Nov 25	5:49		♎
544	Feb 16	21:53	℞	♍
544	Sep 5	18:31		♎
550	Nov 6	21:47		♏
551	May 26	6:32	℞	♎
551	Aug 19	22:16		♏
557	Feb 15	19:14		♐
557	Mar 22	3:18	℞	♏
557	Nov 16	18:59		♐
564	Mar 18	3:41		♑
564	Apr 20	20:08	℞	♐
564	Dec 17	17:58		♑
572	Feb 7	21:10		♒
572	Aug 17	4:60	℞	♑
572	Nov 27	8:55		♒
579	Apr 18	11:58		♓
579	Jul 25	17:35	℞	♒
580	Feb 4	14:31		♓
587	Apr 10	6:32		♈
587	Oct 16	1:22	℞	♓
588	Jan 28	11:02		♈
594	Jun 6	19:37		♉
594	Oct 9	4:35	℞	♈
595	Mar 27	4:59		♉
601	Jul 15	17:46		♊
601	Oct 31	23:16	℞	♉
602	May 1	20:16		♊
608	Jul 24	21:01		♋
608	Dec 28	1:16	℞	♊
609	May 11	23:47		♋
614	Oct 23	20:08		♌
614	Nov 19	8:37	℞	♋
615	Jul 18	10:49		♌
621	Sep 9	18:54		♍
622	Mar 22	20:03	℞	♌
622	Jun 21	13:55		♍
627	Nov 4	4:57		♎
628	Mar 14	17:25	℞	♍
628	Aug 21	0:03		♎
634	Oct 22	22:04		♏
641	Jan 13	12:26		♐
641	Apr 29	18:33	℞	♏
641	Nov 1	3:40		♐
648	Feb 12	12:59		♑
648	May 30	17:05	℞	♐
648	Dec 1	16:28		♑
656	Jan 22	14:02		♒
656	Oct 3	2:46	℞	♑
656	Oct 16	13:23		♒
663	Mar 28	3:54		♓
663	Aug 21	19:36	℞	♒
664	Jan 18	20:28		♓
671	Mar 25	1:13		♈
671	Nov 23	19:18	℞	♓
671	Dec 25	3:42		♈
678	May 19	20:28		♉
678	Nov 2	8:15	℞	♈
679	Mar 9	23:07		♉
685	Jun 25	15:07		♊
685	Nov 24	11:10	℞	♉
686	Apr 14	6:30		♊
692	Jul 8	15:35		♋
693	Jan 20	18:35	℞	♊
693	Apr 20	20:43		♋
698	Sep 19	19:53		♌
698	Dec 25	2:36	℞	♋
699	Jul 3	12:30		♌
705	Aug 27	7:18		♍
711	Oct 19	13:19		♎
712	Apr 7	3:54	℞	♍
712	Aug 3	21:15		♎
717	Dec 27	11:37		♏
718	Mar 16	14:58	℞	♎
718	Oct 9	7:06		♏
724	Dec 25	18:52		♐
725	May 25	8:14	℞	♏
725	Oct 15	18:09		♐
732	Jan 24	5:35		♑
732	Jun 25	20:06	℞	♐
732	Nov 14	23:20		♑
739	Mar 21	1:00		♒
739	Jun 24	2:41	℞	♑
740	Jan 6	13:51		♒
747	Mar 10	6:02		♓
747	Sep 18	1:59	℞	♒
747	Dec 29	4:20		♓
754	May 22	20:45		♈
754	Aug 22	10:04	℞	♓
755	Mar 8	22:14		♈
762	May 3	5:30		♉
762	Nov 30	23:26	℞	♈
763	Feb 14	3:08		♉
769	Jun 9	2:11		♊
769	Dec 20	2:15	℞	♉
770	Mar 24	19:01		♊
776	Jun 24	4:26		♋
782	Aug 31	15:55		♌
783	Jan 18	10:25	℞	♋
783	Jun 17	23:31		♌
788	Nov 8	4:50		♍
789	Jan 2	4:23	℞	♌
789	Aug 13	2:09		♍
795	Oct 4	17:12		♎
796	May 3	19:33	℞	♍
796	Jul 10	17:28		♎
801	Dec 5	20:18		♏
802	Apr 10	15:06	℞	♎
802	Sep 23	20:29		♏
808	Dec 9	15:14		♐
809	Jun 18	12:47	℞	♏
809	Sep 25	14:15		♐
816	Jan 7	16:07		♑
816	Jul 20	16:35	℞	♐
816	Oct 25	4:31		♑
823	Feb 26	20:26		♒
823	Jul 20	7:36	℞	♑
823	Dec 20	5:24		♒
831	Feb 21	17:25		♓
831	Oct 26	15:30	℞	♒
831	Nov 23	5:57		♓
838	Apr 29	8:24		♈
838	Sep 18	4:14	℞	♓
839	Feb 19	1:58		♈
845	Jul 13	4:38		♉
845	Aug 28	22:16	℞	♈
846	Apr 16	18:39		♉
853	May 23	9:42		♊
859	Aug 28	23:10		♋
859	Nov 14	23:42	℞	♊
860	Jun 7	23:39		♋
866	Aug 14	5:22		♌
867	Feb 11	5:53	℞	♋
867	May 28	18:48		♌
872	Oct 12	3:49		♍
873	Jan 31	19:51	℞	♌
873	Jul 27	23:59		♍
879	Sep 19	10:22		♎
885	Nov 18	15:36		♏
886	May 3	9:32	℞	♎
886	Sep 6	2:56		♏
892	Nov 23	22:32		♐
893	Aug 2	19:23	℞	♏
893	Aug 14	2:19		♐
899	Dec 22	22:22		♑
907	Feb 9	16:50		♒
907	Aug 15	17:01	℞	♑
907	Nov 30	16:04		♒
914	Apr 20	0:23		♓
914	Jul 24	3:48	℞	♒
915	Feb 5	16:12		♓
922	Apr 11	6:03		♈
922	Oct 14	16:09	℞	♓
923	Jan 30	2:57		♈
929	Jun 11	17:32		♉
929	Oct 3	13:47	℞	♈
930	Mar 31	4:09		♉
936	Jul 24	7:40		♊
936	Oct 20	5:06	℞	♉
937	May 7	10:57		♊
943	Aug 5	12:49		♋
943	Dec 13	4:00	℞	♊
944	May 22	11:23		♋
950	Jul 29	8:35		♌
951	Mar 21	1:16	℞	♋
951	Apr 25	0:21		♌
956	Sep 23	12:37		♍
957	Feb 26	5:20	℞	♌
957	Jul 10	10:12		♍
962	Nov 21	5:36		♎
963	Feb 20	18:50	℞	♍
963	Sep 3	22:33		♎
969	Nov 2	18:01		♏
970	Jun 3	4:25	℞	♎
970	Aug 11	17:57		♏
976	Jan 27	16:42		♐
976	Apr 12	9:58	℞	♏
976	Nov 8	18:01		♐
983	Feb 20	15:56		♑
983	May 20	3:43	℞	♐
983	Dec 7	12:58		♑
991	Jan 23	18:08		♒
991	Sep 21	20:52	℞	♑
991	Oct 27	16:09		♒
998	Mar 28	13:44		♓
998	Aug 19	7:50	℞	♒
999	Jan 19	3:24		♓
1006	Mar 25	22:57		♈
1006	Nov 20	5:40	℞	♓
1006	Dec 29	3:56		♈
1013	May 23	3:17		♉
1013	Oct 29	2:15	℞	♈
1014	Mar 13	16:19		♉
1020	Jul 1	22:21		♊
1020	Nov 16	10:07	℞	♉
1021	Apr 20	18:57		♊

Uranus Ingresses –500 (501 BC)—2100

1027 Jul 18 7:31 ♋
1028 Jan 7 19:19 ℞ ♊
1028 May 3 5:28 ♋
1033 Oct 9 0:06 ♌
1033 Dec 4 2:44 ℞ ♋
1034 Jul 13 21:12 ♌
1040 Sep 6 18:04 ♍
1041 Mar 27 13:28 ℞ ♌
1041 Jun 16 6:56 ♍
1046 Oct 30 10:23 ♎
1047 Mar 21 1:34 ℞ ♍
1047 Aug 17 7:36 ♎
1053 Jan 22 21:31 ♏
1053 Feb 14 4:43 ℞ ♎
1053 Oct 17 21:32 ♏
1060 Jan 2 17:51 ♐
1060 May 13 19:32 ℞ ♏
1060 Oct 22 8:24 ♐
1067 Jan 28 18:39 ♑
1067 Jun 18 14:51 ℞ ♐
1067 Nov 20 5:39 ♑
1074 Mar 22 21:06 ♒
1074 Jun 20 1:14 ℞ ♑
1075 Jan 7 8:58 ♒
1082 Mar 10 4:06 ♓
1082 Sep 16 3:30 ℞ ♒
1082 Dec 29 5:32 ♓
1089 May 22 19:51 ♈
1089 Aug 20 9:37 ℞ ♓
1090 Mar 8 19:27 ♈
1097 May 4 17:04 ♉
1097 Nov 25 12:00 ℞ ♈
1098 Feb 17 13:58 ♉
1104 Jun 14 5:54 ♊
1104 Dec 11 16:05 ℞ ♉
1105 Apr 1 13:45 ♊
1111 Jul 2 11:21 ♋
1112 Feb 7 21:22 ℞ ♊
1112 Apr 6 8:00 ♋
1117 Sep 12 0:01 ♌
1118 Jan 4 11:17 ℞ ♋
1118 Jun 28 2:41 ♌
1124 Aug 22 14:46 ♍
1130 Oct 13 13:23 ♎
1131 Apr 16 23:12 ℞ ♍
1131 Jul 27 13:32 ♎
1136 Dec 15 21:16 ♏
1137 Mar 29 12:37 ℞ ♎
1137 Oct 1 12:21 ♏
1143 Dec 15 4:03 ♐
1144 Jun 11 1:01 ℞ ♏
1144 Oct 1 21:60 ♐
1151 Jan 10 5:40 ♑
1151 Jul 17 17:37 ℞ ♐
1151 Oct 29 13:39 ♑
1158 Feb 27 4:35 ♒
1158 Jul 20 2:44 ℞ ♑
1158 Dec 20 15:55 ♒
1166 Feb 21 14:44 ♓
1166 Oct 29 11:19 ℞ ♒
1166 Nov 20 20:15 ♓
1173 Apr 29 21:15 ♈
1173 Sep 17 14:23 ℞ ♓
1174 Feb 19 21:27 ♈
1180 Jul 22 5:25 ♉
1180 Aug 19 17:11 ℞ ♈
1181 Apr 19 4:09 ♉
1188 May 28 21:18 ♊
1189 Jan 11 2:00 ℞ ♉
1189 Mar 4 3:58 ♊
1194 Sep 16 20:06 ♋
1194 Oct 26 2:36 ℞ ♊
1195 Jun 16 17:08 ♋
1201 Aug 24 14:00 ♌
1202 Jan 26 19:00 ℞ ♋
1202 Jun 10 20:31 ♌
1207 Oct 28 8:06 ♍
1208 Jan 15 14:52 ℞ ♌
1208 Aug 6 20:47 ♍
1214 Sep 27 14:35 ♎
1215 May 27 18:19 ℞ ♍
1215 Jun 19 1:37 ♎
1220 Nov 25 12:57 ♏
1221 Apr 23 19:44 ℞ ♎
1221 Sep 13 10:42 ♏
1227 Nov 27 22:40 ♐
1228 Jul 17 15:26 ℞ ♏
1228 Aug 29 16:07 ♐
1234 Dec 23 14:40 ♑
1242 Feb 7 13:42 ♒
1242 Aug 16 21:55 ℞ ♑
1242 Nov 28 4:55 ♒
1249 Apr 16 22:01 ♓
1249 Jul 25 20:13 ℞ ♒
1250 Feb 3 8:45 ♓
1257 Apr 10 8:12 ♈
1257 Oct 13 17:42 ℞ ♓
1258 Jan 29 12:37 ♈
1264 Jun 13 18:38 ♉
1264 Sep 29 5:35 ℞ ♈
1265 Apr 1 12:12 ♉
1271 Aug 4 12:27 ♊
1271 Oct 8 1:45 ℞ ♉
1272 May 12 12:58 ♊
1278 Aug 15 20:37 ♋
1278 Nov 28 21:05 ℞ ♊
1279 May 31 14:10 ♋
1285 Aug 8 9:48 ♌
1286 Feb 19 17:52 ℞ ♋
1286 May 20 13:49 ♌
1291 Oct 6 15:00 ♍
1292 Feb 9 2:50 ℞ ♌
1292 Jul 22 5:35 ♍
1297 Dec 10 15:03 ♎
1298 Jan 28 7:49 ℞ ♍
1298 Sep 12 23:46 ♎
1304 Nov 9 21:06 ♏
1305 May 20 0:30 ℞ ♎
1305 Aug 24 1:40 ♏
1311 Feb 4 7:12 ♐
1311 Apr 5 5:15 ℞ ♏
1311 Nov 13 7:48 ♐
1318 Feb 21 8:55 ♑
1318 May 19 18:11 ℞ ♐
1318 Dec 7 18:43 ♑
1326 Jan 22 2:16 ♒
1326 Oct 2 19:59 ℞ ♑
1326 Oct 17 11:24 ♒
1333 Mar 25 20:04 ♓
1333 Aug 23 7:23 ℞ ♒
1334 Jan 16 12:37 ♓
1341 Mar 24 14:24 ♈
1341 Nov 20 23:21 ℞ ♓
1341 Dec 27 0:35 ♈
1348 May 24 4:22 ♉
1348 Oct 25 13:47 ℞ ♈
1349 Mar 15 0:59 ♉
1355 Jul 9 15:40 ♊
1355 Nov 7 2:20 ℞ ♉
1356 Apr 26 16:20 ♊
1362 Jul 27 6:36 ♋
1362 Dec 23 21:23 ℞ ♊
1363 May 14 20:12 ♋
1369 Jul 25 0:37 ♌
1375 Sep 19 16:16 ♍
1376 Mar 4 8:04 ℞ ♌
1376 Jul 4 12:27 ♍
1381 Nov 13 13:45 ♎
1382 Feb 28 23:37 ℞ ♍
1382 Aug 29 10:28 ♎
1388 Oct 25 9:56 ♏
1395 Jan 8 8:03 ♐
1395 May 5 16:13 ℞ ♏
1395 Oct 27 19:19 ♐
1402 Jan 30 3:48 ♑
1402 Jun 17 7:18 ℞ ♐
1402 Nov 21 4:19 ♑
1409 Mar 20 7:39 ♒
1409 Jun 23 5:14 ℞ ♑
1410 Jan 5 23:36 ♒
1417 Mar 7 5:32 ♓
1417 Sep 21 18:18 ℞ ♒
1417 Dec 24 20:02 ♓
1424 May 20 15:33 ♈
1424 Aug 22 22:56 ℞ ♓
1425 Mar 7 18:51 ♈
1432 May 5 16:49 ♉
1432 Nov 23 19:50 ℞ ♈
1433 Feb 19 14:29 ♉
1439 Jun 19 20:50 ♊
1439 Dec 3 12:42 ℞ ♉
1440 Apr 7 17:38 ♊
1446 Jul 9 20:36 ♋
1447 Jan 20 3:53 ℞ ♊
1447 Apr 22 21:53 ♋
1452 Sep 29 13:30 ♌
1452 Dec 13 10:05 ℞ ♋
1453 Jul 9 8:27 ♌
1459 Sep 3 19:56 ♍
1460 Apr 3 16:45 ℞ ♌
1460 Jun 8 19:40 ♍
1465 Oct 25 20:08 ♎
1466 Mar 26 9:32 ℞ ♍
1466 Aug 12 8:49 ♎
1472 Jan 1 12:14 ♏
1472 Mar 9 15:12 ℞ ♎
1472 Oct 10 4:20 ♏
1478 Dec 21 2:38 ♐
1479 May 31 13:17 ℞ ♏
1479 Oct 10 6:12 ♐
1486 Jan 11 6:08 ♑
1486 Jul 14 0:36 ℞ ♐
1486 Oct 30 19:48 ♑
1493 Feb 25 2:50 ♒
1493 Jul 20 21:35 ℞ ♑
1493 Dec 18 14:19 ♒
1500 May 22 3:19 ♓
1500 Jun 18 17:30 ℞ ♒
1501 Feb 18 12:41 ♓
1508 Apr 27 11:32 ♈
1508 Sep 20 22:19 ℞ ♓
1509 Feb 17 20:11 ♈
1515 Jul 21 12:44 ♉
1515 Aug 22 12:26 ℞ ♈
1516 Apr 19 3:32 ♉
1523 Jun 2 19:29 ♊
1524 Jan 2 14:57 ℞ ♉
1524 Mar 13 9:24 ♊
1530 Jun 23 12:45 ♋
1536 Sep 5 11:52 ♌
1537 Jan 11 10:43 ℞ ♋
1537 Jun 22 14:24 ♌
1542 Dec 2 2:05 ♍
1542 Dec 10 3:12 ℞ ♌
1543 Aug 18 14:43 ♍
1549 Oct 8 11:50 ♎
1550 Apr 25 3:06 ℞ ♍
1550 Jul 19 9:44 ♎
1555 Dec 6 9:36 ♏
1556 Apr 10 21:49 ℞ ♎
1556 Sep 22 17:14 ♏
1562 Dec 3 16:05 ♐
1563 Jul 3 3:26 ℞ ♏
1563 Sep 13 19:15 ♐
1569 Dec 25 2:52 ♑
1570 Aug 27 19:29 ℞ ♐
1570 Sep 21 16:08 ♑
1577 Feb 6 12:53 ♒
1577 Aug 19 8:47 ℞ ♑
1577 Nov 26 7:40 ♒
1584 Apr 11 14:30 ♓
1584 Aug 1 9:31 ℞ ♒
1585 Jan 30 19:24 ♓
1592 Apr 7 11:20 ♈
1592 Oct 18 21:45 ℞ ♓
1593 Jan 25 13:13 ♈
1599 Jun 12 15:09 ♉
1599 Oct 2 19:32 ℞ ♈
1600 Mar 31 8:43 ♉
1606 Aug 9 15:15 ♊
1606 Oct 2 19:10 ℞ ♉
1607 May 15 17:47 ♊
1613 Aug 23 6:58 ♋
1613 Nov 20 13:51 ℞ ♊
1614 Jun 5 18:33 ♋
1620 Aug 16 6:09 ♌
1621 Feb 6 20:28 ℞ ♋
1621 May 31 22:39 ♌
1626 Oct 17 14:28 ♍
1627 Jan 27 2:07 ℞ ♌
1627 Jul 31 22:03 ♍
1633 Sep 21 0:04 ♎
1639 Nov 15 16:40 ♏
1640 May 9 7:19 ℞ ♎
1640 Aug 31 6:12 ♏
1646 Feb 12 20:38 ♐
1646 Mar 25 4:48 ℞ ♏
1646 Nov 15 15:03 ♐
1653 Feb 19 18:37 ♑
1653 May 19 19:59 ℞ ♐
1653 Dec 6 9:09 ♑
1660 Apr 28 7:51 ♒
1660 May 9 3:43 ℞ ♑
1661 Jan 18 18:00 ♒
1668 Mar 19 16:51 ♓
1668 Aug 29 18:07 ℞ ♒
1669 Jan 10 6:50 ♓
1675 Jun 24 17:28 ♈
1675 Jul 15 11:47 ℞ ♓
1676 Mar 19 22:21 ♈
1683 May 21 18:40 ♉
1683 Oct 28 21:31 ℞ ♈
1684 Mar 11 23:29 ♉
1690 Jul 10 4:11 ♊
1690 Nov 4 12:30 ℞ ♉
1691 Apr 28 0:10 ♊
1697 Jul 31 1:13 ♋
1697 Dec 16 18:36 ℞ ♊
1698 May 18 21:40 ♋
1704 Jul 31 7:25 ♌
1705 Mar 11 21:27 ℞ ♋
1705 May 3 2:35 ♌
1710 Sep 27 0:14 ♍
1711 Feb 23 0:47 ℞ ♌
1711 Jul 13 22:54 ♍
1716 Nov 22 23:49 ♎
1717 Feb 18 8:53 ℞ ♍
1717 Sep 4 13:38 ♎
1723 Oct 29 13:24 ♏
1724 Jun 18 19:48 ℞ ♎
1724 Jul 27 0:33 ♏
1730 Jan 9 8:46 ♐
1730 May 4 21:03 ℞ ♏
1730 Oct 28 8:56 ♐
1737 Jan 25 14:51 ♑
1737 Jun 21 13:05 ℞ ♐
1737 Nov 16 16:22 ♑
1744 Mar 12 7:33 ♒
1744 Jun 30 22:09 ℞ ♑
1744 Dec 31 5:20 ♒
1752 Feb 29 5:19 ♓
1752 Oct 3 4:49 ℞ ♒
1752 Dec 13 10:01 ♓
1759 May 13 0:29 ♈
1759 Sep 1 1:45 ℞ ♓
1760 Mar 1 17:57 ♈
1767 May 3 0:34 ♉
1767 Nov 29 0:45 ℞ ♈
1768 Feb 15 12:59 ♉
1774 Jun 19 10:40 ♊
1774 Dec 1 23:41 ℞ ♉
1775 Apr 8 13:21 ♊
1781 Jul 12 23:49 ♋
1782 Jan 12 3:49 ℞ ♊
1782 Apr 28 11:59 ♋
1787 Oct 14 5:43 ♌
1787 Nov 28 0:27 ℞ ♋
1788 Jul 14 10:57 ♌
1794 Sep 9 13:59 ♍
1795 Mar 20 16:21 ℞ ♌
1795 Jun 21 15:46 ♍
1800 Nov 1 8:01 ♎
1801 Mar 18 1:50 ℞ ♍
1801 Aug 18 13:47 ♎
1807 Jan 7 2:40 ♏
1807 Mar 4 21:41 ℞ ♎
1807 Oct 13 13:58 ♏
1813 Dec 20 12:47 ♐
1814 Jun 2 2:27 ℞ ♏
1814 Oct 9 1:03 ♐
1821 Jan 6 14:48 ♑
1821 Jul 22 21:09 ℞ ♐
1821 Oct 23 15:36 ♑
1828 Feb 18 16:16 ♒
1828 Jul 31 21:37 ℞ ♑
1828 Dec 10 15:00 ♒
1835 Apr 29 9:52 ♓
1835 Jul 13 6:02 ℞ ♒
1836 Feb 11 3:34 ♓
1843 Apr 20 5:24 ♈
1843 Oct 1 3:29 ℞ ♓
1844 Feb 10 10:57 ♈
1850 Jul 8 15:39 ♉
1850 Sep 3 0:51 ℞ ♈
1851 Apr 15 23:30 ♉
1858 Jun 2 1:28 ♊
1859 Jan 1 7:41 ℞ ♉
1859 Mar 14 3:43 ♊
1865 Jun 27 2:39 ♋
1866 Feb 17 2:41 ℞ ♊
1866 Mar 27 12:10 ♋
1871 Sep 14 18:60 ♌
1871 Dec 31 12:33 ℞ ♋
1872 Jun 29 2:58 ♌
1878 Aug 25 17:48 ♍
1884 Oct 14 14:35 ♎
1885 Apr 11 18:13 ℞ ♍
1885 Jul 29 1:22 ♎
1890 Dec 10 6:57 ♏
1891 Apr 5 2:55 ℞ ♎
1891 Sep 26 15:33 ♏
1897 Dec 2 9:57 ♐
1898 Jul 3 23:07 ℞ ♏
1898 Sep 11 2:16 ♐
1904 Dec 20 13:35 ♑
1912 Jan 30 22:40 ♒
1912 Sep 4 16:51 ℞ ♑
1912 Nov 12 8:41 ♒
1919 Apr 1 1:47 ♓
1919 Aug 16 22:07 ℞ ♒
1920 Jan 22 18:32 ♓
1927 Mar 31 17:26 ♈
1927 Nov 4 10:30 ℞ ♓
1928 Jan 13 8:47 ♈
1934 Jun 6 15:42 ♉

Uranus Ingresses –500 (501 BC)—2100

1934 Oct 10 0:37 ℞ ♈	1968 Sep 28 16:09 ♎	1996 Jan 12 7:13 ♒	2032 Dec 12 6:08 ℞ ♊	2065 Jan 10 19:39 ♐
1935 Mar 28 2:58 ♉	1969 May 20 20:58 ℞ ♍	2003 Mar 10 20:54 ♓	2033 May 22 13:27 ♋	2065 May 1 9:22 ℞ ♏
1941 Aug 7 15:33 ♊	1969 Jun 24 10:30 ♎	2003 Sep 15 3:48 ℞ ♒	2039 Aug 6 10:11 ♌	2065 Oct 28 20:53 ♐
1941 Oct 5 2:08 ℞ ♉	1974 Nov 21 9:30 ♏	2003 Dec 30 9:15 ♓	2040 Feb 25 7:21 ℞ ♋	2072 Jan 22 11:16 ♑
1942 May 15 4:05 ♊	1975 May 1 17:50 ℞ ♎	2010 May 28 1:50 ♈	2040 May 15 22:32 ♌	2072 Jun 25 10:51 ℞ ♐
1948 Aug 30 15:41 ♋	1975 Sep 8 5:14 ♏	2010 Aug 14 3:31 ℞ ♓	2045 Oct 6 7:21 ♍	2072 Nov 12 4:47 ♑
1948 Nov 12 13:27 ℞ ♊	1981 Feb 17 8:53 ♐	2011 Mar 12 0:53 ♈	2046 Feb 8 18:42 ℞ ♌	2079 Mar 2 16:53 ♒
1949 Jun 10 4:08 ♋	1981 Mar 20 23:27 ℞ ♏	2018 May 15 15:24 ♉	2046 Jul 22 22:39 ♍	2079 Jul 13 12:53 ℞ ♑
1955 Aug 24 18:04 ♌	1981 Nov 16 12:04 ♐	2018 Nov 6 18:51 ℞ ♈	2051 Dec 8 20:32 ♎	2079 Dec 23 6:21 ♒
1956 Jan 28 1:58 ℞ ♋	1988 Feb 15 0:08 ♑	2019 Mar 6 8:36 ♉	2052 Feb 1 3:21 ℞ ♍	2087 Feb 18 22:38 ♓
1956 Jun 10 1:48 ♌	1988 May 27 1:22 ℞ ♐	2025 Jul 7 7:58 ♊	2052 Sep 11 8:04 ♎	2094 Apr 28 18:08 ♈
1961 Nov 1 15:59 ♍	1988 Dec 2 15:34 ♑	2025 Nov 8 2:09 ℞ ♉	2058 Nov 3 9:18 ♏	2094 Sep 16 16:36 ℞ ♓
1962 Jan 10 5:56 ℞ ♌	1995 Apr 1 12:08 ♒	2026 Apr 26 1:00 ♊	2059 Jun 1 19:40 ℞ ♎	2095 Feb 19 2:56 ♈
1962 Aug 10 1:18 ♍	1995 Jun 9 1:47 ℞ ♑	2032 Aug 3 18:34 ♋	2059 Aug 11 18:29 ♏	

Saturn Ingresses –500 (501 BC)—2100

-499 Jul 13 20:18 ♋	-436 Oct 30 23:15 ♍	-371 Sep 23 15:50 ♏	-304 Aug 5 2:38 ℞ ♑	-242 Jan 20 20:07 ♓
-497 Sep 4 7:53 ♌	-435 Jan 22 11:24 ℞ ♌	-369 Dec 24 4:43 ♐	-304 Nov 24 4:05 ♒	-240 Mar 13 14:19 ♈
-496 Feb 2 20:35 ℞ ♋	-435 Jul 22 10:15 ♍	-368 Jun 13 11:48 ℞ ♏	-301 Feb 1 17:55 ♓	-238 Apr 25 12:09 ♉
-496 May 25 16:31 ♌	-433 Oct 7 20:41 ♎	-368 Sep 20 7:51 ♐	-299 Mar 25 7:57 ♈	-236 Jun 2 12:38 ♊
-494 Aug 5 14:42 ♍	-430 Oct 7 11:04 ♏	-366 Dec 23 20:46 ♑	-297 May 6 21:59 ♉	-234 Jul 13 19:28 ♋
-492 Oct 21 1:00 ♎	-427 Jan 7 23:23 ♐	-363 Mar 16 16:34 ♒	-295 Jun 13 20:37 ♊	-232 Aug 31 22:55 ♌
-491 Apr 23 12:59 ℞ ♍	-427 May 20 11:30 ℞ ♏	-363 Jul 13 10:17 ℞ ♑	-293 Jul 25 12:54 ♋	-231 Feb 4 7:11 ℞ ♋
-491 Jul 13 14:40 ♎	-427 Oct 8 20:06 ♐	-363 Dec 10 12:19 ♒	-292 Jan 24 23:32 ℞ ♊	-231 May 22 3:31 ♌
-489 Oct 21 7:45 ♏	-424 Jan 5 19:03 ♑	-360 Feb 13 20:51 ♓	-292 Apr 5 8:10 ♋	-230 Nov 19 17:44 ♍
-486 Jan 28 18:45 ♐	-422 Apr 7 18:28 ♒	-358 Apr 4 23:20 ♈	-291 Sep 14 21:42 ♌	-230 Dec 30 22:21 ℞ ♌
-486 Apr 24 11:45 ℞ ♏	-422 Jun 17 11:35 ℞ ♑	-356 May 16 13:03 ♉	-290 Jan 15 9:58 ℞ ♋	-229 Jul 30 13:51 ♍
-486 Oct 24 15:47 ♐	-422 Dec 24 12:51 ♒	-356 Dec 29 9:12 ℞ ♈	-290 Jun 6 19:59 ♌	-227 Oct 11 11:25 ♎
-483 Jan 18 16:23 ♑	-419 Feb 24 17:22 ♓	-355 Jan 1 21:19 ♉	-288 Aug 10 12:08 ♍	-226 May 24 11:08 ℞ ♍
-483 Jul 27 13:57 ℞ ♐	-417 Apr 16 20:51 ♈	-354 Jun 24 15:14 ♊	-286 Oct 24 4:07 ♎	-226 Jun 13 17:04 ♎
-483 Oct 11 9:27 ♑	-417 Nov 22 9:13 ℞ ♓	-354 Dec 25 18:17 ℞ ♉	-285 Apr 17 10:24 ℞ ♍	-224 Oct 8 5:23 ♏
-480 Jan 6 17:01 ♒	-417 Dec 12 23:25 ♈	-353 Mar 5 1:04 ♊	-285 Jul 18 2:59 ♎	-221 Jan 8 21:39 ♐
-478 Mar 9 0:40 ♓	-415 May 28 18:50 ♉	-352 Aug 5 2:37 ♋	-283 Oct 20 17:42 ♏	-221 May 18 23:16 ℞ ♏
-476 Apr 29 0:14 ♈	-415 Nov 18 6:10 ℞ ♈	-352 Dec 31 19:59 ℞ ♊	-280 Jan 28 7:36 ♐	-221 Oct 9 14:52 ♐
-476 Oct 16 18:03 ℞ ♓	-414 Feb 9 16:03 ♉	-351 Apr 23 15:42 ♋	-280 Apr 23 19:47 ℞ ♏	-218 Jan 5 21:30 ♑
-475 Jan 13 15:52 ♈	-413 Jul 7 9:43 ♊	-350 Sep 30 23:16 ♌	-280 Oct 23 9:37 ♐	-216 Apr 13 19:09 ♒
-474 Jun 12 1:05 ♉	-413 Dec 3 7:30 ℞ ♉	-350 Dec 24 17:04 ℞ ♋	-277 Jan 19 8:59 ♑	-216 Jun 7 20:16 ℞ ♑
-474 Oct 26 21:30 ℞ ♈	-412 Mar 23 13:17 ♊	-349 Jun 19 3:24 ♌	-277 Jul 25 5:32 ℞ ♐	-216 Dec 26 20:30 ♒
-473 Feb 28 0:43 ♉	-411 Aug 19 14:57 ♋	-347 Aug 21 0:05 ♍	-277 Oct 13 8:44 ♑	-213 Mar 2 6:49 ♓
-472 Jul 22 2:59 ♊	-411 Dec 12 3:21 ℞ ♊	-345 Nov 6 1:38 ♎	-274 Jan 8 19:42 ♒	-211 Apr 24 16:07 ♈
-472 Nov 11 3:21 ℞ ♉	-410 May 8 15:33 ♋	-344 Mar 24 2:36 ℞ ♍	-272 Mar 13 23:30 ♓	-211 Oct 22 13:27 ℞ ♓
-471 Apr 8 8:59 ♊	-409 Nov 4 9:41 ♌	-344 Aug 3 10:44 ♎	-272 Oct 26 21:58 ℞ ♒	-210 Jan 7 20:04 ♈
-470 Sep 9 2:05 ♋	-409 Nov 17 18:02 ℞ ♋	-342 Nov 1 3:26 ♏	-272 Nov 9 9:01 ♓	-209 Jun 9 16:37 ♉
-470 Nov 18 3:60 ℞ ♊	-408 Jun 30 13:09 ♌	-339 Nov 4 18:46 ♐	-270 May 8 23:52 ♈	-209 Oct 28 8:58 ℞ ♈
-469 May 22 15:04 ♋	-406 Sep 1 18:14 ♍	-336 Feb 1 23:31 ♑	-270 Sep 29 4:60 ℞ ♓	-208 Feb 25 18:41 ♉
-467 Jul 13 3:25 ♌	-404 Nov 22 2:13 ♎	-336 Jun 28 16:20 ℞ ♐	-269 Jan 27 1:32 ♈	-207 Jul 20 8:42 ♊
-465 Sep 14 12:52 ♍	-403 Mar 1 21:43 ℞ ♍	-336 Oct 31 8:07 ♑	-268 Jun 25 5:39 ♉	-207 Nov 11 20:56 ℞ ♉
-464 Apr 18 10:57 ℞ ♌	-403 Aug 18 17:02 ♎	-333 Jan 20 1:56 ♒	-268 Oct 6 6:12 ℞ ♈	-206 Apr 6 13:42 ♊
-464 May 18 12:19 ♍	-401 Nov 14 3:14 ♏	-331 Mar 25 22:12 ♓	-267 Mar 11 11:47 ♉	-205 Sep 5 6:31 ♋
-463 Dec 20 8:17 ♎	-400 Jun 6 21:10 ℞ ♎	-331 Sep 17 14:55 ℞ ♒	-266 Aug 9 1:32 ♊	-205 Nov 21 7:28 ℞ ♊
-462 Jan 28 23:57 ℞ ♍	-400 Jul 31 15:20 ♏	-331 Dec 13 14:55 ♓	-266 Oct 19 23:32 ℞ ♉	-204 May 18 20:13 ♋
-462 Sep 1 21:38 ♎	-398 Nov 17 16:14 ♐	-329 May 23 23:60 ♈	-265 Apr 19 20:21 ♊	-202 Jul 8 11:43 ♌
-460 Nov 27 10:48 ♏	-395 Feb 18 6:08 ♑	-329 Sep 7 15:56 ℞ ♓	-263 May 31 2:04 ♋	-200 Sep 6 20:18 ♍
-459 May 8 5:40 ℞ ♎	-395 Jun 5 20:35 ℞ ♐	-328 Feb 9 8:18 ♈	-261 Jul 19 20:49 ♌	-198 Nov 26 18:08 ♎
-459 Aug 26 11:16 ♏	-395 Nov 15 20:56 ♑	-327 Jul 16 6:29 ♉	-259 Sep 17 17:21 ♍	-197 Feb 26 9:07 ℞ ♍
-457 Nov 30 17:03 ♐	-392 Feb 1 4:12 ♒	-327 Sep 10 15:41 ℞ ♈	-258 Apr 3 8:44 ℞ ♌	-197 Aug 21 18:17 ♎
-454 Mar 16 12:41 ♑	-390 Apr 8 22:37 ♓	-326 Mar 22 18:25 ♉	-258 May 31 21:35 ♍	-195 Nov 13 18:21 ♏
-454 May 6 20:35 ℞ ♐	-390 Aug 26 22:27 ℞ ♒	-324 Apr 29 9:31 ♊	-257 Dec 25 11:34 ♎	-194 Jun 9 2:32 ℞ ♎
-454 Nov 29 21:14 ♑	-390 Dec 30 22:41 ♓	-322 Jun 10 3:29 ♋	-256 Jan 23 13:09 ℞ ♍	-194 Jul 31 5:10 ♏
-451 Feb 12 23:48 ♒	-388 Jun 13 15:37 ♈	-320 Jul 28 17:04 ♌	-256 Sep 1 18:20 ♎	-192 Nov 16 12:22 ♐
-451 Sep 13 18:58 ℞ ♑	-388 Aug 13 6:39 ℞ ♓	-318 Sep 29 2:19 ♍	-254 Nov 26 8:15 ♏	-189 Feb 18 11:03 ♑
-451 Oct 24 17:07 ♒	-387 Feb 20 16:32 ♈	-317 Mar 8 5:49 ℞ ♌	-253 May 10 1:43 ℞ ♎	-189 Jun 7 12:08 ℞ ♐
-449 Apr 26 8:41 ♓	-385 Apr 3 1:38 ♉	-317 Jun 22 9:00 ♍	-253 Aug 24 19:42 ♏	-189 Nov 16 11:12 ♑
-449 Aug 4 21:60 ℞ ♒	-383 May 10 10:10 ♊	-315 Sep 12 22:19 ♎	-251 Nov 28 10:56 ♐	-186 Feb 2 22:35 ♒
-448 Jan 14 12:05 ♓	-381 Jun 21 1:22 ♋	-313 Dec 10 11:32 ♏	-248 Mar 15 5:19 ♑	-184 Apr 15 15:54 ♓
-446 Mar 4 16:60 ♈	-379 Aug 8 22:30 ♌	-312 Apr 15 17:11 ℞ ♎	-248 May 5 18:41 ℞ ♐	-184 Aug 16 14:56 ℞ ♒
-444 Apr 13 11:43 ♉	-377 Oct 13 8:25 ♍	-312 Sep 9 0:07 ♏	-248 Nov 28 23:22 ♑	-183 Jan 6 21:16 ♓
-442 May 21 17:55 ♊	-376 Feb 15 9:49 ℞ ♌	-310 Dec 10 10:58 ♐	-245 Feb 15 19:06 ♒	-181 Mar 2 20:05 ♈
-440 Jul 1 10:33 ♋	-376 Jul 7 20:05 ♍	-309 Jul 18 3:58 ℞ ♏	-245 Sep 3 12:24 ℞ ♑	-179 Apr 14 8:25 ♉
-438 Aug 21 3:43 ♌	-374 Sep 25 2:31 ♎	-309 Aug 22 4:36 ♐	-245 Nov 2 22:12 ♒	-177 May 23 15:50 ♊
-437 Mar 2 1:28 ℞ ♋	-372 Dec 28 19:22 ♏	-307 Dec 11 4:12 ♑	-243 May 7 3:39 ♓	-175 Jul 2 21:40 ♋
-437 May 2 18:16 ♌	-371 Mar 22 19:15 ℞ ♎	-304 Feb 29 6:10 ♒	-243 Jul 19 23:25 ℞ ♒	-173 Aug 20 22:08 ♌

Saturn Ingresses –500 (501 BC)—2100

Year	Date	Time	℞	Sign
-172	Mar 3	4:28	℞	♋
-172	Apr 30	1:24		♌
-171	Oct 25	16:57		♍
-170	Jan 30	0:12	℞	♌
-170	Jul 18	10:15		♍
-168	Sep 30	1:55		♎
-165	Jan 3	18:00		♏
-165	Mar 17	22:40	℞	♎
-165	Sep 26	21:01		♏
-163	Dec 24	23:58		♐
-162	Jun 12	22:48	℞	♏
-162	Sep 22	6:01		♐
-160	Dec 24	11:42		♑
-157	Mar 20	9:19		♒
-157	Jul 10	5:19	℞	♑
-157	Dec 14	2:53		♒
-154	Feb 18	4:03		♓
-152	Apr 11	20:25		♈
-150	May 26	20:54		♉
-150	Nov 22	14:37	℞	♈
-149	Feb 6	16:10		♉
-148	Jul 5	10:24		♊
-148	Dec 4	14:51	℞	♉
-147	Mar 22	4:43		♊
-146	Aug 17	19:50		♋
-146	Dec 15	11:12	℞	♊
-145	May 6	16:33		♋
-144	Oct 19	2:09		♌
-144	Dec 3	23:03	℞	♋
-143	Jun 27	2:05		♌
-141	Aug 26	19:36		♍
-139	Nov 8	18:50		♎
-138	Mar 21	4:42	℞	♍
-138	Aug 6	17:52		♎
-136	Oct 31	13:04		♏
-133	Feb 27	2:29		♐
-133	Mar 21	5:39	℞	♏
-133	Nov 3	21:40		♐
-130	Jan 30	22:36		♑
-130	Jul 2	13:57	℞	♐
-130	Oct 30	3:58		♑
-127	Jan 20	1:18		♒
-125	Mar 29	21:42		♓
-125	Sep 12	6:02	℞	♒
-125	Dec 19	18:57		♓
-123	Jun 3	2:38		♈
-123	Aug 25	14:08	℞	♓
-122	Feb 16	8:13		♈
-120	Mar 31	20:30		♉
-118	May 10	14:21		♊
-116	Jun 20	1:26		♋
-114	Aug 7	15:53		♌
-112	Oct 7	18:07		♍
-111	Feb 22	4:18	℞	♌
-111	Jul 2	12:28		♍
-109	Sep 18	4:49		♎
-107	Dec 12	23:15		♏
-106	Apr 13	8:59	℞	♎
-106	Sep 11	16:33		♏
-104	Dec 10	7:36		♐
-103	Jul 19	8:52	℞	♏
-103	Aug 20	17:38		♐
-101	Dec 11	13:31		♑
-98	Mar 2	9:34		♒
-98	Aug 6	6:21	℞	♑
-98	Nov 26	20:23		♒
-95	Feb 4	23:30		♓
-93	Mar 30	14:28		♈
-91	May 13	3:04		♉
-89	Jun 22	5:30		♊
-88	Jan 5	20:03	℞	♉
-88	Feb 25	15:33		♊
-87	Aug 2	5:32		♋
-86	Jan 9	10:20	℞	♊
-86	Apr 19	0:33		♋
-85	Sep 24	7:55		♌
-84	Jan 5	5:23	℞	♋
-84	Jun 13	11:45		♌
-82	Aug 14	21:60		♍
-80	Oct 25	4:47		♎
-79	Apr 15	15:15	℞	♍
-79	Jul 19	3:35		♎
-77	Oct 19	23:25		♏
-74	Jan 22	14:41		♐
-74	May 1	18:56	℞	♏
-74	Oct 20	18:04		♐
-71	Jan 15	14:21		♑
-71	Aug 3	1:40	℞	♐
-71	Oct 5	18:12		♑
-68	Jan 7	8:02		♒
-66	Mar 14	11:05		♓
-66	Oct 30	6:57	℞	♒
-66	Nov 8	3:28		♓
-64	May 11	20:04		♈
-64	Sep 24	8:55	℞	♓
-63	Jan 30	13:55		♈
-62	Jul 4	13:17		♉
-62	Sep 26	13:33	℞	♈
-61	Mar 18	5:45		♉
-60	Aug 28	18:15		♊
-60	Sep 27	22:10	℞	♉
-59	Apr 26	20:49		♊
-57	Jun 7	23:32		♋
-55	Jul 25	19:44		♌
-53	Sep 23	19:12		♍
-52	Mar 21	16:57	℞	♌
-52	Jun 11	12:59		♍
-50	Sep 5	6:09		♎
-48	Nov 26	14:42		♏
-47	May 9	21:02	℞	♎
-47	Aug 24	11:55		♏
-45	Nov 27	17:60		♐
-42	Mar 9	13:44		♑
-42	May 14	2:12	℞	♐
-42	Nov 27	9:59		♑
-39	Feb 13	13:51		♒
-39	Sep 9	7:44	℞	♑
-39	Oct 28	20:13		♒
-37	May 6	3:19		♓
-37	Jul 22	19:05	℞	♒
-36	Jan 21	5:38		♓
-34	Mar 15	16:52		♈
-32	Apr 28	2:33		♉
-30	Jun 6	23:59		♊
-28	Jul 17	7:33		♋
-27	Feb 20	19:19	℞	♊
-27	Mar 11	3:11		♋
-26	Sep 4	23:49		♌
-25	Jan 31	8:02	℞	♋
-25	May 26	15:25		♌
-24	Nov 24	8:34		♍
-24	Dec 26	2:10	℞	♌
-23	Jul 31	7:46		♍
-21	Oct 11	2:48		♎
-18	Oct 5	9:46		♏
-15	Jan 2	4:41		♐
-15	May 28	21:42	℞	♏
-15	Oct 2	16:52		♐
-12	Jan 1	1:51		♑
-10	Apr 1	22:47		♒
-10	Jun 23	10:16	℞	♑
-10	Dec 22	4:35		♒
-7	Feb 26	8:33		♓
-5	Apr 23	14:39		♈
-5	Oct 27	9:47	℞	♓
-4	Jan 5	17:28		♈
-3	Jun 10	2:38		♉
-3	Oct 27	6:11	℞	♈
-2	Feb 26	16:30		♉
-1	Jul 24	7:08		♊
-1	Nov 8	16:17	℞	♉
0	Apr 9	4:23		♊
1	Sep 10	23:44		♋
1	Nov 14	12:31	℞	♊
2	May 22	16:41		♋
4	Jul 10	15:41		♌
6	Sep 8	2:58		♍
8	Nov 25	14:10		♎
9	Feb 25	15:38	℞	♍
9	Aug 20	6:44		♎
11	Nov 11	11:40		♏
12	Jun 18	3:43	℞	♎
12	Jul 20	12:01		♏
14	Nov 12	13:05		♐
17	Feb 10	13:12		♑
17	Jun 15	16:49	℞	♐
17	Nov 9	19:46		♑
20	Jan 29	7:17		♒
22	Apr 10	5:41		♓
22	Aug 23	18:44	℞	♒
23	Jan 2	8:24		♓
25	Feb 27	9:46		♈
27	Apr 13	5:08		♉
29	May 22	5:07		♊
31	Jul 2	9:08		♋
33	Aug 18	15:14		♌
34	Mar 7	11:31	℞	♋
34	Apr 25	20:22		♌
35	Oct 22	2:01		♍
36	Feb 3	19:15	℞	♌
36	Jul 14	8:30		♍
38	Sep 25	22:16		♎
40	Dec 22	16:25		♏
41	Mar 30	13:27	℞	♎
41	Sep 19	1:26		♏
43	Dec 16	18:11		♐
44	Jun 29	10:03	℞	♏
44	Sep 6	18:39		♐
46	Dec 16	10:22		♑
49	Mar 7	23:01		♒
49	Jul 24	21:49	℞	♑
49	Dec 3	4:41		♒
52	Feb 11	0:02		♓
54	Apr 5	22:07		♈
56	May 21	8:20		♉
56	Dec 1	23:50	℞	♈
57	Jan 27	19:16		♉
58	Jul 2	3:49		♊
58	Dec 9	20:30	℞	♉
59	Mar 18	3:50		♊
60	Aug 13	22:46		♋
60	Dec 18	7:21	℞	♊
61	May 3	1:45		♋
62	Oct 12	15:27		♌
62	Dec 11	3:02	℞	♋
63	Jun 24	14:21		♌
65	Aug 22	23:57		♍
67	Nov 4	4:25		♎
68	Mar 27	4:44	℞	♍
68	Jul 31	12:30		♎
70	Oct 26	11:37		♏
73	Feb 4	5:41		♐
73	Apr 13	8:35	℞	♏
73	Oct 27	3:13		♐
76	Jan 22	19:01		♑
76	Jul 15	19:01	℞	♐
76	Oct 18	6:15		♑
79	Jan 13	3:34		♒
81	Mar 21	9:44		♓
81	Sep 25	18:58	℞	♒
81	Dec 7	2:27		♓
83	May 23	17:32		♈
83	Sep 6	23:43	℞	♓
84	Feb 10	0:08		♈
85	Jul 29	20:01		♉
85	Aug 26	5:49	℞	♈
86	Mar 26	23:16		♉
88	May 5	8:20		♊
90	Jun 15	18:17		♋
92	Aug 1	16:05		♌
94	Sep 30	16:54		♍
95	Mar 5	16:09	℞	♌
95	Jun 23	15:39		♍
97	Sep 9	23:44		♎
99	Dec 1	23:21		♏
100	Apr 29	19:07	℞	♎
100	Aug 31	6:36		♏
102	Dec 1	8:08		♐
105	Mar 20	1:45		♑
105	May 1	8:05	℞	♐
105	Nov 30	23:25		♑
108	Feb 18	9:32		♒
108	Aug 28	7:42	℞	♑
108	Nov 7	12:44		♒
110	May 16	20:29		♓
110	Jul 9	14:17	℞	♒
111	Jan 25	14:51		♓
113	Mar 20	13:50		♈
115	May 5	2:38		♉
117	Jun 13	23:39		♊
119	Jul 26	1:13		♋
120	Jan 23	12:35	℞	♊
120	Apr 6	6:36		♋
121	Sep 14	0:19		♌
122	Jan 16	17:39	℞	♋
122	Jun 5	11:13		♌
124	Aug 7	0:34		♍
126	Oct 17	10:21		♎
127	May 3	12:04	℞	♍
127	Jul 3	17:19		♎
129	Oct 11	1:29		♏
132	Jan 9	23:16		♐
132	May 17	20:14	℞	♏
132	Oct 9	9:51		♐
135	Jan 6	8:00		♑
137	Apr 16	10:53		♒
137	Jun 5	17:04	℞	♑
137	Dec 28	8:13		♒
140	Mar 4	18:03		♓
142	May 1	16:04		♈
142	Oct 9	23:54	℞	♓
143	Jan 19	6:55		♈
144	Jun 20	16:53		♉
144	Oct 11	8:06	℞	♈
145	Mar 8	16:16		♉
146	Aug 7	8:29		♊
146	Oct 21	13:12	℞	♉
147	Apr 19	3:00		♊
149	May 30	7:60		♋
151	Jul 17	17:54		♌
153	Sep 13	6:40		♍
154	Apr 22	21:31	℞	♌
154	May 13	1:15		♍
155	Dec 4	15:38		♎
156	Feb 16	2:56	℞	♍
156	Aug 24	15:23		♎
158	Nov 14	16:56		♏
159	Jun 5	7:59	℞	♎
159	Aug 2	6:10		♏
161	Nov 15	1:45		♐
164	Feb 15	4:32		♑
164	Jun 9	14:46	℞	♐
164	Nov 12	23:37		♑
167	Feb 1	4:15		♒
169	Apr 14	23:07		♓
169	Aug 16	2:30	℞	♒
170	Jan 6	16:16		♓
172	Mar 3	10:26		♈
174	Apr 17	18:57		♉
176	May 27	5:46		♊
178	Jul 7	13:20		♋
180	Aug 23	21:41		♌
181	Feb 19	23:33	℞	♋
181	May 8	19:33		♌
182	Oct 29	10:34		♍
183	Jan 24	15:25	℞	♌
183	Jul 20	9:15		♍
185	Sep 29	22:30		♎
187	Dec 31	3:30		♏
188	Mar 20	9:51	℞	♎
188	Sep 23	12:33		♏
190	Dec 21	3:39		♐
191	Jun 19	6:19	℞	♏
191	Sep 16	5:19		♐
193	Dec 20	19:42		♑
196	Mar 15	4:07		♒
196	Jul 13	13:43	℞	♑
196	Dec 9	21:33		♒
199	Feb 17	0:03		♓
201	Apr 13	18:04		♈
203	May 31	4:57		♉
203	Nov 14	22:47	℞	♈
204	Feb 14	7:59		♉
205	Jul 11	22:16		♊
205	Nov 25	14:53	℞	♉
206	Mar 30	0:13		♊
207	Aug 25	19:22		♋
207	Dec 6	6:42	℞	♊
208	May 12	5:40		♋
210	Jul 1	8:26		♌
212	Aug 28	3:44		♍
214	Nov 9	10:46		♎
215	Mar 21	22:02	℞	♍
215	Aug 6	20:29		♎
217	Oct 29	22:00		♏
220	Feb 12	1:31		♐
220	Apr 6	18:05	℞	♏
220	Oct 30	9:36		♐
223	Jan 26	8:05		♑
223	Jul 11	16:58	℞	♐
223	Oct 24	8:37		♑
226	Jan 16	23:30		♒
228	Mar 26	7:43		♓
228	Sep 17	5:45	℞	♒
228	Dec 15	6:29		♓
230	Jun 1	1:02		♈
230	Aug 28	22:53	℞	♓
231	Feb 15	17:16		♈
233	Apr 1	18:21		♉
235	May 12	6:36		♊
237	Jun 21	10:15		♋
239	Aug 7	20:20		♌
241	Oct 5	20:23		♍
242	Feb 26	20:36	℞	♌
242	Jun 29	20:19		♍
244	Sep 13	23:26		♎
246	Dec 6	21:04		♏
247	Apr 23	15:33	℞	♎
247	Sep 5	15:47		♏
249	Dec 4	21:27		♐
252	Dec 5	12:37		♑
255	Feb 24	16:60		♒
255	Aug 14	18:02	℞	♑
255	Nov 19	17:28		♒
258	Feb 1	20:14		♓
260	Mar 28	5:21		♈
262	May 13	6:47		♉
264	Jun 22	10:07		♊
264	Dec 30	4:23	℞	♉
265	Mar 1	1:40		♊
266	Aug 3	11:32		♋
267	Jan 6	1:51	℞	♊
267	Apr 20	20:25		♋
268	Sep 23	5:28		♌
269	Jan 3	15:44	℞	♋

Saturn Ingresses –500 (501 BC)—2100

Year	Date	Time	℞	Sign
269	Jun 12	21:26		♌
271	Aug 12	13:34		♍
273	Oct 21	3:04		♎
274	Apr 23	4:33	℞	♍
274	Jul 11	17:55		♎
276	Oct 13	17:07		♏
279	Jan 13	11:00		♐
279	May 12	21:33	℞	♏
279	Oct 13	13:42		♐
282	Jan 9	5:51		♑
282	Aug 25	13:34	℞	♐
282	Sep 14	10:24		♑
285	Jan 1	6:39		♒
287	Mar 10	9:51		♓
289	May 8	4:13		♈
289	Sep 28	10:21	℞	♓
290	Jan 27	4:16		♈
291	Jul 1	8:16		♉
291	Sep 29	7:36	℞	♈
292	Mar 15	7:19		♉
293	Aug 24	9:41		♊
293	Oct 1	17:38	℞	♉
294	Apr 25	9:17		♊
296	Jun 4	20:50		♋
298	Jul 22	7:03		♌
300	Sep 18	3:39		♍
301	Apr 4	23:17	℞	♌
301	May 30	20:16		♍
302	Dec 13	7:23		♎
303	Feb 7	9:40	℞	♍
303	Aug 29	23:31		♎
305	Nov 19	2:57		♏
306	May 26	18:30	℞	♎
306	Aug 11	15:24		♏
308	Nov 19	21:36		♐
311	Feb 24	5:26		♑
311	May 31	3:01	℞	♐
311	Nov 20	18:29		♑
314	Feb 8	20:20		♒
316	Apr 29	5:17		♓
316	Jul 29	19:02	℞	♒
317	Jan 17	11:43		♓
319	Mar 14	23:19		♈
321	Apr 28	15:53		♉
323	Jun 8	3:58		♊
325	Jul 18	3:44		♋
326	Feb 19	3:24	℞	♊
326	Mar 13	19:58		♋
327	Sep 4	5:05		♌
328	Feb 3	10:58	℞	♋
328	May 24	0:13		♌
329	Nov 13	21:13		♍
330	Jan 8	2:41	℞	♌
330	Jul 28	3:15		♍
332	Oct 5	14:48		♎
335	Jan 10	2:16		♏
335	Mar 11	2:48	℞	♎
335	Sep 29	12:49		♏
337	Dec 26	3:21		♐
338	Jun 11	6:43	℞	♏
338	Sep 23	15:30		♐
340	Dec 25	22:29		♑
343	Mar 25	11:55		♒
343	Jul 3	9:39	℞	♑
343	Dec 18	9:09		♒
346	Feb 24	14:09		♓
348	Apr 21	21:01		♈
348	Oct 29	15:08	℞	♓
349	Jan 3	5:34		♈
350	Jun 10	3:35		♉
350	Oct 28	10:52	℞	♈
351	Feb 26	21:33		♉
352	Jul 23	15:18		♊
352	Nov 8	14:53	℞	♉
353	Apr 9	10:56		♊
354	Sep 9	10:28		♋
354	Nov 17	20:33	℞	♊
355	May 21	19:37		♋
357	Jul 7	21:41		♌
359	Sep 3	5:36		♍
361	Nov 15	2:53		♎
362	Mar 12	21:21	℞	♍
362	Aug 12	3:58		♎
364	Nov 2	23:18		♏
367	Nov 5	9:43		♐
370	Feb 2	15:59		♑
370	Jun 28	7:50	℞	♐
370	Nov 2	12:00		♑
373	Jan 24	22:41		♒
375	Apr 8	13:18		♓
375	Aug 27	5:59	℞	♒
376	Jan 1	2:40		♓
378	Feb 28	12:10		♈
380	Apr 14	11:08		♉
382	May 24	17:38		♊
384	Jul 3	5:34		♋
386	Aug 18	18:54		♌
387	Mar 10	3:25	℞	♋
387	Apr 24	5:12		♌
388	Oct 17	15:20		♍
389	Feb 9	2:03	℞	♌
389	Jul 11	2:44		♍
391	Sep 21	16:04		♎
393	Dec 14	15:07		♏
394	Apr 11	15:36	℞	♎
394	Sep 12	18:16		♏
396	Dec 10	8:18		♐
397	Jul 20	7:47	℞	♏
397	Aug 19	21:60		♐
399	Dec 12	15:03		♑
402	Mar 5	10:25		♒
402	Jul 29	13:24	℞	♑
402	Dec 1	4:36		♒
405	Feb 10	20:52		♓
407	Apr 8	9:23		♈
409	May 24	20:30		♉
409	Nov 24	20:10	℞	♈
410	Feb 4	5:06		♉
411	Jul 6	0:22		♊
411	Dec 4	20:19	℞	♉
412	Mar 22	1:05		♊
413	Aug 17	0:24		♋
413	Dec 15	17:10	℞	♊
414	May 5	11:43		♋
415	Oct 12	8:39		♌
415	Dec 13	3:15	℞	♋
416	Jun 23	3:30		♌
418	Aug 19	23:49		♍
420	Oct 27	22:36		♎
421	Apr 8	10:42	℞	♍
421	Jul 22	23:44		♎
423	Oct 20	5:59		♏
426	Jan 22	22:03		♐
426	Apr 29	8:16	℞	♏
426	Oct 20	17:25		♐
429	Jan 17	1:39		♑
429	Jul 26	22:12	℞	♐
429	Oct 10	7:17		♑
432	Jan 12	0:56		♒
434	Mar 23	8:44		♓
434	Sep 22	12:58	℞	♒
434	Dec 11	1:49		♓
436	May 29	20:10		♈
436	Aug 28	23:17	℞	♓
437	Feb 14	7:26		♈
439	Apr 2	6:59		♉
441	May 11	17:29		♊
443	Jun 21	2:13		♋
445	Aug 4	23:51		♌
447	Oct 1	6:44		♍
448	Mar 5	16:60	℞	♌
448	Jun 22	10:39		♍
450	Sep 7	16:44		♎
452	Nov 27	1:17		♏
453	May 6	23:18	℞	♎
453	Aug 24	22:07		♏
455	Nov 27	6:58		♐
458	Mar 12	14:52		♑
458	May 8	6:31	℞	♐
458	Nov 28	15:38		♑
461	Feb 17	22:02		♒
461	Aug 24	15:22	℞	♑
461	Nov 10	1:24		♒
463	Jun 4	20:45		♓
463	Jun 17	17:29	℞	♒
464	Jan 29	19:43		♓
466	Mar 26	16:51		♈
468	May 11	11:17		♉
470	Jun 21	14:44		♊
471	Jan 1	9:27	℞	♉
471	Feb 26	22:57		♊
472	Jul 31	22:29		♋
473	Jan 7	21:46	℞	♊
473	Apr 17	8:33		♋
474	Sep 19	4:06		♌
475	Jan 9	3:46	℞	♋
475	Jun 9	5:01		♌
477	Aug 6	14:17		♍
479	Oct 14	3:17		♎
480	May 12	10:29	℞	♍
480	Jun 22	12:00		♎
482	Oct 6	5:47		♏
485	Jan 3	6:29		♐
485	May 24	21:33	℞	♏
485	Oct 3	23:37		♐
488	Jan 3	20:08		♑
490	Apr 19	16:31		♒
490	May 31	14:12	℞	♑
490	Dec 29	13:07		♒
493	Mar 9	13:58		♓
495	May 11	16:13		♈
495	Sep 22	14:52	℞	♓
496	Jan 31	7:14		♈
497	Jul 9	4:49		♉
497	Sep 17	10:41	℞	♈
498	Mar 20	7:23		♉
500	Apr 30	7:31		♊
502	Jun 9	21:03		♋
504	Jul 24	16:02		♌
506	Sep 18	8:54		♍
507	Apr 5	0:00	℞	♌
507	May 30	7:31		♍
508	Dec 6	23:04		♎
509	Feb 12	18:04	℞	♍
509	Aug 26	2:31		♎
511	Nov 14	14:44		♏
512	Jun 7	5:28	℞	♎
512	Jul 30	9:30		♏
514	Nov 15	0:38		♐
517	Feb 16	5:20		♑
517	Jun 7	17:29	℞	♐
517	Nov 15	3:03		♑
520	Feb 6	7:19		♒
522	Apr 28	15:38		♓
522	Jul 29	20:37	℞	♒
523	Jan 17	14:56		♓
525	Mar 15	22:00		♈
527	May 1	16:57		♉
529	Jun 10	11:43		♊
531	Jul 21	0:28		♋
532	Feb 6	12:13	℞	♊
532	Mar 24	9:51		♋
533	Sep 4	17:39		♌
534	Jan 31	3:42	℞	♋
534	May 25	9:15		♌
535	Nov 11	15:17		♍
536	Jan 10	19:38	℞	♌
536	Jul 25	18:02		♍
538	Oct 2	5:42		♎
540	Dec 29	17:53		♏
541	Mar 22	4:46	℞	♎
541	Sep 23	9:06		♏
543	Dec 20	22:55		♐
544	Jun 20	0:10	℞	♏
544	Sep 14	18:08		♐
546	Dec 22	17:42		♑
549	Mar 22	22:52		♒
549	Jul 3	19:46	℞	♑
549	Dec 16	16:47		♒
552	Feb 27	0:37		♓
554	Apr 27	21:38		♈
554	Oct 15	18:27	℞	♓
555	Jan 14	20:17		♈
556	Jun 19	12:28		♉
556	Oct 12	7:47	℞	♈
557	Mar 7	23:44		♉
558	Aug 7	12:34		♊
558	Oct 21	2:04	℞	♉
559	Apr 19	1:24		♊
561	May 29	2:27		♋
563	Jul 14	2:43		♌
565	Sep 6	2:49		♍
567	Nov 16	22:28		♎
568	Mar 9	15:42	℞	♍
568	Aug 12	1:01		♎
570	Nov 1	15:56		♏
573	Feb 20	18:41		♐
573	Mar 25	22:47	℞	♏
573	Nov 1	23:31		♐
576	Jan 31	5:24		♑
576	Jun 30	16:36	℞	♐
576	Oct 30	2:06		♑
579	Jan 24	18:22		♒
581	Apr 10	7:14		♓
581	Aug 21	10:43	℞	♒
582	Jan 3	11:55		♓
584	Mar 4	8:52		♈
586	Apr 20	13:29		♉
588	May 30	6:22		♊
590	Jul 9	8:50		♋
592	Aug 22	20:31		♌
593	Feb 22	23:57	℞	♋
593	May 5	11:14		♌
594	Oct 21	8:16		♍
595	Feb 4	7:46	℞	♌
595	Jul 13	14:27		♍
597	Sep 20	6:36		♎
599	Dec 11	12:06		♏
600	Apr 15	21:60	℞	♎
600	Sep 9	19:45		♏
602	Dec 8	11:57		♐
605	Dec 10	20:58		♑
608	Mar 5	21:13		♒
608	Jul 28	6:13	℞	♑
608	Dec 2	2:38		♒
611	Feb 15	15:49		♓
613	Apr 15	16:47		♈
613	Nov 19	2:02	℞	♓
613	Dec 16	14:55		♈
615	Jun 6	1:40		♉
615	Nov 3	23:10	℞	♈
616	Feb 22	19:49		♉
617	Jul 20	10:24		♊
617	Nov 13	6:31	℞	♉
618	Apr 7	1:39		♊
619	Sep 4	10:26		♋
619	Nov 24	8:30	℞	♊
620	May 18	3:25		♋
622	Jul 3	19:57		♌
624	Aug 26	18:14		♍
626	Nov 2	18:07		♎
627	Apr 1	12:48	℞	♍
627	Jul 29	11:32		♎
629	Oct 21	9:35		♏
632	Jan 23	17:10		♐
632	Apr 29	11:34	℞	♏
632	Oct 20	9:50		♐
635	Jan 17	21:14		♑
635	Jul 27	18:52	℞	♐
635	Oct 11	7:40		♑
638	Jan 13	11:07		♒
640	Mar 27	11:15		♓
640	Sep 13	9:19	℞	♒
640	Dec 18	13:31		♓
642	Jun 13	3:59		♈
642	Aug 13	17:14	℞	♓
643	Feb 22	10:30		♈
645	Apr 10	12:40		♉
647	May 21	10:27		♊
649	Jun 29	8:52		♋
651	Aug 13	4:34		♌
653	Oct 7	4:05		♍
654	Feb 25	7:22	℞	♌
654	Jun 30	1:43		♍
656	Sep 9	11:52		♎
658	Nov 27	12:15		♏
659	May 8	21:27	℞	♎
659	Aug 24	21:16		♏
661	Nov 25	18:07		♐
664	Mar 9	16:54		♑
664	May 11	5:08	℞	♐
664	Nov 27	15:21		♑
667	Feb 19	20:31		♒
667	Aug 22	20:53	℞	♑
667	Nov 13	7:34		♒
670	Feb 3	2:36		♓
672	Apr 3	5:17		♈
674	May 23	12:24		♉
674	Nov 27	22:46	℞	♈
675	Feb 2	7:52		♉
676	Jul 5	9:50		♊
676	Dec 3	14:20	℞	♉
677	Mar 22	18:55		♊
678	Aug 17	10:13		♋
678	Dec 15	18:38	℞	♊
679	May 5	19:22		♋
680	Oct 8	22:14		♌
680	Dec 15	16:08	℞	♋
681	Jun 21	19:52		♌
683	Aug 16	8:38		♍
685	Oct 20	11:43		♎
686	Apr 25	4:50	℞	♍
686	Jul 9	3:16		♎
688	Oct 9	2:29		♏
691	Jan 5	18:11		♐
691	May 23	14:07	℞	♏
691	Oct 6	5:43		♐
694	Jan 4	13:02		♑
696	Apr 27	17:16		♒
696	May 22	10:58	℞	♑
696	Dec 31	13:01		♒
699	Mar 14	15:26		♓
699	Oct 17	4:03	℞	♒
699	Nov 20	7:33		♓
701	May 21	20:44		♈
701	Sep 10	7:15	℞	♓
702	Feb 9	19:59		♈
704	Mar 30	14:48		♉
706	May 11	2:51		♊
708	Jun 19	5:54		♋
710	Aug 2	20:58		♌
712	Sep 25	2:33		♍
713	Mar 19	17:14	℞	♌
713	Jun 12	23:21		♍
714	Dec 17	5:34		♎

Saturn Ingresses –500 (501 BC)—2100

Year	Date	Time	Sign
715	Feb 3	7:49 ℞	♍
715	Aug 30	9:24	♎
717	Nov 15	4:42	♏
718	Jun 6	14:10 ℞	♎
718	Aug 1	10:31	♏
720	Nov 14	0:04	♐
723	Feb 15	17:06	♑
723	Jun 10	8:56 ℞	♐
723	Nov 15	1:44	♑
726	Feb 6	20:14	♒
728	May 4	19:48	♓
728	Jul 21	19:18 ℞	♒
729	Jan 21	11:41	♓
731	Mar 23	14:36	♈
733	May 11	12:23	♉
735	Jun 23	17:48	♊
735	Dec 30	14:12 ℞	♉
736	Mar 2	1:43	♊
737	Aug 3	12:13	♋
738	Jan 6	17:43 ℞	♊
738	Apr 20	11:41	♋
739	Sep 20	14:55	♌
740	Jan 10	6:35 ℞	♋
740	Jun 9	8:07	♌
742	Aug 5	9:51	♍
744	Oct 8	21:36	♎
747	Jan 8	2:35	♏
747	Mar 13	9:30 ℞	♎
747	Sep 28	2:04	♏
749	Dec 22	15:06	♐
750	Jun 17	16:08 ℞	♏
750	Sep 18	1:22	♐
752	Dec 23	9:26	♑
755	Mar 25	23:43	♒
755	Jul 1	17:10 ℞	♑
755	Dec 19	9:15	♒
758	Mar 2	4:34	♓
760	May 4	10:52	♈
760	Oct 3	12:25 ℞	♓
761	Jan 24	8:46	♈
762	Jul 3	14:36	♉
762	Sep 26	8:08 ℞	♈
763	Mar 18	8:24	♉
765	Apr 28	19:53	♊
767	Jun 8	9:27	♋
769	Jul 22	2:47	♌
771	Sep 13	11:34	♍
773	Nov 22	12:53	♎
774	Mar 3	9:20 ℞	♍
774	Aug 16	21:26	♎
776	Nov 2	7:11	♏
779	Feb 16	17:32	♐
779	Apr 1	6:36 ℞	♏
779	Nov 1	14:12	♐
782	Jan 29	2:38	♑
782	Jul 4	19:36 ℞	♐
782	Oct 28	15:39	♑
785	Jan 23	23:53	♒
787	Apr 13	1:56	♓
787	Aug 19	8:04 ℞	♒
788	Jan 6	13:36	♓
790	Mar 10	0:42	♈
792	Apr 27	23:45	♉
794	Jun 9	22:25	♊
796	Jul 20	3:51	♋
797	Feb 5	15:08 ℞	♊
797	Mar 24	18:47	♋
798	Sep 4	3:43	♌
799	Feb 1	19:19 ℞	♋
799	May 24	10:09	♌
800	Nov 5	13:45	♍
801	Jan 16	10:46 ℞	♌
801	Jul 23	2:46	♍
803	Sep 27	6:33	♎
805	Dec 16	10:55	♏
806	Apr 9	5:02 ℞	♎
806	Sep 13	12:34	♏
808	Dec 8	12:06	♐
811	Dec 10	16:55	♑
814	Mar 5	22:24	♒
814	Jul 27	16:40 ℞	♑
814	Dec 2	11:22	♒
817	Feb 16	6:17	♓
819	Apr 19	14:02	♈
819	Nov 3	1:08 ℞	♓
819	Dec 31	8:22	♈
821	Jun 12	11:35	♉
821	Oct 22	2:42 ℞	♈
822	Mar 2	8:04	♉
823	Aug 1	5:22	♊
823	Oct 28	23:35 ℞	♉
824	Apr 14	17:04	♊
825	Sep 23	10:38	♋
825	Oct 31	16:35 ℞	♊
826	May 26	4:40	♋
828	Jul 9	10:43	♌
830	Aug 31	15:40	♍
832	Nov 4	23:56	♎
833	Mar 26	12:56 ℞	♍
833	Jul 31	16:21	♎
835	Oct 21	2:44	♏
838	Jan 18	22:27	♐
838	May 4	5:15 ℞	♏
838	Oct 17	14:35	♐
841	Jan 13	10:20	♑
841	Aug 4	8:60 ℞	♐
841	Oct 2	17:59	♑
844	Jan 10	16:50	♒
846	Mar 26	0:24	♓
846	Sep 15	12:56 ℞	♒
846	Dec 16	20:58	♓
848	Jun 15	19:04	♈
848	Aug 8	3:10 ℞	♓
849	Feb 23	2:43	♈
851	Apr 14	18:50	♉
853	May 26	18:38	♊
855	Jul 6	19:41	♋
857	Aug 19	19:34	♌
858	Mar 3	21:14 ℞	♋
858	Apr 27	23:35	♌
859	Oct 15	10:40	♍
860	Feb 13	1:13 ℞	♌
860	Jul 7	7:30	♍
862	Sep 13	20:45	♎
864	Nov 28	23:55	♏
865	May 3	19:42 ℞	♎
865	Aug 26	11:17	♏
867	Nov 25	9:23	♐
870	Mar 5	22:13	♑
870	May 15	10:27 ℞	♐
870	Nov 25	19:30	♑
873	Feb 16	19:59	♒
873	Aug 25	20:42 ℞	♑
873	Nov 8	22:15	♒
876	Feb 2	8:26	♓
878	Apr 4	0:55	♈
880	May 25	11:08	♉
880	Nov 19	9:47 ℞	♈
881	Feb 7	19:26	♉
882	Jul 10	12:58	♊
882	Nov 25	4:59 ℞	♉
883	Mar 28	21:58	♊
884	Aug 23	6:37	♋
884	Dec 5	13:46 ℞	♊
885	May 10	7:40	♋
886	Oct 20	9:49	♌
886	Dec 2	20:48 ℞	♋
887	Jun 25	22:44	♌
889	Aug 17	21:38	♍
891	Oct 21	5:55	♎
892	Apr 22	16:60 ℞	♍
892	Jul 8	22:33	♎
894	Oct 7	3:24	♏
896	Dec 30	20:49	♐
897	May 30	3:05 ℞	♏
897	Sep 29	15:59	♐
899	Dec 30	9:32	♑
902	Apr 9	20:27	♒
902	Jun 12	20:14 ℞	♑
902	Dec 27	4:55	♒
905	Mar 10	7:35	♓
907	May 18	11:17	♈
907	Sep 14	7:20 ℞	♓
908	Feb 7	11:50	♈
910	Mar 31	1:44	♉
912	May 12	13:40	♊
914	Jun 22	19:45	♋
916	Aug 5	12:58	♌
918	Sep 28	11:35	♍
919	Mar 12	19:34 ℞	♌
919	Jun 18	9:44	♍
920	Dec 23	1:34	♎
921	Jan 25	20:21 ℞	♍
921	Aug 31	1:41	♎
923	Nov 15	0:27	♏
924	Jun 6	16:53 ℞	♎
924	Jul 29	21:59	♏
926	Nov 11	14:41	♐
929	Feb 9	15:03	♑
929	Jun 16	6:57 ℞	♐
929	Nov 9	13:30	♑
932	Feb 2	17:43	♒
934	Apr 27	18:47	♓
934	Jul 29	20:25 ℞	♒
935	Jan 17	19:00	♓
937	Mar 20	8:59	♈
939	May 10	16:01	♉
941	Jun 23	4:39	♊
941	Dec 27	18:30 ℞	♉
942	Mar 3	15:58	♊
943	Aug 4	15:48	♋
944	Jan 4	15:11 ℞	♊
944	Apr 20	22:55	♋
945	Sep 20	15:28	♌
946	Jan 7	23:18 ℞	♋
946	Jun 9	20:04	♌
948	Aug 3	19:28	♍
950	Oct 6	21:31	♎
952	Dec 29	22:01	♏
953	Mar 22	4:01 ℞	♎
953	Sep 22	13:28	♏
955	Dec 16	4:25	♐
956	Jul 1	11:21 ℞	♏
956	Sep 4	8:50	♐
958	Dec 16	5:21	♑
961	Mar 13	5:51	♒
961	Jul 15	23:12 ℞	♑
961	Dec 9	12:50	♒
964	Feb 23	2:17	♓
966	Apr 27	9:39	♈
966	Oct 15	6:01 ℞	♓
967	Jan 15	10:08	♈
968	Jun 25	9:04	♉
968	Oct 3	19:20 ℞	♈
969	Mar 13	1:14	♉
970	Aug 29	5:18	♊
970	Sep 26	12:52 ℞	♉
971	Apr 26	17:19	♊
973	Jun 6	12:53	♋
975	Jul 21	12:31	♌
977	Sep 11	11:17	♍
979	Nov 19	22:34	♎
980	Mar 5	16:44 ℞	♍
980	Aug 13	17:55	♎
982	Oct 30	6:45	♏
985	Feb 3	11:45	♐
985	Apr 14	4:26 ℞	♏
985	Oct 26	13:33	♐
988	Jan 22	11:57	♑
988	Jul 15	15:44 ℞	♐
988	Oct 18	7:42	♑
991	Jan 17	20:28	♒
993	Apr 4	2:54	♓
993	Aug 29	15:47 ℞	♒
993	Dec 28	22:19	♓
996	Mar 3	20:59	♈
998	Apr 23	22:38	♉
1000	Jun 6	18:12	♊
1002	Jul 18	7:60	♋
1003	Feb 18	18:03 ℞	♊
1003	Mar 14	7:39	♋
1004	Aug 31	17:34	♌
1005	Feb 7	17:22 ℞	♋
1005	May 19	12:24	♌
1006	Oct 30	11:12	♍
1007	Jan 26	2:06 ℞	♌
1007	Jul 19	15:54	♍
1009	Sep 22	7:13	♎
1011	Dec 8	16:16	♏
1012	Apr 21	17:47 ℞	♎
1012	Sep 5	1:37	♏
1014	Dec 1	5:12	♐
1017	Mar 18	17:37	♑
1017	May 2	2:05 ℞	♐
1017	Dec 1	2:57	♑
1020	Feb 23	4:39	♒
1020	Aug 16	9:19 ℞	♑
1020	Nov 17	17:26	♒
1023	Feb 7	15:14	♓
1025	Apr 10	1:59	♈
1027	Jun 3	15:32	♉
1027	Nov 6	20:38 ℞	♈
1028	Feb 20	18:24	♉
1029	Jul 21	20:45	♊
1029	Nov 10	18:26 ℞	♉
1030	Apr 8	13:31	♊
1031	Sep 9	13:31	♋
1031	Nov 18	2:28 ℞	♊
1032	May 20	16:21	♋
1034	Jul 5	14:31	♌
1036	Aug 26	16:44	♍
1038	Oct 30	14:51	♎
1039	Apr 6	19:59 ℞	♍
1039	Jul 24	18:13	♎
1041	Oct 15	3:37	♏
1044	Jan 10	2:28	♐
1044	May 17	16:28 ℞	♏
1044	Oct 9	1:55	♐
1047	Jan 6	9:40	♑
1050	Jan 2	13:15	♒
1052	Mar 17	4:08	♓
1052	Oct 5	6:50 ℞	♒
1052	Nov 30	8:31	♓
1054	May 30	6:38	♈
1054	Aug 29	2:19 ℞	♓
1055	Feb 16	0:19	♈
1057	Apr 7	22:59	♉
1059	May 21	14:46	♊
1061	Jun 30	20:41	♋
1063	Aug 14	6:39	♌
1065	Oct 6	11:18	♍
1066	Feb 26	9:60 ℞	♌
1066	Jun 28	15:59	♍
1068	Sep 5	19:12	♎
1070	Nov 19	22:32	♏
1071	May 24	9:05 ℞	♎
1071	Aug 11	11:51	♏
1073	Nov 15	5:56	♐
1076	Feb 15	2:07	♑
1076	Jun 9	1:44 ℞	♐
1076	Nov 13	9:10	♑
1079	Feb 5	19:05	♒
1081	May 4	10:55	♓
1081	Jul 20	19:34 ℞	♒
1082	Jan 21	9:57	♓
1084	Mar 23	23:39	♈
1086	May 15	5:27	♉
1088	Jun 29	3:18	♊
1088	Dec 13	19:25 ℞	♉
1089	Mar 14	18:10	♊
1090	Aug 12	0:27	♋
1090	Dec 23	3:18 ℞	♊
1091	Apr 30	13:17	♋
1092	Sep 30	16:20	♌
1092	Dec 25	10:20 ℞	♋
1093	Jun 16	20:45	♌
1095	Aug 10	11:14	♍
1097	Oct 12	4:01	♎
1098	May 28	5:12 ℞	♍
1098	Jun 8	2:36	♎
1100	Jan 11	15:14	♏
1100	Mar 8	12:39 ℞	♎
1100	Sep 29	0:25	♏
1102	Dec 22	11:04	♐
1103	Jun 19	22:14 ℞	♏
1103	Sep 16	21:04	♐
1105	Dec 21	23:41	♑
1108	Mar 22	7:23	♒
1108	Jul 5	3:18 ℞	♑
1108	Dec 16	20:08	♒
1111	Mar 1	23:59	♓
1113	May 6	9:52	♈
1113	Oct 1	7:41 ℞	♓
1114	Jan 27	3:29	♈
1115	Jul 11	16:08	♉
1115	Sep 17	15:44 ℞	♈
1116	Mar 22	4:42	♉
1118	May 5	10:47	♊
1120	Jun 14	20:51	♋
1122	Jul 29	2:41	♌
1124	Sep 18	8:52	♍
1125	Apr 5	15:04 ℞	♌
1125	May 28	15:19	♍
1126	Nov 28	17:32	♎
1127	Feb 25	1:19 ℞	♍
1127	Aug 20	20:42	♎
1129	Nov 3	20:28	♏
1132	Feb 13	12:17	♐
1132	Apr 5	3:17 ℞	♏
1132	Oct 30	15:00	♐
1135	Jan 26	10:27	♑
1135	Jul 10	21:27 ℞	♐
1135	Oct 24	21:26	♑
1138	Jan 21	14:40	♒
1140	Apr 9	8:11	♓
1140	Aug 23	4:17 ℞	♒
1141	Jan 3	10:20	♓
1143	Mar 9	13:25	♈
1145	Apr 28	23:19	♉
1147	Jun 12	10:05	♊
1149	Jul 23	10:60	♋
1150	Jan 29	1:22 ℞	♊
1150	Apr 1	15:19	♋
1151	Sep 7	7:16	♌
1152	Jan 29	9:40 ℞	♋
1152	May 26	18:30	♌
1153	Nov 8	0:53	♍
1154	Jan 15	1:45 ℞	♌
1154	Jul 24	5:08	♍
1156	Sep 25	19:38	♎
1158	Dec 13	11:60	♏
1159	Apr 14	16:31 ℞	♎
1159	Sep 10	19:05	♏
1161	Dec 5	2:38	♐
1164	Dec 5	14:27	♑

Saturn Ingresses –500 (501 BC)—2100

Year	Date	Time	℞	Sign
1167	Mar 1	6:14		♒
1167	Aug 5	7:50	℞	♑
1167	Nov 27	5:33		♒
1170	Feb 13	20:09		♓
1172	Apr 17	12:07		♈
1172	Nov 6	16:20	℞	♓
1172	Dec 27	12:46		♈
1174	Jun 13	9:01		♉
1174	Oct 21	18:37	℞	♈
1175	Mar 3	16:39		♉
1176	Aug 4	8:07		♊
1176	Oct 24	0:11	℞	♉
1177	Apr 17	15:04		♊
1179	May 29	16:39		♋
1181	Jul 12	8:13		♌
1183	Sep 2	3:25		♍
1185	Nov 4	20:33		♎
1186	Mar 28	9:34	℞	♍
1186	Jul 30	23:39		♎
1188	Oct 18	9:56		♏
1191	Jan 14	0:31		♐
1191	May 12	5:21	℞	♏
1191	Oct 13	11:58		♐
1194	Jan 9	2:34		♑
1194	Aug 25	10:34	℞	♐
1194	Sep 14	7:35		♑
1197	Jan 5	18:02		♒
1199	Mar 22	7:20		♓
1199	Sep 24	7:19	℞	♒
1199	Dec 10	21:50		♓
1201	Jun 8	20:40		♈
1201	Aug 16	18:05	℞	♓
1202	Feb 20	22:24		♈
1204	Apr 12	18:18		♉
1206	May 26	16:29		♊
1208	Jul 6	0:54		♋
1210	Aug 19	6:50		♌
1211	Mar 8	9:47	℞	♋
1211	Apr 24	17:40		♌
1212	Oct 11	18:04		♍
1213	Feb 17	13:16	℞	♌
1213	Jul 4	6:01		♍
1215	Sep 10	2:16		♎
1217	Nov 23	8:14		♏
1218	May 15	17:45	℞	♎
1218	Aug 17	21:35		♏
1220	Nov 18	18:30		♐
1223	Feb 22	1:21		♑
1223	May 30	22:38	℞	♐
1223	Nov 19	10:26		♑
1226	Feb 11	13:22		♒
1226	Sep 11	8:42	℞	♑
1226	Oct 26	15:04		♒
1228	May 27	0:22		♓
1228	Jun 24	14:03	℞	♒
1229	Jan 29	0:18		♓
1231	Apr 2	8:02		♈
1233	May 25	4:26		♉
1233	Nov 21	5:22	℞	♈
1234	Feb 7	12:48		♉
1235	Jul 11	15:16		♊
1235	Nov 24	16:52	℞	♉
1236	Mar 29	8:34		♊
1237	Aug 25	6:07		♋
1237	Dec 4	6:21	℞	♊
1238	May 11	23:20		♋
1239	Oct 22	9:03		♌
1239	Dec 2	1:43	℞	♋
1240	Jun 25	16:26		♌
1242	Aug 16	23:44		♍
1244	Oct 17	11:06		♎
1245	May 2	4:09	℞	♍
1245	Jul 1	9:19		♎
1247	Jan 29	6:18		♏
1247	Feb 16	17:04	℞	♎
1247	Oct 3	0:36		♏
1249	Dec 25	5:46		♐
1250	Jun 10	9:50	℞	♏
1250	Sep 21	21:04		♐
1252	Dec 24	10:48		♑
1255	Mar 29	17:33		♒
1255	Jun 24	15:08	℞	♑
1255	Dec 21	18:34		♒
1258	Mar 6	8:44		♓
1260	May 13	17:46		♈
1260	Sep 16	23:15	℞	♓
1261	Feb 3	14:25		♈
1263	Mar 29	7:04		♉
1265	May 11	6:41		♊
1267	Jun 21	9:38		♋
1269	Aug 3	0:07		♌
1271	Sep 23	18:18		♍
1272	Mar 20	11:34	℞	♌
1272	Jun 9	1:57		♍
1273	Dec 5	21:48		♎
1274	Feb 13	10:22	℞	♍
1274	Aug 24	5:27		♎
1276	Nov 6	8:53		♏
1279	Nov 3	17:15		♐
1282	Jan 31	4:34		♑
1282	Jun 29	0:41	℞	♐
1282	Oct 31	5:03		♑
1285	Jan 26	20:35		♒
1287	Apr 21	7:23		♓
1287	Aug 5	14:26	℞	♒
1288	Jan 13	16:01		♓
1290	Mar 18	12:24		♈
1292	May 9	6:11		♉
1294	Jun 23	18:53		♊
1294	Dec 24	11:14	℞	♉
1295	Mar 5	20:13		♊
1296	Aug 4	12:53		♋
1296	Dec 31	22:28	℞	♊
1297	Apr 22	6:07		♋
1298	Sep 20	16:46		♌
1299	Jan 7	0:49	℞	♋
1299	Jun 9	13:00		♌
1301	Aug 2	12:34		♍
1303	Oct 3	17:11		♎
1305	Dec 21	20:41		♏
1306	Apr 2	15:52	℞	♎
1306	Sep 17	5:38		♏
1308	Dec 9	22:08		♐
1309	Jul 25	20:44	℞	♏
1309	Aug 13	19:08		♐
1311	Dec 11	12:60		♑
1314	Mar 8	9:40		♒
1314	Jul 23	18:33	℞	♑
1314	Dec 5	12:41		♒
1317	Feb 20	23:08		♓
1319	Apr 27	22:37		♈
1319	Oct 15	6:26	℞	♓
1320	Jan 16	14:35		♈
1321	Jun 27	19:44		♉
1321	Oct 1	17:37	℞	♈
1322	Mar 15	1:38		♉
1324	Apr 27	20:35		♊
1326	Jun 8	3:17		♋
1328	Jul 20	14:33		♌
1330	Sep 9	5:03		♍
1332	Nov 12	5:44		♎
1333	Mar 16	12:39	℞	♍
1333	Aug 7	12:09		♎
1335	Oct 24	0:42		♏
1338	Jan 21	9:38		♐
1338	May 1	8:27	℞	♏
1338	Oct 19	5:57		♐
1341	Jan 15	4:13		♑
1341	Jul 30	23:21	℞	♐
1341	Oct 6	15:38		♑
1344	Jan 14	7:31		♒
1346	Apr 2	17:21		♓
1346	Sep 1	17:25	℞	♒
1346	Dec 27	20:26		♓
1349	Mar 5	16:46		♈
1351	Apr 27	10:38		♉
1353	Jun 10	5:03		♊
1355	Jul 21	19:07		♋
1356	Feb 2	7:01	℞	♊
1356	Mar 27	17:44		♋
1357	Sep 3	5:51		♌
1358	Feb 2	8:24	℞	♋
1358	May 22	18:09		♌
1359	Oct 30	19:44		♍
1360	Jan 25	0:04	℞	♌
1360	Jul 18	4:52		♍
1362	Sep 19	10:31		♎
1364	Dec 2	6:57		♏
1365	Apr 29	2:05	℞	♎
1365	Aug 29	19:41		♏
1367	Nov 26	7:58		♐
1370	Mar 7	6:32		♑
1370	May 13	20:04	℞	♐
1370	Nov 26	18:33		♑
1373	Feb 19	15:48		♒
1373	Aug 19	9:40	℞	♑
1373	Nov 14	15:28		♒
1376	Feb 8	8:10		♓
1378	Apr 13	5:59		♈
1378	Nov 25	5:32	℞	♓
1378	Dec 10	7:14		♈
1380	Jun 8	10:54		♉
1380	Oct 26	5:01	℞	♈
1381	Feb 26	21:18		♉
1382	Jul 30	11:03		♊
1382	Oct 29	18:44	℞	♉
1383	Apr 14	13:39		♊
1384	Sep 22	21:06		♋
1384	Oct 31	8:05	℞	♊
1385	May 25	10:44		♋
1387	Jul 8	6:14		♌
1389	Aug 26	13:57		♍
1391	Oct 27	7:06		♎
1392	Apr 11	3:31	℞	♍
1392	Jul 18	7:34		♎
1394	Oct 9	18:04		♏
1397	Jan 1	15:16		♐
1397	May 27	15:25	℞	♏
1397	Oct 1	11:07		♐
1400	Jan 1	10:46		♑
1402	Apr 23	9:49		♒
1402	May 28	10:48	℞	♑
1403	Jan 1	3:32		♒
1405	Mar 19	2:19		♓
1405	Sep 30	23:17	℞	♒
1405	Dec 5	8:27		♓
1407	Jun 9	5:53		♈
1407	Aug 17	22:28	℞	♓
1408	Feb 21	23:51		♈
1410	Apr 15	16:49		♉
1412	May 29	10:03		♊
1414	Jul 9	14:18		♋
1416	Aug 20	21:54		♌
1417	Mar 3	5:10	℞	♋
1417	Apr 29	3:50		♌
1418	Oct 12	11:39		♍
1419	Feb 19	2:03	℞	♌
1419	Jul 4	11:22		♍
1421	Sep 7	2:46		♎
1423	Nov 18	23:41		♏
1424	May 27	20:09	℞	♎
1424	Aug 7	7:56		♏
1426	Nov 13	14:06		♐
1429	Feb 12	11:13		♑
1429	Jun 12	6:55	℞	♐
1429	Nov 12	7:58		♑
1432	Feb 7	7:52		♒
1434	May 15	8:19		♓
1434	Jul 8	18:04	℞	♒
1435	Jan 27	1:08		♓
1437	Apr 1	10:12		♈
1439	May 26	20:07		♉
1439	Nov 20	8:23	℞	♈
1440	Feb 10	1:26		♉
1441	Jul 13	7:52		♊
1441	Nov 22	2:08	℞	♉
1442	Mar 31	23:46		♊
1443	Aug 28	3:44		♋
1443	Dec 2	20:51	℞	♊
1444	May 13	0:51		♋
1445	Oct 23	11:43		♌
1445	Nov 30	23:15	℞	♋
1446	Jun 26	13:31		♌
1448	Aug 15	3:25		♍
1450	Oct 14	9:22		♎
1451	May 18	20:51	℞	♍
1451	Jun 17	13:18		♎
1453	Jan 7	21:20		♏
1453	Mar 12	1:39	℞	♎
1453	Sep 26	20:23		♏
1455	Dec 19	4:52		♐
1456	Jun 24	10:21	℞	♏
1456	Sep 10	7:43		♐
1458	Dec 19	21:49		♑
1461	Mar 22	20:57		♒
1461	Jul 2	17:39	℞	♑
1461	Dec 17	16:45		♒
1464	Mar 5	8:35		♓
1466	May 17	15:32		♈
1466	Sep 13	7:58	℞	♓
1467	Feb 7	14:48		♈
1469	Apr 3	7:48		♉
1471	May 18	10:41		♊
1473	Jun 27	14:26		♋
1475	Aug 9	10:30		♌
1477	Sep 27	20:52		♍
1478	Mar 13	7:19	℞	♌
1478	Jun 16	10:50		♍
1479	Dec 9	22:48		♎
1480	Feb 11	2:06	℞	♍
1480	Aug 25	1:36		♎
1482	Nov 5	17:41		♏
1485	Feb 15	9:33		♐
1485	Mar 31	22:10	℞	♏
1485	Oct 31	4:06		♐
1488	Jan 27	18:27		♑
1488	Jul 6	0:17	℞	♐
1488	Oct 25	22:48		♑
1491	Jan 25	4:58		♒
1493	Apr 19	22:11		♓
1493	Aug 6	16:37	℞	♒
1494	Jan 13	5:23		♓
1496	Mar 20	8:04		♈
1498	May 14	2:37		♉
1500	Jun 30	4:44		♊
1500	Dec 14	1:33	℞	♉
1501	Mar 16	4:11		♊
1502	Aug 12	15:20		♋
1502	Dec 24	12:00	℞	♊
1503	Apr 30	21:20		♋
1504	Sep 28	3:59		♌
1504	Dec 30	20:28	℞	♋
1505	Jun 14	21:11		♌
1507	Aug 5	9:04		♍
1509	Oct 3	4:36		♎
1511	Dec 18	16:29		♏
1512	Apr 8	4:20	℞	♎
1512	Sep 13	16:49		♏
1514	Dec 6	17:45		♐
1517	Dec 7	16:46		♑
1520	Mar 5	8:55		♒
1520	Jul 27	20:03	℞	♑
1520	Dec 2	16:54		♒
1523	Feb 22	10:20		♓
1525	May 2	7:07		♈
1525	Oct 6	17:38	℞	♓
1526	Jan 23	6:39		♈
1527	Jul 12	15:25		♉
1527	Sep 15	18:14	℞	♈
1528	Mar 22	22:21		♉
1530	May 7	23:43		♊
1532	Jun 17	10:26		♋
1534	Jul 30	3:11		♌
1536	Sep 16	10:34		♍
1537	Apr 13	3:06	℞	♌
1537	May 21	0:29		♍
1538	Nov 19	20:19		♎
1539	Mar 8	15:14	℞	♍
1539	Aug 13	15:06		♎
1541	Oct 25	11:34		♏
1544	Jan 21	15:11		♐
1544	May 2	7:58	℞	♏
1544	Oct 18	8:12		♐
1547	Jan 14	16:00		♑
1547	Aug 4	18:39	℞	♐
1547	Oct 4	2:36		♑
1550	Jan 13	14:17		♒
1552	Apr 3	19:51		♓
1552	Aug 30	4:24	℞	♒
1552	Dec 29	18:42		♓
1555	Mar 10	8:54		♈
1557	May 3	4:02		♉
1559	Jun 18	14:53		♊
1560	Jan 13	11:19	℞	♉
1560	Feb 18	9:14		♊
1561	Jul 30	0:17		♋
1562	Jan 14	4:57	℞	♊
1562	Apr 13	21:28		♋
1563	Sep 12	17:33		♌
1564	Jan 21	5:46	℞	♋
1564	Jun 1	0:59		♌
1565	Nov 10	15:19		♍
1566	Jan 12	8:30	℞	♌
1566	Jul 24	10:39		♍
1568	Sep 21	16:54		♎
1570	Dec 3	1:43		♏
1571	Apr 30	12:24	℞	♎
1571	Aug 30	2:32		♏
1573	Nov 24	5:14		♐
1576	Mar 1	22:36		♑
1576	May 19	19:36	℞	♐
1576	Nov 24	5:24		♑
1579	Feb 19	5:24		♒
1579	Aug 22	19:43	℞	♑
1579	Nov 13	13:31		♒
1582	Feb 9	14:59		♓
1584	Apr 18	0:45		♈
1584	Nov 2	18:17	℞	♓
1584	Dec 31	3:30		♈
1586	Jun 20	7:20		♉
1586	Oct 11	8:33	℞	♈
1587	Mar 10	8:23		♉
1588	Aug 25	20:40		♊
1588	Sep 29	7:47	℞	♉
1589	Apr 26	0:28		♊
1591	Jun 7	2:10		♋
1593	Jul 18	23:44		♌
1595	Sep 5	20:02		♍
1597	Nov 4	13:33		♎
1598	Mar 29	2:13	℞	♍
1598	Jul 29	15:19		♎
1600	Oct 13	13:06		♏
1603	Jan 4	12:34		♐
1603	May 25	18:46	℞	♏
1603	Oct 4	0:48		♐

Saturn Ingresses –500 (501 BC)—2100

Year	Date	Time		Sign
1606	Jan 1	14:55		♑
1608	Apr 24	0:44		♒
1608	May 25	6:46	℞	♑
1608	Dec 31	15:20		♒
1611	Mar 21	2:22		♓
1611	Sep 25	2:20	℞	♒
1611	Dec 10	8:54		♓
1613	Jun 19	23:43		♈
1613	Aug 3	1:55	℞	♓
1614	Feb 25	18:36		♈
1616	Apr 21	7:58		♉
1618	Jun 6	17:23		♊
1620	Jul 17	17:48		♋
1621	Feb 13	21:19	℞	♊
1621	Mar 16	13:11		♋
1622	Aug 30	4:33		♌
1623	Feb 10	10:32	℞	♋
1623	May 16	13:52		♌
1624	Oct 21	8:32		♍
1625	Feb 4	15:16	℞	♌
1625	Jul 11	17:45		♍
1627	Sep 11	7:38		♎
1629	Nov 19	15:54		♏
1630	May 24	1:04	℞	♎
1630	Aug 10	2:12		♏
1632	Nov 11	18:56		♐
1635	Feb 10	6:43		♑
1635	Jun 15	0:26	℞	♐
1635	Nov 10	11:27		♑
1638	Feb 5	10:21		♒
1640	May 17	15:59		♓
1640	Jul 3	12:43	℞	♒
1641	Jan 27	8:51		♓
1643	Apr 5	15:38		♈
1645	Jun 3	13:08		♉
1645	Nov 2	18:53	℞	♈
1646	Feb 22	4:05		♉
1647	Jul 28	11:27		♊
1647	Nov 1	9:49	℞	♉
1648	Apr 12	18:19		♊
1649	Sep 23	13:20		♋
1649	Oct 31	1:02	℞	♊
1650	May 25	19:49		♋
1652	Jul 7	5:46		♌
1654	Aug 25	3:12		♍
1656	Oct 22	0:12		♎
1657	Apr 21	4:45	℞	♍
1657	Jul 9	23:51		♎
1659	Jan 28	6:16		♏
1659	Feb 17	20:05	℞	♎
1659	Oct 2	3:58		♏
1661	Dec 21	1:30		♐
1662	Jun 18	11:14	℞	♏
1662	Sep 14	17:55		♐
1664	Dec 19	19:57		♑
1667	Mar 24	1:26		♒
1667	Jun 30	19:52	℞	♑
1667	Dec 18	15:01		♒
1670	Mar 7	6:30		♓
1672	May 22	13:35		♈
1672	Sep 3	19:53	℞	♓
1673	Feb 11	16:54		♈
1675	Apr 9	21:12		♉
1677	May 25	13:25		♊
1679	Jul 6	12:55		♋
1681	Aug 17	8:51		♌
1682	Mar 12	12:07	℞	♋
1682	Apr 19	0:30		♌
1683	Oct 6	16:42		♍
1684	Feb 26	7:22	℞	♌
1684	Jun 26	16:07		♍
1685	Dec 27	14:27		♎
1686	Jan 20	17:00	℞	♍
1686	Aug 30	5:37		♎
1688	Nov 7	0:02		♏
1691	Feb 14	20:36		♐
1691	Apr 1	10:32	℞	♏
1691	Oct 30	18:24		♐
1694	Jan 24	23:22		♑
1694	Jul 8	20:33	℞	♐
1694	Oct 23	13:36		♑
1697	Jan 22	20:59		♒
1699	Apr 19	23:28		♓
1699	Aug 6	3:00	℞	♒
1700	Jan 13	12:26		♓
1702	Mar 24	1:44		♈
1704	May 20	6:38		♉
1704	Dec 2	3:06	℞	♈
1705	Jan 29	23:28		♉
1706	Jul 10	13:40		♊
1706	Nov 26	5:35	℞	♉
1707	Mar 29	18:37		♊
1708	Aug 26	13:39		♋
1708	Dec 2	22:46	℞	♊
1709	May 12	21:07		♋
1710	Oct 22	19:10		♌
1710	Dec 2	5:02	℞	♋
1711	Jun 26	10:51		♌
1713	Aug 13	23:54		♍
1715	Oct 11	3:00		♎
1717	Dec 26	14:54		♏
1718	Mar 27	17:12	℞	♎
1718	Sep 19	15:35		♏
1720	Dec 8	12:05		♐
1723	Dec 8	12:23		♑
1726	Mar 5	18:30		♒
1726	Jul 26	21:14	℞	♑
1726	Dec 3	4:39		♒
1729	Feb 22	12:31		♓
1731	May 5	12:53		♈
1731	Sep 30	16:52	℞	♓
1732	Jan 27	18:58		♈
1733	Jul 27	21:43		♉
1733	Aug 27	8:14	℞	♈
1734	Mar 28	8:23		♉
1736	May 13	17:21		♊
1738	Jun 24	21:03		♋
1740	Aug 5	10:22		♌
1742	Sep 23	5:10		♍
1743	Mar 24	4:12	℞	♌
1743	Jun 7	11:42		♍
1744	Nov 26	3:47		♎
1745	Feb 26	7:55	℞	♍
1745	Aug 17	11:21		♎
1747	Oct 27	4:21		♏
1750	Jan 19	14:55		♐
1750	May 3	14:16	℞	♏
1750	Oct 17	7:28		♐
1753	Jan 11	5:38		♑
1753	Aug 11	7:53	℞	♐
1753	Sep 26	2:42		♑
1756	Jan 11	1:10		♒
1758	Apr 1	17:28		♓
1758	Sep 2	1:42	℞	♒
1758	Dec 27	15:01		♓
1761	Mar 9	20:10		♈
1763	May 6	8:01		♉
1765	Jun 23	19:51		♊
1765	Dec 23	23:22	℞	♉
1766	Mar 6	21:04		♊
1767	Aug 8	1:21		♋
1767	Dec 29	4:15	℞	♊
1768	Apr 25	8:16		♋
1769	Sep 23	11:57		♌
1770	Jan 3	23:37	℞	♋
1770	Jun 11	8:11		♌
1772	Jul 31	11:10		♍
1774	Sep 27	21:02		♎
1776	Dec 7	11:22		♏
1777	Apr 21	4:57	℞	♎
1777	Sep 3	13:17		♏
1779	Nov 25	21:12		♐
1782	Mar 1	20:54		♑
1782	May 19	19:34	℞	♐
1782	Nov 23	21:06		♑
1785	Feb 17	3:28		♒
1785	Aug 23	22:20	℞	♑
1785	Nov 10	14:28		♒
1788	Feb 9	1:24		♓
1790	Apr 18	15:15		♈
1790	Oct 31	0:09	℞	♓
1791	Jan 2	14:59		♈
1792	Jun 22	21:55		♉
1792	Oct 5	1:32	℞	♈
1793	Mar 12	12:43		♉
1795	Apr 30	9:53		♊
1797	Jun 11	3:01		♋
1799	Jul 23	20:22		♌
1801	Sep 9	23:25		♍
1803	Nov 8	22:04		♎
1804	Mar 24	0:05	℞	♍
1804	Aug 1	21:04		♎
1806	Oct 14	17:59		♏
1809	Jan 2	2:02		♐
1809	May 29	14:22	℞	♏
1809	Sep 30	23:00		♐
1811	Dec 29	19:55		♑
1814	Apr 10	1:08		♒
1814	Jun 11	13:09	℞	♑
1814	Dec 28	2:03		♒
1817	Mar 16	20:00		♓
1817	Oct 5	9:39	℞	♒
1817	Dec 1	10:37		♓
1819	Jun 13	3:04		♈
1819	Aug 12	8:39	℞	♓
1820	Feb 24	6:36		♈
1822	Apr 22	3:44		♉
1824	Jun 8	20:17		♊
1826	Jul 22	20:27		♋
1827	Jan 30	8:12	℞	♊
1827	Mar 31	18:59		♋
1828	Sep 4	15:03		♌
1829	Jan 31	15:19	℞	♋
1829	May 24	4:02		♌
1830	Oct 29	11:14		♍
1831	Jan 27	10:30	℞	♌
1831	Jul 17	18:24		♍
1833	Sep 14	15:35		♎
1835	Nov 22	17:40		♏
1836	May 19	13:20	℞	♎
1836	Aug 13	9:22		♏
1838	Nov 12	11:26		♐
1841	Feb 7	17:35		♑
1841	Jun 18	15:04	℞	♐
1841	Nov 7	18:41		♑
1844	Feb 3	12:17		♒
1846	May 10	7:13		♓
1846	Jul 13	13:03	℞	♒
1847	Jan 25	11:31		♓
1849	Apr 3	15:20		♈
1851	Jun 3	16:14		♉
1851	Nov 4	11:56	℞	♈
1852	Feb 22	17:41		♉
1853	Jul 29	20:10		♊
1853	Oct 30	6:46	℞	♉
1854	Apr 14	22:24		♊
1855	Oct 5	15:59		♋
1855	Oct 20	2:54	℞	♊
1856	May 27	17:15		♋
1858	Jul 10	0:40		♌
1860	Aug 26	4:32		♍
1862	Oct 22	23:08		♎
1863	Apr 22	10:50	℞	♍
1863	Jul 10	8:35		♎
1865	Jan 19	10:45		♏
1865	Feb 27	7:13	℞	♎
1865	Sep 29	23:29		♏
1867	Dec 17	17:29		♐
1868	Jun 28	11:54	℞	♏
1868	Sep 5	22:27		♐
1870	Dec 15	1:03		♑
1873	Mar 13	20:02		♒
1873	Jul 14	1:53	℞	♑
1873	Dec 10	21:46		♒
1876	Feb 29	15:09		♓
1878	May 14	20:17		♈
1878	Sep 15	23:52	℞	♓
1879	Feb 6	0:55		♈
1881	Apr 5	22:12		♉
1883	May 24	13:26		♊
1885	Jul 6	2:11		♋
1887	Aug 18	19:07		♌
1888	Mar 9	19:55	℞	♋
1888	Apr 21	10:06		♌
1889	Oct 7	3:34		♍
1890	Feb 25	8:39	℞	♌
1890	Jun 28	4:54		♍
1891	Dec 27	17:49		♎
1892	Jan 22	12:43	℞	♍
1892	Aug 29	23:08		♎
1894	Nov 6	18:51		♏
1897	Feb 7	14:34		♐
1897	Apr 9	14:26	℞	♏
1897	Oct 27	18:34		♐
1900	Jan 21	8:10		♑
1900	Jul 18	17:32	℞	♐
1900	Oct 17	5:03		♑
1903	Jan 19	22:15		♒
1905	Apr 13	8:39		♓
1905	Aug 17	0:41	℞	♒
1906	Jan 8	12:48		♓
1908	Mar 19	14:23		♈
1910	May 17	7:30		♉
1910	Dec 14	23:08	℞	♈
1911	Jan 20	9:22		♉
1912	Jul 7	6:13		♊
1912	Nov 30	18:18	℞	♉
1913	Mar 26	13:07		♊
1914	Aug 24	17:28		♋
1914	Dec 7	6:49	℞	♊
1915	May 11	21:24		♋
1916	Oct 17	15:36		♌
1916	Dec 7	19:22	℞	♋
1917	Jun 24	13:54		♌
1919	Aug 12	13:52		♍
1921	Oct 7	17:22		♎
1923	Dec 20	4:25		♏
1924	Apr 6	8:36	℞	♎
1924	Sep 13	21:59		♏
1926	Dec 2	22:35		♐
1929	Mar 15	13:48		♑
1929	May 5	4:19	℞	♐
1929	Nov 30	4:23		♑
1932	Feb 24	2:47		♒
1932	Aug 13	11:15	℞	♑
1932	Nov 20	2:10		♒
1935	Feb 14	14:09		♓
1937	Apr 25	6:30		♈
1937	Oct 18	3:41	℞	♓
1938	Jan 14	10:31		♈
1939	Jul 6	5:46		♉
1939	Sep 22	5:18	℞	♈
1940	Mar 20	9:41		♉
1942	May 8	19:40		♊
1944	Jun 20	7:48		♋
1946	Aug 2	14:42		♌
1948	Sep 19	4:36		♍
1949	Apr 3	3:40	℞	♌
1949	May 29	12:58		♍
1950	Nov 20	15:50		♎
1951	Mar 7	12:14	℞	♍
1951	Aug 13	16:44		♎
1953	Oct 22	15:36		♏
1956	Jan 12	18:45		♐
1956	May 14	3:47	℞	♏
1956	Oct 10	15:11		♐
1959	Jan 5	13:33		♑
1962	Jan 3	19:02		♒
1964	Mar 24	4:18		♓
1964	Sep 16	21:05	℞	♒
1964	Dec 16	5:39		♓
1967	Mar 3	21:32		♈
1969	Apr 29	22:24		♉
1971	Jun 18	16:10		♊
1972	Jan 10	3:43	℞	♉
1972	Feb 21	14:53		♊
1973	Aug 1	22:21		♋
1974	Jan 7	20:28	℞	♊
1974	Apr 18	22:34		♋
1975	Sep 17	4:57		♌
1976	Jan 14	13:17	℞	♋
1976	Jun 5	5:09		♌
1977	Nov 17	2:42		♍
1978	Jan 5	0:48	℞	♌
1978	Jul 26	12:02		♍
1980	Sep 21	10:48		♎
1982	Nov 29	10:29		♏
1983	May 6	19:32	℞	♎
1983	Aug 24	11:53		♏
1985	Nov 17	2:10		♐
1988	Feb 13	23:51		♑
1988	Jun 10	5:24	℞	♐
1988	Nov 12	9:26		♑
1991	Feb 6	18:52		♒
1993	May 21	4:58		♓
1993	Jun 30	8:31	℞	♒
1994	Jan 28	23:44		♓
1996	Apr 7	8:50		♈
1998	Jun 9	6:08		♉
1998	Oct 25	18:42	℞	♈
1999	Mar 1	1:26		♉
2000	Aug 10	2:26		♊
2000	Oct 16	0:47	℞	♉
2001	Apr 20	21:60		♊
2003	Jun 4	1:28		♋
2005	Jul 16	12:31		♌
2007	Sep 2	13:49		♍
2009	Oct 29	17:09		♎
2010	Apr 7	18:55	℞	♍
2010	Jul 21	15:09		♎
2012	Oct 5	20:34		♏
2014	Dec 23	16:34		♐
2015	Jun 15	0:39	℞	♏
2015	Sep 18	2:48		♐
2017	Dec 20	4:49		♑
2020	Mar 22	3:58		♒
2020	Jul 1	23:40	℞	♑
2020	Dec 17	5:04		♒
2023	Mar 7	13:35		♓
2025	May 25	3:36		♈
2025	Sep 1	8:09	℞	♓
2026	Feb 14	0:12		♈
2028	Apr 13	3:40		♉
2030	Jun 1	2:34		♊
2032	Jul 14	2:16		♋
2034	Aug 27	2:46		♌
2035	Feb 15	19:39	℞	♋
2035	May 11	20:44		♌
2036	Oct 16	7:34		♍
2037	Feb 11	6:50	℞	♌
2037	Jul 7	2:30		♍
2039	Sep 5	15:14		♎
2041	Nov 11	10:58		♏
2042	Jun 21	10:38	℞	♎
2042	Jul 14	13:50		♏

Saturn Ingresses –500 (501 BC)—2100

Year	Month	Day	Time	Sign
2044	Feb	21	14:15	♐
2044	Mar	25	10:10	℞ ♏
2044	Oct	31	12:52	♐
2047	Jan	24	15:40	♑
2047	Jul	11	3:03	℞ ♐
2047	Oct	22	11:08	♑
2050	Jan	21	13:15	♒
2052	Apr	16	13:53	♓
2052	Aug	9	3:40	℞ ♒
2053	Jan	11	2:51	♓
2055	Mar	22	18:30	♈
2057	May	20	5:60	♉
2057	Nov	29	18:56	℞ ♈
2058	Jan	31	9:13	♉
2059	Jul	12	19:57	♊
2059	Nov	21	10:24	℞ ♉
2060	Mar	31	11:49	♊
2061	Sep	1	7:37	♋
2061	Nov	24	19:09	℞ ♊
2062	May	16	10:49	♋
2064	Jun	28	19:26	♌
2066	Aug	16	7:24	♍
2068	Oct	11	2:55	♎
2070	Dec	25	20:43	♏
2071	Mar	27	18:23	℞ ♎
2071	Sep	18	17:21	♏
2073	Dec	6	2:55	♐
2076	Dec	3	16:01	♑
2079	Feb	28	17:24	♒
2079	Aug	2	12:32	℞ ♑
2079	Nov	27	14:17	♒
2082	Feb	19	2:20	♓
2084	May	1	21:25	♈
2084	Oct	2	7:58	℞ ♓
2085	Jan	24	4:55	♈
2086	Jul	27	23:24	♉
2086	Aug	25	21:54	℞ ♈
2087	Mar	28	5:50	♉
2089	May	15	10:23	♊
2091	Jun	27	23:56	♋
2093	Aug	9	3:51	♌
2095	Sep	26	12:44	♍
2096	Mar	14	20:28	℞ ♌
2096	Jun	12	10:18	♍
2097	Nov	29	0:33	♎
2098	Feb	21	23:60	℞ ♍
2098	Aug	18	17:53	♎
2100	Oct	26	17:03	♏

Jupiter Ingresses –500 (501 BC)—2100

Year	Month	Day	Time	Sign
-500	Jan	6	12:43	℞ ♊
-500	Apr	9	8:42	♋
-500	Sep	9	5:47	♌
-499	Feb	16	10:60	℞ ♋
-499	May	2	22:08	♌
-499	Oct	7	23:20	♍
-498	Mar	22	12:29	℞ ♌
-498	May	31	14:51	♍
-498	Nov	6	8:25	♎
-497	Apr	26	8:59	℞ ♍
-497	Jun	28	8:19	♎
-497	Dec	3	1:36	♏
-496	Jun	14	2:09	℞ ♎
-496	Jul	11	15:13	♏
-496	Dec	24	0:24	♐
-494	Jan	9	23:28	♑
-493	Jan	22	22:49	♒
-492	Feb	2	3:23	♓
-491	Feb	9	10:23	♈
-491	Jun	27	10:10	♉
-491	Oct	24	11:55	℞ ♈
-490	Feb	15	22:16	♉
-490	Jul	7	22:41	♊
-489	Jan	2	17:04	℞ ♉
-489	Feb	16	19:16	♊
-489	Jul	27	20:25	♋
-488	Aug	21	17:47	♌
-487	Sep	19	22:52	♍
-486	Oct	19	11:43	♎
-485	Nov	15	11:09	♏
-484	Dec	6	22:15	♐
-483	Dec	24	7:51	♑
-481	Jan	6	3:29	♒
-480	Jan	14	22:57	♓
-480	May	30	21:38	♈
-480	Sep	20	6:10	℞ ♓
-479	Jan	17	23:17	♈
-479	Jun	4	16:42	♉
-478	Jun	19	10:15	♊
-477	Jul	10	21:08	♋
-476	Aug	5	9:52	♌
-475	Sep	3	19:29	♍
-474	Oct	3	7:24	♎
-473	Oct	30	5:30	♏
-472	Nov	20	16:29	♐
-471	Dec	7	21:06	♑
-470	Dec	19	15:33	♒
-469	May	8	6:46	♓
-469	Aug	11	3:52	℞ ♒
-469	Dec	24	22:51	♓
-468	May	7	4:14	♈
-468	Nov	14	21:16	℞ ♓
-468	Dec	5	22:06	♈
-467	May	17	5:11	♉
-466	Jun	2	14:51	♊
-465	Jun	24	16:51	♋
-464	Jul	20	11:27	♌
-463	Aug	18	22:59	♍
-462	Sep	17	10:17	♎
-461	Oct	14	6:04	♏
-460	Nov	4	11:33	♐
-459	Nov	20	21:39	♑
-458	Apr	15	4:17	♒
-458	Jun	29	15:35	℞ ♑
-458	Nov	30	3:28	♒
-457	Apr	12	14:28	♓
-457	Sep	26	13:54	℞ ♒
-457	Nov	23	21:02	♓
-456	Apr	18	15:17	♈
-455	Apr	30	16:11	♉
-454	May	17	14:15	♊
-453	Jun	8	16:19	♋
-452	Jul	4	9:37	♌
-451	Aug	2	21:31	♍
-450	Sep	1	9:04	♎
-449	Sep	28	0:05	♏
-448	Oct	18	11:35	♐
-447	Mar	16	5:49	♑
-447	May	26	10:10	℞ ♐
-447	Nov	1	17:45	♑
-446	Mar	17	3:01	♒
-446	Aug	14	20:29	℞ ♑
-446	Nov	3	0:57	♒
-445	Mar	23	19:26	♓
-444	Apr	1	8:10	♈
-443	Apr	13	22:57	♉
-442	Apr	30	15:52	♊
-441	May	22	10:02	♋
-440	Jun	17	3:17	♌
-439	Jul	16	22:24	♍
-438	Aug	15	15:00	♎
-437	Jan	25	19:58	♏
-437	Mar	8	23:08	℞ ♎
-437	Sep	10	21:04	♏
-436	Feb	6	9:05	♐
-436	May	3	18:40	℞ ♏
-436	Sep	29	15:32	♐
-435	Feb	15	15:06	♑
-435	Jul	9	16:11	℞ ♐
-435	Oct	7	21:26	♑
-434	Feb	25	0:51	♒
-433	Mar	6	8:15	♓
-432	Mar	15	11:05	♈
-431	Mar	27	13:23	♉
-430	Apr	12	2:48	♊
-430	Sep	8	22:47	♋
-430	Nov	30	20:23	℞ ♊
-429	May	2	16:23	♋
-429	Sep	30	8:44	♌
-428	Jan	10	22:22	℞ ♋
-428	May	27	18:39	♌
-428	Oct	27	9:27	♍
-427	Feb	12	3:34	℞ ♌
-427	Jun	26	12:08	♍
-427	Nov	25	16:31	♎
-426	Mar	16	22:50	℞ ♍
-426	Jul	25	22:50	♎
-426	Dec	21	19:09	♏
-425	Apr	25	13:01	℞ ♎
-425	Aug	19	17:13	♏
-424	Jan	11	8:30	♐
-424	Jun	17	5:26	℞ ♏
-424	Sep	1	17:04	♐
-423	Jan	25	20:38	♑
-422	Feb	7	0:02	♒
-421	Feb	17	8:47	♓
-420	Feb	27	5:41	♈
-420	Aug	5	12:13	♉
-420	Sep	2	22:45	℞ ♈
-419	Mar	8	19:41	♉
-419	Jul	28	17:25	♊
-419	Nov	18	16:33	℞ ♉
-418	Mar	21	12:30	♊
-418	Aug	14	8:05	♋
-417	Jan	9	14:14	℞ ♊
-417	Apr	7	6:47	♋
-417	Sep	7	23:38	♌
-416	Feb	19	23:36	℞ ♋
-416	Apr	29	6:37	♌
-416	Oct	5	17:20	♍
-415	Mar	25	8:16	℞ ♌
-415	May	27	15:12	♍
-415	Nov	4	2:08	♎
-414	Apr	29	16:26	℞ ♍
-414	Jun	23	21:38	♎
-414	Nov	30	20:13	♏
-413	Dec	22	21:55	♐
-411	Jan	8	0:58	♑
-410	Jan	21	3:52	♒
-409	Jan	31	10:30	♓
-408	Feb	8	16:58	♈
-408	Jun	25	10:26	♉
-408	Oct	25	8:37	℞ ♈
-407	Feb	13	22:33	♉
-407	Jul	6	4:29	♊
-406	Jan	5	5:00	℞ ♉
-406	Feb	12	22:30	♊
-406	Jul	26	1:39	♋
-405	Aug	20	19:58	♌
-404	Sep	17	21:11	♍
-403	Oct	17	7:19	♎
-402	Nov	13	7:04	♏
-401	Dec	5	22:55	♐
-400	Dec	22	16:25	♑
-398	Jan	4	20:07	♒
-397	Jan	13	21:06	♓
-397	May	30	19:49	♈
-397	Sep	20	16:12	℞ ♓
-396	Jan	17	22:22	♈
-396	Jun	3	14:16	♉
-395	Jun	18	1:44	♊
-394	Jul	9	4:37	♋
-393	Aug	4	9:47	♌
-392	Sep	1	14:40	♍
-391	Oct	1	2:45	♎
-390	Oct	28	5:35	♏
-389	Nov	20	0:14	♐
-388	Dec	6	13:08	♑
-387	Dec	18	13:51	♒
-386	May	7	4:47	♓
-386	Aug	10	12:20	℞ ♒
-386	Dec	23	23:19	♓
-385	May	7	2:59	♈
-385	Nov	16	17:29	℞ ♓
-385	Dec	4	10:25	♈
-384	May	15	22:30	♉
-383	May	31	23:51	♊
-382	Jun	22	18:13	♋
-381	Jul	19	10:00	♌
-380	Aug	17	0:59	♍
-379	Sep	15	20:53	♎
-378	Oct	13	2:34	♏
-377	Nov	4	15:09	♐
-376	Nov	20	3:12	♑
-375	Apr	14	7:06	♒
-375	Jun	28	18:47	℞ ♑
-375	Nov	29	3:56	♒
-374	Apr	11	7:09	♓
-374	Sep	27	5:34	℞ ♒
-374	Nov	21	15:30	♓
-373	Apr	17	22:21	♈
-372	Apr	28	13:32	♉
-371	May	15	3:43	♊
-370	Jun	6	2:28	♋
-369	Jul	2	22:46	♌
-368	Jul	31	18:54	♍
-367	Aug	30	16:43	♎
-366	Sep	26	16:38	♏
-365	Oct	18	8:35	♐
-364	Mar	14	18:17	♑
-364	May	26	7:24	℞ ♐
-364	Oct	31	12:33	♑
-363	Mar	15	16:18	♒
-363	Aug	15	8:49	℞ ♑
-363	Nov	1	1:33	♒
-362	Mar	22	3:47	♓
-361	Mar	31	10:31	♈
-360	Apr	11	19:57	♉
-359	Apr	28	8:42	♊
-358	May	20	0:00	♋
-357	Jun	15	15:44	♌
-357	Dec	6	18:54	♍
-357	Dec	24	21:02	℞ ♌
-356	Jul	14	10:31	♍
-356	Dec	31	17:39	♎
-355	Jan	28	5:32	℞ ♍
-355	Aug	13	3:04	♎
-354	Jan	20	0:14	♏
-354	Mar	13	19:49	℞ ♎
-354	Sep	8	8:39	♏
-353	Feb	2	20:49	♐
-353	May	7	11:38	℞ ♏
-353	Sep	28	0:12	♐
-352	Feb	14	0:50	♑
-352	Jul	12	5:05	℞ ♐
-352	Oct	4	13:28	♑
-351	Feb	22	21:37	♒
-350	Mar	4	10:40	♓
-349	Mar	14	15:57	♈
-348	Mar	25	18:01	♉
-348	Sep	8	10:53	♊
-348	Sep	26	15:46	℞ ♉
-347	Apr	10	4:05	♊
-347	Sep	6	3:31	♋
-347	Dec	2	14:00	℞ ♊
-346	Apr	30	11:37	♋
-346	Sep	27	16:36	♌
-345	Jan	12	18:08	℞ ♋
-345	May	26	6:33	♌
-345	Oct	25	13:19	♍
-344	Feb	15	8:08	℞ ♌
-344	Jun	23	17:23	♍
-344	Nov	22	16:08	♎
-343	Mar	19	11:43	℞ ♍
-343	Jul	22	22:56	♎
-343	Dec	18	20:11	♏
-342	Apr	28	5:52	℞ ♎
-342	Aug	16	11:44	♏
-341	Jan	8	18:36	♐
-341	Jun	21	9:32	℞ ♏
-341	Aug	29	17:17	♐
-340	Jan	24	18:54	♑
-339	Feb	5	8:57	♒
-338	Feb	16	0:28	♓
-337	Feb	25	23:36	♈
-337	Aug	3	10:36	♉
-337	Sep	5	11:56	℞ ♈
-336	Mar	7	9:44	♉
-336	Jul	26	21:27	♊
-336	Nov	19	9:11	℞ ♉
-335	Mar	19	13:44	♊
-335	Aug	12	6:29	♋
-334	Jan	11	8:12	℞ ♊
-334	Apr	4	6:46	♋
-334	Sep	5	14:53	♌
-333	Feb	23	5:11	℞ ♋
-333	Apr	25	20:59	♌
-333	Oct	4	3:18	♍
-332	Mar	29	15:08	℞ ♌
-332	May	22	7:28	♍
-332	Nov	1	11:47	♎
-331	May	4	17:19	℞ ♍
-331	Jun	17	21:08	♎
-331	Nov	28	11:42	♏
-330	Dec	20	23:24	♐
-328	Jan	7	12:46	♑
-327	Jan	19	23:03	♒
-326	Jan	30	8:40	♓
-325	Feb	7	12:22	♈
-325	Jun	24	20:56	♉
-325	Oct	26	18:34	℞ ♈
-324	Feb	13	3:48	♉
-324	Jul	4	8:02	♊
-323	Jan	9	11:39	℞ ♉
-323	Feb	7	7:19	♊

Jupiter Ingresses –500 (501 BC)—2100

Year	Date	Time	℞	Sign
-323	Jul 23	21:15		♋
-322	Aug 18	11:24		♌
-321	Sep 16	14:49		♍
-320	Oct 15	9:19		♎
-319	Nov 11	20:43		♏
-318	Dec 4	22:18		♐
-317	Dec 22	20:12		♑
-315	Jan 3	22:02		♒
-314	Jan 12	14:22		♓
-314	May 28	19:31		♈
-314	Sep 21	17:10	℞	♓
-313	Jan 15	18:25		♈
-313	Jun 2	7:53		♉
-312	Jun 15	12:52		♊
-311	Jul 6	12:37		♋
-310	Aug 1	20:05		♌
-309	Aug 31	8:27		♍
-308	Sep 29	6:46		♎
-307	Oct 26	19:32		♏
-306	Nov 18	20:35		♐
-305	Dec 6	10:22		♑
-304	Dec 17	5:37		♒
-303	May 5	1:09		♓
-303	Aug 11	12:39	℞	♒
-303	Dec 22	0:21		♓
-302	May 5	0:18		♈
-301	May 14	16:30		♉
-300	May 30	15:15		♊
-299	Jun 21	8:33		♋
-298	Jul 18	0:30		♌
-297	Aug 16	16:24		♍
-296	Sep 14	13:25		♎
-295	Oct 11	20:22		♏
-294	Nov 3	10:05		♐
-293	Nov 19	22:11		♑
-292	Apr 11	15:03		♒
-292	Jul 2	11:27	℞	♑
-292	Nov 27	18:57		♒
-291	Apr 10	0:38		♓
-291	Oct 1	14:21	℞	♒
-291	Nov 18	6:45		♓
-290	Apr 16	23:42		♈
-289	Apr 28	17:25		♉
-288	May 14	7:02		♊
-287	Jun 5	3:11		♋
-286	Jul 1	19:47		♌
-285	Jul 31	12:04		♍
-284	Aug 29	6:54		♎
-283	Sep 25	5:20		♏
-282	Oct 16	21:60		♐
-281	Mar 12	21:02		♑
-281	May 31	4:22	℞	♐
-281	Oct 31	3:40		♑
-280	Mar 14	12:38		♒
-280	Aug 18	2:55	℞	♑
-280	Oct 30	6:12		♒
-279	Mar 21	13:41		♓
-278	Mar 31	1:41		♈
-277	Apr 12	10:31		♉
-276	Apr 27	17:33		♊
-275	May 18	23:48		♋
-275	Nov 8	22:58		♌
-275	Nov 23	0:19	℞	♋
-274	Jun 14	6:41		♌
-274	Nov 28	4:57		♍
-273	Jan 3	12:02	℞	♌
-273	Jul 13	20:08		♍
-273	Dec 25	17:39		♎
-272	Feb 6	7:18	℞	♍
-272	Aug 11	12:35		♎
-271	Jan 16	1:24		♏
-271	Mar 18	19:19	℞	♎
-271	Sep 6	22:12		♏
-270	Jan 31	22:50		♐
-270	May 10	8:50	℞	♏
-270	Sep 26	19:10		♐
-269	Feb 13	3:58		♑
-269	Jul 15	6:14	℞	♐
-269	Oct 4	8:07		♑
-268	Feb 23	13:11		♒
-267	Mar 4	7:12		♓
-266	Mar 14	11:37		♈
-265	Mar 26	6:45		♉
-265	Sep 3	20:13		♊
-265	Oct 4	0:53	℞	♉
-264	Apr 9	3:44		♊
-264	Sep 3	23:06		♋
-264	Dec 5	22:46	℞	♊
-263	Apr 28	18:54		♋
-263	Sep 25	10:34		♌
-262	Jan 16	11:35	℞	♋
-262	May 24	3:04		♌
-262	Oct 23	9:19		♍
-261	Feb 18	23:13	℞	♌
-261	Jun 22	15:59		♍
-261	Nov 21	23:18		♎
-260	Mar 22	8:06	℞	♍
-260	Jul 21	10:09		♎
-260	Dec 17	22:26		♏
-259	Apr 29	21:42	℞	♎
-259	Aug 15	15:47		♏
-258	Jan 8	14:15		♐
-258	Jun 21	22:19	℞	♏
-258	Aug 29	13:08		♐
-257	Jan 24	23:29		♑
-256	Feb 6	14:14		♒
-255	Feb 16	0:03		♓
-254	Feb 25	11:47		♈
-254	Jul 30	2:44		♉
-254	Sep 10	17:03	℞	♈
-253	Mar 7	4:29		♉
-253	Jul 25	19:04		♊
-253	Nov 24	3:37	℞	♉
-252	Mar 17	6:42		♊
-252	Aug 10	4:41		♋
-251	Jan 16	9:60	℞	♊
-251	Mar 31	11:10		♋
-251	Sep 3	15:29		♌
-250	Mar 1	15:33	℞	♋
-250	Apr 20	14:33		♌
-250	Oct 2	11:18		♍
-249	Apr 5	20:35	℞	♌
-249	May 18	3:25		♍
-249	Nov 1	7:18		♎
-248	May 10	0:08	℞	♍
-248	Jun 13	10:24		♎
-248	Nov 27	20:08		♏
-247	Dec 20	17:48		♐
-245	Jan 7	11:03		♑
-244	Jan 20	19:01		♒
-243	Jan 29	21:05		♓
-242	Feb 6	11:52		♈
-242	Jun 23	4:13		♉
-242	Oct 30	0:04	℞	♈
-241	Feb 11	3:33		♉
-241	Jul 3	18:35		♊
-240	Jul 22	9:03		♋
-239	Aug 17	0:51		♌
-238	Sep 15	6:02		♍
-237	Oct 15	2:21		♎
-236	Nov 10	15:47		♏
-235	Dec 3	19:46		♐
-234	Dec 21	19:57		♑
-232	Jan 3	23:04		♒
-231	Jan 11	13:46		♓
-231	May 27	7:25		♈
-231	Sep 24	9:22	℞	♓
-230	Jan 14	8:07		♈
-230	Jun 1	7:34		♉
-229	Jun 15	14:52		♊
-228	Jul 5	13:48		♋
-227	Jul 31	18:59		♌
-226	Aug 30	4:27		♍
-225	Sep 29	0:24		♎
-224	Oct 25	12:18		♏
-223	Nov 17	15:07		♐
-222	Dec 5	9:27		♑
-221	Dec 17	10:13		♒
-220	May 3	21:43		♓
-220	Aug 13	7:31	℞	♒
-220	Dec 21	7:31		♓
-219	May 4	13:33		♈
-218	May 14	8:15		♉
-217	May 30	3:48		♊
-216	Jun 19	14:41		♋
-215	Jul 15	23:50		♌
-214	Aug 14	10:57		♍
-213	Sep 13	7:04		♎
-212	Oct 9	17:23		♏
-211	Nov 1	13:16		♐
-210	Nov 18	8:22		♑
-209	Apr 10	17:57		♒
-209	Jul 3	18:53	℞	♑
-209	Nov 27	10:23		♒
-208	Apr 8	19:38		♓
-208	Oct 1	16:18	℞	♒
-208	Nov 16	14:20		♓
-207	Apr 15	20:10		♈
-206	Apr 27	9:16		♉
-205	May 13	14:03		♊
-204	Jun 2	23:40		♋
-203	Jun 29	9:09		♌
-202	Jul 29	2:05		♍
-201	Aug 28	5:21		♎
-200	Sep 24	17:04		♏
-199	Oct 16	23:03		♐
-198	Mar 13	9:25		♑
-198	May 30	15:14	℞	♐
-198	Oct 31	14:49		♑
-197	Mar 16	1:30		♒
-197	Aug 18	6:33	℞	♑
-197	Nov 1	2:36		♒
-196	Mar 21	20:37		♓
-195	Mar 30	22:21		♈
-194	Apr 11	18:08		♉
-193	Apr 27	11:05		♊
-192	May 17	5:45		♋
-192	Oct 28	21:41		♌
-192	Dec 5	4:34	℞	♋
-191	Jun 12	8:43		♌
-191	Nov 22	4:43		♍
-190	Jan 10	13:21	℞	♌
-190	Jul 12	3:49		♍
-190	Dec 21	12:29		♎
-189	Feb 11	8:57	℞	♍
-189	Aug 11	7:55		♎
-188	Jan 15	3:58		♏
-188	Mar 21	6:27	℞	♎
-188	Sep 6	6:48		♏
-187	Jan 31	11:35		♐
-187	May 11	3:51	℞	♏
-187	Sep 26	14:43		♐
-186	Feb 13	4:30		♑
-186	Jul 15	10:38	℞	♐
-186	Oct 4	9:21		♑
-185	Feb 23	14:18		♒
-184	Mar 4	3:02		♓
-183	Mar 13	22:54		♈
-182	Mar 25	8:13		♉
-182	Aug 29	9:12		♊
-182	Oct 10	9:53	℞	♉
-181	Apr 8	19:14		♊
-181	Sep 2	16:56		♋
-181	Dec 10	9:10	℞	♊
-180	Apr 27	2:16		♋
-180	Sep 23	12:58		♌
-179	Jan 19	17:43	℞	♋
-179	May 22	6:36		♌
-179	Oct 21	15:23		♍
-178	Feb 22	2:30	℞	♌
-178	Jun 20	19:54		♍
-178	Nov 20	7:58		♎
-177	Mar 26	9:24	℞	♍
-177	Jul 20	15:30		♎
-177	Dec 17	10:56		♏
-176	May 2	22:25	℞	♎
-176	Aug 13	18:49		♏
-175	Jan 7	8:25		♐
-175	Jun 25	17:10	℞	♏
-175	Aug 26	17:28		♐
-174	Jan 23	23:06		♑
-173	Feb 5	17:44		♒
-172	Feb 16	5:13		♓
-171	Feb 24	16:20		♈
-171	Jul 26	21:39		♉
-171	Sep 14	15:40	℞	♈
-170	Mar 6	5:23		♉
-170	Jul 24	13:25		♊
-170	Nov 26	11:51	℞	♉
-169	Mar 16	22:03		♊
-169	Aug 10	3:04		♋
-168	Jan 20	10:04	℞	♊
-168	Mar 29	5:07		♋
-168	Sep 2	13:23		♌
-167	Mar 6	6:24	℞	♋
-167	Apr 16	16:31		♌
-167	Oct 1	6:59		♍
-166	Apr 12	1:56	℞	♌
-166	May 12	15:34		♍
-166	Oct 31	0:45		♎
-165	May 20	11:21	℞	♍
-165	Jun 5	18:19		♎
-165	Nov 27	13:06		♏
-164	Dec 19	13:37		♐
-162	Jan 6	12:53		♑
-161	Jan 20	4:08		♒
-160	Jan 30	12:29		♓
-160	Jul 15	9:25		♈
-160	Jul 25	16:12	℞	♓
-159	Feb 6	6:34		♈
-159	Jun 22	21:07		♉
-159	Oct 30	21:29	℞	♈
-158	Feb 10	18:12		♉
-158	Jul 3	10:07		♊
-157	Jul 22	18:50		♋
-156	Aug 16	3:44		♌
-155	Sep 14	3:23		♍
-154	Oct 13	21:35		♎
-153	Nov 10	13:50		♏
-152	Dec 3	0:32		♐
-151	Dec 21	8:55		♑
-149	Jan 3	19:19		♒
-148	Jan 12	14:36		♓
-148	May 27	7:47		♈
-148	Sep 24	16:15	℞	♓
-147	Jan 14	8:05		♈
-147	Jun 1	4:21		♉
-146	Jun 15	4:15		♊
-145	Jul 5	17:58		♋
-144	Jul 30	15:47		♌
-143	Aug 29	0:03		♍
-142	Sep 28	2:04		♎
-141	Oct 26	1:45		♏
-140	Nov 17	17:47		♐
-139	Dec 5	22:09		♑
-138	Dec 18	3:46		♒
-137	May 5	21:48		♓
-137	Aug 13	5:17	℞	♒
-137	Dec 23	0:18		♓
-136	May 4	19:45		♈
-135	May 14	0:32		♉
-134	May 29	7:03		♊
-133	Jun 19	7:40		♋
-132	Jul 14	12:31		♌
-131	Aug 13	3:00		♍
-130	Sep 12	8:28		♎
-129	Oct 10	6:54		♏
-128	Nov 1	14:13		♐
-127	Nov 18	16:54		♑
-126	Apr 11	10:35		♒
-126	Jul 3	2:04	℞	♑
-126	Nov 27	21:27		♒
-125	Apr 10	1:59		♓
-125	Oct 2	14:11	℞	♒
-125	Nov 17	20:33		♓
-124	Apr 15	17:28		♈
-123	Apr 26	21:60		♉
-122	May 12	19:40		♊
-121	Jun 3	0:56		♋
-120	Jun 28	9:08		♌
-119	Jul 28	2:57		♍
-118	Aug 27	7:44		♎
-117	Sep 23	20:26		♏
-116	Oct 15	2:32		♐
-115	Mar 10	14:40		♑
-115	Jun 1	4:57	℞	♐
-115	Oct 29	15:51		♑
-114	Mar 14	2:55		♒
-114	Aug 19	19:36	℞	♑
-114	Oct 29	8:40		♒
-113	Mar 21	4:01		♓
-112	Mar 29	8:02		♈
-111	Apr 10	4:04		♉
-110	Apr 25	19:50		♊
-109	May 16	12:15		♋
-109	Oct 25	21:47		♌
-109	Dec 8	20:50	℞	♋
-108	Jun 10	12:39		♌
-108	Nov 18	16:16		♍
-107	Jan 12	19:56	℞	♌
-107	Jul 10	5:18		♍
-107	Dec 17	20:27		♎
-106	Feb 13	20:32	℞	♍
-106	Aug 9	7:23		♎
-105	Jan 11	20:28		♏
-105	Mar 24	11:02	℞	♎
-105	Sep 5	4:17		♏
-104	Jan 29	21:13		♐
-104	May 12	18:13	℞	♏
-104	Sep 24	9:48		♐
-103	Feb 11	4:35		♑
-103	Jul 16	23:06	℞	♐
-103	Oct 1	18:09		♑
-102	Feb 22	1:11		♒
-101	Mar 3	21:51		♓
-100	Mar 13	22:29		♈
-99	Mar 25	8:14		♉
-99	Aug 28	18:43		♊
-99	Oct 11	10:03	℞	♉
-98	Apr 8	14:36		♊
-98	Sep 2	2:28		♋
-98	Dec 11	15:55	℞	♊
-97	Apr 27	11:21		♋
-97	Sep 23	14:17		♌
-96	Jan 22	16:26	℞	♋
-96	May 21	2:39		♌
-96	Oct 20	8:42		♍
-95	Feb 24	14:55	℞	♌
-95	Jun 19	6:27		♍
-95	Nov 18	21:17		♎
-94	Mar 29	4:10	℞	♍
-94	Jul 18	22:25		♎
-94	Dec 16	3:56		♏
-93	May 6	14:36	℞	♎
-93	Aug 13	2:22		♏

Jupiter Ingresses –500 (501 BC)—2100

Year	Date	Time		Sign
-92	Jan 7	11:40		♐
-92	Jun 28	9:37	℞	♏
-92	Aug 24	18:04		♐
-91	Jan 23	13:59		♑
-90	Feb 5	17:58		♒
-89	Feb 16	11:30		♓
-88	Feb 26	0:33		♈
-88	Jul 27	11:44		♉
-88	Sep 14	6:45	℞	♈
-87	Mar 6	10:04		♉
-87	Jul 24	10:53		♊
-87	Nov 27	3:45	℞	♉
-86	Mar 16	14:30		♊
-86	Aug 9	13:44		♋
-85	Jan 22	14:02	℞	♊
-85	Mar 28	13:57		♋
-85	Sep 2	14:35		♌
-84	Mar 11	16:08	℞	♋
-84	Apr 11	22:45		♌
-84	Sep 30	4:02		♍
-83	Apr 22	2:49	℞	♌
-83	May 3	9:00		♍
-83	Oct 30	1:38		♎
-82	Nov 27	1:38		♏
-81	Dec 20	17:07		♐
-79	Jan 7	4:09		♑
-78	Jan 21	1:09		♒
-77	Jan 31	9:12		♓
-76	Feb 7	20:25		♈
-76	Jun 23	0:54		♉
-76	Oct 31	4:22	℞	♈
-75	Feb 10	15:12		♉
-75	Jul 2	21:33		♊
-74	Jul 21	18:55		♋
-73	Aug 15	22:05		♌
-72	Sep 12	23:16		♍
-71	Oct 13	1:51		♎
-70	Nov 10	6:29		♏
-69	Dec 4	5:49		♐
-68	Dec 21	23:11		♑
-66	Jan 4	13:09		♒
-65	Jan 13	6:36		♓
-65	May 28	20:24		♈
-65	Sep 25	7:22	℞	♓
-64	Jan 15	16:26		♈
-64	Jun 1	3:09		♉
-63	Jun 14	18:35		♊
-62	Jul 5	3:28		♋
-61	Jul 30	23:49		♌
-60	Aug 28	8:49		♍
-59	Sep 27	12:31		♎
-58	Oct 25	13:44		♏
-57	Nov 18	7:07		♐
-56	Dec 5	12:23		♑
-55	Dec 17	17:59		♒
-54	May 5	3:22		♓
-54	Aug 14	13:22	℞	♒
-54	Dec 22	11:37		♓
-53	May 5	9:42		♈
-52	May 13	16:43		♉
-51	May 28	23:48		♊
-50	Jun 19	0:16		♋
-49	Jul 15	4:21		♌
-48	Aug 12	17:34		♍
-47	Sep 11	21:40		♎
-46	Oct 9	18:50		♏
-45	Nov 2	1:42		♐
-44	Nov 18	5:43		♑
-43	Apr 10	14:40		♒
-43	Jul 4	8:28	℞	♑
-43	Nov 27	13:13		♒
-42	Apr 9	22:44		♓
-42	Oct 3	6:46	℞	♒
-42	Nov 17	12:53		♓
-41	Apr 16	20:27		♈
-40	Apr 27	2:29		♉
-39	May 12	21:50		♊
-38	Jun 2	21:25		♋
-37	Jun 28	22:28		♌
-36	Jul 27	10:34		♍
-35	Aug 26	13:18		♎
-34	Sep 23	4:25		♏
-33	Oct 15	16:44		♐
-32	Mar 10	4:49		♑
-32	Jun 1	20:13	℞	♐
-32	Oct 29	15:11		♑
-31	Mar 14	9:22		♒
-31	Aug 19	7:10	℞	♑
-31	Oct 30	1:17		♒
-30	Mar 21	17:07		♓
-29	Mar 30	23:08		♈
-28	Apr 10	16:46		♉
-27	Apr 26	1:29		♊
-26	May 16	6:40		♋
-26	Oct 23	23:30		♌
-26	Dec 11	11:28	℞	♋
-25	Jun 10	19:07		♌
-25	Nov 17	8:54		♍
-24	Jan 16	22:20	℞	♌
-24	Jul 9	5:52		♍
-24	Dec 15	16:13		♎
-23	Feb 16	17:12	℞	♍
-23	Aug 8	11:29		♎
-22	Jan 10	19:27		♏
-22	Mar 25	21:55	℞	♎
-22	Sep 4	20:37		♏
-21	Jan 30	2:17		♐
-21	May 13	11:17	℞	♏
-21	Sep 25	20:41		♐
-20	Feb 13	2:37		♑
-20	Jul 14	21:21	℞	♐
-20	Oct 3	13:47		♑
-19	Feb 23	5:36		♒
-18	Mar 5	1:56		♓
-17	Mar 14	20:47		♈
-16	Mar 24	19:59		♉
-16	Aug 27	18:58		♊
-16	Oct 10	19:59	℞	♉
-15	Apr 7	11:23		♊
-15	Aug 31	6:08		♋
-15	Dec 12	7:15	℞	♊
-14	Apr 25	14:36		♋
-14	Sep 21	9:11		♌
-13	Jan 24	0:49	℞	♋
-13	May 19	16:50		♌
-13	Oct 19	2:54		♍
-12	Feb 27	0:41	℞	♌
-12	Jun 16	20:23		♍
-12	Nov 16	23:52		♎
-11	Mar 29	21:59	℞	♍
-11	Jul 17	0:36		♎
-11	Dec 14	21:57		♏
-10	May 6	4:28	℞	♎
-10	Aug 12	0:01		♏
-9	Jan 6	22:03		♐
-9	Jun 27	3:21	℞	♏
-9	Aug 26	2:11		♐
-8	Jan 24	11:11		♑
-7	Feb 5	19:01		♒
-6	Feb 16	10:39		♓
-5	Feb 25	17:27		♈
-5	Jul 28	16:49		♉
-5	Sep 13	6:31	℞	♈
-4	Mar 5	17:39		♉
-4	Jul 23	10:05		♊
-4	Nov 26	16:14	℞	♉
-3	Mar 15	9:13		♊
-3	Aug 8	5:22		♋
-2	Jan 23	0:23	℞	♊
-2	Mar 26	13:27		♋
-2	Sep 1	4:00		♌
-1	Mar 14	21:45	℞	♋
-1	Apr 9	3:33		♌
-1	Sep 29	18:21		♍
0	Oct 28	18:18		♎
1	Nov 25	20:47		♏
2	Dec 19	14:21		♐
4	Jan 7	2:55		♑
5	Jan 20	0:48		♒
6	Jan 30	9:09		♓
7	Feb 6	20:16		♈
7	Jun 22	23:33		♉
7	Oct 31	14:43	℞	♈
8	Feb 10	13:37		♉
8	Jul 1	21:02		♊
9	Jul 20	18:38		♋
10	Aug 14	21:33		♌
11	Sep 12	21:47		♍
12	Oct 11	22:57		♎
13	Nov 9	2:07		♏
14	Dec 3	0:33		♐
15	Dec 21	18:50		♑
17	Jan 3	11:56		♒
18	Jan 12	10:33		♓
18	May 28	5:33		♈
18	Sep 23	21:12	℞	♓
19	Jan 15	4:22		♈
19	Jun 1	13:29		♉
20	Jun 14	3:08		♊
21	Jul 4	7:43		♋
22	Jul 29	22:20		♌
23	Aug 28	2:20		♍
24	Sep 26	3:32		♎
25	Oct 24	6:11		♏
26	Nov 17	4:41		♐
27	Dec 5	17:36		♑
28	Dec 17	8:15		♒
29	May 5	9:38		♓
29	Aug 11	21:50	℞	♒
29	Dec 22	14:32		♓
30	May 5	10:16		♈
31	May 14	12:49		♉
32	May 28	13:00		♊
33	Jun 18	3:60		♋
34	Jul 13	22:01		♌
35	Aug 12	4:47		♍
36	Sep 10	9:30		♎
37	Oct 8	14:59		♏
38	Nov 1	11:27		♐
39	Nov 19	7:06		♑
40	Apr 12	8:33		♒
40	Jun 29	18:45	℞	♑
40	Nov 28	8:33		♒
41	Apr 10	18:59		♓
41	Sep 26	19:42	℞	♒
41	Nov 21	8:07		♓
42	Apr 17	6:29		♈
43	Apr 28	1:29		♉
44	May 12	8:02		♊
45	Jun 1	18:47		♋
46	Jun 27	10:29		♌
47	Jul 26	20:28		♍
48	Aug 25	4:47		♎
49	Sep 22	6:53		♏
50	Oct 15	9:16		♐
51	Mar 12	3:51		♑
51	May 30	7:27	℞	♐
51	Oct 30	23:54		♑
52	Mar 15	0:13		♒
52	Aug 14	19:13	℞	♑
52	Oct 31	21:30		♒
53	Mar 22	1:43		♓
54	Mar 30	23:53		♈
55	Apr 11	8:32		♉
56	Apr 25	8:19		♊
57	May 15	6:56		♋
57	Oct 22	13:27		♌
57	Dec 11	5:48	℞	♋
58	Jun 9	17:02		♌
58	Nov 16	3:10		♍
59	Jan 16	11:15	℞	♌
59	Jul 9	5:14		♍
59	Dec 15	17:02		♎
60	Feb 16	21:52	℞	♍
60	Aug 7	14:18		♎
61	Jan 10	2:18		♏
61	Mar 24	18:04	℞	♎
61	Sep 4	2:33		♏
62	Jan 29	11:23		♐
62	May 12	3:16	℞	♏
62	Sep 25	5:15		♐
63	Feb 12	11:30		♑
63	Jul 14	9:42	℞	♐
63	Oct 4	2:43		♑
64	Feb 23	13:30		♒
65	Mar 4	8:42		♓
66	Mar 14	2:53		♈
67	Mar 25	1:38		♉
67	Aug 28	7:04		♊
67	Oct 10	12:48	℞	♉
68	Apr 6	16:50		♊
68	Aug 30	12:56		♋
68	Dec 11	5:38	℞	♊
69	Apr 24	20:12		♋
69	Sep 20	15:19		♌
70	Jan 22	23:29	℞	♋
70	May 18	22:26		♌
70	Oct 18	8:17		♍
71	Feb 25	23:32	℞	♌
71	Jun 17	1:09		♍
71	Nov 17	4:03		♎
72	Mar 28	22:35	℞	♍
72	Jul 16	3:33		♎
72	Dec 14	0:26		♏
73	May 5	7:51	℞	♎
73	Aug 11	0:35		♏
74	Jan 5	22:57		♐
74	Jun 26	11:45	℞	♏
74	Aug 24	22:32		♐
75	Jan 23	12:06		♑
76	Feb 5	21:60		♒
77	Feb 15	17:33		♓
78	Feb 25	5:34		♈
78	Jul 29	15:12		♉
78	Sep 10	6:33	℞	♈
79	Mar 6	10:34		♉
79	Jul 24	5:40		♊
79	Nov 25	16:19	℞	♉
80	Mar 15	5:58		♊
80	Aug 7	18:26		♋
81	Jan 21	3:25	℞	♊
81	Mar 26	11:56		♋
81	Aug 31	10:43		♌
82	Mar 13	10:19	℞	♋
82	Apr 8	18:22		♌
82	Sep 28	19:14		♍
83	Oct 28	15:20		♎
84	Nov 24	17:49		♏
85	Dec 18	15:28		♐
87	Jan 6	10:37		♑
88	Jan 20	15:43		♒
89	Jan 30	7:07		♓
90	Feb 7	1:07		♈
90	Jun 23	10:19		♉
90	Oct 28	12:16	℞	♈
91	Feb 11	4:02		♉
91	Jul 2	19:00		♊
92	Jul 20	6:04		♋
93	Aug 13	22:45		♌
94	Sep 11	15:22		♍
95	Oct 11	15:02		♎
96	Nov 8	0:16		♏
97	Dec 2	10:49		♐
98	Dec 21	18:52		♑
100	Jan 4	23:51		♒
101	Jan 14	8:23		♓
101	May 30	21:55		♈
101	Sep 20	1:53	℞	♓
102	Jan 17	15:29		♈
102	Jun 3	2:58		♉
103	Jun 16	0:11		♊
104	Jul 4	14:45		♋
105	Jul 29	18:59		♌
106	Aug 27	18:33		♍
107	Sep 26	22:29		♎
108	Oct 24	9:30		♏
109	Nov 17	19:31		♐
110	Dec 6	20:01		♑
111	Dec 19	20:54		♒
112	May 8	4:37		♓
112	Aug 8	4:59	℞	♒
112	Dec 24	14:59		♓
113	May 7	0:12		♈
113	Nov 17	1:13	℞	♓
113	Dec 3	13:11		♈
114	May 15	13:26		♉
115	May 30	3:29		♊
116	Jun 18	11:51		♋
117	Jul 14	3:33		♌
118	Aug 12	11:38		♍
119	Sep 11	19:37		♎
120	Oct 9	3:56		♏
121	Nov 2	2:00		♐
122	Nov 19	22:26		♑
123	Apr 14	12:13		♒
123	Jun 29	12:24	℞	♑
123	Nov 30	0:50		♒
124	Apr 11	8:45		♓
124	Sep 25	16:20	℞	♒
124	Nov 22	11:31		♓
125	Apr 17	16:04		♈
126	Apr 28	8:58		♉
127	May 13	14:34		♊
128	Jun 2	1:26		♋
129	Jun 27	18:07		♌
130	Jul 27	4:53		♍
131	Aug 26	13:38		♎
132	Sep 22	15:32		♏
133	Oct 15	17:10		♐
134	Mar 12	15:34		♑
134	May 29	20:56	℞	♐
134	Oct 31	8:03		♑
135	Mar 16	8:57		♒
135	Aug 15	6:58	℞	♑
135	Nov 2	11:44		♒
136	Mar 22	11:43		♓
137	Mar 31	13:04		♈
138	Apr 12	0:31		♉
139	Apr 27	1:09		♊
140	May 15	21:34		♋
140	Oct 23	17:42		♌
140	Dec 10	5:50	℞	♋
141	Jun 10	2:26		♌
141	Nov 16	12:05		♍
142	Jan 16	9:12	℞	♌
142	Jul 9	8:30		♍
142	Dec 15	15:20		♎
143	Feb 17	7:36	℞	♍
143	Aug 8	13:25		♎
144	Jan 10	22:25		♏
144	Mar 25	5:09	℞	♎
144	Sep 4	1:38		♏
145	Jan 29	13:11		♐
145	May 12	5:13	℞	♏
145	Sep 25	8:53		♐

Jupiter Ingresses –500 (501 BC)—2100

Year	Date	Time	℞	Sign
146	Feb 12	20:44		♑
146	Jul 13	17:19	℞	♐
146	Oct 4	20:13		♑
147	Feb 24	5:15		♒
148	Mar 5	5:50		♓
149	Mar 15	3:51		♈
150	Mar 26	4:15		♉
150	Sep 1	3:04		♊
150	Oct 6	13:45	℞	♉
151	Apr 8	17:46		♊
151	Sep 1	15:07		♋
151	Dec 11	2:14	℞	♊
152	Apr 25	14:09		♋
152	Sep 21	1:04		♌
153	Jan 22	18:27	℞	♋
153	May 19	3:59		♌
153	Oct 18	6:52		♍
154	Feb 26	12:42	℞	♌
154	Jun 16	18:59		♍
154	Nov 16	21:44		♎
155	Mar 30	17:35	℞	♍
155	Jul 16	18:41		♎
155	Dec 14	22:46		♏
156	May 5	15:16	℞	♎
156	Aug 11	1:16		♏
157	Jan 6	9:58		♐
157	Jun 25	3:51	℞	♏
157	Aug 26	7:53		♐
158	Jan 24	12:58		♑
159	Feb 7	9:08		♒
160	Feb 18	10:30		♓
161	Feb 27	0:12		♈
161	Aug 5	23:24		♉
161	Sep 2	12:20	℞	♈
162	Mar 8	3:19		♉
162	Jul 25	20:17		♊
162	Nov 23	15:07	℞	♉
163	Mar 17	16:17		♊
163	Aug 9	10:02		♋
164	Jan 21	6:01	℞	♊
164	Mar 27	7:56		♋
164	Aug 31	12:16		♌
165	Mar 14	12:27	℞	♋
165	Apr 7	21:00		♌
165	Sep 28	13:35		♍
166	Oct 28	10:21		♎
167	Nov 25	20:35		♏
168	Dec 19	5:51		♐
170	Jan 7	12:14		♑
171	Jan 22	1:23		♒
172	Feb 1	21:12		♓
173	Feb 8	16:58		♈
173	Jun 25	5:57		♉
173	Oct 25	23:20	℞	♈
174	Feb 12	23:05		♉
174	Jul 3	18:20		♊
175	Jul 21	19:30		♋
176	Aug 14	8:25		♌
177	Sep 12	1:52		♍
178	Oct 12	4:56		♎
179	Nov 9	17:24		♏
180	Dec 3	5:12		♐
181	Dec 22	12:38		♑
183	Jan 5	15:51		♒
184	Jan 14	22:13		♓
184	May 30	13:19		♈
184	Sep 18	9:38	℞	♓
185	Jan 17	4:50		♈
185	Jun 2	11:11		♉
186	Jun 15	6:10		♊
187	Jul 4	20:50		♋
188	Jul 29	2:55		♌
189	Aug 27	4:49		♍
190	Sep 26	10:35		♎
191	Oct 24	22:30		♏
192	Nov 17	7:49		♐
193	Dec 6	7:01		♑
194	Dec 19	7:43		♒
195	May 8	22:26		♓
195	Aug 7	9:44	℞	♒
195	Dec 25	5:12		♓
196	May 6	14:06		♈
196	Nov 12	9:55	℞	♓
196	Dec 6	5:59		♈
197	May 15	3:51		♉
198	May 29	17:48		♊
199	Jun 19	0:04		♋
200	Jul 14	11:48		♌
201	Aug 12	15:23		♍
202	Sep 11	19:58		♎
203	Oct 10	3:45		♏
204	Nov 2	4:27		♐
205	Nov 20	6:47		♑
206	Apr 15	14:44		♒
206	Jun 28	3:60	℞	♑
206	Nov 30	19:15		♒
207	Apr 13	8:16		♓
207	Sep 24	3:56	℞	♒
207	Nov 25	18:20		♓
208	Apr 18	16:41		♈
209	Apr 29	9:37		♉
210	May 14	12:44		♊
211	Jun 3	17:49		♋
212	Jun 28	2:18		♌
213	Jul 27	5:18		♍
214	Aug 26	10:16		♎
215	Sep 23	15:21		♏
216	Oct 16	3:20		♐
217	Mar 14	5:39		♑
217	May 27	20:19	℞	♐
217	Nov 1	11:26		♑
218	Mar 18	0:27		♒
218	Aug 11	19:41	℞	♑
218	Nov 5	7:12		♒
219	Mar 25	4:26		♓
220	Apr 2	3:57		♈
221	Apr 13	10:20		♉
222	Apr 28	1:58		♊
223	May 17	10:11		♋
223	Oct 25	1:34		♌
223	Dec 11	5:58	℞	♋
224	Jun 10	2:59		♌
224	Nov 15	23:13		♍
225	Jan 17	8:25	℞	♌
225	Jul 9	2:12		♍
225	Dec 14	23:50		♎
226	Feb 18	7:51	℞	♍
226	Aug 8	8:34		♎
227	Jan 10	21:22		♏
227	Mar 26	9:32	℞	♎
227	Sep 5	5:43		♏
228	Jan 31	6:46		♐
228	May 11	4:49	℞	♏
228	Sep 26	4:42		♐
229	Feb 14	2:21		♑
229	Jul 11	3:19	℞	♐
229	Oct 6	23:59		♑
230	Feb 25	16:49		♒
231	Mar 7	18:42		♓
232	Mar 16	14:23		♈
233	Mar 27	9:38		♉
233	Sep 5	15:58		♊
233	Oct 1	23:59	℞	♉
234	Apr 9	15:48		♊
234	Sep 2	12:58		♋
234	Dec 10	5:25	℞	♊
235	Apr 27	5:05		♋
235	Sep 22	13:03		♌
236	Jan 23	7:42	℞	♋
236	May 19	15:50		♌
236	Oct 18	18:42		♍
237	Feb 25	22:41	℞	♌
237	Jun 17	9:41		♍
237	Nov 17	14:33		♎
238	Mar 29	17:20	℞	♍
238	Jul 17	16:16		♎
238	Dec 15	20:50		♏
239	May 5	2:16	℞	♎
239	Aug 13	7:45		♏
240	Jan 8	9:29		♐
240	Jun 22	19:14	℞	♏
240	Aug 28	9:07		♐
241	Jan 25	10:12		♑
242	Feb 8	2:17		♒
243	Feb 18	23:03		♓
244	Feb 28	8:46		♈
244	Aug 6	23:31		♉
244	Sep 1	16:15	℞	♈
245	Mar 8	8:48		♉
245	Jul 26	0:13		♊
245	Nov 23	16:24	℞	♉
246	Mar 17	20:12		♊
246	Aug 9	13:44		♋
247	Jan 21	4:48	℞	♊
247	Mar 28	15:03		♋
247	Sep 1	18:46		♌
248	Mar 13	7:51	℞	♋
248	Apr 9	5:50		♌
248	Sep 29	0:08		♍
249	Oct 29	0:31		♎
250	Nov 26	12:46		♏
251	Dec 20	21:08		♐
253	Jan 8	0:34		♑
254	Jan 22	10:45		♒
255	Feb 2	5:07		♓
256	Feb 10	1:55		♈
256	Jun 25	17:29		♉
256	Oct 25	11:22	℞	♈
257	Feb 13	12:09		♉
257	Jul 4	4:15		♊
258	Jan 24	2:31	℞	♉
258	Jan 25	18:34		♊
258	Jul 22	3:35		♋
259	Aug 15	13:26		♌
260	Sep 12	3:29		♍
261	Oct 12	3:41		♎
262	Nov 9	15:26		♏
263	Dec 4	5:19		♐
264	Dec 22	17:10		♑
266	Jan 6	2:25		♒
267	Jan 15	16:23		♓
267	Jun 1	20:48		♈
267	Sep 17	15:16	℞	♓
268	Jan 19	10:53		♈
268	Jun 3	11:46		♉
269	Jun 16	2:40		♊
270	Jul 5	11:34		♋
271	Jul 30	10:17		♌
272	Aug 27	4:53		♍
273	Sep 26	5:53		♎
274	Oct 24	18:17		♏
275	Nov 18	10:15		♐
276	Dec 6	20:22		♑
277	Dec 20	10:14		♒
278	May 11	12:11		♓
278	Aug 4	0:30	℞	♒
278	Dec 27	0:48		♓
279	May 9	7:14		♈
279	Nov 5	14:47	℞	♓
279	Dec 14	12:11		♈
280	May 16	12:00		♉
281	May 30	16:20		♊
282	Jun 19	11:35		♋
283	Jul 14	13:10		♌
284	Aug 11	10:36		♍
285	Sep 10	15:01		♎
286	Oct 9	4:18		♏
287	Nov 2	14:45		♐
288	Nov 20	5:02		♑
289	Apr 17	7:57		♒
289	Jun 23	20:00	℞	♑
289	Dec 1	8:16		♒
290	Apr 14	1:39		♓
290	Sep 19	4:18	℞	♒
290	Nov 28	2:59		♓
291	Apr 20	1:41		♈
292	Apr 29	10:24		♉
293	May 14	4:17		♊
294	Jun 3	1:17		♋
295	Jun 28	5:53		♌
296	Jul 26	10:23		♍
297	Aug 25	20:48		♎
298	Sep 23	7:55		♏
299	Oct 17	0:19		♐
300	Mar 16	1:31		♑
300	May 25	16:27	℞	♐
300	Nov 2	11:16		♑
301	Mar 18	23:14		♒
301	Aug 10	6:19	℞	♑
301	Nov 6	13:02		♒
302	Mar 25	17:32		♓
303	Apr 3	10:22		♈
304	Apr 13	11:41		♉
305	Apr 28	0:09		♊
306	May 17	7:56		♋
306	Oct 24	19:17		♌
306	Dec 11	19:25	℞	♋
307	Jun 11	3:51		♌
307	Nov 17	6:07		♍
308	Jan 18	5:53	℞	♌
308	Jul 9	8:25		♍
308	Dec 15	18:30		♎
309	Feb 17	14:58	℞	♍
309	Aug 8	19:57		♎
310	Jan 11	21:48		♏
310	Mar 25	7:51	℞	♎
310	Sep 5	20:38		♏
311	Feb 1	3:26		♐
311	May 11	5:02	℞	♏
311	Sep 27	20:37		♐
312	Feb 15	15:49		♑
312	Jul 10	9:30	℞	♐
312	Oct 7	15:45		♑
313	Feb 25	23:58		♒
314	Mar 7	21:43		♓
315	Mar 17	15:31		♈
316	Mar 27	10:29		♉
316	Sep 5	9:58		♊
316	Oct 2	11:55	℞	♉
317	Apr 9	16:46		♊
317	Sep 2	12:46		♋
317	Dec 10	12:52	℞	♊
318	Apr 27	4:47		♋
318	Sep 22	11:16		♌
319	Jan 23	18:41	℞	♋
319	May 20	12:13		♌
319	Oct 19	14:15		♍
320	Feb 27	15:07	℞	♌
320	Jun 17	1:59		♍
320	Nov 17	7:13		♎
321	Mar 30	14:37	℞	♍
321	Jul 17	5:19		♎
321	Dec 15	12:45		♏
322	May 6	1:21	℞	♎
322	Aug 12	19:22		♏
323	Jan 8	3:57		♐
323	Jun 24	18:11	℞	♏
323	Aug 28	19:15		♐
324	Jan 26	9:19		♑
325	Feb 8	6:37		♒
326	Feb 19	8:25		♓
327	Feb 28	22:22		♈
327	Aug 12	3:23		♉
327	Aug 29	12:31	℞	♈
328	Mar 9	1:36		♉
328	Jul 26	19:36		♊
328	Nov 22	18:40	℞	♉
329	Mar 18	14:48		♊
329	Aug 10	0:49		♋
330	Jan 20	15:09	℞	♊
330	Mar 29	6:31		♋
330	Sep 1	21:50		♌
331	Mar 14	21:26	℞	♋
331	Apr 9	20:33		♌
331	Sep 29	19:19		♍
332	Oct 28	13:49		♎
333	Nov 26	0:57		♏
334	Dec 20	14:58		♐
336	Jan 9	4:31		♑
337	Jan 23	1:40		♒
338	Feb 3	5:14		♓
339	Feb 11	8:55		♈
339	Jun 28	8:54		♉
339	Oct 24	5:08	℞	♈
340	Feb 16	2:25		♉
340	Jul 5	2:56		♊
341	Jan 14	13:16	℞	♉
341	Feb 4	5:56		♊
341	Jul 22	13:54		♋
342	Aug 15	13:13		♌
343	Sep 12	20:15		♍
344	Oct 11	18:45		♎
345	Nov 9	10:16		♏
346	Dec 4	8:06		♐
347	Dec 24	5:20		♑
349	Jan 6	23:02		♒
350	Jan 16	19:36		♓
350	Jun 3	14:14		♈
350	Sep 15	9:36	℞	♓
351	Jan 20	20:28		♈
351	Jun 5	9:59		♉
352	Jun 16	13:09		♊
353	Jul 5	13:01		♋
354	Jul 30	7:24		♌
355	Aug 28	3:18		♍
356	Sep 26	10:10		♎
357	Oct 25	5:44		♏
358	Nov 19	2:45		♐
359	Dec 8	14:25		♑
360	Dec 21	2:31		♒
361	May 12	9:10		♓
361	Aug 3	4:24	℞	♒
361	Dec 27	12:09		♓
362	May 9	11:02		♈
362	Nov 5	22:52	℞	♓
362	Dec 14	9:27		♈
363	May 17	8:04		♉
364	May 30	7:44		♊
365	Jun 19	1:28		♋
366	Jul 14	5:08		♌
367	Aug 12	7:30		♍
368	Sep 10	17:33		♎
369	Oct 9	11:16		♏
370	Nov 2	23:17		♐
371	Nov 21	11:47		♑
372	Apr 17	12:28		♒
372	Jun 23	20:02	℞	♑
372	Dec 1	10:04		♒
373	Apr 13	22:37		♓
373	Sep 19	22:30	℞	♒
373	Nov 27	16:43		♓
374	Apr 19	19:48		♈
375	Apr 30	3:24		♉
376	May 13	21:16		♊
377	Jun 2	17:58		♋

Jupiter Ingresses –500 (501 BC)—2100

Year	Date	Time	℞	Sign
378	Jun 27	21:29		♌
379	Jul 27	0:36		♍
380	Aug 25	9:38		♎
381	Sep 22	20:27		♏
382	Oct 16	13:45		♐
383	Mar 15	2:17		♑
383	May 27	2:40	℞	♐
383	Nov 2	2:20		♑
384	Mar 17	16:29		♒
384	Aug 10	1:30	℞	♑
384	Nov 5	5:02		♒
385	Mar 24	17:25		♓
386	Apr 2	13:44		♈
387	Apr 13	16:17		♉
388	Apr 27	3:43		♊
389	May 16	7:15		♋
389	Oct 23	1:01		♌
389	Dec 12	0:52	℞	♋
390	Jun 9	20:01		♌
390	Nov 15	0:51		♍
391	Jan 19	2:01	℞	♌
391	Jul 8	17:05		♍
391	Dec 14	0:53		♎
392	Feb 20	1:26	℞	♍
392	Aug 6	23:15		♎
393	Jan 9	4:04		♏
393	Mar 26	19:28	℞	♎
393	Sep 3	22:54		♏
394	Jan 30	1:17		♐
394	May 11	22:43	℞	♏
394	Sep 26	3:39		♐
395	Feb 14	7:35		♑
395	Jul 11	3:17	℞	♐
395	Oct 7	9:23		♑
396	Feb 26	5:35		♒
397	Mar 7	12:21		♓
398	Mar 17	10:18		♈
399	Mar 28	5:03		♉
399	Sep 8	23:12		♊
399	Sep 29	1:21	℞	♉
400	Apr 9	5:59		♊
400	Sep 1	20:10		♋
400	Dec 9	13:42	℞	♊
401	Apr 26	6:33		♋
401	Sep 21	3:34		♌
402	Jan 23	19:09	℞	♋
402	May 18	22:37		♌
402	Oct 17	20:27		♍
403	Feb 28	8:40	℞	♌
403	Jun 16	0:16		♍
403	Nov 16	9:22		♎
404	Mar 31	14:10	℞	♍
404	Jul 15	0:19		♎
404	Dec 13	18:16		♏
405	May 6	19:04	℞	♎
405	Aug 10	18:47		♏
406	Jan 6	19:15		♐
406	Jun 24	21:18	℞	♏
406	Aug 27	3:14		♐
407	Jan 25	11:44		♑
408	Feb 8	17:33		♒
409	Feb 18	23:58		♓
410	Feb 28	14:14		♈
410	Aug 18	23:00		♉
410	Aug 20	14:33	℞	♈
411	Mar 9	13:10		♉
411	Jul 27	1:02		♊
411	Nov 22	21:03	℞	♉
412	Mar 17	15:33		♊
412	Aug 8	18:44		♋
413	Jan 20	20:43	℞	♊
413	Mar 27	9:40		♋
413	Aug 31	10:28		♌
414	Mar 18	10:14	℞	♋
414	Apr 4	18:51		♌
414	Sep 28	9:06		♍
415	Oct 28	10:26		♎
416	Nov 25	7:01		♏
417	Dec 20	4:10		♐
419	Jan 8	19:54		♑
420	Jan 23	14:22		♒
421	Feb 2	11:29		♓
422	Feb 10	5:25		♈
422	Jun 26	16:37		♉
422	Oct 24	17:57	℞	♈
423	Feb 14	6:08		♉
423	Jul 4	6:49		♊
424	Jul 20	16:19		♋
425	Aug 13	17:43		♌
426	Sep 11	6:28		♍
427	Oct 11	12:13		♎
428	Nov 8	10:26		♏
429	Dec 3	12:06		♐
430	Dec 23	9:01		♑
432	Jan 6	22:43		♒
433	Jan 15	12:50		♓
433	Jun 1	18:06		♈
433	Sep 15	22:46	℞	♓
434	Jan 19	3:13		♈
434	Jun 3	17:11		♉
435	Jun 15	21:27		♊
436	Jul 3	22:06		♋
437	Jul 28	16:25		♌
438	Aug 26	11:51		♍
439	Sep 25	17:57		♎
440	Oct 23	13:10		♏
441	Nov 17	10:57		♐
442	Dec 7	0:13		♑
443	Dec 20	14:05		♒
444	May 10	9:01		♓
444	Aug 3	16:23	℞	♒
444	Dec 26	0:19		♓
445	May 8	2:06		♈
445	Nov 6	22:45	℞	♓
445	Dec 11	21:31		♈
446	May 16	2:29		♉
447	May 30	2:19		♊
448	Jun 17	17:38		♋
449	Jul 12	16:57		♌
450	Aug 10	14:37		♍
451	Sep 9	21:02		♎
452	Oct 7	13:40		♏
453	Nov 1	4:57		♐
454	Nov 20	0:35		♑
455	Apr 16	20:56		♒
455	Jun 24	17:52	℞	♑
455	Dec 1	8:34		♒
456	Apr 13	3:59		♓
456	Sep 18	13:38	℞	♒
456	Nov 27	6:24		♓
457	Apr 19	6:05		♈
458	Apr 29	12:59		♉
459	May 14	1:31		♊
460	Jun 1	13:16		♋
461	Jun 26	6:35		♌
462	Jul 25	2:07		♍
463	Aug 24	8:58		♎
464	Sep 20	22:48		♏
465	Oct 14	23:11		♐
466	Mar 13	6:38		♑
466	May 27	5:41	℞	♐
466	Oct 31	21:11		♑
467	Mar 17	18:10		♒
467	Aug 10	0:30	℞	♑
467	Nov 5	11:40		♒
468	Mar 24	1:41		♓
469	Apr 1	22:27		♈
470	Apr 12	20:44		♉
471	Apr 26	23:38		♊
472	May 14	16:51		♋
472	Oct 19	16:51		♌
472	Dec 14	2:36	℞	♋
473	Jun 7	22:44		♌
473	Nov 12	3:56		♍
474	Jan 20	15:47	℞	♌
474	Jul 6	20:55		♍
474	Dec 11	18:21		♎
475	Feb 20	20:52	℞	♍
475	Aug 6	11:43		♎
476	Jan 8	19:36		♏
476	Mar 26	10:09	℞	♎
476	Sep 2	22:54		♏
477	Jan 29	9:49		♐
477	May 10	13:52	℞	♏
477	Sep 25	13:52		♐
478	Feb 13	20:56		♑
478	Jul 9	6:54	℞	♐
478	Oct 7	4:16		♑
479	Feb 25	15:49		♒
480	Mar 6	15:24		♓
481	Mar 16	3:55		♈
482	Mar 26	11:08		♉
482	Sep 1	6:01		♊
482	Oct 5	14:46	℞	♉
483	Apr 7	23:15		♊
483	Aug 30	17:04		♋
483	Dec 12	21:44	℞	♊
484	Apr 23	12:21		♋
484	Sep 18	9:49		♌
485	Jan 25	22:38	℞	♋
485	May 16	0:11		♌
485	Oct 15	11:55		♍
486	Mar 1	23:01	℞	♌
486	Jun 13	9:48		♍
486	Nov 14	12:06		♎
487	Apr 2	8:30	℞	♍
487	Jul 14	0:24		♎
487	Dec 13	8:53		♏
488	May 6	17:10	℞	♎
488	Aug 9	8:05		♏
489	Jan 5	18:16		♐
489	Jun 24	6:30	℞	♏
489	Aug 26	0:02		♐
490	Jan 24	13:00		♑
491	Feb 7	15:46		♒
492	Feb 18	16:21		♓
493	Feb 26	23:25		♈
493	Aug 6	9:33		♉
493	Sep 1	1:26	℞	♈
494	Mar 7	13:21		♉
494	Jul 24	13:50		♊
494	Nov 24	13:17	℞	♉
495	Mar 16	2:50		♊
495	Aug 7	14:03		♋
496	Jan 24	12:24	℞	♊
496	Mar 23	14:12		♋
496	Aug 29	7:50		♌
497	Sep 26	6:48		♍
498	Oct 26	7:53		♎
499	Nov 24	4:30		♏
500	Dec 19	3:23		♐
502	Jan 7	22:10		♑
503	Jan 22	19:54		♒
504	Feb 2	19:29		♓
505	Feb 9	13:40		♈
505	Jun 25	19:05		♉
505	Oct 26	10:37	℞	♈
506	Feb 13	9:02		♉
506	Jul 3	15:42		♊
507	Jul 21	1:24		♋
508	Aug 13	0:17		♌
509	Sep 10	9:17		♍
510	Oct 10	11:41		♎
511	Nov 8	8:16		♏
512	Dec 2	12:08		♐
513	Dec 22	15:13		♑
515	Jan 6	12:55		♒
516	Jan 16	10:20		♓
516	Jun 1	17:41		♈
516	Sep 16	4:47	℞	♓
517	Jan 19	4:50		♈
517	Jun 3	18:33		♉
518	Jun 15	18:28		♊
519	Jul 4	11:37		♋
520	Jul 27	21:29		♌
521	Aug 25	10:16		♍
522	Sep 24	14:12		♎
523	Oct 23	12:03		♏
524	Nov 16	16:24		♐
525	Dec 6	14:14		♑
526	Dec 20	12:09		♒
527	May 11	9:42		♓
527	Aug 4	19:37	℞	♒
527	Dec 27	3:56		♓
528	May 8	5:50		♈
528	Nov 6	22:22	℞	♓
528	Dec 12	3:13		♈
529	May 16	2:33		♉
530	May 29	18:39		♊
531	Jun 18	0:49		♋
532	Jul 11	17:35		♌
533	Aug 9	14:49		♍
534	Sep 9	3:25		♎
535	Oct 8	5:57		♏
536	Nov 1	6:26		♐
537	Nov 20	7:26		♑
538	Apr 17	9:18		♒
538	Jun 24	6:56	℞	♑
538	Dec 1	15:02		♒
539	Apr 14	4:48		♓
539	Sep 20	1:14	℞	♒
539	Nov 28	0:23		♓
540	Apr 18	21:23		♈
541	Apr 28	17:51		♉
542	May 12	20:25		♊
543	Jun 1	1:19		♋
544	Jun 24	17:41		♌
545	Jul 23	19:01		♍
546	Aug 23	11:55		♎
547	Sep 21	12:14		♏
548	Oct 14	19:54		♐
549	Mar 13	0:24		♑
549	May 27	18:58	℞	♐
549	Oct 31	19:31		♑
550	Mar 17	13:18		♒
550	Aug 10	21:13	℞	♑
550	Nov 5	0:06		♒
551	Mar 24	15:39		♓
552	Apr 1	5:45		♈
553	Apr 11	20:59		♉
554	Apr 25	17:42		♊
555	May 14	6:05		♋
555	Oct 17	0:59		♌
555	Dec 19	18:42	℞	♋
556	Jun 6	8:48		♌
556	Nov 9	4:34		♍
557	Jan 24	16:51	℞	♌
557	Jul 5	6:02		♍
557	Dec 8	20:10		♎
558	Feb 24	20:54	℞	♍
558	Aug 4	21:09		♎
559	Jan 6	2:34		♏
559	Mar 31	6:05	℞	♎
559	Sep 2	8:20		♏
560	Jan 28	6:52		♐
560	May 13	23:10	℞	♏
560	Sep 23	21:04		♐
561	Feb 12	8:10		♑
561	Jul 12	17:44	℞	♐
561	Oct 4	20:46		♑
562	Feb 24	12:45		♒
563	Mar 6	18:15		♓
564	Mar 15	9:38		♈
565	Mar 25	16:55		♉
565	Aug 28	15:39		♊
565	Oct 9	22:18	℞	♉
566	Apr 7	1:55		♊
566	Aug 29	8:44		♋
566	Dec 15	5:13	℞	♊
567	Apr 23	7:53		♋
567	Sep 18	3:47		♌
568	Jan 29	12:11	℞	♋
568	May 14	9:19		♌
568	Oct 14	2:38		♍
569	Mar 4	23:20	℞	♌
569	Jun 11	8:59		♍
569	Nov 12	22:20		♎
570	Apr 5	18:45	℞	♍
570	Jul 11	16:20		♎
570	Dec 11	16:30		♏
571	May 11	13:57	℞	♎
571	Aug 7	15:37		♏
572	Jan 5	5:04		♐
572	Jun 29	7:57	℞	♏
572	Aug 22	0:34		♐
573	Jan 23	8:28		♑
574	Feb 6	21:22		♒
575	Feb 18	6:13		♓
576	Feb 27	17:41		♈
576	Aug 4	14:40		♉
576	Sep 3	5:25	℞	♈
577	Mar 7	6:48		♉
577	Jul 24	1:10		♊
577	Nov 25	19:36	℞	♉
578	Mar 15	10:00		♊
578	Aug 6	20:25		♋
579	Jan 27	8:39	℞	♊
579	Mar 22	7:25		♋
579	Aug 29	6:49		♌
580	Sep 24	23:09		♍
581	Oct 24	21:18		♎
582	Nov 22	20:21		♏
583	Dec 18	2:35		♐
585	Jan 6	7:09		♑
586	Jan 21	13:31		♒
587	Feb 1	18:17		♓
588	Feb 9	12:52		♈
588	Jun 24	12:46		♉
588	Oct 26	7:30	℞	♈
589	Feb 11	23:08		♉
589	Jul 2	2:47		♊
590	Jul 19	3:32		♋
591	Aug 11	19:13		♌
592	Sep 8	2:29		♍
593	Oct 8	9:59		♎
594	Nov 6	16:60		♏
595	Dec 2	8:02		♐
596	Dec 21	18:41		♑
598	Jan 5	18:04		♒
599	Jan 15	10:27		♓
599	Jun 1	4:32		♈
599	Sep 17	10:29	℞	♓
600	Jan 18	13:38		♈
600	Jun 2	21:02		♉
601	Jun 14	12:02		♊
602	Jul 2	22:53		♋
603	Jul 27	7:23		♌
604	Aug 24	0:39		♍
605	Sep 23	13:27		♎
606	Oct 22	21:40		♏
607	Nov 17	10:26		♐
608	Dec 6	12:06		♑
609	Dec 20	7:32		♒
610	May 10	12:23		♓
610	Aug 6	8:30	℞	♒

Jupiter Ingresses –500 (501 BC)—2100

Year	Date	Time		Sign
610	Dec 26	12:19		♓
611	May 8	8:21		♈
611	Nov 13	20:38	℞	♓
611	Dec 7	22:12		♈
612	May 14	23:55		♉
613	May 28	11:31		♊
614	Jun 16	15:03		♋
615	Jul 11	7:08		♌
616	Aug 8	5:04		♍
617	Sep 7	19:05		♎
618	Oct 6	23:09		♏
619	Nov 1	0:59		♐
620	Nov 19	2:16		♑
621	Apr 14	11:02		♒
621	Jun 28	5:29	℞	♑
621	Nov 30	6:28		♒
622	Apr 12	20:50		♓
622	Sep 23	18:39	℞	♒
622	Nov 25	7:52		♓
623	Apr 18	22:13		♈
624	Apr 27	21:33		♉
625	May 11	23:46		♊
626	May 31	2:10		♋
627	Jun 24	14:35		♌
628	Jul 22	11:37		♍
629	Aug 22	1:08		♎
630	Sep 19	23:01		♏
631	Oct 14	5:56		♐
632	Mar 10	0:31		♑
632	May 31	21:15	℞	♐
632	Oct 30	5:49		♑
633	Mar 16	3:49		♒
633	Aug 13	22:09	℞	♑
633	Nov 3	1:11		♒
634	Mar 23	22:11		♓
635	Apr 1	19:54		♈
636	Apr 11	13:04		♉
637	Apr 25	6:02		♊
638	May 13	9:45		♋
638	Oct 14	13:49		♌
638	Dec 23	4:11	℞	♋
639	Jun 6	1:34		♌
639	Nov 7	13:21		♍
640	Jan 29	11:48	℞	♌
640	Jul 3	14:01		♍
640	Dec 5	22:34		♎
641	Mar 1	0:16	℞	♍
641	Aug 3	2:01		♎
642	Jan 3	9:32		♏
642	Apr 4	4:47	℞	♎
642	Aug 31	15:13		♏
643	Jan 26	8:37		♐
643	May 18	2:24	℞	♏
643	Sep 23	8:04		♐
644	Feb 12	6:12		♑
644	Jul 15	6:19	℞	♐
644	Oct 3	6:20		♑
645	Feb 24	0:43		♒
646	Mar 6	13:27		♓
647	Mar 16	6:38		♈
648	Mar 25	9:44		♉
648	Aug 26	10:43		♊
648	Oct 12	18:36	℞	♉
649	Apr 6	7:07		♊
649	Aug 27	20:12		♋
649	Dec 17	22:14	℞	♊
650	Apr 21	17:38		♋
650	Sep 16	9:17		♌
651	Feb 2	2:49	℞	♋
651	May 12	21:46		♌
651	Oct 13	5:19		♍
652	Mar 8	23:27	℞	♌
652	Jun 8	13:43		♍
652	Nov 11	5:49		♎
653	Apr 9	7:07	℞	♍
653	Jul 9	7:31		♎
653	Dec 10	13:29		♏
654	May 14	1:11	℞	♎
654	Aug 6	1:30		♏
655	Jan 4	18:51		♐
655	Jul 1	17:22	℞	♏
655	Aug 22	3:03		♐
656	Jan 24	10:36		♑
657	Feb 7	4:01		♒
658	Feb 18	10:14		♓
659	Feb 27	12:56		♈
659	Aug 2	4:14		♉
659	Sep 8	9:19	℞	♈
660	Mar 6	9:50		♉
660	Jul 22	9:31		♊
660	Nov 29	2:59	℞	♉
661	Mar 13	7:07		♊
661	Aug 5	0:49		♋
662	Feb 3	9:07	℞	♊
662	Mar 16	7:59		♋
662	Aug 27	9:27		♌
663	Sep 24	5:13		♍
664	Oct 23	12:01		♎
665	Nov 21	22:53		♏
666	Dec 17	16:29		♐
668	Jan 7	4:03		♑
669	Jan 21	11:09		♒
670	Feb 1	10:38		♓
671	Feb 8	17:53		♈
671	Jun 24	0:57		♉
671	Oct 30	5:37	℞	♈
672	Feb 11	3:42		♉
672	Jun 30	15:49		♊
673	Jul 17	16:01		♋
674	Aug 10	8:27		♌
675	Sep 7	17:15		♍
676	Oct 7	2:41		♎
677	Nov 5	11:38		♏
678	Dec 1	4:46		♐
679	Dec 21	17:27		♑
681	Jan 4	17:52		♒
682	Jan 14	8:52		♓
682	May 30	11:44		♈
682	Sep 20	6:54	℞	♓
683	Jan 17	2:31		♈
683	Jun 1	18:50		♉
684	Jun 12	12:53		♊
685	Jun 30	23:20		♋
686	Jul 25	5:51		♌
687	Aug 22	20:23		♍
688	Sep 21	6:50		♎
689	Oct 20	13:37		♏
690	Nov 15	2:48		♐
691	Dec 5	7:35		♑
692	Dec 18	7:48		♒
693	May 7	21:41		♓
693	Aug 7	16:14	℞	♒
693	Dec 24	15:30		♓
694	May 6	18:17		♈
694	Nov 17	19:44	℞	♓
694	Dec 2	14:17		♈
695	May 14	15:35		♉
696	May 27	1:54		♊
697	Jun 14	23:49		♋
698	Jul 9	8:27		♌
699	Aug 6	23:41		♍
700	Sep 6	10:28		♎
701	Oct 5	15:49		♏
702	Oct 30	22:25		♐
703	Nov 19	6:21		♑
704	Apr 13	0:37		♒
704	Jun 30	4:17	℞	♑
704	Nov 29	16:34		♒
705	Apr 12	11:46		♓
705	Sep 24	23:51	℞	♒
705	Nov 24	14:25		♓
706	Apr 18	18:17		♈
707	Apr 28	15:50		♉
708	May 11	10:52		♊
709	May 30	2:25		♋
710	Jun 23	4:33		♌
711	Jul 21	21:36		♍
712	Aug 20	16:00		♎
713	Sep 19	2:01		♏
714	Oct 13	23:25		♐
715	Mar 11	2:05		♑
715	Jun 1	21:29	℞	♐
715	Oct 31	12:16		♑
716	Mar 16	15:23		♒
716	Aug 13	3:40	℞	♑
716	Nov 3	19:52		♒
717	Mar 24	7:36		♓
718	Apr 1	21:32		♈
719	Apr 12	2:32		♉
720	Apr 24	4:03		♊
720	Oct 6	0:01		♋
720	Oct 30	20:24	℞	♊
721	May 11	15:49		♋
721	Oct 10	17:24		♌
721	Dec 28	8:45	℞	♋
722	Jun 3	21:07		♌
722	Nov 4	5:48		♍
723	Feb 3	4:00	℞	♌
723	Jul 2	10:06		♍
723	Dec 4	3:44		♎
724	Mar 4	22:39	℞	♍
724	Aug 1	8:28		♎
725	Jan 1	12:48		♏
725	Apr 6	21:16	℞	♎
725	Aug 30	12:20		♏
726	Jan 25	13:02		♐
726	May 19	10:25	℞	♏
726	Sep 22	18:58		♐
727	Feb 12	2:26		♑
727	Jul 16	18:13	℞	♐
727	Oct 4	2:19		♑
728	Feb 25	1:48		♒
729	Mar 6	11:56		♓
730	Mar 15	21:44		♈
731	Mar 25	14:20		♉
731	Aug 23	19:56		♊
731	Oct 18	7:38	℞	♉
732	Apr 4	22:52		♊
732	Aug 25	20:30		♋
732	Dec 21	7:42	℞	♊
733	Apr 19	18:52		♋
733	Sep 14	15:11		♌
734	Feb 5	18:10	℞	♋
734	May 10	10:42		♌
734	Oct 11	14:10		♍
735	Mar 13	16:38	℞	♌
735	Jun 6	22:24		♍
735	Nov 10	16:49		♎
736	Apr 12	21:54	℞	♍
736	Jul 6	18:17		♎
736	Dec 9	2:50		♏
737	May 17	16:35	℞	♎
737	Aug 3	10:33		♏
738	Jan 3	11:51		♐
738	Jul 6	23:49	℞	♏
738	Aug 17	18:32		♐
739	Jan 23	7:58		♑
740	Feb 7	5:05		♒
741	Feb 17	13:10		♓
742	Feb 26	15:11		♈
742	Jul 29	3:12		♉
742	Sep 13	4:24	℞	♈
743	Mar 6	8:01		♉
743	Jul 22	1:41		♊
743	Dec 2	17:33	℞	♉
744	Mar 11	16:10		♊
744	Aug 3	22:12		♋
745	Feb 8	22:38	℞	♊
745	Mar 11	12:16		♋
745	Aug 26	7:14		♌
746	Sep 23	1:36		♍
747	Oct 23	6:27		♎
748	Nov 20	16:13		♏
749	Dec 16	10:44		♐
751	Jan 6	2:17		♑
752	Jan 21	15:37		♒
753	Jan 31	21:23		♓
754	Feb 8	8:40		♈
754	Jun 23	14:33		♉
754	Oct 31	6:54	℞	♈
755	Feb 10	16:05		♉
755	Jul 1	7:25		♊
756	Jul 17	3:14		♋
757	Aug 9	12:58		♌
758	Sep 6	15:13		♍
759	Oct 6	20:33		♎
760	Nov 4	5:60		♏
761	Nov 30	4:00		♐
762	Dec 21	0:16		♑
764	Jan 5	8:49		♒
765	Jan 14	5:46		♓
765	May 30	8:43		♈
765	Sep 20	16:46	℞	♓
766	Jan 17	1:24		♈
766	Jun 1	16:40		♉
767	Jun 13	5:21		♊
768	Jun 30	7:05		♋
769	Jul 24	4:37		♌
770	Aug 21	14:19		♍
771	Sep 21	2:56		♎
772	Oct 19	19:03		♏
773	Nov 14	21:20		♐
774	Dec 5	14:15		♑
775	Dec 19	22:27		♒
776	May 9	0:03		♓
776	Aug 6	10:05	℞	♒
776	Dec 25	9:07		♓
777	May 7	4:23		♈
777	Nov 16	6:09	℞	♓
777	Dec 4	4:59		♈
778	May 14	12:41		♉
779	May 27	9:21		♊
780	Jun 13	18:31		♋
781	Jul 7	19:01		♌
782	Aug 5	9:49		♍
783	Sep 5	3:36		♎
784	Oct 3	20:45		♏
785	Oct 29	16:13		♐
786	Nov 18	10:27		♑
787	Apr 13	14:09		♒
787	Jun 29	14:43	℞	♑
787	Nov 30	2:22		♒
788	Apr 11	19:43		♓
788	Sep 23	15:29	℞	♒
788	Nov 24	0:55		♓
789	Apr 17	18:32		♈
790	Apr 27	6:55		♉
791	May 10	16:58		♊
792	May 28	1:16		♋
793	Jun 20	23:42		♌
794	Jul 19	16:30		♍
795	Aug 19	12:31		♎
796	Sep 17	0:09		♏
797	Mar 6	13:01		♐
797	Mar 27	13:27	℞	♏
797	Oct 11	22:16		♐
798	Mar 8	4:09		♑
798	Jun 3	16:29	℞	♐
798	Oct 29	8:59		♑
799	Mar 15	12:37		♒
799	Aug 15	20:48	℞	♑
799	Nov 2	0:03		♒
800	Mar 22	11:57		♓
801	Mar 31	4:25		♈
802	Apr 10	9:48		♉
803	Apr 23	9:50		♊
803	Oct 1	10:36		♋
803	Nov 5	1:46	℞	♊
804	May 9	18:28		♋
804	Oct 8	0:44		♌
804	Dec 29	20:38	℞	♋
805	Jun 1	20:14		♌
805	Nov 1	16:14		♍
806	Feb 4	15:00	℞	♌
806	Jun 30	6:13		♍
806	Dec 1	11:44		♎
807	Mar 7	14:17	℞	♍
807	Jul 31	2:23		♎
807	Dec 30	18:58		♏
808	Apr 8	16:29	℞	♎
808	Aug 28	4:07		♏
809	Jan 22	23:28		♐
809	May 21	5:22	℞	♏
809	Sep 20	6:53		♐
810	Feb 9	21:49		♑
810	Jul 18	20:17	℞	♐
810	Sep 30	23:18		♑
811	Feb 23	6:45		♒
812	Mar 5	0:56		♓
813	Mar 14	16:26		♈
814	Mar 24	11:17		♉
814	Aug 22	4:24		♊
814	Oct 18	9:20	℞	♉
815	Apr 4	16:46		♊
815	Aug 25	7:39		♋
815	Dec 22	13:48	℞	♊
816	Apr 18	2:13		♋
816	Sep 12	19:44		♌
817	Feb 6	20:02	℞	♋
817	May 7	23:37		♌
817	Oct 9	11:09		♍
818	Mar 15	15:32	℞	♌
818	Jun 3	17:30		♍
818	Nov 8	8:07		♎
819	Apr 16	8:36	℞	♍
819	Jul 4	4:53		♎
819	Dec 7	17:56		♏
820	May 20	8:03	℞	♎
820	Jul 30	17:08		♏
821	Jan 1	9:24		♐
821	Jul 11	7:10	℞	♏
821	Aug 12	6:10		♐
822	Jan 21	15:54		♑
823	Feb 5	23:18		♒
824	Feb 17	14:58		♓
825	Feb 25	21:06		♈
825	Jul 28	16:36		♉
825	Sep 11	19:34	℞	♈
826	Mar 5	13:12		♉
826	Jul 21	1:40		♊
826	Dec 2	5:20	℞	♉
827	Mar 11	11:39		♊
827	Aug 3	12:32		♋
828	Feb 12	20:38	℞	♊
828	Mar 7	0:41		♋
828	Aug 24	11:30		♌
829	Sep 20	22:45		♍
830	Oct 21	2:57		♎
831	Nov 19	20:12		♏
832	Dec 15	4:17		♐
834	Jan 5	9:33		♑
835	Jan 21	8:03		♒
836	Feb 1	17:03		♓
837	Feb 8	1:19		♈
837	Jun 23	0:19		♉

Jupiter Ingresses –500 (501 BC)—2100

Year	Date	Time	℞	Sign
837	Oct 30	2:41	℞	♈
838	Feb 9	20:30		♉
838	Jun 29	23:54		♊
839	Jul 16	6:31		♋
840	Aug 7	7:25		♌
841	Sep 4	7:32		♍
842	Oct 4	18:03		♎
843	Nov 3	14:13		♏
844	Nov 29	1:19		♐
845	Dec 20	8:47		♑
847	Jan 4	23:56		♒
848	Jan 14	21:59		♓
848	May 30	0:56		♈
848	Sep 19	2:06	℞	♓
849	Jan 16	12:25		♈
849	May 31	17:39		♉
850	Jun 11	20:17		♊
851	Jun 29	14:46		♋
852	Jul 22	8:41		♌
853	Aug 19	18:14		♍
854	Sep 19	8:33		♎
855	Oct 19	2:45		♏
856	Nov 13	7:01		♐
857	Dec 4	1:21		♑
858	Dec 18	9:45		♒
859	May 7	22:03		♓
859	Aug 8	2:39	℞	♒
859	Dec 24	17:28		♓
860	May 5	14:39		♈
861	May 13	1:52		♉
862	May 25	23:09		♊
863	Jun 13	7:50		♋
864	Jul 6	7:21		♌
865	Aug 3	20:56		♍
866	Sep 3	13:24		♎
867	Oct 3	5:16		♏
868	Oct 27	23:39		♐
869	Nov 16	17:45		♑
870	Apr 11	4:05		♒
870	Jun 30	15:12	℞	♑
870	Nov 28	10:36		♒
871	Apr 11	8:20		♓
871	Sep 25	3:13	℞	♒
871	Nov 23	2:19		♓
872	Apr 16	15:25		♈
873	Apr 26	7:33		♉
874	May 9	17:13		♊
875	May 27	21:04		♋
876	Jun 19	12:16		♌
877	Jul 17	22:02		♍
878	Aug 17	13:56		♎
879	Sep 16	2:01		♏
880	Feb 29	8:45		♐
880	Apr 1	8:34	℞	♏
880	Oct 10	4:39		♐
881	Mar 6	5:09		♑
881	Jun 4	2:45	℞	♐
881	Oct 27	22:48		♑
882	Mar 14	10:06		♒
882	Aug 15	5:21	℞	♑
882	Nov 1	0:20		♒
883	Mar 22	18:59		♓
884	Mar 30	15:56		♈
885	Apr 9	21:20		♉
886	Apr 22	16:28		♊
886	Sep 30	3:08		♋
886	Nov 4	19:36	℞	♊
887	May 9	14:33		♋
887	Oct 7	2:50		♌
887	Dec 31	11:53	℞	♋
888	May 31	1:53		♌
888	Oct 30	5:44		♍
889	Feb 6	0:59	℞	♌
889	Jun 28	0:36		♍
889	Nov 28	19:25		♎
890	Mar 9	6:02	℞	♍
890	Jul 28	19:19		♎
890	Dec 28	10:60		♏
891	Apr 10	18:31	℞	♎
891	Aug 27	6:21		♏
892	Jan 22	12:43		♐
892	May 20	23:09	℞	♏
892	Sep 19	2:45		♐
893	Feb 9	7:35		♑
893	Jul 16	19:30	℞	♐
893	Oct 1	0:54		♑
894	Feb 23	4:27		♒
895	Mar 6	2:48		♓
896	Mar 14	16:07		♈
897	Mar 24	3:02		♉
897	Aug 21	18:36		♊
897	Oct 17	2:27	℞	♉
898	Apr 3	18:41		♊
898	Aug 23	18:56		♋
898	Dec 22	22:09	℞	♊
899	Apr 17	6:56		♋
899	Sep 11	18:51		♌
900	Feb 9	10:51	℞	♋
900	May 6	2:52		♌
900	Oct 8	5:14		♍
901	Mar 18	22:19	℞	♌
901	Jun 1	7:15		♍
901	Nov 7	5:24		♎
902	Apr 19	5:49	℞	♍
902	Jul 2	3:35		♎
902	Dec 7	2:04		♏
903	May 23	3:25	℞	♎
903	Jul 30	13:22		♏
904	Jan 2	8:52		♐
904	Jul 11	7:27	℞	♏
904	Aug 12	13:15		♐
905	Jan 22	4:53		♑
906	Feb 6	19:52		♒
907	Feb 18	12:59		♓
908	Feb 27	15:06		♈
908	Jul 30	7:39		♉
908	Sep 10	7:12	℞	♈
909	Mar 5	22:36		♉
909	Jul 21	2:05		♊
909	Dec 2	16:24	℞	♉
910	Mar 11	6:20		♊
910	Aug 3	3:04		♋
911	Feb 17	18:05	℞	♊
911	Mar 3	13:24		♋
911	Aug 24	21:33		♌
912	Sep 20	8:32		♍
913	Oct 20	14:55		♎
914	Nov 19	11:04		♏
915	Dec 15	21:55		♐
917	Jan 5	5:23		♑
918	Jan 21	5:13		♒
919	Feb 1	14:40		♓
920	Feb 8	21:59		♈
920	Jun 22	18:11		♉
920	Oct 30	20:49	℞	♈
921	Feb 9	13:31		♉
921	Jun 29	19:27		♊
922	Jul 16	2:09		♋
923	Aug 8	2:39		♌
924	Sep 4	2:03		♍
925	Oct 4	11:31		♎
926	Nov 3	6:35		♏
927	Nov 29	16:45		♐
928	Dec 20	0:22		♑
930	Jan 4	17:33		♒
931	Jan 14	19:29		♓
931	May 31	0:47		♈
931	Sep 20	5:24	℞	♓
932	Jan 17	15:51		♈
932	May 31	22:57		♉
933	Jun 12	2:13		♊
934	Jun 29	18:00		♋
935	Jul 23	6:47		♌
936	Aug 19	10:51		♍
937	Sep 18	21:16		♎
938	Oct 18	14:58		♏
939	Nov 13	22:38		♐
940	Dec 3	23:24		♑
941	Dec 18	16:15		♒
942	May 8	17:52		♓
942	Aug 7	2:28	℞	♒
942	Dec 25	11:04		♓
943	May 7	9:55		♈
943	Nov 15	21:41	℞	♓
943	Dec 5	2:00		♈
944	May 13	19:32		♉
945	May 26	12:07		♊
946	Jun 13	12:38		♋
947	Jul 7	1:42		♌
948	Aug 3	6:25		♍
949	Sep 2	19:54		♎
950	Oct 2	16:54		♏
951	Oct 28	23:33		♐
952	Nov 17	9:47		♑
953	Apr 13	7:58		♒
953	Jun 27	19:36	℞	♑
953	Nov 29	21:32		♒
954	Apr 13	1:14		♓
954	Sep 20	19:59	℞	♒
954	Nov 26	18:03		♓
955	Apr 19	2:13		♈
956	Apr 27	9:34		♉
957	May 10	7:34		♊
958	May 27	21:30		♋
959	Jun 19	23:46		♌
960	Jul 17	2:49		♍
961	Aug 16	20:45		♎
962	Sep 15	18:04		♏
963	Mar 1	6:60		♐
963	Apr 2	12:14	℞	♏
963	Oct 11	10:47		♐
964	Mar 7	7:49		♑
964	Jun 2	14:55	℞	♐
964	Oct 28	22:01		♑
965	Mar 15	17:52		♒
965	Aug 12	9:45	℞	♑
965	Nov 3	7:28		♒
966	Mar 24	1:48		♓
967	Apr 1	17:39		♈
968	Apr 10	15:01		♉
969	Apr 23	0:41		♊
969	Sep 30	2:23		♋
969	Nov 5	4:10	℞	♊
970	May 9	13:37		♋
970	Oct 6	16:40		♌
971	Jan 1	8:34	℞	♋
971	May 31	18:60		♌
971	Oct 30	19:13		♍
972	Feb 7	21:48	℞	♌
972	Jun 27	17:14		♍
972	Nov 28	12:47		♎
973	Mar 9	21:23	℞	♍
973	Jul 28	15:28		♎
973	Dec 28	9:30		♏
974	Apr 11	2:01	℞	♎
974	Aug 27	6:43		♏
975	Jan 22	15:46		♐
975	May 21	23:40	℞	♏
975	Sep 20	6:41		♐
976	Feb 10	12:52		♑
976	Jul 16	14:51	℞	♐
976	Oct 1	8:50		♑
977	Feb 23	10:03		♒
978	Mar 6	7:49		♓
979	Mar 15	19:59		♈
980	Mar 24	5:41		♉
980	Aug 21	18:40		♊
980	Oct 17	8:49	℞	♉
981	Apr 3	19:56		♊
981	Aug 23	19:07		♋
981	Dec 23	5:48	℞	♊
982	Apr 17	6:29		♋
982	Sep 11	18:46		♌
983	Feb 9	19:56	℞	♋
983	May 6	0:27		♌
983	Oct 8	4:56		♍
984	Mar 18	7:56	℞	♌
984	May 31	3:31		♍
984	Nov 6	4:40		♎
985	Apr 18	16:33	℞	♍
985	Jun 30	22:40		♎
985	Dec 6	0:44		♏
986	May 22	16:25	℞	♎
986	Jul 29	5:36		♏
987	Jan 1	6:46		♐
987	Jul 12	11:53	℞	♏
987	Aug 11	14:08		♐
988	Jan 22	2:44		♑
989	Feb 5	19:14		♒
990	Feb 17	15:35		♓
991	Feb 26	22:25		♈
991	Jul 31	18:11		♉
991	Sep 8	20:57	℞	♈
992	Mar 5	11:22		♉
992	Jul 20	17:26		♊
992	Nov 30	21:00	℞	♉
993	Mar 11	1:08		♊
993	Aug 2	14:15		♋
994	Feb 13	22:26	℞	♊
994	Mar 5	11:04		♋
994	Aug 24	3:26		♌
995	Sep 20	8:38		♍
996	Oct 19	10:11		♎
997	Nov 18	4:25		♏
998	Dec 14	17:29		♐
1000	Jan 5	6:32		♑
1001	Jan 21	13:31		♒
1002	Feb 2	6:30		♓
1003	Feb 9	21:44		♈
1003	Jun 25	1:30		♉
1003	Oct 29	22:17	℞	♈
1004	Feb 12	0:57		♉
1004	Jun 30	16:39		♊
1005	Jul 16	14:40		♋
1006	Aug 8	5:27		♌
1007	Sep 4	20:01		♍
1008	Oct 4	1:04		♎
1009	Nov 2	22:39		♏
1010	Nov 29	18:39		♐
1011	Dec 21	16:06		♑
1013	Jan 5	22:60		♒
1014	Jan 16	13:19		♓
1014	Jun 2	19:47		♈
1014	Sep 16	7:13	℞	♓
1015	Jan 20	1:53		♈
1015	Jun 3	15:29		♉
1016	Jun 13	3:12		♊
1017	Jun 30	4:30		♋
1018	Jul 23	4:32		♌
1019	Aug 20	0:43		♍
1020	Sep 18	10:31		♎
1021	Oct 18	10:20		♏
1022	Nov 14	5:04		♐
1023	Dec 5	18:42		♑
1024	Dec 19	23:55		♒
1025	May 11	13:56		♓
1025	Aug 3	9:08	℞	♒
1025	Dec 27	9:00		♓
1026	May 9	2:12		♈
1026	Nov 7	11:00	℞	♓
1026	Dec 12	22:55		♈
1027	May 15	23:11		♉
1028	May 27	5:10		♊
1029	Jun 13	21:05		♋
1030	Jul 7	5:01		♌
1031	Aug 4	9:02		♍
1032	Sep 3	1:16		♎
1033	Oct 3	1:41		♏
1034	Oct 29	10:55		♐
1035	Nov 18	22:50		♑
1036	Apr 14	9:00		♒
1036	Jun 26	16:34	℞	♑
1036	Nov 30	11:53		♒
1037	Apr 13	14:10		♓
1037	Sep 19	22:05	℞	♒
1037	Nov 27	15:07		♓
1038	Apr 19	10:42		♈
1039	Apr 28	15:26		♉
1040	May 10	11:40		♊
1041	May 28	0:52		♋
1042	Jun 20	3:23		♌
1043	Jul 18	7:19		♍
1044	Aug 17	2:16		♎
1045	Sep 16	0:15		♏
1046	Mar 2	2:51		♐
1046	Apr 1	19:22	℞	♏
1046	Oct 11	16:52		♐
1047	Mar 8	15:40		♑
1047	Jun 3	9:17	℞	♐
1047	Oct 30	4:04		♑
1048	Mar 16	0:02		♒
1048	Aug 12	4:01	℞	♑
1048	Nov 3	16:11		♒
1049	Mar 24	8:51		♓
1050	Apr 2	3:29		♈
1051	Apr 12	4:06		♉
1052	Apr 23	15:45		♊
1052	Oct 2	11:42		♋
1052	Nov 2	20:34	℞	♊
1053	May 10	4:02		♋
1053	Oct 7	10:14		♌
1053	Dec 31	18:30	℞	♋
1054	Jun 1	4:48		♌
1054	Oct 31	1:49		♍
1055	Feb 7	21:56	℞	♌
1055	Jun 28	19:53		♍
1055	Nov 29	10:48		♎
1056	Mar 10	8:30	℞	♍
1056	Jul 28	11:53		♎
1056	Dec 28	3:08		♏
1057	Apr 11	18:27	℞	♎
1057	Aug 27	0:43		♏
1058	Jan 22	11:18		♐
1058	May 22	12:23	℞	♏
1058	Sep 20	2:59		♐
1059	Feb 10	15:02		♑
1059	Jul 17	13:39	℞	♐
1059	Oct 2	14:21		♑
1060	Feb 24	19:37		♒
1061	Mar 6	23:57		♓
1062	Mar 16	17:35		♈
1063	Mar 26	6:59		♉
1063	Aug 25	16:42		♊
1063	Oct 15	5:26	℞	♉
1064	Apr 4	22:32		♊
1064	Aug 24	21:24		♋
1064	Dec 21	21:52	℞	♊
1065	Apr 18	6:10		♋
1065	Sep 12	6:60		♌
1066	Feb 9	7:47	℞	♋
1066	May 6	12:40		♌
1066	Oct 8	6:04		♍
1067	Mar 19	19:50	℞	♌
1067	May 31	20:45		♍
1067	Nov 6	22:37		♎

Jupiter Ingresses –500 (501 BC)—2100

Year	Date	Time		Sign
1068	Apr 19	19:36	℞	♍
1068	Jun 30	4:10		♎
1068	Dec 5	18:27		♏
1069	May 23	16:56	℞	♎
1069	Jul 28	15:03		♏
1070	Jan 1	9:05		♐
1070	Jul 12	0:03	℞	♏
1070	Aug 12	7:55		♐
1071	Jan 22	18:37		♑
1072	Feb 7	23:41		♒
1073	Feb 19	4:55		♓
1074	Feb 28	16:50		♈
1074	Aug 10	6:31		♉
1074	Aug 29	19:36	℞	♈
1075	Mar 8	7:34		♉
1075	Jul 23	12:46		♊
1075	Nov 29	6:47	℞	♉
1076	Mar 12	21:58		♊
1076	Aug 3	10:23		♋
1077	Feb 10	5:53	℞	♊
1077	Mar 9	1:01		♋
1077	Aug 24	7:59		♌
1078	Sep 20	3:09		♍
1079	Oct 20	1:57		♎
1080	Nov 18	0:51		♏
1081	Dec 15	0:19		♐
1083	Jan 6	1:45		♑
1084	Jan 22	19:19		♒
1085	Feb 2	19:44		♓
1086	Feb 10	15:54		♈
1086	Jun 26	3:31		♉
1086	Oct 25	21:53	℞	♈
1087	Feb 13	2:55		♉
1087	Jul 1	20:08		♊
1088	Jul 16	5:58		♋
1089	Aug 7	13:59		♌
1090	Sep 4	2:47		♍
1091	Oct 4	10:07		♎
1092	Nov 2	11:25		♏
1093	Nov 29	10:03		♐
1094	Dec 21	8:32		♑
1096	Jan 6	14:52		♒
1097	Jan 16	3:54		♓
1097	Jun 2	13:44		♈
1097	Sep 14	11:34	℞	♓
1098	Jan 19	15:55		♈
1098	Jun 3	0:06		♉
1099	Jun 13	8:27		♊
1100	Jun 30	8:45		♋
1101	Jul 23	9:43		♌
1102	Aug 20	7:55		♍
1103	Sep 19	19:58		♎
1104	Oct 18	21:36		♏
1105	Nov 14	16:41		♐
1106	Dec 6	5:31		♑
1107	Dec 21	10:10		♒
1108	May 12	6:53		♓
1108	Aug 2	15:45	℞	♒
1108	Dec 27	20:51		♓
1109	May 9	13:54		♈
1109	Nov 5	20:30	℞	♓
1109	Dec 14	14:45		♈
1110	May 16	11:27		♉
1111	May 28	17:57		♊
1112	Jun 14	8:52		♋
1113	Jul 7	13:32		♌
1114	Aug 4	12:55		♍
1115	Sep 4	0:59		♎
1116	Oct 2	23:40		♏
1117	Oct 29	10:21		♐
1118	Nov 19	3:10		♑
1119	Apr 16	2:02		♒
1119	Jun 26	20:07	℞	♑
1119	Dec 2	1:07		♒
1120	Apr 14	9:26		♓
1120	Sep 18	2:19	℞	♒
1120	Nov 29	7:06		♓
1121	Apr 20	9:06		♈
1122	Apr 29	15:32		♉
1123	May 12	11:08		♊
1124	May 28	20:22		♋
1125	Jun 20	15:19		♌
1126	Jul 18	9:59		♍
1127	Aug 17	22:12		♎
1128	Sep 15	19:44		♏
1129	Mar 1	16:38		♐
1129	Apr 2	9:41	℞	♏
1129	Oct 11	19:56		♐
1130	Mar 9	11:18		♑
1130	Jun 2	7:45	℞	♐
1130	Oct 30	22:49		♑
1131	Mar 18	7:19		♒
1131	Aug 10	10:21	℞	♑
1131	Nov 6	22:03		♒
1132	Mar 25	22:06		♓
1133	Apr 3	18:37		♈
1134	Apr 13	17:04		♉
1135	Apr 25	22:23		♊
1135	Oct 8	15:16		♋
1135	Oct 29	16:17	℞	♊
1136	May 10	23:47		♋
1136	Oct 8	1:16		♌
1136	Dec 31	8:29	℞	♋
1137	Jun 1	10:35		♌
1137	Oct 30	22:06		♍
1138	Feb 8	12:02	℞	♌
1138	Jun 28	14:00		♍
1138	Nov 29	0:08		♎
1139	Mar 12	6:36	℞	♍
1139	Jul 29	3:07		♎
1139	Dec 28	20:43		♏
1140	Apr 12	7:51	℞	♎
1140	Aug 26	22:27		♏
1141	Jan 22	18:37		♐
1141	May 22	2:07	℞	♏
1141	Sep 20	15:40		♐
1142	Feb 11	13:00		♑
1142	Jul 15	11:32	℞	♐
1142	Oct 4	10:60		♑
1143	Feb 26	3:27		♒
1144	Mar 8	12:34		♓
1145	Mar 18	6:47		♈
1146	Mar 27	17:13		♉
1146	Aug 29	14:08		♊
1146	Oct 11	3:57	℞	♉
1147	Apr 7	2:52		♊
1147	Aug 26	22:27		♋
1147	Dec 21	18:10	℞	♊
1148	Apr 19	2:44		♋
1148	Sep 12	18:42		♌
1149	Feb 8	19:04	℞	♋
1149	May 7	2:28		♌
1149	Oct 8	13:57		♍
1150	Mar 19	9:14	℞	♌
1150	Jun 1	10:06		♍
1150	Nov 7	8:57		♎
1151	Apr 19	23:35	℞	♍
1151	Jul 2	1:07		♎
1151	Dec 7	10:14		♏
1152	May 22	4:02	℞	♎
1152	Jul 30	1:10		♏
1153	Jan 2	4:60		♐
1153	Jul 8	8:32	℞	♏
1153	Aug 15	17:51		♐
1154	Jan 23	15:25		♑
1155	Feb 8	18:33		♒
1156	Feb 20	20:23		♓
1157	Mar 1	4:33		♈
1157	Aug 13	1:01		♉
1157	Aug 27	2:01	℞	♈
1158	Mar 8	16:05		♉
1158	Jul 23	18:53		♊
1158	Nov 29	4:36	℞	♉
1159	Mar 14	3:52		♊
1159	Aug 4	13:50		♋
1160	Feb 11	1:59	℞	♊
1160	Mar 9	10:43		♋
1160	Aug 24	12:26		♌
1161	Sep 20	10:34		♍
1162	Oct 20	12:53		♎
1163	Nov 19	14:47		♏
1164	Dec 15	15:05		♐
1166	Jan 6	14:57		♑
1167	Jan 23	5:54		♒
1168	Feb 4	4:14		♓
1169	Feb 11	0:27		♈
1169	Jun 26	14:19		♉
1169	Oct 25	10:24	℞	♈
1170	Feb 13	15:08		♉
1170	Jul 2	5:21		♊
1171	Jul 17	14:09		♋
1172	Aug 7	19:54		♌
1173	Sep 4	5:31		♍
1174	Oct 4	9:47		♎
1175	Nov 3	9:34		♏
1176	Nov 29	9:15		♐
1177	Dec 21	11:25		♑
1179	Jan 6	23:21		♒
1180	Jan 17	19:44		♓
1180	Jun 3	20:35		♈
1180	Sep 12	18:35	℞	♓
1181	Jan 20	19:55		♈
1181	Jun 4	0:59		♉
1182	Jun 14	6:23		♊
1183	Jul 1	2:10		♋
1184	Jul 22	20:26		♌
1185	Aug 19	10:46		♍
1186	Sep 18	16:22		♎
1187	Oct 18	15:45		♏
1188	Nov 13	14:54		♐
1189	Dec 5	13:32		♑
1190	Dec 21	7:46		♒
1191	May 14	20:03		♓
1191	Jul 30	8:21	℞	♒
1191	Dec 29	12:53		♓
1192	May 10	8:36		♈
1192	Oct 29	19:19	℞	♓
1192	Dec 19	1:09		♈
1193	May 16	23:36		♉
1194	May 28	22:25		♊
1195	Jun 15	3:10		♋
1196	Jul 6	20:38		♌
1197	Aug 3	10:57		♍
1198	Sep 2	19:34		♎
1199	Oct 2	21:09		♏
1200	Oct 28	16:11		♐
1201	Nov 18	21:10		♑
1202	Apr 17	12:52		♒
1202	Jun 22	19:44	℞	♑
1202	Dec 2	10:58		♒
1203	Apr 16	3:25		♓
1203	Sep 14	7:49	℞	♒
1203	Dec 2	8:38		♓
1204	Apr 20	21:30		♈
1205	Apr 29	21:36		♉
1206	May 12	8:43		♊
1207	May 29	8:36		♋
1208	Jun 19	20:36		♌
1209	Jul 17	13:34		♍
1210	Aug 17	5:48		♎
1211	Sep 16	10:14		♏
1212	Mar 4	13:08		♐
1212	Mar 28	7:42	℞	♏
1212	Oct 11	16:49		♐
1213	Mar 10	3:45		♑
1213	May 30	5:17	℞	♐
1213	Oct 31	1:11		♑
1214	Mar 18	10:25		♒
1214	Aug 7	11:30	℞	♑
1214	Nov 7	10:29		♒
1215	Mar 26	16:34		♓
1216	Apr 3	6:06		♈
1217	Apr 12	22:55		♉
1218	Apr 24	23:36		♊
1218	Oct 6	17:29		♋
1218	Oct 29	22:38	℞	♊
1219	May 10	22:21		♋
1219	Oct 7	21:59		♌
1219	Dec 31	19:44	℞	♋
1220	May 31	9:53		♌
1220	Oct 30	0:25		♍
1221	Feb 7	15:04	℞	♌
1221	Jun 27	17:39		♍
1221	Nov 28	9:21		♎
1222	Mar 10	23:06	℞	♍
1222	Jul 28	12:28		♎
1222	Dec 28	12:43		♏
1223	Apr 11	13:51	℞	♎
1223	Aug 27	13:04		♏
1224	Jan 23	12:54		♐
1224	May 20	2:53	℞	♏
1224	Sep 20	9:38		♐
1225	Feb 11	4:19		♑
1225	Jul 13	10:22	℞	♐
1225	Oct 4	8:36		♑
1226	Feb 25	13:48		♒
1227	Mar 8	18:21		♓
1228	Mar 17	9:50		♈
1229	Mar 26	19:31		♉
1229	Aug 28	15:39		♊
1229	Oct 10	6:40	℞	♉
1230	Apr 6	5:18		♊
1230	Aug 26	0:34		♋
1230	Dec 20	21:17	℞	♊
1231	Apr 19	4:56		♋
1231	Sep 12	19:48		♌
1232	Feb 9	1:04	℞	♋
1232	May 6	2:02		♌
1232	Oct 7	12:60		♍
1233	Mar 18	21:49	℞	♌
1233	May 31	3:37		♍
1233	Nov 6	5:25		♎
1234	Apr 19	18:49	℞	♍
1234	Jun 30	13:14		♎
1234	Dec 6	5:02		♏
1235	May 23	3:47	℞	♎
1235	Jul 29	9:46		♏
1236	Jan 2	0:37		♐
1236	Jul 8	18:28	℞	♏
1236	Aug 13	16:24		♐
1237	Jan 22	14:18		♑
1238	Feb 7	22:04		♒
1239	Feb 20	4:47		♓
1240	Feb 29	17:50		♈
1241	Mar 8	10:00		♉
1241	Jul 23	16:24		♊
1241	Nov 27	0:37	℞	♉
1242	Mar 14	3:24		♊
1242	Aug 4	3:60		♋
1243	Feb 7	22:03	℞	♊
1243	Mar 11	15:07		♋
1243	Aug 24	19:37		♌
1244	Sep 19	10:10		♍
1245	Oct 19	5:48		♎
1246	Nov 18	4:16		♏
1247	Dec 15	7:05		♐
1249	Jan 5	15:18		♑
1250	Jan 22	17:30		♒
1251	Feb 4	2:56		♓
1252	Feb 12	9:16		♈
1252	Jun 27	12:56		♉
1252	Oct 21	15:27	℞	♈
1253	Feb 14	13:10		♉
1253	Jul 2	11:05		♊
1254	Jul 17	7:55		♋
1255	Aug 8	2:18		♌
1256	Sep 3	2:40		♍
1257	Oct 3	2:13		♎
1258	Nov 2	2:59		♏
1259	Nov 29	8:49		♐
1260	Dec 20	20:22		♑
1262	Jan 6	18:06		♒
1263	Jan 17	23:39		♓
1263	Jun 5	22:45		♈
1263	Sep 10	0:14	℞	♓
1264	Jan 22	10:18		♈
1264	Jun 4	6:15		♉
1265	Jun 14	0:16		♊
1266	Jun 30	9:44		♋
1267	Jul 22	20:52		♌
1268	Aug 18	9:20		♍
1269	Sep 17	18:37		♎
1270	Oct 18	1:10		♏
1271	Nov 14	6:59		♐
1272	Dec 5	9:33		♑
1273	Dec 21	4:36		♒
1274	May 15	8:50		♓
1274	Jul 27	15:26	℞	♒
1274	Dec 29	7:59		♓
1275	May 10	20:42		♈
1275	Oct 28	23:22	℞	♓
1275	Dec 19	21:42		♈
1276	May 16	2:05		♉
1277	May 27	18:12		♊
1278	Jun 13	18:54		♋
1279	Jul 6	11:58		♌
1280	Aug 2	5:36		♍
1281	Sep 1	19:37		♎
1282	Oct 2	2:52		♏
1283	Oct 29	1:35		♐
1284	Nov 18	7:07		♑
1285	Apr 17	4:55		♒
1285	Jun 21	4:28	℞	♑
1285	Dec 1	18:32		♒
1286	Apr 15	6:54		♓
1286	Sep 13	10:12	℞	♒
1286	Dec 1	10:02		♓
1287	Apr 20	20:02		♈
1288	Apr 28	17:51		♉
1289	May 11	4:06		♊
1290	May 28	3:31		♋
1291	Jun 19	14:33		♌
1292	Jul 16	5:57		♍
1293	Aug 15	20:18		♎
1294	Sep 14	23:45		♏
1295	Mar 1	14:49		♐
1295	Mar 31	17:47	℞	♏
1295	Oct 11	6:38		♐
1296	Mar 8	9:07		♑
1296	May 30	11:06	℞	♐
1296	Oct 29	16:12		♑
1297	Mar 17	3:51		♒
1297	Aug 7	5:48	℞	♑
1297	Nov 6	2:27		♒
1298	Mar 25	16:15		♓
1299	Apr 3	9:53		♈
1300	Apr 13	4:56		♉
1301	Apr 25	5:52		♊
1301	Oct 7	13:11		♋
1301	Oct 29	7:50	℞	♊
1302	May 11	1:56		♋
1302	Oct 7	20:37		♌
1303	Jan 1	5:34	℞	♋
1303	Jun 1	7:08		♌
1303	Oct 30	14:02		♍

Jupiter Ingresses –500 (501 BC)—2100

Year	Date	Time	℞	Sign
1304	Feb 9	14:43	℞	♌
1304	Jun 27	6:15		♍
1304	Nov 27	13:48		♎
1305	Mar 12	11:48	℞	♍
1305	Jul 27	17:40		♎
1305	Dec 27	11:10		♏
1306	Apr 13	10:33	℞	♎
1306	Aug 26	14:37		♏
1307	Jan 22	14:49		♐
1307	May 22	19:12	℞	♏
1307	Sep 20	13:15		♐
1308	Feb 11	17:60		♑
1308	Jul 14	11:31	℞	♐
1308	Oct 3	20:02		♑
1309	Feb 25	16:47		♒
1310	Mar 9	8:04		♓
1311	Mar 19	6:20		♈
1312	Mar 27	18:44		♉
1312	Sep 1	0:32		♊
1312	Oct 6	20:33	℞	♉
1313	Apr 7	2:50		♊
1313	Aug 26	18:52		♋
1313	Dec 20	4:48	℞	♊
1314	Apr 19	18:02		♋
1314	Sep 12	22:11		♌
1315	Feb 9	10:51	℞	♋
1315	May 6	21:24		♌
1315	Oct 8	3:46		♍
1316	Mar 20	11:15	℞	♌
1316	May 30	0:15		♍
1316	Nov 5	13:12		♎
1317	Apr 22	0:08	℞	♍
1317	Jun 28	20:60		♎
1317	Dec 5	12:15		♏
1318	May 25	9:48	℞	♎
1318	Jul 27	17:45		♏
1319	Jan 1	13:60		♐
1319	Jul 12	3:51	℞	♏
1319	Aug 12	17:44		♐
1320	Jan 23	13:56		♑
1321	Feb 8	7:39		♒
1322	Feb 20	21:33		♓
1323	Mar 2	14:05		♈
1324	Mar 9	5:55		♉
1324	Jul 24	9:53		♊
1324	Nov 26	6:23	℞	♉
1325	Mar 14	17:58		♊
1325	Aug 4	7:16		♋
1326	Feb 8	10:32	℞	♊
1326	Mar 11	7:40		♋
1326	Aug 24	14:17		♌
1327	Sep 20	2:09		♍
1328	Oct 19	1:14		♎
1329	Nov 18	7:50		♏
1330	Dec 15	19:01		♐
1332	Jan 7	8:02		♑
1333	Jan 23	10:24		♒
1334	Feb 4	15:45		♓
1335	Feb 12	14:10		♈
1335	Jun 28	8:01		♉
1335	Oct 23	9:39	℞	♈
1336	Feb 15	4:24		♉
1336	Jul 1	22:09		♊
1337	Jul 16	14:18		♋
1338	Aug 7	7:54		♌
1339	Sep 3	11:48		♍
1340	Oct 2	17:44		♎
1341	Nov 2	1:50		♏
1342	Nov 29	13:27		♐
1343	Dec 22	2:59		♑
1345	Jan 6	23:04		♒
1346	Jan 17	23:29		♓
1346	Jun 5	11:58		♈
1346	Sep 10	22:59	℞	♓
1347	Jan 22	1:28		♈
1347	Jun 4	18:51		♉
1348	Jun 13	11:58		♊
1349	Jun 29	21:14		♋
1350	Jul 22	8:02		♌
1351	Aug 18	19:51		♍
1352	Sep 17	4:10		♎
1353	Oct 17	10:04		♏
1354	Nov 13	16:15		♐
1355	Dec 5	20:04		♑
1356	Dec 20	16:56		♒
1357	May 14	7:32		♓
1357	Jul 29	3:20	℞	♒
1357	Dec 28	21:27		♓
1358	May 10	12:46		♈
1358	Oct 30	7:23	℞	♓
1358	Dec 19	0:35		♈
1359	May 16	22:21		♉
1360	May 27	15:32		♊
1361	Jun 13	14:45		♋
1362	Jul 6	4:07		♌
1363	Aug 2	16:57		♍
1364	Sep 1	2:31		♎
1365	Oct 1	7:02		♏
1366	Oct 28	6:53		♐
1367	Nov 18	17:48		♑
1368	Apr 16	7:08		♒
1368	Jun 22	10:04	℞	♑
1368	Dec 1	14:13		♒
1369	Apr 15	10:28		♓
1369	Sep 13	4:37	℞	♒
1369	Dec 1	20:59		♓
1370	Apr 21	7:27		♈
1371	Apr 30	6:57		♉
1372	May 11	14:14		♊
1373	May 28	5:56		♋
1374	Jun 19	6:06		♌
1375	Jul 16	11:15		♍
1376	Aug 14	20:09		♎
1377	Sep 14	0:14		♏
1378	Feb 25	17:10		♐
1378	Apr 5	5:35	℞	♏
1378	Oct 10	13:01		♐
1379	Mar 8	11:56		♑
1379	Jun 1	17:11	℞	♐
1379	Oct 30	8:07		♑
1380	Mar 17	3:56		♒
1380	Aug 7	6:47	℞	♑
1380	Nov 6	8:01		♒
1381	Mar 26	1:56		♓
1382	Apr 3	22:40		♈
1383	Apr 13	16:05		♉
1384	Apr 24	10:42		♊
1384	Oct 5	8:36		♋
1384	Oct 29	23:37	℞	♊
1385	May 9	19:58		♋
1385	Oct 5	22:09		♌
1386	Jan 1	20:52	℞	♋
1386	May 30	13:55		♌
1386	Oct 28	12:11		♍
1387	Feb 10	11:37	℞	♌
1387	Jun 26	8:30		♍
1387	Nov 26	15:49		♎
1388	Mar 13	1:43	℞	♍
1388	Jul 26	1:07		♎
1388	Dec 26	1:13		♏
1389	Apr 13	5:14	℞	♎
1389	Aug 25	9:59		♏
1390	Jan 21	19:29		♐
1390	May 21	14:42	℞	♏
1390	Sep 19	21:49		♐
1391	Feb 11	7:22		♑
1391	Jul 13	10:38	℞	♐
1391	Oct 4	19:05		♑
1392	Feb 26	6:56		♒
1393	Mar 8	17:32		♓
1394	Mar 18	7:36		♈
1395	Mar 27	9:17		♉
1395	Aug 28	16:52		♊
1395	Oct 10	21:09	℞	♉
1396	Apr 5	3:35		♊
1396	Aug 24	4:37		♋
1396	Dec 22	0:54	℞	♊
1397	Apr 17	1:32		♋
1397	Sep 10	11:11		♌
1398	Feb 11	19:49	℞	♋
1398	May 3	11:12		♌
1398	Oct 5	22:08		♍
1399	Mar 23	20:42	℞	♌
1399	May 27	10:13		♍
1399	Nov 4	16:11		♎
1400	Apr 24	12:16	℞	♍
1400	Jun 27	1:30		♎
1400	Dec 5	1:46		♏
1401	May 26	18:26	℞	♎
1401	Jul 26	20:25		♏
1402	Jan 1	13:06		♐
1402	Jul 12	15:23	℞	♏
1402	Aug 12	12:25		♐
1403	Jan 23	17:53		♑
1404	Feb 9	10:54		♒
1405	Feb 20	19:60		♓
1406	Mar 2	5:22		♈
1407	Mar 9	11:49		♉
1407	Jul 24	4:45		♊
1407	Nov 29	15:57	℞	♉
1408	Mar 13	8:10		♊
1408	Aug 3	6:12		♋
1409	Feb 16	4:49	℞	♊
1409	Mar 4	7:12		♋
1409	Aug 23	14:36		♌
1410	Sep 19	2:50		♍
1411	Oct 19	1:50		♎
1412	Nov 17	8:15		♏
1413	Dec 14	20:28		♐
1415	Jan 6	11:48		♑
1416	Jan 23	17:05		♒
1417	Feb 4	0:59		♓
1418	Feb 12	0:30		♈
1418	Jun 27	12:49		♉
1418	Oct 24	21:43	℞	♈
1419	Feb 14	10:50		♉
1419	Jul 2	10:05		♊
1420	Jul 16	3:04		♋
1421	Aug 6	18:37		♌
1422	Sep 2	19:03		♍
1423	Oct 2	21:18		♎
1424	Nov 1	2:30		♏
1425	Nov 28	14:07		♐
1426	Dec 21	7:42		♑
1428	Jan 7	10:48		♒
1429	Jan 17	19:20		♓
1429	Jun 5	10:60		♈
1429	Sep 11	3:44	℞	♓
1430	Jan 22	4:07		♈
1430	Jun 4	23:00		♉
1431	Jun 14	14:07		♊
1432	Jun 29	17:08		♋
1433	Jul 21	19:18		♌
1434	Aug 17	23:02		♍
1435	Sep 17	2:48		♎
1436	Oct 16	9:00		♏
1437	Nov 12	20:06		♐
1438	Dec 5	8:03		♑
1439	Dec 21	13:53		♒
1440	May 14	8:58		♓
1440	Jul 29	4:10	℞	♒
1440	Dec 29	2:46		♓
1441	May 10	20:27		♈
1441	Oct 29	16:12	℞	♓
1441	Dec 19	19:05		♈
1442	May 17	4:19		♉
1443	May 28	15:23		♊
1444	Jun 13	5:12		♋
1445	Jul 5	9:08		♌
1446	Aug 1	17:27		♍
1447	Sep 1	5:45		♎
1448	Sep 30	18:59		♏
1449	Oct 28	5:19		♐
1450	Nov 19	0:37		♑
1451	Apr 18	2:30		♒
1451	Jun 22	13:08	℞	♑
1451	Dec 3	1:07		♒
1452	Apr 15	19:13		♓
1452	Sep 12	19:34	℞	♒
1452	Dec 2	6:22		♓
1453	Apr 21	7:04		♈
1454	Apr 29	20:23		♉
1455	May 11	16:38		♊
1456	May 26	22:27		♋
1457	Jun 17	17:10		♌
1458	Jul 15	0:26		♍
1459	Jan 4	23:29		♎
1459	Jan 24	22:54	℞	♍
1459	Aug 14	18:00		♎
1460	Feb 6	16:36		♏
1460	Feb 22	3:34	℞	♎
1460	Sep 13	9:27		♏
1461	Feb 24	5:36		♐
1461	Apr 7	1:24	℞	♏
1461	Oct 10	8:06		♐
1462	Mar 8	8:37		♑
1462	Jun 2	2:18	℞	♐
1462	Oct 30	8:33		♑
1463	Mar 18	4:13		♒
1463	Aug 8	15:13	℞	♑
1463	Nov 7	5:31		♒
1464	Mar 25	21:59		♓
1465	Apr 3	11:53		♈
1466	Apr 12	21:22		♉
1467	Apr 24	7:55		♊
1467	Sep 29	17:03		♋
1467	Nov 7	12:14	℞	♊
1468	May 8	9:46		♋
1468	Oct 3	13:09		♌
1469	Jan 5	8:11	℞	♋
1469	May 28	21:40		♌
1469	Oct 26	11:44		♍
1470	Feb 13	17:35	℞	♌
1470	Jun 24	13:23		♍
1470	Nov 24	17:04		♎
1471	Mar 17	6:33	℞	♍
1471	Jul 25	6:26		♎
1471	Dec 25	3:08		♏
1472	Apr 16	9:42	℞	♎
1472	Aug 23	16:03		♏
1473	Jan 20	1:59		♐
1473	May 24	17:17	℞	♏
1473	Sep 18	2:35		♐
1474	Feb 9	22:01		♑
1474	Jul 16	20:30	℞	♐
1474	Oct 2	9:48		♑
1475	Feb 25	5:19		♒
1476	Mar 7	21:28		♓
1477	Mar 17	14:45		♈
1478	Mar 26	16:50		♉
1478	Aug 25	23:28		♊
1478	Oct 14	6:21	℞	♉
1479	Apr 5	8:18		♊
1479	Aug 24	2:54		♋
1479	Dec 25	2:33	℞	♊
1480	Apr 15	21:51		♋
1480	Sep 9	11:38		♌
1481	Feb 14	11:13	℞	♋
1481	May 1	13:29		♌
1481	Oct 4	20:04		♍
1482	Mar 27	11:41	℞	♌
1482	May 24	12:53		♍
1482	Nov 3	10:02		♎
1483	Apr 28	19:03	℞	♍
1483	Jun 23	13:43		♎
1483	Dec 3	15:49		♏
1484	May 30	18:10	℞	♎
1484	Jul 21	18:13		♏
1484	Dec 30	2:41		♐
1486	Jan 21	12:24		♑
1487	Feb 7	13:53		♒
1488	Feb 20	7:54		♓
1489	Feb 28	23:43		♈
1490	Mar 8	8:12		♉
1490	Jul 22	22:11		♊
1490	Nov 29	11:18	℞	♉
1491	Mar 12	22:42		♊
1491	Aug 2	19:56		♋
1492	Aug 21	21:10		♌
1493	Sep 17	1:56		♍
1494	Oct 16	19:57		♎
1495	Nov 16	1:58		♏
1496	Dec 12	18:42		♐
1498	Jan 4	18:23		♑
1499	Jan 22	8:42		♒
1500	Feb 3	23:44		♓
1501	Feb 12	2:27		♈
1501	Jun 27	12:46		♉
1501	Oct 25	5:57	℞	♈
1502	Feb 14	9:28		♉
1502	Jul 2	4:34		♊
1503	Jul 16	12:42		♋
1504	Aug 5	19:03		♌
1505	Sep 1	14:11		♍
1506	Oct 1	17:48		♎
1507	Nov 1	7:05		♏
1508	Nov 28	6:08		♐
1509	Dec 21	9:42		♑
1511	Jan 7	18:05		♒
1512	Jan 19	1:44		♓
1512	Jun 5	10:54		♈
1512	Sep 11	12:45	℞	♓
1513	Jan 22	1:11		♈
1513	Jun 4	11:33		♉
1514	Jun 13	15:58		♊
1515	Jun 29	9:56		♋
1516	Jul 20	6:55		♌
1517	Aug 16	11:30		♍
1518	Sep 15	21:56		♎
1519	Oct 16	14:03		♏
1520	Nov 12	11:01		♐
1521	Dec 5	5:31		♑
1522	Dec 21	12:22		♒
1523	May 14	19:56		♓
1523	Jul 31	3:46	℞	♒
1523	Dec 29	18:22		♓
1524	May 10	5:32		♈
1524	Nov 1	13:03	℞	♓
1524	Dec 17	11:51		♈
1525	May 16	7:04		♉
1526	May 27	11:49		♊
1527	Jun 12	21:04		♋
1528	Jul 3	22:43		♌
1529	Jul 31	6:59		♍
1530	Aug 30	20:44		♎
1531	Sep 30	11:43		♏
1532	Oct 26	23:46		♐
1533	Nov 17	19:43		♑
1534	Apr 15	3:58		♒
1534	Jun 26	11:07	℞	♑
1534	Dec 1	17:34		♒
1535	Apr 15	10:47		♓
1535	Sep 17	2:57	℞	♒
1535	Dec 1	0:47		♓
1536	Apr 20	8:15		♈

Jupiter Ingresses –500 (501 BC)—2100

1537	Apr 29	0:35		♉
1538	May 10	20:43		♊
1539	May 27	0:04		♋
1540	Jun 16	14:23		♌
1540	Dec 2	7:14		♍
1540	Dec 30	6:26	℞	♌
1541	Jul 13	16:43		♍
1541	Dec 28	8:57		♎
1542	Feb 2	12:31	℞	♍
1542	Aug 13	6:27		♎
1543	Jan 28	7:06		♏
1543	Mar 4	13:52	℞	♎
1543	Sep 12	18:55		♏
1544	Feb 19	23:52		♐
1544	Apr 13	9:38	℞	♏
1544	Oct 8	15:45		♐
1545	Mar 5	14:44		♑
1545	Jun 6	1:10	℞	♐
1545	Oct 28	15:04		♑
1546	Mar 16	14:57		♒
1546	Aug 11	21:51	℞	♑
1546	Nov 5	2:50		♒
1547	Mar 26	1:21		♓
1548	Apr 3	0:55		♈
1549	Apr 12	14:33		♉
1550	Apr 23	23:57		♊
1550	Sep 27	14:43		♋
1550	Nov 10	4:53	℞	♊
1551	May 8	18:35		♋
1551	Oct 3	4:31		♌
1552	Jan 8	15:19	℞	♋
1552	May 27	17:57		♌
1552	Oct 24	20:07		♍
1553	Feb 16	15:57	℞	♌
1553	Jun 22	20:38		♍
1553	Nov 22	17:45		♎
1554	Mar 20	16:56	℞	♍
1554	Jul 23	6:11		♎
1554	Dec 23	1:05		♏
1555	Apr 21	0:08	℞	♎
1555	Aug 22	15:07		♏
1556	Jan 19	6:28		♐
1556	May 28	1:06	℞	♏
1556	Sep 16	3:57		♐
1557	Feb 8	16:29		♑
1557	Jul 19	22:49	℞	♐
1557	Sep 30	6:39		♑
1558	Feb 24	13:28		♒
1559	Mar 8	14:56		♓
1560	Mar 17	12:25		♈
1561	Mar 26	13:20		♉
1561	Aug 24	17:47		♊
1561	Oct 16	0:31	℞	♉
1562	Apr 4	20:14		♊
1562	Aug 23	2:40		♋
1562	Dec 27	5:32	℞	♊
1563	Apr 15	13:36		♋
1563	Sep 9	3:22		♌
1564	Feb 19	5:48	℞	♋
1564	Apr 28	14:42		♌
1564	Oct 3	5:38		♍
1565	Apr 2	4:57	℞	♌
1565	May 19	17:26		♍
1565	Nov 1	19:43		♎
1566	May 4	12:07	℞	♍
1566	Jun 18	19:21		♎
1566	Dec 2	9:56		♏
1567	Jun 5	7:05	℞	♎
1567	Jul 19	2:08		♏
1567	Dec 30	11:17		♐
1569	Jan 21	11:04		♑
1570	Feb 7	20:45		♒
1571	Feb 20	15:38		♓
1572	Mar 1	1:41		♈
1572	Aug 11	23:59		♉
1572	Aug 27	9:24	℞	♈
1573	Mar 7	20:52		♉
1573	Jul 21	18:05		♊
1573	Dec 2	2:19	℞	♉
1574	Mar 11	5:37		♊
1574	Aug 1	8:04		♋
1575	Aug 21	3:44		♌
1576	Sep 15	7:58		♍
1577	Oct 15	7:32		♎
1578	Nov 14	23:30		♏
1579	Dec 13	3:58		♐
1581	Jan 4	13:04		♑
1582	Jan 22	7:25		♒
1583	Feb 3	20:03		♓
1584	Feb 11	14:02		♈
1584	Jun 25	7:57		♉
1584	Oct 26	15:27	℞	♈
1585	Feb 11	23:09		♉
1585	Jun 29	22:06		♊
1586	Jul 14	3:31		♋
1587	Aug 4	8:57		♌
1588	Aug 30	4:50		♍
1589	Sep 29	10:21		♎
1590	Oct 30	1:36		♏
1591	Nov 27	2:39		♐
1592	Dec 19	8:07		♑
1594	Jan 5	17:29		♒
1595	Jan 16	23:55		♓
1595	Jun 3	13:02		♈
1595	Sep 14	12:23	℞	♓
1596	Jan 20	15:10		♈
1596	Jun 2	8:09		♉
1597	Jun 11	16:22		♊
1598	Jun 27	10:21		♋
1599	Jul 19	5:33		♌
1600	Aug 14	7:30		♍
1601	Sep 13	15:41		♎
1602	Oct 14	6:11		♏
1603	Nov 11	2:38		♐
1604	Dec 2	22:52		♑
1605	Dec 19	9:14		♒
1606	May 11	16:41		♓
1606	Aug 2	1:43	℞	♒
1606	Dec 27	18:11		♓
1607	May 9	11:59		♈
1607	Nov 4	9:54	℞	♓
1607	Dec 15	8:01		♈
1608	May 14	22:02		♉
1609	May 26	3:52		♊
1610	Jun 11	8:55		♋
1611	Jul 3	3:03		♌
1612	Jul 29	3:03		♍
1613	Aug 28	11:13		♎
1614	Sep 28	1:11		♏
1615	Oct 25	16:15		♐
1616	Nov 15	18:07		♑
1617	Apr 12	6:11		♒
1617	Jun 28	0:09	℞	♑
1617	Nov 29	22:14		♒
1618	Apr 13	21:15		♓
1618	Sep 17	13:22	℞	♒
1618	Nov 29	4:19		♓
1619	Apr 20	3:22		♈
1620	Apr 27	20:56		♉
1621	May 9	12:17		♊
1622	May 25	5:47		♋
1623	Jun 15	7:41		♌
1623	Nov 25	17:34		♍
1624	Jan 6	20:39	℞	♌
1624	Jul 11	1:05		♍
1624	Dec 21	15:33		♎
1625	Feb 8	7:12	℞	♍
1625	Aug 10	15:04		♎
1626	Jan 22	4:44		♏
1626	Mar 9	12:24	℞	♎
1626	Sep 10	13:10		♏
1627	Feb 16	16:15		♐
1627	Apr 16	6:34	℞	♏
1627	Oct 8	0:37		♐
1628	Mar 4	5:54		♑
1628	Jun 5	15:04	℞	♐
1628	Oct 27	15:10		♑
1629	Mar 15	23:17		♒
1629	Aug 10	8:30	℞	♑
1629	Nov 4	18:10		♒
1630	Mar 25	12:18		♓
1631	Apr 3	7:05		♈
1632	Apr 11	10:31		♉
1633	Apr 22	4:38		♊
1633	Sep 22	8:25		♋
1633	Nov 14	11:57	℞	♊
1634	May 6	4:10		♋
1634	Sep 29	9:51		♌
1635	Jan 11	22:47	℞	♋
1635	May 25	9:05		♌
1635	Oct 22	4:19		♍
1636	Feb 21	2:51	℞	♌
1636	Jun 19	3:33		♍
1636	Nov 19	7:56		♎
1637	Mar 23	18:15	℞	♍
1637	Jul 19	20:24		♎
1637	Dec 20	4:14		♏
1638	Apr 23	2:55	℞	♎
1638	Aug 19	21:16		♏
1639	Jan 17	4:41		♐
1639	May 29	23:40	℞	♏
1639	Sep 15	3:05		♐
1640	Feb 8	7:57		♑
1640	Jul 19	21:27	℞	♐
1640	Sep 28	18:13		♑
1641	Feb 23	13:50		♒
1642	Mar 7	15:53		♓
1643	Mar 17	8:08		♈
1644	Mar 24	23:02		♉
1644	Aug 20	20:06		♊
1644	Oct 18	19:08	℞	♉
1645	Apr 2	15:17		♊
1645	Aug 20	8:43		♋
1645	Dec 29	13:51	℞	♊
1646	Apr 12	10:46		♋
1646	Sep 6	12:04		♌
1647	Feb 22	22:43	℞	♋
1647	Apr 24	22:18		♌
1647	Oct 1	16:04		♍
1648	Apr 8	1:38	℞	♌
1648	May 12	19:05		♍
1648	Oct 30	8:04		♎
1649	May 10	13:08	℞	♍
1649	Jun 11	16:11		♎
1649	Nov 30	0:16		♏
1650	Jun 11	6:59	℞	♎
1650	Jul 11	23:06		♏
1650	Dec 28	4:08		♐
1652	Jan 20	7:25		♑
1653	Feb 5	20:23		♒
1654	Feb 18	17:15		♓
1655	Feb 28	3:02		♈
1655	Aug 4	5:19		♉
1655	Sep 4	22:12	℞	♈
1656	Mar 5	17:53		♉
1656	Jul 19	8:36		♊
1656	Dec 3	21:41	℞	♉
1657	Mar 8	10:52		♊
1657	Jul 30	5:04		♋
1658	Aug 19	1:42		♌
1659	Sep 14	5:02		♍
1660	Oct 13	3:05		♎
1661	Nov 12	17:53		♏
1662	Dec 10	22:06		♐
1664	Jan 3	9:21		♑
1665	Jan 20	8:19		♒
1666	Feb 2	2:42		♓
1667	Feb 10	1:10		♈
1667	Jun 24	17:16		♉
1667	Oct 27	21:28	℞	♈
1668	Feb 11	9:21		♉
1668	Jun 28	13:24		♊
1669	Jul 12	16:22		♋
1670	Aug 2	15:46		♌
1671	Aug 29	4:30		♍
1672	Sep 27	4:20		♎
1673	Oct 27	17:58		♏
1674	Nov 24	21:47		♐
1675	Dec 18	9:44		♑
1677	Jan 4	3:15		♒
1678	Jan 15	16:57		♓
1678	Jun 2	5:50		♈
1678	Sep 14	2:47	℞	♓
1679	Jan 19	12:16		♈
1679	Jun 2	6:37		♉
1680	Jun 10	11:57		♊
1681	Jun 25	22:32		♋
1682	Jul 17	8:06		♌
1683	Aug 13	2:06		♍
1684	Sep 11	8:19		♎
1685	Oct 12	4:43		♏
1686	Nov 9	12:55		♐
1687	Dec 2	22:26		♑
1688	Dec 18	19:41		♒
1689	May 11	18:45		♓
1689	Jul 30	19:12	℞	♒
1689	Dec 27	11:08		♓
1690	May 9	1:16		♈
1690	Nov 2	2:19	℞	♓
1690	Dec 15	14:20		♈
1691	May 15	0:29		♉
1692	May 24	17:02		♊
1693	Jun 9	7:53		♋
1694	Jun 30	14:16		♌
1695	Jul 27	9:14		♍
1696	Aug 25	21:05		♎
1697	Sep 25	21:34		♏
1698	Oct 24	2:13		♐
1699	Nov 15	16:39		♑
1700	Apr 12	12:53		♒
1700	Jun 27	18:10	℞	♑
1700	Nov 30	5:42		♒
1701	Apr 14	5:59		♓
1701	Sep 17	1:50	℞	♒
1701	Nov 29	17:26		♓
1702	Apr 20	6:57		♈
1703	Apr 28	15:47		♉
1704	May 8	20:51		♊
1705	May 24	4:23		♋
1706	Jun 13	23:03		♌
1706	Nov 21	6:22		♍
1707	Jan 12	6:42	℞	♌
1707	Jul 10	13:44		♍
1707	Dec 18	18:29		♎
1708	Feb 14	2:52	℞	♍
1708	Aug 9	4:51		♎
1709	Jan 18	7:46		♏
1709	Mar 14	7:15	℞	♎
1709	Sep 9	5:17		♏
1710	Feb 13	16:15		♐
1710	Apr 20	4:19	℞	♏
1710	Oct 6	18:19		♐
1711	Mar 3	8:59		♑
1711	Jun 9	12:02	℞	♐
1711	Oct 27	7:32		♑
1712	Mar 14	17:44		♒
1712	Aug 13	5:23	℞	♑
1712	Nov 2	19:49		♒
1713	Mar 24	14:18		♓
1714	Apr 2	12:17		♈
1715	Apr 11	16:10		♉
1716	Apr 21	8:32		♊
1716	Sep 19	17:18		♋
1716	Nov 17	20:40	℞	♊
1717	May 5	3:52		♋
1717	Sep 27	23:27		♌
1718	Jan 14	8:17	℞	♋
1718	May 24	3:00		♌
1718	Oct 20	20:54		♍
1719	Feb 23	13:54	℞	♌
1719	Jun 18	16:17		♍
1719	Nov 18	23:16		♎
1720	Mar 26	8:60	℞	♍
1720	Jul 18	6:04		♎
1720	Dec 18	17:28		♏
1721	Apr 25	21:44	℞	♎
1721	Aug 18	5:02		♏
1722	Jan 15	17:40		♐
1722	Jun 1	23:28	℞	♏
1722	Sep 13	5:57		♐
1723	Feb 7	1:05		♑
1723	Jul 24	15:38	℞	♐
1723	Sep 26	23:20		♑
1724	Feb 23	14:04		♒
1725	Mar 6	23:39		♓
1726	Mar 16	22:01		♈
1727	Mar 25	16:31		♉
1727	Aug 20	23:48		♊
1727	Oct 21	1:20	℞	♉
1728	Apr 2	7:33		♊
1728	Aug 19	20:39		♋
1728	Dec 30	20:27	℞	♊
1729	Apr 11	16:44		♋
1729	Sep 5	19:21		♌
1730	Feb 25	13:26	℞	♋
1730	Apr 22	20:05		♌
1730	Sep 30	16:27		♍
1731	Apr 15	22:51	℞	♌
1731	May 7	12:38		♍
1731	Oct 30	2:02		♎
1732	May 21	6:43	℞	♍
1732	Jun 1	15:42		♎
1732	Nov 28	15:31		♏
1733	Dec 26	22:19		♐
1735	Jan 19	9:36		♑
1736	Feb 6	8:40		♒
1737	Feb 18	14:18		♓
1738	Feb 28	5:52		♈
1738	Aug 4	17:38		♉
1738	Sep 4	14:14	℞	♈
1739	Mar 6	22:43		♉
1739	Jul 20	10:22		♊
1739	Dec 5	5:05	℞	♉
1740	Mar 8	9:32		♊
1740	Jul 29	22:55		♋
1741	Aug 18	9:48		♌
1742	Sep 13	4:06		♍
1743	Oct 12	21:42		♎
1744	Nov 11	15:41		♏
1745	Dec 10	6:39		♐
1747	Jan 3	7:58		♑
1748	Jan 21	18:57		♒
1749	Feb 2	20:03		♓
1750	Feb 10	19:26		♈
1750	Jun 25	9:17		♉
1750	Oct 27	5:36	℞	♈
1751	Feb 11	21:12		♉
1751	Jun 29	11:53		♊
1752	Jul 12	0:36		♋
1753	Aug 1	12:39		♌
1754	Aug 27	19:31		♍
1755	Sep 26	20:53		♎
1756	Oct 26	18:45		♏
1757	Nov 24	11:00		♐
1758	Dec 18	11:33		♑

Jupiter Ingresses –500 (501 BC)—2100

Year	Date	Time	Sign
1760	Jan 5	14:23	♒
1761	Jan 16	8:07	♓
1761	Jun 3	1:19	♈
1761	Sep 13	6:26 ℞	♓
1762	Jan 20	1:52	♈
1762	Jun 2	10:49	♉
1763	Jun 11	5:01	♊
1764	Jun 25	6:18	♋
1765	Jul 16	9:46	♌
1766	Aug 12	1:49	♍
1767	Sep 11	9:14	♎
1768	Oct 11	8:10	♏
1769	Nov 8	19:02	♐
1770	Dec 2	6:39	♑
1771	Dec 19	4:35	♒
1772	May 10	9:27	♓
1772	Aug 1	19:50 ℞	♒
1772	Dec 26	17:28	♓
1773	May 8	8:44	♈
1773	Nov 5	6:45 ℞	♓
1773	Dec 13	1:56	♈
1774	May 14	11:22	♉
1775	May 25	4:34	♊
1776	Jun 8	18:30	♋
1777	Jun 29	23:26	♌
1778	Jul 16	16:49	♍
1779	Aug 26	3:13	♎
1780	Sep 25	2:37	♏
1781	Oct 23	5:59	♐
1782	Nov 14	19:21	♑
1783	Apr 10	17:04	♒
1783	Jun 30	7:53 ℞	♑
1783	Nov 29	7:27	♒
1784	Apr 12	10:59	♓
1784	Sep 18	3:11 ℞	♒
1784	Nov 27	8:47	♓
1785	Apr 18	21:49	♈
1786	Apr 27	12:11	♉
1787	May 8	18:51	♊
1788	May 22	23:32	♋
1789	Jun 12	11:30	♌
1789	Nov 18	7:36	♍
1790	Jan 13	21:47 ℞	♌
1790	Jul 8	17:55	♍
1790	Dec 15	8:57	♎
1791	Feb 16	7:46 ℞	♍
1791	Aug 8	2:39	♎
1792	Jan 15	11:05	♏
1792	Mar 17	0:35 ℞	♎
1792	Sep 7	1:21	♏
1793	Feb 10	7:07	♐
1793	Apr 22	8:38 ℞	♏
1793	Oct 4	16:58	♐
1794	Mar 1	1:56	♑
1794	Jun 10	12:25 ℞	♐
1794	Oct 25	11:39	♑
1795	Mar 14	6:23	♒
1795	Aug 14	9:21 ℞	♑
1795	Nov 2	5:28	♒
1796	Mar 23	14:52	♓
1797	Apr 1	19:23	♈
1798	Apr 11	1:44	♉
1799	Apr 21	15:34	♊
1799	Sep 19	18:45	♋
1799	Nov 18	4:11 ℞	♊
1800	May 5	2:02	♋
1800	Sep 27	9:38	♌
1801	Jan 15	15:51 ℞	♋
1801	May 23	9:15	♌
1801	Oct 19	18:42	♍
1802	Feb 25	21:00 ℞	♌
1802	Jun 17	4:35	♍
1802	Nov 17	12:26	♎
1803	Mar 30	5:34 ℞	♍
1803	Jul 17	10:02	♎
1803	Dec 18	6:59	♏
1804	Apr 28	13:59 ℞	♎
1804	Aug 16	14:25	♏
1805	Jan 14	20:02	♐
1805	Jun 3	16:40 ℞	♏
1805	Sep 12	7:23	♐
1806	Feb 6	22:45	♑
1806	Jul 24	18:47 ℞	♐
1806	Sep 27	3:22	♑
1807	Feb 24	3:41	♒
1808	Mar 7	21:45	♓
1809	Mar 17	21:50	♈
1810	Mar 26	11:54	♉
1810	Aug 22	3:13	♊
1810	Oct 20	2:17 ℞	♉
1811	Apr 3	15:37	♊
1811	Aug 20	15:29	♋
1812	Jan 1	19:37 ℞	♊
1812	Apr 11	2:24	♋
1812	Sep 4	23:29	♌
1813	Feb 28	23:45 ℞	♋
1813	Apr 20	0:08	♌
1813	Sep 29	11:58	♍
1814	Oct 28	20:16	♎
1815	Nov 28	16:13	♏
1816	Dec 26	11:47	♐
1818	Jan 19	13:27	♑
1819	Feb 6	23:22	♒
1820	Feb 20	9:52	♓
1821	Mar 1	0:29	♈
1821	Aug 7	20:19	♉
1821	Sep 1	12:24 ℞	♈
1822	Mar 7	10:49	♉
1822	Jul 20	13:51	♊
1822	Dec 5	11:08 ℞	♉
1823	Mar 9	7:29	♊
1823	Jul 30	14:23	♋
1824	Aug 17	18:21	♌
1825	Sep 12	10:30	♍
1826	Oct 12	5:27	♎
1827	Nov 12	2:31	♏
1828	Dec 9	20:47	♐
1830	Jan 3	0:58	♑
1831	Jan 21	13:49	♒
1832	Feb 3	15:34	♓
1833	Feb 10	13:51	♈
1833	Jun 24	23:08	♉
1833	Oct 28	5:51 ℞	♈
1834	Feb 11	10:22	♉
1834	Jun 29	4:16	♊
1835	Jul 12	16:50	♋
1836	Aug 1	4:10	♌
1837	Aug 27	10:14	♍
1838	Sep 26	10:39	♎
1839	Oct 27	7:48	♏
1840	Nov 23	23:21	♐
1841	Dec 17	23:41	♑
1843	Jan 5	3:38	♒
1844	Jan 17	0:07	♓
1844	Jun 2	15:18	♈
1844	Sep 14	0:01 ℞	♓
1845	Jan 19	21:23	♈
1845	Jun 2	10:41	♉
1846	Jun 11	8:01	♊
1847	Jun 26	8:19	♋
1848	Jul 16	7:40	♌
1849	Aug 11	18:05	♍
1850	Sep 10	20:20	♎
1851	Oct 11	16:56	♏
1852	Nov 8	5:17	♐
1853	Dec 1	21:45	♑
1854	Dec 19	3:09	♒
1855	May 11	15:22	♓
1855	Aug 2	14:15 ℞	♒
1855	Dec 28	1:41	♓
1856	May 8	21:25	♈
1856	Nov 3	9:38 ℞	♓
1856	Dec 14	22:58	♈
1857	May 15	1:46	♉
1858	May 25	16:45	♊
1859	Jun 10	0:22	♋
1860	Jun 29	19:24	♌
1861	Jul 26	2:14	♍
1862	Aug 25	6:03	♎
1863	Sep 25	6:46	♏
1864	Oct 22	19:58	♐
1865	Nov 15	0:54	♑
1866	Apr 12	0:19	♒
1866	Jun 28	14:25 ℞	♑
1866	Nov 30	8:32	♒
1867	Apr 14	21:49	♓
1867	Sep 15	19:24 ℞	♒
1867	Dec 1	3:47	♓
1868	Apr 20	7:32	♈
1869	Apr 28	16:25	♉
1870	May 9	13:22	♊
1871	May 24	4:17	♋
1872	Jun 12	0:33	♌
1872	Nov 16	6:45	♍
1873	Jan 16	17:06 ℞	♌
1873	Jul 7	18:58	♍
1873	Dec 13	1:56	♎
1874	Feb 19	10:13 ℞	♍
1874	Aug 7	0:53	♎
1875	Jan 13	9:58	♏
1875	Mar 20	17:05 ℞	♎
1875	Sep 7	6:08	♏
1876	Feb 10	9:33	♐
1876	Apr 23	14:27 ℞	♏
1876	Oct 4	11:11	♐
1877	Mar 1	9:13	♑
1877	Jun 10	2:19 ℞	♐
1877	Oct 25	23:30	♑
1878	Mar 15	4:33	♒
1878	Aug 12	9:01 ℞	♑
1878	Nov 3	22:42	♒
1879	Mar 25	17:53	♓
1880	Apr 2	21:05	♈
1881	Apr 11	21:33	♉
1882	Apr 22	2:25	♊
1882	Sep 19	23:38	♋
1882	Nov 18	6:29 ℞	♊
1883	May 5	1:60	♋
1883	Sep 27	0:22	♌
1884	Jan 16	14:12 ℞	♋
1884	May 21	22:47	♌
1884	Oct 18	5:53	♍
1885	Feb 26	1:47 ℞	♌
1885	Jun 15	13:06	♍
1885	Nov 16	1:08	♎
1886	Mar 30	7:46 ℞	♍
1886	Jul 15	20:37	♎
1886	Dec 16	23:50	♏
1887	Apr 29	8:29 ℞	♎
1887	Aug 16	6:32	♏
1888	Jan 14	17:30	♐
1888	Jun 3	3:29 ℞	♏
1888	Sep 11	4:22	♐
1889	Feb 5	23:50	♑
1889	Jul 24	0:09 ℞	♐
1889	Sep 26	3:40	♑
1890	Feb 23	6:25	♒
1891	Mar 8	0:40	♓
1892	Mar 16	23:44	♈
1893	Mar 25	11:56	♉
1893	Aug 20	19:19	♊
1893	Oct 19	17:47 ℞	♉
1894	Apr 2	13:13	♊
1894	Aug 19	10:48	♋
1895	Jan 1	11:47 ℞	♊
1895	Apr 10	19:13	♋
1895	Sep 4	18:36	♌
1896	Mar 1	3:19 ℞	♋
1896	Apr 18	5:05	♌
1896	Sep 28	7:02	♍
1897	Oct 27	15:17	♎
1898	Nov 27	11:17	♏
1899	Dec 26	6:48	♐
1901	Jan 19	8:33	♑
1902	Feb 6	19:31	♒
1903	Feb 20	8:35	♓
1904	Mar 1	3:00	♈
1904	Aug 8	20:11	♉
1904	Aug 31	13:54 ℞	♈
1905	Mar 7	18:28	♉
1905	Jul 21	0:23	♊
1905	Dec 4	22:31 ℞	♉
1906	Mar 9	21:48	♊
1906	Jul 30	23:12	♋
1907	Aug 18	23:15	♌
1908	Sep 12	10:02	♍
1909	Oct 11	23:33	♎
1910	Nov 11	17:04	♏
1911	Dec 10	11:36	♐
1913	Jan 2	19:46	♑
1914	Jan 21	15:13	♒
1915	Feb 4	0:44	♓
1916	Feb 12	7:11	♈
1916	Jun 26	1:32	♉
1916	Oct 26	14:53 ℞	♈
1917	Feb 12	15:59	♉
1917	Jun 29	23:52	♊
1918	Jul 13	5:54	♋
1919	Aug 2	8:39	♌
1920	Aug 27	5:30	♍
1921	Sep 25	23:11	♎
1922	Oct 26	19:16	♏
1923	Nov 24	17:31	♐
1924	Dec 18	6:25	♑
1926	Jan 6	1:01	♒
1927	Jan 18	11:44	♓
1927	Jun 6	10:15	♈
1927	Sep 11	3:43 ℞	♓
1928	Jan 23	2:55	♈
1928	Jun 4	4:51	♉
1929	Jun 12	12:20	♊
1930	Jun 26	22:42	♋
1931	Jul 17	7:52	♌
1932	Aug 11	7:16	♍
1933	Sep 10	5:11	♎
1934	Oct 11	4:55	♏
1935	Nov 9	2:56	♐
1936	Dec 2	8:39	♑
1937	Dec 20	4:06	♒
1938	May 14	7:47	♓
1938	Jul 30	3:02 ℞	♒
1938	Dec 29	18:35	♓
1939	May 11	14:09	♈
1939	Oct 30	0:45 ℞	♓
1939	Dec 20	17:03	♈
1940	May 16	7:55	♉
1941	May 26	12:48	♊
1942	Jun 10	10:36	♋
1943	Jun 30	21:46	♌
1944	Jul 26	1:04	♍
1945	Aug 25	6:06	♎
1946	Sep 25	10:19	♏
1947	Oct 24	3:00	♐
1948	Nov 15	10:38	♑
1949	Apr 12	19:18	♒
1949	Jun 27	18:30 ℞	♑
1949	Nov 30	20:08	♒
1950	Apr 15	8:59	♓
1950	Sep 15	2:23 ℞	♒
1950	Dec 1	19:57	♓
1951	Apr 21	14:57	♈
1952	Apr 28	20:51	♉
1953	May 9	15:34	♊
1954	May 24	4:44	♋
1955	Jun 13	0:07	♌
1955	Nov 17	3:59	♍
1956	Jan 18	2:05 ℞	♌
1956	Jul 7	19:02	♍
1956	Dec 13	2:17	♎
1957	Feb 19	15:38 ℞	♍
1957	Aug 7	2:11	♎
1958	Jan 13	12:52	♏
1958	Mar 20	19:14 ℞	♎
1958	Sep 7	8:52	♏
1959	Feb 10	13:46	♐
1959	Apr 24	14:11 ℞	♏
1959	Oct 5	14:40	♐
1960	Mar 1	13:10	♑
1960	Jun 10	1:53 ℞	♐
1960	Oct 26	3:01	♑
1961	Mar 15	8:02	♒
1961	Aug 12	8:55 ℞	♑
1961	Nov 4	2:49	♒
1962	Mar 25	22:08	♓
1963	Apr 4	3:20	♈
1964	Apr 12	6:53	♉
1965	Apr 22	14:33	♊
1965	Sep 21	4:40	♋
1965	Nov 17	3:09 ℞	♊
1966	May 5	14:52	♋
1966	Sep 27	13:20	♌
1967	Jan 16	3:50 ℞	♋
1967	May 23	8:21	♌
1967	Oct 19	10:52	♍
1968	Feb 27	3:34 ℞	♌
1968	Jun 15	14:44	♍
1968	Nov 15	22:44	♎
1969	Mar 30	21:37 ℞	♍
1969	Jul 15	13:30	♎
1969	Dec 16	15:56	♏
1970	Apr 30	6:45 ℞	♎
1970	Aug 15	17:58	♏
1971	Jan 14	8:50	♐
1971	Jun 5	2:13 ℞	♏
1971	Sep 11	15:33	♐
1972	Feb 6	19:37	♑
1972	Jul 24	16:43 ℞	♐
1972	Sep 25	18:20	♑
1973	Feb 23	9:28	♒
1974	Mar 8	11:12	♓
1975	Mar 18	16:48	♈
1976	Mar 26	10:25	♉
1976	Aug 23	10:25	♊
1976	Oct 16	20:25 ℞	♉
1977	Apr 3	15:43	♊
1977	Aug 20	12:43	♋
1977	Dec 30	23:51 ℞	♊
1978	Apr 12	0:12	♋
1978	Sep 5	8:31	♌
1979	Feb 28	23:36 ℞	♋
1979	Apr 20	8:30	♌
1979	Sep 29	10:24	♍
1980	Oct 27	10:11	♎
1981	Nov 27	2:20	♏
1982	Dec 26	1:58	♐
1984	Jan 19	15:05	♑
1985	Feb 6	15:36	♒
1986	Feb 20	16:06	♓
1987	Mar 2	18:42	♈
1988	Mar 8	15:45	♉
1988	Jul 22	0:00	♊
1988	Nov 30	20:55 ℞	♉
1989	Mar 11	3:27	♊
1989	Jul 30	23:51	♋
1990	Aug 18	7:31	♌

Jupiter Ingresses –500 (501 BC)—2100

Year	Date	Time		Sign
1991	Sep 12	6:01		♍
1992	Oct 10	13:27		♎
1993	Nov 10	8:16		♏
1994	Dec 9	10:55		♐
1996	Jan 3	7:23		♑
1997	Jan 21	15:14		♒
1998	Feb 4	10:53		♓
1999	Feb 13	1:23		♈
1999	Jun 28	9:30		♉
1999	Oct 23	5:50	℞	♈
2000	Feb 14	21:40		♉
2000	Jun 30	7:36		♊
2001	Jul 13	0:04		♋
2002	Aug 1	17:21		♌
2003	Aug 27	9:27		♍
2004	Sep 25	3:24		♎
2005	Oct 26	2:52		♏
2006	Nov 24	4:44		♐
2007	Dec 18	20:12		♑
2009	Jan 5	15:42		♒
2010	Jan 18	2:11		♓
2010	Jun 6	6:28		♈
2010	Sep 9	4:51	℞	♓
2011	Jan 22	17:12		♈
2011	Jun 4	13:57		♉
2012	Jun 11	17:23		♊
2013	Jun 26	1:41		♋
2014	Jul 16	10:31		♌
2015	Aug 11	11:12		♍
2016	Sep 9	11:19		♎
2017	Oct 10	13:21		♏
2018	Nov 8	12:39		♐
2019	Dec 2	18:21		♑
2020	Dec 19	13:08		♒
2021	May 13	22:36		♓
2021	Jul 28	12:44	℞	♒
2021	Dec 29	4:10		♓
2022	May 10	23:23		♈
2022	Oct 28	5:12	℞	♓
2022	Dec 20	14:33		♈
2023	May 16	17:21		♉
2024	May 25	23:16		♊
2025	Jun 9	21:03		♋
2026	Jun 30	5:53		♌
2027	Jul 26	4:50		♍
2028	Aug 24	5:09		♎
2029	Sep 24	6:25		♏
2030	Oct 22	23:15		♐
2031	Nov 15	10:30		♑
2032	Apr 12	0:59		♒
2032	Jun 26	12:59	℞	♑
2032	Nov 30	3:32		♒
2033	Apr 14	22:45		♓
2033	Sep 12	22:30	℞	♒
2033	Dec 1	22:35		♓
2034	Apr 21	9:40		♈
2035	Apr 29	18:58		♉
2036	May 9	14:53		♊
2037	May 24	2:13		♋
2038	Jun 12	15:26		♌
2038	Nov 16	21:21		♍
2039	Jan 16	14:58	℞	♌
2039	Jul 8	0:25		♍
2039	Dec 12	22:05		♎
2040	Feb 20	5:38	℞	♍
2040	Aug 5	22:04		♎
2041	Jan 11	19:33		♏
2041	Mar 21	0:04	℞	♎
2041	Sep 6	0:13		♏
2042	Feb 8	23:53		♐
2042	Apr 24	12:43	℞	♏
2042	Oct 4	9:60		♐
2043	Mar 1	17:06		♑
2043	Jun 9	21:45	℞	♐
2043	Oct 26	11:31		♑
2044	Mar 15	4:28		♒
2044	Aug 9	12:45	℞	♑
2044	Nov 4	17:33		♒
2045	Mar 26	5:09		♓
2046	Apr 4	16:12		♈
2047	Apr 13	21:04		♉
2048	Apr 23	1:44		♊
2048	Sep 23	12:57		♋
2048	Nov 12	14:09	℞	♊
2049	May 5	18:13		♋
2049	Sep 27	10:29		♌
2050	Jan 14	7:28	℞	♋
2050	May 22	21:48		♌
2050	Oct 18	12:45		♍
2051	Feb 26	11:05	℞	♌
2051	Jun 15	11:26		♍
2051	Nov 15	14:43		♎
2052	Mar 30	20:34	℞	♍
2052	Jul 14	0:22		♎
2052	Dec 15	6:52		♏
2053	Apr 30	4:36	℞	♎
2053	Aug 14	7:29		♏
2054	Jan 13	7:59		♐
2054	Jun 4	6:31	℞	♏
2054	Sep 10	18:29		♐
2055	Feb 6	8:35		♑
2055	Jul 23	4:42	℞	♐
2055	Sep 27	6:00		♑
2056	Feb 24	10:59		♒
2057	Mar 8	20:52		♓
2058	Mar 19	6:18		♈
2059	Mar 27	23:46		♉
2059	Aug 27	18:59		♊
2059	Oct 12	3:40	℞	♉
2060	Apr 4	1:53		♊
2060	Aug 20	18:12		♋
2060	Dec 28	9:19	℞	♊
2061	Apr 12	5:04		♋
2061	Sep 4	21:41		♌
2062	Feb 26	23:41	℞	♋
2062	Apr 20	8:54		♌
2062	Sep 28	16:17		♍
2063	Oct 27	15:33		♎
2064	Nov 26	11:60		♏
2065	Dec 25	16:54		♐
2067	Jan 19	9:27		♑
2068	Feb 7	10:27		♒
2069	Feb 20	9:12		♓
2070	Mar 2	8:59		♈
2071	Mar 9	2:50		♉
2071	Jul 22	8:26		♊
2071	Nov 30	14:32	℞	♉
2072	Mar 10	11:51		♊
2072	Jul 30	3:33		♋
2073	Aug 17	10:19		♌
2074	Sep 11	10:19		♍
2075	Oct 10	20:42		♎
2076	Nov 9	18:46		♏
2077	Dec 8	23:30		♐
2079	Jan 2	19:55		♑
2080	Jan 22	1:60		♒
2081	Feb 3	19:34		♓
2082	Feb 12	9:08		♈
2082	Jun 27	18:48		♉
2082	Oct 21	20:15	℞	♈
2083	Feb 14	7:50		♉
2083	Jun 30	15:21		♊
2084	Jul 12	7:28		♋
2085	Jul 31	23:22		♌
2086	Aug 26	12:45		♍
2087	Sep 25	3:40		♎
2088	Oct 25	0:57		♏
2089	Nov 23	2:48		♐
2090	Dec 17	20:51		♑
2092	Jan 5	21:14		♒
2093	Jan 17	14:37		♓
2093	Jun 6	10:40		♈
2093	Sep 6	16:56	℞	♓
2094	Jan 22	16:48		♈
2094	Jun 4	13:20		♉
2095	Jun 12	15:12		♊
2096	Jun 25	20:29		♋
2097	Jul 15	23:44		♌
2098	Aug 10	16:36		♍
2099	Sep 9	9:05		♎
2100	Oct 10	6:25		♏

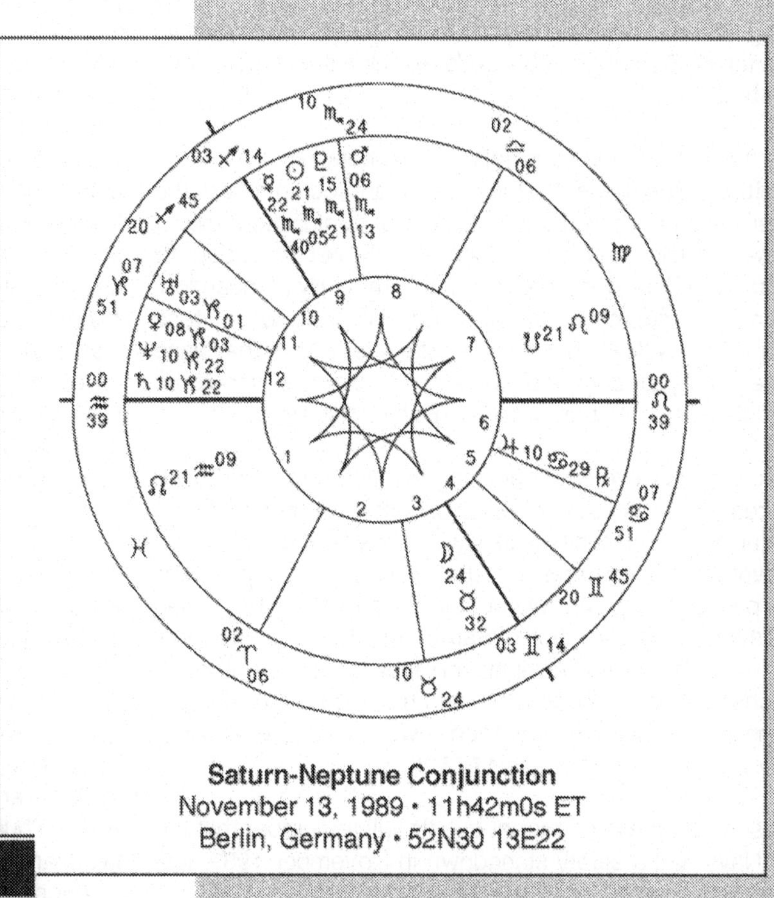

Saturn-Neptune Conjunction
November 13, 1989 • 11h42m0s ET
Berlin, Germany • 52N30 13E22

Part 6

Outer Planet Phenomena

Outer Planet Phenomena: A Commentary on the Tables

by David Dukelow

This part contains three complementary tables. The first lists Outer Planet Conjunctions from 501 BC to AD 2100, the second lists hard aspects and trines occurring between the Outer Planets for each year from 1700 through 2050, and the last gives zero declination and latitude for the same planets also for 1700 through 2050. Let's examine these tables one at a time.

The fewest conjunctions take place between Pluto and Neptune since these are the slowest and outermost of the outer planets. The greatest number of conjunctions occur between Jupiter and Pluto. Jupiter's orbital period is about 12 years, and Pluto's is more than 240 years. By comparison, Pluto just seems to be standing still, making Jupiter's conjunction with Pluto a fairly regular event. Note that since there is no year zero, the year -83, for example, should be read as 84 BC. All times are ET (Ephemeris Time).

History buffs will enjoy examining the first table. For those interested in the current series of Saturn-Uranus-Neptune conjunctions, this table quickly will reveal how rare this kind of event is. For example, the Uranus-Neptune conjunctions just previous to the current ones last occurred in 1821, also in Capricorn. The addition of Saturn, which you can see was not involved with either planet then, makes the current series much more pronounced. The last time all three were in the same sign—it was Scorpio then—was 1307. The last time they were in Capricorn was 1777 BC.

Those with an eye to current events will remember that the US Navy had a safety standdown in November 1989, just when Saturn and Neptune were exactly conjunct. Saturn is often associated with safety, following rules and traditions, and a general reserve, while Neptune has always been known as the King of the Sea. How apt that the Navy's action should just "accidentally" follow the symbolism associated with these planets! The Berlin Wall has fallen too. On another level, Saturn stands for structure; in a negative mode it is constrictive, like a straight jacket. Neptune dissolves. Putting the two together we see the weakening of confining structures. Capricorn is often associated with government and advancement in the social sphere. Most of the governments in Eastern Europe have been going through their Uranus oppositions too. It is no wonder that their expression has had to change so much. We can feel very fortunate that so relatively little blood has been shed given the magnitude of the changes. Finally the hatchets of World War II are being buried. This process will continue and be solidified by the Uranus-Neptune conjunctions in 1993, which may have strong spiritual overtones.

The Jupiter-Saturn conjunctions likewise offer much room for thought. One series of events that comes to mind is the supposed curse that a Native American put on United States presidents—that every one elected in a year that ends in zero would die in office. I don't know whether or not such a curse ever was made, but the conjunctions of Jupiter and Saturn from 1842 through 1961 all took place in earth signs. Earth can be associated with the physical body. Harrison was elected in 1840, Lincoln in 1860, Garfield in 1880, McKinley in 1900, Harding in 1920, Roosevelt in 1940, and Kennedy in 1960—all of them died in office. We can imagine earth signs as being structurally damaged. The attempted assassination of Reagan, who was elected in 1980, was nearly successful. The 1980 conjunction took place, at long last, in an air sign, and he was shot in one of his lungs. Air, so to say, recovers quickly from being punctured by a bullet. We can wonder what will happen to the president who is elected in 2000, when the conjunction again will take place in an earth sign.

The table showing hard aspects and trines between the outer planets is next. This table shows waxing and waning aspects. An example will clarify how to read the table. The first entry reads

1700 Jan 28 3:16 ♃ ♄ 45 16♑37

This means that on Jan 28, 1700, at 3:16 ET, Jupiter was at 16 ♑ 37 and that Saturn followed it by 45°, and so was at 1 ♓ 37. Thus the zodiacal position given is for the first of the two planets. Move ahead in the zodiac from there, passing 0° Aries if necessary, to find the position of the next planet.

This table is useful for many things. For example, note the large number of aspects occurring in air signs in late 1775 and 1776. We can easily connect this with the push for freedom of expression that our country is known for and that was such an issue during our fight for independence. You can "frame" events: find the aspects that happened before or after some event you are researching. Some sharp aspect may suggest to you that you should expand your research to include a larger or smaller period of time. The mid-1960s, for example, were a very hectic time. Perhaps the most prominent event was the Uranus-Pluto conjunction that took place in late 1965. This conjunction took place in Virgo, an earth sign. Remember all of the communes, the "back to the Earth" movement, body painting, and experiential art "happenings?" Undoubtedly much of what took place then appears silly now, but much of it had a spiritual overtone, as the Saturn-Pluto and Saturn-Uranus oppositions indicate, for Saturn was then in Pisces. Knowing this can help us keep

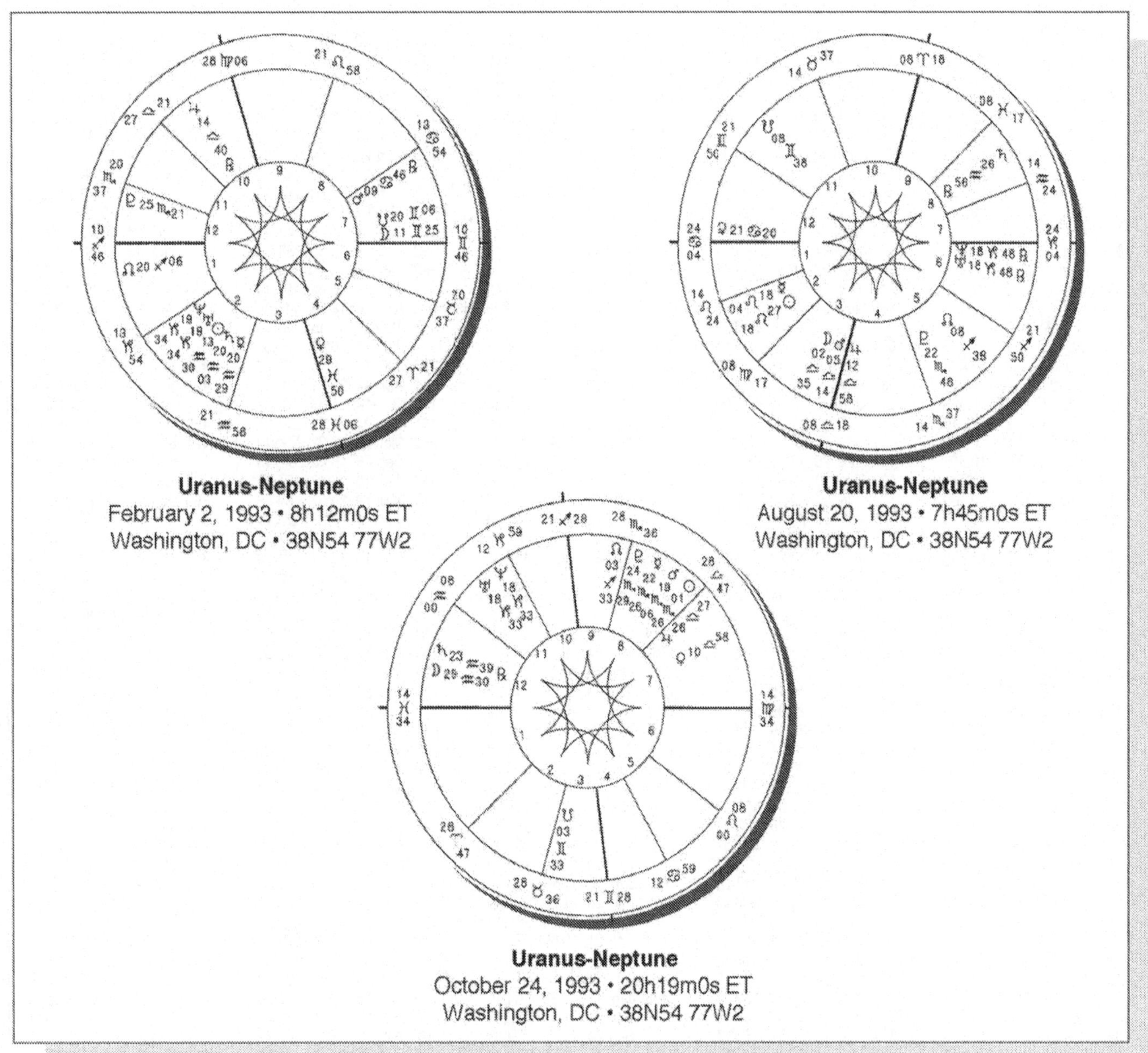

Uranus-Neptune
February 2, 1993 • 8h12m0s ET
Washington, DC • 38N54 77W2

Uranus-Neptune
August 20, 1993 • 7h45m0s ET
Washington, DC • 38N54 77W2

Uranus-Neptune
October 24, 1993 • 20h19m0s ET
Washington, DC • 38N54 77W2

a proper perspective on the events and motivations of that time.

Finally we come to the last table, which shows 0 declinations and 0 latitudes. The ecliptic is the apparent path of the Sun through the constellations. This path moves above and below the celestial equator, the imaginary extension of the Earth's equator into space. Zero declination occurs when a planet crosses the celestial equator. The Sun does this just twice a year, when it passes 0° Aries and again at 0° Libra. The notation dN means that the planet had been below the celestial equator, is now at 0 declination, and will move north of the celestial equator. Likewise, dS means that it is going the other way. Declination is an angular measure, measuring the distance above or below the equatorial plane.

Latitude is different. It also is an angular measure but refers to how far a planet is above or below the ecliptic. Thus the sun always has 0 latitude. The notation IS means that a planet is moving from above the ecliptic to the southern half. Of course IN means the opposite. Mars is included in this listing. This table is useful for helping to gauge the relative strength of various aspects, for when planets are near to 0 latitude, their zodiacal position is, in a sense, less distorted than when they are far above or below the ecliptic.

David Dukelow *was a member of Astro's chart services staff, keying calculation orders, doing phone Astro-Tutorials, training new Astro operators, and writing articles for* ***Astroflash****. A former math teacher, with strong interests in psychology, David had been president of San Diego's "Friends of Jung." He passed away in 1994.*

Outer Planet Conjunctions –500 (501 BC)—2100

♆ ♇

Year	Date	Time	Position
-83	Jul 2	17:56	17♉02
	Oct 27	22:29	16♉38
-82	Apr 3	2:08	16♉05
411	Jul 1	22:52	23♉20
	Nov 12	0:51	22♉53
412	Apr 2	0:07	22♉23
905	May 27	17:14	28♉29
1398	Jul 1	18:05	3♊51
	Dec 5	18:48	3♊19
1399	Apr 2	15:48	2♊55
1891	Aug 2	19:06	8♊38
	Nov 5	19:36	8♊19
1892	Apr 30	17:20	7♊42

♅ ♆

Year	Date	Time	Position
-403	May 15	9:24	1♊35
-232	Jun 25	3:57	18♊43
-61	Jul 24	17:08	5♋21
-60	Feb 7	7:42	4♋28
	Apr 4	12:21	4♋12
110	Aug 20	3:55	21♋53
111	Feb 1	17:31	21♋08
	May 10	4:52	20♋41
281	Sep 8	11:28	8♌09
282	Feb 12	3:58	7♌25
	May 30	5:02	6♌55
452	Sep 13	19:29	23♌56
453	Mar 20	4:09	23♌03
	May 28	11:24	22♌44
623	Sep 22	3:44	9♍39
794	Oct 5	1:52	25♍35
965	Oct 14	6:04	11♎22
1136	Oct 24	12:23	27♎06
1307	Nov 15	2:00	13♏14
1478	Dec 15	8:45	29♏40
1479	Jul 4	10:31	28♏49
	Aug 30	4:58	28♏34
1650	Jan 18	8:00	16♐11
	Jun 13	5:13	15♐35
	Oct 16	8:12	15♐04
1821	Mar 22	3:48	3♑01
	May 3	9:42	2♑51
	Dec 3	16:19	1♑59
1993	Feb 2	8:12	19♑34
	Aug 20	7:45	18♑48
	Oct 24	20:19	18♑33

♅ ♇

Year	Date	Time	Position
-436	Mar 15	0:10	20♑15
	Jun 18	14:16	19♑54
	Dec 11	22:47	19♑16
-322	May 26	9:40	20♉53
-181	Mar 13	8:54	4♒37
	Jul 26	4:35	4♒09
	Dec 14	5:11	3♒38
-69	Aug 21	14:18	1♊45
	Oct 5	10:22	1♊35
-68	May 3	8:17	0♊46
74	Feb 7	11:42	17♒07
185	Jul 17	17:43	12♊04
	Dec 6	16:09	11♊32
186	Apr 14	1:00	11♊01
328	Mar 17	14:34	29♒31
	Sep 22	0:24	28♒51
	Dec 13	14:34	28♒33
439	Jul 3	10:15	22♊40
440	Feb 16	20:47	21♊47
	Mar 1	18:40	21♊43
582	Apr 4	13:20	10♓47
	Sep 20	0:39	10♓12
583	Jan 4	1:14	9♓50
693	Jul 2	11:32	3♋53
836	Apr 8	6:05	21♓22
	Oct 12	9:03	20♓43
837	Jan 4	8:20	20♓25
947	Jul 13	4:41	15♋55
1090	Mar 29	17:18	1♈12
1201	Aug 5	21:15	28♋55
1343	Jun 19	22:45	11♈29
	Aug 24	5:38	11♈16
1344	Mar 10	22:37	10♈33
1455	Oct 2	1:18	13♌35
1456	Jan 21	19:00	13♌08
	Jun 24	23:26	12♌27
1597	May 2	5:03	20♈17
	Nov 24	5:01	19♈35
1598	Jan 22	5:52	19♈23
1710	Sep 7	18:38	28♌53
1850	Jun 26	3:17	29♈40
	Sep 25	11:24	29♈21
1851	Mar 23	21:02	28♈43
1965	Oct 9	20:11	17♍10
1966	Apr 4	20:44	16♍28
	Jun 30	9:49	16♍06

♄ ♅

Year	Date	Time	Position
-463	Oct 29	17:30	26♍21
-462	Apr 18	9:00	24♍56
	Jun 27	2:42	24♍20
-417	Jul 17	20:52	6♈50
	Aug 5	8:46	6♈38
-416	Feb 14	13:29	4♈31
-371	Sep 19	22:06	29♎36
-326	Apr 6	0:11	1♉47
-280	Nov 19	10:41	3♐03
-236	Jun 10	18:24	1♊04
-189	Dec 11	22:30	2♑50
-146	Sep 14	5:13	2♋06
	Nov 28	14:15	1♋18
-145	May 2	23:06	29♊37
-98	Mar 28	23:55	2♒21
	Jul 19	21:34	1♒19
	Nov 27	20:38	0♒05
-55	Aug 24	0:23	3♋37
-7	Feb 3	7:38	27♒08
36	Sep 12	20:35	7♍08
83	Mar 25	12:49	23♓31
127	Oct 29	12:44	11♎47
173	Apr 30	18:41	19♈28
218	Dec 19	14:44	15♏38
219	Jun 3	8:58	14♏17
	Aug 21	8:52	13♏38
263	Jun 17	3:36	16♉39
310	Jan 26	1:38	17♐16
	Jun 25	9:27	16♐01
	Sep 30	17:31	15♐13
353	Aug 18	23:51	15♊17
	Nov 24	20:08	14♊13
354	Apr 8	7:15	12♊44
401	Feb 3	5:47	16♑22
444	Jul 7	9:15	14♋24
492	Jan 20	8:11	13♒09
535	Jul 5	17:32	16♌09
582	Apr 5	7:38	10♓50
626	Aug 15	3:22	20♍42
672	Jun 24	8:48	7♈43
	Aug 29	10:18	7♈03
673	Feb 9	6:28	5♈19
717	Oct 10	3:07	25♎46
763	Apr 6	17:49	2♉22
808	Dec 7	6:59	29♏52
853	May 29	13:23	0♊22
900	Jan 7	2:57	0♑54
943	Aug 3	22:57	29♊55
944	Feb 9	13:49	27♊51
	Mar 5	7:08	27♊35
991	Jan 12	6:04	29♑20
1034	Jun 27	18:33	29♋02
1081	Apr 2	3:09	27♒23
	Sep 18	4:32	25♒48
	Nov 25	21:57	25♒09
1124	Oct 18	11:03	3♍14
1125	Mar 6	10:57	1♍53
	Jun 13	16:01	0♍54
1172	Feb 12	14:06	22♓02
1215	Nov 7	3:07	6♎50
1216	May 7	6:28	5♎13
	Jun 26	1:26	4♎46
1262	Mar 31	18:14	18♈23
1306	Dec 28	19:06	11♏17
1307	May 4	10:24	10♏13
	Sep 2	16:17	9♏12
1352	May 25	3:08	15♉42
1398	Feb 23	4:31	14♐20
	May 3	16:45	13♐46
	Oct 24	9:42	12♐19
1442	Jul 26	21:35	14♊07
	Dec 30	3:13	12♊24
1443	Mar 12	20:00	11♊36
1489	Apr 10	4:30	15♑25
	May 19	21:41	15♑05
	Nov 29	10:17	13♑25
1533	Jun 18	3:31	12♋24
1580	Mar 25	23:41	13♒56
	Aug 18	12:35	12♒39
	Nov 26	7:57	11♒45
1623	Sep 29	19:10	15♌36
1624	Feb 21	0:08	14♌07
	May 20	14:44	13♌10
1671	Mar 5	12:21	10♓26
1714	Oct 12	20:25	18♍54
1761	May 14	9:39	7♈42
	Oct 28	16:31	6♈03
1762	Jan 3	21:59	5♈23
1805	Nov 17	19:48	23♎22
1852	Mar 15	7:25	2♉10
1897	Jan 6	7:10	27♏40
	Jun 1	9:26	26♏26
	Sep 9	10:25	25♏35
1942	May 3	13:20	29♉20
1988	Feb 13	1:00	29♐55
	Jun 26	17:05	28♐47
	Oct 18	13:29	27♐49
2032	Jun 28	11:54	28♊01
2079	Feb 26	21:26	29♑49
	Aug 31	5:24	28♑13
	Oct 21	19:05	27♑47

♄ ♆

Year	Date	Time	Position
-486	Jan 11	5:39	28♏40
	May 25	1:57	27♏53
	Sep 24	15:22	27♏09
-450	May 16	9:59	18♒48
	Jun 25	0:18	18♒32
-449	Jan 3	20:42	17♒13
-414	Apr 12	6:43	6♉35
-379	Jun 25	9:11	24♋27
-344	Dec 19	4:60	14♎04
-343	Mar 6	20:15	13♎36
	Aug 26	13:35	12♎33
-306	Jan 6	5:26	3♑05
-270	Mar 7	17:58	22♓28
-235	May 23	3:20	11♊03
-200	Aug 31	4:25	29♌11
-164	Dec 9	8:55	18♏24
-163	Jul 4	18:25	17♏10
	Aug 2	6:27	17♏00
-127	Apr 21	15:50	8♒48
	Jun 28	7:01	8♒22
	Dec 20	17:58	7♒13
-91	Apr 21	15:08	27♈14
-56	Jul 2	5:36	15♋15
-21	Nov 19	4:40	4♎06
-20	Mar 27	9:33	3♎18
	Jul 29	6:20	2♎30
16	Dec 4	19:24	22♐35
53	Feb 16	17:30	12♓13
88	May 14	15:27	1♊12
123	Aug 10	2:02	19♌08
159	Oct 24	15:12	7♏33
196	Feb 23	13:02	28♑01
	Aug 28	17:08	26♑50
	Oct 23	12:58	26♑29
232	Mar 23	16:07	16♈36
267	Jun 5	8:28	4♋52
302	Oct 1	8:35	23♍20
339	Jan 25	16:46	13♐02
	Jun 8	20:42	12♐14
	Oct 8	18:38	11♐30
375	May 26	1:15	3♓15
	Jul 15	0:01	2♓55
376	Jan 17	0:29	1♓39
411	Apr 24	21:21	20♉57
446	Jul 14	1:33	8♌57
481	Dec 27	21:51	28♎21
482	Mar 28	13:22	27♎49
	Sep 6	8:48	26♎49
519	Jan 18	6:43	17♑28
555	Mar 19	20:07	6♈58
590	Jun 4	10:23	25♊28
625	Sep 16	11:47	13♍41
661	Dec 19	12:23	2♐43
698	May 7	17:54	23♒26
	Jul 11	9:24	23♒01
699	Jan 5	5:09	21♒51
734	May 10	4:28	12♉01
769	Jul 21	22:02	29♋58
804	Dec 11	0:58	18♎47
805	Mar 30	6:27	18♎06
	Aug 20	13:46	17♎11
841	Dec 20	11:02	7♑12
878	Mar 13	12:06	27♓17
913	Jun 12	13:38	16♊22
948	Sep 6	20:54	4♍13
984	Nov 16	22:27	22♏27
1021	Mar 16	10:18	12♒51
	Aug 29	20:01	11♒48
	Nov 20	13:41	11♒16
1057	Apr 22	12:38	1♉53
1092	Jul 4	5:33	20♋02
1127	Oct 31	4:28	8♎24
1164	Feb 18	16:26	27♐48
	Jun 9	7:21	27♐08
	Oct 30	20:41	26♐16
1200	Jun 16	23:19	17♓56
	Jul 19	18:17	17♓43
1201	Feb 2	2:34	16♓22
1236	May 18	23:04	5♊59
1271	Aug 3	22:39	23♌44
1307	Jan 24	10:25	13♏02
	Mar 29	23:53	12♏39
	Sep 28	7:39	11♏31
1344	Jan 30	15:04	1♒57
1380	Mar 29	17:56	21♈28
1415	Jun 22	23:28	10♋09
1450	Sep 28	8:29	28♍04
1486	Dec 31	22:46	17♐07
1523	May 10	8:06	7♓48
	Aug 11	13:10	7♓12
1524	Jan 13	17:11	6♓11
1559	May 21	16:23	26♉27
1594	Aug 7	6:20	14♌28
1629	Dec 19	17:24	3♏00
1630	Apr 21	23:09	2♏14
	Aug 29	11:29	1♏24
1667	Jan 2	11:40	21♑32
1703	Mar 28	1:02	11♈44
1738	Jul 2	7:27	0♋58
1773	Sep 27	9:50	18♍43
1809	Dec 1	15:36	6♐40
1846	Apr 4	1:43	27♒18
	Sep 5	1:36	26♒20
	Dec 11	9:27	25♒42
1882	May 12	17:09	16♉29
1917	Aug 1	5:20	4♌45
1952	Nov 21	13:18	22♎47
1953	May 17	17:29	21♎38
	Jul 22	1:22	21♎12
1989	Mar 3	10:47	11♑55
	Jun 24	3:10	11♑14
	Nov 13	11:42	10♑22
2026	Feb 20	17:01	0♈45
2061	Jun 7	4:08	20♊24
2096	Aug 27	6:43	8♍09

♄ ♇

Year	Date	Time	Position
-493	Dec 8	22:17	23♍15
-492	Feb 4	17:56	22♍56
	Aug 11	2:28	21♍51
-455	Nov 17	6:45	18♐25
-421	Mar 24	6:32	10♒19
	Aug 10	6:12	9♒33
	Dec 1	23:07	8♒54
-389	Jun 13	7:45	16♓47
	Jul 23	18:14	16♓34
-388	Feb 1	16:25	15♓29
-357	May 17	0:52	17♈24
	Nov 19	21:04	16♈22
-356	Jan 8	7:04	16♈05
-325	Apr 28	12:09	17♉13
-293	Jun 4	3:18	23♊28
-260	Oct 31	3:58	22♌32
-259	Jan 13	7:12	22♌06
	Jul 3	13:45	21♌01
-222	Nov 17	9:23	24♏21
-187	Dec 31	21:29	26♑01
-154	Apr 21	20:26	7♓11
	Sep 5	1:15	6♓26
	Dec 28	21:20	5♓48
-122	May 1	0:54	9♈14
-90	Apr 14	9:54	8♉40
-59	Aug 12	19:48	12♊42
	Nov 20	5:59	12♊07
-58	Apr 14	12:12	11♊14
-26	Aug 24	15:11	28♋44
-25	Mar 22	3:48	27♋25
	31	21:53	27♋21
10	Dec 17	8:16	23♎12
11	Mar 31	15:57	22♎38
	Aug 29	22:54	21♎48
47	Dec 7	19:10	9♑11
81	Feb 13	0:21	25♒36
113	Mar 21	2:57	0♈04
144	Jul 6	16:49	1♉15
	Oct 1	4:21	0♉47
145	Mar 7	15:15	29♈53
176	Jun 9	11:51	1♊43
208	Aug 9	3:08	10♋59
209	Feb 16	17:15	9♋47
	Mar 27	15:46	9♋32
243	Aug 26	11:24	17♍08
280	Dec 23	12:48	18♐04
315	Mar 3	18:50	13♒19
347	Jun 3	5:25	21♓30
	Aug 14	13:53	21♓06
348	Feb 1	17:25	20♓09
379	May 24	10:21	22♈36
	Nov 19	7:01	21♈37
380	Jan 19	20:49	21♈16
411	May 3	12:55	22♉03
443	May 23	11:12	26♊21
476	Aug 6	3:43	18♌39
513	Nov 5	20:54	19♏04
549	Mar 3	4:41	28♑17

Outer Planet Conjunctions –500 (501 BC)–2100

Year	Date	Time	Position
	Aug 8	5:22	27♑25
	Nov 11	22:17	26♑53
582	Apr 5	1:53	10♓48
	Oct 20	6:16	9♓43
	Nov 28	17:11	9♓30
614	May 2	21:48	13♈54
646	Apr 18	19:10	13♉21
677	Aug 8	12:25	16♊14
	Dec 3	6:35	15♊34
678	Apr 11	10:59	14♊47
710	Jul 16	20:21	27♋49
745	Nov 13	19:17	14♎43
746	May 6	17:43	13♎44
	Jul 19	7:27	13♎18
783	Jan 17	21:32	8♑52
817	Feb 2	8:43	28♒18
849	Mar 30	23:07	4♈29
881	Mar 27	17:20	4♉45
912	Jun 28	19:50	6♊02
944	Aug 4	1:38	12♋32
978	Sep 10	13:47	11♍11
1016	Jan 1	15:31	13♐35
1051	Feb 3	16:45	14♒15
1083	May 26	6:13	24♓58
	Aug 29	21:36	24♓27
1084	Jan 30	6:36	23♓36
1115	Jun 4	6:36	26♈55
	Nov 9	7:33	26♈04
1116	Feb 6	3:24	25♈34
1147	May 14	0:30	26♉12
1179	May 19	9:30	28♊45
1211	Sep 26	2:10	16♌21
1212	Feb 21	4:54	15♌24
	May 28	7:01	14♌46
1248	Jan 13	12:16	10♏37
	Apr 4	10:58	10♏10
	Sep 21	14:00	9♏13
1284	Dec 27	10:54	26♑24
1318	Mar 8	18:05	12♓48
1350	Apr 21	5:53	17♈24
1382	Apr 10	18:01	17♉07
1413	Jul 22	1:03	19♊01
1414	Jan 11	19:38	18♊01
	Mar 18	11:43	17♊38
1445	Sep 22	1:13	28♋04
1446	Jan 11	4:01	27♋23
	May 25	18:05	26♋32
1480	Sep 25	13:09	3♎46
1518	Jan 13	22:47	4♑20
1552	Apr 4	23:51	0♓07
	Sep 9	7:47	29♒15
	Dec 13	23:43	28♒43
1585	Mar 16	4:55	7♈15
1616	Jul 26	10:25	9♉37
	Sep 24	15:01	9♉18
1617	Mar 22	19:15	8♉18
1648	Jun 24	22:39	9♊13
1680	Jul 13	2:05	13♋17
1713	Sep 23	8:30	5♍02
1750	Nov 21	21:05	4♐00
1786	Mar 27	10:02	14♒11
	Aug 9	4:21	13♒27
	Dec 8	6:44	12♒46
1819	May 5	2:32	27♓04
	Oct 5	6:43	26♓15
1820	Jan 11	17:17	25♓42
1851	Jun 6	21:41	0♉20
	Nov 11	5:52	29♈29
1852	Feb 10	4:21	28♈59
1883	May 22	18:39	29♉46
1914	Oct 4	18:39	2♋14
	Nov 1	8:48	2♋04
1915	May 19	19:55	0♋54
1947	Aug 11	1:20	13♌07
1982	Nov 8	0:39	27♎36
2020	Jan 12	16:23	22♑46
2053	Jun 15	5:40	14♓30
	Jul 10	17:57	14♓21
2054	Feb 2	5:42	13♓13
2086	Apr 8	21:46	19♈54

♃ ♄

Year	Date	Time	Position
-482	Mar 1	6:19	14♑36
-462	Oct 4	22:21	3♎52
-442	Mar 30	15:35	23♉37
-423	Dec 23	15:20	19♑11
-402	Aug 4	21:40	9♎07
-383	Jul 1	9:46	6♊40
-363	Mar 14	19:04	29♑50
-343	Oct 26	3:49	19♎23
-323	May 11	22:33	14♊03
-303	Jan 5	17:58	4♒29
-283	Aug 25	19:58	24♎05
-264	Aug 13	16:25	26♊44
-244	Mar 30	1:43	15♒26
-224	Nov 13	8:53	4♏12
-204	Jun 22	19:35	4♋20
-184	Jan 24	21:00	20♒34
-164	Sep 13	5:25	8♏49
-145	Oct 15	15:08	16♋43
	Dec 7	15:46	15♋32
-144	May 1	18:20	12♋10
-125	Apr 21	22:53	2♓14
-105	Dec 3	0:46	19♏10
-85	Aug 9	21:15	25♋10
-65	Feb 18	13:31	8♓22
-45	Oct 4	15:58	24♏01
-25	Jun 27	16:27	3♌17
-6	May 27	11:26	20♓56
	Sep 29	9:18	17♓25
	Dec 3	16:43	15♓34
14	Dec 24	22:55	4♐52
34	Oct 3	8:08	16♌40
54	Mar 24	6:21	28♓24
74	Oct 27	10:11	10♐03
94	Aug 19	11:56	25♌01
114	Jan 28	13:09	6♈13
134	Jan 19	2:47	21♐17
154	Jul 7	3:01	3♍12
173	May 7	9:53	20♈17
193	Nov 21	5:50	26♐34
213	Oct 11	10:53	16♍11
233	Mar 20	17:06	28♈31
253	Feb 13	16:03	7♑51
273	Aug 27	6:19	23♍31
292	Jun 27	11:05	12♉42
312	Dec 14	17:23	12♑59
332	Nov 29	4:41	5♎35
333	Apr 23	17:25	2♎10
	Jun 16	23:02	0♎57
352	May 7	22:11	20♉58
372	Mar 7	15:02	23♑59
392	Oct 4	1:34	11♎59
411	Aug 29	22:23	4♊08
	Nov 3	11:08	2♊32
412	Mar 12	10:23	29♉13
432	Jan 1	18:30	28♑47
452	Jan 15	8:36	22♎42
	Mar 18	14:39	21♎12
	Aug 4	9:17	17♎54
471	Jun 21	2:27	12♊27
491	Mar 24	8:59	9♒31
511	Nov 1	9:26	28♎29
531	May 2	5:50	20♊00
551	Jan 16	5:11	14♒04
571	Aug 31	22:60	3♏31
590	Aug 1	21:58	2♋52
610	Apr 8	10:41	24♒51
630	Nov 21	22:07	13♏44
650	Jun 13	21:11	10♋15
670	Jan 30	17:20	29♒36
690	Sep 20	12:37	18♏24
709	Sep 17	20:39	22♋53
710	Feb 8	23:58	19♋33
	Apr 3	17:53	18♋20
729	Apr 25	0:29	10♓47
749	Dec 10	3:42	28♏38
769	Jul 27	2:33	0♌38
789	Feb 18	22:55	16♓14
809	Oct 9	11:40	3♐20
829	Jun 8	15:20	8♌32
848	May 19	5:37	28♓13
868	Dec 28	19:38	13♐54
888	Sep 12	17:56	21♌41
908	Mar 18	17:07	4♈46
928	Oct 30	23:38	18♐53
948	Aug 2	12:52	29♌51
967	Jun 30	13:06	17♈34
	Oct 11	10:11	14♈42
968	Jan 9	6:10	12♈09
988	Jan 21	17:39	29♐55
1007	Nov 14	0:59	13♍05
1008	Mar 13	2:54	10♍22
	Jun 7	18:02	8♍27
1027	Apr 26	8:03	25♈25
1047	Nov 24	22:00	5♑08
1067	Sep 25	14:37	21♍25
1087	Mar 4	8:38	3♉22
1107	Feb 16	22:09	16♑27
1127	Aug 14	7:23	29♍18
1146	Jun 11	4:50	17♉30
1166	Dec 18	20:43	21♑42
1186	Nov 15	8:39	12♎04
1206	Apr 23	19:26	25♉46
1226	Mar 12	4:28	2♒58
1246	Sep 28	21:14	19♎07
1265	Aug 1	10:41	9♊42
1286	Jan 7	21:34	8♒02
1306	Jan 2	11:53	0♏49
	Apr 28	13:16	28♎05
	Jul 27	11:41	26♎01
1325	Jun 9	18:05	17♊53
1345	Apr 1	12:08	19♒01
1365	Nov 2	11:47	7♏01
1385	Apr 17	4:11	25♊54
1405	Jan 25	20:06	23♒46
1425	Feb 23	14:35	17♏18
	Mar 27	7:58	16♏33
	Sep 4	7:35	12♏40
1444	Jul 23	3:31	8♋57
1464	Apr 17	8:06	4♓35
1484	Nov 27	17:24	23♏10
1504	Jun 4	5:36	16♋25
1524	Feb 10	6:17	9♓14
1544	Sep 28	2:42	28♏05
1563	Sep 4	17:55	29♋10
1583	May 3	0:36	20♓11
1603	Dec 18	6:55	8♐19
1623	Jul 16	22:42	6♌36
1643	Feb 24	23:14	25♓07
1663	Oct 16	23:49	12♐58
1682	Oct 24	7:38	19♌09
1683	Feb 9	1:18	16♌43
	May 18	5:46	14♌30
1702	May 21	20:57	6♈36
1723	Jan 5	15:15	23♐19
1742	Aug 30	20:52	27♌09
1762	Mar 18	16:41	12♈21
1782	Nov 5	9:26	28♐07
1802	Jul 17	22:48	5♍08
1821	Jun 19	17:13	24♈39
1842	Jan 26	6:12	8♑54
1861	Oct 21	12:26	18♍22
1881	Apr 18	13:37	1♉36
1901	Nov 28	16:29	14♑00
1921	Sep 10	4:14	26♍36
1940	Aug 8	1:24	14♉27
	Oct 20	4:38	12♉28
1941	Feb 15	6:37	9♉07
1961	Feb 19	0:03	25♑12
1980	Dec 31	21:26	9♎30
1981	Mar 4	19:06	8♎06
	Jul 24	4:17	4♎56
2000	May 28	16:05	22♉43
2020	Dec 21	18:22	0♒29
2040	Oct 31	11:50	17♎56
2060	Apr 7	22:32	0♊47
2080	Mar 15	1:34	11♒52
2100	Sep 18	22:36	25♎32

♃ ♅

Year	Date	Time	Position
-490	May 13	16:46	18♉01
-476	Jun 21	15:04	20♋20
-462	Sep 6	1:37	27♍31
-448	Oct 14	16:07	29♏12
-434	Feb 8	15:47	26♑20
-421	May 23	22:38	20♓11
	Sep 20	10:08	18♓20
	Dec 19	18:50	16♓56
-407	Apr 23	21:05	13♉51
-393	May 26	22:46	15♋25
-379	Aug 11	5:59	22♍30
-365	Feb 27	14:15	27♏55
	Apr 11	5:48	27♏19
	Sep 22	4:08	24♏57
-351	Jan 21	11:08	22♑33
-338	May 1	8:11	16♓37
-324	Apr 3	22:00	9♉44
-311	Sep 18	7:22	13♋40
	Dec 27	22:11	12♋16
-310	Apr 24	9:34	10♋36
-297	Dec 7	16:60	20♍29
-296	Feb 16	8:50	19♍32
	Jul 12	16:06	17♍31
-282	Jan 16	21:19	23♏48
	Jun 2	4:15	21♏51
	Aug 20	11:01	20♏44
-268	Jan 6	7:01	18♑46
-255	Apr 13	4:29	13♓02
-241	Mar 15	7:47	5♉41
-228	Aug 18	18:37	9♋04
-214	Oct 29	19:33	15♍40
-213	Apr 13	19:14	13♍25
	May 27	5:08	12♍50
-200	Dec 23	2:27	19♏28
-186	Dec 21	7:46	14♑57
-172	Mar 26	13:17	9♓20
-159	Jul 30	15:50	4♉53
	Sep 30	1:05	3♉58
-158	Feb 21	19:51	1♉45
-145	Jul 26	8:26	4♋26
-131	Oct 2	14:39	10♍48
-117	Dec 1	4:02	15♏07
-103	Dec 3	2:05	11♑08
-89	Mar 12	8:25	5♓44
-76	Jun 30	4:41	1♉10
	Nov 6	6:37	29♈12
-75	Jan 25	21:21	27♈58
-62	Jul 4	7:44	29♊49
-48	Sep 8	23:08	5♍54
-34	Nov 10	17:05	10♏42
-20	Nov 16	18:50	7♑24
-6	Feb 25	4:40	2♓07
7	Jun 8	1:30	27♈17
21	Jun 12	20:00	25♊13
35	Aug 16	7:13	0♍53
49	Oct 21	2:11	6♏14
63	Apr 6	13:30	6♑42
	May 24	11:41	6♑00
	Oct 28	11:48	3♑39
77	Feb 9	12:36	28♒30
90	May 20	13:34	23♈28
104	May 23	10:46	20♊38
118	Jul 23	17:08	25♌51
132	Sep 30	10:55	1♏39
146	Mar 3	7:26	3♑02
	Jul 3	16:02	1♑13
	Oct 3	16:15	29♐52
160	Jan 28	6:16	24♒56
173	May 4	18:05	19♈41
187	May 2	9:45	16♊09
201	Jun 27	18:09	20♌49
215	Sep 8	3:48	26♎55
229	Feb 9	8:31	29♐08
243	Jan 13	5:32	21♒18
256	Apr 18	14:16	15♈52
269	Sep 25	1:25	14♊44
	Oct 19	3:33	14♊23
270	Apr 10	11:06	11♊49
283	Oct 18	20:19	18♌59
284	Feb 10	20:01	17♌25
	May 25	19:35	15♌58
298	Jan 4	3:54	25♎20
	Apr 1	15:28	24♎08
	Aug 11	22:27	22♎19
312	Jan 21	10:31	25♐05
325	Dec 27	15:57	17♒35
339	Apr 4	20:28	12♈07
352	Aug 12	16:33	10♊47
	Dec 6	2:13	9♊05
353	Mar 14	8:39	7♊38
366	Sep 19	12:58	14♌10
380	Dec 2	15:29	20♎42
381	May 28	21:19	18♎16
	Jun 23	13:23	17♎56
395	Jan 1	7:59	20♐58
408	May 28	12:16	16♒57
	Jun 23	13:16	16♒34
	Dec 9	1:43	13♒58
422	Mar 18	14:40	8♈17
435	Jul 17	13:17	6♊33
449	Aug 24	19:16	9♌20
463	Nov 7	2:27	16♎00
477	Dec 13	21:30	16♐53
491	Apr 18	1:02	13♒33
	Aug 7	22:53	11♒50
	Nov 15	17:09	10♒19
505	Mar 1	15:11	4♈27
518	Jun 26	8:39	2♊18
532	Jul 31	21:51	4♌24
546	Oct 14	20:35	11♎13
560	Nov 24	17:48	12♐43
574	Mar 25	12:08	9♒54
588	Feb 12	17:09	0♈41
601	Jun 5	9:07	27♉57
615	Jul 8	10:59	29♋23
629	Sep 20	19:29	6♎15
643	Nov 5	20:46	8♐27
657	Mar 7	3:34	6♒13
671	Jan 24	9:54	26♓55
684	May 15	17:19	23♉38
698	Jun 12	11:49	24♋24
712	Aug 26	12:40	1♎10
726	Oct 15	22:38	4♐09
740	Feb 17	15:46	2♒24
753	Jun 6	10:25	26♓31
	Sep 13	21:35	24♓59
754	Jan 2	6:28	23♓16
767	Apr 28	11:34	19♉28
780	Oct 14	20:25	22♋31
	Dec 14	14:27	21♋41
781	May 14	19:28	19♋31
795	Jan 4	6:32	28♍53
	31	20:26	28♍32
	Jul 29	8:35	26♍06

Outer Planet Conjunctions –500 (501 BC)—2100

Year	Date	Time	Position
809	Feb 13	12:10	2♐49
	May 8	0:45	1♐38
	Sep 18	15:24	29♏45
823	Jan 30	17:49	28♑32
836	May 14	5:37	22♓58
	Oct 18	12:46	20♓31
	Dec 1	5:13	19♓51
850	Apr 9	1:15	15♉21
863	Sep 7	22:13	17♋59
864	Jan 31	13:47	15♋54
	Apr 6	23:25	14♋57
877	Nov 14	18:14	24♍12
878	Mar 30	21:35	22♍22
	Jun 21	19:08	21♍15
892	Jan 13	9:13	28♏31
	Jun 23	16:31	26♏14
	Aug 9	18:50	25♏35
906	Jan 15	11:14	24♑43
919	Apr 25	19:26	19♓19
933	Mar 21	19:49	11♉24
946	Aug 14	4:18	13♋26
960	Oct 17	7:35	19♍19
974	Dec 21	4:21	24♏08
988	Dec 29	1:35	20♑51
1002	Apr 9	14:18	15♓41
1015	Aug 21	5:18	10♉32
	Sep 19	9:11	10♉06
1016	Mar 3	9:52	7♉32
1029	Jul 23	18:44	8♋54
1043	Sep 25	1:05	14♍30
1057	Nov 30	6:30	19♏45
1071	Dec 14	18:43	17♑05
1085	Mar 25	14:51	12♓09
1098	Jul 12	12:23	6♉59
	Oct 30	23:28	5♉17
1099	Feb 7	21:56	3♉44
1112	Jul 3	19:55	4♋23
1126	Sep 2	4:47	9♍34
1140	Nov 10	7:50	15♏19
1154	Nov 28	11:15	13♑20
1168	Mar 10	12:14	8♓30
1181	Jun 20	12:48	3♉12
1195	Jun 14	13:20	29♊52
1209	Aug 9	6:07	4♍37
1223	Oct 21	9:25	10♏48
1237	Nov 8	2:58	9♑30
1251	Feb 24	18:16	4♓57
1264	Jun 1	17:39	29♈29
1278	May 23	19:29	25♊21
1292	Jul 13	21:13	29♌33
1306	Sep 28	11:21	6♏04
1320	Mar 13	6:32	8♑49
	Jun 29	2:49	7♑14
	Oct 15	11:33	5♑40
1334	Feb 10	5:46	1♓20
1347	May 15	13:15	25♈39
1361	May 2	14:46	20♊56
1374	Nov 9	7:42	27♌36
1375	Jan 30	0:36	26♌29
	Jun 15	9:04	24♌36
1389	Feb 13	20:51	4♏06
	Mar 1	7:52	3♏54
	Sep 2	13:28	1♏22
1403	Feb 17	11:52	4♑52
1417	Jan 25	3:22	27♒40
1430	Apr 29	14:32	21♈56
1443	Sep 15	20:39	19♊46
	Nov 11	11:27	18♊57
1444	Apr 9	7:53	16♊41
1457	Oct 4	19:38	22♌46
1458	Apr 2	12:30	20♌17
	21	16:12	20♌01
1471	Dec 22	23:24	29♎41
1472	May 3	7:10	27♎53
	Jul 29	18:30	26♎42

Year	Date	Time	Position
1486	Jan 25	3:02	0♑46
1500	Jan 8	19:39	24♒00
1513	Apr 13	13:41	18♈11
1526	Aug 10	20:22	15♊42
	Dec 27	3:19	13♊38
1527	Mar 8	7:49	12♊33
1540	Sep 8	13:37	17♌57
1554	Nov 24	10:15	24♎58
1569	Jan 6	10:01	26♐43
1582	Dec 22	8:60	20♒26
1596	Mar 27	5:06	14♈28
1609	Jul 17	20:16	11♊37
1623	Aug 15	17:03	13♌08
1637	Oct 29	20:23	20♎12
1651	Dec 18	4:21	22♐36
1665	May 2	2:01	20♒03
	Jul 31	5:24	18♒41
	Nov 29	16:33	16♒51
1679	Mar 11	19:35	10♈48
1692	Jun 26	9:50	7♊29
1706	Jul 23	7:09	8♌15
1720	Oct 6	12:46	15♎22
1734	Nov 29	6:40	18♐30
1748	Apr 9	3:25	16♒40
	Sep 1	16:29	14♒28
	Nov 3	13:12	13♒32
1762	Feb 24	19:07	7♈16
1775	Jun 8	19:45	3♊25
1789	Jun 29	16:21	3♌29
1803	Sep 13	10:27	10♎27
1817	Nov 10	8:37	14♐20
1831	Mar 21	6:35	13♒07
1845	Feb 8	9:26	3♈44
1858	May 23	6:41	29♉26
1872	Jun 5	8:57	28♋44
1886	Aug 18	7:54	5♎30
1900	Oct 20	8:15	10♐06
1914	Mar 4	3:25	9♒32
1927	Jul 15	21:37	3♈24
	Aug 11	11:03	3♈00
1928	Jan 25	6:49	0♈24
1941	May 8	0:22	25♉38
1954	Oct 7	10:02	27♋23
1955	Jan 7	2:01	26♋04
	May 10	20:38	24♋16
1968	Dec 11	15:00	3♎39
1969	Mar 11	19:41	2♎27
	Jul 20	7:58	0♎40
1983	Feb 18	22:43	8♐52
	May 14	20:36	7♐41
	Sep 25	13:56	5♐49
1997	Feb 16	2:23	5♒56
2010	Jun 8	11:26	0♈18
	Sep 19	1:07	28♓43
2011	Jan 4	12:52	27♓02
2024	Apr 21	2:25	21♉50
2037	Sep 8	10:29	23♋03
2038	Feb 19	17:12	20♋39
	Mar 30	21:27	20♋05
2051	Nov 9	6:52	28♍55
2052	May 10	0:20	26♍26
	26	6:19	26♍13
2066	Jan 20	3:53	4♐43
	Jun 24	16:55	2♐34
	Aug 21	5:32	1♐47
2080	Jan 31	17:50	2♒16
2093	May 17	21:30	27♓00
	Oct 21	5:52	24♓35
	Dec 5	19:14	23♓53
	♃♆		
-496	Jan 19	8:60	7♏26
	Apr 10	20:16	6♏39
	Aug 29	23:23	5♏17
-484	Dec 27	19:47	4♐37

Year	Date	Time	Position
-471	Dec 14	15:55	1♑36
-458	Apr 24	23:38	0♒58
	Jun 26	15:43	0♒19
	Nov 23	5:41	28♑43
-445	Mar 17	0:57	28♒29
-432	Feb 27	1:55	25♓54
-420	Jun 26	18:52	25♈56
	Oct 22	8:05	24♈42
-419	Jan 30	18:32	23♈39
-407	Jun 6	12:14	23♉46
-394	May 31	19:39	21♊31
-381	May 27	19:24	19♋14
-369	Oct 3	5:58	19♌05
-368	Mar 8	12:00	17♌37
	May 10	14:20	17♌01
-356	Sep 30	18:37	16♍32
-343	Sep 30	20:45	13♎46
-330	Sep 25	19:51	10♏53
-317	Jan 23	6:41	10♐17
	Jul 10	0:44	8♐36
	Aug 23	13:11	8♐10
-304	Jan 6	9:19	7♑19
-292	Dec 19	8:10	4♒24
-279	Apr 10	1:30	4♓10
-266	Mar 21	10:44	1♈39
-253	Mar 3	15:59	29♈19
-241	Jul 1	3:13	29♉28
-228	Jun 23	0:40	27♊14
-215	Jun 22	2:22	24♋55
-203	Nov 6	7:57	24♌39
-202	Jan 22	11:57	23♌57
	Jun 19	1:37	22♌33
-190	Oct 27	4:49	22♍12
-177	Oct 25	20:14	19♎29
-164	Oct 21	0:07	16♏35
-151	Feb 27	0:15	15♐52
	May 20	23:44	15♐03
	Oct 5	13:47	13♐39
-138	Jan 30	22:11	13♑05
-125	Jan 13	20:14	10♒11
-113	May 11	6:28	9♓54
	Sep 8	11:21	8♓37
	Dec 13	18:41	7♓34
-100	Apr 14	8:38	7♈27
-87	Mar 30	19:48	5♉07
-75	Jul 31	11:50	5♊14
	Dec 8	21:43	3♊55
-74	Mar 7	22:11	3♊00
-62	Jul 18	22:32	3♋00
-49	Jul 18	9:15	0♌42
-36	Jul 18	20:40	28♌17
-24	Nov 27	10:07	27♍53
-23	Mar 15	22:21	26♍53
	Jul 13	10:39	25♍46
-11	Nov 19	17:36	25♎15
2	Nov 15	12:56	22♏23
15	Nov 5	3:40	19♐24
28	Feb 27	11:45	18♑52
41	Feb 7	15:05	16♒04
54	Jan 17	22:53	13♓23
66	May 10	17:24	13♈22
79	Apr 25	15:23	11♉01
92	Apr 12	19:20	8♊49
104	Aug 16	6:41	8♋53
117	Aug 13	8:07	6♌34
130	Aug 15	22:34	4♍08
143	Aug 16	19:05	1♎32
155	Dec 21	3:40	1♏02
156	May 8	0:09	29♎43
	Aug 1	22:27	28♎54
168	Dec 11	3:29	28♏15
181	Dec 2	8:20	25♐17
194	Apr 6	20:56	24♑39
	Jul 2	6:28	23♑45
	Nov 10	15:34	22♑22

Year	Date	Time	Position
207	Mar 6	20:15	21♒59
220	Feb 17	7:32	19♓19
232	Jun 13	11:52	19♈18
	Oct 29	7:44	17♈50
233	Jan 14	7:45	17♈01
245	May 22	22:18	17♉00
258	May 13	23:35	14♊44
270	Sep 23	5:21	14♋44
	Dec 22	14:01	13♋52
271	May 4	5:51	12♋34
283	Sep 11	2:47	12♌29
296	Sep 11	9:25	10♍01
309	Sep 14	19:11	7♎25
322	Sep 11	1:27	4♏40
335	Jan 9	15:53	4♐05
347	Dec 29	4:31	1♑10
360	Dec 13	0:58	28♑14
373	Apr 3	4:59	27♒54
386	Mar 13	17:27	25♓15
399	Feb 22	2:39	22♈49
411	Jun 19	15:37	22♉57
424	Jun 8	10:25	20♊40
437	Jun 4	1:42	18♋24
449	Oct 11	20:26	18♌19
450	Feb 14	18:46	17♌08
	May 25	18:12	16♌11
462	Oct 7	19:42	15♍52
475	Oct 9	15:03	13♎15
488	Oct 7	12:54	10♏29
501	Feb 11	21:33	9♐50
	May 26	11:47	8♐49
	Sep 23	23:05	7♐38
514	Jan 21	21:29	6♑59
527	Jan 7	6:18	4♒04
539	May 6	0:40	3♓42
	Aug 30	23:37	2♓27
	Dec 9	1:19	1♓23
552	Apr 6	0:40	1♈08
565	Mar 19	17:21	28♈40
577	Jul 16	23:07	28♉47
	Dec 18	20:23	27♉12
578	Feb 14	17:35	26♉36
590	Jul 3	6:23	26♊32
603	Jun 30	19:23	24♋14
615	Dec 6	13:41	23♌50
	19	22:48	23♌43
616	Jun 28	9:19	21♌54
628	Nov 4	16:13	21♍39
629	Apr 11	0:13	20♍12
	Jun 13	18:43	19♍36
641	Nov 2	19:06	19♎02
654	Nov 2	2:04	16♏16
667	Oct 25	2:27	13♐22
680	Feb 17	5:50	12♑47
693	Jan 29	14:59	9♒53
706	Jan 9	19:02	7♓08
718	May 2	7:14	7♈01
731	Apr 14	9:04	4♉32
743	Aug 23	12:06	4♊31
	Nov 3	22:29	3♊47
744	Mar 26	6:59	2♊17
756	Jul 28	9:28	2♋23
769	Jul 24	12:27	0♌04
782	Jul 25	7:32	27♌42
794	Dec 11	11:13	27♍20
795	Feb 22	20:13	26♍40
	Jul 24	4:31	25♍15
807	Nov 29	8:35	24♎50
820	Nov 24	22:05	22♏04
833	Nov 19	5:26	19♐09
846	Mar 21	16:39	18♑34
	Jul 9	14:54	17♑27
	Oct 28	16:53	16♑18
859	Feb 23	11:27	15♒47
872	Feb 4	20:14	12♓58

Year	Date	Time	Position
884	May 28	17:48	12♈53
	Nov 15	8:16	11♈03
	Dec 18	0:02	10♈42
897	May 8	1:41	10♉29
910	Apr 25	14:55	8♊09
922	Aug 26	17:04	8♋14
923	Jan 23	0:00	6♋45
	Apr 1	9:55	6♋05
935	Aug 19	15:50	5♌57
948	Aug 19	22:12	3♍33
961	Aug 22	4:31	1♎03
974	Jan 1	18:56	0♏36
	Apr 13	22:34	29♎39
	Aug 17	8:53	28♎28
986	Dec 21	21:17	27♏55
999	Dec 14	15:12	25♐00
1012	Dec 1	7:53	22♑05
1025	Mar 23	21:56	21♒42
1038	Mar 3	20:14	18♓56
1050	Jul 11	21:18	18♈39
	Sep 14	19:02	17♈58
1051	Feb 7	23:16	16♈23
1063	Jun 5	2:44	16♉27
1076	May 23	9:01	14♊07
1088	Oct 14	3:23	13♋57
	Nov 24	2:26	13♋34
1089	May 13	4:36	11♋52
1101	Sep 17	21:59	11♌52
1114	Sep 17	12:49	9♍28
1127	Sep 20	10:23	6♎55
1140	Sep 19	14:08	4♏16
1153	Jan 23	2:35	3♐44
	Jun 11	20:10	2♐24
	Sep 3	15:16	1♐35
1166	Jan 10	14:06	0♑54
1178	Dec 29	4:22	27♑57
1191	Apr 26	11:39	27♒32
	Aug 29	8:12	26♒13
	Nov 30	4:02	25♒14
1204	Mar 29	21:27	24♓54
1217	Mar 10	16:14	22♈19
1229	Jul 3	22:50	22♉22
1242	Jun 19	2:55	20♊04
1255	Jun 13	3:21	17♋46
1267	Oct 23	11:45	17♌40
1268	Jan 26	19:42	16♌46
	Jun 4	14:57	15♌31
1280	Oct 13	17:34	15♍19
1293	Oct 15	10:34	12♎46
1306	Oct 17	11:12	10♏04
1319	Mar 16	16:31	9♐18
	Apr 12	8:20	9♐03
	Oct 11	3:51	7♐16
1332	Feb 7	12:26	6♑43
1345	Jan 23	0:41	3♒49
1358	Jan 2	20:01	0♓58
1370	Apr 24	16:58	0♈45
1383	Apr 6	2:54	28♈13
1395	Aug 9	10:22	28♉08
	Nov 6	13:09	27♉13
1396	Mar 13	5:27	25♉52
1408	Jul 14	14:05	25♊54
1421	Jul 8	18:11	23♋36
1434	Jul 6	22:07	21♌16
1446	Nov 14	8:51	21♍02
1447	Mar 19	20:45	19♍53
	Jun 29	12:06	18♍56
1459	Nov 11	3:11	18♎32
1472	Nov 10	12:24	15♏50
1485	Nov 6	11:03	12♐58
1498	Mar 7	23:19	12♑24
	Jul 14	12:18	11♑06
	Oct 15	19:25	10♑10
1511	Feb 17	7:41	9♒36
1524	Jan 30	12:08	6♓44

Outer Planet Conjunctions –500 (501 BC)–2100

Year	Date	Time	Position
1536	May 21	12:50	6♈31
1549	Apr 29	9:16	4♉00
1562	Apr 12	21:33	1♊37
1574	Aug 9	18:58	1♋40
1587	Aug 1	8:28	29♋20
1600	Jul 31	4:17	26♌59
1613	Jan 4	2:49	26♍29
	23	1:39	26♍19
	Jul 31	4:22	24♍33
1625	Dec 7	2:22	24♎11
1626	May 13	15:31	22♎43
	Jul 16	15:15	22♎08
1638	Dec 4	10:39	21♏32
1651	Nov 30	21:45	18♐40
1664	Nov 16	22:04	15♑45
1677	Mar 11	1:05	15♒17
1690	Feb 21	18:19	12♓29
1702	Jun 26	17:10	12♈10
	Sep 19	13:25	11♈16
1703	Jan 27	2:11	9♈51
1715	May 22	22:23	9♉47
1728	May 7	3:27	7♊21
1740	Sep 9	19:59	7♋21
	Dec 24	12:27	6♋18
1741	Apr 18	19:51	5♋07
1753	Aug 25	0:50	5♌05
1766	Aug 24	10:13	2♍40
1779	Aug 27	3:32	0♎12
1792	Jan 12	18:17	29♎45
	Mar 26	8:00	29♎04
	Aug 24	12:08	27♎39
1804	Dec 30	4:16	27♏10
1817	Dec 25	1:44	24♐21
1830	Dec 15	11:48	21♑25
1843	Apr 9	22:53	20♒57
	Sep 11	23:58	19♒20
	Nov 8	22:53	18♒44
1856	Mar 17	9:22	18♓13
1869	Feb 26	1:47	15♈35
1881	Jun 18	12:20	15♉35
1894	Jun 1	11:32	13♊10
1907	May 22	11:47	10♋50
1919	Sep 24	1:59	10♌49
1920	Mar 8	11:58	9♌12
	Apr 24	13:52	8♌45
1932	Sep 19	4:41	8♍25
1945	Sep 22	9:01	5♎54
1958	Sep 24	16:13	3♏18
1971	Feb 1	6:50	2♐47
	May 22	4:58	1♐44
	Sep 16	5:29	0♐37
1984	Jan 19	17:25	0♑01
1997	Jan 9	11:41	27♑09
2009	May 27	20:13	26♒29
	Jul 10	9:08	26♒02
	Dec 21	8:54	24♒18
2022	Apr 12	14:46	23♓59
2035	Mar 24	16:37	21♈21
2047	Jul 22	20:18	21♉19
	Nov 16	23:24	20♉05
2048	Feb 24	16:32	19♉01
2060	Jun 27	14:06	19♊00
2073	Jun 17	22:57	16♋37
2085	Nov 1	11:13	16♌27
2086	Jan 10	22:33	15♌47
	Jun 9	23:58	14♌19
2098	Oct 16	19:59	14♍09
♃ ♇			
-499	Dec 17	4:24	8♍04
-498	Jan 6	3:47	7♍54
	Jul 14	5:04	6♍11
-486	Dec 30	18:13	11♎35
-485	Mar 5	8:53	10♎59
	Aug 10	2:53	9♎32
-472	Jan 5	15:39	13♏36
	May 19	14:15	12♏21
	Aug 16	21:37	11♏31
-460	Dec 19	1:16	10♐17
-447	Nov 11	1:25	1♑51
-434	Jan 20	5:23	21♑47
-422	Mar 20	10:44	9♒01
-410	Dec 28	6:33	22♒26
-397	Feb 11	3:53	6♓28
-385	Mar 21	8:37	19♓34
-373	Apr 26	20:21	1♈59
-361	Jun 4	23:17	13♈57
	Oct 27	5:57	12♈52
-360	Jan 9	13:55	12♈17
-348	Feb 26	12:12	24♈06
-336	Apr 5	2:10	6♉06
-324	May 12	21:48	18♉34
-312	Jun 24	7:58	1♊53
-300	Aug 25	12:14	16♊33
	Nov 24	0:32	15♊51
-299	Apr 6	14:23	14♊46
-287	Jun 13	0:46	1♋43
-275	Sep 1	21:37	22♋17
-274	Feb 23	15:54	20♋48
	Apr 2	15:47	20♋28
-262	Aug 13	3:25	16♌02
-249	Aug 27	7:26	16♍00
-236	Sep 24	13:30	19♎34
-223	Oct 6	12:47	20♏42
-210	Jan 23	21:13	18♐33
-198	Dec 14	3:03	9♑20
-185	Feb 17	19:08	28♑43
-173	Apr 26	22:50	15♒26
	Jul 27	16:13	14♒40
	Dec 2	8:12	13♒35
-160	Jan 24	16:44	28♒39
-148	Mar 6	6:31	12♓31
-136	Apr 13	17:26	25♓27
-124	May 22	11:51	7♈44
	Nov 8	19:42	6♈25
	Dec 17	19:49	6♈07
-112	Jul 12	20:26	19♈34
	Sep 11	21:30	19♈07
-111	Feb 12	16:29	17♈56
-99	Mar 24	8:27	29♈47
-87	Apr 29	12:19	11♉51
-75	Jun 6	20:58	24♉26
-63	Jul 23	16:05	7♊55
	Dec 31	12:06	6♊40
-62	Feb 25	6:10	6♊14
-50	May 8	10:59	21♊06
-38	Jul 12	2:19	8♋37
-26	Oct 21	11:35	29♋48
	Dec 19	10:10	29♋19
-25	May 30	2:40	27♋55
-13	Sep 20	16:54	24♌47
0	Oct 8	1:32	25♍45
13	Nov 6	0:35	29♎20
26	Nov 15	6:57	29♏34
39	Mar 18	18:60	26♐20
	May 19	13:26	25♐46
	Oct 21	20:43	24♐20
52	Jan 13	5:17	16♑33
64	Mar 21	6:02	5♒22
	Sep 1	20:49	3♒57
	Oct 19	6:51	3♒32
77	Jan 3	9:13	19♒53
89	Feb 19	3:39	4♓45
101	Apr 2	13:51	18♓24
113	May 12	23:01	1♈11
125	Jul 1	8:56	13♈17
	Sep 13	7:07	12♈43
126	Feb 3	12:09	11♈36
138	Mar 14	11:15	23♈30
150	Apr 18	19:05	5♉24
162	May 25	0:43	17♉31
174	Jul 4	17:24	0♊12
186	Sep 5	0:44	13♊46
	Nov 4	7:02	13♊19
187	Apr 10	23:11	12♊04
199	Jun 7	5:33	27♊23
211	Aug 13	19:57	15♋26
224	Jul 7	16:32	5♌30
236	Nov 11	14:20	3♍21
237	Feb 5	13:49	2♍36
	Jun 26	8:36	1♍20
249	Nov 27	7:13	5♎12
250	Apr 5	14:03	4♎02
	Jul 12	17:59	3♎08
262	Dec 22	19:32	8♏38
263	May 31	11:08	7♏09
	Jul 30	9:19	6♏36
275	Dec 23	21:36	8♐02
288	Nov 28	17:54	1♑53
301	Feb 14	16:09	23♑31
313	May 17	11:17	11♒40
	Jun 22	3:51	11♒22
	Dec 9	23:56	9♒53
326	Feb 3	0:33	26♒04
338	Mar 19	23:52	10♓43
350	May 1	13:47	24♓11
362	Jun 19	13:56	6♈44
	Sep 14	20:04	6♈04
363	Jan 24	12:04	5♈02
375	Mar 5	14:58	17♈09
387	Apr 9	15:25	29♈03
399	May 14	9:39	10♉57
411	Jun 20	9:56	23♉07
423	Aug 6	6:58	5♊51
	Nov 27	20:43	4♊59
424	Mar 17	1:32	4♊08
436	May 10	6:05	17♊56
448	Jul 4	2:04	3♋39
460	Sep 17	17:48	22♋08
461	Jan 14	22:30	21♋09
	May 1	23:36	20♋15
473	Aug 9	18:00	13♌03
486	Aug 8	8:15	9♍50
499	Sep 2	4:28	12♎12
512	Sep 25	19:29	15♏14
525	Jan 30	18:36	15♐58
	Jul 7	14:53	14♐31
	Sep 5	19:45	13♐57
537	Dec 29	20:34	9♑05
550	Mar 17	22:35	0♒04
	Aug 23	4:23	28♑40
	Oct 18	20:14	28♑10
563	Jan 7	0:49	16♒02
575	Feb 26	11:03	1♓59
587	Apr 12	7:59	16♓23
599	May 29	21:14	29♓39
	Sep 27	1:56	28♓42
600	Jan 5	3:36	27♓54
612	Feb 20	3:34	10♈24
624	Mar 27	0:32	22♈29
636	Apr 30	1:40	4♉22
648	Jun 3	18:54	16♉16
660	Jul 13	13:37	28♉27
	Dec 23	1:19	27♉13
661	Feb 13	5:05	26♉49
673	Apr 14	10:41	9♊33
685	Jun 2	12:35	23♊37
697	Jul 28	16:40	9♋39
710	Jun 6	5:41	26♋42
722	Sep 9	18:55	20♌20
735	Sep 13	1:38	18♍02
748	Oct 9	18:16	20♎55
761	Nov 1	16:08	23♏34
774	Apr 12	4:08	23♐10
	14	20:30	23♐08
	Oct 25	17:32	21♐20
787	Jan 26	18:24	15♑57
799	Apr 30	0:28	6♒17
	Jun 29	12:24	5♒45
	Nov 30	15:13	4♒23
812	Jan 31	22:09	22♒02
824	Mar 21	2:48	7♓45
836	May 8	13:15	21♓57
	Oct 17	4:03	20♓38
	Dec 6	20:47	20♓14
849	Feb 3	7:49	3♈16
861	Mar 13	13:07	15♈45
873	Apr 16	23:37	27♈47
885	May 20	22:38	9♉38
897	Jun 26	23:02	21♉33
909	Aug 15	5:13	3♊44
	Nov 9	16:11	3♊05
910	Mar 24	11:50	2♊03
922	May 9	21:14	15♊01
934	Jun 26	17:13	29♊19
946	Aug 25	19:01	15♋40
947	Feb 21	10:52	14♋12
	Mar 22	12:58	13♋58
959	Jul 5	14:47	3♌14
971	Oct 15	6:50	27♌38
972	Mar 7	10:27	26♌23
	May 26	20:18	25♌41
984	Oct 17	20:08	26♍15
997	Nov 15	17:30	29♎29
1010	Dec 7	2:48	1♐39
1023	Nov 29	15:37	28♐37
1036	Feb 27	8:36	22♑34
1048	Dec 31	9:03	10♒32
1061	Feb 26	8:20	27♒57
1073	Apr 18	17:34	13♓23
1085	Jun 19	6:00	27♓17
	Aug 22	8:30	26♓46
1086	Jan 19	11:05	25♓33
1098	Mar 2	13:53	8♈36
1110	Apr 8	6:25	21♈00
1122	May 12	10:59	3♉00
1134	Jun 17	13:46	14♉50
1146	Jul 30	9:60	26♉42
	Nov 16	22:29	25♉53
1147	Mar 9	17:35	25♉01
1159	Apr 23	7:10	7♊18
1171	Jun 5	0:07	20♊26
1183	Jul 23	12:37	4♋57
1195	Oct 5	18:31	21♋33
	Dec 21	16:06	20♋56
1196	May 15	11:30	19♋44
1208	Aug 4	11:42	9♌46
1221	Jul 13	22:36	2♍50
1233	Dec 2	12:50	4♎17
1234	Mar 23	0:27	3♎18
	Jul 19	3:21	2♎14
1246	Dec 30	4:41	7♏47
1247	May 8	6:54	6♏36
	Aug 14	6:19	5♏42
1260	Jan 12	18:44	9♐27
1272	Dec 29	23:29	5♑41
1285	Apr 7	17:29	28♑58
	Jul 7	20:15	28♑09
	Nov 14	21:54	26♑58
1298	Jan 27	12:20	16♒37
1310	Mar 25	12:04	3♓43
1322	May 22	3:16	18♓52
	Sep 11	2:18	17♓57
	Dec 28	14:29	17♓03
1335	Feb 16	16:45	0♈54
1347	Mar 26	16:57	13♈52
1359	Apr 30	14:19	26♈13
1371	Jun 5	0:54	8♉09
1383	Jul 14	13:05	19♉55
	Nov 24	14:09	18♉55
1384	Feb 20	4:37	18♉15
1396	Apr 5	16:58	0♊07
1408	May 16	6:09	12♊29
1420	Jun 27	3:40	25♊46
1432	Aug 18	1:05	10♋29
1445	Jun 14	3:02	25♋33
1457	Sep 1	0:44	16♌09
1470	Aug 16	1:22	9♍56
1483	Aug 30	6:21	9♎59
1496	Sep 27	15:52	13♏32
1509	Feb 26	16:48	16♐43
	May 21	0:36	15♐57
	Oct 8	13:18	14♐38
1522	Jan 28	4:28	12♑23
1534	Dec 16	21:02	3♒03
1547	Feb 21	0:35	22♒23
1559	Apr 19	15:13	9♓11
1572	Jan 26	5:37	22♓17
1584	Mar 9	3:37	6♈03
1596	Apr 14	17:32	18♈55
1608	May 20	2:08	1♉10
1620	Jun 26	8:46	13♉04
	Dec 15	9:57	11♉45
1621	Jan 21	1:31	11♉29
1632	Aug 15	5:43	24♉44
	Oct 19	1:40	24♉15
1633	Mar 19	3:45	23♉06
1645	Apr 26	22:18	5♊02
1657	Jun 3	23:57	17♊31
1669	Jul 16	20:18	0♋55
1681	Sep 12	12:41	15♋47
1682	Jan 7	20:38	14♋52
	Apr 25	9:45	14♋00
1694	Jul 6	7:24	1♌14
1706	Sep 27	22:03	22♌19
1719	Sep 13	10:09	16♍51
1732	Sep 30	18:29	17♎32
1745	Oct 31	1:04	21♏07
1758	Nov 10	19:01	21♐38
1771	Feb 25	1:39	18♑48
1784	Jan 10	16:21	9♒02
1796	Mar 14	20:09	28♒03
1808	May 20	19:15	14♓33
	Aug 31	21:01	13♓41
	Dec 27	2:07	12♓41
1821	Feb 18	7:57	27♓31
1833	Mar 30	10:11	11♈10
1845	May 6	2:53	23♈57
1857	Jun 12	6:35	6♉08
1869	Jul 27	2:26	17♉55
	Oct 29	20:05	17♉12
1870	Mar 4	7:56	16♉14
1882	Apr 12	19:53	27♉59
1894	May 18	17:30	9♊59
1906	Jun 26	18:15	22♊31
1918	Aug 10	20:03	6♋03
1931	May 27	3:14	19♋16
1943	Aug 1	8:09	6♌53
1955	Nov 2	23:25	28♌25
1956	Feb 8	2:41	27♌36
	Jun 16	17:44	26♌28
1968	Oct 13	5:12	23♍40
1981	Nov 2	8:26	24♎53
1994	Dec 2	7:25	28♏26
2007	Dec 11	19:26	28♐24
2020	Apr 5	2:15	24♑53
	Jun 30	6:23	24♑06
	Nov 12	21:18	22♑52
2033	Feb 4	21:31	14♒50
2045	Apr 12	8:32	3♓32
2058	Jan 26	1:45	17♓54
2070	Mar 13	8:49	2♈38
2082	Apr 21	17:26	16♈10
2094	May 30	0:15	28♈51

♃ ♄ ♅ ♆ ♇ 0°, 45°, 90°, 120°, 135° and 180° Aspects 1700–2050

Year	Month	Day	Time	Planets	Aspect	Position
1700	Jan	28	3:16	♃ ♄	45	16♑37
	Mar	11	19:47	♄ ♅	120	6♓45
	Jul	4	0:33	♃ ♄	45	29♑18
	Aug	5	17:07	♄ ♅	120	13♓01
	Oct	13	5:44	♃ ♄	45	23♑20
1701	Jan	23	12:08	♃ ♇	180	11♒54
		27	9:08	♄ ♅	120	12♓21
	Mar	5	9:19	♃ ♆	45	21♒35
		26	15:39	♃ ♅	135	26♒18
	Jun	5	4:36	♄ ♇	135	25♓54
	Jul	12	8:55	♄ ♇	135	26♓48
	Aug	22	14:28	♃ ♅	135	3♓12
	Dec	24	4:06	♃ ♅	135	3♓33
1702	Feb	21	13:41	♃ ♅	120	16♓15
	Mar	4	23:59	♄ ♇	135	27♓38
	Apr	7	22:40	♃ ♇	135	27♓09
	May	21	20:57	♃ ♄	0	6♈36
	Jun	26	17:10	♃ ♆	0	12♈10
	Jul	7	1:50	♃ ♇	120	13♈13
	Aug	13	23:07	♃ ♇	120	14♈21
	Sep	19	13:25	♃ ♆	0	11♈16
1703	Jan	27	2:11	♃ ♆	0	9♈51
	Feb	21	2:19	♃ ♇	120	14♈35
	Mar	19	15:35	♃ ♅	90	20♈28
		28	1:02	♄ ♆	0	11♈44
	Apr	13	6:57	♄ ♇	120	13♈46
	Jul	6	9:51	♃ ♇	90	14♉48
	Oct	28	8:01	♃ ♇	90	17♉44
		31	22:10	♄ ♇	120	17♈47
1704	Jan	23	23:56	♄ ♇	120	16♈58
	Mar	2	2:47	♃ ♇	90	16♉05
	Apr	10	15:32	♄ ♅	90	25♈05
	May	8	10:13	♆ ♇	120	15♈26
		11	3:05	♃ ♆	315	0♊32
	Jul	6	19:24	♃ ♅	45	13♊30
		17	3:45	♆ ♇	120	16♈46
	Aug	15	6:38	♃ ♄	315	21♊05
	Oct	14	12:40	♄ ♅	90	3♉32
1705	Feb	12	14:04	♄ ♅	90	0♉52
		22	18:24	♃ ♄	315	16♊41
	Apr	14	18:17	♃ ♄	315	22♊21
		24	14:25	♆ ♇	120	17♈07
	Jun	4	6:56	♃ ♇	45	2♋25
	Jul	29	21:49	♄ ♇	90	18♉49
	Aug	4	6:35	♆ ♇	120	18♈59
		17	20:56	♃ ♆	270	18♋50
		30	10:54	♄ ♇	90	19♉48
1706	Apr	11	2:56	♄ ♇	90	18♉56
		14	19:27	♆ ♇	120	18♈54
	Jul	23	7:09	♃ ♅	0	8♌15
	Aug	18	8:27	♆ ♇	120	21♈07
	Sep	18	15:00	♃ ♆	240	20♌31
		27	22:03	♃ ♇	0	22♌19
	Nov	23	19:57	♃ ♄	270	0♍12
1707	Feb	8	23:19	♃ ♄	270	26♌57
	Apr	7	1:28	♆ ♇	120	20♈46
		15	3:13	♃ ♆	240	21♌04
	May	14	19:45	♃ ♆	240	22♌09
	Jun	2	2:26	♄ ♆	315	7♊42
	Aug	20	22:04	♃ ♆	225	8♍22
		30	9:19	♆ ♇	120	23♈14
	Oct	4	6:16	♃ ♄	270	17♍53
1708	Mar	30	14:49	♆ ♇	120	22♈41
	Sep	2	0:02	♃ ♅	315	4♎38
		9	3:09	♆ ♇	120	25♈19
	Oct	1	19:36	♃ ♇	315	10♎58
	Nov	30	11:24	♃ ♆	180	23♎16
	Dec	29	10:15	♃ ♄	240	27♎51
1709	Mar	25	2:39	♆ ♇	120	24♈38
	Apr	11	5:35	♃ ♄	240	26♎58
		21	11:47	♃ ♆	180	25♎39
	Jun	21	13:38	♄ ♅	45	4♋54
	Aug	10	6:57	♄ ♇	45	11♋08
		27	21:04	♃ ♆	180	27♎49
	Sep	18	22:32	♆ ♇	120	27♈25
	Oct	20	11:32	♅ ♆	240	26♌35
	Nov	22	17:16	♃ ♄	240	15♏43
	Dec	26	13:34	♄ ♇	45	13♋28
1710	Jan	17	15:30	♃ ♅	270	26♏32
		18	3:45	♃ ♄	225	26♏37
		20	15:12	♄ ♅	45	11♋26
		26	18:02	♃ ♇	270	27♏53
	Feb	10	12:15	♅ ♆	240	25♌34
	Mar	12	3:54	♄ ♅	45	9♋19
		20	8:05	♆ ♇	120	26♈37
	Apr	25	12:56	♄ ♇	45	11♋07
	May	11	23:16	♃ ♄	225	27♏33
		23	1:35	♃ ♇	270	26♏08
	Jun	10	5:02	♃ ♅	270	24♏00
	Jul	28	0:58	♃ ♄	240	21♏52
	Sep	7	18:38	♅ ♇	0	28♌53
		21	1:09	♅ ♆	240	29♌40
		28	0:29	♆ ♇	120	29♈30
		29	8:26	♃ ♄	240	28♏40
	Oct	5	2:22	♃ ♇	270	29♏42
		7	18:36	♄ ♆	270	29♋15
		10	11:06	♃ ♅	270	0♐42
	Dec	5	18:39	♃ ♆	135	12♐45
		13	10:10	♃ ♄	225	14♐29
1711	Jan	11	2:58	♄ ♆	270	27♋27
	Feb	17	8:20	♃ ♆	120	27♐54
		25	1:34	♃ ♇	240	29♐06
	Mar	1	8:52	♃ ♅	240	29♐44
		16	3:50	♆ ♇	120	28♈39
		22	23:09	♅ ♆	240	28♌52
	May	29	3:20	♃ ♆	120	1♑18
	Jun	18	12:20	♃ ♅	240	28♐52
		22	1:40	♃ ♇	240	28♐25
	Jul	15	12:45	♄ ♆	270	2♌23
	Aug	24	3:24	♅ ♆	240	2♍25
	Sep	6	21:32	♃ ♄	225	24♐04
	Oct	6	12:27	♆ ♇	120	1♉36
		10	14:15	♃ ♄	225	27♐22
	Nov	1	7:15	♃ ♆	120	0♑53
		8	18:43	♃ ♇	240	2♑17
	Dec	1	4:38	♃ ♅	240	6♑55
1712	Jan	14	10:43	♃ ♇	225	17♑04
		31	5:54	♃ ♅	225	20♑56
	Mar	11	11:54	♆ ♇	120	0♉42
		20	7:07	♃ ♆	90	0♒59
	May	9	15:29	♅ ♆	240	2♍49
	Jul	8	3:04	♃ ♆	90	4♒30
		14	18:54	♅ ♆	240	4♍36
	Oct	13	11:49	♆ ♇	120	3♉42
	Nov	21	5:28	♃ ♆	90	2♒39
1713	Feb	24	18:54	♃ ♄	180	23♒37
	Mar	8	7:50	♆ ♇	120	2♉47
	Apr	3	21:28	♃ ♇	180	2♓12
	May	3	0:18	♃ ♅	180	7♓40
	Aug	11	8:59	♃ ♅	180	10♓37
	Sep	23	8:30	♄ ♇	0	5♍02
		24	6:03	♃ ♄	180	5♓09
		24	19:47	♃ ♇	180	5♓05
	Oct	3	22:33	♄ ♆	240	6♍16
		20	23:09	♆ ♇	120	5♉49
	Dec	13	8:05	♃ ♇	180	6♓25
1714	Jan	9	18:45	♃ ♄	180	11♓00
	Feb	1	13:56	♃ ♅	180	15♓46
		18	0:16	♃ ♆	45	19♓32
	Mar	5	15:40	♆ ♇	120	4♉54
		30	0:31	♄ ♆	240	5♍39
	Jul	23	21:57	♄ ♆	240	9♍09
	Oct	12	20:25	♄ ♅	0	18♍54
		27	22:06	♆ ♇	120	7♉57
	Nov	17	2:41	♄ ♆	225	22♍23
1715	Feb	28	4:03	♄ ♆	225	21♍57
	Mar	3	12:21	♆ ♇	120	7♉02
		7	14:56	♃ ♇	135	21♈55
	Apr	22	15:05	♃ ♅	135	2♉37
		24	16:55	♃ ♄	135	3♉07
	May	6	4:54	♃ ♇	120	5♉52
		22	22:23	♃ ♆	0	9♉47
	Jun	28	13:14	♃ ♅	120	17♉39
	Jul	8	6:51	♃ ♄	120	19♉29
	Sep	11	7:04	♄ ♆	225	26♍19
		12	6:44	♃ ♄	120	26♉27
	Oct	24	16:24	♃ ♅	120	24♉03
	Nov	3	6:45	♆ ♇	120	10♉05
		10	15:12	♅ ♆	225	24♍53
		25	22:10	♃ ♄	135	19♉50
1716	Feb	29	23:25	♆ ♇	120	9♉11
	Mar	1	20:53	♃ ♄	135	20♉27
		7	10:38	♅ ♆	225	24♍21
		21	13:33	♃ ♅	120	23♉44
	Apr	27	12:29	♃ ♄	120	1♊22
	May	25	23:37	♃ ♇	90	7♊54
	Aug	7	23:58	♃ ♅	90	23♊57
	Sep	7	6:15	♃ ♆	315	28♊39
	Oct	13	9:26	♅ ♆	225	27♍57
	Nov	7	23:42	♆ ♇	120	12♉15
		19	8:48	♃ ♅	90	29♊51
	Dec	18	14:47	♃ ♆	315	26♊16
1717	Feb	28	3:01	♆ ♇	120	11♉22
	Apr	14	19:57	♅ ♆	225	27♍44
		21	5:45	♃ ♅	90	27♊30
		24	15:56	♃ ♆	315	28♊05
	Jul	5	14:59	♃ ♄	90	13♋08
	Sep	13	14:43	♃ ♇	45	27♋41
		17	10:47	♅ ♆	225	0♎48
	Nov	12	22:47	♆ ♇	120	14♉26
	Dec	23	5:18	♄ ♇	315	29♎45
1718	Jan	8	4:44	♃ ♄	90	0♌48
		18	4:33	♃ ♇	45	29♋29
	Feb	28	1:01	♆ ♇	120	13♉34
	May	4	11:39	♃ ♇	45	27♋11
		4	15:26	♃ ♄	90	27♋12
		4	23:36	♄ ♇	315	27♎11
		29	10:45	♅ ♆	225	1♎32
	Aug	13	13:59	♅ ♆	225	3♎15
		22	1:10	♃ ♆	270	18♌16
		24	15:38	♃ ♅	45	18♌50
	Sep	19	5:17	♄ ♇	315	29♎57
	Nov	17	2:58	♆ ♇	120	16♉38
1719	Feb	28	18:14	♆ ♇	120	15♉47
	Sep	13	10:09	♃ ♇	0	16♍51
		28	23:13	♃ ♆	240	20♍11
	Nov	20	11:53	♆ ♇	120	18♉51
		29	7:18	♄ ♆	180	18♏37
	Dec	12	17:02	♃ ♆	225	3♎17
1720	Mar	1	7:22	♆ ♇	120	18♉00
		2	4:14	♃ ♆	225	3♎01
	May	28	5:22	♄ ♆	180	20♏50
	Aug	11	9:40	♃ ♄	45	3♎55
		31	10:48	♃ ♆	225	7♎45
	Oct	2	5:54	♄ ♆	180	22♏24
		6	12:46	♃ ♅	0	15♎22
	Nov	22	2:07	♆ ♇	120	21♉06
1721	Jan	26	14:29	♄ ♅	315	4♐52
	Feb	22	4:20	♃ ♇	315	5♏30
	Mar	3	15:54	♆ ♇	120	20♉15
		4	20:31	♃ ♇	315	5♏13
	Jul	5	19:30	♄ ♅	315	0♐49
	Sep	25	3:40	♃ ♇	315	6♏36
	Nov	13	5:01	♄ ♅	315	7♐06
		23	22:22	♆ ♇	120	23♉22
	Dec	10	0:22	♃ ♆	180	22♏56
1722	Mar	6	18:55	♆ ♇	120	22♉30
	Jul	10	21:05	♃ ♆	180	26♏33
	Aug	17	22:11	♃ ♆	180	27♏12
	Nov	14	12:34	♃ ♅	315	11♐36
		25	3:01	♆ ♇	120	25♉38
1723	Jan	5	15:15	♃ ♄	0	23♐19
		17	10:02	♃ ♇	270	25♐52
		28	8:37	♄ ♇	270	25♐43
	Mar	10	14:34	♆ ♇	120	24♉46
	Jul	22	21:60	♄ ♇	270	23♐52
	Nov	18	13:49	♄ ♇	270	27♐47
		25	17:39	♆ ♇	120	27♉56
	Dec	9	11:36	♃ ♆	135	12♑34
1724	Feb	8	12:50	♃ ♆	120	26♑41
		13	12:39	♃ ♇	240	27♑48
	Mar	11	12:31	♃ ♅	270	3♒28
		14	0:57	♆ ♇	120	27♉03
	Apr	30	10:05	♃ ♇	225	10♒54
	Jul	2	4:52	♃ ♇	225	10♒46
	Sep	28	7:48	♃ ♅	270	2♒30
	Nov	6	2:49	♃ ♅	270	4♒53
		24	20:29	♆ ♇	120	0♊15
1725	Jan	5	8:05	♃ ♇	225	15♒40
		12	0:26	♄ ♆	135	14♑08
	Mar	3	1:57	♃ ♆	90	29♒05
		19	0:11	♆ ♇	120	29♉21
	Apr	4	22:47	♃ ♄	315	6♓33
		8	15:04	♃ ♅	240	7♓20
	Jul	18	4:53	♄ ♆	135	18♑19
	Oct	26	7:05	♃ ♅	240	8♓32
	Nov	13	18:27	♄ ♆	135	17♑53
		24	13:08	♆ ♇	120	2♊35
	Dec	18	2:00	♃ ♅	240	11♓37
1726	Mar	8	16:35	♃ ♅	225	28♓01
		23	20:57	♃ ♇	180	1♈41
		24	11:23	♆ ♇	120	1♊40
		25	3:10	♄ ♇	240	1♒39
		25	18:53	♄ ♆	120	1♒42
	May	21	7:47	♄ ♆	120	3♒31
	Jun	13	7:08	♃ ♆	45	19♈22
	Jul	17	16:41	♄ ♇	240	0♒41
	Oct	6	22:58	♃ ♆	45	21♈02
	Nov	23	20:08	♆ ♇	120	4♊55
1727	Jan	7	23:58	♄ ♆	120	3♒47
		22	2:28	♄ ♇	240	5♒26
		24	20:22	♃ ♆	45	18♈32
	Mar	30	9:32	♆ ♇	120	4♊00
	May	21	18:46	♄ ♅	270	15♒09
		28	1:06	♃ ♅	180	14♉54
		29	3:32	♃ ♄	270	15♉10
	Jun	9	13:32	♃ ♇	135	17♉44
	Jul	7	9:32	♄ ♅	270	13♒48
	Nov	22	18:21	♆ ♇	120	7♊16
	Dec	19	5:05	♃ ♇	135	22♉48
1728	Jan	13	5:25	♃ ♅	180	21♉29
	Feb	5	10:33	♃ ♅	180	22♉09
		12	2:47	♃ ♇	135	22♉39
		27	17:58	♅ ♇	315	22♏20
	Mar	15	7:58	♄ ♇	225	21♒55
		17	13:14	♄ ♅	270	22♒09
	Apr	4	18:32	♆ ♇	120	6♊21
		29	18:32	♃ ♇	120	5♊43
	May	3	10:01	♅ ♇	315	20♏38
		7	3:27	♃ ♆	0	7♊21
	Jul	25	9:22	♃ ♄	240	25♊11
	Sep	8	0:43	♄ ♇	225	21♒58
		23	4:39	♃ ♅	135	4♋39
	Oct	5	4:45	♃ ♄	225	5♋36
		9	12:30	♄ ♅	270	20♒28
		21	20:31	♃ ♅	135	6♋10
	Nov	12	1:05	♃ ♄	225	5♋34
		20	7:51	♆ ♇	120	9♊38
1729	Jan	2	15:29	♅ ♇	315	25♏24
		14	19:35	♄ ♇	225	25♒26
		21	10:31	♄ ♅	270	26♒10
		28	3:40	♃ ♄	240	26♊57
	Apr	11	14:16	♆ ♇	120	8♊43
	May	25	12:59	♃ ♇	90	7♋47
		29	16:26	♃ ♄	240	8♋39
	Jun	1	5:36	♃ ♅	135	9♋11
	Jul	17	10:09	♅ ♇	315	22♏53
	Aug	1	1:11	♃ ♄	225	22♋36
		1	22:22	♃ ♅	120	22♋48
		25	22:32	♃ ♆	315	27♋52

♃ ♄ ♅ ♆ ♇ 0°, 45°, 90°, 120°, 135° and 180° Aspects 1700–2050

	Nov	16	6:52	♅♇	315	26♏56
		18	12:35	♆♇	120	12♊00
1730	Feb	13	20:54	♃♅	120	1♌10
		18	19:34	♄♆	90	10♓11
	Mar	20	14:60	♃♄	225	28♋49
	Apr	18	20:31	♆♇	120	11♊06
		26	10:41	♃♅	120	0♌19
	Jun	4	20:30	♃♄	225	5♌41
	Sep	16	0:15	♃♇	45	27♌03
		21	16:38	♃♅	90	28♌13
	Nov	16	9:18	♆♇	120	14♊22
1731	Feb	18	3:50	♃♅	90	5♍38
	Apr	26	12:29	♆♇	120	13♊30
	Jun	13	10:27	♄♅	240	3♈04
		13	13:14	♃♅	90	3♍03
	Aug	31	2:30	♃♆	270	17♍22
	Sep	4	0:42	♄♅	240	2♈02
	Oct	22	7:26	♃♄	180	28♍28
	Nov	13	22:32	♆♇	120	16♊44
1732	Mar	19	5:19	♃♄	180	5♎47
	Apr	19	21:22	♄♅	240	9♈43
	May	3	13:38	♆♇	120	15♊55
	Jun	14	3:28	♄♇	180	15♈15
	Aug	26	3:34	♄♇	180	16♈15
	Sep	18	5:11	♃♄	180	14♎51
		30	18:29	♃♇	0	17♎32
	Oct	10	11:12	♃♆	240	19♎38
		27	19:17	♃♅	45	23♎24
	Nov	10	4:41	♆♇	120	19♊07
		28	13:36	♄♅	240	10♈15
	Dec	15	17:36	♃♆	225	3♏09
1733	Feb	23	4:28	♄♅	240	14♈24
	Apr	5	6:07	♄♇	180	19♈19
	May	9	9:46	♃♆	225	3♏16
		11	23:41	♆♇	120	18♊21
	Jun	13	2:06	♄♅	225	27♈17
	Sep	7	5:37	♃♆	225	6♏53
	Oct	16	10:50	♄♅	225	27♈01
	Nov	7	3:57	♆♇	120	21♊28
1734	Feb	13	15:13	♃♇	315	8♐04
	Apr	25	21:31	♄♅	225	3♉36
	May	10	9:26	♄♆	45	5♉27
		20	18:21	♆♇	120	20♊48
		28	20:11	♃♇	315	5♐39
	Oct	8	0:47	♃♇	315	7♐45
	Nov	3	20:20	♆♇	120	23♊49
		29	6:40	♃♅	0	18♐30
	Dec	1	12:05	♄♆	45	8♉10
		16	7:58	♃♄	135	22♐23
		17	18:22	♃♆	180	22♐42
1735	Jan	16	1:59	♄♆	45	6♉56
		24	20:56	♅♆	180	21♐45
	May	11	10:43	♅♆	180	22♐38
		29	21:30	♆♇	120	23♊16
	Jun	28	22:04	♃♄	135	8♑21
	Oct	31	5:49	♆♇	120	26♊10
	Nov	7	10:29	♃♄	135	9♑56
	Dec	30	19:06	♃♄	120	21♑12
1736	Jan	1	23:32	♅♆	180	24♐35
		30	8:18	♃♇	270	28♑22
	Mar	17	14:15	♃♆	135	8♒40
	Apr	9	12:49	♃♅	315	12♒41
	Jun	7	9:50	♆♇	120	25♊46
		11	18:02	♅♆	180	25♐55
	Aug	2	13:07	♃♆	135	12♒44
		19	1:48	♃♄	120	10♒37
	Sep	6	5:56	♃♅	315	8♒43
	Oct	26	7:28	♆♇	120	28♊30
	Nov	10	4:06	♃♄	120	9♒49
		20	15:33	♃♅	315	11♒11
		30	21:40	♃♆	135	12♒45
	Dec	12	9:15	♅♆	180	27♐26
1737	Feb	2	12:05	♃♆	120	26♒08
		22	3:44	♃♇	240	0♓51
	Mar	16	20:29	♃♄	90	6♓16
	Apr	23	12:50	♃♇	225	14♓29
	May	24	20:32	♄♇	135	13♊40
	Jun	17	9:06	♆♇	120	28♊16
	Jul	12	6:09	♅♆	180	29♐11
	Aug	6	6:59	♃♄	90	22♓35
	Oct	8	2:23	♃♇	225	15♓15
		21	23:19	♆♇	120	0♋49
	Nov	21	22:12	♅♆	180	0♑17
1738	Jan	1	16:37	♃♇	225	18♓14
		13	2:54	♃♄	90	20♓11
	Feb	20	8:28	♃♆	90	28♓10
	Mar	25	20:47	♃♅	270	6♈08
	Jun	27	22:23	♆♇	120	0♋48
		30	21:46	♄♇	120	0♋47
	Jul	2	7:27	♄♆	0	0♋58
		20	17:19	♄♅	180	3♋18
	Aug	18	10:50	♅♆	180	2♑29
	Oct	17	1:58	♆♇	120	3♋06
		24	18:30	♅♆	180	3♑03
	Dec	30	16:22	♄♅	180	6♋30
1739	Jan	7	4:31	♄♇	120	5♋54
	Apr	1	2:29	♃♇	180	5♉28
		18	23:37	♄♇	120	4♋59
		22	10:27	♃♅	240	10♉26
	May	17	23:01	♃♆	45	16♉30
	Jun	2	23:49	♄♅	180	9♋33
		19	15:40	♃♅	225	23♉55
	Jul	9	8:27	♆♇	120	3♋22
	Aug	7	11:17	♃♄	45	2♊52
		30	2:20	♃♄	45	5♊26
	Oct	11	8:18	♆♇	120	5♋22
1740	Jan	18	3:05	♃♅	225	26♉32
	Feb	25	4:27	♃♅	225	28♉29
	Mar	23	23:42	♃♄	45	2♊25
	Jun	19	17:30	♃♇	135	21♊10
	Jul	21	6:49	♆♇	120	5♋59
	Sep	5	5:50	♃♇	120	6♋42
		9	19:59	♃♆	0	7♋21
	Oct	3	3:02	♆♇	120	7♋36
	Nov	25	14:11	♃♇	120	9♋42
	Dec	24	12:27	♃♆	0	6♋18
1741	Apr	18	19:51	♃♆	0	5♋07
	May	15	9:04	♃♇	120	9♋36
	Jun	22	14:29	♃♅	180	17♋29
	Jul	9	5:01	♄♇	90	8♌36
	Aug	6	15:01	♆♇	120	8♋41
	Sep	22	12:29	♆♇	120	9♋44
	Oct	18	9:02	♃♇	90	10♌40
	Dec	16	7:41	♃♇	90	12♌56
1742	Jun	16	17:52	♃♇	90	11♌31
	Aug	24	15:32	♄♆	315	26♌22
		27	14:01	♃♆	315	26♌26
		30	20:52	♃♄	0	27♌09
	Oct	2	17:52	♃♅	135	4♍00
1743	Feb	21	10:44	♃♅	135	10♍11
	Jul	8	14:20	♃♅	135	10♍28
	Aug	29	10:60	♄♅	135	8♍36
	Sep	11	17:31	♃♅	120	23♍18
	Oct	15	11:25	♃♇	45	0♎32
	Dec	31	22:13	♃♆	270	13♎00
1744	Mar	12	0:01	♃♆	270	11♎32
		12	5:56	♄♅	135	15♍00
	Jul	9	19:25	♄♅	135	14♍40
	Sep	7	7:06	♃♆	270	16♎04
	Oct	29	10:22	♄♅	120	27♍27
		30	20:42	♃♅	90	27♎28
1745	Jan	27	1:35	♄♅	120	1♎33
	Feb	17	12:52	♃♆	240	14♏04
	Mar	11	9:23	♃♄	315	14♏02
		17	14:10	♃♆	240	13♏45
	Apr	9	15:08	♃♄	315	11♏49
	Jun	16	10:35	♃♅	90	4♏42
		26	5:39	♃♅	90	4♏24
	Sep	3	0:37	♄♅	120	1♎53
		28	5:19	♄♇	45	4♎56
	Oct	20	5:15	♃♆	240	18♏46
		31	1:04	♃♇	0	21♏07
	Nov	23	15:57	♃♄	315	26♏21
	Dec	23	10:17	♃♆	225	2♐48
1746	Apr	26	12:48	♄♅	120	9♎11
	Jul	7	6:41	♄♅	120	8♎14
	Nov	9	14:31	♄♆	270	20♎55
		25	2:07	♃♅	45	21♐04
1747	Mar	2	13:18	♃♇	315	11♑51
	Jun	23	8:26	♄♆	270	19♎58
	Aug	6	22:51	♃♇	315	9♑04
		8	2:28	♄♆	270	21♎38
	Oct	15	8:40	♃♇	315	10♑25
	Dec	20	8:52	♃♆	180	22♑27
1748	Feb	28	1:17	♃♄	270	8♒36
	Apr	9	3:25	♃♅	0	16♒40
	Sep	1	16:29	♃♅	0	14♒28
	Nov	3	13:12	♃♅	0	13♒32
		24	9:09	♄♅	90	13♏55
1749	Feb	10	0:26	♃♇	270	1♓43
	Mar	7	8:53	♃♆	135	7♓49
		25	15:02	♄♅	90	19♏57
	Apr	22	17:06	♃♄	240	18♓19
	May	19	0:57	♃♆	120	23♓12
	Aug	24	0:37	♃♆	120	26♓28
	Sep	29	5:10	♄♅	90	17♏49
	Oct	18	5:01	♃♄	240	19♓50
	Dec	19	4:03	♄♆	240	27♏01
1750	Jan	22	14:47	♃♆	120	26♓05
	Feb	18	16:02	♃♄	240	1♈44
	Mar	1	23:36	♃♇	240	4♈19
		19	10:38	♃♅	315	8♈28
	Apr	19	8:18	♃♄	225	15♈55
		30	16:26	♃♇	225	18♈35
	Jun	2	6:26	♃♆	90	25♈44
		24	10:54	♄♆	240	26♏26
	Oct	15	4:29	♄♆	240	29♏47
		28	4:60	♃♆	90	29♈52
	Nov	21	21:05	♄♇	0	4♐00
1751	Jan	29	22:32	♃♆	90	28♈10
	Feb	18	16:47	♄♆	225	12♐40
	May	3	4:53	♄♆	225	12♐15
	Jun	25	20:44	♃♅	270	29♉14
	Jul	20	15:27	♃♇	180	4♊11
	Aug	5	21:49	♃♄	180	6♊56
	Oct	22	15:17	♃♄	180	10♊46
	Nov	28	10:19	♃♇	180	6♊35
	Dec	14	7:22	♄♆	225	16♐40
1752	Apr	6	21:53	♃♇	180	8♊59
	May	4	4:53	♃♆	45	14♊28
	Jun	6	20:49	♃♄	180	22♊00
	Jul	23	21:44	♃♅	240	2♋35
	Oct	9	1:21	♃♅	225	14♋51
	Nov	28	15:54	♃♅	225	14♋39
1753	Jun	27	15:07	♃♅	225	22♋16
	Jul	6	20:57	♃♇	135	24♋18
	Aug	25	0:50	♃♆	0	5♌05
	Sep	13	12:27	♃♇	120	8♌59
1754	Jan	30	5:36	♃♇	120	13♌20
	May	31	13:05	♃♇	120	12♌38
	Aug	12	22:40	♃♄	135	26♌46
	Oct	5	10:47	♃♅	180	8♍07
		28	8:58	♃♇	90	12♍20
		28	22:06	♃♄	120	12♍26
	Dec	30	21:55	♃♄	120	18♍38
1755	Feb	14	19:17	♃♇	90	15♍57
	Mar	16	23:12	♃♅	180	12♍08
		18	21:16	♃♄	135	11♍53
	May	29	6:39	♅♇	270	15♓06
	Jun	25	7:58	♃♄	135	12♍15
	Jul	8	3:46	♃♇	90	14♍06
		14	5:58	♃♅	180	15♍04
	Aug	25	16:06	♃♄	120	23♍07
		31	15:37	♅♇	270	13♓32
	Sep	1	17:52	♃♆	315	24♍36
	Dec	11	1:18	♄♅	45	26♑33
1756	Feb	5	9:49	♄♇	315	3♒00
	Mar	28	8:39	♄♆	180	8♒17
	Apr	30	12:20	♅♇	270	18♓07
	May	2	23:54	♃♄	120	10♎12
	Jun	26	11:15	♄♆	180	9♒22
		26	18:12	♃♄	120	9♎21
	Oct	5	21:17	♅♇	270	16♓16
		29	13:04	♃♅	135	0♏36
	Nov	5	10:34	♃♇	45	2♏06
		20	18:55	♃♄	90	5♏22
	Dec	28	23:55	♃♆	270	12♏39
1757	Jan	25	2:30	♄♆	180	11♒58
	Feb	2	15:18	♃♅	120	17♏17
		26	13:25	♃♅	120	18♏34
	Mar	20	21:28	♃♄	90	18♏11
	Apr	6	15:48	♅♇	270	20♓46
	May	29	7:14	♃♆	270	10♏46
	Sep	6	4:17	♃♆	270	14♏02
		19	7:45	♃♄	90	16♏14
	Oct	10	6:56	♃♅	120	20♏13
	Nov	9	20:17	♅♇	270	19♓26
1758	Feb	1	11:41	♃♆	240	14♐02
	Mar	11	1:41	♅♇	270	23♓00
	Jun	17	5:56	♃♆	240	13♐22
	Oct	19	17:54	♃♆	240	17♐19
	Nov	10	19:01	♃♇	0	21♐38
		18	19:39	♃♅	90	23♐20
	Dec	27	23:53	♃♆	225	2♑11
1759	May	8	19:19	♅♆	135	29♓50
	Jul	8	23:39	♅♆	135	1♈09
	Dec	16	16:22	♃♄	45	25♑29
1760	Feb	26	13:32	♃♇	315	12♒11
	Mar	13	7:29	♃♅	45	15♒39
		21	10:55	♃♆	180	17♒20
	Apr	7	16:15	♅♆	135	2♈05
	May	21	18:55	♄♇	270	26♓48
	Aug	15	4:00	♅♆	135	4♈38
	Sep	1	1:09	♃♆	180	20♒15
		20	8:54	♃♅	45	18♒22
		23	2:54	♄♇	270	24♓53
	Oct	11	18:23	♃♅	45	17♒31
	Dec	5	12:00	♃♆	180	21♒57
1761	Mar	5	3:35	♄♇	270	29♓25
		18	0:04	♅♆	135	4♈39
	Apr	13	7:38	♄♆	135	4♈15
	May	14	9:39	♄♅	0	7♈42
		26	17:58	♃♇	270	28♓54
	Sep	13	13:53	♅♆	135	7♈48
		28	14:10	♄♆	135	8♈16
	Oct	4	19:41	♃♇	270	27♓10
		28	16:31	♄♅	0	6♈03
1762	Jan	3	21:59	♄♅	0	5♈23
		22	22:30	♃♇	270	0♈31
	Feb	7	5:52	♄♆	135	7♈55
		24	19:07	♃♅	0	7♈16
		25	11:33	♃♆	135	7♈25
		27	0:07	♅♆	135	7♈23
	Mar	18	16:41	♃♄	0	12♈21
	Apr	25	7:24	♃♆	120	21♈24
	Jun	6	10:26	♃♇	240	0♉49
		7	11:32	♄♆	120	21♈44
	Aug	26	16:05	♄♆	120	24♈16
	Oct	13	2:16	♅♆	135	10♈47
	Dec	13	7:23	♃♇	240	1♉07
1763	Jan	28	16:55	♃♇	240	2♉43
	Feb	6	4:02	♅♆	135	10♈13
	Mar	20	9:36	♄♆	120	24♈07
	Apr	24	3:09	♃♇	225	18♉44
	May	14	20:46	♃♆	90	23♉37
	Jun	1	11:09	♄♇	240	3♉05
		18	14:05	♃♅	315	1♊40
	Nov	23	1:50	♅♆	135	13♈34
		25	3:39	♄♇	240	2♉30
1764	Jan	4	1:55	♅♆	135	13♈16

♃ ♄ ♅ ♆ ♇ 0°, 45°, 90°, 120°, 135° and 180° Aspects 1700–2050

Year	Month	Day	Time	Planets	Aspect	Position
	Mar	17	8:33	♄ ♇	240	5♉47
	Jul	9	20:07	♄ ♇	225	19♉14
		13	14:29	♃ ♇	180	4♋09
		16	11:36	♃ ♄	315	4♋47
	Aug	29	3:19	♃ ♆	45	13♋37
	Oct	9	13:09	♃ ♅	270	19♋16
	Nov	2	18:17	♄ ♇	225	18♉53
	Dec	23	11:04	♃ ♅	270	17♋14
1765	Jan	5	17:10	♃ ♆	45	15♋28
	Apr	16	22:44	♃ ♆	45	13♋08
		27	22:27	♄ ♇	225	22♉49
	Jun	9	11:46	♄ ♆	90	28♉16
		21	12:08	♃ ♅	270	24♋35
	Nov	7	17:36	♃ ♇	135	20♌59
		16	3:39	♄ ♆	90	2♊54
		19	22:50	♃ ♅	240	21♌55
	Dec	18	21:41	♃ ♇	135	22♌16
1766	Jan	4	8:41	♃ ♅	240	21♌16
	Mar	19	4:24	♄ ♆	90	0♊54
	Jul	7	10:19	♄ ♅	315	13♊57
		11	1:41	♃ ♇	135	23♌22
	Aug	8	14:03	♃ ♅	240	29♌15
		24	10:13	♃ ♆	0	2♍40
	Sep	14	23:38	♃ ♇	120	7♍20
	Oct	10	19:36	♃ ♅	225	12♍39
	Nov	12	9:12	♃ ♄	270	18♍22
1767	Apr	2	12:12	♃ ♄	270	15♍00
		14	9:52	♃ ♅	225	13♍56
	Jul	9	19:17	♃ ♅	225	17♍58
	Sep	28	17:39	♃ ♄	270	3♎44
	Oct	26	7:20	♃ ♇	90	9♎37
1768	Jan	15	9:32	♃ ♆	315	22♎02
	Mar	17	12:22	♃ ♆	315	20♎27
	May	16	2:45	♅ ♆	120	4♉37
		18	20:28	♃ ♇	90	13♎33
	Jun	16	17:23	♃ ♇	90	12♎59
	Aug	1	12:22	♄ ♇	180	11♋53
	Sep	1	16:59	♅ ♆	120	7♉14
		3	18:58	♃ ♆	315	22♎19
	Nov	3	20:18	♃ ♅	180	5♏08
	Dec	25	4:05	♃ ♄	240	15♏35
1769	Jan	14	20:33	♄ ♇	180	13♋54
	Apr	20	16:11	♅ ♆	120	7♉00
	May	22	21:54	♄ ♇	180	15♋27
		26	19:54	♃ ♄	240	15♏52
	Jul	22	14:11	♄ ♆	45	22♋54
	Oct	5	17:57	♅ ♆	120	10♉33
	Nov	2	6:07	♃ ♇	45	28♏34
		18	20:56	♃ ♄	240	2♐14
	Dec	31	19:06	♃ ♆	270	11♐42
1770	Jan	13	6:20	♃ ♄	225	14♐16
	Mar	29	20:13	♅ ♆	120	9♉40
	Jun	29	9:59	♃ ♄	225	17♐06
	Aug	11	20:08	♅ ♇	240	15♉36
	Sep	26	10:54	♅ ♇	240	15♉07
	Oct	15	4:53	♄ ♅	270	14♌30
	Nov	7	6:34	♅ ♆	120	13♉34
		22	21:39	♃ ♅	135	27♐56
	Dec	6	23:29	♃ ♄	225	1♑03
1771	Jan	22	3:29	♃ ♅	120	11♑39
		30	6:07	♃ ♆	240	13♑27
	Feb	11	20:07	♄ ♅	270	11♌53
		25	1:39	♃ ♇	0	18♑48
	Mar	6	8:57	♅ ♆	120	12♉32
	Apr	20	14:09	♃ ♆	225	26♑28
	Jun	11	18:48	♃ ♆	225	26♑18
		29	23:17	♅ ♇	240	18♉31
	Aug	8	3:32	♃ ♅	120	19♑40
		13	6:23	♄ ♅	270	19♌43
	Oct	12	11:07	♃ ♅	120	18♑54
	Nov	15	23:32	♅ ♇	240	17♉32
	Dec	24	12:04	♃ ♆	225	1♒10
		25	5:25	♅ ♆	120	16♉10
1772	Jan	25	7:38	♅ ♆	120	15♉48
	Feb	27	1:52	♃ ♅	90	16♒18
	Mar	30	20:08	♃ ♄	180	23♒23
	May	30	22:15	♅ ♇	240	21♉01
	Aug	1	3:04	♃ ♄	180	0♓05
	Sep	1	18:09	♄ ♇	135	4♍03
		24	23:13	♃ ♅	90	23♒41
	Oct	23	5:58	♃ ♅	90	22♒49
	Dec	24	20:09	♅ ♇	240	20♉26
1773	Jan	26	22:26	♃ ♇	315	6♓32
	Feb	14	6:20	♃ ♄	180	10♓48
	Mar	11	10:31	♃ ♆	180	16♓53
		23	12:44	♄ ♇	135	7♍56
	Apr	30	0:26	♅ ♇	240	23♉10
	Jun	16	9:23	♄ ♇	135	7♍33
	Sep	27	9:50	♄ ♆	0	18♍43
	Oct	14	3:34	♄ ♇	120	20♍42
	Dec	6	22:05	♄ ♅	240	25♍23
1774	Feb	14	8:38	♃ ♅	45	9♈15
		20	16:50	♄ ♅	240	24♍21
		24	1:53	♄ ♇	120	24♍06
	Apr	23	1:22	♃ ♇	270	24♈57
	May	26	17:28	♃ ♆	135	2♉46
	Jun	3	13:21	♃ ♄	135	4♉27
	Aug	1	19:32	♄ ♇	120	23♍19
	Sep	29	4:05	♃ ♄	135	15♉10
	Oct	13	8:14	♄ ♅	240	1♎53
	Dec	1	21:54	♃ ♆	135	7♉35
1775	Jan	27	23:12	♃ ♆	135	7♉25
	Apr	9	10:35	♃ ♄	135	19♉26
		14	6:36	♃ ♆	120	20♉31
	May	11	1:29	♃ ♇	240	26♉41
		20	5:09	♄ ♅	240	2♎16
	Jun	3	1:32	♃ ♄	120	2♊05
		8	19:45	♃ ♅	0	3♊25
	Jul	11	14:31	♃ ♇	225	10♊38
	Aug	19	11:54	♄ ♅	240	6♎27
	Nov	28	7:44	♃ ♄	120	18♊02
	Dec	10	11:18	♄ ♅	225	19♎06
1776	Jan	28	21:51	♃ ♇	225	11♊44
	Mar	1	20:45	♃ ♇	225	12♊41
		28	23:47	♄ ♅	225	18♎39
	Apr	9	21:34	♃ ♄	120	17♊45
	May	4	10:01	♃ ♆	90	22♊21
	Sep	14	23:19	♃ ♄	90	20♋23
	Oct	18	0:12	♃ ♄	90	24♋18
		26	9:06	♄ ♅	225	25♎19
		27	19:25	♆ ♇	120	26♍05
	Nov	1	19:40	♃ ♅	315	25♋06
		2	6:60	♄ ♇	90	26♎08
	Dec	16	4:53	♃ ♅	315	23♋18
		16	9:34	♆ ♇	120	27♍04
1777	Apr	19	8:55	♄ ♇	90	0♏08
	Jun	14	21:55	♄ ♅	225	26♎53
		14	23:00	♃ ♄	90	26♋53
		14	23:37	♃ ♅	315	26♋53
		27	13:19	♃ ♇	180	29♋29
	Jul	23	7:52	♅ ♇	225	13♊54
	Aug	14	19:51	♄ ♇	90	28♎23
		17	19:16	♃ ♆	45	10♌41
	Sep	5	22:08	♄ ♅	225	0♏13
	Oct	13	10:16	♆ ♇	120	27♍43
	Dec	2	18:36	♅ ♇	225	13♊23
1778	Jan	4	11:37	♆ ♇	120	29♍18
		17	15:09	♄ ♆	315	14♏13
	May	5	2:07	♄ ♆	315	11♏48
	Jun	21	16:43	♅ ♇	225	16♊20
	Oct	2	11:28	♃ ♇	135	14♍27
		2	21:11	♆ ♇	120	29♍26
		15	0:16	♄ ♆	315	14♏53
		27	0:46	♃ ♅	270	19♍14
1779	Jan	14	15:19	♅ ♇	225	16♊14
		19	18:25	♆ ♇	120	1♎24
	Apr	16	1:39	♃ ♇	135	18♍27
	May	1	11:42	♃ ♅	270	17♍31
		19	13:10	♅ ♇	225	18♊29
	Jun	9	7:57	♃ ♇	135	18♍15
	Jul	7	23:13	♃ ♅	270	21♍22
	Aug	27	3:32	♃ ♆	0	0♎12
	Sep	2	9:19	♃ ♇	120	1♎29
		23	17:49	♆ ♇	120	1♎12
	Oct	11	5:07	♃ ♄	45	9♎48
	Dec	13	7:58	♃ ♅	240	22♎03
1780	Feb	2	16:24	♆ ♇	120	3♎27
	Apr	3	15:24	♃ ♄	45	23♎14
		19	19:49	♃ ♅	240	21♎11
	Jul	2	10:54	♃ ♄	45	17♎44
	Sep	14	5:24	♆ ♇	120	2♎59
		16	22:00	♃ ♅	240	28♎21
	Oct	8	8:30	♃ ♇	90	2♏47
	Nov	21	22:09	♃ ♅	225	12♏29
1781	Jan	3	11:13	♃ ♆	315	20♏52
	Feb	15	1:09	♆ ♇	120	5♎27
	Jun	25	3:18	♃ ♆	315	18♏07
	Aug	16	2:52	♃ ♆	315	19♏06
	Sep	5	21:31	♆ ♇	120	4♎47
	Nov	21	12:13	♄ ♇	45	19♐42
1782	Feb	1	1:50	♃ ♇	45	21♐35
		15	14:23	♄ ♅	180	29♐00
		28	8:22	♆ ♇	120	7♎24
	May	9	19:59	♄ ♅	180	0♑31
	Jun	23	23:13	♃ ♇	45	23♐00
	Aug	28	10:08	♆ ♇	120	6♎36
	Sep	21	20:30	♃ ♇	45	21♐12
	Nov	5	9:26	♃ ♄	0	28♐07
	Dec	12	4:12	♃ ♅	180	5♑58
		30	12:18	♃ ♆	270	10♑12
1783	Jan	5	13:14	♄ ♅	180	4♑56
	Feb	20	23:15	♄ ♆	270	9♑48
	Mar	13	23:48	♆ ♇	120	9♎18
	Jun	27	22:07	♅ ♆	90	7♋29
	Jul	13	2:51	♄ ♅	180	8♑24
		22	8:58	♄ ♆	270	7♑46
	Aug	19	11:16	♆ ♇	120	8♎26
	Nov	16	15:36	♅ ♆	90	11♋31
	Dec	2	15:08	♄ ♅	180	11♑01
		12	17:01	♄ ♆	270	12♑08
1784	Jan	10	16:21	♃ ♇	0	9♒02
		24	22:14	♃ ♆	240	12♒23
	Mar	9	3:09	♃ ♅	135	22♒49
		24	16:25	♃ ♆	225	26♒14
		27	11:45	♆ ♇	120	11♎09
	May	24	21:31	♅ ♆	90	9♋49
	Jun	13	10:23	♃ ♄	315	7♓36
	Aug	8	13:22	♆ ♇	120	10♎16
		25	23:24	♃ ♄	315	2♓51
	Sep	11	16:24	♃ ♅	135	0♓43
	Oct	30	4:34	♃ ♆	225	28♒05
	Nov	5	20:16	♃ ♆	225	28♒18
	Dec	3	1:26	♃ ♅	135	0♓40
		31	15:36	♅ ♆	90	14♋32
1785	Feb	6	14:22	♃ ♅	120	13♓03
		12	23:34	♃ ♄	315	14♓33
	Apr	9	19:37	♃ ♇	315	27♓55
		12	18:15	♆ ♇	120	12♎57
		20	8:38	♅ ♆	90	12♋45
	Jun	22	1:28	♃ ♆	180	11♈49
	Jul	27	19:04	♆ ♇	120	12♎09
	Sep	3	2:18	♃ ♆	180	13♈07
1786	Feb	28	0:43	♃ ♆	180	16♈19
	Mar	3	13:21	♃ ♅	90	17♈05
		27	10:02	♄ ♇	0	14♒11
	Apr	10	1:26	♄ ♆	240	15♒16
	May	3	5:29	♆ ♇	120	14♎40
	Jul	2	1:53	♃ ♇	270	14♉15
		9	19:05	♃ ♄	270	15♉35
		11	18:26	♆ ♇	120	14♎04
		28	19:35	♄ ♆	240	14♒18
	Aug	9	4:21	♄ ♇	0	13♒27
	Dec	6	17:19	♃ ♇	270	12♉45
		7	6:49	♃ ♄	270	12♉41
		8	6:44	♄ ♇	0	12♒46
1787	Feb	3	11:53	♄ ♆	240	18♒53
		21	12:12	♃ ♇	270	14♉49
	Apr	27	14:02	♃ ♄	270	27♉25
	May	15	18:41	♃ ♆	135	1♊38
	Jun	16	4:53	♃ ♅	45	8♊56
	Jul	16	7:37	♃ ♇	240	15♊32
		20	2:31	♃ ♆	120	16♊18
	Sep	5	18:25	♃ ♄	240	24♊09
	Nov	30	15:42	♃ ♄	240	23♊12
	Dec	18	14:10	♃ ♆	120	20♊47
1788	Mar	23	17:53	♄ ♆	225	5♓12
		29	10:08	♃ ♆	120	20♊03
	Jun	4	4:50	♃ ♇	225	2♋40
	Jul	9	14:45	♃ ♄	240	10♋38
	Aug	17	5:16	♃ ♆	90	18♋58
	Sep	3	3:38	♃ ♄	225	22♋14
		30	3:10	♄ ♆	225	5♓22
1789	Jan	17	16:25	♄ ♆	225	8♓18
		22	3:31	♃ ♄	225	23♋46
		25	16:34	♃ ♆	90	23♋18
	Mar	22	21:60	♄ ♅	135	15♓52
	Apr	20	4:55	♃ ♆	90	21♋42
	Jun	29	16:21	♃ ♅	0	3♌29
	Jul	20	20:27	♃ ♄	225	8♌02
	Aug	19	18:32	♄ ♅	135	21♓34
	Sep	2	11:37	♃ ♇	180	17♌32
1790	Feb	10	12:43	♄ ♅	135	21♓54
	Jun	23	13:45	♄ ♇	315	5♈26
	Aug	18	15:39	♃ ♆	45	8♍15
	Sep	5	15:21	♄ ♇	315	3♈58
	Nov	18	20:13	♄ ♅	135	29♓16
	Dec	6	18:31	♄ ♅	135	29♓08
		7	0:32	♃ ♅	315	29♍08
		7	1:56	♃ ♄	180	29♍08
1791	Jan	23	2:49	♃ ♄	180	1♎27
	Mar	6	16:30	♄ ♇	315	5♈56
		27	6:53	♃ ♅	315	25♍20
	Apr	9	15:35	♄ ♅	120	10♈10
	Aug	5	3:09	♃ ♅	315	29♍28
	Sep	5	2:48	♃ ♇	135	5♎28
		17	17:32	♄ ♅	120	17♈02
	Oct	18	4:14	♃ ♄	180	14♎42
	Nov	11	12:56	♃ ♇	120	19♎49
1792	Jan	12	18:17	♃ ♆	0	29♎45
	Feb	23	13:57	♄ ♅	120	16♈11
	Mar	26	8:00	♃ ♆	0	29♎04
	May	2	5:34	♃ ♄	180	24♎32
		11	16:23	♃ ♇	120	23♎31
		27	14:28	♄ ♆	180	27♈30
	Jul	18	19:10	♃ ♇	120	22♎57
	Aug	24	12:08	♃ ♆	0	27♎39
	Sep	14	5:28	♃ ♄	180	1♏21
		19	12:32	♅ ♇	180	21♌39
	Oct	14	9:22	♄ ♆	180	29♈17
	Dec	19	9:22	♃ ♇	90	21♏42
		27	21:49	♃ ♅	270	23♏20
1793	Jan	21	21:03	♅ ♇	180	22♌30
	Mar	24	7:58	♄ ♆	180	1♉21
	Jun	3	11:47	♃ ♇	90	24♏56
	Jul	14	4:45	♃ ♅	270	22♏04
	Aug	13	6:40	♅ ♇	180	23♌52
		21	15:30	♃ ♇	90	23♏41
	Sep	4	12:20	♃ ♅	270	25♏15
	Dec	31	7:57	♃ ♆	315	18♐52
1794	Jan	25	11:12	♃ ♄	135	24♐07
	Feb	8	8:43	♃ ♅	240	26♐43
	Mar	14	2:16	♅ ♇	180	25♌18
	May	4	2:27	♃ ♄	135	3♑22
	Jul	5	2:30	♅ ♇	180	26♌04
		6	20:08	♄ ♇	270	26♉02
		9	5:12	♄ ♅	90	26♉16
		10	6:29	♃ ♅	240	26♐19
	Sep	3	2:14	♄ ♅	90	29♉36
	Nov	10	2:34	♃ ♅	240	2♑52
	Dec	10	13:56	♃ ♇	45	9♑20

♃ ♄ ♅ ♆ ♇ 0°, 45°, 90°, 120°, 135° and 180° Aspects 1700–2050

Year	Month	Day	Time	Planets	Aspect	Position
		10	21:42	♃ ♄	135	9♑24
		11	17:06	♄ ♇	270	24♉21
1795	Jan	15	8:34	♃ ♅	225	17♑36
	Feb	7	17:21	♃ ♄	120	22♑56
	Apr	6	17:52	♄ ♇	270	27♉12
		18	3:06	♃ ♆	270	5♒12
		23	14:22	♄ ♅	90	29♉10
	Jun	19	14:20	♃ ♄	120	6♒26
	Jul	16	15:55	♃ ♆	270	3♒36
	Sep	2	18:52	♃ ♄	135	28♑14
	Oct	16	2:13	♃ ♄	135	28♑21
	Dec	18	11:26	♃ ♆	270	7♒48
		22	10:19	♃ ♄	120	8♒38
1796	Jan	4	6:40	♄ ♅	90	7♊47
	Feb	5	21:14	♄ ♅	90	6♊46
	Mar	14	20:09	♃ ♇	0	28♒03
	Apr	12	18:23	♃ ♅	180	4♓11
		28	20:06	♃ ♆	240	7♓08
	Jul	5	6:25	♄ ♆	135	20♊49
	Aug	29	5:02	♃ ♅	180	8♓15
	Sep	11	0:53	♃ ♆	240	6♓35
		16	16:59	♄ ♇	240	27♊26
	Nov	12	10:54	♄ ♇	240	26♊52
	Dec	11	14:05	♄ ♆	135	24♊44
1797	Jan	5	16:51	♃ ♆	240	10♓22
		15	23:36	♃ ♅	180	12♓23
	Feb	23	5:53	♃ ♄	90	20♓57
	Mar	13	22:39	♃ ♆	225	25♓27
	Apr	25	6:37	♄ ♆	135	24♊28
	Jun	14	15:07	♄ ♇	240	0♋27
		15	20:11	♃ ♇	315	15♈27
	Aug	16	7:22	♄ ♆	120	8♋09
	Oct	18	8:38	♃ ♇	315	13♈22
		28	20:14	♃ ♄	90	12♈05
	Nov	23	21:21	♄ ♆	120	11♋15
	Dec	12	17:58	♃ ♄	90	10♈00
1798	Jan	26	17:21	♃ ♇	315	14♈24
	Apr	7	16:07	♃ ♅	135	29♈11
	May	27	1:15	♃ ♆	180	10♉52
		29	13:43	♄ ♆	120	10♋48
	Jun	8	3:16	♃ ♅	120	13♉33
	Jul	13	17:29	♄ ♇	225	16♋30
	Nov	12	13:22	♃ ♅	120	21♉25
1799	Mar	3	12:51	♃ ♅	120	20♉37
	May	5	2:32	♃ ♇	270	3♊01
		26	17:55	♃ ♄	45	8♊01
	Jul	15	13:57	♃ ♅	90	19♊17
	Aug	30	22:46	♃ ♆	135	27♊40
	Oct	8	10:05	♃ ♇	240	1♋13
	Nov	5	8:08	♃ ♇	240	0♋58
		16	13:36	♃ ♆	135	0♋09
	Dec	13	17:46	♃ ♅	90	26♊58
1800	Mar	31	15:17	♃ ♅	90	24♊25
	May	9	6:37	♃ ♆	135	0♋48
		27	9:14	♃ ♇	240	4♋30
	Jun	21	15:58	♄ ♅	45	8♌11
	Jul	11	15:20	♃ ♆	120	14♋32
		31	9:39	♃ ♇	225	18♋55
	Aug	12	6:49	♄ ♆	90	14♌32
1801	Feb	24	19:10	♄ ♆	90	19♌24
	May	17	8:01	♄ ♆	90	17♌50
	Aug	2	20:40	♃ ♅	45	14♌12
		14	6:16	♃ ♆	90	16♌43
	Oct	2	8:57	♅ ♆	45	2♎43
		13	13:20	♄ ♇	180	3♍50
	Nov	14	19:07	♃ ♇	180	3♍35
1802	Jan	19	23:02	♃ ♇	180	4♍24
	Feb	1	23:02	♅ ♆	45	6♎29
		12	11:09	♄ ♇	180	4♍59
	Jul	17	22:48	♃ ♄	0	5♍08
		26	1:23	♃ ♇	180	6♍41
		31	4:12	♄ ♇	180	6♍36
	Aug	4	9:29	♅ ♆	45	3♎49
1803	Aug	22	20:17	♃ ♆	45	6♎06
	Sep	13	10:27	♃ ♅	0	10♎27
	Nov	2	18:35	♃ ♇	135	21♎15
1804	Sep	30	23:36	♃ ♇	120	7♏58
	Oct	25	23:22	♄ ♆	45	9♎50
	Dec	30	4:16	♃ ♆	0	27♏10
1805	Jan	21	20:46	♃ ♄	315	1♐09
	Feb	27	13:36	♃ ♅	315	5♐28
	Apr	2	18:50	♄ ♆	45	12♎51
	May	14	11:20	♃ ♅	315	2♐33
	Jul	18	12:09	♄ ♆	45	10♎28
	Aug	4	12:43	♃ ♄	315	26♏39
	Sep	27	8:12	♃ ♄	315	2♐14
	Oct	22	5:41	♃ ♅	315	6♐46
	Nov	1	7:39	♃ ♇	90	8♐50
		17	19:48	♄ ♅	0	23♎22
		21	4:33	♄ ♇	135	23♎44
		24	13:09	♅ ♇	135	23♎44
1806	Feb	26	8:40	♅ ♇	135	25♎21
	Apr	1	4:51	♄ ♇	135	26♎13
	Sep	9	2:09	♄ ♇	135	25♎59
	Oct	9	22:10	♅ ♇	135	25♎24
	Dec	26	1:18	♃ ♆	315	16♑15
1807	Feb	6	4:24	♃ ♇	45	26♑02
		24	22:57	♃ ♅	270	0♒10
	Apr	11	11:24	♃ ♄	270	8♒24
		27	13:12	♅ ♇	135	28♎00
	Aug	17	17:56	♃ ♄	270	5♒04
		28	18:04	♅ ♇	135	27♎30
	Oct	23	5:60	♄ ♇	120	11♏29
1808	Feb	1	10:20	♃ ♄	270	21♒31
	Mar	25	23:51	♃ ♅	240	4♓09
		27	20:35	♃ ♆	270	4♓34
	May	20	19:15	♃ ♇	0	14♓33
	Jun	5	14:50	♃ ♅	225	16♓24
		9	22:57	♃ ♄	240	16♓48
	Aug	9	8:52	♃ ♅	225	16♓21
		12	11:15	♃ ♄	240	16♓02
		31	21:00	♃ ♇	0	13♓41
	Dec	27	2:07	♃ ♇	0	12♓41
1809	Feb	23	11:25	♃ ♅	225	24♓37
	Apr	1	13:56	♃ ♄	240	3♈33
		14	0:43	♃ ♆	240	6♈32
	May	24	3:06	♃ ♄	225	15♈24
	Jun	18	1:14	♃ ♆	225	19♈55
	Oct	12	23:28	♃ ♆	225	19♈57
		29	7:37	♃ ♄	225	17♈49
	Dec	1	15:36	♄ ♆	0	6♐40
1810	Feb	26	18:04	♃ ♆	225	23♈59
	Mar	27	19:16	♃ ♄	225	0♉18
		30	21:04	♃ ♇	315	1♉01
	May	15	5:44	♃ ♅	180	11♉46
	Nov	14	0:23	♅ ♇	120	14♏59
		16	16:44	♄ ♇	90	14♐59
1811	Apr	19	11:05	♅ ♇	120	17♏38
	May	20	14:08	♃ ♆	180	10♊09
	Jun	24	19:44	♃ ♇	270	18♊18
	Jul	9	19:02	♃ ♄	180	21♊40
	Aug	21	7:53	♃ ♅	135	0♋07
	Oct	2	21:16	♅ ♇	120	16♏47
	Nov	23	15:54	♃ ♅	135	4♋52
	Dec	31	9:53	♃ ♄	180	0♋11
1812	Apr	3	21:53	♄ ♅	315	7♑52
	May	17	5:10	♃ ♅	135	6♋13
		21	13:07	♃ ♄	180	7♋04
	Jun	24	22:31	♄ ♅	315	4♑49
	Jul	16	20:55	♃ ♇	240	19♋22
		17	1:58	♃ ♅	120	19♋24
	Aug	14	10:42	♃ ♆	135	25♋38
	Sep	22	16:56	♃ ♇	225	3♌11
1813	Jan	14	19:38	♄ ♅	315	11♑58
		31	19:13	♃ ♇	225	3♌04
	Feb	23	21:35	♃ ♆	135	0♌26
	Apr	22	21:30	♃ ♆	135	0♌14
	Jun	3	6:45	♃ ♇	225	5♌37
	Jul	12	23:50	♃ ♆	120	13♌16
	Sep	1	20:49	♃ ♅	90	24♌17
		18	4:25	♃ ♄	135	27♌43
1814	Jan	27	18:27	♃ ♄	135	8♍30
	Mar	19	1:59	♃ ♅	90	2♍24
	May	16	5:31	♃ ♅	90	0♍42
	Aug	1	23:26	♃ ♄	135	11♍34
		18	19:24	♃ ♆	90	15♍00
	Sep	14	18:06	♃ ♇	180	20♍46
		30	10:09	♃ ♄	120	24♍08
1815	Feb	2	15:43	♄ ♆	315	4♒18
		14	11:57	♄ ♇	45	5♒40
	Mar	6	5:55	♃ ♄	120	7♎50
	Aug	14	11:36	♃ ♄	120	8♎05
		24	20:22	♄ ♇	45	7♒22
	Oct	8	17:15	♃ ♅	45	19♎14
	Nov	2	12:46	♄ ♇	45	6♒06
	Dec	28	7:14	♃ ♆	45	5♏14
1816	Jan	2	17:15	♃ ♇	135	6♏02
	Apr	2	15:01	♃ ♇	135	8♏01
		11	10:54	♃ ♆	45	7♏02
	Aug	21	4:33	♃ ♆	45	4♏22
	Sep	13	14:45	♃ ♇	135	8♏09
	Oct	29	8:47	♃ ♄	90	17♏26
	Nov	19	13:25	♃ ♇	120	22♏06
	Dec	20	18:05	♆ ♇	90	22♐05
1817	Apr	7	23:24	♆ ♇	90	24♐16
	May	29	3:26	♃ ♄	90	5♐44
	Aug	29	8:57	♃ ♄	90	2♐24
	Nov	10	8:37	♃ ♅	0	14♐20
		25	4:30	♆ ♇	90	23♐14
	Dec	20	3:57	♃ ♇	90	23♐14
		25	1:44	♃ ♆	0	24♐21
1818	May	10	4:21	♆ ♇	90	26♐03
	Jun	13	14:58	♄ ♅	270	18♓01
	Aug	21	4:53	♄ ♅	270	16♓10
	Nov	2	14:40	♆ ♇	90	24♐37
1819	Feb	24	17:58	♃ ♄	45	4♒00
	Mar	23	20:52	♃ ♅	315	9♒30
	Apr	3	11:45	♃ ♇	45	11♒23
		10	19:14	♄ ♅	270	24♓28
		18	1:12	♃ ♆	315	13♒36
	May	5	2:32	♄ ♇	0	27♓04
		16	21:39	♄ ♆	270	28♓09
	Jun	10	15:22	♆ ♇	90	27♐33
	Jul	6	22:52	♃ ♄	45	15♒43
	Aug	4	17:44	♃ ♇	45	12♒22
		14	16:47	♃ ♆	315	11♒04
	Oct	5	6:43	♄ ♇	0	26♓15
		6	18:18	♄ ♆	270	26♓08
		9	1:01	♆ ♇	90	26♐11
	Nov	8	9:24	♃ ♄	45	9♒19
		18	19:34	♃ ♇	45	10♒36
	Dec	2	19:49	♃ ♆	315	12♒43
		6	13:08	♄ ♅	270	24♓02
1820	Jan	1	8:55	♅ ♇	90	25♐36
		11	17:17	♄ ♇	0	25♓42
		27	13:36	♄ ♅	270	27♓03
	Feb	29	3:04	♄ ♆	270	0♈34
	May	9	23:01	♅ ♇	90	28♐17
	Jul	27	17:35	♆ ♇	90	28♐35
	Aug	26	20:35	♆ ♇	90	28♐09
	Nov	12	9:30	♅ ♇	90	26♐48
1821	Feb	18	7:57	♃ ♇	0	27♓31
	Mar	12	23:40	♃ ♅	270	2♈51
		13	7:13	♃ ♆	270	2♈56
		22	3:48	♅ ♆	0	3♑01
	May	3	9:42	♅ ♆	0	2♑51
	Jun	19	17:13	♃ ♄	0	24♈39
	Aug	1	17:53	♃ ♅	240	29♈42
		2	20:20	♅ ♇	90	29♐40
	Sep	5	0:04	♅ ♇	90	29♐09
		15	1:30	♃ ♅	240	29♈09
	Dec	3	16:19	♅ ♆	0	1♑59
1822	Mar	31	12:48	♃ ♆	240	5♉15
	Apr	9	19:13	♃ ♅	240	7♉23
	May	14	6:58	♃ ♇	315	15♉34
		29	12:33	♄ ♆	240	4♉35
		31	6:53	♃ ♆	225	19♉33
	Jun	7	12:11	♃ ♅	225	21♉12
		11	18:57	♄ ♅	240	6♉02
	Nov	18	19:40	♄ ♅	240	5♉12
	Dec	5	7:38	♄ ♆	240	4♉09
1823	Mar	14	23:42	♄ ♆	240	7♉16
	Apr	20	18:54	♄ ♅	240	11♉36
	Jun	1	16:43	♄ ♇	315	16♉55
	Jul	7	11:34	♄ ♆	225	20♉49
	Aug	8	20:05	♃ ♇	270	1♋51
		9	18:30	♄ ♅	225	23♉13
		24	22:05	♃ ♆	180	4♋49
	Sep	12	3:58	♃ ♅	180	7♋38
		20	14:33	♃ ♄	315	8♋43
	Oct	10	22:15	♄ ♅	225	22♉52
	Nov	12	7:14	♄ ♆	225	20♉30
		28	16:41	♃ ♅	180	9♋41
	Dec	22	13:25	♃ ♆	180	6♋53
1824	Jan	31	9:12	♃ ♄	315	2♋07
	Apr	27	8:55	♄ ♆	225	24♉34
	May	13	11:08	♃ ♆	180	9♋21
	Jun	7	22:25	♄ ♅	225	29♉53
		9	17:35	♃ ♅	180	14♋49
		12	23:06	♃ ♄	315	15♋31
	Aug	30	10:47	♃ ♇	240	2♌38
1825	Jan	12	17:03	♄ ♅	225	1♊15
	Apr	10	9:42	♄ ♅	225	4♊53
	Jul	24	13:12	♃ ♇	225	19♌13
	Aug	17	7:17	♃ ♆	135	24♌21
	Sep	17	7:32	♃ ♅	135	1♍02
	Nov	1	22:25	♃ ♆	120	9♍31
1826	Feb	2	14:07	♃ ♆	120	12♍39
	Mar	11	6:58	♃ ♅	135	8♍08
	Jun	21	2:38	♃ ♅	135	8♍03
	Jul	18	5:16	♃ ♆	120	12♍16
	Aug	29	4:58	♃ ♅	120	20♍33
	Sep	8	20:07	♄ ♇	270	4♋41
	Oct	30	8:42	♃ ♇	180	3♎43
	Nov	9	15:13	♃ ♄	270	5♎42
	Dec	17	1:17	♄ ♇	270	3♋17
1827	Jan	13	14:51	♃ ♆	90	14♎02
		21	16:00	♃ ♆	90	14♎20
	May	3	19:12	♃ ♇	180	5♎44
		22	22:33	♃ ♄	270	4♎38
	Jun	5	9:26	♄ ♇	270	6♋15
	Jul	8	12:42	♃ ♇	180	6♎26
	Aug	5	18:22	♄ ♆	180	14♋04
		26	5:07	♃ ♆	90	13♎40
	Sep	20	2:43	♃ ♄	270	18♎36
	Oct	16	21:01	♃ ♅	90	24♎20
1828	Jan	15	8:32	♄ ♆	180	16♋12
	Feb	14	20:23	♃ ♄	240	14♏05
	Mar	25	12:49	♃ ♄	240	13♏25
	May	29	17:23	♄ ♆	180	17♋59
	Aug	27	3:55	♄ ♅	180	29♋04
	Oct	29	15:47	♃ ♇	135	20♏54
	Dec	21	1:18	♃ ♆	45	2♐24
		23	22:51	♃ ♄	240	3♐00
1829	Jan	5	6:13	♃ ♇	120	5♐30
		10	23:54	♄ ♅	180	1♌41
	Feb	24	11:51	♃ ♄	225	13♐20
	May	5	4:15	♃ ♄	225	13♐33
	Jun	16	16:26	♃ ♇	120	8♐29
	Jul	9	20:29	♄ ♅	180	5♌08
		15	21:18	♃ ♄	240	5♐53
	Aug	4	20:02	♄ ♇	240	8♌27
	Sep	12	9:32	♃ ♇	120	7♐53
	Nov	9	15:45	♃ ♅	45	17♐48
		9	16:22	♃ ♄	240	17♐48
1830	Jan	10	6:39	♃ ♄	225	1♑38
	Feb	3	14:54	♃ ♇	90	6♑53
	Aug	3	4:32	♃ ♇	90	9♑32
		26	4:11	♃ ♄	225	8♑05
	Sep	3	12:36	♄ ♇	225	24♌08

♃ ♄ ♅ ♆ ♇ 0°, 45°, 90°, 120°, 135° and 180° Aspects 1700–2050

Year	Month	Day	Time	Planets	Aspect	Position
		26	11:37	♃ ♇	90	8♑42
	Nov	20	22:19	♃ ♄	225	16♑19
	Dec	15	11:48	♃ ♆	0	21♑25
1831	Mar	21	6:35	♃ ♅	0	13♒07
	May	5	0:10	♄ ♇	225	24♌55
		12	5:16	♄ ♇	225	25♌04
	Sep	15	10:18	♄ ♆	135	7♍19
1832	Jan	6	19:07	♃ ♇	45	23♒40
	Mar	5	17:09	♄ ♆	135	11♍24
		18	3:55	♃ ♄	180	10♓26
		24	3:20	♃ ♆	315	11♓50
	Jul	8	18:19	♄ ♆	135	11♍04
	Oct	4	23:25	♃ ♄	180	21♓18
	Nov	4	5:50	♄ ♆	120	24♍39
1833	Jan	30	3:18	♃ ♄	180	27♓37
	Feb	2	3:33	♄ ♆	120	27♍29
	Mar	4	12:13	♃ ♅	315	4♈57
		30	10:11	♃ ♇	0	11♈10
	Jun	18	5:05	♃ ♆	270	28♈50
	Aug	22	2:26	♄ ♆	120	27♍11
	Oct	14	20:45	♄ ♅	135	3♎43
	Nov	21	4:06	♃ ♆	270	27♈08
1834	Feb	10	21:33	♃ ♆	270	29♈55
	Mar	8	8:23	♄ ♅	135	8♎56
	May	13	19:09	♃ ♄	135	19♉27
	Jun	13	3:35	♃ ♅	270	26♉30
		23	7:24	♃ ♇	315	28♉45
	Jul	2	18:54	♃ ♆	240	0♊45
	Aug	3	6:49	♃ ♄	120	6♊36
		29	5:27	♄ ♅	135	9♎08
	Sep	18	9:27	♃ ♄	120	11♊27
		30	10:59	♄ ♇	180	12♎55
	Dec	7	7:56	♃ ♄	135	5♊32
1835	Feb	3	9:38	♃ ♆	240	1♊45
		9	17:27	♃ ♆	240	1♊59
	Mar	7	14:57	♅ ♇	45	27♒39
		22	8:00	♃ ♄	135	6♊15
	May	17	18:58	♃ ♄	120	17♊17
		24	4:32	♃ ♆	225	18♊43
	Jul	12	18:17	♃ ♅	240	0♋01
		18	1:54	♅ ♇	45	29♒52
	Sep	17	17:27	♃ ♅	225	12♋34
		29	13:05	♃ ♇	270	13♋59
	Oct	25	11:24	♄ ♅	120	26♎41
	Dec	11	11:23	♄ ♆	90	1♏57
		18	4:16	♃ ♇	270	12♋51
		21	5:47	♃ ♅	225	12♋27
		30	17:41	♅ ♇	45	27♒50
1836	Mar	4	18:18	♄ ♆	90	4♏56
	Apr	7	14:30	♄ ♅	120	3♏03
	May	25	7:44	♃ ♇	270	15♋26
	Jun	14	10:24	♃ ♅	225	19♋31
	Jul	28	5:27	♃ ♄	90	29♋08
	Aug	19	13:58	♃ ♆	180	4♌00
	Sep	7	15:45	♄ ♅	120	2♏02
		21	1:29	♄ ♆	90	3♏23
	Oct	17	11:05	♃ ♇	240	14♌41
1837	Jan	13	6:08	♃ ♄	90	15♌39
		26	8:54	♃ ♇	240	14♌01
	May	27	17:04	♃ ♄	90	12♌11
	Jun	24	23:45	♃ ♇	240	16♌50
	Sep	3	11:23	♃ ♇	225	1♍32
		22	15:33	♃ ♅	180	5♍36
1838	Apr	3	11:07	♃ ♅	180	10♍22
	Jun	25	19:59	♃ ♅	180	12♍25
	Aug	26	10:56	♃ ♆	135	23♍22
	Nov	1	22:49	♃ ♆	120	7♎41
		22	9:40	♄ ♇	135	1♐10
	Dec	21	10:29	♃ ♇	180	15♎55
1839	Mar	10	20:25	♃ ♇	180	16♎45
	Apr	15	17:19	♃ ♆	120	12♎23
	Jul	20	20:14	♃ ♆	120	11♎37
		21	23:26	♄ ♇	135	3♐57
	Aug	18	16:04	♄ ♇	135	3♐48
	Sep	2	22:01	♃ ♇	180	18♎37
		7	2:55	♃ ♄	45	19♎25
	Oct	18	3:03	♃ ♅	135	28♎00
	Dec	3	8:27	♄ ♅	90	12♐33
		18	5:31	♃ ♆	90	10♏42
1840	Jan	1	8:59	♃ ♅	120	13♏10
		10	19:58	♄ ♇	120	16♐57
	Mar	30	23:45	♃ ♅	120	17♏43
	Apr	27	22:33	♃ ♆	90	14♏44
	May	20	10:50	♄ ♅	90	19♐52
		26	12:53	♄ ♇	120	19♐27
	Aug	28	6:29	♃ ♆	90	12♏51
	Sep	27	1:48	♃ ♅	120	17♏46
	Oct	10	23:05	♄ ♅	90	17♐16
		27	1:21	♄ ♇	120	18♐39
	Dec	7	16:38	♃ ♇	135	3♐03
1841	Feb	2	0:36	♄ ♆	45	29♐28
	Mar	9	16:45	♃ ♇	120	18♐43
	Apr	18	7:51	♃ ♇	120	19♐38
	May	18	12:49	♄ ♆	45	2♑03
	Oct	30	18:57	♄ ♆	45	29♐17
		31	5:39	♃ ♇	120	19♐37
	Nov	5	11:51	♃ ♅	90	20♐40
	Dec	18	2:22	♃ ♆	45	0♑02
1842	Jan	26	6:12	♃ ♄	0	8♑54
	Mar	31	1:33	♃ ♇	90	20♑10
	Jun	6	3:46	♃ ♇	90	21♑36
	Nov	20	15:51	♃ ♇	90	20♑18
1843	Feb	5	20:43	♄ ♇	90	20♑09
		25	7:08	♃ ♅	45	12♒00
	Apr	9	22:53	♃ ♆	0	20♒57
	Jul	9	21:49	♄ ♇	90	22♑56
	Sep	11	23:58	♃ ♆	0	19♒20
	Nov	8	22:53	♃ ♆	0	18♒44
		15	18:56	♄ ♇	90	21♑24
1844	Feb	12	23:31	♃ ♇	45	6♓14
	Apr	18	12:19	♃ ♄	315	21♓39
1845	Feb	8	9:26	♃ ♅	0	3♈44
	Mar	5	3:40	♃ ♆	315	9♈11
	May	6	2:53	♃ ♇	0	23♈57
	Jul	22	13:44	♅ ♆	315	10♈13
	Sep	21	7:18	♅ ♆	315	8♈40
1846	Feb	27	7:22	♄ ♅	45	23♒26
	Apr	4	1:43	♄ ♆	0	27♒18
	May	28	14:53	♅ ♆	315	13♈10
	Jun	3	8:23	♃ ♆	270	28♉10
		4	10:21	♃ ♅	315	28♉25
		14	21:55	♃ ♄	270	0♊49
	Jul	27	8:13	♄ ♅	45	29♒13
	Aug	4	5:25	♃ ♇	315	10♊56
	Sep	5	1:36	♄ ♆	0	26♒20
	Nov	28	4:19	♅ ♆	315	10♈30
	Dec	6	11:09	♄ ♅	45	25♒23
		11	9:27	♄ ♆	0	25♒42
		24	2:35	♃ ♇	315	8♊59
1847	Mar	17	5:36	♃ ♇	315	9♊45
	Apr	13	22:51	♅ ♆	315	14♈43
	May	3	11:03	♄ ♇	45	10♓49
	Jun	27	8:29	♃ ♆	240	0♋14
	Jul	29	12:27	♄ ♇	45	11♓56
	Aug	15	12:16	♃ ♄	240	10♋53
		30	22:21	♃ ♆	225	13♋45
	Sep	20	15:09	♃ ♅	270	17♋01
1848	Jan	14	8:28	♃ ♅	270	14♋30
		17	12:18	♄ ♇	45	9♓57
		18	21:51	♃ ♆	225	13♋54
	Feb	5	4:33	♃ ♄	240	11♋58
	May	16	5:39	♃ ♆	225	17♋30
	Jun	4	17:21	♃ ♅	270	21♋09
		24	5:39	♃ ♄	240	25♋11
	Jul	6	11:43	♃ ♇	270	27♋50
	Aug	24	0:38	♃ ♄	225	8♌29
	Oct	26	13:21	♃ ♅	240	19♌44
1849	Jan	28	7:01	♃ ♅	240	18♌45
	Mar	19	11:26	♃ ♄	225	13♌08
	Jul	8	5:43	♃ ♄	225	22♌53
		25	1:51	♃ ♅	240	26♌15
	Aug	6	12:57	♃ ♇	240	28♌53
		27	10:24	♃ ♆	180	3♍24
	Sep	27	15:20	♃ ♅	225	10♍05
	Oct	12	10:19	♃ ♇	225	13♍03
1850	Apr	24	10:29	♃ ♇	225	13♍29
	Jun	9	5:51	♃ ♇	225	14♍25
		26	3:17	♅ ♇	0	29♈40
	Sep	25	11:24	♅ ♇	0	29♈21
	Nov	20	20:42	♃ ♄	180	14♎47
	Dec	20	20:26	♃ ♆	135	19♎36
1851	Mar	4	17:49	♃ ♆	135	21♎59
		18	18:01	♃ ♄	180	20♎39
		23	21:02	♅ ♇	0	28♈43
	Apr	8	2:49	♄ ♆	315	23♈11
	Jun	6	21:41	♄ ♇	0	0♉20
	Sep	6	3:31	♃ ♆	135	22♎43
	Oct	11	22:48	♃ ♇	180	0♏03
		18	2:33	♃ ♄	180	1♏23
		23	5:01	♃ ♅	180	2♏30
	Nov	10	11:48	♃ ♆	120	6♏30
		11	5:52	♄ ♇	0	29♈29
1852	Feb	10	4:21	♄ ♇	0	28♈59
	Mar	15	7:25	♄ ♅	0	2♉10
	Jun	20	9:12	♃ ♄	180	13♏55
	Sep	6	2:44	♃ ♄	180	17♏54
	Dec	18	8:35	♃ ♆	90	8♐56
1853	Jan	15	11:01	♃ ♇	135	14♐49
	Feb	13	15:24	♃ ♅	135	19♐56
	May	3	5:05	♃ ♅	135	23♐41
	Jun	27	5:03	♃ ♇	135	17♐33
	Sep	23	7:54	♃ ♇	135	17♐20
	Nov	9	18:58	♃ ♅	135	25♐16
	Dec	6	14:09	♃ ♇	120	1♑03
1854	Jan	8	11:12	♃ ♅	120	8♑36
		14	13:44	♃ ♄	135	10♑00
	Jun	30	1:07	♃ ♄	135	24♑33
	Aug	26	2:12	♄ ♆	270	14♊53
	Nov	25	4:11	♄ ♆	270	13♊10
	Dec	6	3:13	♃ ♄	135	27♑16
		10	20:54	♃ ♆	45	28♑15
		27	8:44	♃ ♇	90	1♒49
1855	Jan	27	11:28	♃ ♄	120	9♒04
	Feb	12	15:59	♃ ♅	90	12♒55
	May	31	21:05	♄ ♆	270	18♊05
	Jun	9	5:06	♄ ♇	315	19♊10
	Aug	21	7:30	♃ ♄	120	27♒39
	Dec	11	14:04	♃ ♄	120	27♒10
1856	Mar	17	9:22	♃ ♆	0	18♓13
		17	22:34	♃ ♇	45	18♓21
		24	6:59	♆ ♇	45	18♓29
	Apr	18	16:50	♃ ♄	90	25♓45
	Jun	29	6:48	♆ ♇	45	20♓26
	Aug	7	10:41	♃ ♄	90	9♈03
		15	5:45	♄ ♅	315	9♋55
1857	Jan	29	12:29	♃ ♅	45	6♈01
		30	16:25	♆ ♇	45	18♓43
	Feb	8	20:53	♃ ♄	90	8♈00
	Jun	12	6:35	♃ ♇	0	6♉08
		20	3:31	♃ ♆	315	7♉41
	Aug	12	19:14	♄ ♆	240	22♋06
	Sep	7	16:04	♆ ♇	45	21♓27
	Dec	10	17:46	♆ ♇	45	19♓55
1858	Feb	28	17:26	♄ ♆	240	21♋53
	May	23	6:41	♃ ♅	0	29♉26
		23	20:33	♄ ♆	240	24♋36
	Sep	7	11:40	♄ ♇	270	7♌25
		17	9:12	♄ ♆	225	8♌29
1859	Feb	6	3:33	♄ ♆	225	8♌15
	Mar	10	20:59	♄ ♇	270	6♌03
	Apr	27	23:37	♃ ♄	45	20♊48
	May	5	2:08	♃ ♇	315	22♊13
		26	20:59	♃ ♆	270	26♊50
		29	9:27	♄ ♇	270	7♌44
	Jul	10	8:08	♄ ♆	225	12♌08
	Oct	1	21:05	♃ ♅	315	22♋35
		26	14:58	♃ ♆	240	24♋48
	Dec	5	23:28	♃ ♆	240	24♋22
1860	Jan	21	4:35	♃ ♅	315	18♋54
	May	22	10:01	♃ ♅	315	22♋26
	Jun	26	23:08	♃ ♆	240	29♋24
	Aug	12	3:23	♃ ♇	270	9♌30
		30	22:25	♃ ♆	225	13♌33
	Nov	12	14:41	♄ ♇	240	8♍17
	Dec	13	20:05	♄ ♅	270	9♍30
1861	Jan	29	13:43	♄ ♅	270	8♍06
	Feb	6	5:41	♄ ♇	240	7♍34
	Aug	16	23:29	♄ ♇	240	10♍26
	Sep	12	2:18	♃ ♇	240	10♍16
	Oct	3	4:02	♄ ♅	270	16♍18
		10	9:42	♃ ♅	270	16♍12
		21	12:26	♃ ♄	0	18♍22
	Nov	24	23:40	♃ ♇	225	24♍02
1862	Mar	3	19:16	♃ ♇	225	23♍46
	May	30	9:19	♄ ♅	270	15♍59
	Jul	16	18:41	♄ ♅	270	18♍40
	Aug	6	14:37	♃ ♇	225	26♍24
	Sep	8	10:06	♃ ♆	180	2♎56
		20	21:11	♄ ♇	225	26♍07
	Nov	5	5:26	♄ ♆	180	1♎27
		25	23:24	♃ ♅	240	19♎18
1863	Mar	11	22:18	♄ ♆	180	3♎03
	May	12	13:05	♃ ♅	240	19♎03
	Aug	27	14:15	♃ ♅	240	24♎34
	Sep	5	1:01	♄ ♆	180	5♎19
	Nov	8	8:44	♃ ♅	225	9♏28
		15	23:11	♃ ♇	180	11♏08
	Dec	20	16:17	♃ ♆	135	18♏19
1864	May	15	3:02	♃ ♆	135	22♏30
	Aug	12	5:57	♅ ♇	315	28♊17
	Sep	11	5:01	♃ ♆	135	22♏26
	Nov	18	11:43	♃ ♆	120	5♐46
	Dec	13	8:44	♄ ♅	240	27♎41
		23	0:38	♃ ♄	315	13♐29
1865	Jan	15	13:07	♅ ♇	315	26♊20
	Feb	24	22:02	♃ ♅	180	25♐26
	Mar	6	5:22	♃ ♇	135	26♐36
	Apr	23	14:16	♄ ♅	240	26♎31
	May	11	21:44	♃ ♇	135	27♐56
		16	4:46	♃ ♅	180	27♐35
		29	20:08	♅ ♇	315	28♊20
	Oct	31	5:20	♄ ♅	240	3♏43
	Nov	6	3:15	♃ ♇	135	28♐13
		28	17:20	♃ ♅	180	2♑54
	Dec	20	9:46	♃ ♆	90	7♑47
1866	Jan	8	23:14	♃ ♇	120	12♑18
	Jul	26	8:37	♄ ♅	240	5♏52
	Aug	23	21:27	♄ ♅	240	7♏16
	Nov	1	7:43	♄ ♇	180	14♏17
1867	Jan	2	1:13	♄ ♅	225	21♏08
		29	7:04	♃ ♇	90	13♒12
	Feb	24	11:51	♃ ♅	135	19♒25
	Mar	16	10:40	♃ ♄	270	23♒58
	Apr	1	21:05	♃ ♆	45	27♒28
	May	12	2:12	♄ ♅	225	20♏48
	Sep	25	23:23	♃ ♆	45	28♒58
	Oct	13	4:53	♃ ♅	135	27♒52
	Nov	2	6:59	♃ ♅	135	27♒48
		5	1:40	♃ ♆	45	27♒54
		24	16:31	♄ ♅	225	27♏19
		26	1:53	♄ ♆	135	27♏29
1868	Jan	25	19:48	♃ ♅	120	9♓51
	Apr	21	9:33	♃ ♇	45	0♈15
	May	6	22:37	♃ ♄	240	3♈36
	Jun	1	21:19	♄ ♆	135	1♐42
	Jul	22	10:60	♄ ♅	225	29♏09
		25	12:38	♃ ♄	225	14♈06
	Aug	11	11:42	♃ ♄	225	14♈07
	Sep	10	23:36	♅ ♆	270	16♋39
		25	5:12	♄ ♆	135	1♐17

♃ ♄ ♅ ♆ ♇ 0°, 45°, 90°, 120°, 135° and 180° Aspects 1700–2050

	Oct	7	5:20	♄ ♅	225	2♐19
	Nov	5	0:16	♃ ♄	240	5♈17
1869	Jan	21	0:14	♅ ♆	270	14♋43
	Feb	1	17:26	♄ ♆	120	14♐56
		17	10:09	♃ ♅	90	13♈46
		26	1:47	♃ ♆	0	15♈35
	Mar	3	6:27	♃ ♄	240	16♈43
	Apr	7	22:22	♄ ♆	120	17♐02
	May	3	3:33	♃ ♄	225	1♉04
	Jul	27	2:26	♃ ♇	0	17♉55
	Aug	10	1:25	♅ ♆	270	19♋30
	Oct	29	20:05	♃ ♇	0	17♉12
	Nov	20	14:32	♄ ♆	120	17♐09
1870	Mar	4	7:56	♃ ♇	0	16♉14
		7	3:42	♅ ♆	270	18♋03
	May	29	1:58	♃ ♅	45	4♊34
	Jun	4	19:29	♃ ♆	315	6♊09
	Jul	6	13:30	♅ ♆	270	21♋44
	Aug	21	6:17	♃ ♄	180	21♊57
	Nov	5	16:14	♃ ♄	180	25♊41
1871	Jan	2	0:51	♄ ♇	135	2♑07
	Jun	11	22:17	♃ ♇	315	4♋07
		24	7:39	♃ ♄	180	6♋55
	Jul	25	0:29	♄ ♇	135	4♑46
	Sep	11	11:48	♃ ♆	270	23♋34
	Oct	14	23:20	♄ ♇	135	4♑23
1872	Feb	10	8:18	♃ ♆	270	21♋43
		24	21:33	♄ ♇	120	18♑01
	Mar	19	9:37	♃ ♄	180	19♋53
	Apr	11	17:05	♃ ♄	180	21♋00
	May	13	20:10	♃ ♆	270	24♋52
	Jun	5	8:57	♃ ♅	0	28♋44
		9	19:04	♄ ♇	120	20♑01
	Sep	17	6:12	♃ ♇	270	20♌42
	Oct	10	23:05	♃ ♆	240	25♌06
	Dec	7	10:52	♄ ♇	120	19♑22
1873	Jan	12	23:13	♄ ♆	90	23♑33
	Mar	3	3:13	♃ ♆	240	24♌28
	Apr	7	13:23	♄ ♅	180	1♒45
	May	23	15:46	♄ ♅	180	2♒37
	Jun	27	21:01	♃ ♆	240	28♌15
	Aug	2	9:32	♄ ♆	90	28♑35
	Sep	2	20:21	♃ ♄	135	11♍42
		9	16:12	♃ ♆	225	13♍11
	Oct	18	3:32	♃ ♇	240	21♍15
		31	0:12	♄ ♆	90	26♑52
	Nov	10	14:31	♃ ♅	315	25♍33
1874	Feb	16	8:50	♄ ♅	180	7♒43
	Mar	22	9:40	♃ ♄	135	26♍15
	May	14	18:43	♃ ♅	315	21♍51
	Jun	19	12:22	♃ ♅	315	23♍16
	Jul	20	3:57	♃ ♄	135	27♍02
	Aug	4	4:12	♄ ♅	180	10♒56
	Sep	14	12:45	♃ ♇	225	7♎37
		17	3:44	♃ ♄	120	8♎11
	Dec	27	19:27	♃ ♆	180	28♎03
1875	Jan	14	3:44	♄ ♅	180	14♒03
	Mar	14	18:07	♄ ♇	90	21♒01
		25	12:33	♃ ♆	180	29♎31
	May	1	4:09	♃ ♄	120	25♎03
	Jul	29	1:24	♃ ♄	120	24♎02
	Aug	4	11:46	♄ ♇	90	23♒35
	Sep	20	17:42	♃ ♆	180	2♏33
	Oct	21	6:51	♄ ♅	180	19♒25
	Nov	19	0:42	♄ ♅	180	19♒58
	Dec	10	23:34	♃ ♅	270	19♏53
		20	9:24	♄ ♇	90	22♒03
		21	15:29	♃ ♇	180	22♏02
		22	20:20	♃ ♄	90	22♏16
1876	Mar	17	16:38	♃ ♄	90	2♐00
	Jun	15	7:39	♃ ♇	180	23♏49
	Aug	29	11:15	♃ ♇	180	24♏35
	Oct	13	21:52	♃ ♄	90	1♐46
		22	0:18	♅ ♇	270	24♌03
	Dec	25	15:38	♃ ♆	135	17♐36
1877	Jan	22	14:21	♃ ♅	240	23♐31
	Feb	12	8:05	♅ ♇	270	22♌38
	Aug	4	0:48	♃ ♅	240	24♐13
		25	5:35	♅ ♇	270	25♌32
	Oct	15	20:07	♃ ♅	240	28♐22
	Nov	23	10:26	♃ ♆	120	5♑28
	Dec	10	3:44	♃ ♇	135	9♑07
1878	Jan	1	1:40	♃ ♅	225	14♑08
	Feb	11	6:45	♃ ♇	120	23♑34
		17	10:10	♄ ♆	45	20♓05
	Dec	17	0:04	♃ ♆	90	7♒17
1879	Jan	10	17:03	♃ ♄	45	12♒41
	Mar	1	23:32	♃ ♇	90	24♒36
		29	5:49	♃ ♅	180	0♓45
	May	7	11:22	♄ ♇	45	10♈43
	Sep	15	22:37	♃ ♅	180	5♓46
	Oct	8	12:51	♄ ♇	45	12♈08
	Dec	31	1:15	♃ ♅	180	8♓53
1880	Jan	23	0:10	♄ ♇	45	10♈30
	Mar	13	9:07	♃ ♆	45	25♓03
	Apr	19	0:12	♄ ♅	135	20♈05
	May	28	17:32	♃ ♇	45	12♈08
	Oct	6	0:42	♄ ♅	135	26♈28
		19	8:55	♃ ♇	45	12♈55
	Nov	4	22:37	♅ ♆	240	12♍55
1881	Jan	7	17:25	♃ ♇	45	11♈35
	Feb	26	16:26	♅ ♆	240	11♍54
	Mar	7	8:54	♄ ♅	135	26♈31
		25	1:11	♃ ♅	135	25♈47
	Apr	18	13:37	♃ ♄	0	1♉36
	May	22	11:44	♃ ♅	120	9♉39
	Jun	18	12:20	♃ ♆	0	15♉35
	Jul	18	15:19	♄ ♅	120	11♉16
		31	6:57	♄ ♅	120	11♉55
	Oct	6	15:13	♅ ♆	240	16♍00
	Dec	4	20:33	♃ ♅	120	18♉24
1882	Feb	8	13:07	♃ ♅	120	17♉38
	Apr	8	10:06	♅ ♆	240	15♍13
		12	19:53	♃ ♇	0	27♉59
		28	13:54	♄ ♅	120	14♉40
	May	12	17:09	♄ ♆	0	16♉29
	Jun	26	1:30	♃ ♅	90	14♊57
	Sep	8	16:51	♅ ♆	240	18♍46
	Nov	16	20:35	♄ ♅	120	22♉33
1883	Jan	11	21:27	♃ ♅	90	23♊16
	Mar	2	11:45	♃ ♅	90	21♊44
		10	12:00	♄ ♅	120	21♉24
	May	22	18:39	♄ ♇	0	29♉46
		25	13:22	♃ ♆	315	4♋07
		28	3:34	♅ ♆	240	19♍13
	Jul	17	12:35	♃ ♇	315	15♋52
		30	14:39	♅ ♆	240	20♍55
	Aug	26	20:31	♃ ♄	315	24♋30
1884	Jul	11	23:13	♃ ♅	45	9♌45
	Sep	12	11:58	♃ ♆	270	23♌16
	Oct	28	18:28	♃ ♇	270	1♍38
	Nov	9	15:27	♅ ♇	240	1♎26
1885	Feb	24	9:04	♃ ♇	270	0♍13
	Mar	29	11:46	♅ ♇	240	0♎33
	Jun	28	11:49	♄ ♅	90	29♊01
	Jul	1	14:57	♃ ♇	270	2♍29
	Sep	21	19:48	♅ ♇	240	3♎03
	Oct	19	11:26	♃ ♆	240	24♍55
	Nov	29	5:50	♃ ♇	240	2♎02
		30	19:44	♄ ♅	90	6♋54
	Dec	25	16:54	♃ ♄	270	4♎59
1886	Mar	17	14:57	♃ ♄	270	1♎38
		19	19:38	♃ ♇	240	1♎21
	Apr	29	20:39	♄ ♅	90	4♋19
	Jul	3	18:31	♄ ♆	315	11♋57
	Aug	9	21:48	♃ ♇	240	3♎58
		18	7:54	♃ ♅	0	5♎30
	Sep	1	4:48	♄ ♇	315	19♋04
		22	21:12	♃ ♆	225	12♎42
	Oct	20	15:14	♃ ♇	225	18♎42
	Nov	7	13:23	♃ ♄	270	22♎31
		25	5:17	♅ ♆	225	11♎14
1887	Feb	3	13:18	♄ ♇	315	17♋07
	Mar	25	20:19	♅ ♆	225	10♎42
	May	12	11:11	♄ ♇	315	18♋15
	Oct	29	6:06	♅ ♆	225	14♎18
1888	Jan	1	13:16	♃ ♆	180	27♏38
		28	20:19	♃ ♅	315	2♐14
		30	18:01	♃ ♄	240	2♐30
	Feb	3	23:15	♃ ♇	180	3♐04
	May	1	19:47	♃ ♇	180	3♐58
		2	6:14	♅ ♆	225	14♎05
		20	5:07	♃ ♄	240	1♐45
	Jun	1	10:16	♃ ♆	180	0♐13
		20	9:20	♃ ♅	315	28♏07
	Sep	21	2:13	♃ ♅	315	1♐25
		26	1:25	♃ ♆	180	2♐12
	Oct	2	9:45	♅ ♆	225	17♎07
		15	16:32	♃ ♇	180	5♐42
	Nov	20	19:40	♅ ♇	225	20♎06
	Dec	20	14:43	♃ ♄	240	19♐59
1889	Feb	13	2:16	♃ ♄	225	1♑18
	Apr	17	19:40	♅ ♇	225	19♎37
	Jun	16	9:57	♅ ♆	225	17♎54
		28	12:59	♃ ♄	225	2♑55
	Aug	28	5:11	♅ ♆	225	19♎33
	Oct	6	3:58	♅ ♇	225	21♎47
	Nov	19	3:28	♄ ♆	270	3♍20
	Dec	29	13:06	♃ ♆	135	17♑16
1890	Jan	3	23:41	♃ ♄	225	18♑32
		11	2:59	♃ ♇	135	20♑12
	Feb	3	0:34	♄ ♆	270	1♍46
		8	3:44	♃ ♅	270	26♑41
	Mar	4	7:54	♃ ♆	120	1♒53
		21	5:06	♃ ♇	120	5♒08
	Jul	27	18:20	♃ ♇	120	7♒36
	Aug	5	9:23	♃ ♆	120	6♒29
		26	14:28	♄ ♆	270	6♍46
	Sep	4	12:31	♄ ♇	270	7♍53
		26	3:45	♄ ♅	45	10♍34
	Nov	14	13:00	♃ ♆	120	5♒46
		22	22:44	♃ ♇	120	7♒01
1891	Jan	26	22:23	♄ ♅	45	16♍22
	Mar	11	17:51	♃ ♅	240	0♓52
		27	16:52	♃ ♆	90	4♓30
	Apr	4	19:12	♃ ♇	90	6♓16
		26	6:23	♃ ♄	180	10♓33
	May	13	3:58	♃ ♅	225	13♓25
	Jun	30	19:42	♄ ♅	45	12♍18
	Aug	2	19:06	♆ ♇	0	8♊38
		10	5:21	♃ ♄	180	16♓16
	Sep	1	2:12	♃ ♅	225	13♓40
	Oct	15	1:31	♃ ♆	90	8♓46
		18	3:29	♃ ♇	90	8♓35
	Nov	5	19:36	♆ ♇	0	8♊19
		9	21:54	♃ ♆	90	8♓12
		10	17:43	♃ ♇	90	8♓14
1892	Feb	8	4:01	♃ ♅	225	21♓05
	Mar	6	21:37	♃ ♄	180	27♓34
	Apr	30	17:20	♆ ♇	0	7♊42
	Jul	29	4:45	♃ ♇	45	24♈32
	Aug	23	18:48	♃ ♇	45	24♈47
	Nov	15	6:38	♄ ♇	240	9♎07
		25	8:53	♄ ♆	240	10♎04
1893	Feb	19	21:43	♃ ♇	45	22♈50
		23	8:04	♃ ♆	45	23♈31
	Apr	3	19:35	♄ ♆	240	9♎05
		13	18:17	♄ ♇	240	8♎19
		30	22:54	♃ ♅	180	8♉37
	Jun	25	20:40	♃ ♄	135	21♉17
	Aug	26	19:52	♄ ♇	240	10♎46
	Sep	20	10:20	♄ ♆	240	13♎34
	Oct	9	4:30	♃ ♄	135	0♊50
1894	Jan	1	8:57	♄ ♇	225	24♎15
	Mar	13	22:29	♄ ♇	225	23♎53
	Apr	29	1:54	♃ ♄	135	5♊32
	May	18	17:30	♃ ♇	0	9♊59
	Jun	1	11:32	♃ ♆	0	13♊10
		24	5:46	♃ ♄	120	18♊25
	Jul	30	16:13	♃ ♅	135	26♊18
	Oct	9	21:56	♄ ♇	225	26♎38
	Nov	8	3:30	♄ ♆	225	0♏10
	Dec	7	1:51	♃ ♄	120	3♋22
		12	6:31	♃ ♅	135	2♋43
1895	May	1	4:44	♃ ♅	135	3♋15
		1	21:43	♃ ♄	120	3♋22
	Jun	15	6:25	♄ ♆	225	0♏50
	Jul	2	2:31	♃ ♅	120	16♋05
	Aug	24	3:42	♃ ♇	315	27♋42
		28	8:14	♄ ♆	225	2♏54
	Sep	21	17:36	♃ ♆	315	3♌04
1896	Feb	26	23:04	♃ ♆	315	0♌15
	May	4	5:55	♃ ♆	315	1♌30
	Jul	8	1:10	♃ ♄	90	12♌29
	Aug	14	12:47	♃ ♅	90	20♌33
1897	Jan	6	7:10	♄ ♅	0	27♏40
	Jun	1	9:26	♄ ♅	0	26♏26
	Aug	15	14:30	♃ ♇	270	14♍35
	Sep	9	10:25	♄ ♅	0	25♏35
		21	20:18	♃ ♆	270	22♍33
1898	Sep	18	21:02	♃ ♅	45	15♎15
		21	1:54	♃ ♇	240	15♎43
	Oct	31	18:09	♃ ♆	240	24♎29
	Nov	11	23:56	♃ ♄	45	26♎52
		26	22:57	♃ ♇	225	29♎54
	Dec	6	13:08	♄ ♇	180	14♐43
1899	Jan	13	5:40	♃ ♆	225	7♏36
	Feb	16	5:50	♄ ♆	180	22♐02
	Mar	28	1:09	♃ ♄	45	8♏39
	Apr	9	10:23	♃ ♆	225	7♏22
	May	2	20:37	♄ ♆	180	22♐57
	Jun	17	19:42	♃ ♇	225	0♏27
	Jul	21	12:21	♃ ♇	225	1♏10
	Aug	3	23:14	♃ ♄	45	2♏19
	Oct	3	14:42	♃ ♆	225	12♏02
	Dec	14	20:23	♄ ♆	180	25♐42
1900	Aug	16	16:01	♄ ♆	180	28♐40
	Oct	4	18:30	♄ ♆	180	29♐16
		20	8:15	♃ ♅	0	10♐06
	Nov	22	10:34	♃ ♇	180	17♐01
1901	Jan	7	5:28	♃ ♆	180	27♐21
		31	13:26	♅ ♇	180	15♐50
	Apr	29	18:24	♅ ♇	180	16♐18
	Nov	28	16:29	♃ ♄	0	14♑00
	Dec	17	3:36	♅ ♇	180	17♐33
1902	Feb	14	8:38	♃ ♇	135	1♒43
	Mar	6	9:49	♃ ♅	315	6♒06
	Apr	21	19:46	♃ ♆	135	14♒10
	Jun	28	12:24	♅ ♇	180	18♐36
		29	12:35	♃ ♆	135	16♒24
	Nov	6	22:49	♅ ♇	180	19♐19
	Dec	26	20:57	♃ ♆	135	17♒16
		31	20:15	♃ ♇	120	18♒18
1903	Feb	12	6:27	♄ ♇	135	2♒45
		24	10:43	♃ ♆	120	0♓59
	May	19	3:41	♃ ♇	90	18♓39
	Jun	2	16:12	♄ ♅	315	9♒11
		29	18:34	♄ ♅	315	8♒05
		30	21:27	♃ ♄	315	23♓01
	Jul	1	3:42	♃ ♅	270	23♓02
	Aug	7	23:18	♄ ♇	135	5♒21
		14	11:02	♃ ♅	270	21♓46
		25	13:15	♃ ♇	90	20♓34
	Sep	13	0:55	♃ ♄	315	18♓12
	Nov	30	6:21	♄ ♇	135	4♒56
1904	Jan	9	15:18	♃ ♇	90	19♓11
	Feb	23	3:35	♄ ♅	315	14♒14
		27	10:39	♃ ♅	270	29♓22
	Mar	1	7:56	♃ ♄	315	0♈03
		14	7:00	♃ ♆	90	3♈08

♃ ♄ ♅ ♆ ♇ 0°, 45°, 90°, 120°, 135° and 180° Aspects 1700–2050

Year	Month	Day	Time	Planets	Aspect	Position
	Apr	1	21:55	♄ ♆	135	18♒14
		10	15:35	♄ ♇	120	18♒57
	Jun	24	23:37	♄ ♆	135	20♒33
		25	19:20	♄ ♇	120	20♒31
	Jul	7	13:25	♃ ♅	240	27♈15
	Oct	9	6:53	♃ ♅	240	26♈27
1905	Jan	15	8:04	♄ ♇	120	20♒06
		23	20:09	♄ ♆	135	21♒05
	Mar	27	2:11	♃ ♅	240	4♉10
		29	22:24	♃ ♇	45	4♉49
	May	26	11:53	♃ ♅	225	18♉22
	Jun	12	10:28	♃ ♆	45	22♉13
	Jul	28	23:21	♃ ♄	270	1♊20
	Dec	19	20:51	♃ ♄	270	28♉14
1906	Mar	1	3:10	♅ ♆	180	7♑42
		14	23:45	♄ ♆	120	7♓37
	May	7	12:45	♅ ♆	180	8♑15
		20	8:03	♃ ♄	270	13♊54
	Jun	26	18:15	♃ ♇	0	22♊31
	Aug	24	14:15	♃ ♅	180	4♋41
		30	16:50	♄ ♆	120	12♓03
	Oct	1	8:35	♃ ♄	240	9♋45
	Dec	6	16:54	♃ ♄	240	8♋49
		15	21:44	♃ ♅	180	7♋42
1907	Jan	9	9:22	♄ ♆	120	11♓04
	Feb	1	6:50	♅ ♆	180	10♑28
	Apr	14	20:41	♄ ♇	90	22♓01
	May	22	11:47	♃ ♆	0	10♋50
		28	16:32	♃ ♅	180	12♋04
	Jun	13	3:50	♅ ♆	180	11♑32
	Aug	4	16:37	♃ ♄	240	26♋55
	Sep	8	17:48	♄ ♇	90	24♓45
		30	9:35	♃ ♄	225	8♌06
	Oct	11	9:21	♃ ♇	315	9♌46
1908	Jan	12	9:41	♅ ♆	180	13♑17
		18	12:41	♄ ♇	90	23♓11
		27	2:51	♃ ♄	225	8♌58
	Feb	3	16:39	♃ ♇	315	7♌58
	Apr	30	12:14	♃ ♄	240	5♌01
	May	12	7:01	♃ ♄	240	6♌16
		31	13:29	♃ ♇	315	8♌56
	Jul	11	14:17	♅ ♆	180	14♑45
	Aug	18	8:52	♃ ♄	225	24♌35
	Sep	3	11:09	♃ ♅	135	28♌05
		21	9:10	♃ ♆	315	1♍53
	Dec	23	19:21	♅ ♆	180	16♑06
1909	Apr	2	3:29	♃ ♅	135	5♍50
		14	5:18	♄ ♆	90	14♈25
	May	29	1:24	♃ ♅	135	5♍39
	Jun	7	1:06	♄ ♅	270	20♈23
	Aug	10	17:24	♅ ♆	180	17♑58
		15	19:57	♃ ♅	120	17♍49
	Sep	27	10:53	♃ ♇	270	26♍54
	Oct	19	1:10	♄ ♆	90	19♈20
	Nov	8	5:27	♄ ♅	270	17♈51
	Dec	2	23:17	♅ ♆	180	18♑54
1910	Jan	24	13:15	♄ ♆	90	17♈31
	Apr	7	8:50	♄ ♅	270	25♈00
	Sep	23	23:12	♅ ♆	180	21♑18
	Oct	2	7:52	♃ ♅	90	21♎16
		3	1:53	♃ ♆	270	21♎26
		28	7:43	♅ ♆	180	21♑34
	Nov	1	4:55	♃ ♇	240	27♎45
		18	9:55	♃ ♄	180	1♏25
1911	Jan	14	9:56	♃ ♇	225	11♏26
	Apr	19	7:40	♃ ♇	225	11♏10
		30	23:35	♃ ♄	180	9♏43
	May	16	2:38	♄ ♇	45	11♉39
	Sep	26	16:44	♃ ♇	225	14♏00
	Oct	18	21:06	♃ ♄	180	18♏28
	Nov	12	3:10	♃ ♆	240	23♏44
1912	Jan	15	13:41	♃ ♆	225	7♐21
	Jun	24	21:18	♃ ♆	225	7♐43
	Jul	23	6:57	♄ ♅	240	1♊33
	Oct	3	0:31	♃ ♆	225	10♐49
		24	12:43	♃ ♅	45	14♐37
	Nov	25	11:09	♄ ♅	240	0♊26
	Dec	28	22:31	♃ ♇	180	28♐53
1913	Mar	16	17:55	♃ ♄	135	14♑09
	Apr	18	0:08	♃ ♄	135	17♑21
	May	28	20:54	♄ ♅	240	7♊27
	Jun	13	13:19	♄ ♆	45	9♊28
1914	Jan	9	6:05	♃ ♆	180	27♑05
		9	18:24	♃ ♄	135	27♑12
		15	1:24	♄ ♆	45	11♊55
	Feb	9	21:28	♄ ♆	45	11♊13
	Mar	4	3:25	♃ ♅	0	9♒32
		16	23:05	♃ ♄	120	12♒13
		26	13:03	♃ ♇	135	14♒06
	Jun	17	17:47	♃ ♄	120	22♒14
	Jul	13	0:01	♄ ♅	225	25♊27
	Aug	15	3:43	♃ ♇	135	16♒48
		27	14:26	♃ ♄	135	15♒14
	Oct	4	18:39	♄ ♇	0	2♋14
	Nov	1	8:48	♄ ♇	0	2♋04
		25	4:15	♃ ♄	135	15♒53
		30	10:32	♃ ♇	135	16♒39
1915	Jan	20	7:52	♃ ♄	120	26♒35
		25	23:32	♄ ♅	225	26♊15
	Feb	5	18:25	♃ ♇	120	0♓25
	Mar	29	5:52	♃ ♆	135	12♓41
	May	17	18:54	♄ ♅	225	0♋40
		19	19:55	♄ ♇	0	0♋54
1916	Feb	15	5:45	♃ ♆	120	0♈38
		17	19:33	♅ ♇	135	16♒22
		18	12:22	♃ ♇	90	1♈22
		18	19:10	♃ ♅	315	1♈26
	Mar	25	2:41	♃ ♄	90	9♈43
	Jul	7	6:52	♃ ♆	90	1♉43
		22	11:37	♅ ♇	135	18♒28
	Sep	20	18:21	♃ ♆	90	4♉16
	Oct	24	13:22	♃ ♄	90	0♉17
1917	Jan	10	19:19	♅ ♇	135	18♒03
		20	2:25	♃ ♄	90	26♈57
	Feb	27	18:36	♃ ♆	90	2♉36
	May	7	16:18	♃ ♇	45	17♉49
	Jun	1	16:54	♃ ♅	270	23♉43
	Aug	1	5:20	♄ ♆	0	4♌45
	Sep	18	18:31	♅ ♇	135	20♒28
	Nov	25	13:03	♅ ♇	135	20♒05
1918	May	29	16:28	♃ ♆	45	19♊50
	Jul	1	15:13	♃ ♅	240	27♊23
		7	9:10	♃ ♄	45	28♊41
	Aug	10	20:03	♃ ♇	0	6♋03
	Sep	2	13:17	♃ ♅	225	10♋11
		7	14:02	♄ ♇	315	21♌29
	Oct	1	17:03	♄ ♅	180	24♌14
	Dec	14	5:00	♃ ♄	45	13♋14
1919	Jan	5	6:16	♃ ♅	225	10♋22
		25	13:38	♄ ♅	180	26♌24
	Mar	29	14:29	♃ ♄	45	6♋55
	Jun	2	1:55	♃ ♅	225	16♋42
	Aug	13	14:44	♄ ♅	180	0♍08
	Sep	24	1:59	♃ ♆	0	10♌49
1920	Mar	8	11:58	♃ ♆	0	9♌12
	Apr	24	13:52	♃ ♆	0	8♌45
		27	0:26	♄ ♅	180	4♍54
	Jun	7	15:37	♄ ♅	180	5♍40
	Jul	25	10:17	♃ ♇	315	22♌55
	Sep	10	16:10	♃ ♅	180	3♍08
1921	Mar	17	11:20	♅ ♇	120	6♓48
	May	3	12:19	♃ ♅	180	8♍56
		25	0:45	♃ ♅	180	9♍28
	Jul	25	1:56	♅ ♇	120	9♓01
	Sep	10	4:14	♃ ♄	0	26♍36
		26	23:24	♃ ♆	315	0♎13
	Oct	12	13:45	♄ ♆	315	0♎35
	Nov	12	14:32	♃ ♇	270	9♎52
1922	Feb	6	5:04	♅ ♇	120	8♓18
	Jun	7	23:39	♃ ♇	270	8♎58
		20	17:38	♃ ♇	270	9♎17
	Sep	17	23:02	♅ ♇	120	11♓06
	Oct	5	20:60	♃ ♅	135	25♎28
		9	2:42	♄ ♇	270	11♎13
	Dec	13	8:42	♃ ♅	120	9♏55
		16	9:57	♃ ♇	240	10♏29
		27	6:43	♅ ♇	120	10♓16
1923	Jan	29	5:56	♃ ♆	270	17♏02
	Apr	20	2:14	♃ ♅	120	16♏00
		25	4:22	♃ ♆	270	15♏23
	Jun	10	4:56	♃ ♇	240	10♏09
	Aug	20	12:08	♃ ♇	240	11♏50
	Sep	14	2:43	♃ ♅	120	15♏23
	Oct	8	4:26	♃ ♆	270	19♏48
	Nov	12	4:60	♃ ♇	225	27♏13
	Dec	5	21:15	♄ ♅	135	28♎42
1924	Feb	16	18:07	♃ ♅	90	16♐20
		23	11:27	♃ ♄	315	17♐12
		29	9:45	♄ ♅	135	2♏03
	Mar	4	22:57	♃ ♆	240	18♐20
	Apr	17	18:11	♃ ♅	90	19♐41
	May	15	3:06	♃ ♆	240	17♐40
	Jul	15	9:02	♃ ♄	315	10♐50
	Oct	13	22:40	♄ ♅	135	3♏22
		23	8:48	♃ ♅	90	18♐05
	Nov	10	16:40	♃ ♄	315	21♐42
		14	20:04	♃ ♆	240	22♐34
1925	Jan	5	18:39	♄ ♇	240	12♏26
		17	9:19	♃ ♆	225	6♑52
	Feb	9	7:11	♃ ♇	180	11♑47
	Apr	24	9:34	♄ ♇	240	11♏35
	May	19	0:01	♄ ♅	135	9♏45
	Aug	11	12:60	♃ ♇	180	13♑58
		27	0:06	♄ ♅	135	9♏18
	Oct	15	19:15	♃ ♇	180	14♑45
		21	18:49	♄ ♇	240	14♏44
	Dec	21	1:06	♄ ♅	120	21♏43
1926	Jan	16	14:43	♄ ♆	270	24♏08
	Feb	11	13:24	♃ ♅	45	8♒36
	Mar	23	17:31	♄ ♅	120	25♏49
	Apr	18	4:13	♃ ♆	180	22♒03
		30	4:43	♃ ♄	270	23♒49
	May	23	11:31	♄ ♆	270	22♏06
	Aug	2	9:54	♃ ♆	180	23♒56
		29	14:29	♃ ♄	270	20♒27
	Oct	30	10:45	♄ ♅	120	26♏03
	Nov	6	4:57	♄ ♆	270	26♏50
	Dec	6	21:54	♄ ♇	225	0♐28
1927	Jan	2	21:39	♃ ♆	180	26♒41
		16	20:60	♃ ♇	135	29♒39
	Feb	17	12:25	♃ ♄	270	6♓59
	Mar	17	19:37	♃ ♇	120	13♓48
	Jun	12	19:19	♄ ♅	120	3♐08
		26	9:15	♃ ♄	240	2♈16
	Jul	15	21:37	♃ ♅	0	3♈24
		31	16:44	♄ ♇	225	1♐03
	Aug	11	11:03	♃ ♅	0	3♈00
		29	14:54	♃ ♄	240	1♈29
	Sep	5	21:20	♄ ♇	225	1♐48
		10	8:35	♄ ♅	120	2♐02
1928	Jan	25	6:49	♃ ♅	0	0♈24
	Mar	18	18:48	♃ ♆	135	12♈01
		31	3:07	♃ ♇	90	14♈59
	Apr	16	4:25	♃ ♄	240	18♈51
	May	18	13:38	♃ ♆	120	26♈25
	Jun	7	22:11	♃ ♄	225	0♉45
	Nov	14	13:38	♃ ♄	225	3♉11
	Dec	2	5:46	♃ ♆	120	1♉23
1929	Jan	12	12:23	♃ ♆	120	0♉58
	Mar	6	17:46	♄ ♆	240	29♐35
	Apr	11	13:41	♃ ♄	225	15♉31
	May	22	20:41	♃ ♅	315	25♉12
		29	8:37	♄ ♆	240	28♐42
	Jun	7	7:29	♃ ♆	90	28♉48
		23	12:19	♃ ♇	45	2♊28
	Dec	29	15:27	♄ ♆	240	3♑26
1930	Feb	22	8:04	♄ ♅	90	9♑15
	Apr	9	5:47	♄ ♅	90	11♑45
	Jul	27	3:56	♃ ♄	180	6♋46
	Sep	5	8:10	♃ ♅	270	14♋35
	Oct	27	6:05	♃ ♆	45	20♋17
	Nov	7	19:28	♃ ♆	45	20♋31
		21	22:41	♆ ♇	315	5♍42
	Dec	12	18:49	♄ ♅	90	11♑28
1931	Jan	11	0:07	♃ ♄	180	14♋54
	Feb	2	3:12	♃ ♅	270	12♋12
		17	8:01	♄ ♇	180	19♑04
		21	12:23	♄ ♆	225	19♑29
	Mar	22	0:48	♆ ♇	315	3♍43
	May	17	21:31	♃ ♅	270	17♋35
		20	5:50	♃ ♆	45	18♋00
		27	3:14	♃ ♇	0	19♋16
		27	23:39	♅ ♆	135	18♈02
	Jun	10	20:14	♃ ♄	180	22♋09
	Jul	8	20:28	♄ ♇	180	20♑18
		21	8:29	♄ ♅	90	19♑22
		23	14:32	♄ ♆	225	19♑12
		28	19:28	♅ ♆	135	19♈23
	Oct	10	20:10	♃ ♅	240	17♌25
		16	18:37	♆ ♇	315	7♍09
		17	0:38	♄ ♅	90	17♑10
	Dec	13	12:30	♄ ♇	180	21♑41
		24	20:55	♄ ♆	225	22♑56
1932	Feb	15	20:08	♃ ♅	240	16♌34
	Apr	21	14:04	♅ ♇	90	20♈02
		26	12:21	♅ ♆	135	20♈18
	May	8	15:08	♆ ♇	315	5♍13
	Jul	9	14:33	♃ ♅	240	23♌14
	Sep	2	9:28	♅ ♇	90	22♈55
		4	4:54	♅ ♆	135	22♈52
		8	15:46	♆ ♇	315	8♍02
		15	1:47	♃ ♅	225	7♍32
		18	2:35	♃ ♇	315	8♍11
		19	4:41	♃ ♆	0	8♍25
	Oct	12	13:20	♃ ♄	135	13♍12
1933	Jan	30	8:10	♃ ♄	135	22♍29
	Mar	8	18:25	♅ ♇	90	21♈23
	Apr	5	12:41	♅ ♆	135	22♈53
	Aug	25	4:01	♃ ♄	135	26♍38
	Oct	3	20:16	♅ ♆	135	26♈02
		26	1:37	♃ ♄	120	9♎50
	Nov	5	3:21	♅ ♇	90	24♈44
1934	Jan	18	3:47	♅ ♇	90	23♈35
	Feb	5	10:54	♃ ♇	270	23♎11
		20	14:11	♃ ♇	270	22♎55
	Mar	7	4:38	♃ ♄	120	22♎00
		17	2:57	♅ ♆	135	25♈36
	Sep	8	12:21	♃ ♄	120	23♎17
		21	4:46	♃ ♇	270	25♎48
	Oct	2	6:32	♃ ♆	315	28♎06
		11	0:32	♃ ♅	180	29♎58
	Nov	2	21:48	♅ ♆	135	29♈02
1935	Feb	23	12:32	♅ ♆	135	28♈28
	May	15	23:41	♄ ♇	135	9♓08
	Jul	1	9:60	♄ ♇	135	10♓09
	Oct	28	3:41	♃ ♇	240	27♏25
	Nov	26	5:59	♃ ♄	90	3♐48
	Dec	18	10:51	♅ ♆	135	1♉47
1936	Jan	1	0:25	♃ ♇	225	11♐39
		16	15:34	♅ ♆	135	1♉34
		24	23:30	♃ ♆	270	16♐25
		26	5:37	♃ ♅	135	16♐39
	Feb	15	3:31	♄ ♇	135	10♓42
	Mar	21	9:47	♄ ♆	180	14♓59
	May	21	22:50	♃ ♅	135	21♐57
		27	1:46	♃ ♄	90	21♐22
	Jul	26	19:01	♃ ♆	270	14♐58
	Sep	20	4:25	♃ ♆	270	16♐55
		28	6:58	♃ ♄	90	17♐54
	Oct	4	23:46	♄ ♆	180	17♓26

♃ ♄ ♅ ♆ ♇ 0°, 45°, 90°, 120°, 135° and 180° Aspects 1700–2050

Year	Month	Day	Time	Planets	Aspect	Position
		28	3:13	♃ ♅	135	22♐43
	Dec	27	14:39	♃ ♅	120	5♑45
1937	Jan	18	2:19	♄ ♆	180	18♓45
	Feb	7	23:17	♄ ♅	45	20♓54
		21	11:37	♃ ♆	240	18♑01
	Mar	26	18:10	♄ ♇	120	26♓32
	Apr	23	2:55	♃ ♇	180	26♑32
	May	29	16:31	♃ ♇	180	27♑00
	Aug	25	17:56	♃ ♆	240	18♑04
	Oct	16	23:27	♄ ♇	120	0♈05
		26	7:10	♃ ♆	240	20♑14
	Dec	18	15:18	♃ ♇	180	29♑40
1938	Jan	4	7:52	♄ ♇	120	29♓20
		15	13:07	♃ ♆	225	6♒00
		31	12:49	♃ ♅	90	9♒48
	Apr	3	17:45	♃ ♄	45	23♒39
	Jun	28	17:13	♃ ♄	45	2♓10
	Dec	7	20:13	♃ ♄	45	26♒16
1939	Mar	4	10:49	♃ ♇	135	14♓32
	Apr	2	5:23	♃ ♆	180	21♓26
	May	8	8:43	♃ ♇	120	29♓22
	Jun	5	14:17	♃ ♅	45	4♈22
	Jul	7	6:24	♅ ♆	120	20♉53
	Aug	14	19:19	♅ ♆	120	21♉53
	Sep	1	21:26	♃ ♅	45	6♈58
	Oct	5	15:25	♃ ♇	120	2♈43
1940	Jan	8	9:54	♃ ♇	120	2♈06
		14	21:34	♃ ♅	45	3♈02
	Mar	26	4:48	♄ ♇	90	0♉41
	May	20	7:23	♃ ♇	90	0♉54
		21	18:38	♄ ♆	135	7♉46
		25	22:05	♅ ♆	120	22♉45
	Jun	22	10:12	♃ ♆	135	7♉49
	Aug	8	1:24	♃ ♄	0	14♉27
	Oct	2	2:56	♅ ♆	120	25♉45
		20	4:38	♃ ♄	0	12♉28
		26	19:40	♃ ♆	135	11♉36
		29	23:13	♄ ♆	135	11♉42
1941	Feb	15	6:37	♃ ♄	0	9♉07
	Mar	3	15:40	♃ ♆	135	11♉42
		14	13:26	♄ ♆	135	11♉24
	May	1	2:24	♅ ♆	120	25♉14
		5	23:33	♃ ♆	120	25♉09
		8	0:22	♃ ♅	0	25♉38
	Jul	8	20:52	♄ ♆	120	25♉12
	Sep	11	17:30	♃ ♇	45	20♊08
	Oct	5	22:23	♄ ♆	120	27♉59
		30	8:34	♃ ♇	45	20♊46
	Nov	5	2:57	♅ ♆	120	28♉59
1942	Apr	7	23:55	♅ ♆	120	27♉59
		16	4:44	♃ ♇	45	18♊28
		20	5:08	♄ ♆	120	27♉42
	May	3	13:20	♄ ♅	0	29♉20
		28	14:47	♃ ♆	90	27♊07
	Sep	11	10:05	♃ ♅	315	19♋35
	Nov	17	8:21	♃ ♄	315	25♋12
	Dec	11	11:37	♅ ♆	120	1♊54
		28	20:41	♃ ♄	315	21♋58
1943	Feb	22	15:56	♃ ♅	315	15♋40
	Mar	11	4:21	♅ ♆	120	1♊00
	Apr	21	17:34	♃ ♅	315	17♋41
	Jul	22	20:19	♄ ♇	45	21♊37
	Aug	1	8:09	♃ ♇	0	6♌53
		7	14:42	♃ ♄	315	8♌16
	Sep	14	20:19	♃ ♆	45	16♌24
	Dec	11	3:18	♄ ♇	45	23♊33
1944	Mar	19	0:13	♃ ♆	45	18♌01
	Apr	4	21:06	♄ ♇	45	21♊27
		21	3:05	♃ ♆	45	17♌08
	Jul	2	10:22	♄ ♆	90	1♋34
	Sep	25	9:45	♃ ♅	270	13♍07
	Dec	3	21:18	♃ ♇	315	25♍09
1945	Jan	8	20:36	♄ ♆	90	6♋26
	Mar	7	20:35	♃ ♇	315	23♍18
	Apr	6	16:01	♄ ♆	90	4♋45
	Jul	28	1:40	♃ ♇	315	24♍42
	Sep	22	9:01	♃ ♆	0	5♎54
	Nov	11	9:29	♃ ♅	240	16♎29
	Dec	20	2:04	♃ ♄	270	23♎15
1946	May	5	4:37	♃ ♄	270	19♎48
	Jun	8	5:47	♃ ♅	240	17♎31
	Jul	30	6:14	♃ ♅	240	20♎21
	Oct	2	23:10	♄ ♅	315	6♌47
		25	20:05	♃ ♅	225	6♏28
	Nov	4	19:49	♃ ♄	270	8♏39
		26	10:49	♃ ♇	270	13♏20
1947	Feb	6	15:50	♃ ♆	315	25♏38
	Mar	4	10:36	♄ ♅	315	2♌46
	May	8	3:01	♃ ♆	315	23♏29
	Jun	30	7:49	♄ ♅	315	7♌54
	Aug	11	1:20	♄ ♇	0	13♌07
	Sep	30	9:45	♃ ♆	315	25♏23
	Dec	29	7:26	♃ ♇	240	14♐33
1948	Jan	26	12:21	♃ ♄	240	20♐20
	Feb	6	13:50	♃ ♅	180	22♐21
	Mar	19	13:24	♃ ♇	225	27♐50
	May	14	15:22	♃ ♇	225	27♐39
	Jun	3	21:43	♃ ♅	180	25♐30
	Jul	9	15:01	♃ ♄	240	21♐10
	Aug	18	18:32	♄ ♆	45	26♌05
	Nov	15	1:40	♃ ♅	180	29♐55
		22	21:21	♃ ♇	225	1♑34
	Dec	13	20:40	♃ ♄	240	6♑12
1949	Jan	21	19:25	♃ ♆	270	15♑10
	Feb	7	14:60	♃ ♄	225	18♑55
	May	31	4:08	♅ ♇	45	29♊25
	Aug	23	23:40	♃ ♄	225	23♑23
	Dec	22	9:47	♃ ♄	225	4♒23
		27	12:02	♅ ♇	45	2♋53
1950	Feb	11	10:43	♃ ♅	135	16♒14
		13	21:20	♃ ♇	180	16♒49
		15	6:17	♃ ♆	240	17♒09
	Mar	24	15:49	♅ ♇	45	1♋02
	Apr	18	22:59	♃ ♆	225	0♓39
		26	6:23	♃ ♅	120	1♓54
	Jul	20	15:19	♃ ♅	120	6♓34
	Sep	7	13:30	♃ ♆	225	0♓54
	Dec	30	10:05	♃ ♆	225	4♓24
1951	Jan	12	4:27	♃ ♅	120	6♓53
	Apr	10	7:45	♃ ♄	180	27♓25
	May	2	15:15	♃ ♇	135	2♈25
		29	16:25	♃ ♅	90	7♈43
	Sep	1	1:10	♃ ♅	90	12♈56
	Oct	3	4:25	♄ ♇	315	5♎56
		15	19:12	♃ ♄	180	7♈29
		25	10:03	♃ ♇	135	6♈21
	Dec	8	2:48	♄ ♅	270	13♎02
1952	Jan	3	3:31	♃ ♇	135	6♈11
	Feb	2	22:47	♃ ♅	90	10♈43
		21	8:37	♃ ♄	180	14♈19
	Mar	16	1:38	♃ ♇	120	19♈33
		21	17:13	♃ ♆	180	20♈52
	Apr	18	12:14	♄ ♅	270	10♎20
	Oct	15	18:51	♄ ♅	270	18♎30
	Nov	21	13:18	♄ ♆	0	22♎47
1953	Mar	30	8:26	♃ ♇	90	21♉03
	May	11	18:44	♃ ♅	45	0♊30
		17	17:29	♄ ♆	0	21♎38
	Jun	3	17:42	♃ ♄	135	5♊53
		5	13:04	♃ ♆	135	6♊18
	Jul	22	1:22	♄ ♆	0	21♎12
	Aug	19	17:48	♃ ♆	120	21♊42
	Nov	16	23:11	♃ ♆	120	24♊44
	Dec	15	21:07	♃ ♄	135	21♊06
1954	Apr	13	3:47	♃ ♄	135	22♊04
		26	10:04	♃ ♆	120	24♊24
	Jun	8	4:49	♃ ♄	120	3♋17
		30	4:14	♃ ♇	45	8♋15
	Jul	15	17:37	♅ ♆	90	23♋19
	Sep	18	3:04	♃ ♆	90	24♋40
	Oct	7	10:02	♃ ♅	0	27♋23
	Dec	2	19:06	♅ ♆	90	27♋20
		23	10:57	♃ ♆	90	27♋51
1955	Jan	7	2:01	♃ ♅	0	26♋04
	Feb	17	15:55	♃ ♄	120	21♋04
	Apr	2	13:42	♃ ♄	120	20♋20
	May	10	20:38	♃ ♅	0	24♋16
		21	23:12	♃ ♆	90	26♋00
	Jun	11	11:09	♅ ♆	90	25♋39
	Aug	24	16:03	♃ ♄	90	15♌33
	Nov	2	23:25	♃ ♇	0	28♌25
	Dec	27	14:28	♄ ♇	270	28♏26
1956	Jan	15	11:39	♃ ♄	90	0♍14
		17	22:34	♄ ♅	240	0♐26
		19	12:11	♅ ♆	90	0♌22
	Feb	8	2:41	♃ ♇	0	27♌36
	May	5	11:53	♅ ♆	90	28♋37
		24	7:38	♄ ♅	240	29♏15
	Jun	16	17:44	♃ ♇	0	26♌28
		22	2:03	♃ ♄	90	27♌18
	Jul	2	5:12	♄ ♇	270	26♏48
	Sep	12	3:43	♃ ♆	45	13♍42
	Oct	7	15:39	♄ ♇	270	29♏43
		20	19:55	♃ ♅	315	21♍46
	Dec	8	19:56	♄ ♅	240	6♐41
1957	Aug	6	12:15	♄ ♅	240	7♐42
	Oct	20	20:59	♄ ♅	240	11♐19
		28	3:58	♃ ♇	315	16♎59
	Dec	31	21:52	♄ ♆	315	19♐26
1958	Feb	16	2:53	♄ ♅	225	23♐53
	May	30	23:22	♄ ♅	225	23♐26
	Sep	24	16:13	♃ ♆	0	3♏18
	Oct	5	11:11	♃ ♄	45	5♏31
	Nov	24	11:23	♃ ♅	270	16♏22
1959	Jan	8	23:27	♄ ♅	225	0♑24
	Feb	5	23:40	♄ ♇	240	3♑23
	Jul	13	11:52	♄ ♇	240	2♑31
	Aug	3	11:37	♄ ♅	225	1♑17
	Nov	4	0:30	♃ ♇	270	5♐51
	Dec	2	14:24	♄ ♅	225	6♑04
		3	11:21	♄ ♇	240	6♑10
1960	Jan	8	6:03	♃ ♅	240	20♐18
		26	14:23	♃ ♆	315	24♐05
	Mar	22	20:28	♃ ♅	225	2♑23
	May	20	9:39	♃ ♅	225	2♑14
	Dec	5	20:46	♃ ♇	240	8♑08
		17	5:53	♃ ♅	225	10♑41
1961	Jan	26	12:15	♄ ♇	225	22♑35
	Feb	5	22:21	♃ ♇	225	22♑21
		19	0:03	♃ ♄	0	25♑12
	Sep	15	8:51	♄ ♇	225	23♑22
	Nov	12	2:56	♄ ♇	225	24♑53
1962	Jan	13	2:41	♃ ♆	270	13♒12
	Mar	14	11:57	♃ ♅	180	27♒27
	May	4	9:13	♃ ♇	180	7♓35
	Jun	2	23:31	♃ ♆	240	11♓20
	Aug	6	13:41	♃ ♆	240	10♓46
		18	22:43	♃ ♇	180	9♓21
	Oct	8	13:56	♃ ♅	180	3♓33
	Dec	7	11:02	♃ ♅	180	5♓18
1963	Jan	16	3:60	♃ ♇	180	11♓54
	Feb	2	14:05	♃ ♆	240	15♓37
		18	21:49	♄ ♆	270	15♒40
	Apr	4	12:29	♃ ♆	225	0♈05
	May	6	22:15	♃ ♄	315	7♈30
	Jul	5	8:20	♃ ♅	135	17♈31
	Aug	10	14:41	♃ ♅	135	19♈29
1964	Mar	11	0:10	♃ ♅	135	22♈29
		31	15:23	♃ ♇	135	27♈14
	May	7	1:35	♃ ♅	120	5♉56
		31	13:04	♃ ♇	120	11♉37
	Jun	18	6:59	♃ ♆	180	15♉27
	Dec	3	16:01	♃ ♆	180	18♉26
		31	1:20	♃ ♇	120	16♉17
1965	Jan	14	18:41	♃ ♇	120	16♉08
	Feb	28	21:20	♃ ♆	180	19♉59
	Apr	1	9:08	♄ ♅	180	11♓37
		23	18:58	♄ ♇	180	13♓56
	Jun	8	21:30	♃ ♅	90	10♊54
		21	19:49	♃ ♇	90	13♊53
	Jul	6	11:56	♃ ♄	270	17♊10
	Aug	17	11:12	♄ ♇	180	15♓19
		28	3:36	♄ ♅	180	14♓33
	Oct	9	20:11	♅ ♇	0	17♍10
1966	Feb	20	4:11	♄ ♇	180	17♓35
		24	13:31	♄ ♅	180	18♓07
	Mar	27	9:18	♄ ♆	240	21♓53
	Apr	4	20:44	♅ ♇	0	16♍28
	May	31	13:12	♃ ♆	135	5♋18
	Jun	30	9:49	♅ ♇	0	16♍06
	Aug	2	21:14	♃ ♆	120	19♋24
	Sep	9	16:14	♃ ♄	240	27♋02
	Nov	8	8:20	♄ ♅	180	23♓12
1967	Jan	6	22:55	♄ ♅	180	24♓24
	Feb	7	0:42	♃ ♄	240	27♋10
	May	10	15:08	♄ ♆	225	8♈06
	Jun	9	16:55	♃ ♇	45	3♌00
		22	23:41	♃ ♅	45	5♌33
	Jul	25	19:16	♃ ♄	240	12♌28
	Sep	7	3:33	♃ ♆	90	21♌54
		21	16:06	♃ ♄	225	24♌53
	Oct	16	18:07	♄ ♆	225	7♈57
1968	Mar	4	20:32	♄ ♆	225	11♈31
		16	1:50	♃ ♄	225	27♌52
	Apr	9	11:31	♃ ♆	90	26♌04
		20	4:23	♃ ♆	90	25♌50
	Aug	12	15:35	♃ ♄	225	10♍32
	Oct	13	5:12	♃ ♇	0	23♍40
	Dec	11	15:00	♃ ♅	0	3♎39
1969	Mar	11	19:41	♃ ♅	0	2♎27
	Jul	17	23:47	♄ ♇	135	7♉56
		20	7:58	♃ ♅	0	0♎40
	Aug	21	17:46	♄ ♇	135	8♉57
	Sep	16	8:34	♃ ♆	45	11♎22
	Dec	30	4:44	♃ ♄	180	2♏05
1970	Mar	8	14:27	♃ ♄	180	5♏32
	Apr	18	6:03	♄ ♇	135	10♉15
	Jul	10	15:13	♄ ♅	135	20♉00
	Sep	7	9:49	♄ ♅	135	22♉37
	Oct	26	19:13	♃ ♇	315	13♏31
	Nov	18	19:20	♃ ♄	180	18♏34
1971	Jan	5	20:50	♃ ♅	315	28♏30
	Feb	1	6:50	♃ ♆	0	2♐47
	May	10	13:03	♄ ♅	135	25♉02
		22	4:58	♃ ♆	0	1♐44
		25	22:15	♄ ♇	120	27♉01
	Jun	12	1:15	♃ ♄	180	29♏11
		25	23:05	♄ ♆	180	0♊52
	Sep	16	5:29	♃ ♆	0	0♐37
	Oct	17	2:59	♃ ♄	180	5♐50
	Nov	27	18:50	♄ ♆	180	2♊53
	Dec	5	13:31	♄ ♅	135	2♊15
		10	8:39	♄ ♇	120	1♊52
1972	Feb	15	12:47	♃ ♇	270	1♑35
	Mar	10	19:16	♄ ♇	120	1♊00
		22	13:11	♄ ♅	135	1♊54
	Apr	19	18:48	♄ ♆	180	4♊46
	Jul	4	8:23	♄ ♅	120	14♊16
		25	22:44	♃ ♇	270	29♐53
	Oct	2	23:40	♅ ♆	45	18♎08
		18	13:32	♃ ♇	270	2♑47
		30	20:26	♄ ♅	120	19♊53
1973	Jan	17	18:28	♃ ♆	315	21♑44
		23	10:54	♃ ♅	270	23♑03
	Feb	17	2:49	♃ ♄	135	28♑39
	Mar	6	2:58	♅ ♆	45	22♎26
		12	2:05	♃ ♇	240	3♒24
	May	12	5:29	♄ ♅	120	19♊47
	Jun	28	17:31	♃ ♄	135	10♒51
	Aug	7	17:15	♅ ♆	45	19♎41

♃ ♄ ♅ ♆ ♇ 0°, 45°, 90°, 120°, 135° and 180° Aspects 1700–2050

Year	Month	Day	Time	Planets	Aspect	Position
	Sep	2	16:41	♃ ♇	240	3♒21
		14	17:19	♄ ♇	90	3♋48
	Oct	7	12:57	♄ ♇	90	4♋40
	Nov	16	20:34	♃ ♇	240	6♒02
1974	Jan	4	18:30	♃ ♄	135	15♒14
	Feb	1	13:20	♃ ♇	225	21♒40
		25	22:01	♃ ♅	240	27♒30
		27	2:14	♃ ♄	120	27♒47
	Apr	19	20:41	♃ ♆	270	9♓14
		25	18:05	♃ ♅	225	10♓21
	May	28	13:15	♄ ♇	90	4♋08
	Aug	22	5:20	♃ ♄	120	14♓46
	Sep	19	4:23	♃ ♅	225	11♓09
	Oct	27	13:10	♃ ♆	270	8♓04
	Dec	2	0:36	♃ ♆	270	9♓21
1975	Jan	10	20:35	♃ ♄	120	15♓04
		22	16:40	♃ ♅	225	17♓23
	Apr	18	8:20	♃ ♇	180	7♈21
	May	4	21:52	♃ ♆	240	11♈08
	Jun	4	3:03	♃ ♄	90	17♈19
	Jul	27	22:25	♃ ♆	225	24♈11
		28	13:03	♄ ♆	135	24♋10
		29	2:51	♃ ♄	90	24♈15
	Sep	3	12:03	♃ ♆	225	24♈04
	Oct	4	18:10	♄ ♅	90	1♌27
		17	14:02	♄ ♅	90	2♌14
1976	Feb	2	7:57	♄ ♆	135	28♋28
	Mar	9	22:35	♃ ♄	90	26♈19
		21	21:13	♃ ♆	225	28♈58
	Apr	18	10:17	♃ ♅	180	5♉24
	May	15	12:49	♄ ♆	135	28♋05
	Jul	2	3:15	♄ ♅	90	3♌04
		11	10:43	♃ ♇	135	24♉04
	Sep	5	3:33	♄ ♆	120	11♌15
	Nov	5	18:60	♃ ♇	135	27♉48
1977	Jan	12	21:54	♄ ♆	120	15♌03
	Feb	24	0:04	♄ ♅	90	11♌45
	Mar	24	10:51	♃ ♇	135	28♉05
	Apr	22	22:26	♄ ♅	90	10♌05
	May	26	12:28	♃ ♇	120	11♊35
	Jun	8	20:42	♃ ♆	180	14♊41
		23	16:14	♄ ♆	120	14♌18
	Jul	14	5:37	♃ ♅	135	22♊41
	Dec	29	11:31	♃ ♅	135	0♋12
1978	Apr	13	20:08	♃ ♅	135	0♋16
	Jun	5	14:15	♃ ♄	45	10♋06
		17	21:51	♃ ♅	120	12♋47
		22	22:59	♃ ♇	90	13♋54
	Jul	18	8:20	♄ ♇	45	29♌04
	Sep	8	10:02	♃ ♆	135	0♌35
1979	Jan	21	4:14	♃ ♆	135	4♌30
	May	27	13:60	♃ ♆	135	4♌30
	Jul	30	4:04	♃ ♅	90	16♌56
	Aug	3	16:28	♃ ♆	120	17♌55
	Sep	14	19:59	♄ ♆	90	17♍47
	Oct	24	21:20	♃ ♇	45	4♍36
1980	Feb	14	5:56	♃ ♇	45	6♍39
	Mar	26	13:33	♄ ♆	90	22♍41
	Jun	17	4:49	♃ ♇	45	4♍00
		22	18:22	♄ ♆	90	21♍01
	Sep	9	13:36	♃ ♆	90	19♍55
	Dec	31	21:26	♃ ♄	0	9♎30
1981	Mar	4	19:06	♃ ♄	0	8♎06
	Jul	24	4:17	♃ ♄	0	4♎56
	Aug	30	7:48	♃ ♅	45	11♎20
	Oct	3	22:30	♄ ♅	45	12♎33
	Nov	2	8:26	♃ ♇	0	24♎53
1982	Apr	3	5:60	♄ ♅	45	19♎22
	Jul	11	5:02	♄ ♅	45	15♎56
	Sep	19	8:36	♃ ♆	45	9♏19
	Nov	8	0:39	♄ ♇	0	27♎36
1983	Feb	18	22:43	♃ ♅	0	8♐52
	May	14	20:36	♃ ♅	0	7♐41
	Sep	25	13:56	♃ ♅	0	5♐49
	Nov	14	23:47	♃ ♇	315	15♐21
1984	Jan	10	19:02	♄ ♆	45	14♏42
		19	17:25	♃ ♆	0	0♑01
		21	11:46	♃ ♄	315	0♑24
	Mar	8	7:11	♄ ♆	45	16♏15
	Sep	24	19:44	♄ ♆	45	13♏43
1985	Feb	17	17:05	♃ ♅	315	2♒30
		27	9:14	♃ ♇	270	4♒37
1986	Jan	2	21:08	♃ ♆	315	18♒39
	Mar	6	7:04	♅ ♇	315	22♐10
		21	19:37	♃ ♇	240	6♓54
	Apr	2	12:50	♃ ♄	270	9♓32
	May	31	2:36	♃ ♇	225	20♓04
	Jun	5	0:14	♃ ♅	270	20♓39
	Jul	1	9:16	♅ ♇	315	19♐35
	Aug	25	4:18	♃ ♇	225	20♓00
	Sep	6	19:52	♃ ♅	270	18♓24
1987	Jan	23	21:13	♅ ♇	315	24♐52
	Feb	8	19:32	♃ ♇	225	24♓58
		12	7:57	♃ ♅	270	25♓45
	Apr	4	23:55	♃ ♆	270	8♈00
	May	23	12:27	♃ ♄	240	19♈05
	Jun	21	16:53	♃ ♅	240	24♈31
	Aug	10	18:22	♃ ♄	225	29♈36
		28	14:44	♃ ♄	225	29♈36
	Sep	1	9:01	♅ ♇	315	22♐43
	Oct	24	13:04	♃ ♅	240	23♈52
	Nov	21	13:39	♃ ♄	240	20♈44
	Dec	9	21:52	♅ ♇	315	26♐20
1988	Jan	17	18:43	♄ ♇	315	27♐21
	Feb	13	1:00	♄ ♅	0	29♐55
	Mar	12	12:20	♃ ♅	240	0♉49
		18	10:59	♃ ♄	240	2♉06
	Apr	22	10:00	♃ ♆	240	10♉10
		27	5:38	♃ ♇	180	11♉19
	May	14	11:06	♃ ♅	225	15♉25
		18	20:00	♃ ♄	225	16♉27
	Jun	21	9:43	♃ ♆	225	24♉03
		26	17:05	♄ ♅	0	28♐47
	Oct	18	13:29	♄ ♅	0	27♐49
1989	Mar	3	10:47	♄ ♆	0	11♑55
	Jun	24	3:10	♄ ♆	0	11♑14
	Jul	18	12:22	♃ ♇	135	27♊22
	Aug	8	19:19	♃ ♅	180	1♋45
	Sep	10	16:20	♃ ♄	180	7♋18
	Oct	1	5:55	♃ ♆	180	9♋38
	Nov	13	11:42	♄ ♆	0	10♑22
		14	6:28	♃ ♄	180	10♋26
		14	20:54	♃ ♆	180	10♋24
	Dec	29	5:46	♃ ♅	180	5♋35
1990	Jan	22	19:50	♃ ♇	135	2♋34
	Mar	28	11:16	♃ ♇	135	2♋24
	May	13	19:32	♃ ♅	180	9♋13
	Jun	6	8:47	♃ ♆	180	13♋56
		13	10:28	♃ ♇	120	15♋27
	Jul	13	12:55	♃ ♄	180	22♋07
1991	Mar	16	1:27	♃ ♄	180	3♌53
	May	17	1:25	♃ ♄	180	6♌51
	Jul	16	21:34	♃ ♇	90	17♌36
	Aug	21	0:07	♃ ♅	135	25♌11
	Sep	7	22:29	♃ ♆	135	29♌05
	Nov	11	10:53	♃ ♅	120	11♍00
1992	Jan	12	13:08	♃ ♅	120	14♍22
	Jul	31	19:50	♃ ♅	120	15♍06
	Aug	9	8:53	♃ ♆	120	16♍47
	Sep	27	2:08	♃ ♄	135	27♍07
	Nov	21	5:51	♃ ♇	45	8♎07
1993	Feb	2	8:12	♅ ♆	0	19♑34
	Mar	20	3:01	♄ ♇	270	25♒23
		23	6:51	♃ ♄	135	10♎43
		26	14:19	♃ ♇	45	10♎18
	Jul	17	15:57	♃ ♇	45	7♎48
	Aug	16	5:42	♃ ♄	135	12♎14
		20	7:45	♅ ♆	0	18♑48
	Sep	16	16:48	♃ ♅	90	18♎17
		17	9:32	♃ ♆	90	18♎25
	Oct	9	6:38	♄ ♇	270	23♒56
		12	19:29	♃ ♄	120	23♎50
		24	20:19	♅ ♆	0	18♑33
1994	Jan	2	2:57	♄ ♇	270	27♒07
	Apr	10	4:15	♄ ♆	315	8♓17
		28	17:57	♃ ♄	120	10♏00
	May	16	7:39	♄ ♅	315	11♓15
	Aug	28	17:10	♃ ♄	120	9♏19
	Sep	23	10:53	♄ ♅	315	7♓25
	Oct	29	18:05	♄ ♆	315	5♓47
	Dec	2	7:25	♃ ♇	0	28♏26
		21	8:43	♄ ♆	315	7♓11
1995	Jan	19	16:22	♃ ♆	45	8♐16
	Feb	20	15:57	♄ ♅	315	13♓22
		27	4:15	♃ ♅	45	13♐42
	Apr	11	7:23	♃ ♅	45	15♐14
	Jun	3	23:03	♃ ♆	45	10♐12
	Sep	12	2:22	♃ ♆	45	7♐55
	Oct	7	16:13	♃ ♅	45	11♐32
	Nov	11	2:31	♃ ♄	90	18♐06
1996	Apr	24	3:13	♃ ♇	315	17♑29
		28	2:41	♄ ♇	240	2♈23
	Jun	1	11:51	♃ ♇	315	16♑28
	Oct	26	3:17	♄ ♇	240	1♈51
	Nov	30	9:13	♃ ♇	315	18♑12
1997	Jan	9	11:41	♃ ♆	0	27♑09
	Feb	16	2:23	♃ ♅	0	5♒56
		19	16:44	♄ ♇	240	5♈31
	Jun	16	21:48	♄ ♇	225	18♈38
	Sep	22	10:57	♄ ♇	225	18♈16
1998	Feb	9	4:07	♃ ♄	45	1♓07
	Mar	10	1:32	♃ ♇	270	8♓04
	Apr	9	9:40	♄ ♇	225	22♈50
		18	21:29	♃ ♆	315	17♓06
	Jun	24	15:35	♃ ♅	315	27♓11
		25	22:28	♄ ♆	270	1♉30
	Sep	4	13:57	♃ ♅	315	24♓34
	Nov	1	1:35	♄ ♆	270	29♈30
1999	Feb	2	16:54	♃ ♅	315	27♓48
	Mar	29	13:55	♃ ♇	240	10♈26
	Apr	6	15:08	♄ ♆	270	4♉07
	May	28	4:33	♃ ♇	225	24♈12
	Jul	18	3:55	♄ ♅	270	15♉37
		21	15:55	♃ ♆	270	3♉06
	Oct	11	6:46	♃ ♆	270	1♉35
	Nov	14	9:37	♄ ♅	270	13♉04
	Dec	5	3:46	♃ ♇	225	25♈26
2000	Jan	26	3:20	♃ ♇	225	27♈13
	Mar	16	17:16	♃ ♆	270	5♉50
	May	13	8:35	♄ ♅	270	20♉46
		20	13:17	♃ ♅	270	20♉49
		28	16:05	♃ ♄	0	22♉43
	Jul	27	11:24	♃ ♆	240	5♊12
	Sep	4	10:54	♃ ♇	180	10♊13
	Oct	13	8:25	♃ ♇	180	10♊55
	Dec	9	14:16	♃ ♆	240	4♊37
2001	Apr	5	14:27	♃ ♆	240	8♊26
	May	6	10:41	♃ ♇	180	14♊40
	Jun	14	8:23	♃ ♆	225	23♊28
		19	12:26	♃ ♅	240	24♊40
		25	7:18	♄ ♆	240	8♊16
	Aug	5	17:04	♄ ♇	180	12♊37
		19	7:40	♃ ♅	225	7♋43
	Nov	2	6:09	♄ ♇	180	13♊49
2002	Jan	18	18:26	♃ ♅	225	8♋21
		23	8:17	♄ ♆	240	8♊16
	Apr	2	2:41	♄ ♆	240	10♊31
	May	17	5:11	♃ ♅	225	13♋43
		26	2:34	♄ ♇	180	16♊36
	Jul	30	2:42	♄ ♆	225	24♊40
	Aug	1	23:24	♃ ♇	135	0♌03
		21	7:18	♄ ♅	240	26♊48
	Sep	11	12:08	♃ ♆	180	8♌36
	Oct	13	14:25	♃ ♄	315	14♌05
		27	23:42	♃ ♇	120	15♌55
	Dec	16	21:37	♄ ♅	240	25♊40
		18	13:41	♃ ♇	120	17♌47
		30	22:29	♄ ♆	225	24♊32
2003	Feb	16	9:12	♃ ♆	180	11♌17
	Mar	27	14:15	♃ ♄	315	8♌09
	May	20	7:09	♄ ♆	225	28♊11
	Jun	3	2:58	♃ ♆	180	13♌06
		24	23:34	♄ ♅	240	2♋42
	Jul	1	12:40	♃ ♇	120	18♌03
		9	2:44	♃ ♄	315	19♌32
	Aug	30	4:38	♃ ♅	180	0♍37
2004	Aug	6	21:23	♃ ♇	90	19♍41
		7	8:26	♄ ♅	225	20♋36
	Sep	15	21:01	♃ ♆	135	28♍00
	Nov	29	8:29	♃ ♆	120	12♎58
2005	Feb	17	20:02	♄ ♅	225	21♋20
	Mar	14	7:46	♃ ♆	120	16♎27
	Jun	12	3:23	♄ ♅	225	25♋46
	Aug	17	19:39	♃ ♆	120	15♎57
	Sep	9	23:34	♄ ♇	135	6♌50
		23	4:56	♃ ♅	135	22♎56
	Nov	27	11:57	♃ ♅	120	6♏54
	Dec	7	23:37	♃ ♇	45	9♏00
		17	5:18	♃ ♄	270	10♏45
2006	Jan	1	8:15	♄ ♇	135	9♌54
		28	1:30	♃ ♆	90	16♏56
	Mar	16	7:02	♃ ♆	90	18♏39
	May	5	3:50	♃ ♅	120	13♏55
		31	9:12	♃ ♇	45	10♏51
	Jun	22	18:44	♃ ♄	270	9♏15
		30	1:24	♄ ♇	135	10♌05
	Jul	25	4:27	♃ ♇	45	9♏30
	Aug	29	9:13	♃ ♅	120	13♏02
		31	9:56	♄ ♆	180	17♌53
	Sep	24	20:34	♃ ♆	90	17♏21
	Oct	25	17:27	♃ ♄	270	23♏32
2007	Jan	22	21:42	♃ ♅	90	12♐26
	Feb	28	12:01	♄ ♆	180	20♌15
	Mar	16	22:44	♃ ♄	240	19♐09
	May	6	7:12	♃ ♄	240	18♐24
		11	3:34	♃ ♅	90	17♐57
	Jun	25	15:57	♄ ♆	180	21♌47
	Aug	6	10:20	♄ ♇	120	26♌34
	Oct	9	18:24	♃ ♅	90	15♐35
	Dec	11	19:26	♃ ♇	0	28♐24
2008	Jan	12	11:58	♃ ♆	45	5♑38
		21	9:16	♃ ♄	240	7♑37
	Mar	18	10:43	♃ ♄	225	18♑24
	Jun	26	7:58	♃ ♄	225	19♑06
	Sep	8	23:18	♃ ♄	240	12♑32
	Nov	4	13:34	♄ ♅	180	18♍58
		21	12:15	♃ ♄	240	20♑19
2009	Jan	27	23:06	♃ ♅	45	5♒15
		30	23:04	♃ ♄	225	5♒58
	Feb	5	11:00	♄ ♅	180	20♍39
	Mar	27	16:51	♃ ♇	315	18♒17
	May	27	20:13	♃ ♆	0	26♒29
	Jul	10	9:08	♃ ♆	0	26♒02
	Sep	15	12:50	♄ ♅	180	24♍43
	Nov	15	14:43	♄ ♇	90	1♎42
	Dec	21	8:54	♃ ♆	0	24♒18
2010	Jan	31	22:07	♄ ♇	90	4♎21
	Apr	26	23:27	♄ ♅	180	28♍46
	May	23	5:38	♃ ♄	180	27♓53
	Jun	8	11:26	♃ ♅	0	0♈18
	Jul	25	1:50	♃ ♇	270	3♈24
		26	17:05	♄ ♅	180	0♎25
	Aug	3	8:01	♃ ♇	270	3♈13
		16	20:45	♃ ♄	180	2♈27
		21	9:56	♄ ♇	90	2♎56
	Sep	19	1:07	♃ ♅	0	28♓43
	Oct	27	10:33	♄ ♆	135	10♎57
2011	Jan	4	12:52	♃ ♅	0	27♓02
	Feb	25	20:29	♃ ♇	270	7♈02
	Mar	24	19:29	♄ ♆	135	14♎40

♃ ♄ ♅ ♆ ♇ 0°, 45°, 90°, 120°, 135° and 180° Aspects 1700–2050

		28	21:56	♃ ♄	180	14♈21
		31	0:44	♃ ♆	315	14♈52
	Jul	7	13:53	♃ ♇	240	5♉58
	Aug	25	0:52	♄ ♆	135	14♎28
	Oct	28	16:46	♃ ♇	240	5♉20
2012	Mar	13	4:31	♃ ♇	240	9♉21
	May	8	2:08	♃ ♅	315	21♉53
		17	23:13	♃ ♇	225	24♉13
	Jun	24	8:15	♅ ♇	270	8♈24
		25	7:59	♃ ♆	270	3♊02
	Jul	21	2:02	♃ ♄	135	8♊18
	Sep	19	6:55	♅ ♇	270	6♈57
	Oct	11	2:42	♄ ♆	120	0♏37
		15	16:57	♃ ♄	135	16♊10
2013	May	20	5:23	♃ ♄	135	21♊37
		20	22:22	♅ ♇	270	11♈14
	Jun	11	23:19	♄ ♆	120	5♏22
	Jul	17	17:33	♃ ♄	120	4♋54
		18	0:17	♃ ♆	240	4♋57
		19	13:29	♄ ♆	120	4♏55
	Aug	7	23:35	♃ ♇	180	9♋26
		21	7:15	♃ ♅	270	12♋04
	Sep	29	2:42	♃ ♆	225	18♋07
	Nov	1	11:14	♅ ♇	270	9♈26
	Dec	13	0:01	♃ ♄	120	18♋28
		17	22:17	♃ ♆	225	17♋55
2014	Jan	31	9:37	♃ ♇	180	12♋17
	Feb	26	7:34	♃ ♅	270	10♋33
	Apr	20	7:26	♃ ♅	270	13♋29
		20	23:06	♃ ♇	180	13♋34
		21	18:39	♅ ♇	270	13♈34
	May	24	17:49	♃ ♄	120	18♋59
	Jun	12	2:15	♃ ♆	225	22♋36
	Sep	25	18:18	♃ ♅	240	15♌00
	Nov	27	16:17	♄ ♇	45	27♏02
	Dec	3	10:44	♄ ♅	135	27♏43
		15	6:15	♅ ♇	270	12♈35
2015	Mar	3	12:28	♃ ♅	240	14♌35
		17	1:51	♅ ♇	270	15♈18
	May	4	6:17	♄ ♅	135	3♐00
	Jun	20	13:09	♄ ♇	45	29♏39
		22	13:45	♃ ♅	240	20♌03
	Aug	3	10:38	♃ ♄	90	28♌17
		4	19:11	♃ ♇	135	28♌34
		13	20:59	♄ ♇	45	28♏24
	Sep	3	3:51	♃ ♅	225	4♍56
		17	6:57	♃ ♆	180	7♍58
	Oct	11	23:38	♃ ♇	120	13♍03
		22	15:57	♄ ♅	135	3♐05
	Nov	26	12:19	♄ ♆	90	7♐02
2016	Mar	16	20:27	♃ ♇	120	17♍13
		23	10:16	♃ ♄	90	16♍24
	May	26	12:29	♃ ♄	90	13♍41
	Jun	18	3:24	♄ ♆	90	12♐02
		26	12:11	♃ ♇	120	16♍29
	Sep	10	13:11	♄ ♆	90	10♐25
	Nov	24	22:43	♃ ♇	90	15♎47
	Dec	25	0:18	♄ ♅	120	20♐34
		26	18:33	♃ ♅	180	20♎34
2017	Mar	3	1:20	♃ ♅	180	22♎11
		30	18:42	♃ ♇	90	19♎17
	May	19	6:20	♄ ♅	120	26♐23
	Aug	4	18:30	♃ ♇	90	17♎31
		11	22:42	♅ ♆	315	28♈30
	Sep	27	14:40	♃ ♆	135	27♎15
		28	4:25	♃ ♅	180	27♎22
	Oct	7	6:23	♅ ♆	315	27♈02
	Nov	11	9:42	♄ ♅	120	25♐38
	Dec	3	2:23	♃ ♆	120	11♏30
		22	14:56	♃ ♄	45	15♏17
2018	Mar	14	11:04	♃ ♄	45	23♏11
	May	25	9:50	♃ ♆	120	16♏20
	Jun	16	10:06	♅ ♆	315	1♉29
	Aug	19	7:49	♃ ♆	120	15♏36
	Sep	3	17:44	♃ ♄	45	17♏33
	Nov	29	4:14	♃ ♇	45	4♐35
	Dec	15	10:43	♅ ♆	315	28♈49
2019	Jan	9	21:32	♃ ♅	135	13♐36
		13	19:02	♃ ♆	90	14♐23
	May	2	3:19	♅ ♆	315	3♉03
	Jun	6	23:23	♃ ♅	135	19♐57
		16	15:19	♃ ♆	90	18♐43
	Sep	21	16:48	♃ ♆	90	17♐00
	Oct	14	5:24	♃ ♅	135	20♐11
	Dec	15	19:01	♃ ♅	120	2♑57
2020	Jan	12	16:23	♄ ♇	0	22♑46
	Apr	5	2:15	♃ ♇	0	24♑53
	Jun	30	6:23	♃ ♇	0	24♑06
	Nov	12	21:18	♃ ♇	0	22♑52
	Dec	21	18:22	♃ ♄	0	0♒29
2021	Jan	4	7:02	♃ ♆	45	3♒32
		17	22:49	♃ ♅	90	6♒44
		20	17:04	♄ ♆	45	3♒56
	Feb	17	19:04	♄ ♅	90	7♒14
	Jun	14	22:08	♄ ♅	90	13♒07
	Dec	24	7:14	♄ ♅	90	11♒06
2022	Feb	23	22:02	♃ ♇	315	12♓38
	Apr	12	14:46	♃ ♆	0	23♓59
	May	11	20:50	♃ ♅	45	0♈10
	Jul	21	11:18	♃ ♄	315	8♈38
	Sep	21	13:09	♃ ♄	315	4♈24
		28	20:04	♃ ♅	45	3♈25
	Dec	24	0:40	♃ ♅	45	0♈19
2023	Mar	21	9:28	♃ ♄	315	16♈35
	May	18	0:57	♃ ♇	270	0♉18
	Jul	22	11:52	♃ ♆	315	12♉34
	Nov	5	21:00	♃ ♆	315	10♉09
2024	Mar	4	3:02	♃ ♆	315	11♉51
	Apr	21	2:25	♃ ♅	0	21♉50
	May	6	11:07	♄ ♇	315	17♓06
	Jun	2	23:59	♃ ♇	240	1♊53
	Aug	7	10:10	♃ ♇	225	15♊31
		19	21:48	♃ ♄	270	17♊27
	Sep	26	0:08	♄ ♇	315	14♓42
	Dec	13	6:27	♃ ♇	225	15♊31
		24	22:01	♃ ♄	270	14♊01
2025	Jan	26	23:58	♄ ♇	315	16♓53
	Apr	17	7:56	♃ ♇	225	18♊45
	Jun	15	14:37	♃ ♄	270	1♋18
		19	3:20	♃ ♆	270	2♋06
	Aug	23	23:59	♃ ♅	315	16♋23
2026	Feb	20	17:01	♄ ♆	0	0♈45
	Jul	18	3:55	♅ ♇	240	4♊30
		20	7:27	♃ ♆	240	4♌22
		20	14:31	♃ ♇	180	4♌26
	Aug	31	22:18	♃ ♄	240	13♌41
	Sep	22	20:27	♃ ♆	225	18♌05
	Oct	31	19:15	♃ ♄	225	24♌18
	Nov	29	12:12	♅ ♇	240	3♊32
2027	Jan	22	10:03	♃ ♄	225	24♌31
	Mar	11	20:21	♃ ♆	225	18♌35
	Apr	3	13:00	♃ ♄	240	17♌08
		12	23:16	♄ ♅	45	18♈20
	Jun	8	1:08	♃ ♆	225	21♌23
		15	7:27	♅ ♇	240	6♊52
	Jul	11	23:17	♃ ♄	240	27♌10
	Sep	10	16:39	♃ ♅	270	9♍57
		18	8:10	♃ ♄	225	11♍35
	Oct	16	2:18	♄ ♅	45	24♈34
		29	3:29	♃ ♇	135	19♍46
2028	Jan	12	6:08	♄ ♅	45	21♈22
		13	7:36	♅ ♇	240	6♊20
	Mar	9	10:09	♃ ♇	135	23♍00
	May	4	5:48	♃ ♄	225	17♍41
		10	2:08	♅ ♇	240	8♊49
	Jun	24	2:25	♄ ♇	270	8♉23
	Jul	16	4:21	♃ ♇	135	22♍56
	Aug	3	5:41	♃ ♄	225	25♍58
	Sep	24	7:30	♃ ♇	120	6♎33
		28	19:19	♃ ♆	180	7♎31
	Oct	27	9:05	♃ ♅	240	13♎38
	Nov	15	13:41	♄ ♇	270	6♉35
2029	Jan	9	3:18	♃ ♅	225	25♎49
	Mar	17	12:58	♃ ♅	225	25♎35
		29	22:32	♄ ♇	270	10♉03
	Oct	10	15:46	♃ ♅	225	3♏26
	Nov	1	0:27	♃ ♇	90	8♏04
	Dec	22	7:05	♃ ♄	180	18♏48
2030	Jan	20	0:50	♃ ♆	135	23♏37
	Apr	12	16:29	♃ ♆	135	26♏16
		24	1:58	♃ ♄	180	25♏08
	May	10	17:54	♄ ♆	315	27♉15
	Oct	7	8:42	♃ ♆	135	26♏54
	Nov	20	1:07	♃ ♄	180	6♐04
	Dec	10	8:05	♃ ♆	120	10♐37
2031	Jan	20	12:02	♃ ♅	180	19♐23
	Mar	21	1:48	♃ ♇	45	28♐00
	May	1	2:57	♃ ♇	45	28♐36
	Jun	11	14:08	♄ ♇	240	13♊29
		20	21:52	♃ ♅	180	23♐25
	Aug	1	8:28	♃ ♄	180	19♐29
	Sep	1	19:58	♅ ♇	225	26♊51
	Oct	6	21:56	♃ ♄	180	23♐02
		27	0:60	♃ ♇	45	26♐16
		30	18:09	♃ ♅	180	26♐56
	Nov	18	4:41	♅ ♇	225	26♊24
2032	Jan	12	1:59	♃ ♆	90	12♑55
	Jun	28	11:54	♄ ♅	0	28♊01
	Jul	10	20:07	♄ ♇	225	29♊36
		22	2:24	♅ ♇	225	29♊21
2033	Jan	6	0:44	♅ ♇	225	28♊57
		28	19:08	♃ ♅	135	13♒09
	Feb	4	21:31	♃ ♇	0	14♒50
		8	6:15	♃ ♄	135	15♒38
		20	5:00	♄ ♇	225	0♋18
	Apr	4	9:17	♃ ♅	120	27♒59
		6	22:48	♄ ♇	225	1♋25
	May	7	10:34	♃ ♆	45	3♓39
	Jun	18	11:51	♅ ♇	225	1♋33
	Aug	3	4:02	♃ ♆	45	5♓05
		8	20:35	♃ ♅	120	4♓26
		25	9:17	♃ ♄	135	2♓20
	Sep	16	10:21	♄ ♆	270	19♋23
	Dec	18	7:46	♃ ♆	45	2♓20
		27	1:29	♃ ♄	135	3♓50
		27	19:36	♃ ♅	120	3♓58
2034	Jan	13	16:02	♄ ♆	270	17♋23
	Feb	17	7:13	♃ ♄	120	15♓01
	Mar	1	13:24	♅ ♇	225	2♋03
	May	3	0:39	♅ ♇	225	3♋15
		6	12:37	♃ ♇	315	3♈16
		7	7:58	♃ ♅	90	3♈26
	Jun	25	15:12	♄ ♆	270	22♋07
	Sep	21	14:49	♃ ♅	90	10♈18
	Nov	2	16:49	♃ ♄	120	5♈12
	Dec	16	15:37	♃ ♄	120	4♈33
2035	Jan	16	11:55	♃ ♅	90	7♈48
	Mar	24	16:37	♃ ♆	0	21♈21
	Apr	25	19:37	♃ ♄	90	29♈03
	Aug	5	14:13	♃ ♇	270	18♉46
	Oct	17	11:16	♄ ♇	180	17♌31
		22	7:47	♃ ♄	90	17♉52
		25	9:54	♃ ♇	270	17♉29
2036	Jan	1	19:29	♄ ♇	180	18♌18
	Feb	22	10:46	♃ ♄	90	14♉26
	Mar	28	19:01	♃ ♇	270	20♉42
	Apr	24	20:50	♃ ♅	45	26♉36
	Jun	28	18:13	♃ ♆	315	11♊37
	Jul	28	0:21	♄ ♇	180	20♌28
	Aug	10	17:02	♃ ♇	240	20♊10
	Sep	12	18:27	♄ ♆	240	26♌22
	Dec	24	7:54	♃ ♇	240	19♊35
2037	Apr	9	5:08	♄ ♆	240	26♌17
		15	22:48	♃ ♇	240	22♊29
	Jun	23	16:43	♄ ♆	240	28♌43
		26	20:59	♃ ♇	225	7♋33
	Aug	31	0:51	♃ ♄	45	21♋31
	Sep	8	10:29	♃ ♅	0	23♋03
		13	20:11	♄ ♅	315	8♍16
	Oct	12	18:22	♃ ♆	270	27♋56
		22	5:43	♄ ♆	225	12♍40
	Nov	16	0:13	♃ ♄	45	29♋47
2038	Jan	2	23:43	♃ ♆	270	26♋19
	Feb	19	17:12	♃ ♅	0	20♋39
	Mar	9	11:52	♄ ♆	225	12♍22
		30	21:27	♃ ♅	0	20♋05
	May	11	13:57	♃ ♄	45	24♋23
	Jun	16	10:13	♃ ♆	270	0♌45
	Aug	17	3:19	♄ ♆	225	16♍20
	Sep	25	17:49	♃ ♇	180	22♌16
	Nov	11	4:52	♃ ♆	240	29♌26
2039	Jan	29	1:25	♃ ♆	240	28♌41
	Mar	4	0:15	♃ ♇	180	24♌21
	Jun	11	9:08	♃ ♇	180	25♌39
	Jul	26	16:05	♃ ♆	240	3♍35
	Oct	1	4:03	♃ ♅	315	17♍45
		1	15:17	♃ ♆	225	17♍51
		3	1:48	♅ ♆	270	2♌49
	Nov	15	22:44	♄ ♇	135	8♎24
2040	Feb	1	0:39	♅ ♆	270	0♌56
	Mar	1	3:45	♄ ♇	135	10♎41
	Aug	29	13:32	♅ ♆	270	5♌45
		31	18:09	♄ ♇	135	10♎40
	Sep	25	12:09	♃ ♇	135	10♎12
	Oct	31	11:50	♃ ♄	0	17♎56
	Dec	7	0:52	♃ ♇	120	25♎01
2041	Mar	18	13:45	♅ ♆	270	4♌11
	Apr	7	17:44	♃ ♇	120	28♎00
	Jul	25	22:39	♅ ♆	270	8♌03
	Aug	21	8:22	♃ ♇	120	27♎21
	Oct	12	2:07	♃ ♆	180	7♏11
		12	14:16	♄ ♇	120	26♎24
	Nov	6	10:34	♃ ♅	270	12♏41
2042	Jan	6	6:37	♄ ♆	180	5♏19
		19	5:17	♃ ♇	90	27♏17
	Mar	10	2:35	♄ ♆	180	6♏06
	Apr	27	7:23	♃ ♇	90	29♏42
	Sep	23	12:29	♃ ♇	90	28♏07
	Oct	29	15:15	♄ ♆	180	9♏01
	Dec	23	6:33	♃ ♅	240	17♐02
2043	Jan	8	1:14	♄ ♅	270	16♏32
		18	0:22	♃ ♆	135	22♐33
	Feb	26	0:42	♃ ♅	225	29♐29
	Mar	28	1:52	♃ ♄	315	2♑46
	May	24	20:25	♄ ♅	270	13♏49
	Jun	13	13:44	♃ ♅	225	29♐33
		30	3:25	♄ ♆	180	12♏02
	Jul	2	23:39	♃ ♆	135	27♐06
		4	6:58	♃ ♄	315	26♐56
	Aug	15	21:35	♄ ♆	180	12♏37
	Oct	6	7:56	♃ ♆	135	26♐57
	Nov	21	18:09	♄ ♅	270	22♏09
	Dec	1	19:50	♃ ♅	225	7♑09
		12	19:55	♃ ♄	315	9♑36
		15	7:16	♃ ♆	120	10♑09
2044	Jan	3	19:25	♃ ♇	45	14♑38
	Nov	4	13:30	♄ ♇	90	0♐28
2045	Jan	8	7:12	♃ ♆	90	12♒06
	Feb	28	11:55	♃ ♅	180	24♒11
	Apr	12	8:32	♃ ♇	0	3♓32
	May	17	21:03	♃ ♄	270	9♓21
	Sep	9	17:46	♃ ♄	270	5♓58
2046	Mar	4	23:11	♃ ♄	270	22♓36
	Apr	7	16:35	♃ ♆	45	0♈43
	Jun	4	16:12	♃ ♅	135	12♈55
	Jul	11	21:32	♃ ♄	240	17♈49
	Sep	5	11:04	♃ ♅	135	17♈43
		12	13:20	♃ ♄	240	17♈01
		22	17:14	♅ ♇	180	3♍45
2047	Feb	10	6:21	♄ ♆	135	1♑37

♃ ♄ ♅ ♆ ♇ 0°, 45°, 90°, 120°, 135° and 180° Aspects 1700–2050

Year	Date	Time	Planets	Aspect	Position
	15	2:35	♅ ♇	180	4♍42
	25	19:10	♃ ♅	135	19♈14
	Mar 1	23:17	♃ ♇	315	20♈07
	10	15:22	♄ ♅	240	3♑41
	Apr 23	17:20	♃ ♅	120	2♉22
	May 1	22:44	♃ ♄	240	4♉20
	9	23:15	♄ ♆	135	4♑03
	Jun 5	11:20	♄ ♅	240	2♑34
	24	0:21	♃ ♄	225	16♉14
	Jul 22	20:18	♃ ♆	0	21♉19
	Aug 16	6:18	♅ ♇	180	5♍54
	Nov 16	23:24	♃ ♆	0	20♉05
	28	20:02	♃ ♄	225	18♉32
	Dec 7	16:34	♄ ♆	135	4♑32
2048	Jan 27	9:03	♄ ♅	240	10♑25
	Feb 24	16:32	♃ ♆	0	19♉01
	Apr 12	0:02	♅ ♇	180	7♍28
	27	10:44	♃ ♄	225	0♊59
	May 23	18:55	♃ ♅	90	7♊04
	28	1:04	♃ ♇	270	8♊04
	Jun 30	2:24	♅ ♇	180	7♍59
	Aug 11	19:26	♄ ♅	240	10♑09
	Dec 18	18:35	♄ ♅	240	15♑57
2049	Jan 31	9:57	♄ ♆	120	21♑04
	Feb 10	9:21	♄ ♇	45	22♑10
	Apr 19	17:60	♄ ♅	225	27♑11
	Jun 1	2:33	♄ ♅	225	26♑53
	18	21:39	♃ ♇	240	9♋22
	21	9:03	♃ ♆	315	9♋56
	30	15:39	♄ ♆	120	25♑13
	Jul 15	12:08	♄ ♇	45	24♑08
	Aug 14	22:27	♃ ♄	180	22♋02
	21	20:41	♃ ♇	225	23♋28
	Nov 5	20:18	♄ ♇	45	22♑13
	Dec 1	10:36	♄ ♆	120	24♑18
2050	Jan 17	17:15	♃ ♄	180	29♋33
	Feb 26	21:30	♄ ♅	225	4♒09
	Mar 15	18:14	♃ ♇	225	24♋21
	Apr 9	14:04	♃ ♇	225	24♋57
	Jun 1	13:48	♃ ♅	45	1♌38
	Jul 1	16:25	♃ ♄	180	7♌28
	Aug 14	22:46	♄ ♅	225	4♒19
	Oct 7	4:52	♃ ♆	270	28♌02

♂ ♃ ♄ ♅ ♆ ♇ 0 Declination/Latitude 1700–2050

Year	Date	Time	Planet	Event
1700	Jan 31	9:30	♆	dN
	May 7	4:19	♂	lS
1701	Feb 4	15:57	♂	dN
	Mar 7	1:32	♂	lN
	Nov 3	6:31	♂	dS
1702	Mar 25	2:49	♂	lS
	May 1	23:53	♃	dN
	5	17:58	♄	dN
	Sep 28	13:34	♄	dS
1703	Jan 10	4:33	♂	dN
	23	0:40	♂	lN
	30	7:28	♄	dN
	Oct 14	9:18	♂	dS
1704	Feb 10	2:31	♂	lS
	Nov 20	6:18	♂	dN
	Dec 10	0:09	♂	lN
1705	Jun 20	3:22	♃	lN
	Sep 24	11:49	♂	dS
	Dec 28	2:06	♂	lS
1706	Jun 7	0:36	♂	dN
	Oct 27	22:13	♂	lN
1707	Sep 5	15:10	♂	dS
	Nov 15	0:47	♂	lS
1708	May 10	12:10	♂	dN
	Aug 23	2:02	♃	dS
	Sep 13	21:32	♂	lN
1709	Aug 16	0:08	♂	dS
	Oct 1	23:16	♂	lS
1710	Apr 18	9:14	♂	dN
	Aug 1	21:44	♂	lN
	16	5:25	♄	lN
1711	Jul 25	3:56	♂	dS
	Aug 19	22:04	♂	lS
	Oct 6	18:27	♃	lS
1712	Mar 27	15:28	♂	dN
	Jun 18	20:05	♂	lN
1713	Jun 24	17:36	♂	dS
	Jul 6	20:56	♂	lS
1714	Mar 7	5:09	♂	dN
	Apr 13	3:58	♃	dN
	May 6	18:42	♂	lN
	Dec 7	19:51	♂	dS
1715	May 24	19:38	♂	lS
	Nov 29	19:31	♄	dS
1716	Feb 14	3:34	♂	dN
	22	1:29	♄	dN
	Mar 23	18:26	♂	lN
	Aug 22	2:27	♄	dS
	Nov 11	8:04	♂	dS
1717	Apr 10	19:23	♂	lS
	29	17:20	♃	lN
	Sep 30	3:37	♅	dS
1718	Jan 20	16:22	♂	dN
	Feb 8	16:37	♂	lN
	May 17	6:32	♅	dN
	Jun 28	3:47	♅	dS
	Oct 21	15:43	♂	dS
1719	Feb 26	18:34	♂	lS
	Dec 8	21:29	♃	dS
	18	20:46	♂	dN
	27	15:20	♂	lN
1720	Feb 25	19:51	♃	dN
	Aug 4	15:32	♃	dS
	Oct 1	12:15	♂	dS
1721	Jan 13	17:15	♂	lS
	Jun 20	20:46	♂	dN
	Nov 13	15:28	♂	lN
1722	Sep 12	17:43	♂	dS
	Dec 1	16:09	♂	lS
1723	May 20	18:19	♂	dN
	Aug 15	20:42	♃	lS
	Oct 1	14:29	♂	lN
1724	Aug 23	12:40	♂	dS
	Oct 18	14:59	♂	lS
1725	Apr 26	12:35	♂	dN
	Aug 18	12:54	♂	lN
	Oct 2	5:00	♄	lS
1726	Mar 27	7:21	♃	dN
	Aug 2	19:20	♂	dS
	Sep 5	13:14	♂	lS
1727	Apr 5	10:37	♂	dN
	Jul 6	12:38	♂	lN
1728	Jul 7	16:54	♂	dS
	23	12:42	♂	lS
1729	Mar 10	13:30	♃	lN
	14	23:21	♂	dN
	May 23	10:52	♂	lN
	Dec 21	9:51	♂	dS
1730	Jun 10	12:06	♂	lS
1731	Feb 22	6:39	♂	dN
	Apr 10	9:15	♂	lN
	Nov 13	10:12	♃	dS
	20	23:36	♂	dS
1732	Mar 13	7:05	♄	lN
	Apr 4	11:57	♃	dN
	27	10:21	♂	lS
	Jul 11	22:39	♃	dS
1733	Jan 30	2:19	♂	dN
	Feb 25	9:14	♂	lN
	May 31	8:33	♅	lS
	Oct 29	2:40	♂	dS
1734	Mar 15	9:23	♂	lS
1735	Jan 2	19:03	♂	dN
	13	8:21	♂	lN
	Jun 25	11:55	♃	lS
	Oct 9	13:50	♂	dS
1736	Jan 31	8:57	♂	lS
	Jul 12	15:51	♂	dN
	Nov 30	6:51	♂	lN
1737	Sep 19	18:27	♂	dS
	Dec 18	7:30	♂	lS
1738	Mar 10	22:28	♃	dN
	May 30	23:44	♂	dN
	Oct 18	6:18	♂	lN
1739	Aug 31	20:08	♂	dS
	Nov 5	6:38	♂	lS
1740	Jan 26	23:19	♄	lN
	May 4	23:14	♂	dN
	Sep 4	5:33	♂	lN
	Nov 24	15:40	♇	dS
1741	Jan 18	4:43	♃	lN
	Feb 12	19:29	♇	dN
	Aug 10	21:40	♂	dS
	Sep 11	14:30	♇	dS
	22	5:57	♂	lS
1742	Apr 13	7:15	♂	dN
	Jul 23	3:34	♂	lN
1743	Jul 19	2:49	♂	dS
	Aug 10	4:32	♂	lS
	Oct 25	10:05	♃	dS
1744	Mar 22	17:36	♂	dN
	Jun 9	3:03	♂	lN
1745	Jan 14	18:54	♂	dS
	Mar 2	4:48	♂	dN
	Jun 13	16:33	♂	dS
	27	3:11	♂	lS
	Sep 28	16:52	♄	dS
1746	Mar 2	5:48	♂	dN
	Apr 27	2:43	♂	lN
	Nov 30	15:59	♂	dS
1747	May 7	10:04	♃	lS
	15	2:14	♂	lS
1748	Feb 8	19:53	♂	dN
	Mar 14	1:22	♂	lN
	Nov 5	21:43	♂	dS
1749	Apr 1	0:51	♂	lS
1750	Jan 14	8:00	♂	dN
	30	0:14	♂	lN
	Feb 22	11:35	♃	dN
	Oct 16	18:03	♂	dS
1751	Feb 17	0:18	♂	lS
	Dec 5	21:24	♂	dN
	17	23:36	♂	lN
1752	Sep 26	19:02	♂	dS
	Nov 28	0:57	♃	lN
1753	Jan 4	0:10	♂	lS
	Jun 11	22:17	♂	dN
	Nov 3	21:53	♂	lN
1754	Sep 7	23:54	♂	dS
	Nov 21	22:38	♂	lS
1755	Mar 7	20:32	♄	lS
	May 14	20:59	♂	dN
	Sep 21	20:57	♂	lN
	Oct 8	17:36	♃	dS
	Nov 12	18:03	♆	lN
1756	Aug 18	13:34	♂	dS
	Oct 8	21:04	♂	lS
1757	Apr 21	8:23	♂	dN
	Aug 8	20:59	♂	lN
1758	Jul 28	5:47	♂	dS
	Aug 26	19:52	♂	lS
1759	Mar 17	3:04	♃	lS
	31	11:30	♂	dN
	Jun 26	19:35	♂	lN
1760	Mar 30	4:23	♅	dN
	Jun 29	21:57	♂	dS
	Jul 13	18:50	♂	lS
	Nov 4	3:46	♅	dS
1761	Jan 10	12:41	♅	dN
	Mar 10	1:10	♂	dN
	Apr 19	7:03	♄	dN
	May 13	18:00	♂	lN
	Jun 30	13:37	♃	dN
	Aug 8	19:10	♃	dS
	Oct 26	2:52	♄	dS
	Dec 12	4:17	♂	dS
1762	Jan 7	17:27	♄	dN
	Feb 3	9:41	♃	dN
	May 31	17:17	♂	lS
1763	Feb 17	3:58	♂	dN
	Mar 31	17:55	♂	lN
	Nov 15	4:17	♂	dS
1764	Apr 17	16:52	♂	lS
	Oct 7	21:41	♃	lN
1765	Jan 24	6:58	♂	dN
	Feb 15	16:13	♂	lN
	Oct 24	2:14	♂	dS
1766	Mar 5	16:17	♂	lS
	Dec 25	7:33	♂	dN
1767	Jan 3	14:20	♂	lN
	Sep 23	5:57	♃	dS
	Oct 4	19:30	♂	dS
1768	Jan 21	15:14	♂	lS
	Jun 27	22:46	♂	dN
	Nov 20	14:25	♂	lN
1769	Jul 11	2:21	♄	lN
	Sep 15	1:06	♂	dS
	Dec 8	14:00	♂	lS
1770	May 24	11:15	♂	dN
	Oct 8	14:03	♂	lN
	Dec 20	3:00	♇	lS
1771	Jan 24	20:12	♃	lS
	Aug 26	23:21	♂	dS
	Oct 26	12:41	♂	lS
1772	Apr 29	14:01	♂	dN
	Aug 25	12:14	♂	lN
1773	May 22	13:52	♃	dN
	Aug 5	14:39	♂	dS
	Sep 12	11:17	♂	lS
	30	19:19	♃	dS
1774	Jan 9	17:29	♃	dN
	Apr 8	7:10	♂	dN
	Jul 13	11:48	♂	lN
	Nov 10	5:42	♄	dS
1775	Mar 18	0:24	♄	dN
	Jul 12	14:25	♂	dS
	31	10:39	♂	lS
	Aug 7	19:18	♄	dS
1776	Mar 17	19:09	♂	dN
	May 30	10:44	♂	lN
	Aug 17	11:33	♃	lN
	Dec 28	0:56	♂	lS
1777	Apr 9	23:51	♂	dN
	May 26	10:50	♂	dS
	Jun 17	10:03	♂	lS
	Oct 28	19:52	♅	lN
1778	Feb 25	4:53	♂	dN
	Apr 17	8:49	♂	lN
	Nov 24	4:14	♂	dS
1779	May 5	8:20	♂	lS
	Sep 7	14:34	♃	dS
	Nov 25	4:18	♆	dS
1780	Feb 3	9:43	♂	dN
	8	0:43	♆	dN
	Mar 4	8:37	♂	lN
	Sep 20	22:43	♆	dS
	Oct 31	16:08	♂	dS
1781	Mar 22	7:16	♂	lS
	May 5	0:03	♆	dN
	Jul 16	14:15	♆	dS
1782	Jan 7	11:39	♂	dN
	20	7:59	♂	lN
	Oct 11	22:13	♂	dS
	Dec 4	0:08	♃	lS
1783	Feb 7	7:00	♂	lS
	Aug 3	16:52	♂	dN
	Sep 23	22:20	♂	dS
	Nov 9	14:07	♂	dN
	Dec 8	6:23	♂	lN
1784	Aug 22	0:43	♄	lS
	Sep 22	1:41	♂	dS
	Dec 25	5:34	♂	lS
1785	Apr 30	12:19	♃	dN
	Jun 4	7:15	♂	dN
	Oct 25	5:41	♂	lN
1786	Sep 3	5:02	♂	dS
	Nov 12	4:12	♂	lS
1787	May 9	4:51	♂	dN
	Sep 12	5:23	♂	lN
1788	Jun 28	7:16	♃	lN
	Aug 13	12:17	♂	dS
	Sep 29	3:47	♂	lS
1789	Apr 16	4:50	♂	dN
	Jul 30	3:05	♂	lN
1790	Jun 19	22:12	♄	dN
	Jul 22	9:32	♂	dS
	Aug 1	9:11	♄	dS
	17	2:36	♂	lS
1791	Feb 27	18:26	♄	dN
	Mar 26	12:58	♂	dN
	Jun 17	2:11	♂	lN
	Aug 22	2:10	♃	dS
1792	Jun 20	15:19	♂	dS
	Jul 4	0:57	♂	lS
1793	Mar 5	2:23	♂	dN
	May 4	2:17	♂	lN
	Dec 4	9:46	♂	dS
1794	May 21	23:52	♂	lS
	Oct 13	15:37	♃	lS
1795	Feb 11	22:24	♂	dN
	Mar 22	1:01	♂	lN
	Nov 9	14:54	♂	dS
1796	Apr 7	22:44	♂	lS
1797	Jan 18	5:26	♂	dN
	Feb 5	23:23	♂	lN
	Apr 12	10:10	♃	dN
	Oct 19	3:51	♂	dS
1798	Feb 23	21:53	♂	lS
	Dec 15	0:34	♂	dN
	21	14:45	♄	lN

♂ ♃ ♄ ♅ ♆ ♇ 0 Declination/Latitude 1700–2050

Year	Month	Day	Time	Planet	Event
		24	22:46	♂	lN
1799	Sep	30	2:28	♂	dS
1800	Jan	11	21:54	♂	lS
	May	9	3:22	♃	lN
	Jun	18	11:53	♂	dN
	Nov	11	21:23	♂	lN
	Dec	16	16:14	♅	dS
1801	Jan	24	6:34	♅	dN
	Sep	11	8:02	♂	dS
		14	14:52	♅	dS
	Nov	29	20:32	♂	lS
1802	May	19	8:48	♂	dN
	Sep	29	20:13	♂	lN
	Dec	6	12:55	♃	dS
1803	Mar	1	3:58	♃	dN
	Aug	4	5:11	♃	dS
		23	1:28	♂	dS
	Oct	17	18:51	♂	lS
1804	Apr	25	8:14	♂	dN
	Aug	16	20:09	♂	lN
	Sep	16	12:29	♄	dS
1805	Aug	1	4:06	♂	dS
	Sep	3	17:52	♂	lS
1806	Apr	4	7:20	♂	dN
	Jul	4	19:15	♂	lN
	Aug	26	12:37	♃	lS
1807	Jul	6	10:13	♂	dS
		22	16:58	♂	lS
1808	Mar	13	20:35	♂	dN
	May	21	17:40	♂	lN
	Dec	18	2:13	♂	dS
1809	Mar	28	5:59	♃	dN
	Jun	8	15:06	♂	lS
1810	Feb	21	3:07	♂	dN
	Apr	8	17:22	♂	lN
	Nov	19	3:10	♂	dS
1811	Apr	26	14:28	♂	lS
1812	Jan	29	18:17	♂	dN
	Feb	24	15:59	♂	lN
	Mar	19	11:19	♃	lN
	Oct	27	14:03	♂	dS
1813	Mar	13	14:20	♂	lS
	Dec	31	19:50	♂	dN
1814	Jan	11	13:50	♂	lN
		24	22:06	♄	lS
	Oct	8	3:42	♂	dS
	Nov	11	21:31	♃	dS
1815	Jan	29	13:12	♂	lS
	Apr	8	16:04	♃	dN
	Jul	9	7:32	♂	dN
		10	20:28	♃	dS
	Nov	29	13:43	♂	lN
1816	Sep	18	8:60	♂	dS
	Dec	16	11:50	♂	lS
1817	Apr	10	12:29	♅	lS
	May	29	10:08	♂	dN
	Oct	16	13:49	♂	lN
1818	Jul	6	10:45	♃	lS
	Aug	30	9:44	♂	dS
	Nov	3	10:29	♂	lS
1819	May	4	17:18	♂	dN
	Sep	3	12:03	♂	lN
1820	Apr	4	14:54	♄	dN
	Aug	9	7:58	♂	dS
	Sep	20	9:19	♂	lS
1821	Mar	11	15:16	♃	dN
	Apr	12	3:60	♂	dN
	Jul	21	10:58	♂	lN
1822	Jul	17	4:37	♂	dS
	Aug	8	8:20	♂	lS
1823	Mar	22	14:29	♂	dN
	Jun	8	10:30	♂	lN
1824	Jan	8	0:30	♂	dS
		28	11:09	♃	lN
	Mar	15	23:54	♂	dN
	Jun	9	5:32	♂	dS

Year	Month	Day	Time	Planet	Event
		25	7:42	♂	lS
1825	Mar	1	1:43	♂	dN
	Apr	25	8:33	♂	lN
	Nov	28	12:22	♂	dS
1826	May	13	6:09	♂	lS
	Oct	24	15:13	♃	dS
1827	Feb	7	14:02	♂	dN
	Mar	13	7:45	♂	lN
	Nov	5	6:20	♂	dS
1828	Mar	30	5:03	♂	lS
	Jun	1	9:05	♄	lN
1829	Jan	12	18:11	♂	dN
		28	7:12	♂	lN
	Oct	15	6:56	♂	dS
1830	Feb	15	4:42	♂	lS
	May	16	12:38	♃	lS
	Dec	1	9:05	♂	dN
		16	5:56	♂	lN
1831	Sep	26	9:06	♂	dS
1832	Jan	3	3:25	♂	lS
	Jun	10	1:02	♂	dN
	Nov	2	4:55	♂	lN
1833	Feb	22	5:56	♃	dN
	Sep	6	13:59	♂	dS
	Oct	25	8:52	♄	dS
	Nov	20	1:52	♂	lS
1834	Apr	13	9:36	♄	dN
	May	13	13:15	♂	dN
	Jul	19	13:03	♄	dS
	Sep	20	4:52	♂	lN
1835	Aug	18	2:15	♂	dS
	Oct	8	1:27	♂	lS
	Dec	8	0:19	♃	lN
1836	Apr	20	3:42	♂	dN
	Aug	7	2:46	♂	lN
1837	Jul	26	12:59	♂	dS
	Aug	25	0:41	♂	lS
1838	Mar	30	8:33	♂	dN
	Jun	25	1:32	♂	lN
	Oct	8	5:51	♃	dS
1839	Jan	14	14:56	♆	lS
	Jun	28	5:47	♂	dS
	Jul	12	22:57	♂	lS
1840	Mar	8	22:21	♂	dN
	May	12	1:51	♂	lN
	Dec	9	11:44	♂	dS
1841	May	29	21:30	♂	lS
1842	Feb	15	23:04	♂	dN
	Mar	25	18:59	♃	lS
		30	0:41	♂	lN
	Nov	13	9:30	♂	dS
1843	Apr	16	20:42	♂	lS
	May	30	10:37	♅	dN
	Jul	10	14:34	♄	lS
	Aug	13	1:38	♅	dS
1844	Jan	23	21:30	♂	dN
	Feb	14	22:47	♂	lN
	Mar	11	22:35	♅	dN
	Jun	29	4:18	♃	dN
	Aug	10	10:31	♃	dS
	Oct	22	13:40	♂	dS
1845	Feb	3	6:19	♃	dN
	Mar	3	19:45	♂	lS
	Dec	23	0:02	♂	dN
1846	Jan	1	22:18	♂	lN
	Oct	3	9:41	♂	dS
1847	Jan	19	19:27	♂	lS
	Jun	26	2:16	♂	dN
	Oct	18	19:47	♃	lN
	Nov	19	21:19	♂	lN
1848	Sep	13	15:56	♂	dS
	Dec	6	18:25	♂	lS
1849	May	19	17:18	♄	dN
		23	0:28	♂	dN
	Sep	7	16:40	♄	dS
	Oct	6	19:47	♂	lN

Year	Month	Day	Time	Planet	Event
1850	Feb	12	8:43	♄	dN
	Aug	25	12:58	♂	dS
	Sep	22	16:05	♃	dS
	Oct	24	16:48	♂	lS
1851	Apr	29	9:41	♂	dN
	Aug	24	19:32	♂	lN
1852	Aug	4	0:36	♂	dS
	Sep	10	15:44	♂	lS
1853	Apr	7	4:02	♂	dN
	Jul	11	18:52	♂	lN
1854	Feb	2	10:43	♃	lS
	Jul	10	12:03	♂	dS
		29	14:44	♂	lS
1855	Mar	17	16:21	♂	dN
	May	29	17:17	♂	lN
	Dec	24	22:22	♂	dS
1856	May	23	2:39	♃	dN
	Jun	15	12:52	♂	lS
	Sep	29	22:59	♃	dS
1857	Jan	10	13:16	♃	dN
	Feb	24	1:22	♂	dN
	Apr	15	16:44	♂	lN
	Nov	11	3:19	♄	lN
		22	4:53	♂	dS
1858	May	3	11:57	♂	lS
1859	Feb	2	2:19	♂	dN
	Mar	3	15:30	♂	lN
	Aug	28	21:09	♃	lN
	Oct	31	2:07	♂	dS
1860	Mar	20	12:08	♂	lS
1861	Jan	5	16:16	♂	dN
		18	13:12	♂	lN
	Sep	12	19:50	♅	lN
	Oct	10	11:20	♂	dS
1862	Feb	5	10:57	♂	lS
	May	15	10:28	♆	dN
		24	23:34	♇	dN
	Jul	24	10:12	♂	dN
	Aug	5	17:27	♇	dS
		22	17:18	♆	dS
	Sep	6	17:41	♃	dS
	Dec	6	13:00	♂	lN
1863	Jan	1	22:60	♄	dS
		15	13:54	♄	dN
	Mar	15	9:34	♆	dN
	Apr	3	6:44	♇	dN
	Sep	3	0:16	♄	dS
		21	15:49	♂	dS
	Oct	4	10:29	♇	dS
	Nov	25	0:13	♆	dS
	Dec	24	9:32	♂	lS
		29	6:24	♆	dN
1864	Feb	20	7:37	♇	dN
	Jun	2	14:56	♂	dN
	Oct	23	13:12	♂	lN
1865	Sep	1	18:52	♂	dS
	Nov	10	8:18	♂	lS
	Dec	15	5:35	♃	lS
1866	May	7	22:18	♂	dN
	Sep	10	11:41	♂	lN
1867	Aug	12	23:34	♂	dS
	Sep	28	7:12	♂	lS
1868	Apr	15	1:42	♂	dN
	May	1	23:04	♃	dN
	Jul	28	10:13	♂	lN
1869	Jul	20	13:52	♂	dS
	Aug	15	6:04	♂	lS
1870	Mar	25	10:21	♂	dN
	Jun	15	10:12	♂	lN
1871	Jan	27	10:37	♂	dS
	Feb	13	13:32	♂	dN
	Jun	18	6:12	♂	dS
	Jul	3	5:28	♂	lS
		9	17:18	♃	lN
1872	Mar	3	22:44	♂	dN
	May	2	8:22	♂	lN

Year	Month	Day	Time	Planet	Event
	Dec	2	2:41	♂	dS
		10	0:12	♄	lS
1873	May	20	4:02	♂	lS
1874	Feb	10	17:10	♂	dN
	Mar	20	6:59	♂	lN
	Aug	21	2:57	♃	dS
	Nov	7	22:23	♂	dS
1875	Apr	7	2:58	♂	lS
1876	Jan	17	17:58	♂	dN
	Feb	5	6:39	♂	lN
	Oct	17	15:57	♂	dS
1877	Feb	22	2:34	♂	lS
	Oct	25	8:54	♃	lS
	Dec	11	21:05	♂	dN
		23	5:55	♂	lN
1878	Sep	28	16:03	♂	dS
1879	Jan	10	1:11	♂	lS
	Mar	20	18:33	♄	dN
	Jun	16	8:10	♂	dN
	Nov	10	4:31	♂	lN
1880	Apr	13	11:05	♃	dN
	Sep	8	21:51	♂	dS
	Nov	26	23:43	♂	lS
1881	May	16	23:60	♂	dN
	Sep	27	4:20	♂	lN
1882	Aug	20	14:25	♂	dS
	Oct	14	23:16	♂	lS
1883	Apr	24	3:14	♂	dN
	May	19	19:27	♃	lN
	Aug	15	2:45	♂	lN
1884	Jul	29	12:43	♂	dS
	Aug	31	22:35	♂	lS
	Nov	14	15:08	♅	dS
1885	Feb	28	1:56	♅	dN
	Apr	2	4:21	♂	dN
	Jul	2	0:56	♂	lN
	Aug	29	3:26	♅	dS
	Dec	4	15:59	♃	dS
1886	Mar	1	12:24	♃	dN
	Jul	3	1:24	♂	dS
		19	20:46	♂	lS
	Aug	2	19:02	♃	dS
1887	Mar	12	18:22	♂	dN
	Apr	17	19:14	♄	lN
	May	20	1:08	♂	lN
	Dec	15	1:29	♂	dS
1888	Jun	5	19:10	♂	lS
1889	Feb	18	23:03	♂	dN
	Apr	6	0:20	♂	lN
	Sep	4	19:47	♃	lS
	Nov	16	7:00	♂	dS
1890	Apr	23	18:31	♂	lS
1891	Jan	27	10:03	♂	dN
	Feb	21	22:13	♂	lN
	Oct	26	0:45	♂	dS
1892	Mar	10	17:32	♂	lS
		27	6:32	♃	dN
	Oct	9	8:30	♄	dS
	Dec	28	19:40	♂	dN
1893	Jan	8	21:33	♂	lN
	Oct	5	17:16	♂	dS
1894	Jan	26	16:49	♂	lS
	Jul	4	10:37	♂	dN
	Nov	26	21:11	♂	lN
1895	Mar	29	6:45	♃	lN
	Sep	16	23:14	♂	dS
	Dec	14	16:10	♂	lS
1896	May	26	20:36	♂	dN
	Oct	13	19:12	♂	lN
1897	Aug	27	22:59	♂	dS
	Oct	31	14:46	♂	lS
	Nov	10	13:13	♃	dS
1898	Apr	8	13:57	♃	dN
	May	2	11:59	♂	dN
	Jul	9	8:39	♃	dS
	Aug	31	18:37	♂	lN

Year	Month	Day	Time	Planet	Event
1899	Aug	7	18:14	♂	dS
	Sep	18	13:26	♂	lS
1900	Apr	11	0:39	♂	dN
	Jul	19	18:26	♂	lN
1901	Feb	15	7:21	♅	lS
	Jul	15	5:26	♂	dS
		16	3:58	♃	lS
	Aug	6	12:25	♂	lS
1902	Mar	21	11:38	♂	dN
	May	24	18:42	♄	lS
	Jun	6	17:01	♂	lN
1903	Jan	2	7:37	♂	dS
	Mar	29	21:52	♂	dN
	Jun	4	15:12	♂	dS
		24	10:52	♂	lS
1904	Feb	28	22:48	♂	dN
	Mar	11	17:05	♃	dN
	Apr	23	16:04	♂	lN
	Nov	26	10:47	♂	dS
1905	May	11	9:33	♂	lS
1906	Feb	6	8:15	♂	dN
	Mar	11	15:12	♂	lN
	Nov	3	16:03	♂	dS
1907	Feb	8	1:31	♃	lN
	Mar	29	9:54	♂	lS
1908	Jan	12	2:42	♂	dN
		27	13:03	♂	lN
	Apr	29	17:09	♄	dN
	Oct	7	9:21	♄	dS
		13	20:08	♂	dS
1909	Jan	24	0:15	♄	dN
	Feb	13	8:57	♂	lS
	Oct	24	6:41	♃	dS
	Nov	25	20:58	♂	dN
	Dec	14	12:39	♂	lN
1910	Sep	24	23:21	♂	dS
1911	Jan	1	7:16	♂	lS
	Jun	9	5:18	♂	dN
	Nov	1	12:43	♂	lN
1912	Sep	5	3:55	♂	dS
	Nov	18	6:17	♂	lS
1913	May	12	5:33	♂	dN
		25	19:54	♃	lS
	Sep	18	11:30	♂	lN
1914	Aug	16	13:48	♂	dS
	Oct	6	5:16	♂	lS
1915	Apr	19	23:50	♂	dN
	Aug	6	9:51	♂	lN
1916	Feb	23	21:34	♃	dN
	Jul	24	18:24	♂	dS
	Aug	23	3:47	♂	lS
	Sep	27	18:40	♄	lN
1917	Mar	29	5:44	♂	dN
	Jun	23	9:45	♂	lN
1918	Jun	25	9:25	♂	dS
	Jul	11	3:01	♂	lS
	Dec	19	7:30	♃	lN
1919	Mar	8	18:50	♂	dN
	May	11	8:06	♂	lN
	Dec	7	23:28	♂	dS
1920	May	28	1:59	♂	lS
	Jun	3	21:24	♆	lN
1921	Feb	14	18:16	♂	dN
	Mar	28	6:25	♂	lN
	Oct	7	16:30	♃	dS
	Nov	11	15:54	♂	dS
		23	1:07	♄	dS
1922	Mar	2	8:53	♄	dN
	Apr	15	0:45	♂	lS
	Aug	18	11:19	♄	dS
1923	Jan	22	12:03	♂	dN
	Feb	13	6:04	♂	lN
	Oct	22	1:38	♂	dS
1924	Mar	2	0:09	♂	lS
	Dec	20	12:22	♂	dN
		31	5:36	♂	lN

♂ ♃ ♄ ♅ ♆ ♇ 0 Declination/Latitude 1700–2050

Year	Month	Day	Time	Planet	Event
1925	Apr	6	11:29	♃	lS
	Oct	1	23:33	♂	dS
1926	Jan	17	22:47	♂	lS
	Jun	23	12:37	♂	dN
	Nov	18	4:10	♂	lN
1927	May	1	22:28	♅	dN
	Jul	7	11:52	♃	dN
	Aug	3	9:38	♃	dS
	Sep	13	5:53	♂	dS
		16	14:03	♅	dS
	Dec	5	21:27	♂	lS
1928	Feb	6	2:31	♃	dN
		21	12:04	♅	dN
	May	21	14:30	♂	dN
	Oct	5	3:26	♂	lN
1929	Aug	24	1:59	♂	dS
	Oct	22	20:52	♂	lS
1930	Apr	28	4:13	♂	dN
	Aug	23	2:27	♂	lN
	Sep	9	7:16	♇	lN
	Oct	30	14:18	♃	lN
1931	Aug	3	9:52	♂	dS
	Sep	9	20:07	♂	lS
	Oct	24	11:01	♄	lS
1932	Apr	6	0:26	♂	dN
	Jul	10	0:30	♂	lN
1933	Jul	8	7:33	♂	dS
		27	18:29	♂	lS
	Sep	22	0:03	♃	dS
1934	Mar	16	13:44	♂	dN
	May	28	0:24	♂	lN
	Dec	21	7:17	♂	dS
1935	Jun	14	16:60	♂	lS
1936	Feb	23	21:30	♂	dN
	Apr	13	23:56	♂	lN
	Nov	20	6:32	♂	dS
1937	Feb	14	18:53	♃	lS
	May	1	16:13	♂	lS
1938	Jan	31	19:03	♂	dN
	Mar	1	22:01	♂	lN
		5	14:08	♄	dN
	Oct	29	12:10	♂	dS
1939	Mar	19	15:18	♂	lS
	May	26	0:46	♃	dN
	Sep	27	19:51	♃	dS
1940	Jan	4	21:25	♂	dN
		13	18:35	♃	dN
		17	21:03	♂	lN
	Oct	9	0:51	♂	dS
1941	Feb	3	14:26	♂	lS
	Jul	17	15:57	♂	dN
	Dec	4	21:07	♂	lN
1942	Sep	9	17:46	♃	lN
		20	6:39	♂	dS
	Dec	22	13:54	♂	lS
1943	Jun	1	23:11	♂	dN
	Oct	22	18:55	♂	lN
	Nov	1	8:33	♆	dS
1944	Mar	7	15:06	♆	dN
	Aug	31	9:01	♂	dS
	Sep	4	14:25	♆	dS
	Nov	8	12:51	♂	lS
1945	May	6	16:36	♂	dN
	Jul	19	9:34	♅	lN
	Sep	6	16:54	♃	dS
		8	17:59	♂	lN
1946	Feb	28	12:41	♄	lN
	Aug	11	10:54	♂	dS
	Sep	26	11:23	♂	lS
1947	Apr	14	22:30	♂	dN
	Jul	27	18:12	♂	lN
1948	Jul	18	17:08	♂	dS
	Aug	13	10:04	♂	lS
	Dec	26	14:41	♃	lS
1949	Mar	24	7:24	♂	dN
	Jun	13	16:51	♂	lN
1950	Jan	13	12:17	♂	dS
	Mar	4	22:13	♂	dN
	Jun	14	8:14	♂	dS
	Jul	1	8:48	♂	lS
1951	Mar	3	19:47	♂	dN
	May	1	15:26	♂	lN
		3	4:38	♃	dN
	Sep	25	4:59	♄	dS
	Nov	30	20:60	♂	dS
1952	May	18	7:21	♂	lS
1953	Feb	9	11:54	♂	dN
	Mar	18	15:00	♂	lN
	Nov	6	6:32	♂	dS
1954	Apr	5	7:25	♂	lS
	Jul	20	3:04	♃	lN
1955	Jan	16	4:42	♂	dN
	Feb	3	13:03	♂	lN
	Oct	17	4:27	♂	dS
1956	Feb	21	6:41	♂	lS
	Dec	8	8:45	♂	dN
		21	12:01	♂	lN
1957	Aug	21	3:35	♃	dS
	Sep	27	6:08	♂	dS
1958	Jan	8	4:54	♂	lS
	Jun	14	7:13	♂	dN
	Nov	8	12:04	♂	lN
1959	Sep	8	11:60	♂	dS
	Nov	26	3:60	♂	lS
1960	May	15	15:29	♂	dN
	Sep	25	11:03	♂	lN
	Nov	5	0:34	♃	lS
1961	Apr	4	19:01	♄	lS
	Aug	19	2:44	♂	dS
	Oct	13	2:57	♂	lS
1962	Apr	22	23:20	♂	dN
	Aug	13	9:20	♂	lN
1963	Apr	14	16:04	♃	dN
	Jul	28	19:44	♂	dS
	Aug	31	1:15	♂	lS
1964	Apr	1	1:54	♂	dN
	Jun	30	9:11	♂	lN
1965	Jun	30	13:14	♂	dS
	Jul	18	0:26	♂	lS
1966	Mar	11	15:09	♂	dN
	May	18	7:56	♂	lN
		30	20:25	♃	lN
	Dec	12	6:04	♂	dS
1967	Apr	12	13:50	♄	dN
	Jun	4	23:54	♂	lS
	Nov	18	9:02	♄	dS
	Dec	20	1:01	♄	dN
1968	Feb	18	18:26	♂	dN
	Apr	4	5:55	♂	lN
	Oct	25	17:12	♅	dS
	Nov	14	11:44	♂	dS
	Dec	4	6:55	♃	dS
1969	Mar	2	7:28	♃	dN
		26	23:24	♅	dN
	Apr	21	22:26	♂	lS
	Aug	2	12:39	♃	dS
		11	1:30	♅	dS
1970	Jan	26	1:43	♂	dN
	Feb	20	5:35	♂	lN
	Oct	24	11:45	♂	dS
1971	Mar	9	21:40	♂	lS
	Dec	27	16:45	♂	dN
1972	Jan	8	5:14	♂	lN
	Sep	14	15:47	♃	lS
	Oct	4	6:34	♂	dS
1973	Jan	24	20:41	♂	lS
	Jul	1	2:19	♂	dN
	Nov	25	3:56	♂	lN
1974	Sep	15	13:04	♂	dS
	Dec	12	19:19	♂	lS
1975	Mar	28	22:43	♃	dN
	May	26	9:02	♂	dN
	Aug	10	15:46	♄	lN
	Oct	13	2:44	♂	lN
1976	Aug	26	12:24	♂	dS
	Oct	29	18:36	♂	lS
1977	May	1	6:25	♂	dN
	Aug	30	2:21	♂	lN
1978	Apr	10	5:27	♃	lN
	Aug	6	4:50	♂	dS
	Sep	16	17:56	♂	lS
1979	Apr	9	21:13	♂	dN
	Jul	18	0:28	♂	lN
1980	Jul	12	5:08	♂	dS
	Aug	3	16:21	♂	lS
	Nov	1	12:52	♄	dS
		10	4:09	♃	dS
1981	Mar	19	9:29	♂	dN
		30	23:43	♄	dN
	Apr	9	17:31	♃	dN
	Jun	3	23:46	♂	lN
	Jul	8	15:38	♃	dS
		29	6:48	♄	dS
	Dec	27	17:06	♂	dS
1982	Apr	11	20:13	♂	dN
	May	26	22:44	♂	dS
	Jun	21	14:54	♂	lS
1983	Feb	26	19:51	♂	dN
	Apr	21	23:34	♂	lN
	Nov	24	10:20	♂	dS
1984	May	8	14:02	♂	lS
	Jul	27	1:46	♃	lS
	Dec	21	3:29	♅	lS
1985	Feb	4	1:56	♂	dN
	Mar	8	22:07	♂	lN
	Nov	1	1:14	♂	dS
1986	Mar	26	12:57	♂	lS
1987	Jan	9	11:08	♂	dN
		24	20:38	♂	lN
	Mar	13	6:31	♃	dN
	Oct	12	8:50	♂	dS
	Nov	12	23:28	♇	dS
1988	Feb	11	11:59	♂	lS
		6	23:18	♇	dN
	Sep	5	6:58	♇	dS
	Nov	17	11:09	♂	dN
	Dec	11	20:35	♂	lN
1989	Sep	22	13:32	♂	dS
	Dec	29	11:31	♂	lS
1990	Feb	19	20:19	♃	lN
	Jun	6	9:21	♂	dN
	Sep	4	5:14	♄	lS
	Oct	29	18:45	♂	lN
1991	Sep	3	17:38	♂	dS
	Nov	16	10:36	♂	lS
1992	May	9	22:30	♂	dN
	Sep	15	17:18	♂	lN
	Oct	22	17:55	♃	dS
1993	Aug	14	1:15	♂	dS
	Oct	3	9:00	♂	lS
1994	Apr	17	20:27	♂	dN
	Aug	3	17:36	♂	lN
1995	Jul	22	23:26	♂	dS
	Aug	21	7:30	♂	lS
1996	Mar	27	2:55	♂	dN
	May	25	3:37	♄	dN
	Jun	6	12:18	♃	lS
		20	16:40	♂	lN
	Aug	30	16:57	♄	dS
1997	Feb	16	5:27	♄	dN
	Jun	21	6:06	♂	dS
	Jul	8	6:34	♂	lS
1998	Mar	6	16:13	♂	dN
	May	8	14:53	♂	lN
	Dec	4	13:45	♂	dS
1999	Feb	24	11:41	♃	dN
	May	26	5:11	♂	lS
2000	Feb	13	14:04	♂	dN
	Mar	25	14:32	♂	lN
	Nov	8	23:24	♂	dS
2001	Apr	12	4:43	♂	lS
	Dec	30	23:32	♃	lN
2002	Jan	20	1:12	♂	dN
	Feb	10	13:06	♂	lN
	Oct	19	14:01	♂	dS
2003	Feb	28	4:22	♂	lS
	Aug	11	5:45	♆	lS
	Dec	17	19:19	♂	dN
		29	11:22	♂	lN
2004	Sep	29	13:27	♂	dS
	Oct	6	19:14	♃	dS
2005	Jan	8	17:10	♄	lN
		15	2:53	♂	lS
	Jun	20	3:22	♂	dN
	Nov	15	11:21	♂	lN
2006	Sep	10	19:54	♂	dS
	Dec	3	1:46	♂	lS
2007	May	20	4:37	♂	dN
	Oct	3	10:47	♂	lN
2008	Apr	17	16:03	♃	lS
	Aug	21	14:30	♂	dS
	Oct	20	0:45	♂	lS
2009	Apr	25	23:30	♂	dN
	Aug	20	9:15	♂	lN
2010	Jul	8	17:49	♃	dN
		31	2:27	♃	dS
		31	17:46	♂	dS
	Sep	6	23:10	♂	lS
		8	13:57	♄	dS
2011	Feb	5	13:48	♃	dN
	Apr	4	21:49	♂	dN
		9	19:34	♅	dN
	Jul	8	8:49	♂	lN
	Oct	16	17:48	♅	dS
2012	Jan	28	3:42	♅	dN
	Jul	5	0:43	♂	dS
		24	22:03	♂	lS
2013	Mar	14	10:50	♂	dN
	May	25	7:52	♂	lN
	Nov	9	5:46	♃	lN
	Dec	17	1:58	♂	dS
2014	Jun	11	21:45	♂	lS
2015	Feb	21	17:30	♂	dN
	Apr	12	5:41	♂	lN
	Nov	18	9:59	♂	dS
2016	Apr	28	20:17	♂	lS
	Sep	21	4:60	♃	dS
2017	Jan	29	12:09	♂	dN
	Feb	27	5:17	♂	lN
	Oct	26	23:01	♂	dS
2018	Mar	16	19:05	♂	lS
	Oct	24	17:45	♇	lS
2019	Jan	2	0:58	♂	dN
		15	4:49	♂	lN
	Oct	7	14:19	♂	dS
2020	Feb	1	18:24	♂	lS
		13	5:56	♄	lS
		26	2:47	♃	lS
	Jul	11	12:19	♂	dN
	Dec	2	3:34	♂	lN
2021	Sep	17	20:33	♂	dS
	Dec	19	17:03	♂	lS
2022	May	25	8:19	♃	dN
		30	9:20	♂	dN
	Sep	26	10:59	♃	dS
	Oct	20	2:16	♂	lN
2023	Jan	13	5:57	♃	dN
	Aug	29	22:10	♂	dS
	Nov	6	16:02	♂	lS
2024	May	4	10:19	♂	dN
	Sep	6	2:05	♂	lN
2025	Aug	8	21:33	♂	dS
	Sep	19	20:40	♃	lN
		23	15:20	♂	lS
2026	Mar	26	21:27	♄	dN
	Apr	12	18:24	♂	dN
		24	4:22	♆	dN
	Jul	25	0:15	♂	lN
	Sep	16	3:01	♆	dS
2027	Feb	26	17:17	♆	dN
	Jul	16	18:50	♂	dS
	Aug	11	14:00	♂	lS
2028	Mar	22	4:40	♂	dN
	Jun	10	23:06	♂	lN
	Sep	5	14:46	♃	dS
2029	Jan	5	6:10	♂	dS
	Mar	17	7:13	♂	dN
	May	19	22:11	♅	lN
	Jun	8	18:39	♂	dS
		28	12:38	♂	lS
2030	Mar	1	16:47	♂	dN
	Apr	28	23:03	♂	lN
	Nov	27	17:18	♂	dS
2031	May	16	11:42	♂	lS
2032	Jan	5	16:23	♃	lS
	Feb	8	6:11	♂	dN
	Mar	15	21:59	♂	lN
	Nov	3	15:01	♂	dS
2033	Apr	2	10:30	♂	lS
2034	Jan	13	15:56	♂	dN
		31	20:18	♂	lN
	May	2	23:19	♃	dN
	Jun	21	15:39	♄	lN
	Oct	14	17:07	♂	dS
2035	Feb	18	9:36	♂	lS
	Dec	4	10:31	♂	dN
		19	19:52	♂	lN
2036	Sep	24	20:40	♂	dS
2037	Jan	5	9:20	♂	lS
	Jun	11	6:54	♂	dN
	Jul	31	8:05	♃	lN
	Nov	5	18:40	♂	lN
2038	Sep	6	2:23	♂	dS
	Nov	23	8:22	♂	lS
2039	May	14	7:42	♂	dN
	Sep	23	17:01	♂	lN
	Oct	15	8:33	♄	dS
2040	May	5	14:55	♄	dN
	Jun	28	6:28	♄	dS
	Aug	16	15:02	♂	dS
		19	22:40	♃	dS
	Oct	10	6:47	♂	lS
2041	Apr	20	19:51	♂	dN
	Aug	10	17:16	♂	lN
2042	Jul	26	2:17	♂	dS
	Aug	28	5:22	♂	lS
2043	Mar	30	23:01	♂	dN
	Jun	28	16:40	♂	lN
	Nov	16	20:00	♃	lS
2044	Jun	26	20:21	♂	dS
	Jul	15	4:24	♂	lS
2045	Mar	9	12:18	♂	dN
	May	15	14:40	♂	lN
	Dec	8	14:01	♂	dS
2046	Apr	15	4:43	♃	dN
	Jun	2	2:59	♂	lS
2047	Feb	16	14:34	♂	dN
	Apr	2	14:10	♂	lN
	Nov	12	17:21	♂	dS
2048	Apr	19	2:06	♂	lS
2049	Jan	23	16:28	♂	dN
	Feb	17	13:16	♂	lN
	Jun	12	3:55	♃	lN
	Jul	15	20:32	♄	lS
	Oct	21	23:31	♂	dS
2050	Mar	7	1:50	♂	lS
	Dec	24	10:24	♂	dN

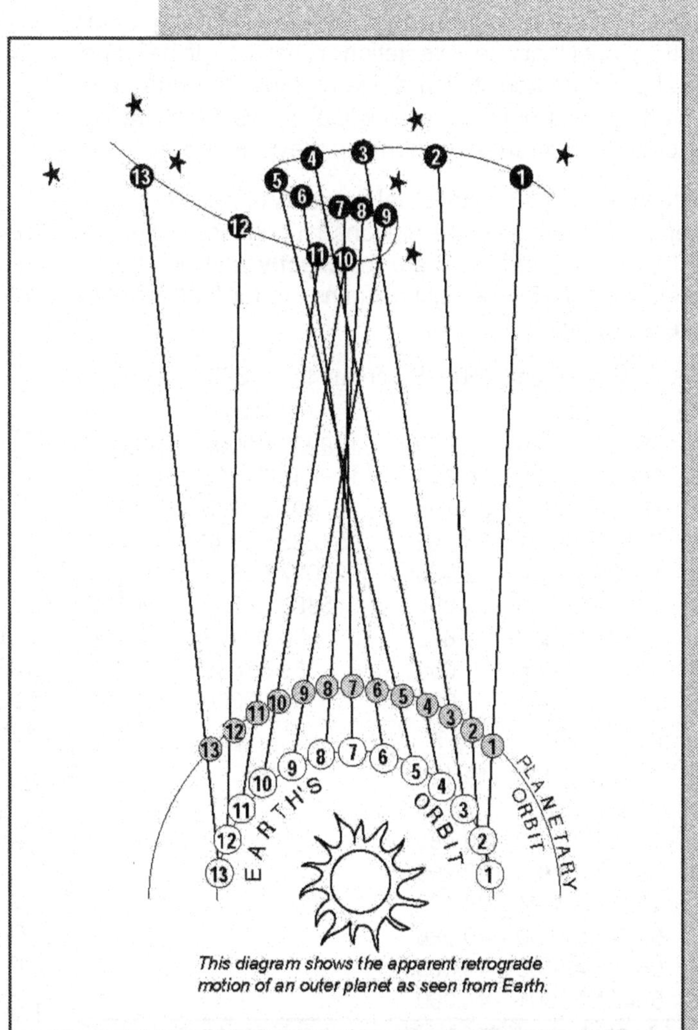

This diagram shows the apparent retrograde motion of an outer planet as seen from Earth.

Part 7

Planetary Stations

Planetary Stations in Longitude 1700–2050

The first number in the Stations Table shows the number of planets that are retrograde as of the date following, along with the planet that was at its station on that date. If the planet was at its retrograde station, the retrograde total was incremented by one from the previous line; if at its direct station, the total was decremented from the previous line.

The following data is a statistical summary of the information tallied when calculating the Stations in Longitude table. The left Total and % columns are for **exactly** that number of planets retrograde; the right columns are for that many **or more** retrograde.

1700 through 2050 Summary for 128200 days				
#Rx	Total	%	Total	%
0	8756.42995	6.830	128200.00000	100.000
1	26445.57750	20.628	119443.57005	93.170
2	38712.08273	30.197	92997.99255	72.541
3	32257.95101	25.162	54285.90982	42.345
4	16139.79144	12.590	22027.95881	17.182
5	4957.35260	3.867	5888.16737	4.593
6	861.29633	.672	930.81478	.726
7	69.51845	.054	69.51845	.054
8	.00000	.000	.00000	.000
Planet	Total	%		
☿	24577.96263	19.172		
♀	9267.83707	7.229		
♂	12159.36470	9.485		
♃	38727.09963	30.208		
♄	46676.53424	36.409		
♅	52544.34290	40.986		
♆	55206.45465	43.063		
♇	56484.33601	44.060		

1900 through 2000 Summary for 36890 days				
#Rx	Total	%	Total	%
0	3346.67197	9.072	36890.00000	100.000
1	7802.89770	21.152	33543.32803	90.928
2	9864.16623	26.739	25740.43033	69.776
3	8601.38954	23.316	15876.26410	43.037
4	5093.72632	13.808	7274.87456	19.720
5	1778.66565	4.822	2181.14824	5.913
6	390.18253	1.058	402.48259	1.091
7	12.30006	.033	12.30006	.033
8	.00000	.000	.00000	.000
Planet	Total	%		
☿	7061.95283	19.143		
♀	2654.75159	7.196		
♂	3484.02512	9.444		
♃	11190.50240	30.335		
♄	13481.22408	36.544		
♅	15210.44763	41.232		
♆	15914.41669	43.140		
♇	16033.50758	43.463		

During the 351 years there were no times when all eight planets were retrograde. There were eight times when seven planets were retrograde:

1703	Nov	19	20:11	☿	♀		♃	♄	♅	♆	♇
		23	6:43	☿D							
1820	Aug	6	1:24	☿	♀		♃	♄	♅	♆	♇
		21	8:03		♀D						
1845	Aug	30	15:40	☿		♂	♃	♄	♅	♆	♇
	Sep	17	8:01			♂D					
1884	Jan	11	20:47	☿		♂	♃	♄	♅	♆	♇
		28	19:60			♆D					
1886	Jan	28	23:12		♀	♂	♃	♄	♅	♆	♇
	Feb	1	19:42							♆D	
1944	Jan	6	6:23	☿		♂	♃	♄	♅	♆	♇
		10	4:37			♂D					
1984	Apr	29	18:38	☿		♂	♃	♄	♅	♆	♇
	May	5	14:07	☿D							
1986	Jul	12	17:02	☿		♂	♃	♄	♅	♆	♇
		15	6:32								♇D

It's not surprising that seven out of these eight times Venus or Mars was the lone "holdout" since they are retrograde only 7.229% and 9.485% of the time, the two lowest percentages of the eight.

At the other end of the spectrum, there were 278 times when no planets were retrograde during the 351 years shown in the table.

For a visual representation of the retrograde motion of the planets, see Figures 25 through 30 in the mandala section of this book.

The most striking orbital/retrograde pattern is that of Venus as shown in Figures 27 and 28. Figure 27 shows almost 8 years of Venus' geocentric orbit starting May 11, 1931. The five-cloverleaf pattern is the result of the five retrograde periods of Venus over an 8-year time span.

A most remarkable characteristic of Venus' orbit is seen in Figure 28. Here Venus' path over a 16-year time span is graphed and the second 8 years almost perfectly retraces the first 8 years. In fact, without having Figure 27 to look at, one would say the path graphed in Figure 28 was unique rather than one 8-year pattern superimposed on top of the previous.

Figures 25 and 26 show Mercury's orbit over a 3- and a 6-year time span, respectively. The loops are the retrograde times. Only if Mercury's orbit had been graphed for more years would we be able to determine if its orbital pattern repeated in a manner analogous to that of Venus.

Figures 29 and 30 show Mars' orbit for 33 and almost 66 years, respectively. It is clear that Mars does not share the remarkable characteristic of Venus' overlapping orbital pattern.

Planetary Stations in Longitude 1700–2050

On Jan 1, 1700, 2 Planets are ℞ – ♅ ♇

3	1700	Jan 7	0:57	☿	℞
2		27	15:27	☿	D
1		Mar 14	23:30	♅	D
2		Apr 3	5:35	♂	℞
1		20	23:03	♇	D
2		May 2	13:10	☿	℞
3		20	11:45	♃	℞
2		26	9:44	☿	D
1		Jun 17	0:18	♂	D
2		25	2:35	♄	℞
3		Jul 11	2:18	♆	℞
4		Aug 12	16:06	♀	℞
5		Sep 2	12:41	☿	℞
4		18	9:52	♃	D
3		24	8:16	♀	D
2		24	21:10	☿	D
3		Oct 21	9:23	♅	℞
2		Nov 11	1:26	♄	D
3		13	23:40	♇	℞
2		Dec 16	5:49	♆	D
3		21	22:50	☿	℞
2	1701	Jan 11	1:03	☿	D
1		Mar 19	16:02	♅	D
2		Apr 13	12:21	☿	℞
1		22	18:36	♇	D
0		May 7	6:56	☿	D
1		Jun 27	2:21	♃	℞
2		Jul 8	10:51	♄	℞
3		13	14:42	♆	℞
4		Aug 16	3:53	☿	℞
3		Sep 8	7:07	☿	D
2		Oct 24	4:04	♃	D
3		26	7:36	♅	℞
4		Nov 15	21:59	♇	℞
3		23	13:54	♄	D
4		Dec 5	20:12	☿	℞
3		18	16:56	♆	D
2		25	15:24	☿	D
3	1702	Mar 23	9:26	♀	℞
2		24	12:46	♅	D
3		26	5:03	☿	℞
2		Apr 18	18:28	☿	D
1		24	15:10	♇	D
0		May 4	20:49	♀	D
1		Jun 8	2:04	♂	℞
2		Jul 16	5:02	♆	℞
3		22	3:01	♄	℞
4		29	11:50	☿	℞
5		Aug 4	9:12	♃	℞
4		10	17:36	♂	D
3		22	6:02	☿	D
4		Oct 31	3:51	♅	℞
5		Nov 17	20:50	♇	℞
6		19	15:24	☿	℞
5		30	2:56	♃	D
4		Dec 6	6:59	♄	D
3		9	9:42	☿	D
2		21	3:32	♆	D
3	1703	Mar 8	16:03	☿	℞
2		29	7:26	♅	D
1		31	18:36	☿	D
0		Apr 26	9:01	♇	D
1		Jul 11	10:22	☿	℞
2		18	17:30	♆	℞
1		Aug 4	13:40	☿	D
2		5	1:36	♄	℞
3		Sep 10	15:26	♃	℞
4		Oct 26	4:31	♀	℞
5		Nov 3	7:05	☿	℞
6		5	2:56	♅	℞
7		19	20:11	♇	℞
6		23	6:43	☿	D
5		Dec 6	8:19	♀	D
4		19	8:02	♄	D
3		23	15:29	♆	D
2	1704	Jan 6	5:05	♃	D
3		Feb 19	17:53	☿	℞
2		Mar 13	4:27	☿	D
1		Apr 2	5:34	♅	D
0		27	5:23	♇	D
1		Jun 21	21:17	☿	℞
0		Jul 16	2:31	☿	D
1		20	7:55	♆	℞
2		Aug 18	6:08	♄	℞
3		24	23:16	♂	℞
4		Oct 14	17:34	♃	℞
5		16	18:27	☿	℞
4		27	6:13	♂	D
3		Nov 6	5:08	☿	D
4		9	1:06	♅	℞
5		20	22:32	♇	℞
4		Dec 25	3:27	♆	D
3		31	17:10	♄	D
4	1705	Feb 2	5:56	☿	℞
3		10	3:26	♃	D
2		23	22:21	☿	D
1		Apr 7	2:40	♅	D
0		29	0:57	♇	D
1		May 31	22:55	♀	℞
2		Jun 2	19:59	☿	℞
1		26	21:01	☿	D
0		Jul 14	1:18	♀	D
1		22	20:57	♆	℞
2		Sep 1	16:01	♄	℞
3		30	1:00	☿	℞
2		Oct 21	3:15	☿	D
3		Nov 14	0:48	♅	℞
4		16	9:33	♃	℞
5		23	0:33	♇	℞
4		Dec 27	14:54	♆	D
3	1706	Jan 14	9:21	♄	D
4		17	0:10	☿	℞
3		Feb 6	23:15	☿	D
2		Mar 16	8:24	♃	D
1		Apr 12	2:03	♅	D
0		30	23:49	♇	D
1		May 14	9:57	☿	℞
0		Jun 7	6:44	☿	D
1		Jul 25	11:45	♆	℞
2		Sep 13	2:09	☿	℞
3		16	4:52	♄	℞
2		Oct 4	22:56	☿	D
3		18	1:06	♂	℞
4		Nov 19	0:41	♅	℞
5		25	4:42	♇	℞
6		Dec 17	8:20	♃	℞
5		30	4:43	♂	D
4		30	4:49	♆	D
5		31	21:20	☿	℞
6	1707	Jan 8	15:20	♀	℞
5		21	6:03	☿	D
4		28	9:09	♄	D
3		Feb 18	19:44	♀	D
2		Apr 17	0:51	♅	D
1		17	21:16	♃	D
2		25	1:33	☿	℞
1		May 2	22:33	♇	D
0		18	21:35	☿	D
1		Jul 28	1:17	♆	℞
2		Aug 26	21:07	☿	℞
1		Sep 18	13:30	☿	D
2		30	18:43	♄	℞
3		Nov 24	0:36	♅	℞
4		27	7:32	♇	℞
5		Dec 15	19:06	☿	℞
4	1708	Jan 1	16:15	♆	D
3		4	17:52	☿	D
4		16	11:41	♃	℞
3		Feb 11	14:26	♄	D
4		Apr 5	7:26	☿	℞
3		21	1:05	♅	D
2		29	0:58	☿	D
1		May 3	23:37	♇	D
0		18	7:46	♃	D
1		Jul 29	13:32	♆	℞
2		Aug 8	8:60	☿	℞
3		10	6:11	♀	℞
2		31	19:26	☿	D
1		Sep 21	23:36	♀	D
2		Oct 14	7:51	♄	℞
3		Nov 25	18:32	♂	℞
4		28	1:15	♅	℞
5		28	12:31	♇	℞
6		28	15:40	☿	℞
5		Dec 18	9:54	☿	D
4	1709	Jan 3	4:60	♆	D
3		Feb 12	5:12	♂	D
4		14	18:21	♃	℞
3		24	23:16	♄	D
4		Mar 18	8:33	☿	℞
3		Apr 10	17:49	☿	D
2		26	1:18	♅	D
1		May 6	1:46	♇	D
0		Jun 18	6:29	♃	D
1		Jul 21	12:57	☿	℞
2		Aug 1	3:36	♆	℞
1		14	12:22	☿	D
2		Oct 28	18:31	♄	℞
3		Nov 12	9:34	☿	℞
4		30	15:55	♇	℞
3		Dec 2	5:20	☿	D
4		3	0:43	♅	℞
3	1710	Jan 5	15:40	♆	D
4		Mar 1	2:32	☿	℞
3		11	9:54	♄	D
4		18	8:34	♃	℞
5		21	0:50	♀	℞
4		23	22:22	☿	D
3		May 1	2:45	♅	D
2		2	11:19	♀	D
1		8	1:42	♇	D
2		Jul 3	7:14	☿	℞
1		19	16:53	♃	D
0		27	11:58	☿	D
1		Aug 3	15:33	♆	℞
2		Oct 26	23:43	☿	℞
3		Nov 12	0:33	♄	℞
2		16	3:09	☿	D
3		Dec 2	19:00	♇	℞
4		8	1:08	♅	℞
5		30	13:33	♂	℞
4	1711	Jan 8	3:10	♆	D
5		Feb 12	9:10	☿	℞
4		Mar 6	12:12	☿	D
3		21	9:16	♂	D
2		25	22:15	♄	D
3		Apr 20	20:29	♃	℞
2		May 6	4:48	♅	D
1		10	4:39	♇	D
2		Jun 14	13:08	☿	℞
1		Jul 8	16:28	☿	D
2		Aug 6	4:43	♆	℞
1		21	3:49	♃	D
2		Oct 10	9:06	☿	℞
3		23	16:54	♀	℞
2		31	1:46	☿	D
3		Nov 25	23:13	♄	℞
2		Dec 3	21:36	♀	D
3		5	0:51	♇	℞
4		12	23:59	♅	℞
3	1712	Jan 10	13:48	♆	D
4		27	0:08	☿	℞
3		Feb 17	9:15	☿	D
2		Apr 8	9:37	♄	D
1		May 10	7:14	♅	D
0		11	4:57	♇	D
1		25	6:47	☿	℞
2		25	19:13	♃	℞
1		Jun 18	6:14	☿	D
2		Aug 7	16:07	♆	℞
3		Sep 22	13:10	☿	℞
2		23	10:12	♃	D
1		Oct 13	23:14	☿	D
2		Dec 6	6:31	♇	℞
3		8	14:09	♄	℞
4		17	0:29	♅	℞
5	1713	Jan 9	19:55	☿	℞
4		12	0:41	♆	D
3		30	12:30	☿	D
4		Feb 2	19:40	♂	℞
3		Apr 22	17:58	♄	D
2		24	12:31	♂	D
3		May 5	19:52	☿	℞
2		13	8:08	♇	D
1		15	11:11	♅	D
2		29	15:49	♀	℞
1		29	16:21	☿	D
2		Jul 2	12:48	♃	℞
1		11	18:13	♀	D
2		Aug 10	6:37	♆	℞
3		Sep 5	11:34	☿	℞
2		27	17:04	☿	D
1		Oct 29	8:56	♃	D
2		Dec 8	15:40	♇	℞
3		21	22:11	♄	℞
4		21	23:09	♅	℞
5		24	17:42	☿	℞
4	1714	Jan 13	21:21	☿	D
3		14	11:34	♆	D
4		Apr 16	16:44	☿	℞
3		May 6	20:22	♄	D
2		10	11:36	☿	D
1		15	12:32	♇	D
0		20	13:59	♅	D
1		Aug 9	18:43	♃	℞
2		12	19:07	♆	℞
3		19	3:53	☿	℞
2		Sep 11	4:17	☿	D
1		Dec 5	11:38	♃	D
2		8	15:15	☿	℞
3		11	0:19	♇	℞
4		27	0:11	♅	℞
3		28	11:09	☿	D
4	1715	Jan 4	0:14	♄	℞
5		6	4:45	♀	℞
4		16	22:54	♆	D
3		Feb 16	8:33	♀	D
4		Mar 15	21:45	♂	℞
5		29	6:26	☿	℞
4		Apr 21	21:13	☿	D
3		May 17	18:36	♇	D
2		20	16:12	♄	D
1		25	18:26	♅	D
0		Jun 1	6:47	♂	D
1		Aug 1	12:56	☿	℞
2		15	9:23	♆	℞
1		25	5:12	☿	D
2		Sep 15	18:34	♃	℞
3		Nov 22	10:47	☿	℞
2		Dec 12	4:56	☿	D
3		13	11:05	♇	℞
4		31	23:11	♅	℞
3	1716	Jan 11	9:42	♃	D
4		16	17:57	♄	℞
3		19	12:30	♆	D
4		Mar 10	14:59	☿	℞
3		Apr 2	19:33	☿	D
2		May 19	1:43	♇	D
1		29	20:54	♅	D
0		Jun 2	6:09	♄	D
1		Jul 13	12:48	☿	℞
0		Aug 6	15:29	☿	D
1		7	20:25	♀	℞
2		16	22:43	♆	℞
1		Sep 19	14:45	♀	D
2		Oct 19	9:55	♃	℞
3		Nov 5	3:05	☿	℞
2		25	1:37	☿	D
3		Dec 14	21:03	♇	℞
4	1717	Jan 5	0:33	♅	℞
3		20	23:58	♆	D
4		28	5:01	♄	℞
3		Feb 15	1:37	♃	D
4		21	15:04	☿	℞
3		Mar 16	4:03	☿	D
4		May 9	23:30	♂	℞
3		21	7:49	♇	D
2		Jun 4	1:38	♅	D
1		15	13:34	♄	D
2		25	1:38	☿	℞
1		Jul 17	15:10	♂	D
0		19	7:03	☿	D
1		Aug 19	11:55	♆	℞
2		Oct 19	15:13	☿	℞
1		Nov 8	23:53	☿	D
2		20	20:20	♃	℞
3		Dec 17	8:50	♇	℞
4	1718	Jan 9	23:24	♅	℞
3		23	13:21	♆	D
4		Feb 5	1:52	☿	℞
5		9	10:10	♄	℞
4		26	20:56	☿	D
5		Mar 18	16:32	♀	℞
4		21	0:03	♃	D
3		Apr 30	1:55	♀	D
2		May 23	16:39	♇	D
3		Jun 6	2:18	☿	℞
2		9	3:51	♅	D
1		28	13:59	♄	D
0		30	3:47	☿	D
1		Aug 22	2:11	♆	℞
2		Oct 2	22:36	☿	℞
1		23	22:09	☿	D
2		Dec 19	20:30	♇	℞
3		21	13:54	♃	℞
4	1719	Jan 15	0:37	♅	℞
5		19	19:18	☿	℞
4		26	0:58	♆	D
3		Feb 9	20:56	☿	D
4		21	10:50	♄	℞
3		Apr 22	7:49	♃	D
4		May 17	16:53	☿	℞
3		25	23:26	♇	D
2		Jun 10	14:13	☿	D
1		14	8:36	♅	D
0		Jul 11	8:56	♄	D
1		28	9:17	♂	℞
2		Aug 24	13:43	♆	℞
3		Sep 16	0:30	☿	℞
2		26	8:55	♂	D
1		Oct 7	18:23	☿	D
2		21	5:40	♀	℞
1		Dec 1	11:22	♀	D
2		22	7:35	♇	℞
3	1720	Jan 3	16:08	☿	℞
4		19	22:57	♅	℞
5		20	16:07	♃	℞
4		24	2:51	☿	D
3		28	13:26	♆	D
4		Mar 4	9:45	♄	℞
5		Apr 27	7:20	☿	℞
4		May 21	3:42	☿	D

Planetary Stations in Longitude 1700–2050

3		22	14:52	♃	D
2		27	9:56	♇	D
1		Jun 18	10:41	♅	D
0		Jul 22	20:29	♄	D
1		Aug 26	2:42	♆	R
2		28	20:15	☿	R
1		Sep 20	9:56	☿	D
2		Dec 17	13:58	☿	R
3		23	21:14	♇	R
2	1721	Jan 6	13:52	☿	D
3		23	23:18	♅	R
2		30	0:35	♆	D
3		Feb 19	4:16	♃	R
4		Mar 16	4:30	♄	R
5		Apr 8	10:44	☿	R
4		May 2	4:42	☿	D
5		27	8:27	♀	R
4		29	19:13	♇	D
3		Jun 22	16:08	♃	D
2		23	15:08	♅	D
1		Jul 9	11:03	♀	D
0		Aug 4	1:37	♄	D
1		11	9:17	☿	R
2		28	13:39	♆	R
1		Sep 3	17:23	☿	D
2		29	10:20	♂	R
3		Dec 1	10:53	☿	R
2		8	5:38	♂	D
1		21	5:18	☿	D
2		26	10:03	♇	R
3	1722	Jan 28	20:51	♅	R
2		Feb 1	11:28	♆	D
3		Mar 21	8:58	☿	R
4		22	22:15	♃	R
5		27	22:19	♄	R
4		Apr 13	19:43	☿	D
3		Jun 1	6:19	♇	D
2		28	17:30	♅	D
1		Jul 24	3:29	♃	D
2		24	14:46	☿	R
1		Aug 16	5:15	♄	D
0		17	12:29	☿	D
1		31	3:27	♆	R
2		Nov 15	5:19	☿	R
1		Dec 5	0:23	☿	D
2		29	1:56	♇	R
3	1723	Jan 3	17:47	♀	R
4		Feb 2	19:38	♅	R
3		3	22:04	♆	D
2		13	21:01	♀	D
3		Mar 4	0:38	☿	R
2		26	22:53	☿	D
3		Apr 8	16:57	♄	R
4		25	20:45	♃	R
3		Jun 3	19:15	♇	D
2		Jul 3	21:24	♅	D
3		6	10:42	☿	R
2		30	14:59	☿	D
1		Aug 25	22:46	♃	D
0		28	4:10	♄	D
1		Sep 2	14:34	♆	R
2		Oct 29	20:01	☿	R
3		Nov 12	6:56	♂	R
2		18	21:60	☿	D
3		Dec 31	16:44	♇	R
2	1724	Jan 28	1:02	♂	D
1		Feb 6	9:01	♆	D
2		7	15:53	♅	R
3		15	5:36	☿	R
2		Mar 8	11:22	☿	D
3		Apr 19	13:43	♄	R
4		May 30	23:53	♃	R
3		Jun 5	9:24	♇	D
4		16	18:17	☿	R
3		Jul 8	0:14	♅	D

2		10	22:25	☿	D
3		Aug 5	11:19	♀	R
4		Sep 4	4:06	♆	R
3		8	0:53	♄	D
2		17	6:06	♀	D
1		28	9:10	♃	D
2		Oct 12	6:05	☿	R
1		Nov 1	20:36	☿	D
2	1725	Jan 2	9:44	♇	R
3		28	19:37	☿	R
2		Feb 7	21:43	♆	D
3		11	12:22	♅	R
2		19	7:17	☿	D
3		May 1	13:48	♄	R
4		28	13:28	☿	R
3		Jun 8	0:49	♇	D
2		21	13:34	☿	D
3		Jul 7	22:28	♃	R
2		13	2:56	♅	D
3		Sep 6	17:07	♆	R
2		19	20:07	♄	D
3		25	10:57	☿	R
2		Oct 16	18:18	☿	D
1		Nov 3	14:33	♃	D
2		Dec 17	6:29	♂	R
3	1726	Jan 5	2:30	♇	R
4		12	14:54	☿	R
3		Feb 2	9:39	☿	D
2		10	8:21	♆	D
3		16	7:50	♅	R
2		Mar 7	10:25	♂	D
3		16	8:49	♀	R
2		Apr 27	16:52	♀	D
3		May 9	2:40	☿	R
4		13	15:44	♄	R
3		Jun 1	23:03	☿	D
2		10	15:11	♇	D
1		Jul 18	5:08	♅	D
2		Aug 15	0:30	♃	R
3		Sep 8	10:23	☿	R
4		9	6:42	♆	R
3		30	12:49	☿	D
2		Oct 1	15:42	♄	D
1		Dec 10	15:20	♃	D
2		27	12:34	☿	R
3	1727	Jan 7	21:30	♇	R
2		16	17:51	☿	D
1		Feb 12	21:25	♆	D
2		21	2:34	♅	R
3		Apr 19	21:27	☿	R
2		May 13	16:43	☿	D
3		26	0:05	♄	R
2		Jun 13	8:40	♇	D
1		Jul 23	5:22	♅	D
2		Aug 22	3:43	☿	R
3		Sep 11	21:38	♆	R
2		14	1:17	☿	D
3		20	15:25	♃	R
2		Oct 13	15:07	♄	D
3		18	18:15	♀	R
2		Nov 29	1:06	♀	D
3		Dec 11	10:16	☿	R
2		31	7:03	☿	D
3	1728	Jan 10	15:01	♇	R
2		16	9:51	♃	D
3		20	18:18	♂	R
2		Feb 15	9:37	♆	D
3		25	21:27	♅	R
4		Mar 31	8:23	☿	R
3		Apr 10	19:43	♂	D
2		24	0:22	☿	D
3		Jun 6	14:59	♄	R
2		14	23:47	♇	D
1		Jul 27	5:55	♅	D
2		Aug 3	13:47	☿	R

1		27	4:05	☿	D
2		Sep 13	9:15	♆	R
3		Oct 24	0:56	♃	R
2		24	14:51	♄	D
3		Nov 24	6:09	☿	R
2		Dec 14	0:15	☿	D
3	1729	Jan 12	9:25	♇	R
2		Feb 16	22:42	♆	D
1		19	20:16	♃	D
2		Mar 1	15:16	♅	R
3		13	14:23	☿	R
2		Apr 5	20:44	☿	D
3		May 25	0:36	♀	R
2		Jun 17	18:03	♇	D
3		19	12:08	♄	R
2		Jul 7	3:21	♀	D
3		16	15:01	☿	R
2		Aug 1	3:41	♅	D
1		9	16:48	☿	D
2		Sep 15	22:58	♆	R
1		Nov 5	18:53	♄	D
2		7	23:02	☿	R
3		25	2:51	♃	R
2		27	20:32	☿	D
3	1730	Jan 15	5:36	♇	R
2		Feb 19	10:28	♆	D
3		24	12:28	☿	R
4		26	18:23	♂	R
5		Mar 6	9:47	♅	R
4		19	3:49	☿	D
3		25	11:40	♃	D
2		May 16	22:20	♂	D
1		Jun 20	10:21	♇	D
2		28	5:47	☿	R
3		Jul 2	17:08	♄	R
2		22	11:08	☿	D
1		Aug 6	2:30	♅	D
2		Sep 18	10:26	♆	R
3		Oct 22	11:52	☿	R
2		Nov 11	18:34	☿	D
1		18	4:11	♄	D
2		Dec 25	19:29	♃	R
3	1731	Jan 1	6:21	♀	R
4		17	23:43	♇	R
5		Feb 7	21:52	☿	R
4		11	8:54	♀	D
3		21	22:15	♆	D
2		Mar 1	19:39	☿	D
3		11	2:50	♅	R
2		Apr 26	16:55	♃	D
3		Jun 9	8:25	☿	R
2		23	5:11	♇	D
1		Jul 3	10:27	☿	D
2		16	4:50	♄	R
1		Aug 10	22:44	♅	D
2		Sep 20	23:16	♆	R
3		Oct 5	20:00	☿	R
2		26	16:60	☿	D
1		Nov 30	19:23	♄	D
2	1732	Jan 20	19:45	♇	R
3		22	14:27	☿	R
4		24	22:25	♃	R
3		Feb 12	18:42	☿	D
2		24	9:50	♆	D
3		Mar 14	20:24	♅	R
4		Apr 15	11:26	♂	R
5		May 19	23:48	☿	R
4		26	22:51	♃	D
3		Jun 12	21:50	☿	D
2		25	0:11	♇	D
1		27	8:20	♂	D
2		Jul 28	23:28	♄	R
3		Aug 3	2:40	♀	R
2		14	20:11	♅	D
1		Sep 14	21:44	♀	D

2		17	22:39	☿	R
3		22	8:59	♆	R
2		Oct 9	13:43	☿	D
1		Dec 12	18:47	♄	D
2	1733	Jan 5	10:58	☿	R
3		22	14:40	♇	R
2		25	23:44	☿	D
3		Feb 23	12:27	♃	R
2		25	20:59	♆	D
3		Mar 19	12:16	♅	R
4		Apr 30	13:23	☿	R
3		May 24	9:54	☿	D
2		Jun 27	0:25	♃	D
1		27	19:54	♇	D
2		Aug 12	2:00	♄	R
1		19	15:21	♅	D
2		31	19:18	☿	R
1		Sep 23	6:13	☿	D
2		24	21:14	♆	R
3		Dec 20	8:52	☿	R
2		26	0:28	♄	D
1	1734	Jan 9	9:59	☿	D
2		25	11:50	♇	R
1		Feb 28	9:21	♆	D
2		Mar 14	1:15	♀	R
3		24	4:43	♅	R
4		27	14:22	♃	R
5		Apr 11	14:26	☿	R
4		25	8:13	♀	D
3		May 5	8:44	☿	D
4		Jun 26	2:33	♂	R
3		30	16:27	♇	D
2		Jul 28	17:07	♃	D
3		Aug 14	9:33	☿	R
2		24	11:31	♅	D
3		26	11:14	♄	R
2		26	11:24	♂	D
1		Sep 6	15:05	☿	D
2		27	8:38	♆	R
3		Dec 4	6:06	☿	R
2		24	0:52	☿	D
1	1735	Jan 8	12:10	♄	D
2		28	6:57	♇	R
1		Mar 2	19:36	♆	D
2		24	9:45	☿	R
3		28	18:46	♅	R
2		Apr 16	21:58	☿	D
3		30	17:16	♃	R
2		Jul 3	14:09	♇	D
3		27	16:23	☿	R
2		Aug 20	12:16	☿	D
1		29	5:31	♅	D
0		30	15:21	♃	D
1		Sep 10	0:16	♄	R
2		29	20:47	♆	R
3		Oct 16	6:13	♀	R
4		Nov 18	0:58	☿	R
3		26	14:31	♀	D
2		Dec 7	19:32	☿	D
1	1736	Jan 22	8:39	♄	D
2		31	4:16	♇	R
1		Mar 4	8:51	♆	D
2		5	22:60	☿	R
3		28	23:35	☿	D
2		Apr 1	10:03	♅	R
3		Jun 5	5:06	♃	R
2		Jul 5	12:55	♇	D
3		8	13:45	☿	R
2		Aug 1	17:32	☿	D
1		Sep 1	23:59	♅	D
2		7	20:43	♂	R
3		23	14:26	♄	R
4		Oct 1	10:17	♆	R
3		3	9:28	♃	D
4		31	16:10	☿	R

3		Nov 12	13:19	♂	D
2		20	16:51	☿	D
3	1737	Feb 2	0:17	♇	R
2		4	12:02	♄	D
3		17	2:15	☿	R
2		Mar 6	20:33	♆	D
1		11	10:38	☿	D
2		Apr 5	22:16	♅	R
3		May 22	16:45	♀	R
4		Jun 19	23:01	☿	R
3		Jul 4	19:25	♀	D
2		8	10:05	♇	D
3		13	5:45	♃	R
2		14	3:50	☿	D
1		Sep 6	16:34	♅	D
2		Oct 3	21:51	♆	R
3		8	4:35	♄	R
4		15	2:56	☿	R
3		Nov 4	15:22	☿	D
2		8	16:30	♃	D
3	1738	Jan 31	15:14	☿	R
4		Feb 4	21:54	♇	R
3		18	20:13	♄	D
2		22	5:27	☿	D
1		Mar 9	9:10	♆	D
2		Apr 10	12:34	♅	R
3		May 31	20:04	☿	R
2		Jun 24	20:42	☿	D
1		Jul 11	10:19	♇	D
2		Aug 20	4:09	♃	R
1		Sep 11	9:22	♅	D
2		28	8:41	☿	R
3		Oct 6	11:58	♆	R
2		19	13:17	☿	D
3		22	16:58	♄	R
4		27	16:18	♂	R
3		Dec 15	18:51	♃	D
4		29	19:10	♀	R
3	1739	Jan 10	6:11	♂	D
4		15	9:59	☿	R
3		Feb 5	7:00	☿	D
4		7	18:40	♇	R
3		8	20:42	♀	D
2		Mar 5	7:24	♄	D
1		11	20:49	♆	D
2		Apr 14	23:12	♅	R
3		May 12	9:42	☿	R
2		Jun 5	6:11	☿	D
1		Jul 14	8:04	♇	D
2		Sep 11	9:06	☿	R
1		15	23:50	♅	D
2		25	14:53	♃	R
1		Oct 3	8:28	☿	D
2		8	23:47	♆	R
3		Nov 6	1:49	♄	R
4		Dec 30	7:27	☿	R
3	1740	Jan 19	14:31	☿	D
2		21	11:03	♃	D
3		Feb 10	15:13	♇	R
2		Mar 13	8:42	♆	D
1		18	20:17	♄	D
2		Apr 18	12:24	♅	R
3		22	2:36	☿	R
2		May 15	22:16	☿	D
1		Jul 16	7:32	♇	D
2		31	18:24	♀	R
3		Aug 24	3:19	☿	R
2		Sep 12	14:05	♀	D
1		15	22:06	☿	D
0		19	14:43	♅	D
1		Oct 10	12:46	♆	R
2		28	14:54	♃	R
3		Nov 19	4:27	♄	R
4		Dec 3	18:05	♂	R
5		13	5:11	☿	R

Planetary Stations in Longitude 1700–2050

4	1741	Jan 2	2:59	☿	D	
5		Feb 12	13:04	♇	℞	
4		20	21:05	♂	D	
3		24	14:28	♃	D	
2		Mar 15	20:30	♆	D	
1		Apr 2	8:22	♄	D	
2		3	10:43	☿	℞	
3		22	21:53	♅	℞	
2		27	3:39	☿	D	
1		Jul 19	5:12	♇	D	
2		Aug 6	14:23	☿	℞	
1		30	2:39	☿	D	
0		Sep 24	3:18	♅	D	
1		Oct 12	22:46	♆	℞	
2		Nov 27	1:26	☿	℞	
3		29	13:45	♃	℞	
4		Dec 3	0:08	♄	℞	
3		16	19:35	☿	D	
4	1742	Feb 15	8:39	♇	℞	
5		Mar 11	17:22	♀	℞	
6		16	14:07	☿	℞	
5		18	7:38	♆	D	
4		30	3:27	♃	D	
3		Apr 8	22:05	☿	D	
2		16	17:38	♄	D	
1		22	23:27	♀	D	
2		27	10:13	♅	℞	
3		Jul 19	17:04	☿	℞	
2		22	4:27	♇	D	
1		Aug 12	17:41	☿	D	
0		Sep 28	15:59	♅	D	
1		Oct 15	10:51	♆	℞	
2		Nov 10	18:52	☿	℞	
1		30	15:24	☿	D	
2		Dec 16	12:39	♄	℞	
3		30	1:23	♃	℞	
4	1743	Jan 7	6:02	♂	℞	
5		Feb 18	5:02	♇	℞	
6		27	10:03	☿	℞	
5		Mar 20	19:41	♆	D	
4		22	3:47	☿	D	
3		29	5:37	♂	D	
2		Apr 30	22:10	♄	D	
1		May 1	3:29	♃	D	
2		1	19:04	♅	℞	
3		Jul 1	9:45	☿	℞	
2		25	2:09	♇	D	
1		25	14:51	☿	D	
0		Oct 3	2:55	♅	D	
1		13	18:03	♀	℞	
2		17	21:19	♆	℞	
3		25	8:27	☿	℞	
2		Nov 14	13:20	☿	D	
1		24	3:42	♀	D	
2		Dec 29	17:23	♄	℞	
3	1744	Jan 29	4:37	♃	℞	
4		Feb 10	17:60	☿	℞	
5		20	23:26	♇	℞	
4		Mar 3	18:35	☿	D	
3		22	5:38	♆	D	
4		May 5	6:17	♅	℞	
3		13	22:01	♄	D	
2		31	8:53	♃	D	
3		Jun 11	14:12	☿	℞	
2		Jul 5	16:53	☿	D	
1		27	0:24	♇	D	
0		Oct 6	13:37	♅	D	
1		7	17:17	☿	℞	
2		19	8:08	♆	℞	
1		28	11:52	☿	D	
2	1745	Jan 10	13:19	♄	℞	
3		24	9:44	☿	℞	
4		Feb 11	5:44	♂	℞	
3		14	16:38	☿	D	
4		22	19:51	♇	℞	

5		27	21:00	♃	℞	
4		Mar 24	19:24	♆	D	
3		May 2	12:34	♂	D	
4		9	15:06	♅	℞	
5		20	8:49	♀	℞	
6		23	6:37	☿	℞	
5		27	17:02	♄	D	
4		Jun 16	5:25	☿	D	
3		Jul 1	10:06	♃	D	
2		2	10:54	♀	D	
1		29	21:50	♇	D	
2		Sep 20	20:42	☿	℞	
1		Oct 10	23:22	♅	D	
0		12	9:04	☿	D	
1		21	20:07	♆	℞	
2	1746	Jan 8	5:56	☿	℞	
3		23	4:22	♄	℞	
2		28	20:44	☿	D	
3		Feb 25	12:06	♇	℞	
2		Mar 27	7:11	♆	D	
3		Apr 1	1:39	♃	℞	
4		May 3	19:45	☿	℞	
5		14	1:27	♅	℞	
4		27	16:16	☿	D	
3		Jun 10	4:11	♄	D	
2		Aug 1	19:59	♇	D	
1		2	3:35	♃	D	
2		Sep 3	18:16	☿	℞	
1		26	2:19	☿	D	
0		Oct 15	8:35	♅	D	
1		24	6:44	♆	℞	
2		Dec 23	3:48	☿	℞	
3		27	8:31	♀	℞	
2	1747	Jan 12	6:13	☿	D	
3		Feb 4	14:10	♄	℞	
2		6	8:57	♀	D	
3		28	6:44	♇	℞	
4		Mar 26	13:32	♂	℞	
3		29	19:43	♆	D	
4		Apr 14	18:35	☿	℞	
5		May 5	12:00	♃	℞	
4		8	13:10	☿	D	
5		18	9:53	♅	℞	
4		Jun 10	13:59	♂	D	
3		23	6:41	♄	D	
2		Aug 4	17:41	♇	D	
3		17	9:39	☿	℞	
2		Sep 4	6:30	♃	D	
1		9	12:28	☿	D	
0		Oct 19	17:10	♅	D	
1		26	20:03	♆	℞	
2		Dec 7	1:12	☿	℞	
1		26	20:30	☿	D	
2	1748	Feb 16	16:25	♄	℞	
3		Mar 1	23:01	♇	℞	
4		26	10:54	☿	℞	
3		31	8:05	♆	D	
2		Apr 19	0:30	☿	D	
3		May 21	19:49	♅	℞	
4		Jun 10	5:34	♃	℞	
3		Jul 5	4:36	♄	D	
4		29	9:45	♀	℞	
5		29	17:41	☿	℞	
4		Aug 6	13:29	♇	D	
3		22	11:38	☿	D	
2		Sep 10	6:31	♀	D	
1		Oct 8	3:10	♃	D	
0		23	1:36	♅	D	
1		28	7:05	♆	℞	
2		Nov 19	20:26	☿	℞	
1		Dec 9	14:43	☿	D	
2	1749	Feb 27	15:23	♄	℞	
3		Mar 4	15:55	♇	℞	
4		8	21:36	☿	℞	
3		Apr 1	0:25	☿	D	

2		2	20:43	♆	D	
3		May 25	18:15	♂	℞	
4		26	3:38	♅	℞	
5		Jul 11	16:23	☿	℞	
4		17	20:25	♄	D	
5		18	8:04	♃	℞	
4		30	16:31	♂	D	
3		Aug 4	19:37	☿	D	
2		9	12:32	♇	D	
1		Oct 27	9:07	♅	D	
2		30	19:29	♆	℞	
3		Nov 3	12:12	☿	℞	
2		13	14:43	♃	D	
1		23	11:42	☿	D	
2	1750	Feb 19	23:10	☿	℞	
3		Mar 7	8:09	♇	℞	
4		9	9:11	♀	℞	
5		11	11:13	♄	℞	
4		14	10:03	☿	D	
3		Apr 5	8:60	♆	D	
2		20	14:34	♀	D	
3		May 30	13:04	♅	℞	
4		Jun 23	3:36	☿	℞	
3		Jul 17	8:52	☿	D	
2		30	5:48	♄	D	
1		Aug 12	8:03	♇	D	
2		25	8:07	♃	℞	
3		Oct 17	23:43	☿	℞	
2		31	16:58	♅	D	
3		Nov 2	5:47	♆	℞	
2		7	10:07	☿	D	
1		Dec 20	19:53	♃	D	
2	1751	Feb 3	11:02	☿	℞	
1		25	3:49	☿	D	
2		Mar 9	23:25	♇	℞	
3		23	6:49	♄	℞	
2		Apr 7	19:44	♆	D	
3		Jun 3	20:22	♅	℞	
4		4	2:38	☿	℞	
3		28	3:43	☿	D	
2		Aug 11	10:55	♄	D	
3		14	3:06	♂	℞	
2		15	5:01	♇	D	
3		Sep 30	11:22	♃	℞	
4		Oct 1	6:23	☿	℞	
5		11	5:38	♀	℞	
4		14	15:07	♂	D	
3		22	8:14	☿	D	
4		Nov 4	18:06	♆	℞	
3		4	23:35	♅	D	
2		21	16:32	♀	D	
3	1752	Jan 18	5:08	☿	℞	
2		26	8:09	♃	D	
1		Feb 8	4:34	☿	D	
2		Mar 11	15:28	♇	℞	
3		Apr 3	1:31	♄	℞	
2		9	7:33	♆	D	
3		May 14	16:44	☿	℞	
4		Jun 7	5:01	♅	℞	
3		7	13:33	☿	D	
2		Aug 16	23:47	♇	D	
1		22	10:13	♄	D	
2		Sep 13	7:37	☿	℞	
1		Oct 5	4:01	☿	D	
2		Nov 2	6:31	♃	℞	
3		6	4:03	♆	℞	
2		8	6:30	♅	D	
3	1753	Jan 1	2:16	☿	℞	
2		21	11:15	☿	D	
1		Mar 1	10:57	♃	D	
2		14	5:44	♇	℞	
1		Apr 11	17:30	♆	D	
2		14	19:47	♄	℞	
3		25	8:03	☿	℞	
4		May 18	1:31	♀	℞	

3		19	4:08	☿	D	
4		Jun 11	12:18	♅	℞	
3		30	2:43	♀	D	
2		Aug 19	20:10	♇	D	
3		27	2:43	☿	℞	
2		Sep 3	7:48	♄	D	
1		18	18:44	☿	D	
2		Oct 10	8:46	♂	℞	
3		Nov 8	14:10	♆	℞	
2		12	12:39	♅	D	
3		Dec 3	21:55	♃	℞	
4		16	0:03	☿	℞	
3		21	3:04	♂	D	
2	1754	Jan 4	22:58	☿	D	
3		Mar 16	20:07	♇	℞	
2		Apr 3	17:14	♃	D	
3		6	13:31	☿	℞	
2		14	6:44	♆	D	
3		26	18:06	♄	℞	
2		30	7:07	☿	D	
3		Jun 15	20:47	♅	℞	
4		Aug 9	14:46	☿	℞	
3		22	13:08	♇	D	
2		Sep 2	0:52	☿	D	
1		15	5:14	♄	D	
2		Nov 11	1:32	♆	℞	
1		16	17:59	♅	D	
2		29	20:39	☿	℞	
1		Dec 19	14:56	☿	D	
2		24	21:55	♀	℞	
3	1755	Jan 3	8:25	♃	℞	
2		Feb 3	21:40	♀	D	
3		Mar 19	7:48	♇	℞	
4		19	14:14	☿	℞	
3		Apr 11	23:41	☿	D	
2		16	17:35	♆	D	
1		May 5	15:56	♃	D	
2		8	19:34	♄	℞	
3		Jun 20	3:56	♅	℞	
4		Jul 22	18:58	☿	℞	
3		Aug 15	18:09	☿	D	
2		25	7:16	♇	D	
1		Sep 27	0:37	♄	D	
2		Nov 13	11:35	♆	℞	
3		13	14:40	☿	℞	
4		20	17:41	♂	℞	
3		20	23:49	♅	D	
2		Dec 3	10:21	☿	D	
3	1756	Feb 2	9:45	♃	℞	
2		6	10:41	♂	D	
3		Mar 1	7:55	☿	℞	
4		20	21:25	♇	℞	
3		24	4:02	☿	D	
2		Apr 18	6:01	♆	D	
3		May 20	2:32	♄	℞	
2		Jun 4	17:14	♃	D	
3		23	12:47	♅	℞	
4		Jul 3	13:28	☿	℞	
5		27	0:55	♀	℞	
4		27	18:09	☿	D	
3		Aug 26	23:26	♇	D	
2		Sep 7	22:54	♀	D	
1		Oct 7	21:08	♄	D	
2		27	4:56	☿	℞	
3		Nov 15	0:00	♆	℞	
2		16	8:09	☿	D	
1		24	4:04	♅	D	
2	1757	Feb 12	14:19	☿	℞	
3		Mar 4	6:12	♃	℞	
2		6	17:44	☿	D	
3		23	7:16	♇	℞	
2		Apr 20	18:34	♆	D	
3		Jun 1	14:00	♄	℞	
4		14	19:34	☿	℞	
5		27	20:16	♅	℞	

4		Jul 5	20:17	♃	D	
3		8	23:03	☿	D	
2		Aug 29	14:58	♇	D	
3		Oct 10	14:24	☿	℞	
2		19	19:03	♄	D	
1		31	6:45	☿	D	
2		Nov 17	10:14	♆	℞	
1		28	9:37	♅	D	
2		Dec 24	22:54	♂	℞	
3	1758	Jan 27	5:09	☿	℞	
2		Feb 17	14:38	☿	D	
3		Mar 7	0:24	♀	℞	
2		15	11:26	♂	D	
3		25	18:02	♇	℞	
4		Apr 5	17:49	♃	℞	
3		18	5:17	♀	D	
2		23	7:33	♆	D	
3		May 26	13:23	☿	℞	
4		Jun 14	6:57	♄	℞	
3		19	12:55	☿	D	
4		Jul 2	5:48	♅	℞	
3		Aug 6	16:37	♃	D	
2		Sep 1	6:05	♇	D	
3		23	18:36	☿	℞	
2		Oct 15	4:17	☿	D	
1		31	22:37	♄	D	
2		Nov 19	21:60	♆	℞	
1		Dec 2	13:50	♅	D	
2	1759	Jan 11	0:54	☿	℞	
1		31	17:47	☿	D	
2		Mar 28	3:44	♇	℞	
1		Apr 25	20:18	♆	D	
2		May 7	2:27	☿	℞	
3		10	12:12	♃	℞	
2		30	22:53	☿	D	
3		Jun 27	8:49	♄	℞	
4		Jul 6	13:43	♅	℞	
3		Sep 3	18:28	♇	D	
4		6	17:07	☿	℞	
3		9	0:34	♃	D	
2		28	22:11	☿	D	
3		Oct 8	17:39	♀	℞	
2		Nov 13	5:58	♄	D	
1		19	5:43	♀	D	
2		22	7:55	♆	℞	
1		Dec 6	18:48	♅	D	
2		25	22:41	☿	℞	
1	1760	Jan 15	2:33	☿	D	
2		28	18:36	♂	℞	
3		Mar 29	12:58	♇	℞	
4		Apr 16	23:08	☿	℞	
3		18	15:23	♂	D	
2		27	7:30	♆	D	
1		May 10	18:02	☿	D	
2		Jun 15	12:18	♃	℞	
3		Jul 9	18:16	♄	℞	
4		9	23:54	♅	℞	
5		Aug 19	9:35	☿	℞	
4		Sep 5	9:08	♇	D	
3		11	9:35	☿	D	
2		Oct 13	3:45	♃	D	
3		Nov 23	19:44	♆	℞	
2		24	17:07	♄	D	
3		Dec 8	20:14	☿	℞	
2		9	23:46	♅	D	
1		28	16:15	☿	D	
2	1761	Mar 29	12:26	☿	℞	
3		31	23:02	♇	℞	
2		Apr 22	3:23	☿	D	
1		29	19:40	♆	D	
2		May 15	18:31	♀	℞	
1		Jun 27	19:05	♀	D	
2		Jul 14	8:11	♅	℞	
3		23	9:37	♄	℞	
4		23	19:25	♃	℞	

Planetary Stations in Longitude 1700–2050

5		Aug 1	18:46	☿	℞
4		25	10:44	☿	D
3		Sep 7	21:31	♇	D
2		Nov 18	21:03	♃	D
3		22	15:50	☿	℞
4		26	4:59	♆	℞
3		Dec 7	12:19	♄	D
2		12	9:59	☿	D
1		14	4:41	♅	D
2	1762	Mar 8	8:26	♂	℞
3		11	20:35	☿	℞
4		Apr 3	6:54	♇	℞
3		4	1:24	☿	D
2		May 2	5:27	♆	D
1		25	13:32	♂	D
2		Jul 14	18:47	☿	℞
3		18	18:27	♅	℞
4		Aug 6	8:19	♄	℞
3		7	21:23	☿	D
4		30	13:40	♃	℞
3		Sep 10	11:09	♇	D
4		Nov 6	8:12	☿	℞
3		26	6:36	☿	D
4		28	14:28	♆	℞
3		Dec 18	10:24	♅	D
2		20	14:10	♄	D
3		22	11:21	♀	℞
2		26	0:37	♃	D
1	1763	Feb 1	10:38	♀	D
2		22	20:21	☿	℞
1		Mar 17	9:37	☿	D
2		Apr 5	14:42	♇	℞
1		May 4	17:47	♆	D
2		Jun 26	8:01	☿	℞
1		Jul 20	13:27	☿	D
2		23	3:03	♅	℞
3		Aug 20	13:12	♄	℞
2		Sep 12	21:24	♇	D
3		Oct 5	9:26	♃	℞
4		20	20:27	☿	℞
3		Nov 10	4:50	☿	D
4		Dec 1	1:31	♆	℞
3		22	16:05	♅	D
2	1764	Jan 2	23:15	♄	D
1		31	11:06	♃	D
2		Feb 6	6:56	☿	℞
1		28	2:21	☿	D
2		Apr 6	19:49	♇	℞
3		28	19:02	♂	℞
2		May 6	3:15	♆	D
3		Jun 6	8:59	☿	℞
2		30	10:29	☿	D
1		Jul 8	11:03	♂	D
2		24	15:47	♀	℞
3		26	12:44	♅	℞
4		Sep 2	22:44	♄	℞
3		5	14:50	♀	D
2		14	10:21	♇	D
3		Oct 3	3:56	☿	℞
2		24	3:07	☿	D
3		Nov 6	19:13	♃	℞
4		Dec 2	11:12	♆	℞
3		25	21:58	♅	D
2	1765	Jan 15	16:36	♄	D
3		20	0:17	☿	℞
2		Feb 10	2:16	☿	D
1		Mar 6	5:09	♃	D
2		Apr 9	2:46	♇	℞
1		May 8	14:48	♆	D
2		17	23:34	☿	℞
1		Jun 10	20:59	☿	D
2		Jul 30	22:25	♅	℞
3		Sep 16	5:57	☿	℞
2		16	20:30	♇	D
3		17	10:57	♄	℞

2		Oct 7	23:26	☿	D
3		Dec 4	23:19	♆	℞
4		8	5:06	♃	℞
3		30	4:29	♅	D
4	1766	Jan 3	21:04	☿	℞
3		24	8:03	☿	D
2		29	15:52	♄	D
3		Mar 4	15:21	♀	℞
2		Apr 8	6:55	♃	D
3		11	5:50	♇	℞
2		15	19:23	♀	D
3		28	13:46	☿	℞
2		May 11	3:12	♆	D
1		22	10:09	☿	D
2		Jul 14	9:54	♂	℞
3		Aug 4	7:44	♅	℞
4		30	1:53	☿	℞
3		Sep 12	9:26	♂	D
2		19	5:29	♇	D
1		21	15:10	☿	D
2		Oct 2	1:00	♄	℞
3		Dec 7	9:13	♆	℞
4		18	18:55	☿	℞
3	1767	Jan 3	10:19	♅	D
4		7	10:32	♃	℞
3		7	19:01	☿	D
2		Feb 12	19:58	♄	D
3		Apr 9	16:52	☿	℞
4		13	9:19	♇	℞
3		May 3	10:52	☿	D
2		9	22:41	♃	D
1		13	15:55	♆	D
2		Aug 8	18:22	♅	℞
3		12	15:04	☿	℞
2		Sep 4	22:49	☿	D
1		21	13:44	♇	D
2		Oct 6	6:30	♀	℞
3		16	14:19	♄	℞
2		Nov 16	19:30	♀	D
3		Dec 2	15:54	☿	℞
4		9	20:60	♆	℞
3		22	10:23	☿	D
2	1768	Jan 7	17:33	♅	D
3		Feb 6	15:03	♃	℞
2		27	4:17	♄	D
3		Mar 21	14:47	☿	℞
2		Apr 14	1:40	☿	D
3		14	13:16	♇	℞
2		May 15	4:38	♆	D
1		Jun 9	0:45	♃	D
2		Jul 24	20:44	☿	℞
3		Aug 12	4:28	♅	℞
2		17	18:12	☿	D
3		Sep 20	13:06	♂	℞
2		22	18:59	♇	D
3		Oct 30	0:27	♄	℞
4		Nov 15	10:26	☿	℞
3		27	13:57	♂	D
2		Dec 5	5:26	☿	D
3		11	7:23	♆	℞
2	1769	Jan 10	23:45	♅	D
3		Mar 4	6:03	☿	℞
4		8	15:15	♃	℞
3		12	16:04	♄	D
2		27	4:37	☿	D
3		Apr 16	16:20	♇	℞
4		May 13	11:40	♀	℞
3		17	17:03	♆	D
2		Jun 25	11:44	♀	D
3		Jul 6	16:48	☿	℞
2		10	3:27	♃	D
1		30	21:00	☿	D
2		Aug 16	16:02	♅	℞
1		Sep 25	2:25	♇	D
2		Oct 30	1:13	☿	℞

3		Nov 13	4:03	♄	℞
2		19	2:59	☿	D
3		Dec 13	18:43	♆	℞
2	1770	Jan 15	7:38	♅	D
3		Feb 15	10:48	☿	℞
2		Mar 9	16:57	☿	D
1		27	4:58	♄	D
2		Apr 10	11:57	♃	℞
3		18	21:13	♇	℞
2		May 20	6:43	♆	D
3		Jun 18	0:35	☿	℞
2		Jul 12	4:52	☿	D
1		Aug 11	6:03	♃	D
2		21	3:41	♅	℞
1		Sep 27	7:07	♇	D
2		Oct 13	11:20	☿	℞
1		Nov 3	1:34	☿	D
2		5	19:07	♂	℞
3		27	1:21	♄	℞
4		Dec 16	3:41	♆	℞
5		20	0:29	♀	℞
4	1771	Jan 19	14:30	♅	D
3		20	14:28	♂	D
2		29	23:24	♀	D
3		30	0:40	☿	℞
2		Feb 20	12:41	☿	D
1		Apr 10	15:22	♄	D
2		20	23:20	♇	℞
3		May 15	15:16	♃	℞
2		22	17:29	♆	D
3		29	20:08	☿	℞
2		Jun 22	20:17	☿	D
3		Aug 25	16:32	♅	℞
2		Sep 13	20:10	♃	D
3		26	16:20	☿	℞
2		29	13:31	♇	D
1		Oct 17	23:19	☿	D
2		Dec 10	16:45	♄	℞
3		18	12:31	♆	℞
4	1772	Jan 13	19:54	☿	℞
3		23	23:12	♅	D
2		Feb 3	14:56	☿	D
3		Apr 22	1:54	♇	℞
2		23	21:45	♄	D
3		May 9	9:25	☿	℞
2		24	6:19	♆	D
1		Jun 2	5:47	☿	D
2		20	23:26	♃	℞
3		Jul 22	6:39	♀	℞
4		Aug 29	5:37	♅	℞
3		Sep 3	6:29	♀	D
4		8	15:54	☿	℞
3		30	17:42	♇	D
2		30	17:55	☿	D
1		Oct 18	8:03	♃	D
2		Dec 11	14:08	♂	℞
3		19	22:47	♆	℞
4		23	1:17	♄	℞
5		27	17:32	☿	℞
4	1773	Jan 16	23:03	☿	D
3		27	7:05	♅	D
2		Mar 1	7:13	♂	D
3		Apr 20	3:55	☿	℞
4		24	0:44	♇	℞
3		May 7	22:55	♄	D
2		13	23:15	☿	D
1		26	16:05	♆	D
2		Jul 29	5:43	♃	℞
3		Aug 22	9:23	☿	℞
4		Sep 2	20:11	♅	℞
3		14	6:32	☿	D
2		Oct 3	0:05	♇	D
1		Nov 24	3:48	♃	D
2		Dec 11	15:12	☿	℞
3		22	7:31	♆	℞

2		31	12:09	☿	D
3	1774	Jan 5	1:29	♄	℞
2		31	17:08	♅	D
3		Mar 2	6:20	♀	℞
4		Apr 1	14:21	☿	℞
3		13	9:11	♀	D
2		25	6:28	☿	D
3		26	0:14	♇	℞
2		May 21	19:08	♄	D
1		29	3:53	♆	D
2		Aug 4	19:37	☿	℞
1		28	9:38	☿	D
2		Sep 4	18:32	♃	℞
3		7	10:16	♅	℞
2		Oct 5	4:29	♇	D
3		Nov 25	11:11	☿	℞
2		Dec 15	5:19	☿	D
3		24	18:47	♆	℞
2		31	7:37	♃	D
3	1775	Jan 14	23:58	♂	℞
4		17	18:48	♄	℞
3		Feb 5	2:27	♅	D
4		Mar 14	19:58	☿	℞
3		Apr 6	0:36	♂	D
2		7	2:32	☿	D
3		27	23:09	♇	℞
2		May 31	15:06	♆	D
1		Jun 4	8:33	♄	D
2		Jul 17	21:04	☿	℞
1		Aug 10	22:44	☿	D
2		Sep 12	2:21	♅	℞
3		Oct 3	19:38	♀	℞
2		7	6:48	♇	D
3		10	5:60	♃	℞
4		Nov 9	4:08	☿	℞
3		14	9:40	♀	D
2		29	1:29	☿	D
3		Dec 27	4:20	♆	℞
4	1776	Jan 30	5:12	♄	℞
3		Feb 5	11:13	♃	D
2		9	14:17	♅	D
3		25	17:46	☿	℞
2		Mar 19	9:24	☿	D
3		Apr 28	21:29	♇	℞
2		Jun 2	2:34	♆	D
1		16	15:23	♄	D
2		28	12:08	☿	℞
1		Jul 22	17:28	☿	D
2		Sep 15	17:15	♅	℞
1		Oct 8	9:16	♇	D
2		22	17:06	☿	℞
3		Nov 11	6:54	♃	℞
2		11	23:32	☿	D
3		Dec 28	16:14	♆	℞
4	1777	Feb 8	2:59	☿	℞
5		10	10:13	♄	℞
4		13	1:05	♅	D
5		19	23:11	♂	℞
4		Mar 2	1:08	☿	D
3		10	23:23	♃	D
4		Apr 30	22:34	♇	℞
3		May 10	15:43	♂	D
4		11	4:34	♀	℞
3		Jun 4	14:42	♆	D
4		9	14:54	☿	℞
3		23	4:19	♀	D
2		29	16:35	♄	D
1		Jul 3	17:00	☿	D
2		Sep 20	10:44	♅	℞
3		Oct 6	1:21	☿	℞
2		10	7:53	♇	D
1		26	21:60	☿	D
2		Dec 12	11:19	♃	℞
3		31	2:56	♆	℞
4	1778	Jan 22	19:28	☿	℞

3		Feb 13	0:05	☿	D
2		17	14:29	♅	D
3		22	12:52	♄	℞
2		Apr 12	18:05	♃	D
3		May 2	20:13	♇	℞
4		21	6:22	☿	℞
3		Jun 7	2:54	♆	D
2		14	4:32	☿	D
1		Jul 12	9:30	♄	D
2		Sep 19	4:07	☿	℞
3		25	2:37	♅	℞
2		Oct 10	18:49	☿	D
1		12	8:51	♇	D
2		Dec 17	12:53	♀	℞
3	1779	Jan 2	14:37	♆	℞
4		6	15:56	☿	℞
5		11	16:23	♃	℞
4		27	4:59	☿	D
3		27	11:32	♀	D
2		Feb 22	2:45	♅	D
3		Mar 6	10:18	♄	℞
4		Apr 7	0:17	♂	℞
5		May 1	19:58	☿	℞
6		4	19:08	♇	℞
5		14	8:02	♃	D
4		25	16:27	☿	D
3		Jun 9	16:32	♆	D
2		20	9:31	♂	D
1		Jul 24	20:13	♄	D
2		Sep 2	0:53	☿	℞
1		24	11:25	☿	D
2		29	21:10	♅	℞
1		Oct 14	8:37	♇	D
2		Dec 21	13:51	☿	℞
3	1780	Jan 5	0:04	♆	℞
2		10	15:09	☿	D
3		Feb 10	20:46	♃	℞
2		26	17:14	♅	D
3		Mar 17	5:36	♄	℞
4		Apr 11	20:44	☿	℞
3		May 5	14:59	☿	D
4		5	15:20	♇	℞
3		Jun 11	3:27	♆	D
2		13	7:13	♃	D
3		Jul 19	21:46	♀	℞
2		Aug 5	3:47	♄	D
3		14	15:15	☿	℞
2		31	21:51	♀	D
1		Sep 6	20:25	☿	D
2		Oct 3	14:25	♅	℞
1		15	9:57	♇	D
2		Dec 4	11:06	☿	℞
1		24	5:56	☿	D
2	1781	Jan 6	8:56	♆	℞
1		Mar 2	7:07	♅	D
2		13	4:32	♃	℞
3		24	15:35	☿	℞
4		28	23:54	♄	℞
3		Apr 17	3:58	☿	D
4		May 7	11:40	♇	℞
5		Jun 12	0:33	♂	℞
4		13	16:38	♆	D
3		Jul 14	14:51	♃	D
4		27	22:15	☿	℞
3		Aug 14	4:56	♂	D
2		17	6:20	♄	D
1		20	17:51	☿	D
2		Oct 8	9:51	♅	℞
1		17	9:44	♇	D
2		Nov 18	6:01	☿	℞
1		Dec 8	0:32	☿	D
2	1782	Jan 8	19:26	♆	℞
3		Feb 27	21:54	♀	℞
2		Mar 6	23:04	♅	D
3		7	4:25	☿	℞

Planetary Stations in Longitude 1700–2050

2		30	5:21	☿	D
3		Apr 9	19:19	♄	℞
2		10	23:26	♀	D
3		15	7:25	♃	℞
4		May 9	7:03	♇	℞
3		Jun 16	2:44	♆	D
4		Jul 9	19:50	☿	℞
3		Aug 2	23:32	☿	D
2		15	20:13	♃	D
1		29	5:55	♄	D
2		Oct 13	4:05	♅	℞
1		19	8:16	♇	D
2		Nov 1	21:19	☿	℞
1		21	21:49	☿	D
2	1783	Jan 11	3:21	♆	℞
3		Feb 18	7:29	☿	℞
2		Mar 11	14:38	♅	D
1		12	16:12	☿	D
2		Apr 21	17:48	♄	℞
3		May 11	2:32	♇	℞
4		20	20:35	♃	℞
3		Jun 18	15:13	♆	D
4		21	5:24	☿	℞
3		Jul 15	10:18	☿	D
4		Aug 29	5:02	♂	℞
3		Sep 10	2:23	♄	D
2		18	19:00	♃	D
3		Oct 1	8:43	♀	℞
4		16	8:10	☿	℞
5		18	0:28	♅	℞
4		21	6:29	♇	D
3		31	22:16	♂	D
2		Nov 5	20:20	☿	D
1		12	0:07	♀	D
2	1784	Jan 13	13:28	♆	℞
3		Feb 1	20:20	☿	℞
2		23	10:53	☿	D
1		Mar 15	8:25	♅	D
2		May 2	15:50	♄	℞
3		12	0:04	♇	℞
4		Jun 1	2:46	☿	℞
3		20	2:12	♆	D
2		25	3:28	☿	D
3		26	6:49	♃	℞
2		Sep 20	21:45	♄	D
3		28	14:04	☿	℞
2		Oct 19	18:17	☿	D
3		21	19:56	♅	℞
2		22	1:28	♇	D
1		23	10:35	♃	D
2	1785	Jan 14	22:14	♆	℞
3		15	14:59	☿	℞
2		Feb 5	12:19	☿	D
1		Mar 20	2:04	♅	D
2		May 8	21:15	♀	℞
3		12	16:25	☿	℞
4		13	18:42	♇	℞
5		14	19:54	♄	℞
4		Jun 5	12:57	☿	D
3		20	20:57	♀	D
2		22	13:07	♆	D
3		Aug 3	13:13	♃	℞
4		Sep 11	14:38	☿	℞
3		Oct 2	20:04	♄	D
2		3	13:34	☿	D
3		20	12:08	♂	℞
2		23	23:35	♇	D
3		26	17:16	♅	℞
2		Nov 29	9:55	♃	D
3		Dec 30	12:24	☿	℞
2	1786	Jan 1	20:48	♂	D
3		17	9:20	♆	℞
2		19	19:44	☿	D
1		Mar 24	21:55	♅	D
2		Apr 23	9:02	☿	℞

3		May 15	14:25	♇	℞
2		17	4:48	☿	D
3		27	5:59	♄	℞
2		Jun 25	1:08	♆	D
3		Aug 25	8:58	☿	℞
4		Sep 9	19:36	♃	℞
3		17	3:21	☿	D
2		Oct 14	18:04	♄	D
1		25	19:57	♇	D
2		31	14:10	♅	℞
3		Dec 14	10:08	☿	℞
4		15	0:55	♀	℞
3	1787	Jan 3	8:06	☿	D
2		5	9:21	♃	D
3		19	19:54	♆	℞
2		24	23:14	♀	D
1		Mar 29	17:26	♅	D
2		Apr 4	16:46	☿	℞
1		28	9:45	☿	D
2		May 17	7:41	♇	℞
3		Jun 8	20:49	♄	℞
2		27	13:11	♆	D
3		Aug 7	20:11	☿	℞
2		31	8:11	☿	D
3		Oct 14	21:18	♃	℞
2		26	18:39	♄	D
1		27	17:00	♇	D
2		Nov 5	12:59	♅	℞
3		28	6:26	☿	℞
4		28	21:01	♂	℞
3		Dec 18	0:36	☿	D
4	1788	Jan 22	7:06	♆	℞
3		Feb 10	7:44	♃	D
2		15	9:15	♂	D
3		Mar 16	19:46	☿	℞
2		Apr 2	15:29	♅	D
1		9	3:53	☿	D
2		May 17	23:00	♇	℞
3		Jun 20	19:03	♄	℞
2		29	2:30	♆	D
3		Jul 17	13:40	♀	℞
4		19	23:03	☿	℞
3		Aug 12	23:30	☿	D
2		29	13:43	♀	D
1		Oct 28	14:16	♇	D
0		Nov 6	23:30	♄	D
1		9	10:60	♅	℞
2		10	23:59	☿	℞
3		15	16:57	♃	℞
2		30	20:23	☿	D
3	1789	Jan 23	17:06	♆	℞
4		Feb 27	15:25	☿	℞
3		Mar 15	13:21	♃	D
2		22	9:29	☿	D
1		Apr 7	12:34	♅	D
2		May 19	15:37	♇	℞
1		Jul 1	13:08	♆	D
2		1	15:59	☿	℞
3		3	23:41	♄	℞
2		25	21:01	☿	D
3		Oct 25	13:39	☿	℞
2		30	9:45	♇	D
3		Nov 14	10:55	♅	℞
2		14	18:18	☿	D
1		19	9:29	♄	D
2		Dec 16	16:34	♃	℞
3	1790	Jan 1	14:38	♂	℞
4		26	2:44	♆	℞
5		Feb 10	23:09	☿	℞
6		25	13:42	♀	℞
5		Mar 5	0:08	☿	D
4		23	9:30	♂	D
3		Apr 8	13:46	♀	D
2		12	12:10	♅	D
1		17	3:35	♃	D

2		May 21	8:06	♇	℞
3		Jun 12	20:39	☿	℞
2		Jul 4	2:34	♆	D
1		6	23:27	☿	D
2		17	11:14	♄	℞
3		Oct 8	22:37	☿	℞
2		29	16:54	☿	D
1		Nov 1	4:24	♇	D
2		19	9:59	♅	℞
1		Dec 2	2:48	♄	D
2	1791	Jan 15	20:34	♃	℞
3		25	14:45	☿	℞
4		28	13:47	♆	℞
3		Feb 15	22:01	☿	D
2		Apr 17	11:02	♅	D
1		May 18	14:37	♃	D
2		23	2:33	♇	℞
3		24	13:16	☿	℞
2		Jun 17	12:10	☿	D
1		Jul 6	13:15	♆	D
2		31	7:55	♄	℞
3		Sep 22	2:07	☿	℞
4		28	21:33	♀	℞
3		Oct 13	14:07	☿	D
2		Nov 2	20:34	♇	D
1		9	14:34	♀	D
2		24	10:05	♅	℞
1		Dec 15	1:03	♄	D
2	1792	Jan 9	10:53	☿	℞
1		30	1:60	☿	D
2		30	22:00	♆	℞
3		Feb 5	23:34	♂	℞
4		15	5:34	♃	℞
3		Apr 21	11:24	♅	D
2		26	13:04	♂	D
3		May 4	2:28	☿	℞
2		23	18:43	♇	℞
3		27	22:55	☿	D
2		Jun 17	16:16	♃	D
1		Jul 8	1:43	♆	D
2		Aug 13	11:16	♄	℞
3		Sep 3	23:49	☿	℞
2		26	7:27	☿	D
1		Nov 3	14:33	♇	D
2		28	10:03	♅	℞
3		Dec 23	8:45	☿	℞
2		27	6:20	♄	D
1	1793	Jan 12	11:22	☿	D
2		Feb 1	8:31	♆	℞
3		Mar 17	16:12	♃	℞
4		Apr 15	0:53	☿	℞
3		26	12:02	♅	D
4		May 6	13:12	♀	℞
3		8	19:30	☿	D
4		25	11:08	♇	℞
3		Jun 18	12:53	♀	D
2		Jul 10	12:28	♆	D
1		19	0:25	♃	D
2		Aug 17	15:22	☿	℞
3		27	19:33	♄	℞
2		Sep 9	17:45	☿	D
1		Nov 5	7:40	♇	D
2		Dec 3	9:53	♅	℞
3		7	6:13	☿	℞
2		27	1:35	☿	D
1	1794	Jan 9	19:48	♄	D
2		Feb 3	17:30	♆	℞
3		Mar 18	10:45	♂	℞
4		27	16:44	☿	℞
5		Apr 20	4:24	♃	℞
4		20	6:34	☿	D
3		May 1	12:55	♅	D
4		27	1:57	♇	℞
3		Jun 3	12:22	♂	D
2		Jul 12	23:17	♆	D

3		30	23:33	☿	℞
2		Aug 20	13:12	♃	D
1		23	17:13	☿	D
2		Sep 11	7:00	♄	℞
1		Nov 7	1:17	♇	D
2		21	1:29	☿	℞
3		Dec 8	10:37	♅	℞
2		10	19:44	☿	D
3		12	13:03	♀	℞
2	1795	Jan 22	10:49	♀	D
1		23	16:45	♄	D
2		Feb 6	4:31	♆	℞
3		Mar 10	3:06	☿	℞
2		Apr 2	6:11	☿	D
1		May 6	15:13	♅	D
2		25	21:29	♃	℞
3		28	15:24	♇	℞
4		Jul 12	22:30	☿	℞
3		15	11:16	♆	D
2		Aug 6	1:40	☿	D
1		Sep 23	15:01	♃	D
2		25	20:49	♄	℞
3		Nov 4	17:20	☿	℞
2		8	19:34	♇	D
1		24	16:43	☿	D
2		Dec 13	9:52	♅	℞
1	1796	Feb 6	19:33	♄	D
2		8	15:04	♆	℞
3		21	4:27	☿	℞
2		Mar 14	15:37	☿	D
1		May 10	16:29	♅	D
2		13	9:16	♂	℞
3		29	8:19	♇	℞
4		Jun 23	9:57	☿	℞
5		Jul 1	14:39	♃	℞
6		15	5:44	♀	℞
5		16	23:10	♆	D
4		17	15:15	☿	D
3		20	13:48	♂	D
2		Aug 27	6:01	♀	D
3		Oct 9	10:53	♄	℞
4		18	4:58	☿	℞
3		28	13:40	♃	D
2		Nov 7	15:05	☿	D
1		9	10:22	♇	D
2		Dec 17	10:53	♅	℞
3	1797	Feb 3	16:09	☿	℞
4		10	1:56	♆	℞
3		20	3:14	♄	D
2		25	9:16	☿	D
1		May 15	20:24	♅	D
2		30	23:08	♇	℞
3		Jun 4	9:14	☿	℞
2		28	10:25	☿	D
1		Jul 19	12:23	♆	D
2		Aug 8	19:18	♃	℞
3		Oct 1	11:46	☿	℞
2		22	13:14	☿	D
3		23	22:57	♄	℞
2		Nov 11	2:06	♇	D
1		Dec 4	12:22	♃	D
2		22	9:45	♅	℞
3	1798	Jan 18	10:06	☿	℞
2		Feb 8	9:53	☿	D
3		12	12:10	♆	℞
4		23	5:33	♀	℞
3		Mar 6	14:10	♄	D
2		Apr 6	4:27	♀	D
3		May 15	23:22	☿	℞
2		20	22:25	♅	D
3		Jun 1	14:54	♇	℞
2		8	20:16	☿	D
1		Jul 21	23:05	♆	D
2		Aug 1	6:43	♂	℞
3		Sep 14	13:08	☿	℞

4		14	18:54	♃	℞
3		30	11:45	♂	D
2		Oct 6	9:05	☿	D
3		Nov 7	6:42	♄	℞
2		12	16:05	♇	D
3		Dec 27	10:57	♅	℞
4	1799	Jan 2	7:12	☿	℞
3		10	10:46	♃	D
2		22	16:29	☿	D
3		Feb 14	21:53	♆	℞
2		Mar 21	2:07	♄	D
3		Apr 26	14:30	☿	℞
2		May 20	10:35	☿	D
1		26	3:39	♅	D
2		Jun 3	3:34	♇	℞
1		Jul 24	12:52	♆	D
2		Aug 28	8:18	☿	℞
1		Sep 19	23:58	☿	D
2		26	9:49	♀	℞
3		Oct 19	15:34	♃	℞
2		Nov 7	4:41	♀	D
1		14	8:28	♇	D
2		21	9:04	♄	℞
3		Dec 17	5:00	☿	℞
4	1800	Jan 1	9:43	♅	℞
3		6	4:05	☿	D
2		Feb 15	4:45	♃	D
3		17	9:23	♆	℞
2		Apr 4	12:48	♄	D
3		7	19:42	☿	℞
2		May 1	13:17	☿	D
1		31	5:60	♅	D
2		Jun 4	15:04	♇	℞
1		Jul 26	23:39	♆	D
2		Aug 10	20:32	☿	℞
1		Sep 3	6:20	☿	D
2		Oct 3	5:09	♂	℞
1		Nov 16	0:32	♇	D
2		21	2:46	♃	℞
3		Dec 1	1:41	☿	℞
4		5	4:29	♄	℞
3		12	10:11	♂	D
2		20	19:59	☿	D
3	1801	Jan 6	11:08	♅	℞
4		Feb 19	17:42	♆	℞
5		Mar 20	19:59	☿	℞
4		21	4:08	♃	D
3		Apr 13	5:37	☿	D
2		18	21:53	♄	D
3		May 5	5:15	♀	℞
2		Jun 5	11:21	♅	D
3		6	3:50	♇	℞
2		17	4:28	♀	D
3		Jul 24	0:57	☿	℞
2		29	11:56	♆	D
1		Aug 16	23:52	☿	D
2		Nov 14	19:47	☿	℞
1		17	15:49	♇	D
0		Dec 4	15:22	☿	D
1		18	15:22	♄	℞
2		22	0:25	♃	℞
3	1802	Jan 11	10:21	♅	℞
4		Feb 22	4:14	♆	℞
5		Mar 3	13:20	☿	℞
4		26	9:48	☿	D
3		Apr 22	15:31	♃	D
2		May 3	3:16	♄	D
3		Jun 7	15:57	♇	℞
2		10	14:06	♅	D
3		Jul 5	19:38	☿	℞
2		30	0:15	☿	D
1		31	22:24	♆	D
2		Oct 29	10:06	☿	℞
3		Nov 15	12:06	♂	℞
2		18	13:08	☿	D

Planetary Stations in Longitude 1700–2050

	Year	Date	Time	Planet	
1		19	7:18	♇	D
2		Dec 11	1:25	♀	℞
3		31	18:06	♄	℞
4	1803	Jan 16	11:12	♅	℞
3		20	22:47	♀	D
4		21	3:20	♃	℞
3		31	9:45	♂	D
4		Feb 14	19:28	☿	℞
5		24	13:46	♆	℞
4		Mar 8	23:15	☿	D
3		May 17	3:30	♄	D
2		24	0:16	♃	D
3		Jun 9	7:49	♇	℞
2		15	18:32	♅	D
3		17	2:04	☿	℞
2		Jul 11	5:39	☿	D
1		Aug 3	8:36	♆	D
2		Oct 12	19:41	☿	℞
1		Nov 2	11:45	☿	D
0		20	17:60	♇	D
1	1804	Jan 13	15:51	♄	℞
2		21	10:15	♅	℞
3		29	10:09	☿	℞
2		Feb 19	19:59	☿	D
3		20	12:23	♃	℞
4		27	0:59	♆	℞
5		May 27	20:05	☿	℞
4		29	19:43	♄	D
5		Jun 9	21:01	♇	℞
4		19	21:18	♅	D
3		20	19:41	☿	D
2		23	0:46	♃	D
3		Jul 13	21:56	♀	℞
2		Aug 4	20:22	♆	D
1		25	22:43	♀	D
2		Sep 24	23:59	☿	℞
1		Oct 16	9:16	☿	D
0		Nov 21	6:54	♇	D
1		Dec 20	7:35	♂	℞
2	1805	Jan 12	5:51	☿	℞
3		25	6:46	♄	℞
4		25	9:56	♅	℞
3		Feb 1	23:02	☿	D
4		28	11:59	♆	℞
3		Mar 10	11:55	♂	D
4		23	4:33	♃	℞
5		May 8	9:07	☿	℞
4		Jun 1	5:32	☿	D
5		11	8:45	♇	℞
4		12	5:18	♄	D
3		25	1:15	♅	D
2		Jul 24	11:57	♃	D
1		Aug 7	7:20	♆	D
2		Sep 7	22:40	☿	℞
1		30	3:17	☿	D
0		Nov 22	19:51	♇	D
1		Dec 27	3:38	☿	℞
0	1806	Jan 16	7:43	☿	D
1		30	7:54	♅	℞
2		Feb 6	14:39	♄	℞
3		21	21:02	♀	℞
4		Mar 2	23:09	♆	℞
3		Apr 4	19:18	♀	D
4		19	5:23	☿	℞
5		25	19:26	♃	℞
4		May 13	0:21	☿	D
5		Jun 12	19:41	♇	℞
4		25	9:11	♄	D
3		30	4:33	♅	D
2		Aug 9	19:40	♆	D
3		21	15:19	☿	℞
2		26	1:23	♃	D
1		Sep 13	14:54	☿	D
0		Nov 24	9:37	♇	D
1		Dec 11	1:14	☿	℞
0		30	21:23	☿	D
1	1807	Jan 23	20:57	♂	℞
2		Feb 4	5:48	♅	℞
3		18	17:57	♄	℞
4		Mar 5	10:18	♆	℞
5		31	18:20	☿	℞
4		Apr 14	19:42	♂	D
3		24	9:27	☿	D
4		May 31	20:42	♃	℞
5		Jun 14	5:40	♇	℞
4		Jul 5	8:01	♅	D
3		8	6:52	♄	D
4		Aug 4	0:39	☿	℞
3		12	6:55	♆	D
2		27	16:21	☿	D
3		Sep 24	22:01	♀	℞
2		29	9:47	♃	D
1		Nov 5	18:22	♀	D
2		24	20:53	☿	℞
1		26	0:14	♇	D
0		Dec 14	15:03	☿	D
1	1808	Feb 9	2:24	♅	℞
2		Mar 1	16:22	♄	℞
3		6	20:40	♆	℞
4		13	2:13	☿	℞
3		Apr 5	7:14	☿	D
4		Jun 14	18:41	♇	℞
5		Jul 7	17:04	♃	℞
4		9	11:13	♅	D
5		16	0:51	☿	℞
4		19	22:16	♄	D
3		Aug 9	3:20	☿	D
2		13	21:12	♆	D
1		Nov 3	9:49	♃	D
2		7	13:20	☿	℞
1		26	12:03	♇	D
0		27	11:36	☿	D
1	1809	Feb 12	22:52	♅	℞
2		24	1:41	☿	℞
3		Mar 2	3:32	♂	℞
4		9	8:24	♆	℞
5		13	13:46	♄	℞
4		18	15:15	☿	D
5		May 2	21:33	♀	℞
4		20	1:25	♂	D
3		Jun 14	19:60	♀	D
4		16	6:53	♇	℞
5		27	14:15	☿	℞
4		Jul 14	13:28	♅	D
3		21	19:43	☿	D
2		Aug 1	8:20	♄	D
3		14	20:27	♃	℞
2		16	8:47	♆	D
3		Oct 22	1:42	☿	℞
2		Nov 11	9:48	☿	D
1		27	23:59	♇	D
0		Dec 10	11:44	♃	D
1	1810	Feb 7	12:03	☿	℞
2		17	18:28	♅	℞
1		Mar 1	7:51	☿	D
2		11	16:56	♆	℞
3		25	9:42	♄	℞
4		Jun 8	15:30	☿	℞
5		17	20:09	♇	℞
4		Jul 2	17:07	☿	D
3		19	15:39	♅	D
2		Aug 13	11:38	♄	D
1		18	21:39	♆	D
2		Sep 20	18:32	♃	℞
3		Oct 5	9:17	☿	℞
2		26	8:06	☿	D
1		Nov 29	9:47	♇	D
2		Dec 8	14:09	♀	℞
1	1811	Jan 16	9:59	♃	D
0		18	11:12	♀	D
1		22	5:15	☿	℞
0		Feb 12	7:37	☿	D
1		22	13:54	♅	℞
2		Mar 14	3:38	♆	℞
3		Apr 6	3:24	♄	℞
4		20	10:13	♂	℞
5		May 20	6:18	☿	℞
4		Jun 13	3:47	☿	D
5		19	5:29	♇	℞
4		Jul 1	21:37	♂	D
3		24	15:40	♅	D
2		Aug 21	8:51	♆	D
1		25	12:42	♄	D
2		Sep 18	11:23	☿	℞
1		Oct 10	4:30	☿	D
2		25	6:34	♃	℞
1		Nov 30	22:14	♇	D
2	1812	Jan 6	2:00	☿	℞
1		26	13:17	☿	D
0		Feb 20	23:00	♃	D
1		27	8:50	♅	℞
2		Mar 15	13:20	♆	℞
3		Apr 16	23:44	♄	℞
4		29	20:21	☿	℞
3		May 23	16:43	☿	D
4		Jun 19	13:12	♇	℞
5		Jul 11	14:01	♀	℞
4		28	16:21	♅	D
3		Aug 22	19:41	♆	D
2		23	15:33	♀	D
3		31	7:27	☿	℞
2		Sep 5	11:43	♄	D
1		22	20:22	☿	D
2		Nov 25	14:06	♃	℞
1		Dec 1	12:01	♇	D
2		19	23:54	☿	℞
1	1813	Jan 9	0:08	☿	D
2		Mar 3	3:04	♅	℞
3		18	0:27	♆	℞
2		25	20:38	♃	D
3		Apr 10	23:06	☿	℞
4		28	22:18	♄	℞
3		May 4	17:08	☿	D
4		Jun 21	0:09	♇	℞
5		Jul 1	1:25	♂	℞
4		Aug 2	14:26	♅	D
5		13	20:48	☿	℞
4		25	7:03	♆	D
3		31	1:07	♂	D
2		Sep 6	4:12	☿	D
1		17	7:60	♄	D
0		Dec 2	23:25	♇	D
1		3	20:55	☿	℞
0		23	15:27	☿	D
1		26	5:53	♃	℞
2	1814	Feb 19	11:54	♀	℞
3		Mar 7	21:32	♅	℞
4		20	11:50	♆	℞
5		23	20:31	☿	℞
4		Apr 2	9:28	♀	D
3		16	7:37	☿	D
2		27	2:21	♃	D
3		May 11	1:36	♄	℞
4		Jun 22	9:57	♇	℞
5		Jul 27	2:43	☿	℞
4		Aug 7	13:46	♅	D
3		19	23:54	☿	D
2		27	16:52	♆	D
1		Sep 29	4:14	♄	D
2		Nov 17	15:31	☿	℞
1		Dec 4	10:58	♇	D
0		7	10:27	☿	D
1	1815	Jan 25	8:50	♃	℞
2		Mar 6	11:27	☿	℞
3		12	14:26	♅	℞
4		22	23:21	♆	℞
3		29	10:20	☿	D
4		May 23	8:08	♄	℞
3		28	10:02	♃	D
4		Jun 23	22:26	♇	℞
5		Jul 8	23:01	☿	℞
4		Aug 2	3:08	☿	D
3		12	9:39	♅	D
2		30	4:10	♆	D
3		Sep 12	22:23	♂	℞
4		22	10:41	♀	℞
3		Oct 11	0:31	♄	D
4		Nov 1	6:23	☿	℞
3		3	8:06	♀	D
2		18	0:29	♂	D
1		21	7:59	☿	D
0		Dec 5	18:44	♇	D
1	1816	Feb 17	15:58	☿	℞
2		24	20:22	♃	℞
1		Mar 10	22:28	☿	D
2		16	8:20	♅	℞
3		24	11:33	♆	℞
4		Jun 3	19:22	♄	℞
5		19	7:01	☿	℞
6		24	8:57	♇	℞
5		27	9:41	♃	D
4		Jul 13	11:24	☿	D
3		Aug 16	7:50	♅	D
2		31	14:43	♆	D
3		Oct 14	16:36	☿	℞
2.		22	1:01	♄	D
1		Nov 4	6:32	☿	D
0		Dec 6	3:60	♇	D
1	1817	Jan 31	5:42	☿	℞
0		Feb 21	18:04	☿	D
1		Mar 20	23:49	♅	℞
2		26	23:22	♆	℞
3		27	16:48	♃	℞
4		Apr 30	14:17	♀	℞
5		May 31	2:43	☿	℞
4		Jun 12	11:46	♀	D
5		16	15:28	♄	℞
4		24	2:59	☿	D
5		25	17:11	♇	℞
4		Jul 28	22:27	♃	D
3		Aug 21	2:05	♅	D
2		Sep 3	4:18	♆	D
3		27	21:46	☿	℞
2		Oct 19	4:20	☿	D
3		30	23:58	♂	℞
2		Nov 3	4:34	♄	D
1		Dec 7	14:11	♇	D
0	1818	Jan 13	18:14	♂	D
1		15	0:54	☿	℞
0		Feb 4	20:16	☿	D
1		Mar 25	16:56	♅	℞
2		29	12:21	♆	℞
3		Apr 30	17:09	♃	℞
4		May 11	16:03	☿	℞
3		Jun 4	12:26	☿	D
4		27	1:59	♇	℞
5		29	17:54	♄	℞
4		Aug 25	23:06	♅	D
3		30	18:21	♃	D
2		Sep 5	15:30	♆	D
3		10	21:28	☿	℞
2		Oct 2	23:02	☿	D
1		Nov 15	11:22	♄	D
2		Dec 6	3:05	♀	℞
1		9	1:40	♇	D
2		29	22:32	☿	℞
1	1819	Jan 15	23:58	♀	D
0		19	4:17	☿	D
1		Mar 30	6:58	♅	℞
2		31	21:49	♆	℞
3		Apr 22	10:21	☿	℞
2		May 16	5:42	☿	D
3		Jun 6	1:20	♃	℞
4		28	10:26	♇	℞
5		Jul 13	2:59	♄	℞
6		Aug 24	15:05	☿	℞
5		30	16:01	♅	D
4		Sep 8	4:24	♆	D
3		16	11:51	☿	D
2		Oct 4	7:08	♃	D
1		Nov 28	0:38	♄	D
2		Dec 7	19:36	♂	℞
1		10	13:28	♇	D
2		13	20:12	☿	℞
1	1820	Jan 2	17:17	☿	D
0		Feb 25	0:53	♂	D
1		Apr 2	9:22	♆	℞
2		2	20:25	☿	℞
3		2	22:12	♅	℞
2		26	12:37	☿	D
3		Jun 28	22:55	♇	℞
4		Jul 9	5:42	♀	℞
5		13	1:21	♃	℞
6		25	19:48	♄	℞
7		Aug 6	1:24	☿	℞
6		21	8:03	♀	D
5		29	15:08	☿	D
4		Sep 3	11:53	♅	D
3		9	16:49	♆	D
2		Nov 8	13:23	♃	D
3		26	16:12	☿	℞
2		Dec 9	20:03	♄	D
1		10	20:40	♇	D
0		16	10:21	☿	D
1	1821	Mar 16	1:39	☿	℞
2		Apr 4	19:36	♆	℞
3		7	11:00	♅	℞
2		8	8:24	☿	D
3		Jun 30	8:50	♇	℞
4		Jul 19	2:60	☿	℞
5		Aug 8	18:23	♄	℞
4		12	4:32	☿	D
5		20	5:48	♃	℞
4		Sep 8	3:37	♅	D
3		12	4:49	♆	D
4		Nov 10	9:13	☿	℞
3		30	6:27	☿	D
2		Dec 12	5:30	♇	D
1		15	18:23	♃	D
0		22	23:08	♄	D
1	1822	Jan 10	7:05	♂	℞
2		Feb 17	2:23	♀	℞
3		26	23:05	☿	℞
2		Mar 21	15:02	☿	D
1		30	23:07	♀	D
0		Apr 1	5:33	♂	D
1		7	5:55	♆	℞
2		12	0:27	♅	℞
3		Jun 30	18:26	☿	℞
4		Jul 1	16:33	♇	℞
3		24	23:44	☿	D
4		Aug 22	22:47	♄	℞
3		Sep 12	21:19	♅	D
2		14	16:38	♆	D
3		25	18:03	♃	℞
4		Oct 24	22:20	☿	℞
3		Nov 14	4:30	☿	D
2		Dec 13	14:34	♇	D
1	1823	Jan 5	9:30	♄	D
0		21	11:38	♃	D
1		Feb 10	8:04	☿	℞
0		Mar 4	6:38	☿	D
1		Apr 9	16:30	♆	℞
2		16	11:51	♅	℞
3		Jun 11	21:33	☿	℞

Planetary Stations in Longitude 1700–2050

4		Jul 2	23:35	♇	℞
3		5	23:40	☿	D
4		Sep 6	8:29	♄	℞
3		17	2:39	♆	D
2		17	11:36	♅	D
3		19	23:48	♀	℞
4		Oct 8	6:41	☿	℞
3		29	2:60	☿	D
4		29	22:30	♃	℞
3		31	22:16	♀	D
2		Dec 15	0:29	♇	D
1	1824	Jan 19	2:04	♄	D
2		25	0:28	☿	℞
1		Feb 15	5:27	☿	D
2		15	10:27	♂	℞
1		25	21:10	♃	D
2		Apr 11	3:30	♆	℞
3		20	0:03	♅	℞
2		May 5	12:57	♂	D
3		22	13:07	☿	℞
2		Jun 15	11:23	☿	D
3		Jul 3	5:29	♇	℞
2		Sep 18	13:47	♆	D
3		19	22:09	♄	℞
4		20	9:34	☿	℞
3		21	2:38	♅	D
2		Oct 11	23:54	☿	D
3		Nov 29	20:45	♃	℞
2		Dec 15	12:04	♇	D
3	1825	Jan 7	20:54	☿	℞
2		28	10:13	☿	D
1		Feb 1	0:13	♄	D
0		Mar 30	9:46	♃	D
1		Apr 13	16:07	♆	℞
2		24	10:26	♅	℞
3		28	7:17	♀	℞
4		May 3	2:32	☿	℞
3		26	23:02	☿	D
2		Jun 10	3:50	♀	D
3		Jul 4	14:59	♇	℞
4		Sep 3	6:30	☿	℞
3		21	0:06	♆	D
2		25	15:08	♅	D
1		25	16:36	☿	D
2		Oct 4	12:11	♄	℞
1		Dec 16	20:31	♇	D
2		22	18:49	☿	℞
3		30	10:15	♃	℞
2	1826	Jan 11	20:19	☿	D
1		Feb 15	5:27	♄	D
2		Mar 30	5:04	♂	℞
3		Apr 14	2:56	☿	℞
4		16	4:06	♆	℞
5		28	22:01	♅	℞
4		May 1	12:42	♃	D
3		7	21:16	☿	D
2		Jun 13	21:38	♂	D
3		Jul 6	0:30	♇	℞
4		Aug 16	21:01	☿	℞
3		Sep 9	1:47	☿	D
2		23	12:23	♆	D
1		30	3:58	♅	D
2		Oct 18	23:58	♄	℞
3		Dec 3	15:56	♀	℞
4		6	16:05	☿	℞
3		18	4:14	♇	D
2		26	11:01	☿	D
1	1827	Jan 13	12:48	♀	D
2		29	10:51	♃	℞
1		Mar 1	15:07	♄	D
2		26	21:23	☿	℞
3		Apr 18	17:22	♆	℞
2		19	9:56	☿	D
3		May 3	7:26	♅	℞
2		Jun 1	15:21	♃	D

3		Jul 7	9:42	♇	℞
4		30	4:12	☿	℞
3		Aug 22	23:31	☿	D
2		Sep 25	22:27	♆	D
1		Oct 4	14:43	♅	D
2		Nov 2	7:59	♄	℞
3		20	11:05	☿	℞
2		Dec 10	5:35	☿	D
1		19	10:09	♇	D
2	1828	Feb 29	3:01	♃	℞
3		Mar 8	9:51	☿	℞
2		15	2:58	♄	D
1		31	11:04	☿	D
2		Apr 20	4:24	♆	℞
3		May 6	18:46	♅	℞
4		30	13:36	♂	℞
3		Jul 1	16:59	♃	D
4		6	21:01	♀	℞
5		7	16:17	♇	℞
6		11	1:53	☿	℞
5		Aug 3	22:49	♂	D
4		4	5:33	☿	D
3		19	0:00	♀	D
2		Sep 27	11:02	♆	D
1		Oct 8	1:55	♅	D
2		Nov 3	2:28	☿	℞
3		15	11:12	♄	℞
2		23	2:49	☿	D
1		Dec 19	18:53	♇	D
2	1829	Feb 19	12:43	☿	℞
1		Mar 13	21:48	☿	D
0		29	14:04	♄	D
1		Apr 1	7:14	♃	℞
2		22	17:42	♆	℞
3		May 11	3:22	♅	℞
4		Jun 22	11:42	☿	℞
5		Jul 8	21:05	♇	℞
4		16	16:43	☿	D
3		Aug 2	9:19	♃	D
2		Sep 29	23:05	♆	D
1		Oct 12	11:31	♅	D
2		17	13:27	☿	℞
1		Nov 7	1:19	☿	D
2		29	9:16	♄	℞
1		Dec 21	5:20	♇	D
2	1830	Feb 3	1:26	☿	℞
3		14	16:58	♀	℞
2		24	16:19	☿	D
1		Mar 28	12:38	♀	D
0		Apr 12	23:28	♄	D
1		25	5:05	♆	℞
2		May 5	16:28	♃	℞
3		15	14:21	♅	℞
4		Jun 3	9:24	☿	℞
3		27	10:08	☿	D
4		Jul 10	6:16	♇	℞
5		Aug 18	14:37	♂	℞
4		Sep 4	11:04	♃	D
5		30	19:29	☿	℞
4		Oct 2	10:45	♆	D
3		16	21:16	♅	D
2		19	12:49	♂	D
1		21	23:19	☿	D
2		Dec 12	23:55	♄	℞
1		22	12:30	♇	D
2	1831	Jan 17	20:01	☿	℞
1		Feb 7	17:41	☿	D
0		Apr 27	5:30	♄	D
1		27	16:34	♆	℞
2		May 14	23:07	☿	℞
3		19	22:07	♅	℞
2		Jun 7	19:38	☿	D
3		11	9:17	♃	℞
4		Jul 11	14:40	♇	℞
5		Sep 13	20:08	☿	℞

6		17	13:31	♀	℞
5		Oct 4	22:45	♆	D
4		5	18:40	☿	D
3		9	7:57	♃	D
2		21	5:59	♅	D
1		29	12:59	♀	D
0		Dec 23	20:14	♇	D
1		26	6:55	♄	℞
2	1832	Jan 1	17:21	☿	℞
1		22	0:57	☿	D
2		Apr 24	15:35	☿	℞
3		29	3:46	♆	℞
2		May 10	6:30	♄	D
1		18	11:22	☿	D
2		23	8:14	♅	℞
3		Jul 11	23:25	♇	℞
4		18	13:49	♃	℞
5		Aug 26	14:36	☿	℞
4		Sep 18	8:35	☿	D
3		Oct 6	9:11	♆	D
4		13	22:24	♂	℞
3		24	14:30	♅	D
2		Nov 13	20:37	♃	D
3		Dec 15	15:04	☿	℞
2		24	1:26	♇	D
1		24	22:48	♂	D
0	1833	Jan 4	13:13	☿	D
1		7	6:60	♄	℞
2		Apr 5	22:52	☿	℞
3		26	0:31	♀	℞
2		29	15:57	☿	D
3		May 1	15:17	♆	℞
2		24	1:26	♄	D
3		27	15:26	♅	℞
2		Jun 7	20:20	♀	D
3		Jul 13	6:37	♇	℞
4		Aug 9	1:55	☿	℞
3		25	12:20	♃	℞
2		Sep 1	13:37	☿	D
3		Oct 8	20:48	♆	D
2		28	22:29	♅	D
3		Nov 29	11:27	☿	℞
2		Dec 19	5:39	☿	D
1		21	0:26	♃	D
0		25	8:11	♇	D
1	1834	Jan 19	22:32	♄	℞
2		Mar 19	1:27	☿	℞
1		Apr 11	9:46	☿	D
2		May 4	3:59	♆	℞
3		Jun 1	0:38	♅	℞
2		6	15:10	♄	D
3		Jul 14	11:03	♇	℞
4		22	5:03	☿	℞
3		Aug 15	5:18	☿	D
4		Sep 30	17:25	♃	℞
3		Oct 11	7:16	♆	D
2		Nov 2	5:31	♅	D
3		13	5:05	☿	℞
4		23	20:03	♂	℞
5		Dec 1	4:10	♀	℞
4		3	1:21	☿	D
3		26	17:45	♇	D
2	1835	Jan 11	1:10	♀	D
1		26	15:22	♃	D
2		Feb 1	8:39	♄	℞
1		9	16:28	♂	D
2		Mar 1	20:45	☿	℞
1		24	15:07	☿	D
2		May 6	15:57	♆	℞
3		Jun 5	7:22	♅	℞
4		19	22:06	♄	D
3		Jul 3	22:20	☿	℞
4		15	18:01	♇	℞
3		28	3:17	☿	D
2		Oct 13	19:09	♆	D

3		27	18:53	☿	℞
4		Nov 3	12:29	♃	℞
3		6	12:34	♅	D
2		16	23:18	☿	D
1		Dec 28	1:51	♇	D
2	1836	Feb 13	4:17	☿	℞
3		13	15:38	♄	℞
2		Mar 1	16:12	♃	D
1		6	5:39	☿	D
2		May 8	5:26	♆	℞
3		Jun 8	16:17	♅	℞
4		14	3:10	☿	℞
3		Jul 1	20:47	♄	D
4		4	12:34	♀	℞
3		8	6:05	☿	D
4		16	1:40	♇	℞
3		Aug 16	15:46	♀	D
4		Oct 10	3:56	☿	℞
3		15	4:51	♆	D
2		30	21:54	☿	D
1		Nov 9	18:34	♅	D
2		Dec 4	5:11	♃	℞
3		27	23:04	♂	℞
2		28	9:32	♇	D
3	1837	Jan 26	19:47	☿	℞
2		Feb 17	3:23	☿	D
3		24	15:58	♄	℞
2		Mar 18	12:34	♂	D
1		Apr 4	0:29	♃	D
2		May 10	17:18	♆	℞
3		25	19:55	☿	℞
4		Jun 12	22:59	♅	℞
3		18	18:57	☿	D
2		Jul 14	12:51	♄	D
3		17	11:32	♇	℞
4		Sep 23	7:34	☿	℞
3		Oct 14	19:10	☿	D
2		17	17:24	♆	D
1		Nov 14	0:15	♅	D
0		Dec 29	13:16	♇	D
1	1838	Jan 3	13:45	♃	℞
2		10	15:50	☿	℞
1		31	7:14	☿	D
2		Feb 12	7:28	♀	℞
3		Mar 8	13:29	♄	℞
2		26	1:44	♀	D
1		May 5	20:36	♃	D
2		6	9:02	☿	℞
3		13	7:50	♆	℞
2		30	5:27	☿	D
3		Jun 17	8:02	♅	℞
4		Jul 18	17:33	♇	℞
3		27	1:21	♄	D
4		Sep 6	5:24	☿	℞
3		28	12:36	☿	D
2		Oct 20	5:23	♆	D
1		Nov 18	5:52	♅	D
2		Dec 25	13:42	☿	℞
1		30	19:03	♇	D
0	1839	Jan 14	16:32	☿	D
1		31	21:32	♂	℞
2		Feb 2	17:16	♃	℞
3		Mar 20	9:22	♄	℞
4		Apr 17	7:11	☿	℞
3		22	15:54	♂	D
2		May 11	1:46	☿	D
3		15	19:54	♆	℞
2		Jun 6	0:13	♃	D
3		21	15:03	♅	℞
4		Jul 19	20:23	♇	℞
3		Aug 8	7:56	♄	D
4		19	21:05	☿	℞
3		Sep 11	23:05	☿	D
4		15	3:24	♀	℞
3		Oct 22	16:47	♆	D

2		27	4:03	♀	D
1		Nov 22	10:16	♅	D
2		Dec 9	11:12	☿	℞
1		29	6:42	☿	D
0	1840	Jan 1	3:49	♇	D
1		Mar 4	12:13	♃	℞
2		28	22:39	☿	℞
3		31	4:22	♄	℞
2		Apr 21	12:38	☿	D
3		May 17	8:00	♆	℞
4		Jun 25	0:08	♅	℞
3		Jul 6	1:03	♃	D
4		20	2:15	♇	℞
5		Aug 1	5:25	☿	℞
4		19	10:47	♄	D
3		24	22:49	☿	D
2		Oct 24	4:56	♆	D
3		Nov 22	6:33	☿	℞
2		25	15:53	♅	D
1		Dec 12	0:48	☿	D
0	1841	Jan 1	11:23	♇	D
1		Mar 11	8:38	☿	℞
2		11	18:24	♂	℞
1		Apr 3	12:01	☿	D
2		6	0:25	♃	℞
3		12	1:12	♄	℞
4		23	17:08	♀	℞
5		May 19	20:20	♆	℞
4		28	17:22	♂	D
3		Jun 5	12:39	♀	D
4		29	7:57	♅	℞
5		Jul 14	4:30	☿	℞
6		21	8:20	♇	℞
5		Aug 6	22:53	♃	D
4		7	7:37	☿	D
3		31	9:43	♄	D
2		Oct 26	15:39	♆	D
3		Nov 5	22:31	☿	℞
2		25	21:43	☿	D
1		29	20:12	♅	D
0	1842	Jan 2	19:05	♇	D
1		Feb 22	9:45	☿	℞
0		Mar 16	21:16	☿	D
1		Apr 23	21:24	♄	℞
2		May 10	17:60	♃	℞
3		22	8:35	♆	℞
4		Jun 25	16:15	☿	℞
5		Jul 3	17:03	♅	℞
4		19	21:35	☿	D
5		22	17:12	♇	℞
4		Sep 9	6:08	♃	D
3		12	5:58	♄	D
4		Oct 20	10:14	☿	℞
3		29	3:40	♆	D
2		Nov 9	20:03	☿	D
3		28	15:42	♀	℞
2		Dec 4	1:17	♅	D
1	1843	Jan 3	23:06	♇	D
0		8	12:58	♀	D
1		Feb 5	21:16	☿	℞
0		27	14:45	☿	D
1		May 3	22:29	♂	℞
2		5	21:46	♄	℞
3		24	21:07	♆	℞
4		Jun 6	15:54	☿	℞
5		16	17:50	♃	℞
4		30	17:06	☿	D
5		Jul 8	1:21	♅	℞
4		13	5:25	♂	D
5		24	1:21	♇	℞
4		Sep 24	4:02	♄	D
5		Oct 3	17:07	☿	℞
4		14	10:16	♃	D
3		24	18:13	☿	D
2		31	13:48	♆	D

Planetary Stations in Longitude 1700–2050

1		Dec	8	6:26	♅	D
0	1844	Jan	5	2:59	♇	D
1			20	15:06	☿	℞
0		Feb	10	15:13	☿	D
1		May	17	2:56	♄	℞
2			17	6:06	☿	℞
3			26	8:51	♆	℞
2		Jun	10	3:06	☿	D
3		Jul	2	4:27	♀	℞
4			11	10:28	♅	℞
5			23	21:24	♃	℞
6			24	5:49	♇	℞
5		Aug	14	7:38	♀	D
6		Sep	15	18:36	☿	℞
5		Oct	5	0:52	♄	D
4			7	14:08	☿	D
3		Nov	2	1:30	♆	D
2			19	1:06	♃	D
1		Dec	11	11:05	♅	D
2	1845	Jan	3	12:07	☿	℞
1			5	9:13	♇	D
0			23	21:41	☿	D
1		Apr	27	21:04	☿	℞
0		May	21	17:13	☿	D
1			28	22:48	♆	℞
2			29	13:05	♄	℞
3		Jul	15	18:58	♅	℞
4			19	12:19	♂	℞
5			25	11:12	♇	℞
6		Aug	29	13:52	☿	℞
7			30	15:40	♃	℞
6		Sep	17	8:01	♂	D
5			21	5:09	☿	D
4		Oct	16	23:21	♄	D
3		Nov	4	11:34	♆	D
2		Dec	15	17:02	♅	D
3			18	9:56	☿	℞
2			26	5:11	♃	D
1	1846	Jan	6	16:24	♇	D
0			7	9:11	☿	D
1		Feb	9	22:25	♀	℞
0		Mar	23	15:15	♀	D
1		Apr	9	1:49	☿	℞
0		May	2	19:26	☿	D
1			31	10:53	♆	℞
2		Jun	11	5:42	♄	℞
3		Jul	20	4:09	♅	℞
4			26	15:34	♇	℞
5		Aug	12	2:20	☿	℞
4		Sep	4	11:49	☿	D
5		Oct	5	12:19	♃	℞
4			29	0:32	♄	D
3		Nov	7	0:12	♆	D
4		Dec	2	6:42	☿	℞
3			19	21:53	♅	D
2			22	1:02	☿	D
1	1847	Jan	8	1:00	♇	D
0			31	13:21	♃	D
1		Mar	22	1:41	☿	℞
0		Apr	14	11:29	☿	D
1		Jun	3	1:32	♆	℞
2			24	3:06	♄	℞
3		Jul	24	12:36	♅	℞
4			25	6:60	☿	℞
5			27	23:50	♇	℞
4		Aug	18	5:41	☿	D
5		Sep	12	16:60	♀	℞
6			25	10:53	♂	℞
5		Oct	24	19:29	♀	D
6		Nov	7	23:09	♃	℞
5			9	12:01	♆	D
4			10	6:31	♄	D
5			16	0:55	☿	℞
4		Dec	2	22:17	♂	D
3			5	20:24	☿	D

2			24	3:55	♅	D
1	1848	Jan	9	5:06	♇	D
2		Mar	3	18:45	☿	℞
1			6	8:49	♃	D
0			26	15:33	☿	D
1		Jun	4	13:30	♆	℞
2		Jul	6	1:53	☿	℞
3			6	8:31	♄	℞
4			27	22:32	♅	℞
5			28	6:37	♇	℞
4			30	6:26	☿	D
5		Oct	29	15:18	☿	℞
4		Nov	10	23:33	♆	D
3			18	18:08	☿	D
2			21	18:30	♄	D
3		Dec	8	10:52	♃	℞
2			27	9:19	♅	D
1	1849	Jan	9	9:27	♇	D
2		Feb	15	0:39	☿	℞
1		Mar	9	4:48	☿	D
0		Apr	8	10:23	♃	D
1			21	9:17	♀	℞
0		Jun	3	4:43	♀	D
1			7	2:55	♆	℞
2			17	8:25	☿	℞
1		Jul	11	12:09	☿	D
2			19	22:55	♄	℞
3			29	9:54	♇	℞
4		Aug	1	7:18	♅	℞
5		Oct	13	0:60	☿	℞
4		Nov	2	16:46	☿	D
5			9	0:24	♂	℞
4			13	12:04	♆	D
3		Dec	4	10:43	♄	D
2			31	15:08	♅	D
3	1850	Jan	7	19:03	♃	℞
2			10	16:06	♇	D
1			24	1:09	♂	D
2			29	15:11	☿	℞
1		Feb	20	1:23	☿	D
0		May	10	5:11	♃	D
1			29	2:40	☿	℞
2		Jun	9	16:00	♆	℞
1			22	2:22	☿	D
2		Jul	30	14:23	♇	℞
3		Aug	2	19:55	♄	℞
4			5	18:11	♅	℞
5		Sep	26	5:23	☿	℞
4		Oct	17	14:18	☿	D
3		Nov	15	23:08	♆	D
4			26	3:17	♀	℞
3		Dec	17	9:28	♄	D
2	1851	Jan	4	21:05	♅	D
1			6	0:50	♀	D
0			11	22:32	♇	D
1			13	10:49	☿	℞
0		Feb	3	4:19	☿	D
1			6	22:07	♃	℞
2		May	9	15:52	☿	℞
1		Jun	2	12:11	☿	D
0			10	6:03	♃	D
1			12	4:24	♆	℞
2		Jul	31	18:41	♇	℞
3		Aug	10	3:39	♅	℞
4			16	22:22	♄	℞
5		Sep	9	4:14	☿	℞
4		Oct	1	8:25	☿	D
3		Nov	18	11:17	♆	D
4		Dec	15	14:43	♂	℞
5			28	8:35	☿	℞
4			30	16:38	♄	D
3	1852	Jan	9	3:14	♅	D
2			13	5:57	♇	D
1			17	12:55	☿	D
0		Mar	4	10:19	♂	D

1			8	23:56	♃	℞
2		Apr	19	11:48	☿	℞
1		May	13	6:48	☿	D
2		Jun	13	17:05	♆	℞
3			29	20:53	♀	℞
2		Jul	10	11:45	♃	D
3		Aug	1	2:26	♇	℞
2			11	23:45	♀	D
3			13	15:10	♅	℞
4			21	20:60	☿	℞
5			30	6:18	♄	℞
4		Sep	13	20:10	☿	D
3		Nov	19	21:05	♆	D
4		Dec	11	6:15	☿	℞
3			31	2:31	☿	D
2	1853	Jan	12	6:43	♄	D
1			12	9:50	♅	D
0			13	9:39	♇	D
1		Apr	1	0:19	☿	℞
2			10	17:11	♃	℞
1			24	15:36	☿	D
2		Jun	16	5:02	♆	℞
3		Aug	2	10:02	♇	℞
4			4	6:27	☿	℞
3			11	11:47	♃	D
4			18	2:13	♅	℞
3			27	21:54	☿	D
4		Sep	13	18:18	♄	℞
3		Nov	22	8:12	♆	D
4			25	1:56	☿	℞
3		Dec	14	20:04	☿	D
2	1854	Jan	14	12:35	♇	D
1			16	16:58	♅	D
2			18	1:15	♂	℞
1			26	3:34	♄	D
2		Feb	7	13:46	♀	℞
3		Mar	14	7:47	☿	℞
2			21	5:23	♀	D
1		Apr	6	13:03	☿	D
0			9	0:53	♂	D
1		May	15	19:44	♃	℞
2		Jun	18	19:31	♆	℞
3		Jul	17	6:56	☿	℞
4		Aug	3	14:40	♇	℞
3			10	9:17	☿	D
4			22	14:06	♅	℞
3		Sep	14	2:12	♃	D
4			28	7:56	♄	℞
5		Nov	8	18:28	☿	℞
4			24	17:34	♆	D
3			28	16:36	☿	D
2	1855	Jan	15	16:30	♇	D
1			21	0:15	♅	D
0		Feb	9	7:03	♄	D
1			25	6:59	☿	℞
0		Mar	19	20:52	☿	D
1		Jun	21	8:02	♆	℞
2			21	22:16	♃	℞
3			28	20:37	☿	℞
2		Jul	23	2:02	☿	D
3		Aug	4	19:42	♇	℞
4			27	2:55	♅	℞
5		Sep	10	6:14	♀	℞
6		Oct	12	21:11	♄	℞
5			19	9:36	♃	D
4			22	10:27	♀	D
5			23	6:55	☿	℞
4		Nov	12	14:45	☿	D
3			27	5:40	♆	D
2	1856	Jan	16	22:12	♇	D
1			25	8:41	♅	D
2		Feb	8	17:11	☿	℞
1			23	14:25	♄	D
2			24	6:17	♂	℞
1		Mar	1	13:19	☿	D

0		May	13	18:12	♂	D
1		Jun	8	22:06	☿	℞
2			22	23:14	♆	℞
1		Jul	2	23:49	☿	D
2			29	4:42	♃	℞
3		Aug	4	22:28	♇	℞
4			30	15:43	♅	℞
5		Oct	5	14:39	☿	℞
6			26	8:43	♄	℞
5			26	13:06	☿	D
4		Nov	24	5:21	♃	D
3			28	17:04	♆	D
2	1857	Jan	17	6:46	♇	D
3			22	10:13	☿	℞
2			28	16:59	♅	D
1		Feb	12	12:57	☿	D
0		Mar	9	0:22	♄	D
1		Apr	19	1:13	♀	℞
2		May	20	12:56	☿	℞
1			31	20:21	♀	D
0		Jun	13	10:35	☿	D
1			25	11:42	♆	℞
2		Aug	6	6:23	♇	℞
3		Sep	4	5:57	♅	℞
4			4	17:49	♃	℞
5			18	16:54	☿	℞
4		Oct	10	9:35	☿	D
5		Nov	9	16:22	♄	℞
4		Dec	1	4:10	♆	D
3			31	6:07	♃	D
4	1858	Jan	6	6:58	☿	℞
3			18	10:43	♇	D
2			26	18:34	☿	D
1		Feb	2	3:03	♅	D
0		Mar	23	11:18	♄	D
1		Apr	10	20:00	♂	℞
2		May	1	2:54	☿	℞
1			24	23:15	☿	D
0		Jun	23	21:21	♂	D
1			28	2:25	♆	℞
2		Aug	7	14:21	♇	℞
3		Sep	1	13:03	☿	℞
4			8	19:55	♅	℞
3			24	1:35	☿	D
4		Oct	10	6:34	♃	℞
5		Nov	23	15:02	♀	℞
6			23	18:23	♄	℞
5		Dec	3	17:42	♆	D
6			21	4:53	☿	℞
5	1859	Jan	3	12:37	♀	D
4			10	5:17	☿	D
3			19	13:39	♇	D
2		Feb	5	11:34	♃	D
1			6	12:44	♅	D
0		Apr	6	22:49	♄	D
1			12	5:20	☿	℞
0		May	5	23:19	☿	D
1		Jun	30	16:14	♆	℞
2		Aug	8	17:57	♇	℞
3			15	2:36	☿	℞
2		Sep	7	9:38	☿	D
3			13	11:23	♅	℞
4		Nov	12	12:26	♃	℞
5		Dec	5	1:57	☿	℞
4			6	5:44	♆	D
5			7	11:21	♄	℞
4			24	20:31	☿	D
3	1860	Jan	20	18:44	♇	D
2		Feb	11	0:13	♅	D
1		Mar	11	1:26	♃	D
2			24	2:18	☿	℞
1		Apr	16	13:35	☿	D
0			20	8:28	♄	D
1		Jun	16	21:20	♂	℞
2			27	13:40	♀	℞

3		Jul	2	4:38	♆	℞
4			27	8:38	☿	℞
5		Aug	8	21:20	♇	℞
4			9	16:26	♀	D
3			18	14:41	♂	D
2			20	5:34	☿	D
3		Sep	17	2:32	♅	℞
4		Nov	17	20:35	☿	℞
3		Dec	7	15:28	☿	D
2			7	18:44	♆	D
3			12	18:42	♃	℞
4			19	21:06	♄	℞
3	1861	Jan	21	0:14	♇	D
2		Feb	14	11:15	♅	D
3		Mar	6	16:55	☿	℞
2			29	16:07	☿	D
1		Apr	12	22:37	♃	D
0		May	4	13:01	♄	D
1		Jul	4	17:19	♆	℞
2			9	5:06	☿	℞
1		Aug	2	9:10	☿	D
2			9	23:34	♇	℞
3		Sep	21	19:20	♅	℞
4		Nov	1	11:31	☿	℞
3			21	12:57	☿	D
2		Dec	10	5:18	♆	D
3	1862	Jan	2	0:57	♄	℞
4			12	0:48	♃	℞
3			22	8:09	♇	D
4		Feb	5	4:47	♀	℞
5			17	21:09	☿	℞
4			19	0:13	♅	D
3		Mar	12	4:00	☿	D
2			18	19:31	♀	D
1		May	14	13:53	♃	D
0			18	10:44	♄	D
1		Jun	20	13:25	☿	℞
2		Jul	7	5:13	♆	℞
1			14	17:53	☿	D
2		Aug	11	5:19	♇	℞
3		Sep	2	11:50	♂	℞
4			26	11:19	♅	℞
5		Oct	15	21:53	☿	℞
4		Nov	5	11:32	☿	D
3			5	14:00	♂	D
2		Dec	12	17:18	♆	D
3	1863	Jan	14	21:48	♄	℞
2			23	12:48	♇	D
3		Feb	1	10:45	☿	℞
4			11	6:36	♃	℞
3			22	23:28	☿	D
2			23	12:15	♅	D
1		Jun	1	1:60	♄	D
2			1	9:25	☿	℞
1			14	16:07	♃	D
0			25	9:42	☿	D
1		Jul	9	18:54	♆	℞
2		Aug	12	12:06	♇	℞
3		Sep	7	19:22	♀	℞
4			29	3:10	☿	℞
5		Oct	1	5:42	♅	℞
4			20	0:60	♀	D
3			20	9:20	☿	D
2		Dec	15	3:15	♆	D
3	1864	Jan	16	5:53	☿	℞
2			24	16:19	♇	D
3			27	10:55	♄	℞
2		Feb	6	1:33	☿	D
1			28	3:03	♅	D
2		Mar	13	8:57	♃	℞
3		May	11	22:49	☿	℞
2		Jun	4	19:12	☿	D
1			13	11:58	♄	D
2		Jul	11	6:12	♆	℞
1			14	20:26	♃	D

Planetary Stations in Longitude 1700–2050

2		Aug 12	17:35	♇	℞
3		Sep 11	3:02	☿	℞
2		Oct 3	4:08	☿	D
3		4	22:23	♅	℞
4		23	21:10	♂	℞
3		Dec 16	14:44	♆	D
4		30	3:29	☿	℞
3	1865	Jan 5	11:48	♂	D
2		19	9:31	☿	D
1		24	19:07	♇	D
2		Feb 7	18:49	♄	℞
1		Mar 3	16:13	♅	D
2		Apr 15	9:25	♃	℞
3		16	17:12	♀	℞
4		22	16:44	☿	℞
3		May 16	12:11	☿	D
2		29	11:36	♀	D
1		Jun 26	15:14	♄	D
2		Jul 13	20:49	♆	℞
3		Aug 13	22:39	♇	℞
2		16	1:29	♃	D
3		24	20:46	☿	℞
2		Sep 16	17:08	☿	D
3		Oct 9	18:20	♅	℞
4		Dec 14	1:12	☿	℞
3		19	1:01	♆	D
2	1866	Jan 2	22:25	☿	D
1		25	23:09	♇	D
2		Feb 19	21:11	♄	℞
1		Mar 8	8:55	♅	D
2		Apr 4	2:23	☿	℞
1		27	18:44	☿	D
2		May 20	14:46	♃	℞
1		Jul 9	12:18	♄	D
2		16	9:29	♆	℞
3		Aug 7	7:14	☿	℞
4		15	0:33	♇	℞
3		30	20:41	☿	D
2		Sep 18	17:30	♃	D
3		Oct 14	12:05	♅	℞
4		Nov 21	3:21	♀	℞
5		27	21:14	☿	℞
6		Dec 1	22:07	♂	℞
5		17	15:23	☿	D
4		21	11:31	♆	D
3	1867	Jan 1	1:01	♀	D
2		27	6:36	♇	D
1		Feb 18	14:46	♂	D
2		Mar 3	21:23	♄	℞
1		12	23:33	♅	D
2		17	7:18	☿	℞
1		Apr 9	14:14	☿	D
2		Jun 27	0:32	♃	℞
3		Jul 19	0:39	♆	℞
4		20	9:03	☿	℞
3		22	3:34	♄	D
2		Aug 13	10:25	☿	D
3		16	6:52	♇	℞
4		Oct 19	9:30	♅	℞
3		24	7:22	♃	D
4		Nov 11	14:20	☿	℞
3		Dec 1	11:26	☿	D
2		24	0:25	♆	D
1	1868	Jan 28	10:45	♇	D
2		Feb 28	4:27	☿	℞
3		Mar 14	18:54	♄	℞
2		16	17:55	♅	D
1		21	20:42	☿	D
2		Jun 25	6:23	♀	℞
3		Jul 1	0:40	☿	℞
4		20	14:46	♆	℞
3		25	5:58	☿	D
2		Aug 2	11:40	♄	D
3		3	6:45	♃	℞
2		7	9:26	♀	D
3		16	14:46	♇	℞
4		Oct 23	4:33	♅	℞
5		25	3:34	☿	℞
4		Nov 14	9:29	☿	D
3		29	2:46	♃	D
2		Dec 25	11:56	♆	D
3	1869	Jan 4	14:42	♂	℞
2		28	13:16	♇	D
3		Feb 10	13:13	☿	℞
2		Mar 4	12:10	☿	D
1		21	10:23	♅	D
0		26	10:31	♂	D
1		26	13:19	♄	℞
2		Jun 12	4:03	☿	℞
1		Jul 6	6:21	☿	D
2		23	4:32	♆	℞
1		Aug 14	16:11	♄	D
2		17	19:29	♇	℞
3		Sep 9	15:58	♃	℞
4		Oct 8	12:02	☿	℞
5		28	3:13	♅	℞
4		29	7:60	☿	D
3		Dec 28	1:06	♆	D
2	1870	Jan 5	5:00	♃	D
3		25	5:28	☿	℞
2		29	17:05	♇	D
3		Feb 2	19:19	♀	℞
2		15	10:50	☿	D
1		Mar 16	9:21	♀	D
0		26	6:46	♅	D
1		Apr 7	8:53	♄	℞
2		May 23	19:50	☿	℞
1		Jun 16	18:09	☿	D
2		Jul 25	18:21	♆	℞
3		Aug 18	23:41	♇	℞
2		26	18:07	♄	D
3		Sep 21	15:02	☿	℞
2		Oct 13	4:59	☿	D
3		15	1:04	♃	℞
4		Nov 1	23:15	♅	℞
3		Dec 30	12:13	♆	D
4	1871	Jan 9	1:52	☿	℞
3		29	15:29	☿	D
2		30	21:49	♇	D
3		Feb 9	2:49	♂	℞
2		10	7:40	♃	D
1		Mar 31	1:30	♅	D
2		Apr 19	5:31	♄	℞
1		30	13:36	♂	D
2		May 4	9:09	☿	℞
1		28	5:33	☿	D
2		Jul 28	7:17	♆	℞
3		Aug 20	1:43	♇	℞
4		Sep 4	12:04	☿	℞
5		5	8:31	♀	℞
4		7	16:27	♄	D
3		26	21:47	☿	D
2		Oct 17	15:22	♀	D
3		Nov 6	22:31	♅	℞
4		16	22:42	♃	℞
5		Dec 23	23:48	☿	℞
4	1872	Jan 2	1:02	♆	D
3		13	1:27	☿	D
2		Feb 1	5:29	♇	D
1		Mar 15	16:25	♃	D
0		Apr 3	23:55	♅	D
1		14	9:15	☿	℞
2		30	6:08	♄	℞
1		May 8	3:35	☿	D
2		Jul 29	20:26	♆	℞
3		Aug 17	2:45	☿	℞
4		20	7:24	♇	℞
3		Sep 9	7:07	☿	D
2		18	13:35	♄	D
3		Nov 10	19:52	♅	℞
4		Dec 6	21:05	☿	℞
5		17	2:20	♃	℞
4		26	16:05	☿	D
3	1873	Jan 3	11:47	♆	D
2		Feb 1	9:56	♇	D
3		Mar 21	22:29	♂	℞
4		27	3:14	☿	℞
3		Apr 8	21:15	♅	D
4		14	9:23	♀	℞
3		17	10:55	♃	D
2		19	15:59	☿	D
3		May 12	8:40	♄	℞
2		27	2:40	♀	D
1		Jun 6	18:08	♂	D
2		Jul 30	10:06	☿	℞
3		Aug 1	7:13	♆	℞
4		21	13:58	♇	℞
3		23	5:08	☿	D
2		Sep 30	8:55	♄	D
3		Nov 15	19:31	♅	℞
4		20	16:09	☿	℞
3		Dec 10	10:37	☿	D
2	1874	Jan 5	23:30	♆	D
3		16	6:16	♃	℞
2		Feb 2	13:29	♇	D
3		Mar 9	15:20	☿	℞
2		Apr 1	16:52	☿	D
1		13	21:11	♅	D
0		May 18	23:10	♃	D
1		24	15:24	♄	℞
2		Jul 12	8:00	☿	℞
3		Aug 3	21:20	♆	℞
2		5	11:33	☿	D
3		22	20:11	♇	℞
2		Oct 12	8:10	♄	D
3		Nov 4	7:38	☿	℞
4		18	16:07	♀	℞
5		20	18:15	♅	℞
4		24	7:49	☿	D
3		Dec 29	13:58	♀	D
2	1875	Jan 8	9:41	♆	D
1		Feb 3	15:37	♇	D
2		15	12:06	♃	℞
3		20	17:57	☿	℞
2		Mar 15	3:21	☿	D
1		Apr 18	19:58	♅	D
2		May 18	22:12	♂	℞
3		Jun 6	5:58	♄	℞
2		18	23:31	♃	D
3		23	18:07	☿	℞
2		Jul 17	23:12	☿	D
1		25	14:32	♂	D
2		Aug 6	8:49	♆	℞
3		24	1:30	♇	℞
4		Oct 18	18:43	☿	℞
3		24	9:13	♄	D
2		Nov 8	6:17	☿	D
3		25	18:36	♅	℞
2	1876	Jan 10	20:03	♆	D
3		Feb 4	6:30	☿	℞
2		4	18:50	♇	D
1		25	21:44	☿	D
2		Mar 17	21:05	♃	℞
1		Apr 22	20:47	♅	D
2		Jun 3	16:04	☿	℞
3		18	2:16	♄	℞
4		22	22:44	♀	℞
3		27	16:53	☿	D
2		Jul 19	7:01	♃	D
1		Aug 5	2:10	♀	D
2		7	22:60	♆	℞
3		24	2:39	♇	℞
4		Oct 1	0:54	☿	℞
3		22	4:18	☿	D
2		Nov 4	11:51	♄	D
3		29	18:22	♅	℞
2	1877	Jan 12	8:49	♆	D
3		18	1:01	☿	℞
2		Feb 5	2:17	♇	D
1		7	23:01	☿	D
2		Apr 20	2:10	♃	℞
1		27	20:29	♅	D
2		May 15	5:48	☿	℞
1		Jun 8	2:24	☿	D
2		Jul 1	5:27	♄	℞
3		Aug 6	0:08	♂	℞
4		10	12:02	♆	℞
3		20	13:60	♃	D
4		25	7:22	♇	℞
5		Sep 14	1:39	☿	℞
4		Oct 5	13:26	♂	D
3		5	23:44	☿	D
2		Nov 16	20:47	♄	D
3		Dec 4	18:50	♅	℞
4	1878	Jan 1	22:19	☿	℞
3		14	19:41	♆	D
2		22	6:11	☿	D
3		31	9:34	♀	℞
2		Feb 6	7:54	♇	D
1		Mar 13	22:37	♀	D
2		Apr 25	21:58	☿	℞
1		May 2	22:02	♅	D
0		19	17:48	☿	D
1		25	17:33	♃	℞
2		Jul 14	15:56	♄	℞
3		Aug 13	2:09	♆	℞
4		26	15:04	♇	℞
5		27	20:15	☿	℞
4		Sep 19	13:52	☿	D
3		23	14:23	♃	D
2		Nov 29	10:42	♄	D
3		Dec 9	18:58	♅	℞
4		16	20:02	☿	℞
3	1879	Jan 5	18:20	☿	D
2		17	8:22	♆	D
1		Feb 7	10:56	♇	D
2		Apr 7	4:57	☿	℞
1		30	22:04	☿	D
0		May 7	22:55	♅	D
1		Jul 2	8:22	♃	℞
2		28	8:44	♄	℞
3		Aug 10	7:43	☿	℞
4		15	16:55	♆	℞
5		27	21:10	♇	℞
4		Sep 2	19:07	☿	D
5		2	22:11	♀	℞
6		Oct 6	20:34	♂	℞
5		15	5:59	♀	D
4		29	7:46	♃	D
5		Nov 30	16:29	☿	℞
4		Dec 12	7:42	♄	D
5		14	19:00	♅	℞
4		16	9:01	♂	D
3		20	10:43	☿	D
2	1880	Jan 19	19:47	♆	D
1		Feb 8	13:15	♇	D
2		Mar 19	7:14	☿	℞
1		Apr 11	15:43	☿	D
0		May 12	1:25	♅	D
1		Jul 22	11:02	☿	℞
2		Aug 8	14:00	♃	℞
3		10	7:42	♄	℞
2		15	11:06	☿	D
3		17	6:38	♆	℞
4		28	2:55	♇	℞
5		Nov 13	10:12	☿	℞
4		Dec 3	6:22	☿	D
3		4	7:45	♃	D
4		18	19:22	♅	℞
3		24	12:22	♄	D
2	1881	Jan 21	9:19	♆	D
1		Feb 8	16:53	♇	D
2		Mar 2	2:10	☿	℞
1		24	20:50	☿	D
2		Apr 12	2:07	♀	℞
1		May 17	4:15	♅	D
0		24	18:10	♀	D
1		Jul 4	4:35	☿	℞
0		28	9:29	☿	D
1		Aug 19	20:08	♆	℞
2		24	13:41	♄	℞
3		29	4:49	♇	℞
4		Sep 14	20:14	♃	℞
5		Oct 28	0:08	☿	℞
4		Nov 17	4:18	☿	D
5		17	14:19	♂	℞
6		Dec 23	19:02	♅	℞
5	1882	Jan 6	22:06	♄	D
4		10	9:25	♃	D
3		23	20:21	♆	D
2		Feb 2	17:36	♂	D
1		10	0:14	♇	D
2		13	9:26	☿	℞
1		Mar 7	11:13	☿	D
0		May 22	7:21	♅	D
1		Jun 15	9:41	☿	℞
0		Jul 9	12:40	☿	D
1		Aug 22	8:05	♆	℞
2		30	9:54	♇	℞
3		Sep 8	0:28	♄	℞
4		Oct 11	9:14	☿	℞
5		19	17:58	♃	℞
4		Nov 1	2:53	☿	D
5		16	4:37	♀	℞
4		Dec 27	2:58	♀	D
5		28	19:60	♅	℞
4	1883	Jan 20	14:35	♄	D
3		26	8:51	♆	D
4		28	0:48	☿	℞
3		Feb 11	5:11	♇	D
2		15	5:12	♃	D
1		18	8:46	☿	D
2		May 27	2:39	☿	℞
1		27	11:36	♅	D
0		Jun 20	1:45	☿	D
1		Aug 24	22:09	♆	℞
2		31	15:42	♇	℞
3		Sep 22	13:31	♄	℞
4		24	12:58	☿	℞
3		Oct 16	0:13	☿	D
4		Nov 21	9:23	♃	℞
5		Dec 23	6:50	♂	℞
6	1884	Jan 2	19:32	♅	℞
7		11	20:47	☿	℞
6		28	19:60	♆	D
5		Feb 1	12:27	☿	D
4		3	14:48	♄	D
3		12	10:11	♇	D
2		Mar 12	14:18	♂	D
1		20	9:42	♃	D
2		May 6	15:43	☿	℞
1		30	12:07	☿	D
0		31	14:54	♅	D
1		Jun 20	14:36	♀	℞
0		Aug 2	18:34	♀	D
1		26	8:42	♆	℞
2		31	22:10	♇	℞
3		Sep 6	10:57	☿	℞
2		28	17:44	☿	D
3		Oct 6	1:48	♄	℞
4		Dec 21	5:20	♃	℞
5		25	18:40	☿	℞
6	1885	Jan 6	20:48	♅	℞
5		14	21:42	☿	D
4		30	7:08	♆	D

Planetary Stations in Longitude 1700–2050

#	Year	Date	Time	Planet	Station
3		Feb 12	13:21	♇	D
2		16	20:42	♄	D
3		Apr 17	13:31	☿	℞
2		21	20:16	♃	D
1		May 11	8:10	☿	D
0		Jun 5	20:05	♅	D
1		Aug 20	2:48	☿	℞
2		28	21:42	♆	℞
3		Sep 2	4:38	♇	℞
2		12	4:23	☿	D
3		Oct 20	12:39	♄	℞
4		Dec 9	16:10	☿	℞
3		29	11:48	☿	D
4	1886	Jan 11	19:50	♅	℞
5		20	8:46	♃	℞
6		25	22:18	♂	℞
7		28	23:12	♀	℞
6		Feb 1	19:42	♆	D
5		13	16:20	♇	D
4		Mar 3	5:53	♄	D
3		11	11:19	♀	D
4		30	4:30	☿	℞
3		Apr 16	20:24	♂	D
2		22	18:39	☿	D
1		May 23	6:15	♃	D
0		Jun 10	23:06	♅	D
1		Aug 2	11:22	☿	℞
0		26	4:27	☿	D
1		31	9:22	♆	℞
2		Sep 3	7:00	♇	℞
3		Nov 3	20:36	♄	℞
4		23	11:37	☿	℞
3		Dec 13	5:52	☿	D
4	1887	Jan 16	20:58	♅	℞
3		Feb 4	6:18	♆	D
2		14	23:16	♇	D
3		19	17:04	♃	℞
4		Mar 12	14:08	☿	℞
3		17	16:39	♄	D
2		Apr 4	17:46	☿	D
1		Jun 16	4:25	♅	D
0		23	5:24	♃	D
1		Jul 15	10:36	☿	℞
0		Aug 8	13:38	☿	D
1		31	12:21	♀	℞
2		Sep 2	22:41	♆	℞
3		4	11:19	♇	℞
2		Oct 12	20:58	♀	D
3		Nov 7	3:41	☿	℞
4		17	23:58	♄	℞
3		27	2:43	☿	D
4	1888	Jan 21	19:12	♅	℞
3		Feb 6	19:07	♆	D
2		16	4:58	♇	D
3		23	15:02	☿	℞
4		Mar 4	11:15	♂	℞
3		17	2:51	☿	D
4		22	6:43	♃	℞
3		31	3:15	♄	D
2		May 22	4:41	♂	D
1		Jun 20	7:01	♅	D
2		25	22:36	☿	℞
1		Jul 20	4:00	☿	D
0		23	14:38	♃	D
1		Sep 4	12:20	♆	℞
2		4	18:11	♇	℞
3		Oct 20	15:30	☿	℞
2		Nov 10	1:01	☿	D
3		30	20:37	♄	℞
4	1889	Jan 25	19:34	♅	℞
5		Feb 6	2:21	☿	℞
4		8	6:39	♆	D
3		16	9:01	♇	D
2		27	20:12	☿	D
3		Apr 9	19:00	♀	℞
2		14	12:12	♄	D
3		24	22:38	♃	℞
2		May 22	10:08	♀	D
3		Jun 6	22:28	☿	℞
2		25	11:39	♅	D
1		30	23:41	☿	D
0		Aug 25	4:59	♃	D
1		Sep 6	1:20	♇	℞
2		7	1:19	♆	℞
3		Oct 3	22:31	☿	℞
2		24	23:13	☿	D
3		Dec 14	10:18	♄	℞
4	1890	Jan 20	20:07	☿	℞
5		30	17:14	♅	℞
4		Feb 10	20:03	♆	D
3		10	20:37	☿	D
2		17	11:07	♇	D
3		Apr 23	9:28	♂	℞
2		28	17:09	♄	D
3		May 18	12:42	☿	℞
4		30	22:12	♃	℞
3		Jun 11	9:46	☿	D
2		30	13:55	♅	D
1		Jul 4	13:14	♂	D
2		Sep 7	7:52	♇	℞
3		9	14:59	♆	℞
4		17	0:05	☿	℞
3		28	11:20	♃	D
2		Oct 8	19:13	☿	D
3		Nov 13	16:39	♀	℞
2		Dec 24	15:45	♀	D
3		27	16:30	♄	℞
4	1891	Jan 4	17:05	☿	℞
3		25	2:56	☿	D
4		Feb 4	16:06	♅	℞
3		13	6:47	♆	D
2		18	14:44	♇	D
3		Apr 29	3:37	☿	℞
2		May 12	17:21	♄	D
1		22	23:47	☿	D
0		Jul 5	17:40	♅	D
1		7	18:27	♃	℞
2		Aug 30	19:30	☿	℞
3		Sep 8	10:27	♇	℞
4		12	3:41	♆	℞
3		22	10:23	☿	D
2		Nov 3	12:41	♃	D
3		Dec 19	14:55	☿	℞
2	1892	Jan 8	14:20	☿	D
3		9	14:21	♄	℞
4		Feb 9	12:42	♅	℞
3		15	19:15	♆	D
2		19	22:04	♇	D
3		Apr 9	8:04	☿	℞
2		May 3	1:43	☿	D
1		25	12:41	♄	D
2		Jun 18	6:22	♀	℞
3		Jul 5	3:28	♂	℞
2		9	19:58	♅	D
1		31	10:44	♀	D
2		Aug 12	8:02	☿	℞
3		14	0:53	♃	℞
2		Sep 3	17:02	♂	D
1		4	17:12	☿	D
2		8	15:55	♇	℞
3		13	18:01	♆	℞
4		Dec 2	11:44	☿	℞
3		9	15:56	♃	D
2		22	6:05	☿	D
3	1893	Jan 21	5:42	♄	℞
4		Feb 13	9:48	♅	℞
3		17	6:12	♆	D
2		20	3:27	♇	D
3		Mar 22	7:30	☿	℞
2		Apr 14	17:28	☿	D
1		Jun 8	1:42	♄	D
0		Jul 14	22:41	♅	D
1		25	12:56	☿	℞
0		Aug 18	11:23	☿	D
1		Sep 9	22:10	♇	℞
2		16	4:38	♆	℞
3		19	21:26	♃	℞
4		Nov 16	5:60	☿	℞
3		Dec 6	1:23	☿	D
2	1894	Jan 15	12:56	♃	D
3		26	12:53	♀	℞
4		Feb 2	16:55	♄	℞
5		18	5:38	♅	℞
4		19	17:21	♆	D
3		21	8:49	♇	D
4		Mar 5	0:07	☿	℞
3		8	23:55	♀	D
2		27	21:14	☿	D
1		Jun 21	5:53	♄	D
2		Jul 7	8:10	☿	℞
1		20	0:34	♅	D
0		31	12:36	☿	D
1		Sep 11	5:54	♇	℞
2		16	0:15	♂	℞
3		18	17:21	♆	℞
4		Oct 24	11:38	♃	℞
5		30	20:29	☿	℞
4		Nov 19	23:07	☿	D
3		21	14:34	♂	D
4	1895	Feb 14	21:42	♄	℞
5		16	5:47	☿	℞
4		20	4:36	♃	D
3		22	5:24	♆	D
2		22	12:06	♇	D
3		23	0:54	♅	℞
2		Mar 10	10:20	☿	D
3		Jun 18	14:54	☿	℞
2		Jul 4	3:44	♄	D
1		12	18:45	☿	D
0		25	1:22	♅	D
1		Aug 29	3:05	♀	℞
2		Sep 12	14:45	♇	℞
3		21	4:45	♆	℞
2		Oct 10	12:46	♀	D
3		14	6:15	☿	℞
2		Nov 3	21:44	☿	D
3		25	17:38	♃	℞
4	1896	Jan 30	20:14	☿	℞
3		Feb 21	6:44	☿	D
2		23	14:13	♇	D
1		24	15:13	♆	D
2		26	21:56	♄	℞
3		27	20:03	♅	℞
2		Mar 24	23:47	♃	D
3		May 29	9:22	☿	℞
2		Jun 22	9:10	☿	D
1		Jul 15	21:09	♄	D
0		29	2:05	♅	D
1		Sep 12	18:54	♇	℞
2		22	16:43	♆	℞
3		26	10:48	☿	℞
2		Oct 17	19:20	☿	D
3		Nov 2	6:48	♂	℞
4		Dec 25	11:31	♃	℞
5	1897	Jan 13	15:48	☿	℞
4		16	8:18	♂	D
3		Feb 3	9:34	☿	D
2		23	21:13	♇	D
1		26	4:31	♆	D
2		Mar 3	14:13	♅	℞
3		9	19:19	♄	℞
4		Apr 7	11:40	♀	℞
3		26	7:56	♃	D
4		May 9	22:30	☿	℞
3		20	2:09	♀	D
2		Jun 2	18:48	☿	D
1		Jul 28	8:15	♄	D
0		Aug 3	0:40	♅	D
1		Sep 9	9:50	☿	℞
2		13	22:29	♇	℞
3		25	4:41	♆	℞
2		Oct 1	13:34	☿	D
3		Dec 28	13:34	☿	℞
2	1898	Jan 17	18:09	☿	D
3		24	12:17	♃	℞
2		Feb 25	4:19	♇	D
1		28	16:11	♆	D
2		Mar 8	8:41	♅	℞
3		21	15:14	♄	℞
4		Apr 20	18:09	☿	℞
3		May 14	13:11	☿	D
2		27	13:06	♃	D
1		Aug 7	23:45	♅	D
0		9	14:56	♄	D
1		23	2:45	☿	℞
0		Sep 15	1:30	☿	D
1		15	3:35	♇	℞
2		27	16:34	♆	℞
3		Nov 11	4:23	♀	℞
4		Dec 9	20:00	♂	℞
5		12	11:14	☿	℞
4		22	4:26	♀	D
3	1899	Jan 1	7:40	☿	D
4		Feb 24	0:31	♃	℞
3		26	11:09	♇	D
2		27	5:54	♂	D
1		Mar 3	5:43	♆	D
2		13	1:52	♅	℞
3		Apr 2	6:16	☿	℞
4		2	12:15	♄	℞
3		25	21:41	☿	D
2		Jun 27	13:54	♃	D
3		Aug 5	12:19	☿	℞
2		12	20:40	♅	D
1		21	16:55	♄	D
0		29	3:29	☿	D
1		Sep 16	11:24	♇	℞
2		30	5:37	♆	℞
3		Nov 26	6:59	☿	℞
2		Dec 16	1:08	☿	D
1	1900	Feb 27	14:50	♇	D
0		Mar 5	16:54	♆	D
1		15	13:22	☿	℞
2		17	19:27	♅	℞
3		27	21:18	♃	℞
2		Apr 7	18:51	☿	D
3		14	6:59	♄	℞
4		Jun 16	22:20	♀	℞
5		Jul 18	12:54	☿	℞
4		29	2:23	♃	D
3		30	2:30	♀	D
2		Aug 11	15:10	☿	D
1		17	18:17	♅	D
0		Sep 2	15:16	♄	D
1		17	19:23	♇	℞
2		Oct 2	17:47	♆	℞
3		Nov 9	23:37	☿	℞
2		29	21:34	☿	D
3	1901	Jan 13	7:04	♂	℞
4		Feb 26	12:18	☿	℞
3		28	18:18	♇	D
2		Mar 8	6:24	♆	D
1		21	2:30	☿	D
2		22	11:26	♅	℞
1		Apr 4	6:52	♂	D
2		26	4:34	♄	℞
3		30	20:41	♃	℞
4		Jun 30	2:52	☿	℞
3		Jul 24	8:17	☿	D
2		Aug 22	13:55	♅	D
1		30	21:46	♃	D
0		Sep 14	14:09	♄	D
1		19	0:36	♇	℞
2		Oct 5	6:56	♆	℞
3		24	12:10	☿	℞
2		Nov 13	19:42	☿	D
3	1902	Jan 25	3:03	♀	℞
4		Feb 9	22:18	☿	℞
3		Mar 2	1:06	♇	D
2		3	18:51	☿	D
1		7	12:46	♀	D
0		10	18:14	♆	D
1		27	3:49	♅	℞
2		May 8	6:18	♄	℞
3		Jun 6	4:31	♃	℞
4		11	4:42	☿	℞
3		Jul 5	6:26	☿	D
2		Aug 27	10:19	♅	D
3		Sep 20	6:48	♇	℞
2		26	10:54	♄	D
1		Oct 4	11:13	♃	D
2		7	17:36	♆	℞
3		7	19:60	☿	℞
2		28	18:06	☿	D
3	1903	Jan 24	15:15	☿	℞
2		Feb 14	18:20	☿	D
3		18	15:34	♂	℞
2		Mar 3	7:12	♇	D
1		13	5:33	♆	D
2		31	17:50	♅	℞
1		May 9	15:26	♂	D
2		20	12:08	♄	℞
3		22	19:39	☿	℞
2		Jun 15	17:24	☿	D
3		Jul 14	4:20	♃	℞
4		Aug 27	17:36	♀	℞
3		Sep 1	4:19	♅	D
4		20	22:22	☿	℞
5		21	12:39	♇	℞
4		Oct 8	8:06	♄	D
3		9	4:36	♀	D
4		10	6:36	♆	℞
3		12	14:40	☿	D
2		Nov 9	17:32	♃	D
3	1904	Jan 8	11:56	☿	℞
2		28	23:48	☿	D
1		Mar 3	13:41	♇	D
0		14	17:03	♆	D
1		Apr 4	9:09	♅	℞
2		May 2	9:34	☿	℞
1		26	5:57	☿	D
2		31	23:27	♄	℞
3		Aug 20	5:28	♃	℞
4		Sep 2	18:37	☿	℞
3		4	23:11	♅	D
4		21	20:45	♇	℞
3		25	6:46	☿	D
4		Oct 11	17:47	♆	℞
3		19	6:57	♄	D
2		Dec 15	19:58	♃	D
3		22	9:50	☿	℞
2	1905	Jan 11	10:26	☿	D
1		Mar 4	18:30	♇	D
0		17	2:34	♆	D
1		Apr 2	20:46	♂	℞
2		6	3:54	♀	℞
3		8	21:20	♅	℞
4		13	11:35	☿	℞
3		May 7	5:35	☿	D
2		18	18:04	♀	D
3		Jun 13	15:10	♄	℞
2		17	7:24	♂	D
3		Aug 16	8:22	☿	℞
2		Sep 8	15:02	☿	D
1		9	15:17	♅	D

Planetary Stations in Longitude 1700–2050

2			23	7:12	♇	℞
3			25	19:20	♃	℞
4		Oct	14	5:22	♆	℞
3			31	9:03	♄	D
4		Dec	6	6:57	☿	℞
3			26	1:35	☿	D
2	1906	Jan	21	14:25	♃	D
1		Mar	5	21:26	♇	D
0			19	15:17	♆	D
1			26	8:03	☿	℞
2		Apr	13	11:54	♅	℞
1			18	19:32	☿	D
2		Jun	26	14:36	♄	℞
3		Jul	29	14:38	☿	℞
2		Aug	22	11:16	☿	D
1		Sep	14	8:12	♅	D
2			24	14:12	♇	℞
3		Oct	16	16:57	♆	℞
4			30	0:16	♃	℞
5		Nov	9	15:36	♀	℞
4			12	17:09	♄	D
5			20	1:40	☿	℞
4		Dec	9	20:29	☿	D
3			20	16:26	♀	D
2	1907	Feb	25	21:40	♃	D
1		Mar	7	4:17	♇	D
2			8	22:19	☿	℞
1			22	1:59	♆	D
0			31	21:51	☿	D
1		Apr	17	22:43	♅	℞
2		Jun	5	6:42	♂	℞
3		Jul	9	22:15	♄	℞
4			11	11:17	☿	℞
3		Aug	4	15:18	☿	D
2			9	3:28	♂	D
1		Sep	18	22:04	♅	D
2			25	20:53	♇	℞
3		Oct	19	4:32	♆	℞
4		Nov	3	16:40	☿	℞
3			23	17:56	☿	D
2			25	4:06	♄	D
3		Dec	1	1:21	♃	℞
4	1908	Feb	20	2:21	☿	℞
3		Mar	7	11:14	♇	D
2			13	9:32	☿	D
1			23	15:01	♆	D
0			30	13:16	♃	D
1		Apr	21	12:18	♅	℞
2		Jun	14	14:51	♀	℞
3			21	19:46	☿	℞
2		Jul	16	0:22	☿	D
3			22	12:46	♄	℞
2			27	18:25	♀	D
1		Sep	22	13:26	♅	D
2			26	2:05	♇	℞
3		Oct	17	3:10	☿	℞
4			20	17:12	♆	℞
3		Nov	6	16:32	☿	D
2		Dec	6	21:04	♄	D
3			30	14:22	♃	℞
4	1909	Feb	2	15:51	☿	℞
3			24	4:54	☿	D
2		Mar	8	19:56	♇	D
1			26	2:12	♆	D
2		Apr	25	22:27	♅	℞
1		May	1	14:52	♃	D
2		Jun	2	16:03	☿	℞
1			26	16:25	☿	D
2		Aug	5	9:32	♄	℞
3			23	2:21	♂	℞
2		Sep	27	1:29	♅	D
3			27	10:44	♇	℞
4			30	8:35	☿	℞
3		Oct	21	14:21	☿	D
4			23	5:03	♆	℞

3			24	7:16	♂	D
2		Dec	19	21:52	♄	D
3	1910	Jan	17	10:53	☿	℞
4			22	17:24	♀	℞
5			29	18:10	♃	℞
4		Feb	7	6:52	☿	D
3		Mar	5	1:55	♀	D
2			10	1:16	♇	D
1			28	16:14	♆	D
2		Apr	30	10:52	♅	℞
3		May	14	5:30	☿	℞
2		Jun	1	21:15	♃	D
1			7	1:50	☿	D
2		Aug	19	12:50	♄	℞
3		Sep	13	8:37	☿	℞
4			28	20:28	♇	℞
3		Oct	1	15:05	♅	D
2			5	9:16	☿	D
3			25	17:30	♆	℞
4	1911	Jan	1	8:26	☿	℞
3			2	5:19	♄	D
2			21	14:44	☿	D
3		Mar	1	8:49	♃	℞
2			11	5:18	♇	D
1			31	4:41	♆	D
2		Apr	24	23:09	☿	℞
3		May	4	20:18	♅	℞
2			18	18:37	☿	D
1		Jul	2	21:31	♃	D
2		Aug	25	7:54	♀	℞
3			27	2:25	☿	℞
4		Sep	2	20:57	♄	℞
3			18	22:23	☿	D
4			30	4:37	♇	℞
3		Oct	6	1:53	♅	D
2			6	20:24	♀	D
3			18	8:38	♂	℞
4			28	4:02	♆	℞
5		Dec	16	6:10	☿	℞
4			29	16:25	♂	D
3	1912	Jan	5	3:33	☿	D
2			15	20:23	♄	D
1		Mar	11	12:47	♇	D
2		Apr	1	12:12	♃	℞
1			1	16:37	♆	D
2			5	8:26	☿	℞
1			29	0:53	☿	D
2		May	8	7:34	♅	℞
1		Aug	2	14:57	♃	D
2			8	12:59	☿	℞
1		Sep	1	2:11	☿	D
2			16	8:37	♄	℞
3			30	13:09	♇	℞
2		Oct	9	13:43	♅	D
3			29	16:52	♆	℞
4		Nov	29	2:15	☿	℞
3		Dec	18	20:24	☿	D
2	1913	Jan	28	18:13	♄	D
1		Mar	12	20:19	♇	D
2			18	12:57	☿	℞
3		Apr	3	19:46	♀	℞
2			4	4:57	♆	D
1			10	20:05	☿	D
2		May	5	19:02	♃	℞
3			12	16:33	♅	℞
2			16	9:38	♀	D
3		Jul	21	15:04	☿	℞
2		Aug	14	16:14	☿	D
1		Sep	4	14:56	♃	D
2			30	21:49	♄	℞
3		Oct	1	19:27	♇	℞
2			13	23:23	♅	D
3		Nov	1	3:02	♆	℞
4			12	19:29	☿	℞
5			26	21:11	♂	℞

4		Dec	2	16:26	☿	D
3	1914	Feb	11	20:52	♄	D
2			12	23:35	♂	D
3		Mar	1	9:48	☿	℞
2			14	5:02	♇	D
1			24	2:24	☿	D
0		Apr	6	14:48	♆	D
1		May	17	2:40	♅	℞
2		Jun	11	9:57	♃	℞
3		Jul	3	6:58	☿	℞
2			27	12:10	☿	D
3		Oct	3	3:15	♇	℞
2			9	10:25	♃	D
3			15	11:42	♄	℞
2			18	9:40	♅	D
3			27	8:47	☿	℞
4		Nov	3	13:17	♆	℞
5			7	3:11	♀	℞
4			16	14:28	☿	D
3		Dec	18	4:29	♀	D
4	1915	Feb	12	18:23	☿	℞
3			26	3:25	♄	D
2		Mar	6	17:42	☿	D
1			15	12:31	♇	D
0		Apr	9	3:32	♆	D
1		May	21	10:48	♅	℞
2		Jun	14	10:38	☿	℞
1		Jul	8	13:04	☿	D
2			19	9:49	♃	℞
3		Oct	4	14:45	♇	℞
4			10	17:22	☿	℞
3			22	18:11	♅	D
4			29	22:59	♄	℞
3			31	13:01	☿	D
4		Nov	5	23:53	♆	℞
3			14	19:30	♃	D
4		Dec	31	22:29	♂	℞
5	1916	Jan	27	10:28	☿	℞
4		Feb	17	16:12	☿	D
3		Mar	11	13:52	♄	D
2			15	16:59	♇	D
1			21	14:43	♂	D
0		Apr	10	13:13	♆	D
1		May	24	20:13	♅	℞
2			25	2:33	☿	℞
3		Jun	12	7:48	♀	℞
2			18	1:03	☿	D
1		Jul	25	10:48	♀	D
2		Aug	25	9:35	♃	℞
3		Sep	22	20:28	☿	℞
4		Oct	5	1:23	♇	℞
3			14	10:01	☿	D
2			26	3:18	♅	D
3		Nov	7	10:37	♆	℞
4			12	5:11	♄	℞
3		Dec	20	23:37	♃	D
4	1917	Jan	10	6:49	☿	℞
3			30	20:44	☿	D
2		Mar	16	23:12	♇	D
1			26	1:54	♄	D
0		Apr	13	1:02	♆	D
1		May	5	15:48	☿	℞
2			29	3:27	♅	℞
1			29	12:11	☿	D
2		Sep	5	17:38	☿	℞
1			28	2:56	☿	D
2			30	16:05	♃	℞
3		Oct	6	12:13	♇	℞
2			30	10:32	♅	D
3		Nov	9	22:28	♆	℞
4			26	4:38	♄	℞
5		Dec	25	4:44	☿	℞
4	1918	Jan	14	6:34	☿	D
5			20	7:51	♀	℞
4			26	12:48	♃	D

5		Feb	3	23:02	♂	℞
4		Mar	2	15:24	♀	D
3			18	6:19	♇	D
2		Apr	9	13:34	♄	D
1			15	11:59	♆	D
2			16	15:29	☿	℞
1			25	16:44	♂	D
0		May	10	9:46	☿	D
1		Jun	2	12:30	♅	℞
2		Aug	19	8:33	☿	℞
1		Sep	11	12:31	☿	D
2		Oct	7	19:13	♇	℞
3		Nov	3	13:52	♃	℞
2			3	18:27	♅	D
3			12	9:19	♆	℞
4		Dec	9	2:06	☿	℞
5			9	21:31	♄	℞
4			28	21:11	☿	D
3	1919	Mar	2	16:36	♃	D
2			19	17:34	♇	D
3			29	9:01	☿	℞
2		Apr	18	1:29	♆	D
1			21	21:58	☿	D
0			23	21:11	♄	D
1		Jun	6	19:13	♅	℞
2		Aug	1	16:02	☿	℞
3			22	21:51	♀	℞
2			25	10:48	☿	D
1		Oct	4	11:46	♀	D
2			9	4:02	♇	℞
1		Nov	8	0:36	♅	D
2			14	21:40	♆	℞
3			22	21:13	☿	℞
4		Dec	5	9:37	♃	℞
3			12	15:40	☿	D
4			23	8:08	♄	℞
5	1920	Mar	10	20:51	☿	℞
6			15	3:05	♂	℞
5			20	2:48	♇	D
4		Apr	2	22:40	☿	D
3			4	1:37	♃	D
2			19	13:37	♆	D
1		May	7	0:05	♄	D
0			31	22:26	♂	D
1		Jun	10	4:07	♅	℞
2		Jul	13	14:06	☿	℞
1		Aug	6	17:37	☿	D
2		Oct	9	14:25	♇	℞
3		Nov	5	12:47	☿	℞
2			11	7:16	♅	D
3			16	8:24	♆	℞
2			25	12:50	☿	D
3	1921	Jan	3	21:37	♃	℞
4			4	10:53	♄	℞
5		Feb	21	23:12	☿	℞
4		Mar	16	8:56	☿	D
3			21	10:01	♇	D
4		Apr	1	11:20	♀	℞
3			22	2:07	♆	D
2		May	6	1:48	♃	D
1			14	0:28	♀	D
0			20	21:37	♄	D
1		Jun	14	10:56	♅	℞
2			25	0:27	☿	℞
1		Jul	19	5:33	☿	D
2		Oct	11	1:06	♇	℞
3			20	0:01	☿	℞
2		Nov	9	11:18	☿	D
1			15	12:50	♅	D
2			18	20:57	♆	℞
3	1922	Jan	17	5:56	♄	℞
4		Feb	2	23:30	♃	℞
5			5	11:36	☿	℞
4			27	3:12	☿	D
3		Mar	22	18:41	♇	D

2		Apr	24	15:22	♆	D
3		May	8	6:10	♂	℞
2		Jun	3	13:08	♄	D
3			5	22:38	☿	℞
2			6	4:49	♃	D
3			18	19:50	♅	℞
2			29	23:28	☿	D
1		Jul	17	2:13	♂	D
2		Oct	3	6:17	☿	℞
3			12	14:08	♇	℞
2			24	9:18	☿	D
3		Nov	4	15:21	♀	℞
2			19	18:06	♅	D
3			21	6:47	♆	℞
2		Dec	15	17:08	♀	D
3	1923	Jan	20	5:59	☿	℞
4			29	18:45	♄	℞
3		Feb	10	4:20	☿	D
4		Mar	5	18:50	♃	℞
3			24	2:07	♇	D
2		Apr	27	2:19	♆	D
3		May	17	12:31	☿	℞
2		Jun	10	9:10	☿	D
1			16	21:42	♄	D
2			23	2:42	♅	℞
1		Jul	7	8:21	♃	D
2		Sep	16	7:09	☿	℞
1		Oct	8	4:48	☿	D
2			14	0:01	♇	℞
3		Nov	23	16:52	♆	℞
2			23	23:29	♅	D
3	1924	Jan	4	3:15	☿	℞
2			24	11:25	☿	D
3		Feb	11	1:17	♄	℞
2		Mar	24	12:43	♇	D
3		Apr	6	1:28	♃	℞
4			27	4:28	☿	℞
3			28	15:26	♆	D
2		May	21	0:21	☿	D
3		Jun	10	0:51	♀	℞
4			26	12:03	♅	℞
3			29	0:44	♄	D
2		Jul	23	3:34	♀	D
3			24	11:02	♂	℞
2		Aug	7	2:11	♃	D
3			29	1:50	☿	℞
2		Sep	20	19:04	☿	D
1			22	9:15	♂	D
2		Oct	14	9:40	♇	℞
3		Nov	25	2:49	♆	℞
2			27	4:03	♅	D
3		Dec	18	1:01	☿	℞
2	1925	Jan	6	23:27	☿	D
3		Feb	22	4:52	♄	℞
2		Mar	25	23:07	♇	D
3		Apr	8	11:03	☿	℞
2		May	1	1:22	♆	D
1			2	4:15	☿	D
2			10	15:30	♃	℞
3		Jun	30	19:13	♅	℞
2		Jul	11	21:18	♄	D
3		Aug	11	13:28	☿	℞
2		Sep	4	0:34	☿	D
1			9	7:18	♃	D
2		Oct	15	20:16	♇	℞
3		Nov	27	12:23	♆	℞
2		Dec	1	9:02	♅	D
3			1	21:30	☿	℞
2			21	15:44	☿	D
3	1926	Jan	17	22:11	♀	℞
2		Feb	28	4:47	♀	D
3		Mar	6	4:54	♄	℞
4			21	12:55	☿	℞
3			27	8:09	♇	D
2		Apr	13	21:35	☿	D

Planetary Stations in Longitude 1700–2050

1		May 3	13:13	♆	D
2		Jun 16	8:35	♃	℞
3		Jul 5	5:02	♅	℞
2		24	9:38	♄	D
3		24	17:05	☿	℞
2		Aug 17	16:55	☿	D
3		Sep 29	5:43	♂	℞
2		Oct 14	4:49	♃	D
3		17	8:51	♇	℞
4		Nov 15	15:19	☿	℞
5		29	23:02	♆	℞
4		Dec 5	11:23	☿	D
3		5	13:52	♅	D
2		7	2:25	♂	D
3	1927	Mar 4	7:34	☿	℞
4		18	0:49	♄	℞
3		27	2:33	☿	D
2		28	16:02	♇	D
1		May 5	23:55	♆	D
2		Jul 6	10:50	☿	℞
3		9	12:32	♅	℞
4		24	13:10	♃	℞
3		30	15:42	☿	D
2		Aug 5	18:59	♄	D
3		20	11:43	♀	℞
2		Oct 2	2:51	♀	D
3		18	23:13	♇	℞
4		30	5:20	☿	℞
3		Nov 19	9:17	☿	D
2		19	18:49	♃	D
3		Dec 2	8:53	♆	℞
2		9	18:16	♅	D
3	1928	Feb 15	14:36	☿	℞
2		Mar 8	16:44	☿	D
3		28	20:37	♄	℞
2		28	23:46	♇	D
1		May 7	12:31	♆	D
2		Jun 16	16:11	☿	℞
1		Jul 10	19:22	☿	D
2		12	22:35	♅	℞
1		Aug 17	0:18	♄	D
2		30	9:19	♃	℞
3		Oct 12	14:32	☿	℞
4		19	12:08	♇	℞
3		Nov 2	7:52	☿	D
4		12	4:13	♂	℞
5		Dec 3	20:48	♆	℞
4		12	23:57	♅	D
3		25	20:33	♃	D
2	1929	Jan 27	12:02	♂	D
3		29	5:48	☿	℞
2		Feb 19	14:07	☿	D
3		Mar 30	3:03	♀	℞
2		30	11:51	♇	D
3		Apr 9	16:02	♄	℞
2		May 9	23:43	♆	D
1		11	15:02	♀	D
2		28	9:18	☿	℞
1		Jun 21	8:28	☿	D
2		Jul 17	6:26	♅	℞
1		Aug 29	0:57	♄	D
2		Sep 25	18:24	☿	℞
3		Oct 5	9:56	♃	℞
2		17	5:16	☿	D
3		21	2:07	♇	℞
4		Dec 6	7:27	♆	℞
3		17	4:20	♅	D
4	1930	Jan 13	1:46	☿	℞
3		31	9:17	♃	D
2		Feb 2	17:43	☿	D
1		Mar 31	23:40	♇	D
2		Apr 21	14:31	♄	℞
3		May 8	22:19	☿	℞
2		12	11:55	♆	D
1		Jun 1	18:38	☿	D
2		Jul 21	16:09	♅	℞
3		Sep 8	16:32	☿	℞
2		9	23:55	♄	D
1		30	22:53	☿	D
2		Oct 22	13:33	♇	℞
3		Nov 2	3:50	♀	℞
4		8	3:21	♃	℞
5		Dec 8	20:17	♆	℞
4		13	6:24	♀	D
5		18	13:45	♂	℞
4		21	10:18	♅	D
5		27	23:38	☿	℞
4	1931	Jan 17	2:52	☿	D
3		Mar 7	8:40	♃	D
2		8	13:52	♂	D
1		Apr 2	11:25	♇	D
2		19	19:52	☿	℞
3		May 3	14:28	♄	℞
2		13	14:33	☿	D
1		15	1:10	♆	D
2		Jul 26	0:36	♅	℞
3		Aug 22	8:33	☿	℞
2		Sep 14	9:44	☿	D
1		21	19:54	♄	D
2		Oct 24	1:48	♇	℞
3		Dec 9	17:30	♃	℞
4		11	6:19	♆	℞
5		11	21:11	☿	℞
4		25	15:29	♅	D
3		31	16:55	☿	D
4	1932	Mar 31	10:27	☿	℞
3		Apr 2	22:59	♇	D
2		8	14:10	♃	D
1		24	0:45	☿	D
2		May 14	16:47	♄	℞
1		16	12:32	♆	D
2		Jun 7	17:36	♀	℞
1		Jul 20	20:23	♀	D
2		29	10:14	♅	℞
3		Aug 3	17:13	☿	℞
2		27	10:03	☿	D
1		Oct 2	17:39	♄	D
2		24	17:44	♇	℞
3		Nov 24	16:40	☿	℞
4		Dec 12	16:31	♆	℞
3		14	10:55	☿	D
2		28	21:01	♅	D
3	1933	Jan 8	2:22	♃	℞
4		21	1:28	♂	℞
5		Mar 13	19:43	☿	℞
4		Apr 4	7:29	♇	D
3		5	23:36	☿	D
2		12	2:18	♂	D
1		May 10	10:21	♃	D
0		19	1:36	♆	D
1		27	2:19	♄	℞
2		Jul 16	16:37	☿	℞
3		Aug 2	19:44	♅	℞
2		9	19:32	☿	D
1		Oct 14	17:14	♄	D
2		26	8:09	♇	℞
3		Nov 8	8:48	☿	℞
2		28	7:42	☿	D
3		Dec 15	2:59	♆	℞
2	1934	Jan 2	3:06	♅	D
3		15	11:46	♀	℞
4		Feb 7	6:19	♃	℞
5		24	20:17	☿	℞
4		25	17:43	♀	D
3		Mar 19	8:26	☿	D
2		Apr 5	19:22	♇	D
1		May 21	11:53	♆	D
2		Jun 8	17:06	♄	℞
1		10	13:41	♃	D
2		28	4:57	☿	℞
1		Jul 22	10:21	☿	D
2		Aug 7	5:25	♅	℞
3		Oct 22	20:44	☿	℞
2		26	17:18	♄	D
3		28	0:34	♇	℞
2		Nov 12	5:59	☿	D
3		Dec 17	11:49	♆	℞
2	1935	Jan 6	8:35	♅	D
3		Feb 8	7:25	☿	℞
4		27	12:11	♂	℞
3		Mar 2	1:37	☿	D
4		10	2:48	♃	℞
3		Apr 7	7:55	♇	D
2		May 17	21:38	♂	D
1		24	0:16	♆	D
2		Jun 9	5:07	☿	℞
3		21	14:28	♄	℞
2		Jul 3	6:25	☿	D
1		11	15:39	♃	D
2		Aug 11	15:49	♅	℞
3		18	1:42	♀	℞
2		Sep 29	17:46	♀	D
3		Oct 6	3:54	☿	℞
2		27	4:11	☿	D
3		29	14:19	♇	℞
2		Nov 7	21:60	♄	D
3		Dec 19	21:25	♆	℞
2	1936	Jan 10	15:20	♅	D
3		23	1:06	☿	℞
2		Feb 13	1:57	☿	D
1		Apr 7	23:25	♇	D
2		10	17:49	♃	℞
3		May 19	19:26	☿	℞
2		25	11:08	♆	D
1		Jun 12	16:36	☿	D
2		Jul 3	18:52	♄	℞
1		Aug 11	14:59	♃	D
2		15	2:35	♅	℞
3		Sep 18	5:33	☿	℞
2		Oct 10	0:17	☿	D
3		30	5:20	♇	℞
2		Nov 19	7:08	♄	D
3		Dec 21	5:56	♆	℞
4	1937	Jan 5	22:03	☿	℞
3		13	21:33	♅	D
2		26	8:11	☿	D
3		Mar 27	19:07	♀	℞
2		Apr 9	13:47	♇	D
3		14	14:42	♂	℞
4		30	10:04	☿	℞
3		May 9	5:56	♀	D
4		15	13:03	♃	℞
3		24	6:16	☿	D
2		27	23:14	♆	D
1		Jun 27	10:09	♂	D
2		Jul 17	5:19	♄	℞
3		Aug 19	13:49	♅	℞
4		Sep 1	1:08	☿	℞
3		13	23:18	♃	D
2		23	15:38	☿	D
3		Oct 31	20:08	♇	℞
2		Dec 1	23:03	♄	D
3		20	19:55	☿	℞
4		23	16:58	♆	℞
3	1938	Jan 9	19:30	☿	D
2		18	4:54	♅	D
1		Apr 11	1:55	♇	D
2		11	14:12	☿	℞
1		May 5	7:54	☿	D
0		30	10:14	♆	D
1		Jun 21	15:30	♃	℞
2		Jul 30	23:14	♄	℞
3		Aug 14	13:51	☿	℞
4		24	2:09	♅	℞
3		Sep 6	22:40	☿	D
2		Oct 19	5:46	♃	D
3		30	16:22	♀	℞
4		Nov 2	12:20	♇	℞
5		Dec 4	16:46	☿	℞
4		10	19:53	♀	D
3		14	21:34	♄	D
2		24	11:10	☿	D
3		26	2:28	♆	℞
2	1939	Jan 22	12:06	♅	D
3		Mar 24	13:17	☿	℞
2		Apr 12	15:17	♇	D
1		16	23:26	☿	D
0		Jun 1	22:38	♆	D
1		22	18:34	♂	℞
2		Jul 27	18:54	☿	℞
3		29	21:01	♃	℞
4		Aug 14	1:03	♄	℞
3		20	17:08	☿	D
2		23	23:59	♂	D
3		28	14:27	♅	℞
4		Nov 4	8:07	♇	℞
5		18	11:05	☿	℞
4		24	21:17	♃	D
3		Dec 8	6:24	☿	D
2		28	1:12	♄	D
3		28	14:15	♆	℞
2	1940	Jan 26	20:26	♅	D
3		Mar 6	5:32	☿	℞
2		29	2:57	☿	D
1		Apr 13	3:15	♇	D
0		Jun 3	11:47	♆	D
1		5	10:05	♀	℞
2		Jul 8	14:17	☿	℞
1		18	13:13	♀	D
0		Aug 1	18:42	☿	D
1		27	7:44	♄	℞
2		Sep 1	4:01	♅	℞
3		4	13:00	♃	℞
4		Nov 1	1:40	☿	℞
5		5	1:31	♇	℞
4		21	4:05	☿	D
5		Dec 30	0:05	♆	℞
4		31	1:20	♃	D
3	1941	Jan 9	12:20	♄	D
2		30	5:02	♅	D
3		Feb 17	10:57	☿	℞
2		Mar 11	15:53	☿	D
1		Apr 14	18:26	♇	D
0		Jun 5	22:54	♆	D
1		19	21:17	☿	℞
0		Jul 14	1:16	☿	D
1		Sep 5	17:36	♅	℞
2		6	18:34	♂	℞
3		10	17:40	♄	℞
4		Oct 10	8:01	♃	℞
5		15	11:30	☿	℞
4		Nov 5	2:41	☿	D
5		6	20:46	♇	℞
4		10	8:33	♂	D
5	1942	Jan 1	10:33	♆	℞
6		13	0:42	♀	℞
5		23	7:01	♄	D
6		Feb 1	1:16	☿	℞
5		3	14:51	♅	D
4		5	10:02	♃	D
3		22	12:08	☿	D
2		23	6:02	♀	D
1		Apr 16	11:02	♇	D
2		May 31	16:03	☿	℞
1		Jun 8	11:44	♆	D
0		24	15:54	☿	D
1		Sep 10	7:42	♅	℞
2		25	5:39	♄	℞
3		28	16:13	☿	℞
2		Oct 20	0:22	☿	D
3		Nov 8	14:42	♇	℞
4		12	14:25	♃	℞
5	1943	Jan 3	21:21	♆	℞
6		15	20:47	☿	℞
5		Feb 5	14:51	☿	D
4		6	7:52	♄	D
3		8	0:54	♅	D
2		Mar 12	2:12	♃	D
1		Apr 18	3:04	♇	D
2		May 12	5:14	☿	℞
1		Jun 5	1:29	☿	D
0		10	22:06	♆	D
1		Aug 15	16:37	♀	℞
2		Sep 11	15:23	☿	℞
3		14	22:36	♅	℞
2		27	9:15	♀	D
1		Oct 3	18:41	☿	D
2		9	18:17	♄	℞
3		28	5:16	♂	℞
4		Nov 10	9:01	♇	℞
5		Dec 13	23:26	♃	℞
6		30	18:32	☿	℞
7	1944	Jan 6	6:23	♆	℞
6		10	4:37	♂	D
5		19	23:21	☿	D
4		Feb 12	12:15	♅	D
3		20	13:18	♄	D
2		Apr 13	2:11	♃	D
1		18	19:23	♇	D
2		22	0:34	☿	℞
1		May 15	19:40	☿	D
0		Jun 12	10:25	♆	D
1		Aug 24	8:26	☿	℞
0		Sep 16	6:47	☿	D
1		18	13:31	♅	℞
2		Oct 23	5:38	♄	℞
3		Nov 11	5:11	♇	℞
4		Dec 13	16:11	☿	℞
3	1945	Jan 2	12:46	☿	D
4		7	16:35	♆	℞
5		12	4:52	♃	℞
4		Feb 15	23:25	♅	D
3		Mar 5	22:43	♄	D
4		25	11:24	♀	℞
5		Apr 3	12:13	☿	℞
4		20	10:22	♇	D
3		27	3:47	☿	D
2		May 6	21:04	♀	D
1		14	17:27	♃	D
0		Jun 14	20:50	♆	D
1		Aug 6	18:11	☿	℞
0		30	9:02	☿	D
1		Sep 23	5:56	♅	℞
2		Nov 6	13:02	♄	℞
3		13	1:54	♇	℞
4		27	12:01	☿	℞
5		Dec 4	22:50	♂	℞
4		17	6:11	☿	D
5	1946	Jan 10	1:16	♆	℞
6		Feb 11	8:27	♃	℞
5		20	12:14	♅	D
4		21	21:12	♂	D
5		Mar 16	18:56	☿	℞
4		20	9:30	♄	D
3		Apr 9	0:38	☿	D
2		22	3:52	♇	D
1		Jun 14	18:06	♃	D
0		17	8:19	♆	D
1		Jul 19	18:56	☿	℞
0		Aug 12	21:03	☿	D
1		Sep 27	22:01	♅	℞
2		Oct 28	4:52	♀	℞
3		Nov 11	4:43	☿	℞
4		15	0:42	♇	℞
5		20	15:22	♄	℞

Planetary Stations in Longitude 1700–2050

4		Dec 1	2:32	☿	D
3		8	9:33	♀	D
4	1947	Jan 12	12:25	♆	℞
3		Feb 25	0:30	♅	D
4		27	17:35	☿	℞
5		Mar 14	11:37	♃	℞
4		22	8:06	☿	D
3		Apr 3	19:38	♄	D
2		23	20:48	♇	D
1		Jun 19	18:47	♆	D
2		Jul 1	9:13	☿	℞
1		15	22:54	♃	D
0		25	14:38	☿	D
1		Oct 2	16:06	♅	℞
2		25	17:25	☿	℞
1		Nov 15	0:41	☿	D
2		16	21:42	♇	℞
3		Dec 4	11:35	♄	℞
4	1948	Jan 8	13:49	♂	℞
5		14	22:02	♆	℞
6		Feb 11	3:24	☿	℞
5		29	14:23	♅	D
4		Mar 4	0:19	☿	D
3		29	12:33	♂	D
4		Apr 15	8:35	♃	℞
3		17	3:20	♄	D
2		24	16:58	♇	D
3		Jun 3	2:02	♀	℞
4		11	11:16	☿	℞
3		21	7:29	♆	D
2		Jul 5	13:04	☿	D
1		16	5:25	♀	D
0		Aug 16	0:40	♃	D
1		Oct 6	9:51	♅	℞
2		8	1:23	☿	℞
1		28	23:06	☿	D
2		Nov 17	20:18	♇	℞
3		Dec 17	0:21	♄	℞
4	1949	Jan 16	9:36	♆	℞
5		24	20:17	☿	℞
4		Feb 14	23:45	☿	D
3		Mar 5	4:09	♅	D
2		Apr 26	14:01	♇	D
1		May 1	8:35	♄	D
2		20	15:34	♃	℞
3		23	2:17	☿	℞
2		Jun 16	0:09	☿	D
1		23	20:46	♆	D
0		Sep 18	18:48	♃	D
1		21	3:50	☿	℞
2		Oct 11	5:14	♅	℞
1		12	19:45	☿	D
2		Nov 19	18:24	♇	℞
3		Dec 30	4:05	♄	℞
4	1950	Jan 8	16:54	☿	℞
5		10	13:36	♀	℞
6		18	19:19	♆	℞
5		29	5:03	☿	D
6		Feb 12	5:49	♂	℞
5		20	18:04	♀	D
4		Mar 9	19:25	♅	D
3		Apr 28	8:40	♇	D
2		May 3	15:52	♂	D
3		3	16:07	☿	℞
2		15	9:23	♄	D
1		27	12:29	☿	D
0		Jun 26	8:05	♆	D
1		27	0:15	♃	℞
2		Sep 4	0:14	☿	℞
1		26	11:59	☿	D
2		Oct 16	0:18	♅	℞
1		24	6:35	♃	D
2		Nov 21	15:57	♇	℞
3		Dec 23	14:48	☿	℞
4	1951	Jan 12	1:18	♄	℞
3		12	15:35	☿	D
4		21	5:29	♆	℞
3		Mar 14	10:41	♅	D
4		Apr 14	17:50	☿	℞
3		30	5:20	♇	D
2		May 8	11:50	☿	D
1		29	3:37	♄	D
0		Jun 28	21:52	♆	D
1		Aug 4	6:54	♃	℞
2		13	7:51	♀	℞
3		17	14:05	☿	℞
2		Sep 9	20:22	☿	D
1		25	0:59	♀	D
2		Oct 20	20:56	♅	℞
3		Nov 23	16:29	♇	℞
2		30	4:09	♃	D
3		Dec 7	11:57	☿	℞
2		27	6:38	☿	D
3	1952	Jan 23	16:29	♆	℞
4		24	17:55	♄	℞
3		Mar 18	4:12	♅	D
4		25	11:07	♂	℞
5		26	13:55	☿	℞
4		Apr 19	1:33	☿	D
3		30	23:21	♇	D
2		Jun 10	2:46	♂	D
1		10	13:20	♄	D
0		30	9:24	♆	D
1		Jul 29	20:31	☿	℞
0		Aug 22	16:55	☿	D
1		Sep 9	19:40	♃	℞
2		Oct 24	16:47	♅	℞
3		Nov 20	6:44	☿	℞
4		24	17:04	♇	℞
3		Dec 10	1:29	☿	D
2	1953	Jan 5	7:52	♃	D
3		25	0:58	♆	℞
4		Feb 5	2:31	♄	℞
5		Mar 9	3:45	☿	℞
4		22	21:22	♅	D
5		23	3:53	♀	℞
4		Apr 1	3:36	☿	D
3		May 2	20:21	♇	D
2		4	12:34	♀	D
1		Jun 23	17:26	♄	D
0		Jul 2	22:13	♆	D
1		11	17:26	☿	℞
0		Aug 4	21:21	☿	D
1		Oct 15	2:57	♃	℞
2		29	14:19	♅	℞
3		Nov 3	21:50	☿	℞
2		23	22:56	☿	D
3		26	20:45	♇	℞
4	1954	Jan 27	10:50	♆	℞
3		Feb 10	9:27	♃	D
4		17	6:16	♄	℞
5		20	7:34	☿	℞
4		Mar 14	15:07	☿	D
3		27	17:32	♅	D
2		May 4	17:45	♇	D
3		23	12:48	♂	℞
4		Jun 23	2:10	☿	℞
3		Jul 5	8:34	♆	D
2		6	15:53	♄	D
1		17	6:51	☿	D
0		29	15:20	♂	D
1		Oct 18	8:26	☿	℞
2		25	16:37	♀	℞
3		Nov 3	10:58	♅	℞
2		7	21:31	☿	D
3		17	3:03	♃	℞
4		28	23:45	♇	℞
3		Dec 5	22:39	♀	D
4	1955	Jan 29	19:19	♆	℞
5		Feb 3	20:55	☿	℞
4		25	10:18	☿	D
5		Mar 1	6:20	♄	℞
4		16	20:39	♃	D
3		Apr 1	12:51	♅	D
2		May 6	18:30	♇	D
3		Jun 3	22:46	☿	℞
2		27	23:11	☿	D
1		Jul 7	19:40	♆	D
0		19	7:30	♄	D
1		Oct 1	13:59	☿	℞
0		22	19:23	☿	D
1		Nov 8	9:29	♅	℞
2		Dec 1	4:48	♇	℞
3		18	4:31	♃	℞
4	1956	Jan 18	15:52	☿	℞
5		Feb 1	6:32	♆	℞
4		8	12:10	☿	D
5		Mar 12	3:29	♄	℞
4		Apr 5	11:22	♅	D
3		17	13:00	♃	D
2		May 7	19:59	♇	D
3		14	12:13	☿	℞
4		31	18:04	♀	℞
3		Jun 7	8:34	☿	D
2		Jul 9	6:09	♆	D
1		13	21:20	♀	D
0		30	18:36	♄	D
1		Aug 10	16:19	♂	℞
2		Sep 13	14:08	☿	℞
1		Oct 5	14:21	☿	D
0		10	10:07	♂	D
1		Nov 12	6:51	♅	℞
2		Dec 2	7:16	♇	℞
3	1957	Jan 1	13:23	☿	℞
4		16	9:22	♃	℞
3		21	19:56	☿	D
4		Feb 2	15:52	♆	℞
5		Mar 24	0:46	♄	℞
4		Apr 10	8:21	♅	D
5		25	5:32	☿	℞
4		May 9	19:51	♇	D
3		19	1:05	☿	D
2		19	2:20	♃	D
1		Jul 11	17:51	♆	D
0		Aug 11	23:57	♄	D
1		27	8:04	☿	℞
0		Sep 19	3:37	☿	D
1		Nov 17	6:28	♅	℞
2		Dec 4	10:31	♇	℞
3		16	11:06	☿	℞
2	1958	Jan 5	8:39	☿	D
3		8	2:47	♀	℞
4		Feb 5	3:16	♆	℞
5		15	14:59	♃	℞
4		18	6:18	♀	D
5		Apr 4	19:39	♄	℞
6		6	14:25	☿	℞
5		15	8:28	♅	D
4		30	6:58	☿	D
3		May 11	22:02	♇	D
2		Jun 19	1:44	♃	D
1		Jul 14	5:53	♆	D
2		Aug 9	18:47	☿	℞
1		24	0:32	♄	D
0		Sep 2	7:43	☿	D
1		Oct 10	9:47	♂	℞
2		Nov 22	4:50	♅	℞
3		30	7:16	☿	℞
4		Dec 6	15:43	♇	℞
3		20	1:27	☿	D
2		20	6:46	♂	D
3	1959	Feb 7	13:36	♆	℞
4		Mar 18	22:10	♃	℞
5		19	18:35	☿	℞
4		Apr 12	1:53	☿	D
5		16	15:32	♄	℞
4		20	6:58	♅	D
3		May 13	21:52	♇	D
2		Jul 16	16:52	♆	D
1		20	8:00	♃	D
2		22	21:03	☿	℞
3		Aug 10	23:16	♀	℞
2		15	22:06	☿	D
1		Sep 5	1:02	♄	D
0		22	17:15	♀	D
1		Nov 14	0:37	☿	℞
2		27	4:47	♅	℞
1		Dec 3	21:26	☿	D
2		8	20:27	♇	℞
3	1960	Feb 10	0:07	♆	℞
4		Mar 1	15:10	☿	℞
3		24	8:05	☿	D
4		Apr 20	4:56	♃	℞
3		24	7:47	♅	D
4		27	14:07	♄	℞
3		May 15	0:49	♇	D
4		Jul 3	13:16	☿	℞
3		18	6:56	♆	D
2		27	18:25	☿	D
1		Aug 20	16:41	♃	D
0		Sep 15	22:48	♄	D
1		Oct 27	14:03	☿	℞
0		Nov 16	19:27	☿	D
1		20	17:04	♂	℞
2		Dec 1	4:21	♅	℞
3		10	4:39	♇	℞
2	1961	Feb 6	2:51	♂	D
3		11	11:33	♆	℞
4		12	23:33	☿	℞
3		Mar 6	23:16	☿	D
4		20	20:13	♀	℞
3		Apr 29	7:51	♅	D
2		May 2	4:16	♀	D
3		9	16:21	♄	℞
2		17	4:24	♇	D
3		25	18:36	♃	℞
4		Jun 14	17:07	☿	℞
3		Jul 8	19:37	☿	D
2		20	18:49	♆	D
1		Sep 23	15:28	♃	D
0		27	19:32	♄	D
1		Oct 10	22:42	☿	℞
0		31	18:02	☿	D
1		Dec 6	4:28	♅	℞
2		12	11:55	♇	℞
3	1962	Jan 27	15:31	☿	℞
4		Feb 13	20:08	♆	℞
3		17	21:36	☿	D
2		May 4	8:57	♅	D
1		19	9:39	♇	D
2		21	23:23	♄	℞
3		26	9:10	☿	℞
2		Jun 19	7:46	☿	D
3		Jul 2	8:59	♃	℞
2		23	8:12	♆	D
3		Sep 24	1:53	☿	℞
2		Oct 9	16:26	♄	D
1		15	15:05	☿	D
2		23	4:15	♀	℞
1		29	10:32	♃	D
0		Dec 3	11:27	♀	D
1		11	5:13	♅	℞
2		14	21:46	♇	℞
3		26	6:12	♂	℞
4	1963	Jan 11	11:47	☿	℞
3		Feb 1	1:58	☿	D
4		16	6:06	♆	℞
3		Mar 16	17:22	♂	D
4		May 6	22:30	☿	℞
3		9	10:17	♅	D
2		21	15:41	♇	D
1		30	18:52	☿	D
2		Jun 3	9:39	♄	℞
1		Jul 25	19:14	♆	D
2		Aug 9	15:26	♃	℞
3		Sep 6	23:10	☿	℞
2		29	8:04	☿	D
1		Oct 21	16:23	♄	D
0		Dec 5	10:11	♃	D
1		16	5:12	♅	℞
2		17	7:08	♇	℞
3		26	9:40	☿	℞
2	1964	Jan 15	11:43	☿	D
3		Feb 18	14:30	♆	℞
4		Apr 16	21:51	☿	℞
3		May 10	16:09	☿	D
2		13	11:27	♅	D
1		22	21:29	♇	D
2		29	10:29	♀	℞
3		Jun 15	3:26	♄	℞
2		Jul 11	13:01	♀	D
1		27	7:02	♆	D
2		Aug 19	14:15	☿	℞
1		Sep 11	17:49	☿	D
2		14	19:01	♃	℞
1		Nov 1	20:45	♄	D
2		Dec 9	7:05	☿	℞
3		18	18:39	♇	℞
4		20	6:46	♅	℞
3		29	2:15	☿	D
2	1965	Jan 10	9:34	♃	D
3		28	22:39	♂	℞
4		Feb 20	1:24	♆	℞
5		Mar 29	14:53	☿	℞
4		Apr 19	21:56	♂	D
3		22	4:01	☿	D
2		May 18	14:32	♅	D
1		25	5:22	♇	D
2		Jun 28	5:32	♄	℞
1		Jul 29	17:42	♆	D
2		Aug 1	21:56	☿	℞
1		25	16:25	☿	D
2		Oct 19	19:33	♃	℞
1		Nov 14	3:17	♄	D
2		23	2:16	☿	℞
1		Dec 12	20:41	☿	D
2		21	5:06	♇	℞
3		25	6:07	♅	℞
4	1966	Jan 5	16:21	♀	℞
3		Feb 15	6:57	♃	D
2		15	18:41	♀	D
3		22	10:42	♆	℞
4		Mar 12	2:19	☿	℞
3		Apr 4	4:25	☿	D
2		May 23	16:38	♅	D
1		27	11:13	♇	D
2		Jul 11	13:03	♄	℞
3		14	20:15	☿	℞
2		Aug 1	4:30	♆	D
1		7	23:43	☿	D
2		Nov 6	17:56	☿	℞
3		21	10:23	♃	℞
2		26	15:34	♄	D
1		26	17:50	☿	D
2		Dec 23	15:38	♇	℞
3		30	7:31	♅	℞
4	1967	Feb 23	4:27	☿	℞
5		24	22:06	♆	℞
6		Mar 8	17:45	♂	℞
5		17	14:28	☿	D
4		21	9:16	♃	D
3		May 26	9:29	♂	D
2		28	21:37	♅	D
1		29	20:30	♇	D
2		Jun 26	6:51	☿	℞

Planetary Stations in Longitude 1700–2050

1		Jul	20	12:02	☿	D
2			25	4:09	♄	℞
1		Aug	3	15:20	♆	D
2			8	14:29	♀	℞
1		Sep	20	9:35	♀	D
2		Oct	21	5:16	☿	℞
1		Nov	10	16:17	☿	D
0		Dec	9	10:28	♄	D
1			22	10:03	♃	℞
2			26	4:48	♇	℞
3	1968	Jan	4	6:15	♅	℞
4		Feb	6	16:41	☿	℞
5			27	8:55	♆	℞
4			28	8:37	☿	D
3		Apr	21	23:27	♃	D
2		May	31	4:02	♇	D
1		Jun	2	0:37	♅	D
2			6	5:17	☿	℞
1			30	6:10	☿	D
0		Aug	5	1:17	♆	D
1			7	2:23	♄	℞
2		Oct	3	11:41	☿	℞
1			24	14:18	☿	D
0		Dec	21	11:39	♄	D
1			27	17:06	♇	℞
2	1969	Jan	8	7:29	♅	℞
3			20	10:57	☿	℞
4			20	12:30	♃	℞
3		Feb	10	9:39	☿	D
4			28	20:21	♆	℞
5		Mar	18	11:50	♀	℞
6		Apr	27	11:25	♂	℞
5			29	19:21	♀	D
6		May	17	19:07	☿	℞
5			23	8:20	♃	D
4		Jun	2	14:01	♇	D
3			7	6:35	♅	D
2			10	15:48	☿	D
1		Jul	8	6:08	♂	D
0		Aug	7	14:56	♆	D
1			21	5:44	♄	℞
2		Sep	16	12:42	☿	℞
1		Oct	8	9:54	☿	D
2		Dec	30	8:08	♇	℞
1	1970	Jan	3	21:07	♄	D
2			4	8:11	☿	℞
3			13	6:10	♅	℞
2			24	16:39	☿	D
3		Feb	19	21:59	♃	℞
4		Mar	3	9:01	♆	℞
5		Apr	28	10:52	☿	℞
4		May	22	6:48	☿	D
3		Jun	5	2:24	♇	D
2			12	9:41	♅	D
1			23	9:45	♃	D
0		Aug	10	2:22	♆	D
1			30	7:28	☿	℞
2		Sep	4	13:58	♄	℞
1			22	0:18	☿	D
2		Oct	20	15:57	♀	℞
1		Dec	1	0:04	♀	D
2			19	5:59	☿	℞
3	1971	Jan	1	22:00	♇	℞
2			8	4:37	☿	D
1			17	13:02	♄	D
2			18	6:55	♅	℞
3		Mar	5	18:08	♆	℞
4			23	11:34	♃	℞
5		Apr	9	17:11	☿	℞
4		May	3	10:26	☿	D
3		Jun	7	15:17	♇	D
2			17	14:51	♅	D
3		Jul	11	6:31	♂	℞
2			24	19:10	♃	D
1		Aug	12	15:15	♆	D
2			12	19:14	☿	℞
1		Sep	5	6:03	☿	D
0			9	13:52	♂	D
1			19	2:18	♄	℞
2		Dec	3	2:33	☿	℞
1			22	20:48	☿	D
2	1972	Jan	4	14:45	♇	℞
3			23	5:27	♅	℞
2			31	10:23	♄	D
3		Mar	7	5:19	♆	℞
4			21	18:39	☿	℞
3		Apr	14	3:29	☿	D
4			25	0:19	♃	℞
5		May	27	3:15	♀	℞
4		Jun	9	5:45	♇	D
3			21	17:28	♅	D
2		Jul	9	4:56	♀	D
3			24	23:03	☿	℞
2		Aug	14	3:10	♆	D
1			17	22:39	☿	D
0			25	8:02	♃	D
1		Oct	2	16:26	♄	℞
2		Nov	15	20:27	☿	℞
1		Dec	5	16:23	☿	D
2	1973	Jan	6	6:57	♇	℞
3			27	5:31	♅	℞
2		Feb	13	12:50	♄	D
3		Mar	4	12:58	☿	℞
4			9	14:33	♆	℞
3			27	8:19	☿	D
4		May	30	22:11	♃	℞
3		Jun	11	20:12	♇	D
2			26	22:01	♅	D
3		Jul	6	17:01	☿	℞
2			30	21:48	☿	D
1		Aug	16	16:06	♆	D
2		Sep	19	23:20	♂	℞
1			28	13:27	♃	D
2		Oct	17	5:51	♄	℞
3			30	10:30	☿	℞
2		Nov	19	14:15	☿	D
1			26	0:07	♂	D
2	1974	Jan	3	6:07	♀	℞
3			9	0:54	♇	℞
4		Feb	1	2:57	♅	℞
3			13	7:29	♀	D
4			15	19:46	☿	℞
3			27	21:14	♄	D
2		Mar	9	22:17	☿	D
3			12	1:21	♆	℞
2		Jun	14	13:17	♇	D
3			17	22:38	☿	℞
2		Jul	2	0:16	♅	D
3			7	16:14	♃	℞
2			12	1:57	☿	D
1		Aug	19	3:38	♆	D
2		Oct	13	19:49	☿	℞
3			31	14:57	♄	℞
2		Nov	3	12:13	♃	D
1			3	12:52	☿	D
2	1975	Jan	11	17:40	♇	℞
3			30	10:48	☿	℞
4		Feb	6	1:49	♅	℞
3			20	19:28	☿	D
2		Mar	14	8:33	♄	D
3			14	10:03	♆	℞
4		May	29	16:01	☿	℞
3		Jun	17	4:04	♇	D
2			22	15:19	☿	D
1		Jul	7	3:59	♅	D
2		Aug	6	5:22	♀	℞
3			14	19:32	♃	℞
2			21	14:54	♆	D
1		Sep	18	1:47	♀	D
2			26	23:47	☿	℞
1		Oct	18	10:16	☿	D
2		Nov	6	12:02	♂	℞
3			14	19:25	♄	℞
2		Dec	10	12:40	♃	D
3	1976	Jan	14	6:43	☿	℞
4			14	11:42	♇	℞
3			20	21:28	♂	D
2		Feb	3	22:58	☿	D
3			10	22:12	♅	℞
4		Mar	15	20:40	♆	℞
3			27	19:59	♄	D
4		May	9	5:05	☿	℞
3		Jun	2	1:21	☿	D
2			18	21:43	♇	D
1		Jul	11	6:06	♅	D
0		Aug	23	2:05	♆	D
1		Sep	8	22:05	☿	℞
2			19	18:40	♃	℞
1		Oct	1	4:00	☿	D
2		Nov	27	18:47	♄	℞
3		Dec	28	4:35	☿	℞
2	1977	Jan	15	10:57	♃	D
3			16	7:06	♇	℞
2			17	8:02	☿	D
3		Feb	14	19:51	♅	℞
4		Mar	16	3:02	♀	℞
5			18	7:36	♆	℞
4		Apr	11	5:42	♄	D
5			20	2:10	☿	℞
4			27	9:49	♀	D
3		May	13	20:52	☿	D
2		Jun	21	13:22	♇	D
1		Jul	16	8:42	♅	D
2		Aug	22	14:20	☿	℞
1			25	12:08	♆	D
0		Sep	14	15:05	☿	D
1		Oct	24	10:14	♃	℞
2		Dec	11	12:12	♄	℞
3			12	2:12	☿	℞
4			12	19:13	♂	℞
3			31	22:03	☿	D
4	1978	Jan	19	0:47	♇	℞
5		Feb	19	15:26	♅	℞
4			20	1:25	♃	D
3		Mar	2	9:57	♂	D
4			20	18:48	♆	℞
5		Apr	1	16:18	☿	℞
4			25	6:49	☿	D
3			25	12:17	♄	D
2		Jun	24	7:43	♇	D
1		Jul	21	10:04	♅	D
2		Aug	4	23:08	☿	℞
1			28	0:55	♆	D
0			28	15:42	☿	D
1		Oct	18	3:59	♀	℞
2		Nov	25	20:31	♃	℞
3			25	21:42	☿	℞
2			28	13:10	♀	D
1		Dec	15	15:57	☿	D
2			24	21:13	♄	℞
3	1979	Jan	21	20:47	♇	℞
4		Feb	24	11:59	♅	℞
5		Mar	15	1:16	☿	℞
6			23	7:36	♆	℞
5			26	0:56	♃	D
4		Apr	7	5:22	☿	D
3		May	9	14:54	♄	D
2		Jun	27	1:27	♇	D
3		Jul	17	22:43	☿	℞
2			26	10:60	♅	D
1		Aug	11	1:33	☿	D
0			30	11:15	♆	D
1		Nov	9	13:56	☿	℞
0			29	12:42	☿	D
1		Dec	26	14:59	♃	℞
2	1980	Jan	6	22:43	♄	℞
3			16	6:18	♂	℞
4			24	15:50	♇	℞
5		Feb	26	1:34	☿	℞
6			29	6:41	♅	℞
5		Mar	19	13:60	☿	D
6			24	17:43	♆	℞
5		Apr	6	8:28	♂	D
4			26	8:48	♃	D
3		May	22	11:51	♄	D
4			24	20:11	♀	℞
5		Jun	28	11:13	☿	℞
4			28	20:10	♇	D
3		Jul	6	21:16	♀	D
2			22	16:38	☿	D
1			30	11:40	♅	D
0		Aug	31	23:39	♆	D
1		Oct	23	1:59	☿	℞
0		Nov	12	10:57	☿	D
1	1981	Jan	18	16:59	♄	℞
2			24	19:23	♃	℞
3			26	12:52	♇	℞
4		Feb	8	12:32	☿	℞
3		Mar	2	7:06	☿	D
4			5	1:48	♅	℞
5			27	6:09	♆	℞
4		May	27	18:27	♃	D
3		Jun	5	2:13	♄	D
4			9	11:36	☿	℞
3		Jul	1	16:13	♇	D
2			3	12:59	☿	D
1		Aug	4	10:50	♅	D
0		Sep	3	11:08	♆	D
1		Oct	6	9:16	☿	℞
0			27	9:11	☿	D
1		Dec	31	19:46	♀	℞
2	1982	Jan	23	6:04	☿	℞
3			29	8:19	♇	℞
4			31	3:47	♄	℞
3		Feb	10	20:38	♀	D
2			13	7:19	☿	D
3			20	19:14	♂	℞
4			24	5:42	♃	℞
5		Mar	9	19:42	♅	℞
6			29	16:39	♆	℞
5		May	11	18:36	♂	D
6			21	2:06	☿	℞
5		Jun	13	23:21	☿	D
4			18	11:06	♄	D
3			27	18:17	♃	D
2		Jul	4	13:12	♇	D
1		Aug	9	10:22	♅	D
0		Sep	5	23:37	♆	D
1			19	11:04	☿	℞
0		Oct	11	5:22	☿	D
1	1983	Jan	7	3:00	☿	℞
0			27	13:26	☿	D
1		Feb	1	5:53	♇	℞
2			12	11:18	♄	℞
3		Mar	14	13:05	♅	℞
4			27	23:56	♃	℞
5		Apr	1	4:28	♆	℞
6		May	1	16:37	☿	℞
5			25	12:49	☿	D
4		Jul	1	12:32	♄	D
3			7	11:26	♇	D
2			29	7:05	♃	D
3		Aug	3	19:44	♀	℞
2			14	7:12	♅	D
3		Sep	2	6:42	☿	℞
2			8	11:01	♆	D
1			15	17:23	♀	D
0			24	20:50	☿	D
1		Dec	22	0:54	☿	℞
0	1984	Jan	11	0:38	☿	D
1		Feb	4	2:06	♇	℞
2			24	14:37	♄	℞
3		Mar	18	6:14	♅	℞
4		Apr	2	14:06	♆	℞
5			5	12:23	♂	℞
6			11	20:24	☿	℞
7			29	18:38	♃	℞
6		May	5	14:07	☿	D
5		Jun	19	18:17	♂	D
4		Jul	9	8:23	♇	D
3			13	6:17	♄	D
4		Aug	14	19:35	☿	℞
3			18	5:41	♅	D
2			29	23:03	♃	D
1		Sep	7	4:03	☿	D
0			9	22:15	♆	D
1		Dec	4	21:47	☿	℞
0			24	16:12	☿	D
1	1985	Feb	5	23:58	♇	℞
2		Mar	7	12:39	♄	℞
3			13	18:18	♀	℞
4			22	22:03	♅	℞
5			24	19:01	☿	℞
6		Apr	5	1:27	♆	℞
5			17	5:24	☿	D
4			25	0:10	♀	D
5		Jun	4	22:25	♃	℞
4		Jul	12	8:41	♇	D
3			25	19:34	♄	D
4			28	0:53	☿	℞
3		Aug	20	22:49	☿	D
2			23	0:20	♅	D
1		Sep	12	9:18	♆	D
0		Oct	3	8:18	♃	D
1		Nov	18	16:10	☿	℞
0		Dec	8	11:24	☿	D
1	1986	Feb	8	20:16	♇	℞
2		Mar	7	10:57	☿	℞
3			19	9:28	♄	℞
4			27	14:18	♅	℞
3			30	8:43	☿	D
4		Apr	7	12:53	♆	℞
5		Jun	8	23:26	♂	℞
6		Jul	9	20:28	☿	℞
7			12	17:02	♃	℞
6			15	6:32	♇	D
5		Aug	3	0:49	☿	D
4			7	4:51	♄	D
3			12	7:46	♂	D
2			27	21:17	♅	D
1		Sep	14	19:40	♆	D
2		Oct	15	16:34	♀	℞
3		Nov	2	6:48	☿	℞
2			8	9:28	♃	D
1			22	9:04	☿	D
0			26	2:47	♀	D
1	1987	Feb	11	16:56	♇	℞
2			18	16:08	☿	℞
1		Mar	12	21:23	☿	D
2			31	4:44	♄	℞
3		Apr	1	4:36	♅	℞
4			10	0:14	♆	℞
5		Jun	21	3:45	☿	℞
4		Jul	15	7:52	☿	D
3			18	6:11	♇	D
2		Aug	19	8:54	♄	D
3			19	21:08	♃	℞
2		Sep	1	14:24	♅	D
1			17	8:24	♆	D
2		Oct	16	16:47	☿	℞
1		Nov	6	7:40	☿	D
0		Dec	15	12:23	♃	D
1	1988	Feb	2	6:19	☿	℞
2			14	14:50	♇	℞
1			23	17:31	☿	D

Planetary Stations in Longitude 1700–2050

No.	Year	Date	Time	Planet	Station
2		Apr 4	19:26	♅	℞
3		11	2:09	♄	℞
4		11	13:18	♆	℞
5		May 22	13:27	♀	℞
6		31	22:44	☿	℞
5		Jun 24	22:41	☿	D
4		Jul 4	14:10	♀	D
3		20	4:22	♇	D
4		Aug 26	14:41	♂	℞
3		30	10:07	♄	D
2		Sep 5	9:42	♅	D
1		18	18:20	♆	D
2		24	13:59	♃	℞
3		28	21:38	☿	℞
2		Oct 20	5:23	☿	D
1		28	5:07	♂	D
2	1989	Jan 16	1:46	☿	℞
1		20	6:13	♃	D
0		Feb 5	20:08	☿	D
1		16	9:47	♇	℞
2		Apr 9	8:54	♅	℞
3		13	23:37	♆	℞
4		22	23:38	♄	℞
5		May 12	11:53	☿	℞
4		Jun 5	8:08	☿	D
3		Jul 23	3:55	♇	D
2		Sep 10	1:15	♅	D
1		11	7:11	♄	D
2		11	20:58	☿	℞
1		21	6:54	♆	D
0		Oct 3	23:49	☿	D
1		29	0:04	♃	℞
2		Dec 29	8:51	♀	℞
3		30	23:30	☿	℞
2	1990	Jan 20	4:33	☿	D
1		Feb 8	9:17	♀	D
2		19	6:31	♇	℞
1		24	19:15	♃	D
2		Apr 13	22:22	♅	℞
3		16	12:57	♆	℞
4		23	6:55	☿	℞
5		May 4	22:44	♄	℞
4		17	2:03	☿	D
3		Jul 26	1:25	♇	D
4		Aug 25	14:09	☿	℞
3		Sep 14	18:30	♅	D
2		17	12:07	☿	D
1		23	5:11	♄	D
0		23	18:38	♆	D
1		Oct 20	19:30	♂	℞
2		Nov 30	5:04	♃	℞
3		Dec 14	21:09	☿	℞
2	1991	Jan 1	12:50	♂	D
1		3	17:53	☿	D
2		Feb 22	1:28	♇	℞
1		Mar 30	13:16	♃	D
2		Apr 4	18:10	☿	℞
3		18	10:34	♅	℞
4		19	0:12	♆	℞
3		28	9:50	☿	D
4		May 17	4:06	♄	℞
3		Jul 28	23:48	♇	D
4		Aug 1	10:36	♀	℞
5		7	23:59	☿	℞
4		31	14:36	☿	D
3		Sep 13	8:57	♀	D
2		19	8:38	♅	D
1		26	7:14	♆	D
0		Oct 5	3:58	♄	D
1		Nov 28	17:02	☿	℞
0		Dec 18	11:13	☿	D
1		30	21:35	♃	℞
2	1992	Feb 24	21:33	♇	℞
3		Mar 17	0:33	☿	℞
2		Apr 9	6:27	☿	D
3		20	12:15	♆	℞
4		21	23:20	♅	℞
3		30	19:39	♃	D
4		May 28	13:37	♄	℞
5		Jul 20	0:55	☿	℞
4		30	21:35	♇	D
3		Aug 13	2:54	☿	D
2		Sep 22	23:46	♅	D
1		27	18:36	♆	D
0		Oct 16	2:07	♄	D
1		Nov 11	9:50	☿	℞
2		28	23:31	♂	℞
1		Dec 1	7:32	☿	D
2	1993	Jan 28	23:10	♃	℞
1		Feb 15	7:44	♂	D
2		26	14:29	♇	℞
3		27	22:55	☿	℞
4		Mar 11	9:29	♀	℞
3		22	13:45	☿	D
2		Apr 22	14:14	♀	D
3		22	22:33	♆	℞
4		26	10:04	♅	℞
3		Jun 1	1:10	♃	D
4		10	5:29	♄	℞
5		Jul 1	15:30	☿	℞
4		25	20:51	☿	D
3		Aug 2	19:29	♇	D
2		Sep 27	12:30	♅	D
1		30	6:10	♆	D
2		Oct 25	22:41	☿	℞
1		28	3:40	♄	D
0		Nov 15	5:40	☿	D
1	1994	Feb 11	8:31	☿	℞
2		28	13:51	♃	℞
3		Mar 1	10:01	♇	℞
2		5	5:50	☿	D
3		Apr 25	10:38	♆	℞
4		30	22:19	♅	℞
5		Jun 12	17:49	☿	℞
6		23	3:58	♄	℞
5		Jul 2	3:34	♃	D
4		6	19:44	☿	D
3		Aug 5	17:08	♇	D
2		Oct 2	1:48	♅	D
1		2	17:49	♆	D
2		9	6:45	☿	℞
3		13	5:42	♀	℞
2		30	4:07	☿	D
1		Nov 9	8:37	♄	D
0		23	16:58	♀	D
1	1995	Jan 2	21:28	♂	℞
2		26	1:17	☿	℞
1		Feb 16	5:08	☿	D
2		Mar 4	2:34	♇	℞
1		24	17:19	♂	D
2		Apr 1	12:04	♃	℞
3		27	22:15	♆	℞
4		May 5	7:49	♅	℞
5		24	9:03	☿	℞
4		Jun 17	6:59	☿	D
5		Jul 6	7:47	♄	℞
4		Aug 2	16:45	♃	D
3		8	13:33	♇	D
4		Sep 22	9:16	☿	℞
3		Oct 5	3:57	♆	D
2		6	12:59	♅	D
1		14	0:48	☿	D
0		Nov 21	19:49	♄	D
1	1996	Jan 9	21:52	☿	℞
0		30	10:18	☿	D
1		Mar 5	20:18	♇	℞
2		Apr 29	9:53	♆	℞
3		May 3	22:41	☿	℞
4		4	15:38	♃	℞
5		8	19:37	♅	℞
6		20	6:09	♀	℞
5		27	19:03	☿	D
4		Jul 2	6:52	♀	D
5		18	20:30	♄	℞
4		Aug 10	12:35	♇	D
3		Sep 3	14:38	♃	D
4		4	5:48	☿	℞
3		26	17:10	☿	D
2		Oct 6	15:56	♆	D
1		10	0:56	♅	D
0		Dec 3	12:40	♄	D
1		23	19:47	☿	℞
0	1997	Jan 12	20:42	☿	D
1		Feb 6	0:38	♂	℞
2		Mar 8	12:54	♇	℞
3		Apr 15	0:02	☿	℞
2		27	19:10	♂	D
3		May 1	23:21	♆	℞
2		8	18:06	☿	D
3		13	4:07	♅	℞
4		Jun 10	0:25	♃	℞
5		Aug 1	16:57	♄	℞
4		13	8:31	♇	D
5		17	19:50	☿	℞
4		Sep 10	1:44	☿	D
3		Oct 8	4:38	♃	D
2		9	1:30	♆	D
1		14	10:49	♅	D
2		Dec 7	16:57	☿	℞
1		16	10:30	♄	D
2		26	21:22	♀	℞
1		27	11:42	☿	D
0	1998	Feb 5	21:27	♀	D
1		Mar 11	4:55	♇	℞
2		27	19:43	☿	℞
1		Apr 20	7:32	☿	D
2		May 4	10:40	♆	℞
3		17	15:02	♅	℞
4		Jul 18	1:50	♃	℞
5		31	2:29	☿	℞
6		Aug 15	19:10	♄	℞
5		16	6:08	♇	D
4		23	22:36	☿	D
3		Oct 11	14:05	♆	D
2		18	21:25	♅	D
1		Nov 13	13:03	♃	D
2		21	11:47	☿	℞
1		Dec 11	6:31	☿	D
0		29	15:46	♄	D
1	1999	Mar 10	9:12	☿	℞
2		13	21:34	♇	℞
3		18	13:42	♂	℞
2		Apr 2	9:20	☿	D
3		May 7	0:52	♆	℞
4		21	22:26	♅	℞
3		Jun 4	6:12	♂	D
4		Jul 12	23:34	☿	℞
5		30	1:43	♀	℞
4		Aug 6	3:28	☿	D
3		19	1:46	♇	D
4		25	2:39	♃	℞
5		30	1:24	♄	℞
4		Sep 11	0:25	♀	D
3		Oct 14	1:37	♆	D
2		23	6:14	♅	D
3		Nov 5	3:00	☿	℞
2		25	3:56	☿	D
1		Dec 20	14:49	♃	D
0	2000	Jan 12	5:00	♄	D
1		Feb 21	12:47	☿	℞
0		Mar 14	20:40	☿	D
1		15	11:50	♇	℞
2		May 8	12:31	♆	℞
3		25	8:22	♅	℞
4		Jun 23	8:33	☿	℞
3		Jul 17	13:21	☿	D
2		Aug 20	22:42	♇	D
3		Sep 12	11:35	♄	℞
4		29	12:53	♃	℞
3		Oct 15	14:13	♆	D
4		18	13:42	☿	℞
3		26	15:25	♅	D
2		Nov 8	2:29	☿	D
1	2001	Jan 25	0:25	♄	D
0		25	8:39	♃	D
1		Feb 4	1:59	☿	℞
0		25	15:42	☿	D
1		Mar 9	1:08	♀	℞
2		18	2:37	♇	℞
1		Apr 20	4:35	♀	D
2		May 11	1:14	♆	℞
3		11	16:09	♂	℞
4		29	15:12	♅	℞
5		Jun 4	5:23	☿	℞
4		28	5:50	☿	D
3		Jul 19	22:46	♂	D
2		Aug 23	16:07	♇	D
3		Sep 27	0:05	♄	℞
4		Oct 1	19:24	☿	℞
3		18	1:50	♆	D
2		23	0:24	☿	D
1		30	22:56	♅	D
2		Nov 2	15:36	♃	℞
3	2002	Jan 18	20:51	☿	℞
2		Feb 8	1:33	♄	D
1		8	17:29	☿	D
0		Mar 1	15:16	♃	D
1		20	14:54	♇	℞
2		May 13	12:12	♆	℞
3		15	18:51	☿	℞
4		Jun 3	0:12	♅	℞
3		8	15:13	☿	D
2		Aug 26	11:00	♇	D
3		Sep 14	19:39	☿	℞
2		Oct 6	19:27	☿	D
3		10	18:36	♀	℞
4		11	13:02	♄	℞
3		20	13:54	♆	D
2		Nov 4	6:28	♅	D
1		21	7:14	♀	D
2		Dec 4	12:23	♃	℞
3	2003	Jan 2	18:20	☿	℞
2		23	1:09	☿	D
3		30	1:00	♆	℞
2		31	23:00	♆	D
1		Feb 22	7:42	♄	D
2		Mar 23	5:12	♇	℞
1		Apr 4	3:05	♃	D
2		26	11:60	☿	℞
3		May 16	0:48	♆	℞
2		20	7:34	☿	D
3		Jun 7	6:59	♅	℞
4		Jul 29	7:38	♂	℞
5		Aug 28	13:42	☿	℞
4		29	3:34	♇	D
3		Sep 20	8:53	☿	D
2		27	7:53	♂	D
1		Oct 23	1:55	♆	D
2		25	23:43	♄	℞
1		Nov 8	12:45	♅	D
2		Dec 17	16:02	☿	℞
3	2004	Jan 3	23:58	♃	℞
2		6	13:45	☿	D
1		Mar 7	16:52	♄	D
2		24	15:08	♇	℞
3		Apr 6	20:28	☿	℞
2		30	13:06	☿	D
1		May 5	3:08	♃	D
2		17	12:14	♆	℞
3		17	22:29	♀	℞
4		Jun 10	15:48	♅	℞
3		29	23:16	♀	D
4		Aug 10	0:34	☿	℞
3		30	19:38	♇	D
2		Sep 2	13:10	☿	D
1		Oct 24	11:57	♆	D
2		Nov 8	6:55	♄	℞
1		11	19:12	♅	D
2		30	12:18	☿	℞
1		Dec 20	6:30	☿	D
2	2005	Feb 2	2:27	♃	℞
3		Mar 20	0:15	☿	℞
2		22	2:55	♄	D
3		27	2:28	♇	℞
2		Apr 12	7:47	☿	D
3		May 19	23:37	♆	℞
2		Jun 5	7:22	♃	D
3		14	22:39	♅	℞
4		Jul 23	3:01	☿	℞
3		Aug 16	3:52	☿	D
2		Sep 2	10:51	♇	D
3		Oct 1	22:05	♂	℞
2		26	23:25	♆	D
3		Nov 14	5:43	☿	℞
2		16	0:09	♅	D
3		22	9:02	♄	℞
2		Dec 4	2:25	☿	D
1		10	4:05	♂	D
2		24	9:38	♀	℞
1	2006	Feb 3	9:20	♀	D
2		Mar 2	20:30	☿	℞
3		4	18:03	♃	℞
2		25	13:43	☿	D
3		29	12:39	♇	℞
2		Apr 5	12:56	♄	D
3		May 22	13:07	♆	℞
4		Jun 19	7:41	♅	℞
5		Jul 4	19:34	☿	℞
4		6	7:20	♃	D
3		29	0:41	☿	D
2		Sep 4	23:21	♇	D
3		Oct 28	19:17	☿	℞
2		29	7:58	♆	D
1		Nov 18	0:26	☿	D
0		20	6:10	♅	D
1		Dec 6	4:08	♄	℞
2	2007	Feb 14	4:39	☿	℞
1		Mar 8	4:46	☿	D
2		31	22:44	♇	℞
3		Apr 6	1:24	♃	℞
2		19	21:25	♄	D
3		May 25	1:10	♆	℞
4		Jun 15	23:41	☿	℞
5		23	14:44	♅	℞
4		Jul 10	2:16	☿	D
5		27	17:29	♀	℞
4		Aug 7	2:06	♃	D
3		Sep 7	14:54	♇	D
2		8	16:15	♀	D
3		Oct 12	4:01	☿	℞
2		31	20:08	♆	D
1		Nov 1	22:60	☿	D
2		15	8:26	♂	℞
1		24	10:16	♅	D
2		Dec 19	14:11	♄	℞
3	2008	Jan 28	20:32	☿	℞
2		30	22:34	♂	D
1		Feb 19	2:58	☿	D
2		Apr 2	9:22	♇	℞
1		May 3	3:08	♄	D
2		9	12:12	♃	℞
3		26	15:49	☿	℞
4		26	16:16	♆	℞
3		Jun 19	14:32	☿	D
4		27	0:02	♅	℞

Planetary Stations in Longitude 1700–2050

3		Sep 8	4:17	♃	D
2		9	3:13	♇	D
3		24	7:18	☿	℞
2		Oct 15	20:07	☿	D
1		Nov 2	6:40	♆	D
0		27	16:09	♅	D
1		Dec 31	18:09	♄	℞
2	2009	Jan 11	16:45	☿	℞
1		Feb 1	7:12	☿	D
2		Mar 6	17:18	♀	℞
3		Apr 4	17:34	♇	℞
2		17	19:25	♀	D
3		May 7	5:01	☿	℞
2		17	2:08	♄	D
3		29	4:31	♆	℞
2		31	1:23	☿	D
3		Jun 15	7:51	♃	℞
4		Jul 1	7:38	♅	℞
5		Sep 7	4:46	☿	℞
4		11	16:56	♇	D
3		29	13:15	☿	D
2		Oct 13	4:36	♃	D
1		Nov 4	18:11	♆	D
0		Dec 1	20:28	♅	D
1		20	13:27	♂	℞
2		26	14:39	☿	℞
3	2010	Jan 13	15:58	♄	℞
2		15	16:53	☿	D
1		Mar 10	17:10	♂	D
2		Apr 7	2:33	♇	℞
3		18	4:07	☿	℞
2		May 11	22:28	☿	D
1		30	18:10	♄	D
2		31	18:50	♆	℞
3		Jul 5	16:50	♅	℞
4		23	12:04	♃	℞
5		Aug 20	19:60	☿	℞
4		Sep 12	23:10	☿	D
3		14	4:35	♇	D
4		Oct 8	7:06	♀	℞
3		Nov 7	6:05	♆	D
2		18	16:55	♃	D
1		18	21:19	♀	D
0		Dec 6	1:51	♅	D
1		10	12:05	☿	℞
0		30	7:22	☿	D
1	2011	Jan 26	6:11	♄	℞
2		Mar 30	20:49	☿	℞
3		Apr 9	8:49	♇	℞
2		23	10:05	☿	D
3		Jun 3	7:29	♆	℞
2		13	3:52	♄	D
3		Jul 10	0:36	♅	℞
4		Aug 3	3:51	☿	℞
3		26	22:04	☿	D
4		30	9:18	♃	℞
3		Sep 16	18:23	♇	D
2		Nov 9	18:55	♆	D
3		24	7:20	☿	℞
2		Dec 10	7:05	♅	D
1		14	1:44	☿	D
0		25	22:09	♃	D
1	2012	Jan 24	0:55	♂	℞
2		Feb 7	14:04	♄	℞
3		Mar 12	7:50	☿	℞
2		Apr 4	10:12	☿	D
3		10	16:22	♇	℞
2		14	3:54	♂	D
3		May 15	14:34	♀	℞
4		Jun 4	21:06	♆	℞
3		25	8:02	♄	D
2		27	15:08	♀	D
3		Jul 13	9:50	♅	℞
4		15	2:17	☿	℞
3		Aug 8	5:41	☿	D
2		Sep 18	5:06	♇	D
3		Oct 4	13:19	♃	℞
4		Nov 6	23:05	☿	℞
3		11	7:54	♆	D
2		26	22:49	☿	D
1		Dec 13	12:03	♅	D
0	2013	Jan 30	11:38	♃	D
1		Feb 18	17:04	♄	℞
2		23	9:42	☿	℞
1		Mar 17	20:04	☿	D
2		Apr 12	19:33	♇	℞
3		Jun 7	8:27	♆	℞
4		26	13:09	☿	℞
3		Jul 8	5:13	♄	D
4		17	17:21	♅	℞
3		20	18:23	☿	D
2		Sep 20	15:27	♇	D
3		Oct 21	10:30	☿	℞
4		Nov 7	5:04	♃	℞
3		10	21:13	☿	D
2		13	18:44	♆	D
1		Dec 17	17:40	♅	D
2		21	21:54	♀	℞
1	2014	Jan 31	20:50	♀	D
2		Feb 6	21:44	☿	℞
1		28	14:01	☿	D
2		Mar 1	16:25	♂	℞
3		2	16:20	♄	℞
2		6	10:43	♃	D
3		Apr 14	23:45	♇	℞
2		May 20	1:32	♂	D
3		Jun 7	11:58	☿	℞
4		9	19:52	♆	℞
3		Jul 1	12:51	☿	D
2		20	20:37	♄	D
3		22	2:54	♅	℞
2		Sep 23	0:35	♇	D
3		Oct 4	17:03	☿	℞
2		25	19:18	☿	D
1		Nov 16	7:07	♆	D
2		Dec 8	20:42	♃	℞
1		21	22:46	♅	D
2	2015	Jan 21	15:55	☿	℞
1		Feb 11	14:58	☿	D
2		Mar 14	15:03	♄	℞
1		Apr 8	16:58	♃	D
2		17	3:52	♇	℞
3		May 19	1:50	☿	℞
2		Jun 11	22:34	☿	D
3		12	9:10	♆	℞
4		Jul 25	9:30	♀	℞
5		26	10:39	♅	℞
4		Aug 2	5:54	♄	D
3		Sep 6	8:30	♀	D
4		17	18:11	☿	℞
3		25	6:56	♇	D
2		Oct 9	14:59	☿	D
1		Nov 18	16:33	♆	D
0		Dec 26	3:54	♅	D
1	2016	Jan 5	13:06	☿	℞
2		8	4:41	♃	℞
1		25	21:51	☿	D
2		Mar 25	10:02	♄	℞
3		Apr 17	12:15	♂	℞
4		18	7:24	♇	℞
5		28	17:21	☿	℞
4		May 9	12:16	♃	D
3		22	13:21	☿	D
4		Jun 13	20:44	♆	℞
3		29	23:39	♂	D
4		Jul 29	21:07	♅	℞
3		Aug 13	9:51	♄	D
4		30	13:05	☿	℞
3		Sep 22	5:32	☿	D
2		26	15:00	♇	D
1		Nov 20	4:40	♆	D
2		Dec 19	10:56	☿	℞
1		29	9:30	♅	D
0	2017	Jan 8	9:44	☿	D
1		Feb 6	6:54	♃	℞
2		Mar 4	9:10	♀	℞
3		Apr 6	5:07	♄	℞
4		9	23:15	☿	℞
3		15	10:19	♀	D
4		20	12:46	♇	℞
3		May 3	16:34	☿	D
2		Jun 9	14:04	♃	D
3		16	11:11	♆	℞
4		Aug 3	5:32	♅	℞
5		13	1:02	☿	℞
4		25	12:10	♄	D
3		Sep 5	11:31	☿	D
2		28	19:34	♇	D
1		Nov 22	14:22	♆	D
2		Dec 3	7:35	☿	℞
1		23	1:52	☿	D
0	2018	Jan 2	14:12	♅	D
1		Mar 9	4:47	♃	℞
2		23	0:20	☿	℞
1		Apr 15	9:22	☿	D
2		18	1:48	♄	℞
3		22	15:23	♇	℞
4		Jun 18	23:28	♆	℞
5		26	21:06	♂	℞
4		Jul 10	17:04	♃	D
5		26	5:03	☿	℞
6		Aug 7	16:50	♅	℞
5		19	4:26	☿	D
4		27	14:06	♂	D
3		Sep 6	11:10	♄	D
2		Oct 1	2:02	♇	D
3		5	19:06	♀	℞
2		Nov 16	10:52	♀	D
3		17	1:34	☿	℞
2		25	1:10	♆	D
1		Dec 6	21:23	☿	D
0	2019	Jan 6	20:27	♅	D
1		Mar 5	18:20	☿	℞
0		28	14:00	☿	D
1		Apr 10	17:02	♃	℞
2		24	18:46	♇	℞
3		30	0:55	♄	℞
4		Jun 21	14:37	♆	℞
5		Jul 7	23:16	☿	℞
4		Aug 1	3:59	☿	D
3		11	13:39	♃	D
4		12	2:27	♅	℞
3		Sep 18	8:48	♄	D
2		Oct 3	6:38	♇	D
3		31	15:42	☿	℞
2		Nov 20	19:13	☿	D
1		27	12:34	♆	D
0	2020	Jan 11	1:49	♅	D
1		Feb 17	0:55	☿	℞
0		Mar 10	3:50	☿	D
1		Apr 25	18:52	♇	℞
2		May 11	4:10	♄	℞
3		13	6:46	♀	℞
4		14	14:33	♃	℞
5		Jun 18	4:60	☿	℞
6		23	4:33	♆	℞
5		25	6:49	♀	D
4		Jul 12	8:28	☿	D
5		Aug 15	14:27	♅	℞
6		Sep 9	22:24	♂	℞
5		13	0:42	♃	D
4		29	5:13	♄	D
3		Oct 4	13:31	♇	D
4		14	1:06	☿	℞
3		Nov 3	17:51	☿	D
2		14	0:37	♂	D
1		29	0:38	♆	D
0	2021	Jan 14	8:37	♅	D
1		30	15:53	☿	℞
0		Feb 21	0:53	☿	D
1		Apr 27	20:01	♇	℞
2		May 23	9:20	♄	℞
3		29	22:35	☿	℞
4		Jun 20	15:06	♃	℞
3		22	22:01	☿	D
4		25	19:23	♆	℞
5		Aug 20	1:41	♅	℞
6		Sep 27	5:11	☿	℞
5		Oct 6	18:27	♇	D
4		11	2:18	♄	D
3		18	5:31	♃	D
2		18	15:18	☿	D
1		Dec 1	13:24	♆	D
2		19	10:37	♀	℞
3	2022	Jan 14	11:42	☿	℞
2		18	15:27	♅	D
1		29	8:47	♀	D
0		Feb 4	4:14	☿	D
1		Apr 29	18:34	♇	℞
2		May 10	11:49	☿	℞
1		Jun 3	8:01	☿	D
2		4	21:48	♄	℞
3		28	7:57	♆	℞
4		Jul 28	20:39	♃	℞
5		Aug 24	13:54	♅	℞
6		Sep 10	3:39	☿	℞
5		Oct 2	9:09	☿	D
4		8	21:54	♇	D
3		23	4:09	♄	D
4		30	13:27	♂	℞
3		Nov 23	23:03	♃	D
2		Dec 4	0:16	♆	D
3		29	9:33	☿	℞
2	2023	Jan 12	20:57	♂	D
1		18	13:13	☿	D
0		22	22:59	♅	D
1		Apr 21	8:36	☿	℞
2		May 1	17:06	♇	℞
1		15	3:18	☿	D
2		Jun 17	17:29	♄	℞
3		30	21:09	♆	℞
4		Jul 23	1:34	♀	℞
5		Aug 23	20:01	☿	℞
6		29	2:39	♅	℞
5		Sep 4	1:21	♀	D
6		4	14:12	♃	℞
5		15	20:22	☿	D
4		Oct 11	1:08	♇	D
3		Nov 4	7:04	♄	D
2		Dec 6	13:24	♆	D
3		13	7:10	☿	℞
2		31	2:42	♃	D
1	2024	Jan 2	3:09	☿	D
0		27	7:36	♅	D
1		Apr 1	22:16	☿	℞
0		25	12:55	☿	D
1		May 2	17:43	♇	℞
2		Jun 29	19:08	♄	℞
3		Jul 2	10:43	♆	℞
4		Aug 5	4:57	☿	℞
3		28	21:15	☿	D
4		Sep 1	15:18	♅	℞
5		Oct 9	7:06	♃	℞
4		12	0:31	♇	D
3		Nov 15	14:21	♄	D
4		26	2:43	☿	℞
5		Dec 6	23:34	♂	℞
4		7	23:45	♆	D
3		15	20:58	☿	D
2	2025	Jan 30	16:23	♅	D
1		Feb 4	9:42	♃	D
0		24	2:01	♂	D
1		Mar 2	0:37	♀	℞
2		15	6:47	☿	℞
1		Apr 7	11:09	☿	D
0		13	1:03	♀	D
1		May 4	15:24	♇	℞
2		Jul 4	21:35	♆	℞
3		13	4:08	♄	℞
4		18	4:46	☿	℞
3		Aug 11	7:31	☿	D
4		Sep 6	4:52	♅	℞
3		Oct 14	2:51	♇	D
4		Nov 9	19:03	☿	℞
5		11	16:43	♃	℞
4		28	3:53	♄	D
3		29	17:40	☿	D
2		Dec 10	12:25	♆	D
1	2026	Feb 4	2:34	♅	D
2		26	6:49	☿	℞
1		Mar 11	3:31	♃	D
0		20	19:34	☿	D
1		May 6	15:31	♇	℞
2		Jun 29	17:37	☿	℞
3		Jul 7	10:57	♆	℞
2		23	22:59	☿	D
3		26	19:58	♄	℞
4		Sep 10	18:28	♅	℞
5		Oct 3	7:17	♀	℞
4		16	2:38	♇	D
5		24	7:14	☿	℞
4		Nov 13	15:55	☿	D
3		14	0:29	♀	D
2		Dec 10	23:32	♄	D
1		12	22:20	♆	D
2		13	0:58	♃	℞
3	2027	Jan 10	13:00	♂	℞
2		Feb 8	12:30	♅	D
3		9	17:37	☿	℞
2		Mar 3	12:33	☿	D
1		Apr 1	14:09	♂	D
0		13	2:13	♃	D
1		May 8	12:53	♇	℞
2		Jun 10	18:16	☿	℞
1		Jul 4	19:41	☿	D
2		9	22:44	♆	℞
3		Aug 9	18:07	♄	℞
4		Sep 15	9:10	♅	℞
5		Oct 7	14:38	☿	℞
4		18	3:48	♇	D
3		28	14:12	☿	D
2		Dec 15	9:09	♆	D
1		24	2:48	♄	D
2	2028	Jan 12	8:55	♃	℞
3		24	11:03	☿	℞
2		Feb 12	23:50	♅	D
1		14	12:39	☿	D
2		May 9	9:30	♇	℞
3		10	23:04	♀	℞
2		13	20:01	♃	D
3		21	8:44	☿	℞
4		30	6:03	♅	℞
3		31	17:59	♅	D
2		Jun 14	6:07	☿	D
1		22	22:14	♀	D
2		Jul 11	13:06	♆	℞
3		Aug 22	22:19	♄	℞
4		Sep 19	0:02	♅	℞
5		19	16:35	☿	℞
4		Oct 11	10:29	☿	D
3		19	3:40	♇	D
2		Dec 16	20:46	♆	D
1	2029	Jan 5	12:40	♄	D
2		7	7:57	☿	℞
1		27	18:41	☿	D

Planetary Stations in Longitude 1700–2050

2		Feb 10	13:08	♃	℞
3		14	8:17	♂	℞
2		16	10:52	♅	D
3		May 1	23:07	☿	℞
2		5	19:01	♂	D
3		11	4:14	♇	℞
2		25	19:22	☿	D
1		Jun 13	21:08	♃	D
2		Jul 14	2:12	♆	℞
3		Sep 2	12:19	☿	℞
4		6	8:36	♄	℞
5		23	16:22	♅	℞
4		25	2:03	☿	D
3		Oct 21	3:52	♇	D
4		Dec 16	23:49	♀	℞
3		19	8:25	♆	D
4		22	5:52	☿	℞
3	2030	Jan 11	5:47	☿	D
2		19	3:55	♄	D
1		26	21:34	♀	D
0		Feb 20	23:23	♅	D
1		Mar 13	14:35	♃	℞
2		Apr 13	2:35	☿	℞
1		May 6	20:16	☿	D
2		12	23:10	♇	℞
1		Jul 15	1:28	♃	D
2		16	16:30	♆	℞
3		Aug 16	1:21	☿	℞
2		Sep 8	9:29	☿	D
3		20	21:31	♄	℞
4		28	8:28	♅	℞
3		Oct 23	3:03	♇	D
4		Dec 6	2:48	☿	℞
3		21	20:41	♆	D
2		25	21:16	☿	D
1	2031	Feb 2	2:26	♄	D
0		25	11:25	♅	D
1		Mar 26	0:45	☿	℞
2		29	0:36	♂	℞
3		Apr 15	12:05	♃	℞
2		18	11:17	☿	D
3		May 14	20:24	♇	℞
2		Jun 13	11:58	♂	D
3		Jul 19	6:13	♆	℞
4		20	17:09	♀	℞
5		29	6:49	☿	℞
4		Aug 16	4:60	♃	D
3		22	4:30	☿	D
2		Sep 1	17:58	♀	D
3		Oct 3	2:43	♅	℞
4		5	10:52	♄	℞
3		24	23:11	♇	D
4		Nov 19	21:17	☿	℞
3		Dec 9	16:25	☿	D
2		24	7:42	♆	D
1	2032	Feb 16	7:01	♄	D
0		Mar 1	1:35	♅	D
1		7	16:23	☿	℞
0		30	14:30	☿	D
1		May 15	15:50	♇	℞
2		19	14:49	♃	℞
3		Jul 10	2:35	☿	℞
4		20	20:45	♆	℞
3		Aug 3	6:53	☿	D
2		Sep 17	19:54	♃	D
3		Oct 6	19:53	♅	℞
4		18	22:28	♄	℞
3		25	21:07	♇	D
4		Nov 2	11:58	☿	℞
3		22	14:02	☿	D
2		Dec 25	21:04	♆	D
3	2033	Feb 18	21:21	☿	℞
4		27	15:42	♀	℞
3		Mar 1	16:04	♄	D
2		5	14:42	♅	D

1		13	2:59	☿	D
0		Apr 10	15:28	♀	D
1		May 17	12:56	♇	℞
2		26	23:49	♂	℞
3		Jun 21	10:06	☿	℞
4		25	21:53	♃	℞
3		Jul 15	14:21	☿	D
4		23	10:28	♆	℞
3		Aug 1	14:26	♂	D
4		Oct 11	16:05	♅	℞
5		16	22:04	☿	℞
4		23	7:20	♃	D
3		27	16:37	♇	D
4		Nov 2	7:05	♄	℞
3		6	12:41	☿	D
2		Dec 28	7:37	♆	D
3	2034	Feb 2	11:23	☿	℞
2		23	22:55	☿	D
1		Mar 10	6:49	♅	D
0		16	2:31	♄	D
1		May 19	6:57	♇	℞
2		Jun 2	5:25	☿	℞
1		26	5:25	☿	D
2		Jul 25	22:33	♆	℞
3		Aug 3	3:43	♃	℞
4		Sep 30	3:01	☿	℞
5		30	19:38	♀	℞
6		Oct 16	10:17	♅	℞
5		21	10:24	☿	D
4		29	13:40	♇	D
3		Nov 11	14:03	♀	D
4		16	12:02	♄	℞
3		29	2:26	♃	D
2		Dec 30	20:11	♆	D
3	2035	Jan 17	6:45	☿	℞
2		Feb 7	1:26	☿	D
1		Mar 14	21:31	♅	D
0		30	13:14	♄	D
1		May 13	18:42	☿	℞
2		20	22:57	♇	℞
1		Jun 6	14:54	☿	D
2		Jul 28	12:30	♆	℞
3		Aug 15	10:02	♂	℞
4		Sep 9	14:16	♃	℞
5		13	2:29	☿	℞
4		Oct 5	4:54	☿	D
3		15	8:33	♂	D
4		21	8:03	♅	℞
3		31	11:32	♇	D
4		Nov 30	11:08	♄	℞
5	2036	Jan 1	4:26	☿	℞
4		2	6:35	♆	D
3		5	4:00	♃	D
2		21	9:43	☿	D
1		Mar 18	15:30	♅	D
0		Apr 12	22:38	♄	D
1		23	13:19	☿	℞
2		May 8	15:59	♀	℞
1		17	8:30	☿	D
2		21	15:34	♇	℞
1		Jun 20	14:13	♀	D
2		Jul 30	0:20	♆	℞
3		Aug 25	19:49	☿	℞
2		Sep 17	17:22	☿	D
3		Oct 14	1:39	♃	℞
4		25	3:24	♅	℞
3		Nov 1	7:51	♇	D
4		Dec 13	2:60	♄	℞
5		15	2:07	☿	℞
4	2037	Jan 3	17:47	♆	D
3		3	22:59	☿	D
2		Feb 9	7:43	♃	D
1		Mar 23	8:27	♅	D
2		Apr 5	0:07	☿	℞
1		27	4:58	♄	D

0		28	15:57	☿	D
1		May 23	7:46	♇	℞
2		Aug 1	13:59	♆	℞
3		8	5:47	☿	℞
2		31	20:08	☿	D
3		Oct 12	23:10	♂	℞
4		30	1:60	♅	℞
3		Nov 3	3:33	♇	D
4		16	2:18	♃	℞
5		28	22:02	☿	℞
6		Dec 14	12:48	♀	℞
5		18	16:14	☿	D
4		23	6:32	♂	D
5		26	11:37	♄	℞
4	2038	Jan 6	5:35	♆	D
3		24	10:21	♀	D
2		Mar 15	17:53	♃	D
3		18	6:09	☿	℞
2		28	4:28	♅	D
1		Apr 10	12:13	☿	D
0		May 11	6:24	♄	D
1		25	2:17	♇	℞
2		Jul 21	6:60	☿	℞
3		Aug 4	1:59	♆	℞
2		14	8:50	☿	D
3		Nov 3	22:02	♅	℞
2		4	20:17	♇	D
3		12	14:57	☿	℞
2		Dec 2	12:31	☿	D
3		17	8:41	♃	℞
4	2039	Jan 8	11:57	♄	℞
3		8	17:02	♆	D
4		Mar 1	4:13	☿	℞
3		23	19:21	☿	D
2		Apr 1	23:33	♅	D
1		17	14:53	♃	D
0		May 25	3:07	♄	D
1		26	19:16	♇	℞
2		Jul 2	21:49	☿	℞
3		18	8:37	♀	℞
2		27	3:08	☿	D
3		Aug 6	16:00	♆	℞
2		30	10:16	♀	D
3		Oct 27	3:55	☿	℞
2		Nov 6	13:52	♇	D
3		8	21:05	♅	℞
2		16	10:39	☿	D
3		23	20:49	♂	℞
2	2040	Jan 11	5:11	♆	D
3		16	13:19	♃	℞
4		21	4:14	♄	℞
3		Feb 9	11:49	♂	D
4		12	13:40	☿	℞
3		Mar 5	11:21	☿	D
2		Apr 5	21:45	♅	D
1		May 18	3:59	♃	D
2		27	13:20	♇	℞
1		Jun 6	17:56	♄	D
2		13	0:20	☿	℞
1		Jul 7	2:22	☿	D
2		Aug 8	5:26	♆	℞
3		Oct 9	12:06	☿	℞
2		30	9:07	☿	D
1		Nov 7	6:00	♇	D
2		12	17:55	♅	℞
1	2041	Jan 12	16:38	♆	D
2		26	6:15	☿	℞
3		Feb 1	16:02	♄	℞
4		14	20:23	♃	℞
3		16	10:28	☿	D
4		25	6:08	♀	℞
3		Apr 8	5:09	♀	D
2		10	19:06	♅	D
3		May 24	15:39	☿	℞
4		29	3:28	♇	℞

3		Jun 17	13:42	☿	D
2		18	6:15	♃	D
1		20	1:12	♄	D
2		Aug 10	19:57	♆	℞
3		Sep 22	14:45	☿	℞
2		Oct 14	5:53	☿	D
1		Nov 9	0:07	♇	D
2		17	17:17	♅	℞
3		Dec 28	5:40	♂	℞
4	2042	Jan 10	2:49	☿	℞
3		15	6:21	♆	D
3		30	15:33	☿	D
3		Feb 13	22:52	♄	℞
4		Mar 18	2:48	♃	℞
3		18	19:52	♂	D
2		Apr 15	18:58	♅	D
3		May 5	5:14	☿	℞
2		29	1:32	☿	D
3		30	16:33	♇	℞
2		Jul 2	23:49	♄	D
1		19	12:50	♃	D
2		Aug 13	9:12	♆	℞
3		Sep 5	11:22	☿	℞
2		27	22:20	☿	D
3		28	8:43	♀	℞
2		Nov 9	4:06	♀	D
1		10	19:18	♇	D
2		22	15:17	♅	℞
3		Dec 25	0:45	☿	℞
2	2043	Jan 14	1:51	☿	D
1		17	17:07	♆	D
2		Feb 25	23:42	♄	℞
3		Apr 16	6:19	☿	℞
4		20	4:04	♃	℞
3		20	17:50	♅	D
2		May 10	0:21	☿	D
3		Jun 1	8:35	♇	℞
2		Jul 15	18:08	♄	D
3		Aug 15	21:59	♆	℞
4		19	1:34	☿	℞
3		20	18:36	♃	D
2		Sep 11	7:05	☿	D
1		Nov 12	11:23	♇	D
2		27	15:39	♅	℞
3		Dec 8	21:59	☿	℞
2		28	16:47	☿	D
1	2044	Jan 20	5:47	♆	D
2		31	23:12	♂	℞
3		Mar 8	22:27	♄	℞
4		28	1:32	☿	℞
3		Apr 20	13:35	☿	D
2		21	23:37	♂	D
1		24	18:52	♅	D
2		May 6	9:03	♀	℞
3		24	14:04	♃	℞
4		Jun 1	23:08	♇	℞
3		18	6:38	♀	D
2		Jul 27	7:30	♄	D
3		31	8:23	☿	℞
4		Aug 17	12:40	♆	℞
3		24	4:13	☿	D
2		Sep 22	14:54	♃	D
1		Nov 13	4:04	♇	D
2		21	16:53	☿	℞
3		Dec 1	14:48	♅	℞
2		11	11:33	☿	D
1	2045	Jan 21	16:19	♆	D
2		Mar 10	14:43	☿	℞
3		20	18:14	♄	℞
2		Apr 2	15:11	☿	D
1		29	18:22	♅	D
2		Jun 3	16:32	♇	℞
3		Jul 1	0:38	♃	℞
4		13	5:39	☿	℞
3		Aug 6	9:29	☿	D

2		8	15:03	♄	D
3		20	0:19	♆	℞
2		Oct 28	4:37	♃	D
3		Nov 5	8:08	☿	℞
2		14	17:30	♇	D
1		25	8:56	☿	D
2		Dec 6	16:03	♅	℞
3		12	1:30	♀	℞
2	2046	Jan 21	22:59	♀	D
1		24	3:38	♆	D
2		Feb 21	18:02	☿	℞
3		Mar 11	2:12	♂	℞
2		16	2:13	☿	D
3		Apr 1	14:47	♄	℞
2		May 4	19:52	♅	D
1		28	15:33	♂	D
2		Jun 5	7:21	♇	℞
3		24	14:59	☿	℞
2		Jul 18	19:52	☿	D
3		Aug 8	4:15	♃	℞
2		20	19:13	♄	D
3		22	13:27	♆	℞
4		Oct 19	18:57	☿	℞
3		Nov 9	7:28	☿	D
2		16	8:44	♇	D
1		Dec 4	1:09	♃	D
2		11	16:11	♅	℞
1	2047	Jan 26	14:55	♆	D
2		Feb 5	7:02	☿	℞
1		26	21:06	☿	D
2		Apr 13	11:48	♄	℞
1		May 9	20:10	♅	D
2		Jun 5	12:06	☿	℞
3		6	20:49	♇	℞
2		29	12:37	☿	D
3		Jul 15	23:48	♀	℞
4		Aug 25	1:18	♆	℞
3		28	2:09	♀	D
2		Sep 1	18:31	♄	D
3		14	12:38	♃	℞
4		Oct 3	0:47	☿	℞
3		24	5:22	☿	D
2		Nov 17	23:51	♇	D
3		Dec 16	17:23	♅	℞
2	2048	Jan 10	2:20	♃	D
3		20	1:49	☿	℞
2		29	1:27	♆	D
1		Feb 9	22:46	☿	D
2		Apr 24	7:55	♄	℞
3		30	16:54	♂	℞
2		May 13	22:38	♅	D
3		16	1:33	☿	℞
4		Jun 7	8:15	♇	℞
3		8	21:58	☿	D
2		Jul 10	22:40	♂	D
3		Aug 26	15:02	♆	℞
2		Sep 12	16:58	♄	D
3		15	1:10	☿	℞
2		Oct 7	0:31	☿	D
3		18	15:59	♃	℞
2		Nov 18	16:51	♇	D
3		Dec 20	17:44	♅	℞
4	2049	Jan 2	23:15	☿	℞
3		23	6:20	☿	D
2		30	13:26	♆	D
1		Feb 14	0:26	♃	D
2		22	20:44	♀	℞
1		Apr 5	18:38	♀	D
2		26	18:21	☿	℞
3		May 6	9:13	♄	℞
2		19	0:48	♅	D
1		20	13:58	☿	D
2		Jun 8	19:10	♇	℞
3		Aug 28	19:22	☿	℞
4		29	3:14	♆	℞

Planetary Stations in Longitude 1700–2050

3		Sep 20	14:11	☿	D
2		24	15:36	♄	D
1		Nov 20	9:35	♇	D
2		20	12:42	♃	℞
3		Dec 17	21:00	☿	℞
4		25	18:13	♅	℞
3	2050	Jan 6	18:53	☿	D
2		Feb 2	1:16	♆	D
1		Mar 20	9:09	♃	D
2		Apr 8	2:29	☿	℞
1		May 1	19:11	☿	D
2		18	14:30	♄	℞
1		24	4:15	♅	D
2		Jun 10	9:54	♇	℞
3		Jul 15	6:05	♂	℞
4		Aug 11	6:23	☿	℞
5		31	16:37	♆	℞
4		Sep 3	18:43	☿	D
3		13	11:03	♂	D
4		25	22:22	♀	℞
3		Oct 6	12:44	♄	D
2		Nov 6	18:46	♀	D
1		21	22:06	♇	D
2		Dec 1	17:20	☿	℞
1		21	11:34	☿	D
2		21	13:18	♃	℞
3		30	18:45	♅	℞

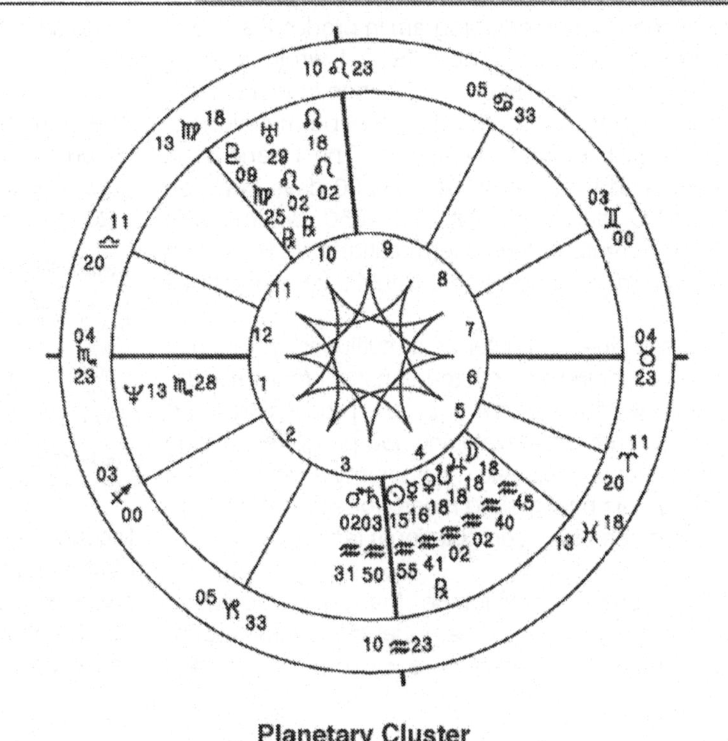

Planetary Cluster
February 5, 1962 • 0h0m0s EST
Washington, DC • 38N54 77W2

This chart shows the Aquarian alignment of February 1962 that has caused much discussion among astrologers.

Part 8

Planetary Clusters

Planetary Clusters

The 1560 occurrences of 5 or more planets being within a 20° arc between January 1, 1700, and December 31, 2050, were calculated by the Phenomena program in productive use at Astro Computing Services since 1983. I wrote a small computer program to generate the 638 lines of input to the Phenomena program that specified the 638 permutations of 10 planets taken 5 or more at a time. The Phenomena program evaluated for each of the 128,200 days between January 1, 1700, and December 31, 2050, whether the planets in one or more of those permutations were within a 20° arc. As you might suspect, that would take a long time!

Fortunately, my Prime computer as a multiuser system has the capability of running a compute-intensive program in the background while other users who are processing chart orders, calculating charts, developing new programs, writing letters, editing manuscripts, etc., get priority attention. The program ran, in this background mode, for several days, to accomplish this herculean computational task!

There was still a challenge left for me. Many of the combinations that the Phenomena program identified were redundant. For example, if 6 planets were within a 20° arc then there would also be six combinations of 5 planets. That is easy to understand—take each planet in turn, from the combination of six and you will end up with six combinations of 5.

After eliminating the redundancies, there were 1560 unique occurrences of 5 or more planets coming into an arc of 20° or less. There were no occurrences of 8 or more planets within a 20° arc. The following table summarizes the results.

Combinations		Average Time		Minimum Time		Maximum Time	
5 w/☽	1092	1.81013	1d19h26m	.00556	0d 0h 8m	3.33611	3d 8h 4m
5 wo/☽	303	12.72746	12d17h27m	.14444	0d 3h28m	37.25069	37d 6h 1m
6 w/☽	127	1.78560	1d18h51m	.32361	0d 7h46m	2.74514	2d17h53m
6 wo/☽	28	8.76582	8d18h22m	.10764	0d 2h35m	23.72639	23d17h26m
7 w/☽	8	1.66389	1d15h56m	.68611	0d16h28m	2.52986	2d12h43m
7 wo/☽	2	3.78264	3d18h46m	3.09028	3d 2h10m	4.47431	4d11h23m
Total	1560						

I accumulated statistics for combinations with and without the Moon. Otherwise, the minimum, average and maximum time spans would be meaningless, skewed either by the Moon's rapid motion, or obscuring meaningful results due to that same rapid motion!

Ten Occurrences of 7 Planets Clustered within a 20° Arc

Starting Position					Planets in Zodiacal Sequence	Dy	Hr	Mn	Ending Position				Planets in Zodiacal Sequence
1762	Mar	24	18:04	23♓48	☽ ☿ ♀ ☉ ♅ ♄ ♃	1	19	29	Mar	26	13:33	26♓28	☿ ♀ ☉ ♅ ♄ ♃ ☽
1821	Apr	1	5:26	21♓10	☽ ♂ ♀ ♇ ☿ ♃ ☉	1	13	34	Apr	2	19:00	24♓57	♂ ♇ ☿ ♀ ♃ ☉ ☽
1821	Apr	1	12:53	25♓51	☽ ♀ ♇ ☿ ♃ ☉ ♄	1	11	51	Apr	3	0:44	28♓36	♇ ☿ ♀ ♃ ☉ ♄ ☽
1821	Apr	4	10:07	26♓13	♂ ☿ ♇ ♀ ♃ ☉ ♄	3	2	10	Apr	7	12:16	27♓21	☿ ♂ ♇ ♀ ♃ ♄ ☉
1831	Jan	13	22:38	21♑33	☽ ♆ ☉ ♃ ♀ ♅ ☿	1	15	11	Jan	15	13:49	22♑34	♆ ☉ ♃ ♀ ♅ ☿ ☽
1850	Apr	11	17:24	11♈27	☽ ♄ ☿ ☉ ♅ ♇ ♀	0	16	28	Apr	12	9:52	12♈17	♄ ☿ ☽ ☉ ♅ ♇ ♀
1882	May	3	0:20	12♉27	☉ ☿ ♄ ♆ ♇ ♀ ♃	4	11	23	May	7	11:43	15♉49	♄ ♆ ☉ ☿ ♇ ♃ ♀
1962	Feb	3	20:16	28♑20	☽ ♂ ♄ ☉ ♀ ☿ ♃	1	15	5	Feb	5	11:20	2♒44	♂ ♄ ☉ ☿ ♀ ♃ ☽
1994	Jan	10	17:06	4♑29	☽ ♂ ♀ ☉ ♆ ♅ ☿	2	12	43	Jan	13	5:49	18♑27	♂ ♆ ♀ ♅ ☉ ☿ ☽
2032	Jun	7	19:54	14♊49	☽ ☉ ♀ ♄ ♅ ♂ ☿	1	23	3	Jun	9	18:56	19♊29	☉ ♀ ♄ ♅ ♂ ☿ ☽

The first zodiacal position shown is the position of the first planet in the sequence which is listed in zodiacal order. The time span or duration that the planets remain within the 20° arc is shown as days, hours and minutes. The second zodiacal position is that of the first planet in the sequence when the planets are about to leave the 20° arc. Again, the planets are shown in zodiacal order.

Looking at the first entry in the above table, one sees the Moon as the leading planet in the entry sequence. One day, 19 hours and 29 minutes later the Moon has passed the other 6 planets to become the trailing planet and the one to break the 20° cluster of this grouping.

5 or More Planets Within 20° Arc 1700-2050

	Starting Position				Planets in Zodiacal Sequence						Dy	Hr	Mn		Ending Position				Planets in Zodiacal Sequence					
1701	Mar	9	13:18	16♓44	☽	♄	☿	☉	♆		1	18	0	1701	Mar	11	7:18	17♓26	♄	☉	☿	♆	☽	
	Jun	20	10:60	24♊32	☿	♀	☉	♂	♅		20	6	40		Jul	10	17:39	15♋46	♅	☉	♂	♀	☿	
	Jul	4	16:53	25♊25	☽	☉	♀	♅	♂		2	20	21		Jul	7	13:14	15♋00	☉	♅	♂	♀	☽	
	Jul	5	11:43	6♋07	☽	☉	♅	♀	♂	☿	2	1	31		Jul	7	13:14	15♋00	☉	♅	♂	♀	☿	☽
	Jul	5	11:43	6♋07	☽	♅	♀	♂	☿		2	2	30		Jul	7	14:13	15♋34	♅	♂	♀	☿	☽	
	Aug	3	17:24	1♌55	☽	♂	☉	♇	♀		1	15	27		Aug	5	8:52	5♌53	♂	♇	☉	♀	☽	
1702	Feb	26	16:29	6♓52	☽	☉	☿	♃	♄		1	20	41	1702	Feb	28	13:10	9♓32	☉	☿	♃	♄	☽	
	Mar	9	22:12	18♓54	☉	♃	♄	☿	♆		4	15	53		Mar	14	14:05	21♓19	♃	☉	♄	♆	☿	
	Mar	26	23:46	19♓32	☽	♃	♄	☉	♆		2	2	39		Mar	29	2:25	24♓49	♃	♄	☉	♆	☽	
	Mar	27	19:34	29♓28	☽	♄	☉	♆	☿		1	18	40		Mar	29	14:14	0♈41	♄	☉	♆	☿	☽	
	Apr	3	12:21	26♓07	♃	♄	♆	☉	☿		3	20	7		Apr	7	8:28	27♓01	♃	♄	♆	☿	☉	
	Apr	19	4:35	29♓45	♃	♄	☿	♆	♀		21	11	36		May	10	16:10	4♈24	♃	♄	♆	♀	☿	
	Apr	23	7:33	20♓33	☽	♃	♄	☿	♆		2	13	51		Apr	25	21:24	1♈15	♃	♄	☿	♆	☽	
	Apr	23	21:15	27♓24	☽	♃	♄	☿	♆	♀	2	0	9		Apr	25	21:24	1♈15	♃	♄	☿	♆	♀	☽
	Apr	23	21:15	27♓24	☽	♄	☿	♆	♀		2	5	38		Apr	26	2:53	3♈58	♄	☿	♆	♀	☽	
	May	21	7:53	29♓39	☽	♃	♄	♆	♀		2	6	46		May	23	14:39	6♈46	♄	♃	♆	♀	☽	
	Dec	25	5:10	19♓28	♂	☽	♄	♃	♆		1	9	23		Dec	26	14:33	20♓26	♂	♄	♃	♆	☽	
1703	Jan	21	7:55	19♓44	☽	♄	♂	♃	♆		2	19	6	1703	Jan	24	3:02	4♈51	♄	♃	♆	♂	☽	
	Mar	10	3:60	28♓17	♀	☿	♄	♆	♃		4	22	19		Mar	15	2:19	29♓25	☿	♀	♄	♆	♃	
	Mar	12	10:24	21♓09	☉	☿	♀	♄	♆		9	18	56		Mar	22	5:21	23♓16	☿	☉	♄	♆	♀	
	Mar	17	3:16	20♓22	☽	☉	☿	♀	♄		1	23	55		Mar	19	3:11	25♓58	☿	☉	♀	♄	☽	
	Mar	17	5:01	21♓20	☽	☉	☿	♀	♄	♆	1	22	10		Mar	19	3:11	25♓58	☿	☉	♀	♄	♆	☽
	Mar	17	5:01	21♓20	☽	☉	♀	♄	♆		2	2	0		Mar	19	7:02	27♓58	☉	♀	♄	♆	☽	
	Mar	17	21:11	0♈03	☽	♀	♄	♆	♃		2	10	35		Mar	20	7:46	10♈46	♄	♀	♆	♃	☽	
	Mar	22	11:15	1♈07	☉	♄	♆	♀	♃		14	23	28		Apr	6	10:42	12♈05	♆	♄	☉	♃	♀	
	Apr	14	16:34	6♈39	☽	♆	♄	☉	♃		2	1	55		Apr	16	18:29	12♈29	♆	♄	☉	♃	☽	
	Jun	15	17:34	7♋18	☽	♂	☿	♅	♀		2	11	17		Jun	18	4:52	16♋49	♂	☿	♅	♀	☽	
	Jul	13	20:17	17♋32	☽	☉	♅	♂	☿		2	1	29		Jul	15	21:46	22♋30	☉	♅	♂	☿	☽	
	Jul	29	2:13	25♋28	♅	☿	☉	♂	♇		4	11	34		Aug	2	13:47	25♋44	♅	☿	☉	♇	♂	
1704	Jul	29	22:48	16♋39	☽	☿	♀	♅	☉		2	0	49	1704	Jul	31	23:37	20♋41	☿	♅	♀	☉	☽	
	Jul	30	20:12	27♋11	☽	♀	♅	☉	♇		1	22	26		Aug	1	18:38	0♌05	♅	♀	☉	♇	☽	
	Aug	5	1:44	27♋21	☿	♅	♀	☉	♇		8	15	15		Aug	13	16:59	0♌48	♅	☿	♀	♇	☉	
1705	May	24	13:21	24♊18	☽	☿	♃	♀	♂		1	17	14	1705	May	26	6:35	26♊13	☿	♃	♀	♂	☽	
	Jun	20	6:07	15♊59	☽	☿	☉	♀	♃		1	21	43		Jun	22	3:50	20♊27	☿	☉	♀	♃	☽	
1706	Apr	12	4:19	9♈13	☽	♆	♀	☉	☿		1	22	55	1706	Apr	14	3:14	18♈53	♆	♀	☉	☿	☽	
	May	12	4:60	18♉12	☽	☉	♄	♀	☿		1	15	42		May	13	20:42	22♉30	☉	♄	♀	☿	☽	
	Jul	11	1:49	29♋56	☽	♃	♅	♀	♇		2	0	4		Jul	13	1:53	6♌02	♃	♅	♀	♇	☽	
	Jul	23	19:36	0♌19	☉	☿	♅	♃	♇		12	12	39		Aug	5	8:14	9♌03	♅	♃	☉	♇	☿	
	Aug	7	11:12	0♌46	☽	♅	♃	☉	♇		2	5	7		Aug	9	16:19	9♌19	♅	♃	☉	♇	☽	
1707	Jul	1	20:22	8♌26	☽	♅	♂	♇	♃		1	15	51	1707	Jul	3	12:12	11♌30	♅	♂	♇	♃	☽	
	Jul	18	21:50	11♌35	☿	♅	♇	♂	♃		3	3	5		Jul	22	0:55	12♌34	♅	☿	♇	♃	♂	
	Jul	29	21:37	17♌28	☽	♇	☿	♃	♂		1	19	22		Jul	31	16:59	22♌16	♇	☿	♃	♂	☽	
	Aug	26	15:15	12♌34	♀	♅	☽	♇	☉		0	19	27		Aug	27	10:42	13♌34	♀	♅	♇	☉	☽	
	Sep	24	6:54	10♍29	☽	☿	♃	♀	☉		1	20	27		Sep	26	3:21	14♍32	☿	♃	♀	☉	☽	
	Oct	24	4:18	13♎57	☽	♀	☉	☿	♂		2	20	51		Oct	27	1:09	28♎56	♀	☉	☿	♂	☽	
1708	Aug	15	10:18	14♌35	☽	♅	☉	♇	☿		1	15	0	1708	Aug	17	1:18	18♌40	♅	☉	♇	☿	☽	
	Aug	29	8:38	19♌25	♅	☿	♇	☉	♀		3	19	40		Sep	2	4:19	19♌39	♅	☿	♇	♀	☉	
	Sep	11	15:31	12♌01	☽	♅	♇	☿	♀		1	22	37		Sep	13	14:08	20♌18	♅	♇	♀	☿	☽	
1709	Jun	8	6:55	13♊11	♀	☉	☽	☿	♄		1	0	2	1709	Jun	9	6:57	14♊25	♀	☉	☿	♄	☽	
	Jul	29	5:24	5♌45	☉	♀	☿	♅	♇		10	9	56		Aug	8	15:20	8♌40	☿	☉	♅	♇	♀	
	Aug	5	3:20	4♌21	☽	☿	☉	♅	♀		1	16	23		Aug	6	19:43	9♌52	☿	☉	♅	♀	☽	
	Aug	5	5:55	5♌58	☽	☿	☉	♅	♀	♇	1	13	48		Aug	6	19:43	9♌52	☿	☉	♅	♇	♀	☽
	Aug	5	5:55	5♌58	☽	☉	♅	♀	♇		1	20	48		Aug	7	2:43	14♌16	☉	♅	♇	♀	☽	
	Sep	2	14:44	19♌50	☽	♅	♇	☿	☉		1	14	36		Sep	4	5:20	24♌13	♅	♇	☿	☉	☽	
	Oct	3	22:21	17♎58	☽	☿	♂	♃	♀		1	22	36		Oct	5	20:57	26♎02	☿	♂	♃	♀	☽	
1710	Apr	26	10:32	7♈59	☽	♂	♀	☿	♆		1	19	59	1710	Apr	28	6:31	9♈59	♂	♀	☿	♆	☽	
	Aug	23	6:14	9♌35	☽	☿	♅	♇	☉		2	13	53		Aug	25	20:08	27♌34	☿	♅	♇	☉	☽	
	Dec	18	20:30	6♐38	☽	♃	☿	♀	☉		2	1	28		Dec	20	21:58	16♐10	♃	♀	☿	☉	☽	
1711	Aug	13	14:48	11♌46	☽	☿	☉	♇	♅		2	5	46	1711	Aug	15	20:34	22♌13	☉	☿	♇	♅	☽	
1712	Jan	7	22:31	10♑20	☽	♃	☉	♂	☿		1	17	57	1712	Jan	9	16:28	15♑57	♃	☉	♂	☿	☽	
	Aug	1	10:35	26♋39	☽	♀	☉	☿	♄		2	6	22		Aug	3	16:57	4♌18	♀	☉	♄	☿	☽	
	Aug	3	0:09	15♌39	☽	♄	☿	♇	♅		1	17	18		Aug	4	17:26	17♌04	♄	☿	♇	♅	☽	
	Aug	3	21:37	11♌28	☉	♄	☿	☽	♇		0	9	53		Aug	4	7:30	11♌51	☉	♄	☿	♇	☽	
	Aug	8	14:42	15♌59	☉	♄	☿	♇	♅		6	1	8		Aug	14	15:50	18♌20	♄	☉	♇	♅	☿	
	Aug	9	16:02	11♌39	♀	☉	♄	☿	♇		3	20	23		Aug	13	12:25	16♌24	♀	♄	☉	♇	☿	
	Aug	13	9:50	16♌16	♀	♄	☉	♇	☿	♅	0	2	35		Aug	13	12:25	16♌24	♀	♄	☉	♇	♅	☿
	Aug	13	9:50	16♌16	♀	♄	☉	♇	♅		19	16	24		Sep	2	2:14	20♌40	♄	♇	♅	☉	♀	
	Aug	30	10:30	17♌20	☽	♄	♇	☉	♅		1	20	10		Sep	1	6:40	20♌34	♄	♇	♅	☉	☽	
	Aug	30	10:34	17♌22	☽	♄	♇	☉	♅	♀	1	20	5		Sep	1	6:40	20♌34	♄	♇	♅	☉	♀	☽
	Aug	30	10:34	17♌22	☽	♇	☉	♅	♀		2	18	3		Sep	2	4:37	2♍26	♇	♅	☉	♀	☽	
	Oct	24	9:37	20♌28	☽	♂	♄	♇	♅		2	1	0		Oct	26	10:37	26♌13	♂	♄	♇	♅	☽	
	Nov	20	19:45	21♌26	☽	♄	♇	♂	♅		2	2	58		Nov	22	22:43	27♌44	♄	♇	♂	♅	☽	
1713	Aug	20	16:30	21♌11	☽	☉	♄	♇	♅		2	9	4	1713	Aug	23	1:34	29♌39	☉	♄	♇	♅	☽	

5 or More Planets Within 20° Arc 1700-2050

Year	Mo	Day	Time	Starting Position	Planets in Zodiacal Sequence						Dy	Hr	Mn	Year	Mo	Day	Time	Ending Position	Planets in Zodiacal Sequence					
	Sep	19	10:44	4♍34	♄	♇	♅	☽	☿		0	6	44		Sep	19	17:28	4♍36	♄	♇	♅	☿	☽	
	Oct	14	12:55	24♌30	☽	♇	♄	♀	♅		2	14	1		Oct	17	2:55	5♍43	♇	♄	♀	♅	☽	
1714	Mar	14	17:34	5♓42	☽	♀	☉	♃	☿		2	4	48	1714	Mar	16	22:22	19♓11	♀	☉	♃	☿	☽	
	Mar	15	12:41	17♓51	☽	☉	♃	☿	♂		1	20	48		Mar	17	9:29	26♓07	♃	☉	☿	♂	☽	
	Mar	16	9:43	18♓32	♀	☉	♃	☿	☽	♂	0	12	39		Mar	16	22:22	19♓11	♀	☉	♃	☿	♂	☽
	Mar	16	9:43	18♓32	♀	☉	♃	☿	♂		9	15	50		Mar	26	1:33	28♓13	♃	♀	☉	♂	☿	
	Apr	9	2:44	17♈57	♀	☉	♂	♆	☿		27	8	29		May	6	11:13	1♉43	☿	♆	☉	♂	♀	
	Apr	13	20:19	16♈10	☽	☉	♀	♂	♆		2	0	14		Apr	15	20:33	25♈26	☉	♀	♂	♆	☽	
	Apr	14	3:26	20♈34	☽	☉	♀	♂	♆	☿	1	17	7		Apr	15	20:33	25♈26	☉	♀	♂	♆	☿	☽
	Apr	14	3:26	20♈34	☽	♀	♂	♆	☿		1	18	42		Apr	15	22:08	26♈23	♀	♂	♆	☿	☽	
	May	12	6:03	1♉02	☽	☿	♆	♂	☉		0	6	3		May	12	12:06	1♉16	☿	☽	♆	♂	☉	
	Jul	23	10:09	24♌04	☿	♀	♇	♄	♅		23	18	33		Aug	16	4:43	5♍41	♇	♄	♅	☿	♀	
	Aug	10	22:27	25♌04	☽	♇	♄	☿	♅		2	13	27		Aug	13	11:53	5♍35	♇	♄	♅	☿	☽	
	Aug	11	7:59	29♌50	☽	♇	♄	☿	♅	♀	2	3	55		Aug	13	11:53	5♍35	♇	♄	♅	☿	♀	☽
	Aug	11	7:59	29♌50	☽	♄	☿	♅	♀		2	16	2		Aug	14	0:00	11♍34	♄	♅	☿	♀	☽	
	Aug	20	12:55	26♌59	☉	♇	♄	♅	☿		30	18	26		Sep	20	7:22	6♍53	♇	☿	♄	♅	☉	
	Sep	7	3:28	24♌33	☽	☿	♇	☉	♄		2	10	12		Sep	9	13:40	3♍25	☿	♇	♄	☉	☽	
	Sep	7	7:51	26♌44	☽	☿	♇	☉	♄	♅	2	5	49		Sep	9	13:40	3♍25	☿	♇	♄	☉	♅	☽
	Sep	7	7:51	26♌44	☽	♇	☉	♄	♅		2	12	7		Sep	9	19:58	6♍32	♇	♄	☉	♅	☽	
	Nov	1	4:53	0♍58	☽	♇	♂	♅	♄		2	6	50		Nov	3	11:42	8♍05	♇	♂	♅	♄	☽	
1715	Aug	28	23:40	4♍42	☽	☉	♇	♅	♄		1	18	23	1715	Aug	30	18:04	6♍38	☉	♇	♅	♄	☽	
	Sep	10	8:33	1♍23	♀	☿	♇	☉	♅		12	6	46		Sep	22	15:19	8♍56	♇	♀	♅	☿	☉	
	Sep	12	11:54	6♍28	☿	♇	☉	♅	♄		10	3	25		Sep	22	15:19	8♍56	♇	♅	☿	♄	☉	
	Sep	14	16:30	6♍45	♀	♇	☿	☉	♅	♄	7	22	49		Sep	22	15:19	8♍56	♇	♀	♅	☿	♄	☉
	Sep	14	16:30	6♍45	♀	♇	☿	♅	♄		10	1	24		Sep	24	17:53	9♍00	♇	♀	♅	♄	☿	
	Sep	14	16:30	6♍45	♀	☿	☉	♅	♄		17	21	48		Oct	2	14:18	22♍46	♅	♄	♀	☉	☿	
	Sep	25	12:38	8♍05	☽	♇	♀	♅	♄		1	17	5		Sep	27	5:43	9♍05	♇	♀	♅	♄	☽	
	Sep	25	17:53	10♍48	☽	♀	♅	♄	☿		2	14	37		Sep	28	8:30	22♍31	♅	♀	♄	☿	☽	
	Sep	25	20:22	12♍05	☽	♀	♅	♄	☿	☉	2	12	7		Sep	28	8:30	22♍31	♅	♀	♄	☉	☿	☽
	Sep	25	20:22	12♍05	☽	♀	♄	☿	☉		2	14	51		Sep	28	11:14	23♍52	♀	♄	☉	☿	☽	
1716	May	20	19:13	20♉47	☽	☿	☉	♃	♂		1	18	42	1716	May	22	13:55	27♉51	☿	☉	♃	♂	☽	
	Sep	14	14:45	6♍45	☽	♇	☉	♅	☿		1	19	18		Sep	16	10:03	10♍45	♇	☉	♅	☿	☽	
	Sep	15	10:49	17♍59	☽	☉	♅	☿	♄		2	1	6		Sep	17	11:55	24♍38	☉	♅	☿	♄	☽	
	Nov	8	11:16	11♍17	☽	♇	♅	♀	♂		1	15	12		Nov	10	2:27	12♍18	♇	♅	♀	♂	☽	
	Nov	9	11:54	24♍34	☽	♅	♀	♂	♄		1	23	35		Nov	11	11:29	29♍31	♅	♀	♂	♄	☽	
1717	May	9	14:37	28♈44	☽	♀	♆	☿	☉		2	4	23	1717	May	11	19:01	10♉07	♀	♆	☉	☿	☽	
	Jul	7	15:32	29♊56	☽	♃	☉	☿	♀		2	5	38		Jul	9	21:09	14♋06	♃	☿	☉	♀	☽	
	Sep	5	3:52	10♍02	☽	☉	♇	☿	♅		1	13	14		Sep	6	17:06	12♍27	♇	☉	☿	♅	☽	
	Sep	7	15:46	27♍58	☿	♅	♀	☽	♄		0	4	33		Sep	7	20:20	28♍17	☿	♅	♀	♄	☽	
1718	Jul	27	12:36	22♋41	☿	☽	☉	♂	♃		0	20	50	1718	Jul	28	9:26	24♋25	☿	☉	♂	♃	☽	
	Oct	21	9:52	25♍08	☽	♂	♀	♅	☿		1	22	4		Oct	23	7:55	3♎31	♂	♀	♅	☿	☽	
1719	Nov	10	11:06	28♎10	☽	☿	♄	☉	♀		2	12	54	1719	Nov	13	0:01	16♏38	♀	♄	☿	☉	☽	
1720	Aug	30	7:10	6♍56	☉	♀	♂	♇	☿		20	0	21	1720	Sep	19	7:31	12♍45	☿	♇	♂	☉	♀	
	Sep	1	19:31	28♌35	☽	☉	♀	♂	♇		2	9	5		Sep	4	4:36	11♍41	☉	♀	♂	♇	☽	
	Sep	2	8:33	6♍00	☽	☉	♀	♂	♇	☿	1	20	3		Sep	4	4:36	11♍41	☉	♀	♂	♇	☿	☽
	Sep	2	8:33	6♍00	☽	♀	♂	♇	☿		2	0	13		Sep	4	8:46	14♍10	♀	♂	♇	☿	☽	
	Sep	19	15:14	24♍19	♂	☉	♀	♃	♅		18	16	49		Oct	8	8:03	6♎28	♂	☉	♅	♃	♀	
	Sep	30	14:10	17♍31	☽	♇	☿	♂	☉		1	12	59		Oct	2	3:09	19♍41	♇	☿	♂	☉	☽	
	Oct	1	2:52	25♍02	☽	♂	☉	♃	♅		1	21	59		Oct	3	0:51	3♎01	♂	☉	♃	♅	☽	
	Oct	1	7:19	27♍42	☽	♂	☉	♃	♅	♀	1	17	32		Oct	3	0:51	3♎01	♂	☉	♃	♅	♀	☽
	Oct	1	7:19	27♍42	☽	☉	♃	♅	♀		2	5	31		Oct	3	12:50	10♎25	☉	♃	♅	♀	☽	
	Oct	3	20:30	25♍12	☿	♂	☉	♃	♅		24	17	18		Oct	28	13:48	16♎45	♅	♂	♃	☉	☿	
	Oct	30	1:29	16♎49	☽	♅	♃	♂	☉		0	0	41		Oct	30	2:10	16♎50	♅	☽	♃	♂	☉	
	Oct	30	5:43	19♎26	☽	♃	♂	☉	☿		0	18	16		Oct	30	23:59	20♎39	♃	♂	☽	☉	☿	
	Oct	31	7:23	5♏31	☽	☉	☿	♀	♄		1	14	5		Nov	1	21:28	9♏39	☉	☿	♄	♀	☽	
1721	Dec	16	16:27	22♏35	☽	♃	♀	♄	☿		1	11	55	1721	Dec	18	4:22	24♏38	♃	♀	♄	☿	☽	
1722	Sep	11	2:43	10♍36	☿	☉	☽	♇	♂		0	19	28	1722	Sep	11	22:11	12♍08	☿	☉	♇	♂	☽	
	Oct	9	20:19	10♎08	☽	☉	♂	♅	☿		2	5	45		Oct	12	2:04	18♎24	☉	♂	♅	☿	☽	
	Dec	7	9:28	29♏55	☽	♂	☉	♃	♄		1	12	44		Dec	8	22:12	1♐02	♂	☉	♃	♄	☽	
	Dec	21	15:02	9♐33	☿	♂	♃	♄	☉		2	0	20		Dec	23	15:23	11♐36	♂	☿	♃	♄	☉	
1723	Jan	4	12:29	9♐25	☽	♂	♃	♄	☿		2	6	57	1723	Jan	6	19:26	21♐55	♂	♄	♃	☿	☽	
	Dec	26	15:26	26♐28	☿	♄	☉	♀	♃		5	0	16		Dec	31	15:43	2♑43	♄	☿	☉	♃	♀	
	Dec	26	21:38	26♐31	☽	☿	♄	☉	♃		1	17	38		Dec	28	15:16	29♐35	☿	♄	☉	♃	☽	
	Dec	26	22:05	26♐46	☽	☿	♄	☉	♃	♀	1	17	11		Dec	28	15:16	29♐35	☿	♄	☉	♃	♀	☽
	Dec	26	22:05	26♐46	☽	♄	☉	♃	♀		1	22	8		Dec	28	20:14	2♑23	♄	☉	♃	♀	☽	
1724	Oct	16	15:50	18♎10	☽	☉	♅	♂	☿		2	7	56	1724	Oct	18	23:46	25♎47	☉	♅	☿	♂	☽	
	Dec	16	2:33	20♐58	♂	☿	☉	☽	♄		1	1	57		Dec	17	4:30	21♐47	♂	☿	☉	♄	☽	
1725	Feb	11	14:22	4♒25	☽	♂	☿	☉	♃		1	15	44	1725	Feb	13	6:05	6♒13	♂	☿	☉	♃	☽	
	Mar	11	11:50	11♒03	☽	☿	♀	♂	♃		2	17	22		Mar	14	5:12	27♒56	☿	♀	♂	♃	☽	
	Jun	9	8:59	28♉57	☽	♆	♀	☉	☿		1	12	35		Jun	10	21:34	2♊08	♆	♀	☿	☉	☽	
1726	Apr	1	14:45	29♓29	☽	♃	☉	☿	♀		1	20	41	1726	Apr	3	11:26	4♈15	♃	☉	☿	♀	☽	
1727	Jan	20	21:26	15♑18	☽	♀	☉	♂	♄		3	5	25	1727	Jan	24	2:52	3♒41	☉	♀	♄	♂	☽	
1728	Jun	6	1:31	25♉25	☽	☿	♆	♃	☉		2	14	54	1728	Jun	8	16:25	8♊34	♆	☿	♃	☉	☽	

5 or More Planets Within 20° Arc 1700-2050

	Starting Position				Planets in Zodiacal Sequence						Dy	Hr	Mn		Ending Position				Planets in Zodiacal Sequence					
	Jun	6	8:30	24♉18	♀	☽	☿	♆	♃		1	8	17		Jun	7	16:47	25♉56	♀	♆	☿	♃	☽	
	Jun	11	18:15	0♊52	♀	♆	♃	☿	☉		1	5	6		Jun	12	23:21	2♊20	♀	♆	♃	☉	☿	
	Oct	2	17:47	0♎10	☽	♇	☉	☿	♀		1	19	54		Oct	4	13:41	7♎59	♇	☉	☿	♀	☽	
	Nov	1	17:41	8♏42	☽	☉	♅	♀	☿		1	11	11		Nov	3	4:52	11♏02	☉	♅	♀	☿	☽	
1729	May	26	13:00	20♉13	☽	♂	☿	☉	♆		2	6	34	1729	May	28	19:34	27♉15	♂	☉	☿	♆	☽	
1730	Mar	17	5:04	6♓22	☽	☿	♄	♀	☉		0	9	50	1730	Mar	17	14:53	6♓47	☿	☽	♄	♀	☉	
	May	16	15:17	22♉01	☽	☉	☿	♀	♆		2	2	31		May	18	17:48	27♉24	☉	☿	♀	♆	☽	
1731	Jun	5	13:12	14♊14	☉	♆	♂	☽	☿		0	20	33	1731	Jun	6	9:45	14♊56	♆	☉	♂	☿	☽	
	Oct	29	3:07	15♎13	☽	♇	☿	♀	☉		0	23	34		Oct	30	2:41	16♎12	♇	☿	☽	♀	☉	
	Nov	28	7:49	21♏32	☽	☿	☉	♅	♀		2	6	50		Nov	30	14:39	2♐20	☿	♅	☉	♀	☽	
1732	Sep	19	21:37	27♍07	☉	☽	♃	☿	♇		1	3	41	1732	Sep	21	1:18	28♍15	☉	♃	☿	♇	☽	
	Oct	17	2:24	3♎58	☽	☿	♇	♃	☉		2	1	17		Oct	19	3:41	8♎20	☿	♇	♃	☉	☽	
1733	Jun	11	12:32	13♊20	☽	♀	♆	☉	♂		1	19	5	1733	Jun	13	7:37	19♊31	♆	♀	☉	♂	☽	
	Jul	10	9:09	4♋40	☽	☉	☿	♂	♀		2	13	14		Jul	12	22:24	20♋23	☉	♂	☿	♀	☽	
1734	Apr	3	23:10	12♈53	☽	☉	♀	♄	☿		1	1	0	1734	Apr	5	0:10	13♈41	♀	☉	☽	♄	☿	
	Dec	9	10:30	7♐12	♀	☉	♅	♃	☿		15	23	58		Dec	25	10:28	13♐31	☿	♅	♃	♀	☉	
	Dec	22	19:21	4♐01	☽	☿	♅	♃	♀		2	11	28		Dec	25	6:49	13♐29	☿	♅	♃	♀	☽	
	Dec	23	10:21	11♐29	☽	☿	♅	♃	♀	☉	1	20	28		Dec	25	6:49	13♐29	☿	♅	♃	♀	☉	☽
	Dec	23	10:21	11♐29	☽	♅	♃	♀	☉		2	9	51		Dec	25	20:12	20♐06	♅	♃	♀	☉	☽	
1737	May	29	21:05	10♊52	☽	♄	♆	♀	☿		1	21	1	1737	May	31	18:06	14♊34	♄	♆	♀	☿	☽	
	May	30	13:57	9♊03	☉	♄	☽	♆	♀		0	19	14		May	31	9:11	9♊49	☉	♄	♆	♀	☽	
	Jun	26	11:47	14♊44	☽	♀	♄	♆	☉		0	7	13		Jun	26	18:60	15♊02	♀	♄	☽	♆	☉	
	Oct	22	22:47	17♎46	☽	♂	☉	♇	☿		1	18	37		Oct	24	17:24	24♎55	♂	♇	☉	☿	☽	
	Nov	19	17:20	22♎35	☽	♀	♇	☿	♂		1	14	42		Nov	21	8:02	27♎01	♀	♇	☿	♂	☽	
1738	Apr	17	13:03	10♈24	☽	♃	☿	☉	♀		1	4	21	1738	Apr	18	17:25	11♈52	♃	☽	☿	☉	♀	
	May	19	17:29	9♊24	☽	♀	☿	♄	♆		1	22	25		May	21	15:54	12♊25	♀	☿	♄	♆	☽	
	May	31	14:44	9♊48	☉	♀	☿	♄	♆		13	14	24		Jun	14	5:08	21♊15	☿	☉	♄	♆	♀	
	Jun	16	1:27	10♊22	☽	☿	☉	♄	♆		2	9	36		Jun	18	11:02	19♊06	☿	☉	♄	♆	☽	
	Jun	17	6:53	25♊00	☽	☉	♄	♆	♀		1	20	49		Jun	19	3:43	27♊31	☉	♄	♆	♀	☽	
1739	Jul	4	8:04	23♊31	☽	☿	♆	☉	♄		2	8	56	1739	Jul	6	16:60	1♋32	☿	♆	♄	☉	☽	
	Oct	22	4:58	15♎48	☿	♀	☉	♂	♇		24	20	44		Nov	16	1:43	6♏48	♇	♂	☉	☿	♀	
	Oct	30	19:35	16♎58	☽	☿	♇	♀	☉		2	17	34		Nov	2	13:08	4♏37	☿	♇	☉	♀	☽	
	Oct	31	4:35	22♎00	☽	☿	♇	♀	☉	♂	2	8	34		Nov	2	13:08	4♏37	☿	♇	☉	♀	♂	☽
	Oct	31	4:35	22♎00	☽	♇	♀	☉	♂		2	11	21		Nov	2	15:56	6♏16	♇	☉	♀	♂	☽	
	Nov	30	5:02	28♏18	☽	♂	☉	♀	☿		1	19	12		Dec	2	0:14	4♐35	♂	☉	♀	☿	☽	
	Dec	30	3:28	4♑46	☽	☉	♅	♀	☿		1	15	46		Dec	31	19:14	9♑47	☉	♅	♀	☿	☽	
1740	Jun	22	15:60	14♊56	☽	☿	♃	☉	♆		2	4	56	1740	Jun	24	20:56	22♊20	♃	☿	☉	♆	☽	
1741	Jun	13	0:26	16♊43	☽	☿	♀	☉	♆		1	22	59	1741	Jun	14	23:26	23♊14	☿	☉	♀	♆	☽	
	Jun	17	17:50	26♊25	☉	♀	☿	♆	♃		14	1	28		Jul	1	19:18	7♋25	♆	☉	♀	♃	☿	
	Jul	11	20:42	7♋09	☽	♆	☉	♃	♀		0	12	44		Jul	12	9:26	7♋48	♆	☽	☉	♃	♀	
	Jul	12	18:27	19♋03	☽	☉	♃	♀	♄		1	19	1		Jul	14	13:29	22♋00	☉	♃	♀	♄	☽	
1742	Apr	3	22:58	23♓59	☽	♂	☿	♀	☉		1	11	19	1742	Apr	5	10:17	26♓09	♂	☿	♀	☉	☽	
	Jul	31	9:01	3♌17	☽	☉	☿	♃	♄		1	22	33		Aug	2	7:34	9♌41	☉	☿	♃	♄	☽	
	Aug	28	13:22	14♌57	☽	☿	♃	♄	☉		2	3	45		Aug	30	17:07	23♌25	☿	♃	♄	☉	☽	
	Nov	25	9:35	13♏01	☽	♇	♀	☿	☉		1	16	48		Nov	27	2:24	14♏45	♇	☿	♀	☽	☉	
1743	Jan	24	4:47	15♑25	☽	♅	☉	☿	♀		2	6	33	1743	Jan	26	11:20	23♑46	♅	☉	♀	☿	☽	
	Oct	18	23:09	11♏21	☽	♇	♀	☿	♂		1	23	24		Oct	20	22:33	15♏45	♇	♀	☿	♂	☽	
	Nov	14	12:18	1♏46	☽	♀	☿	♇	☉		1	19	4		Nov	16	7:22	4♏07	♀	☿	♇	☉	☽	
1744	Jan	14	7:55	17♑59	☽	☉	♅	☿	♂		2	8	29	1744	Jan	16	16:24	26♑00	☉	♅	☿	♂	☽	
	Jul	8	15:01	26♊36	☽	☿	♀	♆	☉		1	12	44		Jul	10	3:45	29♊40	☿	♀	♆	☉	☽	
1745	Nov	22	1:28	9♏55	☽	♇	♃	☿	☉		2	5	13	1745	Nov	24	6:41	22♏05	♇	♃	☉	☿	☽	
1746	Mar	22	17:47	27♓00	☿	♀	☉	☽	♂		0	20	35	1746	Mar	23	14:22	28♓41	☿	♀	☉	♂	☽	
	May	19	19:33	20♉49	☽	☿	☉	♂	♀		0	7	11		May	20	2:44	21♉11	☿	☽	☉	♂	♀	
1747	Nov	2	13:01	6♏05	☽	☉	♀	☿	♇		1	16	45	1747	Nov	4	5:46	11♏28	☉	♀	☿	♇	☽	
1748	Jan	29	10:22	23♑07	☿	☽	♃	☉	♅		1	1	8	1748	Jan	30	11:30	24♑44	☿	♃	☉	♅	☽	
	Jun	25	16:17	2♋40	☽	☉	♂	♆	☿		1	23	48		Jun	27	16:05	6♋12	☉	♂	♆	☿	☽	
	Aug	22	7:14	9♌26	☽	☿	♂	♀	☉		2	3	39		Aug	24	10:54	15♌15	☿	♂	♀	☉	☽	
	Dec	17	4:51	14♏03	☽	♀	♄	♇	☿		1	13	35		Dec	18	18:27	16♏07	♀	♄	♇	☿	☽	
1749	Jul	14	5:39	18♋37	☽	☉	♆	♀	☿		2	2	7	1749	Jul	16	7:46	23♋45	☉	♆	♀	☿	☽	
	Oct	13	6:58	10♏12	☽	☿	♄	♀	♇		1	22	30		Oct	15	5:28	14♏37	☿	♄	♀	♇	☽	
	Nov	9	15:36	11♏11	☽	☉	♄	☿	♇		2	5	18		Nov	11	20:54	19♏39	☉	♄	☿	♇	☽	
1750	Jul	3	10:14	6♋45	☽	☉	☿	♂	♆		1	23	56	1750	Jul	5	10:09	13♋08	☉	☿	♂	♆	☽	
	Nov	23	13:58	14♏12	☿	♀	☉	♇	♄		23	8	31		Dec	16	22:29	4♐59	♇	♄	♀	☿	☉	
	Nov	27	4:30	14♏38	☽	☿	♀	♇	♄		2	8	34		Nov	29	13:04	23♏03	☿	♀	♇	♄	☽	
	Nov	27	5:05	14♏56	☽	☿	♀	♇	♄	☉	2	7	58		Nov	29	13:04	23♏03	☿	♀	♇	♄	☉	☽
	Nov	27	5:05	14♏56	☽	♀	♇	♄	☉		2	14	39		Nov	29	19:45	26♏27	♀	♇	♄	☉	☽	
1751	Jan	27	6:39	5♒25	☽	☉	♀	♅	☿		1	16	50	1751	Jan	28	23:29	8♒48	☉	♀	♅	☿	☽	
1752	Jul	9	22:30	27♊55	☽	♃	☿	♀	☉		1	10	38	1752	Jul	11	9:08	29♊51	♃	♀	☿	☉	☽	
	Dec	5	2:30	5♐40	☽	♇	☉	☿	♄		1	22	55		Dec	7	1:25	9♐15	♇	☉	♄	☿	☽	
1754	Feb	20	18:32	17♒02	☽	♀	☿	☉	♅		2	9	30	1754	Feb	23	4:02	25♒25	♀	☿	☉	♅	☽	
	Jul	4	22:32	0♌34	☿	♆	♀	♃	♂		8	6	27		Jul	13	4:60	5♌39	♆	☿	♀	♃	♂	
	Jul	20	22:17	10♌26	☽	♃	☿	♀	♂		2	4	14		Jul	23	2:31	22♌19	♃	☿	♀	♂	☽	
	Dec	12	11:09	0♐27	☽	♂	☿	♇	☉		1	23	2		Dec	14	10:11	8♐22	♂	☿	♇	☉	☽	

5 or More Planets Within 20° Arc 1700-2050

				Starting Position	Planets in Zodiacal Sequence	Dy	Hr	Mn					Ending Position	Planets in Zodiacal Sequence
1756	Aug	24	1:45	11♌12	☽ ♆ ♀ ☿ ☉	0	6	39	1756	Aug	24	8:24	11♌28	♆ ☽ ♀ ☿ ☉
	Dec	20	5:43	8♐53	☽ ♇ ☿ ♂ ☉	1	22	58		Dec	22	4:41	18♐48	♇ ☿ ♂ ☉ ☽
1757	Jan	20	8:51	21♑24	♂ ☉ ☽ ☿ ♄	0	11	35	1757	Jan	20	20:26	21♑46	♂ ☉ ☿ ♄ ☽
	Mar	16	21:06	14♒49	☽ ♄ ☿ ♀ ♂	1	14	50		Mar	18	11:56	17♒57	♄ ☿ ♂ ♀ ☽
	Mar	17	21:59	29♒40	☽ ☿ ♂ ♀ ♅	1	12	36		Mar	19	10:36	1♓18	☿ ♂ ♀ ♅ ☽
	Dec	9	22:31	0♐31	☽ ♃ ☿ ☉ ♇	1	14	52		Dec	11	13:24	3♐48	♃ ☿ ☉ ♇ ☽
1758	Nov	27	11:07	5♐14	☉ ☿ ♇ ♂ ♃	23	12	30	1758	Dec	20	23:37	23♐04	♇ ☉ ♃ ♂ ☿
	Nov	30	11:37	5♐54	☽ ☉ ☿ ♇ ♃	1	20	13		Dec	2	7:50	10♐10	☉ ☿ ♇ ♃ ☽
	Nov	30	14:26	7♐26	☽ ☉ ☿ ♇ ♃ ♂	1	17	24		Dec	2	7:50	10♐10	☉ ☿ ♇ ♃ ♂ ☽
	Nov	30	14:26	7♐26	☽ ☿ ♇ ♃ ♂	2	0	42		Dec	2	15:07	14♐14	☿ ♇ ♃ ♂ ☽
	Dec	8	4:29	7♐39	♀ ☉ ♇ ☿ ♃	12	19	8		Dec	20	23:37	23♐04	♇ ♀ ☉ ♃ ☿
	Dec	19	13:26	21♐57	♀ ♇ ☉ ♃ ☿ ♂	1	10	11		Dec	20	23:37	23♐04	♇ ♀ ☉ ♃ ♂ ☿
	Dec	19	13:26	21♐57	♀ ♇ ☉ ♃ ♂	1	10	35		Dec	21	0:01	23♐04	♇ ♀ ☉ ♃ ♂
	Dec	19	13:26	21♐57	♀ ☉ ♃ ☿ ♂	3	18	19		Dec	23	7:45	26♐42	♀ ♃ ☉ ♂ ☿
	Dec	28	16:51	17♐01	☽ ♇ ♃ ♀ ☉	1	22	40		Dec	30	15:31	23♐25	♇ ♃ ♀ ☉ ☽
	Dec	29	15:40	29♐48	☽ ♃ ♀ ☉ ♂	1	16	15		Dec	31	7:55	2♑57	♃ ♀ ☉ ♂ ☽
1759	Feb	26	7:47	6♓01	♂ ♄ ☉ ♀ ♅	7	12	25	1759	Mar	5	20:12	7♓38	♄ ♂ ☉ ♅ ♀
	Feb	26	15:30	28♒40	☽ ♂ ♄ ☉ ♀	1	20	50		Feb	28	12:20	6♓59	♄ ♂ ☉ ♀ ☽
	Feb	27	3:17	6♓04	☽ ♂ ♄ ☉ ♀ ♅	1	9	3		Feb	28	12:20	6♓59	♄ ♂ ☉ ♀ ♅ ☽
	Feb	27	3:17	6♓04	☽ ♂ ☉ ♀ ♅	1	10	19		Feb	28	13:36	7♓47	♂ ☉ ♀ ♅ ☽
	Mar	13	2:16	6♓51	☿ ♄ ♂ ☉ ♅	7	3	46		Mar	20	6:02	9♓21	♄ ☿ ♂ ♅ ☉
	Mar	27	6:40	16♓18	☽ ♅ ♂ ☿ ☉	2	1	20		Mar	29	7:59	27♓46	♅ ♂ ☿ ☉ ☽
1760	Mar	16	4:54	10♓49	☽ ♄ ☉ ☿ ♅	1	23	56	1760	Mar	18	4:50	20♓02	♄ ☉ ♅ ☿ ☽
1761	Feb	27	0:18	8♓41	☉ ♃ ☿ ♂ ♄	10	22	19	1761	Mar	9	22:36	12♓26	♃ ☉ ♄ ♂ ☿
	Mar	4	4:58	13♓53	☉ ☿ ♂ ♄ ♅	19	20	29		Mar	24	1:27	1♈46	♄ ☉ ♅ ♂ ☿
	Mar	6	4:43	8♓35	☽ ♃ ☉ ☿ ♂	1	18	16		Mar	7	22:59	11♓57	♃ ☉ ☿ ♂ ☽
	Mar	6	6:31	9♓34	☽ ♃ ☉ ☿ ♂ ♄	1	16	27		Mar	7	22:59	11♓57	♃ ☉ ☿ ♄ ♂ ☽
	Mar	6	6:31	9♓34	☽ ☉ ☿ ♂ ♄	2	3	20		Mar	8	9:51	18♓05	☉ ☿ ♄ ♂ ☽
	Mar	6	14:40	14♓01	☽ ☉ ☿ ♂ ♄ ♅	1	19	11		Mar	8	9:51	18♓05	☉ ☿ ♄ ♂ ♅ ☽
	Mar	6	14:40	14♓01	☽ ☿ ♂ ♄ ♅	2	16	1		Mar	9	6:41	29♓56	♄ ♂ ☿ ♅ ☽
	Apr	2	1:11	2♈53	♄ ♅ ☉ ♂ ☿	5	23	21		Apr	8	0:32	3♈37	♄ ♅ ☉ ☿ ♂
	Apr	4	5:31	0♈46	☽ ♄ ♅ ☉ ♂	1	15	7		Apr	5	20:39	3♈21	♄ ♅ ☉ ♂ ☽
	Apr	4	7:21	1♈48	☽ ♄ ♅ ☉ ♂ ☿	1	13	18		Apr	5	20:39	3♈21	♄ ♅ ☉ ☿ ♂ ☽
	Apr	4	7:21	1♈48	☽ ♅ ☉ ♂ ☿	1	17	22		Apr	6	0:43	5♈44	♅ ☉ ☿ ♂ ☽
	Jun	2	2:25	28♉09	☽ ☿ ♂ ☉ ♀	1	17	59		Jun	3	20:24	4♊25	☿ ♂ ☉ ♀ ☽
1762	Feb	25	3:32	19♓48	☽ ☿ ♅ ♃ ♄	2	1	31	1762	Feb	27	5:03	25♓15	☿ ♅ ♃ ♄ ☽
	Mar	12	3:11	21♓33	☉ ☿ ♅ ♃ ♄	16	22	39		Mar	29	1:51	24♓51	☿ ☉ ♅ ♄ ♃
	Mar	15	15:31	21♓38	♀ ☉ ☿ ♅ ♃	13	10	19		Mar	29	1:51	24♓51	☿ ♀ ☉ ♅ ♃
	Mar	15	23:00	22♓01	♀ ☉ ☿ ♅ ♃ ♄	13	2	50		Mar	29	1:51	24♓51	☿ ♀ ☉ ♅ ♄ ♃
	Mar	15	23:00	22♓01	♀ ☉ ☿ ♅ ♄	15	4	22		Mar	31	3:22	23♓55	☿ ♅ ☉ ♀ ♄
	Mar	15	23:00	22♓01	♀ ☉ ♅ ♃ ♄	30	15	22		Apr	15	14:22	10♈02	♅ ♄ ♃ ☉ ♀
	Mar	24	8:14	18♓46	☽ ☿ ♀ ☉ ♅	2	5	19		Mar	26	13:33	26♓28	☿ ♀ ☉ ♅ ☽
	Mar	24	16:41	23♓06	☽ ☿ ♀ ☉ ♅ ♄	1	20	52		Mar	26	13:33	26♓28	☿ ♀ ☉ ♅ ♄ ☽
	Mar	24	16:41	23♓06	☽ ♀ ☉ ♅ ♄	2	15	7		Mar	27	7:48	6♈09	♀ ☉ ♅ ♄ ☽
	Mar	24	18:04	23♓48	☽ ☿ ♀ ☉ ♅ ♄ ♃	1	19	29		Mar	26	13:33	26♓28	☿ ♀ ☉ ♅ ♄ ♃ ☽
	Mar	24	18:04	23♓48	☽ ♀ ☉ ♅ ♄ ♃	2	13	44		Mar	27	7:48	6♈09	♀ ☉ ♅ ♄ ♃ ☽
	Mar	24	18:04	23♓48	☽ ☉ ♅ ♄ ♃	2	14	41		Mar	27	8:45	6♈39	☉ ♅ ♄ ♃ ☽
	Apr	21	14:54	0♈31	☽ ☿ ♅ ♄ ♃	2	1	38		Apr	23	16:31	6♈51	☿ ♅ ♄ ♃ ☽
1763	Jan	12	10:33	2♑04	☽ ♇ ☿ ♀ ☉	0	2	57	1763	Jan	12	13:29	2♑11	♇ ☽ ☿ ♀ ☉
	May	12	7:15	12♉32	☽ ☉ ☿ ♃ ♂	2	11	0		May	14	18:16	23♉35	☉ ♃ ☿ ♂ ☽
	Aug	17	12:50	6♌03	♀ ♂ ☿ ☉ ♆	7	7	39		Aug	24	20:29	11♌53	♂ ♀ ♆ ☉ ☿
1765	May	19	6:47	22♉37	☽ ♀ ♄ ☉ ☿	1	22	34	1765	May	21	5:21	25♉44	♀ ♄ ☉ ☿ ☽
	Jul	13	10:26	11♋08	☿ ☉ ♂ ♃ ♀	18	1	35		Jul	31	12:01	3♌21	♃ ☉ ♂ ☿ ♀
	Jul	16	18:35	10♋05	☽ ☿ ☉ ♂ ♃	2	19	35		Jul	19	14:10	24♋05	☿ ☉ ♃ ♂ ☽
	Jul	17	6:07	15♋49	☽ ☿ ☉ ♂ ♃ ♀	2	8	4		Jul	19	14:10	24♋05	☿ ☉ ♃ ♂ ♀ ☽
	Jul	17	6:07	15♋49	☽ ☉ ♂ ♃ ♀	2	14	13		Jul	19	20:20	27♋14	☉ ♃ ♂ ♀ ☽
	Aug	2	3:40	9♌45	♂ ☉ ☿ ♀ ♆	7	7	29		Aug	9	11:09	14♌25	♂ ☉ ♆ ♀ ☿
1766	Sep	30	17:12	0♍02	☽ ♆ ♃ ♀ ☿	1	23	38	1766	Oct	2	16:49	4♍04	♆ ♃ ♀ ☿ ☽
	Dec	30	6:51	19♐34	☽ ☿ ♀ ☉ ♇	2	3	20	1767	Jan	1	10:12	0♑58	☿ ♀ ♇ ☉ ☽
1767	Mar	29	22:16	8♈08	☽ ☉ ☿ ♅ ♀	1	12	15		Mar	31	10:31	10♈28	☉ ♅ ☿ ♀ ☽
	Jul	28	3:53	0♍59	☽ ☿ ♆ ♀ ♃	1	22	15		Jul	30	2:09	3♍49	☿ ♆ ♃ ♀ ☽
	Aug	23	3:43	15♌48	☽ ☉ ♂ ♆ ☿	3	2	35		Aug	26	6:18	2♍41	☉ ☿ ♆ ♂ ☽
	Sep	21	15:02	12♍12	☽ ☿ ♂ ☉ ♃	2	5	57		Sep	23	20:60	18♍51	☿ ♂ ☉ ♃ ☽
1768	Sep	10	0:60	5♍19	☽ ♆ ☿ ☉ ♀	1	19	32	1768	Sep	11	20:32	7♍37	♆ ☿ ☉ ♀ ☽
	Oct	10	9:41	13♎05	☽ ☉ ♃ ☿ ♀	2	6	1		Oct	12	15:41	19♎49	☉ ♃ ☿ ♀ ☽
1769	Aug	30	22:40	1♍57	☽ ☿ ☉ ♆ ♂	2	0	45	1769	Sep	1	23:25	9♍11	☿ ♆ ☉ ♂ ☽
	Dec	25	12:03	5♐23	☽ ♃ ♂ ♀ ☿	2	3	49		Dec	27	15:52	10♐50	♃ ♂ ♀ ☿ ☽
1770	Apr	24	17:45	22♈00	☽ ☿ ☉ ♅ ♀	1	19	17	1770	Apr	26	13:02	27♈38	☿ ☉ ♅ ♀ ☽
	Dec	27	15:25	5♑48	♃ ☉ ☿ ♇ ♀	10	22	55	1771	Jan	7	14:20	8♑20	♃ ☉ ♇ ♀ ☿
1771	Jan	14	2:34	3♑50	☽ ♃ ♀ ♇ ☉	2	5	24		Jan	16	7:58	10♑20	♃ ♀ ♇ ☉ ☽
	Oct	7	22:45	9♎11	☽ ♀ ☉ ☿ ♂	1	13	57		Oct	9	12:42	12♎28	♀ ☿ ☉ ♂ ☽
	Nov	5	17:29	29♎08	☽ ☿ ☉ ♀ ♂	1	14	33		Nov	7	8:02	1♏58	☿ ☉ ♀ ♂ ☽
	Dec	5	14:18	4♐02	☽ ♂ ☉ ☿ ♀	2	2	37		Dec	7	16:55	12♐09	♂ ☉ ☿ ♀ ☽

5 or More Planets Within 20° Arc 1700-2050

				Starting Position	Planets in Zodiacal Sequence							Dy	Hr	Mn					Ending Position	Planets in Zodiacal Sequence						
1772	Jan	4	8:13	13♑38	☉	♇	♀	☿	♃			6	6	31	1772	Jan	10	14:44	19♑12	♇	☉	♃	☿	♀		
	Jan	4	21:29	13♑04	☽	☉	♇	♀	☿			1	20	0		Jan	6	17:29	16♑04	☉	♇	♀	☿	☽		
	Jan	4	22:48	13♑46	☽	☉	♇	♀	☿	♃		1	18	41		Jan	6	17:29	16♑04	☉	♇	♃	♀	☿	☽	
	Jan	4	22:48	13♑46	☽	♇	♀	☿	♃			2	0	32		Jan	6	23:20	19♑04	♇	♃	♀	☿	☽		
	Jan	25	2:09	18♑31	♂	♇	☿	☉	♃			5	0	7		Jan	30	2:17	19♑50	♇	♂	☿	♃	☉		
	Feb	1	22:37	22♑44	☽	☿	♂	♃	☉			0	16	34		Feb	2	15:11	23♑26	☿	♂	☽	♃	☉		
	Jul	31	11:45	24♌33	☽	☿	♀	♄	♆			1	11	40		Aug	1	23:25	26♌15	♀	☿	♄	♆	☽		
1773	Aug	18	13:48	0♍17	☽	♄	♀	♆	☿			2	10	29	1773	Aug	21	0:18	14♍04	♄	♆	♀	☿	☽		
	Sep	15	2:57	2♍31	☽	☿	♄	♆	☉			1	18	36		Sep	16	21:34	7♍28	☿	♄	♆	☉	☽		
1774	Apr	9	17:54	3♈16	♂	☽	☉	♃	☿			1	12	45	1774	Apr	11	6:39	4♈27	♂	☉	♃	☿	☽		
1775	May	27	15:52	16♉04	☽	♃	♅	☿	☉			2	18	41	1775	May	30	10:32	1♊14	♃	♅	☉	☿	☽		
	Sep	23	23:17	20♍30	☽	♆	☉	☿	♄			1	19	44		Sep	25	19:01	22♍51	♆	☉	♄	☿	☽		
1776	May	16	22:22	16♉09	☽	♂	☉	☿	♅			1	13	27	1776	May	18	11:50	18♉01	♂	☉	☿	♅	☽		
	Jun	14	12:56	3♊53	☽	♂	♅	♀	☉			1	19	0		Jun	16	7:56	7♊55	♅	♂	♀	☉	☽		
	Jul	13	22:32	1♋55	☽	♃	♀	☿	☉			2	2	17		Jul	16	0:50	8♋26	♃	♀	☿	☉	☽		
	Jul	14	21:30	28♊08	♂	♃	☽	♀	☿			0	8	1		Jul	15	5:31	28♊22	♂	♃	♀	☿	☽		
	Sep	12	8:37	14♍08	☽	☉	♆	♀	☿			2	9	20		Sep	14	17:57	22♍25	☉	♆	♀	☿	☽		
1778	Jan	28	15:40	25♑30	♀	♇	☉	☽	☿			0	12	41	1778	Jan	29	4:21	26♑10	♀	♇	☉	☿	☽		
	Apr	26	18:45	2♉55	☽	☉	♀	♂	☿			1	16	7		Apr	28	10:52	8♉10	☉	♀	♂	☿	☽		
	May	15	6:26	24♉25	☉	♂	♀	♅	☿			18	21	15		Jun	3	3:40	11♊02	☿	☉	♂	♅	♀		
	May	25	16:48	25♉08	☽	☉	♂	♅	☿			2	1	29		May	27	18:17	6♊25	☉	♂	☿	♅	☽		
	May	26	2:22	1♊11	☽	☉	♂	♅	☿	♀		1	15	55		May	27	18:17	6♊25	☉	♂	☿	♅	♀	☽	
	May	26	2:22	1♊11	☽	♂	♅	☿	♀			1	19	1		May	27	21:23	8♊21	♂	☿	♅	♀	☽		
1779	Jan	16	8:57	11♑18	☽	♀	☿	☉	♇			0	15	42	1779	Jan	17	0:39	11♑19	♀	☽	☿	☉	♇		
	Sep	9	23:56	13♍05	☽	☉	☿	♆	♃			1	18	32		Sep	11	18:28	18♍48	☉	☿	♆	♃	☽		
	Sep	16	13:28	14♍29	♀	☿	☉	♆	♃			28	22	55		Oct	15	12:23	2♎00	♆	♃	☿	♀	☉		
	Oct	7	22:31	21♍09	☽	☿	♆	♃	♀			2	4	7		Oct	10	2:38	1♎48	♆	☿	♃	♀	☽		
	Oct	8	4:31	24♍44	☽	☿	♆	♃	♀	☉		1	22	7		Oct	10	2:38	1♎48	♆	☿	♃	♀	☉	☽	
	Oct	8	4:31	24♍44	☽	☿	♃	♀	☉			1	23	17		Oct	10	3:48	2♎29	☿	♃	♀	☉	☽		
	Nov	7	15:47	7♏51	☽	☉	♀	☿	♄			2	6	47		Nov	9	22:35	17♏26	☉	♀	☿	♄	☽		
1781	Jun	21	13:04	26♊33	☽	♅	☉	♀	☿			1	5	45	1781	Jun	22	18:49	28♊49	♅	☉	♀	☽	☿		
1782	Dec	22	4:04	18♐16	☿	♀	☉	♄	♃			22	17	47	1783	Jan	13	21:51	5♑54	♄	♃	☉	☿	♀		
1783	Jan	1	20:43	20♐45	☽	♄	☿	♀	♃			2	5	54		Jan	4	2:37	4♑46	♄	☿	♃	♀	☽		
	Jan	1	21:54	21♐29	☽	♄	☿	♃	♀	☉		2	4	43		Jan	4	2:37	4♑46	♄	☿	♃	♀	☉	☽	
	Jan	1	21:54	21♐29	☽	☿	♃	♀	☉			2	11	14		Jan	4	9:07	8♑48	☿	♃	♀	☉	☽		
	Feb	1	7:46	6♒04	☽	♇	☉	♀	☿			1	6	20		Feb	2	14:06	8♒11	♇	☉	♀	☽	☿		
1784	Jan	22	5:60	29♑34	☽	☉	♇	♃	☿			1	13	53	1784	Jan	23	19:53	3♒34	☉	♇	♃	☿	☽		
	Jul	15	13:21	3♋32	☽	☿	♅	♀	☉			2	2	49		Jul	17	16:10	8♋57	☿	♅	♀	☉	☽		
	Aug	15	12:19	17♌44	☽	☉	♀	☿	♂			2	8	19		Aug	17	20:37	25♌26	☉	♀	♂	☿	☽		
	Sep	14	14:41	21♍25	☽	☉	♂	♀	♆			1	21	3		Sep	16	11:45	24♍11	☉	♂	♀	♆	☽		
	Sep	29	20:13	6♎56	♂	☉	♆	♀	☿			8	20	46		Oct	8	16:59	12♎18	♆	♂	☉	☿	♀		
	Oct	12	14:21	29♍53	☽	♆	♂	☿	☉			2	15	0		Oct	15	5:22	12♎33	♆	☿	♂	☉	☽		
1785	Jan	11	0:13	20♑36	☽	☉	♄	☿	♇			1	12	1	1785	Jan	12	12:14	22♑49	☉	♄	♇	☿	☽		
1786	Jan	28	19:57	22♑38	☽	♀	♄	☉	♇			1	21	0	1786	Jan	30	16:57	28♑46	♀	♄	☉	♇	☽		
	Mar	29	14:10	3♈05	☽	☉	♀	☿	♃			1	19	38		Mar	31	9:48	10♈50	☉	♀	♃	☿	☽		
	Apr	27	15:09	27♈15	☽	♃	☉	♀	☿			1	12	18		Apr	29	3:27	0♉23	♃	☉	☿	♀	☽		
	Oct	20	19:43	13♎13	☽	♆	☿	☉	♂			1	23	37		Oct	22	19:20	17♎00	♆	☉	☿	♂	☽		
1787	Feb	16	10:57	7♒46	☽	♇	☿	♄	☉			2	1	2	1787	Feb	18	11:59	14♒43	♇	☿	♄	☉	☽		
	Feb	17	9:11	0♒34	♂	♇	☿	☽	♄			0	1	25		Feb	17	10:36	0♒36	♂	♇	☿	♄	☽		
	Mar	15	12:14	3♒34	☽	♀	♇	♂	♄			2	1	14		Mar	17	13:28	10♒21	♀	♇	♂	♄	☽		
	Oct	9	22:56	1♎06	☽	♀	☉	♆	☿			2	20	43		Oct	12	19:40	17♎57	♀	♆	☉	☿	☽		
1788	Feb	6	14:10	9♒42	☽	☿	♇	☉	♄			2	3	27	1788	Feb	8	17:37	15♒54	♇	☿	☉	♄	☽		
	Aug	1	7:08	29♋59	☽	♅	☉	☿	♀			1	9	21		Aug	2	16:29	1♌11	♅	☉	☿	♀	☽		
1789	Jan	25	10:37	26♑56	☽	♂	☉	☿	♇			1	23	48	1789	Jan	27	10:25	0♒37	♂	☉	☿	♇	☽		
	Mar	14	23:43	4♓51	♀	♂	☿	♄	☉			5	22	29		Mar	20	22:12	10♓45	☿	♂	♀	♄	☉		
	Mar	23	9:34	25♒55	☽	☿	♂	♀	♄			2	23	4		Mar	26	8:38	11♓22	☿	♂	♄	♀	☽		
	Mar	24	23:33	14♓46	☽	♂	♄	♀	☉			1	8	22		Mar	26	7:55	16♓06	♂	♄	♀	☽	☉		
	Jul	6	19:29	15♋00	☉	♀	☿	♅	♃			12	12	15		Jul	19	7:44	20♋23	☿	☉	♅	♃	♀		
	Jul	21	20:49	18♋15	☽	☿	☉	♅	♃			1	9	17		Jul	23	6:06	18♋48	☿	☉	♅	♃	☽		
	Jul	22	6:12	24♋00	☽	☉	♅	♃	♀			1	20	11		Jul	24	2:22	1♌29	☉	♅	♃	♀	☽		
1790	Nov	5	8:14	23♎09	☽	☿	♆	♀	☉			1	11	51	1790	Nov	6	20:05	25♎50	☿	♆	♀	☉	☽		
1791	Jan	4	5:48	7♑54	☽	☉	♀	☿	♂			1	23	42	1791	Jan	6	5:30	15♑57	☉	♀	☿	♂	☽		
	Jan	19	15:30	29♑37	☉	♀	♂	☿	♇			20	1	46		Feb	8	17:16	8♒58	☿	☉	♇	♂	♀		
	Feb	2	5:48	0♒47	☽	☉	☿	♇	♂			2	10	19		Feb	4	16:07	13♒21	☿	☉	♇	♂	☽		
	Feb	2	5:56	0♒51	☽	☉	☿	♇	♂	♀		2	10	10		Feb	4	16:07	13♒21	☿	☉	♇	♂	♀	☽	
	Feb	2	5:56	0♒51	☽	☉	♇	♂	♀			2	15	16		Feb	4	21:12	16♒06	☉	♇	♂	♀	☽		
	Mar	6	12:10	15♓55	☉	♂	♀	☽	♄			0	2	22		Mar	6	14:32	16♓01	☉	♂	♀	♄	☽		
	Apr	1	18:05	21♓57	☽	☿	♂	♄	☉			2	16	34		Apr	4	10:39	4♈40	☿	♂	♄	☉	☽		
	Oct	18	22:30	7♎19	☿	♃	☉	♀	♆			11	22	2		Oct	30	20:31	17♎24	♃	♀	☿	♆	☉		
	Oct	25	14:41	7♎34	☽	☿	♃	♀	♆			1	23	52		Oct	27	14:34	16♎43	♃	☿	♀	♆	☽		
	Oct	25	22:56	12♎30	☽	☿	♃	♀	♆	☉		1	15	38		Oct	27	14:34	16♎43	♃	☿	♀	♆	☉	☽	
	Oct	25	22:56	12♎30	☽	☿	♀	♆	☉			1	18	14		Oct	27	17:10	18♎20	☿	♀	♆	☉	☽		
1792	Oct	15	20:08	21♎50	☽	☉	♆	♃	♀			1	16	20	1792	Oct	17	12:28	24♎50	☉	♆	♃	♀	☽		

5 or More Planets Within 20° Arc 1700-2050

				Starting Position	Planets in Zodiacal Sequence						Dy	Hr	Mn					Ending Position	Planets in Zodiacal Sequence					
1793	Apr	10	12:53	19♈03	☽	☉	♂	♄	☿		1	17	2	1793	Apr	12	5:54	22♈45	☉	♂	♄	☿	☽	
	May	8	15:36	29♈38	☽	☿	♄	☉	♂		0	18	33		May	9	10:09	0♉12	☿	♄	☽	☉	♂	
	Jun	6	22:56	26♉32	☽	☿	♀	♂	☉		1	20	48		Jun	8	19:44	0♊30	☿	♀	♂	☉	☽	
1795	May	18	23:48	20♉27	☿	☉	♄	☽	♂		0	14	23	1795	May	19	14:11	21♉43	☿	☉	♄	♂	☽	
	Aug	13	3:30	0♌16	☽	☿	♀	♂	☉		1	17	8		Aug	14	20:38	3♌17	☿	♀	♂	☉	☽	
	Aug	22	10:07	13♌19	♂	☿	♀	☉	♅		12	10	42		Sep	3	20:49	21♌14	♂	♀	♅	☿	☉	
	Sep	11	20:16	2♍05	☽	♅	♀	☉	☿		1	10	22		Sep	13	6:38	4♍41	♅	♀	☽	☉	☿	
1796	Feb	8	15:55	16♒04	☽	☉	♃	♇	☿		1	20	13	1796	Feb	10	12:08	20♒12	♃	☉	♇	☿	☽	
1797	Jun	6	21:30	16♊31	☉	♀	♄	☿	♂		12	12	11	1797	Jun	19	9:41	24♊38	☿	☉	♄	♀	♂	
	Jun	23	18:05	19♊39	☽	☿	♄	☉	♀		1	12	23		Jun	25	6:28	22♊15	☿	♄	☉	♀	☽	
	Jun	24	7:18	27♊48	☽	♄	☉	♀	♂		1	14	36		Jun	25	21:54	1♋55	♄	☉	♀	♂	☽	
	Aug	21	22:23	24♌21	☽	♂	☉	♅	☿		0	21	46		Aug	22	20:09	25♌52	♂	☉	☽	♅	☿	
1798	Nov	6	14:42	24♎29	☽	♀	☿	♆	☉		1	23	58	1798	Nov	8	14:40	3♏51	♀	♆	☿	☉	☽	
1799	Aug	30	20:48	6♍08	☽	☉	♂	♅	☿		1	13	18	1799	Sep	1	10:05	8♍54	☉	♂	♅	☿	☽	
	Sep	27	21:23	14♍44	☽	☿	♅	♂	☉		1	15	6		Sep	29	12:29	19♍00	☿	♅	♂	☉	☽	
	Oct	27	9:27	15♎09	☽	♀	♂	☉	☿		1	11	43		Oct	28	21:09	17♎44	♀	♂	☉	☿	☽	
1800	Aug	19	16:57	15♌29	♄	☽	☉	♀	☿		1	9	5	1800	Aug	21	2:02	15♌40	♄	☉	♀	☿	☽	
	Oct	19	19:53	26♎12	☉	☿	☽	♀	♆		0	0	15		Oct	19	20:08	26♎13	☉	☿	♆	♀	☽	
1801	Jul	12	5:33	2♌58	☽	♃	☿	♄	♂		2	6	23	1801	Jul	14	11:56	10♌00	♃	☿	♄	♂	☽	
	Aug	8	17:30	5♌55	☽	☿	♃	☉	♄		2	2	12		Aug	10	19:42	11♌01	☿	♃	☉	♄	☽	
	Dec	3	9:35	7♏59	☽	♀	♆	☿	♂		2	3	35		Dec	5	13:10	18♏29	♀	♆	☿	♂	☽	
1802	Aug	27	8:59	23♌22	☽	☿	☉	♄	♃		2	11	59	1802	Aug	29	20:58	2♍50	☿	☉	♄	♃	☽	
1803	Aug	19	11:07	19♍04	☽	♄	♂	♃	♅		1	19	22	1803	Aug	21	6:30	20♍34	♄	♂	♃	♅	☽	
	Aug	30	23:48	19♍40	☿	♄	♂	♃	♅		10	0	18		Sep	10	0:06	22♍58	♄	☿	♃	♅	♂	
	Sep	15	21:31	20♍58	☽	☉	♄	♅	♃		1	22	25		Sep	17	19:57	23♍56	☉	♄	♅	♃	☽	
	Sep	16	10:06	27♍12	☽	♅	♃	☿	♂		2	20	3		Sep	19	6:09	10♎48	♅	♃	☿	♂	☽	
	Sep	22	4:25	22♍17	♀	♄	☉	♅	♃		18	21	36		Oct	11	2:02	26♍48	♄	♅	♀	♃	☉	
	Oct	7	10:53	11♎21	♀	♅	☉	♃	♂		0	22	45		Oct	8	9:39	12♎00	♅	♀	☉	♃	♂	
	Oct	13	20:55	29♍34	☽	♅	♃	♀	☉		2	18	45		Oct	16	15:40	12♎31	♅	♃	☉	♀	☽	
	Oct	15	7:45	16♎45	☽	♃	☉	♀	♂		1	3	29		Oct	16	11:13	17♎32	♃	☉	♀	☽	♂	
	Oct	15	11:24	18♎33	☽	☉	♀	♂	☿		2	1	51		Oct	17	13:15	23♎13	☉	♀	☿	♂	☽	
	Oct	22	8:13	12♎52	♅	♃	☉	♀	☿		2	10	3		Oct	24	18:16	13♎01	♅	♃	☿	☉	♀	
	Nov	13	7:58	7♏33	☽	☉	♆	♂	♀		2	22	16		Nov	16	6:13	22♏59	☉	♆	♂	♀	☽	
	Dec	13	18:06	15♐42	☽	☿	♂	☉	♀		1	23	44		Dec	15	17:50	20♐49	♂	☿	☉	♀	☽	
1804	Oct	2	20:09	29♍04	☽	♄	☉	♅	☿		2	6	58	1804	Oct	5	3:07	7♎19	♄	☉	♅	☿	☽	
	Nov	30	13:20	20♏06	☽	♃	♆	☉	☿		0	17	7		Dec	1	6:27	21♏13	♃	♆	☽	☉	☿	
1805	Aug	26	10:48	26♍58	☽	♀	☿	♄	♂		1	15	32	1805	Aug	28	2:20	29♍15	♀	☿	♄	♂	☽	
	Aug	26	13:23	28♍27	☽	☿	♄	♂	♅		1	16	56		Aug	28	6:19	1♎26	☿	♄	♂	♅	☽	
	Aug	27	11:28	28♍30	♀	☿	☽	♄	♂	♅	0	14	52		Aug	28	2:20	29♍15	♀	☿	♄	♂	♅	☽
	Aug	27	11:28	28♍30	♀	☿	♄	♂	♅		12	23	22		Sep	9	10:50	6♎10	☿	♀	♄	♅	♂	
	Sep	24	6:07	16♎09	☽	♄	♅	♀	♂		1	6	34		Sep	25	12:41	17♎01	♄	♅	☽	♀	♂	
	Oct	20	22:05	7♎05	☽	☿	♄	♅	☉		2	13	8		Oct	23	11:13	20♎24	☿	♄	♅	☉	☽	
	Oct	24	2:22	18♏23	☽	♆	♂	♃	♀		2	7	48		Oct	26	10:10	26♏57	♆	♂	♃	♀	☽	
	Nov	17	23:38	25♏14	☉	♆	☿	♃	♂		3	13	57		Nov	21	13:35	27♏54	♆	☉	☿	♃	♂	
	Nov	20	18:45	23♏03	☽	♆	☉	☿	♃		2	1	0		Nov	22	19:45	27♏57	♆	☉	☿	♃	☽	
	Nov	21	3:35	27♏36	☽	♆	☉	☿	♃	♂	0	10	0		Nov	21	13:35	27♏54	♆	☉	☽	☿	♃	♂
	Nov	21	3:35	27♏36	☽	☉	☿	♃	♂		1	20	55		Nov	23	0:30	0♐20	☉	☿	♃	♂	☽	
1806	Mar	6	22:43	8♓18	☿	♂	♇	☉	♀		11	18	5	1806	Mar	18	16:49	10♓53	♇	♂	♀	☉	☿	
	Mar	18	13:44	7♓18	☽	♇	♂	♀	☉		1	21	23		Mar	20	11:07	10♓56	♇	♀	♂	☉	☽	
	Mar	18	21:28	11♓16	☽	♂	♀	☉	☿		2	6	24		Mar	21	3:52	19♓51	♀	♂	☉	☿	☽	
	Oct	11	9:49	9♎36	☽	☿	☉	♅	♄		1	19	42		Oct	13	5:31	15♎44	☿	☉	♅	♄	☽	
	Oct	21	16:05	10♎50	♀	♅	☉	☿	♄		2	6	2		Oct	23	22:07	13♎39	♀	♅	☉	♄	☿	
	Nov	8	22:07	25♎52	☽	♅	♄	♀	☉		1	11	38		Nov	10	9:45	27♎21	♅	♄	♀	☽	☉	
1807	Sep	4	19:44	17♎11	☽	♀	♅	♄	♂		1	19	37	1807	Sep	6	15:22	23♎41	♀	♅	♄	♂	☽	
	Oct	14	18:26	20♎29	☉	♀	♅	☿	♄		2	7	42		Oct	17	2:08	20♎45	♀	☉	♅	☿	♄	
1808	Feb	12	5:22	22♒24	☉	♃	☿	♂	♇		11	14	52	1808	Feb	23	20:14	26♒54	♃	☉	♇	♂	☿	
	Feb	25	20:56	0♓29	☽	☉	♇	♂	☿		2	7	14		Feb	28	4:10	8♓27	☉	♇	♂	☿	☽	
	May	23	15:41	12♉15	☽	♀	♂	☿	☉		1	22	8		May	25	13:49	15♉16	♀	♂	☿	☉	☽	
	Oct	20	1:16	1♏33	☽	♅	♀	☿	♄		1	13	3		Oct	21	14:19	4♏55	♅	♀	☿	♄	☽	
	Oct	20	19:31	13♏05	☽	♀	☿	♄	♆		1	19	40		Oct	22	15:11	20♏20	♀	♄	☿	♆	☽	
	Nov	17	8:26	14♏03	☽	♄	☉	☿	♆		1	23	24		Nov	19	7:49	24♏02	☿	♄	☉	♆	☽	
	Nov	17	10:37	6♏35	♅	☽	♄	☉	☿		0	17	38		Nov	18	4:15	6♏37	♅	♄	☿	☉	☽	
1809	Dec	5	9:12	17♏07	☽	♀	☿	♆	♄		1	13	57	1809	Dec	6	23:09	20♏54	♀	☿	♆	♄	☽	
	Dec	5	19:13	23♏19	☽	☿	♆	♄	☉		1	22	37		Dec	7	17:50	2♐48	☿	♆	♄	☉	☽	
1810	Apr	3	23:50	12♈37	☽	☉	♀	♃	♂		1	17	16	1810	Apr	5	17:07	15♈15	☉	♀	♃	♂	☽	
	Apr	21	19:28	25♈33	☿	☉	♃	♀	♂		15	18	49		May	7	14:18	9♉58	♃	☉	♂	☿	♀	
	May	2	21:47	3♉28	☽	♃	☉	☿	♂		2	1	12		May	4	22:59	9♉20	♃	☉	☿	♂	☽	
	May	2	23:17	4♉17	☽	♃	☉	☿	♂	♀	1	23	41		May	4	22:59	9♉20	♃	☉	☿	♂	♀	☽
	May	2	23:17	4♉17	☽	☉	☿	♂	♀		2	9	1		May	5	8:19	14♉08	☉	☿	♂	♀	☽	
	Nov	26	10:45	26♏06	☿	☽	☉	♆	♄		1	8	35		Nov	27	19:20	28♏14	☿	☉	♆	♄	☽	
1811	Nov	15	4:45	10♏34	☽	♅	☿	☉	♀		2	6	8	1811	Nov	17	10:53	19♏29	♅	☿	☉	♀	☽	
	Nov	15	23:10	20♏16	☽	☿	☉	♀	♆		1	19	45		Nov	17	18:55	23♏52	☿	☉	♀	♆	☽	
	Nov	29	12:52	6♐28	☉	♆	☿	♀	♄		10	1	9		Dec	9	14:01	11♐08	♆	☉	♄	☿	♀	

5 or More Planets Within 20° Arc 1700-2050

	Starting Position				Planets in Zodiacal Sequence							Dy	Hr	Mn		Ending Position				Planets in Zodiacal Sequence						
	Dec	15	11:11	18♐31	☽	☉	♄	☿	♀			1	21	40		Dec	17	8:51	24♐35	☉	♄	☿	♀	☽		
1812	Jul	7	14:44	1♋16	☽	☉	☿	♃	♂			2	17	56	1812	Jul	10	8:40	17♋51	☉	♃	☿	♂	☽		
	Aug	5	12:40	22♋51	☽	♃	♀	♂	☉			1	4	9		Aug	6	16:49	23♋58	♃	♀	☽	♂	☉		
1814	Sep	12	13:21	0♍17	☽	☿	♂	☉	♃			2	11	43	1814	Sep	15	1:04	15♍33	☿	♂	♃	☉	☽		
	Nov	26	22:10	26♏58	♀	♅	☉	☿	♆			9	3	20		Dec	6	1:30	27♏19	☿	♅	♀	☉	♆		
	Dec	9	7:33	27♏26	☿	♅	♀	☉	♆			1	5	6		Dec	10	12:39	27♏54	☿	♅	♀	♆	☉		
	Dec	9	23:37	27♏21	☽	☿	♅	♀	☉			0	13	2		Dec	10	12:39	27♏54	☿	♅	☽	♀	☉		
	Dec	9	23:50	27♏27	☽	☿	♅	♀	☉	♆		0	12	49		Dec	10	12:39	27♏54	☿	♅	☽	♀	♆	☉	
	Dec	9	23:50	27♏27	☽	☿	♅	♀	♆			1	17	26		Dec	11	17:16	28♏33	☿	♅	♀	♆	☽		
	Dec	9	23:50	27♏27	☽	♅	♀	☉	♆			2	3	45		Dec	12	3:35	3♐43	♅	♀	♆	☉	☽		
1815	Mar	10	23:01	17♓25	☽	☉	♇	☿	♀			1	22	0	1815	Mar	12	21:01	21♓20	♇	☉	☿	♀	☽		
	Oct	2	21:38	8♎10	☽	☉	♃	♀	☿			1	10	47		Oct	4	8:26	10♎14	☉	♃	♀	☽	☿		
1816	Aug	22	22:52	24♌47	☽	☉	☿	♀	♂			1	18	13	1816	Aug	24	17:05	1♍20	☉	☿	♀	♂	☽		
	Nov	17	23:22	5♏33	☽	☿	♂	♃	☉			1	16	6		Nov	19	15:29	10♏16	☿	♂	♃	☉	☽		
	Dec	1	5:28	21♏26	♂	♃	☿	☉	♅			7	3	6		Dec	8	8:34	26♏13	♃	♂	☿	♅	☉		
	Dec	17	10:01	5♐26	☽	♅	♆	☿	☉			1	22	6		Dec	19	8:08	12♐32	♅	♆	☿	☉	☽		
1817	Jan	13	13:19	2♐57	☽	♃	♅	♂	♆			1	12	3	1817	Jan	15	1:22	3♐43	♃	♅	♆	♂	☽		
	Nov	27	14:10	3♐19	☿	☉	♅	♃	♆			21	3	25		Dec	18	17:35	16♐38	♅	♃	♆	☉	☿		
	Dec	7	11:26	0♐21	☽	☉	♅	☿	♃			2	8	50		Dec	9	20:15	16♐05	♅	☉	♃	☿	☽		
	Dec	7	16:44	3♐42	☽	☉	♅	☿	♃	♆		2	3	32		Dec	9	20:15	16♐05	♅	☉	♃	☿	♆	☽	
	Dec	7	16:44	3♐42	☽	☉	☿	♃	♆			2	5	57		Dec	9	22:41	17♐35	☉	♃	☿	♆	☽		
	Dec	19	19:24	7♐38	♀	♅	♃	♆	☉			9	10	39		Dec	29	6:03	17♐15	♅	♀	♆	♃	☉		
1818	Jan	4	8:33	7♐08	☽	♅	♆	♃	♀			2	1	27	1818	Jan	6	9:60	17♐43	♅	♆	♃	♀	☽		
	Jan	5	12:56	24♐41	☽	♆	♃	♀	☉			0	2	19		Jan	5	15:15	24♐47	♆	☽	♃	♀	☉		
	Mar	6	4:41	4♓33	☽	♄	♀	☉	♇			1	21	42		Mar	8	2:23	9♓36	♄	♀	☉	♇	☽		
	Mar	13	18:09	4♓45	☿	♄	☉	♀	♇			6	15	54		Mar	20	10:04	11♓05	♄	☿	♇	☉	♀		
	Nov	27	18:46	29♏27	☽	♂	☉	☿	♅			1	14	18		Nov	29	9:04	3♐33	♂	☉	☿	♅	☽		
	Nov	28	5:41	5♐27	☉	☽	☿	♅	♆			1	8	34		Nov	29	14:15	6♐49	☉	☿	♅	♆	☽		
	Dec	2	4:52	5♐36	♂	☉	♅	☿	♆			4	22	51		Dec	7	3:43	9♐11	♂	☉	♅	♆	☿		
	Dec	19	16:32	18♐22	♂	♅	♆	☉	♀			14	2	3	1819	Jan	2	18:35	21♐37	♅	♆	♂	♀	☉		
	Dec	26	5:14	13♐54	☽	♅	♂	♆	☉			1	18	56	1818	Dec	28	0:10	21♐16	♅	♂	♆	☉	☽		
	Dec	26	6:18	14♐35	☽	♅	♂	♆	☉	♀		1	17	52		Dec	28	0:10	21♐16	♅	♂	♆	♀	☉	☽	
	Dec	26	6:18	14♐35	☽	♂	♆	☉	♀			1	23	13		Dec	28	5:30	24♐41	♂	♆	♀	☉	☽		
	Dec	27	12:26	3♑46	☽	♀	☉	♃	☿			0	1	9		Dec	27	13:35	3♑47	♀	☽	☉	♃	☿		
1819	Jan	11	20:58	22♐08	♅	♀	♆	♂	☿			9	4	36	1819	Jan	21	1:34	22♐37	♅	♀	♆	☿	♂		
	Jan	23	0:00	19♐01	☽	♅	♆	♀	☿			1	13	56		Jan	24	13:56	22♐48	♅	♆	♀	☿	☽		
	Jan	23	8:38	24♐22	☽	♆	♀	☿	♂			1	12	47		Jan	24	21:25	27♐33	♆	♀	☿	♂	☽		
	Mar	24	23:30	20♓32	☽	♄	♇	☉	☿			1	0	22		Mar	25	23:53	22♓35	♄	♇	☉	☽	☿		
	Apr	20	7:13	6♓46	☽	♀	♂	♄	♇			2	9	58		Apr	22	17:11	19♓54	♀	♂	♄	♇	☽		
	Nov	20	0:08	7♐16	♀	☿	♅	☽	♆			0	1	4		Nov	20	1:13	7♐19	♀	☿	♅	♆	☽		
	Dec	10	3:01	17♐16	☉	♅	♆	♀	☿			9	20	52		Dec	19	23:53	24♐51	♅	☉	♆	☿	♀		
	Dec	16	18:24	17♐35	☽	☉	♅	♆	☿			1	20	23		Dec	18	14:47	24♐46	♅	☉	♆	☿	☽		
	Dec	17	0:14	21♐07	☽	☉	♅	♆	☿	♀		1	14	33		Dec	18	14:47	24♐46	♅	☉	♆	☿	♀	☽	
	Dec	17	0:14	21♐07	☽	☉	♆	☿	♀			1	16	32		Dec	18	16:46	26♐00	☉	♆	☿	♀	☽		
1820	Mar	14	1:27	16♓21	☽	☉	♇	♄	☿			1	22	38	1820	Mar	16	0:04	25♓21	☉	♇	♄	☿	☽		
	Dec	2	0:53	9♐50	☉	☿	♂	♅	♆			7	19	43		Dec	9	20:36	10♐07	☿	☉	♂	♅	♆		
	Dec	5	6:01	8♐04	☽	☉	☿	♂	♅			1	22	9		Dec	7	4:10	13♐34	☿	☉	♂	♅	☽		
	Dec	5	9:29	9♐57	☽	☉	☿	♂	♅	♆		1	18	41		Dec	7	4:10	13♐34	☿	☉	♂	♅	♆	☽	
	Dec	5	9:29	9♐57	☽	☉	♂	♅	♆			1	21	33		Dec	7	7:02	15♐10	☉	♂	♅	♆	☽		
1821	Jan	2	20:39	24♐27	☽	♅	♆	☉	♂			1	20	22	1821	Jan	4	17:01	29♐53	♅	♆	☉	♂	☽		
	Jan	8	6:56	28♐39	☿	♅	♆	☉	♂			2	0	32		Jan	10	7:28	0♑13	♅	♆	☿	☉	♂		
	Mar	4	1:36	10♓43	☽	☉	♇	☿	♃			1	14	16		Mar	5	15:51	14♓48	☉	♇	♃	☿	☽		
	Mar	4	20:18	22♓28	☽	♇	♃	☿	♄			1	16	28		Mar	6	12:46	27♓54	♇	♃	☿	♄	☽		
	Mar	14	12:07	23♓37	☉	♇	♃	☿	♄			24	0	9		Apr	7	12:16	27♓21	☿	♇	♃	♄	☉		
	Mar	22	2:19	15♓03	♀	♂	♇	☉	♃			17	19	43		Apr	8	22:02	28♓44	♇	♂	♀	♃	☉		
	Mar	23	6:17	16♓43	♂	♇	☉	♃	☿			15	6	0		Apr	7	12:16	27♓21	☿	♂	♇	♃	☉		
	Mar	23	8:55	16♓38	♀	♂	♇	☉	♃	☿		15	3	21		Apr	7	12:16	27♓21	☿	♂	♇	♀	♃	☉	
	Mar	23	8:55	16♓38	♀	♂	♇	♃	☿			26	3	25		Apr	18	12:20	28♓57	♇	☿	♂	♃	♀		
	Mar	30	15:07	25♓37	♀	♇	☿	♃	☉	♄		7	21	9		Apr	7	12:16	27♓21	☿	♇	♀	♃	♄	☉	
	Mar	30	15:07	25♓37	♀	♇	♃	☉	♄			9	6	55		Apr	8	22:02	28♓44	♇	♀	♃	♄	☉		
	Mar	30	15:07	25♓37	♀	♇	☿	♃	♄			18	21	13		Apr	18	12:20	28♓57	♇	☿	♃	♄	♀		
	Mar	31	11:38	10♓04	☽	♂	♀	♇	☿			2	7	22		Apr	2	19:00	24♓57	♂	♇	☿	♀	☽		
	Mar	31	23:29	17♓27	☽	♂	♀	♇	☿	♃		1	19	31		Apr	2	19:00	24♓57	♂	♇	☿	♀	♃	☽	
	Mar	31	23:29	17♓27	☽	♀	♇	☿	♃			2	1	15		Apr	3	0:44	28♓36	♇	☿	♀	♃	☽		
	Apr	1	5:26	21♓10	☽	♂	♀	♇	☿	♃	☉	1	13	34		Apr	2	19:00	24♓57	♂	♇	☿	♀	♃	☉	☽
	Apr	1	5:26	21♓10	☽	♀	♇	☿	♃	☉		1	19	18		Apr	3	0:44	28♓36	♇	☿	♀	♃	☉	☽	
	Apr	1	5:26	21♓10	☽	♀	☿	♃	☉			1	19	18		Apr	3	0:45	28♓36	☿	♀	♃	☉	☽		
	Apr	1	12:53	25♓51	☽	♀	♇	☿	♃	☉	♄	1	11	51		Apr	3	0:44	28♓36	♇	☿	♀	♃	☉	♄	☽
	Apr	1	12:53	25♓51	☽	♀	☿	♃	☉	♄		1	11	52		Apr	3	0:45	28♓36	☿	♀	♃	☉	♄	☽	
	Apr	1	12:53	25♓51	☽	♀	♃	☉	♄			1	13	58		Apr	3	2:51	29♓56	♀	♃	☉	♄	☽		
	Apr	4	10:07	26♓13	♂	☿	♇	♀	♃	☉	♄	3	2	10		Apr	7	12:16	27♓21	☿	♂	♇	♀	♃	♄	☉
	Apr	4	10:07	26♓13	♂	♇	♀	♃	☉	♄		4	11	56		Apr	8	22:02	28♓44	♇	♂	♀	♃	♄	☉	
	Apr	4	10:07	26♓13	♂	♀	♃	☉	♄			9	7	31		Apr	13	17:37	3♈27	♂	♃	♀	♄	☉		

5 or More Planets Within 20° Arc 1700-2050

	Starting Position				Planets in Zodiacal Sequence							Dy	Hr	Mn	Ending Position					Planets in Zodiacal Sequence						
	Apr	4	10:07	26♓13	♂	☿	♇	♀	♃	♄		14	2	13		Apr	18	12:20	28♓57	♇	☿	♂	♃	♄	♀	
	Apr	4	10:07	26♓13	♂	☿	♇	♃	♄			23	13	31		Apr	27	23:38	29♓10	♇	☿	♃	♂	♄		
	Apr	4	10:07	26♓13	♂	☿	♀	♃	♄			26	18	54		May	1	5:01	14♈37	♃	☿	♂	♄	♀		
	Apr	28	21:53	25♓08	☽	♇	☿	♃	♂			1	14	41		Apr	30	12:34	29♓13	♇	☿	♃	♂	☽		
	Apr	29	4:40	29♓19	☽	☿	♃	♂	♄			2	8	27		May	1	13:07	14♈42	♃	☿	♂	♄	☽		
	Apr	30	3:08	13♈17	☽	☿	♃	♂	♄	♀		1	1	53		May	1	5:01	14♈37	♃	☿	♂	♄	☽	♀	
	Apr	30	3:08	13♈17	☽	☿	♂	♄	♀			1	11	22		May	1	14:30	15♈33	☿	♂	♄	♀	☽		
	Dec	22	23:25	13♐08	☽	☿	☉	♆	♅			1	21	54		Dec	24	21:19	16♐46	☿	♆	☉	♅	☽		
1822	Dec	13	4:13	16♐31	☽	♀	☉	♆	♅			2	0	59	1822	Dec	15	5:12	20♐40	♀	☉	♆	♅	☽		
	Dec	18	3:35	16♐49	☿	♀	☉	♆	♅			24	4	6	1823	Jan	11	7:42	5♑32	♆	♅	☉	♀	☿		
	Dec	25	18:58	3♑31	☉	♀	♆	♅	♂			1	21	2	1822	Dec	27	15:60	4♑59	♆	☉	♀	♅	♂		
1823	Jan	10	22:32	4♑18	☽	♆	♅	☉	♀			0	23	56	1823	Jan	11	22:27	5♑33	♆	♅	☽	☉	♀		
	Jan	10	23:55	4♑59	☽	♆	♅	☉	♀	☿		0	7	46		Jan	11	7:42	5♑32	♆	♅	☽	☉	♀	☿	
	Jan	10	23:55	4♑59	☽	♅	☉	♀	☿			1	22	56		Jan	12	22:52	8♑21	♅	☉	♀	☿	☽		
	Jan	12	0:12	17♑02	☽	☉	♀	☿	♂			2	4	12		Jan	14	4:24	23♑16	☉	♀	☿	♂	☽		
	Feb	10	16:24	16♒00	☽	☉	♂	♀	☿			2	4	7		Feb	12	20:30	23♒23	☉	♂	☿	♀	☽		
	Mar	12	16:33	20♓13	☽	☉	♂	♇	♀			1	16	44		Mar	14	9:17	23♓01	☉	♂	♇	♀	☽		
	Apr	9	17:19	29♓02	☽	☿	♇	♂	☉			1	14	9		Apr	11	7:29	0♈58	♇	☿	♂	☉	☽		
	Dec	31	11:21	29♐34	☽	♆	☉	♅	☿			2	8	1	1824	Jan	2	19:22	7♑18	♆	☉	♅	☿	☽		
1824	Jul	24	20:55	11♋48	☽	♃	☿	♀	☉			2	5	34		Jul	27	2:29	25♋17	♃	♀	☉	☿	☽		
	Nov	22	18:37	24♐40	☽	♀	♆	♅	♂			2	5	21		Nov	24	23:59	2♑55	♀	♆	♅	♂	☽		
	Dec	20	3:45	24♐52	☽	☉	♆	☿	♅			1	23	59		Dec	22	3:45	0♑20	☉	♆	♅	☿	☽		
1825	Jan	17	9:49	7♑05	☽	♆	♅	☿	☉			1	20	23	1825	Jan	19	6:12	10♑03	♆	♅	☿	☉	☽		
	May	9	4:52	18♉14	☉	♂	☿	♀	♄			11	11	28		May	20	16:19	19♉41	☿	♀	☉	♂	♄		
	May	16	16:09	10♉13	☽	☿	☉	♂	♀			2	9	54		May	19	2:02	20♉25	☿	☉	♀	♂	☽		
	May	17	9:43	19♉16	☽	☿	☉	♂	♀	♄		1	16	19		May	19	2:02	20♉25	☿	☉	♀	♂	♄	☽	
	May	17	9:43	19♉16	☽	☉	♂	♀	♄			2	7	9		May	19	16:52	28♉20	♀	☉	♂	♄	☽		
1826	Jan	5	21:47	29♐45	♀	☿	♆	☉	♅			6	3	23	1826	Jan	12	1:10	1♑23	☿	♀	♆	♅	☉		
	Jan	6	20:16	26♐05	☽	♀	☿	♆	☉			1	21	20		Jan	8	17:36	2♑07	☿	♀	♆	☉	☽		
	Jan	7	2:43	29♐49	☽	♀	☿	♆	☉	♅		1	14	53		Jan	8	17:36	2♑07	☿	♀	♆	☉	♅	☽	
	Jan	7	2:43	29♐49	☽	♀	♆	☉	♅			1	17	12		Jan	8	19:55	3♑25	♀	♆	☉	♅	☽		
	Mar	8	8:21	13♓21	☽	☿	♀	☉	♇			2	2	57		Mar	10	11:19	19♓13	☿	♀	☉	♇	☽		
1827	Jun	24	2:22	28♊15	☽	☉	♂	♄	☿			2	3	33	1827	Jun	26	5:55	3♋48	☉	♂	♄	☿	☽		
	Aug	20	20:47	6♌59	☽	♀	♂	☿	☉			2	4	40		Aug	23	1:27	14♌24	☿	♂	♀	☉	☽		
	Oct	20	8:36	22♎26	☽	♃	☉	♀	☿			1	15	4		Oct	21	23:40	25♎27	♃	☉	♀	☿	☽		
1828	Jan	15	20:36	8♑04	☽	☿	♆	☉	♅			1	19	39	1828	Jan	17	16:15	15♑58	☿	♆	☉	♅	☽		
	Aug	8	20:46	26♋11	☽	♄	☿	♀	☉			0	19	42		Aug	9	16:28	26♋58	♄	♀	☿	☽	☉		
1829	Jan	6	14:25	11♑26	☿	☉	♆	☽	♅			0	4	4	1829	Jan	6	18:29	11♑42	☿	☉	♆	♅	☽		
	Jun	30	20:13	4♋24	☽	☉	☿	♀	♂			2	1	45		Jul	2	21:58	10♋39	☉	☿	♀	♂	☽		
	Jul	1	14:24	14♋07	☽	☿	♀	♂	♄			1	15	34		Jul	3	5:58	14♋46	☿	♀	♂	♄	☽		
	Jul	30	16:14	6♌25	☽	☉	♄	♂	♀			1	5	48		Jul	31	22:02	7♌56	♄	☉	♂	☽	♀		
1830	Dec	26	0:22	3♑47	☉	♀	☿	♆	♃			20	23	19	1831	Jan	15	23:41	22♑35	♆	☉	♃	♀	☿		
1831	Jan	6	5:51	19♑04	♀	♆	♃	☿	♅			9	17	49		Jan	15	23:41	22♑35	♆	♃	♀	♅	☿		
	Jan	10	5:11	19♑17	☉	♆	♀	♃	☿	♅		5	18	29		Jan	15	23:41	22♑35	♆	☉	♃	♀	♅	☿	
	Jan	10	5:11	19♑17	☉	♆	♀	♃	♅			15	0	33		Jan	25	5:45	22♑56	♆	♃	☉	♅	♀		
	Jan	10	5:11	19♑17	☉	♀	♃	☿	♅			21	4	34		Jan	31	9:46	0♒40	☿	♃	♅	☉	♀		
	Jan	12	20:42	7♑57	☽	☉	♆	♀	♃			2	17	7		Jan	15	13:49	22♑34	♆	☉	♃	♀	☽		
	Jan	13	18:43	19♑29	☽	♆	☉	♃	♀	♅		1	19	6		Jan	15	13:49	22♑34	♆	☉	♃	♀	♅	☽	
	Jan	13	18:43	19♑29	☽	☉	♃	♀	♅			1	23	26		Jan	15	18:10	24♑56	☉	♃	♀	♅	☽		
	Jan	13	22:38	21♑33	☽	♆	☉	♃	♀	♅	☿	1	15	11		Jan	15	13:49	22♑34	♆	☉	♃	♀	♅	☿	☽
	Jan	13	22:38	21♑33	☽	☉	♃	♀	♅	☿		1	19	31		Jan	15	18:10	24♑56	☉	♃	♀	♅	☿	☽	
	Jan	13	22:38	21♑33	☽	♃	♀	♅	☿			2	2	25		Jan	16	1:03	28♑42	♃	♀	♅	☿	☽		
	Jan	19	5:58	22♑42	♆	☉	♃	♀	♅	☿		5	23	46		Jan	25	5:45	22♑56	♆	♃	☉	☿	♅	♀	
	Jan	19	5:58	22♑42	♆	☉	♃	♅	☿			14	12	47		Feb	2	18:45	23♑15	♆	☿	♃	♅	☉		
	Feb	10	6:10	21♑04	☽	♆	☿	♃	♅			1	17	33		Feb	11	23:44	23♑34	♆	☿	♃	♅	☽		
	Aug	7	18:34	12♌28	☽	☉	♂	☿	♄			1	16	35		Aug	9	11:10	16♌03	☉	♂	♄	☿	☽		
	Oct	4	17:24	26♍47	☽	☿	♂	☉	♀			1	13	17		Oct	6	6:41	26♍43	☿	♂	☉	♀	☽		
1833	Mar	21	3:07	26♓32	☽	☉	♃	♇	☿			2	1	55	1833	Mar	23	5:02	2♈21	☉	♃	♇	☿	☽		
	Apr	18	8:46	8♈04	☽	♇	♃	☿	☉			1	20	36		Apr	20	5:22	11♈39	♇	♃	☿	☉	☽		
1834	Feb	6	22:06	27♑43	☽	♆	♀	☿	☉			1	19	32	1834	Feb	8	17:38	29♑50	♆	♀	☿	☉	☽		
	Feb	7	7:02	2♒17	☽	♀	☿	☉	♅			2	15	36		Feb	9	22:38	14♒22	♀	☿	☉	♅	☽		
1835	Oct	21	18:47	24♎28	☽	♄	☉	♀	♂			1	11	9	1835	Oct	23	5:56	26♎25	♄	☉	♀	♂	☽		
1836	Jan	17	10:06	13♑31	☽	♂	☉	♆	☿			1	20	5	1836	Jan	19	6:10	20♑37	♂	☉	♆	☿	☽		
1837	Apr	3	21:20	25♓19	☽	♀	☿	☉	♇			2	2	33	1837	Apr	5	23:53	4♈50	♀	☿	♇	☉	☽		
1838	Jan	25	2:59	21♑24	☽	☿	☉	♆	♂			0	21	20	1838	Jan	26	0:19	22♑06	☿	☽	☉	♆	♂		
	Feb	24	2:50	29♒34	☽	☉	♂	♅	♀			1	18	27		Feb	25	21:17	6♓31	♂	☉	♅	♀	☽		
	Mar	5	5:18	24♒21	☿	♅	♂	☉	♀			13	7	46		Mar	18	13:04	7♓31	♀	♅	☿	♂	☉		
	Mar	25	7:53	26♓05	☽	♂	☿	☉	♇			1	12	59		Mar	26	20:52	29♓15	♂	☿	☉	♇	☽		
	Oct	16	18:08	2♎57	☽	♃	♀	☿	☉			1	19	2		Oct	18	13:09	4♎43	♃	♀	☿	☽	☉		
	Nov	16	4:20	10♏26	☽	♀	☉	☿	♄			2	6	13		Nov	18	10:32	18♏21	♀	☉	♄	☿	☽		
1839	Oct	6	22:10	5♎34	☽	☿	♀	☉	♃			2	0	13	1839	Oct	8	22:22	9♎37	☿	♀	☉	♃	☽		
1840	Mar	3	17:18	7♓31	☽	☉	♅	☿	♂			1	23	42	1840	Mar	5	16:60	15♓14	☉	♅	☿	♂	☽		
	Apr	1	21:10	2♈00	☽	☉	♇	♂	☿			2	5	5		Apr	4	2:16	14♈23	☉	♇	☿	♂	☽		

5 or More Planets Within 20° Arc 1700-2050

				Starting Position	Planets in Zodiacal Sequence							Dy	Hr	Mn					Ending Position	Planets in Zodiacal Sequence						
	May	29	21:43	18♉30	☽	♀	☿	♂	☉			1	18	9		May	31	15:52	25♉20	♀	☿	♂	☉	☽		
1841	Dec	24	3:51	15♐05	♀	☿	♃	☉	♄			24	5	41	1842	Jan	17	9:33	6♑57	♃	♄	♀	☿	☉		
1842	Jan	9	9:51	23♐46	☽	♃	♀	♄	☿			2	15	44		Jan	12	1:35	5♑45	♃	♄	♀	☿	☽		
	Jan	9	20:41	29♐16	☽	♃	♀	♄	☿	☉		2	4	54		Jan	12	1:35	5♑45	♃	♄	♀	☿	☉	☽	
	Jan	9	20:41	29♐16	☽	♀	♄	☿	☉			2	8	4		Jan	12	4:45	7♑19	♄	♀	☿	☉	☽		
	Mar	10	19:45	4♓02	☽	☿	☉	♀	♅			1	18	20		Mar	12	14:05	5♓08	☿	☉	♀	♅	☽		
	May	10	5:13	15♉51	☽	☿	☉	♂	♀			1	21	7		May	12	2:20	20♉55	☉	☿	♂	♀	☽		
	Dec	31	17:34	8♑59	☽	☉	☿	♄	♃			1	18	20	1843	Jan	2	11:55	11♑31	☉	☿	♄	♃	☽		
1844	Jan	20	15:23	10♒49	☽	☿	♆	♀	♃			1	20	20	1844	Jan	22	11:43	15♒10	☿	♆	♀	♃	☽		
	Jul	15	11:01	15♋36	☿	☽	☉	♂	♀			1	8	34		Jul	16	19:34	18♋29	☿	☉	♂	♀	☽		
1845	Mar	5	14:54	10♒22	☽	♄	♆	♀	☿			1	16	2	1845	Mar	7	6:56	13♒56	♄	♆	♀	☿	☽		
	Mar	23	17:10	2♈57	☉	☿	♅	♃	♇			11	6	41		Apr	3	23:51	6♈40	♅	☉	♃	♇	☿		
	Mar	28	5:31	24♓39	♀	♅	☉	☿	♃			1	23	26		Mar	30	4:57	27♓06	♀	♅	☉	♃	☿		
	Apr	4	3:23	3♈13	♀	♅	☉	♃	♇			13	11	0		Apr	17	14:22	7♈25	♅	♃	♀	♇	☉		
	Apr	5	6:32	26♓35	☽	♀	♅	☉	♃			2	7	54		Apr	7	14:26	6♈52	♅	♀	♃	☉	☽		
	Apr	5	18:37	3♈15	☽	♀	♅	☉	♃	♇		1	19	49		Apr	7	14:26	6♈52	♅	♀	♃	☉	♇	☽	
	Apr	5	18:37	3♈15	☽	♀	☉	♃	♇			1	21	9		Apr	7	15:45	7♈34	♀	♃	☉	♇	☽		
	Apr	6	9:05	11♈09	☽	☉	♃	♇	☿			2	1	22		Apr	8	10:27	17♈21	♃	☉	♇	☿	☽		
1846	Feb	24	9:32	15♒26	☽	♄	♆	☿	☉			1	20	18	1846	Feb	26	5:50	23♒18	♄	♆	☿	☉	☽		
	Feb	25	1:26	25♒29	☽	♆	☿	☉	♀			1	8	52		Feb	26	10:17	26♒04	♆	☿	☉	♀	☽		
	Feb	28	7:51	23♒33	♄	♆	☿	☉	♀			4	16	44		Mar	5	0:36	24♒06	♄	♆	♀	☿	☉		
	Mar	27	2:16	4♈03	☽	☉	♅	♇	☿			1	16	11		Mar	28	18:26	7♈42	☉	♅	♇	☿	☽		
1847	Feb	7	14:21	11♒32	☿	☉	♆	♀	♄			13	14	15	1847	Feb	21	4:36	28♒00	♆	☉	♄	☿	♀		
	Feb	14	13:34	12♒22	☽	☿	☉	♆	♄			2	7	37		Feb	16	21:11	27♒38	☉	♆	☿	♄	☽		
	Feb	15	2:16	20♒23	☽	☿	☉	♆	♄	♀		1	18	56		Feb	16	21:11	27♒38	☉	♆	☿	♄	♀	☽	
	Feb	15	2:16	20♒23	☽	☿	♆	♄	♀			1	19	15		Feb	16	21:31	27♒50	♆	☿	♄	♀	☽		
	Mar	17	11:30	4♈45	☽	♅	☿	♀	♇			1	21	57		Mar	19	9:27	13♈16	♅	☿	♀	♇	☽		
1848	Mar	31	20:56	28♒40	☽	♆	♀	☿	♄			1	13	47	1848	Apr	2	10:42	1♓35	♆	♀	☿	♄	☽		
	Apr	30	21:45	6♈44	☽	♀	♅	☿	♇			2	4	14		May	3	1:59	19♈36	♅	♀	☿	♇	☽		
	Jul	28	21:07	17♋27	☽	☿	♃	☉	♀			1	19	41		Jul	30	16:48	22♋28	☿	♃	☉	♀	☽		
	Aug	28	21:25	1♍33	☿	☉	☽	♀	♂			1	9	13		Aug	30	6:37	4♍16	☿	☉	♀	♂	☽		
	Sep	27	5:35	2♎21	☽	☉	♂	♀	☿			1	23	15		Sep	29	4:50	6♎10	☉	♂	♀	☿	☽		
1849	Apr	21	12:48	11♈17	☽	☿	♅	♇	☉			2	2	13	1849	Apr	23	15:01	22♈06	☿	♅	♇	☉	☽		
1850	Mar	28	22:06	7♈53	☉	♄	♀	♅	♇			14	11	46	1850	Apr	12	9:52	12♈17	♄	☉	♅	♇	♀		
	Apr	7	4:27	5♈50	☿	♄	☉	♅	♀			5	5	25		Apr	12	9:52	12♈17	♄	☿	☉	♅	♀		
	Apr	8	9:16	8♈07	☿	♄	☉	♅	♀	♇		4	0	35		Apr	12	9:52	12♈17	♄	☿	☉	♅	♇	♀	
	Apr	8	9:16	8♈07	☿	♄	☉	♅	♇			12	7	37		Apr	20	16:53	13♈19	♄	♅	♇	☉	☿		
	Apr	8	9:16	8♈07	☿	☉	♅	♀	♇			15	16	19		Apr	24	1:35	26♈40	♅	♇	☉	☿	♀		
	Apr	11	7:22	5♈56	☽	♄	☿	☉	♅			1	23	18		Apr	13	6:41	12♈24	♄	☿	☉	♅	☽		
	Apr	11	11:28	8♈11	☽	♄	☿	☉	♅	♇		1	19	13		Apr	13	6:41	12♈24	♄	☿	☉	♅	♇	☽	
	Apr	11	11:28	8♈11	☽	☿	☉	♅	♇			2	6	11		Apr	13	17:40	18♈42	☿	☉	♅	♇	☽		
	Apr	11	17:24	11♈27	☽	♄	☿	☉	♅	♇	♀	0	16	28		Apr	12	9:52	12♈17	♄	☿	☽	☉	♅	♇	♀
	Apr	11	17:24	11♈27	☽	☿	☉	♅	♇	♀		2	0	16		Apr	13	17:40	18♈42	☿	☉	♅	♇	♀	☽	
	Apr	11	17:24	11♈27	☽	☉	♅	♇	♀			2	9	4		Apr	14	2:28	23♈47	☉	♅	♇	♀	☽		
	Dec	4	12:35	10♐40	♂	☉	☿	☽	♀			0	18	47		Dec	5	7:22	11♐15	♂	☉	☿	♀	☽		
1851	Mar	31	17:30	9♈08	☿	☉	♄	♇	♅			17	17	17	1851	Apr	18	10:46	24♈30	♄	☉	♇	♅	☿		
	Apr	1	13:33	8♈54	☽	☿	☉	♄	♇			1	23	6		Apr	3	12:40	13♈10	☉	☿	♄	♇	☽		
	Apr	1	14:07	9♈11	☽	☿	☉	♄	♇	♅		1	22	33		Apr	3	12:40	13♈10	☉	☿	♄	♇	♅	☽	
	Apr	1	14:07	9♈11	☽	☿	♄	♇	♅			2	2	28		Apr	3	16:34	15♈13	☿	♄	♇	♅	☽		
	Apr	29	15:47	18♈42	☽	♄	♇	♅	☉			2	4	5		May	1	19:52	26♈11	♄	♇	♅	☉	☽		
	May	10	18:15	11♈25	♂	♀	♄	♇	♅			31	11	7		Jun	11	5:22	0♉24	♇	♄	♅	♂	♀		
	May	26	9:51	11♈31	☽	♂	♄	♇	♀			2	16	21		May	29	2:12	25♈17	♂	♄	♇	♀	☽		
	May	26	11:16	12♈15	☽	♂	♄	♇	♀	♅		2	14	56		May	29	2:12	25♈17	♂	♄	♇	♅	♀	☽	
	May	26	11:16	12♈15	☽	♄	♇	♀	♅			2	22	35		May	29	9:50	29♈26	♄	♇	♅	♀	☽		
	Jun	23	19:07	24♈14	☽	♇	♄	♅	♂			2	1	54		Jun	25	21:01	0♉37	♇	♄	♅	♂	☽		
	Oct	23	15:20	15♎41	☽	☿	☉	♃	♀			1	19	22		Oct	25	10:42	22♎43	☿	☉	♃	♀	☽		
1852	Mar	22	14:27	21♈58	☽	♇	♅	♄	♀			2	7	55	1852	Mar	24	22:21	29♈42	♇	♅	♄	♀	☽		
	Apr	4	2:57	14♈30	☉	♇	☿	♅	♄			37	6	1		May	11	8:58	0♉46	♇	☿	♅	♄	☉		
	Apr	18	8:59	16♈17	☽	☉	♇	♅	♄			2	20	25		Apr	21	5:23	0♉19	♇	☉	♅	♄	☽		
	Apr	19	0:56	24♈11	☽	☉	♇	♅	♄	☿		2	4	27		Apr	21	5:23	0♉19	♇	☉	♅	♄	☿	☽	
	Apr	19	0:56	24♈11	☽	☉	♅	♄	☿			2	6	28		Apr	21	7:24	1♉19	☉	♅	♄	☿	☽		
	May	15	22:27	19♈48	☽	♇	☿	♅	♄			2	14	21		May	18	12:48	0♉56	♇	☿	♅	♄	☽		
	Nov	11	15:21	18♏39	☽	☉	♃	☿	♂			1	11	22		Nov	13	2:43	20♏55	☉	♃	☿	♂	☽		
1853	Mar	8	3:51	27♒32	☽	♀	♂	♆	☉			1	23	23	1853	Mar	10	3:14	2♓52	♀	♂	♆	☉	☽		
	Mar	8	23:28	8♓07	☽	♂	♆	☉	☿			1	0	47		Mar	10	0:16	10♓07	♂	♆	☉	☽	☿		
	Apr	8	8:12	3♈03	♂	♀	☽	☉	☿			0	13	30		Apr	8	21:42	3♈29	♂	♀	☉	☿	☽		
	Apr	8	9:25	17♈17	☽	☉	☿	♇	♅			1	22	4		Apr	10	7:29	20♈20	☉	☿	♇	♅	☽		
	Apr	15	6:54	17♈40	♀	☿	☉	♇	♅			0	12	46		Apr	15	19:41	17♈42	☿	♀	☉	♇	♅		
	Apr	18	21:48	11♈12	♂	☿	♀	☉	♇			6	0	36		Apr	24	22:24	14♈37	☿	♂	♀	♇	☉		
	Apr	24	10:41	28♈58	♀	♇	☉	♅	♄			18	4	7		May	12	14:48	1♉44	♇	♅	♄	♀	☉		
	Apr	28	7:53	18♈25	♂	♇	♀	☉	♅			2	8	57		Apr	30	16:50	20♈13	♂	♇	♀	♅	☉		
	May	5	18:30	18♈50	☽	☿	♂	♇	♅			1	20	15		May	7	14:45	20♈51	☿	♂	♇	♅	☽		
	May	6	3:38	23♈24	☽	♂	♇	♅	♀			1	21	4		May	8	0:42	25♈46	♂	♇	♅	♀	☽		

5 or More Planets Within 20° Arc 1700-2050

				Starting Position	Planets in Zodiacal Sequence						Dy	Hr	Mn					Ending Position	Planets in Zodiacal Sequence						
	May	6	8:10	25♈41	☽	♇	♅	♀	☉		2	4	28		May	8	12:38	1♉39	♇	♅	♀	☉	☽		
	May	6	17:57	0♉33	☽	♇	♅	♀	☉	♄	1	18	42		May	8	12:38	1♉39	♇	♅	♀	☉	♄	☽	
	May	6	17:57	0♉33	☽	♅	♀	☉	♄		2	9	43		May	9	3:39	9♉02	♅	♀	☉	♄	☽		
1854	Feb	26	19:18	2♓47	☽	☉	♀	♆	☿		1	21	48	1854	Feb	28	17:07	9♓27	♀	☉	♆	☿	☽		
1855	Jan	17	15:22	16♑44	☽	☿	☉	♀	♃		2	1	32	1855	Jan	19	16:54	28♑22	☿	☉	♃	♀	☽		
	Jan	18	1:09	25♑37	☿	☉	♀	♃	♂		20	7	3		Feb	7	8:12	11♒39	♃	☉	☿	♀	♂		
	Jan	18	5:30	25♑45	☽	☿	☉	♀	♃	♂	1	11	24		Jan	19	16:54	28♑22	☿	☉	♃	♀	♂	☽	
	Jan	18	5:30	25♑45	☽	☉	♀	♃	♂		1	12	40		Jan	19	18:10	29♑11	☉	♃	♀	♂	☽		
	Feb	14	2:05	24♒52	☉	♂	♀	☿	♆		20	11	42		Mar	6	13:47	15♓17	☿	☉	♆	♂	♀		
	Feb	16	14:40	24♒57	☽	☉	♂	♀	♆		1	14	8		Feb	18	4:48	29♒01	☉	♂	♀	♆	☽		
	Feb	16	15:12	25♒18	☽	☉	♂	♀	♆	☿	1	13	36		Feb	18	4:48	29♒01	☉	♂	♀	♆	☿	☽	
	Feb	16	15:12	25♒18	☽	♂	♀	♆	☿		2	8	50		Feb	19	0:02	10♓51	♂	♆	♀	☿	☽		
	Apr	17	21:12	25♈33	♂	☉	♇	☽	♅		0	4	5		Apr	18	1:17	25♈40	♂	☉	♇	♅	☽		
	Apr	30	23:45	26♈18	☿	♇	♂	☉	♅		13	5	23		May	14	5:09	3♉39	♇	♂	♅	☉	☿		
	May	14	11:42	3♉05	☽	♇	♂	♅	☉		0	14	48		May	15	2:30	3♉40	♇	☽	♂	♅	☉		
	May	14	14:10	4♉28	☽	♂	♅	☉	☿		2	10	58		May	17	1:08	17♉08	♂	♅	☉	☿	☽		
1856	Apr	2	8:24	2♓01	☽	♀	♆	☿	♃		2	7	52	1856	Apr	4	16:16	17♓03	♀	♆	♃	☿	☽		
	May	3	18:02	1♉36	☽	♇	☉	♅	☿		1	8	5		May	5	2:07	4♉25	♇	☉	♅	☽	☿		
	Jun	30	19:15	19♊05	☽	☿	♀	♄	☉		2	0	9		Jul	2	19:24	26♊04	☿	♄	♀	☉	☽		
1857	Apr	7	21:25	14♈44	☿	☉	♃	♂	♇		14	9	28	1857	Apr	22	6:53	24♈38	♃	☉	♇	♂	☿		
	Apr	23	21:19	27♈44	☽	☉	♇	♂	☿		1	19	12		Apr	25	16:30	5♉08	♇	☉	♂	☿	☽		
	Apr	24	1:16	3♉48	☉	♇	♂	☿	♅		3	23	25		Apr	28	0:40	5♉11	♇	☉	♂	♅	☿		
	Apr	24	6:53	3♉48	☽	☉	♇	♂	☿	♅	1	9	38		Apr	25	16:30	5♉08	♇	☉	♂	☿	♅	☽	
	Apr	24	6:53	3♉48	☽	☉	♂	☿	♅		1	10	4		Apr	25	16:56	5♉24	☉	♂	☿	♅	☽		
	Apr	24	12:22	7♉17	☽	♂	☿	♅	♀		1	23	10		Apr	26	11:31	17♉03	♂	☿	♅	♀	☽		
	Apr	26	23:11	6♉38	☉	♂	☿	♅	♀		5	8	42		May	2	7:53	11♉50	☉	♂	♅	♀	☿		
	Apr	30	13:18	5♉15	♇	☉	♂	♅	♀		7	14	57		May	8	4:14	5♉25	♇	☉	♀	♅	♂		
	May	23	2:42	24♉42	☽	♅	☉	♂	☿		1	9	4		May	24	11:45	25♉33	♅	☉	♂	☿	☽		
	Jul	19	18:05	6♋56	☽	♂	♄	☿	☉		2	1	49		Jul	21	19:54	16♋19	♂	♄	☿	☉	☽		
1858	Mar	14	4:21	6♓42	☽	☿	♆	☉	♀		2	4	55	1858	Mar	16	9:16	16♓48	☿	♆	☉	♀	☽		
	Apr	13	19:50	21♈39	☽	☉	♀	♇	☿		1	14	30		Apr	15	10:20	25♈09	☉	♇	♀	☿	☽		
	Apr	14	10:18	0♉25	☽	♀	♇	☿	♃		1	17	23		Apr	16	3:41	5♉51	♇	♀	☿	♃	☽		
	Apr	15	22:37	7♉20	♀	☿	♃	☽	♅		0	8	9		Apr	16	6:46	7♉45	♀	☿	♃	♅	☽		
	Apr	22	18:21	2♉18	☉	♇	♀	☿	♃		8	12	4		May	1	6:26	6♉12	♇	☉	♃	☿	♀		
	Apr	28	15:19	8♉01	☉	♀	♃	☿	♅		14	9	29		May	13	0:48	20♉37	☿	☉	♃	♅	♀		
	May	12	10:18	8♉48	☽	☿	☉	♃	♅		2	1	16		May	14	11:34	19♉46	☿	☉	♃	♅	☽		
	May	13	5:38	20♉51	☽	☉	♃	♅	♀		1	11	59		May	14	17:37	23♉35	☉	♃	♅	♀	☽		
1859	Jun	29	17:45	25♊10	☽	♃	☉	♂	☿		1	23	34	1859	Jul	1	17:19	4♋56	♃	☉	♂	☿	☽		
	Aug	25	14:16	17♌59	♄	♂	♀	☉	☿		7	8	0		Sep	1	22:15	18♌54	♄	♂	☿	♀	☉		
	Aug	26	19:16	12♌58	☽	♄	♂	♀	☉		1	16	21		Aug	28	11:38	18♌21	♄	♂	♀	☉	☽		
	Aug	27	1:10	16♌40	☽	♄	♂	♀	☉	☿	1	10	28		Aug	28	11:38	18♌21	♄	♂	♀	☉	☿	☽	
	Aug	27	1:10	16♌40	☽	♂	♀	☉	☿		1	17	22		Aug	28	18:32	22♌40	♂	♀	☉	☿	☽		
1860	Aug	15	21:22	8♌42	☽	♃	☿	☉	♄		1	11	16	1860	Aug	17	8:38	10♌38	♃	☿	☉	♄	☽		
1861	May	8	3:22	27♈29	☽	☿	♇	♀	☉		2	10	44	1861	May	10	14:06	6♉45	☿	♇	♀	☉	☽		
	Jul	8	8:53	16♋06	☉	☽	♀	♂	☿		1	8	26		Jul	9	17:18	17♋23	☉	♂	♀	☿	☽		
	Aug	6	22:01	19♌14	☽	♂	♃	♀	♄		1	14	44		Aug	8	12:45	22♌01	♂	♃	♄	♀	☽		
	Aug	25	5:53	21♌28	☿	☉	♂	♃	♄		20	23	5		Sep	15	4:58	10♍56	♃	♄	♂	☉	☿		
	Sep	3	10:19	20♌51	☽	♃	♂	☿	☉		2	15	5		Sep	6	1:24	8♍58	♃	♂	☉	☿	☽		
	Sep	3	13:21	22♌38	☽	♃	♂	☿	☉	♄	2	12	3		Sep	6	1:24	8♍58	♃	♂	♄	☉	☿	☽	
	Sep	3	13:21	22♌38	☽	♂	☿	☉	♄		2	14	5		Sep	6	3:26	10♍13	♂	♄	☉	☿	☽		
1863	Oct	10	4:36	29♍07	♀	♄	♂	☉	☿		2	0	58	1863	Oct	12	5:35	28♍24	♀	♄	♂	☿	☉		
	Oct	11	2:26	27♍17	☽	♀	♄	♂	☉		1	3	9		Oct	12	5:35	28♍24	♀	♄	☽	♂	☉		
	Oct	11	3:43	27♍58	☽	♀	♄	♂	☉	☿	1	1	52		Oct	12	5:35	28♍24	♀	♄	☽	♂	☿	☉	
	Oct	11	3:43	27♍58	☽	♀	♄	♂	☿		1	13	43		Oct	12	17:26	28♍15	♀	♄	♂	☿	☽		
	Oct	11	3:43	27♍58	☽	♄	♂	☉	☿		2	11	5		Oct	13	14:48	10♎00	♄	☿	♂	☉	☽		
	Oct	12	8:52	13♎35	☽	♂	☿	☉	♃		1	14	26		Oct	13	23:18	14♎44	☿	♂	☉	♃	☽		
	Nov	9	17:58	26♎52	☽	☿	♂	♃	☉		2	2	42		Nov	11	20:40	5♏49	♂	☿	♃	☉	☽		
1864	Jul	2	6:49	20♊34	☽	☿	♅	♀	☉		2	1	31	1864	Jul	4	8:20	26♊17	♅	☿	♀	☉	☽		
1865	Apr	25	12:17	4♉09	☽	☉	♇	☿	♀		1	12	45	1865	Apr	27	1:03	6♉46	☉	♇	☿	♀	☽		
	Oct	18	12:24	12♎32	☽	☿	☉	♄	♂		3	0	18		Oct	21	12:41	28♎06	☿	☉	♄	♂	☽		
	Dec	25	16:26	19♐00	♀	♂	☿	☉	♃		9	1	7	1866	Jan	3	17:33	23♐12	☿	♂	♀	♃	☉		
1866	Jan	14	7:42	23♐40	☽	☿	♂	♃	♀		2	5	50		Jan	16	13:33	2♑39	☿	♂	♃	♀	☽		
	Jan	15	4:52	4♑53	☽	♂	♃	♀	☉		1	17	23		Jan	16	22:15	7♑29	♂	♃	♀	☉	☽		
	Mar	16	11:09	19♓42	☽	☉	♀	☿	♆		1	21	13		Mar	18	8:22	27♓32	☉	♀	♆	☿	☽		
	Apr	15	4:09	23♈15	☽	☿	☉	♀	♇		0	4	36		Apr	15	8:45	23♈15	☿	☉	☽	♀	♇		
1867	Oct	27	19:15	6♏59	☽	♀	♂	♄	☿		2	5	28	1867	Oct	30	0:44	15♏03	♀	♂	♄	☿	☽		
	Oct	27	22:35	4♏03	☉	☽	♀	♂	♄		1	7	27		Oct	29	6:02	5♏22	☉	♀	♂	♄	☽		
	Nov	10	13:35	17♏43	☉	♄	♀	♂	☿		13	14	21		Nov	24	3:56	26♏30	☿	♄	☉	♂	♀		
	Nov	25	8:09	22♏39	☽	☿	♄	☉	♂		1	9	59		Nov	26	18:08	23♏41	☿	♄	☉	☽	♂		
1868	Apr	19	22:39	25♓20	☽	♃	♂	☿	♆		1	22	54	1868	Apr	21	21:33	0♈21	♃	♂	☿	♆	☽		
	Jul	18	11:52	6♋03	☽	♅	☿	♀	☉		1	20	34		Jul	20	8:26	14♋02	♅	☿	♀	☉	☽		
1869	Apr	10	6:24	0♈25	☽	☿	♀	♆	☉		2	1	31	1869	Apr	12	7:55	5♈18	☿	♀	♆	☉	☽		
	Apr	10	16:59	5♈41	☽	♀	♆	☉	♃		2	12	45		Apr	13	5:44	16♈29	♀	♆	☉	♃	☽		

5 or More Planets Within 20° Arc 1700-2050

	Starting Position				Planets in Zodiacal Sequence						Dy	Hr	Mn		Ending Position				Planets in Zodiacal Sequence					
	Apr	12	20:02	6♈12	☿	♀	♆	☉	♃		15	5	41		Apr	28	1:43	17♈47	♆	♃	♀	☿	☉	
	Apr	23	8:40	26♈12	☿	♃	♀	☉	♇		11	22	7		May	5	6:47	1♉34	♃	♀	☉	♇	☿	
	May	9	22:58	29♈27	☽	♃	♇	☉	♀		1	21	14		May	11	20:12	3♉07	♃	♇	☉	♀	☽	
	May	11	2:10	13♉35	☽	♇	☉	♀	☿		1	13	45		May	12	15:55	16♉38	♇	☉	♀	☽	☿	
1870	Apr	1	5:52	28♓57	☿	♂	☉	☽	♆		0	14	2	1870	Apr	1	19:53	0♈01	☿	♂	☉	♆	☽	
	Apr	30	14:05	7♉55	☽	☉	♇	☿	♃		2	0	17		May	2	14:22	11♉57	☉	♇	♃	☿	☽	
	May	28	14:38	17♉00	☽	♇	♂	♃	☉		0	23	7		May	29	13:45	17♉56	♇	♂	☽	♃	☉	
	Jun	25	8:34	22♉26	☽	♀	♂	♃	☿		1	21	52		Jun	27	6:26	25♉37	♀	♂	♃	☿	☽	
	Dec	22	5:21	26♐12	☽	☉	♄	♀	☿		1	16	32		Dec	23	21:53	1♑03	♄	☉	♀	☿	☽	
1871	Jul	16	10:32	9♋07	☽	♃	☉	♅	☿		1	12	55	1871	Jul	17	23:28	12♋16	♃	☉	♅	☽	☿	
1872	Apr	7	22:03	17♈06	☽	☉	♆	♂	☿		1	17	52	1872	Apr	9	15:55	20♈06	☉	♆	♂	☿	☽	
	May	6	3:40	29♈16	☽	☿	☉	♂	♇		0	19	10		May	6	22:50	29♈19	☿	☽	☉	♇	♂	
	Jun	3	23:35	19♉11	☽	♇	☿	♀	♂		1	1	19		Jun	5	0:54	19♉55	♇	☿	☽	♀	♂	
	Jun	5	14:33	25♉09	☿	♀	☽	♂	☉		0	13	42		Jun	6	4:15	26♉06	☿	♀	♂	☉	☽	
	Jul	5	11:11	10♋22	☽	♀	☉	☿	♅		1	21	58		Jul	7	9:09	13♋01	♀	☉	☿	♅	☽	
	Jul	7	0:28	15♋08	☉	☿	☽	♅	♃		0	14	6		Jul	7	14:34	15♋42	☉	☿	♅	♃	☽	
	Jul	9	12:51	15♋40	♀	☉	♅	☿	♃		4	7	14		Jul	13	20:06	20♋58	♀	☉	♅	♃	☿	
	Aug	3	0:32	25♋50	☽	♅	☉	♃	♀		2	5	22		Aug	5	5:54	2♌15	♅	♃	☉	♀	☽	
1874	Jan	17	8:31	14♑10	☽	☿	♀	☉	♄		1	17	13	1874	Jan	19	1:44	18♑50	☿	♀	☉	♄	☽	
	Aug	10	11:46	27♋37	☽	☿	♂	♅	☉		1	19	11		Aug	12	6:57	0♌47	☿	♂	♅	☉	☽	
1875	Oct	28	5:40	23♎29	☽	☉	☿	♃	♀		2	15	55	1875	Oct	30	21:35	5♏33	☿	☉	♃	♀	☽	
1876	Apr	24	4:09	2♉41	☽	♆	☉	☿	♇		1	9	16	1876	Apr	25	13:25	2♉51	♆	☉	☿	♇	☽	
	Aug	19	0:49	19♌39	☽	♅	♂	☉	☿		0	15	10		Aug	19	15:59	20♌46	♅	♂	☉	☽	☿	
1877	Mar	13	14:29	3♓09	☿	☽	♀	♄	☉		1	14	25	1877	Mar	15	4:54	5♓41	☿	♀	♄	☉	☽	
	Apr	13	0:23	14♈32	☽	♀	☉	☿	♆		1	21	28		Apr	14	21:51	19♈14	♀	☉	☿	♆	☽	
	May	11	20:38	3♉59	☽	♆	☉	♀	♇		1	14	19		May	13	10:58	5♉40	♆	☉	♇	♀	☽	
	May	13	0:19	19♉34	☽	☉	♀	♇	☿		1	18	6		May	14	18:25	24♉01	☉	♇	♀	☿	☽	
1878	May	1	22:41	4♉41	☽	♆	☉	☿	♇		1	19	53	1878	May	3	18:35	7♉28	♆	☉	☿	♇	☽	
	Sep	25	4:24	11♍58	☽	♀	☿	♂	☉		1	13	26		Sep	26	17:50	15♍41	☿	♀	♂	☉	☽	
	Oct	24	13:19	11♎01	☽	♂	♀	☿	☉		1	21	57		Oct	26	11:15	20♎12	♂	♀	☉	☿	☽	
1880	Apr	7	22:25	28♓42	☽	♃	☿	☉	♄		1	19	34	1880	Apr	9	17:59	1♈37	☿	♃	♄	☉	☽	
	May	5	20:10	7♈05	☽	♃	☿	♄	♀		0	11	6		May	6	7:16	7♈39	♃	☽	☿	♄	♀	
	May	7	0:54	21♈57	☽	♄	☿	♀	♆		1	16	28		May	8	17:22	22♈30	♄	☿	♀	♆	☽	
	May	15	23:31	6♉51	☿	♀	♆	☉	♇		7	9	13		May	23	8:44	12♉33	♆	♀	☿	♇	☉	
	Sep	4	9:58	8♍44	☽	♅	☉	♀	♂		1	9	56		Sep	5	19:54	9♍39	♅	☉	☽	♀	♂	
1881	Apr	20	0:24	0♉03	☉	♄	♃	♆	♀		25	18	42	1881	May	15	19:06	5♉02	♄	♀	♃	♆	☉	
	Apr	27	8:04	23♈45	☽	♄	♃	☉	♆		2	5	48		Apr	29	13:52	3♉00	♄	♃	☉	♆	☽	
	Apr	27	13:17	26♈38	☽	♄	♃	☉	♆	♀	2	0	35		Apr	29	13:52	3♉00	♄	♃	☉	♆	♀	☽
	Apr	27	13:17	26♈38	☽	♃	☉	♆	♀		2	2	58		Apr	29	16:15	4♉16	♃	☉	♆	♀	☽	
	Apr	27	23:51	17♈49	☿	☽	♄	♃	☉		0	11	14		Apr	28	11:05	18♈36	☿	♄	♃	☉	☽	
	Apr	28	8:50	7♉23	☽	☉	♆	♀	♇		1	18	5		Apr	30	2:55	9♉53	☉	♆	♀	♇	☽	
	May	1	12:02	23♈54	☿	♄	♃	☉	♆		14	7	4		May	15	19:06	5♉02	♄	♃	♆	☿	☉	
	May	1	15:51	24♈11	☿	♄	♃	☉	♆	♀	14	3	15		May	15	19:06	5♉02	♄	♀	♃	♆	☿	☉
	May	1	15:51	24♈11	☿	♃	☉	♆	♀		15	5	57		May	16	21:48	6♉06	♀	♃	♆	☿	☉	
	May	1	15:51	24♈11	☿	♄	♃	♆	♀		15	9	57		May	17	1:49	5♉11	♄	♀	♃	♆	☿	
	May	8	17:33	7♉37	☿	♀	♆	☉	♇		4	2	9		May	12	19:42	7♉42	♀	♆	☿	☉	♇	
	May	14	6:44	7♉44	♃	♆	☿	☉	♇		4	10	22		May	18	17:06	8♉46	♃	♆	♇	☉	☿	
	May	24	16:26	24♈46	☽	♀	♄	♃	♆		2	8	30		May	27	0:56	4♉58	♀	♄	♃	♆	☽	
	Jun	14	15:33	8♉26	♄	♀	♃	♆	♇		23	12	57		Jul	8	4:30	10♉33	♄	♆	♃	♇	♀	
	Jun	15	15:13	25♈30	♂	♄	♀	♃	♆		22	13	17		Jul	8	4:30	10♉33	♄	♂	♆	♃	♀	
	Jun	21	0:23	26♈06	☽	♂	♄	♆	♃		1	22	37		Jun	22	22:60	0♉51	♂	♄	♆	♃	☽	
	Jun	21	0:42	26♈16	☽	♂	♄	♆	♃	♀	1	22	18		Jun	22	22:60	0♉51	♂	♄	♆	♃	♀	☽
	Jun	21	0:42	26♈16	☽	♄	♆	♃	♀		2	14	39		Jun	23	15:21	9♉18	♄	♆	♃	♀	☽	
	Jun	21	23:39	8♉34	☽	♄	♆	♃	♀	♇	1	15	42		Jun	23	15:21	9♉18	♄	♆	♃	♀	♇	☽
	Jun	21	23:39	8♉34	☽	♆	♃	♀	♇		2	4	15		Jun	24	3:54	15♉45	♆	♃	♀	♇	☽	
	Jul	4	0:47	8♉48	♂	♄	♆	♃	♀	♇	4	3	43		Jul	8	4:30	10♉33	♄	♂	♆	♃	♇	♀
	Jul	4	0:47	8♉48	♂	♆	♃	♀	♇		9	4	22		Jul	13	5:09	15♉16	♂	♆	♃	♇	♀	
	Jul	4	0:47	8♉48	♂	♄	♆	♃	♇		34	5	56		Aug	7	6:43	12♉10	♄	♆	♃	♇	♂	
	Jul	18	15:36	1♉10	☽	♄	♆	♂	♃		2	9	26		Jul	21	1:03	11♉24	♄	♆	♂	♃	☽	
	Jul	19	6:13	9♉02	☽	♄	♆	♂	♃	♇	1	18	50		Jul	21	1:03	11♉24	♄	♆	♂	♃	♇	☽
	Jul	19	6:13	9♉02	☽	♆	♂	♃	♇		2	4	32		Jul	21	10:44	16♉21	♆	♂	♃	♇	☽	
	Aug	15	13:43	9♉17	☽	♄	♆	♃	♇		1	19	30		Aug	17	9:13	12♉23	♄	♆	♃	♇	☽	
	Sep	11	22:35	9♉17	☽	♄	♆	♃	♇		1	17	49		Sep	13	16:24	12♉05	♄	♆	♃	♇	☽	
	Oct	9	8:05	9♉02	☽	♄	♆	♃	♇		1	14	45		Oct	10	22:50	10♉36	♄	♆	♃	♇	☽	
1882	Feb	22	17:20	7♉23	☽	♄	♆	♃	♇		1	12	15	1882	Feb	24	5:34	7♉38	♄	♆	♃	♇	☽	
	Mar	22	3:37	7♉38	☽	♄	♆	♃	♇		1	15	29		Mar	23	19:06	10♉19	♄	♆	♃	♇	☽	
	Apr	15	6:25	8♉31	♀	♄	♆	♇	♃		22	5	18		May	7	11:43	15♉49	♄	♆	♇	♃	♀	
	Apr	17	18:01	25♈33	☽	☉	♀	♄	♆		1	15	46		Apr	19	9:47	29♈13	☉	♄	♀	♆	☽	
	Apr	18	14:54	8♉06	☽	♀	♄	♆	♇		1	19	59		Apr	20	10:53	13♉38	♄	♀	♆	♇	☽	
	Apr	18	16:51	9♉15	☽	♀	♄	♆	♇	♃	1	18	3		Apr	20	10:53	13♉38	♄	♀	♆	♇	♃	☽
	Apr	18	16:51	9♉15	☽	♀	♆	♇	♃		1	20	31		Apr	20	13:22	15♉02	♀	♆	♇	♃	☽	
	Apr	28	18:01	8♉19	☉	♄	♆	♀	♇		8	17	42		May	7	11:43	15♉49	♄	♆	☉	♇	♀	
	Apr	29	19:00	6♉23	☿	☉	♄	♆	♀		7	16	43		May	7	11:43	15♉49	♄	♆	☉	☿	♀	

5 or More Planets Within 20° Arc 1700-2050

Year	Month	Day	Time	Starting Position	Planets in Zodiacal Sequence	Dy	Hr	Mn	Year	Month	Day	Time	Ending Position	Planets in Zodiacal Sequence
	Apr	30	17:15	8♉21	☿ ☉ ♄ ♆ ♀ ♇	6	18	28		May	7	11:43	15♉49	♄ ♆ ☉ ☿ ♇ ♀
	Apr	30	17:15	8♉21	☿ ☉ ♆ ♀ ♇	7	4	5		May	7	21:20	16♉18	♆ ☉ ☿ ♇ ♀
	Apr	30	17:15	8♉21	☿ ☉ ♄ ♆ ♇	13	7	25		May	14	0:40	16♉32	♆ ♄ ☉ ♇ ☿
	May	2	13:50	12♉21	☿ ♄ ♆ ♇ ♀ ♃	4	21	53		May	7	11:43	15♉49	♄ ♆ ☿ ♇ ♃ ♀
	May	2	13:50	12♉21	☿ ♆ ♇ ♀ ♃	5	7	30		May	7	21:20	16♉18	♆ ☿ ♇ ♃ ♀
	May	2	13:50	12♉21	☿ ♄ ♆ ♇ ♃	11	10	50		May	14	0:40	16♉32	♆ ♄ ♇ ♃ ☿
	May	3	0:20	12♉27	☉ ☿ ♄ ♆ ♇ ♀ ♃	4	11	23		May	7	11:43	15♉49	♄ ♆ ☉ ☿ ♇ ♃ ♀
	May	3	0:20	12♉27	☉ ☿ ♆ ♇ ♀ ♃	4	21	0		May	7	21:20	16♉18	♆ ☉ ☿ ♇ ♃ ♀
	May	3	0:20	12♉27	☉ ☿ ♇ ♀ ♃	8	5	49		May	11	6:09	20♉25	☉ ♇ ☿ ♃ ♀
	May	3	0:20	12♉27	☉ ☿ ♄ ♆ ♇ ♃	11	0	20		May	14	0:40	16♉32	♆ ♄ ☉ ♇ ♃ ☿
	May	3	0:20	12♉27	☉ ☿ ♄ ♇ ♃	11	1	53		May	14	2:13	16♉39	♄ ☉ ♇ ♃ ☿
	May	3	0:20	12♉27	☉ ♄ ♆ ♇ ♃	18	23	5		May	21	23:25	16♉49	♆ ♄ ♇ ☉ ♃
	May	16	1:14	8♉42	☽ ♆ ♄ ☉ ♇	2	0	41		May	18	1:55	16♉41	♆ ♄ ☉ ♇ ☽
	May	16	12:60	15♉34	☽ ♆ ♄ ☉ ♇ ♃	1	12	55		May	18	1:55	16♉41	♆ ♄ ☉ ♇ ♃ ☽
	May	16	12:60	15♉34	☽ ♄ ☉ ♇ ♃	1	13	47		May	18	2:47	17♉10	♄ ☉ ♇ ♃ ☽
	May	17	0:31	22♉13	☽ ☉ ♇ ♃ ☿	1	21	21		May	18	21:52	27♉48	☉ ♇ ♃ ☿ ☽
	May	17	10:32	27♉58	☽ ♇ ♃ ☿ ♀	0	15	23		May	18	1:55	28♉44	♇ ♃ ☽ ☿ ♀
	Dec	9	0:16	27♏25	☽ ☿ ♀ ☉ ♂	2	15	3		Dec	11	15:19	11♐36	♀ ☿ ♂ ☉ ☽
1883	Apr	29	23:18	9♉16	☉ ♆ ☿ ♄ ♇	7	9	22	1883	May	7	8:40	16♉25	☉ ♆ ♄ ♇ ☿
	May	6	11:26	9♉24	☽ ☉ ♆ ♄ ♇	1	21	13		May	8	8:38	17♉23	☉ ♆ ♄ ♇ ☽
	May	6	21:34	15♉45	☽ ☉ ♆ ♄ ♇ ☿	0	11	5		May	7	8:40	16♉25	☉ ♆ ☽ ♄ ♇ ☿
	May	6	21:34	15♉45	☽ ♆ ♄ ♇ ☿	1	12	52		May	8	10:26	18♉29	♆ ♄ ♇ ☿ ☽
	Jun	3	0:04	11♉13	☽ ♀ ♆ ♇ ♄	1	14	51		Jun	4	14:55	14♉57	♀ ♆ ♇ ♄ ☽
	Jun	4	5:19	29♉06	☽ ♇ ♄ ☉ ☿	1	10	40		Jun	5	15:59	0♊05	♇ ♄ ☉ ☿ ☽
	Jun	16	17:33	12♉57	♂ ♆ ♀ ♇ ♄	7	2	33		Jun	23	20:07	18♉06	♂ ♆ ♇ ♄ ♀
	Jun	30	13:13	14♉36	☽ ♆ ♂ ♇ ♄	1	19	19		Jul	2	8:33	20♉21	♆ ♂ ♇ ♄ ☽
	Jul	1	11:28	27♉50	☽ ♇ ♄ ♀ ☿	1	14	31		Jul	3	1:59	0♊38	♇ ♄ ♀ ☿ ☽
1884	Mar	29	20:58	15♉53	☽ ♆ ♀ ♇ ♄	1	14	24	1884	Mar	31	11:22	19♉20	♆ ♀ ♇ ♄ ☽
	Apr	26	11:35	18♉47	☽ ♆ ☿ ♇ ♄	1	10	11		Apr	27	21:47	20♉17	♆ ☿ ♇ ♄ ☽
	May	10	20:22	20♉31	☉ ♆ ♇ ☿ ♄	2	17	41		May	13	14:03	20♉52	♆ ☉ ☿ ♇ ♄
	May	23	12:53	12♉44	☽ ♆ ☿ ♇ ☉	1	21	5		May	25	9:58	21♉18	♆ ☿ ♇ ☉ ☽
	May	24	3:55	22♉13	☽ ☿ ♇ ☉ ♄	1	9	34		May	25	13:29	23♉32	☿ ♇ ☉ ♄ ☽
1885	Feb	14	3:13	5♒39	♀ ☿ ☽ ♂ ☉	0	23	38	1885	Feb	15	2:51	6♒52	♀ ☿ ♂ ☉ ☽
	Mar	15	4:20	6♓08	☽ ♀ ♂ ☉ ☿	2	4	2		Mar	17	8:22	14♓29	♀ ♂ ☉ ☿ ☽
	May	13	18:44	11♉26	☽ ♆ ☉ ♀ ♇	2	3	32		May	15	22:16	23♉06	♆ ☉ ♀ ♇ ☽
	Jun	10	6:03	12♉03	☽ ♂ ♆ ☿ ♇	2	4	6		Jun	12	10:09	24♉06	♆ ♂ ♇ ☿ ☽
1886	Jun	1	0:41	20♉25	☽ ♆ ☿ ♇ ☉	1	20	4	1886	Jun	2	20:45	25♉55	♆ ☿ ♇ ☉ ☽
	Sep	27	3:39	23♍37	☽ ☿ ☉ ♅ ♃	2	4	19		Sep	29	7:58	6♎05	☉ ☿ ♅ ♃ ☽
	Sep	27	20:28	17♍53	♀ ☽ ☿ ☉ ♅	0	6	33		Sep	28	3:01	18♍14	♀ ☿ ☉ ♅ ☽
	Oct	3	13:58	25♍00	♀ ♅ ☉ ☿ ♃	1	8	42		Oct	4	22:40	26♍42	♀ ♅ ☉ ♃ ☿
1887	Feb	22	20:25	3♓22	☽ ☉ ☿ ♂ ♀	1	21	39	1887	Feb	24	18:04	5♓51	☉ ♂ ☿ ♀ ☽
	May	16	21:35	13♉21	☿ ♂ ☉ ♆ ♇	16	5	43		Jun	2	3:18	28♉03	♆ ♂ ♇ ☉ ☿
	May	21	5:22	9♉49	☽ ☿ ♂ ♆ ☉	2	20	20		May	24	1:42	25♉39	♂ ♆ ☿ ☉ ☽
	May	21	12:28	13♉27	☽ ☿ ♂ ♆ ☉ ♇	2	13	14		May	24	1:42	25♉39	♂ ♆ ☿ ☉ ♇ ☽
	May	21	12:28	13♉27	☽ ☿ ♆ ☉ ♇	2	17	6		May	24	5:34	27♉43	♆ ☿ ☉ ♇ ☽
	Sep	17	9:48	21♍41	☽ ☉ ☿ ♀ ♅	1	13	56		Sep	18	23:44	25♍43	☉ ♀ ☿ ♅ ☽
1888	May	10	12:03	14♉09	☽ ☿ ☉ ♆ ♇	2	9	10	1888	May	12	21:13	22♉31	☉ ☿ ♆ ♇ ☽
	Jun	7	21:07	27♉28	☽ ♆ ♇ ♀ ☉	1	22	5		Jun	9	19:11	0♊31	♆ ♇ ♀ ☉ ☽
	Jul	9	14:19	17♋07	♀ ☿ ☉ ☽ ♄	0	0	51		Jul	9	15:10	17♋07	☿ ♀ ☉ ☽ ♄
1889	Apr	29	11:54	2♉39	☽ ☉ ♀ ☿ ♂	2	6	55	1889	May	1	18:49	10♉26	♀ ☉ ☿ ♂ ☽
	Apr	30	4:34	11♉10	☽ ♀ ☿ ♂ ♆	0	9	42		Apr	30	14:16	11♉11	♀ ☽ ☿ ♂ ♆
	Apr	30	11:51	14♉52	☽ ☿ ♂ ♆ ♇	2	4	23		May	2	16:14	21♉04	☿ ♂ ♆ ♇ ☽
	May	1	10:30	11♉13	☉ ☿ ♂ ☽ ♆	0	10	45		May	1	21:15	11♉39	☉ ☿ ♂ ♆ ☽
	May	5	7:29	14♉58	☉ ☿ ♂ ♆ ♇	10	2	49		May	15	10:18	24♉44	☉ ♆ ♂ ♇ ☿
	May	28	9:58	22♉53	☽ ♆ ♇ ☉ ♂	2	11	26		May	30	21:25	2♊18	♆ ♇ ☉ ♂ ☽
1890	Apr	22	0:59	15♉38	☿ ♀ ♆ ☽ ♇	0	2	24	1890	Apr	22	3:23	15♉49	☿ ♀ ♆ ♇ ☽
	May	18	11:09	22♉55	☽ ☉ ♆ ♇ ☿	2	2	42		May	20	13:51	29♉27	☉ ♆ ♇ ☿ ☽
	May	19	1:36	0♊35	☽ ♆ ♇ ☿ ♀	1	21	18		May	20	22:54	4♊05	♆ ♇ ☿ ♀ ☽
	Jun	15	15:38	4♊25	☽ ☿ ♆ ♇ ☉	0	15	55		Jun	16	7:32	5♊03	♆ ☿ ♇ ☽ ☉
1891	May	8	5:29	16♉54	☽ ☉ ☿ ♆ ♇	1	13	51	1891	May	9	19:20	18♉51	☉ ☿ ♆ ♇ ☽
	Sep	3	8:55	29♌10	♂ ♀ ☉ ☽ ♄	0	17	46		Sep	4	2:42	29♌39	♂ ♀ ☉ ♄ ☽
	Sep	4	7:24	7♍34	♀ ☉ ♄ ☽ ☿	0	12	40		Sep	4	20:04	8♍13	♀ ☉ ♄ ☿ ☽
	Sep	9	23:39	3♍23	♂ ♀ ☉ ♄ ☿	14	8	26		Sep	24	8:05	12♍29	♂ ☿ ♄ ☉ ♀
	Oct	31	23:31	29♎30	☽ ♅ ☉ ☿ ♀	1	21	4		Nov	2	20:35	2♏17	♅ ☉ ☿ ♀ ☽
1893	May	15	15:03	20♉23	☽ ☉ ♀ ♇ ♆	1	17	25	1893	May	17	8:28	26♉37	☉ ♀ ♇ ♆ ☽
	May	24	20:34	20♉43	☿ ☉ ♇ ♀ ♆	16	1	16		Jun	9	21:50	9♊32	♇ ♆ ☉ ☿ ♀
1894	May	17	11:12	22♉36	☿ ☉ ♃ ♇ ♆	18	0	39	1894	Jun	4	11:51	10♊22	♇ ♆ ☉ ♃ ☿
	Jun	2	14:44	23♉26	☽ ♇ ☉ ♆ ♃	2	11	26		Jun	5	2:10	10♊22	♇ ♆ ♃ ☉ ☽
	Jun	3	15:45	8♊48	☽ ♇ ☉ ♆ ♃ ☿	0	20	6		Jun	4	11:51	10♊22	♇ ♆ ☉ ♃ ☽ ☿
	Jun	3	15:45	8♊48	☽ ☉ ♆ ♃ ☿	1	15	5		Jun	5	6:50	13♊18	♆ ♃ ☉ ☿ ☽
	Jun	30	11:34	29♉50	☽ ♀ ♇ ♆ ♃	1	12	55		Jul	2	0:28	2♊39	♀ ♇ ♆ ♃ ☽
	Oct	27	23:31	24♎58	☽ ♀ ♄ ☉ ♅	1	18	4		Oct	29	17:35	28♎22	♀ ♄ ☉ ♅ ☽
	Nov	9	8:10	0♏18	♄ ♀ ♅ ☉ ☿	3	18	42		Nov	13	2:52	0♏45	♄ ☿ ♅ ♀ ☉

5 or More Planets Within 20° Arc 1700-2050

	Starting Position				Planets in Zodiacal Sequence	Dy	Hr	Mn		Ending Position				Planets in Zodiacal Sequence
	Nov	25	16:23	13♏26	☽ ☿ ♅ ♀ ☉	1	6	46		Nov	26	23:09	14♏44	☿ ♅ ☽ ♀ ☉
1895	Mar	31	9:15	8♊40	☽ ♇ ♆ ♂ ♃	1	13	58	1895	Apr	1	23:13	10♊03	♇ ♆ ♂ ♃ ☽
	May	24	12:36	2♊58	☽ ☉ ♇ ♆ ☿	0	3	21		May	24	15:57	3♊11	☉ ☽ ♇ ♆ ☿
	Oct	17	23:00	20♎12	☽ ♂ ☉ ♄ ☿	1	13	38		Oct	19	12:38	23♎13	♂ ☉ ♄ ☿ ☽
	Nov	11	19:19	0♏10	☿ ♂ ♄ ☉ ♅	13	8	45		Nov	25	4:04	12♏40	♄ ♂ ☿ ♅ ☉
	Nov	15	1:28	0♏23	☽ ☿ ♂ ♄ ♅	1	19	48		Nov	16	21:15	6♏32	☿ ♄ ♂ ♅ ☽
	Nov	15	5:10	2♏37	☽ ☿ ♂ ♄ ♅ ☉	1	16	5		Nov	16	21:15	6♏32	☿ ♄ ♂ ♅ ☉ ☽
	Nov	15	5:10	2♏37	☽ ♂ ♄ ♅ ☉	2	0	59		Nov	17	6:09	11♏45	♄ ♂ ♅ ☉ ☽
1896	Jun	3	13:15	3♊33	♀ ♇ ☉ ♆ ☿	20	5	41	1896	Jun	23	18:56	12♊43	♇ ☿ ♆ ♀ ☉
	Jun	9	15:55	29♉14	☽ ♀ ♇ ♆ ☉	2	14	10		Jun	12	6:05	12♊28	♇ ♀ ♆ ☉ ☽
	Jun	9	18:27	0♊33	☽ ♀ ♇ ♆ ☉ ☿	2	11	39		Jun	12	6:05	12♊28	♇ ♀ ♆ ☿ ☉ ☽
	Jun	9	18:27	0♊33	☽ ♀ ♆ ☉ ☿	2	15	11		Jun	12	9:38	14♊24	♀ ♆ ☿ ☉ ☽
	Aug	8	7:39	4♌26	☽ ☉ ♃ ☿ ♀	2	8	56		Aug	10	16:35	18♌29	☉ ♃ ♀ ☿ ☽
1897	Nov	5	0:25	10♏56	☿ ☉ ♂ ♅ ♄	24	19	37	1897	Nov	29	20:02	29♏51	♅ ♄ ♂ ☉ ☿
	Nov	23	2:55	13♏03	☽ ♅ ♂ ☉ ♄	2	9	21		Nov	25	12:16	29♏35	♅ ♂ ♄ ☉ ☽
	Nov	23	14:16	20♏15	☽ ♅ ♂ ☉ ♄ ☿	1	22	1		Nov	25	12:16	29♏35	♅ ♂ ♄ ☉ ☿ ☽
	Nov	23	14:16	20♏15	☽ ♂ ☉ ♄ ☿	2	2	38		Nov	25	16:53	2♐30	♂ ♄ ☉ ☿ ☽
	Nov	25	2:16	13♏17	♀ ♅ ♂ ☉ ♄	17	5	15		Dec	12	7:31	0♐36	♅ ♀ ♄ ♂ ☉
1898	Jun	17	8:14	6♊06	☽ ☿ ♇ ♆ ☉	2	9	42	1898	Jun	19	17:55	14♊33	♇ ☿ ♆ ☉ ☽
	Nov	14	9:11	27♏01	☽ ♅ ☿ ♄ ♀	1	18	55		Nov	16	4:06	3♐12	♅ ☿ ♄ ♀ ☽
	Nov	14	11:11	22♏08	☉ ☽ ♅ ☿ ♄	1	0	30		Nov	15	11:41	23♏10	☉ ♅ ☿ ♄ ☽
	Nov	18	10:50	26♏10	☉ ♅ ♄ ☿ ♀	7	22	57		Nov	26	9:47	3♐50	♅ ☉ ♀ ♄ ☿
	Dec	12	1:00	0♐04	☽ ♀ ♅ ♄ ☉	1	13	45		Dec	13	14:45	3♐26	♀ ♅ ♄ ☉ ☽
1899	Jan	8	20:15	5♐07	☽ ♅ ♀ ♄ ☿	1	10	43	1899	Jan	10	6:58	6♐25	♅ ♀ ♄ ☿ ☽
	Jun	7	5:23	4♊10	☽ ☿ ♇ ☉ ♆	2	5	19		Jun	9	10:42	11♊46	☿ ♇ ☉ ♆ ☽
	Oct	28	21:30	16♏20	♀ ♃ ☿ ♂ ♅	13	9	23		Nov	11	6:54	20♏19	♃ ♀ ♂ ♅ ☿
	Nov	1	1:31	8♏26	☉ ♃ ♀ ☿ ♂	4	17	0		Nov	5	18:31	13♏09	☉ ♃ ♀ ♂ ☿
	Nov	3	8:39	9♏50	☽ ☉ ♃ ♀ ☿	1	17	20		Nov	5	1:59	12♏27	☉ ♃ ♀ ☿ ☽
	Nov	3	9:07	10♏05	☽ ☉ ♃ ♀ ☿ ♂	1	16	52		Nov	5	1:59	12♏27	☉ ♃ ♀ ♂ ☿ ☽
	Nov	3	9:07	10♏05	☽ ♃ ♀ ☿ ♂	2	4	42		Nov	5	13:50	19♏03	♃ ♀ ♂ ☿ ☽
	Nov	3	21:16	16♏40	☽ ♃ ♀ ♂ ☿ ♅	1	16	34		Nov	5	13:50	19♏03	♃ ♀ ♂ ☿ ♅ ☽
	Nov	3	21:16	16♏40	☽ ♀ ♂ ☿ ♅	2	6	6		Nov	6	3:22	26♏39	♀ ♂ ☿ ♅ ☽
	Nov	4	23:49	1♐15	☽ ♂ ☿ ♅ ♄	1	13	44		Nov	6	13:32	2♐23	♂ ☿ ♅ ♄ ☽
	Nov	9	14:35	17♏00	☉ ♃ ♀ ♂ ♅	8	17	3		Nov	18	7:37	21♏52	♃ ☉ ♅ ♂ ♀
	Nov	10	6:09	1♐47	♀ ♂ ♅ ☿ ♄	21	5	34		Dec	1	11:43	8♐20	♅ ☿ ♂ ♄ ♀
	Nov	24	6:23	1♐47	☉ ♅ ♂ ♀ ☿	7	5	20		Dec	1	11:43	8♐20	♅ ☉ ☿ ♂ ♀
	Nov	25	23:10	3♐30	☉ ♅ ♂ ♀ ☿ ♄	5	12	33		Dec	1	11:43	8♐20	♅ ☉ ☿ ♂ ♄ ♀
	Nov	25	23:10	3♐30	☉ ♂ ♀ ☿ ♄	8	20	5		Dec	4	19:15	12♐28	☉ ☿ ♂ ♄ ♀
	Nov	25	23:10	3♐30	☉ ♅ ♂ ☿ ♄	15	4	32		Dec	11	3:42	7♐58	☿ ♅ ☉ ♄ ♂
	Dec	2	8:22	1♐21	☽ ♅ ☉ ☿ ♂	1	23	17		Dec	4	7:39	8♐30	♅ ☉ ☿ ♂ ☽
	Dec	2	13:31	4♐16	☽ ♅ ☉ ☿ ♂ ♄	1	18	8		Dec	4	7:39	8♐30	♅ ☉ ☿ ♂ ♄ ☽
	Dec	2	13:31	4♐16	☽ ☉ ☿ ♂ ♄	2	0	32		Dec	4	14:03	12♐15	☉ ☿ ♂ ♄ ☽
	Dec	2	23:60	10♐13	☽ ☉ ☿ ♂ ♄ ♀	1	14	3		Dec	4	14:03	12♐15	☉ ☿ ♂ ♄ ♀ ☽
	Dec	2	23:60	10♐13	☽ ☿ ♂ ♄ ♀	1	20	8		Dec	4	20:08	15♐49	☿ ♂ ♄ ♀ ☽
1900	May	29	4:37	5♊58	☿ ☉ ☽ ♇ ♆	1	0	1	1900	May	30	4:38	8♊10	☿ ☉ ♇ ♆ ☽
	Dec	20	7:15	7♐59	☽ ☿ ♅ ♃ ☉	1	23	7		Dec	22	6:23	13♐11	☿ ♅ ♃ ☉ ☽
1901	May	18	8:23	26♉41	☉ ☽ ☿ ♀ ♇	1	7	46	1901	May	19	16:09	27♉58	☉ ♀ ☿ ♇ ☽
	May	30	6:59	8♊09	☉ ♀ ♇ ☿ ♆	3	17	45		Jun	3	0:44	11♊44	☉ ♇ ♀ ♆ ☿
	Jun	16	0:02	16♊28	☽ ♇ ☉ ♆ ♀	0	17	34		Jun	16	17:36	17♊21	♇ ☉ ☽ ♆ ♀
	Nov	14	10:44	22♐39	♂ ☽ ♀ ♃ ♄	1	12	49		Nov	15	23:32	23♐48	♂ ♀ ♃ ♄ ☽
1902	Jan	1	8:55	9♑31	☿ ☉ ♄ ♃ ♂	12	7	28	1902	Jan	13	16:23	19♑12	♄ ☉ ♃ ☿ ♂
	Jan	8	15:01	3♑10	☽ ☉ ♄ ☿ ♃	2	20	38		Jan	11	11:39	18♑56	♄ ☉ ♃ ☿ ☽
	Jan	9	16:05	16♑02	☽ ☉ ♄ ☿ ♃ ♂	1	19	35		Jan	11	11:39	18♑56	♄ ☉ ♃ ☿ ♂ ☽
	Jan	9	16:05	16♑02	☽ ☉ ☿ ♃ ♂	1	22	26		Jan	11	14:31	20♑28	☉ ♃ ☿ ♂ ☽
	Feb	8	6:42	15♒14	☽ ☉ ♀ ♂ ☿	1	21	32		Feb	10	4:14	20♒31	☉ ♀ ♂ ☿ ☽
	Jun	7	6:11	15♊33	☉ ♇ ☽ ♆ ☿	0	9	40		Jun	7	15:50	15♊56	☉ ♇ ♆ ☿ ☽
	Jun	23	17:03	11♊27	♂ ♇ ♆ ☉ ☿	0	18	4		Jun	24	11:08	11♊59	♂ ♇ ☿ ♆ ☉
	Jul	3	11:49	11♊33	☽ ♂ ♇ ☿ ♆	1	19	9		Jul	5	6:58	18♊45	♇ ♂ ☿ ♆ ☽
	Jul	10	9:09	11♊48	♀ ♇ ♂ ☿ ♆	11	15	22		Jul	22	0:31	19♊05	♇ ♀ ♂ ♆ ☿
	Jul	31	5:25	17♊01	☽ ♇ ♆ ♀ ♂	1	12	9		Aug	1	17:34	19♊16	♇ ♆ ♂ ♀ ☽
	Nov	30	11:12	0♐38	☿ ☉ ♀ ☽ ♅	0	21	14		Dec	1	8:26	2♐02	☿ ☉ ♀ ♅ ☽
	Dec	30	4:51	7♑34	☉ ☽ ♀ ☿ ♄	1	12	44		Dec	31	17:35	9♑08	☉ ♀ ☿ ♄ ☽
1903	Jan	28	10:30	4♒31	☽ ☉ ☿ ♀ ♃	2	1	19	1903	Jan	30	11:49	9♒26	☉ ☿ ♀ ♃ ☽
1904	May	14	3:41	7♉10	☽ ♀ ☿ ☉ ♂	1	18	7	1904	May	15	21:47	10♉09	♀ ☿ ☉ ♂ ☽
	Jun	12	7:41	0♊53	☽ ♀ ♂ ♇ ☉	2	14	12		Jun	14	21:53	16♊56	♀ ♂ ♇ ☉ ☽
	Jun	13	8:40	15♊07	☽ ♂ ♇ ☉ ♆	1	17	27		Jun	15	2:07	19♊27	♂ ♇ ☉ ♆ ☽
	Jun	13	10:26	15♊07	♀ ☽ ♂ ♇ ☉ ♆	1	11	27		Jun	14	21:53	16♊56	♀ ♂ ♇ ☉ ♆ ☽
	Jun	13	10:26	15♊07	♀ ♂ ♇ ☉ ♆	19	15	17		Jul	3	1:43	20♊41	♇ ♂ ♆ ♀ ☉
	Jun	20	6:13	8♊28	☿ ♇ ♂ ♀ ☉	12	19	31		Jul	3	1:43	20♊41	♇ ♂ ☿ ♀ ☉
	Jun	24	11:21	15♊32	☿ ♇ ♂ ♀ ☉ ♆	8	14	22		Jul	3	1:43	20♊41	♇ ♂ ☿ ♆ ♀ ☉
	Jun	24	11:21	15♊32	☿ ♇ ♂ ♀ ♆	9	19	18		Jul	4	6:39	20♊42	♇ ♂ ☿ ♆ ♀
	Jun	24	11:21	15♊32	☿ ♂ ♀ ☉ ♆	19	17	37		Jul	14	4:59	6♋15	♆ ♂ ☉ ♀ ☿
	Jul	11	19:39	29♊59	☽ ♆ ♂ ☉ ♀	1	19	23		Jul	13	15:02	6♋14	♆ ♂ ☉ ♀ ☽

5 or More Planets Within 20° Arc 1700-2050

				Starting Position	Planets in Zodiacal Sequence	Dy	Hr	Mn					Ending Position	Planets in Zodiacal Sequence
	Jul	11	22:05	1♋26	☽ ♆ ♂ ☉ ♀ ☿	1	16	57		Jul	13	15:02	6♋14	♆ ♂ ☉ ♀ ☿ ☽
	Jul	11	22:05	1♋26	☽ ♂ ☉ ♀ ☿	1	21	10		Jul	13	19:15	8♋49	♂ ☉ ♀ ☿ ☽
1905	May	2	22:20	22♈47	☽ ☿ ♀ ☉ ♃	2	1	15	1905	May	4	23:36	27♈24	☿ ♀ ♃ ☉ ☽
	Dec	24	20:08	14♐15	☽ ☿ ♀ ☉ ♅	1	9	59		Dec	26	6:08	14♐59	☿ ♀ ☉ ♅ ☽
1906	Feb	21	21:25	15♒04	☽ ☉ ☿ ♀ ♄	3	3	32	1906	Feb	25	0:57	5♓27	♄ ☉ ♀ ☿ ☽
	May	23	18:19	6♊22	☽ ♃ ♂ ♇ ♀	2	10	4		May	26	4:23	15♊15	♃ ♂ ♇ ♀ ☽
	May	23	19:36	1♊44	☉ ☽ ♃ ♂ ♇	1	8	19		May	25	3:54	3♊01	☉ ♃ ♂ ♇ ☽
	May	26	2:38	18♊47	♂ ♇ ♀ ☽ ♆	0	9	20		May	26	11:58	19♊03	♂ ♇ ♀ ♆ ☽
	Jun	2	20:38	4♊00	☿ ☉ ♃ ♇ ♂	17	7	37		Jun	20	4:15	21♊01	♃ ♇ ☉ ♂ ☿
	Jun	11	4:22	19♊19	☉ ♇ ☿ ♂ ♆	9	16	44		Jun	20	21:06	22♊23	♇ ☉ ♂ ♆ ☿
	Jun	13	4:09	19♊24	♃ ☉ ♇ ☿ ♂ ♆	7	0	6		Jun	20	4:15	21♊01	♃ ♇ ☉ ♂ ♆ ☿
	Jun	13	4:09	19♊24	♃ ☉ ♇ ♂ ♆	17	17	8		Jun	30	21:17	22♊37	♇ ♃ ☉ ♆ ♂
	Jun	20	19:49	15♊59	☽ ♃ ♇ ☉ ♂	2	3	8		Jun	22	22:56	21♊39	♃ ♇ ☉ ♂ ☽
	Jun	21	3:14	19♊41	☽ ♃ ♇ ☉ ♂ ♆	1	19	42		Jun	22	22:56	21♊39	♃ ♇ ☉ ♂ ♆ ☽
	Jun	21	3:14	19♊41	☽ ♇ ☉ ♂ ♆	1	21	15		Jun	23	0:29	22♊26	♇ ☉ ♂ ♆ ☽
	Jun	21	10:52	23♊29	☽ ☉ ♂ ♆ ☿	2	7	5		Jun	23	17:56	1♋19	☉ ♂ ♆ ☿ ☽
1907	Jul	22	8:39	12♋59	♆ ♀ ♃ ☉ ☿	4	23	56	1907	Jul	27	8:36	13♋09	♆ ♀ ♃ ☿ ☉
	Aug	6	10:59	12♋03	☽ ♆ ☿ ♃ ♀	1	5	17		Aug	7	16:16	13♋33	♆ ☽ ☿ ♃ ♀
	Aug	7	10:50	23♋46	☽ ☿ ♃ ♀ ☉	2	0	6		Aug	9	10:55	27♋41	☿ ♃ ♀ ☉ ☽
1908	May	31	7:41	23♊17	☽ ♇ ☿ ♂ ♆	1	16	18	1908	Jun	1	23:59	23♊58	♇ ☿ ♂ ♆ ☽
	May	31	17:38	28♊27	☽ ☿ ♂ ♆ ♀	2	4	26		Jun	2	22:04	5♋04	☿ ♂ ♆ ♀ ☽
	Jun	22	12:00	0♋37	☉ ♆ ☿ ♂ ♀	16	3	16		Jul	8	15:16	10♋18	☿ ♀ ♆ ☉ ♂
	Jun	28	0:32	28♊22	☽ ☉ ♆ ☿ ♀	2	11	10		Jun	30	11:43	8♋15	☉ ♆ ☿ ♀ ☽
	Jun	28	11:10	3♋48	☽ ☉ ♆ ☿ ♀ ♂	2	0	33		Jun	30	11:43	8♋15	☉ ♆ ☿ ♀ ♂ ☽
	Jun	28	11:10	3♋48	☽ ♆ ☿ ♀ ♂	2	12	52		Jul	1	0:02	14♋22	♆ ☿ ♀ ♂ ☽
	Jul	4	9:35	24♊44	♇ ☉ ☿ ♆ ♀	2	23	1		Jul	7	8:36	24♊48	♇ ☿ ♀ ♆ ☉
	Aug	25	13:32	16♌46	☽ ♃ ♂ ☉ ☿	2	12	35		Aug	28	2:07	26♌42	♃ ♂ ☉ ☿ ☽
1909	Apr	18	18:43	8♈05	☽ ♄ ☿ ♀ ☉	1	19	24	1909	Apr	20	14:06	15♈12	♄ ♀ ☿ ☉ ☽
	Jun	17	10:46	18♊54	☽ ☿ ♇ ☉ ♀	1	15	34		Jun	19	2:20	21♊00	☿ ♇ ☉ ♀ ☽
1910	Oct	1	14:28	17♍32	☽ ♀ ☿ ♂ ☉	2	7	48	1910	Oct	3	22:16	26♍13	♀ ☿ ♂ ☉ ☽
	Oct	15	15:06	4♎09	☿ ♀ ♂ ☉ ♃	28	14	8		Nov	13	5:14	0♏19	♃ ♂ ♀ ☉ ☿
	Oct	30	15:26	9♎37	☽ ♂ ♃ ☿ ♀	3	4	12		Nov	2	19:38	27♎29	♂ ♃ ☿ ♀ ☽
	Oct	31	6:00	16♎56	☽ ♂ ♃ ☿ ♀ ☉	2	13	37		Nov	2	19:38	27♎29	♂ ♃ ☿ ♀ ☉ ☽
	Oct	31	6:00	16♎56	☽ ♃ ☿ ♀ ☉	2	14	53		Nov	2	20:53	28♎06	♃ ☿ ♀ ☉ ☽
	Dec	31	10:45	6♑18	☽ ☉ ♀ ♅ ☿	2	0	7	1911	Jan	2	10:51	10♑57	☉ ♀ ♅ ☿ ☽
1912	Jun	14	5:22	8♊21	☽ ♀ ☿ ☉ ♇	2	1	54	1912	Jun	16	7:16	19♊19	♀ ☿ ☉ ♇ ☽
	Dec	7	18:18	4♐03	☽ ♂ ☉ ☿ ♃	1	18	20		Dec	9	12:38	6♐35	♂ ☿ ☉ ♃ ☽
1914	Jan	14	13:43	16♑47	☿ ♀ ☉ ♃ ♅	21	13	12	1914	Feb	5	2:55	3♒25	♃ ♅ ♀ ☉ ☿
	Jan	24	14:03	13♑46	☽ ♀ ♃ ☿ ☉	2	23	2		Jan	27	13:06	1♒24	♃ ♀ ☉ ☿ ☽
	Jan	24	20:42	17♑23	☽ ♀ ♃ ☿ ☉ ♅	2	16	24		Jan	27	13:06	1♒24	♃ ♀ ☉ ♅ ☿ ☽
	Jan	24	20:42	17♑23	☽ ♀ ☿ ☉ ♅	2	20	3		Jan	27	16:45	3♒17	♀ ☉ ♅ ☿ ☽
	May	25	16:04	9♊58	☽ ☿ ♄ ♀ ♇	2	5	33		May	27	21:38	18♊02	☿ ♄ ♇ ♀ ☽
1915	Apr	10	23:36	10♓18	☽ ♀ ♃ ♂ ☿	1	9	4	1915	Apr	12	8:40	12♓36	♀ ♃ ♂ ☽ ☿
	Jun	12	15:56	19♊13	☽ ☉ ♇ ♄ ☿	1	22	34		Jun	14	14:30	22♊27	☉ ♇ ♄ ☿ ☽
	Jun	30	16:55	17♊48	♀ ♇ ☿ ♄ ☉	15	3	17		Jul	15	20:12	2♋14	♇ ☿ ♀ ♄ ☉
	Jul	9	18:34	17♊21	☽ ♀ ☿ ♇ ♄	2	18	52		Jul	12	13:25	0♋56	☿ ♇ ♀ ♄ ☽
	Jul	10	14:25	27♊14	☽ ♀ ☿ ♇ ♄ ☉	1	23	0		Jul	12	13:25	0♋56	☿ ♇ ♀ ♄ ☉ ☽
	Jul	10	14:25	27♊14	☽ ♀ ♇ ♄ ☉	2	1	24		Jul	12	15:49	2♋10	♇ ♀ ♄ ☉ ☽
	Aug	9	5:32	25♋33	☽ ♆ ♀ ☿ ☉	2	0	9		Aug	11	5:41	0♌50	♆ ♀ ☿ ☉ ☽
1916	Jun	29	14:40	28♊24	☽ ♇ ☉ ♀ ♄	2	2	0	1916	Jul	1	16:40	2♋59	♇ ☉ ♀ ♄ ☽
	Jul	10	15:42	29♊50	☿ ♇ ♀ ☉ ♄	5	13	57		Jul	16	5:40	3♋20	♇ ♀ ☿ ♄ ☉
	Jul	28	6:01	14♋48	☽ ♄ ♆ ☿ ☉	2	8	1		Jul	30	14:02	22♋24	♄ ♆ ☉ ☿ ☽
1917	Feb	20	11:23	13♒05	☽ ♀ ♅ ☉ ♂	1	13	38	1917	Feb	22	1:01	16♒54	♀ ♅ ☉ ♂ ☽
	Mar	21	17:29	10♓32	☽ ♀ ☿ ♂ ☉	2	6	40		Mar	24	0:09	24♓13	♀ ☿ ♂ ☉ ☽
	May	19	10:22	7♉51	☽ ♂ ♃ ☿ ☉	1	19	24		May	21	5:46	12♉08	♂ ♃ ☿ ☉ ☽
	May	19	22:13	14♉34	☽ ♃ ☿ ☉ ♀	2	0	12		May	21	22:24	21♉12	♃ ☿ ☉ ♀ ☽
	Jul	18	3:55	14♋14	☽ ☉ ☿ ♄ ♆	2	18	48		Jul	20	22:43	27♋36	☉ ♄ ♆ ☿ ☽
	Jul	19	8:25	28♋34	☽ ♄ ☿ ♆ ♀	2	2	0		Jul	21	10:24	3♌22	♄ ♆ ☿ ♀ ☽
1919	Jun	27	16:31	2♋28	☽ ☉ ♇ ♃ ☿	1	15	22	1919	Jun	29	7:53	6♋10	♇ ☉ ♃ ☿ ☽
	Aug	23	2:36	26♋54	☽ ♂ ♃ ♆ ☿	1	18	27		Aug	24	21:03	1♌02	♂ ♃ ♆ ☿ ☽
1920	Jul	15	16:34	20♋34	☽ ☉ ♀ ☿ ♆	1	13	58	1920	Jul	17	6:32	24♋21	☉ ♀ ☿ ♆ ☽
	Jul	26	11:24	3♌08	☉ ☿ ♀ ♆ ♃	1	11	56		Jul	27	23:20	3♌27	☿ ☉ ♆ ♀ ♃
	Aug	15	5:34	22♌04	☉ ♃ ♀ ☽ ♄	0	9	41		Aug	15	15:15	22♌27	☉ ♃ ♀ ♄ ☽
	Sep	11	3:51	29♌58	☽ ♃ ♄ ☉ ☿	1	16	10		Sep	12	20:01	3♍35	♃ ♄ ☉ ☿ ☽
1921	Jul	4	13:17	27♊45	☽ ♇ ♂ ☉ ☿	2	1	0	1921	Jul	6	14:18	8♋34	♇ ♂ ☉ ☿ ☽
	Sep	1	21:57	5♍35	☽ ☉ ☿ ♃ ♄	1	15	58		Sep	3	13:54	10♍30	☉ ☿ ♃ ♄ ☽
	Oct	27	13:29	18♍27	☽ ♂ ♄ ♃ ♀	1	20	24		Oct	29	9:53	24♍55	♂ ♄ ♃ ♀ ☽
1922	Oct	19	9:04	8♎23	☽ ♄ ☿ ☉ ♃	1	14	37	1922	Oct	20	23:42	12♎40	♄ ☿ ☉ ♃ ☽
1923	Jul	12	8:37	28♊58	☽ ♀ ☿ ♇ ☉	2	0	24	1923	Jul	14	9:02	5♋06	♀ ♇ ☿ ☉ ☽
	Jul	13	1:42	8♋05	☽ ☿ ♇ ☉ ♂	1	18	0		Jul	14	19:42	11♋00	♇ ☿ ☉ ♂ ☽
	Aug	10	22:32	27♋53	☽ ♀ ♂ ☉ ♆	2	11	35		Aug	13	10:07	11♌59	♀ ♆ ♂ ☉ ☽
	Nov	8	7:30	10♏07	☽ ☿ ☉ ♃ ♀	1	11	12		Nov	9	18:42	12♏35	☿ ☉ ♃ ♀ ☽
1924	Jun	30	16:58	21♊48	☽ ☿ ☉ ♀ ♇	3	0	15	1924	Jul	3	17:13	7♋59	♀ ☿ ☉ ♇ ☽

5 or More Planets Within 20° Arc 1700-2050

Year	Mo	Day	Time	Starting Position	Planets in Zodiacal Sequence						Dy	Hr	Mn	Year	Mo	Day	Time	Ending Position	Planets in Zodiacal Sequence					
1925	Jun	20	20:21	24♊24	☽	☉	☿	♇	♀		2	6	1	1925	Jun	23	2:22	1♋06	☉	☿	♇	♀	☽	
	Jul	21	11:02	4♌10	☽	♂	♆	♀	☿		2	19	27		Jul	24	6:29	17♌36	♂	♆	♀	☿	☽	
	Aug	18	19:16	17♌04	☽	♆	☉	♂	☿		2	2	44		Aug	20	22:01	22♌31	♆	☉	♂	☿	☽	
1926	Feb	11	7:32	1♒50	☽	♃	♀	☿	☉		1	18	46	1926	Feb	13	2:18	8♒57	♃	♀	☿	☉	☽	
	Sep	5	9:34	22♌04	☽	♀	♆	☿	☉		1	21	42		Sep	7	7:16	24♌36	♀	♆	☿	☉	☽	
	Dec	3	20:16	23♏56	☽	☿	♄	☉	♀		1	0	25		Dec	4	20:41	25♏13	☿	♄	☽	☉	♀	
1927	Feb	3	11:42	13♒39	☉	☿	☽	♀	♃		0	7	49	1927	Feb	3	19:31	13♒59	☉	☿	♀	♃	☽	
	Mar	3	13:24	8♓24	☽	♃	☉	☿	♅		1	11	4		Mar	5	0:27	10♓43	♃	☉	☿	♅	☽	
	Dec	22	9:55	9♐34	☽	♂	♄	☿	☉		1	4	52		Dec	23	14:47	10♐47	♂	♄	☿	☽	☉	
1928	Apr	18	4:35	29♓20	☽	♅	♀	☿	♃		1	16	52	1928	Apr	19	21:28	4♈51	♅	♀	☿	♃	☽	
	Apr	18	19:24	8♈30	☽	♀	☿	♃	☉		1	11	18		Apr	20	6:43	10♈42	♀	☿	♃	☉	☽	
	Aug	14	23:14	14♌06	☽	☿	☉	♆	♀		2	5	3		Aug	17	4:17	24♌00	☉	☿	♆	♀	☽	
1929	Nov	29	12:45	17♏55	☽	♀	☉	♂	☿		2	0	27	1929	Dec	1	13:12	22♏47	♀	☉	♂	☿	☽	
	Dec	2	23:12	10♐19	☉	♂	☿	☽	♄		0	0	56		Dec	3	0:08	10♐21	☉	♂	☿	♄	☽	
	Dec	29	3:50	16♐58	☽	♀	♂	♄	☉		2	20	38	1930	Jan	1	0:28	1♑05	♀	♂	♄	☉	☽	
1930	Jan	27	22:53	17♑18	☽	♂	☿	♀	☉		2	4	16		Jan	30	3:09	23♑09	☿	♂	♀	☉	☽	
	Mar	29	14:19	0♈41	☽	☿	☉	♅	♀		2	6	32		Mar	31	20:51	9♈42	☿	☉	♅	♀	☽	
1931	Jul	15	5:56	18♋15	☽	♇	☉	♃	☿		1	6	12	1931	Jul	16	12:08	20♋30	♇	☉	♃	☽	☿	
	Sep	10	19:35	27♌50	☽	♆	☿	☉	♀		1	20	51		Sep	12	16:26	6♍02	♆	☿	☉	♀	☽	
1932	Feb	4	22:29	24♑55	☽	♄	☿	♂	☉		1	19	2	1932	Feb	6	17:31	28♑05	♄	☿	♂	☉	☽	
	Aug	30	8:37	17♌41	☽	☿	♃	☉	♆		1	15	37		Sep	1	0:14	20♌43	☿	♃	♆	☉	☽	
1934	Jan	23	2:53	2♒26	☉	☿	♄	♂	♀		16	13	21	1934	Feb	8	16:14	13♒33	♀	♄	☉	☿	♂	
	Aug	6	20:50	5♋45	☽	♂	♀	♇	☿		2	14	13		Aug	9	11:03	16♋21	♂	♀	♇	☿	☽	
	Nov	5	13:49	22♎28	☽	♃	☿	♀	☉		2	9	32		Nov	7	23:21	4♏42	☿	♃	♀	☉	☽	
1935	Feb	3	13:33	12♒05	☽	☉	♄	☿	♀		1	12	42	1935	Feb	5	2:15	15♒21	☉	♄	☿	♀	☽	
	Aug	28	17:27	1♍03	☽	☉	♆	♀	☿		2	3	42		Aug	30	21:09	6♍33	☉	♆	♀	☿	☽	
1936	Apr	21	1:13	24♈02	☽	☉	♅	☿	♂		1	21	23	1936	Apr	22	22:36	2♉36	☉	♅	♂	☿	☽	
	Jun	17	16:59	6♊17	☽	☿	♀	♂	☉		0	7	0		Jun	17	23:59	6♊34	☿	☽	♀	♂	☉	
	Jul	12	11:53	6♋45	☿	♂	☉	♀	♇		13	4	7		Jul	25	16:01	19♋45	♂	♇	☉	☿	♀	
	Jul	17	5:34	6♋53	☽	♂	☿	☉	♇		2	3	42		Jul	19	9:16	15♋38	♂	☿	☉	♇	☽	
	Jul	17	10:24	9♋37	☽	♂	☿	☉	♇	♀	1	22	52		Jul	19	9:16	15♋38	♂	☿	☉	♇	♀	☽
	Jul	17	10:24	9♋37	☽	☿	☉	♇	♀		2	10	32		Jul	19	20:56	21♋57	☿	♇	☉	♀	☽	
1937	Apr	11	1:18	18♈29	☽	☉	♀	☿	♅		1	13	55	1937	Apr	12	15:13	22♈18	☉	♀	♅	☿	☽	
1938	Apr	1	19:32	24♈38	☽	♀	☿	♅	♂		1	14	40	1938	Apr	3	10:12	27♈21	♀	☿	♅	♂	☽	
	Sep	22	8:25	8♍40	☽	♂	☿	♆	☉		1	12	10		Sep	23	20:35	10♍09	♂	☿	♆	☉	☽	
1939	Aug	13	18:18	0♌05	☽	♇	♀	☿	☉		1	9	57	1939	Aug	15	4:15	1♌39	♇	♀	☿	☉	☽	
	Sep	12	8:44	2♍54	☽	☿	☉	♀	♆		2	0	14		Sep	14	8:58	13♍19	☿	☉	♀	♆	☽	
1940	Mar	12	12:28	28♈52	☽	♄	♀	♂	♅		1	16	36	1940	Mar	14	5:04	29♈18	♄	♀	♂	♅	☽	
	May	5	17:21	25♈03	☽	♃	☿	♄	☉		1	21	6		May	7	14:28	27♈59	♃	☿	♄	☉	☽	
	May	7	19:17	1♉42	☿	♄	☉	☽	♅		0	2	47		May	7	22:04	1♉55	☿	♄	☉	♅	☽	
	Sep	1	20:25	4♍39	☽	☿	♂	☉	♆		1	15	36		Sep	3	12:01	9♍27	♂	☿	☉	♆	☽	
1941	Apr	25	13:10	4♉56	☉	♀	♄	♃	♅		26	22	38	1941	May	22	11:49	19♉45	♄	♅	♃	☉	♀	
	Apr	26	7:17	2♉54	☽	☉	♀	♄	♃		2	2	16		Apr	28	9:33	7♉42	☉	♀	♄	♃	☽	
	Apr	26	11:30	4♉59	☽	☉	♀	♄	♃	♅	1	22	3		Apr	28	9:33	7♉42	☉	♀	♄	♃	♅	☽
	Apr	26	11:30	4♉59	☽	♀	♄	♃	♅		2	3	23		Apr	28	14:53	10♉21	♀	♄	♃	♅	☽	
	Apr	27	5:18	26♈30	☿	☉	♀	☽	♄		0	6	44		Apr	27	12:02	27♈04	☿	☉	♀	♄	☽	
	Apr	30	21:38	3♉58	☿	☉	♀	♄	♃		16	13	13		May	17	10:51	19♉06	♄	☉	♃	♀	☿	
	May	1	12:34	5♉16	☿	☉	♀	♄	♃	♅	15	22	18		May	17	10:51	19♉06	♄	☉	♅	♃	♀	☿
	May	1	12:34	5♉16	☿	☉	♀	♃	♅		19	18	16		May	21	6:50	26♉24	♅	♃	☉	♀	☿	
	May	24	9:28	12♉48	☽	♄	♅	♃	☉		2	7	14		May	26	16:43	20♉17	♄	♅	♃	☉	☽	
	May	25	6:24	23♉09	☽	♅	♃	☉	♀		1	23	10		May	27	5:34	26♉45	♅	♃	☉	♀	☽	
1942	Feb	22	3:23	21♉51	☽	♂	♄	♅	♃		1	17	47	1942	Feb	23	21:10	22♉33	♄	♂	♅	♃	☽	
	Mar	21	16:55	24♉28	☽	♄	♅	♂	♃		1	5	22		Mar	22	22:18	24♉38	♄	♅	☽	♂	♃	
	Jun	12	4:08	1♊37	♅	☽	♄	☉	☿		1	4	9		Jun	13	8:17	1♊41	♅	♄	☽	☿	☉	
	Oct	8	10:54	0♎10	♆	♀	♂	☉	☿		5	22	5		Oct	14	8:59	0♎23	♆	♀	☿	♂	☉	
	Oct	8	13:56	24♍39	☽	♆	♀	♂	☉		1	21	8		Oct	10	11:04	0♎15	♆	♀	♂	☉	☽	
	Oct	8	22:51	29♍36	☽	♆	♀	♂	☉	☿	1	12	13		Oct	10	11:04	0♎15	♆	♀	♂	☉	☿	☽
	Oct	8	22:51	29♍36	☽	♀	♂	☉	☿		2	1	6		Oct	10	23:56	7♎45	♀	♂	☉	☿	☽	
	Nov	7	3:28	24♎05	☽	☿	♂	♀	☉		2	0	29		Nov	9	3:57	3♏19	☿	♂	♀	☉	☽	
1943	Jun	1	15:25	25♉13	☽	☿	♅	☉	♄		1	18	3	1943	Jun	3	9:28	27♉07	☿	♅	☉	♄	☽	
	Jul	31	14:51	1♌32	☽	♃	♇	☉	☿		2	3	40		Aug	2	18:31	6♌55	♇	♃	☉	☿	☽	
1944	Jun	17	1:49	9♊35	☿	♅	♀	☉	♄		4	16	42	1944	Jun	21	18:31	10♊13	♅	☿	♀	♄	☉	
	Jun	19	1:48	7♊39	☽	♅	☿	♀	☉		1	16	59		Jun	20	18:47	10♊10	♅	☿	♀	☉	☽	
	Jun	19	5:46	9♊52	☽	♅	☿	♀	☉	♄	1	13	0		Jun	20	18:47	10♊10	♅	☿	♀	☉	♄	☽
	Jun	19	5:46	9♊52	☽	☿	♀	☉	♄		2	3	25		Jun	21	9:11	17♊53	☿	♀	☉	♄	☽	
	Jul	20	3:24	26♋11	☽	☉	♀	♇	☿		1	12	29		Jul	21	15:53	28♋43	☉	♀	♇	☽	☿	
	Aug	19	12:58	3♍56	☽	♃	♀	☿	♂		1	19	48		Aug	21	8:46	5♍34	♃	♀	☿	♂	☽	
	Aug	20	19:46	12♍40	♀	☽	☿	♂	♆		1	6	35		Aug	22	2:21	14♍14	♀	☿	♂	♆	☽	
1945	Oct	4	13:37	22♍35	☽	♆	♃	☉	☿		2	19	38	1945	Oct	7	9:15	6♎28	♆	♃	☉	☿	☽	
1946	Jun	30	8:29	24♋20	☽	♄	☿	♇	♀		1	8	4	1946	Jul	1	16:33	25♋54	♄	☿	♇	☽	♀	
	Jul	27	17:48	23♋51	☽	♄	☉	♇	☿		1	18	44		Jul	29	12:32	29♋28	♄	☉	♇	☿	☽	
	Aug	29	6:08	4♎50	☽	♆	♂	♀	♃		1	18	18		Aug	31	0:25	7♎13	♆	♂	♀	♃	☽	
	Nov	21	21:42	8♏59	☽	♃	♀	☿	☉		1	23	41		Nov	23	21:22	12♏48	♃	♀	☿	☉	☽	

5 or More Planets Within 20° Arc 1700-2050

				Starting Position	Planets in Zodiacal Sequence						Dy	Hr	Mn					Ending Position	Planets in Zodiacal Sequence					
	Nov	22	23:10	21♏46	☽	♀	☿	☉	♂		0	0	26		Nov	22	23:36	21♏47	♀	☽	☿	☉	♂	
1947	Aug	5	10:10	22♋57	☿	♀	☉	♄	♇		22	7	47	1947	Aug	27	17:57	13♌37	♇	♄	♀	☿	☉	
	Aug	14	16:02	25♋33	☽	☿	♇	♄	♀		2	8	19		Aug	17	0:22	10♌58	☿	♇	♄	♀	☽	
	Aug	15	1:18	1♌23	☽	☿	♇	♄	♀	☉	1	23	3		Aug	17	0:22	10♌58	☿	♇	♄	♀	☉	☽
	Aug	15	1:18	1♌23	☽	♇	♄	♀	☉		2	2	49		Aug	17	4:07	13♌18	♇	♄	♀	☉	☽	
	Sep	14	17:19	19♍49	☽	☉	♀	☿	♆		1	14	22		Sep	16	7:40	22♍36	☉	♀	☿	♆	☽	
1948	Jul	5	9:52	23♊15	☽	♀	♅	☿	☉		1	13	58	1948	Jul	6	23:50	26♊18	♀	♅	☿	☉	☽	
	Aug	4	16:35	4♌18	☿	☽	☉	♇	♄		1	10	40		Aug	6	3:16	7♌17	☿	☉	♇	♄	☽	
	Dec	30	4:12	5♑38	☽	☉	♃	☿	♂		1	22	39	1949	Jan	1	2:51	10♑23	☉	♃	☿	♂	☽	
1949	Mar	27	18:48	16♓46	☽	☿	♀	♂	☉		2	10	29		Mar	30	5:17	25♓33	☿	♀	♂	☉	☽	
1950	Oct	10	3:34	27♍04	☽	☿	♀	☉	♆		1	19	53	1950	Oct	11	23:28	3♎46	☿	♀	♆	☉	☽	
1951	Mar	9	1:30	15♓31	☿	☉	♃	☽	♂		0	6	54	1951	Mar	9	8:24	16♓03	☿	☉	♃	♂	☽	
	Nov	25	14:27	0♎46	♂	♄	♀	☽	♆		0	7	26		Nov	25	21:52	0♎57	♂	♄	♀	♆	☽	
1952	Jun	21	21:13	24♊59	☽	♀	☉	♅	☿		2	6	22	1952	Jun	24	3:35	2♋21	♀	☉	♅	☿	☽	
1953	Jul	11	22:28	18♋22	♂	♅	☉	☽	☿		0	19	10	1953	Jul	12	17:39	18♋51	♅	♂	☉	☿	☽	
	Sep	6	11:54	23♌35	☽	♇	♂	☿	☉		0	0	8		Sep	6	12:02	23♌35	♇	☽	♂	☿	☉	
1954	Jun	2	14:11	0♋50	☽	♃	☿	♀	♅		1	12	55	1954	Jun	4	3:05	2♋23	♃	☿	♀	♅	☽	
	Jun	30	2:36	2♋22	☽	☉	♃	☿	♅		1	21	19		Jul	1	23:55	8♋40	♃	☉	☿	♅	☽	
	Oct	25	17:54	20♎55	☽	♆	☉	♄	☿		2	2	52		Oct	27	20:46	26♎06	♆	☉	☿	♄	☽	
	Nov	23	16:11	10♏50	☽	☿	♄	♀	☉		2	0	1		Nov	25	16:13	14♏32	♄	♀	☿	☉	☽	
1955	Jul	18	21:44	17♋29	☽	☉	♅	♂	♃		2	1	7	1955	Jul	20	22:51	27♋26	☉	♅	♂	♃	☽	
	Jul	19	1:58	7♋50	☿	♀	☽	☉	♅		0	14	8		Jul	19	16:05	8♋47	☿	♀	☉	♅	☽	
	Jul	23	0:57	18♋24	♀	♅	☉	♂	♃		18	9	27		Aug	10	10:24	29♋11	♅	♀	♃	☉	♂	
	Jul	25	5:34	18♋51	☿	♀	♅	☉	♂		14	17	7		Aug	8	22:41	29♋06	♅	♀	☉	♂	☿	
	Jul	25	5:51	18♋53	☿	♀	♅	☉	♂	♃	14	16	50		Aug	8	22:41	29♋06	♅	♀	♃	☉	♂	☿
	Jul	25	5:51	18♋53	☿	♀	☉	♂	♃		22	8	22		Aug	16	14:13	13♌48	♃	♀	☉	♂	☿	
	Aug	2	13:06	5♌54	☿	☉	♃	♂	♇		14	1	7		Aug	16	14:13	13♌48	♃	☉	♂	♇	☿	
	Aug	6	9:13	6♌02	♀	♃	☉	☿	♂	♇	10	5	0		Aug	16	14:13	13♌48	♃	♀	☉	♂	♇	☿
	Aug	6	9:13	6♌02	♀	☉	☿	♂	♇		17	13	0		Aug	23	22:14	26♌35	♇	♀	♂	☉	☿	
	Aug	6	9:13	6♌02	♀	♃	☉	♂	♇		24	17	36		Aug	31	2:49	16♌56	♃	♇	♂	♀	☉	
	Aug	16	8:29	2♌57	☽	♃	♀	☉	♂		2	4	43		Aug	18	13:12	14♌13	♃	♀	♂	☉	☽	
	Aug	16	14:08	6♌21	☽	♃	♀	☉	♂	♇	1	23	4		Aug	18	13:12	14♌13	♃	♀	♂	☉	♇	☽
	Aug	16	14:08	6♌21	☽	♀	☉	♂	♇		2	12	1		Aug	19	2:09	21♌43	♀	♂	☉	♇	☽	
	Aug	17	4:23	14♌52	☽	♀	♂	☉	♇	☿	1	21	46		Aug	19	2:09	21♌43	♀	♂	☉	♇	☿	☽
	Aug	17	4:23	14♌52	☽	♂	☉	♇	☿		2	3	14		Aug	19	7:37	24♌50	♂	☉	♇	☿	☽	
	Oct	15	2:30	12♎35	☽	☿	☉	♆	♀		1	20	53		Oct	16	23:23	16♎14	☿	☉	♆	♀	☽	
1957	Jul	27	17:18	11♌55	☽	♂	☿	♇	♀		2	3	11	1957	Jul	29	20:29	24♌05	♂	♇	☿	♀	☽	
	Oct	13	6:39	11♎52	☿	♂	♃	☉	♆		14	19	47		Oct	28	2:26	16♎58	♃	♂	♆	☉	☿	
	Oct	21	18:03	8♎05	☽	♃	♂	☿	☉		1	21	20		Oct	23	15:23	16♎01	♃	♂	☿	☉	☽	
	Oct	22	0:40	12♎11	☽	♃	♂	☿	☉	♆	1	14	42		Oct	23	15:23	16♎01	♃	♂	☿	☉	♆	☽
	Oct	22	0:40	12♎11	☽	♂	☿	☉	♆		1	20	15		Oct	23	20:55	19♎23	♂	☿	☉	♆	☽	
1958	Aug	26	11:12	12♌43	♀	♅	☿	♇	☉		0	15	32	1958	Aug	27	2:44	13♌20	♅	♀	☿	♇	☉	
	Sep	10	22:17	12♌34	☽	♅	☿	♀	♇		1	12	1		Sep	12	10:18	14♌15	♅	☿	♇	♀	☽	
	Sep	12	1:20	28♌47	☽	☿	♇	♀	☉		1	14	39		Sep	13	15:59	2♍39	♇	☿	♀	☉	☽	
	Oct	12	17:46	17♎03	☽	☉	☿	♆	♃		1	12	56		Oct	14	6:42	20♎25	☉	☿	♆	♃	☽	
	Oct	18	7:08	18♎15	♀	☉	☿	♆	♃		14	2	51		Nov	1	9:59	4♏40	♆	♀	☉	♃	☿	
	Nov	9	20:39	26♎57	☽	♆	♃	♀	☉		1	20	31		Nov	11	17:10	5♏03	♆	♃	☉	♀	☽	
	Dec	9	23:07	6♐53	☽	☉	☿	♀	♄		1	22	16		Dec	11	21:23	15♐12	☿	☉	♀	♄	☽	
1959	Jul	8	4:35	9♌45	☽	☿	♅	♂	♀		1	19	35	1959	Jul	10	0:10	13♌13	☿	♅	♂	♀	☽	
	Jul	8	9:33	12♌24	☽	♅	♂	♀	♇		1	17	33		Jul	10	3:06	14♌49	♅	♂	♀	♇	☽	
	Jul	9	3:05	12♌25	☿	♅	☽	♂	♀	♇	0	21	5		Jul	10	0:10	13♌13	☿	♅	♂	♀	♇	☽
	Jul	9	3:05	12♌25	☿	♅	♂	♀	♇		6	1	20		Jul	15	4:25	15♌07	♅	☿	♂	♇	♀	
	Sep	1	10:49	17♌58	☽	♅	☿	♇	♀		1	12	9		Sep	2	22:58	18♌09	♅	☿	♇	♀	☽	
	Sep	1	11:24	18♌17	☽	☿	♇	♀	☉		2	3	34		Sep	3	14:58	27♌17	☿	♇	♀	☉	☽	
	Nov	29	7:43	21♏26	☽	☿	♂	☉	♃		1	12	16		Nov	30	19:59	24♏34	☿	♂	☉	♃	☽	
	Dec	28	9:29	15♐54	☽	♂	♃	☿	☉		1	11	10		Dec	29	20:38	18♐16	♃	♂	☿	☉	☽	
1960	Jan	25	5:32	22♐16	☽	♃	♀	♂	♄		1	11	9	1960	Jan	26	16:40	24♐06	♃	♀	♂	♄	☽	
	Aug	21	6:25	15♌37	☽	☿	♅	☉	♇		2	3	29		Aug	23	9:54	21♌59	♅	☿	☉	♇	☽	
1961	Jan	15	22:36	11♑57	☽	♃	♄	☉	☿		1	16	51	1961	Jan	17	15:27	17♑58	♃	♄	☉	☿	☽	
	Aug	12	11:42	17♌13	☿	☉	♅	☽	♇		0	15	43		Aug	13	3:25	18♌33	☿	☉	♅	♇	☽	
	Nov	6	17:27	24♎04	☽	♀	☿	♆	☉		1	17	59		Nov	8	11:26	26♎33	♀	☿	♆	☉	☽	
	Dec	6	14:09	26♏29	☽	♀	☿	☉	♂		2	0	43		Dec	8	14:52	4♐21	♀	☿	☉	♂	☽	
1962	Jan	5	22:34	7♑16	☽	♂	♀	☉	☿		1	14	9	1962	Jan	7	12:43	10♑26	♂	♀	☉	☿	☽	
	Jan	6	4:06	10♑17	♀	☽	☉	☿	♄		1	11	23		Jan	7	15:29	12♑08	♀	☉	☿	♄	☽	
	Jan	7	12:43	10♑26	♂	♀	☉	☿	♄		0	16	49		Jan	8	5:32	10♑58	♂	♀	☉	♄	☿	
	Jan	21	17:10	29♑49	♀	☉	♄	♃	☿		4	14	59		Jan	26	8:09	2♒40	♄	♀	☉	♃	☿	
	Jan	27	16:09	2♒49	♄	☉	♀	♃	☿		13	15	13		Feb	10	7:23	4♒25	♄	☿	♃	☉	♀	
	Jan	29	0:38	26♑57	♂	♄	☉	♀	♃		12	6	44		Feb	10	7:23	4♒25	♄	♂	♃	☉	♀	
	Feb	2	2:18	0♒06	♂	♄	☉	♀	♃	☿	8	5	5		Feb	10	7:23	4♒25	♄	♂	☿	♃	☉	♀
	Feb	2	2:18	0♒06	♂	☉	♀	♃	☿		11	10	4		Feb	13	12:22	8♒27	☿	♂	♃	☉	♀	
	Feb	2	2:18	0♒06	♂	♄	☉	♃	☿		11	22	33		Feb	14	0:51	4♒51	♄	☿	♂	♃	☉	
	Feb	3	16:40	26♑08	☽	♂	♄	☉	♀		1	18	40		Feb	5	11:20	2♒44	♂	♄	☉	♀	☽	
	Feb	3	20:10	28♑17	☽	♂	♄	☉	♀	☿	1	15	10		Feb	5	11:20	2♒44	♂	♄	☉	☿	♀	☽

5 or More Planets Within 20° Arc 1700-2050

	Starting Position				Planets in Zodiacal Sequence	Dy	Hr	Mn		Ending Position				Planets in Zodiacal Sequence
	Feb	3	20:10	28♑17	☽ ♄ ☉ ♀ ☿	1	16	59		Feb	5	13:09	3♒52	♄ ☉ ☿ ♀ ☽
	Feb	3	20:16	28♑20	☽ ♂ ♄ ☉ ♀ ☿ ♃	1	15	5		Feb	5	11:20	2♒44	♂ ♄ ☉ ☿ ♀ ♃ ☽
	Feb	3	20:16	28♑20	☽ ♄ ☉ ♀ ☿ ♃	1	16	54		Feb	5	13:09	3♒52	♄ ☉ ☿ ♀ ♃ ☽
	Feb	3	20:16	28♑20	☽ ☉ ♀ ☿ ♃	2	11	8		Feb	6	7:24	15♒21	☿ ☉ ♃ ♀ ☽
	Mar	3	18:03	4♒59	☽ ♄ ☿ ♂ ♃	1	11	23		Mar	5	5:26	6♒57	♄ ☿ ♂ ♃ ☽
	Nov	25	12:01	12♏48	☽ ♀ ♆ ☉ ☿	0	9	8		Nov	25	21:10	13♏24	♀ ♆ ☽ ☉ ☿
1963	Aug	18	23:43	21♌19	☽ ♀ ☉ ♅ ♇	1	19	2	1963	Aug	20	18:45	24♌29	♀ ☉ ♅ ♇ ☽
	Sep	16	17:51	10♍06	☽ ♇ ☉ ♀ ☿	1	18	45		Sep	18	12:37	12♍22	♇ ☉ ☿ ♀ ☽
1964	May	10	10:50	29♈48	☽ ☿ ♂ ♃ ☉	1	10	51	1964	May	11	21:41	1♉35	☿ ♂ ♃ ☉ ☽
	Sep	4	18:53	23♌55	☽ ☿ ♅ ☉ ♇	2	7	5		Sep	7	1:59	5♍51	☿ ♅ ♇ ☉ ☽
1965	Mar	2	3:07	26♒39	☽ ♀ ♄ ☉ ☿	2	3	49	1965	Mar	4	6:56	3♓42	♀ ♄ ☉ ☿ ☽
	Jul	29	18:32	24♌43	☽ ☿ ♀ ♅ ♇	1	16	44		Jul	31	11:16	0♍00	☿ ♀ ♅ ♇ ☽
	Sep	23	16:22	10♍25	☽ ♅ ♇ ☿ ☉	1	18	20		Sep	25	10:41	16♍19	♅ ♇ ☿ ☉ ☽
1966	Feb	20	3:12	27♒35	☽ ☉ ☿ ♂ ♄	2	3	41	1966	Feb	22	6:53	3♓12	☉ ☿ ♄ ♂ ☽
	Mar	21	4:36	19♓00	☽ ♄ ☉ ☿ ♂	1	20	29		Mar	23	1:05	21♓22	♄ ☿ ☉ ♂ ☽
	Aug	13	17:32	12♋13	☽ ♃ ♂ ♀ ☿	2	0	49		Aug	15	18:22	22♋09	♃ ♂ ♀ ☿ ☽
	Sep	8	18:38	29♌44	♀ ☿ ☉ ♇ ♅	9	5	39		Sep	18	0:18	11♍10	♀ ♇ ♅ ☉ ☿
	Sep	13	9:40	0♍09	☽ ♀ ♇ ♅ ☉	1	19	15		Sep	15	4:56	7♍41	♀ ♇ ♅ ☉ ☽
	Sep	13	14:36	3♍17	☽ ♀ ♇ ♅ ☉ ☿	1	14	19		Sep	15	4:56	7♍41	♀ ♇ ♅ ☉ ☿ ☽
	Sep	13	14:36	3♍17	☽ ♇ ♅ ☉ ☿	2	7	14		Sep	15	21:51	18♍25	♇ ♅ ☉ ☿ ☽
	Nov	12	0:04	11♏04	☽ ☉ ♀ ♆ ☿	2	2	45		Nov	14	2:49	21♏17	☉ ♆ ♀ ☿ ☽
1967	Aug	27	10:08	3♍27	☉ ☿ ♀ ♇ ♅	5	19	30	1967	Sep	2	5:39	3♍48	♀ ☉ ☿ ♇ ♅
	Sep	3	17:15	0♍04	☽ ♀ ☉ ☿ ♇	1	9	13		Sep	5	2:28	2♍09	♀ ☉ ♇ ☽ ☿
	Sep	3	23:36	3♍55	☽ ☉ ♇ ☿ ♅	1	22	46		Sep	5	22:21	12♍39	☉ ♇ ☿ ♅ ☽
1968	Apr	25	22:01	16♈52	☽ ♄ ♀ ☉ ☿	0	12	52	1968	Apr	26	10:53	18♈01	♄ ♀ ☽ ☉ ☿
	Jun	24	5:16	13♊47	☽ ☿ ♂ ☉ ♀	2	11	36		Jun	26	16:51	23♊44	☿ ♂ ☉ ♀ ☽
	Aug	19	2:17	7♍31	☿ ♃ ♀ ♇ ♅	17	11	25		Sep	5	13:42	15♍38	♃ ♇ ♅ ♀ ☿
	Aug	23	19:21	28♌21	☽ ☉ ♃ ☿ ♀	1	19	6		Aug	25	14:27	2♍26	☉ ♃ ☿ ♀ ☽
	Aug	24	1:44	1♍52	☽ ♃ ☿ ♀ ♇	2	8	3		Aug	26	9:47	13♍27	♃ ☿ ♀ ♇ ☽
	Aug	24	12:29	7♍50	☽ ♃ ☿ ♀ ♇ ♅	1	21	18		Aug	26	9:47	13♍27	♃ ☿ ♀ ♇ ♅ ☽
	Aug	24	12:29	7♍50	☽ ☿ ♀ ♇ ♅	2	10	26		Aug	26	22:55	21♍00	☿ ♇ ♀ ♅ ☽
	Aug	25	1:16	1♍54	☉ ♃ ☽ ☿ ♀ ♇	0	13	11		Aug	25	14:27	2♍26	☉ ♃ ☿ ♀ ♇ ☽
	Aug	25	1:16	1♍54	☉ ♃ ☿ ♀ ♇	6	8	56		Aug	31	10:12	8♍03	☉ ♃ ♇ ♀ ☿
	Aug	31	15:03	8♍15	☉ ♃ ♇ ♀ ♅	1	1	45		Sep	1	16:49	9♍17	☉ ♃ ♇ ♅ ♀
	Sep	21	0:18	9♍31	☽ ♃ ♇ ☉ ♅	2	3	49		Sep	23	4:07	19♍27	♃ ♇ ♅ ☉ ☽
	Oct	18	13:17	11♍13	☽ ♂ ♇ ♃ ♅	1	22	11		Oct	20	11:28	17♍53	♂ ♇ ♃ ♅ ☽
	Nov	15	3:05	13♍34	☽ ♇ ♃ ♅ ♂	2	6	34		Nov	17	9:38	24♍40	♇ ♃ ♅ ♂ ☽
1969	Apr	15	17:09	13♈05	☽ ♀ ☉ ♄ ☿	0	12	8	1969	Apr	16	5:18	14♈08	♀ ☽ ☉ ♄ ☿
	Aug	16	11:39	15♍12	☿ ♇ ☽ ♅ ♃	0	10	20		Aug	16	21:59	15♍51	☿ ♇ ♅ ♃ ☽
	Sep	12	5:36	23♍57	☽ ♇ ♅ ♃ ☿	1	15	0		Sep	13	20:36	24♍47	♇ ♅ ♃ ☿ ☽
	Sep	17	20:34	24♍46	☉ ♇ ♅ ♃ ☿	18	6	15		Oct	6	2:49	25♍36	♇ ☿ ♅ ☉ ♃
	Oct	8	20:40	15♍06	☽ ♀ ♇ ☿ ♅	2	1	53		Oct	10	22:33	21♍47	♀ ♇ ☿ ♅ ☽
	Oct	9	18:03	26♍23	☽ ☿ ♅ ☉ ♃	1	20	45		Oct	11	14:48	0♎45	☿ ♅ ♃ ☉ ☽
1970	Apr	7	12:29	2♉12	☿ ☽ ♀ ♄ ♂	1	11	6	1970	Apr	8	23:36	4♉47	☿ ♀ ♄ ♂ ☽
	Sep	28	18:50	15♍13	☽ ♂ ☿ ♇ ☉	1	20	31		Sep	30	15:21	17♍25	♂ ☿ ♇ ☉ ☽
	Sep	30	6:32	19♍02	☿ ♇ ☽ ☉ ♅	0	13	20		Sep	30	19:52	19♍42	☿ ♇ ☉ ♅ ☽
	Oct	30	0:53	3♏28	☽ ☉ ☿ ♃ ♀	1	22	3		Oct	31	22:56	8♏06	☉ ☿ ♃ ♀ ☽
	Oct	31	4:51	9♏46	☿ ♃ ☽ ♀ ♆	1	0	7		Nov	1	4:57	11♏23	☿ ♃ ♀ ♆ ☽
	Nov	2	16:51	9♏51	☉ ☿ ♃ ♀ ♆	13	3	52		Nov	15	20:44	14♏18	♀ ♃ ☉ ♆ ☿
	Dec	25	5:48	11♏46	♂ ♀ ☽ ♃ ♆	0	17	42		Dec	25	23:30	12♏15	♂ ♀ ♃ ♆ ☽
1971	Jan	21	18:34	24♏14	☽ ♂ ♃ ♆ ♀	1	23	24	1971	Jan	23	17:58	0♐26	♂ ♃ ♆ ♀ ☽
	Sep	19	8:14	22♍48	☽ ☉ ♇ ♀ ♅	2	2	37		Sep	21	10:51	27♍48	☉ ♇ ♀ ♅ ☽
	Sep	26	16:27	23♍15	☿ ♇ ☉ ♀ ♅	7	4	36		Oct	3	21:03	29♍57	♇ ☿ ☉ ♅ ♀
	Nov	18	4:25	26♏24	☽ ♆ ♃ ☿ ♀	2	3	1		Nov	20	7:26	2♐36	♆ ♃ ☿ ♀ ☽
	Dec	16	1:18	3♐25	☽ ♆ ☿ ♃ ☉	0	3	21		Dec	16	4:39	3♐34	♆ ☽ ☿ ♃ ☉
1972	Jun	10	19:19	10♊34	☽ ♄ ☉ ☿ ♀	1	9	53	1972	Jun	12	5:12	11♊30	♄ ☉ ♀ ☿ ☽
	Sep	27	13:36	27♍48	♂ ♇ ☉ ☿ ♅	7	0	3		Oct	4	13:39	2♎16	♇ ♂ ☉ ♅ ☿
	Oct	6	1:22	28♍20	☽ ♇ ♂ ☉ ♅	1	23	1		Oct	8	0:23	2♎24	♇ ♂ ☉ ♅ ☽
	Nov	2	12:45	1♎10	☽ ♀ ♇ ♅ ♂	1	19	46		Nov	4	8:31	3♎21	♇ ♀ ♅ ♂ ☽
1973	May	31	17:55	3♊48	☽ ☉ ♄ ☿ ♀	1	20	28	1973	Jun	2	14:23	11♊54	☉ ♄ ♀ ☿ ☽
	Sep	26	11:50	2♎10	☽ ☉ ♇ ☿ ♅	1	15	56		Sep	28	3:47	4♎19	♇ ☉ ♅ ☿ ☽
1974	Jan	23	3:43	29♑27	☽ ☉ ♀ ☿ ♃	1	22	53	1974	Jan	25	2:36	2♒45	♀ ☉ ☿ ♃ ☽
	Oct	14	0:58	0♎28	☽ ♇ ♀ ☉ ♂	1	20	49		Oct	15	21:47	7♎18	♇ ♀ ♂ ☉ ☽
	Oct	14	12:53	7♎41	☽ ♀ ☉ ♂ ♅	2	2	30		Oct	16	15:22	17♎32	♀ ♂ ☉ ♅ ☽
	Oct	15	10:14	20♎28	☽ ♂ ☉ ♅ ☿	1	13	40		Oct	16	23:54	22♎26	♂ ☉ ♅ ☿ ☽
	Oct	18	2:59	19♎24	♀ ♂ ☉ ♅ ☿	23	15	5		Nov	10	18:04	29♎01	☿ ♅ ♂ ☉ ♀
	Nov	25	6:25	19♏05	♂ ☿ ☉ ♀ ♆	3	6	27		Nov	28	12:52	21♏21	♂ ☿ ☉ ♆ ♀
	Dec	11	23:46	29♏34	☽ ♂ ♆ ☿ ☉	1	17	59		Dec	13	17:45	1♐59	♂ ♆ ☿ ☉ ☽
	Dec	12	17:39	9♐11	☽ ♆ ☿ ☉ ♀	0	10	53		Dec	13	4:33	9♐46	♆ ☽ ☿ ☉ ♀
1976	Jul	26	9:47	25♋12	☽ ☉ ♄ ♀ ☿	2	5	10	1976	Jul	28	14:56	5♌38	☉ ♄ ♀ ☿ ☽
	Aug	26	16:31	20♍09	☽ ♀ ☿ ♂ ♇	1	16	11		Aug	28	8:43	24♍37	♀ ☿ ♂ ♇ ☽
	Oct	23	3:04	19♎45	☿ ☽ ☉ ♅ ♂	0	19	49		Oct	23	22:53	21♎09	☿ ☉ ♅ ♂ ☽
	Nov	21	5:14	23♏09	☽ ☉ ♂ ☿ ♆	1	20	4		Nov	23	1:19	0♐53	☉ ♂ ☿ ♆ ☽

5 or More Planets Within 20° Arc 1700-2050

Year	Month	Day	Time	Starting Position	Planets in Zodiacal Sequence						Dy	Hr	Mn	Year	Month	Day	Time	Ending Position	Planets in Zodiacal Sequence					
1978	Oct	31	17:08	6♏21	☽	☉	♅	♀	☿		1	16	16	1978	Nov	2	9:24	9♏36	☉	♅	♀	☿	☽	
	Oct	31	22:07	9♏11	☽	♅	♀	☿	♂		1	22	41		Nov	2	20:48	16♏18	♅	♀	☿	♂	☽	
	Nov	4	15:32	11♏52	☉	♅	♀	☿	♂		0	3	28		Nov	4	18:60	12♏00	☉	♅	♀	♂	☿	
	Nov	29	19:56	0♐19	☽	☉	♆	☿	♂		1	23	37		Dec	1	19:32	9♐15	☉	♆	☿	♂	☽	
1979	Aug	20	21:03	7♌14	☽	☿	♃	♀	☉		2	0	49	1979	Aug	22	21:52	11♌18	☿	♃	♀	☉	☽	
	Sep	20	4:59	13♍36	☽	♄	☉	☿	♀		2	2	44		Sep	22	7:43	18♍43	♄	☉	☿	♀	☽	
	Sep	21	21:49	28♍19	☉	☽	☿	♀	♇		1	7	34		Sep	23	5:24	29♍36	☉	♀	☿	♇	☽	
1980	Sep	8	17:12	8♍26	☽	☉	♃	☿	♄		2	12	38	1980	Sep	11	5:50	18♍39	☉	♃	♄	☿	☽	
1981	May	3	6:08	29♈27	☽	♂	☉	☿	♀		1	19	38	1981	May	5	1:46	7♉18	♂	☉	♀	☿	☽	
	Aug	31	1:18	24♍49	☽	☿	♄	♃	♀		1	21	11		Sep	1	22:29	28♍27	☿	♄	♃	♀	☽	
	Aug	31	15:52	2♎32	☽	♄	♃	♀	♇		2	3	2		Sep	2	18:54	8♎51	♄	♃	♀	♇	☽	
	Sep	4	16:49	2♎40	☿	♄	♃	♀	♇		8	6	27		Sep	12	23:16	10♎01	♄	♃	☿	♇	♀	
	Sep	28	1:21	3♎30	☽	☉	♄	♃	♇		1	20	59		Sep	29	22:20	6♎40	☉	♄	♃	♇	☽	
	Sep	28	15:33	10♎53	☽	♄	♃	♇	☿		1	17	32		Sep	30	9:05	12♎07	♄	♃	♇	☿	☽	
	Oct	9	12:35	13♎15	♄	☉	♃	♇	☿		19	14	45		Oct	29	3:20	15♎37	♄	☿	♃	♇	☉	
	Oct	25	9:48	4♎35	☽	♄	☿	♃	♇		2	12	44		Oct	27	22:32	15♎29	♄	☿	♃	♇	☽	
	Oct	26	1:17	12♎32	☽	♄	☿	♃	♇	☉	1	21	15		Oct	27	22:32	15♎29	♄	☿	♃	♇	☉	☽
	Oct	26	1:17	12♎32	☽	☿	♃	♇	☉		2	2	55		Oct	28	4:12	18♎19	☿	♃	♇	☉	☽	
1982	Jun	28	13:47	10♎26	☽	♂	♄	♇	♃		1	18	28	1982	Jun	30	8:15	12♎41	♂	♄	♇	♃	☽	
	Jul	25	23:38	11♎36	☽	♄	♇	♂	♃		1	23	20		Jul	27	22:58	16♎46	♄	♇	♂	♃	☽	
	Oct	15	18:12	6♎40	☽	♀	☉	♄	♇		2	13	17		Oct	18	7:29	20♎18	♀	☉	♄	♇	☽	
	Oct	16	15:09	4♎54	☿	♀	☽	☉	♄		0	12	44		Oct	17	3:52	5♎22	☿	♀	☉	♄	☽	
	Oct	18	13:10	6♎47	☿	♀	☉	♄	♇		21	13	38		Nov	9	2:48	27♎38	♇	♄	☿	☉	♀	
	Nov	11	12:59	13♏55	☿	☉	♃	♀	♅		19	1	26		Nov	30	14:24	24♏37	♃	♅	☉	☿	♀	
	Nov	14	3:04	3♏56	☽	☿	♃	☉	♀		3	0	40		Nov	17	3:44	21♏40	♃	☿	☉	♀	☽	
	Nov	14	22:19	14♏07	☽	☿	♃	☉	♀	♅	2	5	25		Nov	17	3:44	21♏40	♃	☿	☉	♀	♅	☽
	Nov	14	22:19	14♏07	☽	☿	☉	♀	♅		2	8	21		Nov	17	6:40	23♏08	☿	☉	♀	♅	☽	
	Dec	14	19:25	16♐08	☽	☉	♆	♀	☿		2	10	8		Dec	17	5:34	24♐57	☉	♆	♀	☿	☽	
1983	Nov	3	14:03	23♎00	☽	♇	♄	☉	☿		1	22	22	1983	Nov	5	12:25	29♎59	♇	♄	☉	☿	☽	
	Nov	30	23:28	8♐11	☉	♅	♃	☿	♆		3	3	1		Dec	4	2:29	9♐29	♅	☉	♃	♆	☿	
	Dec	4	6:04	8♐18	☽	♅	☉	♃	♆		1	15	38		Dec	5	21:42	9♐35	♅	☉	♃	♆	☽	
	Dec	4	8:55	9♐51	☽	☉	♃	♆	☿		1	20	13		Dec	6	5:08	13♐30	☉	♃	♆	☿	☽	
1984	Jan	1	11:33	20♐14	☽	♃	♆	☿	☉		2	2	26	1984	Jan	3	13:59	26♐29	♃	♆	☿	☉	☽	
	Jan	9	18:42	10♐30	♀	♅	♃	♆	☿		6	3	58		Jan	15	22:40	11♐56	♅	♀	♃	♆	☿	
	Jan	29	2:29	24♐58	☽	♆	♃	♀	☿		2	1	40		Jan	31	4:09	0♑24	♆	♃	♀	☿	☽	
	Oct	24	5:15	26♎55	☽	☉	♇	☿	♄		1	16	28		Oct	25	21:43	2♏06	♇	☉	☿	♄	☽	
	Nov	24	12:35	23♐12	☽	☿	♆	♀	♃		1	15	35		Nov	26	4:10	25♐47	☿	♆	♃	♀	☽	
	Dec	21	1:47	11♐04	☽	♅	☿	☉	♆		1	16	58		Dec	22	18:45	14♐48	☿	♅	☉	♆	☽	
1985	Dec	1	16:33	27♏40	♀	♄	☿	☉	♅		10	0	5	1985	Dec	11	16:38	29♏35	☿	♄	♀	♅	☉	
	Dec	10	14:24	28♏13	☽	☿	♄	♀	♅		1	10	14		Dec	12	0:38	29♏45	☿	♄	♀	♅	☽	
	Dec	10	14:50	28♏30	☽	☿	♄	♀	♅	☉	1	1	47		Dec	11	16:38	29♏35	☿	♄	♀	☽	♅	☉
	Dec	10	14:50	28♏30	☽	♄	♀	♅	☉		1	14	55		Dec	12	5:45	2♐58	♄	♀	♅	☉	☽	
	Dec	25	3:02	13♐20	☿	♅	♀	☉	♆		6	1	51		Dec	31	4:53	19♐27	♅	☿	♆	♀	☉	
1986	Jan	9	1:14	28♐28	☽	♆	☿	♀	☉		1	17	44	1986	Jan	10	18:58	3♑57	♆	☿	♀	☉	☽	
	Feb	8	2:31	6♒59	☽	☉	♀	☿	♃		2	12	49		Feb	10	15:20	21♒36	☉	♀	♃	☿	☽	
	Dec	29	17:37	17♐43	☽	♅	☿	♆	☉		1	16	28		Dec	31	10:06	23♐34	♅	☿	♆	☉	☽	
1987	Jan	26	2:05	16♐36	☽	♄	♀	♅	♆		1	10	33	1987	Jan	27	12:38	18♐06	♄	♀	♅	♆	☽	
	Aug	22	22:16	12♌01	☽	♀	☉	♂	☿		3	8	4		Aug	26	6:21	2♍11	♂	☉	♀	☿	☽	
	Oct	22	9:24	24♎21	☽	☉	♇	☿	♀		1	22	42		Oct	24	8:07	0♏23	☉	☿	♇	♀	☽	
	Nov	22	12:53	16♐22	☽	♄	♀	♅	♆		1	16	56		Nov	24	5:49	21♐03	♄	♀	♅	♆	☽	
	Dec	14	13:21	17♐08	☿	☉	♄	♅	♆		17	20	27	1988	Jan	1	9:48	25♐31	♄	♅	♆	☉	☿	
	Dec	19	7:11	6♐54	☽	♄	☿	☉	♅		2	12	56	1987	Dec	21	20:07	24♐16	♄	♅	☿	☉	☽	
	Dec	20	0:30	17♐20	☽	♄	☿	♅	☉	♆	1	19	37		Dec	21	20:07	24♐16	♄	♅	☿	☉	♆	☽
	Dec	20	0:30	17♐20	☽	☿	♅	☉	♆		2	0	5		Dec	22	0:35	27♐04	♅	☿	☉	♆	☽	
1988	Feb	13	0:28	19♐17	☽	♂	♄	♅	♆		1	18	38	1988	Feb	14	19:07	24♐52	♂	♅	♄	♆	☽	
	Mar	11	12:56	22♐13	☽	♅	♄	♆	♂		2	1	1		Mar	13	13:57	0♑50	♅	♄	♆	♂	☽	
	Dec	8	21:30	12♐53	☽	☉	☿	♅	♄		1	22	27		Dec	10	19:58	19♐00	☉	☿	♅	♄	☽	
	Dec	9	8:41	19♐05	☽	☿	♅	♄	♆		1	21	36		Dec	11	6:17	24♐54	☿	♅	♄	♆	☽	
	Dec	10	23:18	19♐08	☉	☿	♅	♄	♆		17	4	38		Dec	28	3:55	1♑31	♅	♄	☉	♆	☿	
1989	Jan	5	19:48	20♐06	☽	♀	♅	♄	♆		1	21	23	1989	Jan	7	17:11	26♐12	♀	♅	♄	♆	☽	
	Jan	6	6:04	25♐54	☽	♅	♄	♆	☉		1	21	17		Jan	8	3:20	2♑11	♅	♄	♆	☉	☽	
	Oct	28	16:14	24♎43	☽	♂	☿	☉	♇		1	20	47		Oct	30	13:01	26♎52	♂	☿	☉	♇	☽	
	Nov	2	7:20	20♐05	☽	♀	♅	♄	♆		2	8	31		Nov	4	15:51	29♐13	♀	♅	♄	♆	☽	
	Nov	30	14:45	3♑15	☽	♅	♆	♄	♀		0	21	41		Dec	1	12:26	3♑57	♅	♆	♄	☽	♀	
	Dec	15	16:52	23♐42	☉	♅	♆	☿	♄		13	9	56		Dec	29	2:48	5♑35	♅	☉	♆	♄	☿	
	Dec	27	5:39	25♐02	☽	☉	♅	♆	♄		2	9	52		Dec	29	15:31	5♑37	♅	☉	♆	♄	☽	
	Dec	28	1:00	5♑08	☽	♅	☉	♆	♄	☿	1	1	48		Dec	29	2:48	5♑35	♅	☉	♆	♄	☽	☿
	Dec	28	1:00	5♑08	☽	☉	♆	♄	☿		1	19	8		Dec	29	20:08	8♑06	☉	♆	♄	☿	☽	
1990	Jan	1	3:33	5♑46	♅	☉	♆	♄	☿		15	22	49	1990	Jan	17	2:22	6♑42	♅	☿	♆	♄	☉	
	Jan	12	9:18	12♑27	♆	☿	♄	☉	♀		7	15	39		Jan	20	0:56	9♑42	☿	♆	♄	♀	☉	
	Jan	21	14:40	6♑58	♅	☿	♆	♄	♀		19	22	34		Feb	10	13:13	8♑00	♅	♆	♄	♀	☿	
	Jan	23	9:43	22♐51	☽	♂	♅	☿	♆		1	21	39		Jan	25	7:23	26♐55	♂	♅	☿	♆	☽	
	Jan	23	20:12	28♐17	☽	♅	☿	♆	♄		2	6	9		Jan	26	2:21	7♑13	♅	☿	♆	♄	☽	

5 or More Planets Within 20° Arc 1700-2050

	Starting Position				Planets in Zodiacal Sequence	Dy	Hr	Mn		Ending Position				Planets in Zodiacal Sequence
	Jan	24	9:40	5♑21	☽ ♅ ☿ ♆ ♄ ♀	1	16	41		Jan	26	2:21	7♑13	♅ ☿ ♆ ♄ ♀ ☽
	Jan	24	9:40	5♑21	☽ ☿ ♆ ♄ ♀	2	1	24		Jan	26	11:04	12♑00	☿ ♆ ♄ ♀ ☽
	Jan	27	20:35	28♐45	♂ ♅ ☿ ♆ ♄	13	16	38		Feb	10	13:13	8♑00	♅ ♂ ♆ ♄ ☿
	Feb	1	7:12	1♑57	♂ ♅ ♆ ☿ ♄ ♀	9	6	1		Feb	10	13:13	8♑00	♅ ♂ ♆ ♄ ♀ ☿
	Feb	1	7:12	1♑57	♂ ♆ ☿ ♄ ♀	10	7	48		Feb	11	15:00	9♑26	♂ ♆ ♄ ♀ ☿
	Feb	1	7:12	1♑57	♂ ♅ ♆ ♄ ♀	28	15	59		Mar	1	23:12	8♑49	♅ ♆ ♄ ♂ ♀
	Feb	20	11:02	1♑18	☽ ♅ ♆ ♂ ♄	2	3	11		Feb	22	14:13	8♑32	♅ ♆ ♂ ♄ ☽
	Feb	20	15:41	3♑43	☽ ♅ ♆ ♂ ♄ ♀	1	22	32		Feb	22	14:13	8♑32	♅ ♆ ♂ ♄ ♀ ☽
	Feb	20	15:41	3♑43	☽ ♆ ♂ ♄ ♀	2	8	10		Feb	22	23:50	13♑50	♆ ♂ ♄ ♀ ☽
	Dec	15	7:44	3♑47	♀ ♅ ☿ ♆ ♄	7	6	2		Dec	22	13:46	4♑35	☿ ♅ ♀ ♆ ♄
	Dec	15	18:15	23♐31	☉ ♀ ♅ ☿ ♆	11	7	48		Dec	27	2:03	28♐33	☿ ☉ ♅ ♆ ♀
	Dec	16	17:41	19♐42	☽ ☉ ♀ ♅ ☿	2	6	56		Dec	19	0:37	26♐50	☉ ☿ ♀ ♅ ☽
	Dec	17	1:32	23♐34	☽ ☉ ♀ ♅ ☿ ♆	1	23	5		Dec	19	0:37	26♐50	☉ ☿ ♀ ♅ ♆ ☽
	Dec	17	1:32	23♐34	☽ ♀ ♅ ☿ ♆	2	20	41		Dec	19	22:14	7♑37	☿ ♅ ♀ ♆ ☽
	Dec	17	22:51	4♑04	☽ ♀ ♅ ☿ ♆ ♄	1	23	23		Dec	19	22:14	7♑37	☿ ♅ ♀ ♆ ♄ ☽
	Dec	17	22:51	4♑04	☽ ♀ ♅ ♆ ♄	2	2	11		Dec	20	1:02	9♑01	♅ ♀ ♆ ♄ ☽
	Dec	27	3:21	5♑06	☉ ♅ ♆ ♀ ♄	9	1	21	1991	Jan	5	4:42	9♑59	♅ ♆ ☉ ♄ ♀
1991	Jan	14	11:40	7♑15	☽ ♅ ♆ ☉ ♄	1	22	42		Jan	16	10:22	10♑39	♅ ♆ ☉ ♄ ☽
	Jul	13	6:35	11♌14	☽ ☿ ♃ ♂ ♀	1	18	8		Jul	15	0:43	16♌53	☿ ♃ ♂ ♀ ☽
	Aug	10	0:41	15♌53	☽ ☉ ♃ ☿ ♀	1	12	42		Aug	11	13:23	18♌23	☉ ♃ ♀ ☿ ☽
	Nov	6	9:42	12♏44	☽ ☉ ♂ ♇ ☿	1	18	49		Nov	8	4:31	15♏16	☉ ♂ ♇ ☿ ☽
1992	Jan	4	11:20	26♐21	♂ ☽ ☉ ♅ ♆	0	18	2	1992	Jan	5	5:22	26♐54	♂ ♅ ☉ ♆ ☽
	Jan	7	12:28	26♐28	☿ ♂ ♅ ☉ ♆	7	18	15		Jan	15	6:43	4♑22	♂ ☿ ♅ ♆ ☉
	Jan	30	19:44	27♐20	☽ ♀ ♅ ♂ ♆	2	18	49		Feb	2	14:33	10♑12	♀ ♅ ♆ ♂ ☽
	Feb	1	5:09	13♑48	☽ ♅ ♂ ♆ ☿	1	1	41		Feb	2	6:51	15♑34	♅ ♆ ♂ ☽ ☿
1993	Jan	20	23:51	10♑57	☽ ♅ ♆ ☿ ☉	2	6	57	1993	Jan	23	6:47	18♑59	♅ ♆ ☿ ☉ ☽
	Nov	12	11:09	0♏05	☽ ♃ ♀ ☿ ☉	0	11	3		Nov	12	22:11	0♏33	♃ ♀ ☽ ☿ ☉
	Nov	13	6:40	5♏15	♀ ☿ ☽ ☉ ♇	0	22	54		Nov	14	5:34	6♏27	♀ ☿ ☉ ♇ ☽
	Dec	12	4:31	4♐07	☽ ☿ ♀ ☉ ♂	1	20	40		Dec	14	1:12	10♐38	☿ ♀ ☉ ♂ ☽
	Dec	27	1:27	0♑17	♀ ☿ ☉ ♂ ♆	24	13	45	1994	Jan	20	15:11	21♑12	♆ ♂ ☉ ♀ ☿
	Dec	27	8:47	1♑19	☿ ♂ ☉ ♆ ♅	24	6	25		Jan	20	15:11	21♑12	♆ ♅ ♂ ☉ ☿
	Dec	27	21:45	1♑20	♀ ☿ ♂ ☉ ♆ ♅	23	17	26		Jan	20	15:11	21♑12	♆ ♅ ♂ ☉ ♀ ☿
	Dec	27	21:45	1♑20	♀ ☿ ♂ ☉ ♅	24	15	57		Jan	21	13:43	22♑48	♅ ♂ ☉ ♀ ☿
	Dec	27	21:45	1♑20	♀ ♂ ☉ ♆ ♅	31	22	33		Jan	28	20:18	21♑30	♆ ♅ ♂ ☉ ♀
1994	Jan	10	10:42	0♑49	☽ ♂ ♀ ☉ ♆	2	19	6		Jan	13	5:49	18♑27	♂ ♆ ♀ ☉ ☽
	Jan	10	13:01	2♑09	☽ ♂ ♀ ☉ ♆ ♅	2	16	48		Jan	13	5:49	18♑27	♂ ♆ ♀ ♅ ☉ ☽
	Jan	10	13:01	2♑09	☽ ♀ ☉ ♆ ♅	2	21	21		Jan	13	10:22	20♑56	♆ ♀ ♅ ☉ ☽
	Jan	10	17:06	4♑29	☽ ♂ ♀ ☉ ♆ ♅ ☿	2	12	43		Jan	13	5:49	18♑27	♂ ♆ ♀ ♅ ☉ ☿ ☽
	Jan	10	17:06	4♑29	☽ ♀ ☉ ♆ ♅ ☿	2	17	17		Jan	13	10:22	20♑56	♆ ♀ ♅ ☉ ☿ ☽
	Jan	10	17:06	4♑29	☽ ♀ ☉ ♅ ☿	2	19	44		Jan	13	12:50	22♑16	♀ ♅ ☉ ☿ ☽
	Feb	10	6:42	17♒28	☽ ☉ ♀ ♄ ☿	2	1	27		Feb	12	8:10	23♒23	☉ ♀ ♄ ☿ ☽
	Feb	16	15:09	15♒12	♂ ☉ ♄ ♀ ☿	0	7	14		Feb	16	22:23	15♒27	♂ ☉ ♄ ☿ ♀
	Oct	7	17:37	6♏21	☿ ♃ ♀ ☽ ♇	0	10	20		Oct	8	3:57	6♏25	☿ ♃ ♀ ♇ ☽
	Nov	3	7:54	7♏17	☽ ♀ ☉ ♃ ♇	1	10	38		Nov	4	18:32	9♏13	♀ ☉ ♃ ♇ ☽
	Dec	1	14:04	19♏09	☽ ♃ ♇ ☿ ☉	1	22	21		Dec	3	12:25	28♏29	♇ ♃ ☿ ☉ ☽
1995	Jan	1	2:46	5♑29	☽ ☉ ☿ ♆ ♅	1	19	17	1995	Jan	2	22:03	12♑03	☉ ♆ ☿ ♅ ☽
	Feb	25	20:17	20♑04	☽ ♀ ♆ ♅ ☿	1	18	8		Feb	27	14:25	24♑37	♆ ♀ ♅ ☿ ☽
	Dec	17	15:22	8♑34	☿ ♂ ♆ ♀ ♅	16	2	3	1996	Jan	2	17:26	24♑45	♆ ♂ ♅ ☿ ♀
	Dec	21	20:60	26♐18	☽ ♃ ☉ ☿ ♂	1	9	9	1995	Dec	23	6:09	27♐29	♃ ☉ ☿ ♂ ☽
	Dec	22	16:36	8♑50	☽ ☿ ♂ ♆ ♅	1	22	46		Dec	24	15:22	18♑27	♂ ☿ ♆ ♅ ☽
	Dec	22	20:31	11♑21	☽ ☿ ♂ ♆ ♅ ♀	1	18	51		Dec	24	15:22	18♑27	♂ ☿ ♆ ♅ ♀ ☽
	Dec	22	20:31	11♑21	☽ ☿ ♆ ♅ ♀	1	20	12		Dec	24	16:43	19♑17	☿ ♆ ♅ ♀ ☽
	Dec	31	11:49	9♑19	☉ ♂ ♆ ☿ ♅	23	9	59	1996	Jan	23	21:48	22♑09	☿ ♆ ♅ ☉ ♂
1996	Jan	19	6:33	10♑25	☽ ♆ ☿ ☉ ♅	2	5	57		Jan	21	12:31	24♑44	☿ ♆ ♅ ☉ ☽
	Jan	19	19:55	18♑56	☽ ♆ ☿ ☉ ♅ ♂	1	16	35		Jan	21	12:31	24♑44	☿ ♆ ♅ ☉ ♂ ☽
	Jan	19	19:55	18♑56	☽ ♆ ☉ ♅ ♂	1	17	44		Jan	21	13:39	25♑27	♆ ♅ ☉ ♂ ☽
	Mar	17	22:31	7♓37	☽ ☿ ♂ ♄ ☉	2	11	22		Mar	20	9:53	22♓30	☿ ♂ ♄ ☉ ☽
1997	Jan	8	20:04	13♑43	☽ ☉ ♃ ♆ ♅	1	18	27	1997	Jan	10	14:31	20♑24	☉ ♆ ♃ ♅ ☽
	Jan	21	18:43	14♑28	♀ ♆ ♃ ☉ ♅	16	4	23		Feb	6	23:06	28♑13	♆ ♃ ♀ ♅ ☉
	Jan	28	20:34	14♑53	☿ ♀ ♆ ♃ ♅	20	4	35		Feb	18	1:10	28♑36	♆ ♅ ♃ ☿ ♀
	Feb	5	6:50	13♑26	☽ ☿ ♆ ♀ ♃	2	6	13		Feb	7	13:03	27♑35	☿ ♆ ♃ ♀ ☽
	Feb	5	9:53	15♑19	☽ ☿ ♆ ♀ ♃ ♅	2	3	10		Feb	7	13:03	27♑35	☿ ♆ ♃ ♅ ♀ ☽
	Feb	5	9:53	15♑19	☽ ♆ ♀ ♃ ♅	2	4	13		Feb	7	14:06	28♑14	♆ ♃ ♅ ♀ ☽
	Feb	6	5:21	27♑28	☽ ♆ ♃ ♀ ♅ ☉	0	17	46		Feb	6	23:06	28♑13	♆ ♃ ♀ ♅ ☽ ☉
	Feb	6	5:21	27♑28	☽ ♃ ♀ ♅ ☉	1	17	54		Feb	7	23:14	4♒03	♃ ♅ ♀ ☉ ☽
	Feb	10	10:54	1♒45	☿ ♃ ♅ ♀ ☉	3	16	29		Feb	14	3:23	5♒29	♃ ♅ ☿ ♀ ☉
	Dec	2	22:49	15♑45	☽ ♂ ♀ ♆ ♅	1	17	39		Dec	4	16:29	19♑26	♂ ♀ ♆ ♅ ☽
	Dec	30	13:09	19♑37	☽ ♆ ♀ ♅ ♂	2	2	7	1998	Jan	1	15:16	28♑58	♆ ♀ ♅ ♂ ☽
	Dec	31	10:38	2♒08	☽ ♀ ♅ ♂ ♃	1	11	47		Jan	1	22:25	3♒11	♀ ♅ ♂ ♃ ☽
1998	Jan	26	2:59	18♑33	☿ ♀ ♆ ☉ ♅	3	12	51		Jan	29	15:50	19♑32	♀ ☿ ♆ ♅ ☉
	Jan	26	17:37	16♑34	☽ ☿ ♀ ♆ ☉	1	15	28		Jan	28	9:06	19♑57	♀ ☿ ♆ ☉ ☽
	Jan	26	21:06	18♑35	☽ ☿ ♀ ♆ ☉ ♅	1	12	0		Jan	28	9:06	19♑57	♀ ☿ ♆ ☉ ♅ ☽
	Jan	26	21:06	18♑35	☽ ☿ ♆ ☉ ♅	1	15	38		Jan	28	12:44	22♑09	☿ ♆ ☉ ♅ ☽

5 or More Planets Within 20° Arc 1700-2050

	Starting Position				Planets in Zodiacal Sequence						Dy	Hr	Mn		Ending Position				Planets in Zodiacal Sequence					
	Feb	26	13:09	5♓14	☽	♃	☉	☿	♂		0	2	51		Feb	26	15:60	5♓20	♃	☽	☉	☿	♂	
	Mar	27	18:11	1♈30	☽	☉	♂	♄	☿		1	18	46		Mar	29	12:57	8♈38	☉	♂	☿	♄	☽	
	Nov	19	22:05	27♏22	☉	♀	☽	♇	☿		1	1	56		Nov	21	0:01	28♏28	☉	♀	♇	☿	☽	
1999	Jan	17	14:04	26♑09	☽	☉	♆	♅	♀		1	17	27	1999	Jan	19	7:31	28♑46	☉	♆	♅	♀	☽	
2000	Apr	30	9:15	29♈06	♀	☿	☉	♃	♄		18	22	14	2000	May	19	7:29	20♉31	♃	♄	♀	☉	☿	
	May	2	23:15	26♈38	☽	♀	☿	☉	♃		1	22	27		May	4	21:42	4♉40	♀	☿	☉	♃	☽	
	May	3	3:60	29♈27	☽	♀	☿	☉	♃	♄	1	17	42		May	4	21:42	4♉40	♀	☿	☉	♃	♄	☽
	May	3	3:60	29♈27	☽	☿	☉	♃	♄		2	3	19		May	5	7:19	10♉34	☿	☉	♃	♄	☽	
	May	3	21:43	10♉04	☽	☉	♃	♄	♂		1	17	30		May	5	15:13	15♉25	☉	♃	♄	♂	☽	
	May	5	15:41	11♉18	☿	☉	♃	♄	♂		13	1	14		May	18	16:55	20♉23	♃	♄	☉	☿	♂	
	May	16	8:49	18♉46	♀	♃	♄	☉	☿	♂	2	8	6		May	18	16:55	20♉23	♃	♄	♀	☉	☿	♂
	May	16	8:49	18♉46	♀	♄	☉	☿	♂		3	11	30		May	19	20:19	21♉36	♄	♀	☉	♂	☿	
	Jun	1	1:48	20♉53	☽	♄	♃	♀	☉		1	12	11		Jun	2	13:58	23♉20	♄	♃	♀	☉	☽	
	Jun	30	23:51	27♊54	☽	☉	♂	♀	☿		2	4	33		Jul	3	4:24	11♋06	♂	☉	☿	♀	☽	
2001	Jan	24	7:43	1♒57	☽	☉	♆	♅	☿		2	1	24	2001	Jan	26	9:07	6♒16	♆	☉	♅	☿	☽	
	Dec	13	15:08	6♐32	☽	♀	♇	☉	☿		2	4	47		Dec	15	19:55	15♐26	♇	♀	☉	☿	☽	
2002	Jan	13	11:10	21♑59	☽	♀	☉	♆	☿		1	20	58	2002	Jan	15	8:08	25♑00	☉	♀	♆	☿	☽	
	Jan	23	19:39	3♒38	☉	♀	♆	☿	♅		6	22	23		Jan	30	18:02	4♒01	☿	♆	☉	♀	♅	
	Feb	11	2:40	8♒49	☽	♆	☉	♅	♀		0	3	4		Feb	11	5:43	8♒59	♆	☽	☉	♅	♀	
	May	13	5:20	1♊11	☽	☿	♄	♂	♀		2	6	12		May	15	11:32	9♊59	☿	♄	♂	♀	☽	
2003	Jun	28	0:09	15♊55	☽	♀	☿	♄	☉		2	8	0	2003	Jun	30	8:08	24♊37	♀	☿	♄	☉	☽	
2004	Feb	19	1:43	12♒37	☽	♆	☿	☉	♅		1	11	54	2004	Feb	20	13:37	13♒33	♆	☿	☉	♅	☽	
2005	Jan	7	16:02	7♐27	☽	♂	♇	☿	♀		1	12	10	2005	Jan	9	4:11	10♐00	♂	♇	☿	♀	☽	
	Feb	7	12:37	28♑50	☽	♀	☿	♆	☉		1	23	4		Feb	9	11:42	8♒33	♀	♆	☿	☉	☽	
2006	Aug	21	23:48	8♌46	☽	♀	♄	☿	☉		2	1	54	2006	Aug	24	1:42	13♌45	♀	♄	☿	☉	☽	
	Oct	30	18:52	4♏48	♂	☉	♀	♃	☿		16	22	17		Nov	16	17:09	9♏13	☿	♂	☉	♃	♀	
	Nov	19	8:26	8♏55	☽	☿	♂	☉	♃		1	16	33		Nov	21	0:59	9♏51	☿	♂	☉	♃	☽	
	Nov	19	16:19	12♏57	☽	♂	☉	♃	♀		2	3	49		Nov	21	20:08	19♏57	♂	☉	♃	♀	☽	
	Dec	18	22:06	6♐51	☽	♂	☿	♇	☉		1	19	7		Dec	20	17:13	10♐19	♂	☿	♇	☉	☽	
2007	Aug	12	2:04	8♌28	☽	☿	☉	♄	♀		2	11	3	2007	Aug	14	13:07	20♌00	☿	☉	♀	♄	☽	
	Dec	8	23:49	8♐17	☽	☿	☉	♃	♇		2	5	14		Dec	11	5:03	15♐12	☿	☉	♃	♇	☽	
2009	Jan	24	12:01	14♑38	☽	♂	☿	♃	☉		2	9	18	2009	Jan	26	21:19	23♑14	♂	☿	♃	☉	☽	
	Feb	22	10:44	4♒19	☽	☿	♃	♂	♆		2	5	33		Feb	24	16:17	11♒42	♃	☿	♂	♆	☽	
	Mar	25	8:33	18♓48	☽	♅	☿	☉	♀		1	20	32		Mar	27	5:05	23♓25	♅	☿	☉	♀	☽	
2010	Jan	13	12:03	3♑35	☽	♇	☿	☉	♀		0	3	24	2010	Jan	13	15:27	3♑45	♇	☽	☿	☉	♀	
	Feb	13	8:11	16♒06	☽	☉	♆	♀	♃		2	12	50		Feb	15	21:01	26♒12	♆	☉	♀	♃	☽	
	Mar	6	12:45	8♓46	☿	♃	☉	♅	♀		2	10	20		Mar	8	23:05	11♓47	♃	☿	☉	♅	♀	
	Mar	14	7:39	6♓24	☽	♃	☿	☉	♅		2	5	59		Mar	16	13:38	13♓37	♃	☉	♅	☿	☽	
	Mar	15	10:29	19♓50	☽	☉	☿	♅	♀		2	4	21		Mar	17	14:50	26♓35	♅	☉	☿	♀	☽	
2011	Mar	3	12:57	28♒05	☽	♆	♂	☉	☿		0	10	36	2011	Mar	3	23:33	28♒56	♆	☽	♂	☉	☿	
	Apr	2	1:53	25♓22	☽	♂	♅	☉	♃		2	4	27		Apr	4	6:20	1♈19	♅	♂	☉	♃	☽	
	Apr	7	6:21	1♈29	♅	♂	♃	☉	☿		4	17	36		Apr	11	23:57	1♈45	♅	♂	♃	☿	☉	
	Apr	21	3:16	29♓57	♀	♅	☿	♂	♃		10	14	25		May	1	17:41	2♈46	♅	♀	☿	♃	♂	
	Apr	29	20:15	1♈19	☽	♅	♀	☿	♂		1	19	15		May	1	15:30	2♈46	♅	♀	☿	♂	☽	
	Apr	29	21:43	2♈03	☽	♅	♀	☿	♂	♃	1	17	47		May	1	15:30	2♈46	♅	♀	☿	♃	♂	☽
	Apr	29	21:43	2♈03	☽	♀	☿	♂	♃		2	15	51		May	2	13:34	13♈48	♀	☿	♃	♂	☽	
	Sep	27	1:56	28♍09	☽	☿	☉	♀	♄		1	18	51		Sep	28	20:47	5♎23	☉	☿	♀	♄	☽	
2013	Jan	10	9:24	0♑18	☽	♀	♇	☿	☉		1	13	4	2013	Jan	11	22:29	3♑28	♀	♇	☿	☉	☽	
	Feb	9	23:55	17♒17	☽	☉	♆	♂	☿		1	20	15		Feb	11	20:11	23♒16	☉	♆	♂	☿	☽	
	Feb	25	15:40	29♒28	♀	♆	☉	♂	☿		5	22	1		Mar	3	13:41	3♓13	♆	♀	☉	☿	♂	
	Mar	10	6:02	29♒50	☽	♆	☿	♀	☉		1	17	38		Mar	11	23:40	3♓32	♆	☿	♀	☉	☽	
	Mar	12	3:04	17♓32	♀	☉	☽	♂	♅		1	0	16		Mar	13	3:20	18♓48	♀	☉	♂	♅	☽	
	Apr	8	22:59	2♈08	☽	♅	☉	♂	♀		2	2	55		Apr	11	1:54	9♈14	♅	☉	♂	♀	☽	
	May	9	4:39	9♉28	☽	♂	☿	☉	♀		2	3	41		May	11	8:19	15♉28	♂	☿	☉	♀	☽	
2014	Jan	1	4:46	6♑49	☽	☉	♇	☿	♀		1	14	22	2014	Jan	2	19:08	11♑19	♇	☉	☿	♀	☽	
	Nov	21	10:52	15♏51	☽	☿	♄	☉	♀		1	23	40		Nov	23	10:32	22♏37	☿	♄	☉	♀	☽	
	Dec	21	14:52	23♐42	☽	☉	☿	♇	♀		1	22	18		Dec	23	13:10	1♑37	☉	☿	♇	♀	☽	
2015	Aug	14	14:46	21♌26	☽	☉	♀	♃	☿		0	2	28	2015	Aug	14	17:14	21♌36	☉	☽	♀	♃	☿	
2017	Dec	16	20:23	9♐36	☽	☿	♀	☉	♄		2	2	18	2017	Dec	18	22:41	14♐29	☿	♀	☉	♄	☽	
2018	Feb	15	13:35	23♒18	☽	☿	☉	♀	♆		2	1	33	2018	Feb	17	15:07	28♒54	☉	☿	♀	♆	☽	
2019	Jan	5	15:39	0♑45	☿	☽	♄	☉	♇		0	23	28	2019	Jan	6	15:07	2♑13	☿	♄	☉	♇	☽	
	Aug	29	7:55	19♌51	☽	☿	☉	♂	♀		2	6	34		Aug	31	14:29	4♍30	☿	☉	♂	♀	☽	
	Dec	26	1:44	2♑11	☽	☉	♃	♄	♇		1	19	31		Dec	27	21:16	5♑43	♃	☉	♄	♇	☽	
	Dec	30	16:50	2♑20	☿	♃	☉	♄	♇		17	6	20	2020	Jan	16	23:10	10♑19	♃	♇	♄	☉	☿	
2020	Jan	23	22:33	22♑13	☽	♇	♄	☉	☿		0	13	11		Jan	24	11:44	23♑10	♇	♄	☽	☉	☿	
	Mar	17	10:20	9♑38	☽	♂	♃	♇	♄		2	15	30		Mar	20	1:50	22♑32	♂	♃	♇	♄	☽	
	Apr	14	13:08	20♑14	☽	♇	♃	♄	♂		1	23	34		Apr	16	12:41	24♑58	♇	♃	♄	♂	☽	
2021	Jan	3	12:52	13♑22	☉	☿	♇	♄	♃		14	5	39	2021	Jan	17	18:31	24♑44	♇	☉	♄	♃	☿	
	Jan	12	15:45	15♑29	☽	☉	♇	♄	♃		2	2	46		Jan	14	18:31	24♑38	♇	☉	♄	♃	☽	
	Jan	12	18:14	16♑56	☽	☉	♇	♄	♃	☿	2	0	17		Jan	14	18:31	24♑38	♇	☉	♄	♃	☿	☽
	Jan	12	18:14	16♑56	☽	☉	♄	♃	☿		2	0	37		Jan	14	18:51	24♑50	☉	♄	♃	☿	☽	
	Jan	22	22:32	17♑54	♀	♇	☉	♄	♃		11	23	36		Feb	3	22:08	25♑18	♇	♀	♄	♃	☉	
	Feb	4	19:55	4♒04	♀	♄	♃	☉	☿		10	14	38		Feb	15	10:33	6♒58	♄	☿	♃	♀	☉	

5 or More Planets Within 20° Arc 1700-2050

Year	Month	Day	Time	Starting Position	Planets in Zodiacal Sequence	Dy	Hr	Mn	Year	Month	Day	Time	Ending Position	Planets in Zodiacal Sequence
	Feb	9	11:22	22♑04	☽ ♇ ♄ ♀ ♃	1	17	43		Feb	11	5:05	25♑32	♇ ♄ ♀ ♃ ☽
	Feb	9	22:31	28♑24	☽ ♄ ♀ ♃ ☿	2	2	36		Feb	12	1:07	6♒34	♄ ♃ ♀ ☿ ☽
	Feb	10	4:16	1♒38	☽ ♄ ♀ ♃ ☿ ☉	1	20	51		Feb	12	1:07	6♒34	♄ ♃ ♀ ☿ ☉ ☽
	Feb	10	4:16	1♒38	☽ ♀ ♃ ☿ ☉	2	8	17		Feb	12	12:33	12♒47	♃ ♀ ☿ ☉ ☽
	Feb	12	11:01	25♑34	♇ ♄ ♃ ♀ ☿	1	14	13		Feb	14	1:13	25♑37	♇ ♄ ♃ ☿ ♀
2022	Jan	2	15:38	10♑29	☽ ☉ ♀ ♇ ☿	1	13	14	2022	Jan	4	4:52	13♑48	☉ ♀ ♇ ☿ ☽
	Jan	31	2:15	25♑23	☽ ☿ ♇ ☉ ♄	0	4	38		Jan	31	6:52	25♑24	☿ ♇ ☽ ☉ ♄
	Mar	30	15:29	19♓54	☽ ♃ ♆ ☿ ☉	1	10	14		Apr	1	1:43	21♓19	♃ ♆ ☽ ☿ ☉
	Apr	25	22:31	6♓55	☽ ♂ ♀ ♆ ♃	1	16	40		Apr	27	15:11	9♓27	♂ ♀ ♆ ♃ ☽
2024	Feb	7	10:56	13♑28	☽ ♀ ♂ ♇ ☿	1	20	33	2024	Feb	9	7:29	20♑54	♀ ♂ ♇ ☿ ☽
	Mar	9	15:14	8♓58	☽ ♄ ☉ ♆ ☿	1	2	35		Mar	10	17:49	11♓06	♄ ☉ ☽ ♆ ☿
	May	7	6:53	5♉36	☽ ♀ ☉ ♅ ♃	1	19	36		May	9	2:29	11♉51	♀ ☉ ♅ ♃ ☽
	May	26	10:50	15♉41	☿ ♅ ♃ ♀ ☉	9	1	32		Jun	4	12:22	24♉22	♅ ♃ ☿ ♀ ☉
	Jun	4	23:60	24♉56	☽ ♃ ☿ ☉ ♀	2	0	2		Jun	7	0:01	2♊49	♃ ☿ ☉ ♀ ☽
2025	Feb	27	23:25	8♓51	☽ ☉ ♄ ☿ ♆	1	12	19	2025	Mar	1	11:44	11♓08	☉ ♄ ☿ ♆ ☽
	Mar	9	21:17	19♓33	☉ ♄ ♆ ☿ ♀	25	13	5		Apr	4	10:22	24♓54	♄ ♀ ☿ ♆ ☉
	Mar	27	15:23	11♓57	☽ ♄ ♀ ♆ ☿	2	3	54		Mar	29	19:17	24♓14	♄ ♀ ♆ ☿ ☽
	Mar	28	0:35	17♓35	☽ ♄ ♀ ♆ ☿ ☉	1	18	42		Mar	29	19:17	24♓14	♄ ♀ ♆ ☿ ☉ ☽
	Mar	28	0:35	17♓35	☽ ♀ ♆ ☿ ☉	2	1	27		Mar	30	2:02	28♓29	♀ ♆ ☿ ☉ ☽
	Apr	24	10:41	17♓24	☽ ♀ ♄ ♆ ☿	2	0	40		Apr	26	11:21	27♓23	♄ ♀ ♆ ☿ ☽
2026	Jan	10	5:41	13♑00	☿ ♂ ☉ ♀ ♇	24	4	35	2026	Feb	3	10:16	3♒46	♇ ♂ ☉ ♀ ☿
	Jan	17	6:56	9♑42	☽ ☿ ♂ ☉ ♀	3	0	49		Jan	20	7:45	27♑37	♂ ☿ ☉ ♀ ☽
	Jan	17	13:52	13♑14	☽ ☿ ♂ ☉ ♀ ♇	2	17	53		Jan	20	7:45	27♑37	♂ ☿ ☉ ♇ ♀ ☽
	Jan	17	13:52	13♑14	☽ ☿ ☉ ♀ ♇	2	21	41		Jan	20	11:33	29♑38	☿ ☉ ♇ ♀ ☽
	Feb	18	23:23	10♓42	♀ ☿ ☽ ♄ ♆	0	23	40		Feb	19	23:03	11♓56	♀ ☿ ♄ ♆ ☽
	Mar	2	11:49	11♓54	☉ ☿ ♀ ♆ ♄	7	11	12		Mar	9	23:01	14♓22	☿ ☉ ♆ ♄ ♀
	Mar	18	20:07	25♓23	☽ ☉ ♆ ♄ ♀	1	17	44		Mar	20	13:51	29♓58	☉ ♆ ♄ ♀ ☽
	Apr	14	15:56	17♓14	☽ ☿ ♆ ♂ ♄	2	12	17		Apr	17	4:13	2♈48	♆ ☿ ♂ ♄ ☽
2027	Aug	31	13:21	5♍23	☽ ♃ ☉ ♀ ☿	1	12	39	2027	Sep	2	1:59	8♍05	♃ ☉ ♀ ☿ ☽
2028	Jan	26	1:39	29♑27	☽ ☉ ♇ ♂ ☿	2	7	26	2028	Jan	28	9:05	6♒48	♇ ☉ ☿ ♂ ☽
	Mar	24	12:58	16♓15	☽ ☿ ♂ ☉ ♆	2	1	47		Mar	26	14:45	21♓13	☿ ♂ ♆ ☉ ☽
	May	23	19:07	26♉26	☽ ☉ ♅ ☿ ♀	2	3	31		May	25	22:39	5♊14	☉ ♅ ♀ ☿ ☽
	May	30	2:16	23♉45	♂ ☉ ♅ ♀ ☿	15	21	38		Jun	14	23:54	4♊25	♀ ♂ ☿ ♅ ☉
	Jun	19	18:19	21♉11	☽ ♀ ♂ ☿ ♅	2	9	13		Jun	22	3:32	3♊11	♀ ☿ ♂ ♅ ☽
2029	Apr	13	16:50	21♈50	☽ ☉ ♀ ☿ ♄	2	0	46	2029	Apr	15	17:35	26♈02	☉ ♀ ♄ ☿ ☽
	May	12	22:27	15♉25	☽ ♄ ☉ ☿ ♀	0	3	22		May	13	1:48	15♉35	♄ ☽ ☿ ☉ ♀
2030	May	31	4:29	28♉07	☽ ♄ ♂ ☉ ♅	1	20	46	2030	Jun	2	1:14	0♊07	♄ ♂ ☉ ♅ ☽
	Jun	7	10:41	28♉32	☿ ♄ ♂ ☉ ♅	4	21	7		Jun	12	7:48	1♊25	♄ ☿ ♂ ♅ ☉
2032	May	26	8:05	3♊44	♀ ☉ ☿ ♂ ♄	16	1	49	2032	Jun	11	9:54	21♊02	☉ ♀ ♄ ♂ ☿
	May	26	19:29	6♊06	☉ ☿ ♂ ♄ ♅	15	14	25		Jun	11	9:54	21♊02	☉ ♄ ♅ ♂ ☿
	May	28	7:50	6♊11	♀ ☉ ☿ ♂ ♄ ♅	14	2	4		Jun	11	9:54	21♊02	☉ ♀ ♄ ♅ ♂ ☿
	May	28	7:50	6♊11	♀ ☿ ♂ ♄ ♅	17	8	39		Jun	14	16:29	26♊14	♄ ♅ ♀ ♂ ☿
	May	28	7:50	6♊11	♀ ☉ ♂ ♄ ♅	34	4	43		Jul	1	12:33	28♊12	♅ ♄ ☉ ♂ ♀
	Jun	7	4:49	6♊45	☽ ☉ ♀ ♄ ♅	2	14	7		Jun	9	18:56	19♊29	☉ ♀ ♄ ♅ ☽
	Jun	7	5:08	6♊55	☽ ☉ ♀ ♄ ♅ ♂	2	13	48		Jun	9	18:56	19♊29	☉ ♀ ♄ ♅ ♂ ☽
	Jun	7	5:08	6♊55	☽ ♀ ♄ ♅ ♂	2	18	9		Jun	9	23:17	21♊43	♀ ♄ ♅ ♂ ☽
	Jun	7	19:54	14♊49	☽ ☉ ♀ ♄ ♅ ♂ ☿	1	23	3		Jun	9	18:56	19♊29	☉ ♀ ♄ ♅ ♂ ☿ ☽
	Jun	7	19:54	14♊49	☽ ♀ ♄ ♅ ♂ ☿	2	3	23		Jun	9	23:17	21♊43	♀ ♄ ♅ ♂ ☿ ☽
	Jun	7	19:54	14♊49	☽ ♄ ♅ ♂ ☿	2	11	3		Jun	10	6:57	25♊39	♄ ♅ ♂ ☿ ☽
	Jul	5	23:51	26♊03	☽ ♅ ♄ ☉ ♂	1	19	50		Jul	7	19:41	28♊34	♅ ♄ ☉ ♂ ☽
	Jul	9	3:51	17♋31	☉ ♂ ♀ ☽ ☿	0	5	55		Jul	9	9:46	17♋45	☉ ♂ ♀ ☿ ☽
2033	Jan	30	8:03	2♒40	☽ ☉ ♃ ♇ ☿	2	0	15	2033	Feb	1	8:17	12♒47	☉ ♃ ♇ ☿ ☽
	Jun	26	6:09	27♊05	☽ ♅ ☉ ♄ ☿	1	20	49		Jun	28	2:58	2♋08	♅ ☉ ♄ ☿ ☽
2034	Jan	20	3:23	26♑40	☽ ☉ ♀ ♇ ☿	1	20	27	2034	Jan	21	23:51	2♒01	☉ ♀ ♇ ☿ ☽
	May	19	5:42	14♊01	☽ ☿ ♂ ♀ ♅	1	22	6		May	21	3:48	22♊19	☿ ♂ ♀ ♅ ☽
	May	20	12:09	27♊58	♂ ♀ ☽ ♅ ♄	1	2	24		May	21	14:33	28♊41	♂ ♀ ♅ ♄ ☽
2035	Apr	7	11:35	4♈38	☽ ☉ ☿ ♆ ♃	2	10	55	2035	Apr	9	22:30	19♈54	☉ ♆ ☿ ♃ ☽
	Jul	4	0:25	21♊55	☽ ☿ ♀ ♅ ☉	1	17	26		Jul	5	17:51	28♊13	☿ ♀ ♅ ☉ ☽
	Aug	3	8:46	6♌00	☽ ♀ ♄ ☉ ☿	1	14	19		Aug	4	23:06	9♌25	♄ ♀ ☉ ☿ ☽
2037	Feb	13	8:36	4♒58	☽ ☿ ♀ ♇ ☉	2	16	31	2037	Feb	16	1:07	16♒46	☿ ♀ ♇ ☉ ☽
	Apr	14	10:32	10♈57	☽ ☉ ☿ ♆ ♀	2	16	18		Apr	17	2:50	24♈01	☿ ♆ ☉ ♀ ☽
2038	Jul	30	23:44	24♋56	☽ ♅ ☉ ♃ ☿	1	12	20	2038	Aug	1	12:04	25♋23	♅ ☉ ♃ ☿ ☽
	Aug	4	1:37	21♋55	♀ ♅ ♃ ☉ ☿	4	3	23		Aug	8	4:60	25♋47	♅ ♀ ☿ ♃ ☉
	Aug	28	21:49	15♌42	☽ ♃ ☿ ♀ ☉	1	4	24		Aug	30	2:13	16♌50	♃ ☿ ♀ ☽ ☉
	Sep	28	3:22	26♍01	☽ ♀ ☉ ☿ ♂	1	17	30		Sep	29	20:52	2♎03	♀ ☉ ♂ ☿ ☽
	Nov	25	20:26	23♏23	☽ ♂ ☿ ☉ ♀	1	11	26		Nov	27	7:52	25♏46	☿ ♂ ☉ ♀ ☽
2040	Aug	28	21:03	20♍21	☿ ♀ ♃ ♂ ♄	23	16	28	2040	Sep	21	13:30	9♎21	♃ ♄ ☿ ♂ ♀
	Sep	7	5:15	21♍52	☽ ☿ ♃ ♄ ♀	2	18	17		Sep	9	23:32	6♎53	♃ ☿ ♄ ♀ ☽
	Sep	7	12:03	25♍24	☽ ☿ ♃ ♄ ♀ ♂	2	11	29		Sep	9	23:32	6♎53	♃ ☿ ♄ ♀ ♂ ☽
	Sep	7	12:03	25♍24	☽ ☿ ♄ ♀ ♂	2	16	42		Sep	10	4:45	9♎42	☿ ♄ ♀ ♂ ☽
2041	Oct	23	6:29	10♎14	☽ ☿ ♀ ♄ ☉	2	1	2	2041	Oct	25	7:31	15♎05	☿ ♀ ♄ ☉ ☽
	Oct	29	15:58	20♎59	♀ ☿ ♄ ☉ ♃	13	10	35		Nov	12	2:33	0♏05	♄ ♀ ☿ ♃ ☉
	Nov	22	0:43	10♏05	☽ ♃ ♀ ☿ ☉	2	1	39		Nov	24	2:22	16♏33	♃ ♀ ☉ ☿ ☽

5 or More Planets Within 20° Arc 1700-2050

	Starting Position				Planets in Zodiacal Sequence						Dy	Hr	Mn		Ending Position				Planets in Zodiacal Sequence					
2043	Mar	9	21:12	29♒11	☽	♇	♂	☿	☉		0	20	32	2043	Mar	10	17:44	0♓03	♇	☽	♂	☿	☉	
	May	7	6:46	20♈17	☽	♀	♂	☿	♆		1	13	32		May	8	20:19	23♈57	♀	☿	♂	♆	☽	
	May	7	17:37	27♈04	☽	☿	♂	♆	☉		1	13	13		May	9	6:50	0♉38	☿	♂	♆	☉	☽	
	Jun	4	19:16	6♉47	☽	♆	♂	☿	♀		1	15	12		Jun	6	10:28	11♉22	♆	♂	☿	♀	☽	
2045	Feb	4	3:46	15♒29	☿	☉	♃	♇	♂		5	7	26	2045	Feb	9	11:11	19♒40	♃	☉	☿	♇	♂	
	Feb	9	11:39	11♒55	♀	♃	☉	☿	♇		9	6	57		Feb	18	18:36	21♒53	♃	♀	☉	♇	☿	
	Feb	15	14:22	12♒06	☽	♀	♃	☉	♇		2	11	27		Feb	18	1:48	21♒43	♃	♀	☉	♇	☽	
	Feb	15	23:54	16♒49	☽	♀	♃	☉	♇	☿	2	1	54		Feb	18	1:48	21♒43	♃	♀	☉	♇	☿	☽
	Feb	15	23:54	16♒49	☽	♀	☉	♇	☿		2	4	1		Feb	18	3:55	22♒48	♀	☉	♇	☿	☽	
	Feb	16	17:10	25♒22	☽	☉	♇	☿	♂		2	2	2		Feb	18	19:12	0♓32	☉	♇	☿	♂	☽	
	Mar	17	21:04	18♓05	☽	♀	☉	☿	♂		2	12	0		Mar	20	9:04	29♓31	☿	☉	♀	♂	☽	
	Apr	17	0:30	23♈53	☽	☉	♂	♀	♆		1	21	31		Apr	18	22:01	29♈16	☉	♂	♀	♆	☽	
	May	15	4:55	4♉47	☽	☿	♆	♂	☉		2	4	25		May	17	9:20	15♉01	♆	☿	♂	☉	☽	
2046	Mar	6	13:05	2♓59	☽	♇	☿	☉	♃		1	18	42	2046	Mar	8	7:47	3♓59	♇	☿	☉	♃	☽	
	Aug	30	20:35	24♌52	☽	♀	♅	☉	☿		1	0	34		Aug	31	21:09	26♌44	♀	♅	☉	☽	☿	
2047	Jan	27	19:45	26♒00	☿	☽	♀	♇	♂		1	14	7	2047	Jan	29	9:52	27♒49	☿	♇	♀	♂	☽	
	Apr	22	4:00	29♈13	☿	☉	♃	♆	♂		5	20	12		Apr	28	0:13	3♉24	♃	☉	☿	♆	♂	
	Apr	24	15:39	28♈29	☽	♃	☉	☿	♆		2	1	42		Apr	26	17:21	3♉05	♃	☉	☿	♆	☽	
	Apr	24	21:04	1♉09	☽	♃	☉	☿	♆	♂	1	20	17		Apr	26	17:21	3♉05	♃	☉	☿	♆	♂	☽
	Apr	24	21:04	1♉09	☽	☉	☿	♆	♂		2	3	35		Apr	27	0:39	6♉43	☉	☿	♆	♂	☽	
2048	Mar	14	11:22	4♓33	☿	♀	♇	☽	☉		0	3	17	2048	Mar	14	14:38	4♓46	☿	♀	♇	☉	☽	
	May	12	3:60	14♉21	☽	♀	♆	☉	♃		2	4	35		May	14	8:34	20♉21	♀	♆	☉	♃	☽	
	May	12	16:40	20♉40	☽	♆	☉	♃	☿		1	18	4		May	14	10:45	21♉25	♆	☉	♃	☿	☽	
	May	14	22:42	21♉05	♀	♆	☉	♃	☿		17	1	36		Jun	1	0:18	22♉04	♆	☿	♃	☉	♀	
2049	Jun	29	9:40	29♊21	☽	☿	☉	♃	♂		2	4	22	2049	Jul	1	14:03	5♋15	☿	☉	♃	♂	☽	
	Sep	24	1:42	27♌19	☽	♀	☿	♂	♅		2	17	35		Sep	26	19:17	10♍52	♀	☿	♂	♅	☽	
	Sep	25	8:07	12♍43	☽	☿	♂	♅	☉		1	22	28		Sep	27	6:35	16♍46	☿	♂	♅	☉	☽	

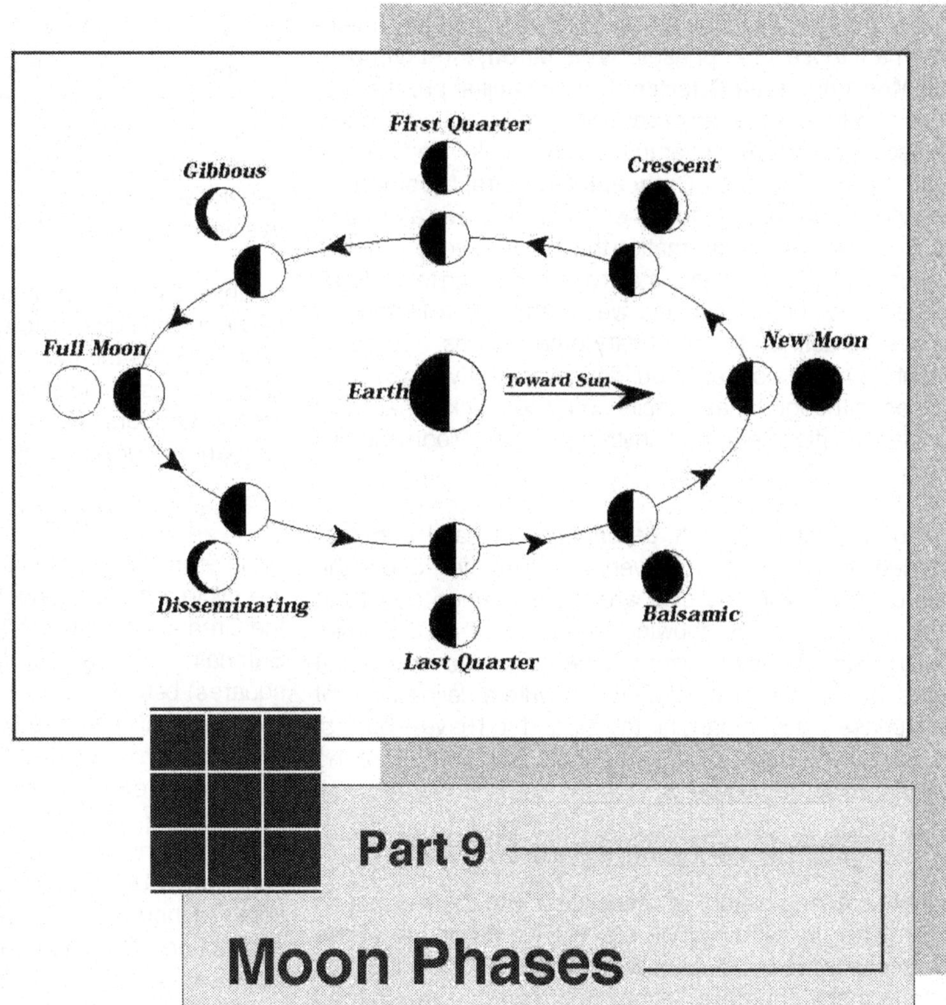

Part 9

Moon Phases

The Lunar Cycle: An 8-Fold Cycle of Transformation

by Maria Kay Simms

The only constant in life is change. Nothing is static. From the tiniest cell to the most complex organism, the cycle continues on—life, growth, deterioration, death and life, again. In planetary symbolism we associate the Moon with change, in reflection of her constantly changing faces in the waxing and waning of her cycle.

Four of the Moon's faces are well known, and many calendars mark those lunar phases: **New Moon, First Quarter, Full Moon** and **Last Quarter**. Not as familiar are the four cross quarter phases, as described by the great astrologer-philosopher Dane Rudhyar in his 1967 book *The Lunation Cycle*. These four are: **Crescent, Gibbous, Disseminating** and **Balsamic**. All together, then, we have a cycle of eight— a cycle of transformation that we can see reflected in our lives. We have a basic natal "type" according to the lunar phase in our birth chart and we go through a lifetime of phases as defined by secondary progressions. To some extent we might also relate our day-to-day activities to lunar phases, although lunar transits go by so quickly that most people pay little attention to anything but New Moon and Full Moon.

I've found that Rudhyar's descriptions of natal and progressed lunar phases "work" very well in my life—and in the lives of most everyone else whom I've queried about the subject. Neil's tables showing the dates of all 8 phases should make it easy for you to check and see how well it works for you, too. He asked me to write a delineation of each phase to accompany his tables, and so I have—but first I have a few thoughts I'd like to share with you about the symbolism of the number 8.

Eight: Transformation, Rebirth and Power

Eight has a long history of association with transformation and rebirth. In astrology we say the eighth house of the horoscope is the house of death and rebirth. The baptismal fonts in many churches—symbols of rebirth—are shaped like an octagon. Before Christianity, eight was a symbol of the Egyptian god Thoth who poured water of purification on the heads of new initiates. Ritual circumcision, as a mark of the covenant with God, is traditionally performed on the eighth day of life.

Rudhyar briefly links ancient Hindu, Chinese and Christian Gnostic symbolism of the number 8 with release of power in the dynamic interplay between two moving factors, but gives no specific reference. Numerologists consider eight to be a power number, and so do astrologers. Consider the 8-fold aspect series on which the lunar cycle is based. These "hard" aspects—conjunction, square and opposition, semisquare and sesquiquadrate—are considered to be the most powerful of all aspects in regard to physical manifestation. I'd like very much to hear from any readers who have additional material on the origins of this obviously very ancient symbolism of 8.

A Cycle of Relationship

It is important to note that in discussing the lunar cycle we are not just talking about the Moon in your chart. We are talking about the Moon **in relation** to the Sun. The lunar cycle is a cycle of relationship. Rudhyar says, "Relationship generates power; without relationship there is no power available for release."

Rudhyar says that the point of basic crisis in the relationship between two polar factors is the square—thus the four-fold cross which is the foundation of both the 8-fold and the 12-fold divisions of the circle. "But four more points, bisecting the four quarters, are necessary to mark the positions (or the moments) of greatest momentum and most critical release."

An 8-Fold Solar Cycle

It is interesting that in the 8 ancient pagan holidays, which are the cycle of transformation through the seasons of the year, the Greater Sabbats are Imbolc, Beltane, Lughnasad and Samhain. These four fall at the cross-quarters (semi-squares) between the four-fold cross of the equinoxes and solstices that mark the beginning of each season. These solar holidays, based on the 8-fold aspect series of the Sun to the vernal equinox, celebrate the cycle of nature. Yet their mythology is such a close match in meaning to Rudhyar's interpretations of the lunar phases that I have wondered if he might have used them as a framework for his interpretations—although I could find nothing in his book to suggest a connection. They **do** connect in symbolism, however, and the meaning of one cycle contributes much to the understanding of the other. Because of that I will include some commentary on the Sabbats in my paragraphs on each lunar phase.

The cycle of the 8 seasonal Sabbats—the Wheel of the Year—is the interplay of relationship between the Sun and Earth. Earthly forms change in response to the energy of the Sun. Seeds germinate, sprout, grow, mature, wither, die, are dormant, are warmed by the Sun and then the cycle begins again. The lunar cycle is the interplay of relationship between Sun and Moon, as the Moon reflects the light of the Sun through her constantly changing faces. Here, however, it is important to realize the true partner in this relationship—Earth! The phases of the Moon as we know them exist only in reference to our vantage point on Earth. The phases tell us nothing about the Moon herself, but only about the state of the relationship between her, the satellite of Earth, and the Sun.

The Moon, then, serves us earthlings by telling us about relationship—but what relationship? Not our relationships with other people—although certainly many of our life events and accompanying development are worked out through our interactions with others. The true relationship at issue here is our relationship with ourselves, the inner relationship of form and energy (spirit).

It seems that some concept of dualism is necessary for our perception within the universe. For our purpose here, let's symbolically assign the Sun the role of spirit, of divine **energy**, while Earth represents matter, or **form**. Let's **not** assign either one to an arbitrary category of "good" or "bad" but, rather, perceive them as equally important. Without form, energy is pointless, has no purpose. Without energy, form is inert and lifeless.

Now, what does all this symbolically mean to us in terms of understanding our birth charts and, consequently, our lives? Let's imagine the Sun saying, "I am light and vitality. Receive my energy that together we might have life and purpose for being." Our earthly forms might answer, "But you are too bright! I can't even look at you directly without hurting my eyes. If I try to take in all your energy all the time, I'll burn out. Give it to me in measured doses that I can handle and give me some time to rest!"

And what then, says the Moon? She might say, "Let me serve you. I will mediate for you by reflecting the light of the Sun in softer hues. I am approachable—you can easily gaze on me, and I will show you the light in progressive stages and help you understand the flow of the life energies within you. Let me show you the seasons of your life!"

Moon and Mother Earth have long been linked with feminine characteristics and the Goddess, while Sun has been associated with masculine characteristics and God. (This is not a universal idea. Some mythologies include Sun goddesses

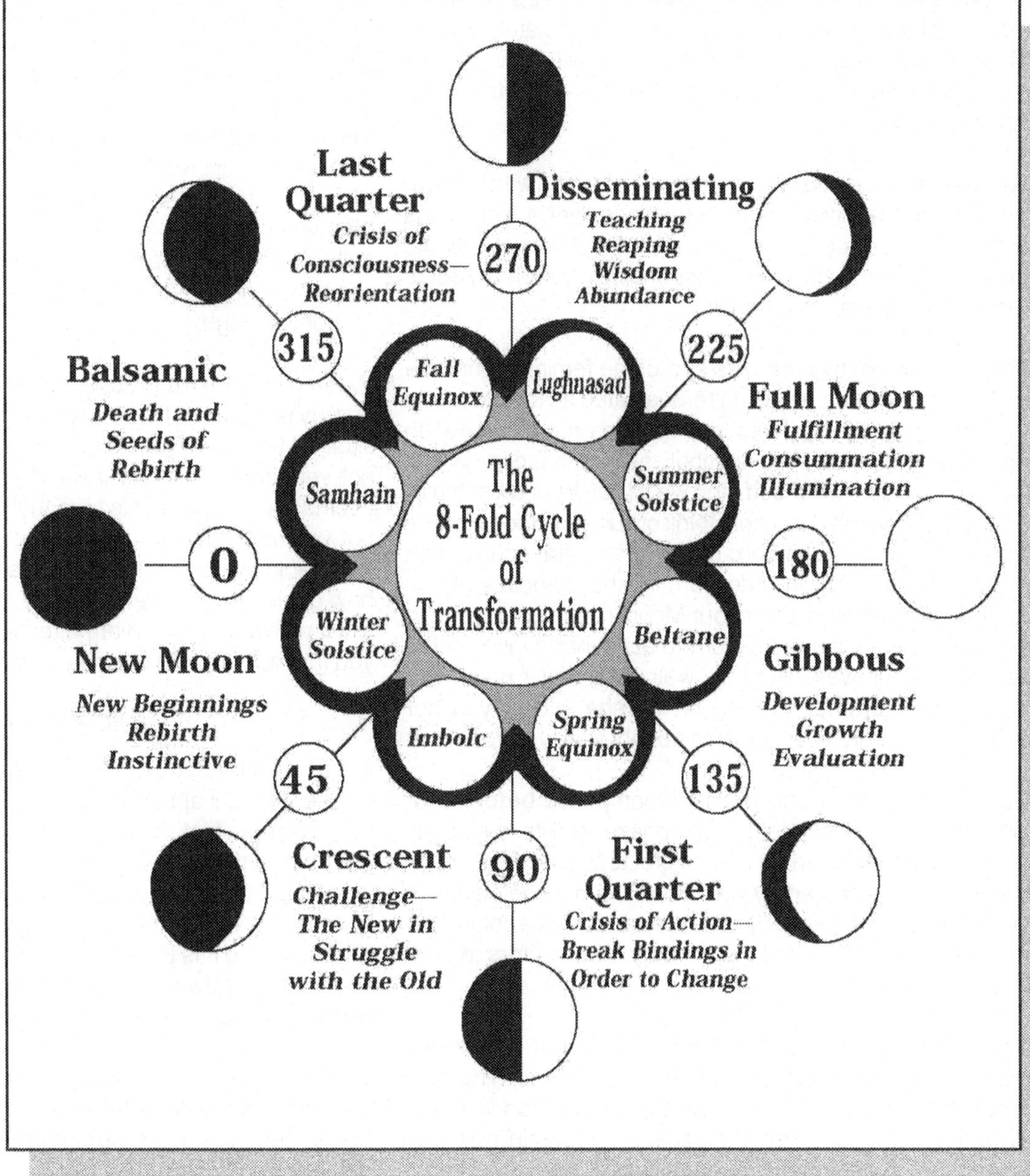

and the "man in the Moon" idea came from somewhere!) The concept of the Goddess as the more approachable mediator is not new, either—even within patriarchal Christianity which denies her divinity. Countless prayers have been offered to Mary as interceder.

The Moon as mediator, reflecting or making **objective** the message of the Sun, is an intellectual concept. Now, in astrology we think of Mercury (a "masculine" planet) as intellect, and by that we mean the rational, logical thought processes of mind. But this is only **one** aspect of mind. Even the most logical, scientific procedures begin with a hunch—an **intuitive** thought. This is the realm of the Moon! Our first thoughts of the Moon usually emphasize her nurturing qualities, her changeableness—but we must not overlook her importance as a symbol of mind. Our culture has devalued the aspect of mind which is more closely associated with the Moon by the very words used to describe the intuitive aspect of intellect—**sub**conscious or **un**conscious—as if this function was inferior.

We have also associated the principle of action with masculine and responsiveness with feminine, yet if conscious actions tend to proceed in response to intuitive motivations, then who is acting and who is responding? Which aspect of mind, then, is more powerful?

The value of intuitive qualities and of the feminine principle in general is fortunately being re-evaluated as the old world view of patriarchy begins to lose its hold on our culture. In any case, the relationship symbolized by the lunar cycle is the relationship **within self**, and we all carry our own "male" and "female" within. We might think of our Sun (and Mercury, his messenger) as symbolic of the basic, vital energy with which we are to act in order to fulfill the purposes of this lifetime. We can then look to our Moon in her relationship to our Sun for the intuitive wisdom to act in harmony with the seasons of our lives. So mark well—and never underestimate—the power of your Moon as she shows you her changing faces in reflection of the bright vitality of your Sun.

Look in the table for the closest Moon phase **before** your birthday. This is your natal Moon phase, and its mythology and symbolism should be meaningful to you in terms of the life purpose suggested by your Sun. The brief delineations given here are, of course, generalized, and will be colored by the sign of your Sun and modified by other factors in your chart.

Your progressed lunar phase should give you insight into major transformative cycles within your lifetime. The progressed lunar phase is the aspect of Progressed Moon to Progressed Sun. It is found, in general, by counting one day forward in the ephemeris for each year of life—you should also be able to figure this out from the table. A complete progressed Moon cycle, from New Moon to New Moon again takes approximately 29 years, with each phase lasting around 3-1/2 years. A brief commentary on each of the 8 phases in the cycle of transformation follows:

New Moon

This is the dark of the Moon. Conjunct the Sun, she is, of course, not visible in the night sky. In the cycle of the seasons, Yule or Winter Solstice represents the rebirth of the light. Here, during the longest night of the year, the Goddess goes forth into the other world to give birth to the Sun Child, and hope for new light is reborn, in joy and celebration. This mythology has been carried out in many religious traditions, including Christianity, in the choice of Winter Solstice for the birth of the son—Jesus. Also, Lucina the Sun Goddess, who rekindles the Sun and brings new light, is known today as Santa Lucia with the wreath of candles on her head.

The New Moon-born individual projects the self on the world with a sense of creative new beginning brought forth largely through instinct or sheer impulse. Here is one who operates best when meeting the challenge of the moment dynamically, often dramatically, who moves forward with the urge to get things going—but may not yet have the process well thought through.

When you are at Progressed New Moon, some new creative energy is released that marks the beginning of a major new cycle of your life. But it is not yet firmly established, and it is not yet certain just how it will develop. Often an event (or events) will occur at this time that "marks" the new cycle—but you may not even be aware of its importance until you look back on it later. This is a time of gradual awakening to new goals. It is not yet a definite break with the past, but it is a time when old familiar patterns seem to lack vitality and you instinctively feel a sense of creative new beginnings.

Crescent

In the monthly lunar cycle this is the time when the first silvery crescent of light appears in the night sky—the newborn light begins to manifest. At the time of the yearly seasonal holiday known as Imbolc or Candlemas (February 2) the newborn Sun God is seen as a small child nursing at the breast of the Mother. New beginnings are nurtured, seeds stir beneath the earth, and it is time to think of spring cleaning as winter and death are swept away. The energy is directed toward blessing and empowering new beginnings.

You who are born at Crescent Moon feel a strong impulse toward action, yet seem forever to be involved in intense challenges. In one way or another you are trying to break with traditions of the past. You may be involved in change from one class to another, or perhaps in the attempt to break away from family expectations, or to improve your status. In some way or another you represent the new in perpetual struggle against the old.

At the time of your Progressed Crescent Moon the new beginnings that were released at Progressed New Moon begin to crystallize and take form. You are challenged to carry forward, but in order to do so, you may have to break from something in the past.

First Quarter

Half of the Moon is now visible at night, a balance between dark and light. In the yearly solar cycle this corresponds to Spring Equinox or Eostar, when days and nights are of equal length. It is the point of equilibrium just before life bursts forth, the chains of winter are broken, and light will reign as the days grow longer. Rituals of this holiday often involve the action of breaking bindings in order to symbolically empower self-change. The God and Goddess are young children at play, and holiday festivals affirm the child within and celebrate new birth with brightly colored eggs.

This phase of the lunar cycle has been called the crisis of action. You who are born during this phase may feel that your life is one crisis after another. You are attracted to action, noise, and movement because you sense in yourself a constant urge to get going—to progress—even if the end goal you are moving toward is just a bit hazy. You feel that you have to clear away old forms or structures that you perceive as obstacles so that you can create new ones. You are strong willed and are likely to develop skills in management.

Progressed First Quarter brings a crisis of action in the new direction that you are establishing in your life. This is the time to make it happen—to be aggressive in pursuing your goals. If there is anything from your past that is holding you back, this is the time to resolve that issue and clear it away once and for all.

Gibbous

The Moon in the sky is increasing in light, but not yet full. The seasonal correspondence is to Beltane or May Eve, the time of sacred marriage which honors the life-giving fertility of the blooming earth. The maiden Goddess now comes of age, blooming with self-discovery, and is pursued by the God in fun and courtship. Celebrations include weaving the web of life around a Maypole and leaping the Beltane fires for luck and future fulfillment of wishes.

You who are Gibbous-born give much attention to self-discovery. You are developing your capacity for personal growth in your desire to make your lives something of value. You constantly evaluate—constantly ask "why"—where you are going, how you are growing, what you are doing that has significance. Nothing is taken for granted. It is important to you to make things clear, to discover better ways of doing things. You could become caught up in working for a cause.

At the Progressed Gibbous Moon you are challenged to perfect the methods of your new direction in life. You could call this the period of apprenticeship. Your new direction is established but not yet fulfilled. This is a stage of development in which you must analyze and evaluate your growth and reorganize or improve your techniques so that you can grow beyond technique and reach out for true fulfillment.

Full Moon

The Moon now shines opposite in the zodiac from the Sun, reflecting his light in all her fullness. In correspondence with the seasonal cycle it is now Midsummer, or Summer Solstice. At the longest day, light triumphs, yet at the same time begins its decline into the dark. From here on, the light will wane. This is the symbolic sacrifice of the Sun King who embraces the Queen of Summer in fulfillment of love that is also death, for his energy must go into the form of the harvest grain, which will die in order to feed new life. It is a season of fulfillment, consummation, abundance—and yet, at the same time, a recognition of the other side, the ending that approaches but is not yet real.

As the Full Moon stands at polar opposite to the Sun, so will the Full Moon-born be strongly involved in issues of relationship. Long before the realization sets in that the true completion is within self, you may go through considerable crises in your relationships with others. Perhaps more than with other phase-types, it is through relationships that you will achieve objectivity and clarity about your own purpose. And it is the discovery of purpose that is paramount. Fulfillment—even abundance—is not enough. You must find illumination, a worthwhile reason for your life.

Progressed Full Moon is a fulfillment or climax of the new direction that began about 14-15 years ago at your Progressed New Moon. It's a high period. The new structures you've been building work! Now what? As at Summer Solstice, the light triumphs, but does that also mean that now there's only one way to go—into decline? Is further growth possible? A bit scary, isn't it? It is important at this time to pause for illumination, to consider the meaning or purpose for what you are doing. And also to integrate any opposing issues from within or without. If there is no illumination, your vitality and enthusiasm for what you are doing are likely to wane and the structures begin to crumble as your direction loses clarity. But if what you have built is truly meaningful, you have much to give back to the world in the coming phase.

Disseminating

The round Moon is now a bit flat on one side, but still bright in the sky. This phase corresponds to the solar festival of Lughnasad which, in the beginning of August, celebrates the first fruits of the fertile harvest that assures life's survival. The full harvest is nearly ready, but not yet completely certain, still vulnerable to weather and change. It is a time of waiting and maturing, with energy directed toward prosperity, growth in wisdom and the reaping of plenty. The Sun King dies when the grain is reaped, and the Earth Mother becomes the reaper, feeding on the energy of life that new life may grow.

Illumination is reached at Full Moon, and at Disseminating Moon it is spread. You who are born at this phase like to communicate ideas that are meaningful to you. You are a natural communicator, a born teacher. If a particular cause has become important to you, you could be quite a crusader. The main purpose for your life—what you live for—is to share your wisdom, your beliefs, your interests.

During the period of your Progressed Disseminating Moon it is time to share with the world the fruits of your achievements of your Full Moon culmination and, more importantly, the wisdom of your illumination. This is the time to teach what you've learned.

Last Quarter

Once again the Moon is half light and half dark—as in the solar cycle at Autumn Equinox, the days and nights are equal. At this balance point, however, it is light that must give way to increased darkness. It is harvest and a time of joy and thanksgiving, yet it is also a time of leave-taking and sorrow for the approaching decline of life. The Goddess mourns her fallen consort, yet the festival emphasis is on the message of rebirth in the harvest seeds and plenty.

Last Quarter is the time of crisis in consciousness and you who are born under this phase know deep inside yourself that somehow you do not "fit in" with the accepted way. You are likely to seem different on the surface (to others) than what is really germinating inside. You could even seem inflexible to others, for you will, on the surface, stick to established structures and patterns because you are not yet ready to "come out" with your inner reorientation. At times when your progressions may indicate you are ready, a "new you" may come suddenly to the surface, surprising others who did not realize the changes that were going on inside you.

At Progressed Last Quarter you will experience some crisis in consciousness that will lead you away from the dominant activities of your current progressed lunar cycle and will begin to prepare you for a new direction at the next Progressed New Moon. You may begin to resist previous ways of doing things because it seems that somehow they no longer serve you. What was to be accomplished since the last New Moon has been done. Deep inside you something new is germinating, even though on the surface you may not show this to others.

Balsamic

Only a sliver of light now remains in the night sky—the waning Crescent Moon. The Balsamic Moon corresponds to the festival of Samhain in the solar cycle, a holiday that is more popularly known as Halloween. This is said to be the time when the veil between the visible and invisible worlds is thin, when souls who are leaving this physical plane pass out, and souls who are reincarnating pass in. Darkness is increasing, the Goddess reigns as the elder Wise Woman or Crone (model for the secular Halloween witch), and the God has passed into the underworld to become the seed of his own rebirth. Winter approaches, but it is understood that death or rest is a natural and necessary part of the cycle, in order that life may continue.

As Balsamic-born, you could be one who seems somehow out-of-sync with the majority, one about whom it could be said "listens to the beat of a different drummer." You may have a sense of the prophet about you. You are sure that you have a special destiny. You are not too clear on just what it is or where you are going, but you are ready to flow with it.

Many experience the Progressed Balsamic Moon period as a true "dark-of-the-Moon," but it should not be looked upon as a fallow period when nothing is accomplished. You will probably try several new starts in your attempt to reach out for your new cycle. Some of them will fall by the wayside, but others—or one—will prove to be the successful conception of the new cycle. Do not mourn for what has ended—it has served its purpose. Have the faith to know that every ending is the seed of a new beginning. The wheel keeps turning!

The 8 Phases of the Moon 1900–2020

Month	Day	Time	Position	Phase
Jan 1900	1	13:52	10♑45	0
	4	20:40	29♒05	45
	8	5:40	17♈32	90
	11	21:12	6♊15	135
	15	19:07	25♋14	180
	19	21:35	14♍24	225
	23	23:53	3♏34	270
	27	17:43	22♐23	315
	31	1:23	10♒45	0
Feb 1900	3	6:00	29♓00	45
	6	16:23	17♉28	90
	10	12:09	6♋20	135
	14	13:50	25♌27	180
	18	17:04	14♎37	225
	22	16:44	3♐38	270
	26	6:28	22♑14	315
Mar 1900	1	11:25	10♓27	0
	4	16:12	28♈39	45
	8	5:34	17♊13	90
	12	5:03	6♌11	135
	16	8:12	25♍18	180
	20	9:47	14♏21	225
	24	5:36	3♑08	270
	27	16:04	21♒32	315
	30	20:30	9♈41	0
Apr 1900	3	3:40	27♉56	45
	6	20:55	16♋36	90
	10	22:46	5♍36	135
	15	1:02	24♎37	180
	18	23:00	13♐26	225
	22	14:33	2♒00	270
	25	23:14	20♓16	315
	29	5:23	8♉26	0
May 1900	2	16:35	26♊48	45
	6	13:39	15♌33	90
	10	16:15	4♎31	135
	14	15:37	23♏21	180
	18	8:42	11♑56	225
	21	20:31	0♓17	270
	25	5:12	18♈31	315
	28	14:50	6♊47	0
Jun 1900	1	6:47	25♋18	45
	5	6:59	14♍08	90
	9	8:41	3♏02	135
	13	3:39	21♐39	180
	16	15:39	9♒59	225
	20	0:57	28♓13	270
	23	11:18	16♉30	315
	27	1:27	4♋55	0
	30	22:03	23♌36	45
Jul 1900	5	0:13	12♎30	90
	8	23:29	1♐17	135
	12	13:22	19♑42	180
	15	21:06	7♓52	225
	19	5:31	26♈03	270
	22	18:50	14♊27	315
	26	13:43	3♌04	0
	30	14:09	21♍55	45
Aug 1900	3	16:45	10♏51	90
	7	12:21	29♐30	135
	10	21:30	17♒45	180
	14	2:34	5♈49	225
	17	11:46	24♉05	270
	21	4:46	12♋39	315
	25	3:52	1♍28	0
	29	6:42	20♎27	45
Sep 1900	2	7:56	9♐22	90
	5	23:21	27♑54	135
	9	5:06	16♓03	180
	12	9:30	4♉08	225
	15	20:57	22♊32	270
	19	17:46	11♌18	315
	23	19:57	0♎19	0
	27	23:03	19♏22	45
Oct 1900	1	21:10	8♑13	90
	5	8:55	26♒39	135
	8	13:18	14♈48	180
	11	19:04	3♊00	225
	15	9:51	21♋35	270
	19	10:06	10♍34	315
	23	13:27	29♎41	0
	27	14:16	18♐43	45
	31	8:17	7♒28	90
Nov 1900	3	17:46	25♓52	135
	6	23:00	14♉06	180
	10	7:53	2♋29	225
	14	2:37	21♌17	270
	18	5:18	10♎26	315
	22	7:17	29♏33	0
	26	3:34	18♑27	45
	29	17:35	7♓05	90
Dec 1900	3	2:38	25♈30	135
	6	10:38	13♊53	180
	9	23:54	2♌30	225
	13	22:42	21♍31	270
	18	2:02	10♏44	315
	22	0:01	29♐43	0
	25	14:45	18♒24	45
	29	1:48	6♈56	90
Jan 1901	1	12:05	25♉25	135
	5	0:13	14♋00	180
	8	18:30	2♍50	225
	12	20:38	22♎00	270
	16	22:13	11♐08	315
	20	14:36	29♑53	0
	24	0:18	18♓21	45
	27	9:52	6♉48	90
	30	22:37	25♊24	135
Feb 1901	3	15:30	14♌09	180
	7	14:37	3♎10	225
	11	18:12	22♏22	270
	15	15:52	11♑18	315
	19	2:45	29♒47	0
	22	9:05	18♈05	45
	25	18:38	6♊30	90
Mar 1901	1	10:30	25♋10	135
	5	8:04	14♍05	180
	9	10:41	3♏11	225
	13	13:06	22♐17	270
	17	5:59	10♒58	315
	20	12:53	29♓14	0
	23	17:49	17♉25	45
	27	4:39	5♋50	90
	30	23:57	24♌35	135
Apr 1901	4	1:20	13♎35	180
	8	4:53	2♐40	225
	12	3:57	21♑33	270
	15	16:39	10♓01	315
	18	21:37	28♈09	0
	22	3:02	16♊18	45
	25	16:15	4♌45	90
	29	15:00	23♍35	135
May 1901	3	18:19	12♏36	180
	7	19:53	1♑32	225
	11	14:38	20♒11	270
	15	0:37	8♈29	315
	18	5:38	26♉34	0
	21	13:04	14♋46	45
	25	5:39	3♍18	90
	29	7:16	22♎12	135
Jun 1901	2	9:53	11♐09	180
	6	7:15	29♑52	225
	9	22:00	18♓19	270
	13	6:55	6♉33	315
	16	13:33	24♊40	0
	20	0:24	12♌58	45
	23	20:59	1♎39	90
	27	23:58	20♏35	135
Jul 1901	1	23:18	9♑22	180
	5	15:37	27♒53	225
	9	3:20	16♈12	270
	12	12:35	4♊26	315
	15	22:10	22♋40	0
	19	13:33	11♍09	45
	23	13:58	29♎59	90
	27	16:07	18♐53	135
	31	10:34	7♒30	180
Aug 1901	3	22:11	25♓50	225
	7	8:02	14♉06	270
	10	18:46	2♋24	315
	14	8:27	20♌50	0
	18	4:57	9♎32	45
	22	7:52	28♏30	90
	26	7:04	17♑20	135
	29	20:21	5♓46	180
Sep 1901	2	4:19	23♈59	225
	5	13:27	12♊16	270
	9	2:43	0♌43	315
	12	21:19	19♍23	0
	16	22:24	8♏20	45
	21	1:33	27♐22	90
	24	20:37	16♒05	135
	28	5:36	4♈23	180
Oct 1901	1	11:17	22♉34	225
	4	20:52	10♋55	270
	8	13:39	29♌34	315
	12	13:11	18♎30	0
	16	16:54	7♐38	45
	20	17:58	26♑39	90
	24	8:57	15♓15	135
	27	15:06	3♉30	180
	30	20:01	21♊42	225
Nov 1901	3	7:24	10♌11	270
	7	4:25	29♍04	315
	11	7:34	18♏14	0
	15	10:53	7♑24	45
	19	8:23	26♒20	90
	22	20:17	14♈51	135
	26	1:18	3♊06	180
	29	7:08	21♋23	225
Dec 1901	2	21:50	10♍03	270
	6	22:55	29♎09	315
	11	2:53	18♐23	0
	15	2:58	7♒28	45
	18	20:35	26♓16	90
	22	6:41	14♉45	135
	25	12:16	3♋02	180
	28	20:57	21♌28	225
Jan 1902	1	16:08	10♎20	270
	5	19:44	29♏34	315
	9	21:14	18♑43	0
	13	16:30	7♓35	45
	17	6:38	26♈15	90
	20	16:11	14♊42	135
	24	0:06	3♌05	180
	27	13:26	21♍42	225
	31	13:08	10♏45	270
Feb 1902	4	16:32	29♐57	315
	8	13:21	18♒52	0
	12	3:35	7♈31	45
	15	14:56	26♉01	90
	19	1:09	14♋28	135
	22	13:03	3♍00	180
	26	7:59	21♎48	225
Mar 1902	2	10:39	10♐56	270
	6	11:18	29♑58	315
	10	2:50	18♓37	0
	13	12:41	7♉01	45
	16	22:13	25♊24	90
	20	10:22	13♌53	135
	24	3:21	2♎34	180
	28	3:15	21♏31	225
Apr 1902	1	6:24	10♑36	270
	5	2:59	29♒24	315
	8	13:50	17♈48	0
	11	20:25	6♊01	45
	15	5:26	24♋19	90
	18	20:44	12♍52	135
	22	18:49	1♏42	180
	26	21:36	20♐42	225
	30	22:58	9♒38	270
May 1902	4	15:26	28♓13	315
	7	22:45	16♉25	0
	11	3:34	4♋31	45
	14	13:40	22♌49	90
	18	8:57	11♎29	135
	22	10:46	0♐24	180
	26	13:41	19♑21	225
	30	12:00	8♓07	270
Jun 1902	3	1:00	26♈31	315
	6	6:11	14♊36	0
	9	11:03	2♌40	45
	12	23:54	21♍02	90
	16	23:06	9♏50	135
	21	2:17	28♐46	180
	25	3:03	17♒37	225
	28	21:52	6♈13	270
Jul 1902	2	8:18	24♉30	315
	5	12:59	12♋33	0
	8	19:54	0♍41	45
	12	12:47	19♎13	90
	16	14:45	8♐06	135
	20	16:45	27♑00	180
	24	13:53	15♓42	225
	28	5:15	4♉11	270
	31	14:14	22♊25	315
Aug 1902	3	20:17	10♌31	0
	7	7:08	28♍50	45
	11	4:24	17♏34	90
	15	7:14	6♑31	135
	19	6:03	25♒19	180
	22	22:50	13♈52	225
	26	11:04	2♊16	270
	29	19:59	20♋31	315
Sep 1902	2	5:19	8♍48	0
	5	21:22	27♎21	45
	9	22:15	16♐16	90
	13	23:55	5♒14	135
	17	18:23	23♓55	180
	21	6:38	12♉20	225
	24	16:32	0♋41	270
	28	2:57	19♌03	315
Oct 1902	1	17:09	7♎35	0
	5	14:32	26♏25	45
	9	17:21	15♑29	90
	13	16:17	4♓23	135
	17	6:01	22♈56	180
	20	14:11	11♊15	225
	23	22:58	29♋36	270
	27	12:31	18♍09	315
	31	8:14	6♏59	0
Nov 1902	4	9:44	26♐03	45
	8	12:30	15♒11	90
	12	7:50	4♈00	135
	15	17:06	22♉25	180
	18	22:24	10♋39	225
	22	7:47	29♌05	270
	26	1:36	17♎52	315
	30	2:04	6♐56	0
Dec 1902	4	5:29	26♑08	45
	8	6:27	15♓15	90
	11	21:53	3♉57	135
	15	3:47	22♊15	180
	18	8:09	10♌29	225
	21	20:00	29♍02	270
	25	18:14	18♏02	315
	29	21:25	7♑15	0
Jan 1903	3	0:11	26♒27	45
	6	21:57	15♈26	90
	10	9:52	4♊00	135

The 8 Phases of the Moon 1900–2020

Month	Day	Time	Position	Phase
	13	14:17	22♋14	180
	16	20:06	10♍32	225
	20	11:49	29♎16	270
	24	13:23	18♐24	315
	28	16:38	7♒36	0
Feb 1903	1	16:30	26♓40	45
	5	10:12	15♉27	90
	8	19:44	3♋54	135
	12	0:58	22♌09	180
	15	10:23	10♎34	225
	19	6:23	29♏26	270
	23	9:25	18♑36	315
	27	10:19	7♓40	0
Mar 1903	3	5:37	26♈29	45
	6	19:14	15♊03	90
	10	4:00	3♌25	135
	13	12:13	21♍45	180
	17	2:32	10♏20	225
	21	2:08	29♐18	270
	25	4:40	18♒22	315
	29	1:26	7♈11	0
Apr 1903	1	15:28	25♉44	45
	5	1:51	14♋07	90
	8	11:39	2♍28	135
	12	0:18	20♎56	180
	15	19:37	9♐39	225
	19	21:30	28♑38	270
	23	21:49	17♓33	315
	27	13:31	6♉07	0
	30	22:45	24♊24	45
May 1903	4	7:26	12♌40	90
	7	19:46	1♎04	135
	11	13:18	19♏40	180
	15	12:44	8♑30	225
	19	15:18	27♒27	270
	23	12:08	16♈11	315
	26	22:50	4♊29	0
	30	4:38	22♋36	45
Jun 1903	2	13:24	10♍49	90
	6	5:12	29♎20	135
	10	3:08	18♐04	180
	14	5:13	6♒58	225
	18	6:44	25♓51	270
	21	23:26	14♉23	315
	25	6:11	2♋31	0
	28	10:33	20♌33	45
Jul 1903	1	21:02	8♎49	90
	5	16:33	27♏27	135
	9	17:43	16♑19	180
	13	20:31	5♓14	225
	17	19:24	24♈01	270
	21	8:10	12♊23	315
	24	12:46	0♌26	0
	27	17:48	18♍30	45
	31	7:15	6♏54	90
Aug 1903	4	6:10	25♐41	135
	8	8:54	14♒38	180
	12	10:15	3♈31	225
	16	5:23	22♉10	270
	19	15:16	10♋27	315
	22	19:51	28♌31	0
	26	3:24	16♎43	45
	29	20:34	5♐18	90
Sep 1903	2	22:05	24♑14	135
	7	0:20	13♓12	180
	10	22:06	2♉00	225
	14	13:14	20♊32	270
	17	21:54	8♌49	315
	21	4:31	27♍01	0
	24	16:01	15♏25	45
	28	13:08	4♑14	90
Oct 1903	2	15:57	23♒16	135
	6	15:24	12♈11	180
	10	8:10	0♊51	225
	13	19:57	19♋18	270
	17	5:13	7♍39	315
	20	15:30	26♎04	0
	24	7:49	14♐44	45
	28	8:33	3♒45	90
Nov 1903	1	10:46	22♓50	135
	5	5:27	11♉37	180
	8	17:02	0♋07	225
	12	2:46	18♌32	270
	15	14:12	7♎02	315
	19	5:10	25♏42	0
	23	2:28	14♑38	45
	27	5:37	3♓48	90
Dec 1903	1	5:05	22♈50	135
	4	18:13	11♊26	180
	8	1:38	29♋47	225
	11	10:53	18♍14	270
	15	1:31	6♏54	315
	18	21:26	25♐48	0
	22	22:57	14♒56	45
	27	2:22	4♈10	90
	30	21:29	23♉02	135
Jan 1904	3	5:47	11♋26	180
	6	10:55	29♌43	225
	9	21:10	18♎12	270
	13	15:28	7♐03	315
	17	15:47	26♑08	0
	21	19:34	15♓22	45
	25	20:41	4♉29	90
	29	11:10	23♊09	135
Feb 1904	1	16:33	11♌25	180
	4	21:28	29♍40	225
	8	9:56	18♏14	270
	12	7:54	7♑12	315
	16	11:05	26♒22	0
	20	14:10	15♈32	45
	24	11:08	4♊26	90
	27	22:08	22♋55	135
Mar 1904	2	2:48	11♍07	180
	5	9:23	29♎24	225
	9	1:01	18♐03	270
	13	2:08	7♒05	315
	17	5:39	26♓13	0
	21	5:09	15♉10	45
	24	21:37	3♋50	90
	28	6:49	22♌10	135
	31	12:44	10♎23	180
Apr 1904	3	22:26	28♏44	225
	7	17:53	17♑29	270
	11	20:54	6♓32	315
	15	21:53	25♈29	0
	19	16:11	14♊10	45
	23	4:55	2♌36	90
	26	13:58	20♍54	135
	29	22:36	9♏09	180
May 1904	3	12:32	27♐38	225
	7	11:50	16♒28	270
	11	14:40	5♈27	315
	15	10:58	24♉10	0
	19	0:03	12♋35	45
	22	10:19	0♍52	90
	25	20:31	19♎10	135
	29	8:55	7♐32	180
Jun 1904	2	3:43	26♑10	225
	6	5:53	15♓04	270
	10	6:15	3♉55	315
	13	21:10	22♊23	0
	17	6:03	10♌36	45
	20	15:10	28♍49	90
	24	3:31	17♏10	135
	27	20:23	5♑42	180
Jul 1904	1	19:50	24♒29	225
	5	22:54	13♈26	270
	9	19:18	2♊06	315
	13	5:27	20♋22	0
	16	11:37	8♍28	45
	19	20:48	26♎42	90
	23	12:08	15♐10	135
	27	9:42	3♒54	180
	31	12:23	22♓49	225
Aug 1904	4	14:03	11♉43	270
	8	6:09	0♋14	315
	11	12:58	18♌23	0
	14	17:58	6♎28	45
	18	4:27	24♏47	90
	21	23:29	13♑26	135
	26	1:02	2♓21	180
	30	4:27	21♈21	225
Sep 1904	3	2:58	10♊10	270
	6	15:32	28♋35	315
	9	20:43	16♍42	0
	13	2:06	4♏51	45
	16	15:13	23♐18	90
	20	14:15	12♒10	135
	24	17:50	1♈14	180
	28	19:10	20♉13	225
Oct 1904	2	13:52	8♋56	270
	6	0:13	27♌19	315
	9	5:25	15♎29	0
	12	12:52	3♐46	45
	16	5:54	22♑27	90
	20	8:17	11♓31	135
	24	10:56	0♉36	180
	28	8:04	19♊29	225
	31	23:13	8♌07	270
Nov 1904	4	8:44	26♍31	315
	7	15:37	14♏49	0
	11	2:53	3♑18	45
	15	0:35	22♒14	90
	19	4:17	11♈25	135
	23	3:12	0♊25	180
	26	19:20	19♋08	225
	30	7:38	7♍41	270
Dec 1904	3	17:34	26♎09	315
	7	3:46	14♐38	0
	10	20:20	3♒23	45
	14	22:07	22♓32	90
	19	0:20	11♉42	135
	22	18:01	0♋30	180
	26	5:27	19♌02	225
	29	15:46	7♎32	270
Jan 1905	2	3:18	26♏05	315
	5	18:17	14♑47	0
	9	16:29	3♓47	45
	13	20:11	23♈01	90
	17	18:44	12♊02	135
	21	7:14	0♌37	180
	24	14:57	18♍59	225
	28	0:20	7♏26	270
	31	14:40	26♐05	315
Feb 1905	4	11:06	15♒00	0
	8	13:30	4♈09	45
	12	16:20	23♉19	90
	16	10:28	12♋06	135
	19	18:52	0♍29	180
	23	0:14	18♎44	225
	26	10:04	7♐09	270
Mar 1905	2	4:13	25♑56	315
	6	5:19	14♓59	0
	10	9:04	4♉08	45
	14	8:59	23♊07	90
	17	23:10	11♌42	135
	21	4:55	29♍55	180
	24	9:39	18♏05	225
	27	21:35	6♑33	270
	31	19:52	25♒26	315
Apr 1905	4	23:23	14♈31	0
	9	1:31	3♊32	45
	12	21:41	22♋18	90
	16	8:54	10♍42	135
	19	13:38	28♎49	180
	22	19:41	16♐59	225
	26	11:14	5♒32	270
	30	12:49	24♓29	315
May 1905	4	15:50	13♉29	0
	8	14:21	2♋18	45
	12	6:46	20♌52	90
	15	16:08	9♎08	135
	18	21:36	27♏14	180
	22	6:56	15♑30	225
	26	2:50	4♓10	270
	30	5:51	23♈08	315
Jun 1905	3	5:56	11♊58	0
	7	0:00	0♌34	45
	10	13:04	18♍57	90
	13	21:51	7♏10	135
	17	5:51	25♐21	180
	20	19:59	13♒46	225
	24	19:46	2♈35	270
	28	22:01	21♉29	315
Jul 1905	2	17:50	10♋08	0
	6	7:21	28♌32	45
	9	17:46	16♎48	90
	13	3:20	5♐03	135
	16	15:32	23♑23	180
	20	10:57	12♓01	225
	24	13:09	0♉56	270
	28	12:54	19♊45	315
Aug 1905	1	4:02	8♌13	0
	4	13:27	26♍28	45
	7	22:16	14♏42	90
	11	10:10	3♑03	135
	15	3:31	21♒37	180
	19	3:31	10♈28	225
	23	6:10	29♉25	270
	27	2:29	18♋08	315
	30	13:13	6♍28	0
Sep 1905	2	19:26	24♎38	45
	6	4:09	12♐53	90
	9	19:43	1♒26	135
	13	18:10	20♓16	180
	17	20:52	9♉16	225
	21	22:13	28♊14	270
	25	14:51	16♌51	315
	28	21:59	5♎05	0
Oct 1905	2	2:32	23♏14	45
	5	12:54	11♑37	90
	9	8:55	0♓24	135
	13	11:03	19♈26	180
	17	14:04	8♊32	225
	21	12:50	27♋27	270
	25	2:02	16♍00	315
	28	6:58	4♏12	0
	31	11:54	22♐24	45
Nov 1905	4	1:39	10♒59	90
	8	1:47	0♈00	135
	12	5:11	19♉10	180
	16	6:15	8♋14	225
	20	1:34	27♌04	270
	23	12:04	15♎33	315
	26	16:47	3♐47	0
	30	0:25	22♑09	45
Dec 1905	3	18:37	10♓57	90
	7	21:22	0♉08	135
	11	23:25	19♊17	180
	15	20:41	8♌14	225
	19	12:09	26♍57	270
	22	21:16	15♏23	315
	26	4:04	3♑44	0
	29	16:19	22♒19	45
Jan 1906	2	14:52	11♈20	90
	6	18:03	0♊33	135
	10	16:36	19♋34	180
	14	8:54	8♍18	225
	17	20:49	26♎52	270
	21	6:17	15♐19	315

The 8 Phases of the Moon 1900–2020

	24	17:09	3♒50	0
	28	10:50	22♓38	45
Feb 1906	1	12:31	11♉46	90
	5	14:03	0♋53	135
	9	7:46	19♌40	180
	12	18:54	8♎10	225
	16	4:23	26♏36	270
	19	15:54	15♑07	315
	23	7:57	3♓48	0
	27	6:31	22♈46	45
Mar 1906	3	9:28	11♊54	90
	7	7:49	0♌51	135
	10	20:17	19♍21	180
	14	3:14	7♏38	225
	17	11:58	25♐59	270
	21	2:50	14♒35	315
	24	23:52	3♈26	0
	29	1:42	22♉28	45
Apr 1906	2	4:02	11♋31	90
	5	22:16	0♍13	135
	9	6:12	18♎29	180
	12	10:48	6♐37	225
	15	20:37	24♑57	270
	19	15:20	13♓39	315
	23	16:07	2♉35	0
	27	19:08	21♊36	45
May 1906	1	19:07	10♌29	90
	5	9:08	28♍57	135
	8	14:10	17♏03	180
	11	18:37	5♑08	225
	15	7:03	23♒32	270
	19	5:19	12♈19	315
	23	8:01	1♊16	0
	27	10:02	20♋11	45
	31	6:23	8♍53	90
Jun 1906	3	17:00	27♎11	135
	6	21:12	15♐13	180
	10	3:36	3♒20	225
	13	19:34	21♓50	270
	17	20:31	10♉42	315
	21	23:06	29♊37	0
	25	22:03	18♌24	45
	29	14:19	6♎54	90
Jul 1906	2	22:58	25♏06	135
	6	4:27	13♑11	180
	9	14:26	1♓26	225
	13	10:13	20♈05	270
	17	12:35	9♊00	315
	21	12:59	27♋50	0
	25	7:24	16♍26	45
	28	19:56	4♏48	90
Aug 1906	1	4:24	23♐00	135
	4	13:00	11♒13	180
	8	3:30	29♓40	225
	12	2:48	18♉28	270
	16	5:03	7♋24	315
	20	1:27	26♌07	0
	23	14:47	14♎32	45
	27	0:42	2♐50	90
	30	10:41	21♑08	135
Sep 1906	2	23:36	9♓34	180
	6	18:55	28♈15	225
	10	20:54	17♊13	270
	14	21:17	6♌07	315
	18	12:33	24♍40	0
	21	21:20	12♏58	45
	25	6:11	1♑16	90
	28	19:02	19♒44	135
Oct 1906	2	12:48	8♈25	180
	6	12:31	27♉20	225
	10	15:39	16♋25	270
	14	12:31	5♍15	315
	17	22:43	23♎39	0
	21	4:26	11♐52	45
	24	13:50	0♒15	90
	28	6:21	18♓56	135
Nov 1906	1	4:46	7♉51	180
	5	7:35	26♊59	225
	9	9:45	16♌05	270
	13	2:13	4♎48	315
	16	8:36	23♏05	0
	19	13:17	11♑19	45
	23	0:39	29♒49	90
	26	21:06	18♈43	135
	30	23:07	7♊51	180
Dec 1906	5	2:44	27♋04	225
	9	1:45	16♍05	270
	12	14:12	4♏40	315
	15	18:54	22♐55	0
	19	0:37	11♒13	45
	22	15:04	29♓53	90
	26	15:06	18♉57	135
	30	18:44	8♋11	180
Jan 1907	3	20:09	27♌19	225
	7	14:47	16♎10	270
	11	0:41	4♐39	315
	14	5:57	22♑56	0
	17	14:27	11♓21	45
	21	8:42	0♉11	90
	25	11:21	19♊21	135
	29	13:45	8♌31	180
Feb 1907	2	10:29	27♍27	225
	6	0:52	16♏06	270
	9	10:01	4♑31	315
	12	17:43	22♒53	0
	16	6:18	11♈26	45
	20	4:35	0♊24	90
	24	7:59	19♋34	135
	28	6:23	8♍31	180
Mar 1907	3	21:30	27♎10	225
	7	8:42	15♐38	270
	10	18:42	4♒03	315
	14	6:05	22♓31	0
	17	23:31	11♉14	45
	22	1:10	0♋16	90
	26	2:52	19♌19	135
	29	19:44	7♎58	180
Apr 1907	2	5:52	26♏21	225
	5	15:21	14♑41	270
	9	3:18	3♓08	315
	12	19:06	21♈43	0
	16	17:22	10♊34	45
	20	20:38	29♋36	90
	24	18:35	18♍25	135
	28	6:05	6♏48	180
May 1907	1	12:46	24♐59	225
	4	21:53	13♒16	270
	8	12:35	1♈46	315
	12	8:59	20♉29	0
	16	11:00	9♋25	45
	20	13:27	28♌22	90
	24	6:50	16♎57	135
	27	14:18	5♐08	180
	30	19:18	23♑12	225
Jun 1907	3	5:20	11♓29	270
	6	23:20	0♉04	315
	10	23:50	18♊55	0
	15	3:20	7♌53	45
	19	2:55	26♍41	90
	22	16:13	15♏04	135
	25	21:27	3♑08	180
	29	2:27	21♒12	225
Jul 1907	2	14:34	9♈32	270
	6	12:13	28♉16	315
	10	15:17	17♋12	0
	14	17:30	6♍06	45
	18	13:11	24♎45	90
	21	23:41	13♐02	135
	25	4:29	1♒05	180
	28	11:02	19♓12	225
Aug 1907	1	2:26	7♉41	270
	5	3:27	26♊34	315
	9	6:36	15♌31	0
	13	5:14	4♎18	45
	16	21:05	22♏49	90
	20	6:17	11♑05	135
	23	12:15	29♒12	180
	26	21:53	17♈29	225
	30	17:28	6♊10	270
Sep 1907	3	20:34	25♋10	315
	7	21:04	14♍04	0
	11	14:53	2♏43	45
	15	3:40	21♐09	90
	18	12:56	9♒27	135
	21	21:34	27♓44	180
	25	11:43	16♉15	225
	29	11:37	5♋10	270
Oct 1907	3	14:31	24♌13	315
	7	10:21	13♎00	0
	10	23:21	1♐30	45
	14	10:02	19♑54	90
	17	20:34	8♓19	135
	21	9:17	26♈49	180
	25	4:53	15♊37	225
	29	7:51	4♌44	270
Nov 1907	2	8:06	23♍45	315
	5	22:39	12♏22	0
	9	7:39	0♑45	45
	12	17:15	19♒10	90
	16	6:12	7♈44	135
	20	0:04	26♉31	180
	24	0:46	15♋35	225
	28	4:21	4♍47	270
Dec 1907	2	0:26	23♎40	315
	5	10:22	12♐08	0
	8	16:37	0♒27	45
	12	2:16	18♓54	90
	15	18:44	7♉39	135
	19	17:55	26♊42	180
	23	21:34	15♌55	225
	27	23:10	5♎04	270
	31	15:00	23♏48	315
Jan 1908	3	21:43	12♑08	0
	7	2:44	0♓25	45
	10	13:53	18♈57	90
	14	10:37	7♊53	135
	18	13:37	27♋05	180
	22	17:01	16♍18	225
	26	15:01	5♏17	270
	30	3:28	23♐51	315
Feb 1908	2	8:36	12♒07	0
	5	14:11	0♈24	45
	9	4:28	19♉02	90
	13	5:14	8♋07	135
	17	9:05	27♌19	180
	21	9:24	16♎22	225
	25	3:24	5♐08	270
	28	13:38	23♑35	315
Mar 1908	2	18:57	11♓49	0
	6	3:07	0♉10	45
	9	21:42	18♊56	90
	14	0:52	8♌03	135
	18	2:28	27♍06	180
	21	22:11	15♏54	225
	25	12:32	4♑28	270
	28	21:46	22♒49	315
Apr 1908	1	5:02	11♈04	0
	4	17:36	29♉33	45
	8	16:31	18♋26	90
	12	19:37	7♍29	135
	16	16:55	26♎17	180
	20	7:46	14♐49	225
	23	19:07	3♒12	270
	27	4:38	21♓31	315
	30	15:33	9♉52	0
May 1908	4	9:28	28♊30	45
	8	11:23	17♌27	90
	12	12:09	6♎21	135
	16	4:32	24♏53	180
	19	15:00	13♑12	225
	23	0:17	1♓27	270
	26	11:28	19♈47	315
	30	3:15	8♊18	0
Jun 1908	3	2:07	27♋05	45
	7	4:56	16♍01	90
	11	2:09	4♏44	135
	14	13:55	23♐04	180
	17	20:54	11♒12	225
	21	5:26	29♓25	270
	24	19:37	17♉50	315
	28	16:31	6♋32	0
Jul 1908	2	18:41	25♌26	45
	6	20:25	14♎19	90
	10	13:48	2♐52	135
	13	21:48	21♑02	180
	17	2:38	9♓05	225
	20	12:02	27♈20	270
	24	6:14	15♊55	315
	28	7:17	4♌47	0
Aug 1908	1	10:22	23♍44	45
	5	9:40	12♏32	90
	8	23:34	0♑58	135
	12	4:59	19♒03	180
	15	9:26	7♈07	225
	18	21:26	25♉29	270
	22	19:50	14♋16	315
	26	22:59	3♍16	0
	31	0:43	22♎12	45
Sep 1908	3	20:51	10♐55	90
	7	7:55	29♑16	135
	10	12:23	17♓22	180
	13	18:32	5♉32	225
	17	10:34	24♊07	270
	21	12:16	13♌06	315
	25	14:59	2♎07	0
	29	13:35	21♏00	45
Oct 1908	3	6:13	9♑38	90
	6	15:32	27♒58	135
	9	21:03	16♈10	180
	13	6:59	4♊32	225
	17	3:35	23♋22	270
	21	6:44	12♍28	315
	25	6:46	1♏28	0
	29	1:02	20♐13	45
Nov 1908	1	14:16	8♒46	90
	4	23:16	27♓09	135
	8	7:58	15♉32	180
	11	23:09	4♋11	225
	15	23:41	23♌14	270
	20	2:06	12♎22	315
	23	21:53	1♐14	0
	27	11:15	19♑50	45
	30	21:44	8♓19	90
Dec 1908	4	8:07	26♈48	135
	7	21:44	15♊25	180
	11	18:24	4♌21	225
	15	21:12	23♍32	270
	19	21:05	12♏36	315
	23	11:50	1♑17	0
	26	20:38	19♒43	45
	30	5:40	8♈10	90
Jan 1909	2	19:04	26♉47	135
	6	14:13	15♋39	180
	10	15:10	4♍46	225
	14	18:11	23♎58	270
	18	14:19	12♐53	315
	22	0:12	1♒21	0
	25	5:44	19♓39	45
	28	15:07	8♉05	90
Feb 1909	1	8:34	26♊52	135

The 8 Phases of the Moon 1900–2020

Month	Day	Time	Position	Phase
	5	8:25	15♌55	180
	9	11:29	5♎06	225
	13	12:47	24♏12	270
	17	4:42	12♑54	315
	20	10:52	1♓11	0
	23	15:15	19♈23	45
	27	2:49	7♊53	90
Mar 1909	3	0:20	26♋48	135
	7	2:56	15♍55	180
	11	5:40	5♏01	225
	15	3:42	23♐56	270
	18	15:46	12♒25	315
	21	20:11	0♈35	0
	25	1:47	18♉47	45
	28	16:49	7♋22	90
Apr 1909	1	17:28	26♌21	135
	5	20:28	15♎25	180
	9	20:38	4♐21	225
	13	14:30	23♑01	270
	16	23:55	11♓20	315
	20	4:51	29♈28	0
	23	13:40	17♊45	45
	27	8:36	6♌26	90
May 1909	1	10:56	25♍25	135
	5	12:08	14♏20	180
	9	8:01	3♑02	225
	12	21:45	21♒29	270
	16	6:11	9♈43	315
	19	13:42	27♉55	0
	23	2:56	16♋20	45
	27	1:28	5♍07	90
	31	3:51	24♎03	135
Jun 1909	4	1:25	12♐46	180
	7	16:13	1♒14	225
	11	2:43	19♓31	270
	14	11:56	7♉45	315
	17	23:28	26♊05	0
	21	17:30	14♌39	45
	25	18:43	3♎31	90
	29	19:32	22♏22	135
Jul 1909	3	12:17	10♑54	180
	6	22:15	29♒09	225
	10	6:58	17♈21	270
	13	18:31	5♊40	315
	17	10:45	24♋11	0
	21	9:09	12♍56	45
	25	11:45	1♏52	90
	29	9:32	20♐36	135
Aug 1909	1	21:14	8♒56	180
	5	3:34	27♓03	225
	8	12:10	15♉16	270
	12	3:04	3♋45	315
	15	23:55	22♌28	0
	20	1:39	11♎23	45
	24	3:55	0♐20	90
	27	21:42	18♑56	135
	31	5:08	7♓08	180
Sep 1909	3	9:40	25♈14	225
	6	19:45	13♊33	270
	10	14:28	2♌13	315
	14	15:09	21♍08	0
	18	18:26	10♏11	45
	22	18:31	29♐06	90
	26	8:12	17♒36	135
	29	13:05	5♈44	180
Oct 1909	2	17:53	23♉53	225
	6	6:44	12♋22	270
	10	5:12	1♍15	315
	14	8:13	20♎21	0
	18	10:40	9♐25	45
	22	7:03	28♑15	90
	25	17:36	16♓40	135
	28	22:07	4♉51	180
Nov 1909	1	5:06	23♊09	225
	4	21:38	11♌50	270
	8	23:11	0♎55	315
	13	2:18	20♏05	0
	17	1:19	9♑04	45
	20	17:29	27♒46	90
	24	2:34	16♈11	135
	27	8:52	4♊29	180
	30	19:36	22♋59	225
Dec 1909	4	16:13	11♍54	270
	8	19:30	1♏06	315
	12	19:59	20♐11	0
	16	13:46	9♒00	45
	20	2:18	27♓35	90
	23	11:45	16♉02	135
	26	21:30	4♋30	180
	30	12:59	23♌13	225
Jan 1910	3	13:27	12♎19	270
	7	16:19	1♐31	315
	11	11:51	20♑24	0
	15	0:09	8♓59	45
	18	10:20	27♈28	90
	21	21:38	16♊00	135
	25	11:51	4♌39	180
	29	8:23	23♍34	225
Feb 1910	2	11:27	12♏46	270
	6	11:27	1♑49	315
	10	1:13	20♒26	0
	13	9:10	8♈48	45
	16	18:32	27♉14	90
	20	8:35	15♋51	135
	24	3:36	4♍40	180
	28	4:31	23♎43	225
Mar 1910	4	7:52	12♐52	270
	8	3:21	1♒41	315
	11	12:12	20♓03	0
	14	17:41	8♉16	45
	18	3:37	26♊40	90
	21	20:56	15♌22	135
	25	20:21	4♎18	180
	29	23:43	23♏24	225
Apr 1910	3	0:47	12♑23	270
	6	15:37	0♓57	315
	9	21:25	19♈08	0
	13	2:21	7♊17	45
	16	14:04	25♋42	90
	20	10:53	14♍29	135
	24	13:23	3♏29	180
	28	16:21	22♐29	225
May 1910	2	13:29	11♒15	270
	6	0:46	29♓37	315
	9	5:33	17♉43	0
	12	11:39	5♋51	45
	16	2:13	24♌20	90
	20	2:20	13♎11	135
	24	5:39	2♐10	180
	28	5:32	21♑00	225
	31	22:24	9♓33	270
Jun 1910	4	7:44	27♈48	315
	7	13:16	15♊53	0
	10	22:02	4♌07	45
	14	16:19	22♍42	90
	18	18:46	11♏37	135
	22	20:12	0♑30	180
	26	15:22	19♒07	225
	30	4:39	7♈30	270
Jul 1910	3	13:34	25♉43	315
	6	21:20	13♋53	0
	10	10:03	2♍15	45
	14	8:24	21♎00	90
	18	11:19	9♐56	135
	22	8:37	28♑39	180
	25	22:47	17♓04	225
	29	9:35	5♉22	270
Aug 1910	1	19:22	23♊38	315
	5	6:37	11♌57	0
	9	0:14	0♎32	45
	13	2:01	19♏26	90
	17	3:07	8♑20	135
	20	19:14	26♒52	180
	24	5:07	15♈09	225
	27	14:33	3♊25	270
	31	2:18	21♋48	315
Sep 1910	3	18:06	10♍20	0
	7	16:49	29♎10	45
	11	20:10	18♐12	90
	15	17:38	6♒59	135
	19	4:52	25♓22	180
	22	11:41	13♉35	225
	25	20:54	1♋54	270
	29	11:38	20♌27	315
Oct 1910	3	8:32	9♎15	0
	7	11:10	28♏18	45
	11	13:40	17♑22	90
	15	6:52	6♓03	135
	18	14:24	24♈20	180
	21	19:34	12♊32	225
	25	5:48	0♌56	270
	29	0:28	19♍43	315
Nov 1910	2	1:56	8♏46	0
	6	5:53	27♐57	45
	10	5:29	16♒57	90
	13	18:58	5♈32	135
	17	0:25	23♉47	180
	20	5:31	12♋02	225
	23	18:14	0♍35	270
	27	17:13	19♎36	315
Dec 1910	1	21:11	8♐49	0
	5	23:20	27♑58	45
	9	19:05	16♓51	90
	13	6:02	5♉22	135
	16	11:05	23♊38	180
	19	17:58	11♌59	225
	23	10:36	0♎44	270
	27	13:08	19♏55	315
	31	16:21	9♑08	0
Jan 1911	4	14:21	28♒08	45
	8	6:20	16♈52	90
	11	16:02	5♊20	135
	14	22:26	23♋40	180
	18	9:02	12♍10	225
	22	6:21	1♏07	270
	26	10:12	20♐21	315
	30	9:45	9♒24	0
Feb 1911	3	2:42	28♓10	45
	6	15:28	16♉45	90
	10	1:07	5♋11	135
	13	10:37	23♌37	180
	17	2:26	12♎19	225
	21	3:44	1♐24	270
	25	6:06	20♑32	315
Mar 1911	1	0:31	9♓19	0
	4	12:39	27♈50	45
	7	23:01	16♊16	90
	11	9:54	4♌43	135
	14	23:58	23♍17	180
	18	21:17	12♏10	225
	23	0:26	1♑16	270
	26	23:18	20♒11	315
	30	12:38	8♈42	0
Apr 1911	2	20:51	27♉00	45
	6	5:55	15♋19	90
	9	19:17	3♍49	135
	13	14:36	22♎33	180
	17	16:04	11♐31	225
	21	18:36	0♒32	270
	25	13:17	19♓13	315
	28	22:25	7♉30	0
May 1911	2	4:00	25♊38	45
	5	13:14	13♌55	90
	9	6:12	2♎30	135
	13	6:10	21♏22	180
	17	9:17	10♑21	225
	21	9:23	29♒12	270
	25	0:13	17♈41	315
	28	6:24	5♊48	0
	31	10:59	23♋52	45
Jun 1911	3	22:04	12♍11	90
	7	19:08	0♏54	135
	11	21:51	19♐50	180
	16	0:02	8♒44	225
	19	20:51	27♓26	270
	23	8:35	15♉45	315
	26	13:20	3♋48	0
	29	18:50	21♌53	45
Jul 1911	3	9:20	10♎19	90
	7	9:57	29♏10	135
	11	12:53	18♑05	180
	15	12:13	6♓53	225
	19	5:31	25♈26	270
	22	15:10	13♊40	315
	25	20:12	1♌44	0
	29	4:38	19♍57	45
Aug 1911	1	23:29	8♏34	90
	6	2:06	27♐30	135
	10	2:55	16♒22	180
	13	22:13	5♈01	225
	17	12:11	23♉27	270
	20	20:57	11♋42	315
	24	4:14	29♌53	0
	27	17:18	18♎18	45
	31	16:21	7♐08	90
Sep 1911	4	18:55	26♑06	135
	8	15:57	14♓52	180
	12	6:44	3♉23	225
	15	17:51	21♊45	270
	19	3:15	10♌04	315
	22	14:37	28♍28	0
	26	9:08	17♏09	45
	30	11:08	6♑10	90
Oct 1911	4	11:47	25♒08	135
	8	4:11	13♈46	180
	11	14:32	2♊09	225
	14	23:46	20♋30	270
	18	11:27	8♍58	315
	22	4:09	27♎38	0
	26	3:37	16♐36	45
	30	6:41	5♒44	90
Nov 1911	3	4:08	24♓37	135
	6	15:48	13♉07	180
	9	22:29	1♋25	225
	13	7:20	19♌48	270
	16	22:45	8♎28	315
	20	20:49	27♏26	0
	24	23:30	16♑35	45
	29	1:42	5♓44	90
Dec 1911	2	19:18	24♈31	135
	6	2:52	12♊52	180
	9	7:27	1♌07	225
	12	17:46	19♍36	270
	16	13:40	8♏30	315
	20	15:40	27♐39	0
	24	19:06	16♒53	45
	28	18:47	5♈56	90
Jan 1912	1	8:32	24♉35	135
	4	13:30	12♋51	180
	7	18:13	1♍06	225
	11	7:43	19♎44	270
	15	7:38	8♐49	315
	19	11:10	28♑02	0
	23	12:53	17♓11	45
	27	8:51	6♉05	90
	30	19:29	24♊34	135
Feb 1912	2	23:58	12♌48	180
	6	7:12	1♎09	225
	10	0:51	19♏56	270
	14	3:17	9♑05	315

The 8 Phases of the Moon 1900–2020

	18	5:44	28♒14	0
	22	3:41	17♈10	45
	25	19:27	5♊51	90
	29	4:22	24♋14	135
Mar 1912	3	10:42	12♍31	180
	6	22:14	1♏00	225
	10	19:55	19♐54	270
	14	22:55	9♒01	315
	18	22:09	27♓57	0
	22	15:05	16♉38	45
	26	3:02	5♋06	90
	29	12:01	23♌26	135
Apr 1912	1	22:05	11♎49	180
	5	14:38	0♐27	225
	9	15:24	19♑24	270
	13	17:06	8♓24	315
	17	11:40	27♈05	0
	20	23:25	15♊30	45
	24	8:47	3♌48	90
	27	19:32	22♍09	135
May 1912	1	10:19	10♏40	180
	5	7:34	29♐26	225
	9	9:56	18♒23	270
	13	8:49	7♈12	315
	16	22:14	25♉38	0
	20	5:42	13♋50	45
	23	14:11	2♍03	90
	27	3:57	20♎29	135
	30	23:29	9♐08	180
Jun 1912	4	0:17	28♑00	225
	8	2:36	16♓55	270
	11	21:38	5♉33	315
	15	6:24	23♊46	0
	18	11:19	11♌49	45
	21	20:39	0♎03	90
	25	14:04	18♏36	135
	29	13:34	7♑24	180
Jul 1912	3	16:13	26♒19	225
	7	16:47	15♈09	270
	11	7:40	3♊36	315
	14	13:13	21♋41	0
	17	17:38	9♍44	45
	21	5:18	28♎03	90
	25	2:23	16♐45	135
	29	4:28	5♒40	180
Aug 1912	2	6:56	24♓35	225
	6	4:17	13♉19	270
	9	15:38	1♋38	315
	12	19:58	19♌42	0
	16	1:55	7♎49	45
	19	16:56	26♏18	90
	23	17:09	15♑10	135
	27	19:59	4♓08	180
	31	20:01	23♈00	225
Sep 1912	4	13:23	11♊37	270
	7	22:33	29♋54	315
	11	3:49	18♍02	0
	14	12:59	6♏19	45
	18	7:55	25♐01	90
	22	10:14	14♒02	135
	26	11:34	3♈00	180
	30	7:16	21♉45	225
Oct 1912	3	20:48	10♋15	270
	7	5:34	28♌35	315
	10	13:41	16♎53	0
	14	3:16	5♐25	45
	18	2:06	24♑20	90
	22	4:58	13♓26	135
	26	2:30	2♉19	180
	29	16:55	20♊54	225
Nov 1912	2	3:38	9♌21	270
	5	13:45	27♍47	315
	9	2:05	16♏19	0
	12	20:39	5♑07	45
	16	22:43	24♒14	90
	21	0:01	13♈19	135
	24	16:12	2♊02	180
	28	1:43	20♋29	225
Dec 1912	1	11:05	8♍55	270
	4	23:54	27♎30	315
	8	17:07	16♐17	0
	12	16:29	5♒19	45
	16	20:06	24♓33	90
	20	17:44	13♉31	135
	24	4:30	2♋02	180
	27	10:38	20♌21	225
	30	20:12	8♎48	270
Jan 1913	3	12:27	27♏33	315
	7	10:28	16♑33	0
	11	13:21	5♓45	45
	15	16:01	24♈56	90
	19	8:57	13♊43	135
	22	15:40	2♌03	180
	25	20:28	20♍18	225
	29	7:34	8♏49	270
Feb 1913	2	3:31	27♐43	315
	6	5:22	16♒51	0
	10	9:13	6♈03	45
	14	8:34	25♉04	90
	17	21:15	13♋38	135
	21	2:03	1♍52	180
	24	7:31	20♎06	225
	27	21:15	8♐42	270
Mar 1913	3	20:42	27♑41	315
	8	0:22	16♓51	0
	12	2:06	5♉55	45
	15	20:58	24♊41	90
	19	6:54	13♌05	135
	22	11:56	1♎16	180
	25	19:43	19♏34	225
	29	12:58	8♑14	270
Apr 1913	2	15:06	27♒16	315
	6	17:48	16♈19	0
	10	15:02	5♊08	45
	14	5:39	23♋40	90
	17	14:35	11♍58	135
	20	21:33	0♏11	180
	24	8:58	18♐34	225
	28	6:09	7♒21	270
May 1913	2	9:20	26♓21	315
	6	8:24	15♉12	0
	10	0:18	3♋44	45
	13	11:45	22♌06	90
	16	21:09	10♎22	135
	20	7:18	28♏39	180
	23	23:19	17♑11	225
	28	0:04	6♓03	270
Jun 1913	1	2:02	24♈58	315
	4	19:57	13♊33	0
	8	7:01	1♌52	45
	11	16:37	20♍07	90
	15	3:38	8♏25	135
	18	17:54	26♐51	180
	22	14:50	15♒33	225
	26	17:41	4♈28	270
	30	16:24	23♉14	315
Jul 1913	4	5:06	11♋36	0
	7	12:37	29♌46	45
	10	21:37	17♎59	90
	14	11:09	6♐23	135
	18	6:06	24♑59	180
	22	7:15	13♓51	225
	26	9:59	2♉47	270
	30	4:27	21♊23	315
Aug 1913	2	12:58	9♌36	0
	5	18:26	27♍41	45
	9	4:03	15♏57	90
	12	20:56	4♑30	135
	16	20:27	23♒20	180
	20	23:50	12♈19	225
	25	0:18	1♊11	270
	28	14:43	19♋40	315
	31	20:38	7♍48	0
Sep 1913	4	1:36	25♎55	45
	7	13:06	14♐17	90
	11	9:57	3♒03	135
	15	12:46	22♓03	180
	19	15:37	11♉05	225
	23	12:30	29♊52	270
	26	23:57	18♌16	315
	30	4:57	6♎25	0
Oct 1913	3	11:02	24♏38	45
	7	1:46	13♑11	90
	11	2:32	2♓10	135
	15	6:07	21♈17	180
	19	5:47	10♊14	225
	22	22:53	28♋56	270
	26	8:44	17♍20	315
	29	14:29	5♏34	0
Nov 1913	1	23:25	23♐57	45
	5	18:34	12♒45	90
	9	21:55	1♈55	135
	13	23:11	20♉59	180
	17	18:08	9♋48	225
	21	7:57	28♌25	270
	24	17:31	16♎51	315
	28	1:41	5♐14	0
Dec 1913	1	15:13	23♑51	45
	5	14:59	12♓54	90
	9	18:21	2♉06	135
	13	15:00	21♊02	180
	17	4:57	9♌40	225
	20	16:16	28♍12	270
	24	2:46	16♏42	315
	27	14:59	5♑17	0
	31	10:09	24♒09	45
Jan 1914	4	13:09	13♈22	90
	8	13:53	2♊28	135
	12	5:09	21♋10	180
	15	14:46	9♍38	225
	19	0:30	28♎06	270
	22	13:08	16♐42	315
	26	6:34	5♒29	0
	30	6:57	24♓34	45
Feb 1914	3	10:32	13♉47	90
	7	7:05	2♋41	135
	10	17:35	21♌10	180
	14	0:02	9♎28	225
	17	9:23	27♏53	270
	21	1:19	16♑35	315
	25	0:02	5♓33	0
Mar 1914	1	3:23	24♈43	45
	5	5:03	13♊48	90
	8	21:18	2♌28	135
	12	4:18	20♍46	180
	15	9:08	8♏57	225
	18	19:39	27♐22	270
	22	15:39	16♒11	315
	26	18:09	5♈15	0
	30	21:26	24♉20	45
Apr 1914	3	19:41	13♋12	90
	7	8:24	1♍41	135
	10	13:28	19♎50	180
	13	18:31	7♐59	225
	17	7:52	26♑28	270
	21	7:46	15♓22	315
	25	11:22	4♉24	0
	29	12:02	23♊19	45
May 1914	3	6:29	11♌59	90
	6	16:43	0♎18	135
	9	21:31	18♏23	180
	13	4:46	6♑35	225
	16	22:12	25♒10	270
	21	0:39	14♈07	315
	25	2:35	3♊03	0
	28	23:11	21♋45	45
Jun 1914	1	14:03	10♍13	90
	4	22:58	28♎27	135
	8	5:18	16♐34	180
	11	16:37	4♒53	225
	15	14:20	23♓37	270
	19	17:14	12♉33	315
	23	15:33	1♋18	0
	27	7:37	19♌48	45
	30	19:24	8♎08	90
Jul 1914	4	4:19	26♏20	135
	7	14:00	14♑35	180
	11	6:28	3♓06	225
	15	7:32	21♈57	270
	19	8:51	10♊49	315
	23	2:38	29♋24	0
	26	14:17	17♍44	45
	29	23:51	5♏59	90
Aug 1914	2	10:16	24♐16	135
	6	0:41	12♒42	180
	9	22:18	1♈27	225
	14	0:56	20♉23	270
	17	23:16	9♋10	315
	21	12:26	27♌35	0
	24	20:17	15♎48	45
	28	4:52	4♐02	90
	31	18:17	22♑29	135
Sep 1914	4	14:01	11♓11	180
	8	15:30	0♉07	225
	12	17:48	19♊06	270
	16	12:32	7♌47	315
	19	21:33	26♍05	0
	23	2:48	14♏14	45
	26	12:03	2♑33	90
	30	5:37	21♒13	135
Oct 1914	4	5:59	10♈10	180
	8	9:09	29♉14	225
	12	9:33	18♋13	270
	16	0:37	6♍48	315
	19	6:34	25♎02	0
	22	11:00	13♐12	45
	25	22:44	1♒41	90
	29	20:46	20♓36	135
Nov 1914	2	23:49	9♉43	180
	7	2:15	28♊50	225
	10	23:37	17♌44	270
	14	11:29	6♎15	315
	17	16:02	24♏28	0
	20	21:55	12♑45	45
	24	13:39	1♓27	90
	28	15:14	20♈34	135
Dec 1914	2	18:20	9♊45	180
	6	17:55	28♋47	225
	10	11:32	17♍35	270
	13	21:13	6♏02	315
	17	2:35	24♐19	0
	20	12:08	12♒47	45
	24	8:25	1♈42	90
	28	11:38	20♉55	135
Jan 1915	1	12:20	10♋01	180
	5	7:27	28♌53	225
	8	21:13	17♎32	270
	12	6:15	5♐58	315
	15	14:42	24♑23	0
	19	5:23	13♓04	45
	23	5:32	2♉09	90
	27	8:12	21♊19	135
	31	4:41	10♌14	180
Feb 1915	3	18:35	28♍52	225
	7	5:11	17♏21	270
	10	15:22	5♑49	315
	14	4:31	24♒25	0
	18	0:31	13♈17	45
	22	2:58	2♊25	90

The 8 Phases of the Moon 1900–2020

	26	3:13	21♋27	135
Mar 1915	1	18:33	10♍06	180
	5	3:35	28♎29	225
	8	12:28	16♐52	270
	12	1:21	5♒24	315
	15	19:42	24♓09	0
	19	19:56	13♉08	45
	23	22:48	2♋14	90
	27	19:21	21♌03	135
	31	5:38	9♎26	180
Apr 1915	3	11:14	27♏37	225
	6	20:12	15♑57	270
	10	12:45	4♓34	315
	14	11:36	23♈27	0
	18	14:12	12♊28	45
	22	15:39	1♌26	90
	26	7:56	20♍01	135
	29	14:19	8♏11	180
May 1915	2	18:34	26♐16	225
	6	5:23	14♒37	270
	10	1:42	3♈20	315
	14	3:31	22♉16	0
	18	6:21	11♋14	45
	22	4:50	0♍02	90
	25	17:10	18♎24	135
	28	21:33	6♐27	180
Jun 1915	1	2:38	24♑32	225
	4	16:32	12♓58	270
	8	16:04	1♉46	315
	12	18:57	20♊43	0
	16	19:51	9♌34	45
	20	14:24	28♍10	90
	23	23:56	16♏25	135
	27	4:27	4♑27	180
	30	12:17	22♒37	225
Jul 1915	4	5:54	11♈11	270
	8	7:37	0♊04	315
	12	9:31	18♋57	0
	16	6:37	7♍39	45
	19	21:09	26♎05	90
	23	5:30	14♐17	135
	26	12:11	2♒25	180
	30	0:04	20♓45	225
Aug 1915	2	21:27	9♉29	270
	7	0:00	28♊25	315
	10	22:52	17♌12	0
	14	15:03	5♎44	45
	18	2:17	24♏04	90
	21	11:16	12♑19	135
	24	21:40	0♓37	180
	28	14:18	19♈11	225
Sep 1915	1	14:57	8♊05	270
	5	16:39	27♋01	315
	9	10:53	15♍40	0
	12	22:04	4♏03	45
	16	7:21	22♐21	90
	19	18:31	10♒44	135
	23	9:35	29♓16	180
	27	6:58	18♉05	225
Oct 1915	1	9:44	7♋08	270
	5	8:46	26♌02	315
	8	21:42	14♎31	0
	12	4:55	2♐47	45
	15	13:52	21♑08	90
	19	4:19	9♓42	135
	23	0:15	28♈31	180
	27	1:37	17♊33	225
	31	4:40	6♌40	270
Nov 1915	3	23:36	25♍28	315
	7	7:52	13♏49	0
	10	12:53	2♑03	45
	13	23:03	20♒30	90
	17	17:22	9♈17	135
	21	17:36	28♉20	180
	25	21:10	17♋32	225
	29	22:11	6♍37	270
Dec 1915	3	12:42	25♎16	315
	6	18:04	13♐33	0
	9	22:59	1♒48	45
	13	11:38	20♓23	90
	17	9:47	9♉23	135
	21	12:52	28♊35	180
	25	15:53	17♌47	225
	29	12:59	6♎44	270
Jan 1916	2	0:03	25♏16	315
	5	4:46	13♑32	0
	8	11:33	1♓52	45
	12	3:37	20♈37	90
	16	5:01	9♊45	135
	20	8:29	28♋58	180
	24	7:59	18♍01	225
	28	0:35	6♏46	270
	31	9:55	25♐12	315
Feb 1916	3	16:06	13♒31	0
	7	2:17	1♈59	45
	10	22:20	20♉52	90
	15	1:36	10♋03	135
	19	2:28	29♌08	180
	22	20:39	17♎55	225
	26	9:24	6♐28	270
	29	18:45	24♑52	315
Mar 1916	4	3:58	13♓16	0
	7	18:38	1♉53	45
	11	18:33	20♊52	90
	15	21:28	9♌59	135
	19	17:27	28♍47	180
	23	6:09	17♏17	225
	26	16:22	5♑41	270
	30	3:06	24♒05	315
Apr 1916	2	16:21	12♈36	0
	6	11:58	1♊21	45
	10	14:35	20♋23	90
	14	14:47	9♍19	135
	18	5:07	27♎50	180
	21	13:30	16♐06	225
	24	22:38	4♒24	270
	28	11:40	22♓50	315
May 1916	2	5:29	11♉28	0
	6	5:36	0♋21	45
	10	8:47	19♌21	90
	14	4:42	8♎03	135
	17	14:11	26♏19	180
	20	19:55	14♑26	225
	24	5:17	2♓41	270
	27	21:19	21♈13	315
	31	19:37	9♊59	0
Jun 1916	4	22:36	28♋56	45
	8	23:59	17♍49	90
	12	15:26	6♏18	135
	15	21:42	24♐24	180
	19	2:30	12♒28	225
	22	13:16	0♈45	270
	26	8:50	19♉23	315
	30	10:43	8♋17	0
Jul 1916	4	14:00	27♌13	45
	8	11:55	15♎57	90
	11	23:49	4♐17	135
	15	4:40	22♑20	180
	18	10:09	10♓25	225
	21	23:33	28♈49	270
	25	22:47	17♊36	315
	30	2:15	6♌34	0
Aug 1916	3	3:08	25♍26	45
	6	21:06	14♏01	90
	10	6:52	2♑17	135
	13	12:00	20♒22	180
	16	19:42	8♈34	225
	20	12:53	27♉08	270
	24	15:05	16♋05	315
	28	17:24	5♍02	0
Sep 1916	1	14:00	23♎46	45
	5	4:26	12♐16	90
	8	13:33	0♒33	135
	11	20:31	18♓45	180
	15	7:59	7♉08	225
	19	5:35	25♊56	270
	23	8:58	14♌59	315
	27	7:34	3♎51	0
	30	23:14	22♏27	45
Oct 1916	4	11:00	10♑53	90
	7	20:44	29♒15	135
	11	7:01	17♈38	180
	14	23:34	6♊17	225
	19	1:09	25♋19	270
	23	3:09	14♍23	315
	26	20:37	3♏06	0
	30	7:45	21♐34	45
Nov 1916	2	17:51	9♒59	90
	6	5:20	28♓29	135
	9	20:18	17♉07	180
	13	18:23	6♋04	225
	17	22:00	25♌15	270
	21	20:30	14♎13	315
	25	8:50	2♐47	0
	28	16:28	21♑08	45
Dec 1916	2	1:55	9♓35	90
	5	16:21	28♈14	135
	9	12:44	17♊09	180
	13	15:08	6♌19	225
	17	18:06	25♍30	270
	21	12:13	14♏20	315
	24	20:31	2♑44	0
	28	2:00	21♒02	45
	31	12:07	9♈31	90
Jan 1917	4	6:29	28♉21	135
	8	7:42	17♋29	180
	12	11:38	6♍44	225
	16	11:42	25♎48	270
	20	1:52	14♐28	315
	23	7:40	2♒45	0
	26	12:40	21♓01	45
	30	1:01	9♉36	90
Feb 1917	2	23:42	28♊36	135
	7	3:28	17♌48	180
	11	5:43	6♎57	225
	15	1:53	25♏50	270
	18	13:10	14♑20	315
	21	18:09	2♓34	0
	25	0:37	20♈51	45
	28	16:44	9♊33	90
Mar 1917	4	18:50	28♋38	135
	8	21:58	17♍46	180
	12	20:16	6♏42	225
	16	12:33	25♐21	270
	19	22:09	13♒44	315
	23	4:05	1♈58	0
	26	14:01	20♉21	45
	30	10:36	9♋10	90
Apr 1917	3	14:00	28♌15	135
	7	13:49	17♎10	180
	11	7:19	5♐50	225
	14	20:12	24♑18	270
	18	5:21	12♓36	315
	21	14:01	0♉53	0
	25	4:55	19♊25	45
	29	5:22	8♌19	90
May 1917	3	7:36	27♍17	135
	7	2:43	15♏58	180
	10	15:32	4♑23	225
	14	1:48	22♒41	270
	17	11:50	10♈59	315
	21	0:47	29♉23	0
	24	21:00	18♋05	45
	28	23:33	7♍02	90
Jun 1917	1	22:50	25♎50	135
	5	13:07	14♐16	180
	8	21:54	2♒29	225
	12	6:39	20♓42	270
	15	18:58	9♉04	315
	19	13:02	27♊39	0
	23	13:36	16♌29	45
	27	16:08	5♎24	90
Jul 1917	1	11:41	24♏02	135
	4	21:41	12♑18	180
	8	3:31	0♓23	225
	11	12:12	18♈35	270
	15	4:05	7♊05	315
	19	3:00	25♋51	0
	23	5:52	14♍47	45
	27	6:40	3♏39	90
	30	22:29	22♐09	135
Aug 1917	3	5:11	10♒17	180
	6	9:35	28♓20	225
	9	19:57	16♉37	270
	13	16:04	5♋18	315
	17	18:21	24♌14	0
	21	21:07	13♎12	45
	25	19:08	1♐59	90
	29	7:42	20♑23	135
Sep 1917	1	12:28	8♓29	180
	4	17:24	26♈35	225
	8	7:05	15♊03	270
	12	7:10	3♌56	315
	16	10:27	22♍58	0
	20	11:02	11♏54	45
	24	5:41	0♑36	90
	27	15:51	18♒57	135
	30	20:31	7♈06	180
Oct 1917	4	4:08	25♉21	225
	7	22:14	14♋04	270
	12	0:53	3♍08	315
	16	2:41	22♎10	0
	19	23:30	11♐00	45
	23	14:38	29♑37	90
	26	23:37	17♓59	135
	30	6:19	6♉16	180
Nov 1917	2	18:30	24♊46	225
	6	17:04	13♌43	270
	10	20:10	2♎52	315
	14	18:28	21♏50	0
	18	10:35	10♑32	45
	21	22:29	29♒04	90
	25	7:54	17♈30	135
	28	18:41	5♊59	180
Dec 1917	2	12:25	24♋46	225
	6	14:14	13♍54	270
	10	15:43	3♏02	315
	14	9:17	21♐50	0
	17	20:30	10♒22	45
	21	6:07	28♓50	90
	24	17:43	17♉22	135
	28	9:52	6♋07	180
Jan 1918	1	8:41	25♌09	225
	5	11:50	14♎21	270
	9	10:08	3♐21	315
	12	22:36	21♑57	0
	16	5:41	10♓18	45
	19	14:38	28♈44	90
	23	5:48	17♊26	135
	27	3:14	6♌23	180
	31	5:25	25♍33	225
Feb 1918	4	7:52	14♏42	270
	8	2:06	3♑31	315
	11	10:05	21♒53	0
	14	14:47	10♈07	45
	18	0:57	28♉34	90
	21	20:16	17♋25	135
	25	21:35	6♍29	180
Mar 1918	2	0:47	25♎38	225
	6	0:44	14♐38	270

The 8 Phases of the Moon 1900–2020

Month	Day	Time	Position	Phase
	9	14:47	3♒14	315
	12	19:52	21♓26	0
	16	0:31	9♉37	45
	19	13:30	28♊08	90
	23	12:32	17♌04	135
	27	15:33	6♎09	180
	31	17:22	25♏11	225
Apr 1918	4	13:33	13♑58	270
	8	0:12	2♓21	315
	11	4:34	20♈29	0
	14	11:24	8♊42	45
	18	4:08	27♋19	90
	22	5:40	16♍17	135
	26	8:05	5♏17	180
	30	6:30	24♐06	225
May 1918	3	22:26	12♒39	270
	7	7:09	0♈54	315
	10	13:01	19♉03	0
	13	23:41	7♋22	45
	17	20:14	26♌05	90
	21	22:45	15♎02	135
	25	22:32	3♐52	180
	29	16:12	22♑27	225
Jun 1918	2	4:20	10♓49	270
	5	12:53	29♈02	315
	8	22:03	17♊16	0
	12	13:23	5♌45	45
	16	13:12	24♍34	90
	20	15:05	13♏27	135
	24	10:38	2♑05	180
	27	23:12	20♒27	225
Jul 1918	1	8:43	8♈41	270
	4	18:48	26♉57	315
	8	8:22	15♋21	0
	12	4:24	4♍01	45
	16	6:25	22♎54	90
	20	6:05	11♐42	135
	23	20:35	0♒09	180
	27	4:45	18♓20	225
	30	13:14	6♉33	270
Aug 1918	3	2:11	24♊56	315
	6	20:30	13♌32	0
	10	20:32	2♎22	45
	14	23:16	21♏20	90
	18	19:24	10♑01	135
	22	5:02	28♒17	180
	25	10:21	16♈24	225
	28	19:27	4♊39	270
Sep 1918	1	12:03	23♋14	315
	5	10:44	12♍03	0
	9	13:27	1♏03	45
	13	15:02	20♐00	90
	17	6:58	8♒34	135
	20	13:01	26♓45	180
	23	17:26	14♉52	225
	27	4:39	3♋16	270
Oct 1918	1	1:06	22♌03	315
	5	3:05	11♎04	0
	9	6:23	0♐09	45
	13	5:00	19♑03	90
	16	17:07	7♓32	135
	19	21:35	25♈41	180
	23	3:09	13♊54	225
	26	17:35	2♌30	270
	30	17:35	21♍29	315
Nov 1918	3	21:01	10♏38	0
	7	22:16	29♐42	45
	11	16:46	18♒30	90
	15	2:27	6♈55	135
	18	7:33	25♉10	180
	21	16:04	13♋33	225
	25	10:25	2♍21	270
	29	13:01	21♎31	315
Dec 1918	3	15:19	10♐40	0
	7	12:07	29♑35	45

Month	Day	Time	Position	Phase
	11	2:31	18♓15	90
	14	11:35	6♉41	135
	17	19:17	25♊04	180
	21	8:04	13♌39	225
	25	6:31	2♎40	270
	29	9:56	21♏53	315
Jan 1919	2	8:24	10♑54	0
	5	23:38	29♒36	45
	9	10:55	18♈09	90
	12	21:04	6♊38	135
	16	8:44	25♋11	180
	20	2:30	13♍59	225
	24	4:22	3♏08	270
	28	6:13	22♐17	315
	31	23:07	11♒03	0
Feb 1919	4	9:14	29♓31	45
	7	18:52	17♉58	90
	11	7:18	6♋31	135
	14	23:38	25♌15	180
	18	22:17	14♎13	225
	23	1:48	3♐24	270
	26	23:50	22♑20	315
Mar 1919	2	11:11	10♓50	0
	5	17:47	29♈07	45
	9	3:14	17♊30	90
	12	18:39	6♌09	135
	16	15:41	25♍00	180
	20	18:00	14♏05	225
	24	20:34	3♑09	270
	28	13:51	21♒50	315
	31	21:05	10♈06	0
Apr 1919	4	2:05	28♉16	45
	7	12:39	16♋39	90
	11	7:27	5♍22	135
	15	8:25	24♎19	180
	19	11:57	13♐22	225
	23	11:21	2♒15	270
	27	0:24	20♓42	315
	30	5:30	8♉49	0
May 1919	3	10:46	26♊57	45
	6	23:34	15♌22	90
	10	21:51	4♎10	135
	15	1:01	23♏09	180
	19	2:53	12♑05	225
	22	22:04	0♓44	270
	26	8:17	19♈02	315
	29	13:12	7♊06	0
Jun 1919	1	20:17	25♋16	45
	5	12:22	13♍47	90
	9	13:40	2♏39	135
	13	16:28	21♐36	180
	17	14:22	10♒20	225
	21	5:33	28♓48	270
	24	14:32	17♉01	315
	27	20:53	5♋08	0
Jul 1919	1	7:12	23♌24	45
	5	3:17	12♎03	90
	9	6:13	0♐59	135
	13	6:02	19♑48	180
	16	22:59	8♓20	225
	20	11:03	26♈40	270
	23	20:13	14♊54	315
	27	5:22	3♌08	0
	30	20:09	21♍35	45
Aug 1919	3	20:11	10♏25	90
	7	22:36	29♐21	135
	11	17:39	17♒59	180
	15	5:51	6♈21	225
	18	15:56	24♉38	270
	22	2:28	12♋57	315
	25	15:37	1♍22	0
	29	11:34	20♎04	45
Sep 1919	2	14:22	9♐03	90
	6	14:02	27♑55	135
	10	3:54	16♓24	180

Month	Day	Time	Position	Phase
	13	12:18	4♉39	225
	16	21:32	22♊57	270
	20	10:30	11♌24	315
	24	4:34	0♎05	0
	28	5:18	19♏02	45
Oct 1919	2	8:37	8♑06	90
	6	4:12	26♒52	135
	9	13:39	15♈13	180
	12	19:34	3♊25	225
	16	5:05	21♋47	270
	19	21:31	10♍27	315
	23	20:39	29♎23	0
	28	0:18	18♐32	45
Nov 1919	1	1:43	7♒35	90
	4	17:10	26♓14	135
	7	23:35	14♉31	180
	11	4:31	2♋44	225
	14	15:41	21♌13	270
	18	12:21	10♎07	315
	22	15:20	29♏17	0
	26	18:51	18♑28	45
	30	16:47	7♓26	90
Dec 1919	4	5:00	26♈00	135
	7	10:03	14♊15	180
	10	15:43	2♌33	225
	14	6:03	21♍12	270
	18	6:52	10♏18	315
	22	10:55	29♐33	0
	26	11:24	18♒39	45
	30	5:25	7♈28	90
Jan 1920	2	15:39	25♉58	135
	5	21:05	14♋15	180
	9	5:24	2♍40	225
	13	0:09	21♎31	270
	17	3:37	10♐44	315
	21	5:27	29♑53	0
	25	1:11	18♓47	45
	28	15:38	7♉26	90
Feb 1920	1	1:08	25♊53	135
	4	8:42	14♌15	180
	7	21:31	2♎50	225
	11	20:49	21♏51	270
	16	0:17	11♑02	315
	19	21:35	29♒58	0
	23	12:17	18♈36	45
	26	23:49	7♊06	90
Mar 1920	1	9:49	25♋32	135
	4	21:13	14♍01	180
	8	15:33	2♏47	225
	12	17:57	21♐52	270
	16	18:52	10♒54	315
	20	10:56	29♓33	0
	23	21:10	17♉57	45
	27	6:45	6♋18	90
	30	18:32	24♌45	135
Apr 1920	3	10:55	13♎23	180
	7	10:19	2♐18	225
	11	13:24	21♑21	270
	15	10:23	10♓09	315
	18	21:43	28♈32	0
	22	4:34	16♊45	45
	25	13:27	5♌02	90
	29	4:17	23♍33	135
May 1920	3	1:47	12♏19	180
	7	4:17	1♑18	225
	11	5:51	20♒13	270
	14	22:45	8♈48	315
	18	6:25	27♉00	0
	21	11:19	15♋05	45
	24	21:07	3♍21	90
	28	15:52	21♎59	135
Jun 1920	1	17:18	10♐52	180
	5	20:16	29♑49	225
	9	18:58	18♓35	270
	13	8:21	6♉59	315

Month	Day	Time	Position	Phase
	16	13:41	25♊04	0
	19	18:24	13♌07	45
	23	6:50	1♎29	90
	27	5:34	20♏14	135
Jul 1920	1	8:41	9♑11	180
	5	9:48	28♒02	225
	9	5:06	16♈40	270
	12	15:47	4♊57	315
	15	20:25	23♋00	0
	19	2:58	11♍07	45
	22	19:20	29♎38	90
	26	21:04	18♐31	135
	30	23:19	7♒26	180
Aug 1920	3	21:01	26♓10	225
	7	12:51	14♉41	270
	10	21:57	2♋55	315
	14	3:44	21♌02	0
	17	14:03	9♎20	45
	21	10:52	28♏03	90
	25	13:44	17♑01	135
	29	13:03	5♓52	180
Sep 1920	2	6:26	24♈28	225
	5	19:05	12♊53	270
	9	3:57	1♌09	315
	12	12:52	19♍26	0
	16	4:20	7♏59	45
	20	4:55	26♐55	90
	24	6:52	15♒55	135
	28	1:57	4♈38	180
Oct 1920	1	14:45	23♉06	225
	5	0:54	11♋29	270
	8	11:09	29♌52	315
	12	0:51	18♎24	0
	15	21:44	7♐14	45
	20	0:29	26♑19	90
	23	23:52	15♓17	135
	27	14:09	3♉52	180
	30	22:43	22♊13	225
Nov 1920	3	7:35	10♌35	270
	6	20:51	29♍09	315
	10	16:05	17♏58	0
	14	17:17	7♑03	45
	18	20:13	26♒13	90
	22	16:00	15♈04	135
	26	1:42	3♊31	180
	29	7:11	21♋47	225
Dec 1920	2	16:29	10♍13	270
	6	9:57	29♎00	315
	10	10:04	18♐04	0
	14	13:24	7♒17	45
	18	14:40	26♓25	90
	22	6:30	15♉08	135
	25	12:39	3♋27	180
	28	16:59	21♌42	225
Jan 1921	1	4:35	10♎15	270
	5	2:26	29♏14	315
	9	5:27	18♑26	0
	13	8:23	7♓38	45
	17	6:31	26♈38	90
	20	18:42	15♊12	135
	23	23:08	3♌26	180
	27	4:43	21♍44	225
	30	20:02	10♏25	270
Feb 1921	3	21:17	29♐32	315
	8	0:37	18♒44	0
	12	0:50	7♈47	45
	15	18:53	26♉35	90
	19	4:30	15♋00	135
	22	9:32	3♍14	180
	25	18:33	21♎38	225
Mar 1921	1	14:03	10♐28	270
	5	16:56	29♑35	315
	9	18:09	18♓39	0
	13	13:56	7♉28	45

The 8 Phases of the Moon 1900–2020

	17	3:49	26♊01	90
	20	12:30	14♌22	135
	23	20:19	2♎40	180
	27	10:04	21♏12	225
	31	9:13	10♑07	270
Apr 1921	4	11:49	29♒10	315
	8	9:05	17♈59	0
	11	23:38	6♊32	45
	15	10:11	24♋54	90
	18	19:44	13♍13	135
	22	7:49	1♏38	180
	26	2:32	20♐19	225
	30	4:09	9♒16	270
May 1921	4	4:45	28♓10	315
	7	21:01	16♉44	0
	11	6:41	5♋01	45
	14	15:25	23♌16	90
	18	3:21	11♎38	135
	21	20:15	0♐12	180
	25	19:12	19♑00	225
	29	21:45	7♓56	270
Jun 1921	2	19:01	26♈40	315
	6	6:15	14♊59	0
	9	12:20	3♌06	45
	12	20:59	21♍18	90
	16	12:18	9♏47	135
	20	9:41	28♐30	180
	24	11:31	17♒23	225
	28	13:17	6♈16	270
Jul 1921	2	6:29	24♉49	315
	5	13:36	12♋57	0
	8	18:03	0♍59	45
	12	4:16	19♎15	90
	15	23:18	7♐53	135
	20	0:08	26♑43	180
	24	3:00	15♓39	225
	28	2:20	4♉27	270
	31	15:32	22♊51	315
Aug 1921	3	20:17	10♌55	0
	7	1:10	28♍59	45
	10	14:14	17♏23	90
	14	12:47	6♑10	135
	18	15:28	25♒07	180
	22	17:11	14♈02	225
	26	12:51	2♊43	270
	29	23:03	21♋02	315
Sep 1921	2	3:33	9♍07	0
	5	10:46	27♎19	45
	9	3:29	15♐54	90
	13	4:49	4♒51	135
	17	7:20	23♓51	180
	21	5:40	12♉41	225
	24	21:18	1♋16	270
	28	6:06	19♌34	315
Oct 1921	1	12:26	7♎47	0
	4	23:28	26♏11	45
	8	20:12	15♑00	90
	12	23:03	4♓04	135
	16	23:00	23♈02	180
	20	16:23	11♊44	225
	24	4:32	0♌14	270
	27	13:45	18♍36	315
	30	23:39	7♏01	0
Nov 1921	3	15:26	25♐41	45
	7	15:54	14♒43	90
	11	18:23	3♈50	135
	15	13:39	22♉40	180
	19	1:44	11♋12	225
	22	11:41	29♌39	270
	25	22:56	18♎09	315
	29	13:26	6♐48	0
Dec 1921	3	10:15	25♑44	45
	7	13:20	14♓55	90
	11	13:12	3♉59	135
	15	2:51	22♊36	180
	18	10:36	10♌59	225
	21	19:54	29♍26	270
	25	10:13	18♏06	315
	29	5:39	6♑59	0
Jan 1922	2	6:52	26♒07	45
	6	10:24	15♈21	90
	10	5:55	4♊14	135
	13	14:36	22♋39	180
	16	19:53	10♍56	225
	20	6:00	29♎25	270
	23	23:53	18♐14	315
	27	23:48	7♒17	0
Feb 1922	1	3:30	26♓30	45
	5	4:52	15♉37	90
	8	19:43	4♋17	135
	12	1:17	22♌33	180
	15	6:10	10♎48	225
	18	18:18	29♏20	270
	22	15:50	18♑15	315
	26	18:48	7♓24	0
Mar 1922	2	22:02	26♈33	45
	6	19:21	15♊27	90
	10	6:34	3♌55	135
	13	11:14	22♍06	180
	16	17:33	10♏21	225
	20	8:43	28♐58	270
	24	9:29	17♒58	315
	28	13:03	7♈04	0
Apr 1922	1	12:57	26♉01	45
	5	5:45	14♋40	90
	8	15:02	3♍00	135
	11	20:44	21♎10	180
	15	5:58	9♐29	225
	19	0:54	28♑11	270
	23	3:44	17♓12	315
	27	5:04	6♉09	0
	30	23:54	24♊50	45
May 1922	4	12:56	13♌16	90
	7	21:54	1♎32	135
	11	6:06	19♏46	180
	14	19:27	8♑11	225
	18	18:17	27♒00	270
	22	21:12	15♈58	315
	26	18:04	4♊41	0
	30	7:42	23♋06	45
Jun 1922	2	18:10	11♍24	90
	6	4:08	29♎40	135
	9	15:58	18♐00	180
	13	10:09	6♒36	225
	17	12:03	25♓29	270
	21	12:47	14♉20	315
	25	4:20	2♋49	0
	28	13:40	21♌03	45
Jul 1922	1	22:52	9♎17	90
	5	10:51	27♏37	135
	9	3:07	16♑07	180
	13	2:05	4♓53	225
	17	5:11	23♈50	270
	21	2:05	12♊31	315
	24	12:47	0♌49	0
	27	19:14	18♍56	45
	31	4:22	7♏10	90
Aug 1922	3	19:16	25♐38	135
	7	16:19	14♒21	180
	11	18:47	3♈17	225
	15	20:46	22♉12	270
	19	13:23	10♋45	315
	22	20:34	28♌56	0
	26	1:38	17♎02	45
	29	11:55	5♐21	90
Sep 1922	2	6:32	24♑00	135
	6	7:47	12♓55	180
	10	11:20	1♉57	225
	14	10:20	20♊48	270
	17	23:19	9♌16	315
	21	4:38	27♍24	0
	24	9:54	15♏34	45
	27	22:40	4♑02	90
Oct 1922	1	21:24	22♒54	135
	6	0:58	11♈59	180
	10	2:42	1♊01	225
	13	21:55	19♋46	270
	17	8:32	8♍11	315
	20	13:40	26♎23	0
	23	20:48	14♐40	45
	27	13:26	3♒21	90
	31	15:40	22♓26	135
Nov 1922	4	18:37	11♉34	180
	8	16:17	0♋29	225
	12	7:53	19♌09	270
	15	17:29	7♎35	315
	19	0:06	25♏53	0
	22	10:55	14♑22	45
	26	8:15	3♓18	90
	30	12:00	22♈31	135
Dec 1922	4	11:24	11♊32	180
	8	4:04	0♌17	225
	11	16:41	18♍52	270
	15	2:32	7♏21	315
	18	12:20	25♐49	0
	22	4:22	14♒33	45
	26	5:53	3♈41	90
	30	8:21	22♉52	135
Jan 1923	3	2:34	11♋42	180
	6	14:27	0♍16	225
	10	0:55	18♎46	270
	13	12:12	7♐18	315
	17	2:41	25♑58	0
	21	0:24	14♓57	45
	25	3:59	4♉10	90
	29	2:54	23♊11	135
Feb 1923	1	15:53	11♌47	180
	4	23:55	0♎10	225
	8	9:16	18♏36	270
	11	23:14	7♑13	315
	15	19:07	26♒06	0
	19	21:11	15♈13	45
	24	0:06	4♊22	90
	27	18:38	23♋10	135
Mar 1923	3	3:24	11♍32	180
	6	8:54	29♎46	225
	9	18:31	18♐10	270
	13	12:12	6♒54	315
	17	12:51	25♓55	0
	21	16:30	15♉03	45
	25	16:42	4♋01	90
	29	7:14	22♌35	135
Apr 1923	1	13:10	10♎47	180
	4	17:49	28♏56	225
	8	5:23	17♑22	270
	12	3:10	6♓12	315
	16	6:29	25♈15	0
	20	8:48	14♊15	45
	24	5:20	3♌01	90
	27	16:48	21♍24	135
	30	21:30	9♏30	180
May 1923	4	3:16	27♐39	225
	7	18:18	16♒09	270
	11	19:31	5♈04	315
	15	22:39	24♉03	0
	19	21:36	12♋52	45
	23	14:25	1♍26	90
	26	23:54	19♎41	135
	30	5:07	7♐46	180
Jun 1923	2	13:58	26♑00	225
	6	9:19	14♓39	270
	10	12:13	3♉35	315
	14	12:42	22♊26	0
	18	7:20	11♌02	45
	21	20:46	29♍26	90
	25	5:29	17♏38	135
	28	13:05	5♑48	180
Jul 1923	2	2:35	24♒12	225
	6	1:57	12♈59	270
	10	4:21	1♊54	315
	14	0:45	20♋34	0
	17	14:51	8♍59	45
	21	1:32	27♎17	90
	24	10:55	15♐31	135
	27	22:33	3♒50	180
	31	17:23	22♓27	225
Aug 1923	4	19:23	11♉22	270
	8	19:31	0♋12	315
	12	11:17	18♌43	0
	15	21:10	6♎59	45
	19	6:07	25♏14	90
	22	17:42	13♑35	135
	26	10:30	2♓09	180
	30	10:03	21♈00	225
Sep 1923	3	12:48	9♊59	270
	7	9:37	28♋44	315
	10	20:53	17♍06	0
	14	3:24	5♏17	45
	17	12:04	23♐34	90
	21	3:17	12♒07	135
	25	1:16	0♈57	180
	29	3:49	19♉58	225
Oct 1923	3	5:29	8♋59	270
	6	22:37	27♌38	315
	10	6:06	15♎54	0
	13	10:43	4♐04	45
	16	20:54	22♑28	90
	20	16:33	11♓15	135
	24	18:26	0♉19	180
	28	21:36	19♊26	225
Nov 1923	1	20:49	8♌24	270
	5	10:23	26♍59	315
	8	15:27	15♏12	0
	11	20:15	3♑25	45
	15	9:41	22♒00	90
	19	9:33	11♈02	135
	23	12:58	0♊13	180
	27	14:23	19♋19	225
Dec 1923	1	10:09	8♍12	270
	4	20:53	26♎41	315
	8	1:31	14♐56	0
	11	8:50	3♒18	45
	15	2:38	22♓06	90
	19	5:14	11♉17	135
	23	7:33	0♋27	180
	27	5:17	19♌26	225
	30	21:07	8♎10	270
Jan 1924	3	6:17	26♏37	315
	6	12:48	14♑57	0
	10	0:35	3♓30	45
	13	22:45	22♈30	90
	18	1:58	11♊43	135
	22	0:57	0♌44	180
	25	17:44	19♍30	225
	29	5:53	8♏04	270
Feb 1924	1	15:13	26♐30	315
	5	1:39	15♒00	0
	8	18:47	3♈45	45
	12	20:09	22♉52	90
	16	21:55	11♋59	135
	20	16:07	0♍46	180
	24	3:42	19♎16	225
	27	13:15	7♐41	270
Mar 1924	2	0:29	26♑10	315
	5	15:58	14♓49	0
	9	14:01	3♉45	45
	13	16:51	22♊51	90
	17	15:32	11♌47	135
	21	4:30	0♎18	180
	24	11:45	18♏34	225

The 8 Phases of the Moon 1900–2020

	27	20:25	6♑54	270
	31	10:50	25♒27	315
Apr 1924	4	7:18	14♈15	0
	8	8:47	3♊15	45
	12	11:12	22♋16	90
	16	5:51	10♍58	135
	19	14:11	29♎14	180
	22	18:53	17♐21	225
	26	4:28	5♒40	270
	29	22:40	24♓19	315
May 1924	3	23:00	13♉12	0
	8	1:57	2♋12	45
	12	2:14	21♌04	90
	15	16:39	9♎33	135
	18	21:53	27♏39	180
	22	2:14	15♑42	225
	25	14:17	4♓04	270
	29	12:04	22♈49	315
Jun 1924	2	14:34	11♊45	0
	6	16:49	0♌40	45
	10	13:37	19♍22	90
	14	0:32	7♏40	135
	17	4:42	25♐42	180
	20	10:47	13♒48	225
	24	2:16	2♈17	270
	28	2:53	21♉07	315
Jul 1924	2	5:35	10♋02	0
	6	5:02	28♌50	45
	9	21:46	17♎21	90
	13	6:34	5♐34	135
	16	11:49	23♑38	180
	19	21:19	11♓52	225
	23	16:36	0♉30	270
	27	18:53	19♊25	315
	31	19:42	8♌16	0
Aug 1924	4	14:44	26♍54	45
	8	3:41	15♏18	90
	11	12:08	3♑31	135
	14	20:19	21♒43	180
	18	10:15	10♈10	225
	22	9:11	28♉58	270
	26	11:37	17♋56	315
	30	8:37	6♍40	0
Sep 1924	2	22:33	25♎08	45
	6	8:46	13♐28	90
	9	18:35	1♒46	135
	13	7:00	20♓12	180
	17	1:47	8♉53	225
	21	3:35	27♊52	270
	25	4:23	16♌49	315
	28	20:16	5♎25	0
Oct 1924	2	5:31	23♏44	45
	5	14:30	12♑04	90
	9	3:05	0♓33	135
	12	20:21	19♈13	180
	16	19:41	8♊10	225
	20	22:55	27♋16	270
	24	20:16	16♍09	315
	28	6:57	4♏35	0
	31	12:57	22♐50	45
Nov 1924	3	22:19	11♒14	90
	7	14:30	29♓55	135
	11	12:31	18♉51	180
	15	15:12	8♋00	225
	19	17:39	27♌08	270
	23	10:34	15♎53	315
	26	17:16	4♐12	0
	29	22:00	22♑26	45
Dec 1924	3	9:11	10♓57	90
	7	5:16	29♈51	135
	11	7:04	18♊59	180
	15	10:47	8♌13	225
	19	10:12	27♍16	270
	22	22:59	15♏51	315
	26	3:46	4♑07	0
	29	9:20	22♒25	45
Jan 1925	1	23:26	11♈04	90
	5	23:09	0♊08	135
	10	2:48	19♋22	180
	14	4:32	8♍31	225
	17	23:33	27♎23	270
	21	9:36	15♐52	315
	24	14:45	4♒08	0
	27	22:54	22♓32	45
	31	16:43	11♉20	90
Feb 1925	4	19:10	0♋29	135
	8	21:49	19♌39	180
	12	19:01	8♎35	225
	16	9:42	27♏13	270
	19	18:50	15♑38	315
	23	2:12	3♓58	0
	26	14:17	22♈29	45
Mar 1925	2	12:07	11♊25	90
	6	15:30	0♌34	135
	10	14:21	19♍31	180
	14	5:57	8♏09	225
	17	17:22	26♐37	270
	21	3:10	15♒00	315
	24	14:03	3♈25	0
	28	6:54	22♉05	45
Apr 1925	1	8:12	11♋06	90
	5	10:08	0♍07	135
	9	3:33	18♎46	180
	12	14:07	7♐09	225
	15	23:40	25♑28	270
	19	11:17	13♓53	315
	23	2:28	2♉25	0
	27	0:12	21♊13	45
May 1925	1	3:20	10♌14	90
	5	1:42	29♍03	135
	8	13:43	17♏26	180
	11	20:42	5♑37	225
	15	5:46	23♒52	270
	18	20:00	12♈20	315
	22	15:48	1♊01	0
	26	17:27	19♋55	45
	30	20:05	8♍52	90
Jun 1925	3	13:56	27♎27	135
	6	21:48	15♐38	180
	10	2:56	3♒42	225
	13	12:44	21♓58	270
	17	6:14	10♉31	315
	21	6:17	29♊21	0
	25	9:45	18♌18	45
	29	9:43	7♎07	90
Jul 1925	2	23:27	25♏31	135
	6	4:54	13♑35	180
	9	9:49	1♓39	225
	12	21:34	19♈58	270
	16	18:46	8♊41	315
	20	21:40	27♋37	0
	25	0:12	16♍32	45
	28	20:23	5♏12	90
Aug 1925	1	7:12	23♐30	135
	4	11:59	11♒34	180
	7	18:14	29♓41	225
	11	9:11	18♉10	270
	15	9:55	7♋02	315
	19	13:15	26♌01	0
	23	12:25	14♎50	45
	27	4:46	3♐23	90
	30	14:07	21♑40	135
Sep 1925	2	19:53	9♓48	180
	6	5:04	28♈04	225
	10	0:12	16♊46	270
	14	3:15	5♌47	315
	18	4:13	24♍43	0
	21	22:39	13♏24	45
	25	11:51	1♑53	90
	28	21:07	20♒12	135
Oct 1925	2	5:23	8♈30	180
	5	19:00	27♉00	225
	9	18:34	15♋56	270
	13	21:41	5♍02	315
	17	18:06	23♎51	0
	21	7:40	12♐24	45
	24	18:38	0♒50	90
	28	5:02	19♓16	135
	31	17:17	7♉46	180
Nov 1925	4	12:23	26♊34	225
	8	15:13	15♌42	270
	12	15:52	4♎45	315
	16	6:58	23♏25	0
	19	16:24	11♑50	45
	23	2:06	0♓16	90
	26	14:47	18♈51	135
	30	8:11	7♊37	180
Dec 1925	4	8:31	26♋41	225
	8	12:11	15♍54	270
	12	8:43	4♏49	315
	15	19:05	23♐19	0
	19	1:34	11♒39	45
	22	11:09	0♈06	90
	26	3:16	18♉51	135
	30	2:02	7♋52	180
Jan 1926	3	5:32	27♌06	225
	7	7:23	16♎15	270
	10	23:36	5♐00	315
	14	6:35	23♑21	0
	17	11:37	11♓37	45
	20	22:31	0♉08	90
	24	18:51	19♊03	135
	28	21:36	8♌14	180
Feb 1926	2	1:05	27♍26	225
	5	23:25	16♏26	270
	9	12:08	5♑00	315
	12	17:21	23♒15	0
	15	22:44	11♈31	45
	19	12:36	0♊08	90
	23	13:00	19♋10	135
	27	16:51	8♍21	180
Mar 1926	3	17:28	27♎23	225
	7	11:50	16♐10	270
	10	22:11	4♒35	315
	14	3:20	22♓48	0
	17	11:07	11♉07	45
	21	5:12	29♊51	90
	25	8:09	18♌56	135
	29	10:00	7♎58	180
Apr 1926	2	6:11	26♏45	225
	5	20:50	15♑19	270
	9	6:02	3♓38	315
	12	12:57	21♈52	0
	16	0:57	10♊17	45
	19	23:23	29♋08	90
	24	2:30	18♍10	135
	28	0:17	6♏58	180
May 1926	1	15:39	25♐30	225
	5	3:13	13♒52	270
	8	12:32	2♈09	315
	11	22:56	20♉28	0
	15	16:13	9♋04	45
	19	17:49	27♌59	90
	23	18:51	16♎52	135
	27	11:49	5♐25	180
	30	22:45	23♑44	225
Jun 1926	3	8:09	11♓59	270
	6	18:59	0♉17	315
	10	10:09	18♊46	0
	14	8:28	7♌31	45
	18	11:14	26♍27	90
	22	8:54	15♏10	135
	25	21:13	3♑31	180
	29	4:32	21♒40	225
Jul 1926	2	13:03	9♈52	270
	6	2:48	28♉17	315
	9	23:07	16♋57	0
	14	0:58	5♍50	45
	18	2:55	24♎44	90
	21	20:49	13♐18	135
	25	5:14	1♒30	180
	28	10:13	19♓34	225
	31	19:25	7♉48	270
Aug 1926	4	13:09	26♊23	315
	8	13:49	15♌15	0
	12	16:56	4♎12	45
	16	16:39	23♏02	90
	20	6:59	11♑30	135
	23	12:38	29♒37	180
	26	17:00	17♈41	225
	30	4:41	6♊03	270
Sep 1926	3	2:42	24♋51	315
	7	5:45	13♍51	0
	11	7:49	2♏49	45
	15	4:27	21♐35	90
	18	15:51	9♒58	135
	21	20:19	28♓05	180
	25	2:11	16♉15	225
	28	17:48	4♋50	270
Oct 1926	2	19:17	23♌50	315
	6	22:14	12♎54	0
	10	21:20	1♐49	45
	14	14:28	20♑29	90
	17	23:56	8♓51	135
	21	5:16	27♈03	180
	24	14:45	15♊26	225
	28	10:57	4♌16	270
Nov 1926	1	14:06	23♍24	315
	5	14:35	12♏26	0
	9	9:24	1♑14	45
	12	23:02	19♒49	90
	16	8:00	8♈13	135
	19	16:21	26♉35	180
	23	7:01	15♋14	225
	27	7:15	4♍17	270
Dec 1926	1	9:53	23♎27	315
	5	6:12	12♐21	0
	8	20:05	1♒00	45
	12	6:47	19♓30	90
	15	17:00	7♉59	135
	19	6:09	26♊35	180
	23	2:19	15♌30	225
	27	4:59	4♎41	270
	31	5:12	23♏46	315
Jan 1927	3	20:28	12♑29	0
	7	5:38	0♓56	45
	10	14:44	19♈22	90
	14	3:49	7♊59	135
	17	22:27	26♋50	180
	21	23:02	15♍56	225
	26	2:05	5♏07	270
	29	22:37	24♐02	315
Feb 1927	2	8:54	12♒31	0
	5	14:38	0♈49	45
	8	23:54	19♉14	90
	12	16:55	7♋59	135
	16	16:18	27♌00	180
	20	19:13	16♎10	225
	24	20:43	5♐15	270
	28	13:00	23♑57	315
Mar 1927	3	19:25	12♓14	0
	6	23:48	0♉25	45
	10	11:03	18♊53	90
	14	8:06	7♌45	135
	18	10:24	26♍50	180
	22	13:15	15♏55	225
	26	11:35	4♑49	270
	29	23:56	23♒18	315
Apr 1927	2	4:24	11♈26	0
	5	9:47	29♉37	45

The 8 Phases of the Moon 1900–2020

	9	0:21	18♋10	90
	13	0:36	7♍06	135
	17	3:36	26♎08	180
	21	4:06	15♐04	225
	24	22:21	3♒44	270
	28	7:54	22♓02	315
May 1927	1	12:40	10♉09	0
	4	21:02	28♊23	45
	8	15:27	17♌02	90
	12	17:34	5♎59	135
	16	19:03	24♏54	180
	20	15:28	13♑37	225
	24	5:34	2♓04	270
	27	13:58	20♈17	315
	30	21:06	8♊26	0
Jun 1927	3	9:46	26♋49	45
	7	7:49	15♍34	90
	11	10:14	4♏30	135
	15	8:20	23♐14	180
	18	23:43	11♒43	225
	22	10:30	0♈00	270
	25	19:32	18♉14	315
	29	6:32	6♋32	0
Jul 1927	2	23:57	25♌05	45
	7	0:53	13♎56	90
	11	2:00	2♐47	135
	14	19:23	21♑20	180
	18	5:52	9♓37	225
	21	14:44	27♈50	270
	25	1:58	16♊08	315
	28	17:37	4♌38	0
Aug 1927	1	15:31	23♍23	45
	5	18:05	12♏18	90
	9	16:22	1♑04	135
	13	4:37	19♒26	180
	16	11:19	7♈35	225
	19	19:55	25♉49	270
	23	10:26	14♋17	315
	27	6:46	3♍00	0
	31	8:14	21♎56	45
Sep 1927	4	10:45	10♐54	90
	8	5:03	29♑33	135
	11	12:54	17♓47	180
	14	17:35	5♉54	225
	18	3:30	24♊13	270
	21	21:50	12♌54	315
	25	22:11	1♎50	0
	30	1:31	20♏54	45
Oct 1927	4	2:02	9♑51	90
	7	16:10	28♒24	135
	10	21:15	16♈34	180
	14	1:58	4♊44	225
	17	14:32	23♋13	270
	21	12:40	12♍07	315
	25	15:38	1♏14	0
	29	18:23	20♐20	45
Nov 1927	2	15:16	9♒12	90
	6	2:07	27♓40	135
	9	6:36	15♉52	180
	12	13:20	4♋10	225
	16	5:28	22♌52	270
	20	6:50	11♎57	315
	24	10:09	1♐08	0
	28	9:39	20♑10	45
Dec 1927	2	2:15	8♓54	90
	5	11:27	27♈20	135
	8	17:32	15♊38	180
	12	3:51	4♌07	225
	16	0:04	23♍02	270
	20	3:20	12♏14	315
	24	4:14	1♑21	0
	27	22:32	20♒11	45
	31	11:22	8♈48	90
Jan 1928	3	20:46	27♉15	135
	7	6:08	15♋42	180
	10	21:06	4♍24	225
	14	21:14	23♎29	270
	19	0:16	12♐41	315
	22	20:19	1♒35	0
	26	9:05	20♓11	45
	29	19:26	8♉40	90
Feb 1928	2	6:29	27♊11	135
	5	20:11	15♌48	180
	9	16:12	4♎41	225
	13	19:05	23♏51	270
	17	19:25	12♑54	315
	21	9:41	1♓32	0
	24	17:59	19♈54	45
	28	3:21	8♊18	90
Mar 1928	2	17:00	26♋53	135
	6	11:27	15♍40	180
	10	11:58	4♏41	225
	14	15:20	23♐48	270
	18	11:13	12♒37	315
	21	20:30	0♈59	0
	25	2:09	19♉11	45
	28	11:55	7♋34	90
Apr 1928	1	4:44	26♌13	135
	5	3:39	15♎07	180
	9	6:50	4♐10	225
	13	8:09	23♑09	270
	16	23:22	11♓42	315
	20	5:25	29♈53	0
	23	10:20	18♊01	45
	26	21:42	6♌23	90
	30	18:00	25♍08	135
May 1928	4	20:12	14♏05	180
	8	23:19	3♑05	225
	12	20:51	21♒51	270
	16	8:25	10♈12	315
	19	13:14	28♉17	0
	22	19:06	16♋25	45
	26	9:12	4♍51	90
	30	8:53	23♎41	135
Jun 1928	3	12:14	12♐39	180
	7	12:32	1♒29	225
	11	5:51	20♓02	270
	14	15:20	8♉17	315
	17	20:42	26♊22	0
	21	5:02	14♌34	45
	24	22:48	3♎08	90
	29	1:02	22♏02	135
Jul 1928	3	2:49	10♑55	180
	6	22:34	29♒33	225
	10	12:16	17♈58	270
	13	21:11	6♊11	315
	17	4:36	24♋20	0
	20	16:44	12♍41	45
	24	14:38	1♏25	90
	28	17:39	20♐21	135
Aug 1928	1	15:31	9♒06	180
	5	6:18	27♓34	225
	8	17:24	15♉53	270
	12	3:03	4♋08	315
	15	13:49	22♌27	0
	19	6:51	11♎01	45
	23	8:22	29♏56	90
	27	9:49	18♑51	135
	31	2:34	7♓26	180
Sep 1928	3	12:58	25♈45	225
	6	22:35	14♊03	270
	10	10:05	2♌26	315
	14	1:21	20♍58	0
	17	23:35	9♏48	45
	22	2:58	28♐51	90
	26	0:56	17♒41	135
	29	12:43	6♈07	180
Oct 1928	2	19:52	24♉21	225
	6	5:06	12♋42	270
	9	19:31	1♍15	315
	13	15:57	20♎04	0
	17	18:20	9♐08	45
	21	21:07	28♑13	90
	25	14:49	16♓57	135
	28	22:44	5♉16	180
Nov 1928	1	4:01	23♊29	225
	4	14:07	11♌55	270
	8	8:25	0♎42	315
	12	9:36	19♏46	0
	16	13:36	8♑58	45
	20	13:36	28♒00	90
	24	3:29	16♈37	135
	27	9:06	4♊54	180
	30	14:07	23♋09	225
Dec 1928	4	2:32	11♍43	270
	8	1:12	0♏43	315
	12	5:06	19♐57	0
	16	7:33	9♒07	45
	20	3:44	28♓02	90
	23	14:55	16♉34	135
	26	19:55	4♋50	180
	30	2:31	23♌10	225
Jan 1929	2	18:45	11♎55	270
	6	21:04	1♐05	315
	11	0:29	20♑19	0
	14	22:55	9♓19	45
	18	15:15	28♈04	90
	22	1:00	16♊32	135
	25	7:09	4♌51	180
	28	17:18	23♍20	225
Feb 1929	1	14:11	12♏15	270
	5	17:59	1♑28	315
	9	17:55	20♒31	0
	13	11:22	9♈17	45
	17	0:23	27♉52	90
	20	9:55	16♋18	135
	23	18:59	4♍42	180
	27	10:14	23♎21	225
Mar 1929	3	11:09	12♐24	270
	7	13:41	1♒30	315
	11	8:37	20♓18	0
	14	21:13	8♉49	45
	18	7:42	27♊14	90
	21	18:16	15♌39	135
	25	7:47	4♎11	180
	29	4:31	23♏00	225
Apr 1929	2	7:29	12♑04	270
	6	6:41	0♓59	315
	9	20:33	19♈30	0
	13	5:07	7♊47	45
	16	14:09	26♋06	90
	20	3:06	14♍33	135
	23	21:48	3♏14	180
	27	22:50	22♐10	225
May 1929	2	1:26	11♒09	270
	5	20:33	29♓50	315
	9	6:08	18♉07	0
	12	11:54	6♋15	45
	15	20:56	24♌31	90
	19	13:24	13♎04	135
	23	12:50	1♐53	180
	27	15:50	20♑51	225
	31	16:13	9♓42	270
Jun 1929	4	7:29	28♈11	315
	7	13:57	16♊18	0
	10	18:30	4♌21	45
	14	5:15	22♍39	90
	18	1:48	11♏20	135
	22	4:15	0♑15	180
	26	6:39	19♒09	225
	30	3:54	7♈52	270
Jul 1929	3	15:59	26♉12	315
	6	20:47	14♋15	0
	10	2:03	2♍20	45
	13	16:05	20♎45	90
	17	16:20	9♐34	135
	21	19:21	28♑30	180
	25	19:08	17♓19	225
	29	12:56	5♉54	270
Aug 1929	1	22:47	24♊09	315
	5	3:40	12♌13	0
	8	11:40	0♎25	45
	12	6:02	19♏02	90
	16	8:31	7♑59	135
	20	9:43	26♒52	180
	24	5:37	15♈34	225
	27	20:02	4♊02	270
	31	4:51	22♋17	315
Sep 1929	3	11:48	10♍29	0
	7	0:18	28♎54	45
	10	22:57	17♐44	90
	15	1:41	6♒44	135
	18	23:16	25♓32	180
	22	14:40	14♉06	225
	26	2:07	2♋30	270
	29	11:25	20♌50	315
Oct 1929	2	22:20	9♎14	0
	6	16:17	27♏55	45
	10	18:05	16♑57	90
	14	19:06	5♓57	135
	18	12:06	24♈38	180
	21	22:57	13♊04	225
	25	8:21	1♌26	270
	28	19:49	19♍55	315
Nov 1929	1	12:01	8♏35	0
	5	11:04	27♐33	45
	9	14:10	16♒42	90
	13	12:04	5♈38	135
	17	0:14	24♉10	180
	20	7:13	12♋30	225
	23	16:05	0♍54	270
	27	7:11	19♎34	315
Dec 1929	1	4:49	8♐31	0
	5	7:16	27♑41	45
	9	9:42	16♓51	90
	13	3:44	5♉40	135
	16	11:38	24♊03	180
	19	16:19	12♌18	225
	23	2:28	0♎47	270
	26	21:59	19♏40	315
	30	23:42	8♑50	0
Jan 1930	4	3:10	28♒03	45
	8	3:11	17♈08	90
	11	17:16	5♊47	135
	14	22:21	24♋03	180
	18	2:58	12♍18	225
	21	16:07	0♏55	270
	25	15:41	19♐58	315
	29	19:08	9♒11	0
Feb 1930	2	21:06	28♓19	45
	6	17:26	17♉13	90
	10	4:15	5♋43	135
	13	8:39	23♌56	180
	16	15:33	12♎15	225
	20	8:45	1♐00	270
	24	10:55	20♑07	315
	28	13:33	9♓15	0
Mar 1930	4	11:56	28♈11	45
	8	4:01	16♊52	90
	11	12:56	5♌14	135
	14	18:59	23♍28	180
	18	6:00	11♏55	225
	22	3:13	0♑46	270
	26	6:09	19♒52	315
	30	5:47	8♈48	0
Apr 1930	2	23:13	27♉29	45
	6	11:25	15♋56	90
	9	20:14	4♍15	135
	13	5:49	22♎35	180
	16	21:46	11♐10	225

The 8 Phases of the Moon 1900–2020

Month	Day	Time	Position	Phase
	20	22:09	0♒05	270
	25	0:02	19♓04	315
	28	19:09	7♉45	0
May 1930	2	7:23	26♊10	45
	5	16:53	14♌27	90
	9	3:19	2♎46	135
	12	17:30	21♏15	180
	16	14:10	9♑58	225
	20	16:22	28♒54	270
	24	15:38	17♈43	315
	28	5:37	6♊10	0
	31	13:28	24♋21	45
Jun 1930	3	21:57	12♍34	90
	7	11:16	0♏58	135
	11	6:12	19♐35	180
	15	6:35	8♒26	225
	19	9:01	27♓20	270
	23	4:33	15♉59	315
	26	13:47	4♋13	0
	29	18:54	22♌17	45
Jul 1930	3	4:03	10♎30	90
	6	20:59	29♏02	135
	10	20:01	17♑48	180
	14	22:35	6♓43	225
	18	23:29	25♈34	270
	22	14:52	14♊03	315
	25	20:42	2♌09	0
	29	1:06	20♍12	45
Aug 1930	1	12:27	8♏31	90
	5	9:05	27♐13	135
	9	10:58	16♒07	180
	13	13:40	5♈04	225
	17	11:31	23♉49	270
	20	23:14	12♋11	315
	24	3:37	0♍15	0
	27	9:20	18♎22	45
	30	23:57	6♐52	90
Sep 1930	3	23:52	25♑44	135
	8	2:48	14♓44	180
	12	3:19	3♉38	225
	15	21:13	22♊17	270
	19	6:36	10♌36	315
	22	11:42	28♍44	0
	25	20:28	17♏02	45
	29	14:58	5♑44	90
Oct 1930	3	17:13	24♒46	135
	7	18:56	13♈47	180
	11	15:13	2♊35	225
	15	5:12	21♋08	270
	18	14:01	9♍28	315
	21	21:48	27♎46	0
	25	10:53	16♐18	45
	29	9:22	5♒14	90
Nov 1930	2	12:24	24♓22	135
	6	10:28	13♉17	180
	10	1:27	1♋56	225
	13	12:28	20♌25	270
	16	22:29	8♎51	315
	20	10:22	27♏23	0
	24	4:25	16♑10	45
	28	6:18	5♓18	90
Dec 1930	2	7:55	24♈25	135
	6	0:40	13♊10	180
	9	10:37	1♌38	225
	12	20:07	20♍06	270
	16	8:41	8♏41	315
	20	1:24	27♐26	0
	24	0:22	16♒28	45
	28	3:59	5♈42	90
Jan 1931	1	2:02	24♉42	135
	4	13:15	13♋14	180
	7	19:39	1♍34	225
	11	5:09	20♎01	270
	14	21:02	8♐45	315
	18	18:36	27♑43	0
	22	21:15	16♓54	45
	27	0:06	6♉06	90
	30	17:26	24♊53	135
Feb 1931	3	0:26	13♌13	180
	6	5:18	1♎28	225
	9	16:10	19♏57	270
	13	11:40	8♑49	315
	17	13:11	27♒55	0
	21	17:03	17♈07	45
	25	16:42	6♊08	90
Mar 1931	1	5:42	24♋41	135
	4	10:36	12♍54	180
	7	15:55	1♏07	225
	11	5:15	19♐40	270
	15	4:17	8♒37	315
	19	7:51	27♓45	0
	23	9:51	16♉49	45
	27	5:04	5♋34	90
	30	15:11	23♌57	135
Apr 1931	2	20:06	12♎07	180
	6	3:31	0♐23	225
	9	20:15	19♑01	270
	13	22:06	8♓01	315
	18	1:00	27♈03	0
	21	22:43	15♊51	45
	25	13:40	4♌23	90
	28	22:37	22♍40	135
May 1931	2	5:15	10♏51	180
	5	16:08	29♐12	225
	9	12:48	17♒56	270
	13	15:56	6♈55	315
	17	15:28	25♉45	0
	21	7:55	14♋18	45
	24	19:39	2♍40	90
	28	4:54	20♎55	135
	31	14:33	9♐10	180
Jun 1931	4	5:57	27♑39	225
	8	6:19	16♓30	270
	12	8:31	5♉25	315
	16	3:02	24♊01	0
	19	14:38	12♌21	45
	23	0:23	0♎36	90
	26	11:07	18♏53	135
	30	0:47	7♑17	180
Jul 1931	3	21:08	25♒57	225
	7	23:52	14♈52	270
	11	23:03	3♊39	315
	15	12:20	22♋03	0
	18	20:15	10♍13	45
	22	5:16	28♎27	90
	25	18:26	16♐50	135
	29	12:48	5♒26	180
Aug 1931	2	13:34	24♓17	225
	6	16:28	13♉14	270
	10	11:29	1♋52	315
	13	20:27	20♌06	0
	17	2:08	8♎13	45
	20	11:37	26♏29	90
	24	4:05	15♑02	135
	28	3:10	3♓51	180
Sep 1931	1	6:30	22♈51	225
	5	7:21	11♊46	270
	8	22:16	0♌17	315
	12	4:27	18♍27	0
	15	9:24	6♏34	45
	18	20:38	24♐57	90
	22	17:06	13♒43	135
	26	19:45	2♈45	180
	30	22:52	21♉48	225
Oct 1931	4	20:15	10♋38	270
	8	8:04	29♌05	315
	11	13:06	17♎15	0
	14	18:58	5♐28	45
	18	9:20	24♑02	90
	22	9:51	13♓02	135
	26	13:34	2♉10	180
	30	13:43	21♊10	225
Nov 1931	3	7:18	9♌54	270
	6	17:20	28♍20	315
	9	22:56	16♏35	0
	13	7:29	4♑57	45
	17	2:14	23♒46	90
	21	5:31	12♈56	135
	25	7:10	2♊03	180
	29	2:39	20♋55	225
Dec 1931	2	16:51	9♍33	270
	6	2:26	28♎00	315
	9	10:16	16♐23	0
	12	23:18	4♒59	45
	16	22:43	24♓02	90
	21	2:15	13♉15	135
	24	23:24	2♋12	180
	28	13:51	20♌52	225
Jan 1932	1	1:23	9♎25	270
	4	11:44	27♏55	315
	7	23:29	16♑29	0
	11	18:09	5♓20	45
	15	20:55	24♈31	90
	19	21:57	13♊38	135
	23	13:44	2♌21	180
	26	23:45	20♍50	225
	30	9:32	9♏18	270
Feb 1932	2	21:51	27♐52	315
	6	14:45	16♒37	0
	10	14:41	5♈40	45
	14	18:16	24♉52	90
	18	15:12	13♋46	135
	22	2:08	2♍15	180
	25	8:49	20♎33	225
	28	18:03	8♐57	270
Mar 1932	3	9:33	27♑37	315
	7	7:45	16♓32	0
	11	10:51	5♉40	45
	15	12:41	24♊44	90
	19	5:19	13♌24	135
	22	12:38	1♎41	180
	25	17:30	19♏51	225
	29	3:44	8♑15	270
Apr 1932	1	23:13	27♒00	315
	6	1:21	16♈02	0
	10	4:41	5♊06	45
	14	3:16	23♋58	90
	17	16:17	12♍26	135
	20	21:27	0♏34	180
	24	2:19	18♐41	225
	27	15:14	7♒08	270
May 1932	1	14:40	25♓59	315
	5	18:12	15♉01	0
	9	19:11	3♋55	45
	13	14:02	22♌35	90
	17	0:28	10♎53	135
	20	5:09	28♏58	180
	23	12:01	17♑07	225
	27	4:55	5♓40	270
	31	7:05	24♈36	315
Jun 1932	4	9:16	13♊31	0
	8	6:24	2♌14	45
	11	21:40	20♍42	90
	15	6:37	8♏56	135
	18	12:38	27♐02	180
	21	23:23	15♒19	225
	25	20:36	4♈01	270
	29	23:31	22♉57	315
Jul 1932	3	22:20	11♋43	0
	7	14:59	0♍15	45
	11	3:07	18♎35	90
	14	11:56	6♐48	135
	17	21:07	25♑01	180
	21	12:58	13♓31	225
	25	13:42	2♉22	270
	29	15:18	21♊15	315
Aug 1932	2	9:42	9♌51	0
	5	21:54	28♍13	45
	9	7:41	16♏29	90
	12	17:51	4♑46	135
	16	7:42	23♒12	180
	20	4:47	11♈56	225
	24	7:22	0♊54	270
	28	6:10	19♋43	315
	31	19:55	8♍10	0
Sep 1932	4	4:10	26♎24	45
	7	12:49	14♐40	90
	11	1:54	3♒07	135
	14	21:06	21♓49	180
	18	22:17	10♉46	225
	23	0:47	29♊47	270
	26	20:02	18♌30	315
	30	5:30	6♎50	0
Oct 1932	3	10:57	25♏01	45
	6	20:06	13♑21	90
	10	13:18	2♓01	135
	14	13:18	20♈59	180
	18	16:27	10♊05	225
	22	17:14	29♋06	270
	26	8:45	17♍44	315
	29	14:56	5♏59	0
Nov 1932	1	19:22	24♐10	45
	5	6:51	12♒40	90
	9	4:33	1♈35	135
	13	7:28	20♉43	180
	17	10:09	9♋52	225
	21	7:58	28♌49	270
	24	20:09	17♎22	315
	28	0:44	5♐35	0
Dec 1932	1	6:23	23♑52	45
	4	21:45	12♓34	90
	8	23:06	1♉41	135
	13	2:21	20♊53	180
	17	2:21	9♌57	225
	20	20:22	28♍46	270
	24	6:11	17♏15	315
	27	11:23	5♑32	0
	30	20:32	23♒58	45
Jan 1933	3	16:24	12♈53	90
	7	19:33	2♊05	135
	11	20:36	21♋12	180
	15	16:12	10♍06	225
	19	6:16	28♎45	270
	22	15:15	17♐11	315
	25	23:20	5♒34	0
	29	13:31	24♓13	45
Feb 1933	2	13:17	13♉16	90
	6	16:03	2♋27	135
	10	13:01	21♌22	180
	14	3:23	10♎00	225
	17	14:09	28♏29	270
	21	0:06	16♑55	315
	24	12:44	5♓29	0
	28	8:11	24♈18	45
Mar 1933	4	10:24	13♊25	90
	8	10:55	2♌26	135
	12	2:46	21♍05	180
	15	12:11	9♏28	225
	18	21:05	27♐49	270
	22	9:35	16♒19	315
	26	3:21	5♈01	0
	30	3:06	23♉58	45
Apr 1933	3	5:57	13♋02	90
	7	2:53	1♍51	135
	10	13:38	20♎14	180
	13	19:28	8♐24	225
	17	4:18	26♑42	270
	20	20:20	15♓17	315
	24	18:39	4♉07	0
	28	21:01	23♊06	45

The 8 Phases of the Moon 1900–2020

May 1933	2	22:39	12♌03	90
	6	15:22	0♎38	135
	9	22:05	18♏48	180
	13	2:21	6♑52	225
	16	12:51	25♒11	270
	20	8:39	13♈52	315
	24	10:07	2♊46	0
	28	13:01	21♋44	45
Jun 1933	1	11:53	10♍31	90
	5	0:36	28♎54	135
	8	5:05	16♐57	180
	11	9:59	5♒00	225
	14	23:26	23♓24	270
	18	22:32	12♉11	315
	23	1:23	1♋07	0
	27	2:39	19♌59	45
	30	21:41	8♎36	90
Jul 1933	4	7:27	26♏51	135
	7	11:51	14♑53	180
	10	19:16	3♓02	225
	14	12:24	21♈35	270
	18	13:54	10♊27	315
	22	16:03	29♋22	0
	26	13:44	18♍05	45
	30	4:44	6♏33	90
Aug 1933	2	13:10	24♐46	135
	5	19:32	12♒53	180
	9	6:53	1♈13	225
	13	3:50	19♉56	270
	17	6:25	8♋53	315
	21	5:48	27♌42	0
	24	22:37	16♎17	45
	28	10:14	4♐38	90
	31	19:07	22♑54	135
Sep 1933	4	5:05	11♓12	180
	7	21:08	29♈46	225
	11	21:30	18♊40	270
	15	23:30	7♌39	315
	19	18:21	26♍21	0
	23	6:06	14♏45	45
	26	15:37	3♑05	90
	30	2:34	21♒29	135
Oct 1933	3	17:08	10♈02	180
	7	14:02	28♉51	225
	11	16:46	17♋55	270
	15	16:15	6♍51	315
	19	5:45	25♎24	0
	22	13:20	13♐42	45
	25	22:21	2♒04	90
	29	12:31	20♓39	135
Nov 1933	2	8:00	9♉27	180
	6	9:04	28♊31	225
	10	12:18	17♌40	270
	14	7:44	6♎30	315
	17	16:24	24♏53	0
	20	21:35	13♑08	45
	24	7:39	1♓35	90
	28	1:37	20♈23	135
Dec 1933	2	1:31	9♊26	180
	6	5:03	28♋38	225
	10	6:24	17♍46	270
	13	21:20	6♏27	315
	17	2:53	24♐44	0
	20	7:46	13♒00	45
	23	20:09	1♈35	90
	27	17:57	20♉34	135
	31	20:54	9♋46	180
Jan 1934	5	0:07	28♌58	225
	8	21:36	17♎57	270
	12	8:55	6♐29	315
	15	13:37	24♑44	0
	18	20:10	13♓04	45
	22	11:51	1♉47	90
	26	12:57	20♊54	135
	30	16:32	10♌07	180

Feb 1934	3	16:26	29♍10	225
	7	9:22	17♏56	270
	10	18:47	6♑22	315
	14	0:44	24♒39	0
	17	10:30	13♈05	45
	21	6:05	1♊56	90
	25	9:13	21♋05	135
Mar 1934	1	10:26	10♍09	180
	5	5:05	28♎57	225
	8	18:06	17♐29	270
	12	3:21	5♒52	315
	15	12:09	24♓14	0
	19	2:15	12♉48	45
	23	1:45	1♋45	90
	27	4:46	20♌50	135
	31	1:15	9♎39	180
Apr 1934	3	14:26	28♏08	225
	7	0:49	16♑31	270
	10	11:16	4♓54	315
	13	23:57	23♈21	0
	17	18:59	12♊04	45
	21	21:21	1♌04	90
	25	21:52	19♍59	135
	29	12:46	8♏30	180
May 1934	2	21:32	26♐46	225
	6	6:41	15♒03	270
	9	19:19	3♈28	315
	13	12:30	22♉03	0
	17	12:09	10♋53	45
	21	15:20	29♌52	90
	25	11:43	18♎34	135
	28	21:42	6♐51	180
Jun 1934	1	3:40	24♑58	225
	4	12:53	13♓12	270
	8	4:26	1♉41	315
	12	2:12	20♊26	0
	16	4:58	9♌22	45
	20	6:37	28♍15	90
	23	22:33	16♏44	135
	27	5:08	4♑52	180
	30	9:59	22♒55	225
Jul 1934	3	20:28	11♈11	270
	7	15:33	29♉48	315
	11	17:06	18♋41	0
	15	20:30	7♍38	45
	19	18:53	26♎23	90
	23	7:11	14♐44	135
	26	12:09	2♒48	180
	29	17:27	20♓53	225
Aug 1934	2	6:27	9♉16	270
	6	5:18	28♊03	315
	10	8:46	17♌02	0
	14	10:04	5♎55	45
	18	4:33	24♏33	90
	21	14:35	12♑50	135
	24	19:37	0♓56	180
	28	2:57	19♈07	225
	31	19:40	7♊41	270
Sep 1934	4	21:42	26♋39	315
	9	0:20	15♍38	0
	12	21:31	4♏25	45
	16	12:26	22♐57	90
	19	21:38	11♒15	135
	23	4:19	29♓27	180
	26	15:18	17♉50	225
	30	12:30	6♋39	270
Oct 1934	4	15:57	25♌44	315
	8	15:05	14♎39	0
	12	7:21	3♐17	45
	15	19:29	21♑45	90
	19	5:09	10♓08	135
	22	15:01	28♈31	180
	26	7:03	17♊11	225
	30	8:22	6♌14	270

Nov 1934	3	10:41	25♍20	315
	7	4:44	14♏05	0
	10	16:21	2♑36	45
	14	2:40	21♒03	90
	17	13:58	9♈33	135
	21	4:27	28♉11	180
	25	2:04	17♋07	225
	29	5:39	6♍19	270
Dec 1934	3	4:34	25♎20	315
	6	17:25	13♐55	0
	10	1:22	2♒18	45
	13	10:52	20♓45	90
	17	0:59	9♉24	135
	20	20:54	28♊18	180
	24	23:01	17♌28	225
	29	2:08	6♎41	270
Jan 1935	1	20:41	25♏31	315
	5	5:20	13♑57	0
	8	10:57	2♓15	45
	11	20:55	20♈44	90
	15	14:54	9♊33	135
	19	15:45	28♋39	180
	23	19:38	17♍53	225
	27	19:59	6♏58	270
	31	10:29	25♐38	315
Feb 1935	3	16:28	13♒56	0
	6	21:23	2♈11	45
	10	9:25	20♉43	90
	14	7:41	9♋42	135
	18	11:17	28♌53	180
	22	13:44	18♎01	225
	26	10:15	6♐54	270
Mar 1935	1	21:44	25♑23	315
	5	2:41	13♓36	0
	8	8:52	1♉52	45
	12	0:31	20♊31	90
	16	2:17	9♌34	135
	20	5:32	28♍41	180
	24	4:14	17♏36	225
	27	20:51	6♑15	270
	31	6:30	24♒37	315
Apr 1935	3	12:11	12♈49	0
	6	21:38	1♊09	45
	10	17:42	19♋56	90
	14	20:59	8♍59	135
	18	21:10	27♎54	180
	22	15:11	16♐33	225
	26	4:21	5♒01	270
	29	13:23	23♓18	315
May 1935	2	21:37	11♉33	0
	6	11:54	0♋02	45
	10	11:55	18♌54	90
	14	14:17	7♎51	135
	18	9:57	26♏32	180
	21	23:17	14♑57	225
	25	9:45	3♓15	270
	28	19:30	21♈32	315
Jun 1935	1	7:52	9♊54	0
	5	3:29	28♋33	45
	9	5:50	17♍29	90
	13	5:28	6♏17	135
	16	20:20	24♐44	180
	20	5:33	12♒58	225
	23	14:22	1♈11	270
	27	2:18	19♉31	315
	30	19:45	8♋04	0
Jul 1935	4	19:52	26♌54	45
	8	22:29	15♎49	90
	12	18:31	4♐28	135
	16	5:01	22♑45	180
	19	11:07	10♓51	225
	22	19:42	29♈03	270
	26	11:08	17♊32	315
	30	9:33	6♌18	0
Aug 1935	3	12:15	25♍14	45

	7	13:23	14♏06	90
	11	5:42	2♑38	135
	14	12:44	20♒48	180
	17	17:12	8♈51	225
	21	3:18	27♉09	270
	24	22:59	15♋50	315
	29	1:01	4♍46	0
Sep 1935	2	3:57	23♎46	45
	6	2:26	12♐35	90
	9	15:25	1♒01	135
	12	20:19	19♓08	180
	16	1:04	7♉14	225
	19	14:23	25♊43	270
	23	14:09	14♌37	315
	27	17:30	3♎40	0
Oct 1935	1	18:30	22♏39	45
	5	13:40	11♑23	90
	9	0:05	29♒46	135
	12	4:39	17♈56	180
	15	11:55	6♊12	225
	19	5:37	24♋54	270
	23	8:08	13♍59	315
	27	10:16	3♏04	0
	31	7:38	21♐57	45
Nov 1935	3	23:12	10♒36	90
	7	8:16	29♓00	135
	10	14:42	17♉17	180
	14	2:25	5♋47	225
	18	0:36	24♌44	270
	22	3:48	13♎55	315
	26	2:36	2♐55	0
	29	19:16	21♑39	45
Dec 1935	3	7:28	10♓13	90
	6	16:48	28♈39	135
	10	3:11	17♊08	180
	13	20:24	5♌55	225
	17	21:58	25♍03	270
	21	23:43	14♏12	315
	25	17:50	3♑01	0
	29	5:29	21♒35	45
Jan 1936	1	15:15	10♈03	90
	5	2:36	28♉35	135
	8	18:15	17♋19	180
	12	16:37	6♍19	225
	16	19:41	25♎31	270
	20	18:22	14♐32	315
	24	7:18	3♒09	0
	27	14:41	21♓30	45
	30	23:36	9♉56	90
Feb 1936	3	14:23	28♊36	135
	7	11:19	17♌32	180
	11	13:12	6♎39	225
	15	15:46	25♏48	270
	19	10:23	14♑37	315
	22	18:43	2♓59	0
	25	23:32	21♈13	45
	29	9:28	9♊38	90
Mar 1936	4	4:19	28♋26	135
	8	5:14	17♍29	180
	12	8:22	6♏36	225
	16	8:35	25♐36	270
	19	22:59	14♒10	315
	23	4:14	2♈22	0
	26	8:47	20♉32	45
	29	21:22	9♋01	90
Apr 1936	2	19:56	27♌54	135
	6	22:47	16♎57	180
	11	0:49	5♐58	225
	14	21:22	24♑44	270
	18	8:14	13♓07	315
	21	12:33	1♉13	0
	24	19:03	19♊25	45
	28	11:16	7♌59	90
May 1936	2	12:28	26♍55	135
	6	15:02	15♏53	180

The 8 Phases of the Moon 1900–2020

	10	13:53	4♑43	225
	14	6:12	23♒16	270
	17	15:00	11♈30	315
	20	20:35	29♉37	0
	24	6:44	17♋55	45
	28	2:46	6♍35	90
Jun 1936	1	5:11	25♎31	135
	5	5:23	14♐21	180
	8	23:37	2♒57	225
	12	12:05	21♓19	270
	15	20:33	9♉31	315
	19	5:15	27♊44	0
	22	19:58	16♌11	45
	26	19:23	4♎58	90
	30	21:26	23♏52	135
Jul 1936	4	17:35	12♑31	180
	8	6:44	0♓54	225
	11	16:28	19♈09	270
	15	2:19	7♊24	315
	18	15:19	25♋47	0
	22	10:46	14♍25	45
	26	12:36	3♏19	90
	30	12:41	22♐09	135
Aug 1936	3	3:48	10♒37	180
	6	12:26	28♓50	225
	9	21:00	17♉03	270
	13	9:36	5♋26	315
	17	3:21	24♌02	0
	21	3:00	12♎52	45
	25	5:49	1♐50	90
	29	2:28	20♑34	135
Sep 1936	1	12:38	8♓52	180
	4	18:12	27♈00	225
	8	3:14	15♊17	270
	11	19:27	3♌51	315
	15	17:42	22♍41	0
	19	20:17	11♏41	45
	23	22:13	0♑41	90
	27	14:39	19♒18	135
	30	21:01	7♈30	180
Oct 1936	4	1:29	25♉38	225
	7	12:29	14♋03	270
	11	8:35	2♍51	315
	15	10:21	21♎53	0
	19	13:49	11♐00	45
	23	12:54	29♑56	90
	27	1:25	18♓27	135
	30	5:58	6♉38	180
Nov 1936	2	11:23	24♊52	225
	6	1:29	13♌28	270
	10	1:13	2♎28	315
	14	4:42	21♏39	0
	18	6:21	10♑45	45
	22	1:19	29♒34	90
	25	11:13	18♈01	135
	28	16:12	6♊16	180
Dec 1936	2	0:23	24♋39	225
	5	18:20	13♍28	270
	9	20:49	2♏38	315
	13	23:25	21♐49	0
	17	20:43	10♒46	45
	21	11:30	29♓27	90
	24	20:36	17♉54	135
	28	4:01	6♋16	180
	31	16:19	24♌51	225
Jan 1937	4	14:22	13♎50	270
	8	17:52	3♐04	315
	12	16:47	22♑06	0
	16	8:31	10♓49	45
	19	20:02	29♈22	90
	23	6:02	17♊50	135
	26	17:16	6♌22	180
	30	10:29	25♍08	225
Feb 1937	3	12:04	14♏16	270
	7	14:10	3♑25	315

	11	7:35	22♒11	0
	14	18:07	10♈40	45
	18	3:50	29♉06	90
	21	15:56	17♋38	135
	25	7:44	6♍18	180
Mar 1937	1	5:53	25♎15	225
	5	9:17	14♐24	270
	9	7:42	3♒20	315
	12	19:32	21♓49	0
	16	2:24	10♉06	45
	19	11:46	28♊28	90
	23	2:44	17♌04	135
	26	23:13	5♎53	180
	31	1:12	24♏55	225
Apr 1937	4	3:53	13♑58	270
	7	21:35	2♓39	315
	11	5:10	20♈54	0
	14	10:16	9♊03	45
	17	20:34	27♋24	90
	21	14:51	16♍05	135
	25	15:24	5♏00	180
	29	18:53	24♐01	225
May 1937	3	18:37	12♒54	270
	7	8:01	1♈20	315
	10	13:18	19♉27	0
	13	18:26	7♋33	45
	17	6:50	25♌57	90
	21	4:38	14♎42	135
	25	7:38	3♐40	180
	29	9:46	22♑36	225
Jun 1937	2	5:24	11♓15	270
	5	15:51	29♈32	315
	8	20:43	17♊36	0
	12	3:29	5♌45	45
	15	19:03	24♍14	90
	19	20:01	13♏05	135
	23	23:00	2♑01	180
	27	21:25	20♒46	225
Jul 1937	1	13:03	9♈15	270
	4	22:08	27♉28	315
	8	4:13	15♋34	0
	11	14:02	3♍50	45
	15	9:37	22♎28	90
	19	12:29	11♐24	135
	23	12:46	0♒13	180
	27	6:20	18♓47	225
	30	18:47	7♉09	270
Aug 1937	3	3:54	25♊23	315
	6	12:37	13♌37	0
	10	2:48	2♎03	45
	14	2:29	20♏53	90
	18	5:06	9♑50	135
	22	0:47	28♒30	180
	25	13:33	16♈55	225
	28	23:55	5♊14	270
Sep 1937	1	10:16	23♋33	315
	4	22:54	11♍58	0
	8	18:17	0♏40	45
	12	20:57	19♐40	90
	16	21:04	8♒34	135
	20	11:33	27♓05	180
	23	20:23	15♉22	225
	27	5:44	3♋42	270
	30	18:25	22♌10	315
Oct 1937	4	11:58	10♎50	0
	8	12:20	29♏48	45
	12	15:47	18♑54	90
	16	11:53	7♓42	135
	19	21:48	26♈05	180
	23	3:58	14♊20	225
	26	13:26	2♌43	270
	30	5:32	21♍23	315
Nov 1937	3	4:16	10♏20	0
	7	7:48	29♐30	45
	11	9:34	18♒35	90

	15	1:28	7♈16	135
	18	8:10	25♉35	180
	21	13:08	13♋49	225
	25	0:05	2♍19	270
	28	20:24	21♎12	315
Dec 1937	2	23:11	10♐23	0
	7	2:52	29♑36	45
	11	1:13	18♓35	90
	14	13:45	7♉10	135
	17	18:53	25♊26	180
	21	0:21	13♌44	225
	24	14:20	2♎23	270
	28	14:52	21♏29	315
Jan 1938	1	18:59	10♑44	0
	5	19:49	29♒51	45
	9	14:13	18♈41	90
	13	0:37	7♊11	135
	16	5:54	25♋28	180
	19	13:51	13♍51	225
	23	8:09	2♏41	270
	27	11:28	21♐53	315
	31	13:35	11♒02	0
Feb 1938	4	9:48	29♓56	45
	8	0:33	18♉36	90
	11	10:01	7♋02	135
	14	17:15	25♌22	180
	18	5:33	13♎55	225
	22	4:25	2♐54	270
	26	7:55	22♑04	315
Mar 1938	2	5:40	11♓00	0
	5	20:51	29♈38	45
	9	8:36	18♊08	90
	12	18:23	6♌32	135
	16	5:16	24♍58	180
	19	23:01	13♏41	225
	24	1:06	2♑45	270
	28	2:16	21♒45	315
	31	18:52	10♈24	0
Apr 1938	4	5:32	28♉48	45
	7	15:10	17♋09	90
	11	2:35	5♍34	135
	14	18:21	24♎08	180
	18	17:14	13♐00	225
	22	20:15	2♒02	270
	26	17:38	20♓49	315
	30	5:28	9♉13	0
May 1938	3	12:37	27♊25	45
	6	21:24	15♌41	90
	10	11:44	4♎09	135
	14	8:39	22♏54	180
	18	10:51	11♑50	225
	22	12:36	0♓45	270
	26	5:58	19♈20	315
	29	14:00	7♊32	0
Jun 1938	1	19:00	25♋36	45
	5	4:33	13♍52	90
	8	22:46	2♏27	135
	12	23:47	21♐19	180
	17	2:47	10♒15	225
	21	1:52	29♓02	270
	24	15:39	17♉27	315
	27	21:10	5♋32	0
Jul 1938	1	1:46	23♌34	45
	4	13:47	11♎55	90
	8	12:05	0♐39	135
	12	15:05	19♑35	180
	16	16:32	8♓28	225
	20	12:19	27♈07	270
	23	23:18	15♊25	315
	27	3:54	3♌28	0
	30	10:07	21♍35	45
Aug 1938	3	2:00	10♏05	90
	7	3:28	28♐58	135
	11	5:57	17♒54	180
	15	4:11	6♈40	225

	18	20:31	25♉13	270
	22	5:45	13♋28	315
	25	11:18	1♍35	0
	28	21:07	19♎53	45
Sep 1938	1	17:29	8♐36	90
	5	20:21	27♑36	135
	9	20:09	16♓28	180
	13	14:09	5♉07	225
	17	3:12	23♊34	270
	20	12:04	11♌52	315
	23	20:34	0♎09	0
	27	11:29	18♏42	45
Oct 1938	1	11:45	7♑38	90
	5	13:58	26♒40	135
	9	9:37	15♈26	180
	12	22:59	3♊57	225
	16	9:24	22♋21	270
	19	19:30	10♍45	315
	23	8:43	29♎17	0
	27	5:06	18♐08	45
	31	7:45	7♒14	90
Nov 1938	4	7:33	26♓14	135
	7	22:24	14♉51	180
	11	7:22	3♋15	225
	14	16:20	21♌38	270
	18	5:20	10♎13	315
	22	0:05	29♏02	0
	26	0:56	18♑07	45
	30	4:00	7♓18	90
Dec 1938	4	0:15	26♈11	135
	7	10:22	14♊40	180
	10	16:04	2♌57	225
	14	1:17	21♍23	270
	17	18:24	10♏10	315
	21	18:07	29♐14	0
	25	21:21	18♒27	45
	29	22:54	7♈35	90
Jan 1939	2	15:07	26♉20	135
	5	21:30	14♋40	180
	9	1:51	2♍54	225
	12	13:11	21♎26	270
	16	10:39	10♐24	315
	20	13:27	29♑36	0
	24	16:32	18♓48	45
	28	15:00	7♉48	90
Feb 1939	1	3:27	26♊23	135
	4	7:55	14♌37	180
	7	13:18	2♎53	225
	11	4:12	21♏32	270
	15	5:07	10♑37	315
	19	8:29	29♒48	0
	23	9:03	18♈51	45
	27	3:26	7♊39	90
Mar 1939	2	13:09	26♋04	135
	5	18:01	14♍16	180
	9	2:36	2♏38	225
	12	21:38	21♐25	270
	17	0:20	10♒31	315
	21	1:50	29♓34	0
	24	22:05	18♉22	45
	28	12:16	6♋56	90
	31	20:53	25♌15	135
Apr 1939	4	4:18	13♎31	180
	7	17:29	2♐00	225
	11	16:12	20♑53	270
	15	18:50	9♓54	315
	19	16:35	28♈43	0
	23	7:39	17♊16	45
	26	18:25	5♌37	90
	30	3:44	23♍55	135
May 1939	3	15:16	12♏18	180
	7	9:21	0♑56	225
	11	10:41	19♒51	270
	15	11:34	8♈45	315
	19	4:25	27♉19	0

The 8 Phases of the Moon 1900–2020

Month	Day	Time	Position	Phase
	22	14:32	15♋36	45
	25	23:21	3♍50	90
	29	10:54	22♎11	135
Jun 1939	2	3:11	10♐42	180
	6	1:38	29♑28	225
	10	4:07	18♓24	270
	14	1:51	7♉08	315
	17	13:37	25♊28	0
	20	20:02	13♌35	45
	24	4:36	1♎47	90
	27	19:27	20♏14	135
Jul 1939	1	16:16	8♑55	180
	5	17:50	27♒48	225
	9	19:49	16♈41	270
	13	13:32	5♊15	315
	16	21:03	23♋25	0
	20	1:36	11♍28	45
	23	11:34	29♎43	90
	27	6:09	18♐19	135
	31	6:37	7♒10	180
Aug 1939	4	9:32	26♓06	225
	8	9:18	14♉56	270
	11	22:57	3♋21	315
	15	3:54	21♌26	0
	18	8:39	9♎30	45
	21	21:21	27♏54	90
	25	19:31	16♑41	135
	29	22:09	5♓39	180
Sep 1939	3	0:13	24♈36	225
	6	20:25	13♊20	270
	10	6:55	1♌40	315
	13	11:23	19♍46	0
	16	18:16	7♏58	45
	20	10:35	26♐34	90
	24	11:42	15♒32	135
	28	14:27	4♈34	180
Oct 1939	2	13:21	23♉27	225
	6	5:28	12♋04	270
	9	14:24	0♍23	315
	12	20:31	18♎37	0
	16	7:05	7♐01	45
	20	3:25	25♑50	90
	24	6:18	14♓56	135
	28	6:42	3♉57	180
Nov 1939	1	0:41	22♊41	225
	4	13:12	11♌13	270
	7	22:24	29♍37	315
	11	7:55	18♏01	0
	14	23:11	6♑41	45
	18	23:22	25♒43	90
	23	2:06	14♈53	135
	26	21:55	3♊45	180
	30	10:30	22♋19	225
Dec 1939	3	20:40	10♍47	270
	7	7:45	29♎18	315
	10	21:46	17♐57	0
	14	18:06	6♒51	45
	18	21:04	26♓03	90
	22	21:19	15♉08	135
	26	11:29	3♋48	180
	29	19:36	22♌12	225
Jan 1940	2	4:56	10♎39	270
	5	18:56	29♏18	315
	9	13:53	18♑10	0
	13	14:45	7♓17	45
	17	18:21	26♈30	90
	21	14:18	15♊24	135
	24	23:22	3♌50	180
	28	4:50	22♍07	225
	31	14:48	10♏35	270
Feb 1940	4	8:16	29♐22	315
	8	7:45	18♒24	0
	12	11:19	7♈36	45
	16	12:56	26♉43	90
	20	4:08	15♋23	135
	23	9:56	3♍39	180
	26	14:46	21♎52	225
Mar 1940	1	2:35	10♐22	270
	4	23:40	29♑16	315
	9	2:23	18♓23	0
	13	5:46	7♉31	45
	17	3:25	26♊24	90
	20	14:53	14♌51	135
	23	19:34	3♎01	180
	27	1:37	21♏15	225
	30	16:20	9♑49	270
Apr 1940	3	16:42	28♒46	315
	7	20:19	17♈52	0
	11	20:35	6♊48	45
	15	13:46	25♋26	90
	18	23:08	13♍45	135
	22	4:37	1♏54	180
	25	13:25	20♐11	225
	29	7:49	8♒50	270
May 1940	3	10:27	27♓50	315
	7	12:07	16♉46	0
	11	7:30	5♋27	45
	14	20:51	23♌53	90
	18	5:45	12♎08	135
	21	13:33	0♐20	180
	25	2:18	18♑43	225
	29	0:41	7♓30	270
Jun 1940	2	3:40	26♈27	315
	6	1:05	15♊10	0
	9	15:17	3♌37	45
	13	1:59	21♍54	90
	16	11:45	10♏09	135
	19	23:02	28♐28	180
	23	16:36	17♒02	225
	27	18:13	5♈54	270
Jul 1940	1	19:18	24♉46	315
	5	11:28	13♋16	0
	8	21:17	1♍31	45
	12	6:36	19♎45	90
	15	18:15	8♐04	135
	19	9:56	26♑33	180
	23	8:23	15♓19	225
	27	11:30	4♉15	270
	31	8:55	22♊59	315
Aug 1940	3	20:09	11♌18	0
	7	2:55	29♍27	45
	10	12:01	17♏41	90
	14	2:32	6♑09	135
	17	23:03	24♒51	180
	22	1:17	13♈47	225
	26	3:33	2♊44	270
	29	20:42	21♋19	315
Sep 1940	2	4:15	9♍32	0
	5	9:26	27♎39	45
	8	19:32	15♐58	90
	12	13:45	4♒38	135
	16	14:41	23♓34	180
	20	18:20	12♉37	225
	24	17:47	1♋31	270
	28	7:12	20♌00	315
Oct 1940	1	12:41	8♎11	0
	4	17:51	26♏21	45
	8	6:19	14♑49	90
	12	4:42	3♓42	135
	16	8:15	22♈49	180
	20	10:22	11♊53	225
	24	6:04	0♌41	270
	27	16:58	19♍08	315
	30	22:03	7♏20	0
Nov 1940	3	4:53	25♐38	45
	6	21:08	14♒19	90
	10	23:12	3♈25	135
	15	2:24	22♉35	180
	19	0:35	11♋32	225
	22	16:36	0♍15	270
	26	2:19	18♎41	315
	29	8:42	7♐00	0
Dec 1940	2	19:05	25♑29	45
	6	16:01	14♓25	90
	10	19:48	3♉38	135
	14	19:38	22♊42	180
	18	12:50	11♌28	225
	22	1:45	0♎05	270
	25	11:32	18♏33	315
	28	20:56	7♑00	0
Jan 1941	1	12:28	25♒44	45
	5	13:40	14♈51	90
	9	16:21	4♊03	135
	13	11:04	22♋54	180
	16	23:25	11♍28	225
	20	10:02	29♎59	270
	23	21:05	18♐30	315
	27	11:03	7♒08	0
	31	8:15	26♓05	45
Feb 1941	4	11:43	15♉17	90
	8	10:58	4♋19	135
	12	0:27	22♌55	180
	15	8:48	11♎18	225
	18	18:08	29♏43	270
	22	7:42	18♑18	315
	26	3:02	7♓08	0
Mar 1941	2	4:43	26♈13	45
	6	7:43	15♊21	90
	10	2:39	4♌09	135
	13	11:47	22♍31	180
	16	17:26	10♏44	225
	20	2:52	29♐07	270
	23	20:03	17♒48	315
	27	20:14	6♈46	0
	31	23:46	25♉52	45
Apr 1941	5	0:12	14♋50	90
	8	15:06	3♍23	135
	11	21:15	21♎35	180
	15	1:51	9♐42	225
	18	13:03	28♑06	270
	22	10:20	16♓53	315
	26	13:24	5♉55	0
	30	15:54	24♊54	45
May 1941	4	12:49	13♌39	90
	8	0:32	2♎02	135
	11	5:16	20♏07	180
	14	10:45	8♑14	225
	18	1:17	26♒42	270
	22	2:07	15♈35	315
	26	5:19	4♊34	0
	30	4:43	23♋23	45
Jun 1941	2	21:57	11♍56	90
	6	7:33	0♏12	135
	9	12:34	18♐16	180
	12	20:57	6♒28	225
	16	15:46	25♓05	270
	20	18:30	14♉00	315
	24	19:23	2♋51	0
	28	14:35	21♌29	45
Jul 1941	2	4:24	9♎53	90
	5	13:06	28♏06	135
	8	20:18	16♑14	180
	12	9:12	4♓37	225
	16	8:08	23♈23	270
	20	10:41	12♊18	315
	24	7:39	1♌00	0
	27	22:20	19♍27	45
	31	9:20	7♏46	90
Aug 1941	3	18:33	26♐00	135
	7	5:39	14♒19	180
	10	23:53	2♈55	225
	15	1:40	21♉50	270
	19	2:12	10♋42	315
	22	18:34	29♌15	0
	26	4:57	17♎34	45
	29	14:04	5♐49	90
Sep 1941	2	1:22	24♑11	135
	5	17:36	12♓45	180
	9	16:44	1♉35	225
	13	19:32	20♊36	270
	17	16:51	9♌23	315
	21	4:39	27♍48	0
	24	11:29	16♏01	45
	27	20:09	4♑19	90
Oct 1941	1	11:01	22♒52	135
	5	8:33	11♈42	180
	9	10:54	0♊45	225
	13	12:53	19♋47	270
	17	6:30	8♍30	315
	20	14:20	26♎48	0
	23	19:04	14♐59	45
	27	5:04	3♒24	90
	31	0:22	22♓12	135
Nov 1941	4	2:00	11♉16	180
	8	5:16	0♋25	225
	12	4:54	19♌25	270
	15	18:52	8♎02	315
	19	0:04	26♏16	0
	22	4:45	14♑30	45
	25	17:53	3♓05	90
	29	17:26	22♈07	135
Dec 1941	3	20:51	11♊19	180
	7	22:36	0♌27	225
	11	18:48	19♍21	270
	15	5:45	7♏52	315
	18	10:19	26♐07	0
	21	17:19	14♒28	45
	25	10:44	3♈16	90
	29	13:09	22♉27	135
Jan 1942	2	15:42	11♋38	180
	6	13:53	0♍38	225
	10	6:05	19♎22	270
	13	15:17	7♐49	315
	16	21:32	26♑09	0
	20	8:51	14♓41	45
	24	6:36	3♉39	90
	28	9:49	22♊51	135
Feb 1942	1	9:13	11♌53	180
	5	2:29	0♎40	225
	8	14:53	19♏13	270
	12	0:04	7♑39	315
	15	10:03	26♒06	0
	19	2:38	14♈50	45
	23	3:40	3♊54	90
	27	5:37	23♋00	135
Mar 1942	3	0:20	11♍48	180
	6	12:21	0♏18	225
	9	22:01	18♐42	270
	13	8:55	7♒09	315
	16	23:50	25♓46	0
	20	21:21	14♉38	45
	25	0:02	3♋43	90
	28	23:04	22♌38	135
Apr 1942	1	12:33	11♎09	180
	4	20:07	29♏25	225
	8	4:43	17♑43	270
	11	18:42	6♓14	315
	15	14:34	24♈59	0
	19	15:41	13♊57	45
	23	18:11	2♌57	90
	27	13:15	21♍38	135
	30	22:00	9♏54	180
May 1942	4	2:52	28♐01	225
	7	12:13	16♒18	270
	11	5:54	4♈54	315
	15	5:46	23♉46	0
	19	8:36	12♋44	45
	23	9:11	1♍36	90
	27	0:02	20♎05	135

The 8 Phases of the Moon 1900–2020

	30	5:29	8♐10	180
Jun 1942	2	9:47	26♑13	225
	5	21:27	14♓33	270
	9	18:45	3♉17	315
	13	21:02	22♊12	0
	17	23:29	11♌07	45
	21	20:45	29♍49	90
	25	7:59	18♏08	135
	28	12:10	6♑09	180
Jul 1942	1	17:58	24♒15	225
	5	8:59	12♈42	270
	9	9:15	1♊32	315
	13	12:04	20♋27	0
	17	11:59	9♍16	45
	21	5:13	27♎49	90
	24	14:11	16♐02	135
	27	19:14	4♒06	180
	31	4:15	22♓20	225
Aug 1942	3	23:04	10♉57	270
	8	1:15	29♊52	315
	12	2:28	18♌45	0
	15	22:07	7♎26	45
	19	11:31	25♏51	90
	22	19:58	14♑05	135
	26	3:47	2♓17	180
	29	17:09	20♈43	225
Sep 1942	2	15:42	9♊32	270
	6	18:18	28♋31	315
	10	15:53	17♍18	0
	14	6:25	5♏49	45
	17	16:57	24♐10	90
	21	2:38	12♒29	135
	24	14:35	0♈55	180
	28	8:49	19♉36	225
Oct 1942	2	10:27	8♋36	270
	6	11:37	27♌35	315
	10	4:07	16♎13	0
	13	13:50	4♐36	45
	16	22:59	22♑57	90
	20	11:19	11♓26	135
	24	4:06	0♉07	180
	28	3:01	19♊04	225
Nov 1942	1	6:18	8♌12	270
	5	4:09	27♍07	315
	8	15:19	15♏35	0
	11	21:36	3♑52	45
	15	6:57	22♒17	90
	18	22:49	10♈58	135
	22	20:25	29♉55	180
	26	22:55	19♋04	225
Dec 1942	1	1:37	8♍14	270
	4	18:59	27♎00	315
	8	2:00	15♐21	0
	11	6:49	3♒36	45
	14	17:48	22♓07	90
	18	13:31	11♉00	135
	22	15:04	0♋09	180
	26	18:51	19♌23	225
	30	18:37	8♎27	270
Jan 1943	3	7:44	27♏04	315
	6	12:38	15♑20	0
	9	18:03	3♓37	45
	13	7:49	22♈15	90
	17	7:12	11♊18	135
	21	10:48	0♌32	180
	25	12:50	19♍41	225
	29	8:14	8♏33	270
Feb 1943	1	18:27	27♐02	315
	4	23:29	15♒17	0
	8	7:18	3♈40	45
	12	0:40	22♉26	90
	16	2:53	11♋34	135
	20	5:45	0♍43	180
	24	3:23	19♎39	225
	27	18:23	8♐17	270

Mar 1943	3	3:31	26♑41	315
	6	10:34	14♓59	0
	9	22:09	3♉28	45
	13	19:30	22♊21	90
	17	22:52	11♌28	135
	21	22:08	0♎25	180
	25	14:15	19♏03	225
	29	1:52	7♑30	270
Apr 1943	1	11:29	25♒52	315
	4	21:53	14♈15	0
	8	14:08	2♊52	45
	12	15:04	21♋50	90
	16	17:13	10♍50	135
	20	11:11	29♎30	180
	23	22:13	17♐52	225
	27	7:52	6♒11	270
	30	19:08	24♓33	315
May 1943	4	9:44	13♉03	0
	8	6:53	1♋49	45
	12	9:53	20♌48	90
	16	8:39	9♎37	135
	19	21:13	28♏00	180
	23	4:33	16♑11	225
	26	13:34	4♓25	270
	30	3:21	22♈51	315
Jun 1943	2	22:34	11♊30	0
	6	23:50	0♌23	45
	11	2:36	19♍19	90
	14	20:57	7♏55	135
	18	5:14	26♐06	180
	21	10:32	14♒11	225
	24	20:08	2♈25	270
	28	13:09	20♉58	315
Jul 1943	2	12:44	9♋45	0
	6	16:08	28♌42	45
	10	16:29	17♎32	90
	14	6:41	5♐58	135
	17	12:22	24♑03	180
	20	17:13	12♓06	225
	24	4:39	0♉25	270
	28	1:24	19♊07	315
Aug 1943	1	4:07	8♌03	0
	5	6:55	26♍59	45
	9	3:37	15♏41	90
	12	14:46	4♑01	135
	15	19:34	22♒05	180
	19	1:34	10♈13	225
	22	16:05	28♉41	270
	26	16:31	17♋33	315
	30	20:00	6♍34	0
Sep 1943	3	19:41	25♎25	45
	7	12:33	14♐01	90
	10	22:05	2♒19	135
	14	3:40	20♓28	180
	17	12:25	8♉44	225
	21	7:07	27♊26	270
	25	10:07	16♌28	315
	29	11:30	5♎27	0
Oct 1943	3	6:32	24♏11	45
	6	20:10	12♑42	90
	10	5:28	1♓02	135
	13	13:23	19♈20	180
	17	2:29	7♊51	225
	21	1:42	26♋47	270
	25	5:01	15♍55	315
	29	2:00	4♏47	0
Nov 1943	1	16:07	23♐22	45
	5	3:23	11♒50	90
	8	13:39	0♈17	135
	12	1:27	18♉47	180
	15	20:02	7♋35	225
	19	22:43	26♌44	270
	23	23:44	15♎49	315
	27	15:23	4♐31	0
Dec 1943	1	1:15	22♑58	45

	4	11:04	11♓26	90
	7	23:30	0♉00	135
	11	16:25	18♊46	180
	15	16:21	7♌50	225
	19	20:04	27♍03	270
	23	17:02	16♏00	315
	27	3:50	4♑31	0
	30	10:34	22♒52	45
Jan 1944	2	20:05	11♈19	90
	6	11:50	0♊03	135
	10	10:10	19♋03	180
	14	13:29	8♍16	225
	18	15:32	27♎26	270
	22	8:09	16♐11	315
	25	15:25	4♒33	0
	28	20:29	22♓49	45
Feb 1944	1	7:09	11♉19	90
	5	3:03	0♋12	135
	9	5:30	19♌21	180
	13	9:03	8♎33	225
	17	7:42	27♏32	270
	20	20:42	16♑06	315
	24	1:59	4♓21	0
	27	7:12	22♈35	45
Mar 1944	1	20:41	11♊10	90
	5	20:40	0♌10	135
	10	0:28	19♍19	180
	14	1:23	8♏21	225
	17	20:05	27♐07	270
	21	6:35	15♒32	315
	24	11:37	3♈43	0
	27	19:01	21♉59	45
	31	12:35	10♋41	90
Apr 1944	4	15:16	29♌44	135
	8	17:22	18♎45	180
	12	14:01	7♐32	225
	16	4:59	26♑05	270
	19	14:10	14♓23	315
	22	20:44	2♉35	0
	26	8:11	20♊58	45
	30	6:07	9♌46	90
May 1944	4	9:13	28♍46	135
	8	7:29	17♏34	180
	11	23:23	6♑07	225
	15	11:12	24♒29	270
	18	20:21	12♈44	315
	22	6:13	1♊01	0
	25	22:52	19♋34	45
	30	0:07	8♍27	90
Jun 1944	3	1:25	27♎20	135
	6	18:58	15♐54	180
	10	6:24	4♒14	225
	13	15:57	22♓29	270
	17	2:28	10♉46	315
	20	17:00	29♊12	0
	24	14:46	17♌56	45
	28	17:27	6♎51	90
Jul 1944	2	15:34	25♏35	135
	6	4:27	13♑58	180
	9	12:09	2♓08	225
	12	20:39	20♈19	270
	16	9:59	8♊43	315
	20	5:43	27♋22	0
	24	7:15	16♍15	45
	28	9:24	5♏09	90
Aug 1944	1	3:49	23♐45	135
	4	12:40	11♒59	180
	7	17:49	0♈04	225
	11	2:52	18♉18	270
	14	20:10	6♋52	315
	18	20:25	25♌44	0
	22	23:32	14♎43	45
	26	23:39	3♐34	90
	30	14:28	22♑04	135
Sep 1944	2	20:21	10♓13	180

	6	0:41	28♈18	225
	9	12:03	16♊40	270
	13	9:41	5♌28	315
	17	12:38	24♍29	0
	21	14:59	13♏29	45
	25	12:07	2♑17	90
	28	23:53	20♒43	135
Oct 1944	2	4:22	8♈51	180
	5	9:59	27♉02	225
	9	1:12	15♋37	270
	13	2:28	4♍38	315
	17	5:35	23♎44	0
	21	5:11	12♐41	45
	24	22:48	1♒24	90
	28	8:27	19♓48	135
	31	13:36	8♉01	180
Nov 1944	3	22:40	26♊24	225
	7	18:29	15♌14	270
	11	21:37	4♎23	315
	15	22:30	23♏27	0
	19	17:53	12♑18	45
	23	7:53	0♓55	90
	26	16:52	19♈20	135
	30	0:52	7♊42	180
Dec 1944	3	15:02	26♋21	225
	7	14:57	15♍24	270
	11	17:45	4♏35	315
	15	14:35	23♐31	0
	19	4:58	12♒11	45
	22	15:54	0♈42	90
	26	1:57	19♉11	135
	29	14:39	7♋47	180
Jan 1945	2	10:19	26♌41	225
	6	12:48	15♎52	270
	10	13:20	4♐58	315
	14	5:07	23♑41	0
	17	14:40	12♓09	45
	20	23:48	0♉35	90
	24	12:35	19♊11	135
	28	6:42	8♌00	180
Feb 1945	1	6:52	27♍04	225
	5	9:56	16♏15	270
	9	6:51	5♑10	315
	12	17:34	23♒40	0
	15	23:30	11♈56	45
	19	8:38	0♊21	90
	23	1:13	19♋04	135
	27	0:07	8♍03	180
Mar 1945	3	2:49	27♎10	225
	7	4:30	16♐15	270
	10	21:10	4♒56	315
	14	3:51	23♓13	0
	17	8:15	11♉23	45
	20	19:12	29♊49	90
	24	15:45	18♌38	135
	28	17:45	7♎41	180
Apr 1945	1	20:39	26♏45	225
	5	19:19	15♑38	270
	9	7:58	4♓06	315
	12	12:30	22♈14	0
	15	17:40	10♊23	45
	19	7:47	28♋53	90
	23	7:36	17♍47	135
	27	10:33	6♏48	180
May 1945	1	11:23	25♐43	225
	5	6:02	14♒22	270
	8	15:45	2♈40	315
	11	20:22	20♉45	0
	15	4:19	8♋58	45
	18	22:13	27♌35	90
	23	0:05	16♎30	135
	27	1:49	5♐24	180
	30	22:45	24♑07	225
Jun 1945	3	13:15	12♓34	270
	6	21:40	0♉47	315

The 8 Phases of the Moon 1900–2020

Month	Day	Time	Position	Phase
	10	4:26	18♊55	0
	13	16:31	7♌16	45
	17	14:06	26♍00	90
	21	16:33	14♏54	135
	25	15:08	3♑40	180
	29	7:08	22♒10	225
Jul 1945	2	18:13	10♈28	270
	6	3:07	28♉40	315
	9	13:36	16♋57	0
	13	6:24	5♍29	45
	17	7:01	24♎19	90
	21	8:26	13♐12	135
	25	2:26	1♒47	180
	28	13:28	20♓05	225
	31	22:30	8♉19	270
Aug 1945	4	9:27	26♊37	315
	8	0:32	15♌06	0
	11	21:56	3♎50	45
	16	0:27	22♏47	90
	19	23:12	11♑34	135
	23	12:03	29♒59	180
	26	19:08	18♈09	225
	30	3:45	6♊24	270
Sep 1945	2	17:55	24♋53	315
	6	13:44	13♍35	0
	10	14:54	2♏31	45
	14	17:39	21♐32	90
	18	12:29	10♒13	135
	21	20:46	28♓29	180
	25	1:37	16♉37	225
	28	11:24	4♋58	270
Oct 1945	2	5:22	23♌39	315
	6	5:23	12♎36	0
	10	8:43	1♐41	45
	14	9:39	20♑41	90
	18	0:14	9♓16	135
	21	5:32	27♈28	180
	24	10:12	15♊39	225
	27	22:30	4♌09	270
	31	20:19	23♍03	315
Nov 1945	4	23:11	12♏11	0
	9	2:13	1♑19	45
	12	23:35	20♒14	90
	16	10:43	8♈44	135
	19	15:13	26♉56	180
	22	21:42	15♋15	225
	26	13:29	3♍57	270
	30	14:37	23♎03	315
Dec 1945	4	18:07	12♐15	0
	8	18:04	1♒19	45
	12	11:05	20♓05	90
	15	20:25	8♉32	135
	19	2:18	26♊50	180
	22	12:12	15♌18	225
	26	8:01	4♎12	270
	30	11:14	23♏25	315
Jan 1946	3	12:30	12♑33	0
	7	7:19	1♓24	45
	10	20:27	20♈01	90
	14	5:47	8♊28	135
	17	14:47	26♋54	180
	21	5:14	15♍34	225
	25	5:00	4♏38	270
	29	8:11	23♐50	315
Feb 1946	2	4:44	12♒45	0
	5	17:57	1♈21	45
	9	4:28	19♉50	90
	12	15:17	8♋19	135
	16	4:28	26♌54	180
	19	23:57	15♎45	225
	24	2:37	4♐53	270
	28	3:15	23♑56	315
Mar 1946	3	18:02	12♓34	0
	7	2:41	0♉56	45
	10	12:03	19♊19	90
	14	1:19	7♌52	135
	17	19:11	26♍35	180
	21	19:15	15♏34	225
	25	22:38	4♑40	270
	29	18:55	23♒29	315
Apr 1946	2	4:38	11♈50	0
	5	10:29	0♊02	45
	8	20:05	18♋23	90
	12	12:25	6♍59	135
	16	10:47	25♎50	180
	20	13:46	14♐52	225
	24	15:19	3♒50	270
	28	6:57	22♓23	315
May 1946	1	13:16	10♉33	0
	4	18:11	28♊40	45
	8	5:14	17♌01	90
	12	1:01	5♎42	135
	16	2:53	24♏38	180
	20	6:06	13♑37	225
	24	4:02	2♓23	270
	27	15:56	20♈44	315
	30	20:50	8♊49	0
Jun 1946	3	2:29	26♋55	45
	6	16:07	15♍20	90
	10	15:23	4♏08	135
	14	18:42	23♐05	180
	18	19:25	11♒56	225
	22	13:12	0♈30	270
	25	22:53	18♉45	315
	29	4:06	6♋49	0
Jul 1946	2	12:01	24♌59	45
	6	5:16	13♎32	90
	10	7:17	2♐26	135
	14	9:23	21♑19	180
	18	5:44	10♓00	225
	21	19:52	28♈25	270
	25	4:50	16♊38	315
	28	11:54	4♌47	0
	31	23:29	23♍07	45
Aug 1946	4	20:56	11♏51	90
	9	0:01	0♑48	135
	12	22:26	19♒35	180
	16	13:51	8♈05	225
	20	1:17	26♉25	270
	23	10:50	14♋42	315
	26	21:08	3♍00	0
	30	13:34	21♎34	45
Sep 1946	3	14:49	10♐29	90
	7	16:37	29♑26	135
	11	10:00	18♓03	180
	14	20:56	6♉25	225
	18	6:45	24♊45	270
	21	18:02	13♌08	315
	25	8:46	1♎41	0
	29	6:31	20♏31	45
Oct 1946	3	9:54	9♑35	90
	7	8:21	28♒28	135
	10	20:41	16♈56	180
	14	4:12	5♊13	225
	17	13:28	23♋34	270
	21	3:35	12♍08	315
	24	23:32	0♏57	0
	29	1:41	20♐02	45
Nov 1946	2	4:41	9♒10	90
	5	22:53	27♓56	135
	9	7:11	16♉17	180
	12	12:38	4♋32	225
	15	22:35	22♌58	270
	19	16:33	11♎45	315
	23	17:24	0♐50	0
	27	21:26	20♑03	45
Dec 1946	1	21:48	9♓07	90
	5	12:04	27♈46	135
	8	17:52	16♊03	180
	11	22:50	4♌19	225
	15	10:58	22♍52	270
	19	9:18	11♏53	315
	23	13:06	1♑07	0
	27	15:48	20♒18	45
	31	12:23	9♈14	90
Jan 1947	3	23:49	27♉47	135
	7	4:47	16♋03	180
	10	11:07	4♍22	225
	14	2:56	23♎06	270
	18	5:01	12♐16	315
	22	8:35	1♒29	0
	26	7:26	20♓30	45
	30	0:07	9♉16	90
Feb 1947	2	9:56	27♊43	135
	5	15:51	16♌01	180
	9	1:33	4♎28	225
	12	21:58	23♏21	270
	17	1:41	12♑33	315
	21	2:00	1♓36	0
	24	19:56	20♈23	45
	28	9:12	8♊57	90
Mar 1947	3	18:37	27♋21	135
	7	3:16	15♍43	180
	10	17:57	4♏19	225
	14	18:28	23♐20	270
	18	21:08	12♒26	315
	22	16:34	1♈13	0
	26	5:38	19♉44	45
	29	16:16	8♋08	90
Apr 1947	2	2:33	26♌31	135
	5	15:29	15♎00	180
	9	11:38	3♐47	225
	13	14:24	22♑49	270
	17	13:56	11♓43	315
	21	4:20	0♉14	0
	24	13:16	18♊31	45
	27	22:18	6♌48	90
May 1947	1	10:49	25♍14	135
	5	4:54	13♏52	180
	9	5:30	2♑45	225
	13	8:08	21♒44	270
	17	3:43	10♈24	315
	20	13:44	28♉42	0
	23	19:43	16♋50	45
	27	4:36	5♍04	90
	30	20:33	23♎35	135
Jun 1947	3	19:27	12♐22	180
	7	22:17	1♒18	225
	11	22:58	20♓09	270
	15	14:41	8♉39	315
	18	21:27	26♊47	0
	22	2:01	14♌50	45
	25	12:26	3♎06	90
	29	8:28	21♏46	135
Jul 1947	3	10:39	10♑40	180
	7	13:13	29♒34	225
	11	10:55	18♈18	270
	14	23:22	6♊39	315
	18	4:16	24♋43	0
	21	9:18	12♍46	45
	24	22:54	1♏11	90
	28	22:46	20♐00	135
Aug 1947	2	1:50	8♒57	180
	6	2:04	27♓47	225
	9	20:22	16♉23	270
	13	6:27	4♋40	315
	16	11:13	22♌44	0
	19	18:48	10♎56	45
	23	12:41	29♏32	90
	27	15:02	18♑30	135
	31	16:34	7♓25	180
Sep 1947	4	13:05	26♈09	225
	8	3:57	14♊40	270
	11	12:51	2♌56	315
	14	19:29	21♍08	0
	18	7:27	9♏32	45
	22	5:42	28♐23	90
	26	8:33	17♒25	135
	30	6:41	6♈16	180
Oct 1947	3	22:41	24♉52	225
	7	10:30	13♋18	270
	10	19:43	1♍39	315
	14	6:11	20♎03	0
	17	23:35	8♐45	45
	22	1:11	27♑47	90
	26	2:32	16♓50	135
	29	20:07	5♉33	180
Nov 1947	2	7:28	24♊02	225
	5	17:04	12♌26	270
	9	4:19	0♎55	315
	12	20:01	19♏36	0
	16	18:38	8♑34	45
	20	21:44	27♒44	90
	24	20:05	16♈42	135
	28	8:46	5♊16	180
Dec 1947	1	16:04	23♋37	225
	5	0:56	12♍02	270
	8	15:43	0♏43	315
	12	12:54	19♐39	0
	16	15:07	8♒49	45
	20	17:44	28♓00	90
	24	12:13	16♉51	135
	27	20:27	5♋15	180
	31	1:15	23♌31	225
Jan 1948	3	11:13	12♎00	270
	7	6:21	0♐52	315
	11	7:45	20♑00	0
	15	11:13	9♓14	45
	19	11:33	28♈19	90
	23	1:58	16♊59	135
	26	7:12	5♌15	180
	29	11:43	23♍29	225
Feb 1948	2	0:32	12♏05	270
	5	23:42	1♑06	315
	10	3:02	20♒18	0
	14	5:14	9♈26	45
	18	1:55	28♉20	90
	21	12:56	16♋49	135
	24	17:16	5♍01	180
	27	23:52	23♎19	225
Mar 1948	2	16:36	12♐01	270
	6	18:29	1♒06	315
	10	21:15	20♓13	0
	14	20:03	9♉10	45
	18	12:28	27♊50	90
	21	21:25	16♌11	135
	25	3:11	4♎23	180
	28	13:42	22♏47	225
Apr 1948	1	10:25	11♑36	270
	5	13:16	0♓40	315
	9	13:17	19♈36	0
	13	7:14	8♊16	45
	16	19:42	26♋43	90
	20	4:23	15♍00	135
	23	13:29	3♏17	180
	27	4:50	21♐50	225
May 1948	1	4:48	10♒43	270
	5	6:51	29♓41	315
	9	2:31	18♉22	0
	12	15:16	6♋47	45
	16	0:55	25♌04	90
	19	11:03	13♎22	135
	23	0:37	1♐47	180
	26	20:43	20♑28	225
	30	22:43	9♓23	270
Jun 1948	3	22:22	28♈12	315
	7	12:56	16♊39	0
	10	21:12	4♌51	45
	14	5:41	23♍04	90
	17	18:35	11♏26	135

The 8 Phases of the Moon 1900–2020

Month	Day	Time	Position	Phase
	21	12:55	0♑02	180
	25	12:53	18♒51	225
	29	15:23	7♈45	270
Jul 1948	3	11:25	26♉25	315
	6	21:09	14♋40	0
	10	2:30	2♍44	45
	13	11:30	20♎57	90
	17	3:58	9♐28	135
	21	2:32	28♑14	180
	25	4:57	17♓08	225
	29	6:12	6♉01	270
Aug 1948	1	22:05	24♊31	315
	5	4:13	12♌38	0
	8	8:37	0♎41	45
	11	19:41	19♏00	90
	15	15:53	7♑42	135
	19	17:32	26♒37	180
	23	20:25	15♈35	225
	27	18:47	4♊22	270
	31	6:53	22♋46	315
Sep 1948	3	11:22	10♍51	0
	6	16:52	28♎59	45
	10	7:06	17♐28	90
	14	6:42	6♒21	135
	18	9:43	25♓22	180
	22	10:42	14♉19	225
	26	5:07	3♋01	270
	29	14:44	21♌21	315
Oct 1948	2	19:42	9♎30	0
	6	4:05	27♏49	45
	9	22:11	16♑31	90
	14	0:20	5♓34	135
	18	2:24	24♈37	180
	21	23:16	13♊28	225
	25	13:42	2♌03	270
	28	22:35	20♍25	315
Nov 1948	1	6:03	8♏44	0
	4	18:38	27♐16	45
	8	16:47	16♒12	90
	12	19:56	5♈21	135
	16	18:32	24♉19	180
	20	10:04	13♋00	225
	23	21:23	1♍31	270
	27	7:18	19♎58	315
	30	18:45	8♐29	0
Dec 1948	4	12:18	27♑17	45
	8	13:58	16♓25	90
	12	15:54	5♉34	135
	16	9:11	24♊21	180
	19	19:35	12♌50	225
	23	5:13	1♎18	270
	26	17:31	19♏53	315
	30	9:45	8♑38	0
Jan 1949	3	8:16	27♒39	45
	7	11:52	16♈53	90
	11	10:19	5♊53	135
	14	22:00	24♋26	180
	18	4:40	12♍46	225
	21	14:08	1♏14	270
	25	5:38	19♐56	315
	29	2:43	8♒53	0
Feb 1949	2	5:06	28♓03	45
	6	8:06	17♉14	90
	10	1:49	6♋01	135
	13	9:09	24♌21	180
	16	14:05	12♎35	225
	20	0:43	1♐04	270
	23	19:46	19♑53	315
	27	20:55	8♓57	0
Mar 1949	4	0:46	28♈08	45
	8	0:43	17♊08	90
	11	14:01	5♌41	135
	14	19:03	23♍53	180
	18	0:14	12♏05	225
	21	13:11	0♑36	270
	25	11:45	19♒30	315
	29	15:11	8♈36	0
Apr 1949	2	17:27	27♉39	45
	6	13:02	16♋24	90
	9	23:19	4♍46	135
	13	4:09	22♎54	180
	16	11:14	11♐08	225
	20	3:28	29♑43	270
	24	4:59	18♓41	315
	28	8:03	7♉42	0
May 1949	2	6:14	26♊31	45
	5	21:33	15♌02	90
	9	6:31	3♎18	135
	12	12:51	21♏27	180
	15	23:14	9♑46	225
	19	19:23	28♒27	270
	23	22:25	17♈26	315
	27	22:24	6♊16	0
	31	15:26	24♋50	45
Jun 1949	4	3:28	13♍11	90
	7	12:35	1♏25	135
	10	21:46	19♐39	180
	14	12:32	8♒06	225
	18	12:30	26♓55	270
	22	14:55	15♉50	315
	26	10:02	4♋27	0
	29	22:11	22♌48	45
Jul 1949	3	8:08	11♎03	90
	6	18:36	29♏20	135
	10	7:42	17♑42	180
	14	3:28	6♓21	225
	18	6:02	25♈16	270
	22	5:40	14♊04	315
	25	19:33	2♌30	0
	29	3:53	20♍42	45
Aug 1949	1	12:58	8♏55	90
	5	1:46	27♐18	135
	8	19:34	15♒53	180
	12	19:56	4♈45	225
	16	22:59	23♉42	270
	20	18:32	12♋23	315
	24	3:59	0♍39	0
	27	9:54	18♎47	45
	30	19:17	7♐04	90
Sep 1949	3	11:21	25♑37	135
	7	10:00	14♓26	180
	11	13:15	3♉27	225
	15	14:29	22♊24	270
	19	5:54	10♌57	315
	22	12:21	29♍09	0
	25	17:20	17♏18	45
	29	4:19	5♑41	90
Oct 1949	3	0:26	24♒28	135
	7	2:53	13♈30	180
	11	6:13	2♊36	225
	15	4:06	21♋28	270
	18	16:16	9♍57	315
	21	21:23	28♎09	0
	25	3:04	16♐22	45
	28	17:05	4♒57	90
Nov 1949	1	17:20	23♓57	135
	5	21:09	13♉08	180
	9	21:45	2♋10	225
	13	15:48	20♌56	270
	17	2:02	9♎24	315
	20	7:30	27♏39	0
	23	15:41	16♑02	45
	27	10:02	4♓50	90
Dec 1949	1	13:13	24♈02	135
	5	15:14	13♊10	180
	9	11:14	2♌04	225
	13	1:48	20♍44	270
	16	11:24	9♏11	315
	19	18:56	27♐34	0
	23	7:29	16♒09	45
	27	6:32	5♈11	90
	31	10:10	24♉25	135
Jan 1950	4	7:48	13♋24	180
	7	22:45	2♍05	225
	11	10:32	20♎38	270
	14	20:42	9♐08	315
	18	8:00	27♑40	0
	22	2:08	16♓29	45
	26	4:40	5♉40	90
	30	5:59	24♊47	135
Feb 1950	2	22:17	13♌31	180
	6	8:41	2♎00	225
	9	18:33	20♏27	270
	13	6:32	9♑00	315
	16	22:53	27♒43	0
	20	22:21	16♈43	45
	25	1:53	5♊54	90
	28	23:11	24♋48	135
Mar 1950	4	10:34	13♍17	180
	7	17:31	1♏35	225
	11	2:39	19♐58	270
	14	17:41	8♒35	315
	18	15:21	27♓28	0
	22	18:11	16♉33	45
	26	20:10	5♋36	90
	30	13:12	24♌16	135
Apr 1950	2	20:49	12♎32	180
	6	1:45	0♐42	225
	9	11:43	19♑03	270
	13	6:41	7♓46	315
	17	8:26	26♈46	0
	21	11:46	15♊48	45
	25	10:40	4♌39	90
	29	0:02	23♍07	135
May 1950	2	5:20	11♏15	180
	5	10:03	29♐20	225
	8	22:32	17♒45	270
	12	21:30	6♈34	315
	17	0:55	25♉34	0
	21	2:13	14♋28	45
	24	21:29	3♍07	90
	28	8:07	21♎26	135
	31	12:43	9♐29	180
Jun 1950	3	19:14	27♑37	225
	7	11:36	16♓09	270
	11	13:29	5♉03	315
	15	15:53	23♊58	0
	19	13:32	12♌41	45
	23	5:13	1♎11	90
	26	14:15	19♏24	135
	29	19:59	7♑29	180
Jul 1950	3	6:11	25♒45	225
	7	2:54	14♈26	270
	11	5:48	3♊22	315
	15	5:06	22♋09	0
	18	22:21	10♍42	45
	22	10:51	29♎04	90
	25	19:35	17♐16	135
	29	4:18	5♒29	180
Aug 1950	1	19:32	23♓58	225
	5	19:56	12♉48	270
	9	21:48	1♋43	315
	13	16:49	20♌21	0
	17	5:34	8♎45	45
	20	15:36	27♏02	90
	24	1:33	15♑20	135
	27	14:51	3♓45	180
	31	11:24	22♈29	225
Sep 1950	4	13:54	11♊27	270
	8	13:09	0♌18	315
	12	3:29	18♍48	0
	15	12:10	7♏05	45
	18	20:54	25♐22	90
	22	9:41	13♒49	135
	26	4:22	2♈31	180
	30	5:12	21♉28	225
Oct 1950	4	7:53	10♋31	270
	8	3:38	29♌17	315
	11	13:34	17♎40	0
	14	19:14	5♐52	45
	18	4:18	24♑13	90
	21	21:09	12♓54	135
	25	20:47	1♉52	180
	29	23:52	20♊59	225
Nov 1950	3	1:01	10♌02	270
	6	16:59	28♍43	315
	9	23:26	17♏00	0
	13	3:51	5♑12	45
	16	15:06	23♒42	90
	20	12:28	12♈37	135
	24	15:15	1♊47	180
	28	18:08	20♋57	225
Dec 1950	2	16:22	9♍55	270
	6	4:52	28♎30	315
	9	9:29	16♐44	0
	12	14:57	5♒01	45
	16	5:57	23♓43	90
	20	7:03	12♉50	135
	24	10:23	2♋03	180
	28	10:46	21♌08	225
Jan 1951	1	5:12	9♎58	270
	4	15:09	28♏27	315
	7	20:10	16♑44	0
	11	4:57	5♓10	45
	15	0:23	24♈02	90
	19	3:25	13♊15	135
	23	4:47	2♌22	180
	27	0:52	21♍16	225
	30	15:14	9♏56	270
Feb 1951	3	0:11	28♐21	315
	6	7:54	16♒43	0
	9	21:34	5♈20	45
	13	20:56	24♉21	90
	17	23:47	13♋31	135
	21	21:13	2♍26	180
	25	12:04	21♎05	225
	28	23:00	9♐33	270
Mar 1951	4	8:44	27♑58	315
	7	20:51	16♓29	0
	11	15:44	5♉16	45
	15	17:40	24♊20	90
	19	18:28	13♌21	135
	23	10:50	2♎00	180
	26	20:40	20♏23	225
	30	5:35	8♑43	270
Apr 1951	2	17:43	27♒10	315
	6	10:52	15♈50	0
	10	10:09	4♊44	45
	14	12:56	23♋46	90
	18	10:17	12♍35	135
	21	21:30	0♏58	180
	25	3:36	19♐08	225
	28	12:18	7♒24	270
May 1951	2	3:51	25♓57	315
	6	1:36	14♉44	0
	10	3:42	3♋41	45
	14	5:32	22♌38	90
	17	22:42	11♎13	135
	21	5:45	29♏23	180
	24	10:05	17♑26	225
	27	20:17	5♓43	270
	31	15:34	24♈22	315
Jun 1951	4	16:41	13♊15	0
	8	19:37	2♌12	45
	12	18:52	20♍59	90
	16	7:59	9♏23	135
	19	12:36	27♐25	180
	22	17:20	15♒28	225
	26	6:22	3♈51	270
	30	5:03	22♉37	315

The 8 Phases of the Moon 1900–2020

Jul 1951	4	7:48	11♋32	0
	8	9:25	0♍25	45
	12	4:57	19♎03	90
	15	14:59	7♐19	135
	18	19:18	25♑21	180
	22	2:21	13♓29	225
	25	19:00	2♉01	270
	29	20:16	20♊53	315
Aug 1951	2	22:40	9♌49	0
	6	20:54	28♍34	45
	10	12:23	17♏04	90
	13	20:55	5♑17	135
	17	3:00	23♒25	180
	20	13:50	11♈44	225
	24	10:21	0♊27	270
	28	12:57	19♋25	315
Sep 1951	1	12:50	8♍16	0
	5	6:17	26♎53	45
	8	18:17	15♐17	90
	12	3:07	3♒33	135
	15	12:39	21♓52	180
	19	4:09	10♉25	225
	23	4:14	29♊20	270
	27	6:30	18♌21	315
Oct 1951	1	1:57	7♎05	0
	4	14:15	25♏33	45
	8	0:01	13♑54	90
	11	10:47	2♓19	135
	15	0:51	20♈52	180
	18	21:16	9♊41	225
	22	23:56	28♋46	270
	26	23:52	17♍45	315
	30	13:55	6♏20	0
Nov 1951	2	21:53	24♐40	45
	6	6:59	13♒03	90
	9	20:53	1♈39	135
	13	15:53	20♉28	180
	17	16:39	9♋31	225
	21	20:02	28♌42	270
	25	15:56	17♎34	315
	29	1:01	6♐00	0
Dec 1951	2	6:23	24♑16	45
	5	16:21	12♓44	90
	9	9:58	1♉31	135
	13	9:31	20♊34	180
	17	12:59	9♌47	225
	21	14:38	28♍55	270
	25	5:57	17♏38	315
	28	11:44	5♑56	0
	31	16:36	24♒12	45
Jan 1952	4	4:43	12♈46	90
	8	2:09	1♊44	135
	12	4:55	20♋56	180
	16	8:19	10♍09	225
	20	6:10	29♎08	270
	23	17:44	17♐41	315
	26	22:27	5♒56	0
	30	4:45	24♓15	45
Feb 1952	2	20:02	12♉56	90
	6	20:50	2♋01	135
	11	0:29	21♌14	180
	15	0:45	10♎17	225
	18	18:02	29♏02	270
	22	3:31	17♑28	315
	25	9:16	5♓43	0
	28	18:37	24♈08	45
Mar 1952	3	13:44	12♊56	90
	7	16:42	2♌04	135
	11	18:14	21♍08	180
	15	13:23	9♏55	225
	19	2:40	28♐27	270
	22	11:49	16♒48	315
	25	20:13	5♈07	0
	29	9:46	23♉39	45
Apr 1952	2	8:49	12♋34	90
	6	11:54	1♍37	135
	10	8:54	20♎26	180
	13	22:35	8♐56	225
	17	9:08	27♑18	270
	20	19:20	15♓38	315
	24	7:28	4♉03	0
	28	1:53	22♊43	45
May 1952	2	3:58	11♌42	90
	6	4:48	0♎36	135
	9	20:16	19♏07	180
	13	5:28	7♑23	225
	16	14:40	25♒39	270
	20	2:54	14♈02	315
	23	19:28	2♊35	0
	27	18:36	21♋23	45
	31	21:47	10♍21	90
Jun 1952	4	18:38	29♎03	135
	8	5:07	17♐21	180
	11	11:22	5♒27	225
	14	20:28	23♓41	270
	18	11:33	12♉09	315
	22	8:46	0♋51	0
	26	11:16	19♌46	45
	30	13:12	8♎40	90
Jul 1952	4	5:38	27♏11	135
	7	12:34	15♑19	180
	10	17:29	3♓22	225
	14	3:43	21♈38	270
	17	22:19	10♊14	315
	21	23:31	29♋06	0
	26	3:01	18♍04	45
	30	1:51	6♏50	90
Aug 1952	2	14:34	25♐13	135
	5	19:40	13♒17	180
	9	0:50	1♈22	225
	12	13:27	19♉45	270
	16	11:55	8♋32	315
	20	15:21	27♌31	0
	24	17:03	16♎27	45
	28	12:04	5♐06	90
	31	22:22	23♑25	135
Sep 1952	4	3:20	11♓32	180
	7	10:20	29♈43	225
	11	2:36	18♊18	270
	15	4:26	7♌16	315
	19	7:22	26♍17	0
	23	5:08	15♏07	45
	26	20:31	3♑41	90
	30	5:50	22♒00	135
Oct 1952	3	12:16	10♈13	180
	6	22:45	28♉37	225
	10	19:33	17♋26	270
	14	23:04	6♍32	315
	18	22:43	25♎30	0
	22	15:34	14♐11	45
	26	4:05	2♒41	90
	29	13:42	21♓05	135
Nov 1952	1	23:10	9♉29	180
	5	14:40	28♊08	225
	9	15:43	17♌11	270
	13	18:19	6♎20	315
	17	12:56	25♏08	0
	21	1:04	13♑40	45
	24	11:35	2♓09	90
	27	22:42	20♈39	135
Dec 1952	1	12:42	9♊17	180
	5	9:51	28♋13	225
	9	13:22	17♍26	270
	13	12:41	6♏28	315
	17	2:03	25♐05	0
	20	10:21	13♒30	45
	23	19:52	1♈58	90
	27	9:40	20♉36	135
	31	5:06	9♋29	180
Jan 1953	4	6:55	28♌38	225
	8	10:09	17♎51	270
	12	5:07	6♐43	315
	15	14:09	25♑09	0
	18	19:55	13♓27	45
	22	5:43	1♉55	90
	25	23:17	20♊43	135
	29	23:45	9♌48	180
Feb 1953	3	3:33	29♍01	225
	7	4:10	18♏06	270
	10	19:01	6♑46	315
	14	1:11	25♒03	0
	17	6:03	13♈17	45
	20	17:45	1♊49	90
	24	15:34	20♋45	135
	28	18:59	9♍54	180
Mar 1953	4	21:36	29♎01	225
	8	18:27	17♐54	270
	12	6:10	6♒23	315
	15	11:05	24♓34	0
	18	17:01	12♉48	45
	22	8:11	1♋25	90
	26	9:35	20♌26	135
	30	12:55	9♎32	180
Apr 1953	3	12:01	28♏26	225
	7	4:59	17♑05	270
	10	14:42	5♓26	315
	13	20:09	23♈35	0
	17	5:09	11♊54	45
	21	0:41	0♌37	90
	25	3:48	19♍39	135
	29	4:21	8♏33	180
May 1953	2	22:53	27♐13	225
	6	12:21	15♒40	270
	9	21:18	3♈56	315
	13	5:06	22♉08	0
	16	18:46	10♋35	45
	20	18:21	29♌25	90
	24	20:50	18♎22	135
	28	17:03	7♐03	180
Jun 1953	1	6:56	25♑29	225
	4	17:36	13♓47	270
	8	3:08	2♉02	315
	11	14:55	20♊22	0
	15	9:55	8♌59	45
	19	12:01	27♍54	90
	23	12:02	16♏43	135
	27	3:30	5♑11	180
	30	13:10	23♒26	225
Jul 1953	3	22:04	11♈38	270
	7	9:39	29♉58	315
	11	2:29	18♋30	0
	15	2:08	7♍18	45
	19	4:48	26♎13	90
	23	1:19	14♐54	135
	26	12:21	3♒12	180
	29	18:45	21♓19	225
Aug 1953	2	3:17	9♉32	270
	5	18:16	28♊00	315
	9	16:10	16♌45	0
	13	18:42	5♎42	45
	17	20:08	24♏36	90
	21	12:58	13♑10	135
	24	20:21	1♓21	180
	28	0:54	19♈26	225
	31	10:47	7♊43	270
Sep 1953	4	6:03	26♋24	315
	8	7:48	15♍22	0
	12	10:52	4♏23	45
	16	9:50	23♐14	90
	19	23:14	11♒42	135
	23	4:16	29♓51	180
	26	8:54	17♉58	225
	29	21:52	6♋27	270
Oct 1953	3	21:19	25♌22	315
	8	0:41	14♎27	0
	12	2:04	3♐27	45
	15	21:45	22♑15	90
	19	8:26	10♓40	135
	22	12:56	28♈50	180
	25	19:52	17♊06	225
	29	13:10	5♌49	270
Nov 1953	2	15:33	24♍55	315
	6	17:58	14♏02	0
	10	15:52	2♑58	45
	14	7:53	21♒39	90
	17	17:02	10♈04	135
	20	23:13	28♉21	180
	24	10:28	16♋51	225
	28	8:17	5♍49	270
Dec 1953	2	11:33	25♎00	315
	6	10:48	14♐02	0
	10	4:00	2♒49	45
	13	16:31	21♓23	90
	17	1:46	9♉50	135
	20	11:44	28♊19	180
	24	4:26	17♌04	225
	28	5:44	6♎12	270
Jan 1954	1	7:44	25♏22	315
	5	2:22	14♑13	0
	8	14:28	2♓47	45
	12	0:22	21♈16	90
	15	11:29	9♊48	135
	19	2:37	28♋30	180
	23	0:30	17♍28	225
	27	3:29	6♏40	270
	31	2:31	25♐41	315
Feb 1954	3	15:56	14♒18	0
	6	23:37	2♈40	45
	10	8:30	21♉05	90
	13	22:54	9♋43	135
	17	19:18	28♌36	180
	21	20:51	17♎42	225
	25	23:29	6♐50	270
Mar 1954	1	18:30	25♑39	315
	5	3:12	14♓01	0
	8	8:09	2♉13	45
	11	17:52	20♊38	90
	15	12:14	9♌23	135
	19	12:43	28♍23	180
	23	15:46	17♏28	225
	27	16:14	6♑27	270
	31	6:59	25♒02	315
Apr 1954	3	12:25	13♈13	0
	6	16:53	1♊21	45
	10	5:06	19♋48	90
	14	3:11	8♍38	135
	18	5:49	27♎40	180
	22	8:03	16♐39	225
	26	4:58	5♒26	270
	29	16:05	23♓48	315
May 1954	2	20:23	11♉53	0
	6	2:34	0♋02	45
	9	18:18	18♌34	90
	13	19:08	7♎28	135
	17	21:47	26♏26	180
	21	21:05	15♑15	225
	25	13:50	3♓48	270
	28	22:43	22♈02	315
Jun 1954	1	4:03	10♊08	0
	4	13:43	28♋24	45
	8	9:14	17♍03	90
	12	11:31	5♏57	135
	16	12:06	24♐48	180
	20	6:56	13♒25	225
	23	19:46	1♈47	270
	27	4:11	19♉59	315
	30	12:26	8♋10	0
Jul 1954	4	2:33	26♌36	45
	8	1:34	15♎22	90
	12	3:46	4♐16	135

The 8 Phases of the Moon 1900–2020

Month	Day	Time	Position	Phase
	16	0:30	22♑57	180
	19	14:14	11♓22	225
	23	0:14	29♈37	270
	26	9:53	17♊52	315
	29	22:20	6♌14	0
Aug 1954	2	17:12	24♍52	45
	6	18:51	13♏45	90
	10	19:19	2♑37	135
	14	11:03	21♒07	180
	17	20:10	9♈22	225
	21	4:51	27♉36	270
	24	17:09	15♋59	315
	28	10:21	4♍35	0
Sep 1954	1	9:35	23♎25	45
	5	12:29	12♐24	90
	9	9:39	1♒10	135
	12	20:20	19♓31	180
	16	2:12	7♉41	225
	19	11:12	25♊59	270
	23	3:02	14♌33	315
	27	0:51	3♎23	0
Oct 1954	1	3:17	22♏25	45
	5	5:31	11♑27	90
	8	22:28	0♓06	135
	12	5:10	18♈21	180
	15	9:42	6♊30	225
	18	20:31	24♋55	270
	22	16:15	13♍44	315
	26	17:47	2♏47	0
	30	21:24	21♐55	45
Nov 1954	3	20:55	10♒55	90
	7	9:49	29♓27	135
	10	14:30	17♉40	180
	13	19:46	5♋54	225
	17	9:33	24♌30	270
	21	9:00	13♎31	315
	25	12:31	2♐43	0
	29	14:31	21♑51	45
Dec 1954	3	9:56	10♓42	90
	6	20:03	29♈11	135
	10	0:57	17♊26	180
	13	8:48	5♌49	225
	17	2:22	24♍37	270
	21	4:41	13♏47	315
	25	7:34	2♑59	0
	29	5:21	21♒58	45
Jan 1955	1	20:29	10♈40	90
	5	5:37	29♉07	135
	8	12:45	17♋28	180
	12	0:34	6♍02	225
	15	22:14	25♎00	270
	20	1:45	14♐13	315
	24	1:07	3♒16	0
	27	17:20	22♓00	45
	31	5:06	10♉33	90
Feb 1955	3	14:57	29♊01	135
	7	1:43	17♌31	180
	10	18:24	6♎15	225
	14	19:40	25♏21	270
	18	21:59	14♑29	315
	22	15:55	3♓16	0
	26	2:52	21♈44	45
Mar 1955	1	12:41	10♊10	90
	5	0:28	28♋40	135
	8	15:42	17♍18	180
	12	13:20	6♏12	225
	16	16:36	25♐19	270
	20	15:23	14♒15	315
	24	3:43	2♈44	0
	27	10:53	21♉00	45
	30	20:10	9♋21	90
Apr 1955	3	10:41	27♌55	135
	7	6:35	16♎41	180
	11	8:13	5♐40	225
	15	11:01	24♑42	270
	19	5:09	13♓23	315
	22	13:07	1♉38	0
	25	18:20	19♊46	45
	29	4:23	8♌06	90
May 1955	2	22:09	26♍43	135
	6	22:15	15♏36	180
	11	1:40	4♑36	225
	15	1:43	23♒28	270
	18	15:31	11♈55	315
	21	20:59	0♊01	0
	25	2:01	18♋07	45
	28	14:02	6♍28	90
Jun 1955	1	11:21	25♎12	135
	5	14:09	14♐08	180
	9	16:33	3♒04	225
	13	12:37	21♓44	270
	16	23:22	10♉01	315
	20	4:12	28♊05	0
	23	10:39	16♌12	45
	27	1:44	4♎40	90
Jul 1955	1	2:22	23♏30	135
	5	5:29	12♑26	180
	9	4:25	1♓12	225
	12	20:31	19♈42	270
	16	5:44	7♊56	315
	19	11:35	26♋02	0
	22	20:55	14♍16	45
	26	16:00	2♏53	90
	30	18:46	21♐49	135
Aug 1955	3	19:31	10♒41	180
	7	13:42	29♓17	225
	11	2:33	17♉40	270
	14	11:39	5♋55	315
	17	19:59	24♌08	0
	21	9:35	12♎34	45
	25	8:52	1♐23	90
	29	11:42	20♑22	135
Sep 1955	2	8:00	9♓05	180
	5	21:21	27♈32	225
	9	8:00	15♊52	270
	12	18:12	4♌12	315
	16	6:20	22♍37	0
	20	1:10	11♏19	45
	24	3:41	0♑20	90
	28	4:13	19♒16	135
Oct 1955	1	19:18	7♈50	180
	5	4:36	26♉10	225
	8	14:04	14♋31	270
	12	2:30	3♍00	315
	15	19:33	21♎40	0
	19	19:31	10♐38	45
	23	23:05	29♑46	90
	27	19:41	18♓37	135
	31	6:04	7♉02	180
Nov 1955	3	12:30	25♊19	225
	6	21:56	13♌43	270
	10	13:42	2♎23	315
	14	12:02	21♏20	0
	18	15:26	10♑31	45
	22	17:29	29♒38	90
	26	9:51	18♈22	135
	29	16:50	6♊42	180
Dec 1955	2	21:51	24♋57	225
	6	8:36	13♍27	270
	10	4:34	2♏20	315
	14	7:08	21♐31	0
	18	10:56	10♒45	45
	22	9:40	29♓46	90
	25	22:31	18♉22	135
	29	3:44	6♋39	180
Jan 1956	1	9:03	24♌56	225
	4	22:41	13♎34	270
	8	22:55	2♐39	315
	13	3:02	21♑54	0
	17	4:12	11♓02	45
	20	22:59	29♈53	90
	24	9:31	18♊23	135
	27	14:41	6♌39	180
	30	22:16	25♍01	225
Feb 1956	3	16:08	13♏49	270
	7	19:16	3♑00	315
	11	21:38	22♒09	0
	15	18:18	11♈03	45
	19	9:22	29♉43	90
	22	18:48	18♋08	135
	26	1:42	6♍27	180
	29	13:29	24♎57	225
Mar 1956	4	11:54	13♐54	270
	8	15:25	3♒03	315
	12	13:37	21♓58	0
	16	5:18	10♉36	45
	19	17:14	29♊05	90
	23	2:49	17♌28	135
	26	13:12	5♎51	180
	30	6:21	24♏32	225
Apr 1956	3	8:07	13♑33	270
	7	9:31	2♓32	315
	11	2:39	21♈11	0
	14	13:46	9♊35	45
	17	23:28	27♋55	90
	21	10:32	16♍18	135
	25	1:41	4♏50	180
	29	0:00	23♐39	225
May 1956	3	2:56	12♒39	270
	7	0:44	1♈26	315
	10	13:05	19♉50	0
	13	20:32	8♋02	45
	17	5:16	26♌16	90
	20	19:08	14♎43	135
	24	15:26	3♐25	180
	28	17:18	22♑19	225
Jun 1956	1	19:14	11♓14	270
	5	13:03	29♈49	315
	8	21:30	18♊02	0
	12	2:37	6♌06	45
	15	11:57	24♍20	90
	19	5:39	12♏54	135
	23	6:14	1♑44	180
	27	9:13	20♒40	225
Jul 1956	1	8:41	9♈28	270
	4	22:54	27♉53	315
	8	4:38	15♋59	0
	11	9:09	4♍01	45
	14	20:47	22♎21	90
	18	18:37	11♐04	135
	22	21:29	0♒00	180
	26	23:15	18♓54	225
	30	19:32	7♉34	270
Aug 1956	3	6:50	25♊54	315
	6	11:25	13♌57	0
	9	17:20	2♎04	45
	13	8:45	20♏34	90
	17	9:57	9♑27	135
	21	12:38	28♒25	180
	25	11:24	17♈13	225
	29	4:13	5♊47	270
Sep 1956	1	13:38	24♋04	315
	4	18:58	12♍12	0
	8	4:19	0♏29	45
	12	0:13	19♐13	90
	16	3:05	8♒13	135
	20	3:20	27♓08	180
	23	21:57	15♉50	225
	27	11:26	4♋19	270
	30	20:17	22♌38	315
Oct 1956	4	4:25	10♎55	0
	7	18:47	29♏28	45
	11	18:45	18♑26	90
	15	21:11	7♓29	135
	19	17:25	26♈18	180
	23	7:21	14♊52	225
	26	18:03	3♌18	270
	30	4:00	21♍43	315
Nov 1956	2	16:44	10♏15	0
	6	12:37	29♐05	45
	10	15:10	18♒13	90
	14	15:21	7♈15	135
	18	6:45	25♉55	180
	21	16:09	14♋20	225
	25	1:13	2♍45	270
	28	13:57	21♎20	315
Dec 1956	2	8:13	10♐09	0
	6	8:43	29♑13	45
	10	11:52	18♓25	90
	14	8:33	7♉21	135
	17	19:07	25♊51	180
	21	1:02	14♌09	225
	24	10:10	2♎36	270
	28	2:55	21♏22	315
Jan 1957	1	2:14	10♑25	0
	5	5:19	29♒37	45
	9	7:07	18♈47	90
	12	23:44	7♊32	135
	16	6:22	25♋52	180
	19	10:44	14♍07	225
	22	21:48	2♏38	270
	26	18:52	21♐35	315
	30	21:25	10♒45	0
Feb 1957	4	0:36	29♓57	45
	7	23:24	18♉57	90
	11	12:07	7♋31	135
	14	16:38	25♌44	180
	17	21:49	13♎59	225
	21	12:19	2♐37	270
	25	12:52	21♑40	315
Mar 1957	1	16:13	10♓49	0
	5	17:06	29♈52	45
	9	11:51	18♊39	90
	12	21:41	7♌03	135
	16	2:22	25♍14	180
	19	10:34	13♏34	225
	23	5:05	2♑18	270
	27	7:34	21♒22	315
	31	9:19	10♈24	0
Apr 1957	4	6:03	29♉13	45
	7	20:33	17♋45	90
	11	5:07	6♍03	135
	14	12:10	24♎17	180
	18	0:47	12♐44	225
	21	23:01	1♒33	270
	26	1:40	20♓34	315
	29	23:54	9♉23	0
May 1957	3	15:30	27♊55	45
	7	2:30	16♌16	90
	10	11:36	4♎32	135
	13	22:35	22♏52	180
	17	16:03	11♑28	225
	21	17:04	0♓21	270
	25	18:13	19♈15	315
	29	11:39	7♊49	0
Jun 1957	1	22:16	26♋07	45
	5	7:10	14♍21	90
	8	18:22	2♏40	135
	12	10:02	21♐10	180
	16	7:57	9♒54	225
	20	10:23	28♓49	270
	24	8:34	17♉33	315
	27	20:54	5♋54	0
Jul 1957	1	3:39	24♌02	45
	4	12:10	12♎14	90
	8	2:34	0♐40	135
	11	22:50	19♑20	180
	16	0:06	8♓12	225
	20	2:18	27♈06	270

The 8 Phases of the Moon 1900–2020

	23	20:32	15♊41	315
	27	4:29	3♌52	0
	30	9:10	21♍56	45
Aug 1957	2	18:56	10♏11	90
	6	13:03	28♐47	135
	10	13:09	17♒37	180
	14	16:05	6♈35	225
	18	16:17	25♉26	270
	22	6:24	13♋53	315
	25	11:33	1♍59	0
	28	16:13	20♎04	45
Sep 1957	1	4:35	8♐28	90
	5	2:23	27♑16	135
	9	4:56	16♓15	180
	13	7:19	5♉14	225
	17	4:02	24♊00	270
	20	14:52	12♌22	315
	23	19:19	0♎29	0
	27	1:55	18♏42	45
	30	17:50	7♑18	90
Oct 1957	4	18:45	26♒16	135
	8	21:43	15♈20	180
	12	21:08	4♊16	225
	16	13:44	22♋56	270
	19	22:50	11♍17	315
	23	4:44	29♎31	0
	26	14:52	17♐56	45
	30	10:48	6♒45	90
Nov 1957	3	13:42	25♓53	135
	7	14:32	14♉55	180
	11	9:06	3♋43	225
	14	22:00	22♌17	270
	18	7:11	10♎41	315
	21	16:20	29♏06	0
	25	7:06	17♑45	45
	29	6:58	6♓48	90
Dec 1957	3	9:55	25♈59	135
	7	6:16	14♊53	180
	10	19:22	3♌29	225
	14	5:46	21♍59	270
	17	16:39	10♏30	315
	21	6:12	29♐07	0
	25	2:03	18♒01	45
	29	4:53	7♈13	90
Jan 1958	2	5:29	26♉19	135
	5	20:09	15♋00	180
	9	4:38	3♍25	225
	12	14:02	21♎52	270
	16	3:42	10♐31	315
	19	22:08	29♑21	0
	23	22:37	18♓26	45
	28	2:17	7♉40	90
	31	22:37	26♊34	135
Feb 1958	4	8:06	15♌01	180
	7	13:45	3♎17	225
	10	23:34	21♏44	270
	14	16:36	10♑29	315
	18	15:39	29♒29	0
	22	19:02	18♈40	45
	26	20:52	7♊46	90
Mar 1958	2	12:27	26♋26	135
	5	18:28	14♍41	180
	8	23:18	2♏53	225
	12	10:48	21♐21	270
	16	7:24	10♒12	315
	20	9:50	29♓17	0
	24	13:19	18♉24	45
	28	11:19	7♋17	90
	31	23:03	25♌43	135
Apr 1958	4	3:45	13♎52	180
	7	9:35	2♐04	225
	10	23:50	20♑36	270
	14	23:48	9♓31	315
	19	3:24	28♈34	0
	23	4:02	17♊30	45
	26	21:36	6♌08	90
	30	7:05	24♍26	135
May 1958	3	12:24	12♏34	180
	6	20:45	0♑48	225
	10	14:38	19♒25	270
	14	17:02	8♈23	315
	18	19:01	27♉19	0
	22	14:56	16♋00	45
	26	4:39	4♍26	90
	29	13:30	22♎40	135
Jun 1958	1	20:56	10♐50	180
	5	9:06	29♑12	225
	9	6:59	17♓56	270
	13	10:02	6♉53	315
	17	8:00	25♊38	0
	20	22:47	14♌05	45
	24	9:45	2♎23	90
	27	19:20	20♏37	135
Jul 1958	1	6:05	8♑54	180
	4	23:01	27♒26	225
	9	0:21	16♈18	270
	13	1:46	5♊10	315
	16	18:34	23♋42	0
	20	4:53	11♍59	45
	23	14:20	0♏13	90
	27	1:42	18♐32	135
	30	16:47	7♒00	180
Aug 1958	3	14:44	25♓45	225
	7	17:50	14♉42	270
	11	15:45	3♋27	315
	15	3:34	21♌49	0
	18	10:40	9♎59	45
	21	19:45	28♏14	90
	25	9:54	16♑42	135
	29	5:54	5♓24	180
Sep 1958	2	7:52	24♈20	225
	6	10:25	13♊19	270
	10	4:05	1♌57	315
	13	12:03	20♍11	0
	16	17:22	8♏20	45
	20	3:18	26♐40	90
	23	21:08	15♒20	135
	27	21:44	4♈16	180
Oct 1958	2	1:26	23♉21	225
	6	1:21	12♋17	270
	9	15:12	0♍49	315
	12	20:52	19♎01	0
	16	1:57	7♐12	45
	19	14:07	25♑41	90
	23	12:12	14♓35	135
	27	15:42	3♉43	180
	31	18:08	22♊49	225
Nov 1958	4	14:20	11♌40	270
	8	1:30	0♎08	315
	11	6:34	18♏22	0
	14	13:08	6♑40	45
	18	5:00	25♒21	90
	22	6:52	14♈28	135
	26	10:17	3♊39	180
	30	8:58	22♋39	225
Dec 1958	4	1:25	11♍23	270
	7	11:14	29♎51	315
	10	17:24	18♐09	0
	14	3:20	6♒38	45
	17	23:53	25♓33	90
	22	3:39	14♉47	135
	26	3:55	3♋52	180
	29	21:37	22♌41	225
Jan 1959	2	10:51	11♎18	270
	5	20:33	29♏46	315
	9	5:34	18♑13	0
	12	20:34	6♓54	45
	16	21:27	26♈01	90
	21	0:19	15♊13	135
	24	19:33	4♌05	180
	28	8:21	22♍40	225
	31	19:07	11♏10	270
Feb 1959	4	5:55	29♐40	315
	7	19:23	18♒17	0
	11	16:03	7♈11	45
	15	19:21	26♉22	90
	19	18:56	15♋23	135
	23	8:54	4♍00	180
	26	17:36	22♎23	225
Mar 1959	2	2:55	10♐47	270
	5	16:05	29♑20	315
	9	10:52	18♓07	0
	13	12:08	7♉10	45
	17	15:11	26♊17	90
	21	10:30	15♌04	135
	24	20:03	3♎26	180
	28	1:52	21♏39	225
	31	11:07	9♑59	270
Apr 1959	4	3:48	28♒38	315
	8	3:30	17♈34	0
	12	6:52	6♊38	45
	16	7:33	25♋34	90
	19	22:50	14♍08	135
	23	5:14	2♏19	180
	26	9:48	20♐25	225
	29	20:39	8♒47	270
May 1959	3	17:25	27♓32	315
	7	20:12	16♉31	0
	11	22:51	5♋29	45
	15	20:09	24♌14	90
	19	8:10	12♎37	135
	22	12:56	0♐41	180
	25	18:11	18♑47	225
	29	8:14	7♓13	270
Jun 1959	2	8:39	26♈04	315
	6	11:54	15♊02	0
	10	11:43	3♌51	45
	14	5:23	22♍26	90
	17	15:09	10♏41	135
	20	20:00	28♐44	180
	24	3:55	16♒55	225
	27	22:13	5♈30	270
Jul 1959	2	0:47	24♉25	315
	6	2:01	13♋17	0
	9	21:48	1♍56	45
	13	12:02	20♎21	90
	16	20:45	8♐34	135
	20	3:34	26♑42	180
	23	15:53	15♓03	225
	27	14:22	3♉48	270
	31	17:03	22♊44	315
Aug 1959	4	14:34	11♌28	0
	8	5:52	29♍57	45
	11	17:10	18♏17	90
	15	2:15	6♑31	135
	18	12:51	24♒50	180
	22	6:30	13♈25	225
	26	8:03	2♊21	270
	30	8:57	21♋15	315
Sep 1959	3	1:56	9♍50	0
	6	12:49	28♎11	45
	9	22:07	16♐28	90
	13	9:11	4♒50	135
	17	0:52	23♓24	180
	20	23:32	12♉15	225
	25	2:23	1♋16	270
	29	0:11	20♌07	315
Oct 1959	2	12:31	8♎34	0
	5	19:42	26♏49	45
	9	4:23	15♑08	90
	12	18:55	3♓42	135
	16	15:59	22♈32	180
	20	18:08	11♊36	225
	24	20:22	0♌40	270
	28	14:29	19♍25	315
	31	22:42	7♏46	0
Nov 1959	4	3:33	25♐58	45
	7	13:24	14♒23	90
	11	8:21	3♈12	135
	15	9:42	22♉17	180
	19	13:02	11♋27	225
	23	13:04	0♍29	270
	27	3:25	19♎08	315
	30	8:47	7♐24	0
Dec 1959	3	13:22	25♑38	45
	7	2:12	14♓13	90
	11	1:27	3♉15	135
	15	4:49	22♊28	180
	19	6:52	11♌37	225
	23	3:29	0♎33	270
	26	14:39	19♏05	315
	29	19:10	7♑20	0
Jan 1960	2	1:53	25♒40	45
	5	18:54	14♈27	90
	9	21:07	3♊38	135
	13	23:51	22♋49	180
	17	22:28	11♍50	225
	21	15:01	0♏35	270
	25	0:16	19♐02	315
	28	6:16	7♒20	0
	31	17:08	25♓51	45
Feb 1960	4	14:27	14♉47	90
	8	17:37	3♋59	135
	12	17:24	23♌01	180
	16	11:10	11♎48	225
	19	23:48	0♐21	270
	23	8:51	18♑45	315
	26	18:24	7♓10	0
Mar 1960	1	10:26	25♈51	45
	5	11:06	14♊54	90
	9	13:12	3♌59	135
	13	8:26	22♍47	180
	16	20:54	11♏17	225
	20	6:41	29♐40	270
	23	17:17	18♒05	315
	27	7:38	6♈39	0
	31	4:35	25♉29	45
Apr 1960	4	7:05	14♋31	90
	8	6:27	3♍26	135
	11	20:28	21♎57	180
	15	4:23	10♐12	225
	18	12:57	28♑29	270
	22	2:29	16♓58	315
	25	21:45	5♉40	0
	29	22:27	24♊35	45
May 1960	4	1:01	13♌34	90
	7	20:32	2♎16	135
	11	5:43	20♏32	180
	14	10:45	8♑38	225
	17	19:55	26♒53	270
	21	13:04	15♈28	315
	25	12:27	4♊17	0
	29	15:09	23♋14	45
Jun 1960	2	16:02	12♍06	90
	6	7:19	0♏35	135
	9	13:02	18♐40	180
	12	17:18	6♒43	225
	16	4:36	25♓01	270
	20	1:25	13♉43	315
	24	3:27	2♋37	0
	28	6:06	21♌32	45
Jul 1960	2	3:49	10♎15	90
	5	15:23	28♏35	135
	8	19:37	16♑36	180
	12	1:10	4♓41	225
	15	15:43	23♈07	270
	19	15:39	11♊56	315
	23	18:31	0♌52	0
	27	18:55	19♍43	45
	31	12:39	8♏17	90

The 8 Phases of the Moon 1900–2020

Aug 1960	3	21:49	26♐31	135
	7	2:41	14♒35	180
	10	11:17	2♈48	225
	14	5:37	21♉25	270
	18	7:40	10♋21	315
	22	9:16	29♌16	0
	26	5:32	17♎58	45
	29	19:23	6♐26	90
Sep 1960	2	3:52	24♑40	135
	5	11:19	12♓53	180
	9	0:09	1♉19	225
	12	22:20	20♊08	270
	17	1:04	9♌08	315
	20	23:13	27♍58	0
	24	14:22	16♏32	45
	28	1:13	4♑55	90
Oct 1960	1	10:48	23♒15	135
	4	22:17	11♈41	180
	8	15:59	0♊22	225
	12	17:26	19♋23	270
	16	18:57	8♍24	315
	20	12:03	27♎06	0
	23	22:15	15♐30	45
	27	7:34	3♒53	90
	30	19:41	22♓23	135
Nov 1960	3	11:58	11♉04	180
	7	10:29	0♋01	225
	11	13:48	19♌11	270
	15	12:06	8♎08	315
	18	23:47	26♏39	0
	22	6:21	14♑58	45
	25	15:42	3♓23	90
	29	7:15	22♈05	135
Dec 1960	3	4:25	11♊01	180
	7	6:43	0♌10	225
	11	9:39	19♍22	270
	15	3:28	8♏10	315
	18	10:47	26♐32	0
	21	15:42	14♒48	45
	25	2:30	3♈19	90
	28	21:52	22♉12	135
Jan 1961	1	23:06	11♋19	180
	6	2:57	0♍34	225
	10	3:03	19♎39	270
	13	16:29	8♐16	315
	16	21:30	26♑32	0
	20	2:49	14♓49	45
	23	16:14	3♉27	90
	27	15:16	22♊28	135
	31	18:47	11♌41	180
Feb 1961	4	21:05	0♎50	225
	8	16:50	19♏42	270
	12	3:14	8♑11	315
	15	8:11	26♒25	0
	18	15:40	14♈46	45
	22	8:35	3♊30	90
	26	10:33	22♋36	135
Mar 1961	2	13:35	11♍45	180
	6	11:39	0♏40	225
	10	2:58	19♐18	270
	13	12:06	7♒41	315
	16	18:51	25♓57	0
	20	5:56	14♉24	45
	24	2:49	3♋14	90
	28	6:06	22♌20	135
Apr 1961	1	5:48	11♎16	180
	4	22:24	29♏54	225
	8	10:16	18♑21	270
	11	19:43	6♓40	315
	15	5:38	25♈01	0
	18	21:17	13♊35	45
	22	21:50	2♌31	90
	27	0:09	21♍30	135
	30	18:41	10♏10	180
May 1961	4	6:12	28♐32	225
	7	15:58	16♒50	270
	11	2:55	5♈11	315
	14	16:55	23♉38	0
	18	13:29	12♋21	45
	22	16:19	1♍19	90
	26	15:30	20♎08	135
	30	4:38	8♐32	180
Jun 1961	2	12:19	26♑43	225
	5	21:19	14♓57	270
	9	10:41	3♉21	315
	13	5:17	21♊57	0
	17	6:08	10♌49	45
	21	9:02	29♍45	90
	25	3:54	18♏21	135
	28	12:38	6♑34	180
Jul 1961	1	18:06	24♒38	225
	5	3:33	12♈52	270
	8	20:05	1♊23	315
	12	19:12	20♋10	0
	16	22:30	9♍07	45
	20	23:14	27♎58	90
	24	13:54	16♐25	135
	27	19:51	4♒31	180
	31	0:40	22♓34	225
Aug 1961	3	11:48	10♉53	270
	7	8:06	29♊34	315
	11	10:36	18♌31	0
	15	13:39	7♎28	45
	19	10:52	26♏13	90
	22	22:22	14♑34	135
	26	3:14	2♓39	180
	29	9:00	20♈47	225
Sep 1961	1	23:06	9♊15	270
	5	23:14	28♋08	315
	10	2:50	17♍10	0
	14	3:01	6♏04	45
	17	20:24	24♐42	90
	21	6:08	13♒01	135
	24	11:34	1♈11	180
	27	19:54	19♉27	225
Oct 1961	1	14:10	8♋09	270
	5	17:06	27♌13	315
	9	18:53	16♎14	0
	13	14:31	5♐01	45
	17	4:35	23♑34	90
	20	13:55	11♓56	135
	23	21:31	0♉14	180
	27	10:07	18♊45	225
	31	8:59	7♌42	270
Nov 1961	4	12:28	26♍51	315
	8	9:59	15♏46	0
	12	0:40	4♑24	45
	15	12:13	22♒54	90
	18	22:23	11♈21	135
	22	9:44	29♉51	180
	26	3:49	18♋39	225
	30	6:19	7♍48	270
Dec 1961	4	7:40	26♎55	315
	7	23:52	15♐39	0
	11	10:09	4♒08	45
	14	20:06	22♓37	90
	18	8:17	11♉11	135
	22	0:42	29♊56	180
	26	0:13	18♌59	225
	30	3:57	8♎13	270
Jan 1962	3	1:20	27♏11	315
	6	12:36	15♑43	0
	9	19:34	4♓05	45
	13	5:02	22♈32	90
	16	20:25	11♊15	135
	20	18:17	0♌13	180
	24	21:23	19♍25	225
	28	23:37	8♏35	270
Feb 1962	1	16:37	27♐21	315
	5	0:10	15♒43	0
	8	5:18	3♈58	45
	11	15:43	22♉27	90
	15	11:11	11♋18	135
	19	13:18	0♍25	180
	23	16:53	19♎36	225
	27	15:50	8♐35	270
Mar 1962	3	5:08	27♑09	315
	6	10:31	15♓23	0
	9	15:35	3♉35	45
	13	4:39	22♊08	90
	17	4:13	11♌06	135
	21	7:56	0♎13	180
	25	9:08	19♏14	225
	29	4:11	8♑00	270
Apr 1962	1	14:50	26♒24	315
	4	19:45	14♈33	0
	8	2:47	2♊48	45
	11	19:51	21♋26	90
	15	22:15	10♍27	135
	20	0:34	29♎28	180
	23	21:40	18♐15	225
	27	13:00	6♒47	270
	30	22:10	25♓04	315
May 1962	4	4:25	13♉14	0
	7	15:20	1♋35	45
	11	12:45	20♌21	90
	15	15:49	9♎20	135
	19	14:32	28♏08	180
	23	6:59	16♑40	225
	26	19:06	5♓02	270
	30	4:05	23♈16	315
Jun 1962	2	13:27	11♊31	0
	6	5:28	0♌02	45
	10	6:22	18♍54	90
	14	7:55	7♏47	135
	18	2:03	26♐22	180
	21	14:00	14♒42	225
	24	23:43	2♈57	270
	28	9:57	21♉13	315
Jul 1962	1	23:53	9♋38	0
	5	21:04	28♌20	45
	9	23:40	17♎15	90
	13	22:13	6♐01	135
	17	11:41	24♑25	180
	20	19:47	12♓36	225
	24	4:19	0♉48	270
	27	17:15	19♊11	315
	31	12:24	7♌49	0
Aug 1962	4	13:35	26♍41	45
	8	15:55	15♏37	90
	12	10:51	4♑15	135
	15	20:10	22♒30	180
	19	1:32	10♈36	225
	22	10:27	28♉51	270
	26	3:19	17♋25	315
	30	3:09	6♍16	0
Sep 1962	3	6:14	25♎16	45
	7	6:45	14♐10	90
	10	22:03	2♒42	135
	14	4:12	20♓52	180
	17	8:31	8♉58	225
	20	19:36	27♊21	270
	24	16:52	16♌09	315
	28	19:40	5♎12	0
Oct 1962	2	22:17	24♏14	45
	6	19:55	13♑05	90
	10	8:01	1♓32	135
	13	12:34	19♈42	180
	16	17:57	7♊53	225
	20	8:48	26♋29	270
	24	9:49	15♍30	315
	28	13:05	4♏38	0
Nov 1962	1	13:09	23♐38	45
	5	7:15	12♒24	90
	8	17:05	0♈49	135
	11	22:04	19♉02	180
	15	6:45	7♋25	225
	19	2:10	26♌16	270
	23	5:15	15♎26	315
	27	6:30	4♐32	0
Dec 1962	1	2:26	23♑25	45
	4	16:48	12♓04	90
	8	1:48	0♉29	135
	11	9:28	18♊52	180
	14	23:08	7♌29	225
	18	22:43	26♍32	270
	23	1:40	15♏44	315
	26	22:59	4♑42	0
	30	13:52	23♒24	45
Jan 1963	3	1:02	11♈55	90
	6	10:55	0♊24	135
	9	23:09	18♋59	180
	13	18:18	7♍51	225
	17	20:35	27♎01	270
	21	21:25	16♐07	315
	25	13:42	4♒52	0
	28	23:38	23♓20	45
Feb 1963	1	8:50	11♉46	90
	4	21:18	0♋21	135
	8	14:52	19♌08	180
	12	14:37	8♎10	225
	16	17:39	27♏20	270
	20	14:57	16♑15	315
	24	2:06	4♓45	0
	27	8:16	23♈01	45
Mar 1963	2	17:18	11♊25	90
	6	9:25	0♌05	135
	10	7:49	19♍01	180
	14	10:17	8♏07	225
	18	12:08	27♐10	270
	22	5:11	15♒52	315
	25	12:10	4♈08	0
	28	16:36	22♉17	45
Apr 1963	1	3:15	10♋41	90
	4	23:18	29♌28	135
	9	0:57	18♎28	180
	13	3:53	7♐31	225
	17	2:53	26♑23	270
	20	15:51	14♓51	315
	23	20:29	2♉58	0
	27	1:28	21♊05	45
	30	15:08	9♌33	90
May 1963	4	14:31	28♍25	135
	8	17:24	17♏24	180
	12	18:33	6♑19	225
	16	13:37	24♒58	270
	19	23:31	13♈15	315
	23	4:00	1♊19	0
	26	11:34	19♋31	45
	30	4:56	8♍05	90
Jun 1963	3	6:33	26♎59	135
	7	8:31	15♐53	180
	11	5:59	4♒37	225
	14	20:54	23♓04	270
	18	5:20	11♉16	315
	21	11:46	29♊23	0
	24	23:18	17♌43	45
	28	20:24	6♎25	90
Jul 1963	2	22:51	25♏19	135
	6	21:56	14♑06	180
	10	14:32	2♓37	225
	14	1:58	20♈56	270
	17	10:44	9♊08	315
	20	20:43	27♋24	0
	24	12:55	15♍55	45
	28	13:13	4♏45	90
Aug 1963	1	14:54	23♐38	135
	5	9:31	12♒15	180
	8	21:07	0♈35	225

The 8 Phases of the Moon 1900–2020

	12	6:22	18♉50	270
	15	17:04	7♋09	315
	19	7:35	25♌37	0
	23	4:28	14♎20	45
	27	6:54	3♐18	90
	31	6:07	22♑08	135
Sep 1963	3	19:34	10♓34	180
	7	3:03	28♈47	225
	10	11:43	17♊03	270
	14	1:33	5♌31	315
	17	20:51	24♍14	0
	21	21:43	13♏11	45
	26	0:39	2♑13	90
	29	20:01	20♒57	135
Oct 1963	3	4:44	9♈15	180
	6	9:47	27♉25	225
	9	19:28	15♋47	270
	13	13:04	4♍28	315
	17	12:43	23♎25	0
	21	16:02	12♐32	45
	25	17:21	1♒34	90
	29	8:24	20♓11	135
Nov 1963	1	13:56	8♉25	180
	4	18:34	26♊37	225
	8	6:37	15♌08	270
	12	4:07	4♎03	315
	16	6:51	23♏11	0
	20	10:08	12♑22	45
	24	7:56	1♓19	90
	27	19:23	19♈50	135
	30	23:55	8♊03	180
Dec 1963	4	6:09	26♋22	225
	7	21:34	15♍03	270
	11	22:29	4♏10	315
	16	2:07	23♐23	0
	20	2:29	12♒28	45
	23	19:55	1♈16	90
	27	5:22	19♉44	135
	30	11:04	8♋01	180
Jan 1964	2	20:34	26♌29	225
	6	15:58	15♎22	270
	10	19:07	4♐35	315
	14	20:44	23♑43	0
	18	16:02	12♓36	45
	22	5:29	1♉13	90
	25	14:46	19♊40	135
	28	23:23	8♌05	180
Feb 1964	1	13:19	26♍43	225
	5	12:43	15♏45	270
	9	16:00	4♑56	315
	13	13:02	23♒52	0
	17	2:43	12♈28	45
	20	13:25	0♊57	90
	23	23:59	19♋24	135
	27	12:40	7♍57	180
Mar 1964	2	7:35	26♎45	225
	6	10:00	15♐52	270
	10	10:56	4♒54	315
	14	2:14	23♓32	0
	17	11:16	11♉54	45
	20	20:40	0♋16	90
	24	9:32	18♌47	135
	28	2:49	7♎27	180
Apr 1964	1	2:25	26♏23	225
	5	5:46	15♑28	270
	9	2:28	4♓16	315
	12	12:38	22♈38	0
	15	18:42	10♊49	45
	19	4:10	29♋08	90
	22	20:00	17♍42	135
	26	17:50	6♏31	180
	30	20:34	25♐30	225
May 1964	4	22:20	14♒27	270
	8	14:25	3♈00	315
	11	21:02	21♉10	0
	15	1:58	9♋16	45
	18	12:43	27♌35	90
	22	7:59	16♎15	135
	26	9:29	5♐09	180
	30	12:47	24♑07	225
Jun 1964	3	11:08	12♓53	270
	6	23:24	1♉15	315
	10	4:23	19♊19	0
	13	9:51	7♌24	45
	16	23:02	25♍47	90
	20	21:52	14♏34	135
	25	1:09	3♑30	180
	29	2:15	22♒22	225
Jul 1964	2	20:31	10♈57	270
	6	6:25	29♉12	315
	9	11:31	17♋16	0
	12	19:03	5♍26	45
	16	11:48	23♎57	90
	20	13:35	12♐50	135
	24	15:58	1♒45	180
	28	12:55	20♓27	225
Aug 1964	1	3:30	8♉54	270
	4	12:31	27♊08	315
	7	19:17	15♌17	0
	11	6:20	3♎36	45
	15	3:20	22♏19	90
	19	6:27	11♑18	135
	23	5:25	0♓06	180
	26	21:27	18♈38	225
	30	9:16	7♊01	270
Sep 1964	2	18:44	25♋18	315
	6	4:35	13♍36	0
	9	20:26	2♏10	45
	13	21:24	21♐06	90
	17	23:31	10♒05	135
	21	17:31	28♓45	180
	25	4:59	17♉09	225
	28	15:02	5♋30	270
Oct 1964	2	2:07	23♌54	315
	5	16:20	12♎27	0
	9	13:36	1♐17	45
	13	16:57	20♑23	90
	17	15:53	9♓18	135
	21	4:46	27♈49	180
	24	12:39	16♊08	225
	27	21:59	4♌31	270
	31	11:48	23♍05	315
Nov 1964	4	7:17	11♏54	0
	8	9:08	1♑00	45
	12	12:21	20♒09	90
	16	7:01	8♈58	135
	19	15:43	27♉21	180
	22	21:20	15♋37	225
	26	7:11	4♍04	270
	30	0:48	22♎51	315
Dec 1964	4	1:19	11♐56	0
	8	5:19	1♒10	45
	12	6:02	20♓15	90
	15	20:42	8♉56	135
	19	2:42	27♊14	180
	22	7:36	15♌30	225
	25	19:27	4♎03	270
	29	17:27	23♏03	315
Jan 1965	2	21:07	12♑17	0
	7	0:03	1♓29	45
	10	21:00	20♈26	90
	14	8:40	8♊59	135
	17	13:38	27♋15	180
	20	19:42	15♍34	225
	24	11:08	4♏16	270
	28	12:55	23♐24	315
Feb 1965	1	16:36	12♒37	0
	5	15:51	1♈39	45
	9	8:53	20♉25	90
	12	18:46	8♋52	135
	16	0:27	27♌08	180
	19	9:43	15♎33	225
	23	5:40	4♐24	270
	27	9:16	23♑34	315
Mar 1965	3	9:56	12♓37	0
	7	4:21	1♉23	45
	10	17:53	19♊57	90
	14	3:11	8♌20	135
	17	11:24	26♍40	180
	21	1:31	15♏13	225
	25	1:37	4♑12	270
	29	4:24	23♒16	315
Apr 1965	2	0:21	12♈03	0
	5	13:54	0♊34	45
	9	0:40	18♋57	90
	12	10:41	7♍19	135
	15	23:03	25♎45	180
	19	18:36	14♐29	225
	23	21:07	3♒29	270
	27	20:59	22♓22	315
May 1965	1	11:56	10♉53	0
	4	21:17	29♊11	45
	8	6:20	17♌27	90
	11	18:26	5♎50	135
	15	11:53	24♏26	180
	19	12:00	13♑17	225
	23	14:41	2♓14	270
	27	10:43	20♈55	315
	30	21:13	9♊13	0
Jun 1965	3	3:27	27♋21	45
	6	12:12	15♍34	90
	10	3:38	4♏03	135
	14	2:00	22♐48	180
	18	4:38	11♒44	225
	22	5:37	0♈35	270
	25	21:48	19♉05	315
	29	4:53	7♋14	0
Jul 1965	2	9:29	25♌17	45
	5	19:37	13♎32	90
	9	15:10	2♐11	135
	13	17:02	21♑04	180
	17	19:44	9♓59	225
	21	17:54	28♈44	270
	25	6:45	17♊06	315
	28	11:45	5♌10	0
	31	16:37	23♍14	45
Aug 1965	4	5:48	11♏38	90
	8	5:17	0♑27	135
	12	8:23	19♒24	180
	16	9:02	8♈16	225
	20	3:51	26♉55	270
	23	14:11	15♋13	315
	26	18:51	3♍18	0
	30	2:03	21♎30	45
Sep 1965	2	19:28	10♐06	90
	6	21:40	29♑04	135
	10	23:32	18♓01	180
	14	20:38	6♉48	225
	18	11:59	25♊21	270
	21	20:59	13♌39	315
	25	3:18	1♎51	0
	28	14:46	20♏15	45
Oct 1965	2	12:38	9♑06	90
	6	15:35	28♒10	135
	10	14:14	17♈04	180
	14	6:50	5♊43	225
	17	19:00	24♋11	270
	21	4:10	12♍33	315
	24	14:12	0♏57	0
	28	7:04	19♐39	45
Nov 1965	1	8:26	8♒42	90
	5	10:06	27♓47	135
	9	4:16	16♉33	180
	12	16:06	5♋04	225
	16	1:54	23♌30	270
	19	12:57	11♎59	315
	23	4:10	0♐40	0
	27	2:20	19♑38	45
Dec 1965	1	5:25	8♓49	90
	5	4:11	27♈49	135
	8	17:22	16♊25	180
	12	0:59	4♌48	225
	15	9:52	23♍13	270
	19	0:21	11♏53	315
	22	21:03	0♑49	0
	26	23:00	19♒59	45
	31	1:47	9♈11	90
Jan 1966	3	20:41	28♉02	135
	7	5:17	16♋28	180
	10	10:12	4♍43	225
	13	20:00	23♎12	270
	17	14:45	12♐03	315
	21	15:47	1♒10	0
	25	19:12	20♓23	45
	29	19:49	9♉28	90
Feb 1966	2	10:35	28♊08	135
	5	15:58	16♌24	180
	8	20:24	4♎38	225
	12	8:53	23♏12	270
	16	7:38	12♑11	315
	20	10:50	1♓21	0
	24	13:14	20♈29	45
	28	10:16	9♊23	90
Mar 1966	3	21:28	27♋51	135
	7	1:46	16♍02	180
	10	8:04	4♏18	225
	14	0:20	22♐58	270
	18	1:54	12♒01	315
	22	4:47	1♈07	0
	26	3:58	20♉03	45
	29	20:44	8♋42	90
Apr 1966	2	5:44	27♌02	135
	5	11:14	15♎13	180
	8	21:16	3♐35	225
	12	17:29	22♑21	270
	16	20:12	11♓23	315
	20	20:36	0♉18	0
	24	15:04	18♊59	45
	28	3:50	7♌25	90
May 1966	1	12:23	25♍40	135
	4	21:01	13♏56	180
	8	11:46	2♑26	225
	12	11:19	21♒17	270
	16	13:30	10♈13	315
	20	9:43	28♉55	0
	23	23:00	17♋21	45
	27	8:51	5♍37	90
	30	18:41	23♎53	135
Jun 1966	3	7:41	12♐17	180
	7	3:10	0♒56	225
	11	4:59	19♓50	270
	15	4:59	8♉39	315
	18	20:09	27♊07	0
	22	4:52	15♌20	45
	25	13:23	3♎32	90
	29	1:54	21♏53	135
Jul 1966	2	19:37	10♑27	180
	6	19:09	29♒15	225
	10	21:43	18♈10	270
	14	18:16	6♊50	315
	18	4:31	25♋07	0
	21	10:07	13♍12	45
	24	19:00	1♏25	90
	28	11:02	19♐55	135
Aug 1966	1	9:06	8♒40	180
	5	11:22	27♓35	225
	9	12:56	16♉29	270
	13	5:20	5♋01	315
	16	11:48	23♌10	0
	19	16:15	11♎13	45

The 8 Phases of the Moon 1900–2020

Month	Day	Time	Position	Phase
	23	3:02	29♏33	90
	26	22:50	18♑14	135
	31	0:14	7♓09	180
Sep 1966	4	3:17	26♈09	225
	8	2:08	14♊59	270
	11	14:39	3♌24	315
	14	19:14	21♍31	0
	18	0:33	9♏39	45
	21	14:25	28♐09	90
	25	13:44	17♒02	135
	29	16:48	6♈05	180
Oct 1966	3	18:12	25♉05	225
	7	13:09	13♋49	270
	10	23:00	2♍11	315
	14	3:52	20♎21	0
	17	11:54	8♐40	45
	21	5:35	27♑23	90
	25	7:37	16♓27	135
	29	10:01	5♉32	180
Nov 1966	2	7:26	24♊25	225
	5	22:19	13♌03	270
	9	7:16	1♎26	315
	12	14:27	19♏45	0
	16	2:34	8♑17	45
	20	0:21	27♒14	90
	24	3:35	16♈24	135
	28	2:41	5♊25	180
Dec 1966	1	18:45	24♋08	225
	5	6:23	12♍40	270
	8	16:12	1♏07	315
	12	3:14	19♐38	0
	15	20:16	8♒25	45
	19	21:41	27♓33	90
	23	23:54	16♉43	135
	27	17:44	5♋32	180
	31	4:33	24♌03	225
Jan 1967	3	14:19	12♎31	270
	7	2:23	1♐05	315
	10	18:07	19♑49	0
	14	16:10	8♓48	45
	18	19:42	28♈02	90
	22	18:32	17♊03	135
	26	6:41	5♌37	180
	29	13:38	23♍57	225
Feb 1967	1	23:03	12♏24	270
	5	14:10	1♑05	315
	9	10:44	20♒00	0
	13	12:49	9♈08	45
	17	15:57	28♉18	90
	21	10:04	17♋05	135
	24	17:44	5♍26	180
	27	22:46	23♎39	225
Mar 1967	3	9:11	12♐06	270
	7	3:45	0♒53	315
	11	4:30	19♓55	0
	15	8:18	9♉04	45
	19	8:32	28♊03	90
	22	22:10	16♌36	135
	26	3:21	4♎47	180
	29	8:25	22♏57	225
Apr 1967	1	20:59	11♑26	270
	5	19:05	0♓18	315
	9	22:21	19♈22	0
	14	0:50	8♊24	45
	17	20:48	27♋09	90
	21	7:18	15♍30	135
	24	12:04	3♏37	180
	27	18:49	21♐49	225
May 1967	1	10:33	10♒22	270
	5	11:44	29♓17	315
	9	14:56	18♉18	0
	13	13:35	7♋06	45
	17	5:18	25♌38	90
	20	14:19	13♎53	135
	23	20:23	2♐00	180
	27	6:15	20♑17	225
	31	1:52	8♓57	270
Jun 1967	4	4:49	27♈54	315
	8	5:14	16♊44	0
	11	22:51	5♌19	45
	15	11:12	23♍40	90
	18	20:14	11♏54	135
	22	4:57	0♑06	180
	25	19:07	18♒32	225
	29	18:40	7♈19	270
Jul 1967	3	21:16	26♉14	315
	7	17:01	14♋53	0
	11	5:43	3♍15	45
	14	15:53	21♎31	90
	18	2:07	9♐47	135
	21	14:40	28♑09	180
	25	9:50	16♓46	225
	29	12:15	5♉41	270
Aug 1967	2	12:18	24♊31	315
	6	2:49	12♌58	0
	9	11:35	1♎12	45
	12	20:45	19♏27	90
	16	9:13	7♑49	135
	20	2:27	26♒24	180
	24	2:25	15♈15	225
	28	5:36	4♊14	270
Sep 1967	1	1:41	22♋57	315
	4	11:38	11♍15	0
	7	17:47	29♎25	45
	11	3:06	17♐42	90
	14	18:48	6♒16	135
	18	17:00	25♓05	180
	22	20:08	14♉07	225
	26	21:44	3♋06	270
	30	13:39	21♌42	315
Oct 1967	3	20:24	9♎56	0
	7	1:26	28♏06	45
	10	12:11	16♑30	90
	14	7:56	5♓17	135
	18	10:11	24♈21	180
	22	13:43	13♊28	225
	26	12:04	2♌23	270
	30	0:37	20♍54	315
Nov 1967	2	5:49	9♏07	0
	5	11:19	27♐21	45
	9	1:00	15♒56	90
	13	0:59	4♈57	135
	17	4:53	24♉09	180
	21	5:53	13♋13	225
	25	0:24	2♍02	270
	28	10:50	20♎31	315
Dec 1967	1	16:10	8♐47	0
	5	0:01	27♑09	45
	8	17:58	15♓58	90
	12	21:03	5♉09	135
	16	23:22	24♊19	180
	20	19:52	13♌15	225
	24	10:48	1♎56	270
	27	20:25	20♏24	315
	31	3:39	8♑46	0
Jan 1968	3	15:43	27♒20	45
	7	14:23	16♈21	90
	11	18:06	5♊35	135
	15	16:12	24♋35	180
	19	7:38	13♍18	225
	22	19:38	1♏51	270
	26	5:39	20♐20	315
	29	16:30	8♒50	0
Feb 1968	2	10:05	27♓38	45
	6	12:21	16♉47	90
	10	13:55	5♋54	135
	14	6:43	24♌38	180
	17	17:32	13♎07	225
	21	3:28	1♐34	270
	24	15:08	20♑05	315
	28	6:56	8♓45	0
Mar 1968	3	5:54	27♈44	45
	7	9:21	16♊53	90
	11	7:02	5♌47	135
	14	18:53	24♍16	180
	18	2:06	12♏33	225
	21	11:08	0♑54	270
	25	1:43	19♒29	315
	28	22:49	8♈19	0
Apr 1968	2	1:20	27♉22	45
	6	3:28	16♋24	90
	9	20:54	5♍04	135
	13	4:52	23♎20	180
	16	9:54	11♐28	225
	19	19:35	29♑48	270
	23	14:02	18♓28	315
	27	15:22	7♉25	0
May 1968	1	18:41	26♊26	45
	5	17:55	15♌17	90
	9	7:38	3♎44	135
	12	13:05	21♏51	180
	15	17:41	9♑56	225
	19	5:45	28♒18	270
	23	4:13	17♈05	315
	27	7:30	6♊04	0
	31	9:05	24♋58	45
Jun 1968	4	4:47	13♍37	90
	7	15:40	1♏56	135
	10	20:14	19♐59	180
	14	2:24	8♒05	225
	17	18:14	26♓35	270
	21	19:49	15♉28	315
	25	22:25	4♋23	0
	29	20:34	23♌07	45
Jul 1968	3	12:42	11♎37	90
	6	21:50	29♏51	135
	10	3:18	17♑55	180
	13	12:59	6♓10	225
	17	9:12	24♈50	270
	21	12:04	13♊46	315
	25	11:50	2♌35	0
	29	5:42	21♍09	45
Aug 1968	1	18:35	9♏32	90
	5	3:16	27♐45	135
	8	11:33	15♒58	180
	12	2:11	4♈25	225
	16	2:14	23♉16	270
	20	4:20	12♋12	315
	23	23:57	0♍53	0
	27	13:17	19♎19	45
	30	23:35	7♐38	90
Sep 1968	3	9:22	25♑56	135
	6	22:08	14♓21	180
	10	18:08	3♉04	225
	14	20:32	22♊04	270
	18	20:13	10♌57	315
	22	11:09	29♍30	0
	25	20:16	17♏49	45
	29	5:07	6♑07	90
Oct 1968	2	17:36	24♒35	135
	6	11:47	13♈17	180
	10	12:16	2♊15	225
	14	15:06	21♋20	270
	18	11:21	10♍09	315
	21	21:45	28♎33	0
	25	3:40	16♐48	45
	28	12:40	5♒10	90
Nov 1968	1	5:11	23♓51	135
	5	4:25	12♉49	180
	9	7:26	1♋58	225
	13	8:54	21♌03	270
	17	1:19	9♎46	315
	20	8:02	28♏04	0
	23	12:29	16♑18	45
	26	23:31	4♓48	90
	30	20:32	23♈43	135
Dec 1968	4	23:08	12♊53	180
	9	2:11	2♌05	225
	13	0:50	21♍05	270
	16	13:38	9♏41	315
	19	18:19	27♐56	0
	22	23:36	16♒13	45
	26	14:15	4♈54	90
	30	15:04	24♉00	135
Jan 1969	3	18:28	13♋13	180
	7	19:13	2♍20	225
	11	14:01	21♎11	270
	15	0:06	9♐40	315
	18	4:59	27♑56	0
	21	13:24	16♓21	45
	25	8:24	5♉12	90
	29	11:17	24♊23	135
Feb 1969	2	12:56	13♌31	180
	6	9:29	2♎26	225
	10	0:09	21♏05	270
	13	9:03	9♑30	315
	16	16:26	27♒50	0
	20	5:34	16♈25	45
	24	4:31	5♊24	90
	28	7:24	24♋32	135
Mar 1969	4	5:18	13♍28	180
	7	20:38	2♏06	225
	11	7:45	20♐34	270
	14	17:16	8♒57	315
	18	4:52	27♓25	0
	21	23:10	16♉10	45
	26	0:49	5♋12	90
	30	1:51	24♌11	135
Apr 1969	2	18:45	12♎51	180
	6	5:00	1♐13	225
	9	13:59	19♑32	270
	13	1:43	7♓58	315
	16	18:16	26♈34	0
	20	17:02	15♊26	45
	24	19:45	4♌26	90
	28	17:30	23♍14	135
May 1969	2	5:14	11♏37	180
	5	11:37	29♐47	225
	8	20:12	18♒02	270
	12	11:16	6♈33	315
	16	8:27	25♉17	0
	20	10:15	14♋13	45
	24	12:16	3♍08	90
	28	5:53	21♎44	135
	31	13:19	9♐54	180
Jun 1969	3	17:44	27♑57	225
	7	3:40	16♓13	270
	10	22:26	4♉50	315
	14	23:09	23♊41	0
	19	2:06	12♌37	45
	23	1:45	1♎25	90
	26	15:16	19♏49	135
	29	20:04	7♑52	180
Jul 1969	3	0:40	25♒55	225
	6	13:18	14♈17	270
	10	11:33	3♊01	315
	14	14:12	21♋57	0
	18	16:08	10♍50	45
	22	12:10	29♎30	90
	25	22:30	17♐46	135
	29	2:46	5♒49	180
Aug 1969	1	9:28	23♓57	225
	5	1:39	12♉28	270
	9	2:40	1♋20	315
	13	5:17	20♌17	0
	17	4:05	9♎05	45
	20	20:04	27♏36	90
	24	4:44	15♑51	135
	27	10:33	3♓58	180
	30	20:54	22♈17	225

The 8 Phases of the Moon 1900–2020

Month	Day	Time	Position	Phase
Sep 1969	3	16:58	11♊00	270
	7	19:35	29♋59	315
	11	19:56	18♍53	0
	15	14:01	7♏33	45
	19	2:25	25♐59	90
	22	11:14	14♒16	135
	25	20:22	2♈35	180
	29	11:19	21♉08	225
Oct 1969	3	11:06	10♋04	270
	7	13:37	29♌06	315
	11	9:40	17♎54	0
	14	22:31	6♐24	45
	18	8:32	24♑48	90
	21	19:09	13♓13	135
	25	8:45	1♉46	180
	29	4:40	20♊35	225
Nov 1969	2	7:14	9♌42	270
	6	7:35	28♍43	315
	9	22:12	17♏21	0
	13	6:34	5♑43	45
	16	15:46	24♒07	90
	20	5:23	12♈43	135
	23	23:54	1♊32	180
	28	0:21	20♋36	225
Dec 1969	2	3:51	9♍48	270
	6	0:13	28♎42	315
	9	9:43	17♐09	0
	12	15:17	5♒26	45
	16	1:10	23♓55	90
	19	18:26	12♉42	135
	23	17:36	1♋44	180
	27	20:57	20♌57	225
	31	22:53	10♎06	270
Jan 1970	4	14:36	28♏50	315
	7	20:36	17♑09	0
	11	1:27	5♓25	45
	14	13:19	23♈58	90
	18	10:22	12♊55	135
	22	12:56	2♌06	180
	26	16:28	21♍19	225
	30	14:39	10♏18	270
Feb 1970	3	2:29	28♐51	315
	6	7:14	17♒05	0
	9	13:19	5♈23	45
	13	4:11	24♉03	90
	17	4:39	13♋06	135
	21	8:19	2♍18	180
	25	8:56	21♎21	225
Mar 1970	1	2:34	10♐06	270
	4	12:09	28♑30	315
	7	17:43	16♓44	0
	11	2:39	5♉07	45
	14	21:16	23♊53	90
	19	0:03	12♌59	135
	23	1:53	2♎01	180
	26	21:31	20♏48	225
	30	11:05	9♑20	270
Apr 1970	2	20:10	27♒40	315
	6	4:10	15♈57	0
	9	17:09	4♊26	45
	13	15:44	23♋18	90
	17	18:52	12♍20	135
	21	16:22	1♏09	180
	25	6:34	19♐38	225
	28	17:19	8♒00	270
May 1970	2	3:16	26♓19	315
	5	14:52	14♉41	0
	9	8:40	3♋19	45
	13	10:27	22♌15	90
	17	11:34	11♎09	135
	21	3:38	29♏41	180
	24	13:17	17♑57	225
	27	22:32	6♓12	270
	31	10:25	24♈33	315
Jun 1970	4	2:22	13♊04	0
	8	0:58	1♌50	45
	12	4:07	20♍47	90
	16	1:27	9♏30	135
	19	12:28	27♐48	180
	22	19:00	15♒56	225
	26	4:02	4♈09	270
	29	18:40	22♉35	315
Jul 1970	3	15:18	11♋16	0
	7	17:33	0♍10	45
	11	19:44	19♎04	90
	15	12:40	7♐36	135
	18	19:59	25♑46	180
	22	1:00	13♓49	225
	25	11:00	2♉05	270
	29	5:09	20♊40	315
Aug 1970	2	5:59	9♌32	0
	6	9:32	28♍30	45
	10	8:51	17♏19	90
	13	21:59	5♑43	135
	17	3:16	23♒49	180
	20	8:19	11♈54	225
	23	20:35	0♊17	270
	27	18:40	19♋04	315
	31	22:02	8♍04	0
Sep 1970	5	0:07	27♎02	45
	8	19:39	15♐44	90
	12	6:15	4♒04	135
	15	11:10	22♓12	180
	18	17:51	10♉23	225
	22	9:43	28♊58	270
	26	11:21	17♌57	315
	30	14:32	7♎01	0
Oct 1970	4	12:51	25♏53	45
	8	4:43	14♑30	90
	11	14:10	2♓51	135
	14	20:22	21♈04	180
	18	6:24	9♊28	225
	22	2:48	28♋17	270
	26	6:21	17♍25	315
	30	6:29	6♏25	0
Nov 1970	2	23:55	25♐09	45
	6	12:48	13♒42	90
	9	22:23	2♈07	135
	13	7:29	20♉30	180
	16	22:27	9♋09	225
	20	23:14	28♌13	270
	25	2:05	17♎23	315
	28	21:15	6♐14	0
Dec 1970	2	9:52	24♑49	45
	5	20:36	13♓18	90
	9	7:32	1♉49	135
	12	21:04	20♊26	180
	16	17:44	9♌22	225
	20	21:10	28♍35	270
	24	20:51	17♏39	315
	28	10:43	6♑17	0
	31	19:22	24♒43	45
Jan 1971	4	4:56	13♈11	90
	7	18:25	1♊49	135
	11	13:21	20♋40	180
	15	14:49	9♍48	225
	19	18:09	29♎01	270
	23	13:31	17♐54	315
	26	22:56	6♒21	0
	30	4:52	24♓39	45
Feb 1971	2	14:31	13♉06	90
	6	7:40	1♋52	135
	10	7:42	20♌55	180
	14	11:23	10♎07	225
	18	12:14	29♏12	270
	22	3:27	17♑51	315
	25	9:49	6♓09	0
	28	14:39	24♈22	45
Mar 1971	4	2:02	12♊51	90
	7	23:23	1♌45	135
	12	2:34	20♍52	180
	16	5:20	9♏58	225
	20	2:31	28♐50	270
	23	14:28	17♒19	315
	26	19:24	5♈29	0
	30	1:04	23♉41	45
Apr 1971	2	15:47	12♋15	90
	6	16:48	1♍14	135
	10	20:11	20♎18	180
	14	19:39	9♐12	225
	18	12:58	27♑51	270
	21	22:47	16♓10	315
	25	4:02	4♉19	0
	28	12:34	22♊35	45
May 1971	2	7:35	11♌16	90
	6	10:31	0♎15	135
	10	11:24	19♏10	180
	14	6:28	7♑49	225
	17	20:16	26♒16	270
	21	5:09	14♈31	315
	24	12:33	2♊42	0
	28	1:36	21♋06	45
Jun 1971	1	0:43	9♍54	90
	5	3:19	28♎50	135
	9	0:04	17♐32	180
	12	14:30	5♒58	225
	16	1:25	24♓16	270
	19	10:44	12♉31	315
	22	21:58	0♋49	0
	26	16:20	19♌25	45
	30	18:12	8♎18	90
Jul 1971	4	18:33	27♏08	135
	8	10:37	15♑38	180
	11	20:47	3♓53	225
	15	5:47	22♈06	270
	18	17:02	10♊25	315
	22	9:16	28♋56	0
	26	8:26	17♍43	45
	30	11:08	6♏39	90
Aug 1971	3	8:09	25♐21	135
	6	19:43	13♒41	180
	10	2:26	1♈50	225
	13	10:56	20♉03	270
	17	1:31	8♋31	315
	20	22:54	27♌15	0
	25	1:13	16♎12	45
	29	2:57	5♐08	90
Sep 1971	1	20:17	23♑44	135
	5	4:03	11♓57	180
	8	8:43	0♉03	225
	11	18:24	18♊21	270
	15	13:16	7♌02	315
	19	14:43	26♍00	0
	23	17:54	15♏03	45
	27	17:18	3♑57	90
Oct 1971	1	7:08	22♒27	135
	4	12:20	10♈37	180
	7	16:51	28♉46	225
	11	5:30	17♋15	270
	15	4:38	6♍10	315
	19	8:00	25♎17	0
	23	9:45	14♐20	45
	27	5:55	3♒09	90
	30	16:53	21♓37	135
Nov 1971	2	21:20	9♉48	180
	6	3:58	28♊05	225
	9	20:52	16♌48	270
	13	23:06	5♎55	315
	18	1:46	25♏03	0
	22	0:11	14♑02	45
	25	16:37	2♓45	90
	29	1:53	21♈11	135
Dec 1971	2	7:49	9♊28	180
	5	18:37	27♋58	225
	9	16:03	16♍55	270
	13	19:21	6♏08	315
	17	19:03	25♐11	0
	21	12:47	14♒00	45
	25	1:36	2♈36	90
	28	10:46	21♉03	135
	31	20:20	9♋30	180
Jan 1972	4	12:31	28♌15	225
	8	13:31	17♎22	270
	12	15:45	6♐32	315
	16	10:53	25♑25	0
	19	23:26	14♓00	45
	23	9:29	2♉29	90
	26	20:21	20♊59	135
	30	10:59	9♌39	180
Feb 1972	3	8:22	28♍36	225
	7	11:12	17♏47	270
	11	10:35	6♑48	315
	15	0:29	25♒26	0
	18	8:29	13♈48	45
	21	17:21	2♊11	90
	25	7:21	20♋48	135
	29	3:13	9♍39	180
Mar 1972	4	4:24	28♎42	225
	8	7:06	17♐49	270
	12	2:31	6♒37	315
	15	11:35	25♓00	0
	18	16:41	13♉11	45
	22	2:12	1♋34	90
	25	20:05	20♌17	135
	29	20:06	9♎14	180
Apr 1972	2	23:02	28♏18	225
	6	23:45	17♑16	270
	10	14:52	5♓50	315
	13	20:32	24♈00	0
	17	0:55	12♊07	45
	20	12:46	0♌32	90
	24	10:21	19♍20	135
	28	12:45	8♏19	180
May 1972	2	15:09	27♐18	225
	6	12:27	16♒04	270
	9	23:51	4♈26	315
	13	4:09	22♉30	0
	16	10:03	10♋38	45
	20	1:17	29♌08	90
	24	1:45	18♎00	135
	28	4:28	6♐56	180
Jun 1972	1	4:12	25♑46	225
	4	21:22	14♓19	270
	8	6:23	2♉33	315
	11	11:31	20♊38	0
	14	20:41	8♌51	45
	18	15:42	27♍29	90
	22	17:50	16♏23	135
	26	18:47	5♑14	180
	30	14:11	23♒52	225
Jul 1972	4	3:26	12♈15	270
	7	11:49	0♊26	315
	10	19:40	18♋37	0
	14	9:11	7♍01	45
	18	7:46	25♎46	90
	22	10:06	14♐41	135
	26	7:24	3♒24	180
	29	21:45	21♓50	225
Aug 1972	2	8:03	10♉07	270
	5	17:31	28♊22	315
	9	5:27	16♌43	0
	12	23:44	5♎20	45
	17	1:10	24♏14	90
	21	2:00	13♑07	135
	24	18:22	1♓40	180
	28	3:59	19♈56	225
	31	12:49	8♊12	270
Sep 1972	4	0:50	26♋35	315
	7	17:29	15♍10	0
	11	16:16	4♏01	45

The 8 Phases of the Moon 1900–2020

	15	19:14	23♐02	90
	19	16:54	11♒50	135
	23	4:07	0♈14	180
	26	10:18	18♉25	225
	29	19:17	6♋44	270
Oct 1972	3	10:47	25♌19	315
	7	8:09	14♎09	0
	11	10:23	3♐12	45
	15	12:55	22♑16	90
	19	6:22	10♓58	135
	22	13:26	29♈15	180
	25	18:04	17♊25	225
	29	4:42	5♌52	270
Nov 1972	2	0:05	24♍40	315
	6	1:22	13♏44	0
	10	5:04	2♑54	45
	14	5:01	21♒56	90
	17	18:19	10♈31	135
	20	23:07	28♉44	180
	24	4:17	16♋59	225
	27	17:45	5♍36	270
Dec 1972	1	16:54	24♎37	315
	5	20:25	13♐49	0
	9	22:45	2♒59	45
	13	18:36	21♓52	90
	17	4:56	10♉22	135
	20	9:46	28♊37	180
	23	17:18	17♌00	225
	27	10:28	5♎47	270
	31	12:37	24♏57	315
Jan 1973	4	15:43	14♑10	0
	8	13:58	3♓10	45
	12	5:28	21♈53	90
	15	14:38	10♊20	135
	18	21:29	28♋40	180
	22	8:51	17♍12	225
	26	6:06	6♏09	270
	30	9:36	25♐22	315
Feb 1973	3	9:24	14♒25	0
	7	2:06	3♈10	45
	10	14:06	21♉43	90
	13	23:48	10♋09	135
	17	10:08	28♌37	180
	21	2:15	17♎19	225
	25	3:11	6♐23	270
Mar 1973	1	5:41	25♑30	315
	5	0:08	14♓17	0
	8	11:32	2♉46	45
	11	21:26	21♊11	90
	15	8:55	9♌39	135
	18	23:34	28♍14	180
	22	20:40	17♏05	225
	26	23:47	6♑11	270
	30	22:56	25♒06	315
Apr 1973	3	11:46	13♈35	0
	6	19:15	1♊51	45
	10	4:29	20♋10	90
	13	18:33	8♍41	135
	17	13:51	27♎25	180
	21	15:05	16♐22	225
	25	17:59	5♒23	270
	29	12:34	24♓03	315
May 1973	2	20:56	12♉18	0
	6	2:17	0♋25	45
	9	12:07	18♌43	90
	13	5:23	7♎19	135
	17	4:59	26♏09	180
	21	8:18	15♑08	225
	25	8:41	4♓00	270
	28	22:54	22♈27	315
Jun 1973	1	4:35	10♊33	0
	4	9:33	28♋37	45
	7	21:12	16♍57	90
	11	18:01	5♏39	135
	15	20:35	24♐35	180
	19	23:13	13♒30	225
	23	19:46	2♈11	270
	27	6:49	20♉29	315
	30	11:39	8♋32	0
Jul 1973	3	17:50	26♌38	45
	7	8:26	15♎05	90
	11	8:42	3♐54	135
	15	11:57	22♑51	180
	19	11:23	11♓38	225
	23	3:58	0♉10	270
	26	13:20	18♊24	315
	29	19:00	6♌30	0
Aug 1973	2	3:52	24♍43	45
	5	22:27	13♏20	90
	10	1:07	2♑16	135
	14	2:17	21♒09	180
	17	21:06	9♈48	225
	21	10:23	28♉13	270
	24	19:29	16♋28	315
	28	3:26	4♍41	0
	31	16:29	23♎07	45
Sep 1973	4	15:23	11♐57	90
	8	18:24	0♒57	135
	12	15:17	19♓42	180
	16	5:14	8♉12	225
	19	16:11	26♊34	270
	23	2:16	14♌55	315
	26	13:55	3♎20	0
	30	8:12	22♏02	45
Oct 1973	4	10:33	11♑04	90
	8	11:29	0♓02	135
	12	3:10	18♈39	180
	15	12:55	7♊02	225
	18	22:33	25♋24	270
	22	10:45	13♍53	315
	26	3:17	2♏34	0
	30	2:51	21♐33	45
Nov 1973	3	6:30	10♒42	90
	7	3:35	29♓35	135
	10	14:27	18♉03	180
	13	21:10	6♋21	225
	17	6:35	24♌46	270
	20	22:01	13♎27	315
	24	19:56	2♐24	0
	28	23:10	21♑35	45
Dec 1973	3	1:29	10♓45	90
	6	18:17	29♈30	135
	10	1:35	17♊51	180
	13	6:40	6♌07	225
	16	17:13	24♍37	270
	20	12:49	13♏30	315
	24	15:08	2♑40	0
	28	19:02	21♒55	45
Jan 1974	1	18:07	10♈57	90
	5	7:18	29♉34	135
	8	12:37	17♋51	180
	11	17:47	6♍08	225
	15	7:04	24♎45	270
	19	6:57	13♐49	315
	23	11:03	3♒04	0
	27	12:31	22♓12	45
	31	7:40	11♉03	90
Feb 1974	3	18:22	29♊33	135
	6	23:25	17♌48	180
	10	6:40	6♎09	225
	14	0:04	24♏55	270
	18	2:58	14♑04	315
	22	5:34	3♓13	0
	26	2:41	22♈07	45
Mar 1974	1	18:03	10♊47	90
	5	3:29	29♋11	135
	8	10:04	17♍27	180
	11	21:20	5♏55	225
	15	19:16	24♐49	270
	19	22:46	13♒57	315
	23	21:25	2♈52	0
	27	13:35	21♉30	45
	31	1:45	9♋58	90
Apr 1974	3	11:09	28♌19	135
	6	21:01	16♎41	180
	10	13:34	5♐18	225
	14	14:58	24♑17	270
	18	16:35	13♓16	315
	22	10:17	1♉55	0
	25	21:51	20♊18	45
	29	7:40	8♌37	90
May 1974	2	18:23	26♍58	135
	6	8:55	15♏27	180
	10	6:41	4♑14	225
	14	9:29	23♒13	270
	18	7:41	12♈00	315
	21	20:35	0♊24	0
	25	4:23	18♋36	45
	28	13:04	6♍49	90
Jun 1974	1	2:29	25♎14	135
	4	22:10	13♐54	180
	8	23:41	2♒47	225
	13	1:46	21♓41	270
	16	20:05	10♉17	315
	20	4:56	28♊30	0
	23	10:14	16♌34	45
	26	19:21	4♎48	90
	30	12:33	23♏21	135
Jul 1974	4	12:41	12♑10	180
	8	15:38	1♓05	225
	12	15:29	19♈54	270
	16	6:08	8♊20	315
	19	12:07	26♋27	0
	22	16:35	14♍29	45
	26	3:52	2♏48	90
	30	1:15	21♐31	135
Aug 1974	3	3:58	10♒27	180
	7	6:00	29♓22	225
	11	2:47	18♉04	270
	14	14:26	6♋25	315
	17	19:02	24♌29	0
	21	0:40	12♎36	45
	24	15:39	1♐05	90
	28	16:34	19♑59	135
Sep 1974	1	19:26	8♓58	180
	5	18:42	27♈49	225
	9	12:02	16♊26	270
	12	21:38	4♌44	315
	16	2:46	22♍52	0
	19	11:40	11♏09	45
	23	7:09	29♐53	90
	27	9:58	18♒55	135
Oct 1974	1	10:39	7♈52	180
	5	5:52	26♉37	225
	8	19:46	15♋09	270
	12	4:39	3♍29	315
	15	12:26	21♎46	0
	19	2:16	10♐19	45
	23	1:54	29♑17	90
	27	4:32	18♓23	135
	31	1:20	7♉14	180
Nov 1974	3	15:49	25♊51	225
	7	2:48	14♌19	270
	10	12:38	2♎44	315
	14	0:54	21♏16	0
	17	20:16	10♑06	45
	21	22:40	29♒15	90
	25	23:14	18♈19	135
	29	15:11	7♊01	180
Dec 1974	3	0:59	25♋28	225
	6	10:11	13♍54	270
	9	22:39	2♏29	315
	13	16:26	21♐17	0
	17	16:32	10♒22	45
	21	19:44	29♓34	90
	25	16:52	18♉31	135
	29	3:52	7♋02	180
Jan 1975	1	10:00	25♌22	225
	4	19:05	13♎48	270
	8	11:28	2♐33	315
	12	10:20	21♑35	0
	16	13:15	10♓47	45
	20	15:15	29♈57	90
	24	8:16	18♊43	135
	27	15:10	7♌03	180
	30	19:34	25♍17	225
Feb 1975	3	6:24	13♏47	270
	7	3:01	2♑42	315
	11	5:18	21♒51	0
	15	8:32	11♈02	45
	19	7:39	0♊02	90
	22	20:40	18♋36	135
	26	1:15	6♍49	180
Mar 1975	1	6:16	25♎02	225
	4	20:21	13♐38	270
	8	20:30	2♒39	315
	12	23:48	21♓47	0
	17	0:59	10♉49	45
	20	20:05	29♊35	90
	24	6:04	17♌59	135
	27	10:37	6♎08	180
	30	18:25	24♏26	225
Apr 1975	3	12:26	13♑08	270
	7	14:40	2♓09	315
	11	16:40	21♈10	0
	15	13:52	9♊59	45
	19	4:42	28♋31	90
	22	13:14	16♍48	135
	25	19:56	4♏59	180
	29	7:59	23♐24	225
May 1975	3	5:44	12♒11	270
	7	8:23	1♈10	315
	11	7:06	19♉59	0
	14	23:15	8♋32	45
	18	10:30	26♌53	90
	21	19:24	15♎07	135
	25	5:51	3♐25	180
	28	22:43	21♑58	225
Jun 1975	1	23:23	10♓50	270
	6	0:47	29♈43	315
	9	18:50	18♊19	0
	13	5:57	6♌38	45
	16	14:59	24♍51	90
	20	1:51	13♏09	135
	23	16:55	1♑36	180
	27	14:17	20♒19	225
Jul 1975	1	16:38	9♈13	270
	5	15:16	27♉59	315
	9	4:11	16♋21	0
	12	11:18	4♍30	45
	15	19:47	22♎42	90
	19	9:47	11♐07	135
	23	5:29	29♑46	180
	27	6:25	18♓37	225
	31	8:49	7♉32	270
Aug 1975	4	3:35	26♊10	315
	7	11:58	14♌22	0
	10	16:49	2♎26	45
	14	2:24	20♏42	90
	17	20:06	9♑18	135
	21	19:48	28♒08	180
	25	22:44	17♈06	225
	29	23:20	5♊59	270
Sep 1975	2	13:57	24♋29	315
	5	19:19	12♍36	0
	8	23:56	0♏42	45
	12	12:00	19♐06	90
	16	9:26	7♒54	135
	20	11:51	26♓54	180
	24	14:32	15♉55	225

The 8 Phases of the Moon 1900–2020

Month	Day	Time	Position	Phase
	28	11:47	4♋44	270
Oct 1975	1	22:57	23♌08	315
	5	3:24	11♎16	0
	8	9:45	29♏30	45
	12	1:16	18♑06	90
	16	1:58	7♓05	135
	20	5:07	26♈11	180
	24	5:02	15♊10	225
	27	22:08	3♌52	270
	31	7:23	22♍15	315
Nov 1975	3	13:06	10♏29	0
	6	22:49	28♐54	45
	10	18:22	17♒44	90
	14	21:13	6♈53	135
	18	22:29	25♉58	180
	22	17:36	14♋48	225
	26	6:53	3♍23	270
	29	16:04	21♎49	315
Dec 1975	3	0:51	10♐13	0
	6	15:07	28♑52	45
	10	14:40	17♓55	90
	14	17:47	7♉07	135
	18	14:40	26♊03	180
	22	4:16	14♌41	225
	25	14:53	3♎11	270
	29	1:36	21♏42	315
Jan 1976	1	14:41	10♑19	0
	5	10:02	29♒12	45
	9	12:40	18♈23	90
	13	13:37	7♊30	135
	17	4:48	26♋12	180
	20	13:39	14♍38	225
	23	23:05	3♏05	270
	27	12:26	21♐42	315
	31	6:21	10♒30	0
Feb 1976	4	6:25	29♓34	45
	8	10:06	18♉47	90
	12	6:50	7♋41	135
	15	16:44	26♌08	180
	18	22:35	14♎24	225
	22	8:17	2♐50	270
	26	0:52	21♑33	315
	29	23:26	10♓31	0
Mar 1976	5	2:37	29♈39	45
	9	4:39	18♊45	90
	12	20:36	7♌24	135
	16	2:54	25♍39	180
	19	7:43	13♏50	225
	22	18:55	2♑17	270
	26	15:02	21♒05	315
	30	17:09	10♈07	0
Apr 1976	3	20:42	29♉13	45
	7	19:02	18♋05	90
	11	7:03	6♍31	135
	14	11:50	24♎39	180
	17	17:26	12♐49	225
	21	7:15	1♒19	270
	25	6:47	20♓11	315
	29	10:20	9♉13	0
May 1976	3	11:20	28♊09	45
	7	5:18	16♌47	90
	10	14:56	5♎04	135
	13	20:05	23♏10	180
	17	4:01	11♑23	225
	20	21:23	29♒58	270
	24	23:32	18♈54	315
	29	1:48	7♊49	0
Jun 1976	1	22:15	26♋31	45
	5	12:21	14♍57	90
	8	21:12	3♏11	135
	12	4:16	21♐19	180
	15	15:52	9♒39	225
	19	13:16	28♓22	270
	23	16:21	17♉18	315
	27	14:51	6♋04	0
Jul 1976	1	6:13	24♌32	45
	4	17:29	12♎50	90
	8	2:55	1♐04	135
	11	13:10	19♑20	180
	15	5:29	7♓51	225
	19	6:30	26♈42	270
	23	8:14	15♊36	315
	27	1:39	4♌09	0
	30	12:30	22♍27	45
Aug 1976	2	22:07	10♏43	90
	6	9:13	29♐01	135
	9	23:44	17♒29	180
	13	21:09	6♈13	225
	18	0:13	25♉11	270
	21	22:39	13♋58	315
	25	11:01	2♍22	0
	28	18:29	20♎33	45
Sep 1976	1	3:36	8♐50	90
	4	17:24	27♑17	135
	8	12:53	15♓59	180
	12	14:34	4♉57	225
	16	17:21	23♊57	270
	20	11:33	12♌37	315
	23	19:56	0♎54	0
	27	1:25	19♏04	45
	30	11:13	7♑25	90
Oct 1976	4	4:41	26♒05	135
	8	4:56	15♈02	180
	12	8:40	4♊09	225
	16	8:59	23♋07	270
	19	23:18	11♍42	315
	23	5:10	29♎55	0
	26	10:12	18♐08	45
	29	22:06	6♒37	90
Nov 1976	2	19:51	25♓31	135
	6	23:15	14♉41	180
	11	1:59	3♋49	225
	14	22:40	22♌42	270
	18	10:08	11♎12	315
	21	15:11	29♏27	0
	24	21:30	17♑45	45
	28	13:00	6♓26	90
Dec 1976	2	14:39	25♈34	135
	6	18:15	14♊46	180
	10	17:23	3♌48	225
	14	10:15	22♍34	270
	17	20:11	11♏02	315
	21	2:09	29♐21	0
	24	11:40	17♒48	45
	28	7:48	6♈43	90
Jan 1977	1	11:33	25♉57	135
	5	12:11	15♋03	180
	9	6:24	3♍53	225
	12	19:56	22♎31	270
	16	5:34	10♐59	315
	19	14:12	29♑24	0
	23	4:41	18♓04	45
	27	5:12	7♉10	90
	31	8:13	26♊21	135
Feb 1977	4	3:57	15♌14	180
	7	17:13	3♎50	225
	11	4:08	22♏19	270
	14	14:41	10♑48	315
	18	3:38	29♒22	0
	21	23:46	18♈15	45
	26	2:51	7♊24	90
Mar 1977	2	2:45	26♋25	135
	5	17:14	15♍01	180
	9	2:17	3♏24	225
	12	11:35	21♐47	270
	16	0:22	10♒18	315
	19	18:33	29♓02	0
	23	19:24	18♉03	45
	27	22:27	7♋08	90
	31	18:11	25♌55	135
Apr 1977	4	4:10	14♎17	180
	7	10:11	2♐29	225
	10	19:15	20♑48	270
	14	11:26	9♓24	315
	18	10:36	28♈17	0
	22	13:47	17♊19	45
	26	14:43	6♌15	90
	30	6:24	24♍48	135
May 1977	3	13:04	12♏58	180
	6	17:39	1♑04	225
	10	4:09	19♒23	270
	14	0:24	8♈06	315
	18	2:52	27♉03	0
	22	5:39	16♋01	45
	26	3:21	4♍46	90
	29	15:41	23♎09	135
Jun 1977	1	20:32	11♐13	180
	5	1:33	29♑17	225
	8	15:08	17♓42	270
	12	15:08	6♉31	315
	16	18:23	25♊28	0
	20	18:37	14♌18	45
	24	12:45	2♎53	90
	27	22:42	21♏08	135
Jul 1977	1	3:25	9♑11	180
	4	10:54	27♒21	225
	8	4:40	15♈54	270
	12	7:03	4♊49	315
	16	8:37	23♋42	0
	20	4:59	12♍22	45
	23	19:39	0♏49	90
	27	4:25	19♐02	135
	30	10:53	7♒09	180
Aug 1977	2	22:38	25♓30	225
	6	20:41	14♉15	270
	10	23:27	3♋12	315
	14	21:32	21♌58	0
	18	13:26	10♎29	45
	22	1:05	28♏50	90
	25	10:04	17♑05	135
	28	20:11	5♓24	180
Sep 1977	1	13:14	23♈59	225
	5	14:34	12♊55	270
	9	15:47	1♌51	315
	13	9:24	20♍29	0
	16	20:48	8♏52	45
	20	6:19	27♐11	90
	23	17:08	15♒33	135
	27	8:18	4♈07	180
Oct 1977	1	6:30	22♉58	225
	5	9:22	12♋01	270
	9	7:39	0♍54	315
	12	20:31	19♎24	0
	16	4:03	7♐41	45
	19	12:47	26♑01	90
	23	3:00	14♓36	135
	26	23:36	3♉27	180
	31	1:31	22♊31	225
Nov 1977	4	3:59	11♌37	270
	7	22:35	0♎25	315
	11	7:10	18♏47	0
	14	12:10	7♑01	45
	17	21:53	25♒27	90
	21	16:29	14♈15	135
	25	17:32	3♊21	180
	29	20:53	22♋32	225
Dec 1977	3	21:17	11♍36	270
	7	12:01	0♏16	315
	10	17:33	18♐34	0
	13	22:05	6♒48	45
	17	10:38	25♓23	90
	21	9:32	14♉25	135
	25	12:50	3♋37	180
	29	15:07	22♌48	225
Jan 1978	2	12:08	11♎45	270
	5	23:33	0♐17	315
	9	4:01	18♑32	0
	12	10:28	6♓52	45
	16	3:04	25♈38	90
	20	5:02	14♊47	135
	24	7:56	3♌59	180
	28	6:58	23♍00	225
	31	23:52	11♏46	270
Feb 1978	4	9:10	0♑12	315
	7	14:55	18♒29	0
	11	1:20	6♈58	45
	14	22:11	25♉52	90
	19	1:17	15♋02	135
	23	1:27	4♍04	180
	26	19:41	22♎51	225
Mar 1978	2	8:35	11♐24	270
	5	17:30	29♑47	315
	9	2:37	18♓10	0
	12	18:04	6♉48	45
	16	18:22	25♊48	90
	20	20:36	14♌53	135
	24	16:21	3♎40	180
	28	5:17	22♏10	225
	31	15:12	10♑33	270
Apr 1978	4	1:30	28♒56	315
	7	15:16	17♈27	0
	11	11:39	6♊14	45
	15	13:56	25♋14	90
	19	13:39	14♍08	135
	23	4:12	2♏39	180
	26	12:30	20♐55	225
	29	21:03	9♒11	270
May 1978	3	10:08	27♓37	315
	7	4:48	16♉17	0
	11	5:04	5♋09	45
	15	7:40	24♌07	90
	19	3:39	12♎49	135
	22	13:17	1♐05	180
	25	18:32	19♑11	225
	29	3:31	7♓25	270
Jun 1978	1	20:10	25♈58	315
	5	19:02	14♊45	0
	9	21:35	3♌41	45
	13	22:45	22♍33	90
	17	14:30	11♏02	135
	20	20:31	29♐08	180
	24	0:46	17♒10	225
	27	11:45	5♈28	270
Jul 1978	1	8:05	24♉08	315
	5	9:51	13♋01	0
	9	12:39	1♍57	45
	13	10:50	20♎41	90
	16	22:47	9♐02	135
	20	3:06	27♑04	180
	23	8:25	15♓08	225
	26	22:32	3♉34	270
	30	22:06	22♊22	315
Aug 1978	4	1:02	11♌19	0
	8	1:52	0♎11	45
	11	20:07	18♏47	90
	15	5:31	7♑03	135
	18	10:15	25♒07	180
	21	18:25	13♈20	225
	25	12:18	1♊57	270
	29	14:13	20♋53	315
Sep 1978	2	16:10	9♍50	0
	6	13:02	28♎35	45
	10	3:21	17♐05	90
	13	11:54	5♒20	135
	16	19:02	23♓33	180
	20	7:21	11♉59	225
	24	5:08	0♋48	270
	28	8:00	19♌51	315
Oct 1978	2	6:41	8♎43	0
	5	22:26	27♏19	45

The 8 Phases of the Moon 1900–2020

Month	Day	Time	Position	Phase
	9	9:39	15♑45	90
	12	19:08	4♓06	135
	16	6:10	22♈32	180
	19	23:21	11♊13	225
	24	0:35	0♌15	270
	28	2:26	19♍19	315
	31	20:07	8♏03	0
Nov 1978	4	6:49	26♐30	45
	7	16:19	14♒54	90
	11	4:13	3♈25	135
	14	20:01	22♉06	180
	18	18:06	11♋03	225
	22	21:25	0♍13	270
	26	20:10	19♎13	315
	30	8:20	7♐46	0
Dec 1978	3	15:13	26♑06	45
	7	0:35	14♓33	90
	10	15:49	3♉14	135
	14	12:31	22♊10	180
	18	14:35	11♌19	225
	22	17:42	0♎31	270
	26	11:57	19♏21	315
	29	19:37	7♑44	0
Jan 1979	2	0:37	26♒01	45
	5	11:16	14♈31	90
	9	6:14	3♊23	135
	13	7:09	22♋30	180
	17	11:00	11♍44	225
	21	11:24	0♏49	270
	25	1:10	19♐28	315
	28	6:20	7♒44	0
	31	11:32	26♓00	45
Feb 1979	4	0:37	14♉36	90
	7	23:16	3♋35	135
	12	2:40	22♌47	180
	16	5:12	11♎56	225
	20	1:18	0♐48	270
	23	11:53	19♑16	315
	26	16:46	7♓29	0
Mar 1979	1	23:57	25♈48	45
	5	16:24	14♊30	90
	9	18:03	3♌34	135
	13	21:15	22♍42	180
	17	19:44	11♏37	225
	21	11:23	0♑15	270
	24	20:32	18♒36	315
	28	3:00	6♈51	0
	31	13:35	25♉15	45
Apr 1979	4	9:58	14♋03	90
	8	13:10	3♍07	135
	12	13:16	22♎02	180
	16	6:24	10♐41	225
	19	18:31	29♑06	270
	23	3:49	17♓24	315
	26	13:16	5♉43	0
	30	4:18	24♊14	45
May 1979	4	4:26	13♌08	90
	8	6:56	2♎06	135
	12	2:02	20♏46	180
	15	14:03	9♑09	225
	18	23:58	27♒26	270
	22	10:37	15♈45	315
	26	0:01	4♊10	0
	29	20:00	22♋51	45
Jun 1979	2	22:38	11♍47	90
	6	22:13	0♏36	135
	10	11:56	19♐01	180
	13	20:01	7♒12	225
	17	5:02	25♓26	270
	20	17:59	13♉48	315
	24	11:59	2♋23	0
	28	12:24	21♌13	45
Jul 1979	2	15:24	10♎09	90
	6	10:47	28♏47	135
	9	20:00	17♑01	180
	13	1:41	5♓06	225
	16	11:00	23♈19	270
	20	3:05	11♊50	315
	24	1:41	0♌36	0
	28	4:52	19♍32	45
Aug 1979	1	5:58	8♏25	90
	4	21:08	26♐53	135
	8	3:22	15♒00	180
	11	8:12	3♈05	225
	14	19:03	21♉23	270
	18	14:55	10♋04	315
	22	17:11	29♌01	0
	26	20:27	18♎00	45
	30	18:10	6♐46	90
Sep 1979	3	6:03	25♑09	135
	6	10:59	13♓16	180
	9	16:33	1♉24	225
	13	6:16	19♊52	270
	17	6:05	8♌46	315
	21	9:47	27♍49	0
	25	10:26	16♏46	45
	29	4:21	5♑26	90
Oct 1979	2	14:18	23♒48	135
	5	19:36	11♈58	180
	9	3:34	0♊15	225
	12	21:25	18♋57	270
	17	0:14	8♍02	315
	21	2:24	27♎06	0
	24	22:37	15♐55	45
	28	13:07	4♒31	90
	31	22:31	22♓54	135
Nov 1979	4	5:48	11♉13	180
	7	17:54	29♊43	225
	11	16:25	18♌41	270
	15	20:02	7♎51	315
	19	18:04	26♏48	0
	23	9:19	15♑29	45
	26	21:09	4♓01	90
	30	7:13	22♈29	135
Dec 1979	3	18:09	10♊59	180
	7	11:42	29♋46	225
	11	14:00	18♍55	270
	15	15:40	8♏04	315
	19	8:24	26♐50	0
	22	19:07	15♒20	45
	26	5:12	3♈49	90
	29	17:08	22♉23	135
Jan 1980	2	9:03	11♋07	180
	6	8:08	0♍09	225
	10	11:50	19♎23	270
	14	9:37	8♐22	315
	17	21:20	26♑55	0
	21	4:35	15♓17	45
	24	13:59	3♉44	90
	28	4:59	22♊25	135
Feb 1980	1	2:22	11♌22	180
	5	5:12	0♎33	225
	9	7:36	19♏42	270
	13	1:00	8♑28	315
	16	8:52	26♒50	0
	19	14:04	15♈05	45
	23	0:15	3♊32	90
	26	19:15	22♋21	135
Mar 1980	1	21:00	11♍26	180
	6	0:35	0♏36	225
	9	23:50	19♐34	270
	13	13:26	8♒07	315
	16	18:57	26♓21	0
	19	23:52	14♉32	45
	23	12:32	3♋02	90
	27	11:39	21♌58	135
	31	15:15	11♎03	180
Apr 1980	4	16:42	0♐04	225
	8	12:07	18♑48	270
	11	22:57	7♓12	315
	15	3:47	25♈20	0
	18	10:28	13♊32	45
	22	3:00	2♌08	90
	26	5:06	21♍07	135
	30	7:36	10♏06	180
May 1980	4	5:10	28♐53	225
	7	20:51	17♒25	270
	11	6:04	5♈42	315
	14	12:01	23♉50	0
	17	22:23	12♋08	45
	21	19:17	0♍52	90
	25	22:18	19♎50	135
	29	21:28	8♐38	180
Jun 1980	2	14:29	27♑11	225
	6	2:54	15♓33	270
	9	11:46	3♉46	315
	12	20:39	22♊00	0
	16	12:02	10♌29	45
	20	12:33	29♍19	90
	24	14:19	18♏12	135
	28	9:03	6♑48	180
Jul 1980	1	21:32	25♒10	225
	5	7:28	13♈25	270
	8	17:26	1♊40	315
	12	6:47	20♋04	0
	16	3:23	8♍45	45
	20	5:51	27♎40	90
	24	4:51	16♐26	135
	27	18:54	4♒52	180
	31	3:26	23♓04	225
Aug 1980	3	12:01	11♉17	270
	7	0:36	29♊39	315
	10	19:10	18♌17	0
	14	19:59	7♎09	45
	18	22:29	26♏06	90
	22	17:56	14♑46	135
	26	3:43	3♓03	180
	29	9:19	21♈11	225
Sep 1980	1	18:08	9♊26	270
	5	10:36	28♋00	315
	9	10:01	16♍52	0
	13	13:02	5♏53	45
	17	13:55	24♐49	90
	21	5:42	13♒24	135
	24	12:09	1♈35	180
	27	16:29	19♉42	225
Oct 1980	1	3:19	8♋06	270
	5	0:12	26♌55	315
	9	2:50	15♎58	0
	13	5:41	5♐03	45
	17	3:48	23♑56	90
	20	16:16	12♓26	135
	23	20:53	0♉36	180
	27	2:04	18♊49	225
	30	16:34	7♌25	270
Nov 1980	3	17:20	26♍27	315
	7	20:43	15♏36	0
	11	21:13	4♑39	45
	15	15:48	23♒27	90
	19	1:49	11♈54	135
	22	6:40	0♊07	180
	25	14:59	18♋30	225
	29	9:59	7♍21	270
Dec 1980	3	13:00	26♎32	315
	7	14:36	15♐40	0
	11	11:03	4♒34	45
	15	1:48	23♓15	90
	18	10:47	11♉41	135
	21	18:09	0♋03	180
	25	7:20	18♌40	225
	29	6:33	7♎42	270
Jan 1981	2	9:37	26♏55	315
	6	7:25	15♑54	0
	9	22:48	4♓37	45
	13	10:11	23♈09	90
	16	19:54	11♊37	135
	20	7:40	0♌10	180
	24	2:17	19♍01	225
	28	4:20	8♏10	270
Feb 1981	1	5:26	27♐16	315
	4	22:15	16♒02	0
	8	8:34	4♈30	45
	11	17:50	22♉56	90
	15	5:58	11♋28	135
	18	22:59	0♍13	180
	22	22:16	19♎13	225
	27	1:15	8♐22	270
Mar 1981	2	22:56	27♑17	315
	6	10:32	15♓46	0
	9	16:57	4♉02	45
	13	1:51	22♊24	90
	16	17:32	11♌03	135
	20	15:23	29♍56	180
	24	17:35	18♏59	225
	28	19:35	8♑02	270
Apr 1981	1	13:02	26♒43	315
	4	20:20	14♈58	0
	8	0:50	3♊06	45
	11	11:11	21♋29	90
	15	6:43	10♍13	135
	19	8:00	29♎10	180
	23	10:56	18♐12	225
	27	10:15	7♒04	270
	30	23:34	25♓31	315
May 1981	4	4:20	13♉37	0
	7	9:09	1♋43	45
	10	22:23	20♌09	90
	14	21:18	8♎58	135
	19	0:04	27♏56	180
	23	1:31	16♑50	225
	26	21:01	5♓30	270
	30	7:09	23♈47	315
Jun 1981	2	11:33	11♊50	0
	5	18:43	0♌00	45
	9	11:34	18♍32	90
	13	12:54	7♏25	135
	17	15:05	26♐19	180
	21	13:05	15♒03	225
	25	4:26	3♈31	270
	28	12:57	21♉43	315
Jul 1981	1	19:04	9♋50	0
	5	6:03	28♌08	45
	9	2:40	16♎48	90
	13	5:05	5♐43	135
	17	4:40	24♑31	180
	20	21:53	13♓04	225
	24	9:41	1♉24	270
	27	18:21	19♊36	315
	31	3:53	7♌51	0
Aug 1981	3	19:29	26♍21	45
	7	19:27	15♏11	90
	11	21:22	4♑06	135
	15	16:37	22♒45	180
	19	4:47	11♈07	225
	22	14:16	29♉23	270
	26	0:45	17♋42	315
	29	14:44	6♍10	0
Sep 1981	2	11:05	24♎53	45
	6	13:26	13♐51	90
	10	13:06	2♒44	135
	14	3:10	21♓13	180
	17	11:03	9♉28	225
	20	19:48	27♊45	270
	24	9:20	16♌14	315
	28	4:08	4♎57	0
Oct 1981	2	4:40	23♏54	45
	6	7:46	12♑58	90
	10	3:40	1♓45	135
	13	12:50	20♈06	180
	16	18:05	8♊17	225

The 8 Phases of the Moon 1900–2020

	20	3:41	26♋40	270
	23	20:57	15♍22	315
	27	20:14	4♏19	0
	31	23:29	23♐27	45
Nov 1981	5	1:10	12♒32	90
	8	16:40	1♈12	135
	11	22:27	19♉27	180
	15	3:06	7♋40	225
	18	14:55	26♌11	270
	22	12:04	15♎06	315
	26	14:39	4♐16	0
	30	18:09	23♑28	45
Dec 1981	4	16:23	12♓27	90
	8	4:09	0♉59	135
	11	8:42	19♊14	180
	14	14:45	7♌32	225
	18	5:48	26♍13	270
	22	6:27	15♏19	315
	26	10:11	4♑33	0
	30	10:57	23♒40	45
Jan 1982	3	4:46	12♈29	90
	6	14:22	0♊57	135
	9	19:54	19♋14	180
	13	5:00	7♍41	225
	16	23:59	26♎32	270
	21	3:00	15♐44	315
	25	4:57	4♒54	0
	29	0:44	23♓47	45
Feb 1982	1	14:29	12♉25	90
	4	23:42	0♋51	135
	8	7:58	19♌14	180
	11	21:22	7♎50	225
	15	20:22	26♏50	270
	19	23:43	16♑00	315
	23	21:14	4♓56	0
	27	11:24	23♈33	45
Mar 1982	2	22:16	12♊00	90
	6	8:37	0♌27	135
	9	20:46	18♍57	180
	13	15:07	7♏43	225
	17	17:16	26♐47	270
	21	18:27	15♒48	315
	25	10:18	4♈26	0
	28	19:44	22♉48	45
Apr 1982	1	5:09	11♋09	90
	4	17:39	29♌37	135
	8	10:19	18♎15	180
	12	9:25	7♐09	225
	16	12:43	26♑12	270
	20	9:51	14♓59	315
	23	20:30	3♉21	0
	27	2:49	21♊32	45
	30	12:08	9♌49	90
May 1982	4	3:29	28♍21	135
	8	0:46	17♏07	180
	12	3:13	6♑05	225
	16	5:12	25♒01	270
	19	21:44	13♈34	315
	23	4:41	1♊44	0
	26	9:41	19♋49	45
	29	20:07	8♍07	90
Jun 1982	2	14:53	26♎44	135
	6	16:00	15♐37	180
	10	19:21	4♒34	225
	14	18:07	23♓21	270
	18	6:46	11♉43	315
	21	11:53	29♊47	0
	24	17:11	17♌51	45
	28	5:57	6♎13	90
Jul 1982	2	4:20	24♏58	135
	6	7:32	13♑55	180
	10	9:01	2♓47	225
	14	3:48	21♈23	270
	17	13:56	9♊39	315
	20	18:58	27♋43	0
	24	2:07	15♍52	45
	27	18:23	4♏23	90
	31	19:55	23♐16	135
Aug 1982	4	22:35	12♒12	180
	8	20:06	0♈56	225
	12	11:09	19♉25	270
	15	20:17	7♋40	315
	19	2:46	25♌48	0
	22	13:18	14♎07	45
	26	9:50	2♐50	90
	30	13:00	21♑50	135
Sep 1982	3	12:29	10♓41	180
	7	5:08	29♈15	225
	10	17:20	17♊40	270
	14	2:45	5♌58	315
	17	12:10	24♍16	0
	21	3:28	12♏50	45
	25	4:08	1♑46	90
	29	6:32	20♒47	135
Oct 1982	3	1:09	9♈30	180
	6	13:10	27♉57	225
	9	23:27	16♋20	270
	13	10:22	4♍45	315
	17	0:05	23♎18	0
	20	20:51	12♐08	45
	25	0:09	1♒15	90
	28	23:31	20♓13	135
Nov 1982	1	12:57	8♉46	180
	4	21:14	27♊07	225
	8	6:39	15♌32	270
	11	20:11	4♎06	315
	15	15:11	22♏56	0
	19	16:44	12♑02	45
	23	20:06	1♓13	90
	27	15:15	20♈03	135
Dec 1982	1	0:22	8♊28	180
	4	6:09	26♋45	225
	7	15:54	15♍13	270
	11	9:10	4♏00	315
	15	9:19	23♐04	0
	19	13:16	12♒19	45
	23	14:17	1♈26	90
	27	5:21	20♉07	135
	30	11:33	8♋27	180
Jan 1983	2	16:26	26♌42	225
	6	4:01	15♎15	270
	10	1:38	4♐14	315
	14	5:09	23♑27	0
	18	8:15	12♓40	45
	22	5:34	1♉37	90
	25	17:29	20♊11	135
	28	22:27	8♌26	180
Feb 1983	1	4:17	26♍44	225
	4	19:18	15♏24	270
	8	20:46	4♑31	315
	13	0:33	23♒44	0
	17	0:10	12♈45	45
	20	17:33	1♊31	90
	24	3:30	19♋57	135
	27	8:59	8♍12	180
Mar 1983	2	17:49	26♎35	225
	6	13:17	15♐24	270
	10	16:44	4♒32	315
	14	17:44	23♓35	0
	18	12:38	12♉21	45
	22	2:26	0♋54	90
	25	11:39	19♌15	135
	28	19:28	7♎33	180
Apr 1983	1	9:00	26♏04	225
	5	8:39	15♑00	270
	9	11:31	4♓03	315
	13	7:59	22♈50	0
	16	22:02	11♊21	45
	20	8:59	29♋43	90
	23	18:44	18♍03	135
	27	6:32	6♏26	180
May 1983	1	1:28	25♐07	225
	5	3:44	14♒06	270
	9	3:55	2♈58	315
	12	19:26	21♉30	0
	16	5:12	9♋47	45
	19	14:18	28♌03	90
	23	2:00	16♎24	135
	26	18:49	4♐57	180
	30	18:27	23♑46	225
Jun 1983	3	21:08	12♓43	270
	7	17:38	1♉24	315
	11	4:38	19♊43	0
	14	11:09	7♌50	45
	17	19:47	26♍03	90
	21	10:44	14♏30	135
	25	8:33	3♑14	180
	29	10:58	22♒09	225
Jul 1983	3	12:13	11♈00	270
	7	4:53	29♉32	315
	10	12:19	17♋41	0
	13	17:00	5♍44	45
	17	2:51	23♎59	90
	20	21:55	12♐36	135
	24	23:28	1♒29	180
	29	2:17	20♓25	225
Aug 1983	2	0:53	9♉11	270
	5	14:09	27♊35	315
	8	19:19	15♌40	0
	12	0:01	3♎44	45
	15	12:48	22♏08	90
	19	11:55	10♑56	135
	23	15:00	29♒55	180
	27	16:03	18♈49	225
	31	11:23	7♊29	270
Sep 1983	3	22:01	25♋49	315
	7	2:36	13♍55	0
	10	9:27	2♏07	45
	14	2:25	20♐43	90
	18	4:27	9♒42	135
	22	6:37	28♓42	180
	26	4:16	17♉31	225
	29	20:06	6♋06	270
Oct 1983	3	5:13	24♌26	315
	6	11:17	12♎38	0
	9	22:15	1♐03	45
	13	19:43	19♑54	90
	17	22:45	8♓59	135
	21	21:54	27♈56	180
	25	15:06	16♊38	225
	29	3:38	5♌08	270
Nov 1983	1	12:45	23♍31	315
	4	22:22	11♏56	0
	8	14:43	0♑37	45
	12	15:50	19♒41	90
	16	17:47	8♈48	135
	20	12:30	27♉37	180
	24	0:50	16♋10	225
	27	10:51	4♍37	270
	30	21:42	23♎07	315
Dec 1983	4	12:27	11♐47	0
	8	10:09	0♒45	45
	12	13:10	19♓56	90
	16	12:20	8♉58	135
	20	2:01	27♊36	180
	23	9:59	16♌00	225
	26	18:53	4♎26	270
	30	9:03	23♏05	315
Jan 1984	3	5:17	12♑00	0
	7	6:55	1♓09	45
	11	9:49	20♈21	90
	15	5:08	9♊14	135
	18	14:06	27♋40	180
	21	19:10	15♍56	225
	25	4:49	4♏24	270
	28	23:08	23♐13	315
Feb 1984	1	23:47	12♒19	0
	6	3:08	1♈31	45
	10	4:00	20♉36	90
	13	19:07	9♋16	135
	17	0:42	27♌32	180
	20	5:04	15♎45	225
	23	17:13	4♐17	270
	27	15:32	23♑14	315
Mar 1984	2	18:32	12♓22	0
	6	21:06	1♉29	45
	10	18:28	20♊23	90
	14	5:54	8♌51	135
	17	10:11	27♍01	180
	20	16:12	15♏14	225
	24	7:59	3♑52	270
	28	9:12	22♒53	315
Apr 1984	1	12:10	11♈57	0
	5	11:46	0♊53	45
	9	4:52	19♋32	90
	12	13:56	7♍50	135
	15	19:12	26♎00	180
	19	4:45	14♐19	225
	23	0:27	3♒02	270
	27	3:02	22♓02	315
May 1984	1	3:46	10♉57	0
	4	22:47	29♊38	45
	8	11:51	18♌04	90
	11	20:18	6♎18	135
	15	4:30	24♏32	180
	18	18:38	12♑59	225
	22	17:46	1♓48	270
	26	20:03	20♈44	315
	30	16:49	9♊26	0
Jun 1984	3	6:39	27♋52	45
	6	16:43	16♍08	90
	10	2:18	4♏23	135
	13	14:43	22♐45	180
	17	9:36	11♒22	225
	21	11:11	0♈15	270
	25	11:32	19♉04	315
	29	3:19	7♋34	0
Jul 1984	2	12:29	25♌47	45
	5	21:05	13♎59	90
	9	9:13	2♐20	135
	13	2:21	20♑52	180
	17	1:26	9♓39	225
	21	4:02	28♈34	270
	25	1:05	17♊16	315
	28	11:52	5♌34	0
	31	17:45	23♍40	45
Aug 1984	4	2:34	11♏54	90
	7	18:09	0♑24	135
	11	15:44	19♒08	180
	15	17:48	8♈03	225
	19	19:41	26♉59	270
	23	12:37	15♋33	315
	26	19:26	3♍43	0
	29	23:56	21♎48	45
Sep 1984	2	10:31	10♐08	90
	6	5:54	28♑49	135
	10	7:02	17♓45	180
	14	10:13	6♉46	225
	18	9:32	25♊38	270
	21	22:29	14♌06	315
	25	3:12	2♎14	0
	28	8:22	20♏23	45
Oct 1984	1	21:53	8♑53	90
	5	20:54	27♒47	135
	9	23:59	16♈52	180
	14	1:47	5♊54	225
	17	21:15	24♋40	270
	21	7:22	13♍04	315
	24	12:09	1♏16	0

The 8 Phases of the Moon 1900–2020

	27	19:51	19♐34	45
	31	13:08	8♒18	90
Nov 1984	4	15:02	27♓23	135
	8	17:44	16♉30	180
	12	15:42	5♋26	225
	16	7:00	24♌06	270
	19	16:02	12♎31	315
	22	22:58	0♐50	0
	26	10:37	19♑22	45
	30	8:01	8♓18	90
Dec 1984	4	11:20	27♈30	135
	8	10:54	16♊32	180
	12	3:31	5♌18	225
	15	15:26	23♍51	270
	19	1:10	12♏19	315
	22	11:48	0♑49	0
	26	4:19	19♒35	45
	30	5:28	8♈43	90
Jan 1985	3	7:56	27♉53	135
	7	2:17	16♋44	180
	10	13:33	5♍16	225
	13	23:28	23♎44	270
	17	11:16	12♐18	315
	21	2:29	1♒00	0
	25	0:04	19♓58	45
	29	3:30	9♉11	90
Feb 1985	2	2:42	28♊12	135
	5	15:20	16♌47	180
	8	22:35	5♎07	225
	12	7:58	23♏33	270
	15	22:41	12♑12	315
	19	18:44	1♓05	0
	23	20:29	20♈11	45
	27	23:42	9♊20	90
Mar 1985	3	18:13	28♋07	135
	7	2:14	16♍27	180
	10	7:23	4♏40	225
	13	17:35	23♐05	270
	17	11:40	11♒50	315
	21	12:00	0♈49	0
	25	15:42	19♉56	45
	29	16:12	8♋55	90
Apr 1985	2	6:12	27♌27	135
	5	11:33	15♎38	180
	8	16:31	3♐47	225
	12	4:42	22♑13	270
	16	2:20	11♓03	315
	20	5:23	0♉05	0
	24	8:05	19♊05	45
	28	4:26	7♌50	90
May 1985	1	15:10	26♍11	135
	4	19:54	14♏17	180
	8	2:20	2♑27	225
	11	17:35	20♒57	270
	15	18:23	9♈51	315
	19	21:42	28♉50	0
	23	20:49	17♋39	45
	27	12:57	6♍11	90
	30	22:03	24♎25	135
Jun 1985	3	3:51	12♐31	180
	6	13:14	0♒46	225
	10	8:20	19♓24	270
	14	11:08	8♉20	315
	18	11:59	27♊11	0
	22	6:11	15♌46	45
	25	18:54	4♎08	90
	29	3:51	22♏21	135
Jul 1985	2	12:09	10♑33	180
	6	1:43	28♒57	225
	10	0:50	17♈43	270
	14	3:37	6♊39	315
	17	23:57	25♋19	0
	21	13:14	13♍43	45
	24	23:40	1♏59	90
	28	9:42	20♐15	135
	31	21:42	8♒36	180
Aug 1985	4	16:17	27♓13	225
	8	18:30	16♉08	270
	12	18:58	5♋00	315
	16	10:06	23♌29	0
	19	19:20	11♎44	45
	23	4:37	0♐00	90
	26	16:47	18♑23	135
	30	9:28	6♓57	180
Sep 1985	3	9:00	25♈48	225
	7	12:17	14♊49	270
	11	8:53	3♌34	315
	14	19:21	21♍55	0
	18	1:47	10♏06	45
	21	11:04	28♐24	90
	25	2:24	16♒58	135
	29	0:09	5♈48	180
Oct 1985	3	3:08	24♉51	225
	7	5:05	13♋53	270
	10	21:29	2♍31	315
	14	4:34	20♎47	0
	17	9:39	8♐58	45
	20	20:14	27♑23	90
	24	15:37	16♓10	135
	28	17:38	5♉15	180
Nov 1985	1	21:20	24♊24	225
	5	20:07	13♌21	270
	9	9:02	1♎54	315
	12	14:21	20♏09	0
	15	19:43	8♑24	45
	19	9:04	26♒59	90
	23	8:46	16♈00	135
	27	12:43	5♊13	180
Dec 1985	1	14:05	24♋20	225
	5	9:02	13♍10	270
	8	19:41	1♏40	315
	12	0:55	19♐56	0
	15	8:26	8♒19	45
	19	1:59	27♓06	90
	23	4:55	16♉18	135
	27	7:31	5♋29	180
	31	4:30	24♌26	225
Jan 1986	3	19:48	13♎09	270
	7	5:27	1♐37	315
	10	12:23	19♑58	0
	13	23:58	8♓31	45
	17	22:14	27♈31	90
	22	1:59	16♊45	135
	26	0:32	5♌45	180
	29	16:28	24♍28	225
Feb 1986	2	4:42	13♏02	270
	5	14:33	1♑30	315
	9	0:56	19♒59	0
	12	17:58	8♈44	45
	16	19:56	27♉51	90
	20	21:44	16♋58	135
	24	15:03	5♍43	180
	28	2:17	24♎12	225
Mar 1986	3	12:18	12♐37	270
	6	23:39	1♒06	315
	10	14:53	19♓44	0
	14	13:20	8♉40	45
	18	16:39	27♊47	90
	22	14:42	16♌41	135
	26	3:03	5♎10	180
	29	10:33	23♏26	225
Apr 1986	1	19:31	11♑46	270
	5	9:38	0♓19	315
	9	6:09	19♈06	0
	13	8:20	8♊07	45
	17	10:36	27♋08	90
	21	4:27	15♍47	135
	24	12:47	4♏03	180
	27	17:56	22♐10	225
May 1986	1	3:23	10♒28	270
	4	21:18	29♓06	315
	8	22:11	18♉01	0
	13	1:27	7♋01	45
	17	1:01	25♌51	90
	20	15:06	14♎18	135
	23	20:46	2♐25	180
	27	1:16	20♑28	225
	30	12:55	8♓49	270
Jun 1986	3	10:54	27♈34	315
	7	14:01	16♊32	0
	11	15:53	5♌26	45
	15	12:01	24♍06	90
	18	23:10	12♏24	135
	22	3:43	0♑27	180
	25	9:34	18♒32	225
	29	0:54	7♈00	270
Jul 1986	3	2:09	25♉52	315
	7	4:56	14♋48	0
	11	3:35	3♍34	45
	14	20:11	22♎05	90
	18	5:27	10♐19	135
	21	10:41	28♑23	180
	24	19:52	16♓37	225
	28	15:35	5♉16	270
Aug 1986	1	18:24	24♊12	315
	5	18:37	13♌02	0
	9	13:05	1♎39	45
	13	2:22	20♏04	90
	16	11:03	8♑17	135
	19	18:55	26♒29	180
	23	8:58	14♈56	225
	27	8:39	3♊47	270
	31	10:59	22♋45	315
Sep 1986	4	7:11	11♍28	0
	7	21:06	29♎56	45
	11	7:42	18♐17	90
	14	17:19	6♒36	135
	18	5:35	25♓01	180
	22	1:02	13♉44	225
	26	3:18	2♋45	270
	30	3:24	21♌41	315
Oct 1986	3	18:56	10♎16	0
	7	4:30	28♏37	45
	10	13:29	16♑57	90
	14	1:42	5♓25	135
	17	19:23	24♈07	180
	21	19:30	13♊06	225
	25	22:26	2♌12	270
	29	19:11	21♍04	315
Nov 1986	2	6:03	9♏31	0
	5	12:13	27♐47	45
	8	21:12	16♒10	90
	12	13:22	4♈52	135
	16	12:12	23♉50	180
	20	15:05	13♋00	225
	24	16:51	2♍07	270
	28	9:43	20♎51	315
Dec 1986	1	16:43	9♐12	0
	4	21:13	27♑26	45
	8	8:02	15♓56	90
	12	4:42	4♉51	135
	16	7:05	24♊01	180
	20	10:16	13♌14	225
	24	9:18	2♎16	270
	27	22:25	20♏52	315
	31	3:11	9♑08	0
Jan 1987	3	8:17	27♒25	45
	6	22:35	16♈05	90
	10	23:06	5♊10	135
	15	2:31	24♋24	180
	19	3:36	13♍31	225
	22	22:46	2♏23	270
	26	9:00	20♐52	315
	29	13:46	9♒07	0
Feb 1987	1	21:48	27♓30	45
	5	16:22	16♉20	90
	9	19:04	5♋30	135
	13	20:59	24♌37	180
	17	17:59	13♎32	225
	21	8:57	2♐11	270
	24	17:49	20♑35	315
	28	0:52	8♓54	0
Mar 1987	3	13:29	27♈26	45
	7	11:59	16♊23	90
	11	14:54	5♌30	135
	15	13:14	24♍25	180
	19	5:03	13♏04	225
	22	16:23	1♑31	270
	26	1:41	19♒52	315
	29	12:47	8♈18	0
Apr 1987	2	6:29	26♉59	45
	6	7:49	15♋59	90
	10	9:05	4♍58	135
	14	2:32	23♎38	180
	17	13:13	12♐00	225
	20	22:16	0♒18	270
	24	9:39	18♓41	315
	28	1:35	7♉15	0
May 1987	1	23:50	26♊04	45
	6	2:27	15♌03	90
	10	0:36	3♎51	135
	13	12:51	22♏14	180
	16	19:33	10♑24	225
	20	4:03	28♒38	270
	23	18:38	17♈06	315
	27	15:14	5♊49	0
	31	16:43	24♋42	45
Jun 1987	4	18:54	13♍38	90
	8	13:00	2♏13	135
	11	20:50	20♐24	180
	15	1:22	8♒27	225
	18	11:03	26♓42	270
	22	5:20	15♉17	315
	26	5:38	4♋07	0
	30	8:34	23♌03	45
Jul 1987	4	8:35	11♎52	90
	7	22:33	0♐16	135
	11	3:34	18♑20	180
	14	8:03	6♓22	225
	17	20:18	24♈43	270
	21	18:07	13♊27	315
	25	20:38	2♌22	0
	29	22:53	21♍17	45
Aug 1987	2	19:25	9♏58	90
	6	6:04	28♐16	135
	9	10:18	16♒19	180
	12	16:42	4♈26	225
	16	8:26	22♉57	270
	20	9:11	11♋50	315
	24	12:00	0♍48	0
	28	11:19	19♎38	45
Sep 1987	1	3:49	8♐12	90
	4	12:38	26♑27	135
	7	18:14	14♓35	180
	11	4:07	2♉54	225
	14	23:45	21♊37	270
	19	2:21	10♌37	315
	23	3:09	29♍34	0
	26	21:51	18♏16	45
	30	10:40	6♑44	90
Oct 1987	3	19:29	25♒03	135
	7	4:13	13♈22	180
	10	18:39	1♊55	225
	14	18:07	20♋51	270
	18	20:51	9♍56	315
	22	17:29	28♎46	0
	26	6:53	17♐19	45
	29	17:11	5♒45	90
Nov 1987	2	3:39	24♓11	135
	5	16:47	12♉44	180

The 8 Phases of the Moon 1900–2020

	9	12:12	1♋33	225
	13	14:39	20♌41	270
	17	15:24	9♎44	315
	21	6:34	28♏24	0
	24	15:21	16♑48	45
	28	0:38	5♓14	90
Dec 1987	1	13:59	23♈50	135
	5	8:02	12♊38	180
	9	8:07	1♌42	225
	13	11:42	20♍55	270
	17	8:31	9♏51	315
	20	18:26	28♐20	0
	24	0:14	16♒38	45
	27	10:02	5♈06	90
	31	2:56	23♉53	135
Jan 1988	4	1:41	12♋54	180
	8	4:54	2♍07	225
	12	7:05	21♎17	270
	15	23:11	10♐01	315
	19	5:27	28♑21	0
	22	10:19	16♓36	45
	25	21:54	5♉09	90
	29	18:33	24♊04	135
Feb 1988	2	20:52	13♌14	180
	7	0:30	2♎26	225
	10	23:02	21♏26	270
	14	11:08	9♑58	315
	17	15:55	28♒12	0
	20	21:49	16♈29	45
	24	12:16	5♊07	90
	28	12:22	24♋08	135
Mar 1988	3	16:02	13♍18	180
	7	16:59	2♏21	225
	11	10:57	21♐05	270
	14	20:39	9♒29	315
	18	2:03	27♓42	0
	21	10:35	16♉02	45
	25	4:42	4♋45	90
	29	7:16	23♌49	135
Apr 1988	2	9:22	12♎51	180
	6	5:29	1♐38	225
	9	19:22	20♑09	270
	13	4:23	8♓28	315
	16	12:01	26♈43	0
	20	0:27	15♊09	45
	23	22:33	3♌58	90
	28	1:42	23♍00	135
May 1988	1	23:42	11♏48	180
	5	14:26	0♑18	225
	9	1:24	18♒39	270
	12	11:08	6♈56	315
	15	22:11	25♉16	0
	19	15:23	13♋51	45
	23	16:50	2♍46	90
	27	18:15	21♎39	135
	31	10:54	10♐12	180
Jun 1988	3	21:01	28♑28	225
	7	6:22	16♓43	270
	10	17:54	5♉03	315
	14	9:15	23♊32	0
	18	7:19	12♌16	45
	22	10:24	1♎13	90
	26	8:12	19♏56	135
	29	19:47	8♑15	180
Jul 1988	3	2:38	26♒23	225
	6	11:37	14♈36	270
	10	1:50	3♊02	315
	13	21:54	21♋41	0
	17	23:50	10♍35	45
	22	2:15	29♎30	90
	25	19:43	18♐03	135
	29	3:26	6♒14	180
Aug 1988	1	8:34	24♓18	225
	4	18:23	12♉34	270
	8	12:05	1♋09	315

	12	12:32	20♌00	0
	16	16:08	9♎00	45
	20	15:52	27♏50	90
	24	5:28	16♑16	135
	27	10:57	4♓23	180
	30	15:54	22♈29	225
Sep 1988	3	3:51	10♊52	270
	7	1:33	29♋39	315
	11	4:50	18♍40	0
	15	7:16	7♏40	45
	19	3:19	26♐24	90
	22	14:14	14♒47	135
	25	19:08	2♈55	180
	29	1:32	21♉08	225
Oct 1988	2	16:59	9♋43	270
	6	18:25	28♌43	315
	10	21:50	17♎48	0
	14	20:40	6♐43	45
	18	13:02	25♑22	90
	21	22:38	13♓45	135
	25	4:37	1♉59	180
	28	14:13	20♊23	225
Nov 1988	1	10:12	9♌13	270
	5	13:46	28♍22	315
	9	14:21	17♏24	0
	13	8:21	6♑11	45
	16	21:36	24♒46	90
	20	7:10	13♈11	135
	23	15:54	1♊35	180
	27	6:22	20♋14	225
Dec 1988	1	6:50	9♍18	270
	5	9:55	28♎29	315
	9	5:37	17♐22	0
	12	18:44	5♒59	45
	16	5:41	24♓30	90
	19	16:26	13♉00	135
	23	5:30	1♋37	180
	27	1:41	20♌31	225
	31	4:58	9♎44	270
Jan 1989	4	5:01	28♏49	315
	7	19:23	17♑29	0
	11	4:23	5♓56	45
	14	13:59	24♈24	90
	18	3:09	13♊00	135
	21	21:34	1♌50	180
	25	22:40	20♍57	225
	30	2:03	10♏10	270
Feb 1989	2	21:49	29♐03	315
	6	7:38	17♒30	0
	9	13:45	5♈48	45
	12	23:16	24♉14	90
	16	15:58	12♋58	135
	20	15:33	1♍59	180
	24	19:04	21♎09	225
	28	20:09	10♐13	270
Mar 1989	4	11:43	28♑53	315
	7	18:20	17♓10	0
	10	23:08	5♉22	45
	14	10:12	23♊49	90
	18	7:04	12♌40	135
	22	9:59	1♎45	180
	26	12:51	20♏50	225
	30	10:22	9♑42	270
Apr 1989	2	22:35	28♒09	315
	6	3:34	16♈19	0
	9	9:00	4♊29	45
	12	23:14	23♋01	90
	16	23:50	11♍57	135
	21	3:14	1♏00	180
	25	3:05	19♐53	225
	28	20:47	8♒32	270
May 1989	2	6:43	26♓50	315
	5	11:47	14♉57	0
	8	19:53	3♋11	45
	12	14:20	21♌50	90

	16	17:05	10♎48	135
	20	18:17	29♏42	180
	24	13:52	18♑22	225
	28	4:02	6♓49	270
	31	12:53	25♈02	315
Jun 1989	3	19:54	13♊12	0
	7	8:22	1♌34	45
	11	7:00	20♍20	90
	15	9:41	9♏16	135
	19	6:58	27♐59	180
	22	21:58	16♒26	225
	26	9:10	4♈44	270
	29	18:19	22♉58	315
Jul 1989	3	5:00	11♋15	0
	6	22:44	29♌49	45
	11	0:20	18♎42	90
	15	1:01	7♐32	135
	18	17:43	26♑04	180
	22	4:22	14♓21	225
	25	13:32	2♉35	270
	29	0:29	20♊53	315
Aug 1989	1	16:07	9♌22	0
	5	14:47	28♍09	45
	9	17:29	17♏06	90
	13	15:00	5♑50	135
	17	3:08	24♒12	180
	20	10:12	12♈22	225
	23	18:41	0♊36	270
	27	8:53	19♋04	315
	31	5:45	7♍48	0
Sep 1989	4	7:50	26♎46	45
	8	9:50	15♐44	90
	12	3:41	4♒22	135
	15	11:51	22♓37	180
	18	16:40	10♉44	225
	22	2:11	29♊03	270
	25	20:39	17♌45	315
	29	21:48	6♎43	0
Oct 1989	4	1:03	25♏47	45
	8	0:53	14♑44	90
	11	15:09	3♓17	135
	14	20:33	21♈28	180
	18	0:59	9♊38	225
	21	13:20	28♋07	270
	25	12:09	17♍03	315
	29	15:28	6♏11	0
Nov 1989	2	17:33	25♐17	45
	6	14:12	14♒09	90
	10	1:27	2♈38	135
	13	5:52	20♉50	180
	16	12:13	9♋07	225
	20	4:45	27♌50	270
	24	6:48	16♎58	315
	28	9:42	6♐08	0
Dec 1989	2	8:35	25♑09	45
	6	1:27	13♓54	90
	9	10:48	2♉21	135
	12	16:31	20♊38	180
	16	2:53	9♌08	225
	19	23:55	28♍04	270
	24	3:14	17♏17	315
	28	3:21	6♑22	0
	31	21:35	25♒12	45
Jan 1990	4	10:41	13♈49	90
	7	19:47	2♊16	135
	11	4:58	20♋42	180
	14	20:37	9♍26	225
	18	21:18	28♎32	270
	22	23:42	17♐42	315
	26	19:21	6♒35	0
	30	8:21	25♓11	45
Feb 1990	2	18:33	13♉40	90
	6	5:10	2♋09	135
	9	19:17	20♌47	180

	13	16:08	9♎42	225
	17	18:49	28♏51	270
	21	18:31	17♑52	315
	25	8:55	6♓30	0
	28	17:15	24♈51	45
Mar 1990	4	2:06	13♊14	90
	7	15:42	1♌49	135
	11	10:59	20♍37	180
	15	11:47	9♏38	225
	19	14:31	28♐43	270
	23	10:20	17♒31	315
	26	19:49	5♈53	0
	30	1:05	24♉04	45
Apr 1990	2	10:25	12♋25	90
	6	3:47	1♍05	135
	10	3:19	20♎00	180
	14	6:05	9♐02	225
	18	7:03	27♑59	270
	21	22:34	16♓33	315
	25	4:28	4♉43	0
	28	8:50	22♊49	45
May 1990	1	20:19	11♌11	90
	5	17:23	29♍57	135
	9	19:32	18♏54	180
	13	22:04	7♑52	225
	17	19:46	26♒38	270
	21	7:28	15♈00	315
	24	11:48	3♊03	0
	27	17:27	21♋10	45
	31	8:12	9♍38	90
Jun 1990	4	8:17	28♎28	135
	8	11:02	17♐24	180
	12	11:11	6♒14	225
	16	4:49	24♓48	270
	19	14:00	13♉02	315
	22	18:56	1♋05	0
	26	3:38	19♌18	45
	29	22:08	7♎54	90
Jul 1990	4	0:07	26♏47	135
	8	1:24	15♑39	180
	11	21:25	4♓18	225
	15	11:05	22♈43	270
	18	19:27	10♊54	315
	22	2:55	29♋04	0
	25	15:53	17♍27	45
	29	14:02	6♏12	90
Aug 1990	2	16:29	25♐07	135
	6	14:20	13♒52	180
	10	5:18	2♈20	225
	13	15:55	20♉38	270
	17	1:15	8♋54	315
	20	12:40	27♌15	0
	24	6:23	15♎51	45
	28	7:35	4♐45	90
Sep 1990	1	8:46	23♑40	135
	5	1:47	12♓15	180
	8	11:54	0♉35	225
	11	20:54	18♊51	270
	15	8:40	7♌15	315
	19	0:47	25♍50	0
	22	23:07	14♏41	45
	27	2:07	3♑43	90
Oct 1990	1	0:17	22♒34	135
	4	12:03	11♈00	180
	7	18:33	29♉14	225
	11	3:32	17♋34	270
	14	18:43	6♍10	315
	18	15:38	25♎00	0
	22	17:39	14♐04	45
	26	20:27	3♒10	90
	30	14:24	21♓54	135
Nov 1990	2	21:49	10♉13	180
	6	2:34	28♊25	225
	9	13:03	16♌52	270
	13	8:06	5♎41	315

The 8 Phases of the Moon 1900–2020

	17	9:06	24♏45	0
	21	12:51	13♑57	45
	25	13:12	3♓00	90
	29	2:53	21♈37	135
Dec 1990	2	7:51	9♊52	180
	5	12:54	28♋07	225
	9	2:05	16♍44	270
	13	0:55	5♏45	315
	17	4:23	24♐58	0
	21	7:01	14♒09	45
	25	3:17	3♈04	90
	28	13:50	21♉34	135
	31	18:36	9♋50	180
Jan 1991	4	1:51	28♌11	225
	7	18:36	16♎58	270
	11	20:32	6♐07	315
	15	23:51	25♑20	0
	19	22:32	14♓21	45
	23	14:22	3♉05	90
	26	23:35	21♊31	135
	30	6:11	9♌51	180
Feb 1991	2	17:05	28♍21	225
	6	13:53	17♏16	270
	10	17:21	6♑28	315
	14	17:33	25♒31	0
	18	10:44	14♈16	45
	21	22:59	2♊49	90
	25	8:33	21♋14	135
	28	18:26	9♍40	180
Mar 1991	4	9:59	28♎19	225
	8	10:33	17♐21	270
	12	13:13	6♒27	315
	16	8:11	25♓14	0
	19	20:03	13♉43	45
	23	6:04	2♋07	90
	26	17:13	20♌33	135
	30	7:18	9♎05	180
Apr 1991	3	3:50	27♏54	225
	7	6:46	16♑57	270
	11	6:16	5♓52	315
	14	19:39	24♈21	0
	18	3:28	12♊37	45
	21	12:40	0♌55	90
	25	2:17	19♍24	135
	28	20:59	8♏04	180
May 1991	2	21:48	26♐59	225
	7	0:47	15♒59	270
	10	19:49	4♈39	315
	14	4:37	22♉54	0
	17	10:08	11♋01	45
	20	19:47	29♌18	90
	24	12:32	17♎51	135
	28	11:38	6♐39	180
Jun 1991	1	14:49	25♑37	225
	5	15:31	14♓29	270
	9	6:11	2♉56	315
	12	12:07	21♊02	0
	15	17:03	9♌06	45
	19	4:20	27♍25	90
	23	0:40	16♏05	135
	27	2:59	5♑00	180
Jul 1991	1	5:50	23♒55	225
	5	2:51	12♈37	270
	8	14:14	0♊56	315
	11	19:07	18♋59	0
	15	1:02	7♍05	45
	18	15:12	25♎30	90
	22	15:06	14♐19	135
	26	18:25	3♒16	180
	30	18:21	22♓05	225
Aug 1991	3	11:26	10♉38	270
	6	21:00	28♊54	315
	10	2:29	17♌00	0
	13	10:56	5♎13	45
	17	5:02	23♏49	90
	21	7:34	12♑46	135
	25	9:08	1♓41	180
	29	4:34	20♈22	225
Sep 1991	1	18:17	8♊49	270
	5	3:26	27♋05	315
	8	11:02	15♍18	0
	11	23:32	3♏44	45
	15	22:02	22♐34	90
	20	1:13	11♒36	135
	23	22:41	0♈24	180
	27	13:14	18♉56	225
Oct 1991	1	0:31	7♋21	270
	4	10:29	25♌42	315
	7	21:40	14♎07	0
	11	15:24	2♐49	45
	15	17:34	21♑52	90
	19	18:53	10♓53	135
	23	11:09	29♈33	180
	26	21:23	17♊58	225
	30	7:12	6♌22	270
Nov 1991	2	19:09	24♍52	315
	6	11:12	13♏32	0
	10	10:21	2♑31	45
	14	14:03	21♒42	90
	18	11:36	10♈38	135
	21	22:57	29♉08	180
	25	5:58	17♋27	225
	28	15:22	5♍53	270
Dec 1991	2	6:29	24♎34	315
	6	3:57	13♐31	0
	10	6:59	2♒43	45
	14	9:33	21♓53	90
	18	2:47	10♉40	135
	21	10:24	29♊03	180
	24	15:34	17♌19	225
	28	1:56	5♎49	270
	31	21:10	24♏41	315
Jan 1992	4	23:11	13♑51	0
	9	3:07	3♓06	45
	13	2:33	22♈09	90
	16	16:03	10♊47	135
	19	21:29	29♋04	180
	23	2:32	17♍20	225
	26	15:28	5♏56	270
	30	14:59	24♐58	315
Feb 1992	3	19:01	14♒12	0
	7	20:45	3♈20	45
	11	16:16	22♉12	90
	15	3:08	10♋41	135
	18	8:05	28♌55	180
	21	15:00	17♎14	225
	25	7:57	5♐58	270
	29	10:35	25♑06	315
Mar 1992	4	13:23	14♓14	0
	8	10:56	3♉08	45
	12	2:37	21♊47	90
	15	12:02	10♌10	135
	18	18:19	28♍24	180
	22	5:04	16♏50	225
	26	2:31	5♑41	270
	30	5:58	24♒47	315
Apr 1992	3	5:02	13♈42	0
	6	21:43	2♊20	45
	10	10:07	20♋47	90
	13	19:20	9♍07	135
	17	4:43	27♎26	180
	20	20:39	16♐00	225
	24	21:41	4♒57	270
	28	23:31	23♓55	315
May 1992	2	17:45	12♉34	0
	6	5:48	0♋57	45
	9	15:44	19♌15	90
	13	2:08	7♎34	135
	16	16:04	26♏01	180
	20	13:14	14♑46	225
	24	15:54	3♓43	270
	28	14:30	22♈30	315
Jun 1992	1	3:58	10♊55	0
	4	12:08	29♋07	45
	7	20:48	17♍20	90
	11	9:46	5♏43	135
	15	4:51	24♐20	180
	19	5:58	13♒12	225
	23	8:12	2♈06	270
	27	3:00	20♉43	315
	30	12:19	8♋57	0
Jul 1992	3	17:48	27♌01	45
	7	2:44	15♎14	90
	10	19:27	3♐46	135
	14	19:07	22♑34	180
	18	22:00	11♓30	225
	22	22:13	0♉19	270
	26	13:21	18♊47	315
	29	19:36	6♌54	0
Aug 1992	2	0:02	24♍57	45
	5	11:00	13♏16	90
	9	7:56	1♑59	135
	13	10:28	20♒55	180
	17	12:46	9♈51	225
	21	10:02	28♉35	270
	24	22:03	16♋58	315
	28	2:43	5♍03	0
	31	8:06	23♎10	45
Sep 1992	3	22:40	11♐40	90
	7	23:18	0♒34	135
	12	2:18	19♓34	180
	16	2:03	8♉28	225
	19	19:54	27♊07	270
	23	5:42	15♌27	315
	26	10:41	3♎36	0
	29	19:10	21♏53	45
Oct 1992	3	14:13	10♑37	90
	7	16:59	29♒41	135
	11	18:04	18♈40	180
	15	13:52	7♊28	225
	19	4:13	26♋02	270
	22	13:09	14♍23	315
	25	20:35	2♏41	0
	29	9:54	21♐14	45
Nov 1992	2	9:12	10♒12	90
	6	12:01	29♓20	135
	10	9:21	18♉14	180
	14	0:23	6♋53	225
	17	11:40	25♌23	270
	20	21:23	13♎49	315
	24	9:12	2♐21	0
	28	4:04	21♑11	45
Dec 1992	2	6:18	10♓20	90
	6	7:12	29♈26	135
	9	23:42	18♊10	180
	13	9:56	6♌39	225
	16	19:14	25♍06	270
	20	7:27	13♏40	315
	24	0:44	2♑28	0
	28	0:26	21♒32	45
Jan 1993	1	3:39	10♈44	90
	5	1:12	29♉43	135
	8	12:38	18♋15	180
	11	19:02	6♍35	225
	15	4:02	25♎01	270
	18	20:03	13♐45	315
	22	18:28	2♒46	0
	26	21:09	21♓57	45
	30	23:21	11♉06	90
Feb 1993	3	16:45	29♊53	135
	6	23:56	18♌13	180
	10	4:23	6♎27	225
	13	14:58	24♏55	270
	17	11:09	13♑48	315
	21	13:06	2♓55	0
	25	16:22	22♈05	45
Mar 1993	1	15:48	11♊05	90
	5	5:06	29♋38	135
	8	9:47	17♍50	180
	11	14:37	6♏02	225
	15	4:18	24♐36	270
	19	4:01	13♒34	315
	23	7:15	2♈40	0
	27	8:43	21♉42	45
	31	4:11	10♋28	90
Apr 1993	3	14:18	28♌50	135
	6	18:44	16♎58	180
	10	2:09	5♐13	225
	13	19:40	23♑53	270
	17	21:37	12♓52	315
	21	23:50	1♉52	0
	25	21:31	20♊41	45
	29	12:41	9♌12	90
May 1993	2	21:14	27♍28	135
	6	3:35	15♏38	180
	9	15:05	3♑59	225
	13	12:21	22♒45	270
	17	14:58	11♈42	315
	21	14:07	0♊31	0
	25	6:50	19♋05	45
	28	18:22	7♍25	90
Jun 1993	1	3:07	25♎39	135
	4	13:03	13♐55	180
	8	5:17	2♒26	225
	12	5:37	21♓16	270
	16	7:15	10♉09	315
	20	1:53	28♊46	0
	23	13:32	17♌05	45
	26	22:44	5♎19	90
	30	9:19	23♏36	135
Jul 1993	3	23:46	12♑02	180
	7	20:35	0♓43	225
	11	22:50	19♈37	270
	15	21:54	8♊24	315
	19	11:25	26♋48	0
	22	18:55	14♍58	45
	26	3:26	3♏10	90
	29	17:02	21♐35	135
Aug 1993	2	12:11	10♒12	180
	6	12:46	29♓04	225
	10	15:20	18♉00	270
	14	10:38	6♋39	315
	17	19:29	24♌53	0
	21	0:31	12♎59	45
	24	9:58	1♐15	90
	28	3:15	19♑50	135
Sep 1993	1	2:34	8♓41	180
	5	5:27	27♈40	225
	9	6:27	16♊35	270
	12	21:33	5♌07	315
	16	3:11	23♍16	0
	19	7:46	11♏23	45
	22	19:33	29♐48	90
	26	16:38	18♒36	135
	30	18:55	7♈37	180
Oct 1993	4	21:52	26♉41	225
	8	19:36	15♋32	270
	12	7:07	3♍58	315
	15	11:37	22♎08	0
	18	17:44	10♐22	45
	22	8:53	28♑58	90
	26	9:22	17♓59	135
	30	12:39	7♉06	180
Nov 1993	3	13:02	26♊08	225
	7	6:37	14♌52	270
	10	16:03	3♎17	315
	13	21:35	21♏32	0
	17	6:55	9♑57	45
	21	2:04	28♒47	90
	25	4:53	17♈56	135

The 8 Phases of the Moon 1900–2020

	29	6:32	7♊03	180
Dec 1993	3	2:11	25♋55	225
	6	15:50	14♍33	270
	10	1:01	2♏59	315
	13	9:28	21♐23	0
	16	23:14	10♒02	45
	20	22:27	29♓04	90
	25	1:43	18♉17	135
	28	23:06	7♋15	180
Jan 1994	1	13:12	25♌54	225
	5	0:02	14♎25	270
	8	10:35	2♐55	315
	11	23:11	21♑31	0
	15	18:01	10♓22	45
	19	20:28	29♈33	90
	23	21:42	18♊40	135
	27	13:24	7♌23	180
	30	22:38	25♍49	225
Feb 1994	3	8:07	14♏16	270
	6	21:08	2♑51	315
	10	14:31	21♒38	0
	14	14:09	10♈39	45
	18	17:48	29♉51	90
	22	14:56	18♋46	135
	26	1:16	7♍13	180
Mar 1994	1	7:20	25♎29	225
	4	16:54	13♐53	270
	8	9:03	2♒34	315
	12	7:06	21♓29	0
	16	10:03	10♉35	45
	20	12:15	29♊40	90
	24	4:36	18♌19	135
	27	11:11	6♎33	180
	30	16:02	24♏43	225
Apr 1994	3	2:56	13♑08	270
	6	22:32	1♓53	315
	11	0:18	20♈53	0
	15	3:54	9♊58	45
	19	2:35	28♋49	90
	22	14:55	17♍15	135
	25	19:46	5♏22	180
	29	1:11	23♐30	225
May 1994	2	14:33	11♒57	270
	6	13:38	0♈48	315
	10	17:08	19♉48	0
	14	18:28	8♋43	45
	18	12:51	27♌21	90
	21	22:40	15♎38	135
	25	3:40	3♐43	180
	28	11:13	21♑54	225
Jun 1994	1	4:03	10♓27	270
	5	5:56	29♈21	315
	9	8:27	18♊17	0
	13	5:28	6♌59	45
	16	19:57	25♍26	90
	20	4:50	13♏39	135
	23	11:34	1♑47	180
	26	22:38	20♒05	225
	30	19:32	8♈46	270
Jul 1994	4	22:37	27♉42	315
	8	21:38	16♋29	0
	12	13:37	4♍59	45
	16	1:13	23♎18	90
	19	10:31	11♐32	135
	22	20:17	29♑47	180
	26	12:00	18♓16	225
	30	12:41	7♉07	270
Aug 1994	3	14:43	26♊02	315
	7	8:46	14♌38	0
	10	20:09	2♎58	45
	14	5:58	21♏14	90
	17	16:50	9♑33	135
	21	6:48	28♒00	180
	25	3:41	16♈43	225
	29	6:42	5♊42	270
Sep 1994	2	5:36	24♋32	315
	5	18:34	12♍58	0
	9	2:25	1♏12	45
	12	11:35	19♐29	90
	16	1:03	7♒57	135
	19	20:02	26♓39	180
	23	21:24	15♉37	225
	28	0:24	4♋39	270
Oct 1994	1	19:08	23♌22	315
	5	3:56	11♎41	0
	8	9:36	29♏53	45
	11	19:18	18♑15	90
	15	12:25	6♓55	135
	19	12:19	25♈53	180
	23	16:02	15♊01	225
	27	16:45	4♌02	270
	31	7:30	22♍39	315
Nov 1994	3	13:36	10♏54	0
	6	18:36	29♐07	45
	10	6:15	17♒37	90
	14	3:40	6♈32	135
	18	6:58	25♉42	180
	22	9:58	14♋52	225
	26	7:05	3♍47	270
	29	18:51	22♎19	315
Dec 1994	2	23:55	10♐35	0
	6	6:00	28♑53	45
	9	21:07	17♓34	90
	13	22:33	6♉42	135
	18	2:18	25♊55	180
	22	1:51	14♌59	225
	25	19:07	3♎46	270
	29	5:10	22♏15	315
Jan 1995	1	10:57	10♑33	0
	4	20:04	29♒00	45
	8	15:47	17♈54	90
	12	19:27	7♊08	135
	16	20:27	26♋15	180
	20	15:10	15♍05	225
	24	4:59	3♏44	270
	27	14:33	22♐11	315
	30	22:49	10♒35	0
Feb 1995	3	12:46	29♓13	45
	7	12:55	18♉17	90
	11	16:03	7♋28	135
	15	12:16	26♌21	180
	19	2:00	14♎57	225
	22	13:05	3♐26	270
	25	23:24	21♑53	315
Mar 1995	1	11:49	10♓26	0
	5	7:23	29♈15	45
	9	10:15	18♊23	90
	13	10:27	7♌23	135
	17	1:27	25♍59	180
	20	10:51	14♏22	225
	23	20:11	2♑44	270
	27	8:34	21♒13	315
	31	2:10	9♈54	0
Apr 1995	4	2:33	28♉52	45
	8	5:36	17♋56	90
	12	1:44	6♍42	135
	15	12:09	25♎04	180
	18	18:24	13♐15	225
	22	3:19	1♒33	270
	25	19:00	20♓06	315
	29	17:37	8♉56	0
May 1995	3	20:35	27♊57	45
	7	21:45	16♌52	90
	11	13:51	5♎25	135
	14	20:49	23♏35	180
	18	1:25	11♑40	225
	21	11:37	29♒58	270
	25	7:20	18♈38	315
	29	9:28	7♊34	0
Jun 1995	2	12:22	26♋31	45
	6	10:27	15♍16	90
	9	23:08	3♏39	135
	13	4:05	21♐42	180
	16	8:54	9♒46	225
	19	22:02	28♓09	270
	23	21:36	16♉57	315
	28	0:51	5♋54	0
Jul 1995	2	1:28	24♌44	45
	5	20:03	13♎20	90
	9	6:15	1♐36	135
	12	10:50	19♑38	180
	15	17:56	7♓47	225
	19	11:11	26♈20	270
	23	13:21	15♊14	315
	27	15:14	4♌08	0
	31	12:10	22♍50	45
Aug 1995	4	3:17	11♏18	90
	7	12:07	29♐32	135
	10	18:17	17♒39	180
	14	5:29	5♈59	225
	18	3:05	24♉43	270
	22	5:56	13♋41	315
	26	4:32	2♍29	0
	29	21:03	21♎03	45
Sep 1995	2	9:04	9♐26	90
	5	17:58	27♑42	135
	9	3:38	16♓00	180
	12	20:06	4♉35	225
	16	21:10	23♊31	270
	20	22:43	12♌30	315
	24	16:56	1♎10	0
	28	4:53	19♏36	45
Oct 1995	1	14:37	7♑57	90
	5	1:14	26♒20	135
	8	15:53	14♈54	180
	12	13:37	3♊45	225
	16	16:27	22♋50	270
	20	15:12	11♍45	315
	24	4:37	0♏18	0
	27	12:31	18♐37	45
	30	21:18	6♒59	90
Nov 1995	3	11:13	25♓33	135
	7	7:22	14♉24	180
	11	9:01	3♋29	225
	15	11:41	22♌38	270
	19	6:45	11♎27	315
	22	15:44	29♏52	0
	25	20:53	18♑07	45
	29	6:29	6♓33	90
Dec 1995	3	0:45	25♈22	135
	7	1:28	14♊27	180
	11	4:48	3♌39	225
	15	5:32	22♍45	270
	18	20:40	11♏27	315
	22	2:23	29♐45	0
	25	6:52	18♒00	45
	28	19:07	6♈34	90
Jan 1996	1	17:42	25♉35	135
	5	20:52	14♋48	180
	9	23:23	3♍59	225
	13	20:46	22♎57	270
	17	8:25	11♐30	315
	20	12:52	29♑45	0
	23	19:03	18♓04	45
	27	11:15	6♉48	90
	31	12:57	25♊56	135
Feb 1996	4	15:59	15♌07	180
	8	15:24	4♎09	225
	12	8:38	22♏55	270
	15	18:00	11♑20	315
	18	23:31	29♒36	0
	22	9:30	18♈03	45
	26	5:53	6♊55	90
Mar 1996	1	8:53	26♋04	135
	5	9:24	15♍06	180
	9	4:07	3♏52	225
	12	17:16	22♐25	270
	16	2:04	10♒46	315
	19	10:46	29♓07	0
	23	1:39	17♉43	45
	27	1:32	6♋40	90
	31	3:53	25♌43	135
Apr 1996	4	0:08	14♎31	180
	7	13:33	3♐01	225
	10	23:37	21♑22	270
	14	9:38	9♓43	315
	17	22:50	28♈12	0
	21	18:38	16♊56	45
	25	20:41	5♌55	90
	29	20:43	24♍48	135
May 1996	3	11:49	13♏19	180
	6	20:31	1♑35	225
	10	5:05	19♒49	270
	13	17:45	8♈14	315
	17	11:47	26♉51	0
	21	11:37	15♋41	45
	25	14:14	4♍38	90
	29	10:40	23♎20	135
Jun 1996	1	20:48	11♐37	180
	5	2:17	29♑42	225
	8	11:07	17♓56	270
	12	3:16	6♉26	315
	16	1:37	25♊12	0
	20	3:58	14♌06	45
	24	5:24	2♎59	90
	27	21:39	21♏29	135
Jul 1996	1	3:59	9♑36	180
	4	8:15	27♒38	225
	7	18:56	15♈55	270
	11	14:47	4♊34	315
	15	16:16	23♋26	0
	19	19:12	12♍22	45
	23	17:50	1♏08	90
	27	6:12	19♐29	135
	30	10:36	7♒32	180
Aug 1996	2	15:44	25♓36	225
	6	5:26	14♉02	270
	10	4:39	2♋50	315
	14	7:35	21♌47	0
	18	8:50	10♎41	45
	22	3:37	29♏20	90
	25	13:16	17♑36	135
	28	17:53	5♓41	180
Sep 1996	1	1:40	23♈54	225
	4	19:07	12♊31	270
	8	20:53	1♌28	315
	12	23:08	20♍27	0
	16	20:36	9♏15	45
	20	11:24	27♐46	90
	23	20:02	16♒04	135
	27	2:52	4♈17	180
	30	14:41	22♉42	225
Oct 1996	4	12:05	11♋32	270
	8	15:02	0♍36	315
	12	14:15	19♎32	0
	16	6:36	8♐11	45
	19	18:10	26♑38	90
	23	3:35	15♓01	135
	26	14:12	3♉26	180
	30	6:51	22♊08	225
Nov 1996	3	7:51	11♌10	270
	7	10:02	0♎16	315
	11	4:17	19♏03	0
	14	15:28	7♑33	45
	18	1:10	25♒59	90
	21	12:52	14♈30	135
	25	4:11	3♊10	180
	29	1:49	22♋07	225
Dec 1996	3	5:07	11♍19	270
	7	4:17	0♏20	315

The 8 Phases of the Moon 1900–2020

Month	Day	Time	Position	Phase
	10	16:57	18♐56	0
	14	0:09	7♒17	45
	17	9:32	25♓44	90
	21	0:27	14♉25	135
	24	20:42	3♋20	180
	28	22:29	22♌29	225
Jan 1997	2	1:46	11♎42	270
	5	20:26	0♐33	315
	9	4:27	18♑57	0
	12	9:35	7♓14	45
	15	20:03	25♈44	90
	19	14:37	14♊34	135
	23	15:12	3♌40	180
	27	18:59	22♍53	225
	31	19:41	11♏59	270
Feb 1997	4	9:48	0♑37	315
	7	15:07	18♒53	0
	10	20:14	7♈09	45
	14	8:59	25♉43	90
	18	7:12	14♋41	135
	22	10:28	3♍51	180
	26	13:12	22♎59	225
Mar 1997	2	9:39	11♐51	270
	5	20:25	0♒18	315
	9	1:16	18♓31	0
	12	8:09	6♉48	45
	16	0:07	25♊27	90
	20	1:28	14♌29	135
	24	4:46	3♎35	180
	28	3:40	22♏30	225
	31	19:39	11♑08	270
Apr 1997	4	4:50	29♒28	315
	7	11:03	17♈40	0
	10	21:09	6♊02	45
	14	17:01	24♋47	90
	18	20:05	13♍49	135
	22	20:35	2♏45	180
	26	14:14	21♐23	225
	30	2:38	9♒48	270
May 1997	3	11:48	28♓05	315
	6	20:48	16♉21	0
	10	11:14	4♋50	45
	14	10:56	23♌41	90
	18	13:34	12♎39	135
	22	9:14	1♐19	180
	25	21:47	19♑42	225
	29	7:52	7♓59	270
Jun 1997	1	18:15	26♈17	315
	5	7:05	14♊40	0
	9	2:27	3♌18	45
	13	4:53	22♍14	90
	17	4:51	11♏03	135
	20	19:10	29♐29	180
	24	3:40	17♒41	225
	27	12:43	5♈54	270
Jul 1997	1	1:18	24♉15	315
	4	18:41	12♋48	0
	8	18:39	1♍37	45
	12	21:45	20♎34	90
	16	17:39	9♐13	135
	20	3:21	27♑28	180
	23	9:17	15♓33	225
	26	18:29	3♉47	270
	30	10:08	22♊17	315
Aug 1997	3	8:15	11♌02	0
	7	11:16	29♍59	45
	11	12:43	18♏53	90
	15	4:24	7♑23	135
	18	10:56	25♒32	180
	21	15:49	13♈37	225
	25	2:25	1♊56	270
	28	21:52	20♋37	315
Sep 1997	1	23:53	9♍34	0
	6	3:20	28♎35	45
	10	1:32	17♐23	90
	13	13:49	5♒48	135
	16	18:52	23♓56	180
	20	0:15	12♉05	225
	23	13:36	0♋33	270
	27	13:07	19♌27	315
Oct 1997	1	16:53	8♎33	0
	5	17:58	27♏32	45
	9	12:23	16♑15	90
	12	22:35	4♓38	135
	16	3:47	22♈49	180
	19	11:23	11♊07	225
	23	4:49	29♋49	270
	27	7:32	18♍55	315
	31	10:02	8♏01	0
Nov 1997	4	6:48	26♐53	45
	7	21:44	15♒31	90
	11	7:12	3♈56	135
	14	14:13	22♉15	180
	18	1:50	10♋45	225
	21	23:59	29♌43	270
	26	3:43	18♎55	315
	30	2:15	7♐54	0
Dec 1997	3	18:02	26♑37	45
	7	6:10	15♓10	90
	10	16:08	3♉38	135
	14	2:38	22♊08	180
	17	19:41	10♌55	225
	21	21:44	0♎04	270
	25	23:42	19♏14	315
	29	16:58	8♑01	0
Jan 1998	2	4:07	26♒33	45
	5	14:19	15♈03	90
	9	2:00	3♊36	135
	12	17:25	22♋18	180
	16	16:02	11♍19	225
	20	19:41	0♏33	270
	24	17:51	19♐32	315
	28	6:02	8♒06	0
	31	13:33	26♓28	45
Feb 1998	3	22:54	14♉55	90
	7	13:31	3♋34	135
	11	10:24	22♌29	180
	15	12:56	11♎38	225
	19	15:28	0♐47	270
	23	9:15	19♑33	315
	26	17:27	7♓55	0
Mar 1998	1	22:44	26♈09	45
	5	8:42	14♊34	90
	9	3:14	3♌21	135
	13	4:35	22♍24	180
	17	8:08	11♏32	225
	21	7:39	0♑29	270
	24	21:35	19♒02	315
	28	3:15	7♈15	0
	31	8:04	25♉25	45
Apr 1998	3	20:19	13♋52	90
	7	18:58	2♍45	135
	11	22:25	21♎49	180
	16	0:07	10♐49	225
	19	19:54	29♑33	270
	23	6:56	17♓56	315
	26	11:42	6♉03	0
	29	18:04	24♊13	45
May 1998	3	10:05	12♌47	90
	7	11:50	1♎44	135
	11	14:30	20♏42	180
	15	12:32	9♑29	225
	19	4:36	28♒01	270
	22	13:53	16♈16	315
	25	19:33	4♊23	0
	29	5:24	22♋40	45
Jun 1998	2	1:46	11♍21	90
	6	4:43	0♏18	135
	10	4:19	19♐06	180
	13	21:54	7♒40	225
	17	10:39	26♓03	270
	20	19:26	14♉16	315
	24	3:51	2♋27	0
	27	18:36	20♌54	45
Jul 1998	1	18:44	9♎44	90
	5	20:43	28♏37	135
	9	16:02	17♑15	180
	13	5:05	5♓37	225
	16	15:14	23♈53	270
	20	0:59	12♊08	315
	23	13:45	0♌31	0
	27	9:47	19♍10	45
	31	12:06	8♏05	90
Aug 1998	4	11:31	26♐54	135
	8	2:11	15♒21	180
	11	11:09	3♈35	225
	14	19:50	21♉49	270
	18	8:04	10♋11	315
	22	2:04	28♌48	0
	26	2:30	17♎40	45
	30	5:08	6♐39	90
Sep 1998	3	1:05	25♑21	135
	6	11:22	13♓40	180
	9	17:14	1♉49	225
	13	1:59	20♊05	270
	16	18:03	8♌40	315
	20	17:03	27♍32	0
	24	19:57	16♏34	45
	28	21:12	5♑32	90
Oct 1998	2	13:28	24♒09	135
	5	20:13	12♈23	180
	9	0:35	0♊31	225
	12	11:12	18♋55	270
	16	7:44	7♍44	315
	20	10:10	26♎49	0
	24	13:13	15♐55	45
	28	11:47	4♒51	90
Nov 1998	1	0:38	23♓23	135
	4	5:19	11♉35	180
	7	10:20	29♊48	225
	11	0:29	18♌24	270
	15	1:00	7♎27	315
	19	4:28	26♏38	0
	23	5:22	15♑42	45
	27	0:24	4♓33	90
	30	10:37	23♈01	135
Dec 1998	3	15:20	11♊15	180
	6	23:18	29♋38	225
	10	17:55	18♍28	270
	14	20:49	7♏39	315
	18	22:43	26♐48	0
	22	19:40	15♒45	45
	26	10:47	4♈27	90
	29	19:48	22♉53	135
Jan 1999	2	2:51	11♋15	180
	5	15:32	29♌50	225
	9	14:23	18♎52	270
	13	17:31	8♐05	315
	17	15:47	27♑05	0
	21	7:40	15♓48	45
	24	19:16	4♉21	90
	28	4:50	22♊48	135
	31	16:08	11♌20	180
Feb 1999	4	10:12	0♎08	225
	8	11:59	19♏16	270
	12	13:21	8♑22	315
	16	6:40	27♒08	0
	19	17:24	15♈37	45
	23	2:44	4♊02	90
	26	14:32	22♋32	135
Mar 1999	2	7:00	11♍15	180
	6	5:47	0♏12	225
	10	8:41	19♐19	270
	14	6:44	8♒14	315
	17	18:49	26♓44	0
	21	1:30	14♉59	45
	24	10:19	3♋20	90
	28	1:31	21♌56	135
	31	22:50	10♎46	180
Apr 1999	5	0:43	29♏48	225
	9	2:52	18♑49	270
	12	20:44	7♓30	315
	16	4:23	25♈45	0
	19	8:57	13♊52	45
	22	19:03	2♌12	90
	26	14:03	20♍54	135
	30	14:56	9♏49	180
May 1999	4	17:51	28♐49	225
	8	17:30	17♒41	270
	12	7:10	6♈08	315
	15	12:06	24♉14	0
	18	16:47	12♋18	45
	22	5:35	0♍43	90
	26	4:03	19♎30	135
	30	6:41	8♐26	180
Jun 1999	3	8:25	27♑20	225
	7	4:21	16♓00	270
	10	14:44	4♉17	315
	13	19:04	22♊20	0
	17	1:53	10♌28	45
	20	18:14	28♍59	90
	24	19:16	17♏50	135
	28	21:39	6♑45	180
Jul 1999	2	20:09	25♒30	225
	6	11:58	13♈59	270
	9	20:34	2♊11	315
	13	2:25	20♋17	0
	16	12:53	8♍34	45
	20	9:01	27♎14	90
	24	11:24	16♐08	135
	28	11:26	4♒58	180
Aug 1999	1	5:16	23♓32	225
	4	17:28	11♉54	270
	8	2:05	0♋07	315
	11	11:10	18♌21	0
	15	2:11	6♎50	45
	19	1:48	25♏40	90
	23	3:57	14♑36	135
	26	23:49	3♓17	180
	30	12:34	21♈42	225
Sep 1999	2	22:18	10♊00	270
	6	8:36	28♋19	315
	9	22:03	16♍47	0
	13	17:53	5♏30	45
	17	20:07	24♐29	90
	21	20:13	13♒24	135
	25	10:52	1♈56	180
	28	19:12	20♉13	225
Oct 1999	2	4:03	8♋31	270
	5	17:17	27♌01	315
	9	11:35	15♎44	0
	13	11:46	4♐42	45
	17	15:01	23♑48	90
	21	11:25	12♓37	135
	24	21:03	1♉00	180
	28	2:32	19♊13	225
	31	12:05	7♌37	270
Nov 1999	4	5:00	26♍19	315
	8	3:54	15♏17	0
	12	7:04	4♑27	45
	16	9:04	23♒33	90
	20	1:02	12♈15	135
	23	7:05	0♊32	180
	26	11:44	18♋46	225
	29	23:20	7♍17	270
Dec 1999	3	20:09	26♎12	315
	7	22:33	15♐22	0
	12	2:13	4♒35	45
	16	0:51	23♓36	90
	19	12:55	12♉10	135

The 8 Phases of the Moon 1900–2020

	22	17:32	0♋25	180
	25	23:23	18♌43	225
	29	14:05	7♎24	270
Jan 2000	2	14:28	26♏30	315
	6	18:15	15♑44	0
	10	19:23	4♓51	45
	14	13:35	23♈41	90
	17	23:19	12♊09	135
	21	4:42	0♌26	180
	24	13:26	18♍51	225
	28	7:58	7♏42	270
Feb 2000	1	10:50	26♐53	315
	5	13:04	16♒02	0
	9	9:20	4♈56	45
	12	23:22	23♉33	90
	16	8:33	11♋58	135
	19	16:28	0♍20	180
	23	5:20	18♎54	225
	27	3:55	7♐51	270
Mar 2000	2	7:19	27♑01	315
	6	5:18	15♓57	0
	9	19:57	4♉33	45
	13	7:00	23♊01	90
	16	17:07	11♌25	135
	20	4:45	29♍53	180
	23	22:31	18♏36	225
	28	0:22	7♑38	270
Apr 2000	1	1:49	26♒39	315
	4	18:13	15♈16	0
	8	4:04	3♊38	45
	11	13:31	21♋58	90
	15	1:38	10♍24	135
	18	17:43	28♎59	180
	22	16:17	17♐50	225
	26	19:31	6♒51	270
	30	17:04	25♓39	315
May 2000	4	4:13	14♉00	0
	7	10:49	2♋11	45
	10	20:02	20♌27	90
	14	10:54	8♎57	135
	18	7:36	27♏40	180
	22	9:45	16♑36	225
	26	11:56	5♓32	270
	30	4:56	24♈05	315
Jun 2000	2	12:15	12♊15	0
	5	17:19	0♌20	45
	9	3:30	18♍37	90
	12	21:45	7♏12	135
	16	22:28	26♐03	180
	21	1:51	15♒00	225
	25	1:01	3♈47	270
	28	14:05	22♉10	315
Jul 2000	1	19:21	10♋14	0
	5	0:31	28♌18	45
	8	12:54	16♎39	90
	12	10:50	5♐23	135
	16	13:56	24♑19	180
	20	15:47	13♓13	225
	24	11:03	1♉51	270
	27	21:29	20♊07	315
	31	2:26	8♌12	0
Aug 2000	3	9:16	26♍20	45
	7	1:03	14♏50	90
	11	2:19	3♑44	135
	15	5:14	22♒41	180
	19	3:19	11♈27	225
	22	18:52	29♉58	270
	26	4:07	18♋14	315
	29	10:20	6♍23	0
Sep 2000	1	20:23	24♎41	45
	5	16:28	13♐24	90
	9	19:38	2♒25	135
	13	19:38	21♓18	180
	17	12:55	9♉56	225
	21	1:29	28♊22	270
	24	10:53	16♌41	315
	27	19:54	5♎00	0
Oct 2000	1	10:39	23♏33	45
	5	11:00	12♑30	90
	9	13:41	1♓34	135
	13	8:54	20♈19	180
	16	21:27	8♊49	225
	20	8:00	27♋14	270
	23	18:45	15♍40	315
	27	7:59	4♏12	0
	31	4:15	23♐03	45
Nov 2000	4	7:28	12♒11	90
	8	7:16	1♈11	135
	11	21:16	19♉47	180
	15	5:55	8♋10	225
	18	15:26	26♌36	270
	22	4:41	15♎11	315
	25	23:12	4♐00	0
	30	0:26	23♑06	45
Dec 2000	4	3:56	12♓18	90
	7	23:33	1♉11	135
	11	9:04	19♊38	180
	14	15:03	7♌56	225
	18	0:42	26♍24	270
	21	17:36	15♏10	315
	25	17:23	4♑14	0
	29	21:14	23♒29	45
Jan 2001	2	22:33	12♈37	90
	6	13:59	1♊19	135
	9	20:25	19♋39	180
	13	1:17	7♍55	225
	16	12:36	26♎27	270
	20	9:49	15♐24	315
	24	13:08	4♒37	0
	28	16:23	23♓49	45
Feb 2001	1	14:03	12♉47	90
	5	2:14	1♋20	135
	8	7:13	19♌35	180
	11	12:49	7♎52	225
	15	3:25	26♏30	270
	19	4:33	15♑35	315
	23	8:22	4♓47	0
	27	8:21	23♈48	45
Mar 2001	3	2:04	12♊33	90
	6	12:07	0♌59	135
	9	17:24	19♍12	180
	13	1:48	7♏33	225
	16	20:46	26♐19	270
	21	0:03	15♒26	315
	25	1:22	4♈28	0
	28	20:44	23♉14	45
Apr 2001	1	10:50	11♋46	90
	4	19:58	0♍06	135
	8	3:23	18♎22	180
	11	16:20	6♐50	225
	15	15:32	25♑43	270
	19	18:29	14♓45	315
	23	15:27	3♉32	0
	27	6:00	22♊03	45
	30	17:09	10♌25	90
May 2001	4	2:40	28♍42	135
	7	13:54	17♏04	180
	11	8:12	5♑42	225
	15	10:12	24♒38	270
	19	10:42	13♈31	315
	23	2:47	2♊03	0
	26	13:00	20♋20	45
	29	22:10	8♍35	90
Jun 2001	2	9:30	26♎55	135
	6	1:40	15♐26	180
	10	0:48	4♒13	225
	14	3:29	23♓09	270
	18	0:26	11♉51	315
	21	11:59	0♋10	0
	24	18:47	18♌18	45
	28	3:21	6♎31	90
Jul 2001	1	17:50	24♏57	135
	5	15:05	13♑39	180
	9	17:16	2♓33	225
	13	18:46	21♈25	270
	17	11:56	9♊58	315
	20	19:45	28♋08	0
	24	0:32	16♍12	45
	27	10:09	4♏27	90
	31	4:44	23♐03	135
Aug 2001	4	5:57	11♒56	180
	8	8:52	0♈53	225
	12	7:54	19♉41	270
	15	21:36	8♋06	315
	19	2:56	26♌12	0
	22	7:31	14♎17	45
	25	19:56	2♐40	90
	29	18:40	21♑29	135
Sep 2001	2	21:44	10♓28	180
	6	23:10	29♈25	225
	10	19:01	18♊08	270
	14	5:56	6♌29	315
	17	10:28	24♍36	0
	20	17:00	12♏48	45
	24	9:32	1♑24	90
	28	11:23	20♒24	135
Oct 2001	2	13:50	9♈26	180
	6	12:02	28♉18	225
	10	4:21	16♋56	270
	13	13:35	5♍17	315
	16	19:24	23♎30	0
	20	5:55	11♐55	45
	24	2:59	0♒46	90
	28	6:05	19♓53	135
Nov 2001	1	5:42	8♉52	180
	4	23:28	27♊37	225
	8	12:22	16♌10	270
	11	21:27	4♎33	315
	15	6:41	22♏58	0
	18	22:31	11♑39	45
	22	23:22	0♓44	90
	27	1:34	19♈52	135
	30	20:50	8♊43	180
Dec 2001	4	9:40	27♋18	225
	7	19:53	15♍47	270
	11	6:33	4♏17	315
	14	20:48	22♐56	0
	18	18:02	11♒53	45
	22	20:57	1♈05	90
	26	20:30	20♉08	135
	30	10:42	8♋48	180
Jan 2002	2	19:00	27♌12	225
	6	3:56	15♎39	270
	9	17:46	4♐17	315
	13	13:30	23♑11	0
	17	14:48	12♓19	45
	21	17:48	1♉31	90
	25	13:31	20♊24	135
	28	22:52	8♌51	180
Feb 2002	1	4:05	27♍07	225
	4	13:34	15♏33	270
	8	7:28	4♑21	315
	12	7:42	23♒25	0
	16	10:56	12♈35	45
	20	12:03	1♊40	90
	24	3:31	20♋21	135
	27	9:18	8♍36	180
Mar 2002	2	13:37	26♎47	225
	6	1:26	15♐17	270
	9	23:17	4♒12	315
	14	2:04	23♓19	0
	18	4:47	12♉25	45
	22	2:29	1♋17	90
	25	14:10	19♌45	135
	28	18:26	7♎54	180
Apr 2002	1	0:11	26♏06	225
	4	15:30	14♑41	270
	8	16:21	3♓39	315
	12	19:22	22♈42	0
	16	19:20	11♊37	45
	20	12:49	0♌16	90
	23	21:59	18♍34	135
	27	3:01	6♏41	180
	30	12:07	24♐58	225
May 2002	4	7:17	13♒39	270
	8	9:41	2♈37	315
	12	10:46	21♉32	0
	16	6:19	10♋13	45
	19	19:43	28♌39	90
	23	4:06	16♎52	135
	26	11:52	5♐04	180
	30	1:25	23♑29	225
Jun 2002	3	0:06	12♓16	270
	7	2:29	1♉11	315
	10	23:48	19♊54	0
	14	14:12	8♌21	45
	18	0:30	26♍37	90
	21	9:52	14♏52	135
	24	21:43	3♑11	180
	28	16:01	21♒47	225
Jul 2002	2	17:20	10♈39	270
	6	18:03	29♉29	315
	10	10:27	18♋00	0
	13	20:06	6♍15	45
	17	4:48	24♎27	90
	20	16:36	12♐47	135
	24	9:08	1♒18	180
	28	7:45	20♓04	225
Aug 2002	1	10:23	9♉00	270
	5	7:56	27♊44	315
	8	19:16	16♌04	0
	12	1:28	4♎11	45
	15	10:13	22♏25	90
	19	1:25	10♑55	135
	22	22:30	29♒39	180
	27	0:22	18♈35	225
	31	2:32	7♊32	270
Sep 2002	3	19:59	26♋08	315
	7	3:11	14♍20	0
	10	7:47	2♏26	45
	13	18:09	20♐47	90
	17	13:10	9♒28	135
	21	14:00	28♓25	180
	25	17:17	17♉28	225
	29	17:04	6♋23	270
Oct 2002	3	6:27	24♌53	315
	6	11:19	13♎02	0
	9	16:22	1♐12	45
	13	5:34	19♑43	90
	17	4:17	8♓37	135
	21	7:21	27♈43	180
	25	9:32	16♊48	225
	29	5:29	5♌37	270
Nov 2002	1	15:52	24♍03	315
	4	20:36	12♏15	0
	8	3:59	0♑34	45
	11	20:53	19♒17	90
	15	22:38	8♈23	135
	20	1:35	27♉33	180
	24	0:03	16♋31	225
	27	15:47	5♍13	270
Dec 2002	1	0:55	23♎39	315
	4	7:35	11♐58	0
	7	18:48	0♒29	45
	11	15:50	19♓26	90
	15	19:11	8♉38	135
	19	19:11	27♊42	180
	23	12:19	16♌29	225
	27	0:32	5♎04	270
	30	10:11	23♏32	315

The 8 Phases of the Moon 1900–2020

Jan 2003	2	20:24	12♑01	0
	6	12:24	0♓46	45
	10	13:16	19♈53	90
	14	15:57	9♊04	135
	18	10:49	27♋55	180
	21	22:32	16♍28	225
	25	8:34	4♏57	270
	28	20:07	23♐29	315
Feb 2003	1	10:49	12♒09	0
	5	7:55	1♈05	45
	9	11:12	20♉17	90
	13	10:45	9♋19	135
	16	23:52	27♌54	180
	20	7:26	16♎14	225
	23	16:47	4♐39	270
	27	7:06	23♑16	315
Mar 2003	3	2:36	12♓06	0
	7	3:59	1♉10	45
	11	7:16	20♊18	90
	15	2:12	9♌05	135
	18	10:36	27♍25	180
	21	15:53	15♏37	225
	25	1:52	4♑00	270
	28	19:28	22♒42	315
Apr 2003	1	19:20	11♈39	0
	5	22:55	0♊44	45
	9	23:41	19♋42	90
	13	14:03	8♍14	135
	16	19:37	26♎24	180
	20	0:30	14♐32	225
	23	12:19	2♒56	270
	27	9:27	21♓43	315
May 2003	1	12:16	10♉43	0
	5	15:10	29♊43	45
	9	11:54	18♌27	90
	12	22:54	6♎48	135
	16	3:37	24♏53	180
	19	9:47	13♑01	225
	23	0:32	1♓30	270
	27	0:57	20♈21	315
	31	4:21	9♊20	0
Jun 2003	4	3:55	28♋09	45
	7	20:29	16♍41	90
	11	5:42	4♏55	135
	14	11:17	23♐00	180
	17	20:11	11♒13	225
	21	14:46	29♓49	270
	25	17:25	18♉45	315
	29	18:40	7♋37	0
Jul 2003	3	13:28	26♌13	45
	7	2:33	14♎36	90
	10	11:29	2♐49	135
	13	19:22	20♑59	180
	17	8:21	9♓22	225
	21	7:02	28♈08	270
	25	9:57	17♊04	315
	29	6:54	5♌46	0
Aug 2003	1	20:46	24♍11	45
	5	7:29	12♏29	90
	8	17:20	0♑45	135
	12	4:49	19♒05	180
	15	22:49	7♈41	225
	20	0:49	26♉37	270
	24	1:42	15♋30	315
	27	17:27	4♍02	0
	31	3:09	22♎19	45
Sep 2003	3	12:35	10♐36	90
	7	0:29	29♑00	135
	10	16:37	17♓34	180
	14	15:42	6♉25	225
	18	19:04	25♊27	270
	22	16:12	14♌14	315
	26	3:10	2♎38	0
	29	9:54	20♏51	45
Oct 2003	2	19:10	9♑11	90
	6	10:11	27♒45	135
	10	7:29	16♈35	180
	14	10:17	5♊39	225
	18	12:32	24♋43	270
	22	5:26	13♍24	315
	25	12:51	1♏41	0
	28	18:02	19♐54	45
Nov 2003	1	4:26	8♒20	90
	4	23:28	27♓08	135
	9	1:14	16♉13	180
	13	5:03	5♋23	225
	17	4:16	24♌23	270
	20	17:33	12♎58	315
	23	23:00	1♐14	0
	27	4:14	19♑29	45
	30	17:17	8♓05	90
Dec 2003	4	16:41	27♈06	135
	8	20:38	16♊20	180
	12	22:20	5♌28	225
	16	17:43	24♍21	270
	20	4:35	12♏51	315
	23	9:44	1♑08	0
	26	16:56	19♒30	45
	30	10:04	8♈17	90
Jan 2004	3	12:50	27♉28	135
	7	15:41	16♋40	180
	11	13:08	5♍38	225
	15	4:47	24♎21	270
	18	14:27	12♐49	315
	21	21:06	1♒10	0
	25	8:14	19♓41	45
	29	6:04	8♉40	90
Feb 2004	2	9:50	27♊53	135
	6	8:48	16♌54	180
	10	1:13	5♎37	225
	13	13:41	24♏11	270
	16	23:23	12♑37	315
	20	9:19	1♓04	0
	24	1:47	19♈47	45
	28	3:25	8♊53	90
Mar 2004	3	5:25	27♋58	135
	6	23:15	16♍43	180
	10	10:55	5♏12	225
	13	21:02	23♐37	270
	17	8:03	12♒04	315
	20	22:42	0♈39	0
	24	20:37	19♉32	45
	28	23:49	8♋38	90
Apr 2004	1	22:13	27♌31	135
	5	11:04	16♎00	180
	8	18:53	4♐16	225
	12	3:47	22♑35	270
	15	17:27	11♓04	315
	19	13:22	29♈49	0
	23	15:12	18♊48	45
	27	17:34	7♌47	90
May 2004	1	11:50	26♍26	135
	4	20:34	14♏42	180
	8	1:51	2♑49	225
	11	11:05	21♒05	270
	15	4:29	9♈41	315
	19	4:53	28♉33	0
	23	8:06	17♋32	45
	27	7:58	6♍22	90
	30	22:28	24♎49	135
Jun 2004	3	4:21	12♐56	180
	6	8:47	0♒59	225
	9	20:03	19♓18	270
	13	17:32	8♉01	315
	17	20:28	26♊57	0
	21	22:34	15♌52	45
	25	19:09	4♎32	90
	29	6:37	22♏51	135
Jul 2004	2	11:10	10♑54	180
	5	16:44	28♒58	225
	9	7:35	17♈25	270
	13	8:30	6♊17	315
	17	11:25	25♋13	0
	21	10:34	14♍00	45
	25	3:38	2♏32	90
	28	13:04	20♐47	135
	31	18:06	8♒51	180
Aug 2004	4	2:49	27♓04	225
	7	22:02	15♉42	270
	12	0:46	4♋39	315
	16	1:25	23♌31	0
	19	20:30	12♎10	45
	23	10:13	0♐37	90
	26	18:54	18♑51	135
	30	2:23	7♓03	180
Sep 2004	2	15:52	25♈30	225
	6	15:12	14♊21	270
	10	17:43	3♌20	315
	14	14:30	22♍06	0
	18	5:01	10♏37	45
	21	15:55	29♐00	90
	25	1:24	17♒19	135
	28	13:10	5♈45	180
Oct 2004	2	8:06	24♉28	225
	6	10:13	13♋30	270
	10	10:42	2♍28	315
	14	2:49	21♎06	0
	17	12:52	9♐29	45
	20	22:00	27♑51	90
	24	9:58	16♓20	135
	28	3:08	5♉02	180
Nov 2004	1	2:53	24♊01	225
	5	5:54	13♌09	270
	9	3:08	2♎03	315
	12	14:28	20♏33	0
	15	20:55	8♑50	45
	19	5:51	27♒15	90
	22	21:43	15♈56	135
	26	20:08	4♊55	180
	30	22:52	24♋05	225
Dec 2004	5	0:54	13♍14	270
	8	18:12	2♏00	315
	12	1:30	20♐22	0
	15	6:03	8♒37	45
	18	16:41	27♓07	90
	22	12:59	16♉02	135
	26	15:07	5♋12	180
	30	18:24	24♌25	225
Jan 2005	3	17:47	13♎28	270
	7	7:13	2♐05	315
	10	12:04	20♑21	0
	13	17:02	8♓37	45
	17	6:59	27♈16	90
	21	7:09	16♊21	135
	25	10:33	5♌34	180
	29	11:56	24♍41	225
Feb 2005	2	7:28	13♏33	270
	5	17:51	2♑02	315
	8	22:29	20♒16	0
	12	6:11	8♈38	45
	16	0:17	27♉25	90
	20	2:46	16♋34	135
	24	4:55	5♍41	180
	28	2:21	24♎36	225
Mar 2005	3	17:37	13♐14	270
	7	2:28	1♒37	315
	10	9:12	19♓54	0
	13	21:17	8♉24	45
	17	19:20	27♊18	90
	21	22:14	16♌24	135
	25	21:00	5♎18	180
	29	13:19	23♏57	225
Apr 2005	2	0:51	12♑23	270
	5	9:58	0♓43	315
	8	20:33	19♈06	0
	12	13:39	7♊45	45
	16	14:39	26♋42	90
	20	16:07	15♍40	135
	24	10:07	4♏20	180
	27	21:17	22♐42	225
May 2005	1	6:25	10♒59	270
	4	17:27	29♓20	315
	8	8:47	17♉52	0
	12	6:28	6♋38	45
	16	8:58	25♌36	90
	20	7:31	14♎23	135
	23	20:19	2♐47	180
	27	3:21	20♑57	225
	30	11:48	9♓10	270
Jun 2005	3	1:56	27♈36	315
	6	21:56	16♊16	0
	10	23:04	5♌09	45
	15	1:23	24♍04	90
	18	19:59	12♏40	135
	22	4:15	0♑51	180
	25	8:56	18♒54	225
	28	18:25	7♈08	270
Jul 2005	2	12:11	25♉42	315
	6	12:04	14♋31	0
	10	14:57	3♍27	45
	14	15:21	22♎16	90
	18	5:47	10♐43	135
	21	11:01	28♑47	180
	24	15:26	16♓49	225
	28	3:20	5♉10	270
Aug 2005	1	0:44	23♊53	315
	5	3:06	12♌48	0
	9	5:37	1♎44	45
	13	2:40	20♏28	90
	16	13:39	8♑47	135
	19	17:54	26♒50	180
	23	0:01	14♈58	225
	26	15:19	3♊29	270
	30	15:48	22♋22	315
Sep 2005	3	18:46	11♍21	0
	7	18:37	0♏14	45
	11	11:38	18♐50	90
	14	20:38	7♒07	135
	18	2:02	25♓16	180
	21	11:29	13♉35	225
	25	6:42	2♋18	270
	29	9:15	21♌20	315
Oct 2005	3	10:29	10♎19	0
	7	5:47	29♏04	45
	10	19:02	17♑34	90
	14	3:51	5♓54	135
	17	12:15	24♈13	180
	21	2:09	12♊47	225
	25	1:18	1♌44	270
	29	4:14	20♍50	315
Nov 2005	2	1:26	9♏43	0
	5	15:24	28♐19	45
	9	1:58	16♒46	90
	12	12:18	5♈13	135
	16	0:59	23♉46	180
	19	19:54	12♋35	225
	23	22:12	1♍43	270
	27	23:19	20♎49	315
Dec 2005	1	15:02	9♐31	0
	5	0:13	27♑57	45
	8	9:37	16♓24	90
	11	22:43	5♉00	135
	15	16:17	23♊48	180
	19	15:59	12♌51	225
	23	19:37	2♎05	270
	27	16:51	21♏02	315
	31	3:13	9♑32	0
Jan 2006	3	9:14	27♒51	45
	6	18:58	16♈19	90

The 8 Phases of the Moon 1900–2020

	10	11:29	5♊05	135
	14	9:49	24♋05	180
	18	12:52	13♍17	225
	22	15:15	2♏27	270
	26	7:44	21♐12	315
	29	14:16	9♒32	0
Feb 2006	1	19:09	27♓47	45
	5	6:30	16♉19	90
	9	2:43	5♋12	135
	13	4:45	24♌20	180
	17	8:27	13♎32	225
	21	7:18	2♐31	270
	24	19:40	21♑03	315
	28	0:32	9♓16	0
Mar 2006	3	6:14	27♈31	45
	6	20:17	16♊07	90
	10	19:59	5♌06	135
	14	23:37	24♍15	180
	19	0:52	13♏17	225
	22	19:12	2♑01	270
	26	5:01	20♒24	315
	29	10:16	8♈35	0
Apr 2006	1	18:24	26♉53	45
	5	12:02	15♋34	90
	9	14:20	4♍36	135
	13	16:41	23♎37	180
	17	13:17	12♐23	225
	21	3:30	0♒54	270
	24	12:29	19♓11	315
	27	19:45	7♉24	0
May 2006	1	7:38	25♊48	45
	5	5:14	14♌35	90
	9	8:23	3♎35	135
	13	6:52	22♏23	180
	16	22:09	10♑54	225
	20	9:22	29♒14	270
	23	18:55	17♈30	315
	27	5:27	5♊48	0
	30	22:00	24♋21	45
Jun 2006	3	23:07	13♍13	90
	8	0:48	2♏07	135
	11	18:04	20♐41	180
	15	4:40	8♒58	225
	18	14:09	27♓12	270
	22	1:22	15♉31	315
	25	16:06	3♋58	0
	29	13:37	22♌41	45
Jul 2006	3	16:38	11♎37	90
	7	14:54	0♐22	135
	11	3:03	18♑42	180
	14	10:15	6♓51	225
	17	19:14	25♈04	270
	21	9:02	13♊29	315
	25	4:32	2♌07	0
	29	6:08	21♍00	45
Aug 2006	2	8:47	9♏56	90
	6	2:47	28♐32	135
	9	10:55	16♒44	180
	12	16:13	4♈49	225
	16	1:52	23♉05	270
	19	19:08	11♋39	315
	23	19:11	0♍31	0
	27	22:47	19♎31	45
	31	22:58	8♐24	90
Sep 2006	4	13:01	26♑52	135
	7	18:43	15♓00	180
	10	23:37	3♉07	225
	14	11:16	21♊30	270
	18	8:36	10♌18	315
	22	11:46	29♍20	0
	26	14:31	18♏22	45
	30	11:05	7♑09	90
Oct 2006	3	22:19	25♒34	135
	7	3:14	13♈43	180
	10	9:23	1♊56	225
	14	0:27	20♋31	270
	18	1:38	9♍32	315
	22	5:15	28♎40	0
	26	4:36	17♐37	45
	29	21:26	6♒19	90
Nov 2006	2	7:12	24♓43	135
	5	12:59	12♉58	180
	8	22:11	1♋22	225
	12	17:46	20♌12	270
	16	21:20	9♎23	315
	20	22:19	28♏27	0
	24	16:53	17♑16	45
	28	6:30	5♓53	90
Dec 2006	1	16:04	24♈19	135
	5	0:26	12♊43	180
	8	14:24	1♌21	225
	12	14:33	20♍25	270
	16	17:49	9♏38	315
	20	14:02	28♐32	0
	24	3:39	17♒11	45
	27	14:49	5♈42	90
	31	1:23	24♉13	135
Jan 2007	3	13:59	12♋48	180
	7	9:39	1♍42	225
	11	12:46	20♎54	270
	15	13:09	10♐00	315
	19	4:02	28♑41	0
	22	13:24	17♓08	45
	25	23:03	5♉36	90
	29	11:52	24♊11	135
Feb 2007	2	5:46	12♌59	180
	6	6:28	2♎05	225
	10	9:52	21♏16	270
	14	6:01	10♑09	315
	17	16:15	28♒37	0
	20	22:34	16♈54	45
	24	7:57	5♊19	90
	28	0:13	24♋01	135
Mar 2007	3	23:18	13♍00	180
	8	2:38	2♏08	225
	12	3:55	21♐11	270
	15	19:52	9♒51	315
	19	2:44	28♓07	0
	22	7:33	16♉18	45
	25	18:17	4♋43	90
	29	14:40	23♌32	135
Apr 2007	2	17:16	12♎35	180
	6	20:14	1♐39	225
	10	18:05	20♑29	270
	14	6:35	8♓57	315
	17	11:37	27♈05	0
	20	16:50	15♊14	45
	24	6:37	3♌43	90
	28	6:47	22♍37	135
May 2007	2	10:10	11♏38	180
	6	10:23	0♑32	225
	10	4:28	19♒09	270
	13	14:33	7♈28	315
	16	19:28	25♉33	0
	20	3:08	13♋45	45
	23	21:04	2♍21	90
	27	23:34	21♎18	135
Jun 2007	1	1:05	10♐12	180
	4	21:12	28♑52	225
	8	11:44	17♓19	270
	11	20:35	5♉33	315
	15	3:14	23♊41	0
	18	15:07	12♌01	45
	22	13:16	0♎46	90
	26	16:01	19♏41	135
	30	13:50	8♑25	180
Jul 2007	4	5:25	26♒53	225
	7	16:55	15♈12	270
	11	1:55	3♊25	315
	14	12:05	21♋41	0
	18	5:11	10♍14	45
	22	6:30	29♎06	90
	26	7:31	17♐58	135
	30	0:49	6♒31	180
Aug 2007	2	12:00	24♓50	225
	5	21:21	13♉05	270
	9	8:01	1♋23	315
	12	23:04	19♌51	0
	16	21:13	8♎38	45
	20	23:55	27♏35	90
	24	21:55	16♑21	135
	28	10:36	4♓46	180
	31	18:03	22♈57	225
Sep 2007	4	2:33	11♊12	270
	7	16:24	29♋40	315
	11	12:45	18♍25	0
	15	14:34	7♏23	45
	19	16:49	26♐22	90
	23	11:11	15♒03	135
	26	19:46	3♈20	180
	30	0:44	21♉29	225
Oct 2007	3	10:07	9♋49	270
	7	4:13	28♌31	315
	11	5:02	17♎30	0
	15	8:19	6♐36	45
	19	8:34	25♑35	90
	22	23:17	14♓10	135
	26	4:53	2♉23	180
	29	9:15	20♊34	225
Nov 2007	1	21:19	9♌04	270
	5	19:49	28♍01	315
	9	23:04	17♏10	0
	14	1:27	6♑17	45
	17	22:34	25♒12	90
	21	10:06	13♈42	135
	24	14:31	1♊55	180
	27	20:36	20♋13	225
Dec 2007	1	12:45	8♍56	270
	5	14:37	28♎04	315
	9	17:41	17♐16	0
	13	17:02	6♒18	45
	17	10:19	25♓05	90
	20	19:47	13♉33	135
	24	1:17	1♋50	180
	27	11:14	20♌18	225
	31	7:52	9♎14	270
Jan 2008	4	11:08	28♏27	315
	8	11:38	17♑33	0
	12	6:23	6♓25	45
	15	19:47	25♈02	90
	19	4:48	13♊29	135
	22	13:36	1♌54	180
	26	4:44	20♍36	225
	30	5:04	9♏40	270
Feb 2008	3	7:37	28♐50	315
	7	3:46	17♒44	0
	10	17:14	6♈21	45
	14	3:35	24♉49	90
	17	13:57	13♋17	135
	21	3:32	1♍53	180
	24	23:51	20♎45	225
	29	2:19	9♐52	270
Mar 2008	4	2:20	28♑53	315
	7	17:15	17♓31	0
	11	1:57	5♉53	45
	14	10:47	24♊14	90
	17	23:59	12♌46	135
	21	18:41	1♎31	180
	25	19:03	20♏30	225
	29	21:48	9♑34	270
Apr 2008	2	18:02	28♒22	315
	6	3:56	16♈44	0
	9	9:24	4♊54	45
	12	18:33	23♋13	90
	16	11:24	11♍51	135
	20	10:26	0♏43	180
	24	13:01	19♐43	225
	28	14:13	8♒39	270
May 2008	2	6:09	27♓13	315
	5	12:19	15♉22	0
	8	16:40	3♋27	45
	12	3:48	21♌48	90
	16	0:22	10♎31	135
	20	2:12	29♏27	180
	24	4:52	18♑24	225
	28	2:58	7♓10	270
	31	15:00	25♈31	315
Jun 2008	3	19:24	13♊34	0
	7	0:48	1♌40	45
	10	15:05	20♍06	90
	14	14:46	8♏54	135
	18	17:32	27♐50	180
	22	18:04	16♒40	225
	26	12:11	5♈15	270
	29	21:34	23♉29	315
Jul 2008	3	2:20	11♋32	0
	6	10:36	29♌44	45
	10	4:36	18♎18	90
	14	6:23	7♐11	135
	18	8:00	26♑04	180
	22	4:36	14♓45	225
	25	18:43	3♉10	270
	29	3:07	21♊23	315
Aug 2008	1	10:14	9♌32	0
	4	22:37	27♍54	45
	8	20:21	16♏38	90
	12	22:53	5♑35	135
	16	21:18	24♒21	180
	20	12:53	12♈52	225
	23	23:51	1♊12	270
	27	9:03	19♋28	315
	30	19:59	7♍48	0
Sep 2008	3	13:08	26♎24	45
	7	14:05	15♐19	90
	11	15:37	4♒16	135
	15	9:14	22♓54	180
	18	19:54	11♉16	225
	22	5:05	29♊34	270
	25	16:37	17♌58	315
	29	8:13	6♎33	0
Oct 2008	3	6:06	25♏24	45
	7	9:05	14♑28	90
	11	7:45	3♓22	135
	14	20:03	21♈51	180
	18	2:54	10♊06	225
	21	11:56	28♋27	270
	25	2:48	17♍04	315
	28	23:15	5♏54	0
Nov 2008	2	1:02	24♐59	45
	6	4:04	14♒07	90
	9	22:31	2♈54	135
	13	6:18	21♉15	180
	16	11:11	9♋28	225
	19	21:32	27♌56	270
	23	16:14	16♎45	315
	27	16:56	5♐49	0
Dec 2008	1	20:43	25♑02	45
	5	21:27	14♓08	90
	9	11:30	2♉46	135
	12	16:38	21♊02	180
	15	21:37	9♌18	225
	19	10:30	27♍54	270
	23	9:01	16♏54	315
	27	12:23	6♑08	0
	31	15:17	25♒20	45
Jan 2009	4	11:57	14♈16	90
	7	22:44	2♊47	135
	11	3:28	21♋02	180
	14	10:26	9♍23	225
	18	2:47	28♎08	270

The 8 Phases of the Moon 1900–2020

	22	4:28	17♐17	315
	26	7:56	6♒30	0
	30	7:03	25♓32	45
Feb 2009	2	23:14	14♉15	90
	6	8:30	2♋41	135
	9	14:50	21♌00	180
	13	1:17	9♎28	225
	16	21:38	28♏21	270
	21	1:02	17♑32	315
	25	1:36	6♓35	0
	28	19:17	25♈20	45
Mar 2009	4	7:47	13♊52	90
	7	17:12	2♌16	135
	11	2:39	20♍40	180
	14	17:38	9♏16	225
	18	17:48	28♐16	270
	22	20:37	17♒21	315
	26	16:07	6♈08	0
	30	4:26	24♉37	45
Apr 2009	2	14:35	12♋59	90
	6	1:26	1♍23	135
	9	14:57	19♎53	180
	13	10:54	8♐39	225
	17	13:37	27♑40	270
	21	13:29	16♓34	315
	25	3:24	5♉04	0
	28	11:35	23♊19	45
May 2009	1	20:45	11♌36	90
	5	9:57	0♎03	135
	9	4:03	18♏41	180
	13	4:25	7♑33	225
	17	7:27	26♒32	270
	21	2:57	15♈12	315
	24	12:12	3♊28	0
	27	17:55	21♋34	45
	31	3:23	9♍50	90
Jun 2009	3	19:38	28♎21	135
	7	18:13	17♐07	180
	11	21:14	6♒04	225
	15	22:16	24♓56	270
	19	13:23	13♉24	315
	22	19:36	1♋30	0
	26	0:31	19♌34	45
	29	11:30	7♎52	90
Jul 2009	3	7:20	26♏31	135
	7	9:23	15♑24	180
	11	12:24	4♓20	225
	15	9:54	23♈03	270
	18	21:39	11♊23	315
	22	2:36	29♋27	0
	25	8:17	17♍32	45
	28	22:01	5♏57	90
Aug 2009	1	21:33	24♐45	135
	6	0:56	13♒43	180
	10	1:20	2♈34	225
	13	18:56	21♉09	270
	17	4:42	9♋25	315
	20	10:03	27♌32	0
	23	18:05	15♎44	45
	27	11:43	4♐21	90
	31	14:07	23♑18	135
Sep 2009	4	16:04	12♓15	180
	8	12:06	0♉59	225
	12	2:17	19♊28	270
	15	11:29	7♌46	315
	18	18:45	25♍59	0
	22	6:44	14♏24	45
	26	4:51	3♑15	90
	30	8:10	22♒18	135
Oct 2009	4	6:11	11♈10	180
	7	21:20	29♉44	225
	11	8:57	18♋11	270
	14	18:50	6♍33	315
	18	5:34	24♎59	0
	21	22:46	13♐40	45
	26	0:43	2♒44	90
	30	2:23	21♓48	135
Nov 2009	2	19:15	10♉30	180
	6	5:58	28♊57	225
	9	15:57	17♌23	270
	13	3:42	5♎54	315
	16	19:15	24♏34	0
	20	17:58	13♑33	45
	24	21:40	2♓45	90
	28	19:40	21♈43	135
Dec 2009	2	7:32	10♊15	180
	5	14:50	28♋36	225
	9	0:14	17♍03	270
	12	15:02	5♏43	315
	16	12:03	24♐40	0
	20	14:51	13♒51	45
	24	17:37	3♈03	90
	28	11:17	21♉51	135
	31	19:14	10♋15	180
Jan 2010	4	0:30	28♌32	225
	7	10:41	17♎01	270
	11	5:31	5♐52	315
	15	7:12	25♑01	0
	19	11:10	14♓16	45
	23	10:54	3♉20	90
	27	0:45	21♊58	135
	30	6:19	10♌15	180
Feb 2010	2	11:14	28♍30	225
	5	23:50	17♏04	270
	9	22:57	6♑05	315
	14	2:52	25♒18	0
	18	4:52	14♈25	45
	22	0:43	3♊17	90
	25	11:47	21♋46	135
	28	16:39	9♍59	180
Mar 2010	3	23:15	28♎16	225
	7	15:43	16♐57	270
	11	18:04	6♒03	315
	15	21:02	25♓10	0
	19	19:01	14♉04	45
	23	11:01	2♋43	90
	26	20:27	21♌04	135
	30	2:27	9♎17	180
Apr 2010	2	12:42	27♏40	225
	6	9:38	16♑29	270
	10	13:01	5♓33	315
	14	12:30	24♈27	0
	18	5:42	13♊06	45
	21	18:21	1♌32	90
	25	3:25	19♍50	135
	28	12:20	8♏07	180
May 2010	2	3:38	26♐39	225
	6	4:16	15♒33	270
	10	6:17	4♈30	315
	14	1:05	23♉09	0
	17	13:38	11♋33	45
	20	23:44	29♌51	90
	24	9:50	18♎08	135
	27	23:08	6♐33	180
	31	19:43	25♑15	225
Jun 2010	4	22:14	14♓11	270
	8	21:14	2♉58	315
	12	11:16	21♊24	0
	15	19:50	9♌36	45
	19	4:31	27♍49	90
	22	17:04	16♏11	135
	26	11:31	4♑46	180
	30	12:15	23♒37	225
Jul 2010	4	14:36	12♈31	270
	8	9:54	1♊09	315
	11	19:42	19♋24	0
	15	1:24	7♍29	45
	18	10:12	25♎42	90
	22	2:26	14♐12	135
	26	1:38	3♒00	180
	30	4:25	21♓56	225
Aug 2010	3	5:00	10♉47	270
	6	20:37	29♊16	315
	10	3:09	17♌25	0
	13	7:35	5♎28	45
	16	18:15	23♏47	90
	20	14:46	12♑29	135
	24	17:06	1♓26	180
	28	19:37	20♈23	225
Sep 2010	1	17:23	9♊10	270
	5	5:47	27♋34	315
	8	10:31	15♍41	0
	11	15:42	3♏48	45
	15	5:51	22♐18	90
	19	6:12	11♒13	135
	23	9:18	0♈15	180
	27	9:32	19♉11	225
Oct 2010	1	3:53	7♋52	270
	4	13:55	26♌14	315
	7	18:46	14♎24	0
	11	2:51	2♐42	45
	14	21:28	21♑26	90
	19	0:11	10♓31	135
	23	1:38	29♈33	180
	26	22:00	18♊23	225
	30	12:47	6♌59	270
Nov 2010	2	21:46	25♍22	315
	6	4:53	13♏40	0
	9	17:42	2♑13	45
	13	16:40	21♒12	90
	17	19:37	10♈21	135
	21	17:28	29♉18	180
	25	9:04	17♋59	225
	28	20:38	6♍30	270
Dec 2010	2	6:13	24♎57	315
	5	17:37	13♐28	0
	9	11:58	2♒18	45
	13	14:00	21♓27	90
	17	15:13	10♉34	135
	21	8:15	29♊21	180
	24	18:54	17♌51	225
	28	4:20	6♎19	270
	31	16:17	24♏52	315
Jan 2011	4	9:04	13♑39	0
	8	8:21	2♓42	45
	12	11:33	21♈54	90
	16	9:29	10♊54	135
	19	21:22	29♋27	180
	23	4:01	17♍47	225
	26	12:58	6♏13	270
	30	4:35	24♐55	315
Feb 2011	3	2:32	13♒54	0
	7	4:58	3♈04	45
	11	7:19	22♉13	90
	15	1:07	10♋59	135
	18	8:37	29♌20	180
	21	13:07	17♎33	225
	24	23:27	6♐00	270
	28	19:11	24♑51	315
Mar 2011	4	20:47	13♓56	0
	9	0:03	3♉04	45
	12	23:46	22♊03	90
	16	13:23	10♌37	135
	19	18:11	28♍48	180
	22	22:53	16♏58	225
	26	12:08	5♑29	270
	30	11:26	24♒25	315
Apr 2011	3	14:33	13♈30	0
	7	16:17	2♊30	45
	11	12:06	21♋16	90
	14	22:25	9♍38	135
	18	2:45	27♎44	180
	21	9:48	15♐57	225
	25	2:48	4♒34	270
	29	4:28	23♓32	315
May 2011	3	6:52	12♉31	0
	7	5:01	1♋19	45
	10	20:34	19♌51	90
	14	5:08	8♎05	135
	17	11:10	26♏13	180
	20	22:08	14♑33	225
	24	18:53	3♓16	270
	28	21:27	22♈13	315
Jun 2011	1	21:04	11♊02	0
	5	14:21	29♋36	45
	9	2:12	17♍56	90
	12	10:48	6♏09	135
	15	20:15	24♐23	180
	19	11:52	12♒53	225
	23	11:49	1♈41	270
	27	13:40	20♉35	315
Jul 2011	1	8:55	9♋12	0
	4	21:07	27♌33	45
	8	6:31	15♎47	90
	11	16:48	4♐03	135
	15	6:41	22♑28	180
	19	2:56	11♓08	225
	23	5:03	0♉02	270
	27	4:33	18♊50	315
	30	18:41	7♌16	0
Aug 2011	3	2:36	25♍27	45
	6	11:09	13♏40	90
	10	0:23	2♑04	135
	13	18:59	20♒41	180
	17	19:13	9♈32	225
	21	21:56	28♉30	270
	25	17:45	17♋11	315
	29	3:05	5♍27	0
Sep 2011	1	8:20	23♎34	45
	4	17:40	11♐51	90
	8	10:34	0♒27	135
	12	9:28	19♓17	180
	16	12:16	8♉18	225
	20	13:40	27♊15	270
	24	5:15	15♌49	315
	27	11:10	4♎00	0
	30	15:44	22♏08	45
Oct 2011	4	3:16	10♑34	90
	7	24:00	29♒22	135
	12	2:07	18♈24	180
	16	5:17	7♊30	225
	20	3:31	26♋24	270
	23	15:24	14♍52	315
	26	19:57	3♏03	0
	30	1:51	21♐17	45
Nov 2011	2	16:39	9♒55	90
	6	16:53	28♓56	135
	10	20:17	18♉05	180
	14	21:07	7♋08	225
	18	15:10	25♌55	270
	22	0:47	14♎21	315
	25	6:11	2♐37	0
	28	15:08	21♑02	45
Dec 2011	2	9:53	9♓52	90
	6	12:38	29♈02	135
	10	14:37	18♊11	180
	14	10:48	7♌05	225
	18	0:49	25♍44	270
	21	10:00	14♏10	315
	24	18:08	2♑34	0
	28	7:24	21♒12	45
Jan 2012	1	6:16	10♈13	90
	5	9:39	29♉27	135
	9	7:31	18♋26	180
	12	22:06	7♍06	225
	16	9:09	25♎38	270
	19	19:32	14♐07	315
	23	7:40	2♒42	0
	27	1:58	21♓31	45

The 8 Phases of the Moon 1900–2020

	31	4:11	10♉41	90
Feb 2012	4	5:42	29♊48	135
	7	21:55	18♌32	180
	11	7:32	6♎58	225
	14	17:05	25♏24	270
	18	5:46	13♑58	315
	21	22:36	2♓42	0
	25	21:46	21♈42	45
Mar 2012	1	1:23	10♊52	90
	4	22:54	29♋46	135
	8	9:41	18♍13	180
	11	15:59	6♏29	225
	15	1:26	24♐52	270
	18	17:07	13♒30	315
	22	14:38	2♈22	0
	26	17:19	21♉27	45
	30	19:42	10♋30	90
Apr 2012	3	12:27	29♌09	135
	6	19:20	17♎23	180
	10	0:14	5♐32	225
	13	10:51	23♑55	270
	17	5:57	12♓38	315
	21	7:20	1♉35	0
	25	10:57	20♊38	45
	29	9:59	9♌29	90
May 2012	2	22:38	27♍55	135
	6	3:36	16♏01	180
	9	8:52	4♑08	225
	12	21:48	22♒33	270
	16	20:25	11♈21	315
	20	23:48	0♊21	0
	25	1:28	19♋15	45
	28	20:17	7♍53	90
Jun 2012	1	6:18	26♎10	135
	4	11:13	14♐14	180
	7	18:23	2♒23	225
	11	10:42	20♓54	270
	15	12:18	9♉48	315
	19	15:03	28♊43	0
	23	12:36	17♌27	45
	27	3:31	5♎54	90
	30	12:27	24♏07	135
Jul 2012	3	18:53	12♑14	180
	7	5:25	0♓30	225
	11	1:49	19♈11	270
	15	4:53	8♊07	315
	19	4:25	26♋55	0
	22	21:01	15♍26	45
	26	8:57	3♏47	90
	29	18:10	22♐01	135
Aug 2012	2	3:29	10♒15	180
	5	18:35	28♓44	225
	9	18:56	17♉34	270
	13	21:14	6♋30	315
	17	15:55	25♌08	0
	21	3:52	13♎30	45
	24	13:55	1♐48	90
	28	0:33	20♑07	135
	31	13:59	8♓34	180
Sep 2012	4	10:20	27♈17	225
	8	13:16	16♊17	270
	12	12:39	5♌09	315
	16	2:12	23♍37	0
	19	10:27	11♏53	45
	22	19:42	0♑12	90
	26	8:52	18♒40	135
	30	3:20	7♈22	180
Oct 2012	4	4:23	26♉21	225
	8	7:34	15♋26	270
	12	2:49	4♍11	315
	15	12:04	22♎32	0
	18	17:56	10♐46	45
	22	3:33	29♑09	90
	25	20:19	17♓50	135
	29	19:51	6♉48	180
Nov 2012	2	23:31	25♊57	225
	7	0:37	15♌00	270
	10	15:48	3♎39	315
	13	22:09	21♏57	0
	17	3:08	10♑11	45
	20	14:33	28♒41	90
	24	11:37	17♈36	135
	28	14:47	6♊47	180
Dec 2012	2	18:00	25♋58	225
	6	15:33	14♍55	270
	10	3:37	3♏29	315
	13	8:43	21♐45	0
	16	14:34	10♒03	45
	20	5:20	28♓44	90
	24	6:31	17♉51	135
	28	10:22	7♋06	180
Jan 2013	1	10:20	26♌10	225
	5	3:59	14♎58	270
	8	14:09	3♐28	315
	11	19:45	21♑46	0
	15	4:29	10♓11	45
	18	23:46	29♈04	90
	23	3:20	18♊17	135
	27	4:39	7♌24	180
	30	23:50	26♍16	225
Feb 2013	3	13:57	14♏54	270
	6	23:27	3♑21	315
	10	7:21	21♒43	0
	13	20:47	10♈19	45
	17	20:32	29♉21	90
	21	23:45	18♋31	135
	25	20:27	7♍24	180
Mar 2013	1	10:39	26♎00	225
	4	21:54	14♐29	270
	8	7:59	2♒54	315
	11	19:52	21♓24	0
	15	14:52	10♉11	45
	19	17:28	29♊16	90
	23	17:57	18♌16	135
	27	9:28	6♎52	180
	30	19:17	25♏15	225
Apr 2013	3	4:38	13♑35	270
	6	16:37	2♓02	315
	10	9:36	20♈41	0
	14	9:30	9♊36	45
	18	12:32	28♋38	90
	22	9:05	17♍24	135
	25	19:58	5♏46	180
	29	2:28	23♐57	225
May 2013	2	11:15	12♒13	270
	6	2:26	0♈44	315
	10	0:30	19♉31	0
	14	3:13	8♋30	45
	18	4:36	27♌25	90
	21	21:08	15♎58	135
	25	4:26	4♐08	180
	28	9:05	22♑12	225
	31	18:59	10♓28	270
Jun 2013	4	14:10	29♈07	315
	8	15:57	18♊01	0
	12	18:56	6♌57	45
	16	17:25	25♍43	90
	20	6:29	14♏06	135
	23	11:33	2♑10	180
	26	16:13	20♒13	225
	30	4:55	8♈35	270
Jul 2013	4	4:03	27♉21	315
	8	7:15	16♋18	0
	12	8:15	5♍09	45
	16	3:19	23♎46	90
	19	13:46	12♐03	135
	22	18:17	0♒06	180
	26	0:59	18♓13	225
	29	17:44	6♉45	270
Aug 2013	2	19:42	25♊40	315
	6	21:52	14♌35	0
	10	19:21	3♎19	45
	14	10:57	21♏49	90
	17	19:53	10♑04	135
	21	1:46	28♒11	180
	24	12:26	16♈30	225
	28	9:36	5♊15	270
Sep 2013	1	12:30	24♋14	315
	5	11:37	13♍04	0
	9	4:45	1♏41	45
	12	17:09	20♐06	90
	16	2:01	8♒23	135
	19	11:14	26♓41	180
	23	3:09	15♉16	225
	27	3:57	4♋13	270
Oct 2013	1	5:47	23♌13	315
	5	0:36	11♎56	0
	8	13:05	0♐25	45
	11	23:03	18♑47	90
	15	9:30	7♓12	135
	18	23:39	25♈45	180
	22	20:54	14♊37	225
	26	23:42	3♌43	270
	30	22:53	22♍41	315
Nov 2013	3	12:51	11♏16	0
	6	21:07	29♐37	45
	10	5:58	18♒00	90
	13	19:36	6♈35	135
	17	15:17	25♉26	180
	21	16:39	14♋32	225
	25	19:29	3♍42	270
	29	15:01	22♎33	315
Dec 2013	3	0:23	10♐59	0
	6	5:43	29♑16	45
	9	15:13	17♓43	90
	13	9:07	6♉31	135
	17	9:29	25♊36	180
	21	12:47	14♌49	225
	25	13:49	3♎56	270
	29	5:20	22♏39	315
Jan 2014	1	11:15	10♑57	0
	4	15:41	29♒12	45
	8	3:40	17♈46	90
	12	1:52	6♊46	135
	16	4:53	25♋58	180
	20	7:35	15♍09	225
	24	5:20	4♏08	270
	27	17:13	22♐41	315
	30	21:40	10♒55	0
Feb 2014	3	3:36	29♓13	45
	6	19:23	17♉56	90
	10	20:47	7♋02	135
	14	23:54	26♌13	180
	18	23:42	15♎14	225
	22	17:16	4♐00	270
	26	2:43	22♑25	315
Mar 2014	1	8:01	10♓39	0
	4	17:33	29♈04	45
	8	13:28	17♊54	90
	12	16:19	7♌01	135
	16	17:09	26♍02	180
	20	12:22	14♏49	225
	24	1:47	3♑21	270
	27	10:29	21♒40	315
	30	18:46	9♈59	0
Apr 2014	3	9:04	28♉32	45
	7	8:32	17♋27	90
	11	10:58	6♍29	135
	15	7:43	25♎16	180
	18	21:39	13♐46	225
	22	7:53	2♒07	270
	25	17:38	20♓26	315
	29	6:15	8♉52	0
May 2014	3	1:28	27♊33	45
	7	3:16	16♌30	90
	11	3:36	5♎23	135
	14	19:17	23♏55	180
	18	4:24	12♑10	225
	21	13:00	0♓24	270
	25	1:16	18♈47	315
	28	18:41	7♊21	0
Jun 2014	1	18:02	26♋10	45
	5	20:40	15♍06	90
	9	17:33	3♏48	135
	13	4:13	22♐06	180
	16	9:57	10♒11	225
	19	18:40	28♓24	270
	23	10:21	16♉53	315
	27	8:10	5♋37	0
Jul 2014	1	10:18	24♌31	45
	5	12:00	13♎24	90
	9	4:44	1♐56	135
	12	11:26	20♑03	180
	15	15:45	8♓05	225
	19	2:09	26♈21	270
	22	21:33	15♊00	315
	26	22:43	3♌52	0
	31	1:45	22♍48	45
Aug 2014	4	0:51	11♏36	90
	7	13:38	29♐59	135
	10	18:10	18♒02	180
	13	23:08	6♈07	225
	17	12:27	24♉32	270
	21	11:18	13♋20	315
	25	14:14	2♍19	0
	29	15:53	21♎14	45
Sep 2014	2	11:12	9♐55	90
	5	21:08	28♑14	135
	9	1:39	16♓19	180
	12	9:05	4♉32	225
	16	2:06	23♊09	270
	20	3:42	12♌07	315
	24	6:15	1♎08	0
	28	4:17	19♏58	45
Oct 2014	1	19:34	8♑33	90
	5	4:18	26♒51	135
	8	10:52	15♈05	180
	11	22:12	3♊31	225
	15	19:13	22♋21	270
	19	22:15	11♍27	315
	23	21:58	0♏25	0
	27	14:54	19♐07	45
	31	2:49	7♒36	90
Nov 2014	3	12:12	26♓00	135
	6	22:24	14♉26	180
	10	14:32	3♋07	225
	14	15:17	22♌10	270
	18	17:44	11♎18	315
	22	12:33	0♐07	0
	26	0:14	18♑39	45
	29	10:07	7♓06	90
Dec 2014	2	21:37	25♈38	135
	6	12:28	14♊18	180
	10	9:38	3♌14	225
	14	12:52	22♍26	270
	18	12:27	11♏30	315
	22	1:37	0♑06	0
	25	9:09	18♒29	45
	28	18:33	6♈56	90
Jan 2015	1	9:08	25♉37	135
	5	4:54	14♋31	180
	9	6:23	3♍39	225
	13	9:48	22♎52	270
	17	4:52	11♐44	315
	20	13:15	0♒09	0
	23	18:31	18♓26	45
	27	4:50	6♉55	90
	30	22:59	25♊44	135
Feb 2015	3	23:10	14♌48	180
	8	2:53	4♎00	225

The 8 Phases of the Moon 1900–2020

	12	3:51	23♏06	270
	15	18:18	11♑44	315
	18	23:48	0♓00	0
	22	4:51	18♈14	45
	25	17:15	6♊47	90
Mar 2015	1	15:03	25♋42	135
	5	18:07	14♍50	180
	9	21:02	3♏58	225
	13	17:49	22♐49	270
	17	4:49	11♒16	315
	20	9:37	29♓27	0
	23	16:13	17♉43	45
	27	7:44	6♋19	90
	31	8:43	25♌19	135
Apr 2015	4	12:07	14♎24	180
	8	11:25	3♐19	225
	12	3:46	21♑55	270
	15	13:00	10♓15	315
	18	18:58	28♈25	0
	22	4:35	16♊45	45
	25	23:56	5♌27	90
	30	2:51	24♍28	135
May 2015	4	3:43	13♏23	180
	7	21:55	2♑01	225
	11	10:37	20♒26	270
	14	19:41	8♈42	315
	18	4:14	26♉56	0
	21	18:04	15♋22	45
	25	17:20	4♍11	90
	29	20:06	23♎08	135
Jun 2015	2	16:20	11♐49	180
	6	5:25	0♒13	225
	9	15:43	18♓30	270
	13	1:51	6♉46	315
	16	14:07	25♊07	0
	20	8:52	13♌44	45
	24	11:04	2♎38	90
	28	11:25	21♏28	135
Jul 2015	2	2:21	9♑55	180
	5	11:18	28♒08	225
	8	20:25	16♈21	270
	12	8:38	4♊42	315
	16	1:25	23♋14	0
	20	0:56	12♍02	45
	24	4:05	0♏59	90
	28	0:30	19♐39	135
	31	10:44	7♒56	180
Aug 2015	3	16:56	26♓03	225
	7	2:04	14♉17	270
	10	17:18	2♋46	315
	14	14:55	21♌31	0
	18	17:45	10♎28	45
	22	19:32	29♏24	90
	26	11:43	17♑56	135
	29	18:36	6♓06	180
Sep 2015	1	23:33	24♈12	225
	5	9:55	12♊32	270
	9	4:58	1♌13	315
	13	6:42	20♍10	0
	17	10:19	9♏13	45
	21	9:00	28♐04	90
	24	21:42	16♒31	135
	28	2:52	4♈40	180
Oct 2015	1	8:06	22♉50	225
	4	21:07	11♋19	270
	8	20:19	0♍14	315
	13	0:07	19♎20	0
	17	1:37	8♐22	45
	20	20:32	27♑08	90
	24	7:00	15♓33	135
	27	12:06	3♉45	180
	30	19:23	22♊03	225
Nov 2015	3	12:25	10♌45	270
	7	15:00	29♍52	315
	11	17:48	19♏01	0
	15	15:07	7♑56	45
	19	6:28	26♒36	90
	22	16:01	15♈01	135
	25	22:45	3♊20	180
	29	9:55	21♋51	225
Dec 2015	3	7:41	10♍48	270
	7	11:30	0♏01	315
	11	10:30	19♐03	0
	15	2:49	7♒47	45
	18	15:15	26♓22	90
	22	1:07	14♉51	135
	25	11:13	3♋20	180
	29	3:44	22♌05	225
Jan 2016	2	5:32	11♎14	270
	6	7:44	0♐24	315
	10	1:32	19♑13	0
	13	13:07	7♓46	45
	16	23:27	26♈16	90
	20	10:52	14♊48	135
	24	1:47	3♌29	180
	27	23:55	22♍29	225
Feb 2016	1	3:29	11♏41	270
	5	2:00	0♑41	315
	8	14:40	19♒16	0
	11	22:29	7♈38	45
	15	7:48	26♉03	90
	18	22:01	14♋41	135
	22	18:21	3♍34	180
	26	20:34	22♎41	225
Mar 2016	1	23:12	11♐48	270
	5	17:23	0♒34	315
	9	1:56	18♓56	0
	12	7:20	7♉09	45
	15	17:04	25♊33	90
	19	11:06	14♌17	135
	23	12:02	3♎17	180
	27	15:30	22♏23	225
	31	15:18	11♑20	270
Apr 2016	4	5:35	29♒53	315
	7	11:25	18♈04	0
	10	16:08	6♊13	45
	14	4:00	24♋39	90
	18	2:09	13♍29	135
	22	5:25	2♏31	180
	26	7:20	21♐29	225
	30	3:30	10♒13	270
May 2016	3	14:46	28♓35	315
	6	19:31	16♉41	0
	10	1:33	4♋50	45
	13	17:03	23♌21	90
	17	18:27	12♎16	135
	21	21:16	1♐14	180
	25	19:45	20♑01	225
	29	12:13	8♓33	270
Jun 2016	1	21:35	26♈48	315
	5	3:01	14♊53	0
	8	12:21	3♌08	45
	12	8:11	21♍47	90
	16	11:01	10♏43	135
	20	11:03	29♐33	180
	24	5:13	18♒07	225
	27	18:20	6♈30	270
Jul 2016	1	3:03	24♉43	315
	4	11:02	12♋54	0
	8	1:10	1♍19	45
	12	0:53	20♎07	90
	16	3:03	9♐01	135
	19	22:58	27♑40	180
	23	12:35	16♓05	225
	26	23:01	4♉21	270
	30	8:33	22♊36	315
Aug 2016	2	20:46	10♌58	0
	6	16:12	29♍37	45
	10	18:22	18♏32	90
	14	18:11	7♑22	135
	18	9:28	25♒52	180
	21	18:54	14♈08	225
	25	3:42	2♊22	270
	28	15:38	20♋45	315
Sep 2016	1	9:04	9♍21	0
	5	9:05	28♎14	45
	9	11:50	17♐13	90
	13	8:19	5♒58	135
	16	19:06	24♓20	180
	20	1:15	12♉31	225
	23	9:57	0♋48	270
	27	1:39	19♌23	315
Oct 2016	1	0:13	8♎15	0
	5	3:00	27♏18	45
	9	4:34	16♑19	90
	12	21:20	4♓58	135
	16	4:24	23♈14	180
	19	8:50	11♊24	225
	22	19:15	29♋49	270
	26	15:26	18♍38	315
	30	17:39	7♏44	0
Nov 2016	3	20:51	26♐52	45
	7	19:52	15♒50	90
	11	9:05	4♈24	135
	14	13:53	22♉38	180
	17	18:45	10♋51	225
	21	8:34	29♌28	270
	25	8:49	18♎31	315
	29	12:19	7♐43	0
Dec 2016	3	13:36	26♑49	45
	7	9:04	15♓42	90
	10	19:30	4♉11	135
	14	0:07	22♊26	180
	17	7:44	10♌48	225
	21	1:57	29♍38	270
	25	4:43	18♏49	315
	29	6:54	7♑59	0
Jan 2017	2	4:20	26♒57	45
	5	19:48	15♈40	90
	9	4:50	4♊07	135
	12	11:35	22♋27	180
	15	23:48	11♍02	225
	19	22:15	0♏02	270
	24	1:25	19♐14	315
	28	0:08	8♒15	0
	31	16:30	27♓00	45
Feb 2017	4	4:20	15♉32	90
	7	13:44	3♋59	135
	11	0:34	22♌28	180
	14	18:06	11♎14	225
	18	19:34	0♐20	270
	22	21:09	19♑26	315
	26	14:59	8♓12	0
Mar 2017	2	2:09	26♈41	45
	5	11:34	15♊05	90
	8	23:02	3♌34	135
	12	14:55	22♍13	180
	16	13:12	11♏08	225
	20	15:59	0♑14	270
	24	14:24	19♒08	315
	28	2:58	7♈37	0
	31	9:57	25♉53	45
Apr 2017	3	18:41	14♋12	90
	7	9:25	2♍45	135
	11	6:09	21♎33	180
	15	7:43	10♐32	225
	19	9:58	29♑32	270
	23	4:16	18♓12	315
	26	12:17	6♉27	0
	29	16:58	24♊34	45
May 2017	3	2:48	12♌52	90
	6	21:17	1♎31	135
	10	21:44	20♏24	180
	15	0:35	9♑23	225
	19	0:34	28♒14	270
	22	14:39	16♈41	315
	25	19:46	4♊47	0
	29	0:19	22♋50	45
Jun 2017	1	12:43	11♍13	90
	5	10:43	29♎58	135
	9	13:11	18♐53	180
	13	15:10	7♒47	225
	17	11:34	26♓28	270
	20	22:14	14♉45	315
	24	2:32	2♋47	0
	27	9:01	20♌55	45
Jul 2017	1	0:52	9♎24	90
	5	1:36	28♏15	135
	9	4:08	17♑09	180
	13	3:09	5♓56	225
	16	19:27	24♈26	270
	20	4:11	12♊39	315
	23	9:47	0♌44	0
	26	19:45	19♍00	45
	30	15:24	7♏39	90
Aug 2017	3	17:43	26♐34	135
	7	18:12	15♒25	180
	11	12:40	4♈02	225
	15	1:16	22♉25	270
	18	9:52	10♋39	315
	21	18:31	28♌53	0
	25	8:58	17♎21	45
	29	8:14	6♐11	90
Sep 2017	2	10:36	25♑09	135
	6	7:04	13♓53	180
	9	20:24	2♉20	225
	13	6:26	20♊40	270
	16	16:34	9♌00	315
	20	5:31	27♍27	0
	24	0:48	16♏10	45
	28	2:55	5♑11	90
Oct 2017	2	3:26	24♒08	135
	5	18:41	12♈43	180
	9	3:28	1♊02	225
	12	12:27	19♋22	270
	16	1:25	7♍52	315
	19	19:13	26♎35	0
	23	19:02	15♐34	45
	27	22:23	4♒41	90
	31	19:17	23♓34	135
Nov 2017	4	5:24	11♉59	180
	7	11:08	0♋14	225
	10	20:38	18♌38	270
	14	13:13	7♎21	315
	18	11:43	26♏19	0
	22	14:45	15♑29	45
	26	17:04	4♓38	90
	30	9:28	23♈22	135
Dec 2017	3	15:48	11♊40	180
	6	20:30	29♋55	225
	10	7:53	18♍26	270
	14	4:20	7♏21	315
	18	6:32	26♐31	0
	22	10:20	15♒45	45
	26	9:21	4♈47	90
	29	21:44	23♉22	135
Jan 2018	2	2:25	11♋38	180
	5	8:06	29♌56	225
	8	22:26	18♎36	270
	12	22:30	7♐40	315
	17	2:18	26♑54	0
	21	3:47	16♓03	45
	24	22:22	4♉53	90
	28	8:13	23♊21	135
	31	13:28	11♌37	180
Feb 2018	3	21:50	0♎01	225
	7	15:55	18♏49	270
	11	18:36	7♑59	315
	15	21:06	27♒08	0
	19	17:50	16♈02	45

The 8 Phases of the Moon 1900–2020

Month	Day	Time	Position	Phase
	23	8:10	4♊39	90
	26	17:18	23♋03	135
Mar 2018	2	0:52	11♍23	180
	5	13:14	29♎54	225
	9	11:21	18♐50	270
	13	14:46	7♒58	315
	17	13:13	26♓53	0
	21	4:22	15♉30	45
	24	15:36	3♋57	90
	28	1:31	22♌19	135
	31	12:38	10♎45	180
Apr 2018	4	5:48	29♏24	225
	8	7:19	18♑24	270
	12	9:01	7♓24	315
	16	1:58	26♈02	0
	19	12:15	14♊23	45
	22	21:47	2♌42	90
	26	9:32	21♍06	135
	30	0:59	9♏39	180
May 2018	3	23:01	28♐27	225
	8	2:10	17♒27	270
	12	0:09	6♈14	315
	15	11:49	24♉36	0
	18	18:43	12♋46	45
	22	3:50	1♍02	90
	25	18:15	19♎29	135
	29	14:21	8♐10	180
Jun 2018	2	16:10	27♑04	225
	6	18:33	16♓00	270
	10	12:02	4♉34	315
	13	19:44	22♊44	0
	17	0:55	10♌49	45
	20	10:52	29♍04	90
	24	4:37	17♏39	135
	28	4:54	6♑28	180
Jul 2018	2	8:17	25♒25	225
	6	7:52	14♈13	270
	9	21:21	2♊36	315
	13	2:49	20♋41	0
	16	7:53	8♍45	45
	19	19:53	27♎05	90
	23	17:23	15♐49	135
	27	20:21	4♒45	180
	31	22:32	23♓39	225
Aug 2018	4	18:19	12♉19	270
	8	5:03	0♋37	315
	11	9:59	18♌42	0
	14	16:30	6♎50	45
	18	7:50	25♏20	90
	22	8:50	14♑13	135
	26	11:57	3♓12	180
	30	10:36	22♈01	225
Sep 2018	3	2:39	10♊34	270
	6	12:02	28♋51	315
	9	18:03	17♍00	0
	13	3:38	5♏19	45
	16	23:16	24♐02	90
	21	2:25	13♒04	135
	25	2:54	2♈00	180
	28	20:47	20♉40	225
Oct 2018	2	9:47	9♋09	270
	5	19:10	27♌29	315
	9	3:48	15♎48	0
	12	18:00	4♐21	45
	16	18:03	23♑19	90
	20	20:58	12♓25	135
	24	16:46	1♉13	180
	28	5:53	19♊45	225
	31	16:41	8♌12	270
Nov 2018	4	3:17	26♍39	315
	7	16:03	15♏11	0
	11	11:49	4♑02	45
	15	14:55	23♒11	90
	19	15:08	12♈14	135
	23	5:40	0♊52	180
	26	14:44	19♋17	225
	30	0:20	7♍43	270
Dec 2018	3	13:19	26♎19	315
	7	7:22	15♐07	0
	11	8:14	4♒13	45
	15	11:50	23♓27	90
	19	7:53	12♉21	135
	22	17:50	0♋49	180
	26	0:02	19♌09	225
	29	9:35	7♎36	270
Jan 2019	2	2:08	26♏22	315
	6	1:29	15♑25	0
	10	5:13	4♓39	45
	14	6:47	23♈48	90
	17	22:36	12♊31	135
	21	5:17	0♌52	180
	24	10:09	19♍07	225
	27	21:12	7♏38	270
	31	18:00	26♐34	315
Feb 2019	4	21:05	15♒45	0
	9	0:27	4♈57	45
	12	22:27	23♉55	90
	16	10:53	12♋28	135
	19	15:55	0♍42	180
	22	21:18	18♎57	225
	26	11:29	7♐34	270
Mar 2019	2	12:15	26♑37	315
	6	16:05	15♓47	0
	10	16:24	4♉48	45
	14	10:28	23♊33	90
	17	20:37	11♌58	135
	21	1:44	0♎09	180
	24	9:44	18♏28	225
	28	4:11	7♑12	270
Apr 2019	1	7:15	26♒17	315
	5	8:52	15♈17	0
	9	4:43	4♊03	45
	12	19:07	22♋35	90
	16	4:11	10♍54	135
	19	11:13	29♎07	180
	22	23:36	17♐33	225
	26	22:19	6♒23	270
May 2019	1	1:19	25♓24	315
	4	22:47	14♉11	0
	8	13:51	2♋42	45
	12	1:13	21♌03	90
	15	10:31	9♎19	135
	18	21:13	27♏39	180
	22	14:53	16♑14	225
	26	16:35	5♓09	270
	30	17:23	24♈01	315
Jun 2019	3	10:03	12♊34	0
	6	20:44	0♌52	45
	10	6:00	19♍06	90
	13	16:59	7♏24	135
	17	8:32	25♐53	180
	21	7:08	14♒39	225
	25	9:48	3♈34	270
	29	7:12	22♉17	315
Jul 2019	2	19:17	10♋38	0
	6	2:25	28♌46	45
	9	10:56	16♎58	90
	13	0:59	5♐23	135
	16	21:39	24♑04	180
	20	23:34	12♓58	225
	25	1:19	1♉51	270
	28	19:00	20♊25	315
Aug 2019	1	3:13	8♌37	0
	4	8:08	26♍41	45
	7	17:32	14♏56	90
	11	11:40	3♑32	135
	15	12:30	22♒24	180
	19	15:29	11♈22	225
	23	14:57	0♊12	270
	27	5:06	18♋40	315
	30	10:38	6♍47	0
Sep 2019	2	15:08	24♎52	45
	6	3:12	13♐15	90
	10	1:34	2♒04	135
	14	4:34	21♓05	180
	18	6:20	10♉03	225
	22	2:42	28♊49	270
	25	13:56	17♌12	315
	28	18:28	5♎20	0
Oct 2019	2	0:41	23♏32	45
	5	16:48	12♑09	90
	9	18:28	1♓10	135
	13	21:09	20♈14	180
	17	19:52	9♊08	225
	21	12:40	27♋49	270
	24	22:04	16♍12	315
	28	3:40	4♏25	0
	31	13:43	22♐50	45
Nov 2019	4	10:24	11♒42	90
	8	13:31	0♈50	135
	12	13:36	19♉52	180
	16	7:56	8♋39	225
	19	21:12	27♌14	270
	23	6:15	15♎39	315
	26	15:07	4♐03	0
	30	6:26	22♑44	45
Dec 2019	4	6:59	11♓49	90
	8	9:25	0♉59	135
	12	5:13	19♊52	180
	15	18:33	8♌29	225
	19	4:58	26♍58	270
	22	15:27	15♏28	315
	26	5:14	4♑07	0
	30	1:58	23♒03	45
Jan 2020	3	4:47	12♈15	90
	7	4:41	1♊19	135
	10	19:22	20♋00	180
	14	4:01	8♍26	225
	17	13:00	26♎52	270
	21	2:30	15♐29	315
	24	21:43	4♒22	0
	28	22:40	23♓28	45
Feb 2020	2	1:43	12♉40	90
	5	21:50	1♋33	135
	9	7:34	20♌00	180
	12	12:58	8♎16	225
	15	22:18	26♏41	270
	19	15:46	15♑27	315
	23	15:33	4♓29	0
	27	18:38	23♈38	45
Mar 2020	2	19:59	12♊42	90
	6	11:48	1♌22	135
	9	17:49	19♍37	180
	12	22:06	7♏48	225
	16	9:35	26♐16	270
	20	6:58	15♒08	315
	24	9:29	4♈12	0
	28	12:20	23♉17	45
Apr 2020	1	10:22	12♋09	90
	4	22:19	0♍36	135
	8	2:36	18♎44	180
	11	8:07	6♐54	225
	14	22:57	25♑27	270
	18	23:25	14♓22	315
	23	2:27	3♉24	0
	27	2:47	22♊19	45
	30	20:39	10♌57	90
May 2020	4	5:56	29♍14	135
	7	10:46	17♏20	180
	10	19:25	5♑35	225
	14	14:04	24♒14	270
	18	16:17	13♈10	315
	22	17:40	2♊05	0
	26	13:45	20♋46	45
	30	3:31	9♍12	90
Jun 2020	2	11:52	27♎24	135
	5	19:14	15♐34	180
	9	8:11	3♒57	225
	13	6:25	22♓42	270
	17	8:51	11♉37	315
	21	6:43	0♋21	0
	24	21:43	18♌49	45
	28	8:17	7♎06	90
Jul 2020	1	17:27	25♏19	135
	5	4:46	13♑38	180
	8	22:26	2♓11	225
	12	23:30	21♈03	270
	17	0:32	9♊54	315
	20	17:34	28♋27	0
	24	3:44	16♍43	45
	27	12:34	4♏56	90
	31	0:03	23♐16	135
Aug 2020	3	16:00	11♒46	180
	7	14:08	0♈31	225
	11	16:46	19♉28	270
	15	14:49	8♋13	315
	19	2:43	26♌35	0
	22	9:14	14♎44	45
	25	17:59	2♐59	90
	29	8:48	21♑28	135
Sep 2020	2	5:23	10♓12	180
	6	7:01	29♈09	225
	10	9:27	18♊08	270
	14	3:26	6♌47	315
	17	11:01	25♍01	0
	20	15:44	13♏08	45
	24	1:56	1♑29	90
	27	20:34	20♒11	135
Oct 2020	1	21:06	9♈08	180
	6	0:27	28♉13	225
	10	0:41	17♋10	270
	13	14:30	5♍42	315
	16	19:32	23♎53	0
	20	0:29	12♐05	45
	23	13:24	0♒36	90
	27	11:48	19♓31	135
	31	14:50	8♉38	180
Nov 2020	4	17:21	27♊45	225
	8	13:47	16♌37	270
	12	0:27	5♎04	315
	15	5:08	23♏18	0
	18	12:14	11♑37	45
	22	4:46	0♓20	90
	26	6:21	19♈27	135
	30	9:31	8♊38	180
Dec 2020	4	8:29	27♋39	225
	8	0:38	16♍22	270
	11	9:51	4♏49	315
	14	16:18	23♐08	0
	18	3:04	11♒39	45
	21	23:42	0♈35	90
	26	3:04	19♉48	135
	30	3:29	8♋53	180

Part 10

High Energy Solar System Phenomena

- *Sunspots*
- *Major Magnetic Storms: Ap* 1932-1989*

SUNSPOTS

The energy of the thermonuclear furnace of the Sun, at the core, manifests in all kinds of disturbances—cold areas in the photosphere, called sunspots; hot areas in the chromosphere and corona, called plages; dense ribbons of cold material suspended in the corona, called quiescent prominences; and violent explosions called flares, in which a relatively tiny area of the Sun suddenly emits 10 times more energy than normal for a few minutes or hours. The result of each disturbance is a burst of radiation which reaches the Earth in about 8-1/2 minutes and causes ionospheric disturbances and radio interference. The disturbances also produce charged particles which reach the Earth in a spiral path a day or two later, causing auroras, magnetic storms and further radio interference.

Since sunspots have been observed since ancient times and much work has been done correlating their appearance with planetary cycles, we shall focus our attention on this manifestation of solar activity in hopes that the research-minded reader will be inspired to extend the range of phenomena correlated to sunspots and solar system cycles which might explain their origin.

Galileo's claim to having discovered sunspots with his telescope in 1610 is not now generally credited. The first printed accounts of sunspots sightings were made by the Frisian astronomer Fabricus in 1611 who used his observations to verify the rotation of the solar disk. Chinese astronomers had been recording naked eye sightings of large sunspots since about AD 300.

A sunspot is a dark, sharply defined region on the solar disk with an umbra 2,000 K cooler than the temperature of the Sun's photosphere surrounded by a lighter but still sharply defined penumbra. The average spot is about 37,000 km in diameter, but exceptionally large spots can be larger than 240,000 km across. Most sunspots are found in groups of two or more and their magnetic field is much higher than that of the solar disk as a whole. They rarely last more than two to three weeks.

It wasn't until 1843, when amateur astronomer Heinrich Schwabe published a paper (1844) on his observations of sunspots from 1826 to 1843, that anyone noted in print the fact that sunspots go in cycles. Rudolph Wolf, director of the astronomical observatory in Zurich, Switzerland, was prompted by Schwabe's startling report to devise a quantitative definition for sunspot number. He applied it to the existing historical data to see if Schwabe's 10-year cycle could be found in longer spans of time. Wolf did find such cycles when he examined the data for the years 1700 through 1848. The average cycle length is 11.1 years.

For the mathematically minded, the Wolf sunspot number R is defined as

$$R = k(10g+f)$$

where **f** is the total number of spots regardless of size, g is the number of spot groups, and **k** reconciles the counts from different observatories. It is clear that groups are weighted more heavily than individual spots. Daily counts of sunspots are made routinely at many astronomical observatories and combined according to the above equation and are available from the Zurich observatory or the World Data Center in Boulder, Colorado, as daily numbers, monthly means and yearly means. There is a table of yearly mean values in this book from 1700 through 1988 (See page 200). The validity of Wolf numbers from 1700 to 1748 is poor, from 1749 to 1817 is questionable and from 1818 to 1847 is good. From 1848 on the numbers are based on close observation.

The sunspot cycle length varies from about 8.5 to 14 years between successive minima and from 7.3 to about 17 years between maxima. The beginning of each new cycle is marked by the appearance of new sunspots at high solar latitudes. As the cycle progresses, sunspots appear at successively lower latitudes until most appear within 5° of the solar equator near the end of an 11-year period. The magnetic polarity of a new high latitude group is opposite to that of low latitude groups belonging to the old cycle. This means that a cycle that accounts for polarity is really 22 years long rather than 11.

The beginning of a new cycle usually overlaps the end of the old cycle sometimes by a year or more. An old spot or two near the equator can exist simultaneously with a new high latitude spot or group of spots of opposite magnetic polarity. The precise time of sunspot minima is established only in retrospect. Observations of the movement of sunspots from high latitude toward the equator led to the discovery that the Sun rotates at different speeds at different latitudes—at the equator the rotation period is 25 days, at 30° latitude it is 27.5 days, and at the solar poles it is 35 days. The average rotation period is 27 days and it is this period that is most often referred to in Sun weather literature.

Sunspot cycles have been correlated to rainfall, weather, climate, commodity prices, electromagnetic disturbances, calamities of various types, premature satellite orbit decay, etc. In the case of the *Skylab* which fell to earth on July 11, 1979, in Australia, the problem was one of atmospheric density and drag. At the height of 300 miles the air density can be 10 times greater during sunspot maxima than during minima. A satellite at that 300-mile height could have a 5-

year life if launched two years before a minimum and only six months if launched at a maximum.

If sunspot cycles can be correlated with many other natural and human-based cycles, the question then is how can we predict sunspot cycle variations such as length and intensity?

Astronomers and others have worked at finding planetary harmonics or resonances that correlate to sunspot cycles. The following are some examples that I found in the literature.

Short Period Resonances of the Inner Planets

Period	Earth Years
46 sidereal revolutions of Mercury	11.079
18 sidereal revolutions of Venus	11.074
137 synodic revolutions of Moon	11.077
11 sidereal revolutions of Earth	11.000
6 sidereal revolutions of Mars	11.286

There are more periodicities of sunspot activity than just the 11-year one. Others that have been identified are 5.5, 8.1, 9.7, 100, and 180 years.

Long Period Resonances of the Outer Planets

Period	Earth Years
6 sidereal revolutions of Saturn	176.746
15 sidereal revolutions of Jupiter	177.933
9 synodic periods Jupiter-Saturn	178.734
14 synodic periods Jupiter-Neptune	178.923
13 synodic periods Jupiter-Uranus	179.542
5 synodic periods Saturn-Neptune	179.385
4 synodic periods Saturn-Uranus	181.455

In *Recent Advances* Geoffrey Dean has a very extensive discussion of planetary cycles that have resonances that may be useful in understanding solar cycles. He proposes an original theory that uses the Jupiter/Neptune synodic period of 22.13 years, the Neptune/Pluto midpoint and Neptune-Pluto aspects to account for sunspot cycles including the Maunder minimum (the time from 1645 to 1715 when sunspot activity was just about nil.)

Dean lists 36 cycles that resonate at 21 to 22 years, the complete sunspot period when accounting for the polarity shift between successive cycles. (See Table at right.)

References

Geoffrey Dean and Arthur Mather ed., *Recent Advances in Natal Astrology: A Critical Review 1900-1976* (The Astrological Association, Bromley, Kent, England, 1977).
John R. Herman and Richard A. Goldberg, *Sun, Weather, and Climate* (U.S. Government Printing Office, 1978).
D. Justin Schove, ed., *Sunspot Cycles* (Stroudsburg, Pennsylvania: Hutchinson Ross Publishing Company, 1983).

36 Sunspot Cycles
(From *Recent Advances in Natal Astrology*)

22.68	♄ - ♅	x1/2
22.57	♅ - ♃/♄/♆	x2/3
22.57	♂ - SE	x12
22.55	♃/♄	x4/3
22.52	♇/11	
22.46	♃/♇ - ♄/♅	x1/2
22.43	♃ - ♇	x9/5
22.42	♄ - ♆	x5/8
22.38	♆ - ♇	x1/22
22.34	♃ - ♄	x9/8
22.34	Mass Displ	x1/8
22.29	♄ - ♇	x2/3
22.29	♃ + ♄ - ♆	x5/2
22.26	♅/♆	x1/5
22.25	♄ - ♃/♆	x1/4
22.23	♄ + ♆ - ♅	x5/8
22.21	♄/♆	x4/9
22.19	♃ + ♅ - ♆	x2
22.16	☿ - SE	x92
22.15	♃ + ♆ - ♄	x5/4
22.15	♀ - SE	x36
22.13	♃/♆	
22.11	♄ - SE	x3/4
22.10	♃ - ♅	x8/5
22.08	♆ - SE	x2/15
22.02	♃/♄/♅/♆	x3
22.00	♃/♅/♆	x9/4
22.00	TE - SE	x22
21.99	♆/♇	x1/9
21.81	♄/♅	x1/2
21.45	♃/♄/♆	x8/3
21.42	♃ + ♅ - ♄	x4/3
21.36	♃ - SE	x9/5
21.19	♅ - ♇	x1/6
21.18	♅ - ♃/♄	
21.03	♅ - SE	x1/4

SE = Solar Equator TE = Terrestrial Equator

Yearly Mean Sunspot Numbers

Year	Number		Year	Number		Year	Number		Year	Number		Year	Number	
1700	5		1758	47.6		1816	45.8	MAX	1874	44.7		1932	11.1	
1701	11		1759	54.0		1817	41.1		1875	17.0		1933	5.7	min
1702	16		1760	62.9		1818	30.1		1876	11.3		1934	8.7	
1703	23		1761	85.9	MAX	1819	23.9		1877	12.4		1935	36.1	
1704	36		1762	61.2		1820	15.6		1878	3.4	min	1936	79.7	
1705	58	MAX	1763	45.1		1821	6.6		1879	6.0		1937	114.4	MAX
1706	29		1764	36.4		1822	4.0		1880	32.3		1938	109.6	
1707	20		1765	20.9		1823	1.8	min	1881	54.3		1939	88.8	
1708	10		1766	11.4	min	1824	8.5		1882	59.7		1940	67.8	
1709	8		1767	37.8		1825	16.6		1883	63.7	MAX	1941	47.5	
1710	3		1768	69.8		1826	36.3		1884	63.5		1942	30.6	
1711	0		1769	106.1	MAX	1827	49.6		1885	52.2		1943	16.3	
1712	0	min	1770	100.8		1828	64.2		1886	25.4		1944	9.6	min
1713	2		1771	81.6		1829	67.0		1887	13.1		1945	33.2	
1714	11		1772	66.5		1830	70.9	MAX	1888	6.8		1946	92.6	
1715	27		1773	34.8		1831	47.8		1889	6.3	min	1947	151.6	MAX
1716	47		1774	30.6		1832	27.5		1890	7.1		1948	136.3	
1717	63	MAX	1775	7.0	min	1833	8.5	min	1891	35.6		1949	134.7	
1718	60		1776	19.8		1834	13.2		1892	73.0		1950	83.9	
1719	39		1777	92.5		1835	56.9		1893	85.1	MAX	1951	69.4	
1720	28		1778	154.4	MAX	1836	121.5		1894	78.0		1952	31.5	
1721	26		1779	125.9		1837	138.3	MAX	1895	64.0		1953	13.9	
1722	22		1780	84.8		1838	103.2		1896	41.8		1954	4.4	min
1723	11	min	1781	68.1		1839	85.7		1897	26.2		1955	38.0	
1724	21		1782	38.5		1840	64.6		1898	26.7		1956	141.7	
1725	40		1783	22.8		1841	36.7		1899	12.1		1957	190.2	MAX
1726	78		1784	10.2	min	1842	24.2		1900	9.5		1958	184.8	
1727	122	MAX	1785	24.1		1843	10.7	min	1901	2.7	min	1959	159.0	
1728	103		1786	82.9		1844	15.0		1902	5.0		1960	112.3	
1729	73		1787	132.0	MAX	1845	40.1		1903	24.4		1961	53.9	
1730	47		1788	130.9		1846	61.5		1904	42.0		1962	37.6	
1731	35		1789	118.1		1847	98.5		1905	63.5	MAX	1963	27.9	
1732	11		1790	89.9		1848	124.7	MAX	1906	53.8		1964	10.2	min
1733	5	min	1791	66.6		1849	96.3		1907	62.0		1965	15.1	
1734	16		1792	60.0		1850	66.6		1908	48.5		1966	47.0	
1735	34		1793	46.9		1851	64.5		1909	43.9		1967	93.8	
1736	70		1794	41.0		1852	54.1		1910	18.6		1968	105.9	MAX
1737	81		1795	21.3		1853	39.0		1911	5.7		1969	105.5	
1738	111	MAX	1796	16.0		1854	20.6		1912	3.6		1970	104.5	
1739	101		1797	6.4		1855	6.7		1913	1.4	min	1971	66.6	
1740	73		1798	4.1	min	1856	4.3	min	1914	9.6		1972	68.9	
1741	40		1799	6.8		1857	22.7		1915	47.4		1973	38.0	
1742	20		1800	14.5		1858	54.8		1916	57.1		1974	34.5	
1743	16		1801	34.0		1859	93.8		1917	103.9	MAX	1975	15.5	
1744	5	min	1802	45.0		1860	95.8	MAX	1918	80.6		1976	12.6	min
1745	11		1803	43.1		1861	77.2		1919	63.6		1977	27.5	
1746	22		1804	47.5	MAX	1862	59.1		1920	37.6		1978	92.5	
1747	40		1805	42.2		1863	44.0		1921	26.1		1979	155.4	MAX
1748	60		1806	28.1		1864	47.0		1922	14.2		1980	154.6	
1749	80.9		1807	10.1		1865	30.5		1923	5.8	min	1981	140.4	
1750	83.4	MAX	1808	8.1		1866	16.3		1924	16.7		1982	115.9	
1751	47.7		1809	2.5		1867	7.3	min	1925	44.3		1983	66.6	
1752	47.8		1810	0.0	min	1868	37.6		1926	63.9		1984	45.9	
1753	30.7		1811	1.4		1869	74.0		1927	69.0		1985	17.9	
1754	12.2		1812	5.0		1870	139.0	MAX	1928	77.8	MAX	1986	13.4	min
1755	9.6	min	1813	12.2		1871	111.2		1929	64.9		1987	29.4	
1756	10.2		1814	13.9		1872	101.6		1930	35.7		1988	100.2	
1757	32.4		1815	35.4		1873	66.2		1931	21.2				

Each 'MAX' marks a sunspot cycle maximum and each 'min' a minimum. Through 1944 yearly means were calculated as the average of the 12 monthly means; since 1945 yearly means have been calculated as the average of the daily means.

Daily Sunspot Numbers 1930–1989

Daily Sunspot Numbers 1930

Day	Jan	Feb	Mar	Apr	May	Jun	Jul	Aug	Sep	Oct	Nov	Dec
01	36	47	23	56	52	31	22	17	56	26	57	45
02	41	73	24	59	52	28	36	23	46	30	41	35
03	55	98	28	41	50	28	35	7	48	26	25	33
04	38	111	54	42	41	34	28	7	68	30	26	20
05	49	117	55	58	30	27	26	7	66	44	16	8
06	55	110	50	57	37	34	28	17	73	43	8	7
07	62	111	50	65	24	70	18	17	70	39	8	7
08	68	82	49	35	26	65	18	16	41	37	8	0
09	62	101	53	46	23	62	39	20	40	35	8	8
10	56	66	28	50	19	52	21	20	41	59	15	19
11	65	79	17	56	22	52	15	21	39	53	8	21
12	70	55	30	50	25	42	26	21	33	48	15	17
13	91	47	26	60	25	37	16	23	39	56	0	15
14	89	37	17	45	18	23	24	13	23	38	12	22
15	96	36	28	33	32	21	25	10	28	32	14	22
16	108	22	44	22	41	20	24	9	17	24	21	20
17	107	21	52	20	35	16	29	10	8	11	26	30
18	135	23	44	14	25	15	9	23	0	22	31	52
19	95	17	42	10	31	9	8	23	7	22	43	50
20	63	8	33	26	39	14	9	29	7	11	57	42
21	74	10	31	30	31	8	25	31	8	8	63	33
22	59	13	33	31	33	8	14	28	10	11	66	27
23	63	17	8	28	45	7	22	38	12	18	68	29
24	49	20	24	23	67	10	14	37	18	16	48	42
25	39	16	17	24	46	16	15	41	20	29	58	52
26	34	15	25	25	43	14	16	35	35	37	76	54
27	31	19	36	22	56	32	18	37	33	63	72	33
28	46	26	31	39	38	28	34	43	31	53	67	19
29	60		30	34	52	29	33	53	27	49	61	8
30	67		52	46	48	31	10	50	20	49	51	15
31	62		52		35		22	47		47		15
Mean	65.3	49.9	35.0	38.2	36.8	28.8	21.9	24.9	32.1	34.4	35.6	25.8

1930 Yearly Mean = 35.7

Daily Sunspot Numbers 1931

Day	Jan	Feb	Mar	Apr	May	Jun	Jul	Aug	Sep	Oct	Nov	Dec
01	0	0	34	34	17	13	22	23	34	10	8	19
02	7	8	31	32	8	28	23	35	27	21	14	15
03	0	28	25	29	7	34	23	34	26	14	17	7
04	9	27	33	37	8	36	19	28	18	18	18	0
05	18	23	37	25	8	30	19	28	15	15	24	0
06	11	29	33	31	17	36	16	19	14	15	27	6
07	11	18	29	41	17	32	38	8	15	7	13	12
08	12	27	37	45	26	44	35	0	18	8	12	13
09	14	29	33	46	20	35	28	2	13	7	16	24
10	11	28	33	29	33	47	48	0	24	0	0	29
11	10	20	38	37	33	20	35	8	29	7	0	35
12	9	20	38	36	26	14	26	0	23	0	0	37
13	16	23	43	44	32	0	30	8	27	8	0	38
14	41	19	47	38	17	10	23	0	26	9	0	35
15	43	41	46	37	36	0	8	0	19	8	0	25
16	27	44	41	31	37	0	7	0	27	0	0	22
17	20	47	51	41	29	0	8	11	28	0	8	15
18	22	45	49	22	32	7	7	14	26	0	14	8
19	19	50	38	20	34	0	0	14	11	8	10	8
20	24	64	40	20	22	0	0	10	13	8	16	8
21	24	89	27	38	30	0	7	10	10	10	37	8
22	22	79	25	41	26	7	10	0	22	9	41	15
23	21	100	17	27	35	0	8	0	22	25	33	16
24	16	92	16	29	32	0	8	0	16	18	40	22
25	20	68	8	37	31	0	8	0	7	12	44	31
26	7	76	8	21	35	0	0	8	7	11	42	30
27	8	67	8	19	35	8	7	26	15	11	35	30
28	5	47	14	14	20	10	9	36	17	11	31	15
29	7		16	17	19	25	22	25	10	9	35	9
30	0		9	18	20	23	23	26	11	12	27	11
31	0		27		20		23	30		18		9
Mean	14.6	43.1	30.0	31.2	24.6	15.3	17.4	13.0	19.0	10.0	18.7	17.8

1931 Yearly Mean = 21.2

Daily Sunspot Numbers 1932

Day	Jan	Feb	Mar	Apr	May	Jun	Jul	Aug	Sep	Oct	Nov	Dec
01	13	19	34	8	8	8	21	9	7	7	7	18
02	26	16	46	8	0	0	24	11	7	7	10	13
03	14	17	37	16	0	10	26	9	7	7	13	13
04	8	8	24	9	0	12	31	10	0	0	12	10
05	8	8	22	0	0	12	34	10	0	0	0	8
06	0	8	22	0	0	23	21	9	0	8	0	8
07	0	7	16	0	8	33	14	8	0	7	0	10
08	3	7	10	0	12	39	15	8	0	0	0	11
09	0	0	10	0	14	31	11	0	0	0	0	13
10	7	9	8	0	8	31	10	0	0	0	7	13
11	0	9	0	0	9	32	9	8	0	0	9	15
12	0	7	0	0	9	11	8	0	14	7	9	22
13	0	0	0	0	8	8	9	0	7	8	9	23
14	5	0	0	0	25	8	0	0	0	7	10	16
15	10	0	0	8	38	8	0	0	0	8	9	15
16	15	0	0	8	35	16	0	0	0	8	0	13
17	12	0	9	9	41	16	0	0	0	8	13	18
18	8	0	12	8	40	21	8	0	0	15	23	20
19	7	0	9	0	27	28	0	0	8	21	27	19
20	0	0	7	0	38	26	8	0	0	29	31	16
21	8	0	7	18	30	32	0	0	19	20	25	0
22	19	0	7	34	31	27	7	0	8	19	12	0
23	17	18	0	29	31	31	0	0	0	20	0	0
24	16	23	7	23	34	29	0	13	8	12	0	0
25	26	26	0	31	23	40	0	19	8	11	0	0
26	44	26	8	31	22	30	0	22	0	10	0	0
27	37	39	15	32	18	26	8	26	3	8	0	10
28	18	31	15	27	17	31	8	16	8	8	0	11
29	18	29	8	24	10	22	9	17	8	7	7	10
30	18		8	14	10	24	9	8	7	6	12	9
31	17		7		8		9	8		7		8
Mean	12.1	10.6	11.2	11.2	17.9	22.2	9.6	6.8	4.0	8.9	8.2	11.0

1932 Yearly Mean = 11.1

Daily Sunspot Numbers 1933

Day	Jan	Feb	Mar	Apr	May	Jun	Jul	Aug	Sep	Oct	Nov	Dec
01	0	45	10	9	0	0	0	0	0	0	10	0
02	0	48	10	8	8	7	0	0	7	0	0	0
03	8	67	10	0	0	7	0	0	7	0	0	0
04	15	59	13	0	0	7	0	0	7	0	8	0
05	17	62	11	0	0	7	0	0	0	0	0	0
06	17	67	11	0	0	14	7	0	15	0	0	0
07	19	53	11	0	0	2	17	0	19	0	0	0
08	20	53	14	0	0	0	17	0	12	0	0	0
09	16	47	9	0	3	0	18	0	11	0	0	0
10	18	33	8	0	8	0	14	0	7	8	0	0
11	17	33	7	0	0	0	8	0	0	0	0	8
12	26	16	7	0	0	0	7	7	0	2	0	0
13	42	11	0	0	0	12	0	0	0	0	0	0
14	36	8	0	0	0	16	0	0	0	0	0	0
15	27	0	0	0	0	19	0	0	0	0	0	0
16	14	0	0	0	0	14	0	0	0	0	0	0
17	7	0	0	13	0	10	0	0	0	0	0	0
18	0	0	0	13	0	8	0	0	0	0	0	0
19	0	0	0	20	8	8	0	0	0	0	0	0
20	0	0	0	10	12	8	0	0	0	0	0	0
21	0	0	0	8	12	8	0	0	7	0	0	0
22	0	0	12	0	11	9	0	0	11	0	0	0
23	0	0	14	0	17	0	0	0	11	0	0	0
24	0	0	14	0	12	0	0	0	8	0	0	0
25	0	0	24	0	8	0	0	0	0	0	0	0
26	0	0	29	0	0	0	0	0	0	7	0	0
27	0	8	26	0	0	0	0	0	0	20	0	0
28	9	11	28	0	0	0	0	0	11	19	0	0
29	12		22	7	0	0	0	0	12	14	0	0
30	25		13	0	0	0	0	0	8	13	0	0
31	35		10		0		0	0		10		0
Mean	12.3	22.2	10.1	2.9	3.2	5.2	2.8	0.2	5.1	3.0	0.6	0.3

1933 Yearly Mean = 5.7

Daily Sunspot Numbers 1930–1989

Daily Sunspot Numbers 1934

Day	Jan	Feb	Mar	Apr	May	Jun	Jul	Aug	Sep	Oct	Nov	Dec
01	0	11	0	0	7	0	0	0	0	15	13	27
02	0	9	0	11	0	0	0	0	0	0	14	20
03	0	9	0	12	0	0	0	0	7	0	16	12
04	0	0	6	9	14	0	0	0	0	8	14	14
05	0	10	0	8	17	0	0	0	0	0	12	14
06	0	11	7	0	21	0	8	8	0	0	14	10
07	0	19	9	0	26	0	8	9	0	0	10	13
08	0	8	19	0	34	0	11	9	0	0	8	11
09	0	14	22	0	23	7	11	10	0	0	10	0
10	0	8	12	0	19	0	18	11	7	0	7	0
11	0	9	15	0	10	0	24	12	0	7	7	0
12	8	9	7	0	7	0	24	21	7	8	7	0
13	11	16	0	0	15	0	25	22	7	8	0	0
14	12	17	0	7	21	0	24	24	8	8	0	0
15	13	10	0	21	26	11	20	24	16	9	0	0
16	16	11	0	33	25	27	23	27	9	9	0	0
17	11	11	0	32	35	31	17	17	8	8	0	0
18	4	11	7	29	41	26	18	22	0	8	7	0
19	0	8	0	22	46	25	17	13	0	14	0	0
20	0	0	0	21	37	14	9	0	0	0	0	14
21	0	0	0	22	29	16	8	0	0	0	0	24
22	0	0	0	18	34	10	0	0	0	7	0	21
23	0	0	0	16	33	10	0	7	7	8	0	27
24	0	10	0	19	23	8	8	8	0	0	0	25
25	0	7	7	11	19	8	8	0	0	7	7	47
26	0	0	7	10	17	8	0	0	0	7	11	37
27	0	0	0	16	9	0	0	7	0	7	14	29
28	0	0	0	14	16	0	6	0	9	7	23	35
29	8		7	7	8	0	0	0	14	9	35	31
30	11		7	0	0	0	0	7	21	16	31	36
31	12		0		0		0	0		8		31
Mean	3.4	7.8	4.3	11.3	19.7	6.7	9.3	8.3	4.0	5.7	8.7	15.4

1934 Yearly Mean = 8.7

Daily Sunspot Numbers 1935

Day	Jan	Feb	Mar	Apr	May	Jun	Jul	Aug	Sep	Oct	Nov	Dec
01	34	10	19	0	17	34	41	10	30	71	22	50
02	27	10	16	0	26	39	29	11	36	73	17	57
03	27	9	19	0	46	34	29	22	37	68	42	64
04	22	9	12	7	56	34	24	24	46	52	46	65
05	17	10	18	0	56	31	28	18	47	61	46	53
06	21	29	15	0	56	41	29	28	46	57	41	67
07	19	48	8	0	56	25	22	43	47	53	59	77
08	12	30	8	11	62	46	50	49	47	40	59	79
09	11	24	17	21	54	59	43	26	53	12	67	85
10	9	28	27	22	41	73	38	33	32	7	61	65
11	11	22	34	16	46	74	43	29	23	25	68	77
12	24	26	44	22	41	66	58	38	22	37	68	85
13	24	18	56	34	41	55	62	37	33	65	97	63
14	28	27	72	30	49	41	51	34	29	58	98	59
15	16	22	68	37	32	49	48	29	26	69	111	67
16	16	20	50	22	27	42	49	26	33	68	104	59
17	14	10	43	18	8	38	47	20	34	95	102	58
18	13	7	33	20	0	43	46	29	33	84	94	48
19	10	19	40	11	0	38	51	23	31	79	91	27
20	9	28	34	16	0	67	60	52	20	64	70	27
21	7	21	24	15	0	50	36	55	18	76	71	44
22	14	29	17	16	0	35	32	40	21	67	52	41
23	16	17	12	9	0	29	30	34	45	63	62	47
24	31	17	8	7	17	38	29	35	56	63	45	53
25	32	25	7	7	7	44	23	32	59	65	44	79
26	31	18	8	0	8	51	19	29	69	59	56	62
27	26	20	7	0	8	56	11	13	80	40	58	79
28	26	20	0	0	8	52	8	26	71	28	58	63
29	11		0	8	17	45	0	28	78	24	64	61
30	9		0	16	30	42	8	24	61	13	53	70
31	11		0		38		8	37		13		75
Mean	18.6	20.5	23.1	12.2	27.3	45.7	33.9	30.1	42.1	53.2	64.2	61.5

1935 Yearly Mean = 36.1

Daily Sunspot Numbers 1936

Day	Jan	Feb	Mar	Apr	May	Jun	Jul	Aug	Sep	Oct	Nov	Dec
01	56	45	74	93	29	77	79	66	110	113	118	193
02	70	45	68	100	44	97	74	64	68	98	137	179
03	61	46	60	91	47	65	44	74	77	103	149	176
04	69	43	55	74	57	62	50	65	57	112	144	161
05	63	67	69	85	47	62	52	87	68	122	159	158
06	55	56	60	91	36	66	37	86	65	137	151	146
07	37	61	83	86	46	69	30	89	46	138	127	116
08	37	93	89	76	46	73	47	89	53	122	140	134
09	41	84	88	89	46	64	43	107	42	107	127	104
10	29	73	92	99	40	40	47	89	40	81	150	107
11	34	60	79	91	54	35	49	83	49	81	148	82
12	38	93	67	92	49	40	67	70	70	82	133	76
13	44	69	59	83	71	43	67	88	94	76	139	74
14	62	77	69	86	73	32	76	103	77	92	117	71
15	70	77	56	73	68	19	67	122	64	123	119	40
16	56	91	61	88	67	55	69	93	71	104	95	43
17	58	58	60	88	64	67	67	105	63	105	95	71
18	79	55	66	73	47	60	53	115	66	82	61	88
19	83	56	87	83	36	101	49	89	58	80	60	85
20	87	74	112	75	26	88	43	64	74	85	40	74
21	99	111	104	67	45	119	28	71	80	65	29	86
22	98	97	96	49	49	100	27	63	116	55	40	117
23	104	87	82	56	44	76	30	64	128	63	48	130
24	107	109	53	53	85	71	36	63	90	52	44	149
25	85	90	49	72	71	89	42	90	89	35	70	153
26	72	97	65	77	78	112	49	75	85	40	99	152
27	75	91	78	55	65	103	38	87	95	52	145	164
28	50	85	98	48	68	68	47	89	94	77	218	135
29	49	64	98	32	68	68	59	106	86	86	197	170
30	37		103	21	48	79	61	123	106	95	162	205
31	42		109		78		93	118		95		187
Mean	62.8	74.3	77.1	74.9	54.6	70.0	52.3	87.0	76.0	89.0	115.4	123.4

1936 Yearly Mean = 79.7

Daily Sunspot Numbers 1937

Day	Jan	Feb	Mar	Apr	May	Jun	Jul	Aug	Sep	Oct	Nov	Dec
01	144	211	154	138	89	79	69	176	108	131	104	14
02	156	224	154	128	91	89	91	180	106	170	115	33
03	109	181	109	112	77	92	74	207	124	214	105	34
04	107	152	65	137	56	116	65	197	82	206	67	29
05	83	146	76	147	59	128	91	205	79	175	68	54
06	82	128	71	112	46	121	108	176	85	182	49	50
07	94	98	105	119	47	102	143	135	101	173	34	67
08	103	90	115	94	50	64	185	154	104	157	47	49
09	97	75	107	85	68	73	181	173	119	153	68	56
10	85	85	99	71	103	98	192	183	119	161	85	56
11	97	70	98	82	99	96	202	140	110	148	79	72
12	91	77	59	62	91	134	223	144	100	137	83	70
13	80	87	42	38	102	166	188	114	110	142	100	107
14	93	87	21	28	123	185	215	124	101	138	106	112
15	87	90	20	53	140	191	204	128	99	113	74	141
16	104	101	23	64	183	174	180	119	76	127	69	155
17	108	92	22	63	188	190	152	75	58	127	93	115
18	108	88	37	76	158	194	167	82	82	121	90	109
19	101	111	33	94	158	185	155	88	88	114	74	124
20	128	114	42	127	177	183	149	96	88	89	82	107
21	127	130	62	127	154	186	150	80	73	72	62	86
22	163	190	74	146	194	199	145	103	102	58	62	90
23	155	155	107	144	202	163	139	139	128	63	59	107
24	178	187	94	157	213	133	126	150	120	75	50	116
25	181	162	87	190	171	108	124	137	127	69	61	124
26	200	167	80	157	130	116	115	144	104	59	70	114
27	180	149	118	161	93	91	143	143	80	58	96	125
28	201	150	131	149	71	80	124	130	101	104	64	103
29	200		117	123	83	80	128	110	126	90	68	111
30	233		135	94	103	93	139	109	121	113	47	110
31	233		143		98		131	128		133		112
Mean	132.5	128.5	83.9	109.3	116.7	130.3	145.1	137.7	100.7	124.9	74.4	88.8

1937 Yearly Mean = 114.4

Daily Sunspot Numbers 1930–1989

Daily Sunspot Numbers 1938

Day	Jan	Feb	Mar	Apr	May	Jun	Jul	Aug	Sep	Oct	Nov	Dec
01	117	62	74	83	115	113	119	144	106	130	146	97
02	109	73	67	81	134	100	116	121	124	94	143	82
03	86	68	62	80	160	107	157	121	101	55	162	64
04	76	94	45	80	137	103	151	153	107	90	128	82
05	80	85	43	91	123	91	141	132	120	106	112	58
06	101	128	52	95	138	86	184	133	136	102	167	90
07	102	124	78	95	136	134	175	135	100	92	176	117
08	86	110	71	85	153	139	186	150	88	102	159	106
09	59	101	97	87	156	115	175	158	74	143	138	130
10	92	133	106	103	151	115	183	161	75	152	131	124
11	98	137	134	110	149	106	205	173	67	132	125	129
12	104	161	124	97	143	99	211	132	59	134	134	154
13	106	169	161	119	151	91	229	124	44	121	152	124
14	111	200	149	115	135	88	208	107	48	122	152	151
15	118	171	145	117	131	87	200	102	44	103	161	120
16	134	205	161	133	105	76	173	119	47	78	157	105
17	110	171	140	107	91	76	161	106	46	71	137	76
18	110	174	105	112	87	56	148	100	65	31	115	77
19	104	145	80	100	95	69	151	104	55	20	106	87
20	119	98	77	99	116	76	153	76	57	58	97	89
21	123	109	86	89	106	103	147	65	56	55	78	88
22	122	91	64	75	124	101	118	72	70	46	56	88
23	149	90	71	82	119	98	157	94	86	61	61	81
24	108	92	66	95	172	88	189	86	97	66	79	88
25	94	83	59	92	161	76	202	113	131	91	94	82
26	76	81	34	92	152	72	179	103	150	104	85	73
27	67	97	52	124	126	108	156	91	143	114	110	73
28	76	85	55	144	99	106	151	94	137	138	107	69
29	59		65	144	104	128	151	114	125	148	103	64
30	79		73	105	89	119	139	105	131	159	95	44
31	76		86		91		109	98		155		63
Mean	98.4	119.2	86.5	101.0	127.4	97.5	165.3	115.7	89.6	99.1	122.2	92.7

1938 Yearly Mean = 109.6

Daily Sunspot Numbers 1939

Day	Jan	Feb	Mar	Apr	May	Jun	Jul	Aug	Sep	Oct	Nov	Dec
01	41	79	102	34	163	129	103	67	103	144	81	54
02	42	90	92	85	157	120	97	78	116	143	88	40
03	60	97	70	83	119	113	112	73	124	109	72	43
04	76	67	75	82	141	97	128	94	119	92	61	27
05	58	56	60	74	124	104	130	90	136	90	58	18
06	90	82	52	70	115	124	122	112	136	82	62	17
07	68	76	52	63	133	127	151	106	114	91	66	23
08	78	85	44	86	105	113	167	141	145	91	37	47
09	55	64	61	89	103	116	130	157	159	77	40	45
10	134	44	47	98	128	104	143	151	168	67	46	52
11	118	49	49	102	101	119	131	157	136	56	66	49
12	111	73	55	100	142	102	118	170	150	74	82	56
13	103	86	55	112	121	107	101	159	127	85	84	48
14	84	76	46	126	148	112	97	138	92	68	99	62
15	86	56	58	121	139	101	87	146	96	73	87	58
16	55	62	55	141	118	97	74	122	83	68	111	53
17	71	62	83	109	93	92	85	128	69	79	94	52
18	63	61	112	102	79	91	86	111	67	74	103	61
19	70	62	133	94	79	89	95	110	88	92	75	44
20	74	82	112	125	68	56	113	104	70	95	50	46
21	86	92	89	125	87	68	106	94	89	86	67	46
22	83	96	77	115	85	68	96	86	88	94	66	47
23	77	98	74	152	93	65	80	72	88	94	62	35
24	90	93	66	151	106	74	67	75	107	112	61	41
25	102	112	48	134	107	61	62	58	106	112	58	32
26	86	74	49	134	97	84	53	69	98	100	59	37
27	102	101	41	146	104	109	50	86	105	80	62	32
28	103	92	35	145	138	137	57	85	131	64	61	31
29	72		41	136	172	134	71	69	131	81	43	28
30	76		36	140	157	118	68	76	137	85	43	47
31	76		35		146		46	95		74		34
Mean	80.3	77.4	64.6	109.1	118.3	101.0	97.6	105.8	112.6	88.1	68.1	42.1

1939 Yearly Mean = 88.8

Daily Sunspot Numbers 1940

Day	Jan	Feb	Mar	Apr	May	Jun	Jul	Aug	Sep	Oct	Nov	Dec
01	39	58	91	85	26	38	91	69	130	38	41	27
02	37	59	74	80	28	41	67	60	112	33	41	17
03	42	58	96	65	23	77	77	67	127	29	67	29
04	69	52	116	46	25	80	47	105	97	32	61	45
05	66	55	92	62	19	58	56	103	91	35	67	66
06	61	47	81	58	21	95	44	111	89	44	43	68
07	49	63	77	64	22	94	56	121	68	57	56	89
08	38	64	72	56	32	106	68	119	62	60	67	82
09	47	82	46	41	31	103	97	129	42	53	76	108
10	41	65	47	59	34	107	122	148	49	57	63	142
11	50	41	48	50	36	109	125	128	40	70	60	157
12	29	69	76	53	53	94	126	124	38	77	66	135
13	34	62	74	53	62	104	101	162	37	72	99	158
14	61	89	76	60	93	76	76	128	41	66	70	149
15	47	78	49	74	91	82	62	110	32	70	92	100
16	61	73	70	65	85	59	74	98	50	71	100	79
17	52	51	43	65	77	55	60	109	56	59	88	67
18	64	50	56	59	63	51	62	114	79	71	87	60
19	59	52	78	71	69	46	66	97	100	61	65	29
20	88	65	79	79	61	38	67	126	98	67	47	37
21	71	60	85	94	71	58	52	124	106	64	34	37
22	50	59	92	83	86	61	58	126	93	74	16	38
23	52	44	111	63	85	83	34	116	66	68	25	27
24	34	40	115	64	67	113	34	94	61	41	41	58
25	30	44	101	56	76	108	48	84	53	45	56	51
26	49	51	108	50	57	136	37	71	35	53	53	47
27	50	52	136	62	61	117	50	75	26	52	52	38
28	43	46	125	38	62	120	59	76	37	52	46	34
29	45	95	98	32	62	104	53	89	38	46	42	55
30	50		86	35	53	103	58	89	41	49	31	49
31	56		85		54		66	99		38		38
Mean	50.5	59.4	83.3	60.7	54.4	83.9	67.5	105.5	66.5	55.0	58.4	68.3

1940 Yearly Mean = 67.8

Daily Sunspot Numbers 1941

Day	Jan	Feb	Mar	Apr	May	Jun	Jul	Aug	Sep	Oct	Nov	Dec
01	43	81	46	35	44	37	76	107	50	44	51	70
02	45	69	49	26	38	21	73	97	61	30	53	52
03	45	65	50	21	35	47	79	94	49	31	57	48
04	54	72	48	23	37	53	62	93	53	33	48	47
05	75	85	41	20	40	61	47	87	49	34	39	57
06	74	64	45	11	32	70	53	90	44	42	8	54
07	54	57	47	38	14	61	53	86	47	43	0	31
08	51	43	31	43	12	97	47	57	49	48	7	36
09	58	58	42	51	28	118	59	50	34	41	14	38
10	32	47	40	51	21	95	62	55	37	32	0	52
11	46	36	46	59	23	82	31	68	38	39	0	47
12	28	30	60	46	31	74	25	52	58	43	13	47
13	25	33	37	41	29	62	23	32	77	43	24	46
14	24	29	37	30	22	56	12	16	83	38	38	49
15	8	27	37	17	26	45	8	8	91	48	32	49
16	16	8	48	16	32	22	23	10	103	58	32	41
17	22	21	61	31	38	29	34	13	148	66	23	21
18	29	22	65	29	23	28	56	16	140	63	26	8
19	16	28	70	25	26	28	49	34	132	60	23	7
20	32	40	64	18	28	45	60	48	89	49	37	0
21	34	40	76	20	48	40	65	70	78	45	24	0
22	49	26	56	20	44	36	62	76	88	34	34	8
23	43	15	59	36	58	47	84	73	58	52	46	9
24	40	46	39	34	43	61	99	82	47	42	63	8
25	45	54	47	36	26	59	103	68	63	44	70	10
26	61	46	36	45	26	71	113	66	54	52	81	16
27	56	50	43	34	16	74	123	72	43	63	74	32
28	65	55	40	43	16	82	107	79	35	54	81	53
29	85		34	43	15	94	125	64	35	64	84	40
30	89		17	41	11	98	128	50	43	50	71	36
31	71		28		31		133	48		50		33
Mean	45.6	44.5	46.4	32.8	29.5	59.8	66.9	60.0	65.9	46.3	38.4	33.7

1941 Yearly Mean = 47.5

Daily Sunspot Numbers 1930–1989

Daily Sunspot Numbers 1942

Day	Jan	Feb	Mar	Apr	May	Jun	Jul	Aug	Sep	Oct	Nov	Dec
01	46	27	127	39	51	0	0	21	15	14	54	61
02	41	35	116	35	28	8	18	11	0	17	61	56
03	34	41	56	41	30	8	19	22	28	8	49	46
04	39	67	32	30	31	8	24	23	21	0	40	35
05	67	77	31	32	27	0	49	24	20	0	28	31
06	58	82	20	17	25	14	50	20	14	0	33	15
07	57	79	7	25	25	15	43	19	26	18	31	31
08	81	48	10	28	20	13	34	28	15	17	27	31
09	83	39	0	36	25	10	31	18	14	27	22	26
10	60	34	7	33	29	8	19	12	15	32	25	31
11	61	23	15	44	34	7	16	8	7	29	22	29
12	48	46	18	57	31	0	10	0	10	32	21	25
13	50	46	17	59	40	0	29	7	26	10	24	24
14	37	44	25	67	54	10	0	7	33	9	25	25
15	31	52	26	60	39	8	19	7	32	11	20	25
16	23	37	29	69	52	8	19	17	16	12	8	15
17	15	38	38	71	46	10	18	8	8	10	0	9
18	21	37	53	84	35	14	8	7	8	10	0	8
19	22	40	65	109	34	31	7	0	8	17	0	7
20	18	52	72	105	26	25	15	10	15	19	7	7
21	25	47	83	94	14	28	13	28	25	23	30	7
22	24	41	102	94	11	19	11	27	22	25	31	13
23	31	53	117	82	9	17	0	47	21	17	48	27
24	31	65	106	85	8	15	0	34	11	16	39	22
25	31	68	100	59	8	20	0	36	20	8	37	20
26	10	84	115	79	15	14	8	47	21	13	37	17
27	8	82	79	89	7	20	8	43	14	31	47	12
28	0	93	48	73	15	11	17	34	21	39	33	11
29	11		51	65	0	0	23	26	16	37	56	11
30	22		61	61	0	0	25	19	15	51	66	11
31	20		55		7		17	17		44		11
Mean	35.6	52.8	54.2	60.7	25.0	11.4	17.7	20.2	17.2	19.2	30.7	22.5

1942 Yearly Mean = 30.6

Daily Sunspot Numbers 1943

Day	Jan	Feb	Mar	Apr	May	Jun	Jul	Aug	Sep	Oct	Nov	Dec
01	8	10	46	24	9	9	0	10	0	15	10	22
02	8	11	38	22	13	7	0	17	0	15	10	21
03	8	20	16	22	12	0	0	8	0	17	10	18
04	8	16	10	30	9	0	0	8	0	19	9	17
05	0	7	16	24	8	7	0	18	0	14	8	14
06	16	0	19	24	8	0	0	18	0	13	0	21
07	10	0	37	12	8	0	8	17	19	11	0	29
08	14	25	32	14	8	16	16	27	29	10	0	14
09	12	38	39	19	18	8	34	25	31	13	0	19
10	18	37	39	26	7	8	32	18	26	10	0	24
11	14	37	53	31	7	8	28	19	29	8	0	14
12	13	31	46	33	13	8	30	19	22	0	0	12
13	12	21	44	20	14	19	32	19	0	0	10	11
14	9	29	21	20	17	19	21	26	0	0	13	28
15	0	16	29	28	14	14	19	25	0	0	22	32
16	0	16	11	27	21	18	17	25	0	0	25	32
17	11	11	0	32	37	15	14	32	0	0	25	37
18	19	15	10	35	47	7	13	41	23	7	0	48
19	26	11	11	41	34	0	9	53	20	9	0	30
20	21	20	21	36	20	7	8	49	13	0	0	41
21	25	31	37	38	13	0	8	36	12	0	11	27
22	25	54	25	45	13	0	8	22	10	0	15	22
23	15	62	35	41	10	10	0	20	7	0	13	22
24	25	60	34	36	10	13	8	9	0	9	15	17
25	27	63	28	34	10	10	12	0	0	9	16	12
26	10	61	25	22	10	10	12	0	9	9	13	0
27	8	50	24	20	11	8	17	11	11	9	20	0
28	9	56	20	8	9	7	21	12	13	9	19	0
29	7		26	10	9	0	19	10	13	14	20	0
30	0		25	10	9	0	16	7	14	11	21	0
31	8		33		10		8	0		10		0
Mean	12.4	28.9	27.4	26.1	14.1	7.6	13.2	19.4	10.0	7.8	10.2	18.8

1943 Yearly Mean = 16.3

Daily Sunspot Numbers 1944

Day	Jan	Feb	Mar	Apr	May	Jun	Jul	Aug	Sep	Oct	Nov	Dec
01	7	7	8	0	0	14	0	0	0	42	11	0
02	0	7	0	0	0	8	10	0	21	32	11	0
03	0	0	8	0	0	0	10	7	8	46	12	0
04	0	0	7	0	0	0	7	0	8	41	12	0
05	0	0	0	0	0	0	7	10	0	23	14	7
06	0	0	0	0	0	0	7	20	0	15	14	16
07	0	0	0	0	0	0	0	22	0	8	0	16
08	0	0	0	0	0	8	0	25	0	16	0	19
09	0	0	0	0	0	7	0	29	8	19	0	25
10	0	0	0	0	0	8	8	25	11	17	0	44
11	0	0	0	0	0	7	8	30	14	7	11	39
12	0	0	0	0	0	0	0	28	22	7	16	32
13	0	0	0	0	0	0	0	19	25	0	8	56
14	0	0	7	0	0	0	0	24	23	0	0	37
15	0	0	0	0	0	2	0	14	20	8	0	39
16	0	0	8	0	0	3	0	16	14	22	9	32
17	0	0	14	8	0	8	0	34	12	23	9	31
18	0	0	29	0	0	8	7	31	12	21	11	52
19	0	0	31	0	0	8	7	18	14	12	11	40
20	0	0	33	0	0	8	7	23	20	17	10	54
21	0	0	27	0	0	8	0	8	21	17	11	51
22	8	0	36	0	0	8	8	0	22	18	20	49
23	8	0	36	0	0	8	8	15	20	13	19	39
24	8	0	22	0	7	8	13	14	23	9	24	41
25	8	0	14	0	0	8	7	19	23	11	23	39
26	8	0	14	0	0	7	7	18	22	10	17	31
27	13	0	12	0	0	7	0	14	18	9	17	33
28	18	0	12	0	11	7	14	21	11	14	19	24
29	19	0	15	0	19	0	11	18	9	11	8	17
30	9		7	0	23	0	10	16	28	18	8	8
31	8		0		16		0	0		17		9
Mean	3.7	0.5	11.0	0.3	2.5	5.0	5.0	16.7	14.3	16.9	10.8	28.4

1944 Yearly Mean = 9.6

Daily Sunspot Numbers 1945

Day	Jan	Feb	Mar	Apr	May	Jun	Jul	Aug	Sep	Oct	Nov	Dec
01	6	7	13	50	62	20	14	23	37	87	56	48
02	0	8	23	57	55	10	0	26	35	82	45	38
03	0	18	18	52	52	22	7	24	26	82	37	34
04	0	23	22	50	39	8	8	23	31	67	35	36
05	14	20	26	38	34	22	19	19	25	70	29	32
06	26	10	14	32	43	22	34	17	46	81	44	30
07	29	8	14	28	35	23	18	36	39	93	38	21
08	23	9	15	8	20	8	32	24	47	71	31	27
09	17	14	22	8	34	19	29	30	35	71	37	17
10	17	0	21	7	16	21	51	35	39	64	29	19
11	30	0	22	0	20	35	57	38	38	31	31	20
12	23	0	19	0	8	42	80	53	23	29	33	30
13	20	16	20	7	0	50	100	63	9	41	49	40
14	21	10	11	10	9	53	98	70	16	47	65	42
15	20	14	10	10	22	53	105	71	0	50	66	38
16	18	14	0	20	43	68	99	51	7	50	48	34
17	14	15	8	21	46	70	88	34	19	55	42	46
18	23	13	8	23	50	67	76	34	8	71	52	42
19	17	29	15	32	47	59	87	33	13	98	57	34
20	16	18	15	32	26	64	53	20	20	96	46	23
21	31	7	16	31	27	62	41	0	17	78	39	19
22	41	7	13	31	19	56	35	0	41	57	45	18
23	23	11	14	38	26	48	27	8	66	89	57	20
24	23	12	14	29	32	39	28	16	77	76	54	18
25	16	19	17	52	36	28	31	8	57	59	57	18
26	10	22	21	46	24	25	33	0	53	68	63	18
27	29	16	35	56	31	26	8	0	35	79	53	18
28	25	16	36	55	23	23	19	9	55	86	58	19
29	17		60	71	22	19	18	10	49	68	35	14
30	15		63	67	19	23	17	8	84	65	48	15
31	11		68		28		9	20		71		22
Mean	18.5	12.7	21.5	32.0	30.6	36.2	42.6	25.9	34.9	68.8	46.0	27.4

1945 Yearly Mean = 33.2

Daily Sunspot Numbers 1930–1989

Daily Sunspot Numbers 1946

Day	Jan	Feb	Mar	Apr	May	Jun	Jul	Aug	Sep	Oct	Nov	Dec
01	25	94	96	99	163	20	96	153	115	91	95	84
02	35	103	83	102	150	28	106	154	128	107	88	88
03	34	104	81	102	156	31	91	137	127	73	85	79
04	24	109	92	105	145	26	104	137	97	77	59	104
05	18	110	100	85	150	43	120	128	63	62	63	102
06	12	115	92	97	116	63	120	111	49	64	121	98
07	10	109	71	71	103	54	113	116	49	67	125	111
08	15	102	71	80	82	75	98	100	49	65	126	87
09	19	95	65	83	72	70	87	109	40	57	110	73
10	38	121	78	55	61	48	60	107	50	61	130	103
11	35	115	67	64	52	54	76	99	49	50	138	119
12	21	103	71	71	41	62	91	98	68	68	169	120
13	73	96	57	64	36	68	87	86	92	92	147	99
14	103	79	50	62	40	74	80	108	89	144	167	116
15	109	64	52	52	17	86	78	95	106	115	145	165
16	93	53	49	50	37	81	89	109	101	131	140	150
17	83	58	59	48	66	67	107	90	90	126	159	143
18	59	54	87	65	92	94	124	94	99	127	150	143
19	56	60	106	56	85	68	150	100	100	134	161	141
20	51	45	100	64	89	112	130	107	90	131	141	145
21	58	65	101	58	78	105	110	110	88	128	141	126
22	44	70	103	56	88	108	143	104	101	133	124	138
23	48	67	109	61	88	111	137	115	133	132	153	156
24	59	87	74	58	102	112	146	107	109	123	140	152
25	44	70	55	69	110	99	117	94	139	136	138	148
26	33	90	57	67	101	101	120	80	132	128	127	140
27	45	86	49	78	100	94	171	73	152	130	116	144
28	43	90	60	109	76	94	156	82	129	106	102	154
29	50		60	119	59	75	157	88	105	109	84	132
30	56		87	120	41	83	165	114	93	102	69	116
31	83		94		37		174	119		103		98
Mean	47.6	86.2	76.6	75.7	84.9	73.5	116.2	107.2	94.4	102.3	123.8	121.7

1946 Yearly Mean = 92.6

Daily Sunspot Numbers 1948

Day	Jan	Feb	Mar	Apr	May	Jun	Jul	Aug	Sep	Oct	Nov	Dec
01	124	78	103	164	125	131	157	193	138	126	85	64
02	131	76	110	190	128	127	144	190	142	130	93	70
03	137	79	115	194	130	126	142	198	123	106	93	90
04	124	90	112	181	141	142	114	199	113	96	88	100
05	110	107	108	170	203	175	114	191	103	95	112	80
06	104	106	108	152	238	212	95	208	82	72	88	85
07	117	116	102	163	247	177	112	175	50	63	96	91
08	120	101	90	151	280	173	121	150	75	68	74	92
09	133	79	97	167	283	178	118	130	68	90	79	102
10	112	98	79	173	305	198	135	117	56	112	84	96
11	88	90	103	181	288	172	163	115	73	158	107	92
12	91	81	118	190	307	143	168	110	95	175	110	130
13	96	59	123	219	270	140	170	115	134	200	127	130
14	112	45	130	243	230	151	152	120	132	222	102	128
15	115	63	137	215	192	145	148	138	134	197	85	132
16	112	67	103	200	174	157	133	165	181	205	83	177
17	110	96	83	190	144	172	123	193	208	192	118	192
18	88	96	83	226	116	193	114	184	228	178	123	213
19	102	103	77	228	130	164	104	193	222	162	147	221
20	89	121	61	206	108	134	106	196	213	153	141	210
21	111	106	39	179	99	151	128	218	203	174	123	200
22	116	89	18	184	104	155	132	190	237	188	97	176
23	109	88	41	214	102	160	139	163	221	159	90	188
24	103	71	54	245	115	184	130	159	216	158	90	169
25	106	74	65	215	128	202	154	136	170	102	96	180
26	127	76	66	190	111	198	183	135	159	106	80	170
27	128	64	76	188	126	205	170	121	115	110	68	152
28	118	80	98	166	132	200	158	132	143	112	71	138
29	90	98	136	169	160	216	178	100	124	115	65	146
30	77		166	138	128	152	192	116	141	105	58	140
31	62		138		151		212	146		95		123
Mean	108.5	86.1	94.8	189.7	174.0	167.8	142.2	157.9	143.3	136.3	95.8	138.0

1948 Yearly Mean = 136.3

Daily Sunspot Numbers 1947

Day	Jan	Feb	Mar	Apr	May	Jun	Jul	Aug	Sep	Oct	Nov	Dec
01	76	64	103	168	169	221	145	134	231	221	101	110
02	62	90	134	170	159	206	129	152	196	225	98	91
03	54	85	110	194	177	167	148	196	230	250	74	102
04	53	94	163	194	188	137	136	204	183	275	80	94
05	47	115	175	182	149	136	131	192	196	238	81	94
06	56	110	198	212	158	154	135	204	198	250	76	103
07	87	120	207	226	162	158	166	243	240	179	83	120
08	94	130	210	212	158	132	128	253	272	184	69	107
09	91	153	212	182	154	104	165	297	232	152	72	96
10	102	162	195	171	159	100	167	311	195	140	50	111
11	119	213	206	143	165	100	136	303	185	121	59	105
12	121	206	164	120	171	91	135	283	184	105	90	122
13	115	192	150	92	147	96	163	283	156	84	97	115
14	150	199	115	108	133	96	193	273	140	84	107	131
15	187	166	96	98	114	117	202	269	126	104	192	136
16	174	157	76	75	130	155	197	246	120	106	168	98
17	191	154	59	78	155	190	200	203	145	113	160	127
18	199	130	46	85	169	228	179	174	128	123	175	118
19	192	110	34	87	211	270	210	138	100	130	180	114
20	183	125	47	96	206	251	203	124	88	128	182	138
21	161	100	83	90	224	242	210	100	92	128	190	97
22	155	92	91	81	258	222	195	85	94	146	180	94
23	157	93	121	95	295	219	177	70	102	183	171	92
24	150	96	115	110	300	193	161	78	122	220	180	114
25	135	129	113	222	323	186	153	90	142	229	190	109
26	111	158	111	198	321	151	152	88	167	233	193	170
27	85	156	130	191	290	146	133	117	187	201	160	156
28	72	135	130	216	273	144	123	151	195	169	132	142
29	56		138	214	264	163	105	177	207	127	123	140
30	67		141	185	225	143	105	201	229	117	126	126
31	84		151		233		113	213		107		139
Mean	115.7	133.4	129.8	149.8	201.3	163.9	157.9	188.8	169.4	163.6	128.0	116.5

1947 Yearly Mean = 151.6

Daily Sunspot Numbers 1949

Day	Jan	Feb	Mar	Apr	May	Jun	Jul	Aug	Sep	Oct	Nov	Dec
01	108	135	150	148	82	121	156	150	165	73	120	170
02	99	149	160	155	85	125	124	156	163	115	125	158
03	86	179	144	152	121	116	138	120	168	150	120	145
04	88	199	158	176	122	119	100	108	170	196	122	125
05	75	206	168	176	139	120	67	103	166	194	135	106
06	87	218	172	145	141	125	79	80	172	222	125	97
07	91	220	180	147	132	100	86	58	170	190	128	124
08	94	193	172	151	118	108	61	50	160	190	135	120
09	112	190	162	144	114	83	57	45	153	180	157	122
10	118	180	152	139	103	85	52	34	160	166	128	124
11	109	186	156	104	104	102	59	17	170	183	130	137
12	113	200	180	126	72	86	95	56	167	198	133	143
13	122	222	178	130	60	119	107	82	163	182	143	148
14	123	212	168	141	56	114	91	102	160	145	158	105
15	118	221	172	150	69	85	113	148	162	150	128	107
16	140	224	175	130	80	103	113	163	142	145	136	106
17	145	218	182	160	111	86	105	164	174	125	167	96
18	157	222	196	154	111	85	109	158	205	77	172	102
19	177	220	197	158	110	76	136	155	170	58	149	112
20	169	190	210	160	105	83	144	173	164	73	134	88
21	167	157	221	160	100	92	142	140	130	77	160	92
22	153	133	169	155	111	115	150	190	144	113	140	110
23	155	135	153	177	119	139	171	177	138	118	122	103
24	149	140	126	185	140	137	182	158	122	106	156	119
25	145	137	112	177	120	116	187	148	131	95	143	140
26	128	126	110	160	103	164	164	155	106	71	150	129
27	90	140	114	130	114	197	182	160	88	83	170	107
28	86	152	112	122	98	220	164	152	79	88	152	114
29	80		90	112	119	224	185	145	50	104	188	101
30	90		122	85	120	206	185	133	47	120	180	90
31	119		120		112		196	158		92		105
Mean	119.1	182.3	157.5	147.0	106.2	121.7	125.8	123.8	145.3	131.6	143.5	117.6

1949 Yearly Mean = 134.7

Daily Sunspot Numbers 1930–1989

Daily Sunspot Numbers 1950

Day	Jan	Feb	Mar	Apr	May	Jun	Jul	Aug	Sep	Oct	Nov	Dec
01	101	60	95	72	144	88	70	94	49	41	78	82
02	100	38	75	80	146	84	58	110	59	41	62	80
03	92	33	90	122	132	84	58	106	49	41	57	82
04	84	36	128	133	130	66	66	84	51	50	67	75
05	76	53	134	136	129	58	75	90	31	50	79	61
06	85	43	148	139	139	54	88	83	27	45	94	46
07	84	32	184	151	130	50	98	76	23	54	80	85
08	86	20	187	114	121	70	77	72	24	78	55	108
09	64	29	163	120	108	65	67	70	38	84	61	94
10	83	43	150	109	105	108	68	75	31	79	60	94
11	75	66	156	88	101	102	78	70	28	68	46	96
12	85	72	128	91	71	72	68	74	37	88	48	115
13	83	85	124	95	69	95	67	84	65	75	42	94
14	80	125	133	97	60	101	98	68	85	72	61	79
15	75	144	130	103	47	94	75	80	80	106	81	59
16	70	156	110	120	57	84	89	93	83	103	62	42
17	82	154	100	120	61	83	96	106	85	99	66	26
18	91	166	108	85	79	78	83	93	87	74	58	19
19	110	197	101	90	86	78	102	114	80	50	50	7
20	130	190	90	93	89	66	130	113	65	48	36	0
21	155	170	80	85	92	55	108	103	58	27	22	7
22	163	162	70	70	112	86	125	95	51	20	18	0
23	150	137	76	96	128	107	115	115	44	22	16	0
24	157	113	72	128	162	108	108	103	56	32	13	31
25	140	96	73	138	142	128	96	92	41	30	20	39
26	130	80	80	142	134	113	118	77	45	37	32	56
27	110	73	73	119	131	97	112	76	49	51	64	58
28	111	82	69	160	121	74	110	55	38	55	74	35
29	98		97	153	109	82	112	58	49	95	69	41
30	118		100	154	86	78	106	58	32	107	73	23
31	82		78		72		100	54		80		43
Mean	101.6	94.8	109.7	113.4	106.2	83.6	91.0	85.2	51.3	61.4	54.8	54.1

1950 Yearly Mean = 83.9

Daily Sunspot Numbers 1951

Day	Jan	Feb	Mar	Apr	May	Jun	Jul	Aug	Sep	Oct	Nov	Dec
01	32	97	74	41	62	38	17	64	46	41	45	32
02	22	84	62	27	56	38	16	71	47	44	57	24
03	32	62	50	24	78	37	36	55	48	43	46	20
04	42	53	45	20	51	26	50	57	55	38	53	22
05	42	60	38	40	46	65	32	73	64	31	61	20
06	64	46	50	61	20	103	56	74	84	19	56	34
07	71	43	55	69	26	115	69	83	77	16	62	41
08	75	53	54	78	17	130	86	102	91	25	43	54
09	60	60	33	75	32	138	105	121	108	54	61	42
10	57	70	26	74	84	137	109	132	118	71	62	22
11	54	74	40	84	102	133	112	121	129	81	76	22
12	46	69	61	88	125	147	96	112	123	95	65	28
13	17	63	43	78	155	159	95	82	114	72	41	31
14	26	67	36	103	170	163	92	66	110	52	40	26
15	15	63	26	118	184	158	90	62	100	63	40	40
16	16	54	31	126	212	147	40	58	89	67	50	49
17	30	50	26	130	220	152	45	54	93	56	46	59
18	35	38	35	148	229	157	48	49	98	58	44	63
19	45	36	38	150	204	146	40	66	89	81	42	62
20	40	41	49	132	180	138	33	67	91	78	43	68
21	50	44	59	149	180	134	26	54	104	43	45	76
22	51	51	60	144	154	123	28	62	109	32	52	102
23	63	55	83	140	140	93	70	38	104	21	54	106
24	77	61	110	119	117	63	78	42	80	14	54	66
25	90	67	108	115	114	60	61	24	76	22	54	52
26	105	72	97	103	93	63	52	8	70	41	60	29
27	115	80	84	110	87	48	60	6	63	55	75	27
28	130	65	74	96	81	45	79	8	58	71	59	41
29	120		70	81	51	43	61	24	23	73	55	43
30	125		65	65	48	18	66	15	31	72	31	50
31	111		52		46		58	40		70		68
Mean	59.9	59.9	55.9	92.9	108.5	100.6	61.5	61.0	83.1	51.6	52.4	45.8

1951 Yearly Mean = 69.4

Daily Sunspot Numbers 1952

Day	Jan	Feb	Mar	Apr	May	Jun	Jul	Aug	Sep	Oct	Nov	Dec
01	66	21	0	28	30	12	59	62	89	20	14	13
02	63	7	0	16	18	19	55	42	75	23	12	12
03	58	7	0	21	9	14	39	35	55	22	7	14
04	40	15	0	26	22	7	31	44	36	42	0	16
05	32	27	9	37	32	7	26	46	35	33	9	29
06	18	31	10	33	34	6	12	43	38	37	13	32
07	27	28	10	37	30	26	13	51	35	37	32	38
08	35	26	23	40	27	21	19	49	14	23	30	43
09	47	30	20	32	23	8	44	57	16	26	30	38
10	43	18	30	30	7	17	52	59	17	24	26	28
11	55	0	38	46	7	10	70	43	7	16	23	31
12	57	16	28	28	6	18	66	54	0	15	16	42
13	61	23	35	22	8	20	72	66	7	15	18	47
14	65	35	25	19	15	22	93	50	0	14	22	63
15	72	44	22	7	14	46	90	44	8	11	23	71
16	70	44	18	8	8	36	85	45	10	10	15	67
17	55	53	20	7	10	45	53	50	11	0	28	70
18	53	52	15	17	18	45	43	43	23	0	35	66
19	44	54	9	33	22	55	23	30	17	12	43	66
20	38	35	0	53	36	57	30	22	20	15	47	50
21	33	28	0	62	26	50	25	28	27	25	42	40
22	12	20	0	52	25	55	9	30	29	27	39	35
23	24	26	0	40	32	70	9	54	42	35	35	35
24	30	17	0	27	31	58	9	69	45	33	30	29
25	32	0	23	20	17	56	17	80	38	37	28	18
26	31	0	30	26	10	56	11	74	38	40	17	30
27	27	0	46	16	43	52	19	90	37	34	14	15
28	19	0	60	17	57	66	23	85	31	33	8	0
29	15	0	71	32	49	63	26	89	28	32	0	0
30	22		75	42	36	76	36	83	19	26	7	9
31	17		66		23		60	85		22		16
Mean	40.7	22.7	22.0	29.1	23.4	36.4	39.3	54.9	28.2	23.8	22.1	34.3

1952 Yearly Mean = 31.5

Daily Sunspot Numbers 1953

Day	Jan	Feb	Mar	Apr	May	Jun	Jul	Aug	Sep	Oct	Nov	Dec
01	16	0	0	43	46	15	0	0	7	7	12	0
02	15	7	0	49	40	28	7	7	0	0	11	0
03	20	8	0	50	35	23	7	12	7	7	10	0
04	24	8	0	57	26	51	0	12	7	7	9	0
05	24	8	14	35	9	35	0	11	7	7	0	0
06	35	10	0	35	8	32	7	10	14	13	0	0
07	34	14	7	38	8	36	7	16	9	13	0	9
08	45	8	0	43	0	30	0	12	24	14	0	0
09	50	14	0	30	0	28	9	29	23	12	0	0
10	55	13	0	21	0	26	18	48	28	10	0	0
11	59	13	0	12	0	18	20	73	28	9	0	0
12	59	7	0	0	0	8	16	77	30	14	0	0
13	60	0	7	0	0	7	23	73	18	14	0	0
14	62	0	15	0	0	13	24	65	29	29	0	0
15	60	0	8	0	0	24	38	62	41	23	0	0
16	46	0	7	0	7	33	20	54	42	17	0	0
17	37	0	0	0	8	33	17	47	38	9	0	0
18	30	0	8	7	14	20	21	31	38	0	0	0
19	25	0	10	7	10	25	11	26	34	0	0	0
20	17	0	8	0	10	26	8	24	21	0	7	0
21	14	0	10	0	11	22	14	17	25	7	0	7
22	18	0	10	9	11	20	0	15	16	0	0	0
23	8	0	10	27	11	12	0	8	9	0	0	0
24	8	0	9	33	13	12	0	0	15	7	0	8
25	0	0	9	45	18	15	0	0	18	0	0	9
26	0	0	7	57	11	20	0	0	21	12	0	9
27	0	0	17	66	10	21	0	0	7	9	0	11
28	0	0	25	63	18	7	0	0	8	7	0	10
29	0		32	57	24	8	0	0	7	0	0	9
30	0		47	49	20	7	0	0	7	0	0	7
31	0		50		19		0	0		7		0
Mean	26.5	3.9	10.0	27.8	12.5	21.8	8.6	23.5	19.3	8.2	1.6	2.5

1953 Yearly Mean = 13.9

Daily Sunspot Numbers 1930–1989

Daily Sunspot Numbers 1954

Day	Jan	Feb	Mar	Apr	May	Jun	Jul	Aug	Sep	Oct	Nov	Dec
01	0	0	9	0	0	0	0	8	0	0	0	0
02	0	0	12	0	0	7	0	9	0	7	0	0
03	0	0	11	0	0	0	8	16	0	14	0	0
04	0	0	7	0	0	0	0	9	7	8	0	0
05	0	0	0	0	8	0	0	12	7	7	7	0
06	0	0	0	0	0	0	0	19	0	0	7	0
07	0	0	0	8	0	0	0	14	0	0	8	7
08	0	7	0	8	0	0	7	10	0	0	7	0
09	0	7	0	15	0	0	0	13	0	0	24	0
10	0	0	0	0	0	0	0	23	0	0	38	0
11	7	0	0	0	0	0	0	14	0	0	41	0
12	0	0	8	0	0	0	7	14	0	7	40	0
13	0	0	17	0	0	0	10	8	0	7	39	0
14	0	0	22	0	9	0	15	7	0	15	26	0
15	0	0	36	7	7	0	8	0	7	17	11	11
16	0	0	40	7	0	0	15	0	9	24	7	18
17	0	0	42	0	0	0	7	0	0	22	7	17
18	0	0	39	0	0	0	7	0	0	7	7	16
19	0	0	29	0	0	0	0	0	0	14	7	20
20	0	0	23	8	0	0	0	0	7	14	0	19
21	0	0	17	0	0	0	0	9	0	8	0	12
22	0	0	12	0	0	0	0	15	0	8	0	7
23	0	0	7	0	0	0	0	18	0	14	0	7
24	0	0	7	0	0	0	8	16	0	8	0	14
25	0	0	0	0	0	0	10	11	0	8	0	14
26	0	0	0	0	0	0	7	9	0	7	0	7
27	0	0	0	0	0	0	7	7	0	0	0	0
28	0	0	0	0	0	0	10	0	0	0	0	0
29	0		0	0	0	0	8	0	0	0	0	13
30	0		0	0	0	0	7	0	7	0	0	29
31	0		0		0		7	0		0		25
Mean	0.2	0.5	10.9	1.8	0.8	0.2	4.8	8.4	1.5	7.0	9.2	7.6

1954 Yearly Mean = 4.4

Daily Sunspot Numbers 1955

Day	Jan	Feb	Mar	Apr	May	Jun	Jul	Aug	Sep	Oct	Nov	Dec
01	22	19	23	9	23	26	35	25	89	37	102	99
02	17	28	20	14	21	25	38	20	88	54	92	87
03	12	33	16	8	32	13	38	16	80	58	77	75
04	20	34	15	21	45	22	43	0	85	64	52	86
05	32	32	8	36	44	25	48	26	78	62	50	100
06	40	28	8	30	28	32	60	46	70	60	36	100
07	54	34	8	32	20	26	47	61	74	71	71	84
08	54	24	8	31	17	23	47	77	68	71	84	72
09	35	28	7	19	0	24	39	83	64	79	115	65
10	33	27	0	10	0	27	41	87	52	56	131	74
11	30	27	0	0	9	48	35	85	40	55	150	80
12	29	26	0	0	7	47	35	77	40	61	152	79
13	28	27	0	0	0	40	35	77	40	41	140	71
14	27	10	0	0	0	56	37	60	33	22	130	63
15	17	8	0	7	7	53	29	44	46	7	122	75
16	16	16	0	9	16	62	22	28	25	0	105	68
17	15	9	0	13	29	65	20	16	38	0	90	70
18	11	0	0	0	32	62	7	15	41	0	75	85
19	10	0	0	0	34	61	26	13	29	11	55	89
20	7	0	0	0	45	65	32	17	23	21	60	92
21	8	7	0	8	53	55	11	22	7	23	60	105
22	8	9	0	0	53	37	9	23	0	42	61	85
23	14	19	0	0	50	15	0	23	7	57	63	64
24	22	26	0	8	48	0	0	14	25	86	70	51
25	21	28	0	0	45	0	8	11	30	95	77	53
26	25	28	0	0	45	0	0	26	11	107	81	61
27	25	28	7	10	45	0	11	44	21	98	90	62
28	19	26	0	22	45	8	12	56	24	108	97	65
29	22		7	23	44	11	16	57	21	119	95	72
30	22		15	29	36	23	20	52	32	124	93	81
31	22		10		24		26	62		123		70
Mean	23.1	20.8	4.9	11.3	28.9	31.7	26.7	40.7	42.7	58.5	89.2	76.9

1955 Yearly Mean = 38.0

Daily Sunspot Numbers 1956

Day	Jan	Feb	Mar	Apr	May	Jun	Jul	Aug	Sep	Oct	Nov	Dec
01	54	50	152	82	94	98	164	140	168	170	157	163
02	49	63	120	69	107	105	155	148	158	183	175	177
03	46	60	115	66	138	109	133	146	136	190	187	189
04	41	57	100	66	169	106	153	149	130	187	198	200
05	49	31	112	50	158	117	138	152	142	180	220	213
06	49	32	110	45	162	118	139	149	158	145	274	185
07	53	29	107	63	162	111	163	151	165	145	308	173
08	57	26	104	86	186	90	158	140	157	170	312	157
09	52	31	102	103	180	85	150	140	146	180	260	185
10	32	40	97	145	178	89	157	136	136	176	236	216
11	41	56	87	145	169	87	177	140	170	166	243	229
12	65	80	86	160	154	97	216	148	208	175	262	212
13	85	90	97	178	142	103	192	150	244	154	230	202
14	90	142	122	164	133	112	156	140	251	134	215	210
15	95	168	140	152	110	119	156	143	254	121	230	198
16	118	224	135	155	122	132	144	143	244	110	236	186
17	126	237	138	172	132	120	98	131	234	90	231	190
18	130	270	130	166	144	130	67	173	213	115	180	156
19	128	246	128	155	140	167	65	192	214	134	178	151
20	120	260	122	145	127	161	71	217	223	145	180	143
21	110	208	122	145	144	162	78	224	202	149	183	173
22	100	186	118	130	119	150	86	237	153	160	154	200
23	93	177	130	121	82	139	113	213	139	153	138	219
24	87	156	136	96	102	125	84	232	125	163	120	219
25	103	149	138	104	103	106	90	154	132	165	160	229
26	69	140	140	91	120	70	100	178	136	152	160	229
27	44	125	115	91	115	71	116	203	131	140	125	215
28	48	132	117	67	137	122	104	196	127	150	135	202
29	53	132	122	40	136	135	108	200	143	168	154	187
30	48		116	70	146	162	130	212	158	178	198	171
31	46		113		123		140	182		167		177
Mean	73.6	124.0	118.4	110.7	136.6	116.6	129.1	169.6	173.2	155.3	201.3	192.1

1956 Yearly Mean = 141.7

Daily Sunspot Numbers 1957

Day	Jan	Feb	Mar	Apr	May	Jun	Jul	Aug	Sep	Oct	Nov	Dec
01	160	108	155	140	124	158	185	144	244	236	266	230
02	189	120	164	152	121	163	194	148	225	234	250	217
03	211	102	137	135	118	180	204	162	190	242	232	230
04	224	110	128	160	106	169	235	163	173	217	214	243
05	226	110	124	138	92	159	213	158	171	219	201	266
06	252	123	147	108	138	194	226	163	160	227	182	245
07	224	138	147	138	140	170	192	157	137	234	177	190
08	207	151	144	160	150	145	152	141	172	244	158	197
09	166	157	180	163	162	168	162	121	215	267	192	152
10	153	142	186	150	195	158	135	89	240	264	226	148
11	151	136	210	121	211	140	107	96	245	232	232	151
12	155	132	224	114	204	160	93	116	253	236	231	157
13	134	122	228	143	197	178	97	104	252	244	221	161
14	121	130	175	122	214	158	136	135	251	232	210	167
15	86	142	156	162	210	225	156	157	247	264	177	174
16	100	153	146	181	196	239	184	195	252	268	179	187
17	112	140	150	202	179	252	203	197	258	251	181	205
18	143	132	147	205	185	272	218	196	273	222	185	225
19	170	123	147	207	173	274	223	186	290	217	194	249
20	170	117	122	208	182	272	238	170	302	230	207	284
21	177	123	120	214	205	265	250	138	334	237	234	299
22	193	130	137	218	159	242	255	114	302	241	263	316
23	191	132	152	226	180	232	265	108	268	254	251	343
24	209	134	145	248	186	235	265	110	238	276	238	355
25	184	139	160	251	150	208	227	132	234	240	211	355
26	168	131	170	223	132	212	206	164	215	293	199	337
27	150	141	155	215	132	220	173	181	226	280	201	275
28	141	129	152	221	143	190	158	204	242	317	215	260
29	132		154	177	162	180	142	236	242	334	215	275
30	107		172	155	179	204	159	252	224	317	184	274
31	108		145		179		150	261		299		255
Mean	165.0	130.2	157.4	175.2	164.6	200.7	187.2	158.0	235.8	253.8	210.9	239.4

1957 Yearly Mean = 190.2

Daily Sunspot Numbers 1930–1989

Daily Sunspot Numbers 1958

Day	Jan	Feb	Mar	Apr	May	Jun	Jul	Aug	Sep	Oct	Nov	Dec
01	214	150	109	290	250	200	165	262	200	223	217	241
02	213	168	90	292	246	154	164	250	221	220	212	234
03	200	161	140	245	269	183	190	200	230	207	205	228
04	217	144	185	253	268	203	203	177	240	175	192	221
05	191	177	203	244	267	206	209	198	206	157	177	233
06	192	187	215	238	223	192	214	209	220	140	152	227
07	205	197	220	246	198	185	212	223	175	125	133	242
08	210	181	198	246	177	200	205	230	160	115	114	255
09	232	168	186	204	150	202	193	253	166	116	97	252
10	252	167	181	197	181	200	201	244	219	121	85	258
11	253	171	173	159	166	193	175	253	245	123	84	237
12	255	177	162	140	172	197	130	228	267	135	85	211
13	271	168	154	127	114	178	138	220	265	138	93	198
14	279	174	158	96	103	160	135	202	233	142	97	185
15	291	159	165	99	106	132	135	190	230	160	95	150
16	278	148	155	108	110	100	144	177	206	219	95	142
17	247	147	164	147	116	113	160	163	189	231	80	124
18	230	139	162	168	123	100	181	152	205	243	80	109
19	212	141	155	191	140	114	191	128	187	238	98	80
20	190	160	154	192	132	107	188	131	163	232	106	83
21	171	170	156	212	162	141	196	145	156	212	125	92
22	173	170	163	212	165	157	184	160	172	241	142	114
23	182	173	187	201	171	187	178	192	175	230	155	150
24	137	182	204	181	199	185	170	183	174	190	178	185
25	137	187	180	206	189	191	179	198	161	176	211	218
26	143	174	194	182	170	207	213	180	169	171	237	229
27	169	153	226	192	157	207	238	196	177	164	247	218
28	160	125	292	198	160	193	250	202	208	179	258	183
29	130		302	207	192	200	261	225	217	200	259	168
30	110		338	208	178	159	268	225	201	193	260	175
31	132		342		181		263	210		210		175
Mean	202.5	164.9	190.7	196.0	175.3	171.5	191.4	200.2	201.2	181.5	152.3	187.6

1958 Yearly Mean = 184.8

Daily Sunspot Numbers 1959

Day	Jan	Feb	Mar	Apr	May	Jun	Jul	Aug	Sep	Oct	Nov	Dec
01	221	141	158	243	120	152	147	194	290	65	136	170
02	225	141	151	242	112	133	118	210	256	76	121	165
03	229	140	151	174	113	152	138	213	202	89	97	160
04	231	137	146	159	105	166	158	225	161	101	103	163
05	243	128	152	124	112	162	136	212	148	115	91	142
06	238	114	148	108	138	180	127	207	152	128	98	147
07	247	124	150	107	156	181	120	179	135	130	114	141
08	246	90	155	136	188	192	131	175	136	115	131	145
09	245	87	164	161	238	188	129	170	157	103	136	94
10	224	100	156	177	262	160	127	155	141	91	142	89
11	218	100	148	197	287	172	133	180	155	87	153	82
12	203	101	126	189	276	176	135	160	170	81	154	75
13	192	106	159	178	257	165	160	125	148	78	149	73
14	128	129	173	193	227	170	180	139	151	102	137	88
15	120	133	216	174	204	158	176	144	161	96	127	123
16	143	144	225	153	182	172	190	157	130	116	113	113
17	168	170	228	126	187	161	193	166	87	107	83	107
18	179	170	230	114	198	174	195	174	100	116	73	117
19	202	175	234	117	185	182	184	182	120	111	69	134
20	240	160	238	135	187	173	160	180	149	108	65	133
21	255	163	230	128	151	162	132	200	143	111	70	131
22	278	171	208	138	145	170	94	204	157	129	110	126
23	270	186	194	186	149	188	113	205	143	135	131	122
24	261	190	178	186	143	157	108	217	155	143	151	116
25	255	181	199	203	178	180	118	212	132	137	162	121
26	252	176	190	204	188	184	134	220	110	126	161	124
27	263	163	178	175	177	186	156	231	102	128	157	132
28	239	186	173	172	132	160	181	274	91	129	151	127
29	213		217	160	99	158	182	301	87	129	161	136
30	167		233	141	106	147	193	292	86	131	175	127
31	143		248		131		190	284		141		153
Mean	217.4	143.1	185.7	163.3	172.0	168.7	149.6	199.6	145.2	111.4	124.0	125.0

1959 Yearly Mean = 159.0

Daily Sunspot Numbers 1960

Day	Jan	Feb	Mar	Apr	May	Jun	Jul	Aug	Sep	Oct	Nov	Dec
01	136	173	63	154	97	100	167	75	103	22	76	74
02	141	181	57	143	97	90	157	58	105	34	79	92
03	148	177	62	152	102	109	163	36	80	22	69	101
04	160	156	66	162	96	113	203	30	75	53	67	111
05	168	149	74	156	87	104	168	25	83	70	77	102
06	174	145	79	143	93	109	139	24	100	92	90	104
07	179	123	108	123	125	123	133	56	110	113	116	94
08	171	116	111	112	135	113	134	58	121	110	132	99
09	158	143	109	98	142	129	123	76	138	128	127	97
10	139	143	109	103	149	147	108	94	147	140	137	103
11	143	128	82	114	147	149	95	156	145	133	134	102
12	123	116	68	139	127	151	83	201	147	116	116	101
13	108	106	85	132	135	131	84	235	160	123	122	92
14	118	104	76	149	110	138	89	236	161	106	132	101
15	121	94	84	156	91	144	105	252	151	98	133	108
16	119	84	98	152	101	138	132	244	128	98	121	103
17	117	73	86	124	114	105	136	253	122	103	103	92
18	103	60	85	116	106	91	140	257	153	98	93	82
19	87	44	95	121	108	84	141	228	166	96	83	70
20	94	49	97	116	115	60	137	204	171	92	82	71
21	108	56	115	123	109	56	139	177	177	82	72	63
22	134	64	128	108	118	50	135	168	189	60	66	44
23	138	68	145	106	125	58	127	130	168	54	59	35
24	136	74	123	102	147	68	105	113	157	49	52	37
25	152	89	128	95	148	80	110	131	141	62	42	57
26	209	96	133	96	124	99	92	140	114	72	60	48
27	203	92	138	82	148	116	90	109	97	67	58	70
28	199	87	139	91	142	140	80	98	89	52	57	86
29	193	83	142	92	138	147	94	97	74	72	64	94
30	178		151	100	121	165	82	96	44	82	69	103
31	178		132		111		83	100		68		118
Mean	146.3	106.0	102.2	122.0	119.6	110.2	121.7	134.1	127.2	82.8	89.6	85.6

1960 Yearly Mean = 112.3

Daily Sunspot Numbers 1961

Day	Jan	Feb	Mar	Apr	May	Jun	Jul	Aug	Sep	Oct	Nov	Dec
01	145	58	17	87	102	30	60	39	51	45	0	82
02	133	55	33	60	84	42	65	17	53	47	0	80
03	109	59	49	55	72	48	68	24	54	58	0	77
04	84	75	46	73	55	62	63	23	55	55	10	67
05	78	65	34	86	42	55	44	14	55	48	19	55
06	69	56	41	82	39	49	55	11	57	45	25	38
07	63	52	38	64	37	40	57	14	51	43	48	31
08	58	55	49	66	31	45	60	37	33	46	54	31
09	61	68	49	49	44	58	65	59	45	47	76	31
10	53	61	33	48	46	77	73	84	57	53	67	14
11	43	50	34	47	45	82	85	109	54	58	53	0
12	35	35	15	42	56	72	96	103	62	76	50	0
13	28	30	27	40	52	75	86	103	82	47	49	0
14	25	26	46	41	46	80	113	104	109	44	48	10
15	27	26	42	53	38	123	107	108	114	53	47	8
16	43	24	52	60	31	128	99	98	102	46	31	7
17	53	39	66	78	23	128	92	85	84	39	11	7
18	51	30	51	72	44	128	82	71	73	44	17	10
19	50	26	45	65	47	112	86	72	70	52	10	12
20	45	30	39	56	59	116	85	52	46	38	15	21
21	50	44	46	52	66	128	85	45	41	47	26	21
22	44	49	60	38	71	123	75	39	40	33	24	47
23	35	48	61	36	74	96	81	33	43	16	12	56
24	23	58	76	36	78	87	78	37	74	17	18	77
25	27	53	64	48	72	70	63	49	83	16	29	94
26	43	52	63	60	47	56	62	45	74	13	36	80
27	47	42	88	82	41	51	53	54	67	8	37	70
28	62	25	95	74	38	38	42	36	69	8	38	74
29	81		95	92	36	59	32	54	58	9	53	55
30	65		97	99	41	63	30	58	52	9	75	45
31	66		93		24		34	54		8		38
Mean	57.9	46.1	53.0	61.4	51.0	77.4	70.2	55.8	63.6	37.7	32.6	39.9

1961 Yearly Mean = 53.9

Daily Sunspot Numbers 1930–1989

Daily Sunspot Numbers 1962

Day	Jan	Feb	Mar	Apr	May	Jun	Jul	Aug	Sep	Oct	Nov	Dec
01	29	76	85	37	49	35	54	0	48	51	22	27
02	25	59	77	31	48	34	42	7	57	39	19	29
03	20	57	63	30	46	26	39	7	80	22	17	37
04	10	48	46	24	42	21	30	10	87	18	16	44
05	18	43	27	28	37	26	28	14	88	13	7	46
06	13	39	32	21	41	33	26	11	80	25	12	49
07	11	36	36	23	31	35	21	9	66	37	16	48
08	10	27	25	22	34	38	18	8	58	40	18	29
09	8	15	19	15	37	46	11	7	53	42	16	25
10	15	14	13	10	44	41	13	0	44	51	18	13
11	0	19	7	21	44	40	19	0	50	62	25	13
12	10	8	9	35	46	39	17	15	60	64	33	16
13	20	9	13	55	39	39	29	24	58	72	47	19
14	31	20	15	75	27	40	34	40	53	67	57	24
15	24	22	27	84	15	59	22	50	60	61	60	12
16	24	15	27	90	18	58	28	50	42	51	82	0
17	19	22	29	82	26	70	34	54	33	43	67	14
18	25	28	36	71	29	68	29	46	35	33	58	26
19	29	29	61	71	32	62	14	46	24	29	47	34
20	34	53	75	72	37	44	14	39	24	28	28	45
21	42	65	86	75	45	35	29	37	31	32	23	34
22	63	72	94	78	59	46	29	32	32	41	8	28
23	82	108	84	72	62	33	17	29	38	43	0	23
24	83	124	79	46	62	30	14	36	53	41	13	32
25	88	103	74	39	60	43	12	16	54	43	24	24
26	86	95	71	37	60	46	10	7	55	48	23	14
27	92	108	48	32	57	36	11	7	51	40	16	0
28	85	95	38	41	60	44	15	14	44	31	14	7
29	66		37	40	63	44	9	15	36	15	8	0
30	66		44	34	58	49	8	25	46	20	14	0
31	71		38		48		0	22		23		7
Mean	38.7	50.3	45.6	46.4	43.7	42.0	21.8	21.8	51.3	39.5	26.9	23.2

1962 Yearly Mean = 37.6

Daily Sunspot Numbers 1963

Day	Jan	Feb	Mar	Apr	May	Jun	Jul	Aug	Sep	Oct	Nov	Dec
01	23	30	0	15	23	31	30	65	20	0	45	28
02	29	25	0	25	22	26	22	55	25	7	52	31
03	34	44	8	28	24	15	37	53	34	9	43	30
04	35	53	14	17	20	13	22	51	43	8	37	30
05	23	47	22	23	26	23	9	50	42	0	29	28
06	8	50	32	50	43	8	9	53	31	15	13	25
07	7	48	35	50	46	29	9	38	9	20	10	17
08	8	40	29	63	55	54	10	23	14	32	11	13
09	7	32	32	55	48	68	17	22	15	37	9	32
10	8	21	34	59	64	82	9	20	23	32	0	27
11	8	18	23	48	64	82	10	9	22	40	8	26
12	8	16	18	63	55	87	10	0	28	39	11	18
13	9	9	17	56	54	82	18	7	40	42	7	10
14	33	16	24	45	56	57	22	13	65	51	7	8
15	44	17	15	50	65	54	19	11	84	49	9	7
16	40	16	8	50	66	33	11	18	85	52	16	7
17	40	18	13	41	76	27	11	29	81	50	24	8
18	21	16	19	34	78	25	13	43	73	40	28	17
19	20	20	12	28	68	23	15	36	72	29	25	15
20	16	20	13	19	58	19	11	36	73	37	28	17
21	16	20	13	10	49	19	19	50	77	35	30	14
22	7	20	16	0	37	7	19	68	70	45	34	13
23	17	22	17	0	24	15	25	64	54	50	36	9
24	15	20	19	0	28	24	17	50	38	51	35	16
25	17	16	10	0	18	29	25	37	25	53	32	8
26	7	11	16	0	9	34	16	29	13	52	23	7
27	14	17	15	0	18	31	23	16	0	38	23	0
28	34	0	7	7	36	24	7	21	9	24	21	0
29	25		12	16	32	30	24	16	0	54	27	0
30	23		17	26	37	27	55	23	0	58	28	0
31	18		19		35		65	24		45		0
Mean	19.8	24.4	17.1	29.3	43.0	35.9	19.6	33.2	38.8	35.3	23.4	14.9

1963 Yearly Mean = 27.9

Daily Sunspot Numbers 1964

Day	Jan	Feb	Mar	Apr	May	Jun	Jul	Aug	Sep	Oct	Nov	Dec
01	0	0	27	10	7	8	7	9	7	17	9	0
02	14	0	8	0	0	8	0	20	8	12	8	0
03	8	0	13	13	0	8	0	17	8	0	8	0
04	7	0	7	0	10	8	8	9	0	0	0	0
05	13	0	7	10	14	0	10	8	0	0	0	7
06	17	0	0	11	11	0	8	7	0	14	7	0
07	20	10	15	15	11	14	7	7	7	20	7	0
08	16	13	9	13	10	0	0	0	20	16	7	8
09	13	18	8	10	7	7	0	0	12	11	0	7
10	15	9	0	9	7	7	0	7	11	0	0	10
11	19	7	14	8	7	14	0	8	11	0	0	12
12	20	0	23	7	0	22	0	21	20	0	9	16
13	27	0	40	7	0	12	0	23	18	0	7	10
14	24	8	32	7	9	18	10	36	11	0	17	17
15	22	13	29	7	17	24	12	30	0	0	8	10
16	16	17	28	7	17	23	11	30	0	0	16	17
17	20	21	20	13	23	13	9	19	0	0	15	27
18	7	15	8	7	11	22	8	9	0	12	19	28
19	14	13	10	0	9	24	0	8	0	11	12	30
20	11	23	11	9	7	19	0	7	0	10	19	29
21	11	39	20	19	7	9	0	7	0	0	21	23
22	11	42	32	17	18	0	0	0	0	0	8	26
23	11	54	30	16	13	0	0	0	0	0	0	16
24	18	44	27	23	11	0	0	0	0	7	8	18
25	17	36	23	12	11	0	0	0	0	8	9	19
26	10	34	20	7	14	0	0	0	0	7	0	14
27	9	34	16	0	8	0	0	0	0	9	0	19
28	24	34	14	0	8	0	0	0	0	0	7	28
29	27	28	7	0	8	7	0	0	0	9	0	38
30	22		7	0	9	7	0	0	7	16	0	21
31	11		7		9		7	7		9		19
Mean	15.3	17.7	16.5	8.6	9.5	9.1	3.1	9.3	4.7	6.1	7.4	15.1

1964 Yearly Mean = 10.2

Daily Sunspot Numbers 1965

Day	Jan	Feb	Mar	Apr	May	Jun	Jul	Aug	Sep	Oct	Nov	Dec
01	23	14	16	0	0	9	18	0	20	52	29	13
02	26	13	7	0	14	24	20	0	20	63	28	8
03	31	13	0	0	8	36	19	15	21	60	20	8
04	31	13	8	0	8	38	17	14	22	62	13	8
05	26	10	13	0	7	34	8	0	22	55	13	8
06	19	23	26	0	0	30	17	16	19	39	29	8
07	18	23	26	0	11	32	22	7	23	27	40	8
08	17	17	7	0	15	24	29	31	22	7	46	15
09	11	23	0	0	9	23	33	12	18	8	38	7
10	8	17	12	0	0	9	29	14	15	13	41	7
11	7	17	9	0	0	7	35	16	19	8	40	0
12	0	23	18	9	15	0	30	13	17	9	26	0
13	0	25	16	9	21	0	23	8	17	8	17	14
14	7	16	17	15	15	14	12	7	8	7	16	0
15	8	23	12	27	30	0	11	0	8	0	10	14
16	7	15	9	18	36	0	8	0	16	7	9	22
17	7	8	11	17	55	12	7	0	8	0	7	21
18	20	8	22	8	72	25	0	7	9	0	0	20
19	22	0	17	7	75	16	0	7	7	10	0	18
20	28	0	19	7	72	21	0	7	0	12	0	15
21	23	7	9	9	70	19	0	7	0	15	0	10
22	22	0	0	15	62	14	0	0	0	26	7	11
23	13	0	0	17	50	7	0	0	11	23	0	9
24	19	13	7	10	43	7	0	8	17	16	7	8
25	18	15	17	7	30	7	7	0	13	24	0	12
26	18	22	10	11	22	7	0	8	17	17	7	23
27	34	23	18	10	7	8	7	14	24	17	0	29
28	17	18	12	8	0	23	0	12	23	9	8	64
29	25		9	0	0	18	0	16	37	8	8	64
30	22		9	0	0	14	9	15	50	8	15	44
31	15		8		0		7	22		14		38
Mean	17.5	14.2	11.7	6.8	24.1	15.9	11.9	8.9	16.8	20.1	15.8	17.0

1965 Yearly Mean = 15.1

Daily Sunspot Numbers 1930–1989

Daily Sunspot Numbers 1966

Day	Jan	Feb	Mar	Apr	May	Jun	Jul	Aug	Sep	Oct	Nov	Dec
01	22	7	25	64	50	71	49	78	44	57	43	35
02	21	11	11	58	52	74	49	74	44	55	42	33
03	20	21	14	74	57	41	54	72	25	50	38	30
04	17	17	20	74	61	60	53	68	18	36	38	57
05	11	19	15	59	43	48	48	60	26	40	20	69
06	0	17	15	63	32	47	46	50	30	44	32	68
07	7	17	12	70	29	40	58	33	36	53	48	64
08	13	14	11	65	17	35	68	13	38	48	55	88
09	13	12	15	49	8	33	60	13	39	44	59	86
10	0	12	14	37	0	25	65	0	37	65	63	112
11	0	14	10	29	14	43	52	16	42	66	72	125
12	0	11	0	27	14	34	62	36	38	64	80	130
13	17	18	7	24	23	34	56	30	33	72	68	118
14	30	14	0	29	50	31	42	37	35	64	66	113
15	40	16	10	29	46	22	34	41	38	60	66	107
16	58	13	26	35	47	40	48	40	57	70	52	116
17	51	19	44	40	35	46	42	41	76	70	59	88
18	64	24	53	40	28	40	49	39	83	70	57	76
19	68	29	60	30	35	36	38	33	76	76	65	57
20	64	39	54	41	58	42	65	28	78	96	74	46
21	58	42	50	44	80	33	55	22	89	91	77	37
22	52	50	52	56	72	35	66	38	86	83	78	34
23	42	55	40	69	68	62	56	65	71	75	76	38
24	44	45	31	58	68	66	70	71	67	64	72	45
25	37	39	24	61	64	80	67	89	68	50	74	60
26	23	40	18	54	70	82	74	95	54	47	67	65
27	17	36	10	40	66	76	65	90	48	39	59	48
28	16	33	12	40	60	52	70	84	42	36	41	48
29	21		35	48	42	47	76	89	45	27	37	51
30	28		44	53	56	55	59	76	42	27	37	70
31	19		52		58		62	66		35		68
Mean	28.2	24.4	25.3	48.7	45.3	47.7	56.7	51.2	50.2	57.2	57.2	70.4

1966 Yearly Mean = 47.0

Daily Sunspot Numbers 1967

Day	Jan	Feb	Mar	Apr	May	Jun	Jul	Aug	Sep	Oct	Nov	Dec
01	73	93	172	105	81	138	85	139	123	76	115	131
02	96	88	179	82	79	118	89	126	115	77	122	126
03	124	92	191	63	62	102	92	113	119	95	113	89
04	148	100	172	60	62	104	95	95	121	98	110	79
05	150	72	164	68	68	90	98	103	125	103	91	79
06	148	89	157	72	49	80	97	106	120	98	51	89
07	134	138	137	86	41	59	82	98	109	92	48	126
08	116	109	98	108	18	43	82	119	104	76	27	131
09	111	112	85	88	25	26	84	107	99	80	34	117
10	111	97	92	68	17	21	67	91	95	82	41	114
11	104	96	89	62	25	20	53	94	77	90	38	132
12	97	79	69	51	34	19	60	77	79	65	56	135
13	93	77	53	63	34	19	53	75	65	55	77	137
14	85	58	50	48	40	20	70	66	51	63	95	140
15	60	58	52	51	43	35	87	61	36	47	98	151
16	56	60	58	32	44	41	80	77	39	41	119	160
17	59	60	74	42	44	57	75	95	44	38	121	172
18	72	70	75	58	55	64	78	114	50	50	134	170
19	82	67	73	56	70	67	62	110	59	62	131	129
20	92	74	86	52	80	84	42	113	63	83	116	141
21	125	82	92	64	99	79	63	120	67	80	95	130
22	140	86	108	76	118	83	73	123	62	85	92	105
23	152	84	111	98	145	80	93	122	55	101	103	101
24	122	100	121	83	159	99	98	122	51	93	108	91
25	133	106	131	85	164	96	108	130	61	114	128	111
26	136	123	137	66	174	79	118	125	53	125	109	142
27	130	186	122	66	194	61	123	121	50	125	105	140
28	125	166	129	81	197	80	157	119	71	156	112	165
29	122		133	79	164	65	155	111	66	137	117	141
30	132		132	73	150	89	165	121	74	132	123	124
31	110		125		147		152	129		116		119
Mean	110.9	93.6	111.8	69.5	86.5	67.3	91.5	107.2	76.8	88.2	94.3	126.4

1967 Yearly Mean = 93.8

Daily Sunspot Numbers 1968

Day	Jan	Feb	Mar	Apr	May	Jun	Jul	Aug	Sep	Oct	Nov	Dec
01	119	208	108	122	126	139	55	98	78	75	89	104
02	123	211	110	108	144	134	37	91	82	73	76	109
03	128	199	92	98	143	121	30	92	119	108	76	113
04	137	170	86	96	138	114	26	94	118	119	81	116
05	152	137	77	89	127	115	28	94	111	118	97	118
06	150	114	67	85	142	129	41	95	96	126	92	117
07	164	86	58	79	135	138	54	100	90	135	92	116
08	182	97	67	82	128	119	89	113	106	112	89	122
09	200	95	65	94	122	103	91	98	128	87	105	130
10	198	92	74	104	117	99	99	90	138	70	111	117
11	154	89	85	95	106	87	124	104	145	95	106	101
12	144	76	87	83	82	105	152	116	150	99	94	68
13	139	67	89	60	91	108	147	142	153	70	94	75
14	107	69	67	96	80	114	138	165	113	76	85	81
15	94	87	59	110	95	107	123	172	88	90	84	84
16	78	85	46	114	103	103	129	170	84	88	84	67
17	68	94	59	91	114	113	117	160	81	82	82	77
18	60	78	59	63	136	121	96	148	85	108	77	93
19	58	65	53	53	138	107	102	136	88	112	80	101
20	55	72	60	63	140	103	93	122	84	114	92	102
21	55	79	70	64	142	108	93	138	90	122	84	107
22	69	82	91	68	143	94	86	143	99	134	81	114
23	75	93	113	50	149	101	93	126	118	136	76	114
24	93	119	132	48	165	113	101	108	149	139	67	125
25	90	161	143	64	146	111	124	86	187	138	80	131
26	87	150	141	50	121	107	130	77	184	133	89	140
27	88	126	146	57	139	102	127	67	176	138	87	148
28	140	124	138	82	133	111	118	49	149	118	73	139
29	175	120	127	71	135	94	129	64	137	114	73	139
30	185		154	96	126	88	115	68	91	112	83	119
31	209		134		136		93	63		99		117
Mean	121.8	111.9	92.2	81.2	127.2	110.3	96.1	109.3	117.2	107.7	86.0	109.8

1968 Yearly Mean = 105.9

Daily Sunspot Numbers 1969

Day	Jan	Feb	Mar	Apr	May	Jun	Jul	Aug	Sep	Oct	Nov	Dec
01	68	92	132	156	90	32	125	175	105	99	82	91
02	75	96	111	143	77	47	134	182	94	101	68	107
03	72	98	103	143	70	74	167	177	81	99	83	102
04	98	86	105	122	73	77	160	180	74	99	86	103
05	117	94	108	101	88	116	145	171	71	109	88	95
06	128	101	117	78	71	157	130	153	72	120	98	70
07	146	122	115	82	57	187	123	139	71	123	97	53
08	155	109	108	77	87	190	122	114	67	109	89	43
09	152	102	113	90	81	185	122	108	51	93	94	44
10	150	85	107	85	100	192	120	105	51	85	85	39
11	138	74	101	92	125	195	120	86	67	72	81	28
12	137	64	85	91	149	187	112	70	73	60	76	51
13	124	55	88	122	155	178	98	62	91	57	67	74
14	119	54	90	149	169	166	79	59	95	63	67	94
15	116	70	114	152	146	149	77	62	114	54	68	97
16	116	87	158	144	121	134	75	50	118	47	67	97
17	100	104	170	155	124	105	78	41	123	42	75	99
18	85	101	198	148	117	102	73	35	121	45	86	93
19	73	126	192	128	120	86	66	32	89	50	94	88
20	76	142	196	124	123	97	61	28	65	87	123	96
21	85	169	207	122	163	84	62	39	75	102	127	116
22	105	198	195	90	178	56	60	48	89	113	132	135
23	88	207	157	80	198	43	55	62	91	127	129	122
24	97	215	146	81	205	43	55	68	98	137	119	129
25	103	208	142	81	182	51	53	77	119	141	118	137
26	100	189	149	78	177	28	53	91	127	145	113	131
27	85	171	138	78	145	35	57	104	123	145	109	136
28	79	155	140	72	136	49	79	117	117	131	102	139
29	82		142	68	88	63	95	143	107	120	92	152
30	80		145	72	54	71	109	138	99	104	90	152
31	87		138		50		137	121		87		122
Mean	104.4	120.5	135.8	106.8	120.0	106.0	96.8	98.0	91.3	95.7	93.5	97.9

1969 Yearly Mean = 105.5

Daily Sunspot Numbers 1930–1989

Daily Sunspot Numbers 1970

Day	Jan	Feb	Mar	Apr	May	Jun	Jul	Aug	Sep	Oct	Nov	Dec
01	115	121	137	112	118	102	137	77	98	63	86	91
02	83	96	129	105	118	92	153	68	104	57	82	78
03	78	82	113	121	122	64	155	64	110	43	80	78
04	69	68	107	116	119	63	159	59	115	55	78	76
05	66	72	107	120	113	59	165	65	120	75	67	88
06	57	93	103	115	115	57	161	68	133	53	89	90
07	30	104	111	123	98	58	125	72	136	72	86	91
08	37	102	118	147	87	61	115	82	125	76	69	100
09	59	123	120	172	90	60	104	76	116	78	77	96
10	84	133	125	188	111	92	90	71	103	79	78	110
11	106	175	103	183	132	122	81	75	82	75	97	120
12	138	153	88	163	134	138	74	73	76	80	89	110
13	145	145	104	141	142	153	79	92	73	84	105	90
14	160	124	84	124	145	165	68	94	76	87	117	85
15	155	115	65	106	159	168	61	108	75	87	125	84
16	145	139	48	92	161	153	61	100	68	94	133	68
17	160	142	29	82	169	148	59	99	65	84	135	63
18	168	143	41	68	173	134	56	108	75	76	135	79
19	165	120	48	67	176	105	92	113	98	83	132	95
20	133	125	93	65	146	99	92	117	114	70	128	104
21	118	128	115	64	143	96	120	117	129	69	119	101
22	104	132	122	57	125	96	122	108	109	73	105	97
23	79	164	135	67	106	87	106	101	104	89	96	85
24	73	166	140	90	122	102	110	116	129	100	77	66
25	98	173	142	93	110	126	122	114	114	111	62	75
26	123	143	122	81	125	127	138	109	107	117	65	64
27	130	150	115	88	126	114	153	91	87	142	74	53
28	156	146	110	106	106	113	146	101	85	131	89	50
29	154		103	112	118	124	153	114	81	139	78	59
30	138		111	116	116	127	122	120	77	126	103	74
31	131		101		127		108	111		117		68
Mean	111.5	127.8	102.9	109.5	127.5	106.8	112.5	93.0	99.5	86.6	95.2	83.5

1970 Yearly Mean = 104.5

Daily Sunspot Numbers 1971

Day	Jan	Feb	Mar	Apr	May	Jun	Jul	Aug	Sep	Oct	Nov	Dec
01	68	90	83	58	47	49	95	72	22	63	73	63
02	67	85	93	57	49	61	97	61	19	58	69	65
03	65	81	84	59	54	60	98	58	26	48	62	55
04	69	80	72	56	61	55	95	48	29	37	66	41
05	63	73	63	62	66	43	84	45	42	52	69	59
06	64	78	52	58	66	28	79	38	71	42	64	82
07	67	82	48	59	72	29	74	44	74	43	53	84
08	79	64	44	61	70	38	68	58	59	44	58	86
09	89	45	37	47	69	28	58	62	47	40	56	100
10	80	40	41	54	73	24	45	64	22	37	49	101
11	76	62	49	51	71	26	48	62	16	26	45	102
12	91	57	68	85	74	30	58	60	27	35	46	98
13	82	65	76	103	78	23	54	59	45	33	42	86
14	78	64	71	125	78	32	61	58	60	30	30	84
15	64	69	72	123	76	20	82	52	72	21	28	89
16	67	69	79	109	74	36	93	49	64	24	26	89
17	76	71	79	102	65	40	87	52	80	28	42	111
18	102	81	76	102	56	40	78	63	85	39	45	117
19	109	96	64	110	48	28	104	65	73	42	48	108
20	120	97	53	106	45	35	91	84	60	66	50	102
21	131	101	58	98	43	35	97	102	62	73	62	89
22	125	104	55	82	35	38	116	100	69	74	74	88
23	120	102	51	55	20	49	83	108	61	78	78	88
24	120	101	51	50	20	58	112	97	36	81	86	91
25	112	98	48	48	27	69	112	91	30	87	87	88
26	109	87	50	53	36	88	84	82	26	82	97	76
27	121	85	55	51	49	103	75	57	40	79	102	75
28	109	84	52	49	64	106	72	40	56	69	106	65
29	108		49	45	67	110	70	29	62	62	99	60
30	95		54	36	68	112	72	21	70	52	84	54
31	103		54		63		69	21		59		52
Mean	91.3	79.0	60.7	71.8	57.5	49.8	81.0	61.4	50.2	51.7	63.2	82.2

1971 Yearly Mean = 66.6

Daily Sunspot Numbers 1972

Day	Jan	Feb	Mar	Apr	May	Jun	Jul	Aug	Sep	Oct	Nov	Dec
01	50	53	77	40	28	85	68	103	127	70	75	40
02	47	49	83	43	39	96	74	93	99	65	67	31
03	49	42	86	43	32	105	82	89	79	73	49	28
04	50	44	79	38	34	121	91	85	78	73	30	24
05	54	45	69	42	49	139	104	93	80	67	23	21
06	55	40	64	56	68	115	95	85	81	57	19	18
07	53	45	69	71	79	99	91	65	73	54	8	24
08	50	54	81	73	78	90	82	60	71	52	7	29
09	39	50	79	79	97	79	75	59	59	34	14	42
10	29	52	79	82	94	68	64	47	46	30	12	53
11	22	57	72	74	88	63	62	31	43	34	30	61
12	27	60	73	80	92	52	74	50	36	23	33	64
13	28	71	85	74	106	48	84	55	32	15	30	67
14	37	85	98	63	133	62	80	40	37	8	27	69
15	40	104	110	67	123	88	61	42	45	14	21	71
16	37	129	104	60	125	98	53	57	53	34	25	66
17	45	135	109	55	140	105	59	59	44	30	32	71
18	54	144	104	59	133	95	55	57	38	28	28	58
19	61	158	103	58	127	88	66	57	33	44	42	49
20	69	157	107	65	115	92	56	60	47	60	58	54
21	78	154	107	77	96	100	66	62	60	69	65	67
22	89	157	102	81	79	97	69	85	69	78	69	59
23	105	136	114	83	65	92	65	79	65	85	79	57
24	121	112	109	82	58	88	62	82	77	94	77	48
25	102	93	98	88	56	83	62	71	82	105	65	43
26	91	88	55	83	52	77	77	79	78	111	57	39
27	92	79	34	63	44	79	82	93	77	110	55	34
28	101	85	29	58	44	81	86	118	67	104	61	26
29	102	87	30	38	58	78	102	147	70	89	47	25
30	72		38	22	79	78	108	141	75	98	43	29
31	56		37		85		115	137		93		37
Mean	61.5	88.4	80.1	63.2	80.5	88.0	76.5	76.8	64.0	61.3	41.6	45.3

1972 Yearly Mean = 68.9

Daily Sunspot Numbers 1973

Day	Jan	Feb	Mar	Apr	May	Jun	Jul	Aug	Sep	Oct	Nov	Dec
01	45	14	40	65	24	8	29	36	89	68	31	46
02	53	17	38	79	46	8	31	28	124	66	33	24
03	61	22	35	93	64	16	39	21	130	52	23	24
04	66	21	32	93	77	14	32	28	121	50	20	0
05	74	41	22	75	92	7	42	34	108	44	7	0
06	83	32	32	75	68	16	56	40	84	38	0	0
07	66	34	38	76	82	37	57	42	77	30	0	0
08	62	53	50	71	52	41	50	40	72	22	0	7
09	67	60	53	85	30	31	38	38	75	23	0	8
10	58	61	67	65	25	38	32	27	58	8	0	16
11	52	59	69	62	26	60	23	23	42	0	7	9
12	32	80	85	46	18	58	14	0	22	0	0	9
13	32	83	93	41	7	52	15	0	0	8	9	8
14	20	85	83	37	7	54	10	0	0	10	11	8
15	16	74	73	35	25	48	16	0	13	16	12	17
16	11	54	64	29	33	45	9	0	26	18	13	26
17	27	40	52	16	34	36	28	0	20	19	16	40
18	42	28	44	15	41	18	42	7	16	15	16	43
19	47	18	38	30	42	38	23	7	8	0	22	41
20	60	30	23	37	46	51	8	7	30	0	16	47
21	62	31	20	45	52	75	8	15	39	0	23	51
22	62	32	30	62	56	66	14	10	48	16	29	51
23	60	37	37	73	47	54	0	17	58	28	39	47
24	50	42	29	71	57	51	9	22	63	36	38	51
25	39	44	27	67	64	49	14	28	74	53	46	53
26	27	37	23	67	49	46	8	38	78	59	62	57
27	14	36	32	65	51	43	9	37	78	53	60	26
28	14	36	43	60	32	42	10	47	80	62	61	12
29	13		46	54	29	51	17	56	75	65	64	0
30	16		50	42	21	33	11	64	71	55	59	0
31	14		59		17		22	82		37		0
Mean	43.4	42.9	46.0	57.7	42.4	39.5	23.1	25.6	59.3	30.7	23.9	23.3

1973 Yearly Mean = 38.0

Daily Sunspot Numbers 1930–1989

Daily Sunspot Numbers 1974

Day	Jan	Feb	Mar	Apr	May	Jun	Jul	Aug	Sep	Oct	Nov	Dec
01	12	13	24	22	47	33	79	37	8	61	18	0
02	15	10	14	20	70	41	87	23	8	53	27	0
03	13	7	0	19	85	52	90	12	16	46	39	9
04	12	7	10	22	98	67	93	17	37	60	45	16
05	8	0	14	21	100	62	95	18	40	85	36	17
06	0	0	19	23	102	72	93	26	44	83	25	8
07	0	7	20	28	98	65	78	32	38	84	22	7
08	24	15	14	38	96	59	59	34	32	97	14	0
09	29	21	20	56	88	64	40	43	63	107	7	0
10	43	22	30	66	69	59	26	48	74	114	24	9
11	48	20	37	71	62	48	22	54	80	110	27	21
12	54	22	38	74	49	38	22	67	80	92	24	31
13	45	48	30	77	38	44	28	69	74	76	16	34
14	70	26	39	83	32	41	38	66	67	63	8	33
15	73	45	34	87	23	32	49	59	64	48	16	35
16	64	48	23	77	16	25	54	57	68	41	20	40
17	63	49	20	67	8	25	52	52	71	28	20	36
18	55	47	28	55	0	27	53	44	66	16	18	34
19	53	43	21	45	0	28	47	43	51	9	34	43
20	48	39	15	42	0	20	50	32	31	11	40	40
21	33	35	16	35	0	16	55	28	13	12	40	40
22	36	38	28	25	7	11	58	34	0	9	44	37
23	28	31	25	17	9	11	60	34	7	7	44	28
24	14	29	21	18	7	15	57	28	11	7	37	26
25	0	17	16	19	0	15	59	25	11	8	29	9
26	8	19	10	20	20	8	60	8	13	16	25	8
27	0	37	9	28	18	8	54	8	19	30	23	8
28	8	33	17	15	28	18	51	8	23	27	13	20
29	0		19	22	18	30	42	14	38	22	7	16
30	0		24	16	7	47	41	8	58	22	7	19
31	0		26		30		38	15		16		13
Mean	27.6	26.0	21.3	40.3	39.5	36.0	55.8	33.6	40.2	47.1	25.0	20.5

1974 Yearly Mean = 34.5

Daily Sunspot Numbers 1975

Day	Jan	Feb	Mar	Apr	May	Jun	Jul	Aug	Sep	Oct	Nov	Dec
01	30	0	0	0	26	7	23	37	14	15	0	7
02	30	18	9	0	33	11	18	36	16	8	0	23
03	28	27	14	0	34	8	22	46	19	9	7	20
04	19	27	13	0	32	7	16	78	29	10	18	23
05	18	20	14	0	30	7	23	93	25	8	22	21
06	23	26	14	0	20	7	33	104	24	10	27	18
07	29	34	7	7	14	0	23	102	24	9	30	20
08	29	29	18	17	0	0	19	89	23	16	33	18
09	37	22	20	15	0	0	16	83	17	15	30	8
10	32	18	20	7	8	0	23	80	10	8	26	0
11	30	13	18	0	0	9	29	72	10	8	30	0
12	28	18	15	0	0	0	33	45	16	10	24	0
13	32	9	15	0	0	0	43	52	19	21	22	0
14	13	8	17	0	7	0	46	34	17	26	29	7
15	20	8	24	0	7	8	43	31	8	21	28	7
16	19	8	30	0	8	19	39	26	14	18	28	7
17	16	0	28	0	0	17	25	19	14	16	30	9
18	20	0	22	0	8	12	32	16	18	18	33	8
19	20	0	20	0	0	15	36	8	13	15	36	7
20	23	7	14	0	0	0	28	22	30	10	35	0
21	16	8	9	0	0	7	30	23	27	7	31	0
22	16	0	0	0	8	0	27	7	23	0	23	0
23	15	0	0	7	8	12	19	14	0	0	12	0
24	7	12	0	8	7	20	30	8	0	7	11	18
25	7	9	0	7	0	24	33	11	0	0	9	14
26	7	0	7	7	0	33	30	16	0	0	7	8
27	0	0	0	22	7	38	29	18	0	0	0	0
28	7	0	0	21	13	36	26	10	0	0	0	0
29	7		0	16	0	23	20	10	0	0	0	0
30	7		0	20	0	22	27	21	7	0	0	0
31	0		8		8		34	21		0		0
Mean	18.9	11.5	11.5	5.1	9.0	11.4	28.2	39.7	13.9	9.1	19.4	7.8

1975 Yearly Mean = 15.5

Daily Sunspot Numbers 1976

Day	Jan	Feb	Mar	Apr	May	Jun	Jul	Aug	Sep	Oct	Nov	Dec
01	0	0	0	23	30	0	9	10	17	30	0	0
02	0	0	0	23	23	0	8	16	20	28	0	0
03	0	0	0	21	25	0	10	17	12	30	0	0
04	0	0	0	13	8	0	8	13	11	30	0	0
05	0	0	0	12	21	0	8	16	17	25	0	0
06	0	0	10	9	10	0	10	14	10	24	0	0
07	0	0	12	0	10	0	7	24	9	30	0	7
08	0	0	7	0	9	10	0	27	9	7	0	19
09	0	0	10	8	8	10	0	31	18	14	0	22
10	0	0	12	10	10	7	0	24	22	0	0	19
11	0	0	13	15	16	7	0	23	24	0	0	22
12	20	0	13	17	17	8	0	28	20	13	0	16
13	26	13	13	17	23	8	0	26	18	17	0	12
14	34	16	22	19	30	15	0	15	10	23	0	32
15	20	18	16	19	17	18	0	8	16	25	7	34
16	22	11	11	19	12	15	0	15	14	28	7	36
17	22	8	30	22	18	18	0	19	8	31	14	34
18	20	15	43	27	8	24	0	22	8	24	20	24
19	18	10	47	27	20	23	0	25	7	20	13	15
20	16	12	48	30	20	20	0	20	0	19	12	8
21	11	8	44	37	13	30	0	17	0	15	8	9
22	10	7	36	20	7	31	0	8	0	22	13	9
23	10	0	26	17	15	22	0	9	7	28	11	9
24	0	0	22	16	8	25	0	15	7	30	10	17
25	0	0	22	17	0	18	0	10	16	30	9	22
26	0	0	38	26	7	17	0	14	17	29	9	25
27	7	7	45	23	0	9	0	7	18	24	8	16
28	0	0	43	21	0	11	0	8	18	19	8	17
29	8	0	38	24	0	11	0	9	23	15	8	19
30	8		32	32	0	10	0	10	30	8	0	19
31	0		26		0		0	9		0		12
Mean	8.1	4.3	21.9	18.8	12.4	12.2	1.9	16.4	13.5	20.6	5.2	15.3

1976 Yearly Mean = 12.6

Daily Sunspot Numbers 1977

Day	Jan	Feb	Mar	Apr	May	Jun	Jul	Aug	Sep	Oct	Nov	Dec
01	20	15	0	7	15	44	42	17	22	43	44	20
02	32	19	8	11	14	43	45	15	29	37	40	20
03	25	19	8	10	22	43	42	24	29	47	25	31
04	25	16	8	7	23	49	39	19	25	47	22	47
05	24	18	8	7	18	40	40	23	20	48	25	58
06	13	7	9	8	16	39	40	26	26	55	27	58
07	0	7	8	7	12	41	25	28	25	57	34	55
08	0	26	20	0	19	38	20	25	18	52	27	45
09	0	21	20	0	25	33	17	30	30	47	31	58
10	0	25	19	0	29	29	23	25	40	38	25	75
11	14	28	19	8	34	27	9	23	45	28	26	71
12	22	48	14	12	35	22	8	29	51	33	27	62
13	23	68	8	16	26	20	10	40	48	53	28	44
14	22	61	7	22	33	25	7	40	47	48	31	37
15	24	45	0	29	26	8	0	42	53	54	39	41
16	18	49	0	31	25	8	0	38	56	53	49	39
17	30	47	8	32	20	8	0	36	53	51	51	29
18	26	37	0	29	12	21	0	40	60	50	54	33
19	7	25	0	22	0	33	7	35	59	54	52	40
20	0	14	0	12	11	21	8	33	60	54	38	23
21	15	9	0	20	14	28	8	33	58	42	32	23
22	24	9	10	19	7	40	23	38	42	35	28	17
23	34	9	9	18	7	57	30	15	41	30	24	23
24	35	8	7	8	7	60	38	19	48	29	18	31
25	20	8	14	0	0	74	42	25	46	28	10	35
26	14	8	8	14	7	71	42	34	49	30	9	41
27	0	0	9	8	13	74	37	38	54	38	14	50
28	13	0	16	11	16	65	26	36	61	37	9	45
29	11		16	10	20	50	16	40	64	42	10	58
30	8		8	9	30	45	10	36	60	45	23	64
31	10		8		40		8	31		52		67
Mean	16.4	23.1	8.7	12.9	18.6	38.5	21.4	30.1	44.0	43.8	29.1	43.2

1977 Yearly Mean = 27.5

Daily Sunspot Numbers 1930–1989

Daily Sunspot Numbers 1978

Day	Jan	Feb	Mar	Apr	May	Jun	Jul	Aug	Sep	Oct	Nov	Dec
01	90	128	102	70	85	119	64	42	136	96	109	110
02	94	120	92	68	89	98	61	48	167	112	122	110
03	104	130	95	71	93	78	51	38	159	105	125	117
04	103	142	98	75	92	60	48	62	162	100	129	115
05	91	137	84	94	89	51	54	74	177	73	121	104
06	79	129	75	92	85	31	63	66	177	74	108	122
07	55	122	90	88	75	39	84	58	147	95	112	138
08	39	90	99	105	63	45	105	62	120	103	118	148
09	36	97	94	126	62	36	108	64	109	121	108	152
10	15	102	92	125	60	29	115	67	99	149	120	144
11	20	112	88	120	63	57	127	58	84	158	118	170
12	26	115	78	109	66	62	111	71	72	158	99	188
13	33	96	73	105	74	62	114	93	92	156	90	165
14	37	82	72	91	74	64	109	93	113	170	78	150
15	34	65	74	90	78	89	102	77	133	166	59	140
16	27	64	74	95	91	94	110	52	143	163	77	143
17	26	58	74	99	86	103	98	50	136	143	92	146
18	14	57	74	103	89	115	84	50	156	135	93	132
19	8	56	65	111	84	109	77	42	159	154	85	95
20	8	58	59	115	74	109	76	30	163	151	76	84
21	19	65	77	114	76	154	77	30	171	144	68	68
22	28	73	84	115	74	158	48	36	148	125	77	63
23	40	76	88	119	73	158	38	45	156	116	55	59
24	40	91	85	106	82	154	38	48	163	104	61	65
25	38	94	74	136	85	135	30	55	168	96	85	81
26	49	90	60	115	88	152	13	45	152	102	101	93
27	67	85	52	99	97	143	22	57	142	115	118	110
28	78	88	49	83	93	130	31	57	126	117	118	122
29	90		48	78	103	115	48	59	122	137	111	135
30	103		45	75	107	103	39	72	94	128	103	159
31	118		58		113		36	100		111		177
Mean	51.9	93.6	76.5	99.7	82.7	95.1	70.4	58.1	138.2	125.1	97.9	122.7

1978 Yearly Mean = 92.5

Daily Sunspot Numbers 1980

Day	Jan	Feb	Mar	Apr	May	Jun	Jul	Aug	Sep	Oct	Nov	Dec
01	153	195	181	168	121	152	101	78	208	151	188	171
02	158	178	168	145	149	124	108	63	226	135	218	176
03	148	185	151	133	140	128	97	65	232	139	204	152
04	160	182	136	123	166	141	85	65	233	121	217	146
05	184	178	130	154	192	150	96	53	188	96	201	131
06	207	209	132	179	145	131	98	72	179	116	196	126
07	212	220	120	194	147	149	97	64	136	135	175	108
08	221	203	101	199	157	150	87	90	140	173	201	124
09	249	172	103	229	168	164	84	125	108	186	158	117
10	219	140	69	214	144	177	86	130	119	235	158	145
11	245	148	67	245	142	172	87	181	125	260	144	148
12	210	128	70	251	143	166	98	174	128	256	120	178
13	181	131	71	252	150	161	105	172	133	213	103	185
14	178	140	68	203	166	136	128	193	100	232	108	213
15	146	159	52	182	148	129	161	192	83	224	105	217
16	166	163	36	154	148	134	198	196	98	202	112	237
17	145	132	67	126	173	129	211	190	93	158	109	198
18	130	122	63	127	215	146	241	195	114	142	113	183
19	118	129	119	134	218	166	220	185	137	137	125	166
20	115	125	108	164	230	179	227	179	150	167	112	171
21	121	114	105	143	233	191	229	152	134	155	107	170
22	123	99	130	122	244	196	201	139	147	164	119	178
23	124	100	149	95	246	190	184	154	158	140	112	177
24	120	116	175	112	256	193	155	122	178	127	128	191
25	107	121	176	133	229	179	151	109	168	118	127	200
26	127	152	191	159	220	166	138	101	209	119	140	208
27	120	175	205	150	223	185	117	98	231	134	168	206
28	130	197	221	149	190	188	127	124	181	136	167	206
29	122	181	191	145	185	149	118	158	166	173	148	208
30	145		182	138	150	97	108	184	149	184	153	187
31	164		174		138		81	194		178		182
Mean	159.6	155.0	126.2	164.1	179.9	157.3	136.3	135.4	155.0	164.7	147.9	174.4

1980 Yearly Mean = 154.6

Daily Sunspot Numbers 1979

Day	Jan	Feb	Mar	Apr	May	Jun	Jul	Aug	Sep	Oct	Nov	Dec
01	158	116	116	131	108	121	158	115	165	213	224	122
02	158	113	138	134	106	145	168	96	141	187	157	156
03	191	138	141	135	103	154	205	121	148	167	155	187
04	157	123	142	138	112	178	219	110	157	156	172	218
05	146	134	135	109	113	207	232	93	139	168	166	232
06	173	146	144	91	122	226	249	104	139	168	203	206
07	163	144	146	77	148	222	223	110	170	179	240	212
08	172	142	143	69	157	220	219	132	192	190	280	262
09	165	139	146	61	162	224	191	115	190	210	279	280
10	163	137	140	75	145	205	163	92	177	178	302	260
11	157	137	156	94	148	186	155	84	167	183	295	242
12	159	138	170	107	158	199	145	87	156	189	248	261
13	151	152	169	113	163	172	142	91	175	201	183	235
14	157	163	159	116	203	149	127	112	186	213	218	230
15	178	161	155	117	207	117	121	135	177	198	186	225
16	164	159	130	119	187	103	107	115	163	185	166	215
17	164	160	142	107	184	122	109	124	155	214	238	180
18	146	162	142	98	148	126	109	143	177	224	172	151
19	138	166	138	79	109	110	135	176	195	221	174	138
20	177	181	131	68	107	111	158	187	191	214	153	126
21	192	171	134	68	114	124	151	218	184	209	124	124
22	188	155	140	79	121	108	152	216	178	191	116	111
23	200	127	139	76	117	96	154	206	219	179	142	116
24	209	99	118	72	119	90	143	203	236	161	162	130
25	209	88	114	85	124	120	144	201	252	153	155	143
26	173	108	114	118	123	132	142	182	261	145	141	116
27	167	97	117	125	118	112	146	189	256	136	115	93
28	157	95	114	132	110	128	132	174	239	142	119	98
29	153		123	132	113	124	148	158	235	184	98	121
30	149		135	120	96	154	150	150	233	190	116	139
31	130		147		120		144	168		223		135
Mean	166.6	137.5	138.0	101.5	134.4	149.5	159.4	142.2	188.4	186.2	183.3	176.3

1979 Yearly Mean = 155.4

Daily Sunspot Numbers 1981

Day	Jan	Feb	Mar	Apr	May	Jun	Jul	Aug	Sep	Oct	Nov	Dec
01	159	148	161	153	112	62	149	121	205	216	165	193
02	141	132	182	170	133	59	140	105	183	206	222	197
03	122	150	169	148	156	44	140	112	160	219	218	212
04	113	126	173	151	152	58	112	109	170	189	221	212
05	94	133	141	146	162	55	112	113	195	195	233	219
06	71	172	147	132	192	57	85	102	220	169	199	234
07	95	158	130	152	171	58	66	107	205	171	192	244
08	108	129	142	195	177	46	62	115	208	185	184	249
09	126	124	124	199	168	58	65	121	190	177	134	258
10	120	157	127	199	148	59	99	138	196	144	147	253
11	123	172	130	200	169	72	130	136	164	131	146	263
12	126	185	128	193	183	79	139	140	138	123	160	240
13	123	143	127	197	149	86	153	134	132	171	158	185
14	106	142	128	180	140	99	145	140	148	187	178	159
15	106	124	110	212	141	111	150	153	129	212	139	113
16	81	129	128	197	127	109	161	134	138	223	126	66
17	72	120	109	213	124	119	171	125	129	219	103	80
18	79	131	95	214	119	104	161	148	145	210	108	79
19	78	138	95	203	100	90	151	175	156	189	90	74
20	88	133	120	199	77	71	145	188	137	183	82	57
21	99	131	135	154	99	87	122	222	175	145	82	65
22	99	128	134	122	106	106	129	220	172	145	73	75
23	115	98	130	103	93	119	162	200	137	118	65	86
24	113	124	125	92	96	109	196	178	135	109	59	68
25	115	137	142	119	93	127	213	189	142	101	60	62
26	120	148	133	90	105	127	206	215	153	92	60	100
27	135	175	126	81	99	133	218	222	181	75	77	104
28	142	170	165	72	93	123	208	214	195	92	130	136
29	165		160	100	92	138	159	194	191	131	148	132
30	158		152	106	83	161	156	233	190	152	165	112
31	143		132		92		152	216		156		126
Mean	114.0	141.3	135.5	156.4	127.5	90.9	143.8	158.7	167.3	162.4	137.5	150.1

1981 Yearly Mean = 140.4

Daily Sunspot Numbers 1930–1989

Daily Sunspot Numbers 1982

Day	Jan	Feb	Mar	Apr	May	Jun	Jul	Aug	Sep	Oct	Nov	Dec
01	92	258	168	145	63	70	50	55	115	132	80	88
02	94	241	174	115	57	83	41	68	124	164	88	125
03	112	232	175	151	46	94	33	68	146	143	75	132
04	109	221	177	137	58	104	42	81	176	120	100	137
05	112	219	163	112	63	111	39	97	160	109	100	137
06	86	230	165	117	64	108	32	128	141	55	76	174
07	94	226	146	130	69	115	33	144	117	54	98	175
08	97	232	140	131	89	127	42	150	115	55	86	184
09	98	211	116	132	47	142	61	161	94	54	102	152
10	85	181	122	138	53	147	110	155	81	88	109	166
11	46	158	119	152	58	138	146	157	86	87	112	171
12	52	156	135	142	75	144	187	138	78	92	83	194
13	51	162	155	133	78	139	219	113	81	98	98	172
14	58	142	153	136	58	137	222	100	104	88	116	160
15	81	134	140	127	52	125	246	100	129	71	116	166
16	76	111	156	122	69	128	263	86	133	65	100	140
17	111	120	180	108	76	136	272	93	127	54	108	118
18	139	103	168	91	89	134	270	105	107	33	117	102
19	143	107	167	87	110	134	234	97	117	56	122	79
20	134	119	160	93	112	139	192	77	104	70	118	63
21	134	120	153	91	98	143	138	79	102	95	131	87
22	121	100	146	109	121	146	99	90	95	100	141	88
23	93	97	144	138	107	116	74	71	97	128	120	96
24	70	120	122	145	110	112	27	79	109	145	96	100
25	82	128	152	149	88	92	25	101	118	142	75	122
26	119	136	147	150	117	94	29	98	138	135	73	116
27	125	154	182	126	130	49	22	115	133	131	71	126
28	168	163	179	90	119	36	19	132	132	103	74	120
29	216		169	85	112	32	23	134	144	101	82	98
30	211		162	79	77	38	38	144	160	96	76	79
31	237		132		82		60	120		73		69
Mean	111.2	163.6	153.8	122.0	82.2	110.4	106.1	107.6	118.8	94.7	98.1	127.0

1982 Yearly Mean = 115.9

Daily Sunspot Numbers 1983

Day	Jan	Feb	Mar	Apr	May	Jun	Jul	Aug	Sep	Oct	Nov	Dec
01	60	103	109	53	114	61	62	131	46	29	17	26
02	65	85	93	70	104	72	59	128	56	51	22	23
03	55	88	86	61	94	73	61	105	59	63	37	15
04	63	94	93	53	85	68	87	103	69	74	51	14
05	82	82	113	36	95	77	80	79	84	65	66	17
06	103	71	88	49	88	85	79	49	78	75	74	39
07	109	72	77	64	92	104	79	60	72	87	84	41
08	126	63	68	59	98	100	82	70	68	99	90	48
09	100	39	74	59	110	100	69	69	74	106	70	71
10	83	26	55	64	114	86	59	63	70	121	68	82
11	90	21	49	69	101	73	68	88	65	136	56	76
12	77	18	32	65	114	66	86	103	41	122	43	66
13	89	11	12	64	132	72	85	104	36	100	36	66
14	92	10	24	64	125	88	88	97	36	80	29	52
15	77	24	44	53	130	92	92	93	42	72	28	50
16	89	17	63	54	99	84	93	80	33	61	38	35
17	102	22	74	63	93	79	96	72	35	60	31	46
18	86	32	88	75	99	78	98	71	45	63	36	36
19	93	33	82	110	88	103	96	54	40	46	26	31
20	81	32	82	90	105	117	101	40	32	26	12	25
21	74	39	87	87	110	117	109	52	36	18	18	21
22	73	33	70	83	104	136	114	50	38	22	0	15
23	59	40	66	91	102	143	95	51	42	22	0	20
24	58	50	60	92	111	122	105	35	46	20	0	22
25	75	67	48	123	98	122	85	52	42	18	0	21
26	77	70	70	118	100	110	58	53	50	20	7	23
27	75	88	72	126	85	92	49	51	51	12	10	12
28	89	98	48	146	68	83	40	55	48	15	12	10
29	99		44	142	88	68	73	63	43	16	19	11
30	101		54	137	68	63	89	59	33	15	21	13
31	110		37		60		110	45		16		9
Mean	84.3	51	66.5	80.7	99.2	91.1	82.2	71.8	50.3	55.8	33.3	33.4

1983 Yearly Mean = 66.6

Daily Sunspot Numbers 1984

Day	Jan	Feb	Mar	Apr	May	Jun	Jul	Aug	Sep	Oct	Nov	Dec
01	10	110	74	103	109	48	33	14	45	7	16	19
02	16	82	78	94	89	44	36	17	50	8	14	22
03	17	67	66	88	69	45	61	19	61	11	11	19
04	18	61	54	81	52	34	80	25	58	11	14	19
05	21	66	65	61	38	30	72	18	53	0	12	16
06	29	76	49	70	27	23	61	24	32	0	0	21
07	37	79	51	50	35	34	64	27	21	0	11	18
08	38	94	64	33	54	31	74	32	20	12	13	23
09	50	115	60	36	72	26	63	35	13	14	13	21
10	44	123	46	12	85	31	74	31	10	17	21	15
11	48	118	65	21	94	37	57	29	9	22	27	28
12	51	108	72	28	100	39	54	31	9	16	21	29
13	48	82	79	24	118	41	44	28	9	10	16	28
14	46	77	88	32	111	50	34	27	0	9	15	28
15	44	80	112	59	85	80	30	23	8	14	13	26
16	46	53	117	60	97	83	25	23	12	19	11	30
17	51	51	105	56	83	73	21	18	0	24	11	24
18	49	50	95	73	70	62	26	17	0	25	14	12
19	51	54	90	82	74	51	22	11	10	25	13	11
20	69	54	103	69	70	53	18	16	0	17	27	11
21	76	76	98	68	65	43	12	12	9	19	36	14
22	64	100	87	55	77	48	22	10	10	12	36	12
23	70	121	89	59	83	54	25	19	8	11	41	11
24	70	117	80	80	86	58	38	24	8	9	47	16
25	99	117	97	99	75	44	30	36	7	10	59	21
26	105	101	97	124	87	49	25	49	0	10	44	20
27	99	78	96	121	86	40	9	41	0	8	39	14
28	106	78	98	125	69	41	9	37	0	0	39	16
29	110	88	94	120	74	50	12	34	0	8	30	15
30	102		107	107	70	42	16	27	8	11	20	10
31	82		113		63		12	36		14		10
Mean	57.0	85.4	83.5	69.7	76.4	46.1	37.4	25.5	15.7	12.0	22.8	18.7

1984 Yearly Mean = 45.9

Daily Sunspot Numbers 1985

Day	Jan	Feb	Mar	Apr	May	Jun	Jul	Aug	Sep	Oct	Nov	Dec
01	0	18	13	25	19	10	21	35	7	0	0	0
02	0	22	13	21	15	0	27	25	0	0	0	16
03	0	25	9	23	14	11	30	27	0	0	0	13
04	0	22	0	17	18	26	32	27	0	0	0	0
05	0	20	0	23	16	35	38	20	0	0	16	18
06	0	16	0	19	14	37	43	14	0	0	19	26
07	0	7	0	11	32	38	71	12	0	0	19	15
08	11	16	14	9	44	42	67	12	0	0	18	12
09	14	24	15	9	56	42	82	17	0	0	25	16
10	0	19	13	0	49	58	82	12	0	0	15	15
11	0	13	16	0	49	66	61	12	7	0	17	18
12	13	10	18	0	33	54	45	12	0	0	19	19
13	16	11	14	0	32	45	25	0	9	11	30	18
14	26	13	10	10	32	36	9	0	9	13	44	30
15	25	11	0	0	32	37	8	0	9	15	48	47
16	26	10	11	0	31	27	9	14	9	25	39	66
17	29	12	20	0	38	23	11	12	8	19	43	63
18	26	10	35	10	41	18	11	11	10	20	37	52
19	27	19	27	9	40	10	11	12	10	31	30	40
20	55	27	19	11	37	9	11	10	9	44	28	24
21	59	27	9	17	36	9	10	9	8	50	18	17
22	50	25	15	31	34	9	10	0	7	72	12	11
23	39	16	22	28	32	12	18	0	0	67	10	0
24	33	11	36	30	25	13	12	0	0	63	0	0
25	20	11	30	37	19	12	10	0	0	55	0	0
26	9	11	33	37	13	10	13	8	0	40	0	0
27	8	10	27	31	12	8	12	8	0	27	0	0
28	0	9	36	27	12	8	36	10	0	14	0	0
29	9		25	26	10	9	51	9	7	11	0	0
30	0		29	26	8	11	46	8	7	0	0	0
31	17		23		8		40	9		0		0
Mean	16.5	15.9	17.2	16.2	27.5	24.2	30.7	11.1	3.9	18.6	16.2	17.3

1985 Yearly Mean = 17.9

Daily Sunspot Numbers 1930–1989

Daily Sunspot Numbers 1986

Day	Jan	Feb	Mar	Apr	May	Jun	Jul	Aug	Sep	Oct	Nov	Dec
01	0	18	16	9	15	7	0	12	9	12	44	0
02	0	33	33	10	26	0	0	11	9	14	35	0
03	0	52	34	10	15	0	11	11	8	23	37	0
04	0	55	32	0	12	0	14	11	8	24	37	0
05	0	53	33	0	10	0	18	11	0	24	35	0
06	0	47	33	0	0	0	29	10	11	22	31	0
07	0	52	38	0	0	0	29	8	13	27	24	0
08	0	54	29	9	0	9	29	9	12	20	15	0
09	0	47	22	0	0	0	17	8	10	32	10	12
10	0	35	20	9	0	8	36	0	8	29	9	20
11	0	37	18	13	0	0	39	0	8	23	9	23
12	0	25	13	14	0	0	36	0	0	26	0	22
13	13	22	8	13	0	0	25	0	0	22	14	24
14	16	16	0	26	0	0	16	0	0	0	12	13
15	13	11	10	25	10	0	28	0	0	0	12	0
16	10	0	0	21	12	0	26	9	0	11	12	11
17	0	0	0	13	13	0	28	8	0	16	12	9
18	0	0	0	15	22	0	14	0	0	22	12	0
19	0	0	0	13	27	0	13	0	0	31	12	0
20	0	10	12	16	27	0	18	11	0	39	12	0
21	0	10	13	22	30	0	21	12	0	47	11	11
22	0	10	10	20	27	0	22	12	0	57	10	16
23	0	10	15	42	24	0	14	14	0	71	18	16
24	0	8	14	58	24	0	0	9	0	76	12	13
25	0	11	10	43	22	8	0	9	0	68	0	9
26	7	9	10	43	28	0	0	9	0	60	0	0
27	0	15	11	33	19	0	12	9	0	65	13	0
28	0	10	13	23	18	0	13	9	0	61	0	0
29	0		11	28	19	0	17	9	8	63	8	0
30	10		11	27	13	0	19	9	9	62	0	0
31	10		0		12		17	9		50		11
Mean	2.5	23.2	15.1	18.5	13.7	1.1	18.1	7.4	3.8	35.4	15.2	6.8

1986 Yearly Mean = 13.4

Daily Sunspot Numbers 1987

Day	Jan	Feb	Mar	Apr	May	Jun	Jul	Aug	Sep	Oct	Nov	Dec
01	19	0	13	14	39	15	13	45	33	34	56	17
02	15	0	23	12	40	11	0	47	38	25	57	16
03	13	0	15	10	27	0	0	39	37	31	57	16
04	12	0	16	13	23	0	0	33	38	58	46	15
05	11	0	24	28	24	10	0	31	39	54	47	19
06	10	0	23	47	27	0	0	32	44	48	27	24
07	11	0	24	56	34	0	9	38	56	39	31	34
08	0	0	22	64	25	0	12	45	67	55	43	36
09	0	0	14	69	23	0	13	39	64	50	42	41
10	0	7	11	77	25	0	11	47	59	51	30	34
11	0	0	9	80	26	11	0	56	58	63	28	22
12	0	0	0	80	23	21	0	48	44	53	25	13
13	0	0	0	79	22	14	0	47	25	74	18	20
14	8	8	10	77	13	10	0	49	20	92	23	26
15	9	7	11	78	39	11	13	49	21	101	22	42
16	0	0	11	60	50	12	17	55	24	101	33	40
17	13	0	22	41	68	14	14	46	25	91	46	39
18	13	0	21	36	54	24	17	43	30	86	48	39
19	9	0	12	29	65	13	23	45	35	82	51	28
20	9	0	12	12	46	22	38	51	38	79	49	26
21	14	7	15	19	41	29	67	48	32	61	51	14
22	20	7	17	26	38	38	87	34	23	50	70	24
23	23	0	19	25	40	37	102	39	26	33	83	17
24	14	0	19	35	38	38	92	35	25	22	56	13
25	13	7	16	25	37	38	88	35	12	29	42	25
26	14	9	12	21	37	41	85	34	12	40	47	27
27	13	8	11	11	35	33	77	24	19	70	21	29
28	20	8	12	14	21	41	60	23	22	79	11	28
29	15		13	20	17	25	60	13	26	82	20	30
30	14		15	30	15	14	62	10	26	85	16	42
31	11		15		12		63	20		62		43
Mean	10.4	2.4	14.7	39.6	33.0	17.4	33.0	38.7	33.9	60.6	39.9	27.1

1987 Yearly Mean = 29.4

Daily Sunspot Numbers 1988

Day	Jan	Feb	Mar	Apr	May	Jun	Jul	Aug	Sep	Oct	Nov	Dec
01	47	63	68	110	69	95	139	142	137	109	126	128
02	31	68	66	96	84	96	145	143	144	117	114	114
03	25	68	72	94	76	100	142	146	129	129	121	139
04	23	74	77	74	101	105	129	135	148	128	104	122
05	32	58	64	66	103	125	119	120	128	130	129	149
06	40	43	61	62	77	145	108	123	93	123	124	149
07	58	44	65	84	50	141	103	144	97	128	114	144
08	57	46	67	92	63	151	106	160	88	131	95	111
09	62	50	49	115	74	173	82	171	74	125	110	122
10	68	38	36	107	87	144	78	152	76	146	131	133
11	75	26	20	115	65	108	102	135	81	148	155	152
12	67	14	39	118	56	77	109	133	88	169	159	175
13	76	23	53	120	44	47	103	122	91	150	147	187
14	91	28	62	138	37	53	121	128	94	131	139	213
15	90	33	63	145	44	65	121	121	89	109	156	225
16	83	42	74	157	53	81	111	91	89	108	181	226
17	72	35	99	144	57	76	124	67	79	125	196	232
18	68	55	95	137	44	67	136	47	97	134	175	222
19	73	66	105	108	20	70	105	57	113	133	147	223
20	85	51	85	88	20	77	106	57	153	119	112	218
21	78	27	81	79	25	95	103	40	168	117	145	210
22	66	15	76	72	30	92	106	21	168	109	131	255
23	47	13	74	43	40	91	116	26	190	104	117	235
24	44	23	83	30	48	93	81	43	172	121	116	199
25	33	19	92	40	54	111	76	76	149	124	89	183
26	44	15	93	44	63	107	76	93	151	119	73	174
27	54	31	103	36	66	111	101	142	157	120	69	175
28	67	40	109	41	70	116	117	146	143	119	86	196
29	59	52	104	39	74	121	157	164	111	128	86	194
30	56		108	47	83	121	161	163	106	115	107	178
31	57		120		86		146	151		111		172
Mean	59.0	40.0	76.2	88.0	60.1	101.8	113.8	111.6	120.1	125.1	125.1	179.2

1988 Yearly Mean = 100.2

Daily Sunspot Numbers 1989

Day	Jan	Feb	Mar	Apr	May	Jun	Jul	Aug	Sep	Oct	Nov	Dec
01	148	141	127									
02	173	144	107									
03	146	164	103									
04	120	133	98									
05	155	127	90									
06	142	127	103									
07	165	132	98									
08	155	161	109									
09	165	172	133									
10	190	192	163									
11	211	190	155									
12	229	216	140									
13	206	219	162									
14	189	208	181									
15	177	191	165									
16	164	195	187									
17	155	209	168									
18	160	163	164									
19	140	164	148									
20	126	169	158									
21	114	149	155									
22	165	142	155									
23	171	134	145									
24	142	153	155									
25	144	189	131									
26	152	163	117									
27	157	147	102									
28	172	128	89									
29	169		95									
30	157		78									
31	140		91									
Mean	161.3	165.1	131.4									

The remainder of the 1989 data was not available at press time.

1989 Yearly Mean =

Major Magnetic Storms: Ap* 1932–1989

Ap* is derived from the standard IAGA global magnetic activity index "Ap." The 3-hourly Ap index is produced monthly by the Geophysical Institut, Universität Göttingen, FRG, from locally scaled indices prepared at some 12 or 13 magnetic observatories of a worldwide network mostly in the Northern Hemisphere. Data is available from 1932 to March 31, 1990.

In 1978 the Ap* index was defined by J. H. Allen as the maximum 24-hour value attained by the 8-point running mean of the 3-hourly Ap indices without regard to the UT-day but restricted to separate storms. A "separate storm" was arbitrarily defined to begin when the running mean went above a selected onset level and to continue until it dropped below a selected cutoff level. For Ap data in the tables, these values are both at 40 units. Once a major storm begins, the maximum value attained by the running mean during that event is Ap*. These indices can be used to examine the relative frequency of major magnetic storms since 1932 by month and by year. They are listed by each storm in chronological order and in sequence from largest to smallest.

Solar-Terrestrial Physics data and products in the STP Division of the National Geophysical Data Center and WDC-A for STP are available from:

National Geophysical Data Center
Solar-Terrestrial Physics Division
NOAA/NGDC, E/GC2
325 Broadway
Boulder, Colorado 80303, USA

References

J. H. Allen, et al, "Effects of the March 1989 Solar Activity" (Transactions of the American Geophysical Union, Vol. 70, No. 46, November 14, 1989).

S. I. Akasofu and S. Chapman, *Solar-Terrestrial Physics*, Oxford University Press, 1972.

A. S. Jursa, *Handbook of Geophysics and the Space Environment* (Air Force Geophysics Laboratory, 1985).

P.N. Mayaud, Derivation, Meaning, and Use of Geomagnetic Indices, (geophysical monograph 22, American Geophysical Union, 1980).

Major Magnetic Storms: Ap* 1932–1989 Summary

YEAR	JAN	FEB	MAR	APR	MAY	JUN	JUL	AUG	SEP	OCT	NOV	DEC	TOTAL
1932	0	0	3	0	1	0	0	1	1	1	0	1	8
1933	0	0	1	0	1	0	0	1	1	0	0	0	4
1934	0	0	0	0	0	0	0	0	1	0	0	1	2
1935	0	0	1	1	0	1	0	0	2	2	0	0	7
1936	0	0	0	2	0	2	0	0	0	1	1	1	7
1937	0	1	1	1	2	1	0	2	2	6	0	0	16
1938	3	3	2	3	3	0	3	1	3	2	0	0	23
1939	0	2	1	5	3	1	5	3	3	3	1	1	28
1940	1	0	2	2	1	2	1	0	3	1	3	1	17
1941	1	2	5	2	0	1	1	2	1	2	2	1	20
1942	0	1	5	3	0	0	1	1	2	2	1	0	16
1943	1	1	1	1	2	0	1	5	5	7	4	3	31
1944	0	2	1	1	1	0	0	1	0	1	0	2	9
1945	1	0	4	2	0	1	0	0	1	2	1	1	13
1946	1	3	3	2	4	3	4	2	5	1	0	0	28
1947	1	1	5	1	2	3	1	4	6	4	1	0	29
1948	1	0	2	1	2	0	0	1	0	4	2	0	13
1949	2	1	3	1	3	3	0	1	0	3	3	0	20
1950	1	2	1	2	2	2	2	3	5	4	4	3	31
1951	2	3	5	8	3	1	2	4	7	4	1	5	45
1952	4	7	6	4	5	2	2	0	3	3	2	0	38
1953	3	2	3	0	1	2	2	4	3	3	2	0	25
1954	0	2	2	1	0	0	0	0	2	2	0	0	9
1955	2	0	1	1	1	0	0	0	1	2	1	0	9
1956	5	2	3	3	4	1	1	2	3	2	2	0	28
1957	2	3	4	3	0	4	2	2	5	1	2	2	30
1958	1	1	4	2	4	3	2	3	3	2	0	3	28
1959	1	6	1	3	3	3	3	2	3	3	4	4	36
1960	3	0	2	4	5	3	1	2	2	5	5	3	35
1961	1	2	3	1	0	1	5	3	2	1	2	1	22
1962	1	1	0	1	0	0	2	0	3	1	0	2	11
1963	1	1	1	1	0	1	0	1	5	2	1	0	14
1964	1	0	2	2	0	1	0	0	1	0	0	0	7
1965	0	0	0	1	0	1	0	0	0	0	0	0	2
1966	0	0	3	0	2	0	1	1	2	1	0	1	11
1967	2	2	0	0	4	1	0	0	3	0	0	3	15
1968	0	2	0	1	1	2	0	1	2	2	1	0	12
1969	0	2	2	1	2	0	1	0	1	0	1	0	10
1970	0	0	3	1	2	0	3	1	0	2	1	1	14
1971	1	1	1	2	2	0	0	0	2	0	3	1	13
1972	0	0	1	1	1	1	0	2	1	1	1	1	10
1973	0	3	1	5	2	2	0	1	2	2	1	0	19
1974	1	2	5	6	1	2	2	3	3	4	3	1	33
1975	1	1	2	3	1	0	0	0	0	1	2	0	11
1976	1	0	2	2	1	0	0	0	1	1	0	1	9
1977	0	0	0	2	1	0	1	2	2	1	1	2	12
1978	2	3	2	5	2	4	2	2	3	0	2	1	28
1979	1	1	3	6	0	1	0	3	1	1	0	0	17
1980	0	1	0	0	1	1	1	0	0	2	0	1	7
1981	0	1	3	4	5	1	1	1	1	5	1	0	23
1982	0	10	2	3	3	2	3	3	4	3	3	4	40
1983	1	4	5	3	6	2	1	1	2	2	4	0	31
1984	0	4	2	3	1	1	3	1	4	2	1	0	22
1985	2	2	1	4	0	1	1	1	2	1	2	2	19
1986	1	1	0	0	2	0	0	0	2	1	2	0	9
1987	0	0	0	0	0	0	1	2	3	1	0	0	7
1988	2	1	2	3	1	0	0	0	1	1	0	1	12
1989	3	1	8	2	3	2	0	0	0	0	0	0	19
TOTAL	58	91	126	122	97	66	62	76	126	111	74	55	1064

Major Magnetic Storms: Ap* 1932–1989

All AP* storms persist into the following day but not into the day after. In these tables, UT times represent intervals. i.e., 0000 UT represents 0000 - 0259 UT, and 0300 UT represents 0300 - 0559 UT., etc.

Year	Date	UT	AP*
1932	Mar 10	0900	43
	Mar 28	1500	45
	Mar 30	1200	53
	May 29	0900	124
	Aug 27	1200	65
	Sep 24	1800	44
	Oct 20	1200	41
	Dec 14	0900	40
1933	Mar 19	1800	41
	May 01	0300	91
	Aug 05	0900	47
	Sep 09	0300	56
1934	Sep 24	2100	58
	Dec 03	2100	45
1935	Mar 14	0600	48
	Apr 11	0000	50
	Jun 07	1200	47
	Sep 11	0600	60
	Sep 24	2100	45
	Oct 20	0900	41
	Oct 24	0600	42
1936	Apr 17	2100	43
	Apr 21	1800	60
	Jun 08	1800	42
	Jun 18	1800	72
	Oct 16	1500	52
	Nov 28	2100	63
	Dec 27	1800	41
1937	Feb 02	2100	57
	Mar 31	0300	53
	Apr 27	1800	143
	May 04	1800	73
	May 28	0300	52
	Jun 05	1800	49
	Aug 01	2100	48
	Aug 22	0300	75
	Sep 10	1800	41
	Sep 30	1200	53
	Oct 03	0900	79
	Oct 07	1200	43
	Oct 09	1200	64
	Oct 11	1200	49
	Oct 23	0300	42
	Oct 23	1500	42
1938	Jan 16	2100	130
	Jan 21	2100	130
	Jan 25	0900	146
	Feb 06	0300	53
	Feb 08	1500	51
	Feb 13	2100	40
	Mar 05	0600	41
	Mar 23	0900	65
	Apr 13	1500	72
	Apr 16	0000	136
	Apr 23	0600	42
	May 03	2100	45
	May 11	1500	149
	May 14	0600	50
	Jul 04	0600	40
	Jul 15	0300	72
	Jul 30	0000	44
	Aug 03	2100	63
	Sep 14	2100	104
	Sep 27	2100	72
	Sep 30	1200	63
	Oct 07	1200	102
	Oct 26	1200	40
1939	Feb 06	0600	47
	Feb 24	1500	105
	Mar 28	1500	85
	Apr 10	0000	42
	Apr 17	0000	134
	Apr 19	1200	47
	Apr 22	2100	91
	Apr 24	1500	118
	May 01	0900	81
	May 05	1800	41
	May 06	1200	67
	Jun 13	1800	60
	Jul 03	0000	45
	Jul 04	1800	103
	Jul 19	2100	48
	Jul 20	1500	41
	Jul 21	0900	44
	Aug 11	2100	87
	Aug 16	0900	71
	Aug 22	1200	146
	Sep 02	2100	41
	Sep 17	0300	55
	Sep 19	0900	44
	Oct 03	0600	73
	Oct 13	1800	113
	Oct 16	1200	41
	Nov 13	0300	44
	Dec 06	1800	53
1940	Jan 03	0300	48
	Mar 24	1200	277
	Mar 29	1500	226
	Apr 02	1800	110
	Apr 25	0300	81
	May 24	0300	79
	Jun 14	1200	53
	Jun 25	0000	125
	Jul 13	0900	65
	Sep 26	1500	70
	Sep 27	1800	47
	Sep 30	2100	41
	Oct 07	0600	74
	Nov 12	0900	59
	Nov 25	0900	49
	Nov 29	0300	40
	Dec 20	0900	54
1941	Jan 17	0000	42
	Feb 21	2100	43
	Feb 22	0900	40
	Mar 01	0300	212
	Mar 04	0600	42
	Mar 14	0000	79
	Mar 21	1800	43
	Mar 30	1500	126
	Apr 18	2100	43
	Apr 24	0900	81
	Jun 13	0600	45
	Jul 05	0000	222
	Aug 04	0300	113
	Aug 27	0000	58
	Sep 18	0900	312
	Oct 11	0600	53
	Oct 31	1800	102
	Nov 06	0300	43
	Nov 28	0000	52
	Dec 01	0600	93
1942	Feb 23	1200	54
	Mar 01	0600	136
	Mar 03	0000	41
	Mar 05	1200	58
	Mar 08	1800	43
	Mar 09	0000	40
	Apr 03	2100	71
	Apr 10	2100	43
	Apr 16	1800	50
	Jul 10	2100	47
	Aug 23	0000	42
	Sep 11	1800	60
	Sep 20	2100	40
	Oct 02	0900	67
	Oct 28	1500	98
	Nov 23	2100	67
1943	Jan 20	1500	52
	Feb 17	0300	41
	Mar 29	1200	49
	Apr 10	0900	45
	May 01	0300	63
	May 17	1500	47
	Jul 05	1200	50
	Aug 08	0900	109
	Aug 13	0300	53
	Aug 19	1200	46
	Aug 28	0900	51
	Aug 30	1800	153
	Sep 03	0000	48
	Sep 08	1500	45
	Sep 26	1200	44
	Sep 27	1800	50
	Sep 29	1200	73
	Oct 02	1800	46
	Oct 08	2100	48
	Oct 24	0900	53
	Oct 25	1800	51
	Oct 27	1800	48
	Oct 28	1500	41
	Oct 28	2100	40
	Nov 19	0600	65
	Nov 23	1500	47
	Nov 25	0000	44

Major Magnetic Storms: Ap* 1932–1989

	Date	UT	AP*
	Nov 26	1200	58
	Dec 16	0600	46
	Dec 19	0300	41
	Dec 19	1500	40
1944	Feb 07	0900	48
	Feb 13	1500	52
	Mar 26	1200	71
	Apr 02	0300	90
	May 01	1200	46
	Aug 02	1200	47
	Oct 14	0900	46
	Dec 16	0900	90
	Dec 27	0300	40
1945	Jan 28	2100	51
	Mar 12	0300	51
	Mar 15	0000	57
	Mar 26	0000	52
	Mar 27	1500	61
	Apr 01	0300	59
	Apr 11	0900	44
	Jun 30	2100	42
	Sep 18	0300	45
	Oct 24	0600	66
	Oct 27	2100	40
	Nov 08	2100	43
	Dec 13	1800	81
1946	Jan 03	0900	93
	Feb 07	0900	199
	Feb 14	0600	41
	Feb 20	1800	61
	Mar 10	0300	65
	Mar 25	0000	195
	Mar 28	0300	215
	Apr 14	2100	63
	Apr 23	1200	168
	May 06	1500	51
	May 09	0000	49
	May 10	1800	42
	May 22	0300	54
	Jun 07	0900	53
	Jun 16	0900	40
	Jun 29	0000	46
	Jul 07	0300	40
	Jul 18	1500	47
	Jul 26	1800	212
	Jul 28	2100	60
	Aug 14	0600	53
	Aug 30	1800	55
	Sep 16	1200	47
	Sep 17	2100	136
	Sep 19	0900	40
	Sep 22	0300	214
	Sep 28	0300	100
	Oct 26	2100	63
1947	Jan 25	0000	61
	Feb 16	0900	66
	Mar 03	0900	147
	Mar 08	0900	109
	Mar 15	0000	74
	Mar 23	0900	47
	Mar 28	0000	75
	Apr 17	1200	112
	May 15	1500	42
	May 24	0000	52
	Jun 05	0300	41
	Jun 13	2100	68
	Jun 17	0000	40
	Jul 17	1500	112
	Aug 15	0900	77
	Aug 17	1500	69
	Aug 20	2100	42
	Aug 22	0600	89
	Sep 03	0600	87

	Date	UT	AP*
	Sep 07	0900	47
	Sep 14	0300	62
	Sep 17	0000	55
	Sep 22	1500	53
	Sep 24	1200	142
	Oct 02	0600	78
	Oct 09	1200	63
	Oct 14	0000	45
	Oct 15	0300	47
	Nov 09	0900	76
1948	Jan 02	2100	41
	Mar 01	0000	40
	Mar 15	0000	139
	Apr 21	2100	50
	May 15	2100	75
	May 21	0900	51
	Aug 08	0300	147
	Oct 01	1800	49
	Oct 14	2100	65
	Oct 18	1800	115
	Oct 21	0000	67
	Nov 02	0300	57
	Nov 20	0600	63
1949	Jan 01	2100	47
	Jan 25	0000	156
	Feb 21	1200	48
	Mar 16	1500	45
	Mar 17	0900	50
	Mar 21	2100	100
	Apr 07	1800	101
	May 03	1800	49
	May 12	0600	196
	May 30	1200	54
	Jun 05	0300	62
	Jun 12	0300	40
	Jun 12	1200	40
	Aug 03	0600	72
	Oct 07	0300	75
	Oct 15	0600	163
	Oct 27	1200	51
	Nov 01	1200	40
	Nov 02	0600	41
	Nov 19	1500	60
1950	Jan 24	1200	51
	Feb 20	1500	138
	Feb 23	0900	80
	Mar 19	0000	84
	Apr 01	0000	40
	Apr 05	0000	53
	May 02	2100	45
	May 27	1200	85
	Jun 23	1800	54
	Jun 29	1200	61
	Jul 11	1200	63
	Jul 24	0900	50
	Aug 07	1200	96
	Aug 10	1200	46
	Aug 19	1200	203
	Sep 03	0900	67
	Sep 08	0300	46
	Sep 19	2100	42
	Sep 24	0000	40
	Sep 24	1800	44
	Oct 02	0300	82
	Oct 14	0600	49
	Oct 16	0000	44
	Oct 28	0300	97
	Nov 04	0300	45
	Nov 10	0300	40
	Nov 26	0000	63
	Nov 28	0000	40
	Dec 13	0600	41
	Dec 22	1200	49

	Date	UT	AP*
	Dec 24	1500	40
1951	Jan 22	0000	54
	Jan 31	0300	50
	Feb 23	0000	63
	Feb 27	0000	48
	Feb 27	1500	59
	Mar 07	1200	41
	Mar 08	0600	41
	Mar 09	1500	42
	Mar 13	0900	60
	Mar 22	0600	45
	Apr 04	1500	56
	Apr 05	0900	40
	Apr 06	0600	51
	Apr 12	1800	44
	Apr 18	0600	72
	Apr 20	1500	61
	Apr 21	2100	43
	Apr 24	0600	53
	May 01	1800	81
	May 09	1800	66
	May 26	0900	53
	Jun 17	1500	82
	Jul 01	1800	96
	Jul 31	0300	48
	Aug 01	0900	48
	Aug 12	2100	44
	Aug 21	0000	54
	Aug 25	0300	44
	Sep 11	1500	47
	Sep 12	0600	41
	Sep 13	0000	47
	Sep 16	0300	86
	Sep 20	0600	113
	Sep 25	0600	168
	Sep 26	2100	47
	Oct 07	1500	75
	Oct 09	2100	44
	Oct 17	0000	90
	Oct 28	0300	100
	Nov 13	0900	53
	Dec 08	0000	55
	Dec 09	0900	42
	Dec 22	0300	41
	Dec 27	2100	70
	Dec 31	0600	42
1952	Jan 05	0300	45
	Jan 13	0900	46
	Jan 14	1500	40
	Jan 29	0900	41
	Feb 06	1200	57
	Feb 07	2100	44
	Feb 10	1500	49
	Feb 16	0300	55
	Feb 23	2100	71
	Feb 26	0900	43
	Feb 27	1800	44
	Mar 05	0900	119
	Mar 07	0900	65
	Mar 21	0600	45
	Mar 22	2100	52
	Mar 23	1800	51
	Mar 30	1200	91
	Apr 02	1800	85
	Apr 09	0900	44
	Apr 21	1200	110
	Apr 29	0300	97
	May 07	0600	80
	May 18	1200	43
	May 26	0900	87
	May 27	1800	40
	May 28	1200	48
	Jun 23	0600	40

	Date	UT	AP*
	Jun 29	1800	89
	Jul 05	0900	57
	Jul 20	1800	49
	Sep 01	0000	50
	Sep 07	1800	62
	Sep 29	0300	83
	Oct 04	2100	80
	Oct 25	1800	41
	Oct 30	1500	62
	Nov 26	1800	47
	Nov 27	0300	40
1953	Jan 05	0000	51
	Jan 26	0000	44
	Jan 26	1800	41
	Feb 24	0000	55
	Feb 25	2100	45
	Mar 02	0300	69
	Mar 08	1500	51
	Mar 24	0000	62
	May 16	0300	90
	Jun 02	0300	52
	Jun 29	0900	56
	Jul 23	0300	44
	Jul 26	2100	45
	Aug 11	2100	40
	Aug 24	0000	57
	Aug 26	2100	43
	Aug 29	1800	49
	Sep 03	1500	80
	Sep 18	2100	82
	Sep 22	2100	47
	Oct 15	1200	64
	Oct 16	1800	43
	Oct 18	1200	68
	Nov 12	2100	42
	Nov 15	0600	46
1954	Feb 21	1500	49
	Feb 26	0900	41
	Mar 23	0000	41
	Mar 23	1200	41
	Apr 11	1500	77
	Sep 20	1200	47
	Sep 30	2100	45
	Oct 17	1800	40
	Oct 23	2100	46
1955	Jan 17	0900	85
	Jan 19	0000	53
	Mar 30	2100	57
	Apr 27	1500	75
	May 25	1200	66
	Sep 29	1500	57
	Oct 25	0600	60
	Oct 25	2100	40
	Nov 19	0900	78
1956	Jan 10	1500	47
	Jan 18	0300	42
	Jan 18	1500	41
	Jan 24	0300	44
	Jan 27	0900	47
	Feb 25	0300	104
	Feb 29	0000	40
	Mar 03	0300	103
	Mar 21	0600	60
	Mar 28	1200	41
	Apr 21	1200	111
	Apr 26	2100	186
	Apr 30	0000	50
	May 12	1200	48
	May 16	0300	165
	May 20	0600	46
	May 24	0900	114
	Jun 24	1200	71
	Jul 26	0000	41

	Date	UT	AP*
	Aug 23	2100	88
	Aug 25	0900	48
	Sep 02	0300	84
	Sep 08	0900	81
	Sep 20	1200	44
	Oct 20	0600	42
	Oct 26	1200	56
	Nov 10	1200	77
	Nov 14	1500	108
1957	Jan 21	1200	133
	Jan 29	1200	45
	Feb 04	1200	46
	Feb 12	2100	42
	Feb 23	1500	79
	Mar 02	0000	132
	Mar 10	0000	72
	Mar 27	1200	82
	Mar 29	0300	83
	Apr 05	0900	48
	Apr 09	1800	62
	Apr 18	1500	67
	Jun 03	0600	41
	Jun 04	0300	41
	Jun 25	1800	87
	Jun 30	0900	181
	Jul 01	1800	67
	Jul 05	0000	55
	Aug 29	1800	59
	Aug 31	1200	55
	Sep 04	1200	221
	Sep 13	0000	160
	Sep 14	0600	40
	Sep 22	1200	186
	Sep 29	1200	154
	Oct 14	0000	50
	Nov 06	1500	49
	Nov 26	1200	79
	Dec 11	0300	42
	Dec 31	0600	65
1958	Jan 20	0900	42
	Feb 11	0000	199
	Mar 05	0600	47
	Mar 11	1800	69
	Mar 12	2100	48
	Mar 19	0600	48
	Apr 04	0900	43
	Apr 17	0000	54
	May 13	1200	42
	May 25	1800	40
	May 28	2100	52
	May 31	0900	108
	Jun 06	2100	82
	Jun 21	0900	75
	Jun 28	1800	136
	Jul 08	0600	216
	Jul 21	1500	60
	Aug 17	0600	91
	Aug 23	1800	84
	Aug 27	0000	63
	Sep 04	1200	171
	Sep 16	0300	41
	Sep 25	0300	86
	Oct 24	0000	88
	Oct 27	1800	47
	Dec 04	0600	70
	Dec 13	0000	49
	Dec 17	1500	56
1959	Jan 09	1500	56
	Feb 11	0600	41
	Feb 14	1200	42
	Feb 15	0600	42
	Feb 16	0300	63
	Feb 25	0600	76

Major Magnetic Storms: Ap* 1932–1989

	Date	UT	AP*
	Feb 28	1800	49
	Mar 26	2100	185
	Apr 08	2100	45
	Apr 09	1800	100
	Apr 23	0900	50
	May 11	2100	113
	May 15	0900	56
	May 24	0300	61
	Jun 27	1200	44
	Jun 28	1200	41
	Jun 29	0300	53
	Jul 11	0300	52
	Jul 15	0600	252
	Jul 17	1500	183
	Aug 16	0600	173
	Aug 20	0300	41
	Sep 03	2100	117
	Sep 18	1500	45
	Sep 21	1200	93
	Oct 01	0000	43
	Oct 03	1500	78
	Oct 05	1800	60
	Nov 02	0300	71
	Nov 04	0900	45
	Nov 27	2100	84
	Nov 30	0600	50
	Dec 03	0000	49
	Dec 05	0600	73
	Dec 13	2100	45
	Dec 27	2100	42
1960	Jan 10	0600	47
	Jan 14	0600	50
	Jan 21	0000	49
	Mar 15	2100	56
	Mar 31	2100	251
	Apr 04	1800	43
	Apr 16	1200	40
	Apr 24	1800	67
	Apr 30	0000	174
	May 08	0000	128
	May 11	0000	42
	May 16	1200	47
	May 23	1200	42
	May 28	1800	56
	Jun 04	0300	53
	Jun 27	0000	65
	Jun 29	2100	65
	Jul 15	0900	137
	Aug 16	1200	118
	Aug 29	1200	64
	Sep 02	1200	45
	Sep 04	1200	150
	Oct 01	2100	54
	Oct 04	1200	48
	Oct 06	0900	258
	Oct 25	0900	99
	Oct 27	1800	50
	Nov 03	2100	51
	Nov 12	2100	293
	Nov 15	1200	128
	Nov 21	0600	55
	Nov 24	2100	41
	Dec 01	0000	92
	Dec 15	1200	61
	Dec 27	0300	52
1961	Jan 19	1800	52
	Feb 04	1200	66
	Feb 17	1800	59
	Mar 05	1500	46
	Mar 09	1500	49
	Mar 19	0300	40
	Apr 14	0900	98
	Jun 21	0900	73
	Jul 04	1800	48
	Jul 13	1200	139
	Jul 17	1800	96
	Jul 20	1800	40
	Jul 27	0000	114
	Aug 02	0000	42
	Aug 29	1800	40
	Aug 30	0900	46
	Sep 24	0900	62
	Sep 30	1800	142
	Oct 28	0900	145
	Nov 07	0600	51
	Nov 17	2100	51
	Dec 02	0900	84
1962	Jan 10	0000	52
	Feb 16	0900	43
	Apr 06	2100	59
	Jul 26	0300	50
	Jul 31	1800	40
	Sep 03	0900	51
	Sep 12	0300	60
	Sep 19	0300	41
	Oct 01	0300	45
	Dec 17	1500	56
	Dec 18	1200	45
1963	Jan 30	1800	49
	Feb 09	2100	45
	Mar 10	0300	48
	Apr 30	1500	48
	Jun 06	1800	50
	Aug 19	1800	70
	Sep 14	0000	81
	Sep 16	1200	47
	Sep 22	0300	159
	Sep 24	1800	68
	Sep 27	1800	58
	Oct 24	0000	63
	Oct 29	1200	100
	Nov 07	0900	54
1964	Jan 02	0300	56
	Mar 04	0300	55
	Mar 22	1200	44
	Apr 01	1200	60
	Apr 27	1200	44
	Jun 10	0300	52
	Sep 21	1500	43
1965	Apr 17	1500	69
	Jun 16	0600	75
1966	Mar 13	1800	73
	Mar 23	0000	66
	Mar 28	0600	47
	May 26	0300	80
	May 31	0300	52
	Jul 08	1800	42
	Aug 30	0000	81
	Sep 03	1200	173
	Sep 08	0000	42
	Oct 04	1800	46
	Dec 14	0300	52
1967	Jan 07	1200	69
	Jan 13	1200	80
	Feb 07	1500	61
	Feb 15	2100	66
	May 02	2100	89
	May 25	1200	241
	May 28	0900	79
	May 30	0900	73
	Jun 05	0600	66
	Sep 20	2100	86
	Sep 29	0000	45
	Sep 29	1800	43
	Dec 01	0600	40
	Dec 19	1800	41
	Dec 31	0300	61
1968	Feb 10	1500	69
	Feb 20	0600	42
	Apr 05	1500	57
	May 07	0000	53
	Jun 10	2100	108
	Jun 12	1500	49
	Aug 16	1800	52
	Sep 07	2100	54
	Sep 12	2100	42
	Oct 02	0000	47
	Oct 12	0300	54
	Nov 01	0900	161
1969	Feb 02	1500	78
	Feb 11	0000	61
	Mar 11	1800	45
	Mar 23	1500	117
	Apr 27	1800	59
	May 13	0300	41
	May 14	2100	133
	Jul 26	0900	56
	Sep 29	1200	112
	Nov 08	1800	43
1970	Mar 06	2100	41
	Mar 08	0600	162
	Mar 31	0000	51
	Apr 21	0600	112
	May 27	1800	48
	May 28	0900	40
	Jul 09	0300	97
	Jul 25	0000	92
	Jul 28	2100	45
	Aug 16	2100	124
	Oct 16	0900	44
	Oct 17	0900	54
	Nov 07	0000	57
	Dec 14	0300	66
1971	Jan 27	0300	41
	Feb 25	1200	55
	Mar 12	2100	45
	Apr 09	0600	59
	Apr 14	1500	59
	May 06	0600	59
	May 17	0600	81
	Sep 17	1800	51
	Sep 26	1800	50
	Nov 22	1800	45
	Nov 23	1500	40
	Nov 24	1200	45
	Dec 17	0000	67
1972	Mar 06	1800	61
	Apr 29	0300	46
	May 15	1500	51
	Jun 17	1800	143
	Aug 04	2100	223
	Aug 08	2100	75
	Sep 13	0900	95
	Oct 31	1500	115
	Nov 02	0000	42
	Dec 15	2100	43
1973	Feb 21	1500	59
	Feb 22	1800	56
	Feb 27	0300	45
	Mar 19	0900	94
	Apr 01	1200	118
	Apr 13	0900	68
	Apr 16	0600	70
	Apr 19	1800	50
	Apr 28	2100	62
	May 13	2100	82
	May 20	1500	50
	Jun 10	1800	51
	Jun 28	2100	44
	Aug 23	1500	50
	Sep 09	2100	47
	Sep 22	2100	66
	Oct 02	0900	52
	Oct 29	0000	85
	Nov 24	1200	50
1974	Jan 25	0300	58
	Feb 11	1500	48
	Feb 23	1200	47
	Mar 16	0600	43
	Mar 21	0300	70
	Mar 22	0600	41
	Mar 22	1800	44
	Mar 23	0900	40
	Apr 02	2100	42
	Apr 03	1800	45
	Apr 18	0000	48
	Apr 18	2100	42
	Apr 19	0300	40
	Apr 19	1500	48
	May 04	1200	41
	Jun 11	1200	44
	Jun 26	2100	54
	Jul 05	1500	142
	Jul 23	0300	85
	Aug 03	0600	43
	Aug 19	0900	51
	Aug 22	1200	41
	Sep 15	1200	141
	Sep 21	0900	48
	Sep 25	1500	44
	Oct 12	2100	87
	Oct 14	1500	63
	Oct 16	0900	69
	Oct 20	0000	41
	Nov 08	1800	51
	Nov 11	1500	82
	Nov 13	1500	48
	Dec 09	0300	42
1975	Jan 06	1200	58
	Feb 10	0300	40
	Mar 10	0600	90
	Mar 27	1500	50
	Apr 09	0300	53
	Apr 10	1800	40
	Apr 12	0900	40
	May 05	0600	41
	Oct 08	1200	49
	Nov 02	1800	73
	Nov 22	0300	52
1976	Jan 10	0900	72
	Mar 07	1500	46
	Mar 26	0300	151
	Apr 01	0000	118
	Apr 03	0300	47
	May 02	1200	132
	Sep 20	0000	51
	Oct 15	0900	43
	Dec 29	0000	45
1977	Apr 06	1500	74
	Apr 19	0300	50
	May 02	0000	65
	Jul 29	0000	61
	Aug 05	0000	40
	Aug 05	0600	40
	Sep 19	1200	60
	Sep 21	2100	78
	Oct 27	0900	90
	Nov 14	0300	46
	Dec 02	0000	69
	Dec 11	0600	42
1978	Jan 04	0300	91
	Jan 29	1200	47
	Feb 14	1500	52
	Feb 28	0000	46
	Feb 28	1500	43
	Mar 01	0900	41
	Mar 26	1200	73
	Apr 04	0000	55
	Apr 10	2100	79
	Apr 13	2100	55
	Apr 19	0600	47
	Apr 23	1800	48
	May 01	1200	130
	May 08	2100	85
	Jun 02	0600	96
	Jun 04	0900	50
	Jun 26	0000	45
	Jun 29	2100	52
	Jul 04	0900	103
	Jul 13	2100	51
	Aug 28	0300	128
	Aug 30	1800	51
	Sep 25	0900	43
	Sep 26	0600	45
	Sep 28	1800	121
	Nov 12	0000	52
	Nov 25	0900	66
	Dec 18	0000	47
1979	Jan 04	0300	47
	Feb 21	0300	62
	Mar 10	0300	55
	Mar 22	0600	49
	Mar 28	2100	70
	Apr 01	2100	44
	Apr 03	1500	91
	Apr 05	0000	52
	Apr 21	2100	47
	Apr 25	0000	126
	Apr 29	0300	50
	Jun 06	0900	46
	Aug 13	0600	77
	Aug 20	0600	48
	Aug 29	0300	80
	Sep 17	2100	66
	Oct 07	1200	41
1980	Feb 15	1500	61
	May 11	0600	45
	Jun 11	0600	62
	Jul 25	0900	58
	Oct 10	1500	51
	Oct 22	1800	48
	Dec 19	0300	80
1981	Feb 06	0900	60
	Mar 05	0300	82
	Mar 13	1500	50
	Mar 25	0300	40
	Apr 12	1200	134
	Apr 18	2100	46
	Apr 20	0300	53
	Apr 26	0600	74
	May 08	1500	41
	May 10	1500	78
	May 15	2100	61
	May 17	2100	62
	May 19	2100	43
	Jun 07	0300	53
	Jul 25	0600	161
	Aug 23	0000	56
	Sep 18	1800	47
	Oct 02	1800	43
	Oct 10	1800	51
	Oct 13	2100	73
	Oct 20	1200	78
	Oct 22	0900	80
	Nov 11	1200	58

Major Magnetic Storms: Ap* 1932–1989

Year	Date	UT	AP*
1982	Feb 01	1200	73
	Feb 04	0600	55
	Feb 06	0600	46
	Feb 10	0900	44
	Feb 11	0300	50
	Feb 13	0900	55
	Feb 18	1800	41
	Feb 22	0300	58
	Feb 24	2100	45
	Feb 26	0000	42
	Mar 01	1200	140
	Mar 21	0900	44
	Apr 02	1200	52
	Apr 10	1200	79
	Apr 24	1800	58
	May 02	1800	45
	May 27	0600	58
	May 28	2100	40
	Jun 10	0000	51
	Jun 12	1500	69
	Jul 13	1500	229
	Jul 16	0300	57
	Jul 24	0000	49
	Aug 02	0900	56
	Aug 06	1800	116
	Aug 28	1800	40
	Sep 05	2100	201
	Sep 08	2100	50
	Sep 21	1800	148
	Sep 26	0600	98
	Oct 06	1800	40
	Oct 13	1500	46
	Oct 31	1800	46
	Nov 02	1200	41
	Nov 21	0900	42
	Nov 24	0900	106
	Dec 10	0600	50
	Dec 17	0300	62
	Dec 19	2100	46
	Dec 21	0600	58
1983	Jan 09	1500	86
	Feb 04	1500	157
	Feb 07	0300	46
	Feb 11	1800	41
	Feb 20	1200	46
	Mar 02	0000	85
	Mar 12	0900	60
	Mar 25	0300	51
	Mar 28	0600	45
	Mar 28	2100	40
	Apr 14	1500	66
	Apr 24	0000	61
	Apr 29	0900	42
	May 11	0600	63
	May 13	0600	40
	May 17	0000	64
	May 21	1200	41
	May 22	0300	54
	May 24	0300	79
	Jun 09	1800	41
	Jun 12	2100	69
	Jul 23	1800	42
	Aug 07	1200	73
	Sep 19	0000	53
	Sep 25	1200	41
	Oct 03	2100	43
	Oct 17	1200	61
	Nov 09	0300	46
	Nov 11	0000	40
	Nov 11	0900	50
	Nov 16	1500	41
1984	Feb 04	0000	53
	Feb 13	0600	40
	Feb 13	1500	42
	Feb 14	0300	44
	Mar 01	1200	52
	Mar 28	1200	79
	Apr 04	0300	85
	Apr 08	0300	69
	Apr 25	2100	102
	May 20	1200	45
	Jun 15	1500	52
	Jul 13	0600	72
	Jul 16	1800	45
	Jul 31	2100	74
	Aug 27	1200	49
	Sep 04	0900	83
	Sep 19	0900	43
	Sep 23	0300	115
	Sep 25	1500	48
	Oct 06	1800	47
	Oct 18	1800	76
	Nov 15	2100	125
1985	Jan 08	1800	52
	Jan 28	0000	58
	Feb 05	2100	46
	Feb 27	2100	73
	Mar 05	0300	44
	Apr 08	1800	45
	Apr 20	1800	118
	Apr 27	1500	73
	Apr 30	0600	43
	Jun 09	1500	43
	Jul 12	0000	47
	Aug 12	1500	55
	Sep 15	1800	40
	Sep 19	0900	44
	Oct 05	0300	71
	Nov 02	1200	45
	Nov 29	1500	77
	Dec 19	0300	42
	Dec 30	0000	45
1986	Jan 06	1800	44
	Feb 08	0600	228
	May 02	0900	75
	May 06	0000	66
	Sep 11	2100	92
	Sep 23	0000	43
	Oct 13	1500	49
	Nov 03	2100	68
	Nov 24	2100	54
1987	Jul 28	1200	64
	Aug 25	0900	57
	Aug 31	0600	41
	Sep 10	1200	54
	Sep 25	0600	48
	Sep 29	1200	46
	Oct 27	1800	49
1988	Jan 06	0600	41
	Jan 14	1500	91
	Feb 21	2100	97
	Mar 26	0600	59
	Mar 29	0600	45
	Apr 03	1800	85
	Apr 05	1800	56
	Apr 22	0300	46
	May 05	2100	112
	Sep 11	0600	57
	Oct 10	0000	85
	Dec 17	1800	40
1989	Jan 11	0900	50
	Jan 15	1200	50
	Jan 20	1200	52
	Feb 02	1800	44
	Mar 13	0300	285
	Mar 16	0600	53
	Mar 19	0000	55
	Mar 22	0300	41
	Mar 22	1800	44
	Mar 23	0600	40
	Mar 27	1200	51
	Mar 29	0000	71
	Apr 04	0900	55
	Apr 25	2100	75
	May 04	2100	47
	May 07	0000	46
	May 23	1500	73
	Jun 09	2100	79
	Jun 14	0300	52

Major Magnetic Storms: Ap* 1932–1989 by Severity

Rank	AP*	Date	UT
1	312	41 Sep 18	0900
2	293	60 Nov 12	2100
3	285	89 Mar 13	0300
4	277	40 Mar 24	1200
5	258	60 Oct 6	0900
6	252	59 Jul 15	0600
7	251	60 Mar 31	2100
8	241	67 May 25	1200
9	229	82 Jul 13	1500
10	228	86 Feb 8	0600
11	226	40 Mar 29	1500
12	223	72 Aug 4	2100
13	222	41 Jul 5	0000
14	221	57 Sep 4	1200
15	216	58 Jul 8	0600
16	215	46 Mar 28	0300
17	214	46 Sep 22	0300
18	212	41 Mar 1	0300
19	212	46 Jul 26	1800
20	203	50 Aug 19	1200
21	201	82 Sep 5	2100
22	199	46 Feb 7	0900
23	199	58 Feb 11	0000
24	196	49 May 12	0600
25	195	46 Mar 25	0000
26	186	56 Apr 26	2100
27	186	57 Sep 22	1200
28	185	59 Mar 26	2100
29	183	59 Jul 17	1500
30	181	57 Jun 30	0900
31	174	60 Apr 30	0000
32	173	59 Aug 16	0600
33	173	66 Sep 3	1200
34	171	58 Sep 4	1200
35	168	46 Apr 23	1200
36	168	51 Sep 25	0600
37	165	56 May 16	0300
38	163	49 Oct 15	0600
39	162	70 Mar 8	0600
40	161	68 Nov 1	0900
41	161	81 Jul 25	0600
42	160	57 Sep 13	0000
43	159	63 Sep 22	0300
44	157	83 Feb 4	1500
45	156	49 Jan 25	0000
46	154	57 Sep 29	1200
47	153	43 Aug 30	1800
48	151	76 Mar 26	0300
49	150	60 Sep 4	1200
50	149	38 May 11	1500
51	148	82 Sep 21	1800
52	147	47 Mar 3	0900
53	147	48 Aug 8	0300
54	146	38 Jan 25	0900
55	146	39 Aug 22	1200
56	145	61 Oct 28	0900
57	143	37 Apr 27	1800
58	143	72 Jun 17	1800
59	142	47 Sep 24	1200
60	142	61 Sep 30	1800
61	142	74 Jul 5	1500
62	141	74 Sep 15	1200
63	140	82 Mar 1	1200
64	139	48 Mar 15	0000
65	139	61 Jul 13	1200
66	138	50 Feb 20	1500
67	137	60 Jul 15	0900
68	136	38 Apr 16	0000
69	136	42 Mar 1	0600
70	136	46 Sep 17	2100
71	136	58 Jun 28	1800
72	134	39 Apr 17	0000
73	134	81 Apr 12	1200
74	133	57 Jan 21	1200
75	133	69 May 14	2100
76	132	57 Mar 2	0000
77	132	76 May 2	1200
78	130	38 Jan 16	2100
79	130	38 Jan 21	2100
80	130	78 May 1	1200
81	128	60 May 8	0000
82	128	60 Nov 15	1200
83	128	78 Aug 28	0300
84	126	41 Mar 30	1500
85	126	79 Apr 25	0000
86	125	40 Jun 25	0000
87	125	84 Nov 15	2100
88	124	32 May 29	0900
89	124	70 Aug 16	2100
90	121	78 Sep 28	1800
91	119	52 Mar 5	0900
92	118	39 Apr 24	1500
93	118	60 Aug 16	1200
94	118	73 Apr 1	1200
95	118	76 Apr 1	0000
96	118	85 Apr 20	1800
97	117	59 Sep 3	2100
98	117	69 Mar 23	1500
99	116	82 Aug 6	1800
100	115	48 Oct 18	1800
101	115	72 Oct 31	1500
102	115	84 Sep 23	0300
103	114	56 May 24	0900
104	114	61 Jul 27	0000
105	113	39 Oct 13	1800
106	113	41 Aug 4	0300
107	113	51 Sep 20	0600
108	113	59 May 11	2100
109	112	47 Apr 17	1200
110	112	47 Jul 17	1500
111	112	69 Sep 29	1200
112	112	70 Apr 21	0600
113	112	88 May 5	2100
114	111	56 Apr 21	1200
115	110	40 Apr 2	1800
116	110	52 Apr 21	1200
117	109	43 Aug 8	0900
118	109	47 Mar 8	0900
119	108	56 Nov 14	1500
120	108	58 May 31	0900
121	108	68 Jun 10	2100
122	106	82 Nov 24	0900
123	105	39 Feb 24	1500
124	104	38 Sep 14	2100
125	104	56 Feb 25	0300
126	103	39 Jul 4	1800
127	103	56 Mar 3	0300
128	103	78 Jul 4	0900
129	102	38 Oct 7	1200
130	102	41 Oct 31	1800
131	102	84 Apr 25	2100
132	101	49 Apr 7	1800
133	100	46 Sep 28	0300
134	100	49 Mar 21	2100
135	100	51 Oct 28	0300
136	100	59 Apr 9	1800
137	100	63 Oct 29	1200
138	99	60 Oct 25	0900
139	98	42 Oct 28	1500
140	98	61 Apr 14	0900
141	98	82 Sep 26	0600
142	97	50 Oct 28	0300
143	97	52 Apr 29	0300
144	97	70 Jul 9	0300
145	97	88 Feb 21	2100
146	96	50 Aug 7	1200
147	96	51 Jul 1	1800
148	96	61 Jul 17	1800
149	96	78 Jun 2	0600
150	95	72 Sep 13	0900
151	94	73 Mar 19	0900
152	93	41 Dec 1	0600
153	93	46 Jan 3	0900
154	93	59 Sep 21	1200
155	92	60 Dec 1	0000
156	92	70 Jul 25	0000
157	92	86 Sep 11	2100
158	91	33 May 1	0300
159	91	39 Apr 22	2100
160	91	52 Mar 30	1200
161	91	58 Aug 17	0600
162	91	78 Jan 4	0300
163	91	79 Apr 3	1500
164	91	88 Jan 14	1500
165	90	44 Apr 2	0300
166	90	44 Dec 16	0900
167	90	51 Oct 17	0000
168	90	53 May 16	0300
169	90	75 Mar 10	0600
170	90	77 Oct 27	0900

Major Magnetic Storms: Ap* 1932–1989 by Severity

Rank	AP*	Date	UT
171	89	47 Aug 22	0600
172	89	52 Jun 29	1800
173	89	67 May 2	2100
174	88	56 Aug 23	2100
175	88	58 Oct 24	0000
176	87	39 Aug 11	2100
177	87	47 Sep 3	0600
178	87	52 May 26	0900
179	87	57 Jun 25	1800
180	87	74 Oct 12	2100
181	86	51 Sep 16	0300
182	86	58 Sep 25	0300
183	86	67 Sep 20	2100
184	86	83 Jan 9	1500
185	85	39 Mar 28	1500
186	85	50 May 27	1200
187	85	52 Apr 2	1800
188	85	55 Jan 17	0900
189	85	73 Oct 29	0000
190	85	74 Jul 23	0300
191	85	78 May 8	2100
192	85	83 Mar 2	0000
193	85	84 Apr 4	0300
194	85	88 Apr 3	1800
195	85	88 Oct 10	0000
196	84	50 Mar 19	0000
197	84	56 Sep 2	0300
198	84	58 Aug 23	1800
199	84	59 Nov 27	2100
200	84	61 Dec 2	0900
201	83	52 Sep 29	0300
202	83	57 Mar 29	0300
203	83	84 Sep 4	0900
204	82	50 Oct 2	0300
205	82	51 Jun 17	1500
206	82	53 Sep 18	2100
207	82	57 Mar 27	1200
208	82	58 Jun 6	2100
209	82	73 May 13	2100
210	82	74 Nov 11	1500
211	82	81 Mar 5	0300
212	81	39 May 1	0900
213	81	40 Apr 25	0300
214	81	41 Apr 24	0900
215	81	45 Dec 13	1800
216	81	51 May 1	1800
217	81	56 Sep 8	0900
218	81	63 Sep 14	0000
219	81	66 Aug 30	0000
220	81	71 May 17	0600
221	80	50 Feb 23	0900
222	80	52 May 7	0600
223	80	52 Oct 4	2100
224	80	53 Sep 3	1500
225	80	66 May 26	0300
226	80	67 Jan 13	1200
227	80	79 Aug 29	0300
228	80	80 Dec 19	0300
229	80	81 Oct 22	0900
230	79	37 Oct 3	0900
231	79	40 May 24	0300
232	79	41 Mar 14	0000
233	79	57 Feb 23	1500
234	79	57 Nov 26	1200
235	79	67 May 28	0900
236	79	78 Apr 10	2100
237	79	82 Apr 10	1200
238	79	83 May 24	0300
239	79	84 Mar 28	1200
240	79	89 Jun 9	2100
241	78	47 Oct 2	0600
242	78	55 Nov 19	0900
243	78	59 Oct 3	1500

Rank	AP*	Date	UT
244	78	69 Feb 2	1500
245	78	77 Sep 21	2100
246	78	81 May 10	1500
247	78	81 Oct 20	1200
248	77	47 Aug 15	0900
249	77	54 Apr 11	1500
250	77	56 Nov 10	1200
251	77	79 Aug 13	0600
252	77	85 Nov 29	1500
253	76	47 Nov 9	0900
254	76	59 Feb 25	0600
255	76	84 Oct 18	1800
256	75	37 Aug 22	0300
257	75	47 Mar 28	0000
258	75	48 May 15	2100
259	75	49 Oct 7	0300
260	75	51 Oct 7	1500
261	75	55 Apr 27	1500
262	75	58 Jun 21	0900
263	75	65 Jun 16	0600
264	75	72 Aug 8	2100
265	75	86 May 2	0900
266	75	89 Apr 25	2100
267	74	40 Oct 7	0600
268	74	47 Mar 15	0000
269	74	77 Apr 6	1500
270	74	81 Apr 26	0600
271	74	84 Jul 31	2100
272	73	37 May 4	1800
273	73	39 Oct 3	0600
274	73	43 Sep 29	1200
275	73	59 Dec 5	0600
276	73	61 Jun 21	0900
277	73	66 Mar 13	1800
278	73	67 May 30	0900
279	73	75 Nov 2	1800
280	73	78 Mar 26	1200
281	73	81 Oct 13	2100
282	73	82 Feb 1	1200
283	73	83 Aug 7	1200
284	73	85 Feb 27	2100
285	73	85 Apr 27	1500
286	73	89 May 23	1500
287	72	36 Jun 18	1800
288	72	38 Apr 13	1500
289	72	38 Jul 15	0300
290	72	38 Sep 27	2100
291	72	49 Aug 3	0600
292	72	51 Apr 18	0600
293	72	57 Mar 10	0000
294	72	76 Jan 10	0900
295	72	84 Jul 13	0600
296	71	39 Aug 16	0900
297	71	42 Apr 3	2100
298	71	44 Mar 26	1200
299	71	52 Feb 23	2100
300	71	56 Jun 24	1200
301	71	59 Nov 2	0300
302	71	85 Oct 5	0300
303	71	89 Mar 29	0000
304	70	40 Sep 26	1500
305	70	51 Dec 27	2100
306	70	58 Dec 4	0600
307	70	63 Aug 19	1800
308	70	73 Apr 16	0600
309	70	74 Mar 21	0300
310	70	79 Mar 28	2100
311	69	47 Aug 17	1500
312	69	53 Mar 2	0300
313	69	58 Mar 11	1800
314	69	65 Apr 17	1500
315	69	67 Jan 7	1200
316	69	68 Feb 10	1500

Rank	AP*	Date	UT
317	69	74 Oct 16	0900
318	69	77 Dec 2	0000
319	69	82 Jun 12	1500
320	69	83 Jun 12	2100
321	69	84 Apr 8	0300
322	68	47 Jun 13	2100
323	68	53 Oct 18	1200
324	68	63 Sep 24	1800
325	68	73 Apr 13	0900
326	68	86 Nov 3	2100
327	67	39 May 6	1200
328	67	42 Oct 2	0900
329	67	42 Nov 23	2100
330	67	48 Oct 21	0000
331	67	50 Sep 3	0900
332	67	57 Apr 18	1500
333	67	57 Jul 1	1800
334	67	60 Apr 24	1800
335	67	71 Dec 17	0000
336	66	45 Oct 24	0600
337	66	47 Feb 16	0900
338	66	51 May 9	1800
339	66	55 May 25	1200
340	66	61 Feb 4	1200
341	66	66 Mar 23	0000
342	66	67 Feb 15	2100
343	66	67 Jun 5	0600
344	66	70 Dec 14	0300
345	66	73 Sep 22	2100
346	66	78 Nov 25	0900
347	66	79 Sep 17	2100
348	66	83 Apr 14	1500
349	66	86 May 6	0000
350	65	32 Aug 27	1200
351	65	38 Mar 23	0900
352	65	40 Jul 13	0900
353	65	43 Nov 19	0600
354	65	46 Mar 10	0300
355	65	48 Oct 14	2100
356	65	52 Mar 7	0900
357	65	57 Dec 31	0600
358	65	60 Jun 27	0000
359	65	60 Jun 29	2100
360	65	77 May 2	0000
361	64	37 Oct 9	1200
362	64	53 Oct 15	1200
363	64	60 Aug 29	1200
364	64	83 May 17	0000
365	64	87 Jul 28	1200
366	63	36 Nov 28	2100
367	63	38 Aug 3	2100
368	63	38 Sep 30	1200
369	63	43 May 1	0300
370	63	46 Apr 14	2100
371	63	46 Oct 26	2100
372	63	47 Oct 9	1200
373	63	48 Nov 20	0600
374	63	50 Jul 11	1200
375	63	50 Nov 26	0000
376	63	51 Feb 23	0000
377	63	58 Aug 27	0000
378	63	59 Feb 16	0300
379	63	63 Oct 24	0000
380	63	74 Oct 14	1500
381	63	83 May 11	0600
382	62	47 Sep 14	0300
383	62	49 Jun 5	0300
384	62	52 Sep 7	1800
385	62	52 Oct 30	1500
386	62	53 Mar 24	0000
387	62	57 Apr 9	1800
388	62	61 Sep 24	0900
389	62	73 Apr 28	2100

Rank	AP*	Date	UT
390	62	79 Feb 21	0300
391	62	80 Jun 11	0600
392	62	81 May 17	2100
393	62	82 Dec 17	0300
394	61	45 Mar 27	1500
395	61	46 Feb 20	1800
396	61	47 Jan 25	0000
397	61	50 Jun 29	1200
398	61	51 Apr 20	1500
399	61	59 May 24	0300
400	61	60 Dec 15	1200
401	61	67 Feb 7	1500
402	61	67 Dec 31	0300
403	61	69 Feb 11	0000
404	61	72 Mar 6	1800
405	61	77 Jul 29	0000
406	61	80 Feb 15	1500
407	61	81 May 15	2100
408	61	83 Apr 24	0000
409	61	83 Oct 17	1200
410	60	35 Sep 11	0600
411	60	36 Apr 21	1800
412	60	39 Jun 13	1800
413	60	42 Sep 11	1800
414	60	46 Jul 28	2100
415	60	49 Nov 19	1500
416	60	51 Mar 13	0900
417	60	55 Oct 25	0600
418	60	56 Mar 21	0600
419	60	58 Jul 21	1500
420	60	59 Oct 5	1800
421	60	62 Sep 12	0300
422	60	64 Apr 1	1200
423	60	77 Sep 19	1200
424	60	81 Feb 6	0900
425	60	83 Mar 12	0900
426	59	40 Nov 12	0900
427	59	45 Apr 1	0300
428	59	51 Feb 27	1500
429	59	57 Aug 29	1800
430	59	61 Feb 17	1800
431	59	62 Apr 6	2100
432	59	69 Apr 27	1800
433	59	71 Apr 9	0600
434	59	71 Apr 14	1500
435	59	71 May 6	0600
436	59	73 Feb 21	1500
437	59	88 Mar 26	0600
438	58	34 Sep 24	2100
439	58	41 Aug 27	0000
440	58	42 Mar 5	1200
441	58	43 Nov 26	1200
442	58	63 Sep 27	1800
443	58	74 Jan 25	0300
444	58	75 Jan 6	1200
445	58	80 Jul 25	0900
446	58	81 Nov 11	1200
447	58	82 Feb 22	0300
448	58	82 Apr 24	1800
449	58	82 May 27	0600
450	58	82 Dec 21	0600
451	58	85 Jan 28	0000
452	57	37 Feb 2	2100
453	57	45 Mar 15	0000
454	57	48 Nov 2	0300
455	57	52 Feb 6	1200
456	57	52 Jul 5	0900
457	57	53 Aug 24	0000
458	57	55 Mar 30	2100
459	57	55 Sep 29	1500
460	57	68 Apr 5	1500
461	57	70 Nov 7	0000
462	57	82 Jul 16	0300

Rank	AP*	Date	UT
463	57	87 Aug 25	0900
464	57	88 Sep 11	0600
465	56	33 Sep 9	0300
466	56	51 Apr 4	1500
467	56	53 Jun 29	0900
468	56	56 Oct 26	1200
469	56	58 Dec 17	1500
470	56	59 Jan 9	1500
471	56	59 May 15	0900
472	56	60 Mar 15	2100
473	56	60 May 28	1800
474	56	62 Dec 17	1500
475	56	64 Jan 2	0300
476	56	69 Jul 26	0900
477	56	73 Feb 22	1800
478	56	81 Aug 23	0000
479	56	82 Aug 2	0900
480	56	88 Apr 5	1800
481	55	39 Sep 17	0300
482	55	46 Aug 30	1800
483	55	47 Sep 17	0000
484	55	51 Dec 8	0000
485	55	52 Feb 16	0300
486	55	53 Feb 24	0000
487	55	57 Jul 5	0000
488	55	57 Aug 31	1200
489	55	60 Nov 21	0600
490	55	64 Mar 4	0300
491	55	71 Feb 25	1200
492	55	78 Apr 4	0000
493	55	78 Apr 13	2100
494	55	79 Mar 10	0300
495	55	82 Feb 4	0600
496	55	82 Feb 13	0900
497	55	85 Aug 12	1500
498	55	89 Mar 19	0000
499	55	89 Apr 4	0900
500	54	40 Dec 20	0900
501	54	42 Feb 23	1200
502	54	46 May 22	0300
503	54	49 May 30	1200
504	54	50 Jun 23	1800
505	54	51 Jan 22	0000
506	54	51 Aug 21	0000
507	54	58 Apr 17	0000
508	54	60 Oct 1	2100
509	54	63 Nov 7	0900
510	54	68 Sep 7	2100
511	54	68 Oct 12	0300
512	54	70 Oct 17	0900
513	54	74 Jun 26	2100
514	54	83 May 22	0300
515	54	86 Nov 24	2100
516	54	87 Sep 10	1200
517	53	32 Mar 30	1200
518	53	37 Mar 31	0300
519	53	37 Sep 30	1200
520	53	38 Feb 6	0300
521	53	39 Dec 6	1800
522	53	40 Jun 14	1200
523	53	41 Oct 11	0600
524	53	43 Aug 13	0300
525	53	43 Oct 24	0900
526	53	46 Jun 7	0900
527	53	46 Aug 14	0600
528	53	47 Sep 22	1500
529	53	50 Apr 5	0000
530	53	51 Apr 24	0600
531	53	51 May 26	0900
532	53	51 Nov 13	0900
533	53	55 Jan 19	0000
534	53	59 Jun 29	0300
535	53	60 Jun 4	0300

Major Magnetic Storms: Ap* 1932–1989 by Severity

Rank	AP*	Date	UT
536	53	68 May 7	0000
537	53	75 Apr 9	0300
538	53	81 Apr 20	0300
539	53	81 Jun 7	0300
540	53	83 Sep 19	0000
541	53	84 Feb 4	0000
542	53	89 Mar 16	0600
543	52	36 Oct 16	1500
544	52	37 May 28	0300
545	52	41 Nov 28	0000
546	52	43 Jan 20	1500
547	52	44 Feb 13	1500
548	52	45 Mar 26	0000
549	52	47 May 24	0000
550	52	52 Mar 22	2100
551	52	53 Jun 2	0300
552	52	58 May 28	2100
553	52	59 Jul 11	0300
554	52	60 Dec 27	0300
555	52	61 Jan 19	1800
556	52	62 Jan 10	0000
557	52	64 Jun 10	0300
558	52	66 May 31	0300
559	52	66 Dec 14	0300
560	52	68 Aug 16	1800
561	52	73 Oct 2	0900
562	52	75 Nov 22	0300
563	52	78 Feb 14	1500
564	52	78 Jun 29	2100
565	52	78 Nov 12	0000
566	52	79 Apr 5	0000
567	52	82 Apr 2	1200
568	52	84 Mar 1	1200
569	52	84 Jun 15	1500
570	52	85 Jan 8	1800
571	52	89 Jan 20	1200
572	52	89 Jun 14	0300
573	51	38 Feb 8	1500
574	51	43 Aug 28	0900
575	51	43 Oct 25	1800
576	51	45 Jan 28	2100
577	51	45 Mar 12	0300
578	51	46 May 6	1500
579	51	48 May 21	0900
580	51	49 Oct 27	1200
581	51	50 Jan 24	1200
582	51	51 Apr 6	0600
583	51	52 Mar 23	1800
584	51	53 Jan 5	0000
585	51	53 Mar 8	1500
586	51	60 Nov 3	2100
587	51	61 Nov 7	0600
588	51	61 Nov 17	2100
589	51	62 Sep 3	0900
590	51	70 Mar 31	0000
591	51	71 Sep 17	1800
592	51	72 May 15	1500
593	51	73 Jun 10	1800
594	51	74 Aug 19	0900
595	51	74 Nov 8	1800
596	51	76 Sep 20	0000
597	51	78 Jul 13	2100
598	51	78 Aug 30	1800
599	51	80 Oct 10	1500
600	51	81 Oct 10	1800
601	51	82 Jun 10	0000
602	51	83 Mar 25	0300
603	51	89 Mar 27	1200
604	50	35 Apr 11	0000
605	50	38 May 14	0600
606	50	42 Apr 16	1800
607	50	43 Jul 5	1200
608	50	43 Sep 27	1800
609	50	48 Apr 21	2100
610	50	49 Mar 17	0900
611	50	50 Jul 24	0900
612	50	51 Jan 31	0300
613	50	52 Sep 1	0000
614	50	56 Apr 30	0000
615	50	57 Oct 14	0000
616	50	59 Apr 23	0900
617	50	59 Nov 30	0600
618	50	60 Jan 14	0600
619	50	60 Oct 27	1800
620	50	62 Jul 26	0300
621	50	63 Jun 6	1800
622	50	71 Sep 26	1800
623	50	73 Apr 19	1800
624	50	73 May 20	1500
625	50	73 Aug 23	1500
626	50	73 Nov 24	1200
627	50	75 Mar 27	1500
628	50	77 Apr 19	0300
629	50	78 Jun 4	0900
630	50	79 Apr 29	0300
631	50	81 Mar 13	1500
632	50	82 Feb 11	0300
633	50	82 Sep 8	2100
634	50	82 Dec 10	0600
635	50	83 Nov 11	0900
636	50	89 Jan 11	0900
637	50	89 Jan 15	1200
638	49	37 Jun 5	1800
639	49	37 Oct 11	1200
640	49	40 Nov 25	0900
641	49	43 Mar 29	1200
642	49	46 May 9	0000
643	49	48 Oct 1	1800
644	49	49 May 3	1800
645	49	50 Oct 14	0600
646	49	50 Dec 22	1200
647	49	52 Feb 10	1500
648	49	52 Jul 20	1800
649	49	53 Aug 29	1800
650	49	54 Feb 21	1500
651	49	57 Nov 6	1500
652	49	58 Dec 13	0000
653	49	59 Feb 28	1800
654	49	59 Dec 3	0000
655	49	60 Jan 21	0000
656	49	61 Mar 9	1500
657	49	63 Jan 30	1800
658	49	68 Jun 12	1500
659	49	75 Oct 8	1200
660	49	79 Mar 22	0600
661	49	82 Jul 24	0000
662	49	84 Aug 27	1200
663	49	86 Oct 13	1500
664	49	87 Oct 27	1800
665	48	35 Mar 14	0600
666	48	37 Aug 1	2100
667	48	39 Jul 19	2100
668	48	40 Jan 3	0300
669	48	43 Sep 3	0000
670	48	43 Oct 8	2100
671	48	43 Oct 27	1800
672	48	44 Feb 7	0900
673	48	49 Feb 21	1200
674	48	51 Feb 27	0000
675	48	51 Jul 31	0300
676	48	51 Aug 1	0900
677	48	52 May 28	1200
678	48	56 May 12	1200
679	48	56 Aug 25	0900
680	48	57 Apr 5	0900
681	48	58 Mar 12	2100
682	48	58 Mar 19	0600
683	48	60 Oct 4	1200
684	48	61 Jul 4	1800
685	48	63 Mar 10	0300
686	48	63 Apr 30	1500
687	48	70 May 27	1800
688	48	74 Feb 11	1500
689	48	74 Apr 18	0000
690	48	74 Apr 19	1500
691	48	74 Sep 21	0900
692	48	74 Nov 13	1500
693	48	78 Apr 23	1800
694	48	79 Aug 20	0600
695	48	80 Oct 22	1800
696	48	84 Sep 25	1500
697	48	87 Sep 25	0600
698	47	33 Aug 5	0900
699	47	35 Jun 7	1200
700	47	39 Feb 6	0600
701	47	39 Apr 19	1200
702	47	40 Sep 27	1800
703	47	42 Jul 10	2100
704	47	43 May 17	1500
705	47	43 Nov 23	1500
706	47	44 Aug 2	1200
707	47	46 Jul 18	1500
708	47	46 Sep 16	1200
709	47	47 Mar 23	0900
710	47	47 Sep 7	0900
711	47	47 Oct 15	0300
712	47	49 Jan 1	2100
713	47	51 Sep 11	1500
714	47	51 Sep 13	0000
715	47	51 Sep 26	2100
716	47	52 Nov 26	1800
717	47	53 Sep 22	2100
718	47	54 Sep 20	1200
719	47	56 Jan 10	1500
720	47	56 Jan 27	0900
721	47	58 Mar 5	0600
722	47	58 Oct 27	1800
723	47	60 Jan 10	0600
724	47	60 May 16	1200
725	47	63 Sep 16	1200
726	47	66 Mar 28	0600
727	47	68 Oct 2	0000
728	47	73 Sep 9	2100
729	47	74 Feb 23	1200
730	47	76 Apr 3	0300
731	47	78 Jan 29	1200
732	47	78 Apr 19	0600
733	47	78 Dec 18	0000
734	47	79 Jan 4	0300
735	47	79 Apr 21	2100
736	47	81 Sep 18	1800
737	47	84 Oct 6	1800
738	47	85 Jul 12	0000
739	47	89 May 4	2100
740	46	43 Aug 19	1200
741	46	43 Oct 2	1800
742	46	43 Dec 16	0600
743	46	44 May 1	1200
744	46	44 Oct 14	0900
745	46	46 Jun 29	0000
746	46	50 Aug 10	1200
747	46	50 Sep 8	0300
748	46	52 Jan 13	0900
749	46	53 Nov 15	0600
750	46	54 Oct 23	2100
751	46	56 May 20	0600
752	46	57 Feb 4	1200
753	46	61 Mar 5	1500
754	46	61 Aug 30	0900
755	46	66 Oct 4	1800
756	46	72 Apr 29	0300
757	46	76 Mar 7	1500
758	46	77 Nov 14	0300
759	46	78 Feb 28	0000
760	46	79 Jun 6	0900
761	46	81 Apr 18	2100
762	46	82 Feb 6	0600
763	46	82 Oct 13	1500
764	46	82 Oct 31	1800
765	46	82 Dec 19	2100
766	46	83 Feb 7	0300
767	46	83 Feb 20	1200
768	46	83 Nov 9	0300
769	46	85 Feb 5	2100
770	46	87 Sep 29	1200
771	46	88 Apr 22	0300
772	46	89 May 7	0000
773	45	32 Mar 28	1500
774	45	34 Dec 3	2100
775	45	35 Sep 24	2100
776	45	38 May 3	2100
777	45	39 Jul 3	0000
778	45	41 Jun 13	0600
779	45	43 Apr 10	0900
780	45	43 Sep 8	1500
781	45	45 Sep 18	0300
782	45	47 Oct 14	0000
783	45	49 Mar 16	1500
784	45	50 May 2	2100
785	45	50 Nov 4	0300
786	45	51 Mar 22	0600
787	45	52 Jan 5	0300
788	45	52 Mar 21	0600
789	45	53 Feb 25	2100
790	45	53 Jul 26	2100
791	45	54 Sep 30	2100
792	45	57 Jan 29	1200
793	45	59 Apr 8	2100
794	45	59 Sep 18	1500
795	45	59 Nov 4	0900
796	45	59 Dec 13	2100
797	45	60 Sep 2	1200
798	45	62 Oct 1	0300
799	45	62 Dec 18	1200
800	45	63 Feb 9	2100
801	45	67 Sep 29	0000
802	45	69 Mar 11	1800
803	45	70 Jul 28	2100
804	45	71 Mar 12	2100
805	45	71 Nov 22	1800
806	45	71 Nov 24	1200
807	45	73 Feb 27	0300
808	45	74 Apr 3	1800
809	45	76 Dec 29	0000
810	45	78 Jun 26	0000
811	45	78 Sep 26	0600
812	45	80 May 11	0600
813	45	82 Feb 24	2100
814	45	82 May 2	1800
815	45	83 Mar 28	0600
816	45	84 May 20	1200
817	45	84 Jul 16	1800
818	45	85 Apr 8	1800
819	45	85 Nov 2	1200
820	45	85 Dec 30	0000
821	45	88 Mar 29	0600
822	44	32 Sep 24	1800
823	44	38 Jul 30	0000
824	44	39 Jul 21	0900
825	44	39 Sep 19	0900
826	44	39 Nov 13	0300
827	44	43 Sep 26	1200
828	44	43 Nov 25	0000
829	44	45 Apr 11	0900
830	44	50 Sep 24	1800
831	44	50 Oct 16	0000
832	44	51 Apr 12	1800
833	44	51 Aug 12	2100
834	44	51 Aug 25	0300
835	44	51 Oct 9	2100
836	44	52 Feb 7	2100
837	44	52 Feb 27	1800
838	44	52 Apr 9	0900
839	44	53 Jan 26	0000
840	44	53 Jul 23	0300
841	44	56 Jan 24	0300
842	44	56 Sep 20	1200
843	44	59 Jun 27	1200
844	44	64 Mar 22	1200
845	44	64 Apr 27	1200
846	44	70 Oct 16	0900
847	44	73 Jun 28	2100
848	44	74 Mar 22	1800
849	44	74 Jun 11	1200
850	44	74 Sep 25	1500
851	44	79 Apr 1	2100
852	44	82 Feb 10	0900
853	44	82 Mar 21	0900
854	44	84 Feb 14	0300
855	44	85 Mar 5	0300
856	44	85 Sep 19	0900
857	44	86 Jan 6	1800
858	44	89 Feb 2	1800
859	44	89 Mar 22	1800
860	43	32 Mar 10	0900
861	43	36 Apr 17	2100
862	43	37 Oct 7	1200
863	43	41 Feb 21	2100
864	43	41 Mar 21	1800
865	43	41 Apr 18	2100
866	43	41 Nov 6	0300
867	43	42 Mar 8	1800
868	43	42 Apr 10	2100
869	43	45 Nov 8	2100
870	43	51 Apr 21	2100
871	43	52 Feb 26	0900
872	43	52 May 18	1200
873	43	53 Aug 26	2100
874	43	53 Oct 16	1800
875	43	58 Apr 4	0900
876	43	59 Oct 1	0000
877	43	60 Apr 4	1800
878	43	62 Feb 16	0900
879	43	64 Sep 21	1500
880	43	67 Sep 29	1800
881	43	69 Nov 8	1800
882	43	72 Dec 15	2100
883	43	74 Mar 16	0600
884	43	74 Aug 3	0600
885	43	76 Oct 15	0900
886	43	78 Feb 28	1500
887	43	78 Sep 25	0900
888	43	81 May 19	2100
889	43	81 Oct 2	1800
890	43	83 Oct 3	2100
891	43	84 Sep 19	0900
892	43	85 Apr 30	0600
893	43	85 Jun 9	1500
894	43	86 Sep 23	0000
895	42	35 Oct 24	0600
896	42	36 Jun 8	1800
897	42	37 Oct 23	0300
898	42	37 Oct 23	1500
899	42	38 Apr 23	0600
900	42	39 Apr 10	0000

Major Magnetic Storms: Ap* 1932–1989 by Severity

Rank	AP*	Date	UT
901	42	41 Jan 17	0000
902	42	41 Mar 4	0600
903	42	42 Aug 23	0000
904	42	45 Jun 30	2100
905	42	46 May 10	1800
906	42	47 May 15	1500
907	42	47 Aug 20	2100
908	42	50 Sep 19	2100
909	42	51 Mar 9	1500
910	42	51 Dec 9	0900
911	42	51 Dec 31	0600
912	42	53 Nov 12	2100
913	42	56 Jan 18	0300
914	42	56 Oct 20	0600
915	42	57 Feb 12	2100
916	42	57 Dec 11	0300
917	42	58 Jan 20	0900
918	42	58 May 13	1200
919	42	59 Feb 14	1200
920	42	59 Feb 15	0600
921	42	59 Dec 27	2100
922	42	60 May 11	0000
923	42	60 May 23	1200
924	42	61 Aug 2	0000
925	42	66 Jul 8	1800
926	42	66 Sep 8	0000
927	42	68 Feb 20	0600
928	42	68 Sep 12	2100
929	42	72 Nov 2	0000
930	42	74 Apr 2	2100
931	42	74 Apr 18	2100
932	42	74 Dec 9	0300
933	42	77 Dec 11	0600
934	42	82 Feb 26	0000
935	42	82 Nov 21	0900
936	42	83 Apr 29	0900
937	42	83 Jul 23	1800
938	42	84 Feb 13	1500
939	42	85 Dec 19	0300
940	41	32 Oct 20	1200
941	41	33 Mar 19	1800
942	41	35 Oct 20	0900
943	41	36 Dec 27	1800
944	41	37 Sep 10	1800
945	41	38 Mar 5	0600
946	41	39 May 5	1800
947	41	39 Jul 20	1500
948	41	39 Sep 2	2100
949	41	39 Oct 16	1200
950	41	40 Sep 30	2100
951	41	42 Mar 3	0000
952	41	43 Feb 17	0300
953	41	43 Oct 28	1500
954	41	43 Dec 19	0300
955	41	46 Feb 14	0600
956	41	47 Jun 5	0300
957	41	48 Jan 2	2100
958	41	49 Nov 2	0600
959	41	50 Dec 13	0600
960	41	51 Mar 7	1200
961	41	51 Mar 8	0600
962	41	51 Sep 12	0600
963	41	51 Dec 22	0300
964	41	52 Jan 29	0900
965	41	52 Oct 25	1800
966	41	53 Jan 26	1800
967	41	54 Feb 26	0900
968	41	54 Mar 23	0000
969	41	54 Mar 23	1200
970	41	56 Jan 18	1500
971	41	56 Mar 28	1200
972	41	56 Jul 26	0000
973	41	57 Jun 3	0600
974	41	57 Jun 4	0300
975	41	58 Sep 16	0300
976	41	59 Feb 11	0600
977	41	59 Jun 28	1200
978	41	59 Aug 20	0300
979	41	60 Nov 24	2100
980	41	62 Sep 19	0300
981	41	67 Dec 19	1800
982	41	69 May 13	0300
983	41	70 Mar 6	2100
984	41	71 Jan 27	0300
985	41	74 Mar 22	0600
986	41	74 May 4	1200
987	41	74 Aug 22	1200
988	41	74 Oct 20	0000
989	41	75 May 5	0600
990	41	78 Mar 1	0900
991	41	79 Oct 7	1200
992	41	81 May 8	1500
993	41	82 Feb 18	1800
994	41	82 Nov 2	1200
995	41	83 Feb 11	1800
996	41	83 May 21	1200
997	41	83 Jun 9	1800
998	41	83 Sep 25	1200
999	41	83 Nov 16	1500
1000	41	87 Aug 31	0600
1001	41	88 Jan 6	0600
1002	41	89 Mar 22	0300
1003	40	32 Dec 14	0900
1004	40	38 Feb 13	2100
1005	40	38 Jul 4	0600
1006	40	38 Oct 26	1200
1007	40	40 Nov 29	0300
1008	40	41 Feb 22	0900
1009	40	42 Mar 9	0000
1010	40	42 Sep 20	2100
1011	40	43 Oct 28	2100
1012	40	43 Dec 19	1500
1013	40	44 Dec 27	0300
1014	40	45 Oct 27	2100
1015	40	46 Jun 16	0900
1016	40	46 Jul 7	0300
1017	40	46 Sep 19	0900
1018	40	47 Jun 17	0000
1019	40	48 Mar 1	0000
1020	40	49 Jun 12	0300
1021	40	49 Jun 12	1200
1022	40	49 Nov 1	1200
1023	40	50 Apr 1	0000
1024	40	50 Sep 24	0000
1025	40	50 Nov 10	0300
1026	40	50 Nov 28	0000
1027	40	50 Dec 24	1500
1028	40	51 Apr 5	0900
1029	40	52 Jan 14	1500
1030	40	52 May 27	1800
1031	40	52 Jun 23	0600
1032	40	52 Nov 27	0300
1033	40	53 Aug 11	2100
1034	40	54 Oct 17	1800
1035	40	55 Oct 25	2100
1036	40	56 Feb 29	0000
1037	40	57 Sep 14	0600
1038	40	58 May 25	1800
1039	40	60 Apr 16	1200
1040	40	61 Mar 19	0300
1041	40	61 Jul 20	1800
1042	40	61 Aug 29	1800
1043	40	62 Jul 31	1800
1044	40	67 Dec 1	0600
1045	40	70 May 28	0900
1046	40	71 Nov 23	1500
1047	40	74 Mar 23	0900
1048	40	74 Apr 19	0300
1049	40	75 Feb 10	0300
1050	40	75 Apr 10	1800
1051	40	75 Apr 12	0900
1052	40	77 Aug 5	0000
1053	40	77 Aug 5	0600
1054	40	81 Mar 25	0300
1055	40	82 May 28	2100
1056	40	82 Aug 28	1800
1057	40	82 Oct 6	1800
1058	40	83 Mar 28	2100
1059	40	83 May 13	0600
1060	40	83 Nov 11	0000
1061	40	84 Feb 13	0600
1062	40	85 Sep 15	1800
1063	40	88 Dec 17	1800
1064	40	89 Mar 23	0600

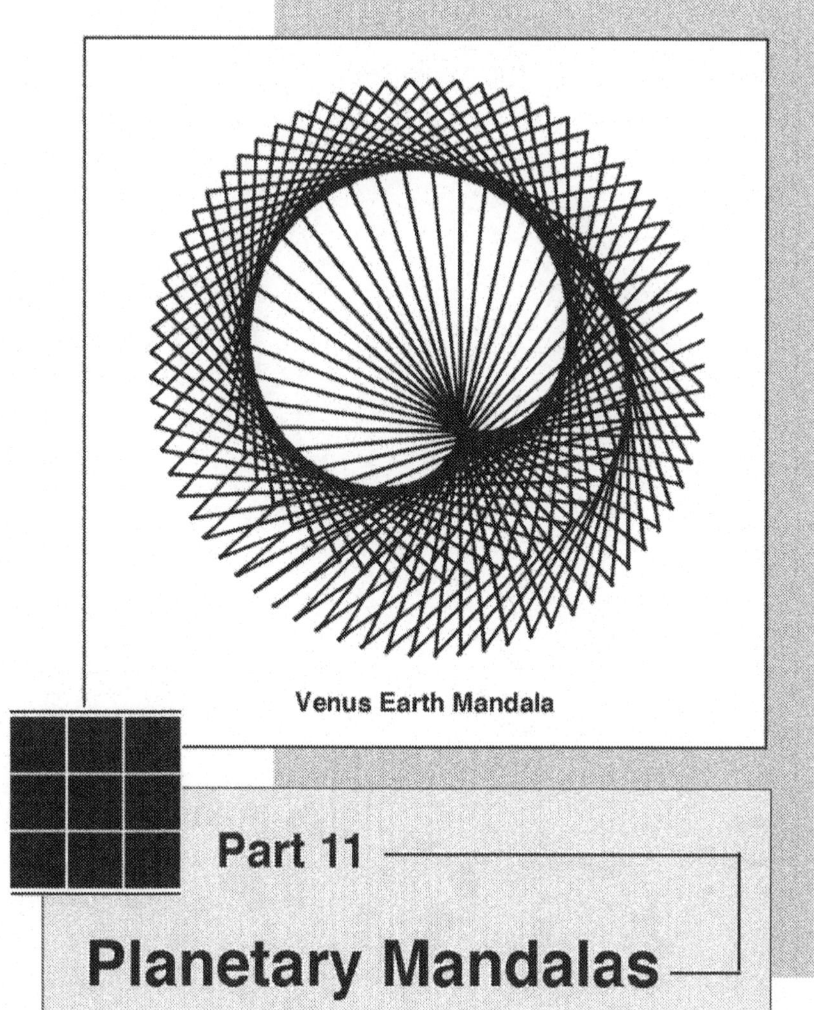
Venus Earth Mandala

Part 11

Planetary Mandalas

Introduction to the Graphs and Mandalas

Figures 1 through 24 Center of Mass.
Figures 25 through 30 Geocentric orbital paths of Mercury, Venus and Mars, showing retrograde motion.
Figures 31 through 48 Planetary Mandalas.
Figures 49 through 60 Nongeocentric orbital paths of solar system planets.
Figures 61 through 96 Planetary Mandalas.
Each figure has a two-line legend. Line 1 shows the start date, end date, number of steps and time interval in days. Line 2 shows the body or bodies and the figure number.

Figures 1 through 24 show the path of the solar system barycenter (center of mass) at 20-year intervals from 1540 through 2020. These plots are the visual representation of the tabular data in the solar system barycenter data in this book, pages 15-19.

Figures 5, 14 and 23 show the three instances of the Sun moving retrograde with respect to the solar system center of mass. See the article for a complete explanation.

Figures 25 through 30 show the geocentric paths of Mercury, Venus and Mars.

The most striking orbital/retrograde pattern is that of Venus as shown in Figures 27 and 28. Figure 27 shows almost 8 years of Venus' geocentric orbit starting May 11, 1931. The five-cloverleaf pattern is the result of the five retrograde periods of Venus over an 8-year time span.

A most remarkable characteristic of Venus' orbital pattern is seen in Figure 28. Here Venus' path over a 16-year time span is graphed and the second 8 years almost perfectly retrace the first 8 years.

Figures 25 and 26 show Mercury's orbit over a 3- and a 6-year time span, respectively. The loops are the retrograde times. Only if Mercury's orbit had been graphed for more years would we be able to determine if its orbital pattern repeated in a pattern analogous to that of Venus.

Figures 29 and 30 show Mars' orbit for 33 and almost 66 years, respectively. It is clear that Mars does not share the remarkable characteristic of Venus' overlapping orbital pattern after a given number of years.

The planetary mandalas shown in Figures 31 through 48 were inspired by the educational film *Infinite Design* which Peggy Lance brought to an early 1970 ISAR conference held in Buena Vista in southern California. I had an "intellectual orgasm" when I saw this film and at my request the film was shown again to a much larger audience. I went home after the conference and did nothing for the next four days except the programming necessary to duplicate as closely as my hardware allowed what I had seen in that film.

On many future occasions when I spoke at astrological conferences, I would bring graphs from that week's work, as well as subsequent enhancements, to show as attention getters before one of my talks. I promised, as a result of numerous requests, to publish a book of mandalas. Even though the 16 pages of mandalas are not a book, this is the delivery on my promise!

The planetary mandalas are constructed by calculating heliocentric orbital positions of two planets over a period of time and connecting, in a straight line, the planets' respective positions for a given instant of time. In the film, the unfolding pattern, starting with the first line, made for a very dramatic presentation. The equipment required for this film, made in the very early 1970s, cost several hundred thousand dollars. Today, one could achieve the same effect on a PC with a color monitor for less than $2,000.

In order to construct a mandala that appears aesthetic and complete, one must judiciously choose the time interval, starting and ending dates, and the planetary pairs. For example, Figure 36 shows the Venus/Jupiter mandala, which I do not find very interesting. The reason for that is when the difference of the distance to the Sun of the two planets is too great, the mandalas that are formed have boring patterns. If the starting and ending time intervals are not wisely selected, the mandalas will be incomplete. If the time interval between successive lines connecting respective positions is too short, the mandala will be too dense and its pattern obscured.

I often asked people who viewed the mandalas to report the subjective impression made on them by the mandala pattern. For example, I see Mercury/Venus, Figure 31, as an insect with two bulbous eyes and a maw of a mouth. I see Venus/Mars, Figure 35, as a spider, in its web, waiting for its next meal! I see in Uranus/Pluto, Figure 47, a creature with two claws extended, ready to clamp on to an unsuspecting victim.

Isn't it striking that Venus/Earth, Figure 34, is a heart pattern?! Venus, the Goddess of love, when joined with Earth, is a heart. Most of the other patterns are more geometric—Jupiter/Uranus, Figure 41, I see as a Mogen-David, the Jewish six-pointed star symbol.

We are living in an age of space travel and it is possible, within the lifetime of some of us living on the planet now, that we will see children of men (and women) born on other planets. When that day comes, Astro Computing Services will be ready to calculate Marsocentric or Venusocentric horoscopes! Before that day arrives, I thought it would be interesting to show the orbital paths of some of our solar system planets as viewed from a planet other than Earth. Figures 49 through 60 are the result.

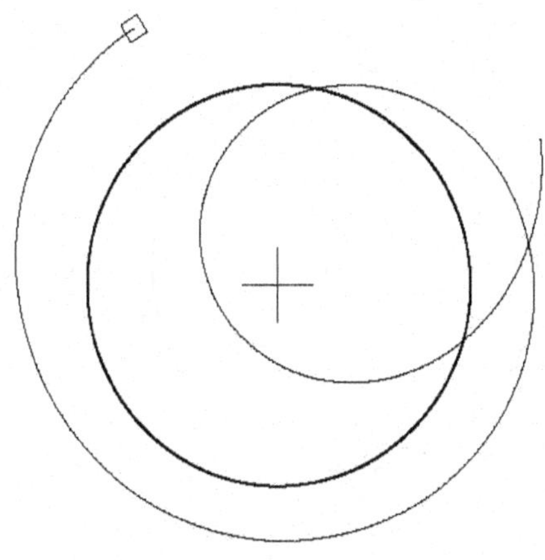

1540 JAN 1 to 1559 DEC 27 366 20.00
CENTER OF MASS Figure 1

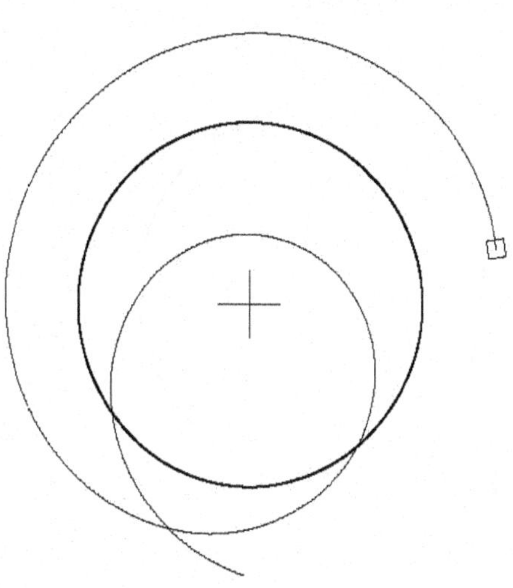

1560 JAN 1 to 1579 DEC 27 366 20.00
CENTER OF MASS Figure 2

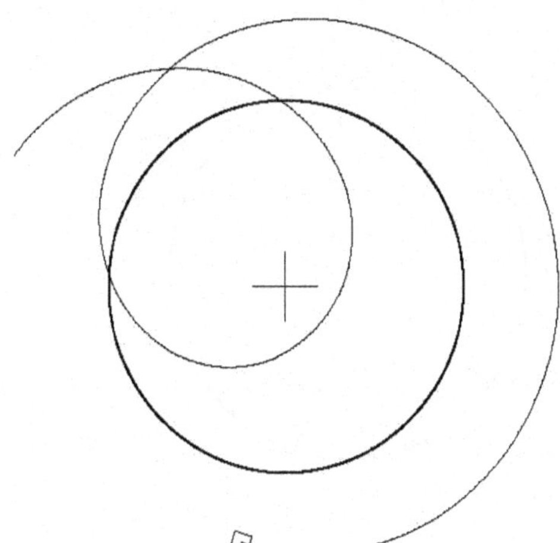

1580 JAN 1 to 1600 JAN 6 366 20.00
CENTER OF MASS Figure 3

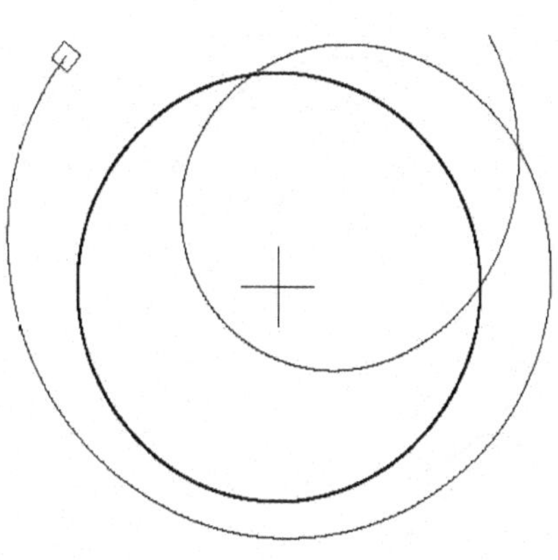

1600 JAN 1 to 1619 DEC 27 366 20.00
CENTER OF MASS Figure 4

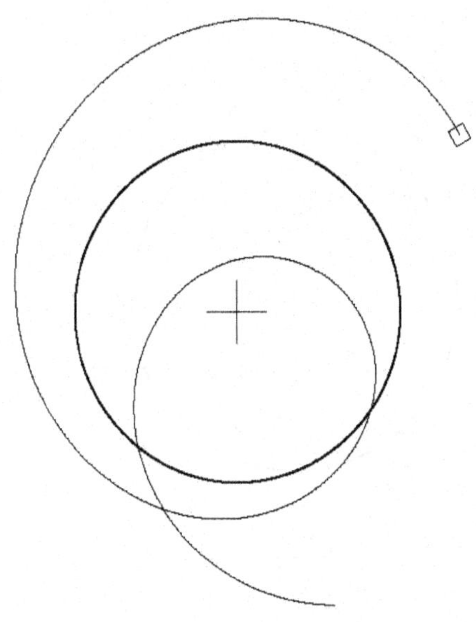

1620 JAN 1 to 1639 DEC 27 366 20.00
CENTER OF MASS Figure 5

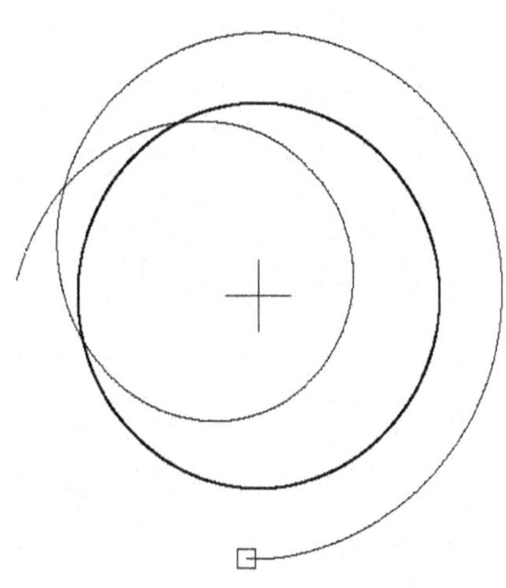

1640 JAN 1 to 1659 DEC 27 366 20.00
CENTER OF MASS Figure 6

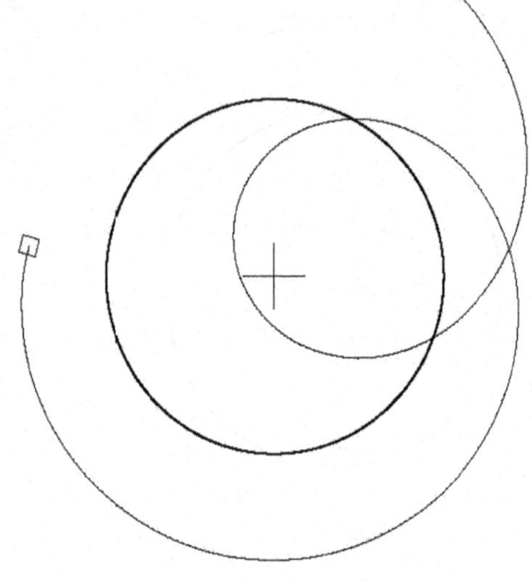

1660 JAN 1 to 1679 DEC 27 366 20.00
CENTER OF MASS Figure 7

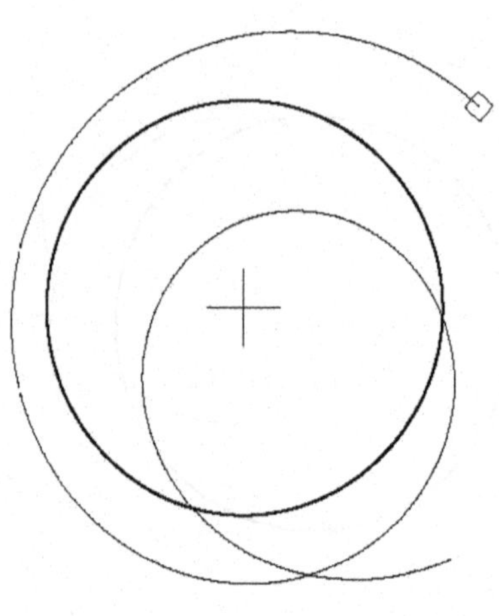

1680 JAN 1 to 1699 DEC 27 366 20.00
CENTER OF MASS Figure 8

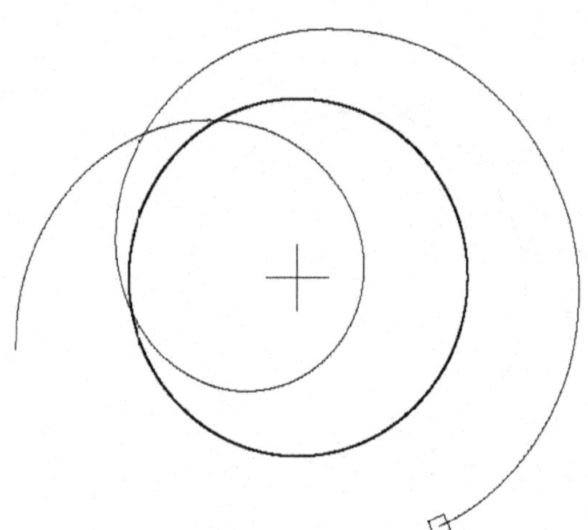

1700 JAN 1 to 1719 DEC 28 366 20.00
CENTER OF MASS Figure 9

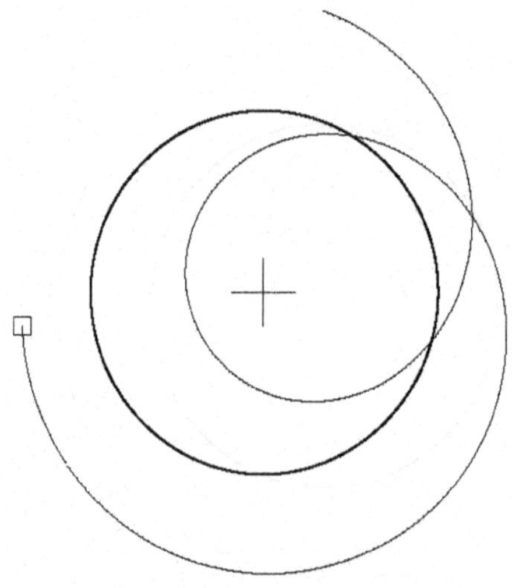

1720 JAN 1 to 1739 DEC 27 366 20.00
CENTER OF MASS Figure 10

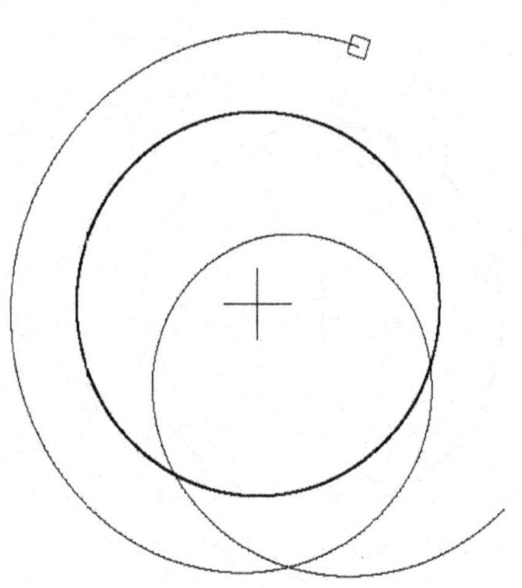

1740 JAN 1 to 1759 DEC 27 366 20.00
CENTER OF MASS Figure 11

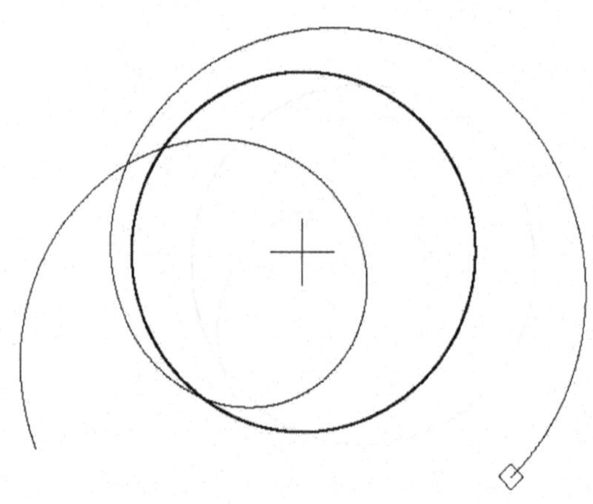

1760 JAN 1 to 1779 DEC 27 366 20.00
CENTER OF MASS Figure 12

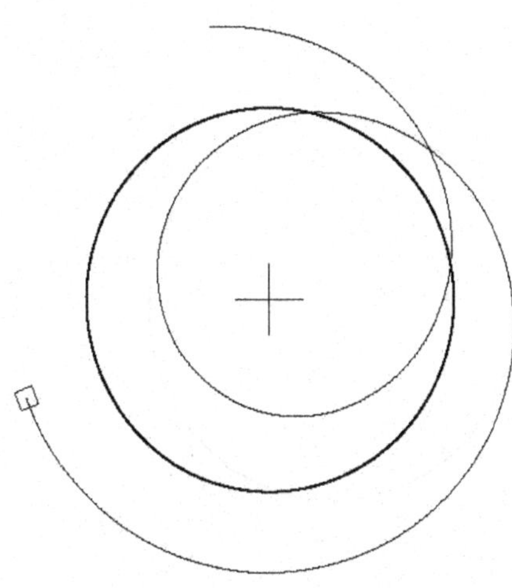

1780 JAN 1 to 1799 DEC 27 366 20.00
CENTER OF MASS Figure 13

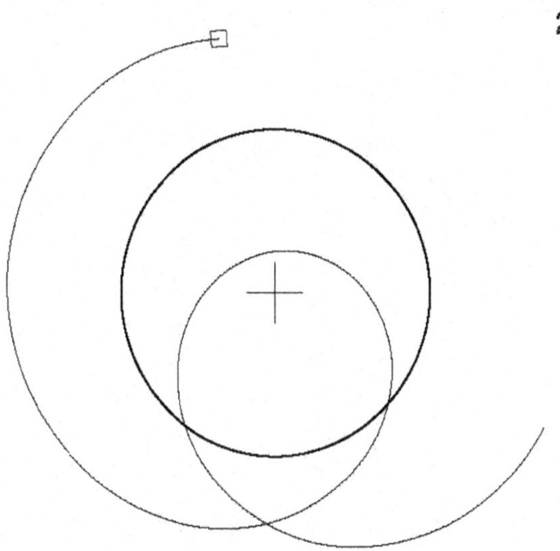

1800 JAN 1 to 1819 DEC 28 366 20.00
CENTER OF MASS Figure 14

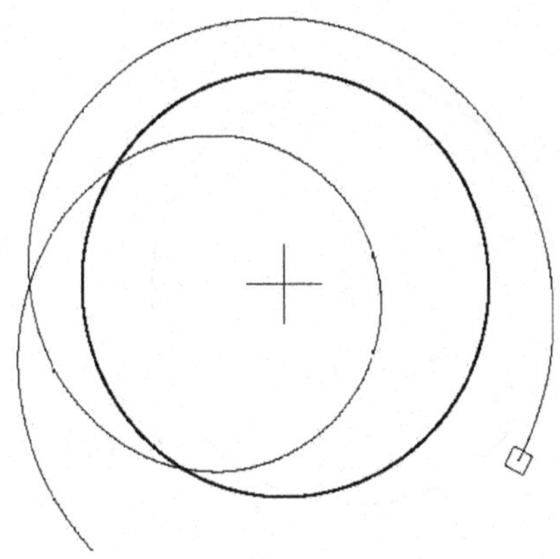

1820 JAN 1 to 1839 DEC 27 366 20.00
CENTER OF MASS Figure 15

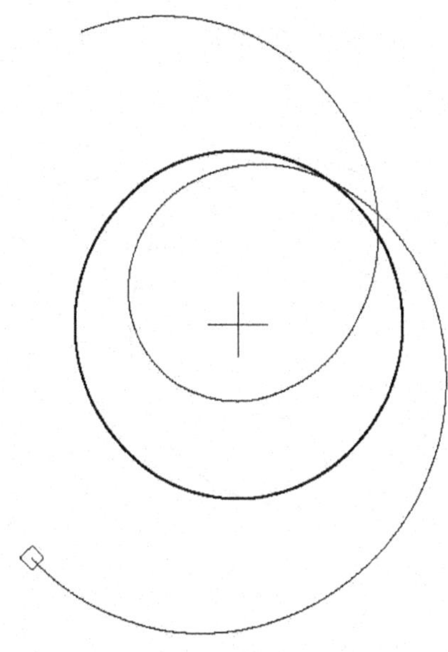

1840 JAN 1 to 1859 DEC 27 366 20.00
CENTER OF MASS Figure 16

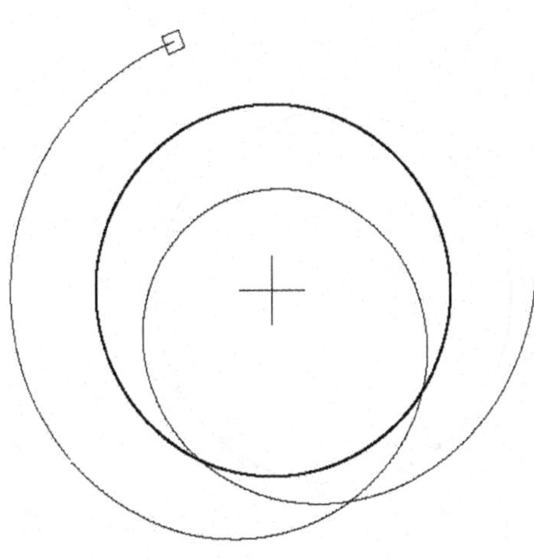

1860 JAN 1 to 1879 DEC 27 366 20.00
CENTER OF MASS Figure 17

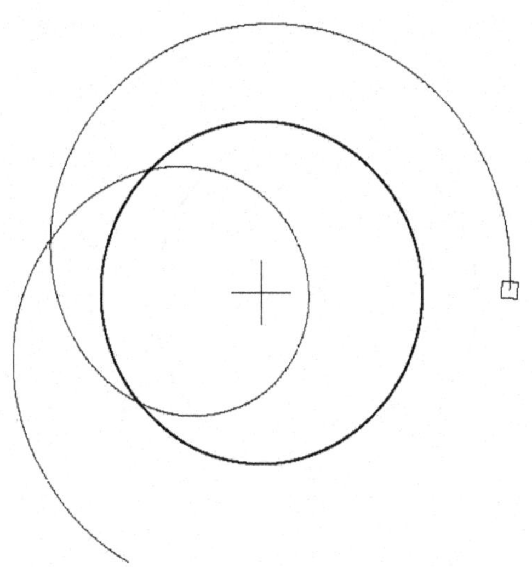

1880 JAN 1 to 1899 DEC 27 366 20.00
CENTER OF MASS Figure 18

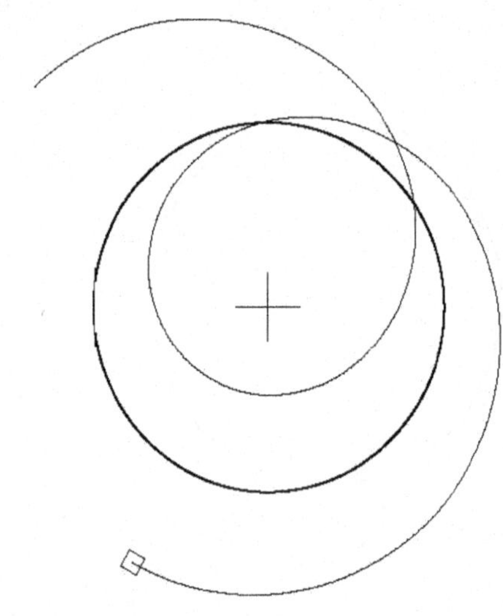

1900 JAN 1 to 1919 DEC 28 366 20.00
CENTER OF MASS Figure 19

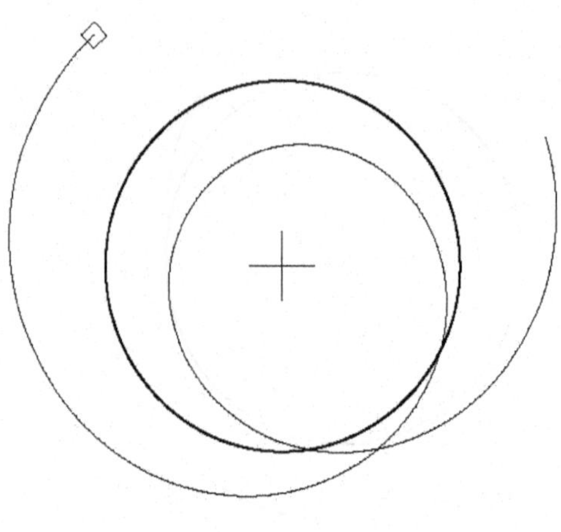

1920 JAN 1 to 1939 DEC 27 366 20.00
CENTER OF MASS Figure 20

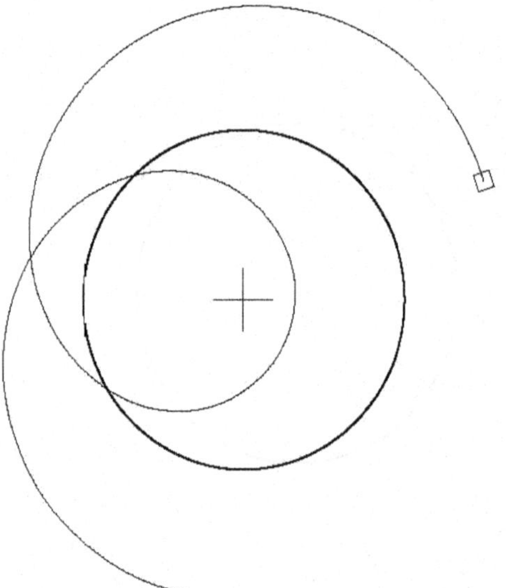

1940 JAN 1 to 1959 DEC 27 366 20.00
CENTER OF MASS Figure 21

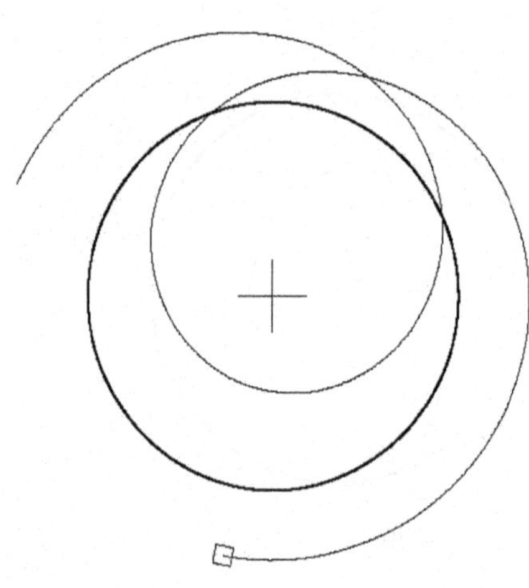

1960 JAN 1 to 1979 DEC 27 366 20.00
CENTER OF MASS Figure 22

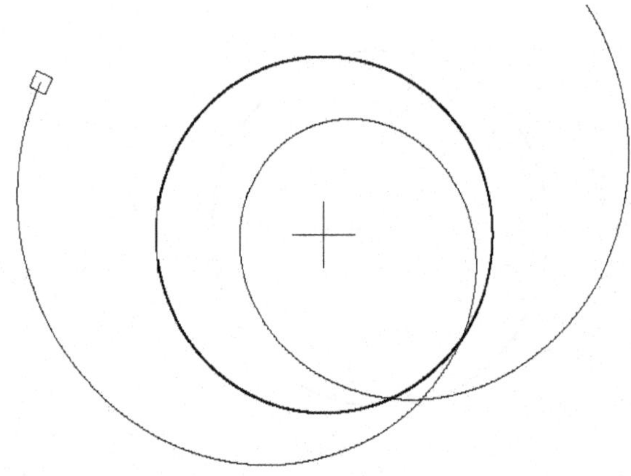

1980 JAN 1 to 1999 DEC 27 366 20.00
CENTER OF MASS Figure 23

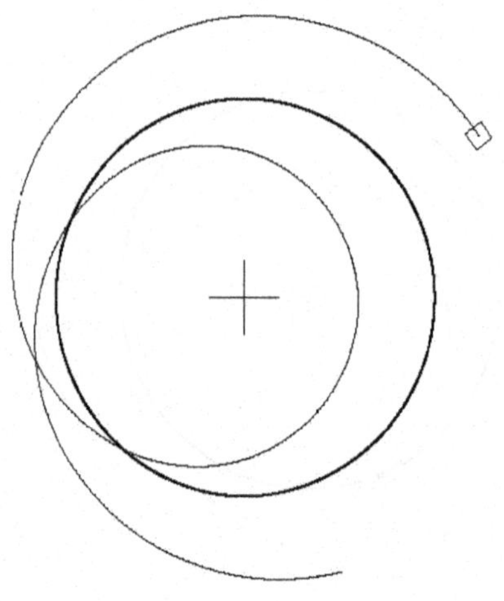

2000 JAN 1 to 2019 DEC 27 366 20.00
CENTER OF MASS Figure 24

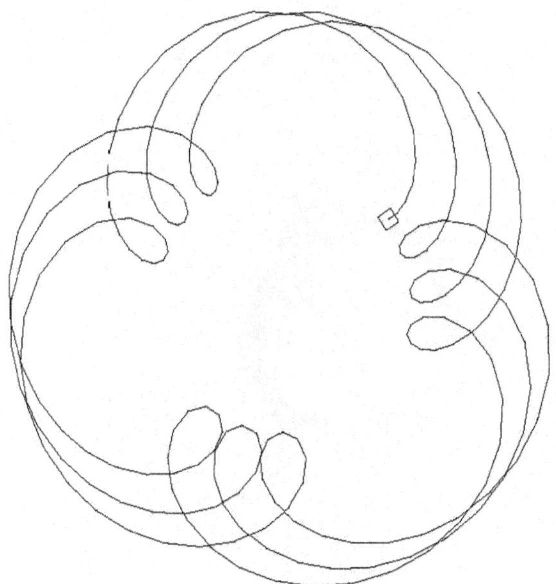

1931 MAY 11 to 1934 MAY 10 220 5.00
MERCURY ORBIT Figure 25

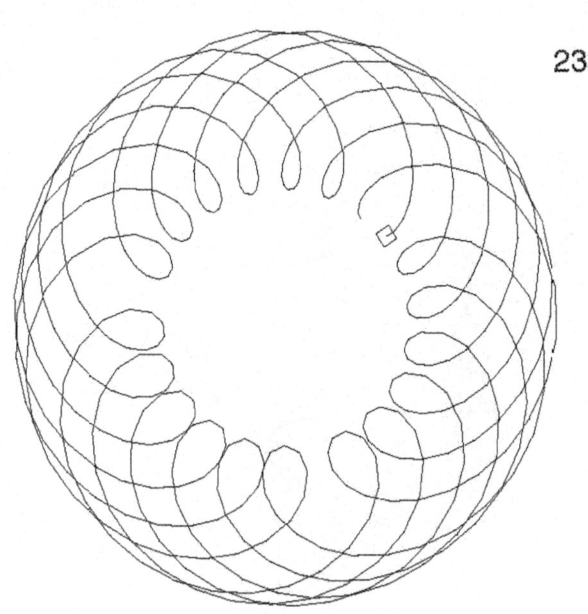

1931 MAY 11 to 1937 MAY 14 440 5.00
MERCURY ORBIT Figure 26

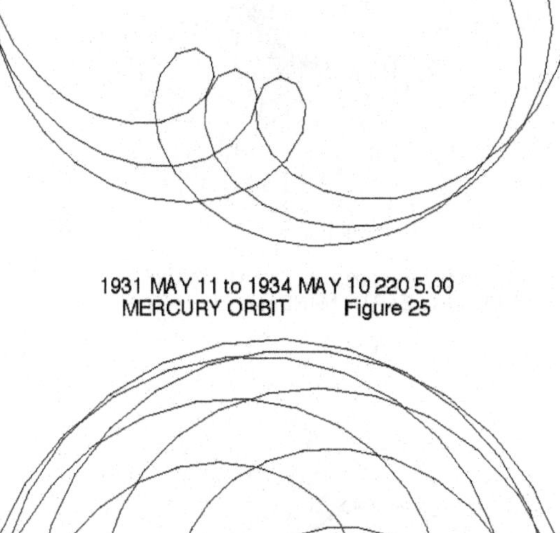

1931 MAY 11 to 1939 MAR 30 300 9.63
VENUS ORBIT Figure 27

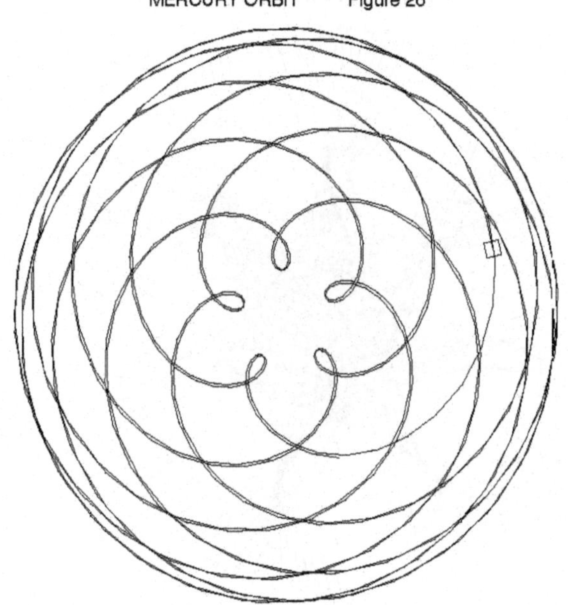

1931 MAY 11 to 1947 FEB 26 600 9.63
VENUS ORBIT Figure 28

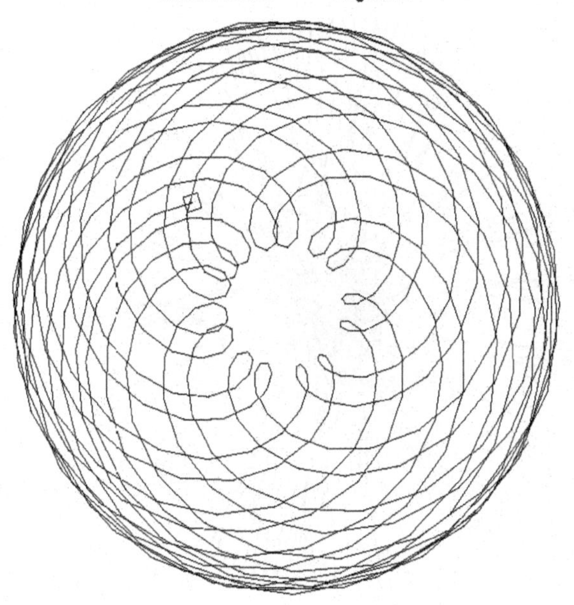

1931 MAY 11 to 1964 FEB 23 500 24.00
MARS ORBIT Figure 29

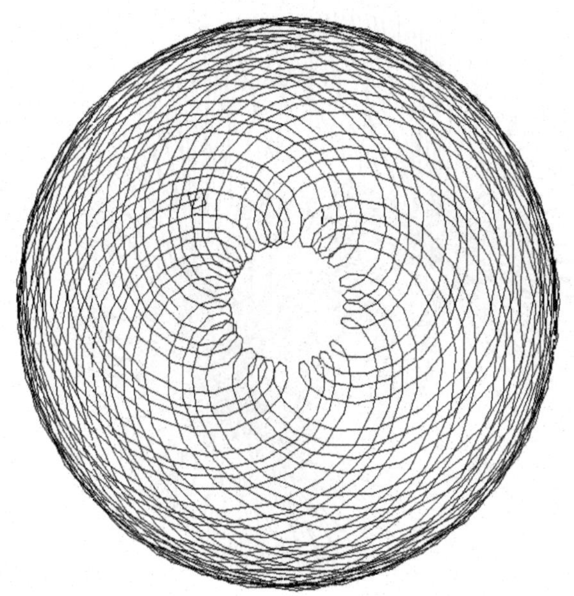

1931 MAY 11 to 1996 DEC 31 1000 24.00
MARS ORBIT Figure 30

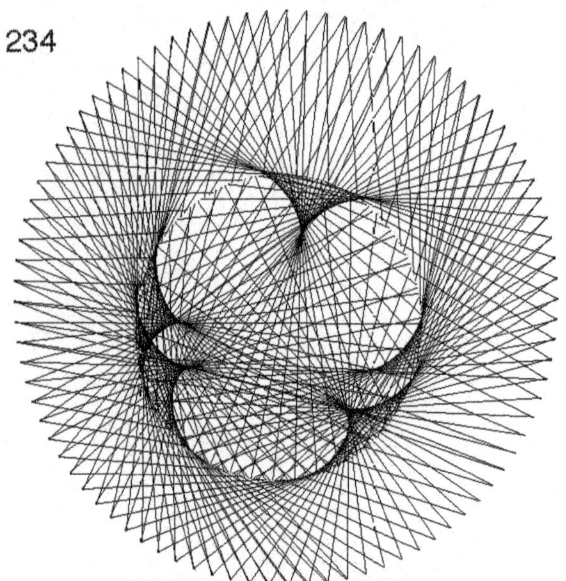

1900 JAN 1 to 1901 SEP 29 250 2.55
MERCURY VENUS MANDALA Figure 31

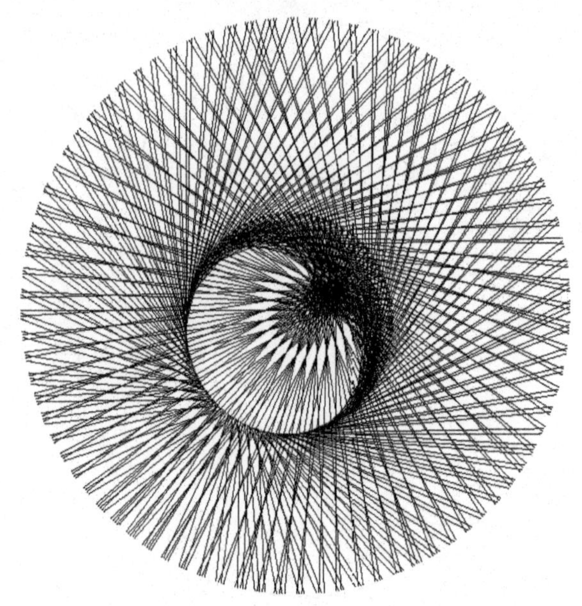

1931 MAY 8 to 2032 MAY 17 370 100.00
MERCURY EARTH MANDALA Figure 32

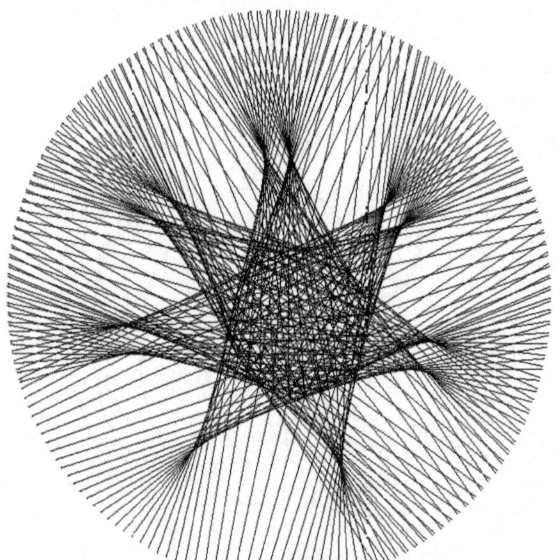

1900 JAN 1 to 1903 APR 12 300 4.00
MERCURY MARS MANDALA Figure 33

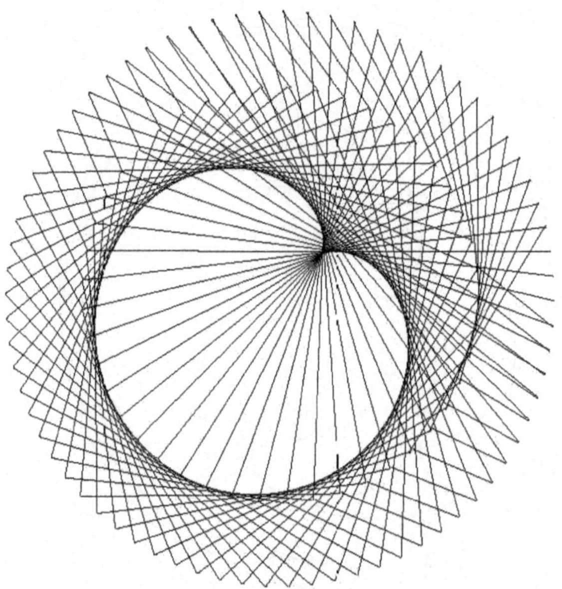

1981 OCT 7 to 1983 SEP 17 143 5.00
VENUS EARTH MANDALA Figure 34

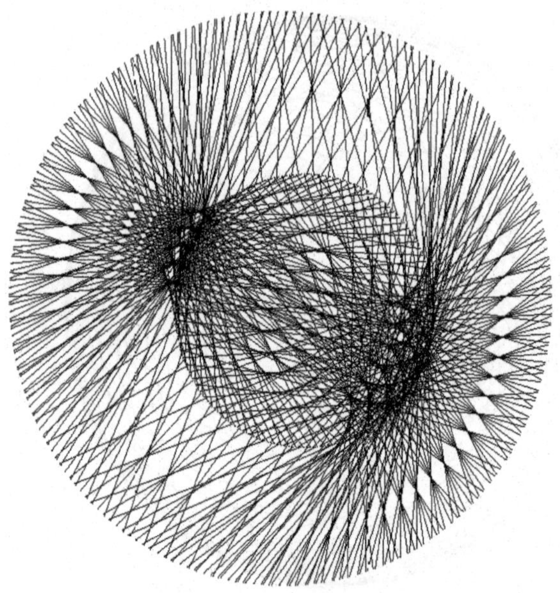

1899 DEC 5 to 1909 OCT 4 360 10.00
VENUS MARS MANDALA Figure 35

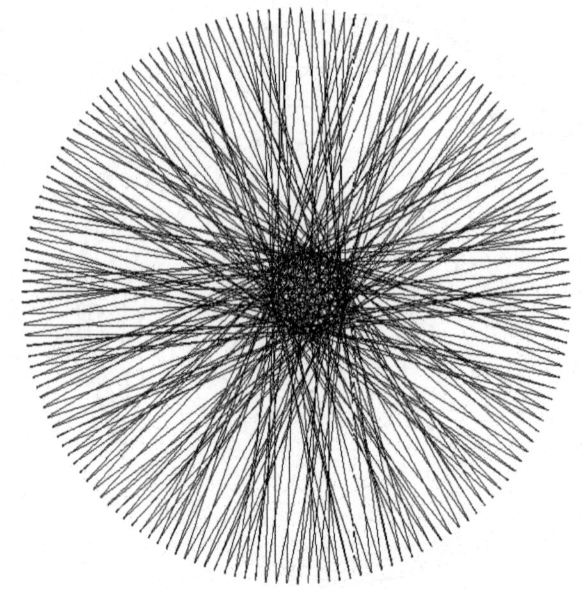

1899 OCT 20 to 1923 JUN 14 320 27.07
VENUS JUPITER MANDALA Figure 36

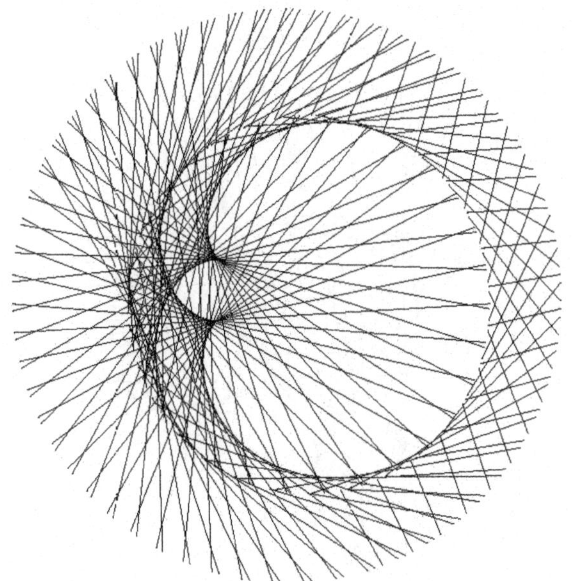

1900 JAN 1 to 1904 NOV 24 150 12.00
EARTH MARS MANDALA Figure 37

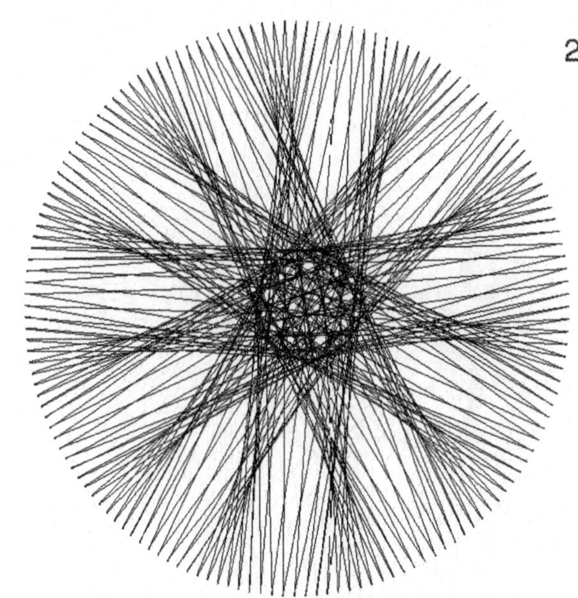

1900 MAY 27 to 1924 JAN 17 300 28.88
EARTH JUPITER MANDALA Figure 38

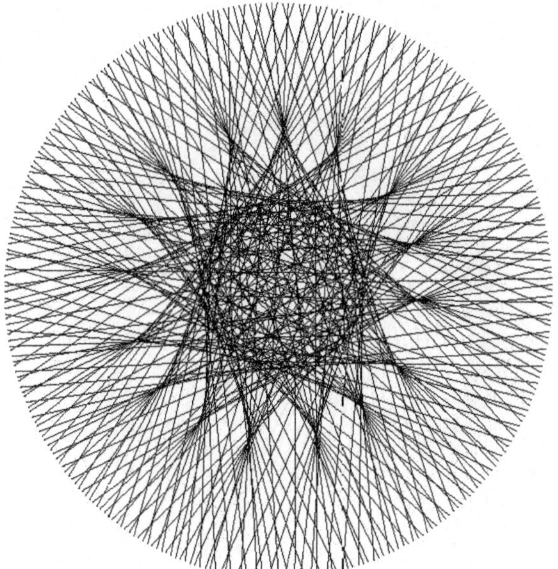

1899 OCT 7 to 1935 MAR 27 320 40.61
MARS JUPITER MANDALA Figure 39

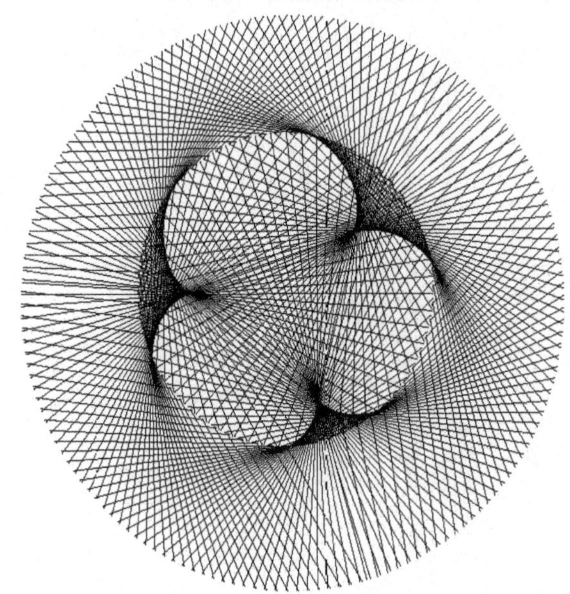

1901 SEP 20 to 1960 JUN 12 300 71.74
JUPITER SATURN MANDALA Figure 40

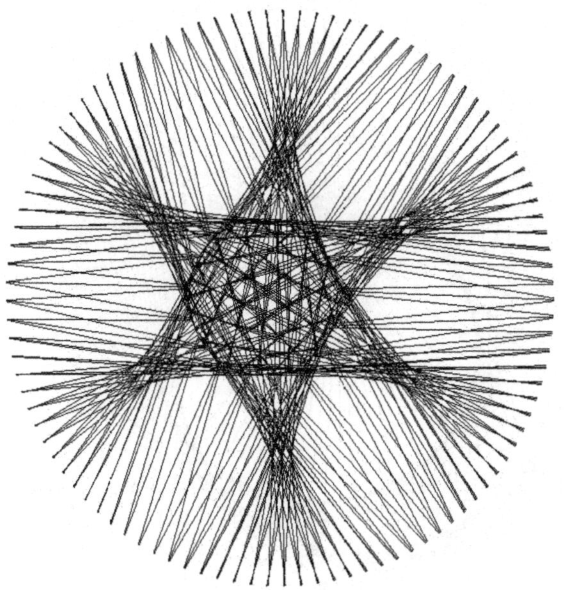

1900 JAN 1 to 2145 AUG 4 300 300.00
JUPITER URANUS MANDALA Figure 41

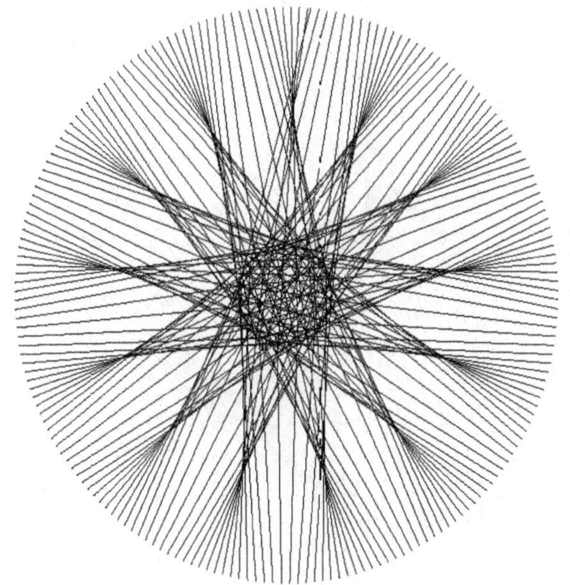

1900 JAN 1 to 2063 JUN 15 200 300.00
JUPITER NEPTUNE MANDALA Fig 42

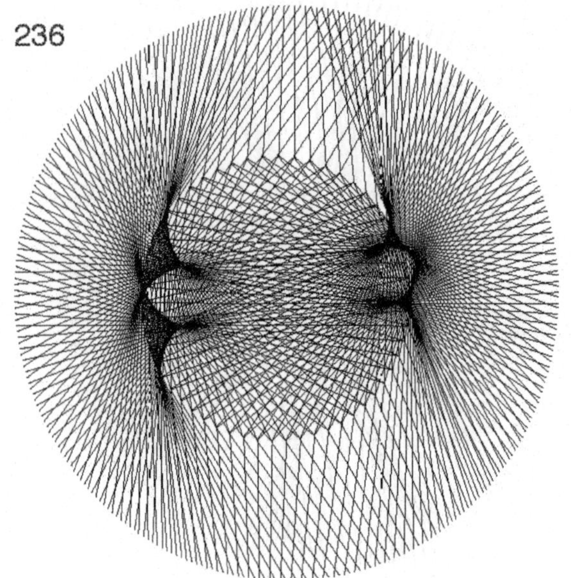

1942 MAR 31 to 2114 DEC 29 330 191.78
SATURN URANUS MANDALA Figure 43

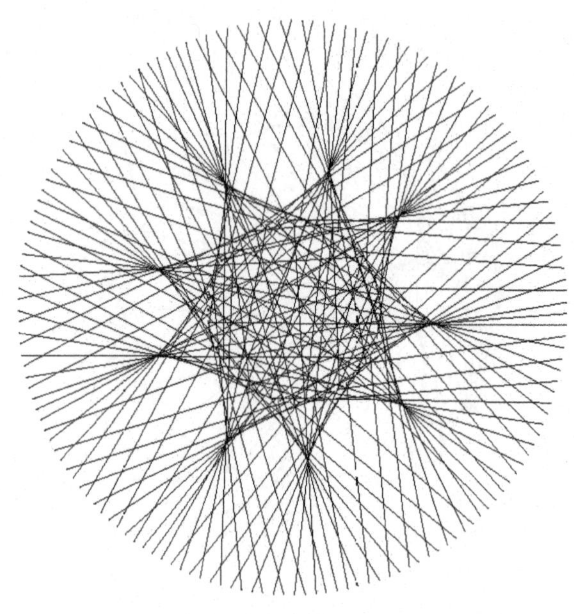

1917 AUG 9 to 2245 FEB 15 160 752.36
SATURN NEPTUNE MANDALA Figure 44

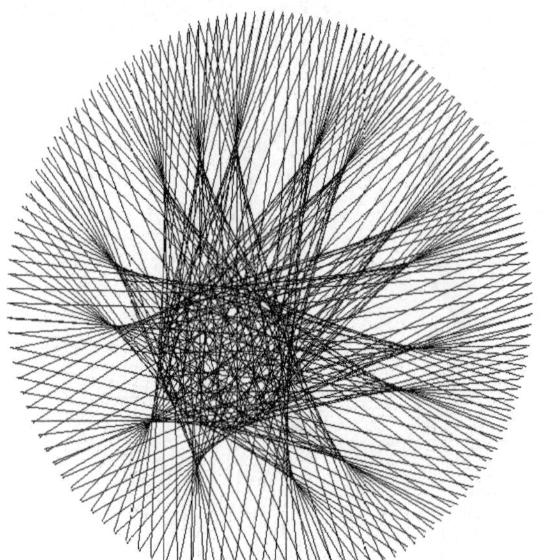

1915 FEB 27 to 2409 JUL 6 300 603.88
SATURN PLUTO MANDALA Figure 45

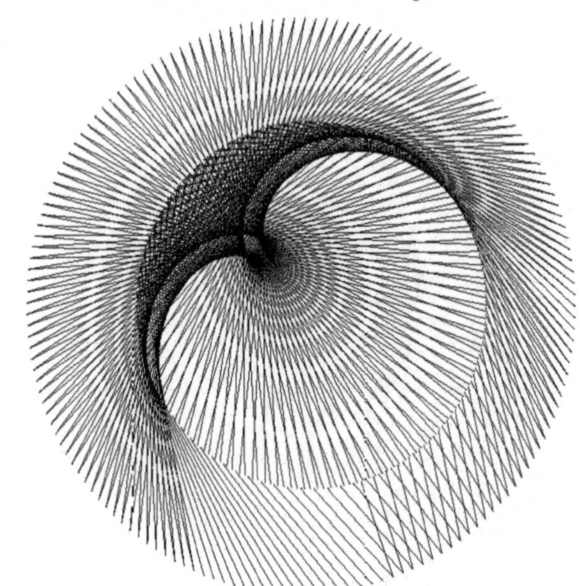

1993 APR 21 to 2301 APR 4 300 376.18
URANUS NEPTUNE MANDALA Figure 46

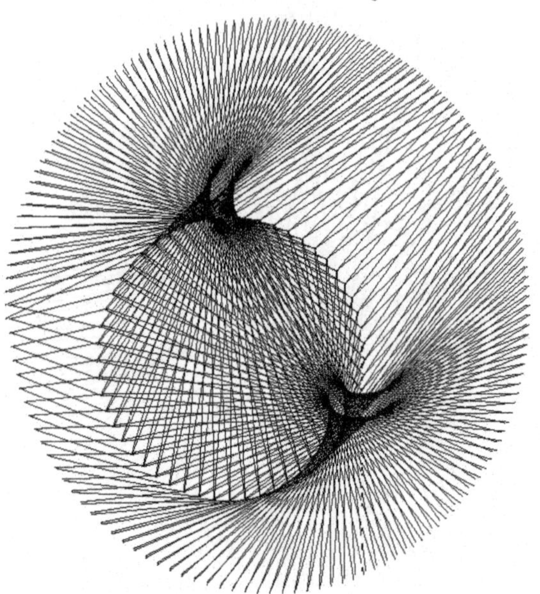

1966 JAN 8 to 2460 JUN 24 320 566.14
URANUS PLUTO MANDALA Figure 47

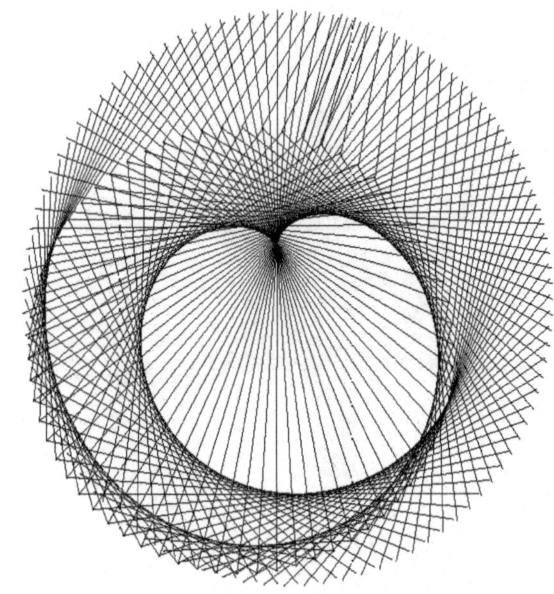

1892 JAN 29 to 2385 AUG 10 200 905.82
NEPTUNE PLUTO MANDALA Figure 48

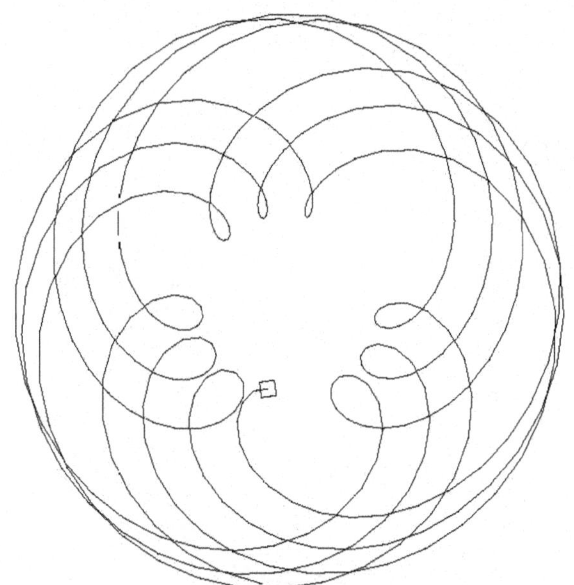

1980 FEB 19 to 1983 NOV 10 341 4.00
VENUS viewed from MERCURY Fig 49

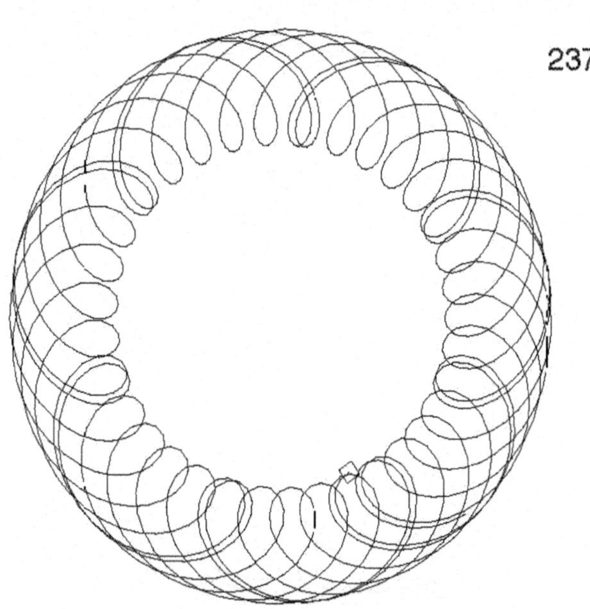

1979 NOV 29 to 1991 MAY 10 1046 4.00
MARS viewed from MERCURY Fig 50

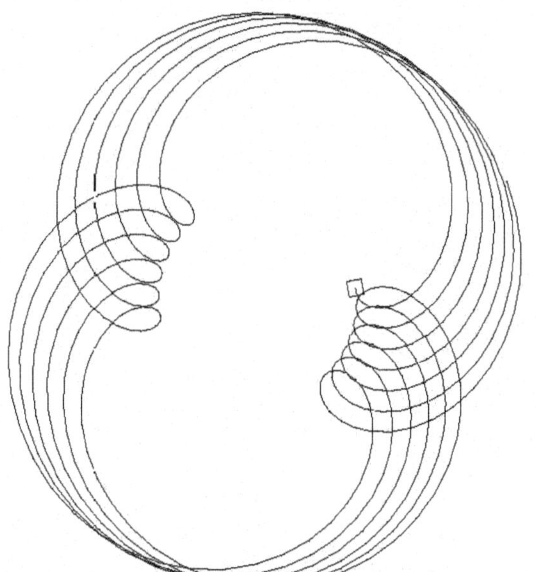

1980 APR 24 to 1991 SEP 22 522 8.00
MARS viewed from VENUS Fig 51

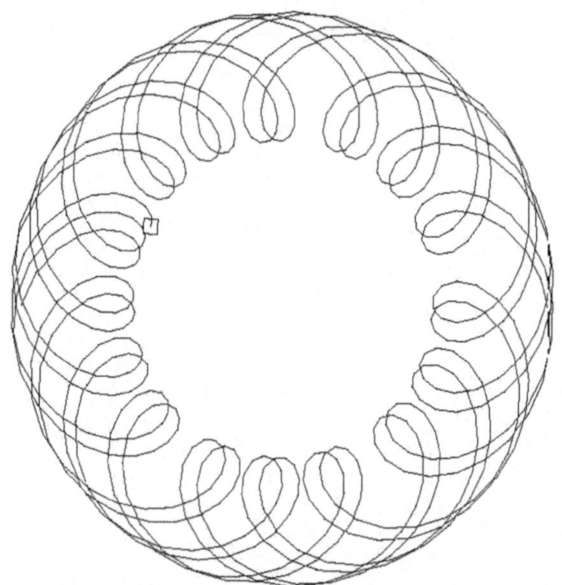

1980 FEB 23 to 2052 JUL 14 662 40.00
MARS viewed from JUPITER Fig 52

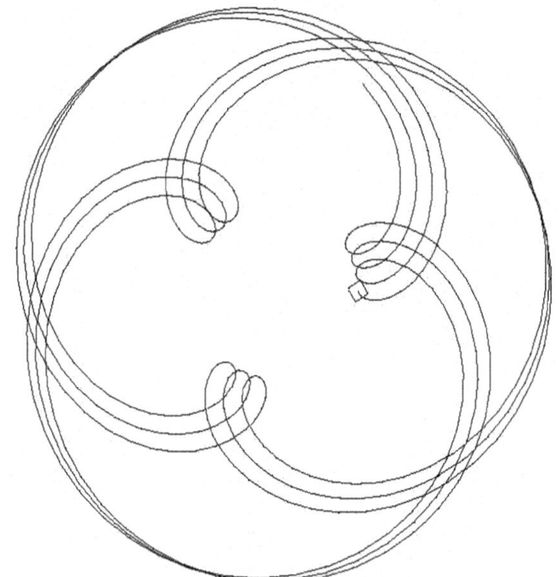

1981 APR 17 to 2165 APR 12 481 140.00
SATURN viewed from JUPITER Fg 53

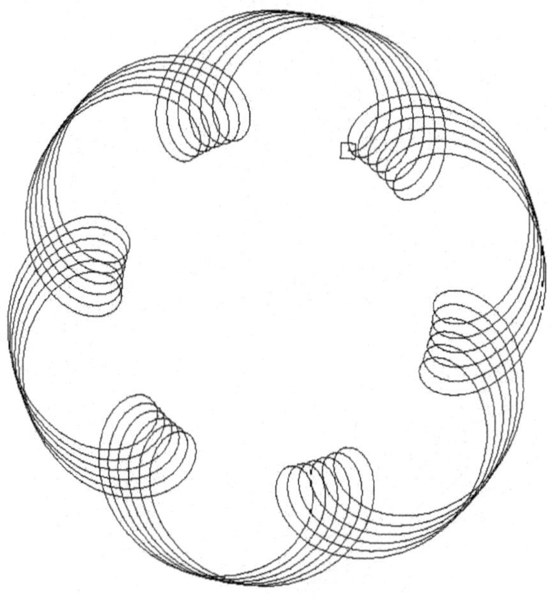

1983 JUN 12 to 2492 FEB 3 1328 140.00
URANUS viewed from JUPITER Fg 54

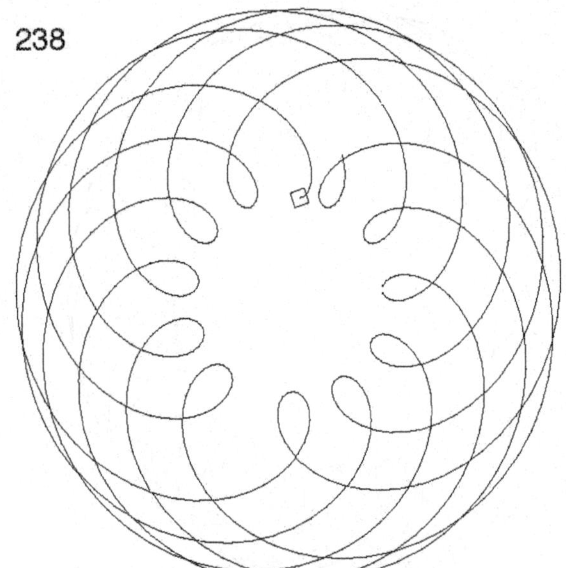

1988 JUN 13 to 2493 AUG 4 616 300.00
URANUS viewed from SATURN Fig 55

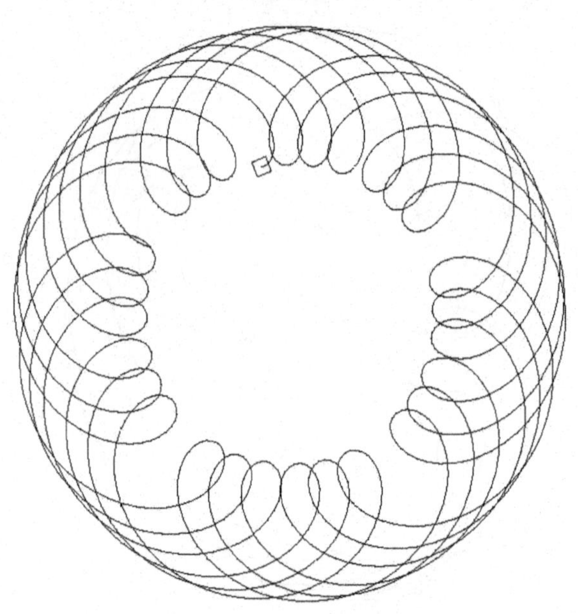

1989 JUL 21 to 2990 OCT 21 1220 300.00
NEPTUNE viewed from SATURN Fg 56

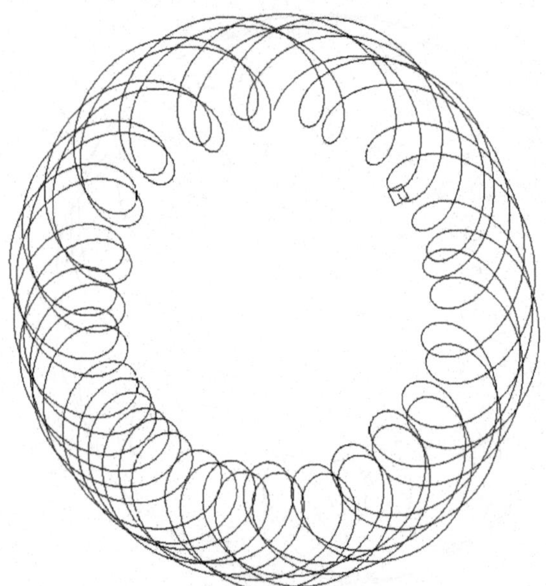

1982 DEC 27 to 3482 OCT 24 1827 300.00
PLUTO viewed from SATURN Fig 57

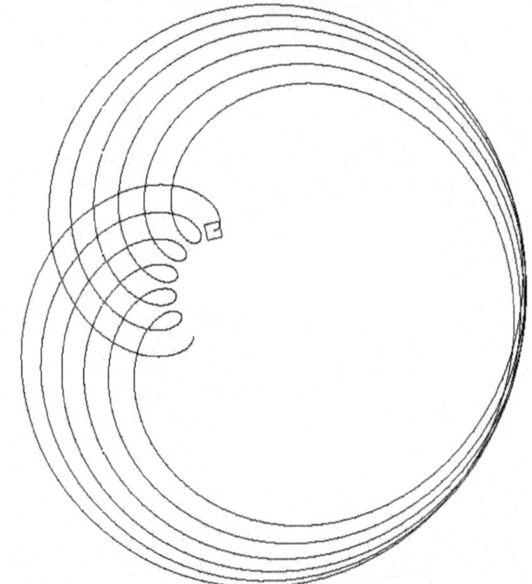

1993 APR 22 to 3022 OCT 5 753 500.00
NEPTUNE seen from URANUS Fig 58

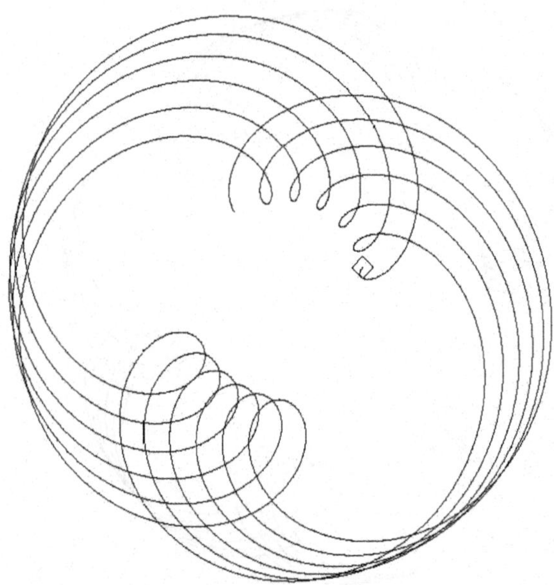

1966 JAN 9 to 3496 JUL 6 1119 500.00
PLUTO viewed from URANUS Fig 59

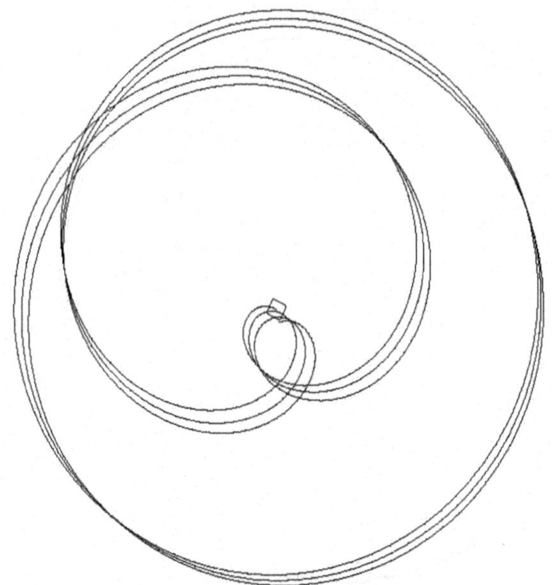

1892 MAR 29 to 3380 JUL 26 605 900.00
PLUTO viewed from NEPTUNE Fig 60

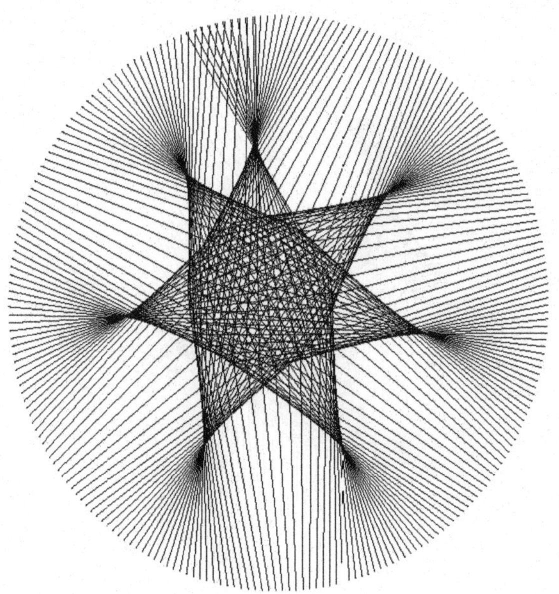

1990 JAN 2 to 1994 OCT 14 250 7.01
VENUS CERES MANDALA Figure 61

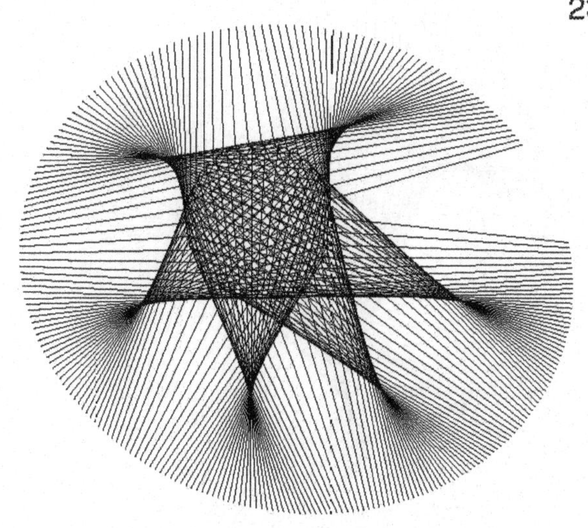

1989 NOV 15 to 1994 FEB 27 250 6.28
VENUS PALLAS MANDALA Figure 62

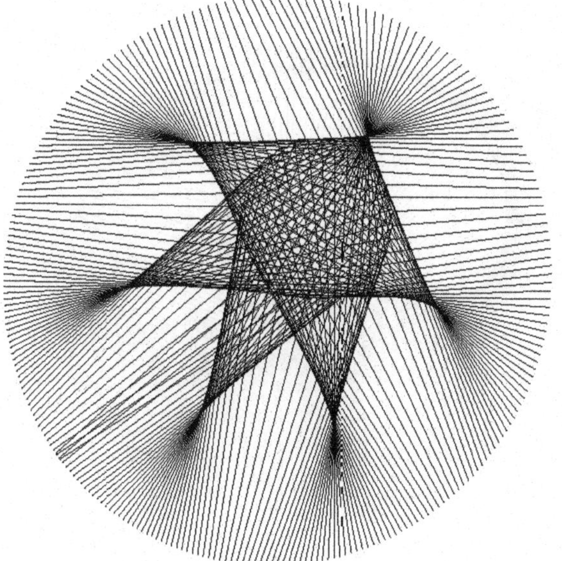

1990 MAR 23 to 1994 AUG 9 250 6.43
VENUS JUNO MANDALA Figure 63

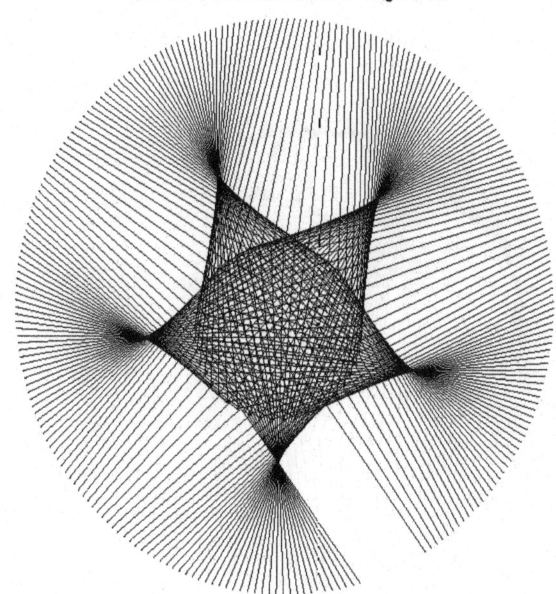

1989 OCT 2 to 1993 MAR 28 250 5.11
VENUS VESTA MANDALA Figure 64

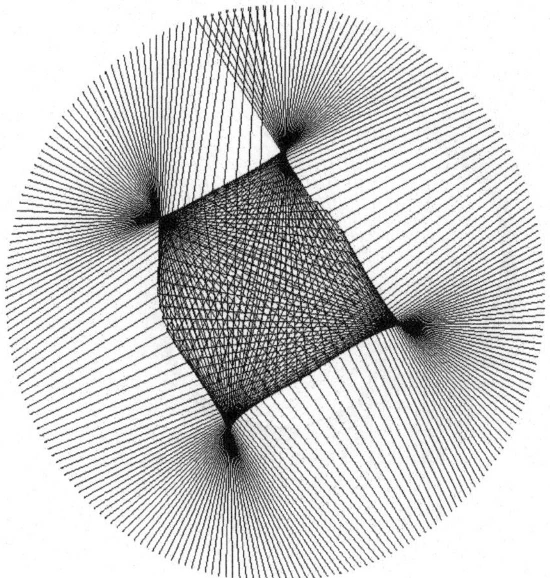

1989 DEC 20 to 1994 OCT 1 250 7.01
EARTH CERES MANDALA Figure 65

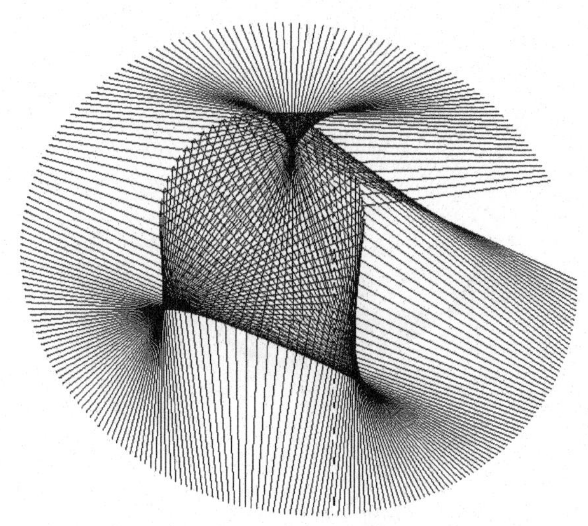

1989 SEP 30 to 1994 JAN 11 250 6.28
EARTH PALLAS MANDALA Figure 66

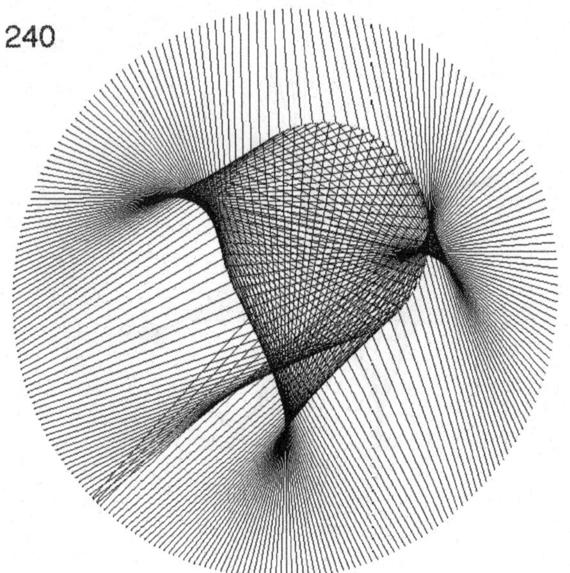

1990 MAY 8 to 1994 SEP 24 250 6.43
EARTH JUNO MANDALA Figure 67

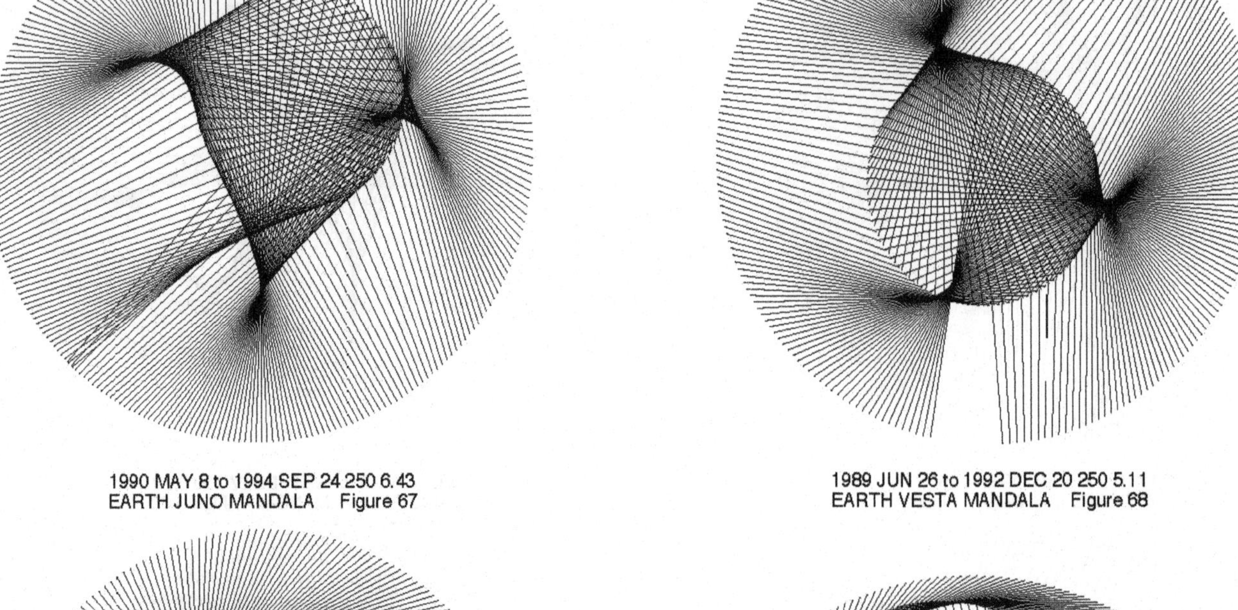

1989 JUN 26 to 1992 DEC 20 250 5.11
EARTH VESTA MANDALA Figure 68

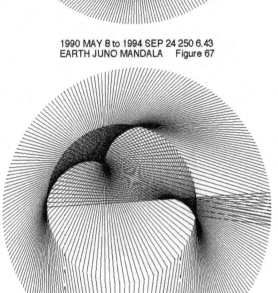

1988 SEP 8 to 1993 JUN 20 250 7.01
MARS CERES MANDALA Figure 69

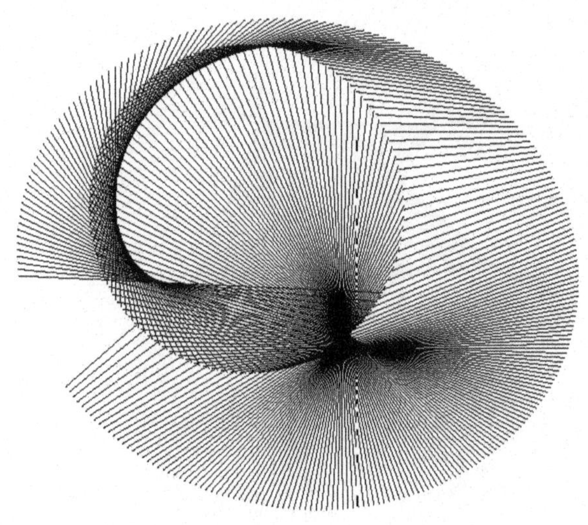

1991 OCT 28 to 1996 FEB 8 250 6.28
MARS PALLAS MANDALA Figure 70

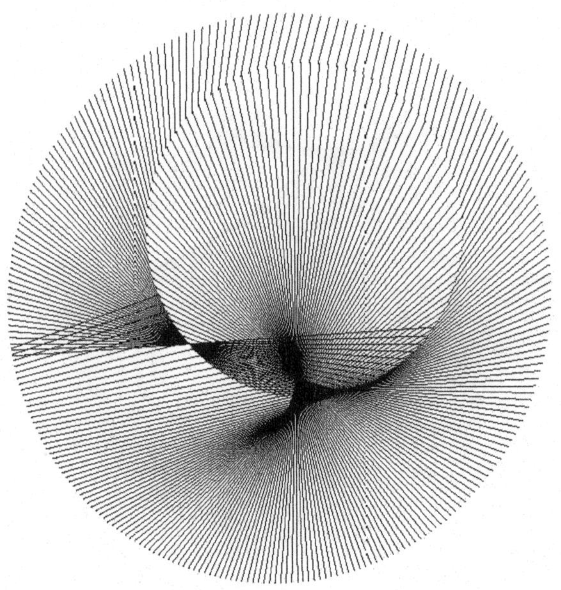

1989 OCT 26 to 1994 MAR 15 250 6.43
MARS JUNO MANDALA Figure 71

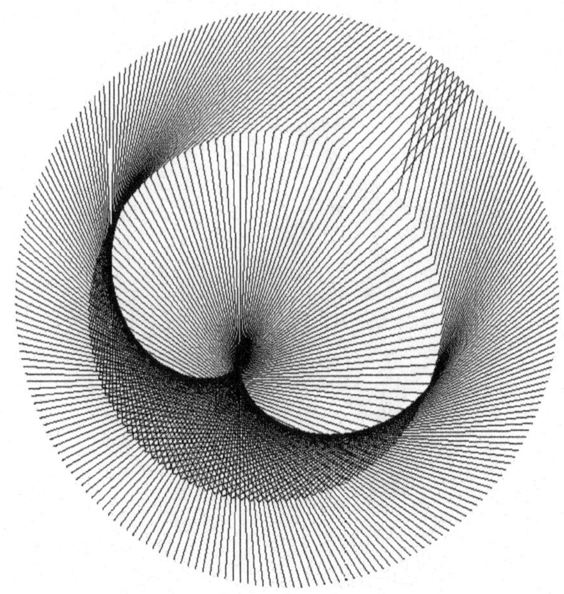

1990 OCT 28 to 1994 JUL 28 250 5.50
MARS VESTA MANDALA Figure 72

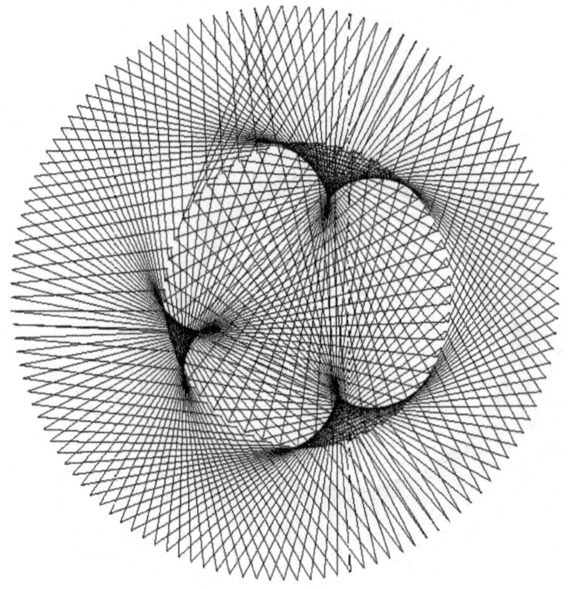

1990 FEB 4 to 2013 SEP 21 250 34.65
JUPITER CERES MANDALA Figure 73

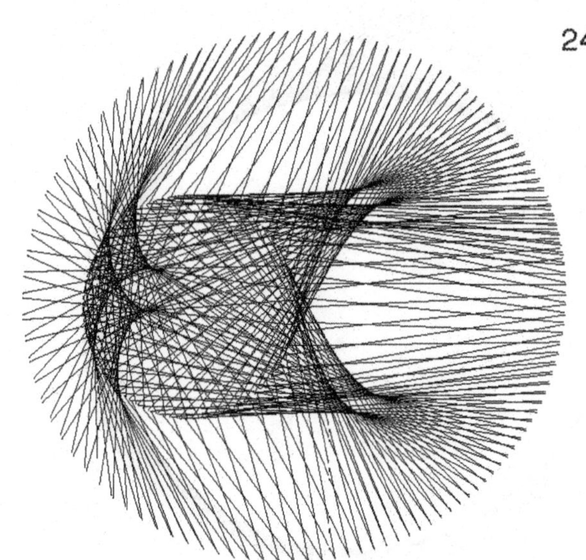

1773 OCT 27 to 1873 JUN 4 250 146.10
CHIRON JUPITER MANDALA Figure 74

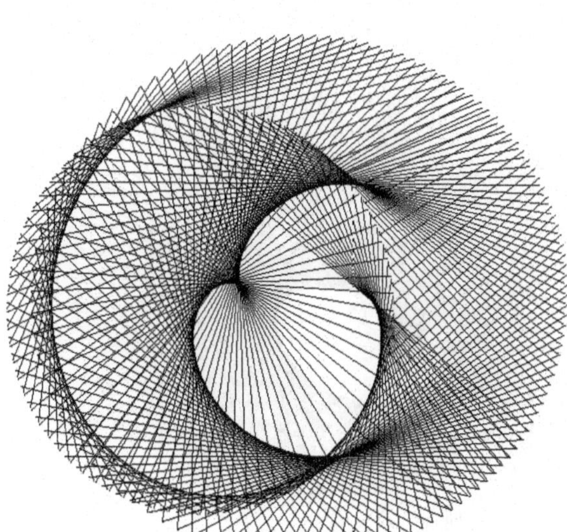

1522 MAY 19 to 1622 JAN 3 250 146.10
CHIRON SATURN MANDALA Figure 75

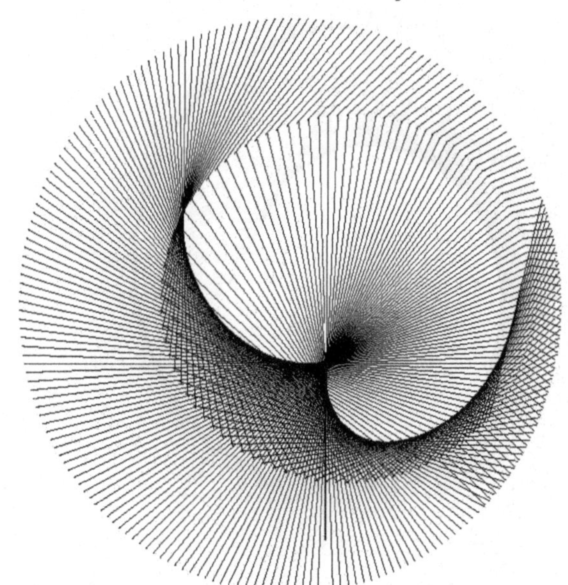

1665 MAY 31 to 1765 JAN 6 250 146.10
CHIRON URANUS MANDALA Figure 76

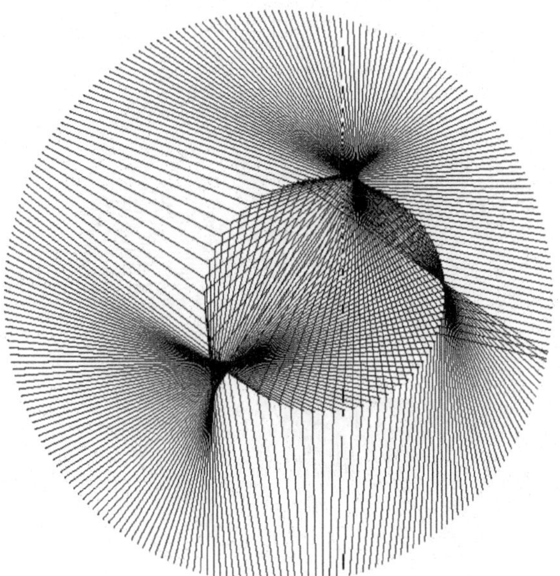

1528 JUL 2 to 1692 AUG 29 250 240.76
CHIRON NEPTUNE MANDALA Figure 77

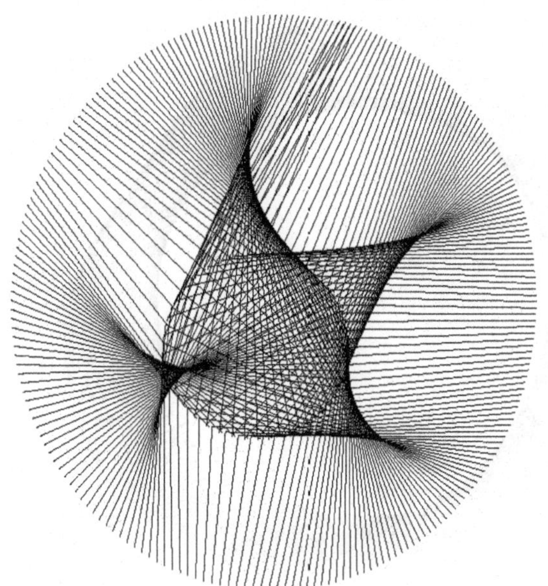

1401 OCT 7 to 1648 OCT 19 250 362.33
CHIRON PLUTO MANDALA Figure 78

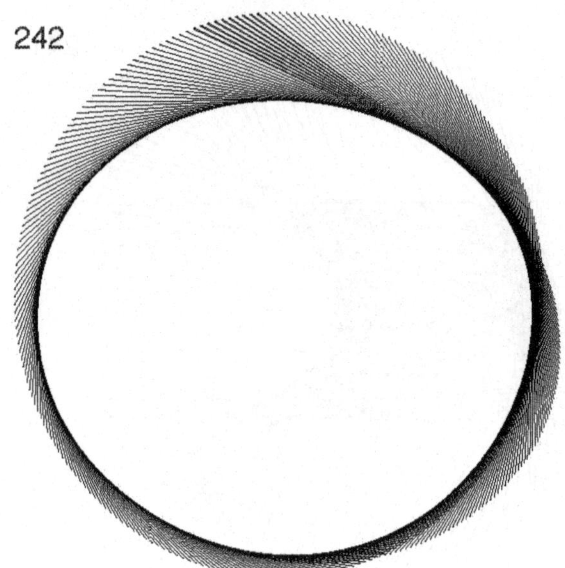

1990 JAN 1 to 1994 OCT 10 250 7.00
CERES PALLAS MANDALA Figure 79

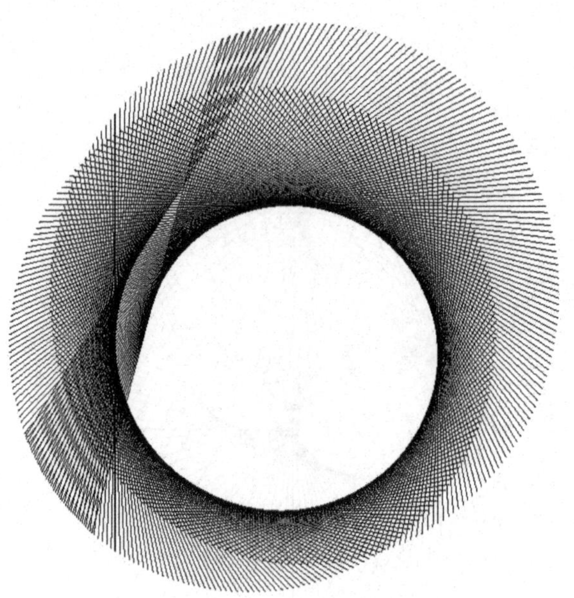

1990 JAN 1 to 1994 OCT 10 250 7.00
CERES JUNO MANDALA Figure 80

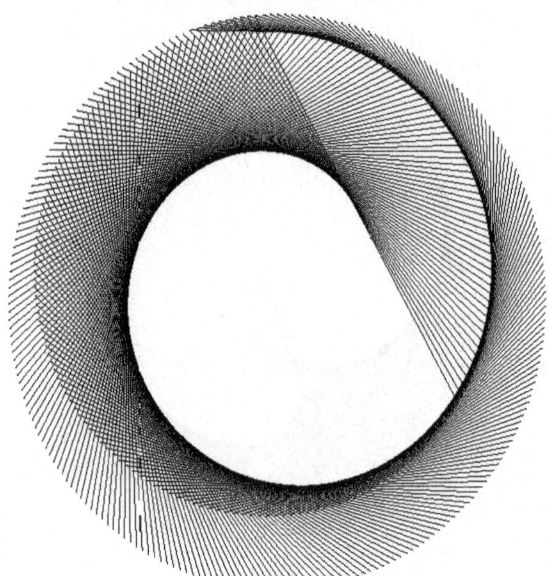

1990 JAN 1 to 1994 OCT 10 250 7.00
CERES VESTA MANDALA Figure 81

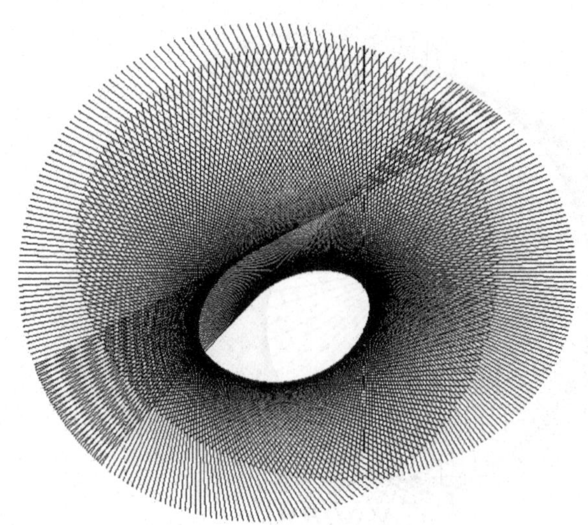

1990 JAN 1 to 1994 OCT 10 250 7.00
PALLAS JUNO MANDALA Figure 82

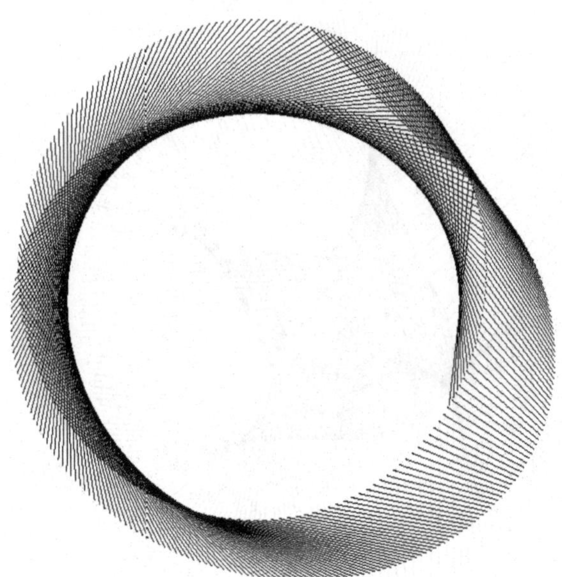

1990 JAN 1 to 1994 OCT 10 250 7.00
PALLAS VESTA MANDALA Figure 83

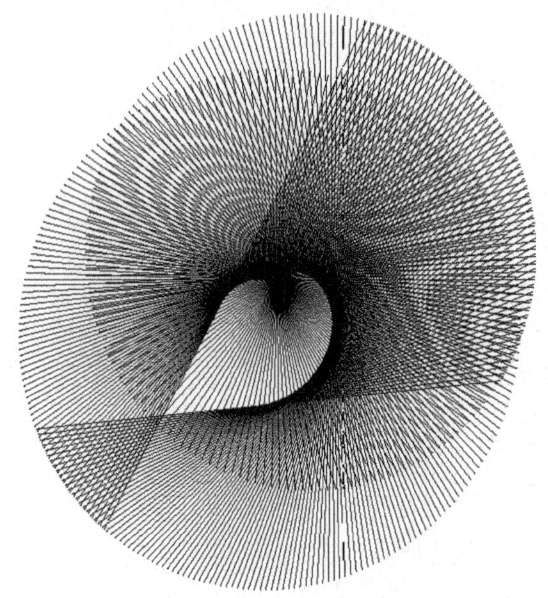

1990 JAN 1 to 1994 OCT 10 250 7.00
JUNO VESTA MANDALA Figure 84

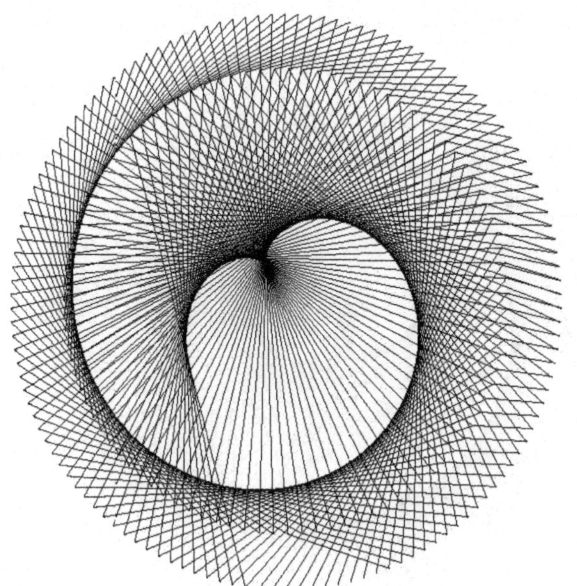

1500 JAN 1 to 2181 JAN 30 250 999.00
CUPIDO HADES MANDALA Figure 85

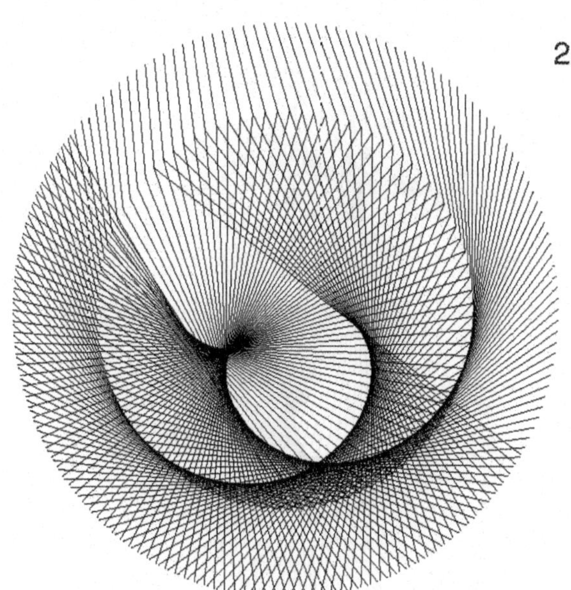

1500 JAN 1 to 2181 JAN 30 250 999.00
CUPIDO ZEUS MANDALA Figure 86

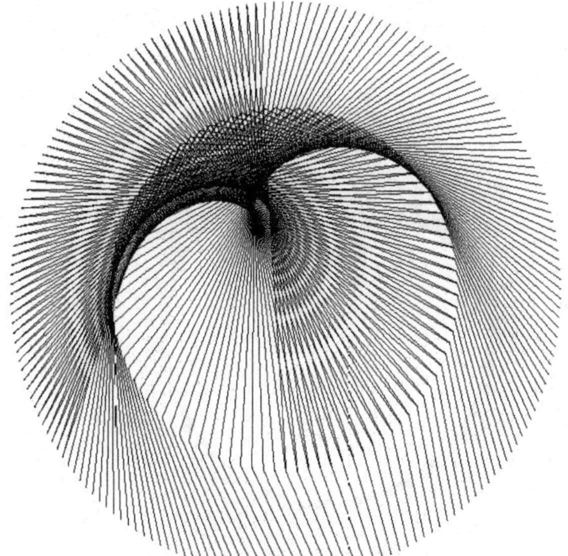

1500 JAN 1 to 2181 JAN 30 250 999.00
CUPIDO KRONOS MANDALA Figure 87

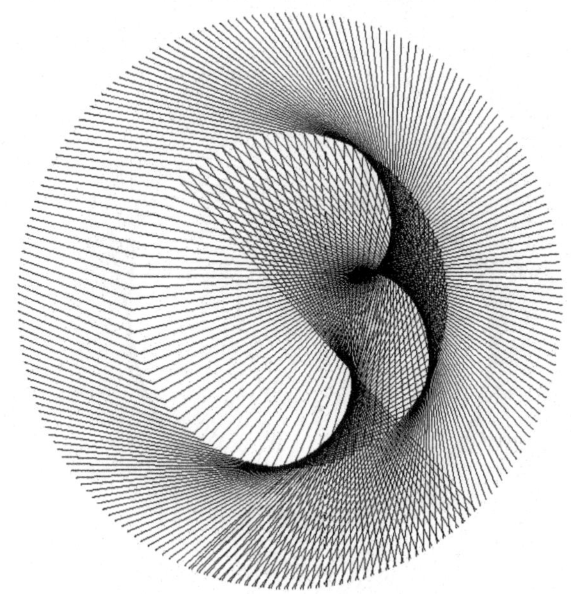

1500 JAN 1 to 2181 JAN 30 250 999.00
CUPIDO APOLLON MANDALA Figure 88

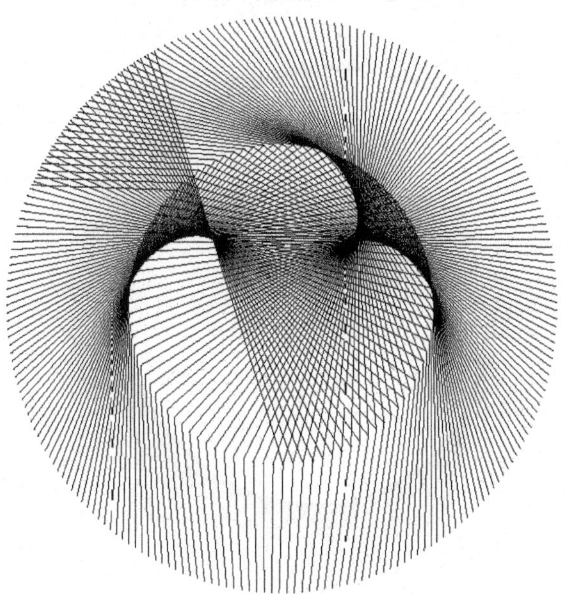

1500 JAN 1 to 2181 JAN 30 250 999.00
CUPIDO ADMETOS MANDALA Figure 89

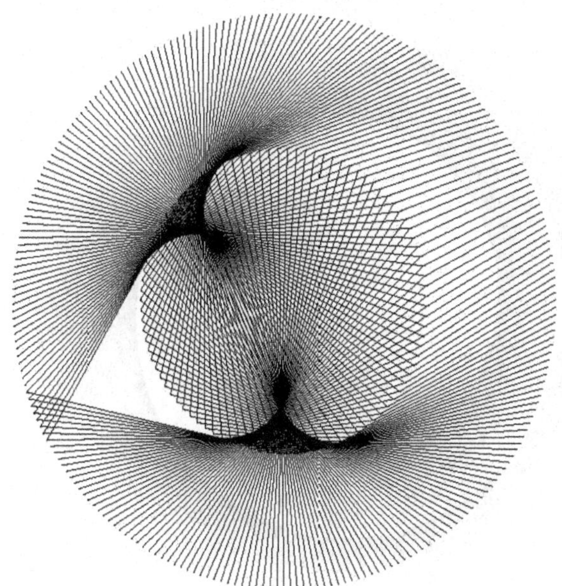

1500 JAN 1 to 2181 JAN 30 250 999.00
CUPIDO VULKANUS MANDALA Fig 90

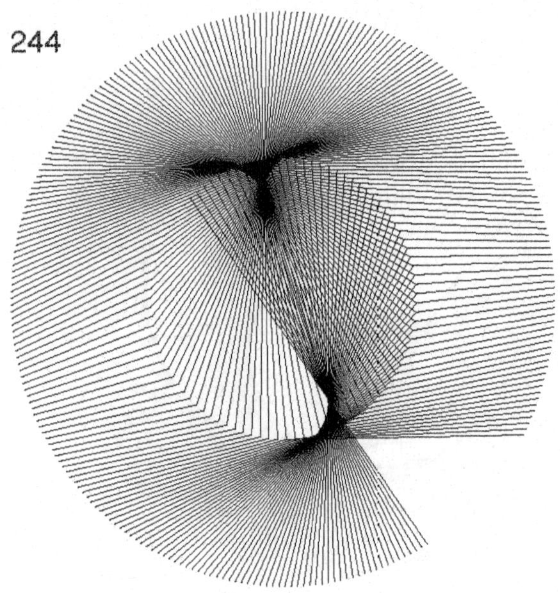

1500 JAN 1 to 2181 JAN 30 250 999.00
CUPIDO POSEIDON MANDALA Fig 91

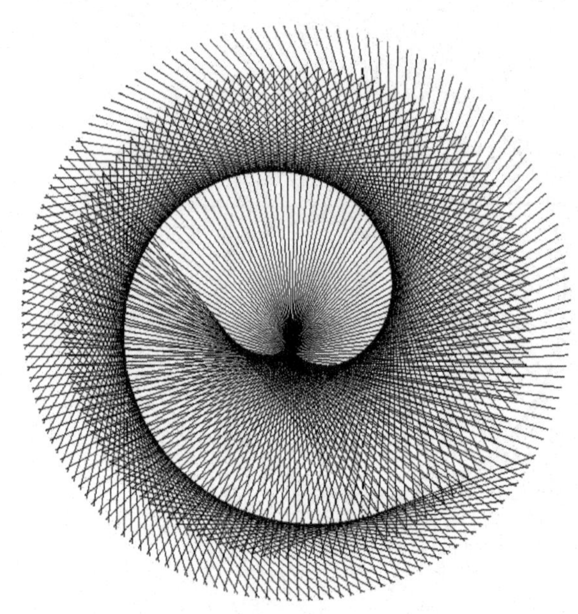

1500 JAN 1 to 2181 JAN 30 250 999.00
HADES ZEUS MANDALA Figure 92

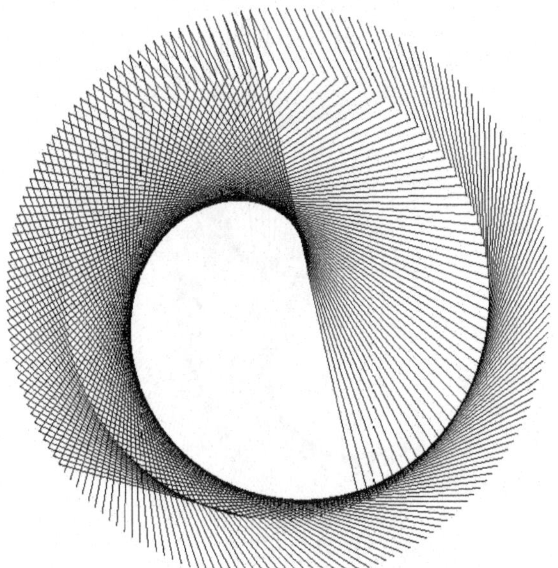

1500 JAN 1 to 2181 JAN 30 250 999.00
HADES KRONOS MANDALA Figure 93

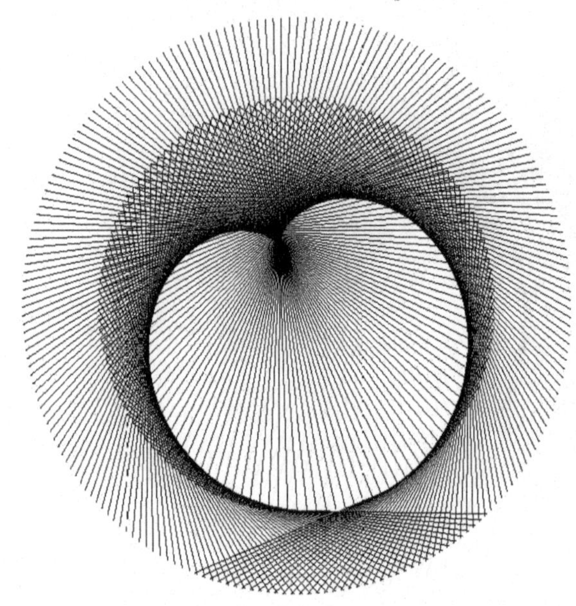

1500 JAN 1 to 2181 JAN 30 250 999.00
HADES APOLLON MANDALA Figure 94

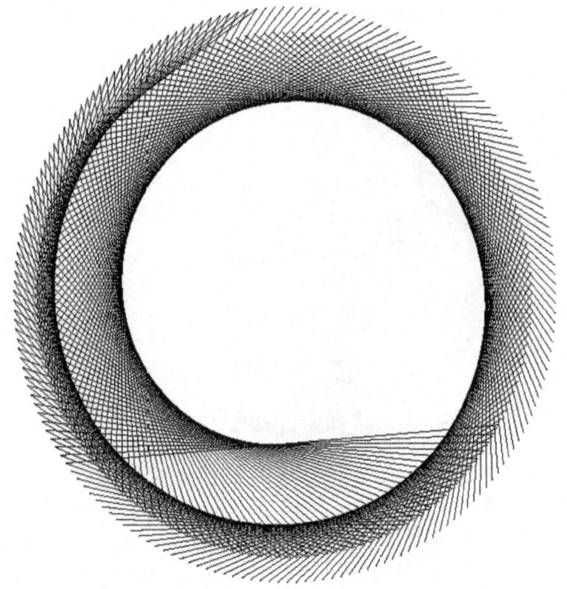

1500 JAN 1 to 2181 JAN 30 250 999.00
ZEUS KRONOS MANDALA Figure 95

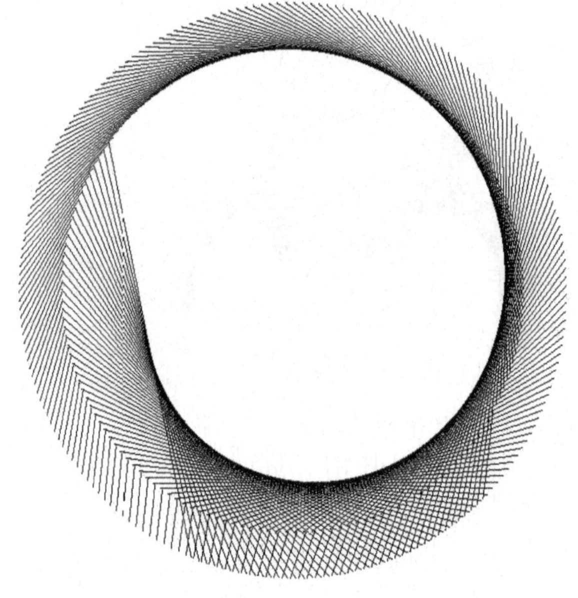

1500 JAN 1 to 2181 JAN 30 250 999.00
ZEUS APOLLON MANDALA Figure 96

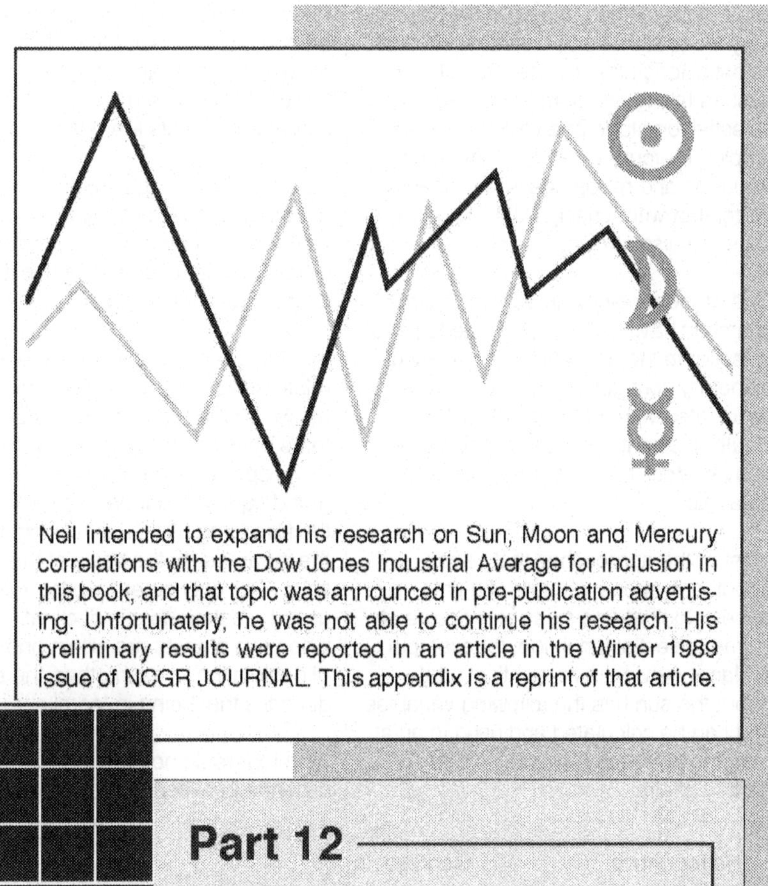

Neil intended to expand his research on Sun, Moon and Mercury correlations with the Dow Jones Industrial Average for inclusion in this book, and that topic was announced in pre-publication advertising. Unfortunately, he was not able to continue his research. His preliminary results were reported in an article in the Winter 1989 issue of NCGR JOURNAL. This appendix is a reprint of that article.

Part 12

Appendix

- ***Planetary Patterns and the Dow Jones Industrial Average***

Planetary Patterns and the Dow Jones Industrial Average

by Neil F. Michelsen

Abstract

The various measures of planetary positions are outlined and the correlation of some of these to the Dow Jones Industrial Average from June 1, 1952 to October 31, 1989 are presented. The main point of the author, based on his preliminary work, is that one measure, such as celestial longitude, by itself, is not as robust as taking two or more measures — celestial longitude and velocity, for example. Mercury when in Sagittarius or Aquarius and retrograde is significantly correlated with a rising DJIA. Other results are also shown.

One of the problems in astrological research is having the appropriate tools to investigate the almost infinite variety of planetary configurations that could be associated with phenomena such as weather, climate, sunspots, political upheaval, stock market prices, time series data, etc.

Most of the approaches that I know about look at one variable at a time, or, at best, look at one class of measure at a time, celestial longitude, for example. A planet moving in an elliptical orbit about the sun has the following variables that can be calculated and used in an attempt to correlate their values with earthly affairs:

Heliocentric	Geocentric	
longitude	longitude	(ecliptic)
latitude	latitude	(ecliptic)
radius vector	radius vector	(not measured on any plane)
—distance from the sun	— distance from earth	
	right ascension	(celestial equator)
	declination	(celestial equator)
	azimuth	(horizon plane)
	altitude	(horizon plane)

Each of the above measures have position, velocity and acceleration. Each of the above measures, with the exception of heliocentric longitude and azimuth are bi-directional. Geo longitude is either direct or retrograde, a planet is either going north or south in latitude, the radius vector is either increasing or decreasing. All of these measures also have station points — the position and time when they change direction. Each body also has nodes — the orbital plane intersection of the body with another plane. Also the measures above and below the reference plane — latitude (ecliptic), altitude(horizon) and declination (equator) can have a zero value as the body actually intersects the reference plane.

When the Sun is at zero Aries it is also at zero degrees declination — it is always within a second or so of zero degrees latitude, of course, since its orbit defines the ecliptic plane.

In addition, astrologers use the angular relationships between two or more planets which they call aspects. Aspect patterns between more than two planets are given special names such as grand trine, grand square, t-square, yod, etc. All of the foregoing use celestial longitude as the measure for the basis of the relationship. The only other "aspect" measure used by astrologers is declination and when two planets are within one degree of declination of each other, the astrologer calls that being in 'parallel'.

Astrologers do not use the true angular distance between planets which can be found by using the formula ArcCos(CosACosD) where A is the longitude difference and D is the latitude difference between the two bodies.

A more sophisticated elaboration of aspects is their generalization into harmonics, angular distances determined by integer division of the 360 degrees of a circle. But, again, the only measure to which they are applied is celestial longitude.

I was scheduled to speak for the Foundation for the Study of Cycles' World Headquarters Chapter's November 14th dinner meeting in Irvine, California, and I didn't have any original material to present even though I had been scheduled six months earlier. Fortunately, I had some tools that allowed me to do some analysis starting on Friday morning, November 10th, that produced results, that if they hold up, are very significant.

The tools I had were:

- curiosity
- computer
- an ability to write programs to ask the computer to answer specific questions
- a suite of programs that enables me to calculate all the variables of planetary movement and position listed above
- a database containing the Dow Jones Industrial averages from 1885 to date

I was motivated along the lines I will shortly describe by an article I read in the October 25th issue of *Personal Finance*, a bi-weekly newsletter edited by Richard E. Band. 'Stocks:The Next Six Months Could Be Hot' by Yale Hirsh pointed out the bear market bottoms of long term significance occurred in October of 1957, 1960, 1962, 1966 and 1974, and that October "massacres" occurred in 1978, 1979 and 1987. He also observed that since 1950, in the six consecutive months November thru April, the Dow has gained 2505.33 points and in the remaining six months has lost 397.72 points! Astounding!

This should be easy to duplicate, I thought, not using calendar dates but the Sun's position. The results I obtained, taken directly from the computer printout, are shown in **Table 1**. I chose June

Table 1

From Jun 1 1952 to Oct 31 1989 Filter=0.99 Trade Days= 9408/ 9408

Up %	Up days	Down %	Down days	Tot days	Ratios %	Ratios Days
3010.78/52%	4944/53%	-2742.87/48%	4464/47%	9408/100%	1.098	1.108

Sun Statistics

	Geo Long	Hel Long	G Lat	H Lat	Declin	Helio RV	Geo RV	Speed
Mean	177.4463	182.7129	0.0000	0.0000	0.6159	1.0003293	1.0003293	0.98523
Std Dev	103.3338	104.6911	0.0001	0.0001	163820 0	0117836	0.0117836	0.02323
Minimum	0.0139	0.0293	-0.0003	-0.0003	-23.4455	0.9832112 0	9832112	0.95291
Maximum	359.9653	359.9977	0.0003	0.0003	23.4455	1.0167608	1.0167608	1.01972

Sun Analysis

Up %	Up days	Down %	Down days	Tot days	Ratios %	Ratios Days
Sun in Aries						
245.63/56%	424/55%	-194.16/44%	345/45%	769/ 8%	1.265	1.229
2765.15/52%	4520/52%	-2548.71/48%	4119/48%	8639/92%	1.085	1.097
Sun in Taurus						
229.88/48%	405/50%	-248.24/52%	411/50%	816/ 9%	0.926	0.985
2780.90/53%	4539/53%	-2494.63/47%	4053/47%	8592/91%	1.115	1.120
Sun in Gemini						
249.64/51%	407/51%	-244.48/49%	396/49%	803/ 9%	1.021	1.028
2761.14/52%	4537/53%	-2498.39/48%	4068/47%	8605/91%	1.105	1.115
Sun in Cancer						
240.29/53%	428/53%	-214.95/47%	384/47%	812/ 9%	1.118	1.115
2770.49/52%	4516/53%	-2527.92/48%	4080/47%	8596/91%	1.096	1.107
Sun in Leo						
254.90/52%	445/53%	-232.42/48%	398/47%	843/ 9%	1.097	1.118
2755.88/52%	4499/53%	-2510.45/48%	4066/47%	8565/91%	1.098	1.106
Sun in Virgo						
249.75/50%	409/51%	-248.20/50%	389/49%	798/ 8%	1.006	1.051
2761.03/53%	4535/53%	-2494.67/47%	4075/47%	8610/92%	1.107	1.113
Sun in Libra						
280.70/47%	411/50%	-312.45/53%	405/50%	816/ 9%	0.898	1.015
2730.08/53%	4533/53%	-2430.42/47%	4059/47%	8592/91%	1.123	1.117
Sun in Scorpio						
279.65/52%	411/53%	-256.51/48%	358/47%	769/ 8%	1.090	1.148
2731.13/52%	4533/52%	-2486.36/48%	4106/48%	8639/92%	1.098	1.104
Sun in Sagittarius						
259.15/56%	407/55%	-205.25/44%	335/45%	742/ 8%	1.263	1.215
2751.63/52%	4537/52%	-2537.62/48%	4129/48%	8666/92%	1.084	1.099
Sun in Capricorn						
243.68/57%	384/54%	-184.66/43%	323/46%	707/ 8%	1.320	1.189
2767.10/52%	4560/52%	-2558.21/48%	4141/48%	8701/92%	1.082	1.101
Sun in Aquarius						
231.90/53%	386/50%	-209.27/47%	382/50%	768/ 8%	1.108	1.010
2778.88/52%	4558/53%	-2533.61/48%	4082/47%	8640/92%	1.097	1.117
Sun in Pisces						
245.60/56%	427/56%	-192.26/44%	338/44%	765/ 8%	1.277	1.263
2765.18/52%	4517/52%	-2550.61/48%	4126/48%	8643/92%	1.084	1.095
Sun longitude .GE. 70 .AND. .LE.158 June thru August						
738.60/52%	1285/53%	-674.34/48%	1157/47%	2442/26%	1.095	1.111
2272.18/52%	3659/53%	-2068.53/48%	3307/47%	6966/74%	1.098	1.106
Sun longitude .GE. 350 .OR. .LT. 40 March and April						
415.64/55%	712/55%	-340.58/45%	592/45%	1304/14%	1.220	1.203
2595.14/52%	4232/52%	-2402.29/48%	3872/48%	8104/86%	1.080	1.093
Sun longitude .GE. 219.AND. .LE. 340 November thru January						
999.49/54%	1590/53%	-842.44/46%	1389/47%	2979/32%	1.186	1.145
2011.29/51%	3354/52%	-1900.44/49%	3075/48%	6429/68%	1.058	1.091
Sun longitude .GE. 40 .AND. .LE. 70 May						
222.45/47%	374/48%	-251.52/53%	411/52%	785/ 8%	0.884	0.910
2788.33/53%	4570/53%	-2491.35/47%	4053/47%	8623/92%	1.119	1.128
Sun longitude .GE. 158 .AND. .LE. 187 September						
226.59/47%	393/51%	-258.10/53%	374/49%	767/ 8%	0.878	1.051
2784.19/53%	4551/53%	-2484.78/47%	4090/47%	8641/92%	1.120	1.113
Sun Velocity faster than 1 degree per day — Speed test						
1084.65/55%	1729/54%	-897.52/45%	1484/46%	3213/34%	1.208	1.165
1926.13/51%	3215/52%	-1845.35/49%	2980/48%	6195/66%	1.044	1.079

* * * * * * * * * * * * * * * *

Up %	Up days	Down %	Down days	Tot days	Ratios %	Ratios Days
Sun latitude .GT. 0						
1507.98/52%	2462/53%	-1371.29/48%	2221/47%	4683/50%	1.100	1.109
1502.80/52%	2482/53%	-1371.59/48%	2243/47%	4725/50%	1.096	1.107

* * * * * * * * * * * * * * * *

Up %	Up days	Down %	Down days	Tot days	Ratios %	Ratios Days
Monday						
502.01/41%	820/45%	-730.49/59%	1004/55%	1824/19%	0.687	0.817
2508.77/55%	4124/54%	-2012.38/45%	3460/46%	7584/81%	1.247	1.192
Tuesday						
631.42/53%	982/51%	-556.05/47%	930/49%	1912/20%	1.136	1.056
2379.36/52%	3962/53%	-2186.83/48%	3534/47%	7496/80%	1.088	1.121
Wednesday						
674.04/58%	1067/56%	-496.60/42%	839/44%	1906/20%	1.357	1.272
2336.74/51%	3877/52%	-2246.27/49%	3625/48%	7502/80%	1.040	1.070
Thursday						
579.91/53%	1007/53%	-512.37/47%	882/47%	1889/20%	1.132	1.142
2430.87/52%	3937/52%	-2230.50/48%	3582/48%	7519/80%	1.090	1.099
Friday						
623.40/58%	1068/57%	-447.36/42%	809/43%	1877/20%	1.394	1.320
2387.38/51%	3876/51%	-2295.51/49%	3655/49%	7531/80%	1.040	1.060

1952 as the starting date for this analysis because that was the first month that the NYSE did not trade on Saturdays and I wanted to compare the astronomical result with something simple like how the market does on each day of the week over a long time span.

The first line of the computer report as shown in Table 1 shows the beginning and ending dates, the filter used, and the number of 'filtered' trade days and the total number of trade days. The filter is used by the program to eliminate any days when the DJIA moves more than that value to see if any result is biased by the huge movement on October 19, 1987, for example. When 4% is used twenty one dates in the time period shown are eliminated. Since no result was significantly changed by using a 4% filter I will show the results using 99%, no filter..

There are five columns of data each with a pair of values separated by a slash. The first column (Up %) shows the cumulative total of the percentage of movement on up days and the percent of the total movement this represents — 3010.78/(3010.78 + 2742.87) = .52 = 52%.

The second column shows the number of trade days when the market closed higher than the preceding day, and what percent of the total trade days for this line this represents.

The third and fourth columns show the same results for down days.

The fifth column shows the total days for both ups and downs for that line.

The sixth double column is simply the ratio of up% to down% and up days to down days. 3010.78/2742.87 = 1.098. 4944/4464 = 1.108.

The program calculates the positions for the assumed market opening time of 9:30 am for the eight values shown — geo and helio longitude and latitude, declination, helio and geo radius vector and the instantaneous velocity in degrees per day. The statistics are calculated for use in formulating different astronomical criteria to correlate to the DJIA.

For each criterion two lines of data are shown: the first if the criterion is met,the second, if it is not met. Obviously, when added together, the respective values should equal the total shown on the fourth line of the table. Sun in Aries has 424 up days, Sun not in Aries has 4520 up days. 424 + 4520 = 4944, the total up days shown in the fourth line of the table.

Examining the results

• Looking at the bottom of the Sun table at the non-astronomical results for Wednesday and Friday, we see that on both of those days the market cumulative up% was 58 vs 52 for the entire time period.

• Only Sun in Capricorn with a cumulative up% of 57 is within one percentage point of this result.

• Now let's look at some results for Mercury in **Table 2**.The double row of asterisks is an attempt at a printer plot to show whether the result on the previous two lines is an anomaly because the phenomenon occurs only in a few periods or whether it is distributed across the entire span of 37 plus years. Since I used only 80 asterisks for a time span of 13698 days (June 1, 1952 thru October 31, 1989) each asterisk represents 171.225 days.

• Most of the Mercury astronomical criteria should be self-explanatory.

• Results of note are the cumulative up percentages of 69, 59, 71 and 69 when Mercury is both retrograde and in Aries, Virgo, Sagittarius and Aquarius, respectively.

• Note also that when Mercury is in Aquarius or Pisces and its latitude is greater than 2 degrees North or less than 2 degrees south and retrograde, its cumulative Up% is 60.

• I have similar results for the Moon. However, since the Moon does not go retrograde an equivalent criterion is whether the moon is moving faster or slower than its mean velocity.

Table 2

From Jun 1 1952 to Oct 31 1989 Filter=0.99 Trade Days= 9408/ 9408

Up %	Up days	Down %	Down days	Tot days	Ratios %	Ratios Days
3010.78/52%	4944/53%	-2742.87/48%	4464/47%		1.098	1.108

Mercury Analysis

	Geo Long	Hel Long	G Lat	H Lat	Declin	Helio RV	Geo RV	Speed
Mean	185.0499	201.8563	-0.4357	-0.6857	-1.2077 0	3951673	1.0379909	0.98607
Std Dev	102.3034	98.0208	2.0499	4.8605	16.4700	0.0557232	0.2736134	0.92351
Minimum	0.0547	0.1226	-4.9694	-7.0048	-25.8560 0	3074960 0	5491129	-1.38644
Maximum	359.9920	359.9886	3.7230	7.0048	25.6585	0.4666988	1.4514873	2.20221

Up %	Up days	Down %	Down days	Tot days	Ratios %	Ratios Days
Mercury direct, second line is Mercury retrograde						
2401.55/52%	3994/53%	-2214.80/48%	3609/47%	7603/81%	1.084	1.107
609.23/54%	950/53%	-528.08/46%	855/47%	1805/19%	1.154	1.111
Mercury at North latitude						
1283.74/52%	2153/52%	-1173.36/48%	1951/48%	4104/44%	1.094	1.104
1727.04/52%	2791/53%	-1569.51/48%	2513/47%	5304/56%	1.100	1.111
Mercury at North declination						
1292.78/51%	2278/52%	-1245.75/49%	2121/48%	4399/47%	1.038	1.074
1718.00/53%	2666/53%	-1497.12/47%	2343/47%	5009/53%	1.148	1.138
Mercury speed .GE. 1 degree per day						
1682.79/52%	2792/53%	-1536.14/48%	2484/47%	5276/56%	1.095	1.124
1327.99/52%	2152/52%	-1206.74/48%	1980/48%	4132/44%	1.100	1.087
Mercury latitude .GE. 1 degree						
775.77/53%	1269/53%	-695.43/47%	1133/47%	2402/26%	1.116	1.120
2235.01/52%	3675/52%	-2047.44/48%	3331/48%	7006/74%	1.092	1.103
Mercury in Capricorn, Aquarius or Pisces and (latitude.GE.1 or .LE. -1)						
592.73/54%	993/53%	-506.44/46%	874/47%	1867/20%	1.170	1.136
2418.05/52%	3951/52%	-2236.44/48%	3590/48%	7541/80%	1.081	1.101
Mercury in Aquarius or Pisces and (latitude. GE.2 or .LE. -2)						
224.93/56%	365/54%	-178.22/44%	309/46%	674/7%	1.262	1.181
2785.85/52%	4579/52%	-2564.65/48%	4155/48%	8734/93%	1.086	1.102
Mercury in Aquarius or Pisces and (latitude.GE.2 or .LE. -2) and Mercury retro						
94.59/60%	146/56%	-63.79/40%	116/44%	262/3%	1.483	1.259
2916.19/52%	4798/52%	-2679.08/48%	4348/48%	9146/97%	1.089	1.103
Mercury retrograde and in Aries						
44.75/69%	84/63%	-20.32/31%	50/37%	134/1%	2.203	1.680
2966.03/52%	4860/52%	-2722.56/48%	4414/48%	9274/99%	1.089	1.101
Mercury retrograde and in Taurus						
36.52/47%	64/50%	-40.61/53%	63/50%	127/1%	0.899	1.016
2974.26/52%	4880/53%	-2702.26/48%	4401/47%	9281/99%	1.101	1.109
Mercury retrograde and in Gemini						
54.09/48%	67/44%	-57.57/52%	86/56%	153/2%	0.940	0.779
2956.69/52%	4877/53%	-2685.30/48%	4378/47%	9255/98%	1.101	1.114
Mercury retrograde and in Cancer						
47.44/53%	77/50%	-42.92/47%	77/50%	154/2%	1.105	1.000
2963.34/52%	4867/53%	-2699.95/48%	4387/47%	9254/98%	1.098	1.109
Mercury retrograde and in Leo						
36.54/49%	88/52%	-37.69/51%	81/48%	169/2%	0.969	1.086
2974.24/52%	4856/53%	-2705.18/48%	4383/47%	9239/98%	1.099	1.108
Mercury retrograde and in Virgo						
52.34/59%	84/56%	-36.78/41%	65/44%	149/2%	1.423	1.292
2958.44/52%	4860/52%	-2706.09/48%	4399/48%	9259/98%	1.093	1.105
Mercury retrograde and in Libra						
59.44/52%	79/48%	-55.48/48%	86/52%	165/2%	1.071	0.919
2951.34/52%	4865/53%	-2687.39/48%	4378/47%	9243/98%	1.098	1.111

	Up %	Up days	Down %	Down days	Tot days	Ratios %	Ratios Days
Mercury retrograde and in Scorpio							
	77.76/46%	78/49%	-92.40/54%	80/51%	158/2%	0.842	0.975
	2933.02/53%	4866/53%	-2650.47/47%	4384/47%	9250/98%	1.107	1.110
Mercury retrograde and in Sagittarius							
	52.51/71%	91/64%	-21.95/29%	51/36%	142/2%	2.392	1.784
	2958.27/52%	4853/52%	-2720.92/48%	4413/48%	9266/98%	1.087	1.100
Mercury retrograde and in Capricorn							
	30.04/42%	63/46%	-40.90/58%	74/54%	137/1%	0.734	0.851
	2980.74/52%	4881/53%	-2701.97/48%	4390/47%	9271/99%	1.103	1.112
Mercury retrograde and in Aquarius							
	67.93/69%	94/60%	-31.23/31%	63/40%	157/2%	2.175	1.492
	2942.85/52%	4850/52%	-2711.64/48%	4401/48%	9251/98%	1.085	1.102
Mercury retrograde and in Pisces							
	49.85/50%	81/51%	-50.21/50%	79/49%	160/2%	0.993	1.025
	2960.93/52%	4863/53%	-2692.66/48%	4385/47%	9248/98%	1.100	1.109
Heliocentric Mercury in Aries, Taurus or Gemini							
	529.91/53%	871/53%	-473.83/47%	787/47%	1658/18%	1.118	1.107
	2480.87/52%	4073/53%	-2269.05/48%	3677/47%	7750/82%	1.093	1.108
Heliocentric Mercury in Cancer, Leo or Virgo							
	568.67/52%	967/52%	-534.00/48%	890/48%	1857/20%	1.065	1.087
	2442.11/53%	3977/53%	-2208.88/47%	3574/47%	7551/80%	1.106	1.113
Heliocentric Mercury in Libra, Scorpio or Sagittarius							
	1001.95/52%	1647/52%	-933.22/48%	1496/48%	3143/33%	1.074	1.101
	2008.83/53%	3297/53%	-1809.65/47%	2968/47%	6265/67%	1.110	1.111
Heliocentric Mercury in Capricorn, Aquarius or Pisces							
	910.25/53%	1459/53%	-801.83/47%	1291/47%	2750/29%	1.135	1.130
	2100.53/52%	3485/52%	-1941.04/48%	3173/48%	6658/71%	1.082	1.098

Table 3

From Jun 1 1952 to Oct 31 1989 Filter=0.99 Trade Days= 9408/ 9408

Up %	Up days	Down %	Down days	Tot days	Ratios %	Ratios Days
3010.78/52%	4944/53%	-2742.87/48%		4464/47%	1.098	1.108

MOON ANALYSIS

	Geo Long	Hel Long	G Lat	H Lat	Declin	Helio RV	Geo RV	Speed
Mean	179.7584	182.7125	-0.0035	0.0000	0.0719	1.0003191 0	0025735	13.17749
Std Dev	103.9924	104.6911	3.6379	0.0092	16.8326	0.0119130	0.0001015	1.05342
Minimum	0.0302	0.0215	-5.3013	-0.0143	-28.6631	0.9806062	0.0023835	11.76605
Maximum	359.9764	359.9764	5.3024	0.0143	28.7256	1.0193813	0.0027186	15.38453

	Up %	Up days	Down %	Down days	Tot days	Ratios %	Ratios Days
Slow Moon in Aries							
	44.30/44%	87/48%	-55.81/56%	94/52%	181/2%	0.794	0.926
	2966.48/52%	4857/53%	-2687.06/48%	4370/47%	9227/98%	1.104	1.111
Slow Moon in Gemini							
	38.76/41%	74/45%	-54.82/59%	92/55%	166/2%	0.707	0.804
	2972.02/53%	4870/53%	-2688.05/47%	4372/47%	9242/98%	1.106	1.114
Fast Moon in Taurus							
	68.19/59%	112/62%	-46.51/41%	68/38%	180/2%	1.466	1.647
	2942.59/52%	4832/52%	-2696.36/48%	4396/48%	9228/98%	1.091	1.099
Fast Moon in Cancer							
	44.99/46%	73/50%	-52.09/54%	73/50%	146/2%	0.864	1.000
	2965.79/52%	4871/53%	-2690.78/48%	4391/47%	9262/98%	1.102	1.109
Fast Moon in Libra							
	60.90/64%	97/63%	-34.92/36%	58/37%	155/2%	1.744	1.672
	2949.88/52%	4847/52%	-2707.95/48%	4406/48%	9253/98%	1.089	1.100
Fast Moon in Scorpio							
	50.23/64%	80/58%	-28.00/36%	59/42%	139/1%	1.794	1.356
	2960.55/52%	4864/52%	-2714.87/48%	4405/48%	9269/99%	1.090	1.104
Fast Moon in Capricorn							
	51.85/58%	88/54%	-38.04/42%	76/46%	164/2%	1.363	1.158
	2958.93/52%	4856/53%	-2704.83/48%	4388/47%	9244/98%	1.094	1.107
Fast Moon in Aquarius							
	46.56/46%	82/47%	-55.72/54%	91/53%	173/2%	0.836	0.901
	2964.22/52%	4862/53%	-2687.15/48%	4373/47%	9235/98%	1.103	1.112

• This is where the statistical information about the mean and standard deviation of longitude, latitude, radius vector and speed is helpful. I defined a slow Moon as one moving slower than the mean speed, 13.17749° per day less 1 standard deviation, 1.05342° per day. Those numbers come directly from Table 3 under the columnar heading "Speed." A fast Moon is one that is moving faster than its mean motion + 1 standard deviation.

• The most striking result in **Table 3** is fast Moon in Libra, followed by fast Moon in Scorpio where the up percentage movement in the DJIA is 1-3/4 times the down percentage movement.

• The only significant result with the slow Moon is when the Moon is in Aries or Gemini. In both cases the percentage movement is strikingly less than the average of 52%.

• There are an infinite number of variables one can look at. For example, I just started using the 35 combinations of Sun with Moon thru Pluto, Moon with Mercury thru Pluto, Venus with Mars thru Pluto and Mars with Jupiter thru Pluto. Taking the the angular separation in longitude in one degree increments gives 35 tables each with 360 entries (0 thru 359 degrees).

• On any given day at market opening, these 35 planet combinations have a given angular separation. One can look up what the up/down % is for each combination to estimate what the market will do for that day.

• The trick is to ask the right kind of questions — select the appropriate criteria — without having to do a mindless evaluation of all possible combinations of criteria.

I have just scratched the surface. I hope I have stimulated you to try some new approaches of your own. I welcome any feedback from you!

Reprinted from NCGR Journal Winter 1989 by permission of the editor

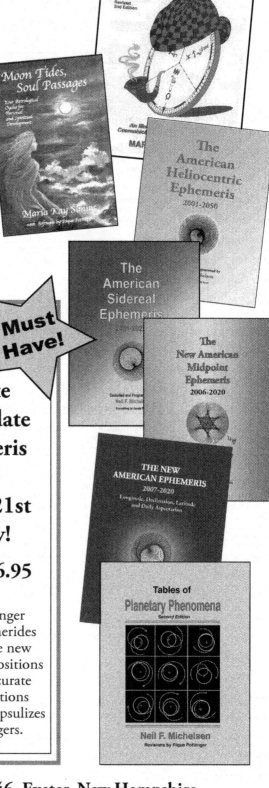

Lightning Source UK Ltd.
Milton Keynes UK
UKOW07f2343120917
309090UK00002B/7/P

9 780976 242246